HANDBOOK OF

MUSIC AND EMOTION

THEORY, RESEARCH, APPLICATIONS

Series in Affective Science
Series Editors
Richard J. Davidson
Paul Ekman
Klaus Scherer

The Nature of Emotion
Fundamental Questions
Edited by Paul Ekman and Richard J. Davidson

Boo!
Culture, Experience, and the Startle Reflex
Ronald Simons

Emotions in Psychopathology
Theory and Research
Edited by William F. Flack Jr. and James D.
Laird

What the Face Reveals
Basic and Applied Studies of Spontaneous
Expression Using the Facial Action Coding
System (FACS)
Edited by Paul Ekman and Erika Rosenberg

Shame
Interpersonal Behavior, Psychopathology, and
Culture
Edited by Paul Gilbert and Bernice Andrews

Affective Neuroscience
The Foundations of Human and Animal
Emotions
Jaak Panksepp

Extreme Fear, Shyness, and Social Phobia
Origins, Biological Mechanisms, and Clinical
Outcomes
Edited by Louis A. Schmidt and Jay Schulkin

Cognitive Neuroscience of Emotion
Edited by Richard D. Lane and Lynn Nadel

The Neuropsychology of Emotion
Edited by Joan C. Borod

Anxiety, Depression, and Emotion
Edited by Richard J. Davidson

Persons, Situations, and Emotions
An Ecological Approach
Edited by Hermann Brandstätter and Andrzej
Eliasz

Emotion, Social Relationships, and Health
Edited by Carol D. Ryff and Burton Singer

Appraisal Processes in Emotion
Theory, Methods, Research
Edited by Klaus R. Scherer, Angela Schorr, and
Tom Johnstone

Music and Emotion
Theory and Research
Edited by Patrik N. Juslin and John A. Sloboda

Nonverbal Behavior in Clinical Settings
Edited by Pierre Philippot, Robert S. Feldman,
and Erik J. Coats

Memory and Emotion
Edited by Daniel Reisberg and Paula Hertel

Psychology of Gratitude
Edited by Robert A. Emmons and
Michael E. McCullough

Thinking about Feeling
Contemporary Philosophers on Emotions
Edited by Robert C. Solomon

Bodily Sensibility
Intelligent Action
Jay Schulkin

Who Needs Emotions?
The Brain Meets the Robot
Edited by Jean-Marc Fellous and
Michael A. Arbib

What the Face Reveals
Basic and Applied Studies of Spontaneous
Expression Using the Facial Action Coding
System (FACS), Second Edition
Edited by Paul Ekman and Erika L. Rosenberg

The Development of Social Engagement
Neurobiological Perspectives
Edited by Peter J. Marshall and Nathan A. Fox

Handbook of Emotion Elicitation and Assessment
Edited by James A. Coan and John J. B. Allen

Emotion and Memory in Development
Biological, Cognitive, and Social Considerations
Edited by Jodi A. Quas and Robyn Fivush

Emotion explained
Edited by Edmund T. Rolls

New handbook of nonverbal behaviour research
Edited by Jinni Harrigan, Robert Rosenthal
and Klaus Scherer

HANDBOOK OF

MUSIC AND EMOTION

THEORY, RESEARCH, APPLICATIONS

PATRIK N. JUSLIN

and

JOHN A. SLOBODA

OXFORD

UNIVERSITY PRESS

OXFORD

UNIVERSITY PRESS

Great Clarendon Street, Oxford OX2 6DP

Oxford University Press is a department of the University of Oxford.
It furthers the University's objective of excellence in research, scholarship,
and education by publishing worldwide in

Oxford New York

Auckland Cape Town Dar es Salaam Hong Kong Karachi
Kuala Lumpur Madrid Melbourne Mexico City Nairobi
New Delhi Shanghai Taipei Toronto

With offices in

Argentina Austria Brazil Chile Czech Republic France Greece
Guatemala Hungary Italy Japan Poland Portugal Singapore
South Korea Switzerland Thailand Turkey Ukraine Vietnam

Oxford is a registered trade mark of Oxford University Press
in the UK and in certain other countries

Published in the United States
by Oxford University Press Inc., New York

British Library Cataloguing in Publication Data
Data available

Library of Congress Cataloging-in-Publication-Data
Data available

Typeset by Cepha Imaging Private Ltd., Bangalore, India
Printed in Great Britain
on acid-free paper by
CPI Antony Rowe,
Chippenham, Wiltshire

ISBN 978–0–19–923014–3

10 9 8 7 6 5 4 3 2 1

FOREWORD

This is an important volume. It is a beautiful joint enterprise by most, or all, of the most prominent researchers currently in the field. It also represents an extremely multi-faceted enterprise. It approaches the topic of music as a source of emotions from a large number of different perspectives and levels of analysis: as an intrapersonal process, as an interpersonal or social phenomenon, and as a product of cultural influences and traditions. The emotions evoked by music are examined in great detail, and the various methods by means of which they can be assessed are discussed, as are the emotions that are involved in composing and performing music. One cannot but be impressed by the range of issues treated, and the efforts put into approaching this multifaceted area in depth.

I think that the domain of music and emotion is crucial for understanding emotion and emotion processes generally – precisely because the processes involved appear to diverge importantly from those that we think are involved in everyday emotions. Everyday emotions are best understood as the outcome of events in the world or the individual's history, which are appraised as relevant to the individual's personal concerns. They have much to do with the relationship between the individual, other people, and the world. Appraisal of relevance to concerns and evoking action impulses to establish or modify individual-environment relationships are almost absent in our appraisal of and emotional response to music. Sometimes those responses appear like mirror-neuron activities that became independent. One may float and move with the music, perhaps more so than one may do in other aesthetic emotions. And perhaps this is so because in listening to music, one is not required to deal with things and with space, but with time – with being and becoming and fading away or decaying.

I think the present volume brings us nearer to realizing the mysteries involved in such confrontations, and closer to understanding them.

Nico Frijda

Acknowledgements

Science is a social enterprise, and a number of people contributed their time and expertise to this joint venture. First and foremost, this handbook would not exist without the authors. We would like to thank them for entering into the project with great enthusiasm, professionalism, and efficiency. It was a pleasure to work with first-rate authors who contributed intellectually stimulating material. Many of the authors also reviewed first drafts of chapters for this book. We are further grateful to a large number of external referees who participated in the review process, including Eckart Altenmüller, Steven Brown, Martin Clayton, Jane Davidson, Steven Dollinger, David Elliott, Andy Evans, Anders Friberg, Simon Frith, Ernest Haakanen, Morris Holbrook, Petr Janata, Tom Johnstone, James Kellaris, Petri Laukka, Colin Martindale, Cathy McKinney, Julie Nagel, Richard Parncutt, Aniruddh Patel, David Rawlings, Bennett Reimer, Bruno Repp, Nikki Rickard, Even Ruud, Suvi Saarikallio, Paul Silvia, Maria Spychiger, Töres Theorell, Bradley Vines, Ulrik Volgsten, Aaron Williamon, and Graham Welch (a number of additional referees preferred to be anonymous). We especially thank Nico Frijda for writing a Foreword, and Graham Welch for providing us with a workspace during our London meeting. We would also like to acknowledge everyone at Oxford University Press who helped with this project - especially our senior commissioning editor, Martin Baum, and our production editor, Marionne Cronin, who were highly supportive of the project at various stages.

Patrik Juslin's work was supported by the Swedish Research Council. He also thanks the members of the music psychology group in Uppsala for several years of fruitful collaboration, and, in particular, Susanne, Lars, and Gun-Mari for their love, patience, and support.

John Sloboda would like to thank the members of the music psychology research group at Keele University, both faculty and students, for support and encouragement, and also Patrik Juslin for uncomplainingly shouldering the greater part of the duties of co-editorship.

August 2009   Patrik Juslin
                                                                                 John Sloboda

Contents

List of contributors   xiii

PART I OVERTURE

1. Introduction: aims, organization, and terminology   3
   PATRIK N. JUSLIN AND JOHN A. SLOBODA

PART II
MULTI-DISCIPLINARY PERSPECTIVES

2. Emotions expressed and aroused by music: philosophical
   perspectives   15
   STEPHEN DAVIES

3. Emotion in culture and history: perspectives
   from musicology   45
   NICHOLAS COOK AND NICOLA DIBBEN

4. At the interface between the inner and outer world:
   psychological perspectives   73
   JOHN A. SLOBODA AND PATRIK N. JUSLIN

5. Towards a neurobiology of musical emotions   99
   ISABELLE PERETZ

6. Exploring the habitus of listening: anthropological
   perspectives   127
   JUDITH BECKER

7. Emotion as social emergence: perspectives
   from music sociology   159
   TIA DENORA

PART III MEASUREMENT

8. Self-report measures and models   187
    MARCEL ZENTNER AND TUOMAS EEROLA

9. Continuous self-report methods   223
    EMERY SCHUBERT

10. Indirect perceptual, cognitive, and behavioural measures   255
    DANIEL VÄSTFJÄLL

11. Psychophysiological measures   279
    DONALD A. HODGES

12. Functional neuroimaging   313
    STEFAN KOELSCH, WALTER A. SIEBEL, AND THOMAS FRITZ

PART IV MUSIC MAKING

13. Emotion and composition in classical music: historiometric
    perspectives   347
    DEAN KEITH SIMONTON

14. The role of structure in the musical expression of emotions   367
    ALF GABRIELSSON AND ERIK LINDSTRÖM

15. Emotion and motivation in the lives of performers   401
    ROBERT H. WOODY AND GARY E. MCPHERSON

16. The role of negative emotions in performance anxiety   425
    DIANNA T. KENNY

17. Expression and communication of emotion in music
    performance   453
    PATRIK N. JUSLIN AND RENEE TIMMERS

PART V MUSIC LISTENING

18. Music in everyday life: the role of emotions   493
    JOHN A. SLOBODA

19. Experimental aesthetics and liking for music   515
    DAVID J. HARGREAVES AND ADRIAN C. NORTH

20. Strong experiences with music   547
    ALF GABRIELSSON

21. Musical expectancy and thrills   575
    DAVID HURON AND ELIZABETH HELLMUTH MARGULIS

22. How does music evoke emotions? Exploring the underlying
    mechanisms   605
    PATRIK N. JUSLIN, SIMON LILJESTRÖM, DANIEL VÄSTFJÄLL,
    AND LARS-OLOV LUNDQVIST

PART VI DEVELOPMENT, PERSONALITY, AND SOCIAL FACTORS

23. Perspectives on music and affect in the early years   645
    SANDRA E. TREHUB, ERIN E. HANNON,
    AND ADENA SCHACHNER

24. Preference, personality, and emotion   669
    PETER J. RENTFROW AND JENNIFER A. McDONALD

25. The influence of affect on music choice   697
    VLADIMIR J. KONEČNI

26. Politics, mediation, social context, and public use   725
    REEBEE GAROFALO

27. Cross-cultural similarities and differences   755
    WILLIAM FORDE THOMPSON AND LAURA-LEE BALKWILL

PART VII APPLICATIONS

28. Music education: the role of affect   791
    SUSAN HALLAM

29. Music therapy   819
    MICHAEL H. THAUT AND BARBARA L. WHEELER

30. Music, health, and well-being   849
    SUZANNE B. HANSER

31. Music as a source of emotion in film   879
    ANNABEL J. COHEN

32. Music and marketing   909
    ADRIAN C. NORTH AND DAVID J. HARGREAVES

PART VIII ENCORE

33. The past, present, and future of music and emotion research   933
    PATRIK N. JUSLIN AND JOHN A. SLOBODA

    Index   957

LIST OF CONTRIBUTORS

Laura-Lee Balkwill Department of Psychology, Queen's University, Canada

Judith Becker School of Music, University of Michigan, USA

Annabel J. Cohen Department of Psychology, University of Prince Edward Island, Canada

Nicholas Cook Faculty of Music, University of Cambridge, UK

Stephen Davies Department of Philosophy, University of Auckland, New Zealand

Tia DeNora Department of Sociology, University of Exeter, UK

Nicola Dibben Department of Music, University of Sheffield, UK

Tuomas Eerola Department of Music, University of Jyväskylä, Finland

Thomas Fritz Department of Neurophysics, Max Planck Institute for Human Cognitive and Brain Sciences, Germany

Alf Gabrielsson Department of Psychology, Uppsala University, Sweden

Reebee Garofalo College of Public and Community Service, University of Massachusetts, Boston, USA

Susan Hallam Institute of Education, University of London, UK

Erin E. Hannon Department of Psychology, University of Nevada Las Vegas, USA

Suzanne B. Hanser Music Therapy Department, Berklee College of Music, USA

David J. Hargreaves School of Education, Roehampton University, UK

Donald A. Hodges School of Music, University of North Carolina at Greensboro, USA

David Huron School of Music, Ohio State University, USA

Patrik N. Juslin Department of Psychology, Uppsala University, Sweden

Dianna T. Kenny Australian Centre for Applied Research in Music Performance, Faculty of Arts, The University of Sydney, Australia

Stefan Koelsch Department of Psychology, University of Sussex, UK

Vladimir J. Konečni Department of Psychology, University of California, San Diego, USA

Simon Liljeström Department of Psychology, Uppsala University, Sweden

Erik Lindström School of Management, Blekinge Institute of Technology, Sweden

Lars-Olov Lundqvist Centre of Rehabilitation Research, Örebro University Hospital, Sweden

Elizabeth Hellmuth Margulis Music Department, University of Arkansas, USA

Jennifer A. McDonald Department of Social and Developmental Psychology, University of Cambridge, UK

Gary E. McPherson School of Music, University of Melbourne, Australia

Adrian C. North School of Life Sciences, Heriot Watt University, UK

Isabelle Peretz Department of Psychology, University of Montreal, Canada

Peter J. Rentfrow Department of Social and Developmental Psychology, University of Cambridge, UK

Adena Schachner Department of Psychology, Harvard University, USA

Emery Schubert School of English, Media, and Performing Arts, University of New South Wales, Australia

Walter A. Siebel Conflict Research Center Wiesbaden, Germany

Dean Keith Simonton Department of Psychology, University of California, Davis, USA

John A. Sloboda School of Psychology, Keele University, UK

Michael H. Thaut Center for Biomedical Research, Colorado State University, USA

Willam Forde Thompson Music, Sound, and Performance Lab, Macquarie University, Australia

Renee Timmers Department of Music, University of Sheffield, UK

Sandra E. Trehub Department of Psychology, University of Toronto, Canada

Daniel Västfjäll Department of Applied Acoustics, Chalmers University of Technology, Sweden

Barbara L. Wheeler School of Music, University of Louisville, USA

Robert H. Woody School of Music, University of Nebraska, Lincoln, USA

Marcel Zentner Department of Psychology, University of York, UK

PART I

OVERTURE

....

CHAPTER 1

INTRODUCTION

AIMS, ORGANIZATION, AND TERMINOLOGY

....

PATRIK N. JUSLIN AND
JOHN A. SLOBODA

THIS volume results from and reflects the enormous interest among both researchers and lay people in the many and complex ways that music may relate to our emotions. Music is often regarded as a 'language of the emotions' (Cooke, 1959). It expresses emotions that listeners perceive, recognize, or are 'moved' by. Furthermore, several studies have suggested that the most common motive for listening to music is to influence emotions—listeners use music to change emotions, to release emotions, to match their current emotion, to enjoy or to comfort themselves, or to relieve stress. Indeed, there is some indication that most people experience music (somehow, somewhere) every day of their lives, often with an accompanying affective reaction of some sort (e.g. nostalgic recognition of a favourite song on the radio while driving a car, frustration directed at the music at the regular shop, joy when listening to the excellent performance at the evening concert, or a sad mood evoked by the soundtrack of a late-night movie).

Yet the fact that music may evoke strong emotions is a mystery, which has fascinated scholars since ancient Greece (Budd, 1985). Why do we react to music with emotions, even though music does not appear to have implications for our life goals? How can 'mere sound' engage us so? To explain how and why music may evoke emotion in listeners is all the more important, since music is already used in a number of applications in society that presume its effectiveness in evoking emotions, such as film music, marketing, and music therapy. Indeed, evidence is slowly accumulating that music has benefits for health, which could be exploited systematically to the extent that we achieve an understanding of the underlying mechanisms. Emotion is also central to the process of creating music, whether in composing or performing music. Numerous musicians have attested to the crucial role of emotions in writing, learning, and interpreting music. In fact, many musicians chose to become musicians because of their valued emotional experiences with music from an early age.

Given the important role of emotion in music, one would expect it to have occupied a central position in music psychology. Yet the topic was neglected during the 1960s, 1970s, and 1980s, and it was only in the last decade that the field received well-deserved attention. (For a discussion of some of the reasons for the slow progress, see Chapter 33, this volume.) The first edited volume in music psychology devoted entirely to emotions in music was published in 2001. *Music and emotion: Theory and research* (Juslin & Sloboda, 2001) sold 5,040 copies (30 March 2009), has been widely cited (258 times on Google Scholar, on 30 March 2009), and arguably contributed to rapid development in the field. We were gratified by the positive response to the book, which many scholars have used as part of their selected readings for students.

Since the publication of *Music and emotion*, the broader field of *affective science*—the multi-disciplinary study of affect in all its forms—has blossomed. Recent years have seen the publication of new journals (e.g. *Emotion, Emotion Review*) and handbooks (e.g. *Handbook of affective sciences*, Davidson, Scherer, & Goldsmith, 2003; *Handbook of emotions*, Lewis, Haviland-Jones, & Barrett, 2008; *Handbook of emotion elicitation and assessment*, Coan & Allen, 2007). The study of affective processes has become a mature field, featuring its own standardized measures, theoretical debates, and subdisciplines. Current publications suggest an increasing diversity and interdisciplinary cross-fertilization. This trend is also reflected in the study of music and emotion: never before has the field featured so many different topics, theories, and methods—as illustrated, for instance, by the diversity of approaches represented at the *International Conference on Music and Emotion* in Durham (September, 2009), where, at time of writing (March 2009), over 120 abstracts had been submitted. Special issues devoted to music and emotion in journals (e.g. Juslin & Zentner, 2002) have confirmed the healthy state of the field.

Although this flurry of research is a cause for celebration, the rapid progress has meant that *Music and emotion* has quickly grown outdated. Several findings of relevance to an understanding of music and emotion have been published in various outlets since work commenced on *Music and emotion* about ten years ago. And so it is time to take stock of the latest developments, and to offer an up-to-date account of the field. In making plans for a revised version, we decided that, rather than merely update *Music and emotion* in a second edition, we would expand the book and turn it into a genuine handbook featuring many new contributions.

The final commentary in *Music and emotion* written by the editors identified a number of shortcomings of the research at that time, and also suggested various future directions for research. Among the issues mentioned were the difficulty of measuring emotions (especially using multiple measures), the narrowness of domains studied (e.g. little developmental and cross-cultural work), and the lack of common definitions of key terms. It was also noted (in the Introduction) that the field had still not reached a stage where it could provide a body of knowledge for application to practical problems. Moreover, in hindsight it seemed clear that certain topics were not sufficiently covered in *Music and emotion* (e.g. musical preferences, psychophysiology, aesthetics, personality). The present handbook is intended to address the issues and shortcomings identified in the commentary, and in reviews of the previous book. The aim is also to provide a volume that, in true handbook fashion, provides useful practical information that can guide researchers, for instance regarding the measurement of emotions. More generally, the handbook provides a representative coverage of approaches that may be said to define the field of music and emotion, in all its breadth and depth. As was the case in the previous book, the purpose of the handbook is both summative and formative: we aim to summarize what is currently known about music and emotion, but we also intend to stimulate further research in promising directions that have been little studied.

The book is organized into eight sections. The first section consists of this introductory chapter, which describes the aims of the book and provides working definitions of key terms and distinctions used throughout the book, largely based on increasingly consensual views in the affective sciences more generally. The definitions and distinctions were circulated among the authors prior to the writing of the book (discussed further below).

The second section offers multi-disciplinary perspectives on music and emotion from philosophy, musicology, psychology, neurobiology, anthropology, and sociology. This part consists of updated and revised chapters from the much-cited second section of *Music and emotion*. Although emotion is primarily a psychological concept— given its focus on mental processes and behaviour—the study of musical emotions often transcends the traditional lines of inquiry. Thus, important insights can also be gleaned from other perspectives represented here, alongside psychology. The chapters in Section II of the book are ordered to reflect both historical primacy (philosophy and musicology are arguably the oldest disciplines to consider music and emotion) and a progression from more individualist perspectives (as epitomized by psychology and biology) to social and cultural perspectives (as reflected in anthropology and sociology). The authors were encouraged to make their chapters accessible to a wide range of readers from different disciplines, and to strive towards consistency across different levels of analysis. Each chapter begins with a description of the discipline and its scientific approach to music and emotion, followed by a tour of 'classic' themes and studies—as well as more recent trends. In a way, Section II provides the intellectual foundations (and challenges) for the study of music and emotion, highlighting the scope and complexity of the phenomenon.

Most work on music and emotion today involves an empirical approach to the topic. Section III of the book contains methodologically oriented chapters on the measurement of emotions through different channels. Emotion is increasingly regarded as a phenomenon that features various subcomponents (e.g. subjective feeling, emotional expression, physiological reaction, action tendencies), which can all be used to measure emotional responses (Juslin & Västfjäll, 2008; Scherer & Zentner, 2001; for a recent review, see Mauss & Robinson, 2009). There continue to be debates concerning whether music can arouse 'genuine', 'everyday', or 'garden variety' emotions, and, if so, which emotions they might be. Thus, an important goal is to improve the ways that responses to music are measured, so that more valid conclusions about the experienced states can be drawn. Accordingly, Section III features scholarly reviews of several kinds of measures of musically induced emotions—self-report ('post performance' vs. 'continuous response' methods), psychophysiological indices (e.g. heart rate, respiration), emotional expression (e.g. facial electromyography), functional neuroimaging (PET, fMRI), and various indirect or implicit measures (e.g. effects on information processing: perception, judgement, and memory). Each chapter both reviews evidence associated with respective types of measure and offers practical guidelines concerning how the measure can be used in music-emotion research. This section highlights a surprisingly broad range of measures that may be used to explore musical emotions. Although self-report will probably remain the most crucial and widely used type of measure (as reflected in this section by the inclusion of two chapters), it is clearly in the interest of the field to expand the methodological toolbox to circumvent the commonly noted problems associated with self-reports. Section III will assist music researchers to be better equipped for a multi-method approach to music and emotion.

Sections IV and V address how emotion enters into different aspects of musical behaviour, both the making of music and its consumption. Hence, Section IV features contributions which explore the musical means that composers and performers may utilize to express emotions, as well as how emotions may affect the creative process itself. Topics addressed include melodic originality and 'arousal potential', biographical antecedents of composers' style development, structural contributions to emotional expression, performers' motivation and interpretation of music, performance anxiety, and musical communication of specific emotions. It is suggested that emotions play an essential part in the lives of those who produce music. Section V focuses on the listener's musical experience, featuring chapters on everyday uses of music, aesthetics, 'peak' experiences, 'thrills', musical expectancy, and modelling of psychological mechanisms. These chapters illustrate—among other things—where, when, and why people listen to music, which emotions (or other sensations such as 'thrills') they tend to experience, and why music might induce both 'everyday emotions' and more refined 'aesthetic' responses in the listener. The final chapter of the section offers a set of theoretical predictions implying that depending on the precise induction mechanism involved, different individual and social factors will play key roles in determining the emotional response (this is followed up in Section VI).

Section VI covers developmental, personality, and social factors. Chapters in this section provide reviews of such topics as the development of affective responses to music, individual differences in personality and music preferences, influences of affect on music choice, public use of music in social manipulation, politics, and mass movements, and cross-cultural studies. These chapters highlight the multitude of personal and social factors that directly or indirectly shape emotional responses in connection with music. As such they will help to extend as well as qualify the empirical findings discussed in the previous sections of the book.

Section VII showcases the most important current applications involving the relationship of music and emotion. A significant trend in recent years has been an increasing emphasis on the practical value or usefulness of music-psychological research in society—on whether and how research may contribute to solving 'real-world' problems (for a discussion, see Sloboda, 2005). Accordingly, this section includes chapters on established as well as new applications in music education, music therapy, health, film music, and marketing. The chapters illustrate the potential importance of research on music and emotion to greater society.

The final section, *Encore*, consists of a commentary by the editors in which they draw together the 'threads' from the previous chapters. The editors comment on the history of the field, summarize the current state of affairs, as well as propose future directions for the field. In particular, the editors try to identify major problems that remain to be tackled and suggest possible ways of resolving them in future research. In predicting future trends, the editors are guided by the findings from a brief questionnaire to the contributors, in which they were able to nominate their 'top priorities' for future research.

As indicated above, the book consists of a combination of revised chapters from *Music and emotion* and new chapters commissioned especially for this volume. Table 1.1 shows an overview of the featured chapters of the book in terms of whether each chapter is an update of a previous chapter, a major revision of a previous chapter, or a new chapter. As can be seen, 22 of the 33 chapters (67 per cent) are new contributions not included in the previous book in any form. With such a large proportion of new material, we felt it was justified to change the title of the book, to reflect its more inclusive approach.

To enhance the quality and coherence of the handbook, the authors received a set of guidelines prior to writing. Among the 'briefs' given to the authors, were that they should:

- State early in the chapter the overall purpose and structure of the chapter
- Use key terms such as *emotion*, *mood*, and *feeling* in accordance with a provided set of working definitions to facilitate integration and clear communication among researchers
- Provide clear definitions of all terms and concepts not covered in the working definitions
- Try as far as possible to avoid scientific jargon
- Try to make the literature review as up to date as possible, through literature searches in appropriate databases; further make the coverage as international as possible and consider the generalizability of theories and findings across different musical traditions
- Emphasize the research questions that are addressed and why they are important
- Discuss theoretical implications and future prospects in the specific area
- Indicate gaps in the literature
- If possible, consider practical implications of research in their area
- Suggest two or three state-of-the-art books or articles for 'further recommended reading'.

The published chapters demonstrate a gratifying willingness on the part of the authors to work coherently within the spirit of these guidelines.

Table 1.1 Overview of chapters featured in the *Handbook of music and emotion*

I.	Overture	
1.	Introduction: aims, organization, and terminology—Juslin & Sloboda	New
II.	Multi-disciplinary perspectives	
2.	Emotions expressed and aroused by music: philosophical perspectives—Davies	Update
3.	Emotion in culture and history: perspectives from musicology—Cook & Dibben	Update
4.	At the interface between the inner and outer world: psychological perspectives—Sloboda and Juslin	Major revision
5.	Towards a neurobiology of musical emotions—Peretz	Major revision
6.	Exploring the habitus of listening: anthropological perspectives—Becker	Update
7.	Emotion as social emergence: perspectives from music sociology—DeNora	Update
III.	Measurement	
8.	Self-report measures and models—Zentner & Eerola	New
9.	Continuous self-report methods—Schubert	New
10.	Indirect perceptual, cognitive, and behavioural measures—Västfjäll	New
11.	Psychophysiological measures—Hodges	New
12.	Functional neuroimaging—Koelsch, Fritz, & Siebel	New
IV.	Music making	
13.	Emotion and composition in classical music: historiometric perspectives—Simonton	Update
14.	The role of structure in the musical expression of emotions—Gabrielsson & Lindström	Update
15.	Emotion and motivation in the lives of performers—Woody & McPherson	New
16.	Negative emotions in music making: performance anxiety—Kenny	New
17.	Expression and communication of emotion in music performance—Juslin & Timmers	Major revision
V.	Music listening	
18.	Music in everyday life: the role of emotions—Sloboda	New
19.	Experimental aesthetics and liking for music—Hargreaves & North	New
20.	Strong experiences with music—Gabrielsson	Major revision
21.	Musical expectancy and thrills—Huron & Margulis	New
22.	How does music evoke emotions? Exploring the underlying mechanisms—Juslin, Liljeström, Västfjäll, & Lundqvist	New
VI.	Development, personality, and social factors	
23.	Music and affect in the early years—Trehub, Hannon, & Schachner	New
24.	Preference, personality, and emotion—Rentfrow & MacDonald	New
25.	The influence of affect on music choice—Konečni	New

26.	Politics, mediation, social context, and public use—Garofalo	New
27.	Cross-cultural similarities and differences—Thompson & Balkwill	New
VII.	Applications	
28.	Music education: the role of affect—Hallam	New
29.	Music therapy—Thaut & Wheeler	New
30.	Music, health, and well-being—Hanser	New
31.	Music as a source of emotion in film—Cohen	Update
32.	Music and marketing—North & Hargreaves	New
VIII.	Encore	
33.	The past, present, and future of music and emotion research—Juslin & Sloboda	New

Note: The right-hand column shows whether each chapter is an update of a previous chapter, a major revision of a previous chapter, or a new chapter.

As noted above, the authors were asked to adhere to a certain terminology in this book. A major problem that has plagued the field of music and emotion is terminological confusion. Researchers have tended to use words such as *affect, emotion, feeling,* and *mood* in different ways, which has made communication and integration difficult. Sometimes, researchers have used the same term to refer to different things. At other times, researchers have used different terms to refer to the same thing. Although we are aware that most researchers have their own preferred terms, for the sake of clear communication it is better to use a common vocabulary, grounded in the growing consensus in 'affective science' more generally (see e.g. Davidson, Scherer, & Goldsmith, 2003, p. xiii; Oatley, Keltner, & Jenkins, 2006, pp. 29–31).

Accordingly, we have provided simple working definitions of 'key terms' in music and emotion for the current handbook (Table 1.2). Authors were asked to use the terms according to this scheme as far as possible in their contributions. We tried to keep the definitions simple in order to not 'prejudge' theoretical issues that may divide different contributors to the book. We recognize that researchers may take radically different views on many of the phenomena covered. Thus, the definitions focus on what *phenomenon* each word refers to, rather than on how the phenomenon should be explained. The important thing in the present context is that the reader will understand what is meant by each term throughout the book.

As seen in Table 1.2, the term *affect* is used as an 'umbrella term' that covers different affective phenomena. Musical affect thus defined comprises anything from music preference, mood, and emotion to aesthetic and even spiritual experiences. This book covers all of this to some extent. This might suggest that the volume should have been termed the *Handbook of music and affect*. However, despite the effort by

Table 1.2 Definitions of key terms as used in the *Handbook of music and emotion*

Affect	This is used as an umbrella term that covers all evaluative—or 'valenced' (positive/negative)—states (e.g. emotion, mood, preference). The term denotes such phenomena in general. If that is not intended, a more precise term (e.g. mood, emotion, preference) is used instead.
Emotion	This term is used to refer to a quite brief but intense affective reaction that usually involves a number of sub-components—subjective feeling, physiological arousal, expression, action tendency, and regulation—that are more or less 'synchronized'. Emotions focus on specific 'objects' and last minutes to a few hours (e.g. happiness, sadness).
Musical emotions	This term is used only as a short term for 'emotions that were somehow induced by music', without any further implications about the precise nature of these emotions. (If an author believes that there are certain emotions that are 'unique' to music in some way, this is explicitly stated.)
Mood	This term is used to denote such affective states that are lower in intensity than emotions, that do not have a clear 'object', and that are much longer lasting than emotions (i.e. several hours to days). Moods do not involve a synchronized response in components like expression and physiology (e.g. gloomy).
Feeling	This term is used to refer to the subjective experience of emotions or moods. Feeling is one component of an emotion that is typically measured via verbal self-report.
Arousal	This term is used to refer to physical activation of the autonomic nervous system. Physiological arousal is one of the components of an emotional response, but could also occur in the absence of emotion (e.g. due to exercise). Arousal is often reflected in the 'feeling' component (i.e. the subjective experience).
Preference	This term is used to refer to longer-term affective evaluations of objects or persons with a low intensity (e.g. liking of a particular type of music).
Personality trait	This term is used to refer to relatively stable affective dispositions, which are characterized by low intensity and a behavioural impact which is usually the result of an interaction with situational factors (e.g. a neurotic personality).
Emotion induction	This term is used to refer to all instances where music evokes an emotion in a listener—regardless of the nature of the process that evoked the emotion.
Emotion perception	This term is used to refer to all instances where a listener perceives or recognizes emotions in music (e.g. 'a sad expression'), without necessarily feeling an emotion him- or herself.
Communication	This term is used to refer to a process where a sender conveys an emotion to a receiver who is able to decode the emotion concerned. Note that the term 'communication' is used regardless of whether the transmitted emotion is 'genuinely felt' or simply 'portrayed' by the performer in a symbolic manner. (Music's potential to convey referential information is separate from the issue of whether the music is the result of felt emotion or a sending intention, or both.)

some researchers to define the field as 'the affective sciences', in practice the field is still referred to as, and recognized mainly in terms of, *emotion* (e.g. 'the study of emotion and emotion-related processes', Coan & Allen, 2007, Preface). This is seen in all the journals in the field: despite their increasingly broad coverage, current journals use the word 'emotion' (e.g. *Motivation and Emotion*, *Cognition & Emotion*, *Emotion*, *Emotion Review*), rather than the word 'affect'. In accordance with this practice, we decided to name this book the *Handbook of music and emotion*, despite its inclusion of a wide range of affective processes.

In the previous book, *Music and emotion*, we saluted two 'giants' in the field who have had a lasting influence: Leonard Meyer (who sadly passed away on 27 December 2007, and whose book, *Emotion and meaning in music* (1956), remains the most cited book in the field) and Alf Gabrielsson (to whom the volume was dedicated to coincide with his retirement). The present volume is instead dedicated to the field itself, comprising hundreds of researchers and scores of institutions (research centres, scholarly bodies, journals), to celebrate a vibrant field approaching its coming of age. It is likely that this volume will become outdated even more quickly than the previous one, but as far as the present field is concerned, that would clearly be a good thing.

Who is this book for? The editors and chapter authors are predominantly teachers and researchers, situated in universities and music conservatoires. It is inevitable (and intended) that our primary audience is the academic community. The book is designed to be a resource for established researchers in the field, a developmental aid for early-career researchers and postgraduate research students, and a compendium of relevant materials to assist students at various levels. However, as was the case for *Music and emotion*, we expect the book to attract interest from practising musicians, and also from lay readers who are fascinated by music and are willing to expend some mental energy in grappling with the many rigorous and systematic approaches that modern academic study offers. If our collective efforts can provide some new insights and effective means to a deeper engagement with this most intimate yet inscrutable activity that so many of us share and value, then we will consider those efforts to have been worthwhile.

REFERENCES

Budd, M. (1985). *Music and the emotions. The philosophical theories.* London: Routledge.

Coan, J. A., & Allen, J. B. (eds) (2007). *Handbook of emotion elicitation and assessment.* Oxford: Oxford University Press.

Cooke, D. (1959). *The language of music.* London: Oxford University Press.

Davidson, R. J., Scherer, K. R., & Goldsmith, H. H. (eds) (2003). *Handbook of affective sciences.* Oxford: Oxford University Press.

Juslin, P. N., & Sloboda, J. A. (eds) (2001). *Music and emotion: Theory and research.* Oxford: Oxford University Press.

Juslin, P. N., & Västfjäll, D. (2008). Emotional responses to music: The need to consider underlying mechanisms. *Behavioral and Brain Sciences, 31*, 559–75.

Juslin, P. N., & Zentner, M. R. (2002). Current trends in the study of music and emotion: Overture. *Musicae Scientiae, Special Issue 2001–2*, 3–21.

Lewis, M., Haviland-Jones, J. M., & Barrett, L. F. (eds) (2008). *Handbook of emotions* (3rd edn). New York: Guilford Press.

Mauss, I., & Robinson, M. (2009). Measures of emotion: A review. *Cognition & Emotion*, 23, 209–37.

Meyer, L. B. (1956). *Emotion and meaning in music*. Chicago, IL: Chicago University Press.

Oatley, K., Keltner, D., & Jenkins, J. M. (2006). *Understanding emotions* (2nd edn). Oxford: Blackwell.

Scherer, K. R. & Zentner, M. R. (2001). Emotional effects of music: Production rules. In P. N. Juslin & J. A. Sloboda (eds), *Music and emotion: Theory and research* (pp. 361–92). Oxford: Oxford University Press.

Sloboda, J. A. (2005). Assessing music psychology research: Values, priorities, and outcomes. In J. A. Sloboda (ed.), *Exploring the musical mind: Cognition, emotion, ability, function* (pp. 395–419). Oxford: Oxford University Press.

PART II

MULTI-DISCIPLINARY PERSPECTIVES

....

EMOTIONS EXPRESSED AND AROUSED BY MUSIC

PHILOSOPHICAL PERSPECTIVES

....

STEPHEN DAVIES

2.1 PHILOSOPHY AND ITS METHODS

....

SOMETIMES philosophy seems to psychologists to be psychologizing in a fashion that is uninformed and unrestrained by empirical data. (And sometimes psychology looks to philosophers like unskilled philosophizing!) As this is the only chapter by a philosopher, I begin with an introduction outlining the nature of academic philosophy.

For most questions, one (or more) of the following strategies supplies the answer: fact-finding, scientific theorizing, calculating, voting, and legislating. The natural and social sciences rely on the first three of these methods. Some questions are not satisfactorily resolved by their use, however. The issues these questions present are neither empirical nor merely matters of opinion—they are 'philosophical'. 'Philosophy' comes to connote the recalcitrant residue of questions which remain after all the (other) branches of knowledge and taste have taken the questions they are equipped to answer. The fact that philosophical questions are immune from empirical data suggests, perhaps, that they arise from deep conceptual confusions or subtleties, and that it is the purpose of philosophy to untangle these knotted skeins.

Some of the questions of philosophy are distinctive to it, such as many of those addressed by metaphysics, ethics, and logic. But also, philosophical queries are generated by consideration of foundational issues in all areas and disciplines, and so there is philosophy of art, of science, of mathematics, of feminism, of medicine, of mind, and so on.

Some classical examples of philosophical questions are these. What is truth? Is causality a natural relation or, instead, merely how constant conjunction sometimes is interpreted by human observers? What is identity? Is more than one consideration (such as merit and need) relevant to justice and, if so, are these different aspects mutually commensurable? How is the good to be characterized? What is time? A few moment's reflection should make clear that the answers cannot be settled by an investigation looking at the sorts of facts tested by science. The usual scientific methods of inquiry typically presuppose certain answers to such questions, and the use of such approaches thereby prejudges the outcome of the study. To take another case, how could science analyse the nature of scientific facts without begging the outcome? And another: if empirical facts under-determine the explanatory theories we apply to them, we cannot choose between theories, as we will want to do in distinguishing pseudo-science and psycho-babble from legitimate disciplines, solely by citing the facts, because what counts as a fact and how it is significant is disputed between the contested theories. Also, if we are indeed enmeshed in some subtle confusion about a topic, we may be confused in how to describe and respond to (further) empirical evidence.

Appeals to the support of empirical data for experimental hypotheses and theories become questionable more often and quickly than is widely recognized. Consider this example: in testing if expressive musical effects are cross-culturally perceivable, Gregory and Varney (1996) noted that the European spring and the Indian monsoon share the same associations with growth and renewal. They compared the responses of European and Indian listeners to excerpts from Vivaldi's 'Spring' and the monsoon *raga*, '*Rag Kirvani*', but found no correlation to support the claim that this expressive effect is cross-culturally recognized. But if music's expressiveness depends as much or more on its dynamic pattern and other sonic effects as on external associations, as seems plausible (and is argued further in Section 2.6.1), and if the dynamic pattern of Europe's spring imitated in Vivaldi's music is unlike that of the Indian monsoon as presented in the *raga*, as seems likely, then the result does not disconfirm the experiment's hypothesis. Rather, it calls into question whether the methods adopted provide tests relevant to that hypothesis.

A quick rejoinder might be that we can also empirically test whether music's expressiveness is purely associational, depends on intrinsic music features alone, or relies on some combination of these two. But I doubt that this is a simple matter. After all, the issue is not whether music comes with associations, but is with the extent to which they are arbitrary and external. It may be that some music attracts the associations it does precisely because it has intrinsic expressive tendencies. And the argument will soon become one not about whether the associations might have been different but instead about whether there are relevant similarities between the different associations that (hypothetically) might have been made. The significance of counterfactual scenarios of this kind is by no means easy to quantify and the attempt to do so is almost certainly bound to stir up theoretical debate and conceptual analysis.

There is a more abstract way of making the point. Instead of assuming, as Gregory and Varney did in their experiment, that music's expressive character is primarily a function of arbitrary, external associations, we could test that assumption. But in doing so we must make new assumptions about which differentia are crucial to determining the outcome of our test. This might seem innocuous if these new assumptions can also be tested empirically, and so on for the further assumptions this new test would rely on, and ditto for the test of the new test, and so on down the chain. But in fact, where hard and disputed cases come up frequently and, as is always the case, more than one theory is compatible with a given set of data, the empirical reliability of any such tests is soon in question. Rather than each successive experiment in the chain confirming the foundation on which its predecessor stands until we descend to the very roots of knowledge, we strike empirically impenetrable bedrock in no time at all.

To say that the philosophical method is non-empirical is not to imply that philosophy is indifferent to the facts of science. Philosophical analyses must be consistent with the facts, or with interpretations of what these are. (For examples of philosophical studies that make extensive reference to relevant scientific literature, see Davies, in press a; Higgins, 2006; Nussbaum, 2007; Robinson, 2005.) But philosophical analyses must go beyond the facts in resolving the problems, paradoxes, and inconsistencies they can seem to generate. What is needed often is not more facts but a clarification of the issues raised by those that are available. The most familiar notions can produce conceptual puzzles, and then it is not more facts but a deepening of our current understanding, or new interpretations of the resident data, that is needed. Sometimes philosophical investigations are suggestive of new empirical questions, and here science takes over again. At other times, a grasp of unexpected conceptual connections or distinctions enables us to overcome the mental cramps that formerly afflicted us.

To bring out their non-empirical nature, philosophical puzzles often describe two things that are alike in their appearance or empirical features but which strike us as conceptually very different, and then asks what makes that difference. For instance, Descartes wondered how he knew he was not presently dreaming, given that he could dream that he was awake. Others have explored how we are to describe the distinction between one's arm's being moved and the action of one's moving one's arm, or how Marcel Duchamp's readymades could be artworks where their lookalike, unappropriated counterparts were not.

It can be that nothing hangs on how we answer the philosophical questions before us. In that case, we will come to see that it is for us to decide which way to go, since there is no truth of the matter to be discovered. And it can be that, on examination, philosophical questions turn out to be nonsensical. But it cannot be assumed from the beginning, however, that all philosophical questions are empty, trivial, or silly. In many cases, how we propose to resolve a philosophical question can have far-reaching implications for other cases, for overall consistency within our folk practices, for the power and fecundity of our explanatory models, and for coherence and consistency in our theories.

Not all philosophical questions are weighty. 'Is the karaoke singer a co-performer with the people on the accompanying DVD?' is a philosophical question that provokes us to consider the individuating conditions of performances and recordings, but it is not in the same league as 'What is the meaning of life?' And not all weighty questions are as exciting as this last. Also, the significance of the topic under discussion is often not apparent in the examples in terms of which it is discussed. These frequently are mundane or commonplace, either because it is appropriate to begin with uncontroversial paradigms or to avoid illustrations that attract attention to themselves, rather than to what is at issue. Philosophers who discuss the expression of emotion in music regularly offer the slow movement of Beethoven's *Eroica* as illustrating musical sadness. This does not mean they deny that other pieces are expressive, or that other emotions can be expressed in music. Instead, it indicates that even such a humdrum case already presents in a graphic form the puzzle that troubles the philosopher.

Sometimes, Anglo-American analytic philosophy, which is the approach of this chapter, is contrasted with Continental philosophy. The differences are largely matters of degree or style. In terms of the philosophy of music, Continental approaches sometimes describe an entire metaphysical system and consider music in order to locate it within that system; or they view music in terms of larger socio-political or psychological models of human behaviour, such as Marxist or psychoanalytic ones; or, again, they approach it from the perspective of general theories that are semiotic, structuralist, or deconstructionist. And when they do focus on music as such, they are likely to emphasize the subjective response and the phenomenology of musical experience. By contrast, analytic philosophy is less theory driven and politically motivated. It is centred on perceived 'problems' or 'questions', rather than on a canon of works by great philosophers. The approach is (often) piecemeal, tackling issues one by one as their relevance emerges. The focus falls on interpersonal judgements and public criteria, rather than the idiosyncratic or personal.

Because it is driven by provocative problem cases, and because the philosopher of music is interested in the listener's states and responses mainly for the light they shed on the music, the philosopher's approach can look narrow and selective. For a start, the philosopher will focus only on those listeners who are positioned (by training or prolonged exposure) to understand and appreciate the music is question—see Section 2.5 below—and only when they listen attentively and without distraction, and then will home in on only those responses that challenge commonsense or philosophical theory in some way.

Here is an example: music often comes charged with contingent but powerful associations, whether private to the individual or widely shared across the culture, and these regularly affect how listeners respond to and describe the music they listen to. Philosophers rarely spend much time on these common reactions, however (but see Davies, 1994, Ch. 1). That is both because, to the extent that the connection is arbitrary, it is unlikely to reveal the music's character and because there is nothing philosophically puzzling about the fact that music affects the listener in this manner.

Other reactions—for instance, ones in which the listener is surprised when the music takes an unexpected course or is bored by its tedious repetitiveness, or in which the listener is intrigued by the performer's unusual interpretation or irritated by careless wrong notes—are directed to the music's or performance's features but are again not philosophically puzzling. A different case—that in which the listener apparently catches the mood of the music, and thereby comes to feel, say, sad, without believing of the music the kinds of things that are usually relevant to a response of sadness, such as that it is unfortunate or regrettable—does attract the attention of the philosopher, however, because it calls into question a widely held theory according to which emotions arise if and only if the appropriate emotion-relevant beliefs are held. The issue now becomes one of whether we should doubt the credibility of listeners who report that their reaction mirrors the music's expressive character, or of whether we can reconcile the response with the theory it seems to contradict, or of whether we should revise or abandon the theory, and if so, for what.

The philosophical discussion of the listener's response to music's expressiveness has been structured to a large extent by the issue just described, as I outline further in subsequent sections. The point to be made here is one about why philosophers circumscribe the topic as they do. Their concerns are more limited than those that psychologists are likely to have. A psychologist may be legitimately interested in how music affects the listener when he or she is not attending to it, is quite unfamiliar with its kind or style, is influenced in his or her reaction by personal or social circumstances not directly dependent on or conditioning of the music's features, is moved by contingent associations borne by the music or that he or she brings to it, and so on. In other words, the psychologist may be as much concerned with what the listener's response reveals about him or her as in what it reveals about the music, or in cataloguing the many indirect as well as direct ways in which the music might affect her.

Moreover, some kinds of studies, such as those that seek universals underpinning our experiences of musical features such as consonance, closure, and expression, require musical 'innocents'. For instance, if one seeks such universals by testing if (or which) expressive musical effects can be recognized cross-culturally, it is important to work with people who are not already habituated to the music in question. (As I explain in Section 2.6.4, a number of cross-cultural studies of music's expressiveness fail in this regard.)

Of special interest, then, are studies on newborns and babies, since they are (largely) free of cultural influence. (For a review of the literature, see Trehub, 2003; for a critical assessment, see McDermott & Hauser, 2005, and Patel, 2008.) Yet the interpretation of experimental data produced by such studies is fraught with difficulty. First, even newborns may have prior exposure to music, and have acquired implicit knowledge of its local grammars and styles. Further, there is the danger of generalizing reactions to four-note 'melodies' and isolated chords to the much wider and richer sonic context in which genuinely musical pieces are found. As well, changes in the direction of attentional focus or of the frontal hemisphere that is activated may signify the positive or negative valence of a response, but it is another thing to characterize that evaluation as an emotional reaction or to equate it with a judgement of overall musical value or goodness. In music, what is experienced as a discord depends at least in part on the musical context and grammar: recall that major thirds were discords in medieval music, that we are generally happy to compromise just intonation for the compensatory advantages of equal temperament, and that scales can contain all manner of intervals even if they inevitably respect the identity of octaves and usually possess a perfect fifth or fourth. And discord plays a role no less essential than that of concord in progressing the musical flow. Indeed, a discord might be deliciously piquant, and enjoyable as such, when it tips the musical direction toward a much later return to the tonic, and even brutally raw, unresolved discords may present qualities to be savoured or be pleasantly shocking. Similarly, in music sad does not equal bad. Personally, I doubt that the minor triad alone, divorced from a tonal and harmonic context, has an expressive leaning either way, but if I am wrong and the isolated minor triad is somehow less enjoyable than a major one, this says nothing about how we should comparatively evaluate works in major and minor keys, and it certainly does not predetermine the overall expressive character of the work.

The philosophical literature on music aesthetics has displayed the kinds of biases also common in other music-focused academic disciplines: a concentration on Western high-art music from 1750–1920, on composers and their works, and on live performances, all from the perspective of the listener rather than the composer, performer, or analyst. To some extent this imbalance is being redressed, with more being written on vocal music generally, on rock music, popular music, and jazz, on non-Western kinds of music, on functional music, on performances and interpretative practice, on recordings, and on electronic and computer music.

2.2 Ways in which music's expression of emotions is philosophically problematic

In what follows, I concentrate on philosophical discussions of music's expressive character. An obvious question asks how music could be expressive of emotion, which is how we seem to experience many pieces, when it is non-sentient. Depending on how we answer this first query, we are led to others. For instance, if we argue that expressive predicates apply only metaphorically to music, we might then be puzzled at the strength of the response music is capable of eliciting from the listener.

The first problem has dominated philosophical discussions about music and emotion over the past three decades. It observes that purely instrumental music is not the kind of thing that can express emotions.[1] Music is not sentient and neither is its relation to occurrent emotions such that it could express them. The second problem concerns

---

[1] The focus falls on instrumental music simply because the problem of music's expressive powers is at its most acute where music is divorced from words, narrative, and drama.

the listener's response, where this mirrors the music's expressive character. When listeners are saddened by the music's sadness, apparently they lack the beliefs that normally underpin such a reaction; for example, they do not think the music suffers, or that the music's expressiveness is unfortunate and regrettable. The third perplexity concerns negative responses elicited by music, such as the sad one just mentioned. Why do listeners enjoy and revisit works that, on their own account, incline them to feel sad? (For a summary of philosophical approaches to these three topics and more besides, see Levinson, 1997.) Before addressing these puzzles, it is useful to examine philosophical theories regarding the nature of the emotions.

2.3 THEORIES OF THE EMOTIONS

It was once thought, by Descartes for instance, that emotions involve the subject's awareness of the perturbations of his or her animal spirits. It was the dynamic structure of this inner motion, along with the feeling of pleasure or displeasure with which it was apprehended, that distinguished the various emotions. Call this the 'hydraulic theory' of the emotions. In this view, emotions are experiences passively undergone by the subject; they are only contingently connected to their causes and to their behavioral manifestations; they are essentially non-cognitive.

In the latter half of the twentieth century, an alternative account, usually called the 'cognitive theory', was developed (see Lyons, 1980; Solomon, 1976).[2] This allows that emotions possess a phenomenological profile, but regards this as only one element among several, all of which are necessary and none of which is sufficient alone for an emotion's occurrence. Emotions may be characterized by physiological changes, but, more importantly, they are object-focused. Emotions are directed toward their objects. This means they are usually outward facing, as when I fear the lion that is before me, though the emotion's object also may be one's own sensations or emotions, as when I am alarmed by how tense I feel or where I am ashamed that I am angry. Moreover, emotions involve the categorization of their objects; for instance, if the emotion is one of fear its object must be viewed as harmful, and if the emotion is one of envy its object must be viewed as something both desirable and not already controlled or possessed. In addition, they include attitudes toward their objects; for example, though I judge you to be injured, my emotional response will depend on whether this is a source of concern, satisfaction, or indifference to me. Also, particular emotions find expression

---

[2] The term 'cognitive' has a somewhat different meaning in philosophical theories of emotion than it has in psychological theories. In the latter, the term implies a focus on underlying information-processing mechanisms, whereas in philosophical theories it refers to beliefs, imaginings, thoughts, intentions, desires, and like states of consciousness.

in typical behaviours; if I pity you I will try to comfort you and to change your situation for the better, and if I fear you I will fight, flee, or seek protection.

Philosophers disagree in the versions of the cognitive theory they espouse. Some insist that emotions require a belief in their objects' existence, while others think that other cognitive attitudes such as make-believe can also play the role of securing the emotion's object. Some hold that emotions can be individuated in terms of their sensational patterns, without reference to the emotion's propositional component, whereas others regard its cognitive ingredient as crucial to its identification. (For a useful summary of the literature, see Deigh, 1994.)

When psychologists rediscovered the mind, toward the end of the twentieth century, they tended to adopt the cognitive theory of the emotions (for example, see Lazarus, 1984, 1991; Oatley, 1992; Oatley & Johnson-Laird, 1987; Ortony, Clore, & Collins, 1988; Scherer, 1988). Nevertheless, the view has been criticized by psychologists (e.g. see Damasio, 1994; Ekman, 1992; LeDoux, 1998; Zajonc, 1980, 1984) and philosophers (e.g. Griffiths, 1997) who are inclined to identify emotions with automatically triggered bodily sensations. There are a number of grounds on which the cognitive theory can be questioned: non-human animals with which humans are evolutionarily continuous display signs of an affective life, though they lack the capacity for complex cognition; the same applies to infant humans; some emotions appear to be basic in having universal displays and reflex-like, pre-reflective characters; some emotions of a phobic, compulsive character occur in the presence of cognitions that should block them.

In this vein, several philosophers (Prinz, 2004; Robinson, 2005) have defended versions of the theory first developed by William James (1884, 1894), according to which emotions are perceptions of changes in the body. Robinson (2005), who applies her theory to the arts, including music, views emotions as bodily changes caused by precognitive affective appraisals of the subject's situation; higher cognitive appraisals enter later, either to confirm or reject the initial assessment, when the emotion is already in place. Yet neo-Jamesian accounts face difficulties of their own. For instance, they typically include startle and shock as emotions but exclude love, along with all emotions that are both episodically experienced and temporally extended. And to the extent that they reduce emotions to sensations, they cannot distinguish appropriately caused genuine cases from drug-induced simulacra. Moreover, in Robinson's account of the emotions induced by music, which are of a few second's duration and constantly change in response to the flux of tension in the music, a listener to the first movement of Beethoven's Ninth Symphony experiences perhaps as many as a thousand emotions, and this seems a long way from the affective phenomenology of the listener's engagement with the music.

It seems reasonable to concede that emotions do not constitute a homogenous class. Some, such as disgust, might be primitive, automatic responses that are not susceptible in their operation to changes in the subject's cognitive state, whereas others, such as patriotism, envy, jealousy, regret, and shame, are marked more by their self-conscious, intellectual content than their sensational character. Even if there is a continuum of cases between these extremes, it is useful to distinguish between emotions (such as hope and remorse) in which the cognitive elements are prominent, malleable, and sophisticated from those (such as lust, fear, and disgust) that involve unconscious appraisals and automatic and inflexible responses. It should also be noted that otherwise similar emotions might come both in crude, non-cognitive forms and in sophisticated, thought-impregnated forms. Reflex fear of a suddenly noticed snake might be of the first kind, while fear that the economy is heading for a downturn will be of the second. And finally we should observe that artworks might elicit emotions of either variety, but those requiring imaginative engagement with narrative fictions almost inevitably elicit cognitively sophisticated responses, though movies and dramas can exploit crude reactions of the startle variety. Though one response to this diversity is to regard the emotions as not forming a natural kind and to question the status as emotions of cognitively sophisticated responses (as in Griffiths, 1997), an appropriate sensitivity to the interplay in our affective lives between evolution and culture can make for a more encompassing, reconciliatory view (as in Goldie, 2000).

Some further distinctions that may be useful are those between emotions and moods and between emotions and mere sensations (or mere feelings). These distinctions are drawn roughly within folk-psychological discourse along the following lines. Moods are not object-directed and involve rather general feelings. There can be moods of dread, depression, and happiness, but not of embarrassment or remorse, because these latter lack a distinctive experiential character and are individuated more in terms of what is cognized about their objects. Meanwhile, emotions may involve bodily sensations but are not reducible to them. A person who sits too close to the fire might experience exactly the same sensations as another who is acutely embarrassed but it is only the latter who feels an emotion.

2.4 CONSTRAINTS ON THE THEORY

Before outlining philosophers' theories of musical expressiveness, it is helpful to consider the desiderata that an acceptable theory must satisfy. We could not account for the interest and value of expression in music, or for the emotional responses music calls from the listener, unless terms like 'sad' and 'happy' retain their usual meanings in connection with music's expressiveness. So a principal task will be to indicate how, despite their manifest differences, music's expressing an emotion parallels the default case in which a person expresses an emotion they feel. In other words, an account explaining and justifying our attribution to music of predicates such as 'sad' and 'happy' must make clear how this non-primary use relates to these words' normal application to the occurrent emotions of sentient creatures.

As I see it, this constraint quickly rules out three approaches to the topic. It will not do to attempt to reduce music's expressiveness to a catalogue of technicalities and compositional devices. Even if it is true that all and only music in minor keys sounds sad, it cannot be that 'sounds sad' *means* 'is in a minor key'. Even if one can make sad music by composing it in the minor key, there must be more to the analysis of music's expressiveness than acknowledgment of this, for it is by no means clear how the music's modality relates to the very different kinds of things that make it true in the standard case that a person is expressing sadness. Musical features ground music's expressiveness, and it is interesting to discover what features those are, but identifying them is, at best, only an initial step toward an informative theory of musical expressiveness.

Another of the disallowed strategies claims that music's expressiveness is metaphorical and declines to unpack the metaphor. The claim here is not merely that, as an optional conceit, music can be described metaphorically. It is, rather, that the music itself is metaphorically expressive. (In its strongest version, the theory denies the possibility of analysing this crucial metaphor; for example, see Goodman, 1968; Scruton, 1997.) While this position obviously locates expressiveness squarely with the music, its meaning is quite mysterious. The idea that musical expression is metaphorical must itself be a metaphor, since metaphor primarily is a linguistic device depending on semantic relations for which there are no musical equivalents. This approach indicates what is puzzling about music's expression of emotions—that it is hard to see how emotion terms could retain their literal sense when predicated of music, though clearly their application to music trades somehow on their literal meaning—but it offers no solution to that puzzle.

Also unacceptable is the theory insisting that music's expressiveness is *sui generis*, that is, of its own kind and not relevantly comparable to the default case in which occurrent emotions are expressed. That approach is not offering a theory, but rather, is rejecting the philosophical enterprise that seeks one. I do not deny that, when it comes to expressiveness, music does its own thing. This is only to be expected: its medium is that of organized sound, not that of a biological organism evolved and educated to engage emotionally with its environment. What I repudiate is the suggestion that an analysis of music's expressiveness can avoid addressing if and how the musical medium realizes a kind of expressiveness that is equivalent to the biological one.

2.5 THE QUALIFIED LISTENER

One assumption common to the theories discussed below should be made explicit: listeners must be suitably qualified if they are to be capable of detecting and appreciating music's expressiveness. (Unprepared listeners may miss, or misidentify, the music's expressive character.) Qualified listeners are at home with the type of music in question, with its genre, style, and idiom. They know when the melody begins and ends, when the piece is over. They can recognize mistakes and can distinguish predictable from unusual continuations. They may not be able to articulate this knowledge, most of which is acquired through unreflective exposure to pieces of the relevant kind. Indeed, the majority of qualified listeners have no formal music education and are not familiar with the musicologist's technical vocabulary (Davies, 1994; Kivy, 1990; Levinson, 1996).

2.6 FIRST PROBLEM: THE EXPRESSION OF EMOTION IN MUSIC

When we say that something expresses an emotion, usually we mean that it publicly betrays or indicates a state that it feels. People's tears express their sadness only if they are experiencing sadness. Therefore, only sentient creatures can express emotions. Musical works are not sentient, so emotions cannot be expressed in them. Yet many of them do express emotions such as sadness and happiness. How could that be?

2.6.1 Music as a symbol

A first theory suggests that music operates as a symbol or sign, the import of which is purely associative and conventional. Though it bears no natural relation to an emotion, it comes to denote or refer to an emotion, and then to characterize it, by virtue of its place within a system. In this view, music picks out and conveys something about emotions after the manner of linguistic utterances; that is, through combining elements according to rules with the function of generating and communicating a semantic or propositional content (Coker, 1972). Musical signs, like linguistic ones, are both unlike and opaque to their referents.

Quasi-vocabularies sometimes have been described for music in its relation to the emotions (Cooke, 1959), and music is highly organized according to quasi-syntactic rules governing the well-formedness of musical strings (Lerdahl & Jackendoff, 1983; Meyer, 1956), yet there is not a semantics in music. Without that, the parallel with linguistic and other symbol systems collapses. It is not the case that music points or refers to emotions that it then goes on to describe. There are no plausible equivalents in music to predication, to propositional closure, or to any of the other functions and operators that are essential to the meaningful use of linguistic and other truth-functional systems.

An alternative theory would have it that music refers to the emotions not within the framework of a symbol system, but as a result of ad hoc, arbitrary designations and associations. For instance, certain musical gestures or phrases happen to be linked saliently with texts expressive of a given emotion and retain that connection over many years, so that purely instrumental music comes to be heard as expressive when it includes the relevant gesture or phrase (Cooke, 1959). Or music of certain kinds is linked with rites or events that otherwise are emotionally charged, and these ties persist, becoming commonplaces of musical expressiveness.

There is no denying that some aspects of music's expressiveness—for instance, the links holding between instruments and moods, as between the oboe and bucolic frames of mind, the organ and religiosity, and the trumpet and regality or bellicosity—seem to be arbitrary and conventional in ways that may depend on historical associations. Such cases notwithstanding, this last account is no more plausible or attractive than the first. It reduces music's expressiveness to something like brute naming; it indicates how music might refer to an emotion but not how it could characterize it.

These theories regard expressive music as referring beyond itself. As with language or signs relying on arbitrary associations, features intrinsic to the music are of interest only in so far as they happen to be relevant to its role as a symbolic vehicle. Though the music mediates contact with the emotion that is symbolized, listeners should not be distracted by its intrinsic qualities from pursuing its referential target. Because it is radically different from the emotions it symbolizes, it is opaque with respect to them, yet the music is of interest only in its symbolic import.

This account is seriously at odds with the phenomenology of listeners' experiences of music's expressiveness. Registering music's expressiveness is more like encountering a person who feels the emotion and shows it than like reading a description of the emotion or than like examining the word 'sad'. While the dinner bell might, through association, lead us to salivate, we do not think of it as tasty. By contrast, we experience the sadness of music as present within it. Emotion is transparently immediate in our experience of music and our awareness of music's expressiveness is not separable from or independent of our following its unfolding in all its detail. Moreover, the listener's connection is not with some general, abstract conception of the emotions, but with a specific and concrete presentation.

Any theory of musical expressiveness must acknowledge and respect the phenomenological vivacity and particularity with which music presents its expressive aspect. Here, then, is a further constraint on acceptable theories of music's expressiveness, and it is one that is failed by the theories discussed so far. Music is not merely a vehicle for referring beyond itself in a fashion that largely ignores the intrinsic and unique character of its individual works.

The semiotic theory can respond to this objection if the link between music and emotion is transparent because natural, not arbitrarily conventional. Here is a first suggestion: there is a synaesthetic quality to certain timbres. The trumpet's upper notes are bright and the clarinet's low register is dark; the tone of the celesta is ethereal, while high string harmonics are brittle. Even if these connections are widely made, however, they lack the temporally extended complexity that could account for music's expressiveness. They might contribute to the work's emotional ambience, but they could not generate it.

A stronger form of natural connection is that of similarity, and this is emphasized in theories regarding music as an iconic or exemplificatory symbol. If music vividly resembles the emotions it expresses—indeed, if it depicts them in virtue of these resemblances—then it would be natural to respond to the symbol much as we respond to that for which it stands. Iconic symbols (such as representational paintings) are more transparent to their referents than are signs that rely on arbitrary associations or symbol systems (such as that of a natural language) to establish the connection. We regularly talk of pictures as if we are in the presence of what they depict, though this is not to say we are deceived by them. We do not react to linguistic descriptions in the same way. Both Langer (1942) and Goodman (1968) have suggested that music is symbolic precisely because it is experienced as resembling or exemplifying what it denotes.

What is it about the emotions that music resembles? Not their thought components if, as was just argued, purely instrumental music is not equipped to convey the contents of proposition. It has been suggested that expressive instrumental music recalls the tones and intonations with which emotions are given vocal expression (Kivy, 1989), but this also is dubious. It is true that blues guitar and jazz saxophone sometimes imitate singing styles, and that singing styles sometimes recall the sobs, wails, whoops, and yells that go with ordinary occasions of expressiveness. For the general run of cases, though, music does not sound very like the noises made by people gripped by emotion.

A more promising comparison is with the prosodic features—contour, phrasing, accent, volume—characteristic of expressive speech. Juslin and others (Juslin & Laukka, 2003; see also Chapter 17, this volume) have demonstrated the contribution made by such features to music's expressive character in a series of experiments based on different instrumental renditions of a given song. (Because of this methodology, Juslin describes the expressive musical features as belonging to the *performance*, not the *song*, but many of these effects can be notated in work-specifying scores, and thereby can belong to works, not only to their performed interpretations.) The standardization of the melody—along with the brevity of the examples, which is typical of almost all psychological experiments on music's expressiveness—neutralizes any expressive contribution from melodic character and melodic transformation, or from large-scale formal effects. Whereas prosody-like musical features generate local, short-lived expressive effects, the sustained expressive mood we experience in many extended musical works is likely to depend more on the large-scale pattern of dynamic movement in the music. And where micro-elements contribute accumulatively to the whole, what then matters is not their resemblance to features of vocal prosody but their input to the music's processional character.[3]

A more significant resemblance to human expression lies in music's dynamic structure than in its sound as such. We experience movement and pattern in music; we hear in music a terrain shaped by ongoing interactions between its parts, which vary in their pitch, complexity, teleological impetus, energy, texture, inertia, tension, and so on. If music resembles an emotion, it does so by sharing the dynamic character displayed either in the emotion's phenomenological profile, as Addis (1999) maintains, or in the public behaviours through which the emotion is standardly exhibited.

---

[3] Trehub, Unyk, and Trainor (1993a) found cross-cultural recognition of lullabies, as distinct from other kinds of song, and suggested that expressive communication is part of what makes lullabies distinctive. This result might be thought to favour the prosodic account of musical expressiveness, because the experimenters found that prosodic features in the style of presentation (see Trehub, Unyk, & Trainor, 1993b) rather than dynamic pattern and structure appeared to be responsible for the expression and its detection. But whereas the prosodic theory holds that music is expressive by imitating prosodic features of natural vocal expressions of basic emotions (by adults, under the force of those emotions), the prosodic features that account for the lullaby effect more likely derive from the inflections of Motherese, a sing-song exaggerated vocal style adopted by mothers of neonates in all cultures. At best, it is not clear whether it is purely musical features of the lullaby or the lullaby's elaboration of Motherese that is responsible for the expressiveness that is recognized. Even if we speculate that music derived originally from Motherese (Dissanayake, 2001), apart from the special case of lullabies it has long since gone its own way.

The first of these suggestions assumes that the phenomenological profile of some emotions is distinctive enough to provide for their individuation. I am doubtful both that cognitively rich emotions, like shame or jealousy, survive being divorced from their cognitive elements and that there is anything to distinguish the internal dynamics of bursting with joy from blowing one's top. Moreover, to suggest that music symbolizes the 'general form of emotions' (Langer, 1942), not particular kinds or their instances, enfeebles the account. It is more promising to compare music with the outward expressions of emotions than with their experiential shape. A number of emotions have standard behavioural expressions that are partly constitutive of their nature, rather than dispensable concomitants, and these have distinctive dynamic appearances. A downcast bearing and slow movements go with sadness, whereas joy is upbeat and lively. Sometimes we can tell what a person is feeling from the carriage of their body, without knowing the cause of their feeling, their cognitive states, or the object of their emotion.

A fatal problem remains in explaining music's expressiveness in terms of this or any other resemblance between music's features and properties displayed by emotions: in the normal case, the pertinent behaviours are expressive only if they stand in the relevant relation to an instance of the appropriate emotion. Someone might always display the behaviour without feeling the way their behaviour leads us to suppose. In that case, no occurrent emotion is expressed. And if a given physiological state is not accompanied by relevant thoughts, attitudes, desires, or behavioural dispositions, the experience of that state would not normally be regarded as an emotion. No matter how powerful the resemblance, the analogy fails to go through, since it cannot be supposed that music experiences or undergoes the emotions expressed in it.

Theories regarding music as a sign or symbol referring to the emotions accept the conclusion of the argument with which I commenced: occurrent emotions cannot be expressed in musical works. They look for some other, more abstract, way music can connect with the affective life. But semiotic theories inevitably leave a gap between music and emotion. In consequence, they do not do justice to the direct and unmediated fashion in which emotional expression imposes itself on our experience of the music.

2.6.2 Experiencing subjects: composers, listeners, and imagined personas

Most theorists accept that only sentient creatures can express occurrent emotions, but deny that this counts against music's expressiveness. They hold that, when emotion is expressed in a piece of music, that piece stands to a sentient being's occurrent emotion as expressing it. Accordingly, they seek a sentient being whose emotion is given expression by the music. The prime candidates are the composer (or performer) or a persona represented in the music. Alternatively, they maintain it is the occurrent feelings of the

listener, ones caused by his or her attention to the music, that license the judgement
that the music is expressive.

The *expression theory* analyses the music's expressiveness as depending on the composer's expressing his or her occurrent emotion through the act of composition. The
chief difficulty for this theory is conveyed by O. K. Bouwsma's aphorism: 'The sadness
is to the music rather like the redness to the apple, than it is like the burp to the cider'
(1950, p. 94). In other words, we experience music's expressiveness not as a residue of
feelings discharged in the compositional process but as resident in its nature.

The expression theory seems to be empirically false: not all expressive music is written by composers who feel emotions and try to express them. A more philosophical
point is this: in the default case, sadness is expressed by weeping and the like, not by
musical composition. The connection between the composer's emotions and the work
he or she writes is by no means as natural or transparent as that between his or her
emotions and the behaviours, like weeping or whooping, that vent them. So, even if
composers sometimes express their emotions in the works they write, this fact, rather
than accounting for the music's expressiveness, needs to be explained. Indeed, on the
most plausible account, the composer appropriates the music's expressiveness in order
to make the connection with his or her own emotions. In other words, the composer
is like the person who expresses his or her feelings not by showing them directly but
by making a mask that wears an appropriate expression. Just as the mask is expressive whether or not it is used in this sophisticated act of self-expression, so too is the
music. If composers occasionally match the expressiveness of the music to their own
feelings, that is possible only because the music can present expressive aspects apart
from its being appropriated in this fashion. (For further critical discussion of the
expression theory, see Davies, 1994, 2003, 2007, Ch. 16; Goldman, 1995; Kivy, 1989;
Tormey, 1971.)

Similar arguments can be ranged against the version of the expression theory that
identifies the performers as the ones who express their emotions through their rendering of the music. Performers need not feel the emotions they present, and when they
do, there is matching rather than direct expression.

The *arousal theory* explains the music's expressiveness as its propensity to evoke the
corresponding emotion in the listener. What makes it true that grass is green is that it
arouses certain experiences in (human) observers under standard conditions; grass's
greenness is its causal power to bring about appropriate experiences. Similarly, what
makes it true that music is sad or happy is its causal power to bring about these or
related responses in the listener (Matravers, 1998).

I doubt that the correspondence between listeners' attributing sadness to music and
their experiencing feelings or emotions of sadness in response to it is sufficient to make
the arousal theory plausible. In the case of colour, the experience inevitably goes with
the judgement and the two are pulled apart only when the observer or the conditions
of observation are abnormal. The 'standard conditions' for music to produce its effects
are those in which a qualified listener pays attention to it. Those conditions are often
satisfied. When they are, the arousal of a response in listeners who correctly judge

the music to be expressive is not nearly as regular as the arousal theory requires. And it is unconvincing to claim that the relevant feelings, or dispositions to them, can be so weak as to escape the listener's notice. In fact, we have a clear sense of the music's expressive character as quite distinct from our (very variable) responses to it. This is not to deny that the music sometimes can cause an emotional reaction. What is denied is that this reaction is what makes it true that the music is expressive. Normally, we regard the connection as reversed: it is because the expressiveness is apparent in the work that we are moved by the music.

Many theorists (but cf. Beever, 1998) would subscribe to the following proposition: if we were never moved by music, we would not find it expressive. This involves no commitment to the arousalist's programme for analysing music's expressiveness, though. Usually the conditional is regarded as reversible: if we never found music expressive, we would not be moved by it. In other words, it identifies the close and mutual dependence of our experience of music and the judgements we make concerning its features; it does not imply that one takes explanatory precedence over the other.

Expression and arousal theories go hunting for an experiencing subject to whom the music might stand, either as the expression of his or her (the composer's) occurrent emotion or as the cause of his or her (the listener's) emotion-like response. Instead of actual persons and emotions, perhaps we should consider imagined ones. In the case of works generating fictional worlds, such as novels and films, we engage imaginatively with characters inhabiting those worlds. Maybe music's expressiveness connects to fictional or make-believe experiences of emotion. There are two possibilities. In the first, listeners imaginatively ascribe emotions to themselves on the basis of their make-believe engagement with the world of the work. In the second, listeners make believe that the work generates a fictional world of which they are external observers; they imagine of the music that it presents a narrative concerning the emotional life of a persona.

Both views are presented by Walton (1988), but it is his version of the first that I consider. He suggests that a passage is expressive of sadness if the listeners imagine of their hearing of it that it is a cognizance of their own feeling of sadness. Listeners take their awareness of their auditory sensations to be an awareness of their own feelings, and it is these feelings that the music can be said to express.

Even if one charitably allows that awareness of music's expressiveness could be as self-centred and introspective as this, the theory remains implausible. Reflecting on one's auditory sensations is not plainly similar to experiencing emotions, so it is difficult to see how what one imagines can be connected back to and controlled by the music, so that, ultimately, it is the music's expressiveness that is revealed.

The thesis that, in hearing expressiveness in music, we sometimes imagine a persona who is subject to a narrative that unfolds in the music, is widely supported (Budd, 1985; Levinson, 1996, Ch. 6, 2006; Ridley, 1995; Robinson, 2005; Vermazen, 1986; Walton, 1988, 1990). The idea could be offered as an heuristic—as a way of helping people recognize the music's expressiveness—or as a claim applying only to particular kinds of works, such as nineteenth-century Romantic symphonies and sonatas. The strongest position insists that this manner of hearing is *always* required for appreciation of music's expressiveness. Levinson (1996, Ch. 6) comes nearest to the strong position by defining musical expressiveness such that a passage is expressive of an emotion if and only if it is heard (by appropriately experienced listeners) as the expression of that emotion by an imagined human subject, the music's persona.

A first objection denies that all qualified listeners imagine a persona as a condition of their awareness of the music's expressiveness. They might be able to say what it would be suitable to imagine, even if they do not imagine it themselves, but they do this in terms of an awareness of the music's expressive character that is not mediated by the imagination. Besides, I contend that what the listener imagines is too little constrained by the course and detail of the music to provide a theory regarding music's expressiveness as an objective property, which is what Levinson intends. In the case of novels and films, a great deal of information about the fictional word is conveyed to the audience, even if its members must entertain the reality of this world. Those data control what is to be imagined, and why and how, in following the story. Because it does not convey a definite propositional or depicted content, and hints at such things (if at all) only in the vaguest and most general fashion, purely instrumental music cannot direct and channel the content of the listener's imagining (Davies, 2003, Ch. 10, 2006). For instance, what is to determine how many personas he or she should make believe, or the background of relations that might hold between different personas? Inevitably, what is imagined reveals more about the listener than about the music's expressiveness.

2.6.3 The contour theory

A final view, the *contour theory*, abandons the attempt to analyse music's expressiveness as depending on its connection to occurrent emotions. It observes that certain behaviours, comportments, and physiognomies are experienced as expressive without giving expression to, or being caused by, occurrent emotions. Some faces, gaits, or movements are happy looking. They present an emotion characteristic in their appearance. St. Bernards and basset hounds are sad-looking dogs, but this is to say nothing about how they feel. The use of emotion terms to name the expressive characteristics of appearances is secondary, but it bears an obvious connection to those terms' primary use: the behaviours that display an emotion characteristic unconnected with an occurrent emotion are the same (or very similar) to the ones that, where the emotion is occurrent, give direct and distinctive expression to it. Only those emotions that can be recognized solely on the basis of the outward expressions that betray them have corresponding emotion characteristics in appearance.

Turning now to music, the contour theory proposes that pieces present emotion characteristics, rather than giving expression to occurrent emotions, and they do so in virtue of resemblances between their own dynamic structures and behaviours or movements that, in humans, present emotion characteristics. The claim is not that music somehow refers beyond itself to occurrent emotions; music is not an iconic symbol of emotions as a result of resembling their outward manifestations. Rather, the claim is that the expressiveness is a property of the music itself. This property resides in the way the music sounds to the attuned listener, just as happy-lookingness can be a property displayed in a creature's face or movements. Because music is a temporal art, its expressive character is revealed only gradually, and can be heard only through sustained attention to its unfolding. It takes as long to hear the music's expressive properties as it takes to hear the passages in which those properties are articulated.[4]

Consider Figure 2.1. The car and the puppet are happy looking, and the dog and the weeping willow are sad looking. These attributions apply to the appearances the depicted items present, not to occurrent emotions. Only the dog is sentient, and there is no reason to think it feels as it looks. (Besides, dogs do not display feelings of

(a)   (b)

(c)   (d)

Fig. 2.1 Appearances with various emotion characteristics: (a) car, (b) puppet, (c) dog, and (d) weeping willow.

[4] In outline, this is the theory presented in Kivy (1989), as well as in Davies (1994). For further discussion of our differences, see Davies (1994) and Kivy (1999). And for critical commentaries, see Goldman (1995), Levinson (1996, 1997), Madell (1996), and Stecker (1999). Kivy's (1989) version of the theory often is called 'cognitivism' as a way of acknowledging his commitment to a cognitive theory of the emotions, especially as these concern the listener's response. His theory of music's expressiveness does not invoke the cognitive theory of the emotions, however, because it denies that the music expresses occurrent emotions. For a related theory and an account of the way musical space and movement maps the human body and its actions, see Nussbaum (2007).

sadness, when they have them, in their *faces*.) These looks present emotion character-istics because they resemble bearings or expressions which, were they shown by people under appropriate circumstances, would express those people's occurrent emotions. I maintain that, when we attribute emotions to music, we are describing the emotional character it presents, just as we do when we call the willow sad or the car happy. In the case of music, this 'appearance' depends on its dynamic topography, as this unfolds through time. In general, music resembles gaits, carriages, or comportments that are typically expressive of human occurrent emotions, rather than facial expressions.

In discussing the theory that regards music as an iconic symbol or depiction of emo-tions, I have already considered objections to the view that music resembles expres-sions of the emotions. I concluded that the resemblance claim is at its most plausible when it compares music's dynamic pattern to that apparent in non-verbal, behav-ioural expressions of emotion. Yet even if this is accepted, a further objection notes that resemblance alone could not ground music's expressiveness. Resemblances, which are symmetrical and, anyway, can be found between music and many things besides expressive appearances, are insufficient to explain why we experience music as power-fully expressive of emotion.

One might reply, as Kivy does, that we are evolutionarily programmed to 'animate' what we perceive. Or one might simply say 'Yet this is how we hear it,' without commit-ting oneself to an account of the mechanisms and triggers that underlie the response. Not just music but many things are experienced as redolent of emotions, despite lack-ing the feature one would assume to be crucial, namely sentience. There can be no denying that crude representations of the human face can be emotionally compelling in their expressive power, though such responses are not strictly entailed by the resem-blances that can be found. Consider the masks of comedy and tragedy, or a simple drawing such as Edvard Munch's 'scream' face.

If these last observations are not fully satisfying, that does not reflect worse on the contour theory than on other analyses. For instance, the arousalist is reduced ultimately to saying 'Simply, this is how music affects us,' and philosophers who regard music as an iconic symbol or as calling on us to make believe a narrative about a persona are no better equipped than the contour theorist to go beyond the perceived resemblances that are central to their accounts of music's expressiveness.

A different line of objection doubts that the contour theory can explain the signifi-cance we attach to expressiveness in music, or the energy with which music engages our emotions. What can we learn from and why should we be moved by mere appearances of emotion that are not expressions of occurrent, deeply felt emotions? One answer draws attention to the fact that music is intentionally and ingeniously designed to be as it is. Though expressiveness is a property of the piece's sounds, we encounter it not as an accident of nature but as deliberately created and used, which adds considerably to its potential importance. Another response could question if it is true that music is valued as a source of knowledge about the emotions, rather than for the experience it provides, where this experience takes in much more than only its expressiveness. (For further discussion and defences, see Davies, 1999.)

2.6.4 Universalism

The contour theory, more than any other, lends itself to the idea that music is a universal 'language of the emotions', that is, to the suggestion that expressiveness can be recognized cross-culturally. If, as some psychologists have claimed (Ekman, 1980, 2003), certain emotions have characteristic appearances that are universally understood, and if music is experienced as expressive as a result of its recalling these same appearances in its dynamic character, then cross-cultural appreciation of music's expressiveness should be possible. And perhaps it is sometimes. When the musical systems of different cultures are parallel (for instance, in their principles of scalar organization and modalities), there may be sufficient transparency to allow members of the one culture to correctly recognize expressiveness in the music of the other culture. Many Westerners can access sub-Saharan African music, and not only because it provided the seeds from which a number of popular Western musical types emerged.

Often, though, the music of one culture is expressively opaque to outsiders. There are several reasons why this can be so. The emotions appropriate to given circumstances can differ, so that one group sees death as an occasion for sadness where another views it as a cause for joyous celebrations. Until one appreciates the belief systems that determine the significance of the social settings in which emotions are situated, and then recognizes the connection of music with all this, it will not be a simple matter to read off expressiveness from foreign music. And even if music's expressiveness implicates 'natural' resemblances to behaviours that are trans-cultural in their import, these then are structured according to historically malleable musical conventions of genre and style, so that they are no longer apparent to those who lack familiarity with the culture's music. To take a crude example, whether a given pitch is 'high', 'middle', or 'low' depends on the range that is deemed available for use, and that can vary arbitrarily from musical type to type. The contour theory, no less than other analyses, supposes that qualified listeners can become such only by immersing themselves in the kinds of music that are their focus, and that listeners have no guaranteed access to the properties of foreign music, including its expressive ones, until they become appropriately experienced.

So far, the experimental work on the cross-cultural study of music is insufficient, inadequate, and inconclusive (Davies, in press b). Though there are some good studies (e.g. Balkwill & Thompson, 1999; see also Chapter 27, this volume), a number of methodological problems are common. The inevitable use of short musical excerpts is likely to be even more invidious in cross-cultural studies of music's expressiveness than in those dealing with listeners already at home with the grammar of the music they are hearing. Most studies compare Western music with some other kind, yet the style of Western music has become globally known through movies and popular music, so the non-Western listeners are not the innocents that the experiments require for genuine two-directionality (e.g. Balkwill, Thompson, & Matsunaga, 2004; Darrow, Haack, & Kuribayashi, 1987; Gregory & Varney, 1996; Hoshino, 1996). Experiments sometimes confuse questions about what the music expresses with ones about what it makes the listeners feel (e.g. Darrow, Haack, & Kuribayashi, 1987; Gregory & Varney, 1996). And, to return to an example mentioned earlier, experiments sometimes assume musical expression depends on arbitrary association (Gregory & Varney, 1996).

2.7 SECOND PROBLEM: MIRRORING RESPONSES TO MUSIC'S EXPRESSIVENESS

People often respond emotionally to musical works. While there is nothing odd about a listener's being moved by the work's beauty, it is strange that he or she should respond with sadness to the sadness it expresses. The listener's sad response appears to lack beliefs of the kind that typically go with sadness. When I am sad because the dog has died, or because it is raining on your parade, or because you are depressed, I believe the death of the dog, or the rain, or your depression, are unfortunate occurrences, but when the sadness of the music makes me feel sad I do not believe there is anything unfortunate about the music. Moreover, the response to another's emotion often does not mirror it. Another's anger is as likely to produce in me fear, or disappointment, or irritation, as it is likely to precipitate my anger. Yet the listener is not as liable to feel pity, or compassion, or evil delight at the music's sadness as he or she is liable to feel sadness. How is the listener's response appropriate to the music?

The problem is not a general one. We can marvel at the music's complexity and be shocked by its discordant novelty. These responses, in taking the music as their object, involve beliefs or thoughts of the kinds that normally accompany marvelling and shock. The problem case is the one in which listeners mirror in their reactions what the music expresses; where they are saddened by sad music, or cheered by happy music.

Kivy (1989) denies the problem's existence: people are mistaken when they claim to be saddened by sad music. They are moved by the music, certainly, but not to sadness. This explains why concert audiences neither display nor act as if they are sad about the music; simply, that is not how they feel. People are not often wrong about the identity of their emotions, however, and Kivy's position will fail so long as some people some-times react to music's expressiveness by mirroring it in their own feelings. For these reasons and by appeal to their own experience, most philosophers reject Kivy's stance (for discussion, see Davies, 1994; Goldman, 1995).

Also untroubled is the view mentioned earlier, according to which emotions corre-spond to brief episodes of bodily change induced by unconscious affective appraisals. Of course, it remains to explain why music is pre-reflectively judged to be expressive, and just why cognition does not overrule this unthinkingly automatic response. (For an attempt to address such issues, see Robinson, 2005; as indicated above, she does so by arguing that the listener is induced to hear a persona as inhabiting the music.)

If the listener believed music expresses a sadness felt by its composer (or performer), there would again be no special puzzle about his or her reaction, for such beliefs are appropriate to a sad response. In this case, however, the object of the response would be not the music but the composer or performer. When we react to a person's emotional state, our response is directed to them, not to their expressive behaviour as such, even if it was this behaviour that alerted us to their condition. This account does not after all address the problem case, that in which the listeners' responses are solely to the music's expressive character. To have this reaction, they need not believe that the music expresses emotions experienced by its composer; it can be sufficient that they acknowledge the music's expressive appearance, without supposing this to be connected to anyone's occurrent emotions.

According to the theory in which a persona is the human subject of the imaginary act of expression we hear as going on in the music, the problem response can be approached as follows: if that response is directed to the persona, then it will be targeted at the music, for it is in the world of the music that the persona is imagined to exist. And if we hear the persona as undergoing the emotional vicissitudes outlined in the music, then we entertain thoughts about the situation of the persona that are appropriate for mirroring reactions. Admittedly, these thoughts are make-believed, not believed, but if this presents no special difficulty in accounting for our reactions to fictional characters, then the response is also unproblematic in the musical case. So long as the cognitive theory of the emotions allows that the cognitive connection between the emotion and its object can be secured by the imagination in some cases, as well as by belief in others, the listener's response can be seen to be consistent with the cognitive theory of the emotions.

Even if we accept this revision of the cognitive theory of the emotions, it might be thought that it is one thing to imagine of the emotion's object that it has emotion-pertinent features that one does not believe it to have, yet quite another to make believe that the emotion's object exists when one does not believe it to do so. There is also the concern mentioned earlier: that it is not clear that what is entertained is sufficiently controlled by what happens in the music to count as belonging to the world of the work. In addition, a point made earlier—that the typical response to another's emotion is not usually a feeling of the same emotion—should apply also to the case in which the 'other' is a fictional concoction.

The arousalist maintains that what makes it true that the music is sad is that it arouses sadness in the listener; the listener's response is not to some expressive property possessed independently by the music. While the arousalist might deny that listeners' responses *mirror* an expressiveness that is independent of their reaction, still he or she must hold that the response correlates with the music's expressiveness by licensing the judgement that the music is expressive of what is felt by the listener. Given this, and also the fact that the causal relation between the music and the listener's response need not be informed by cognitions beyond those involved in tracking the unfolding of the music, a problem remains for the arousalist in characterizing the listener's reaction as emotional.

In a defense of arousalism, Matravers (1998) acknowledges that the crucial response is a feeling, not an emotion as such, because it lacks the cognitive contents that characterize the emotions. For instance, the response feels like sadness or pity, and this makes it true that the music expresses sadness, but the response is not an object-directed, cognitively founded emotion. This explains why listeners are not strongly inclined to act on their feelings; the prime motivators for action are beliefs and desires directed to an emotional object, but these are absent in the musical case. Because only a few feelings have distinctive phenomenologies, music can arouse only rather general feelings, and thereby is capable of expressing only a limited range of emotions.

I endorse this approach, which can be disassociated from arousalism: if the listener does mirror the music's expressiveness, that response is caused by and tracks the music, but does not take the music, or any other thing, as its emotional object, that is, as the subject of emotion-relevant beliefs. Of course, this is not to deny that the music is the focus of attention and perceptual object of the response (which is a point apparently missed by Madell, 2000).

My account can appeal to one resource that is not available to the arousalist, who does not acknowledge the music as expressive independently of its arousing the mirroring response. Earlier I suggested that inanimate appearances often strike us as expressive. To this it can be added that sometimes we find expressive characteristics in appearances highly evocative of responses of the mirroring kind (Davies, 1994), not only in the musical case but also in others. Whether through empathy or sociality, we often 'catch' the mood prevailing around us. Both high-spiritedness and despondency can be 'contagious'. And the same applies sometimes, I claim, when we are confronted with powerfully expressive appearances that are not connected to occurrent emotions. There is no reason why appearances of sadness should make me feel gloomy if I do not think they show how anyone feels (and often they do not do so). This is to say, mere appearances of sadness are not a suitable object for sadness, since they are not thought to be unfortunate and the rest. Nevertheless, if I am roused to an emotion under those circumstances, it will be a mirroring one, because, in the absence of relevant cognitions, it is only through a kind of contagion or osmosis that my feelings are engaged.

The view presented here requires rejection or revision of the cognitive theory of the emotions sketched earlier, since it countenances emotions that lack the appropriate beliefs or make-beliefs, the desires and behavioural dispositions that would follow from these, and the relevant emotional object. But here I can appeal to empirical work that has distinguished emotional contagion, such as I have described, from like states such as empathy and sympathy. (See Brennan, 2004; Hatfield, Cacioppo, & Rapson, 1994; Johnstone & Scherer, 2000; Neumann & Strack, 2000; Wheeler, 1966. For consideration of the musical case, see Juslin & Västfjäll, 2008.) As well, I can cite marketing studies on the effects of ambient music on shoppers' and diners' moods (see Bruner, 1990; North & Hargreaves, 1997), though it should be noted that these involve non-attentional emotional contagion from music to listener rather than the music-focused contagion that is more typical of the case I describe (Davies, in press c).

In the human-to-human case, unconscious facial mimicry is most often identified as the causal route for emotional contagion, though Brennan (2004) assigns this role to pheromones. But if the listener's mirroring response can also be described in terms of emotional contagion, as seems the most promising account, some other process of transmission must be involved, given that music is not experienced as presenting a physiognomy or pheromones. There are several putative candidates. If contagion operates through mimicry, we might expect the listener to adopt bodily postures and attitudes (or posturally relevant muscular proprioceptions) like those apparent in the music's progress (see Janata & Grafton, 2003). Vocal mimicry, in the form of subtle tensing or flexing of vocal muscles, would also be a predictable response to vocal music or to acts of subvocal singing along with instrumental music (see Koelsch et al, 2006). And if the flux of music is felt as an articulated pattern of tensing and relaxing, this is likely to be imaged and mimed within the body, perhaps in ways that are neither subpostural nor subvocal.

2.8 THIRD PROBLEM: NEGATIVE RESPONSES

Yet if we accept that music expressive of negative emotions sometimes produces an echo in feelings experienced by the listener, another problem emerges. People avoid sad experiences where they can, because these are unpleasant. Those who are under no duty to listen to sad music often choose to do so. They report that such music gives rise to a negative emotional response, yet they offer this in praise of the music. Rather than fleeing, they are attracted to the music, and they sometimes return to it, despite predicting that it will again make them feel sad. Given that music lovers are not masochists, how is this to be explained?

For Kivy (1990) there is no problem. Listeners to sad music do not experience negative feelings, or if they do, these are of the ordinary kind—as when one is disappointed in the poverty of the work's ideas or by its execrable execution—and provide reason for avoiding the emotion's object, the work or the performers, in the future.

Those who think that music can lead the listener to a negative, mirroring response cannot avoid the issue, though. Three argumentative strategies are available. The first notes that there can be much to enjoy about musical works that arouse negative emotions; for instance, the work's beauty, the composer's treatment of the medium, and so forth. In addition, because it lacks 'life implications', one can savour and examine one's response, thereby coming to understand the emotion better while being reassured of one's own sensitivity. In this view, the negative elements are outweighed by positive ones. We listen to music that arouses negative emotions because it also does much more, and the overall balance is on the credit side.

The position is not entirely convincing in its present formulation. If we can get the same or similar benefits from works that do not make us feel unhappy, we should prefer them. We should shun skilful, interesting works that make us feel sad in favor of equally skilful and interesting works that make us feel happy. To reply to this objection, the original view can be developed (as in Levinson, 1982) by arguing that at least some of the benefits cannot be obtained from works other than those that are liable to induce negative feelings. The Aristotelian position, according to which we are better off for purging negative feelings in the context of art, pursues this line, as does the theory that our experiences of artworks educate us about the emotions in a setting that insulates us from the practical demands and dangers of the real world. In this connection, it is also often held that the feelings experienced in regard to artworks are muted and undemanding compared to equivalents provoked by real-world situations.

I find that these ways of addressing the objection are more convincing in the discussion of our reactions to narrative and representational art works, not instrumental music. If the response to music lacks the cognitive contents of emotions, it is difficult to see how it could be a source of education or insight, or how it is easier to tolerate than similarly unpleasant feelings caused by real-world phenomena. If music does not generate a contentful fictional world, the reaction to its expressive properties is not less a response to 'real-world' features than is, say, that in which an especially vivid shade of lime green induces sensations of dyspepsia in its observer.

The second approach to the issue derives from Hume (1912), who argued of the experience of tragedy that its negative aspects are transformed to positive ones through the delight taken in the narrative's construction, the natural attractiveness of representation, and so on. It is far from clear, though, what the character of this conversion is, or how feelings such as sad ones could remain sad while becoming intrinsically pleasant. Perhaps what Hume was driving at is better articulated by the third strategy, which offers the strongest possibility for justifying the interest of someone whose sensitivities incline him or her to negative feelings on hearing music in which negative emotions are presented.

Even if we accept that the negative aspects of experience are unpleasant, and that this gives a reason for avoiding them, it is plain that, for many, this reason is not always overriding. For music, that which is negative often is integral to the whole. Provided our desire to understand and appreciate the work is strong enough, we may be prepared to face those negative elements. The experience that results is not just good on balance; it is not as if the work would be better if we could ignore its negative aspects, for then we would not be engaging with it as such. In other words, experience of, and reaction to, music's negative expressiveness, where that expressiveness is important to the work, is something to be accepted if our goal is to understand and, through understanding, to appreciate the music. There is nothing irrational in pursuing that goal, though the experience to which it gives rise can be unpleasant in parts.

There is a different way of getting at the same point. It simply is not true that people always duck the avoidable negative aspects of life. These are recognized as essential components of many things we like and value. They come along with the territory, not solely as something to be endured but also as contributing to its being the territory it is. This is true of the most important components of our lives: intimate personal relationships, child-rearing, self-realization, career. To achieve a fulfilling life, the individual must honestly and seriously face these in all their dimensions, both positive and negative. Yet it also is true of the way we live generally, even apart from the big issues of survival and flourishing. Thousands of amateurs train for endurance races, such as marathons and triathlons. Other hobbies and activities, in which the challenge of the negative is no less central, are pursued with the same passionate commitment by other people, though they are under no compulsion to do so. Against this background, surely it is safe to deny there is a special problem about the fact that people willingly engage with something so rewarding as music, though they know that doing so will expose them to expressions of negative emotions, which are liable to cause feelings that are unpleasant to experience (Davies, 1994, Ch. 6).[5]

[5] I thank the editors, Jerrold Levinson, Jenefer Robinson, and an anonymous referee for comments on this chapter, and Vivian Ward for help with the artwork.

RECOMMENDED FURTHER READING

1. Davies, S. (1994). *Musical meaning and expression*. Ithaca, NY: Cornell University Press.
2. Robinson, J. (2005). *Deeper than reason: Emotion and its role in literature, music, and art*. Oxford: Clarendon Press.
3. Levinson, J. (2006). Musical expressiveness as hearability-as-expression. In M. Kieran (ed.), *Contemporary debates in aesthetics and the philosophy of art* (pp. 192–204). Oxford: Blackwell.

REFERENCES

Addis, L. (1999). *Of mind and music*. Ithaca, NY: Cornell University Press.
Balkwill, L.-L., & Thompson, W. F. (1999). A cross-cultural investigation of the perception of emotion in music: Psychophysical and cultural cues. *Music Perception, 17*, 43–64.
Balkwill, L.-L., Thompson, W. F., and Matsunaga, R. (2004). Recognition of emotion in Japanese, Western, and Hindustani music by Japanese listeners. *Japanese Psychological Research, 46*, 337–49.
Beever, A. (1998). The arousal theory again? *British Journal of Aesthetics, 38*, 82–90.
Bouwsma, O. K. (1950). The expression theory of art. In M. Black (ed.), *Philosophical analysis* (pp. 71–96). Englewood Cliffs, NJ: Prentice-Hall.
Brennan, T. (2004). *The transmission of affect*. Ithaca, NY: Cornell University Press.
Bruner, G. C. (1990). Music, mood, and marketing. *Journal of Marketing, 54*, 94–104.
Budd, M. (1985). *Music and the emotions: The philosophical theories*. London: Routledge.
Coker, W. (1972). *Music and meaning: A theoretical introduction to musical aesthetics*. New York: Free Press.
Cooke, D. (1959). *The language of music*. London: Oxford University Press.
Damasio, A. R. (1994). *Descartes' error: Emotion, reason, and the human brain*. New York: G. P. Putnam.
Darrow, A.-A., Haack, P., & Kuribayashi F. (1987). Descriptors and preferences for Eastern and Western musics by Japanese and American nonmusic majors. *Journal of Research in Music Education, 35*, 237–48.
Davies, S. (1994). *Musical meaning and expression*. Ithaca, NY: Cornell University Press.
Davies, S. (1999). Response to Robert Stecker. *British Journal of Aesthetics, 39*, 282–7.
Davies, S. (2003). *Themes in the philosophy of music*. Oxford: Oxford University Press.

Davies, S. (2006). Artistic expression and the hard case of pure music. In M. Kieran (ed.), *Contemporary debates in aesthetics and the philosophy of art* (pp. 179–91). Oxford: Blackwell.

Davies, S. (2007). *Philosophical perspectives on art*. Oxford: Oxford University Press.

Davies, S. (in press a). Perceiving melodies and perceiving musical colors. *Review of Philosophy and Psychology*.

Davies, S. (in press b). Cross-cultural musical expressiveness: Theory and the empirical programme. In E. Schellekens & P. Goldie (eds), *Philosophical aesthetics and aesthetic psychology*. Oxford: Oxford University Press.

Davies, S. (in press c). Infectious music: Music-listener emotional contagion. In P. Goldie & A. Coplan (eds), *Empathy: Philosophical and psychological perspectives*. Oxford: Oxford University Press.

Deigh, J. (1994). Cognitivism in the theory of the emotions. *Ethics*, 104, 824–54.

Dissanayake, E. (2001). Antecedents of the temporal arts in early mother–infant interaction. In N. L. Wallin, B. Merker, & S. Brown (eds), *The origins of music* (pp. 389–410). Cambridge, MA: MIT Press.

Ekman, P. (1980). Biological and cultural contributions to body and facial movements in the expression of the emotions. In A. O. Rorty (ed.), *Explaining emotions* (pp. 73–101). Los Angeles, CA: University of California Press.

Ekman, P. (1992). Are there basic emotions? A reply to Ortony and Turner. *Psychological Review*, 99, 550–3.

Ekman, P. (2003). *Emotions revealed*. New York: Henry Holt.

Goldie, P. (2000). *The emotions: A philosophical exploration*. Oxford: Oxford University Press.

Goldman, A. H. (1995). Emotion in music (a postscript). *Journal of Aesthetics and Art Criticism*, 53, 59–69.

Goodman, N. (1968). *Languages of art*. Indianapolis, IN: Bobbs-Merrill Company.

Gregory, A. H., & Varney, N. (1996). Cross-cultural comparisons in the affective response to music. *Psychology of Music*, 24, 47–52.

Griffiths, P. (1997). *What emotions really are*. Chicago, IL: University of Chicago Press.

Hatfield, E., Cacioppo, J. T., & Rapson, R. L. (1994). *Emotional contagion*. New York: Cambridge University Press.

Higgins, K. M. (2006). The cognitive and appreciative impact of musical universals. *Revue Internationale de Philosophie*, 60, 487–503.

Hoshino, E. (1996). The feeling of musical mode and its emotional character in a melody. *Psychology of Music*, 24, 29–46.

Hume, D. (1912). Of tragedy. In T. H. Green & T. H. Grose (eds), *Essays moral, political and literary* (Vol. 1, pp. 258–65). London: Longmans, Green & Co (riginally published 1777).

James, W. (1884). What is an emotion? *Mind*, 9, 188–205.

James, W. (1894). The physical basis of emotion. *Psychological Review*, 1, 516–29.

Janata, P., & Grafton, S. T. (2003). Swinging in the brain: Shared neural substrates for behaviors related to sequencing and music. *Nature Neuroscience*, 6, 682–7.

Johnstone, T., & Scherer, K. R. (2000). The communication of emotion. In M. Lewis & J. M. Haviland-Jones (eds), *Handbook of emotions* (2nd edn, pp. 200–35). New York: Guilford Press.

Juslin, P. N., & Laukka, P. (2003). Communication of emotion in vocal expression and music performance: Different channels, same code? *Psychological Bulletin*, 129, 770–814.

Juslin, P. N., & Västfjäll, D. (2008). Emotional responses to music: The need to consider underlying mechanisms. *Behavioral and Brain Sciences*, 31, 559–75.

Kivy, P. (1989). *Sound sentiment*. Philadelphia, PA: Temple University Press.

Kivy, P. (1990). *Music alone: Philosophical reflection on the purely musical experience*. Ithaca, NY: Cornell University Press.

Kivy, P. (1999). Feeling the musical emotions. *British Journal of Aesthetics*, 39, 1–13.

Langer, S. K. (1942). *Philosophy in a new key*. Cambridge, MA: Harvard University Press.

Lazarus, R. S. (1984). On the primacy of cognition. *American Psychologist*, 39, 124–9.

Lazarus, R. S. (1991). *Emotion and adaptation*. New York: Oxford University Press.

LeDoux, J. E. (1998). *The emotional brain*. London: Weidenfeld & Nicolson.

Lerdahl, F., & Jackendoff, R. (1983). *A generative theory of tonal grammar*. Cambridge, MA: MIT Press.

Levinson, J. (1982). Music and negative emotion. *Pacific Philosophical Quarterly*, 63, 327–46.

Levinson, J. (1996). *The pleasures of aesthetics*. Ithaca, NY: Cornell University Press.

Levinson, J. (1997). Emotion in response to art: A survey of the terrain. In M. Hjort & S. Laver (eds), *Emotion and the arts* (pp. 20–34). Oxford: Oxford University Press.

Levinson, J. (2006). Musical expressiveness as hearability-as-expression. In M. Kieran (ed.), *Contemporary debates in aesthetics and the philosophy of art* (pp. 192–204). Oxford: Blackwell.

Lyons, W. (1980). *Emotion*. New York: Cambridge University Press.

Madell, G. (1996). What music teaches about emotion. *Philosophy*, 71, 63–82.

Madell, G. (2000). *Philosophy, music and emotion*. Edinburgh, UK: Edinburgh University Press.

Matravers, D. (1998). *Art and emotion*. Oxford: Clarendon Press.

McDermott, J., & Hauser, M. D. (2005). The origins of music: Innateness, uniqueness, and evolution. *Music Perception*, 23, 29–59.

Meyer, L. B. (1956). *Emotion and meaning in music*. Chicago, IL: Chicago University Press.

Neumann, R., & Strack, F. (2000). 'Mood contagion': the automatic transfer of mood between persons. *Journal of Personality and Social Psychology*, 79, 211–23.

North, A. C., & Hargreaves, D. J. (1997). Music and consumer behaviour. In D. J. Hargreaves & A. C. North (eds) *The social psychology of music* (pp. 268–89). Oxford: Oxford University Press.

Nussbaum, C. O. (2007). *The musical representation: Meaning, ontology, and emotion*. Cambridge, MA: MIT Press.

Oatley, K., & Johnson-Laird, P. N. (1987). Towards a cognitive theory of emotions. *Cognition & Emotion*, 1, 29–50.

Oatley, K. (1992). *Best laid schemes: The psychology of emotions*. Cambridge, UK: Cambridge University Press.

Ortony, A., Clore, G. L., & Collins, A. (1988). *The cognitive structure of the emotions*. Cambridge, UK: Cambridge University Press.

Patel, A. (2008). *Music, language, and the brain*. Oxford: Oxford University Press.

Prinz, J. J. (2004). *Gut reactions: A perceptual theory of the emotions*. Oxford: Oxford University Press.

Ridley, A. (1995). *Music, value and the passions*. Ithaca, NY: Cornell University Press.

Robinson, J. (2005). *Deeper than reason: Emotion and its role in literature, music, and art*. Oxford: Clarendon Press.

Scherer, K. R. (1988). *Facets of emotion: Recent research*. Hillsdale, NJ: Erlbaum.

Scruton, R. (1997). *The aesthetics of music*. Oxford: Clarendon Press.

Solomon, R. C. (1976). *The passions*. Garden City, NY: Anchor Press/Doubleday.

Stecker, R. (1999). Davies on the musical expression of emotion. *British Journal of Aesthetics*, 39, 273–81.

Tormey, A. (1971). *The concept of expression*. Princeton, NJ: Princeton University Press.

Trehub, S. E. (2003). The developmental origins of musicality. *Nature Neuroscience*, 6, 669–73.

Trehub, S. E., Unyk, A. M., & Trainor, L. J. (1993a). Adults identify infant-directed music across cultures. *Infant Behavior & Development, 16,* 193–211.

Trehub, S. E., Unyk, A. M., & Trainor, L. J. (1993b). Maternal singing in cross-cultural perspective. *Infant Behavior & Development, 16,* 285–95.

Vermazen, B. (1986). Expression as expression. *Pacific Philosophical Quarterly, 67,* 196–224.

Walton, K. L. (1988). What is abstract about the art of music? *Journal of Aesthetics and Art Criticism, 46,* 351–64.

Walton, K. L. (1990). *Mimesis as make-believe: On the foundations of the representational arts.* Cambridge, MA: Harvard University Press

Wheeler, L. (1966). Toward a theory of behavioral contagion. *Psychological Review, 73,* 179–92.

Zajonc, R. B. (1980). Feeling and thinking: Preferences need no inferences. *American Psychologist, 35,* 151–75.

Zajonc, R. B. (1984). On the primacy of affect. *American Psychologist, 39,* 117–29.

CHAPTER 3

....

EMOTION IN CULTURE AND HISTORY

PERSPECTIVES FROM MUSICOLOGY

....

NICHOLAS COOK AND NICOLA DIBBEN

3.1 DEFINING MUSICOLOGY

....

WRITING about music may well go back as far as writing itself, but to speak of 'musicology' before about 1800 is to court anachronism. In the centuries before then, there were in the West two broadly distinct traditions of writing about music: on the one hand more or less practical manuals addressed in general to (and generally by) composers and performers, and on the other hand more or less speculative writings that, to modern eyes, can at times resemble cosmology with a musical vocabulary. The emergence of 'musicology' (a term not used in English until the twentieth century, but borrowed from the earlier French term *musicologie*) can, then, be traced to two circumstances: first, the new relationship between compositional theory and practice that resulted from a general growth in historical awareness and the establishment of a canon of 'masterworks'; and second, the increasing systematization of what in the course of the nineteenth century became known (especially in Germany) as the human sciences.

In its original form, and to some extent still in common British parlance, 'musicology' means simply the study of and knowledge about all aspects of music, taking in for example the systematic approaches to musical organization collectively known as 'music theory'. American usage of the term is distinctly narrower: in Joseph Kerman's words, 'the study of the history of Western music in the high-art tradition' (Kerman, 1985, p. 11). In the 1990s, however, the self-imposed limitations of this version of musicology were seriously challenged by the so-called 'New' musicology (a development foreshadowed by Kerman's critique of the traditional discipline's formalist and positivist tendencies). There is, then, no single, universally accepted definition of the discipline's scope.

This poses problems in determining the scope of this chapter. A genuinely inclusive treatment of musicological approaches to emotion would not restrict itself to the work of 'musicologists' in any narrow sense, but might encompass the views of performers, composers, aestheticians, and others who wrote on music before 1800; similarly, it might take in not only present-day musicological writing but also the ethnomusicological, philosophical, psychological, or sociological perspectives that inform it. (It might also recognize the existence of other traditions of systematic thinking about music, other musicologies, outside the Western orbit.) But that would take a book and not a chapter! More modestly, then, we discuss a selection of musicological or music-theoretical approaches to emotion in Western 'art' and popular music, most of them written since 1950, emphasizing in particular those that set out general frameworks within which to understand how specific pieces of music embody, arouse, signify, or otherwise express emotional states.[1] (We recognize, and readers should be aware, that other authors might well have made a different selection.) Bearing in mind the likelihood that many of our readers will be unfamiliar with the discipline, however, we precede this with a whistle-stop tour of thinking about music and emotion since around 1600: this will serve as much to contextualize musicology as to identify issues and points of reference that will be drawn on later in the chapter.

3.2 A HISTORICAL SKETCH

While comparatively little is known of the nature and practice of ancient Greek music, classical writings about music have formed a constant point of reference for subsequent theorists and accordingly exerted a lasting influence. One could almost frame a history

---

[1] The term 'express' and its derivatives are used in musicological and everyday discourse to refer both to the affective character of particular pieces and to the playing of particular performers (through their variation of such musical parameters as dynamics, articulation, timing, and so forth). For an example of the latter approach, which we do not explicitly discuss in this chapter, see Leech-Wilkinson (2007).

of thinking about music and emotion in terms of the two principal functions which the Greeks ascribed to music: on the one hand *mimesis* (the imitation or transformation of an external reality), and on the other *catharsis* (the purification of the soul through affective experience). The first term values music for its representational function, in this sense embracing it within the theory of knowledge, whereas the second locates music's value in the effect it makes upon the experiencing subject. At issue are two fundamentally different conceptions of what sort of thing music is. As might be expected, however, such philosophical concerns did not greatly impinge upon the practice of working musicians, who were less likely to discuss issues of music's affective powers than simply to take them for granted; a comprehensive history of pre-musicological approaches to emotion would have to be extracted from a multitude of oblique references hidden in the nooks and crannies of a wide range of texts.

The rise of opera around 1600, with which we begin this overview, was associated with a long period of ascendancy in the idea of music as *mimesis*. (It is perhaps not irrelevant that the Florentine camerata responsible for this development saw themselves, however misguidedly, as reconstructing the practices of ancient Greek drama.) The function of music in baroque opera is to reflect or heighten the expression of the emotions signified by the words and presented by means of staged action; we can talk of the music 'expressing' emotion just to the extent that the emotion is located not within the music as such, but within an external reality (whether actual or imagined) which the music references. Music, in short, represents reality, just as language does. It is not surprising, then, that baroque musicians borrowed wholesale from contemporary thinking about language, seeking to understand even instrumental music as a form of discourse and, in particular, applying to it the principles of classical rhetoric: an eighteenth-century example is Mattheson (1981), who traced the operation in music of such rhetorical devices as repetition, variation, or counterstatement, seeing them as serving to project or heighten emotional content in the same way that, in language, the devices of rhetoric colour or inflect propositional content. And in each case the aim was persuasion: just as legal or political orators would seek to persuade their listeners of the case being presented, so musicians sought to convince audiences of their emotional veracity. Like actors, musical performers had themselves to feel the emotions they wanted to convey to their listeners: as C. P. E. Bach put it in his *Essay on the true art of playing keyboard instruments*, 'A musician cannot move others unless he too is moved' (Bach, 1974, p. 152).

During the seventeenth and eighteenth centuries, vocal music—that is, music allied to words—was understood as the paradigm case for music in general. It was through heightening verbal signification that music itself acquired meaning; purely instrumental music by contrast had no meaning, or at best signified at second hand, functioning as a more or less pale reflection of texted music. Unsurprisingly, then, music fared badly in the formulation of the eighteenth-century discipline of aesthetics; music can arouse emotions, Kant admitted, but it amounts to no more than 'a play with aesthetic ideas ... by which in the end nothing is thought'. (He added that the pleasure it creates 'is merely bodily, even though it is aroused by ideas of the mind, and ... consists merely in the feeling of health that is produced by an intestinal agitation corresponding to such play'.[2]) It is in this light that the much-vaunted rise around 1800 of autonomous instrumental music has to be understood: the point is not that people did not play purely instrumental music up to that time, but that it was not the paradigm case for music that it became by the middle of the nineteenth century. Lydia Goehr has characterized this conceptual transformation as a conjunction of a '*formalist* move which brought meaning from the music's outside to its inside' and a '*transcendent* move from the worldly and the particular to the spiritual and the universal' (Goehr, 1992, p. 153).

The formalist move to which Goehr refers is most famously represented in the writings of the Viennese critic Eduard Hanslick, the first edition of whose short book, *On the musically beautiful*, appeared in 1854. In describing the 'content' of music as 'tonally moving forms' (Hanslick, 1986, p. 29), Hanslick was claiming that questions about musical meaning, which had long been formulated in terms of representation, should be reformulated as questions about the intrinsic properties of the music itself. The clearest indication of what is at stake here is to be found in those later writers, such as the turn-of-the-century Viennese theorist Heinrich Schenker, who sought to build systems of musical analysis on Hanslickian foundations: commenting on C. P. E. Bach's prescriptions of how the improviser is to excite or soothe the passions, Schenker claims that 'One must not seek in Bach's word "passions" [*Leidenschaften*] what certain aestheticians of the doctrine of affections bring to it . . .[Bach] means by it simply the consequences of a change in diminution: pure musical effects which have nothing in common with the amateurishly misunderstood and so grossly exaggerated ideas of the aestheticians' (Schenker, 1994, p. 5).[3] (This development of the scope of musical analysis, in effect elaborating on the structural potential of 'tonally moving forms', might be seen as a definitive rebuttal of Kant's dismissive reduction of music to the level of intestinal agitation.) It is in this sense that, as Goehr puts it, meaning was brought from the music's outside to its inside.

Released from its representational function, music is no longer seen as describing specific emotions within specific situations (the Count's mounting jealousy in Act 1 of Mozart's *Marriage of Figaro*, say) but rather as abstracting the essence of phenomena; this is the move from the particular to the transcendental of which Goehr speaks. Just as in the work of early Romantic artists like Caspar David Friedrich, personal emotions are subsumed within a generalized aesthetic yearning for the universal and the spiritual; for the influential writer E. T. A. Hoffmann, writing in the early years of the nineteenth century, music's power lay precisely in its ability to transcend the conditions of ordinary existence, a view echoed in Hanslick's statement that the composer creates 'something which has no counterpart in nature and hence none in the other arts, indeed none in this world.' (Hanslick, 1986, p. 74). Seen in this light, music, once the poor relation of the visual and literary arts, could be considered uniquely privileged within the aesthetic hierarchy: the very lack of specificity that formerly consigned it

---

[2] This passage (from Kant's *Critique of judgement*) is quoted and discussed by Kivy, who scornfully encapsulates Kant's image of music as 'the sonic counterpart of Tums for the tummy' (Kivy, 1993, pp. 258–9).

[3] The passage in Bach's *Essay on the true art of playing keyboard instruments* to which Schenker refers is on pp. 438–9 of Mitchell's translation (Bach, 1974).

to a subordinate role was now construed as an infinite suggestiveness. It is precisely because of its lack of direct reference to the specifics of everyday existence that the art historian Walter Pater (1910, p. 135) wrote that 'All art constantly aspires to the condition of music.'

But it is at this point that the story takes a series of unexpected turns, which between them can be seen as accounting for the fragmented and in many ways contradictory nature of present-day thinking about music, and particularly about musical meaning. For no sooner had music made itself independent of the word than the word began to re-establish itself, only this time outside rather than inside the musical text. It was during the nineteenth century that the consumption of music began to be routinely surrounded by a variety of informative and interpretative texts: programme notes and music appreciation texts led to today's CD liners, broadcasts, and news-stall magazines. This development was largely associated with the reception of Beethoven's instrumental music, and in particular the increasingly idiosyncratic, not to say erratic, works of his late period. Some contemporary listeners put their hermetic style down to the composer's now profound deafness. Others felt that behind the music's apparent contradictions (such as the consistent mixing of genres in the Ninth Symphony) there must lie some intention, some deeper message. And so there emerged a plethora of commentaries on the music, each attempting to work from the musical text to the meaning assumed to lie behind it. The most influential of these commentaries understood the music in autobiographical terms. In 1828, for example, Franz Joseph Fröhlich published a review of the Ninth Symphony, interpreting it as the expression of Beethoven's struggle with deafness and his ultimate transmutation of suffering into joy (Wallace, 1986). Fröhlich even brought this interpretation to bear upon the bar-by-bar details of the music: bars 1–30 of the first movement, he explained, represent in succession tender longing, heroic strength, pathos, and a vision of joy—all of them complementary aspects of Beethoven's own, complex personality.

Commentaries of this kind, which maintained their popularity among the concert-going public during the remainder of the nineteenth century, set up a number of striking paradoxes. The first we have already referred to by implication: in Scott Burnham's words, 'music no longer in need of words now seems more than ever in need of words' (Burnham, 1999, p. 194). Second, and related to this, music now vindicated as the most abstract of the arts is explained in the most concrete terms; it is worth observing how the programme music tradition which runs from Berlioz and Liszt to Richard Strauss (and from there, arguably, into film music) in effect brought such explanations back within the music itself, so setting itself up in opposition to the prevailing aesthetic of autonomous instrumental music. And third, meaning now understood as located within the musical text (the very term applied to such commentaries, 'hermeneutics', is borrowed from traditions of Biblical exegesis) is explained through the construction of an authorial persona whose experiences the music represents. Most telling of all, however, is the manner in which music is now construed as an expression of what might be termed bourgeois subjectivity.

As presented in baroque and classical opera, emotion belongs to the public sphere; to put it another way, it is conceived dramatically. The paradigm of nineteenth-century literature, by comparison, is the novel, where emotion subsists in private, subjective experience, to which the various characteristic devices of the novel give the reader access. In the same way, the emotion which nineteenth-century commentators read into Beethoven's music belongs to the private sphere, unmistakably so when Wagner describes the Ninth Symphony as Beethoven's attempt to reach out from the solitude of his deafness: 'When you meet the poor man, who cries to you so longingly, will you pass him on the other side if you find you do not understand his speech at once?' (Wagner, 1899, p. 203). Music is still understood as expression, just as under the principle of *mimesis*, but this now takes the form of self-expression, the attempt of the artist to make contact with others and, so to speak, with himself or—more rarely—herself. And however dated its origins, this is a concept that has never really lost currency in the years since the 1820s, though it is nowadays perhaps most evident in popular music: music videos, for instance, promise the fan a means of intimate access to the star, while the values of authentic self-expression are central to the carefully constructed persona of an artist like Bruce Springsteen (Cavicchi, 1999).[4] It is in the contrast which Adorno once drew between the emotional qualities of Schoenberg's music and the earlier model of dramatic representation, however, that the idea of music as self-expression reaches its apogee: 'Passions are no longer simulated,' he wrote. Instead, 'genuine emotions of the unconscious—of shock, of trauma—are registered without disguise through the medium of music' (Adorno, 1987, pp. 38–9). For the composer, then, and perhaps for the listener too, music provides something akin to the purification of the soul through affective experience that the Greeks associated with it, and so assumes the function of *catharsis*.

Nowadays, formalism and hermeneutics are seen as opposite ends of the critical spectrum. But as we have explained, it was not always so: formalism, the idea that music is autonomous and should be understood in its own terms, was originally associated with the sense of music's other-worldliness and consequent spiritual value. Nor did Hanslick seek to deny music's affective powers, although later formalists often read him this way. (Hence his statement in the foreword to the eighth edition of *On the musically beautiful*—published in 1891, 37 years after the book's first appearance—that 'I share completely the view that the ultimate worth of the beautiful is always based on the immediate manifestness of feeling' (Hanslick, 1986, p. xxii).) He did, however, seek to qualify its ability to represent specific emotions, putting forward an early version of what is nowadays called the cognitive theory of the emotions (Kivy, 1993, pp. 270, 284; see also Chapter 2, this volume). You cannot feel love, Hanslick claims, without thinking of the loved one; the emotion is inextricably tied up with its object. But depending on the circumstances 'its dynamic can appear as readily gentle as stormy, as readily joyful as sorrowful, and yet still be love'. His point is that 'music can only express the various accompanying adjectives and never the substantive, e.g. love itself' (Hanslick,

---

[4] For a study of the bourgeois subject that takes in both Romantic *Lieder* and rock, see Bloomfield (1993); for an example of popular music which problematizes this expressive norm, see Dibben (2001).

1986, p. 9). But how does it do this? In order to answer this question, Hanslick asks another (p. 11):

What, then, from the feelings, can music present, if not their content? Only that same dynamic . . . It can reproduce the motion of a physical process according to the prevailing momentum: fast, slow, strong, weak, rising, falling. Motion is just one attribute, however, one moment of feeling, not the feeling itself.

His conclusion, then, is that it is these purely musical motions, and not the feelings with which they may be associated, that must form the focus of any meaningful theory or criticism of music.

   It would be possible to argue that what Hanslick means is that only when you can fully explain music in *motional* terms is there any point in trying to do so in *emotional* ones. Because you can never fully explain anything in the arts, however, that is a recipe for infinite deferral. At all events, and whatever Hanslick himself may have intended, he laid the foundations for a formalism that grew in strength during the later part of the nineteenth century and survived through the greater part of the twentieth, according to which issues of musical meaning and expression were regarded as off limits for purposes of serious academic discussion. This change in the nature of formalism coincided with the development of increasingly abstract and powerful methods for musical analysis (through the work of not only Schenker but also Riemann and Schoenberg in the first half of the twentieth century, for example, and Babbitt, Forte, and Lerdahl in the second), the aim of which was to provide complete and self-sufficient explanations of music in exclusively structural terms. That did not necessarily entail a denial that music might have affective powers. Lerdahl and Jackendoff (1983, p. 8) specifically state that:

To approach any of the subtleties of musical affect, we assume, requires a better understanding of musical structure. In restricting ourselves to structural considerations, we do not mean to deny the importance of affect in one's experience of music. Rather we hope to provide a stepping stone toward a more interesting account of affect than can at first be envisioned.[5]

But the practical effect is, of course, the indefinite postponement of consideration of music's expressive qualities to which we have already referred. In what follows, we shall consider the viability of the separation that this implies between structural analysis and expressive interpretation. For now it is worth just noting its apparent similarity to the traditional piano teacher's advice formulated by Ralph Kirkpatrick as 'Learn the notes and then put in the expression'; tellingly, Kirkpatrick continues, 'My admonition is to learn the notes and understand their relationships, and then to draw the expression out' (Kirkpatrick, 1984, p. 128).

   By the 1980s there was a growing view that this narrowness of analytical purview, coupled to a parallel reluctance to enter upon aesthetic interpretation on the part of

---

[5] Cf. Edward T. Cone's claim that 'If verbalization of true content—the specific expression uniquely embodied in a work—is possible at all, it must depend on close structural analysis' (Cone, 1982, p. 233).

music historians, had resulted in an apparently unbridgeable schism between the concerns of professional musicologists on the one hand, and those of practically everyone else who had an interest in music on the other: as Kerman put it, 'Along with the preoccupation with structure goes the neglect of other vital matters—not only the whole historical complex ... but also everything else that makes music affective, emotional, expressive' (Kerman, 1985, p. 73). And in this context one can see the 'New' musicology that followed as less new than revisionary, aiming to reinstate something of the more generous purview of musical interpretation as practised in the middle of the nineteenth century. Indeed, one of the vehicles of the 'New' musicology was the revival of a self-styled hermeneutic criticism tacitly modelled on the nineteenth-century version.[6] Leo Treitler has made the acid observation that such criticism is 'not different in form or verisimilitude from the sort of nineteenth-century hermeneutic that interpreted Beethoven's Ninth Symphony in images drawn from Goethe's *Faust*' (Treitler, 1999, p. 370).[7]

There is a crucial difference, however, for the 'New' musicological revival of hermeneutics was supplemented by a strain of social critique deriving primarily from the work of Adorno. It was most conspicuous in the work of Susan McClary, who gained a great deal of notoriety through her critical interpretations of the warhorses of the symphonic repertory: most famously, she likened parts of the Ninth Symphony to a rapist's murderous fantasy (McClary, 1991, pp. 128–9), contrasting what she saw as the violent and misogynous emotions expressed by Beethoven's music with the altogether more accommodating and socialized expression found in the music of the contemporary but (arguably) homosexual Schubert. One might see this as a frivolous or mischievous application of traditional hermeneutical procedures, involving the construction of a clearly unhistorical compositional persona (and McClary has been criticized on precisely these grounds). But that is to miss her substantial point, which is that music serves to express not only personal emotions but also social ideologies, in this case a characteristic attitude to women or, more generally, to sociocultural difference. While many aspects of McClary's work have been subject to critique, the broadened musicological purview represented by her work has been widely accepted. And as a result, the long-marginalized topic of musical meaning has become central to the discipline.

3.3   SOME CLASSIC APPROACHES

As we have seen, one strand which has dominated thinking about musical expression is a reliance on linguistic models. And the notion of a shared musical 'language' is

---

[6] See, for instance, Kramer (1990), along with McClary (1991), one of the key texts of the 'New' musicology; for a brief overview, focusing on issues of gender representation, see Cook (1998a), Chapter 7.

[7] The reference is to the programme note that Wagner drew up for his 1846 performance of the symphony in Dresden.

particularly prominent in baroque music treatises which, influenced by newly rediscovered Greek and Roman doctrines of oratory and rhetoric, provided instruction on
how the composer was to 'move' the 'affections' or emotions of the listener.

A primary aesthetic goal in baroque music was to achieve stylistic unity based on the
representation of a single emotion—a phenomenon exemplified by the da capo aria, so
called because its final section repeated the first one da capo, 'from the top'. Affections
were conceived as typified and static attitudes of mind, expressed in music through
specific figures and compositional techniques identified and discussed in contemporary theoretical sources (one of the earliest was Burmeister's *Musica Autoschediastike* of
1601). The approach derived from the rhetorical concept of *decoratio*, that is, rules and
techniques embellishing the ideas of an oration and infusing it with passion. Applied
to music, devices such as melodic repetition, fugal imitation, and the use of dissonance were invoked in order to explain and justify irregular contrapuntal writing, in
much the same way that nineteenth-century commentators proposed hermeneutical
explanations for the idiosyncrasies of Beethoven's style. Gesturing was also part of
rhetorical delivery (itself an object of study for politicians, ministers, and actors), and
was theorized in the form of treatises on gestures in everyday life, and on rhetorical
delivery and opera acting (Solomon, 1989, from which Figure 3.1 is taken). The precise
bodily gestures and movements associated with the representation of specific attitudes

Fig. 3.1 Gestures with the hand and face: (a) astuteness, (b) beauty, (c) carefulness,
(d) deception, and (e) the negative (from Andrea di Joria, *La mimica degli antichi
investigate nel gestire napoletano*, Napoli, 1832, reproduced in Solomon, 1989).

of mind outlined in these texts seem perversely static and unreal from the standpoint
of nineteenth- and twentieth-century constructions of subjectivity; in the same way,
the da capo aria has long been criticized for the artificial nature of its return to the
opening, as if emotions could be repeated to order. All this reflects a fundamental shift
of conception: whereas the eighteenth-century affection is a rationalized attitude of
mind, the nineteenth-century understood emotion as a personal and spontaneous
expression or experience. (The listeners of Figure 3.2, eyes turned away from the performers or heads buried in hands, embody the migration of emotion from the outer to
the inner world.)

In the later part of the eighteenth century, there was a shift from the earlier emphasis on *decoratio* to a lexicon of affective types or 'topics', as they have been termed by
Ratner (1980); this was linked to an increasingly dynamic view of musical expression,
whereby a single piece might encompass different emotions, or the transition between
one emotion and another. (For contemporary listeners this was one of the most striking
and innovatory features of Mozart's operatic arias and ensembles.) Basing his work on
contemporary treatises as well as the study of musical texts, Ratner showed how classical compositions evoked, often in kaleidoscopic succession, a more or less fixed repertory of melodic, rhythmic, textural, and other types, each of which had its own specific
connotation. Such types might refer, for example, to particular dances (minuet, gigue),

Fig. 3.2 Beethoven playing for his friends (lithograph by Albert Graefle, c. 1877).

styles (the 'brilliant' style, the 'Turkish' style), compositional procedures (the 'learned' style), or extra-musical associations (the hunt).

This notion of an affective lexicon has been further developed by means of semiotic theory, in relation to both 'art' music (Agawu, 1991; Allanbrook, 1983) and popular music (Tagg, 1982); it has also been interpreted in terms of cognitive theory (Gjerdingen, 1988). All such approaches understand expressive meaning as the product of historical usage: music signifies through reference to established syntactical types (the V-I progression and motivic liquidation that encode closure in a Mozart string quartet, say), to other music and its circumstances of performance (the parade ground, for instance, in the case of an orchestral march), or to some kind of extra-musical reality. And it is crucial to such approaches that these meanings were deliberately employed by composers and understood as such by contemporary audiences. For example, Agawu (1991, p. 31) cites a letter from Mozart to his father in which he discusses his compositional strategy in the opera *Die Entführung aus dem Serail*, and the likely impact of particular features on the audience. Mozart refers specifically to his use of the 'Turkish' style to create a comic effect during the scene in which Osmin expresses his rage, as well as to the use of syntactical features such as a change of key and metre at the end of a particular aria in order to surprise his audience.[8]

Because of the assumption that musical meaning results from historical sedimentation, the application of any given lexical approach of this kind is necessarily restricted to a specific repertory. By contrast, the aim of Deryck Cooke's *The language of music*, first published in 1959, is to provide not only a lexicon of but also an explanatory basis for the emotional meanings of European 'art' music in general (and perhaps even, as we shall see, for music as a universal phenomenon). In Cooke's words, his book 'attempts to show that the conception of music as a language capable of expressing certain very definite things is not a romantic aberration, but has been the common unconscious assumption of composers for the past five-and-a-half centuries at least' (Cooke, 1959, p. xi). He locates his basic expressive lexicon in the tonal and intervallic 'tensions' embodied in specific scale steps and the patterns of motion between them, seeing other musical dimensions such as timbre and texture as 'characterizing agents', that is, as merely modifying the tensions established through pitch, time, and dynamics (pp. 37–8). He substantiates his theory by citing large numbers of extracts taken from vocal works, the texts of which embody similar expressive meanings. The assumption is that the emotional associations of particular musical formations apply equally when these formations occur in autonomous instrumental music. After going through this process with each of the different scale steps, he draws up a summary of what he terms

---

[8] Such lexicons had a kind of afterlife in early cinema history, in the form of the cue sheets, manuals, and handbooks that provided guidance to the performers, usually pianists, who accompanied silent films. These volumes contained both transcriptions from the classical repertoire and originally composed music, categorized according to the narrative situations and emotions engendered by it (see also Chapter 31, this volume). One of the earliest anthologies (*Motion picture piano music: Descriptive titles to fit the action, character or scene of moving pictures*, cited in Marks, 1992, p. 68) contains 51 short pieces with titles such as 'Aged Colored Man', 'Aged Persons', 'Ancient Dance', 'Andante', 'Antique Dance', 'Apparitions', all listed alphabetically.

'the basic expressive functions of all twelve notes of our scale', beginning as follows (pp. 89–90):

Tonic: Emotionally neutral; context of finality. *Minor Second*: Semitonal tension down to the tonic, in a minor context: spiritless anguish, context of finality. *Major Second*: As a passing note, emotionally neutral. As a whole-tone tension down to the tonic, in a major context, pleasurable longing, context of finality. *Minor Third*: Concord, but a 'depression' of natural third: stoic acceptance, tragedy. *Major Third*: Concord, natural third: joy . . .

Philip Tagg's (1982; Tagg & Clarida, 2003) application of semiotic theory to popular music is reminiscent of Cooke's approach in both concept and method. He identifies a range of signs in popular music, equating particular emotions, moods, and meanings with particular harmonies, melodies, timbres, and so forth, and referring to them as 'musemes' or minimal units of musical meaning; the term is based on 'phoneme', and is thus a further illustration of the indebtedness of theories of musical emotion to linguistic models.[9] Tagg verifies his interpretations in two ways. The first of these is what he calls 'inter-subjective comparison', by which he simply means establishing the consistency of attributions of meaning to the same music played to different respondents. The second and better known is what he terms 'inter-objective comparison': this means the substitution for a given museme of others drawn from comparable expressive contexts, especially ones involving words, in order to confirm their semantic equivalence. (Again the reference to texted music provides a link with Cooke's method.) Tagg demonstrates his theory through the detailed analysis of specific pieces of music, the most extended examples being his analyses of the *Kojak* TV theme tune and the Abba hit *Fernando*. The readings that result are more complex than Cooke's, in that they do not simply bring to light affective contents but attempt to define an attitude towards the ostensible meaning of the lyrics: in the case of Fernando, for instance, Tagg concludes that the music gives the lie to the revolutionary sympathies expressed by the words.

There are a number of criticisms which can be levelled equally at Cooke and Tagg.[10] One is that both their methods are heavily dependent upon extra-musical aspects, particularly accompanying lyrics or other programmatic elements. Although such elements are obviously important where present, how do we know what happens in music from which they are absent and the connotations of which are therefore less clear (Middleton, 1990, p. 234)? How confident can we be that what applies in the one case applies in the other? (Does music derive its affective meanings from purely historical associations with certain texts, or were those texts associated with the music because of some affective quality inherent in the music?) Related to this is an objection

---

[9] Tagg's concept of sign, however, is broader than Cooke's: as well as 'style indicators', which refer to compositional 'norms', and 'genre synecdoche', referring to a 'foreign' style and hence to the genre and culture to which it belongs, Tagg identifies 'anaphones', which share a structural homology with the sonic, kinetic or tactile events that they signify, and 'episodic markers', which designate structural functions (Tagg, 1992).

[10] See, for example, Middleton (1990), Davies (1994, with many references), and Shepherd and Wicke (1997). See also Scruton (1997, pp. 203–8) for a trenchant critique of the parallel between music and language implicit in Cooke's approach.

which applies to all lexical approaches to musical meaning: the emotional or other signification of musemes may vary according to the musical contexts within which they
are articulated (in other words, it may not be possible to draw so confident a distinction
between the 'semantic' and the 'syntactical' aspects of music).[11] Lexical approaches, in
short, may endow the music with a false semblance of semantic fixity.

Other criticisms, by contrast, apply to one method but not the other. For example,
one problem with Tagg's IOC technique is that it is so laborious, if it is to be done properly, as to verge on the impractical. As Allan Moore (1993, p. 158) puts it, 'it is so time-
consuming that I have never seen it properly undertaken in equivalent studies' (other
than by Tagg, that is to say). Again, Tagg has been criticized for drawing comparisons
between contemporary popular styles and the European 'art' repertory, so implicitly
assuming that they form part of a common cultural tradition (Middleton, 1990, p. 234).
This may be a reasonable assumption in the case of some film and television music:
several commentators have traced the appropriation of semantic elements from late
nineteenth- and early twentieth-century 'art' music by the Hollywood film industry
(Eisler [and Adorno], 1947; Flinn, 1992). Analyses of popular music also sometimes
reveal the influence of 'art' traditions, as in Robert Walser's linkage of heavy metal
music with the ideologies and even some of the performance practices of nineteenth-
century Romanticism (Walser, 1993). However, it would be clearly wrong to claim that
traditions such as blues, rock, rap, or dance music derive primarily from 'art' music. So
it becomes necessary to define just what the relevant frame of reference is for any particular repertory or piece, and that of course raises questions of who is doing the defining and to what ends. Nor is that the only problem. If you set out to identify the different stylistic traditions within which different musemes operate, how are you going to
decide where to stop? (Are there specific musemes applicable to popular music? Or to
pop but not rock? Or just to dance music? house? garage? jungle? Bristol jungle?)

Such problems may not be insoluble in principle, but they are certainly hard to solve
in practice. In such a context, there is something very tempting about Cooke's attempt
to derive the emotional expression of music directly from natural principles. As we
have seen, he explains expression in terms of intervallic tensions, and he explains intervallic tensions in terms of basic acoustic principles, specifically the overtone series.
'That the major third should be found to express pleasure should surprise no one,' he
writes, since it appears 'early on in the harmonic series: it is nature's own basic harmony, and by using it we feel ourselves to be at one with nature' (Cooke, 1959, p. 51).
He admits that tradition builds on tradition, that is, that there is a historical element
in musical meaning, but he insists that traditions arise in the first place because of the
natural principles built into the music (Cooke, 1959, pp. 40–1). In other words, there

---

[11] Cf. Jenefer Robinson's criticism (also voiced, for example, by Anthony Newcomb) that 'most
philosophical theorists of musical expression have either ignored or underemphasized . . . the fact
that the musical expression of complex emotions is not a function of a few isolated measures
here and there, as in Kivy's examples in *The Corded Shell*; rather it is very often a function of the
large-scale formal structures of the piece as a whole. We cannot understand the expression of
complex emotions in music apart from the continuous development of the music itself' (Robinson,
1998, p. 19).

was emotional meaning in music before texts were associated with it. And, of course, principles like the overtone series do not vary from one culture to another. It is in this sense that, although limiting his examples to Western 'art' traditions, Cooke implicitly sets out a universal model of emotion in music: the laws of nature apply in China and in Africa as they do in Europe and America, and therefore the same principles should govern musical expression. Such thinking has become deeply unfashionable, because of its potentially essentializing and ethnocentric nature, and few present-day scholars would probably be prepared to sign up to this aspect of Cooke's theory. (Approaches to emotion and meaning in the ethnomusicological literature, while falling outside the scope of this chapter, are almost invariably rooted in the 'thick' description of specific cultures and contexts.[12]) Perhaps the most telling symptom of Cooke's ethno-centricity, however, lies in the way in which he unquestioningly identifies meaning with the expression of personal emotion—in which he understands it, in short, in terms of bourgeois subjectivity. A strong argument could be made that Cooke's approach, valid as it may be for Schubert or Schumann, is misleading in relation not just to Chinese or African music, but to Monteverdi's and Handel's too.

Despite the difficulties to which we have referred, Cooke's work was important in placing emotion firmly within the musicological agenda, and in attempting to do so on a principled basis. Much the same might be said of Leonard B. Meyer, whose first book, *Emotion and meaning in music*, appeared three years before Cooke's (indeed, Kivy has described it, perhaps rather sweepingly, as 'the book that taught many of us for the first time that you can talk about music without talking nonsense' (Kivy, 1987, p. 153)). Whereas Cooke attempted to ground the emotional expression of music in natural-scientific principles, thereby as it were short-circuiting cultural mediation, Meyer drew upon a range of sources in psychology. His overall interpretation of musical structure, which he continued to develop over the ensuing forty years, is based on Gestalt principles: listeners are drawn to perceive musical patterns as wholes, as tending towards closure, and compositional techniques can be understood as ways of both stimulating and challenging such perceptions. In essence, Meyer sees music as setting up expectations in the listener (or, to put it another way, implications in the music) which are in general fulfilled or realized, but often only after postponement or apparent diversion. And it is here that Meyer's approach to emotion comes in. The basic principle, which Meyer also drew from contemporary psychology, is that 'Emotion or affect is aroused when a tendency to respond is arrested or inhibited' (Meyer, 1956, p. 14). To take a very simple example, a dominant seventh chord implies resolution; the longer resolution is postponed, the more affect will be created, and if when it comes the resolution is to vi (an interrupted cadence), further postponing the return to I, there will be a further heightening of affect. Because the implications created by any given piece of music, and the manner in which they are or are not realized, fall clearly within the domain of structural analysis, the result is that emotion is incorporated within the latter. In effect, the analysis of musical emotion plugs into that of musical structure.

[12] For representative examples—one chapter-length, one book-length—see Tolbert (1994) and Feld (1990). See also Chapter 6, this volume.

For all its neatness, however, this approach creates a number of difficulties. One concerns the relationship between emotions as normally understood—hope, joy, grief, and so on—and the kind of undifferentiated affect or feeling tone (in effect a unidimensional variable) that Meyer's theory predicates. Some commentators have doubted whether Meyer's theory can properly be considered as pertaining to the emotions at all (e.g. Budd, 1985). Davies (1994, p. 288), by contrast, observes that 'for Meyer the possibility of the listener's differentiating the feeling tone is a real one', and he elaborates and justifies Meyer's position by arguing that the feeling tone can itself take on a kind of mimetic function:

There are, within any culture, groups of emotions having a common pattern of behavioral expression. For instance, the dynamics of the behavioral expressions of sadness, grief, disappointment, and regret are similar and can be distinguished from the behavioral expressions of joy, happiness, and enthusiasm. Music can be heard as imitating the dynamics of behavior. As listeners we hear these dynamics and imagine that the music is through them expressive of, say, sadness. In so doing we (imaginatively) make the music the emotional object in terms of which our feeling tone can be differentiated.

In saying this, Davies is invoking the Hanslickian idea that feelings are characterized by specific dynamic qualities. As we saw above, Hanslick argues that music cannot specify love, but through its motional qualities it can specify such adjectival properties as the joyful or sorrowful quality of love. In effect Davies is suggesting that Meyer's undifferentiated affect conveys such adjectival properties, which we are led to attribute to the music itself (that is why it is common, if arguably misleading, to talk of the music being happy or sad, as if it were a sentient being). And since Hanslick's day the idea that music expresses emotion through somehow mirroring the dynamics of our inner life has become a commonplace in writing on the topic; the classic formulation is Langer's claim that 'there are certain aspects of the so-called "inner life"—physical or mental— which have formal properties similar to those of music—patterns of motion and rest, of tension and release, of agreement and disagreement, preparation, fulfilment, excitation, sudden change, etc.' (Langer, 1957, p. 228).[13] When we said that music 'somehow' mirrors the dynamic of inner life, however, we meant to signal a crucial vagueness in such thinking: without entering into details, the problem lies in specifying what sort of entity the 'dynamics of our inner life' might actually be, or how it might be measured. In the absence of adequate answers to these questions, the appeal to such impalpable dynamics has little explanatory force.

A second line of criticism is that Meyer's approach is too narrow and exclusive. Davies, for instance, complains that it 'overemphasizes the status of the unpredictable at the expense of the structural significance of similarity' (Davies, 1994, p. 289), while Keil similarly complains that it ignores the significance of repetition and performance skills (Keil, 1994). Underlying these complaints is a suspicion that, through incorporating them within a psychologically-based theory, Meyer is lending a spurious generality

---

[13] Davies (1994, pp. 123–4) offers a critique, along with an extensive though by no means complete listing of similar claims by other writers (p. 230, n. 33). The basic approach, of course, links with earlier ideas of music 'moving' listeners' affections.

to principles grounded in the modernist aesthetic, with its valorization of innovation and the unique. This charge would be not altogether fair, because the link he makes between psychological principles and musical meaning is not a simple or direct one. For one thing, Meyer recognizes the extent to which listeners' expectations reflect not only the properties of the musical stimulus but also the culturally-specific stylistic codes that are acquired through enculturation. For another, he took pains to explain on the very first page of *Emotion and meaning in music* that the kind of musical meaning we have so far discussed is not the only one: he distinguishes 'embodied' meaning, which is the result of the realization or frustration of expectation, from 'designative' meaning, which involves reference to objects, concepts, or events outside music (a distinction corresponding to Jakobson's 'introversive' and 'extroversive semiosis' (Jakobson, 1971, pp. 704–5)), emphasizing that the latter reflects not just culture-specific associations but the listener's personal experiences and disposition, too. Nevertheless, embodied meanings play a far larger role in Meyer's work than designative ones, and it is not hard to see why, for his theory explains musical meaning (rather than simply acknowledging its existence) only to the extent that it can be reformulated in terms of relationships between musical elements. Or to put it another way, explaining meaning means translating it into music-structural terms; it is a one-way process. There is something symbolic in the fact that Meyer's first book is the only one he wrote specifically about musical emotion and meaning, the others all focusing on issues of structure and style.

3.4 STRUCTURAL AND EXPRESSIVE VOCABULARIES

The basic problem we have diagnosed in Meyer is that of talking about both the emotion and the music in a sustained manner: you may start off talking about the emotion, but you seem to end up talking about the music in more or less the usual way. And of the admittedly limited amount of musicological or music-theoretical work in this area since 1956, much is open to the same criticism. So it is of interest to consider a more recent critique of such work by a professional philosopher. Peter Kivy (1993) takes as his starting point a critical reading of Schumann's Second Symphony by a writer loosely associated with the early stages of the 'New' musicology, Anthony Newcomb (1984). Newcomb's essay is a good example of the revival of a hermeneutical approach to which we previously referred, and indeed sets out to reconstruct a nineteenth-century perception of Schumann's symphony (which was more highly rated in its own time than is generally the case today). Newcomb attempts to achieve this through consideration of the expressive trajectory of the piece, which he characterizes as 'suffering leading to healing or redemption', and relates these affective characteristics to the difficult circumstances of Schumann's life as he sketched the work. He also points out that many other compositions from around the same period exhibit a similar trajectory (an example to which we have already referred being the 'transmutation of suffering into joy' in Beethoven's Ninth Symphony), and suggests that we might think of this as a 'plot archetype', in other words a generic category in terms of which individual instances may be understood.

Kivy (1993) applauds Newcomb's aims (indeed he sees in them the seeds of a 'new music criticism'), but identifies what he sees as serious methodological failings. In particular, Kivy objects that Newcomb is trying to add an additional, interpretative layer to structural analysis, whereas the whole project of interpreting autonomous instrumental music is built on a fallacy. 'Pure' music cannot represent anything, Kivy claims, and therefore the symphony cannot contain the meaning Newcomb ascribes to it; in other words, as soon as Newcomb started talking about Schumann's biography, he stopped talking about the music. (As a musicologist rather than a philosopher, Newcomb might very well reply that nineteenth-century listeners clearly did interpret the music in just this way, and that the question of whether they were philosophically justified in doing so is irrelevant to an exercise in historical reconstruction.) But in that case, you might ask, how *are* we to build emotional expression into music criticism? Kivy (1993, p. 316) replies:

The new way is not to amplify criticism by adding interpretation to analysis but, rather, by amplifying analysis itself. For once one ceases to see expressive properties of music as semantic or representational properties, it becomes clear that they are simply *musical* properties: they are phenomenological properties of music, and as such a proper subject of musical analysis.

In other words, he is saying, when we analyse music we should analyse its expressive properties alongside its structural ones. And he offers some examples of what he has in mind. In Mozart's 'Dissonance' Quartet, he says, the relationship between the dark, anguished character of the introduction (which gives the quartet its soubriquet) and the light, sunny character of the allegro that follows creates an effect of strong, expressive resolution; take away the expression and you weaken the resolution. Or again, there is an expressive difference between a Haydn symphony movement that goes from tonic minor to relative major to tonic minor (that is, from dark to light to dark), and one that ends in the tonic major (so that its overall trajectory is from dark to light). Because these are directly experienced aspects of the music, Kivy concludes, 'an analysis . . . that leaves out the expressive contrast, is incomplete in a musically non-trivial way' (p. 319). But does this solve the problem of how to talk about both the music and the emotion in a sustained manner? The answer turns on whether Kivy has identified expressive properties as distinct from structural ones, or whether he is simply talking about structural properties but giving them expressive names. In the Mozart case, is the effect of resolution created by the passage from dark to light actually different from that created by the passage from the dissonance of the opening to the diatonicism of the main movement? Or are these just different ways of talking about the same thing? (If so, then in what sense are you leaving out the expression in speaking only of dissonance and diatonicism?) Again, in the Haydn case, just what does it mean to speak of the passage from dark to light over and above what it means to speak of the passage from minor to major? If the conclusion is that the one terminology can be simply substituted for the other, then there must be a suspicion at least that Kivy's 'new music criticism' is just the old music criticism with an updated (some music theorists might say outdated) vocabulary.

Of course, it might just be that Kivy applies his expressive terminology in too literal a manner. That, at any rate, is suggested by the comparison with another study, this time a collaboration between a musicologist (Gregory Karl) and a philosopher (Jenefer Robinson), which interprets Shostakovitch's Tenth Symphony as 'a progression from dark to light or struggle to victory' (Karl & Robinson, 1997, p. 166). In using these terms, the authors are not referring to anything as simple as a major or minor mode, or dissonance versus consonance. They are referring to the composite properties of a complex musical structure, and indeed their main purpose is to show how the large-scale musical unfolding of the third movement is central to the construction of its expressive message, which they see as one of hope (and more than that, false hope). While their argument begins with structural analysis and ends with expressive analysis—the same sequential approach that Kivy criticized in Newcomb—it would not be fair to describe Karl and Robinson as simply building expression onto structure, like icing on a cake. The very characterization of complex, large-scale passages as 'light' or 'dark' stimulates the attempt to explain these expressive qualities in terms of the music's structural properties; again, the authors set out what they call the 'cognitive content' of hope (which involves looking forward to and striving towards a happier but uncertain future), and then match the structural properties of the music against these criteria, in effect using them as an analytical framework. In this way their interpretative strategy involves what they describe as 'a complex interplay among a variety of different sorts of observations' (p. 170), both formal and expressive. There is, however, a certain ambiguity at this point. On the one hand, the authors write that 'we consider this dichotomy [between the formal and the expressive] ill-conceived, because often the formal and expressive threads of a work's structure are so finely interwoven as to be inextricable' (p. 176). On the other, they claim that 'the formal and expressive elements of musical structure are so thoroughly interdependent that the formal function of particular passages can often be accurately described only in expressive terms' (p. 177). The second statement seems to start by saying the same as the first but ends up saying the opposite: if you can describe a particular passage in expressive but not structural terms, or for that matter vice versa, then this reinstates the dichotomy between them (an implication which becomes still clearer when the authors continue 'there is no "strictly formal" or purely musical explanation for why our focal passage unfolds as it does in the central section of the third movement').[14] The relationship between structure and expression remains unclear.

[14] Karl and Robinson make a related point in a footnote on p. 173, where they explain that 'a listener schooled in the epic symphonic tradition might expect that the tension of the third movement should be swept away at the beginning of the finale . . . Upon finding this expectation frustrated, he or she may then feel tense, impatient, or bewildered . . . The listener's feelings of impatience or frustration, while poorly mirroring the expressive structure of the work, may nonetheless provide the initial clues that something is amiss . . . providing an impetus to interpretation'. In this way the frustration of expectation which Meyer saw as the source of affect

This issue has been explicitly addressed by another musicologist, Fred Maus. In an article entitled 'Music as Drama' (Maus, 1988), he launches a systematic attack on the sequential, structure-to-expression approach, and then proceeds to offer an analysis of the opening of Beethoven's String Quartet, Op. 95, combining analytical and expressive vocabulary and commenting self-consciously on his analytical strategies as he does so.[15] The conclusion that Maus draws from this analysis—as much an analysis of analysis as of Beethoven—is that music has neither structural nor emotional content. Rather it consists of a series of *events*, which we make sense of by regarding them as the *actions* of imaginary agents, so attributing intentions or motivations to them: his Beethoven analysis, Maus claims, '*explains* events by regarding them as *actions* and suggesting *motivation*, *reasons* why those actions are performed, and the reasons consist of combinations of psychological states' (p. 67). It is this imagined dramatic content that both structural and expressive vocabularies seek to represent, each in their own way, as Maus (1988, p. 69) explains:

the technical language and the dramatic language offer descriptions of *the same events*. That event at the opening of the quartet, according to the analysis, is an outburst and it is also a unison passage with an obscure relation between metrical hierarchy and pitch hierarchy. The technical vocabulary of the analysis describes the actions that make up the piece.

While referring to the same musical content, then, the two vocabularies construct it in different ways, filter it differently, and the analyst can exploit the asymmetries between them in order to gain purchase on the music. It is for this reason, presumably, that Maus observes that 'Both sorts of description—"technical" or music-theoretical, "dramatic" or anthropomorphically evocative—belong, interacting, to the analysis' (p. 63), and Robert Hatten uses the same word when he writes of 'the interaction of expressively significant . . . thematic, motivic, or topical events with structurally significant voice-leading events' (Hatten, 1994, p. 320, n. 8). Hatten's book is, to date, the most comprehensive attempt to incorporate expressive and structural analysis within a coherent critical practice, and it brings together many of the approaches we have described so far. As his reference to topics suggests, Hatten builds on the documentary evidence that historical listeners (his book focuses on Beethoven) not only identified topical references in the music they heard but also saw them as one of the main ways in which it conveyed emotional or other meaning; to this extent Hatten's work, like Agawu's, links with the tradition of understanding emotion as a public, rationalized state, which as we have seen goes back to the baroque affections. Unlike Agawu's work, however, Hatten's also embraces nineteenth-century conceptions of emotion as private, subjective experience, and indeed the book is easily read as a contribution to the hermeneutic tradition (like Newcomb, Hatten claims to be reconstructing historical practices of listening, and his concept of 'expressive genre' corresponds closely

---

functions as an interpretative cue: implicit in this is a distinction between the listener's emotional response and the expressive properties of the music per se. (This distinction bulks large in philosophical writing on the subject, particularly Kivy's, but falls outside the scope of this chapter.)

   [15] For detailed discussion of the relationship between structural and expressive vocabularies in critical writings which draw analogies between music and narrative, see Maus (1997).

to Newcomb's 'plot archetype'). More centrally, it brings together extroversive and introversive approaches within a unified theoretical framework drawn from present-day semiotic theory. The question on which we wish to focus, however, is the extent to which Hatten succeeds in theorizing the interaction between structure and expression to which he refers.

The immediate impression of Hatten's working procedure is that, once again, he starts with structural analysis, and then adds in the interpretation. The first ten pages of his analysis of the first movement of the Quartet Op. 130, for instance, consist of structural analysis, while the final page offers an expressive interpretation in terms of a quasi-Hegelian synthesis of opposed emotions (Hatten, 1994, pp. 134–45). And while he does sometimes begin with a provisional and intuitive identification of the music's expressive content, following this with structural analysis and then a refinement of the expressive interpretation based on that analysis, it is significant that Hatten never goes on to the next stage (that is, returns to and refines the structural analysis on the basis of the expressive one). To this extent the relationship between structure and expression is still an unequal one: as usual in musical analysis, the cards are stacked in favour of structure. In other contexts, however, such as his account of the *Cavatina* from the same quartet, Hatten's treatment is more even-handed. He makes use of vocabulary that applies equally well to structure or expression (undercutting, irruption, or reversal, for example). He mingles structural and expressive vocabulary (1994, p. 213):

A strong wedge motion in m. 5 expands registrally to the apex on the downbeat of m. 6, which is negated as a climax by the more intensely expressive crux created by the unexpected reversal (registral collapse) on the second beat. The 'willed' (basically stepwise) ascent takes on a hopeful character supported by the stepwise bass.

At other times, he offers parallel structural and expressive interpretations; on p. 214 he writes of bar 12 that 'As the vi region of Eb major, C minor would appear to be an appropriate choice in light of the harmonic emphasis it has already received in m. 6. The region could also be motivated by the expressive value of the relative minor as an emotionally troubled opposition to the serenity of the major'.

But most revealing is the way in which he stresses what, in 'purely musical' terms, might be seen as points of abnormality or incoherence, and siezes upon them as interpretative opportunities. For instance, he says of the repeated iv^7 chords on the second beats of bars 15 and 16, following anomalously on cadential six-four chords, that they support:

a construal as 'parenthetical' or outside the normal course of time, thus akin to 'insight' in that it comes without logical necessity or sequential train of thought . . . Interactively interpreting these inflections of meaning, one might understand the resulting trope as 'tragically weighted insight or reflection, expanding an instant that seems frozen within the flow of time' (Hatten, 1994, p. 215).

Expanding the same principle to the scale of the movement's formal unfolding, he provides a figure showing 'unconvincing formal analyses' (1994, p. 209, Figure 8.1): the very incoherence of the movement when understood in purely formal terms becomes a source of its overall expressive meaning, which Hatten sees as a kind of metaphorical blend of tragic insight and faith, each illuminating the other. In this way, expression is not seen as simply a gloss on structure; it works in counterpoint with it.

Writers such as Karl and Robinson, Maus, and Hatten demonstrate that it is possible to use structural and expressive vocabularies together in a way that does not simply map the one onto the other, in the manner of Kivy's 'new music criticism'. It might be going too far to say that any of them succeeds in talking in a sustained manner about both the music and the emotion (even Hatten sometimes gives the impressive of lurching from one to the other). But they manage to do so in flashes, and the result is illuminating.

3.5 CONCLUSION: DISCOURSE AND EMOTION IN MUSIC

In the work of some writers, the distance between technical and 'anthropomorphically evocative' interpretation, to borrow Maus's phrase, becomes much greater. A good illustration is provided by a pair of curiously similar essays: by Charles Fisk on the first movement of Schubert's Sonata in Bb major, D. 960 (Fisk, 1997), and by Marion Guck on—among other things—the second movement of Mozart's G minor Symphony, K. 550 (Guck, 1994). Each begins with a single, portentous moment in the piece:[16] the left hand trill in the seventh bar of Schubert's sonata, and the Cb in bar 53 of the symphony movement. And each constructs out of this moment a similar story: that of an alien element, an 'outsider' who after a succession of vicissitudes becomes accepted within the larger context represented by the piece—is accepted, in other words, as an 'insider'. The link that each author makes between music on the one hand, and on the other the narrative of rejection and acceptance, alterity and assimilation, builds on the expressive properties of the music and at the same time brings new expressive properties, new connotations of positive or negative emotion, to bear upon it. Neither author, of course, is claiming that the original music was in any sense 'about' immigration. Like Newcomb in the case of Schumann's Second Symphony, and Karl and Robinson in the case of Shostakovitch's Tenth, Fisk invokes the circumstances of Schubert's life to add credibility to, or at least to deepen, his interpretation: maybe, he says, the (again arguably) homosexual Schubert felt himself to be an outsider in his own society and so 'took solace, at least unconsciously' from his own parable of integration (Fisk, 1997, p. 200). Whereas Karl and Robinson give the impression of speaking from a position of interpretative authority, however ('Shostakovich, ever mistrustful of happy endings, undercuts its optimistic qualities' (1997, p. 178)), Fisk claims to be doing no more than telling a story, offering 'a naively poetic description of what happens in the music'

---

[16] Both authors use this word: Fisk (1997, p. 184) and Guck (1994, p. 63).

(Fisk, 1997, p. 195), and the personal and provisional nature of his interpretation is highlighted in the title: 'What Schubert's last sonata might hold' (further glossed, on the final page of the article, as 'what Schubert's last sonata holds for me'). Guck similarly introduces her account as 'a story about Cb' (Guck, 1994, p. 67).

Then what, you might ask, is the point of all this? Fisk tells his story in order to substantiate an argument that every listener projects his or her own emotional experiences into the music, which in turn moulds those experiences so that they become in some sense purely musical emotions (Fisk, 1997, p. 182). The limitation of his approach, however, is that he begins with technical analysis, goes on to unfold his narrative (showing how it can be fitted to the framework of the analysis)—and then stops. Guck, by contrast, structures her article through a process of oscillation between technical and expressive interpretation. She begins with her perception of the Cb's portentousness, an observation which (as she puts it) 'incorporates a conceptual structure that is covert' (Guck, 1994, p. 71). The purpose of constructing the parallel narrative, she continues, is that 'the conceptual structure of the immigrant's tale is revealed in the process of its telling'; in other words, the story renders the structure explicit, and so initiates the process of answering the analytical question '*why* is the Cb portentous?'. But to complete the answer it is necessary to return to the musical text, to the plane of technical analysis, understanding and experiencing the music in light of the narrative: as Guck puts it, her story 'suggests a strategy for hearing not only the highlighted events but also the lines of development in which they participate, which is to say that it provides a means of codifying and enriching the hearing of the whole piece' (1994, p. 71). The point of the analysis, in short, is not just to describe how you experience the music, but to *change* how you experience it, in both technical and affective terms.

It is not only Fisk's and Guck's analyses which do this. We mentioned above that Hatten presents his work as, in essence, an exercise in the reconstruction of historical listening practices. However, this is not the only nor necessarily the most productive way of reading it, and indeed Hatten does not embark upon the systematic kind of historical reconstruction of period perception, based on contemporary documentation, that has been attempted for instance by James Johnson (1995). The alternative is to read Hatten's work as a sustained argument about how we might most fruitfully hear Beethoven's music today. Understood this way, Hatten's book becomes an attack on the etiolated listening practices brought about by what he refers to as the 'errors of formalism' (Hatten, 1994, p. 228); by contrast, he is offering a richer, more complex, more human way to hear the music, and one which (as a bonus) perhaps recreates something of the manner in which Beethoven's first listeners heard it. Another way to express this is that it is not simply a matter of hearing emotions out of the music—that is, hearing the meanings that were always there within it—but, so to speak, of hearing them *into* it. And understood this way, analytical and critical practices are less concerned with how the music is than how it might be heard to be; they aim less at proof than at persuasion (as Guck puts it, 'Truth is replaced by the plausibility of the narrative', 1994, p. 72). This is the basis of what we term a 'performative' approach to music and expressive meaning.[17]

---

[17] The concept of the performative derives from speech act theory (Austin, 1962) and is particularly influential in performance and gender studies (see, respectively, Schechner, 1988 and

There is a sense in which writing about music has always been performative, and one of the most common ways of misinterpreting the documents of music history is by reading them as descriptions of actual practice rather than interventions in it. This is obvious in the case of the treatises of the Baroque and Classical periods, which prescribed how their readers were to compose, perform, or understand music (and in some cases the music they were to compose, perform, or understand, too).[18] Equally, musicological knowledge can shape perceptions: John Spitzer (1987) has shown how divergent acounts by different critics of the same piece of music (*Sinfonia Concertante* in Eb, attributed to Mozart) are not simply due to differences in taste, but reflect debate over the work's authenticity. (Not only do critics tend to write more positively when they think the music is by Mozart, Spitzer found, but they tend to focus on the same passages and use the same metaphors in describing them.) And one might equally claim that, to misquote Judith Butler, all the approaches to musical emotion outlined in the previous sections have helped to bring about the very responses and practices which they purport to describe.[19] Or to use the language of social constructionism, discourse about music (by which we mean principally but certainly not exclusively verbal discourse) actively constructs rather than simply reconstructs its expressivity. The very act of saying that a certain piece of music is expressive in a certain sort of way leads you to hear it that way, and so one can think of dominant interpretations of particular compositions (Tovey's interpretation of the first-movement recapitulation of the Ninth Symphony as the embodiment of cosmic catastrophe, for instance, or for that matter McClary's interpretation of the same passage in terms of a rapist's fantasy) as exercises in the creation and not merely the reporting of expressive meaning.

There has always been a strong awareness of the performative value of criticism among writers associated with the 'New' musicology (in particular, Lawrence Kramer and Carolyn Abbate[20]). More generally, and reflecting parallel trends in cultural studies, the ethnomusicologist Philip Bohlman argued in his significantly named article 'Musicology as a political act' (1993) that the discipline as a whole is as much involved in the generation as the analysis of the values and meanings that are ascribed to music.

Seen in this way, the history of musicological approaches to music's affective character forms part of the broader history of emotions, within which affective states are

Butler, 1990). Central to it is the idea that meaning is constructed through performative acts: whereas the meaning of 'the sky is blue' is referential (it refers to an external reality), when you say 'I promise' you are not referring to something but actually *doing* it by virtue of what you say. The term therefore has no direct link with performance in the musical sense (which is not to say that performative approaches do not have much to offer the study of musical performance).

[18] For an example of the role of performance pedagogy in the construction of musical experience, see Blasius (1996). Blasius argues that, along with other discursive domains, early nineteenth-century piano method is a realization of the eighteenth-century project to systematize affect and rhetoric.

[19] '[Gender] identity is performatively constituted by the very "expressions" that are said to be its results' (Butler, 1990, p. 25).

[20] See, in particular, Kramer (1990) and Abbate (1991). More recently, Monson (1996) has applied the same principle to the analysis of jazz performance, arguing that 'emotion is constituted or constructed through social practices . . . Music, it seems to me, is a particularly powerful constructor of emotion . . . a powerful activity that can produce a "community of sentiment" binding performers and audiences into something larger than the individual' (p. 178).

understood to be experienced by individuals in ways which are culturally mediated and historically contingent. For example, the changed conceptions and experiences of music's affective character in France between 1750 and 1850, attested to by Johnson's (1995) account of opera in Paris, formed part of, and arguably helped produce, broader changes in emotional thinking and display (Reddy, 2001). Recent contributions to this musicological strand of the cultural history of emotion include Gary Tomlinson's (2004) observations of a shift in Monteverdi's musical treatment of the 'passions', Penelope Gouk and Helen Hills's (2005) collection of essays, whose historical reach spans the fourteenth to twentieth centuries, and Nicola Dibben's (2006) analysis of the construction of emotions as private, interiorized experiences in the music and videos of Björk. What these studies have in common is their understanding of emotions as historically contingent, and of music (including musical discourse and behaviour) as one of the ways in which emotional displays and experience are produced by culture.

Attempts to develop explicit theoretical models for the attribution of meaning to music, however, are a recent development and arise out of a promising intersection of music theory, psychology, and cognitive science. Lawrence Zbikowski (1999), for instance, has drawn on conceptual blending theory (itself representing the intersection of linguistics and literary theory) in order to analyse three separate settings of the same poem, Müller's *Trockne Blumen*. Without entering into details, the basic idea is that there are aspects of shared structure (what Zbikowski calls a 'common topography') between the words and the music, which enables us to map the one onto the other as we listen to the song.[21] The result is a blending of the attributes of each, which gives rise to emergent meaning—meaning, that is, which is not present in either words or music separately but arises out of their interaction. In this way the affective associations of the words are transferred to the music: as Zbikowski says, 'We can easily imagine outward physical expressions of the miller's torment—facial contortions, hand wringing, pacing—mirroring his internal conflict' (1999, p. 309). And the point is that these become as much properties of the music as of the words,[22] so that once again there is a sense in which we are talking about emotional content even as we analyse musical structure. Up to now such approaches have been principally applied to the analysis of multimedia texts (Cook, 1998b, builds a general theory of multimedia on a similar basis), but there is no reason why this should be the case: you can equally well use them to compare Tovey's and McClary's interpretations of the first movement recapitulation of the Ninth Symphony, demonstrating the manner in which each interpretation creates new meaning (Cook, 2001). Used this way, the conceptual blending approach reveals how meaning is constructed through the interaction between musical texts and

[21] The analysis involves the creation of a graphic diagram or 'conceptual integration framework' (CIN) which shows four interrelated 'spaces'. These are the 'text space' and 'music space', which show the corresponding features on which the mapping is based; the 'generic space', which indicates the dimension within which it takes place; and the 'blended space', where attributes of the text and music spaces are combined to create new meaning. For further explanation of CINs, which derive from the work of Mark Turner and Gilles Fauconnier, see Zbikowski (1999, pp. 310–14).

[22] This links with Fisk's claim, mentioned in the previous section, that listeners' emotions are so moulded by music as to become purely musical emotions.

the invisible web of discourse, ranging from books and CD liners to television and concert-interval chatter, that surrounds them.

Coming from a different direction but converging with the conceptual blending approach is another, drawn this time from psychology—specifically, from James Gibson's (1979) 'ecological' approach to perception (which musicologists and music theorists are only now beginning to explore seriously). Traditional approaches to music perception see it as built up in succession from basic elements such as tones, scale patterns, chords, and so on, with expressive or social meaning representing, to repeat our earlier phrase, the icing on the cake. (This corresponds to the sequential approach we have criticized: first analysing the structure, and then interpreting the meaning.) By contrast, the ecological approach seeks to understand perception in terms of its function, that is to say the means by which any organism grasps and interacts with its environment, and from this perspective the semantic properties of any stimulus, including its affective properties, are just as basic—just as much properties of the music—as any acoustic ones. Affective properties, in short, are not deduced through interpretation of the music, but directly specified by it. But this does not represent a reversion to earlier ideas that meaning is 'locked into the sounds', to borrow Moore's phrase (1993, p. 157), just waiting to be unlocked by listeners, because meaning emerges from a mutual relationship between perceiver and perceived in which any number of personal, historical, or critical influences come into play. It is this mutual relationship that becomes the object of analysis. As represented by Clarke's (1999) study of subject-position in music by Frank Zappa and P. J. Harvey, and subsequent monograph (Clarke, 2005), the aim is very much the same as we have described in the work of Zbikowski: to find a way of talking about music which articulates the emotional properties that keep us listening to it, while at the same time conforming to the requirements for intersubjective intelligibility in the absence of which writing about music becomes a critical free-for-all where anything goes.

New as they may be, at least to musicology, such approaches address an old problem: how to speak about music and emotional meaning at the same time, without changing the subject. In addition, they emphasize the intrinsic reflexivity of critical activity—the way that what we say about music's meaning contributes to bringing that meaning into being. If the further development of musicological approaches to emotion depends on continued cross-fertilization with other disciplines, then (to misquote Butler again) this book may itself contribute to the very thinking we have attempted to describe.

RECOMMENDED FURTHER READING

1. Feld, S. (1990). *Sound and sentiment: Birds, weeping, poetics, and song in Kaluli expression* (2nd edn). Philadelphia, PA: University of Pennsylvania Press.
2. Hatten, R. (1994). *Musical meaning in Beethoven: Markedness, correlation, and interpretation.* Bloomington, IN: Indiana University Press.
3. Zbikowski, L. (2002). *Conceptualizing music: Cognitive structure, theory, and analysis.* Oxford: Oxford University Press.

References

Abbate, C. (1991). *Unsung voices: Opera and musical narrative in the nineteenth century.* Princeton, NJ: Princeton University Press.

Adorno, T. W. (1987). *Philosophy of new music.* London: Sheed & Ward. (Originally published 1973)

Agawu, V. K. (1991). *Playing with signs.* Princeton, NJ: Princeton University Press.

Allanbrook, W. J. (1983). *Rhythmic gesture in Mozart.* Chicago, IL: University of Chicago Press.

Austin, J. L. (1962). *How to do things with words.* Cambridge, MA: Harvard University Press.

Bach, C. P. E. (1974). *Essay on the true art of playing keyboard instruments* (trans. W. J. Mitchell). London: Eulenberg Books. (Originally published 1778)

Blasius, L. D. (1996). The mechanics of sensation and the construction of the Romantic musical experience. In I. Bent (ed.), *Music theory in the age of Romanticism* (pp. 3–24). Cambridge, UK: Cambridge University Press.

Bloomfield, T. (1993). Resisting songs: Negative dialectics in pop. *Popular Music, 12,* 13–31.

Bolhman, P. (1993). Musicology as a political act. *Journal of Musicology, 11,* 411–36.

Budd, M. (1985). *Music and the emotions: The philosophical theories.* London: Routledge.

Burnham, S. (1999). How music matters: Poetic content revisited. In N. Cook & M. Everist (eds), *Rethinking music* (pp. 193–216). Oxford: Oxford University Press.

Butler, J. P. (1990). *Gender trouble: Feminism and the subversion of identity.* London: Routledge.

Cavicchi, D. (1999). *Tramps like us: Music and meaning among Springsteen fans.* Oxford: Oxford University Press.

Clarke, E. F. (1999). Subject-position and the specification of invariants in music by Frank Zappa and P. J. Harvey. *Music Analysis, 18,* 347–74.

Clarke, E. F. (2005). *Ways of listening: An ecological approach to the perception of musical meaning.* Oxford: Oxford University Press.

Cone, E. T. (1982). Schubert's promissary note. *19th-Century Music, 5,* 233–41.

Cook, N. (1998a). *Music: A very short introduction.* Oxford: Oxford University Press.

Cook, N. (1998b). *Analysing musical multimedia.* Oxford: Clarendon Press.

Cook, N. (2001). Theorizing musical meaning. *Music Theory Spectrum, 23,* 170–95.

Cooke, D. (1959). *The language of music.* London: Oxford University Press.

Davies, S. (1994). *Musical meaning and expression.* Ithaca, NY: Cornell University Press.

Dibben, N. (2001). Pulp, pornography and voyeurism. *Journal of the Royal Musical Association, 126,* 83–106.

Dibben, N. (2006). Subjectivity and the construction of emotion in the music of Björk. *Music Analysis, 25,* 1–2, 171–197.

Eisler, H. [and Adorno, T. W.] (1947). *Composing for the films.* London: Dennis Dobson.

Feld, S. (1990). *Sound and sentiment: Birds, weeping, poetics, and song in Kaluli expression* (2nd edn). Philadelphia, PA: University of Pennsylvania Press.

Fisk, C. (1997). What Schubert's last sonata might hold. In J. Robinson (ed.), *Music and meaning* (pp. 179–200). Ithaca, NY: Cornell University Press.

Flinn, C. (1992). *Strains of utopia: Gender, nostalgia, and Hollywood film music.* Princeton, NJ: Princeton University Press.

Gibson, J. J. (1979). *The ecological approach to visual perception.* Boston, MA: Houghton-Mifflin.

Gjerdingen, R. O. (1988). *A classic turn of phrase.* Philadelphia, PA: University of Pennsylvania Press.

Goehr, L. (1992). *The imaginary museum of musical works: An essay in the philosophy of music.* Oxford: Clarendon Press.

Gouk, P. & Hills, H. (2005). *Representing Emotions: New Connections in the Histories of Art, Music and Medicine.* Aldershot, UK: Ashgate.

Guck, M. A. (1994). Rehabilitating the incorrigible. In A. Pople (ed.), *Theory, analysis and meaning in music* (pp. 57–73). Cambridge, UK: Cambridge University Press.

Hanslick, E. (1986). *On the musically beautiful: A contribution towards the revision of the aesthetics of music* (trans. G. Payzant). Indianapolis, IN: Hackett. (Originally published 1854)

Hatten, R. (1994). *Musical meaning in Beethoven: Markedness, correlation, and interpretation.* Bloomington, IN: Indiana University Press.

Jakobson, R. (1971). *Language in relation to other communication systems. Selected writings,* Vol. 2. The Hague, The Netherlands: Mouton.

Johnson, J. H. (1995). *Listening in Paris: A cultural history.* Berkeley, CA: University of California Press.

Karl, G., & Robinson, J. (1997). Shostakovich's Tenth Symphony and the musical expression of cognitively complex emotions. In J. Robinson (Ed.), *Music and meaning* (pp. 154–78). Ithaca, NY: Cornell University Press.

Keil, C. (1994). Motion and feeling through music. In C. Keil & S. Feld (eds), *Music grooves* (pp. 53–76). Chicago, IL: University of Chicago Press.

Kerman, J. (1985). *Musicology.* London: Fontana Press. (*Contemplating music: Challenges to musicology.* Cambridge, MA: Harvard University Press)

Kirkpatrick, R. (1984). *Interpreting Bach's 'Well-Tempered Clavier': A performer's discourse of method.* New Haven, CT: Yale University Press.

Kivy, P. (1987). How music moves. In P. Alperson (ed.), *What is music? An introduction to the philosophy of music* (pp. 149–62). University Park, PA: Pennsylvania State University Press.

Kivy, P. (1993). *The fine art of repetition: Essays in the philosophy of music.* Cambridge, UK: Cambridge University Press.

Kramer, L. (1990). *Music as cultural practice, 1800–1900.* Berkeley, CA: University of California Press.

Langer, S. K. (1957). *Philosophy in a new key.* Cambridge, MA: Harvard University Press. (Originally published 1942)

Leech-Wilkinson, D. (2007). Sound and meaning in recordings of Schubert's 'Die Junge Nonne'. *Musicae Scientiae, 11,* 209–36.

Lerdahl, F., & Jackendoff, R. (1983). *A generative theory of tonal music.* Cambridge, MA: MIT Press.

Marks, M. M. (1992). *Music for the silent film: Contexts and case studies 1895–1924.* Oxford: Oxford University Press.

Mattheson, J. (1981). *Der vollkommene Capellmeister* (trans. E. C. Harris). Ann Arbor, MI: UMI Research Press. (Originally published 1739)

Maus, F. E. (1988). Music as drama. *Music Theory Spectrum, 10,* 56–73.

Maus, F. E. (1997). Narrative, drama and emotion in instrumental music. *The Journal of Aesthetics and Art Criticism, 55,* 293–302.

McClary, S. (1991). *Feminine endings: Music, gender and sexuality.* Minnesota, MN: University of Minnesota Press.

Meyer, L. B. (1956). *Emotion and meaning in music.* Chicago, IL: Chicago University Press.

Middleton, R. (1990). *Studying popular music.* Milton Keynes, UK: Open University Press.

Monson, I. (1996). *Saying something: Jazz improvisation and interaction.* Chicago, IL: University of Chicago Press.

Moore, A. F. (1993). *Rock: The primary text*. Buckingham, UK: Open University Press.

Newcomb, A. (1984). Once more 'between absolute and program music': Schumann's Second Symphony. *19th-Century Music, 7*, 233–50.

Pater, W. (1910). *The Renaissance: Studies in art and poetry*. London: Macmillan. (Originally published 1873)

Ratner, L. G. (1980). *Classic music: Expression, form and style*. New York: Schirmer.

Reddy, W. M. (2001). *The navigation of feeling: A framework for the history of emotions*. Cambridge, UK: Cambridge University Press.

Robinson, J. (1998). The expression and arousal of emotion in music. In P. Alperson (ed.), *Musical worlds: New directions in the philosophy of music* (pp. 13–22). University Park, PA: Pennsylvania State University Press.

Schechner, R. (1988). *Performance theory* (Revised edn). London: Routledge.

Schenker, H. (1994). The art of improvisation (trans. R. Kramer). In H. Schenker (ed. W. Drabkin), *The masterwork in music: A yearbook. Volume 1 (1925)* (pp. 2–19). Cambridge, UK: Cambridge University Press. (Originally published 1925)

Scruton, R. (1997). *The aesthetics of music*. Oxford: Clarendon Press.

Shepherd, J., & Wicke, P. (1997). *Music and cultural theory*. Cambridge, UK: Polity Press.

Solomon, N. (1989). Signs of the times: A look at late 18th-century gesturing. *Early Music, 17*, 551–61.

Spitzer, J. (1987). Musical attribution and critical judgement: The rise and fall of the Sinfonia Concertante for Winds, K. 279b. *Journal of Musicology, 5*, 319–56.

Tagg, P. (1982). Analysing popular music: Theory, method and practice. *Popular Music, 2*, 37–67.

Tagg, P. (1992). Towards a sign typology of music. In R. Dalmonte & M. Baroni (eds), *Secondo Convegno Europeo di Analisi Musicale* (pp. 369–78). Trento, Italy: Università degli studi di Trento.

Tagg, P. & Clarida, B. (2003). *Ten little title tunes: towards a musicology of the mass media*. New York: Mass Media Music Scholars' Press.

Tolbert, E. (1994). The voice of lament: Female vocality and performative efficacy in the Finnish-Karelian itkuvirsi. In L. C. Dunn & N. A. Jones (eds), *Embodied voices: representing female vocality in Western culture* (pp. 179–94). Cambridge, UK: Cambridge University Press.

Tomlinson, G. (2004). Five pictures of pathos. In G. K. Paster, K. Rowe and M. Floyd-Wilson (eds), *Reading the Early Modern Passions* (pp. 192–214). Philadelphia: University of Pennsylvania Press.

Treitler, L. (1999). The historiography of music: Issues of past and present. In N. Cook & M. Everist (eds.), *Rethinking music* (pp. 356–77). Oxford: Oxford University Press.

Wagner, R. (1899). *Prose works, Vol. 8* (trans. W. A. Ellis). London: Reeves.

Wallace, R. (1986). *Beethoven's critics: Aesthetic dilemmas and resolutions during the composer's lifetime*. Cambridge, UK: Cambridge University Press.

Walser, R. (1993). *Running with the Devil: Power, gender and madness in heavy metal music*. Hanover, NH: Weslyan University Press.

Zbikowski, L. M. (1999). The blossoms of 'Trockne Blumen': Music and text in the early nineteenth century. *Music Analysis, 18*, 307–45.

CHAPTER 4

AT THE INTERFACE BETWEEN THE INNER AND OUTER WORLD

PSYCHOLOGICAL PERSPECTIVES

JOHN A. SLOBODA AND
PATRIK N. JUSLIN

PSYCHOLOGY is concerned with the explanation of individual human behaviour and mental processes, and so a psychological approach to music and emotion seeks an explanation for whether, when, how, and why individuals experience emotional reactions to music, and how and why they experience music as expressive of emotions.

The explanations sought by psychologists are essentially causal and organismic. They are causal in the sense that they seek both to discover antecedents to the behaviours requiring explanation and uncover or postulate mechanisms whereby the antecedents interact to bring about the observed behaviours. They are organismic in that the primary interest of psychology is in mechanisms which are internal to the organism. External causes, such as historical or social factors, are only relevant to a psychological framework where there is a route by which these may impact on the internal mechanisms. So, in the study of music and emotion, a central aim of psychology is to understand the mechanisms that intervene between music reaching a person's ears and an emotion being experienced or detected by that person as a result of hearing that music. Other important aims involve understanding the roles of emotion in producing music.

In this chapter, we outline some of the achievements of and challenges for the psychological approach to musical emotions. First, we describe how psychologists have conceptualized and approached the study of emotions in general. Second, we identify some emergent themes in the psychological literature on music and emotion, and illustrate progress in addressing these themes through some studies that we consider, in one way or another, to be exemplary of the discipline. Third and last, we highlight some implications of the research to date, including some directions for future research.

4.1 THE PSYCHOLOGY OF EMOTION

What is an emotion? This question, which was the title of one of William James's (1884) most famous articles, has still not received a definitive answer. One reason for this is that emotions are difficult to define and measure, let alone explain.

4.1.1 Defining emotions

Kleinginna and Kleinginna (1981) identified 92 definitions in textbooks, articles, dictionaries, and other sources, each based on a different set of criteria. However, although psychologists do not agree on a precise definition of emotions, they do agree about the general characteristics (Izard, 2009). Thus, in accordance with the working definition of emotion in Chapter 1 of this volume, and the increasing consensus in the affective sciences more generally (e.g. Davidson, Scherer, & Goldsmith, 2003, p. xiii), we offer the following broad definition:

Emotions are relatively brief, intense, and rapidly changing responses to potentially important events (subjective challenges or opportunities) in the external or internal environment, usually of a social nature, which involve a number of subcomponents (cognitive changes, subjective feelings, expressive behaviour, and action tendencies) that are more or less 'synchronized'.

The concept of 'synchronization' (Juslin & Scherer, 2005, pp. 70–1) or 'coherence' (Ekman, 1992) refers to the idea that emotions organize coordinated responses in different components to prepare the organism for adaptive behaviour and regulation (Levenson, 2003). Although the extent to which various emotion components are synchronized is still debated (Russell, 2003) and certain exceptions may be found (Frijda, 2008), some degree of synchronization has been demonstrated in recent research (e.g. Mauss, Levenson, McCarter, Wilhelm, & Gross, 2005). Hence, multi-component approaches are increasingly popular in the field.

4.1.2 Measuring emotions

Ever since psychology wedded philosophy to science in the late nineteenth century to create a novel discipline distinct from the speculation of the past (Boring, 1950), the issue of how to measure mental phenomena has been at the forefront. Emotion as a scientific construct is inferred from three primary types of evidence: (a) *self-report* (Chapters 8 and 9, this volume), (b) *expressive behaviour* (Chapter 11), and (c) *bodily responses* (Chapters 11 and 12). Recent years have seen the proliferation of an additional set of so-called *implicit measures* (Chapter 10). Each type of measure presents its own set of problems, therefore the best approach might be to use multiple measures whenever practically feasible (for an extensive overview, see Coan & Allen, 2007).

On the other hand, several psychologists believe that self-reported feeling is, and will remain, the most important kind of evidence of emotions, whatever its problems in terms of language or demand characteristics.[1] Feelings as irreducible qualia are the essence of many definitions of emotions (Kleinginna & Kleinginna, 1981), and data concerning the prevalence of feelings represent to a considerable extent what any theory of emotion should explain in the first place (Barrett, Mesquita, Ochsner, & Gross, 2007; Juslin, 2009; see also Chapter 8, this volume).

4.1.3 Explaining emotions

From a psychological point of view, then, emotion is a scientific construct that points to a set of phenomena of feelings, behaviours and bodily reactions that occur together in everyday life. The task of emotion psychology is to describe these phenomena, and to explain them in terms of their underlying processes. The explanations can be formulated at different levels (Dennett, 1987): the *phenomenological* level (e.g. feelings), the *functional* level (e.g. different types of information processing), and the *hardware* level (e.g. brain neurons, hormones, genes).

Psychological explanations of emotions operate primarily at the functional level, though with frequent references to the other levels. Psychological theories of emotion outline the structure of the individual, incoming and stored information that is processed, and dynamic interactions with the environment (Frijda, 2008). Psychologists agree that emotions are biologically based (Buck, 1999), but also acknowledge a range of socio-cultural influences (Mesquita, 2003).

The psychological *mechanisms* that mediate between external events and emotional responses may be of several kinds (Izard, 1993; Juslin & Västfjäll, 2008). However, cognitive appraisals of events in relation to subjective goals, intentions, motives, and concerns of the individual are believed to be frequent sources of emotion in everyday life (Scherer, 1999). This suggests that emotions cannot be explained merely in terms of objectively defined stimuli—the stimuli gain their significance from how they are processed by the individual in a specific context.

---

[1] The term *demand characteristics* refers to cues that convey the researcher's hypothesis to the participant, and therefore may influence the participant's behaviour. Verbal measures are believed to be more sensitive to demand than, say, bodily responses, which are more difficult to control for the individual (see also Chapter 10, this volume).

4.1.4 Distinguishing emotional processes

Most psychologists like to think of an emotion as a sequence of events, although they usually disagree about the precise sequence and about where an emotion episode begins or ends. Part of this difficulty in determining the beginning or end of an emotion episode might reflect that affective processing is really a *continuous* process: several researchers assume that people are always in *some* affective state, even if they may not be aware of it (see Davidson, 1994; Izard, 2009; Barrett et al, 2007). When the state is intense and involves a 'salient stimulus', we tend to call it an 'emotion', whereas when the state is less intense, and its cause is not immediately apparent, we tend to call it a 'mood' (or 'core affect'; Russell, 2003). Thus, it remains unclear whether the distinction between mood and emotion, which is based more on folk theories than on scientific evidence (Beedie, Terry, & Lane, 2005), will survive closer scrutiny.[2]

Another distinction, which may be of more lasting importance, is that between the *perception* of emotions and the *induction*, or experience, of emotions. Although the distinction can often be a matter of degree, these are in principle different and independent processes: for instance, we can perceive or recognize an emotion in a person's face without experiencing it ourselves; and we can experience an emotion to a stimulus without concurrently perceiving any emotion. Wager et al (2008) were able to demonstrate, in an extensive meta-analysis of PET and fMRI studies, that perception and induction of emotions involve 'peak activations' of different areas of the brain, supporting the idea that these are different processes.

The ways that emotions are perceived and experienced help both psychologists and lay people to conceptualize emotions and differentiate between them. In the following, we briefly outline the dominant approaches to conceptualizing emotions in psychology.

4.1.5 Categorical approaches

According to categorical theories, people experience emotion episodes as *categories* that are distinct from each other. Common to this approach is the concept of 'basic emotions'; that is, the idea that there is a limited number of innate and universal emotion categories from which all other emotional states can be derived (Ekman, 1992; Izard, 1977; Lazarus, 1991; Plutchik, 1994; Power & Dalgleish, 1997; Tomkins, 1962). Each category may be defined functionally in terms of a key appraisal of events which have occurred frequently during evolution (Table 4.1).[3] It is further hypothesized that basic emotions (a) have distinct functions that contribute to individual survival, (b) are found in all cultures, (c) are experienced as unique feelings, (d) appear early in

---

[2] For a discussion of how emotions relate to other affective phenomena such as moods and preferences, we refer to Chapter 1 of this volume.

[3] 'Basic' emotions are also sometimes referred to as 'discrete', 'primary', or 'fundamental' emotions.

Table 4.1 Key appraisals for basic emotions adapted from Oatley (1992) and Lazarus (1991)

Emotion	Juncture of plan[a]	Core relational theme[b]
Happiness:	Subgoals being achieved	Making reasonable progress towards a goal
Anger:	Active plan frustrated	A demeaning offense against me and mine
Sadness:	Failure of major plan or loss of active goal	Having experienced an irrevocable loss
Fear:	Self preservation goal threatened or goal conflict	Facing an immediate, concrete, or overwhelming physical danger
Disgust:	Gustatory goal violated	Taking in or being close to an indigestible object or idea (metaphorically speaking)

[a] Adapted from Oatley (1992)
[b] Adapted from Lazarus (1991)

development, (e) involve distinct patterns of physiological changes, (f) can be inferred in other primates, and (g) have distinct facial and vocal expressions.

The notion of basic emotions has been criticized on various grounds. One criticism has been that different theorists have come up with different sets of basic emotions (Ortony & Turner, 1990). However, psychologists adopting an evolutionary perspective on emotions agree that *happiness, anger, sadness, fear* and *disgust* are basic emotions. Another frequent criticism is that basic emotions cannot do justice to the variety of emotions experienced in everyday life. Basic emotion theorists would counter that the irreducible qualia of basic emotions combine with conscious cognitive appraisals to produce a range of complex emotions (Oatley, 1992). Moreover, some theorists postulate as many as 14 (Lazarus, 1991) or 16 (Roseman, Spindel, & Jose, 1990) discrete emotions.

A different, more recent categorical emotion approach is represented by *component process* theories (Scherer, 2001). Such theories continue to assume that there are emotion categories, but instead of proposing a limited number of 'basic' categories, the theories suggest that the categories are as many and as fine-grained as the particular patterns of appraisals they result from. A problem is, however, that not all emotions are aroused through cognitive appraisals. Hence, differences among emotions cannot simply be reduced to patterns of appraisal.

4.1.6 Dimensional approaches

Dimensional theories conceptualize emotions based on their placement along broad affective *dimensions*.[4] The search for the dimensional structure of emotions has a long

---

[4] Dimensional models can be derived from any type of response data, but common sources are similarity ratings of emotion words or facial expressions, which are then analysed using factor analysis or multi-dimensional scaling (Plutchik, 1994, Ch. 3).

history (Wundt, 1897). There are both one-dimensional models (*arousal*; Duffy, 1941) and three-dimensional models (*valence, activation,* and *power*; Osgood et al, 1957), although Russell's (1980) two-dimensional *circumplex model* has been the most influential (see Figure 4.1). This model consists of a circular structure featuring the dimensions of *pleasure* and *arousal*. Within this structure, emotions that are across the circle from one another, such as sadness and happiness, correlate inversely. The circumplex model captures two important aspects of emotions—that they vary in their degree of similarity, and that some emotions may be conceived of as bipolar.

One criticism of the circumplex model is that valence may not be bipolar. Perhaps we can experience positive and negative affect simultaneously. Thus, an alternative version by Watson and Tellegen (1985) uses two independent unipolar dimensions: *positive affectivity* and *negative affectivity* (e.g. Chapter 8, this volume). Another criticism is that dimensional models blur essential psychological distinctions. In the circumplex model, emotions that are placed in the same position in the circular matrix can be quite different. For instance, *angry* and *afraid* are two emotions that are highly correlated in the structure because they are both high in arousal and unpleasantness. Yet they are very different in terms of their implications for the individual (see Table 4.1). Hence, dimensional models tend to lack theoretical depth, unless they are augmented by further assumptions (e.g. Russell, 2003).

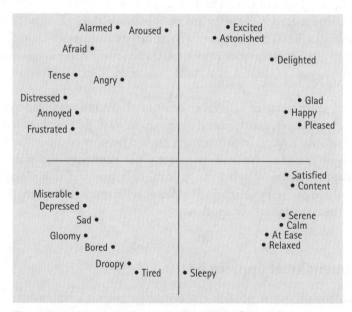

Fig. 4.1 A circumplex model of emotion (from Russell, 1980). (Copyright © 1980 by the American Psychological Association. Reprinted with permission.)

4.1.7 Prototype approaches

Prototype theories posit that language strongly shapes how we conceptualize and categorize information in the world (e.g. Rosch, 1978). It is proposed that membership in a category is determined by the resemblance to *prototypical exemplars*. The prototype itself is an abstract image, which consists of a set of weighted features that represent the exemplar; for instance, robins are seen as more prototypical of birds than ostriches, based on their different features. Similarly, some emotions (e.g. elation) are perhaps better exemplars of joy than others (e.g. relief), depending on their features (e.g. elicitors, appraisals). The prototype approach offers an interesting compromise among categorical and dimensional approaches. An example of a prototype structure is presented in Figure 4.2. The vertical dimension of the structure shows the hierarchical relationships among the categories. The most general level is the 'superordinate' level, which is defined by the positive or negative valence of the emotions within a particular category. The middle level represents the basic-level categories, or prototypes, which anchor our mental representations of all emotions within a category. The 'subordinate' level consists of all other emotions related to the prototype (Shaver, Schwartz, Kirson, & O'Connor, 1987).

Critics of the prototype approach have claimed that people's verbal accounts of emotions are insufficient for capturing the underlying structure of emotions, and that there is disagreement about which emotions qualify as prototypes. However, proponents of the prototype approach accept that boundaries among emotion categories are 'fuzzy', and claim that emotions cannot be defined in terms of a set of necessary and sufficient conditions.

4.2 EMOTION IN MUSIC: EMERGENT THEMES

Although emotions have been studied scientifically for a century, treatises on emotion rarely mention emotional reactions to music (for notable exceptions, see Frijda, 1989; James, 1884; Lazarus, 1991; Oatley, 1992; Zajonc, 1994). This may be part of a general neglect of music within the whole of psychology. Textbooks of psychology provide an informative overview of what is considered 'mainstream' by those responsible for outlining the field of psychology in introductory courses. In Martin, Carlson, and Buskist (2006), an introductory textbook co-written by European and North American authors with a strong focus on recent research, there are entire chapters on both language and emotion, neither of which mention music, except once, in passing. In the subject index to the book, music is referenced three times. By contrast language is referenced 34 times, and emotion 20 times. Still, even this is an advance. General textbooks written in the 1980s and 1990s tended to avoid music entirely.

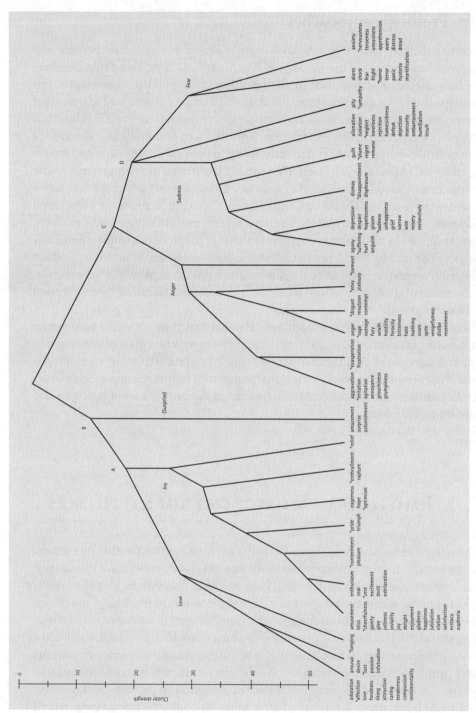

Fig. 4.2 A prototype analysis of emotion words (from Shaver et al, 1987). (Copyright © 1987 by the American Psychological Association. Reprinted with permission.)

We identify the 1990s as a 'turning point', both for the psychological study of emotions and the study of emotions in music. This is partly a function of the increased quantity and quality of relevant research, key themes of which we discuss below. But it may also be a function of increased societal acceptance of emotion and the emotional life as a topic for public discourse. The 1990s was the decade that saw huge public interest in both 'emotional intelligence' (e.g. Goleman, 1995) and the psychological effects of music stimulation (e.g. the 'Mozart effect' of Rauscher, Shaw, & Hy, 1993). Within the psychology of music, the same decade saw the emergence of the study of emotion from its earlier peripheral existence (Gabrielsson, 1993) to a more central, and continuously growing, role (see Chapter 1, this volume). This is reflected in the most recent 'textbook-type' addition to the music psychology literature—the *Oxford handbook of music psychology* (Hallam, Cross, & Thaut, 2009). Its subject index lists 53 separate references to emotion. These are distributed over ten of the 52 chapters. By contrast, the seminal textbook of the 1980s (Deutsch, 1982) has only four brief references to emotion.

We believe that this growing interest in emotion may reflect an increasing awareness that a central question of music psychology—how people experience music—cannot be answered without reference to the role of the emotions. But perhaps more importantly for scientists, the research literature now contains a number of frequently cited studies that have tackled well-defined scientific issues in methodologically replicable and extendable ways, thus offering the possibility of 'normal science' as defined by Kuhn (1962; see also Sloboda 1986/2005). This means that communities of researchers interact around these studies and the issues they raise, using shared paradigms and communication outlets (conferences and journals). The following sections highlight some of these studies and the emerging themes that they have addressed.

4.2.1 Emotional connotations of musical stimuli are consistent and predictable

Studies demonstrating shared patterns of emotion judgements of music across different people have been available for many years (systematic research starting with the seminal studies of Kate Hevner, 1935; see also Chapter 14, this volume). Recent years have seen two important developments. The first of these developments is the appearance of integrative studies (using meta-analysis and related techniques), which combine results from several different studies to provide a more robust and comprehensive account of the music–emotion link than any single study could give.

Two important studies in this regard are Juslin and Laukka (2003) and Västfjäll (2002). Juslin and Laukka conducted a meta-analysis of 41 studies, which revealed that the ascribed emotion of a music performance could be well predicted from a fairly small set of characteristics of the stimulus relating for instance to pitch, speed, intensity, and articulation (a summary appears in Figure 17.2 of Chapter 17, this volume). Västfjäll (2002) reviewed a different set of 41 studies of musical mood induction studies, and found significant commonalities in the choice of musical material, with the same piece (e.g. *Coppèlia* by Delibes) sometimes being used in 12 or more studies to induce a given mood. This suggests common ascription of mood to musical extracts by researchers and therapists.

The second development is the emergence of some well-articulated theoretical frameworks for explaining these specific music–emotion links. In the case of the data analysed by Juslin and Laukka (2003), comparison with results from 104 studies of emotional speech revealed that the same features that underlie the speech–emotion code are also responsible for listeners' judgements in musical experiments. For example, the features of speech that allow us to judge that a speaker is happy are largely the same features that allow us to ascribe that emotion to a music performance. This relationship was predicted by a 'functionalist' framework for music performance proposed several years earlier (Juslin, 1997).

Many other testable predictions follow from this framework. Because speech–emotion codes transcend linguistic cultures, and seem to be biologically inbuilt, then we would expect these codes also to operate across different musical cultures. Such predictions have been confirmed by Adachi, Trehub, and Abe (2004). Secondly, because children are able to accurately detect basic emotions in speech, we would expect the ability to detect these same emotions in music to emerge relatively early in childhood. Indeed, several studies (e.g. Cunningham & Sterling, 1988; Dolgin & Adelson, 1990; Kastner & Crowder, 1990; see also Chapter 23, this volume) suggest that these abilities are reasonably well developed by the age of four.

The studies that found these commonalities have generally featured short pieces of music and have focused on basic emotions. If stimuli get longer, and participants are able to use a wider range of descriptors, agreement might diminish. This would also be expected from theoretical considerations: longer sequences acquire specific cultural and personal meanings as a result of their use in specific contexts, and are more likely to contain changes in the various parameters signaling emotion, thus creating more complex, ambiguous and temporally shifting emotional signals. Such subtle, dynamic changes in expression are perhaps best captured by dimensional models of emotions, which are more amenable to analysis using continuous response methods (Sloboda & Lehmann, 2001; see Chapter 9, this volume).

4.2.2 Music not only expresses emotion that is perceived by listeners, it also evokes emotions in listeners

Although the distinction between perceived emotions and evoked emotions is clear, and has been well articulated in seminal literature (Meyer, 1956), empirical research has not always been careful to distinguish these two quite different ways in which emotion can be manifested through music. Gabrielsson (2002) notes that neither researchers nor subjects always observe the distinction. Listeners might confuse perceived emotions with what they feel themselves. In particular, asking listeners questions such as 'What emotion do you feel?', without further qualification, may be insufficiently precise to be assured that the person is having the emotion concerned. When someone says 'I feel that it might rain,' this means that the person senses or judges (on the basis of external evidence of some sort) that rain is coming. Similarly, when someone is asked about music 'What do you feel?', this may be interpreted as 'what do you sense or judge the emotion of the music to be?' The response 'I feel sadness' may be no more than 'I sense sadness in the music.' This possibility has been used by the philosopher Kivy (1990) and others to argue that music does not generally evoke emotions in listeners, it merely expresses emotions that are perceived by listeners. Kivy labelled this the 'cognitivist' position. The opposing position, that music also evokes emotions, was called the 'emotivist' position.

Some authors have noted that evoked emotion is most reliably inferred when measures other than self-report are taken, which could not possibly arise simply from perceptual judgements (Scherer & Zentner, 2001). Thus, for example, there is no real reason to expect pronounced responses in, say, the autonomic nervous system if a listener merely perceives an emotion in the music. Such arousal would, however, clearly be expected if the listener is experiencing a strong emotion. A few studies that have taken such methodological concerns on board have now been undertaken and prove quite conclusively that music does evoke emotions, and that the strong version of cognitivism is thus untenable. A pioneering contribution in this regard was the study of Krumhansl (1997), who demonstrated that the physiological changes (such as heart rate and skin conductance) that took place while people listened to music of varying emotional character were quite similar to the physiological changes that accompany emotions in non-musical situations. Moreover, different pieces produced different patterns of response. This finding was replicated by Nyklíček, Thayer, and Van Doornen (1997), who used multi-variate techniques to discriminate among four emotions based on cardiorespiratory variables. Rickard (2004) found that more intensely felt self-reported emotions tended to involve more pronounced psychophysiological arousal. These findings are all consistent with the emotivist position: that music may evoke as well as express emotions.

Recent studies further suggest that listeners may be able to distinguish between perception and induction, if properly instructed. Zentner, Grandjean, and Scherer (2008) asked several hundred people to rate a large set of emotions for the frequency with which they perceived and felt each to music. By asking for both types of response simultaneously, they decreased the likelihood that participants could be misconstruing the feeling question as a perception question. Rather clear differences were obtained in the patterns of response. Music was rated as particularly effective in evoking 'peaceful' emotions (e.g. soothed, calm, serene). Other emotions were more likely to be perceived in the music than felt (e.g. energetic, angry, and tense). These results show that there is no simple one-to-one relationship between perceived and felt emotion in regard to music. Indeed, Gabrielsson (2002) argued that the relationship between perception and induction may take several forms such as 'positive', 'negative', 'no systematic relationship', and 'no relation' (see Figure 4.3). Gabrielsson observed that many researchers presume a positive relationship, but that this relationship is far from general.

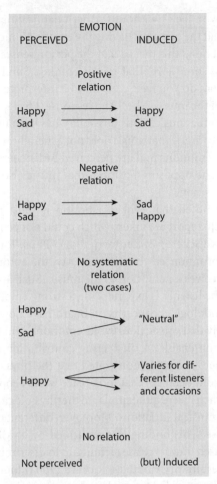

Fig. 4.3 Schematic illustration of the relationship between perceived and induced emotion in music (adapted from Gabrielsson, 2002).

The fact that music can evoke emotions in some circumstances does not prove that it does so in all circumstances. In many cases, only perception of emotion is taking place. In fact, recent estimates suggest that music arouses emotions in only about 55–65 per cent of the musical episodes (Juslin & Laukka, 2004; Juslin, Liljeström, Västfjäll, Barradas, & Silva, 2008). Unfortunately, the literature does not yet contain a clear enough theoretical account of which combination of circumstances and factors are likely to lead to musically induced emotion, and which are not. However, one development that will undoubtedly help this task is the clearer specification of the mechanisms under which emotions might be induced through music (see Chapter 22, this volume). Another promising way to distinguish instances of perceived and evoked emotions, hinted at above, is the use of a broader range of emotion measures.

4.2.3 Musically evoked emotions usually involve 'synchronized' responses at many different levels of the organism

From Darwin (1872) onward, a number of researchers have suggested that emotions involve coordinated changes across different subcomponents, to facilitate the organism's response to environmental demands (e.g. Lazarus, 1991; Mauss et al, 2005; Scherer, 2001). If emotions are defined by the co-occurrence of subcomponents that are more or less 'synchronized', then it becomes important to ask whether research has demonstrated such 'synchronization' in the case of music (Scherer & Zentner, 2001). There are three main categories of subcomponents: autonomic (e.g. changes in physiological parameters such as skin conductance or heart rate), experiential (e.g. changes in the nature and intensity of self-reported feeling), and behavioural (e.g. changes in observable phenomena such as facial expressions).[5]

Quite a number of studies have shown co-occurrence between two of these three categories (see Krumhansl, 1997; Steinbeis, Koelsch, & Sloboda, 2006, for co-occurrence of autonomic and experiential; and Grewe, Nagel, Kopiez, & Altenmuller, 2007, and other studies covered in Chapter 21, this volume, for co-occurrence of experiential and behavioural manifestations of 'thrills' such as piloerection and weeping). Few studies have shown coherence across all three components, however. One such study is that of Lundqvist, Carlsson, Hilmersson, and Juslin (2009), where significant co-occurrence was discovered between felt emotion (happy, sad), facial expressions, and a range of autonomic measures. The results were interpreted as consistent with an account in terms of 'emotional contagion' via music. For example, music with a 'happy' expression produced more zygomatic facial activity (associated with smiling), greater skin conductance, lower finger temperature, higher ratings of felt happiness and lower ratings of felt sadness than music with a 'sad' expression. Though the study was ecologically valid since it used brief pop songs with lyrics, arguably the most commonly encountered type of music in the Western world, further systematic studies, mapping these relationships across a wider range of emotions and types of music, are clearly called for.

One area for specific exploration should be the range of behavioural outcomes associated with musically induced emotion. Emotions in everyday non-musical situations are often connected to immediate behavioural consequences such as approach or avoidance. They tend to be spurs to significant (and often sudden) shifts in behaviour. On the other hand, many music-listening situations are characterized by suppressed or deferred expression of emotion (Chapter 18, this volume). Consider, for instance, the archetypal 'classical concert experience', which seems to be accompanied by behavioural stasis (almost total lack of movement or expressive behaviour).

---

[5] A more recent addition to the types of evidence used to infer emotions is brain activation as revealed by e.g. PET or fMRI (Blood & Zatorre, 2001; see Chapter 12, this volume).

Nonetheless, evidence from a number of sources (including the strong experiences with music reviewed in Chapter 20, this volume) shows that under certain circumstances, music-induced emotions may have profound, even life-changing behavioural consequences (e.g. the lifting of deep depressive states). There is also considerable evidence that music often creates strong action tendencies to move in coordination with the music (e.g. dancing, foot-tapping). This kind of coordination has been discussed under the broad heading of 'entrainment' (Clayton, Sager, & Will, 2005), although the role of emotion has not yet been explored.

In this respect, the traditional folk or modern pop concert is probably a richer environment for the study of emotion-induced behaviours. Such contexts are generally accompanied by highly visible ongoing behavioural manifestations among audience members, directly in response to the music. Indeed, it is somewhat surprising that psychologists appear not to have studied the whole set of behavioural repertoires available to audiences to explicitly signal their emotional reactions to the music (e.g. cheering, booing, applause). Even during classical concerts, these exist in abundance, but appear to have been totally ignored by psychological science, perhaps because much music-psychological research has been carried out in laboratory environments. Still, considering that subjective feelings and expressive behaviours may be more closely tied than subjective feelings and physiological response (Mauss et al, 2005), behavioural measures are clearly worthy of further investigation.

4.2.4 Emotional responses to music occur in a complex interaction between the music, the listener, and the situation

The contexts in which music can be heard are very varied. It is possible to be exposed to the same piece of music in situations as diverse as a shopping mall, a car, or a concert hall. The recent upsurge of interest in everyday musical experience has documented the range of such contexts in considerable detail (see Chapter 18, this volume). It is likely that someone hearing a piece of music in the background while they do their shopping is going to have a different emotional response to someone who has paid money to hear it in a concert. Not only is the level of attention likely to be different, but the emotional ambience of the situation itself will influence the response. In addition, the response is not the same from person to person. Much depends on the personality, level of knowledge, cultural orientation, and personal history of the listener.

Progress has been made in mapping some of the parameters of this interaction. For instance, Sloboda and Lehmann (2001) have shown that even when the music and the listening context are kept constant, and where all the listeners share a similarly high level of musical education (professional musicians working in a conservatoire), there are significant group differences in the time course of perception of emotion in a short piece of music. Pianists, non-pianists, and jurists showed different trajectories in their judgements of 'emotionality' in a Chopin prelude, where their judgements were elicited in real time by a continuous response method.

The effect of extra-musical variables on emotional responses has been shown in a number of experimental studies where the same piece of music is heard in different contexts. Emotional response to music can be influenced both by concurrent context (e.g. Thompson, Graham, & Russo, 2005) or by what preceded it (e.g. Dibben, 2004; see also Chapter 25, this volume). In addition to such experimental studies, correlational data from field studies show a statistical relationship between musical emotions and situations. For example, Juslin et al (2008) have shown that happiness tends to occur when the listener is with friends, whereas nostalgia tends to occur when the listener is alone. This underscores the importance of social contexts in the generation of musical emotion. So far, no experimental study has systematically manipulated all three factors—listener characteristics, music and context—in an attempt to predict specific emotions to music, although such research is currently under way (Chapter 22, this volume).

It is important to emphasize the importance of personal and contextual factors in emotional response, particularly given the cultural prevalence of rather naïve folk theories which hold that music can influence emotional state in the same kind of reliable way that a drug such as caffeine affects arousal. These theories have been used in the rather aggressive marketing of recorded music products (e.g. 'stress busters') but are also implicit in some scientific studies, where it is assumed, sometimes without adequate evidence, that a piece of music that has had a particular emotional effect in some other study will have this same effect in the study under question. However, the field has not yet mapped these variables in a way that provides much theoretical or predictive power. It has also made insufficient distinction between effects of person and contextual factors on the perception of emotion in music, and their effects on the experience of emotional states. It is highly plausible that perception of emotion in music is less vulnerable to these factors than experience of emotion. It is also possible that contextual factors more often attenuate or accentuate a given emotional state than result in radical shifts in emotional state. It would be theoretically and practically useful to delineate the precise variables that would allow the same piece of music to elicit intense happiness in some contexts and intense sadness in others. Such strategically driven research is still too infrequent in the discipline.

4.2.5 Music evokes mainly positive emotions in listeners

Prior to the 1990s, the predominant paradigm for music-psychological research on emotions was experimental. In this paradigm, participants are exposed to experimenter-chosen musical materials under carefully controlled laboratory conditions. This approach is ideal for mapping the parameters of the links between musical materials and the judged emotional content of the music. However, the experimental paradigm is less well suited to studying felt emotions to music, their scope and prevalence.

This is because felt emotions are strongly influenced by the social and personal context in which the music is being experienced.

Progress on these issues has been made by adopting an observational approach, surveying the range of music-induced emotions found in daily life in a more or less representative manner. One approach is to ask people to recall which emotions they have experienced to music over a period of time (e.g. Juslin & Laukka, 2004, Laukka, 2007; Zentner, Grandjean, & Scherer, 2008). However, this approach may be vulnerable to selection and recall bias. A more robust approach is to obtain data on the emotional effects of each occurrence of music exposure as close to the point of exposure as possible. The best-developed technique for doing this is the *experience-sampling methodology* (ESM), introduced to the literature by Czikzentmihalyi (Hektner, Schmidt & Czikzentmihalyi, 2007; see also description in Chapter 18, this volume). There is now strong converging evidence from a number of studies using ESM (e.g. North, Hargreaves, & Hargreaves, 2004; Juslin, Liljeström, Västfjäll, Barradas, & Silva, 2008) that positive emotions predominate in music listening, and—where emotional change over time is measured (as in Sloboda, Ivaldi, & O'Neill, 2001)—the direction is from negative to positive valence in the majority of cases.

In the ESM study by Juslin et al (2008), the emotions most frequently reported to music were *calm-contentment*, *happiness-elation*, and *interest-expectancy*, which together accounted for more than 50 per cent of the emotion episodes reported. Negative emotions such as *anger-irritation*, *anxiety-fear*, and *sadness-melancholy* occurred in less than 5 per cent of the episodes. A particularly important feature of this study was the concurrent measurement of emotional response to non-musical events. In general, positive emotions were more prevalent in musical than in non-musical situations, whereas negative emotions were more prevalent in non-musical than in musical situations. The study by Sloboda et al (2001) showed that where there was emotional change over the course of a musical episode, 87 per cent of these changes were in the direction of greater positivity (i.e. more happy, generous, comforted, secure, and relaxed). Hence, recent research has established, beyond doubt, that the common belief that 'music does you good' is grounded in empirical realities about the prevalence of emotional responses to music.

We can speculate as to why most music yields emotional improvements. It could be that, overall, encouraging valued pleasant emotions has been the intention (whether explicit or implicit) of those that write and perform music. If large amounts of music were designed to make people feel bad, it is hard to imagine that musicians would find it easy to get paid and supported for their work! Nonetheless, a more thoroughgoing analysis of the potential value of negative emotions in music (particularly where such emotions were designed to be felt by the music's producers) would be a very useful contribution, and one which would move our understanding well beyond the extensively studied negative emotion of music performance anxiety, which is a context-driven rather than content-driven emotion (see Chapter 16, this volume). Some indications of the potential value of negative emotions to music come from music therapy, where music is used to trigger emotionally laden memories of past events as sources of reflection on life (Thaut, 1990). Memories are, however, only one of the ways in which musical events may evoke emotions.

4.2.6 Musical emotions are evoked through the activation of one or more mechanisms, each incorporating a distinct type of information processing

The complexity of the music–emotion link has led some researchers to conclude that there cannot be just one mechanism by which music evokes emotion, but a number of different mechanisms (Berlyne, 1971). For instance, Dowling and Harwood (1986) have proposed an influential tripartite categorization of the ways that music may represent and evoke emotion, based on the notions of Charles Pierce, in terms of index, icon, and symbol. *Index* refers to a response due to an 'arbitrary' association between the music and some other event or object; *icon* refers to a response based on some formal similarity between the music and some other emotion-bearing signal such as human movement; and *symbol* refers to a response based on internal, 'syntactic' relationships within the music itself. A somewhat similar approach was proposed by Sloboda (1998/2005) in terms of *episodic associations, iconic associations* and *structural expectancies* (see also Scherer & Zentner, 2001).

However, the most thoroughgoing attempt to exhaustively delineate the various mechanisms to date is offered by Juslin and Västfjäll (2008). They noted first an overall lack of empirical research on underlying mechanisms. Then they proposed six mechanisms (i.e. in addition to cognitive appraisal) through which music may induce emotions: (a) brain stem reflexes, (b) evaluative conditioning, (c) emotional contagion, (d) visual imagery, (e) episodic memory, and (f) musical expectancy. By synthesizing theory and results from different domains, they were able to provide a first set of hypotheses that may help researchers to distinguish among the mechanisms in terms of their information focus, development, key brain regions, cultural impact, induction speed, and degree of volitional influence. The idea is that these hypotheses can guide the construction of designs to confirm the existence of and delineate more precisely the mode of operation of each mechanism (Chapter 22, this volume, offers an updated version of the framework and a summary of the hypotheses).

An implication of this is that before one can understand an emotional response in any given situation, it is necessary to know which of these mechanisms is in operation. As the authors observe, 'differing listeners may activate different mechanisms to the same musical stimulus with resulting difference in response' (p. 573). This may help to explain why the same piece might evoke happiness in one listener but sadness in another. It remains an open question as to whether testing situations may be devised that can isolate the separable effects of these different mechanisms. One approach is the *factorial* experiment where a variable relevant to one (and only one) such mechanism is varied and all other variables of the situation are kept constant. Using such an approach, Steinbeis, Koelsch, and Sloboda (2006) demonstrated that less expected harmonies in a Bach chorale heightened the level of evoked emotionality, and that this was associated with an increase in early negativity of electrodermal response in the seconds immediately following the less expected chords. This provided clear evidence for the mechanism 'musical expectancy' (Meyer, 1956) featured in Juslin and Västfjäll's framework. The listeners' responses to the unexpected chords were relatively immediate and unreflexive. Other mechanisms, however, may be more dependent on volitional control, and are therefore more influenced by the current goals and motives of the listener.

4.2.7 Musical emotions depend to a considerable extent on the goals and motives of the listener

We have already seen how emotions to music are partly determined by factors in the person and the situation, and by mechanisms, such that there can be no automatic 'read off' from a musical stimulus to a reliable and predictable evoked emotion in the listener. One especially significant subset of such instances is the case of the self-conscious use of music by a listener for active goal achievement. The growing literature on such uses of music (see DeNora, 2000; Sloboda, Lamont, & Greasley, 2009) shows how people choose particular pieces of music to accompany a range of daily activities (e.g. travel, physical work, intellectual work, exercise, and emotion/mood management). Different functions have been documented. In using music as *distraction*, people engage unallocated attention and reduce boredom. In *energizing*, people use music to maintain arousal and focus attention on task. Some of the most interesting uses, in relation to understanding the role of emotions, are summarized under the heading *meaning enhancement*. Here, music is used to heighten or strengthen the emotional significance of an event or activity, such as, for instance, when music is chosen to accompany a social ritual like a wedding, a funeral, or a meal with a prospective partner. Many studies have documented how listeners use music to assist with the emotional processing of significant events. For instance, music is used as an aid to reminiscence of valued past experiences (e.g. Hays & Minchiello, 2005), or to lift the stress induced by recent events (e.g. Sloboda, 1999/2005).

What joins all these disparate examples is that the intentions of the listener are paramount in the causal process. In many cases, to obtain a strong emotional effect from a musical stimulus requires an act of will or decision on the part of the listener. This has been acknowledged for some time in the clinical mood-induction literature (Eich, Ng, Macaulay, Percy, & Grebneva, 2007; Västfjäll, 2002). Emotional effects are often only reliable when the participant 'tries hard' to get into the emotion signified through the music. However, even when the listener does not explicitly aim to evoke emotions, the motives for listening to music may influence his or her response by influencing other features of the listening situation, such as choice of music or amount of attention focused on the music.

These effects have mostly been documented somewhat impressionistically to date, primarily through retrospective interviews (Saarikallio, 2007). Concurrent studies, using experimental and quantitative paradigms, or time-sensitive observational techniques such as ESM, are in their infancy, although relevant studies are under way (e.g. Greasley & Lamont, 2006; Van Goethem, 2008). Thus, for instance, Van Goethem (2008) asked participants to monitor their deliberate music listening for a week. They filled out a questionnaire for every music listening episode they had in the week, and reported how their mood changed from before the music to after the music, what their intention to listen to the music had been (did they intend to regulate their mood, or were there other reasons to listen to music?), and noted which strategies were supported by the music. Participants reported that they intended to regulate their mood in half of the occasions. Listening motives may also influence the type of emotion evoked. The study by Juslin et al (2008, Table 4) showed that *sadness-melancholy* was often experienced when the listening motive was 'to influence emotions' or when 'the music could not be avoided'; in contrast, *calm-contentment* was experienced when the listening motive was 'to relax', 'to pass the time', or 'to get some company'. The most common motive in *happiness-elation* episodes was 'to get energized'. Only fine-grained incident-by-incident data collection of this sort will be sufficient to make significant progress in detailed theory building in this domain. A crucial unanswered question is which of the mechanisms outlined by Juslin and Västfjäll (2008) may be mobilized for goal-directed emotional activity by music listeners in everyday life.

4.3 IMPLICATIONS AND DIRECTIONS FOR FUTURE RESEARCH

The psychological research described above represents some significant advances in our understanding of how music evokes emotion. It is now indisputable that people feel real emotions (rather than simply observing or inferring them) while listening to music, and that specific features of the music have a causal role in such emotions. On the other hand, it is equally indisputable that there is no one-to-one mapping between the features of a musical stimulus and an emotional response. It is impossible to predict what emotion a person may feel solely from the musical content. Factors relating to the person and to the context also play a key role. There are distinct mechanisms by which music may have an emotional effect, and carefully constructed experiments may be capable of distinguishing the working of these mechanisms in individual listeners. Some of these mechanisms are activated most strongly when the goals and intentions of the listener are engaged—thus, to a considerable extent, we choose how and when to become fully emotionally engaged with music. In general, we exercise that choice in situations where the emotional effects of music are beneficial to us.

We believe that this body of findings is useful, not only to psychologists, but to researchers in other disciplines, and to musicians and listeners. For musicologists, psychology assists the delineation of those emotional effects that are lawfully attributable to the musical stimulus, and thus helps determine which of these effects are likely to be illuminated by the expertise of music analysts. For performing musicians, psychology helps to explain which aspects of listener response are likely to be influenced by them and what they do, and which may be outside their control. For listeners, psychology helps show that musical emotion is something that they can enhance or diminish by their purposive and deliberate engagement in the musical experience. They are not powerless 'victims' of Orpheus!

Based on the present review of key themes, we are also able to propose several future directions for research. First, research can investigate a wider range of emotional categories and dimensions in studies of how listeners perceive expression in music, to capture more complex, ambiguous, and temporally shifting emotional signals. This can include assessing the role of context (e.g. lyrics, programme notes) in disambiguating the perceived expression. In general, the interplay between the listener, the music, and the context can benefit from further study. The field has not yet mapped these factors in a way that offers much theoretical or predictive power. There is clearly an untapped potential for large-scale experimental and observational studies, which take an inclusive approach to the range of causal factors that shape emotions to music in everyday life. Such studies could be demanding but may be the best route to further significant progress in this field.

Second, there is scope to examine closer the relationship between perceived and evoked emotion in music. What is the relative frequency of each process? How do they affect each other? What, exactly, are the conditions that will lead to induced emotion, rather than mere perception? Are the kinds of emotions usually perceived in music somewhat different from those usually evoked by music? To obtain general and valid answers to these questions, it is necessary to avoid limiting the research focus to laboratory studies using unfamiliar music.

Third, there is a need for systematic studies of the psychological mechanisms that underlie the induction of musical emotions. In particular, experiments that manipulate single mechanisms, or contrast two or more mechanisms, could make a crucial contribution to the field. As noted in Chapter 22 (this volume), the induction process holds the key to many of the unresolved problems in this field. Given the centrality of mechanisms to a theoretically grounded psychological approach, it is somewhat disappointing that relatively few research studies have directly addressed induction mechanisms in their design.

Fourth and finally, further application of time-sensitive observational techniques such as the experience-sampling method can help us to investigate how listeners actively use music to achieve goals, and how these goals and intentions in turn influence which emotions are evoked by the music. A psychological approach implies that to understand human behaviour, we need to understand the goals and functions of the behaviour.

Recommended further reading

1. Hallam, S., Cross, I., & Thaut, M. (eds) (2009). *Oxford handbook of music psychology*. Oxford: Oxford University Press (Chapters 3, 4, 11–15, 35, 40, 42, 44–46, 48, 49).
2. North, A. C., & Hargreaves, D. J. (2008). *The social and applied psychology of music*. Oxford: Oxford University Press (Chapters 3 and 5).
3. Oatley, K., Keltner, D., & Jenkins, J. M. (2006). *Understanding emotions* (2nd edn). Oxford: Blackwell.

References

Adachi, M., Trehub, S. E., & Abe, J. (2004). Perceiving emotion in children's songs across age and culture. *Japanese Psychological Research*, *46*, 322–36.

Barrett, L. F., Mesquita, B., Ochsner, K. N., & Gross, J. J. (2007). The experience of emotion. *Annual Review of Psychology*, *58*, 387–403.

Beedie, C. J., Terry, P. C., & Lane, A. M. (2005). Distinctions between emotion and mood. *Cognition & Emotion*, *19*, 847–78.

Berlyne, D. E. (1971). *Aesthetics and psychobiology*. New York: Appleton Century Crofts.

Blood, A. J., & Zatorre, R. J. (2001). Intensely pleasurable responses to music correlate with activity in brain regions implicated in reward and emotion. *Proceedings of National Academy of Sciences*, *98*, 11818–23.

Boring, E. G. (1950). *A history of experimental psychology* (2d edn). New York: Appleton Century Crofts.

Buck, R. (1999). The biology of affects: A typology. *Psychological Review*, *106*, 301–36.

Clayton, M., Sager, R., & Will, U. (2005). In time with the music: the concept of entrainment and its significance for ethnomusicology. *European Meetings in Ethnomusicology*, *11*, 3–75.

Coan, J. A., & Allen, J. B. (eds) (2007). *Handbook of emotion elicitation and assessment*. Oxford: Oxford University Press.

Cunningham, J. G., & Sterling, R. S. (1988). Developmental changes in the understanding of affective meaning in music. *Motivation and Emotion*, *12*, 399–413.

Darwin, C. (1872). *The expression of the emotions in man and animals*. London: John Murray.

Davidson, R. J. (1994). On emotion, mood, and related affective constructs. In P. Ekman & R. J. Davidson (eds), *The nature of emotion: Fundamental questions* (pp. 51–5). Oxford: Oxford University Press.

Davidson, R. J., Scherer, K. R., & Goldsmith, H. H. (eds) (2003). *Handbook of affective sciences*. Oxford: Oxford University Press.

Dennett, D. C. (1987). *The intentional stance*. Cambridge, MA: MIT Press.

DeNora, T. (2000). *Music in everyday life*. Cambridge, UK: Cambridge University Press.

Deutsch, D. (ed.) (1982). *The psychology of music*. New York: Academic Press.

Dibben, N. J. (2004). The role of peripheral feedback in emotional experience with music. *Music Perception*, *22*, 79–115.

Dolgin, K., & Adelson, E. (1990). Age changes in the ability to interpret affect in sung and instrumentally presented melodies. *Psychology of Music*, *18*, 87–98.

Dowling W. J., & Harwood, D. L. (1986). *Music cognition*. New York: Academic Press.

Duffy, E. (1941). An explanation of 'emotional' phenomena without the use of the concept 'emotion'. *Journal of General Psychology*, *25*, 283–93.

Eich, E., Ng, J. T. W., Macaulay, D., Percy, A. D., & Grebneva, I. (2007). Combining music with thought to change mood. In J. A. Coan & J. J. B. Allen (eds), *Handbook of emotion elicitation and assessment* (pp. 124–36). Oxford: Oxford University Press.

Ekman, P. (1992). An argument for basic emotions. *Cognition & Emotion, 6,* 169–200.

Frijda, N. H. (1989). Aesthetic emotions and reality. *American Psychologist, 44,* 1546–7.

Frijda, N. H. (2008). The psychologist's point of view. In M. Lewis, J. M. Haviland-Jones, & L. F. Barrett (eds), *Handbook of emotions* (3rd edn) (pp. 68–87). New York: Guilford Press.

Gabrielsson, A. (1993). Music and emotion. *ESCOM Newsletter, 4,* 4–9.

Gabrielsson, A. (2002). Emotion perceived and emotion felt: Same or different? *Musicae Scientiae, Special Issue 2001–2,* 123–47.

Goleman, D. (1995). *Emotional intelligence.* New York: Bantam Books.

Greasley, A. E., & Lamont, A. (2006). Music preference in adulthood: Why do we like the music we do? In M. Baroni, A. R. Adessi, R. Caterina, & M. Costa (eds), *Proceedings of the 9th International Conference on Music Perception and Cognition* (pp. 960–6). Bologna, Italy: University of Bologna.

Grewe, O., Nagel, F., Kopiez, R., & Altenmüller, E. (2007). Listening to music as a re-creative process: Physiological, psychological, and psychoacoustical correlates of chills and strong emotions. *Music Perception, 24,* 297–314.

Hallam, S., Cross, I., & Thaut, M. (eds) (2009). *Oxford handbook of music psychology.* Oxford: Oxford University Press.

Hays, T., & Minchiello, V. (2005). The meaning of music in the lives of older people: A qualitative study. *Psychology of Music, 33,* 437–51.

Hektner, J. M., Schmidt, J. A., & Csikszentmihalyi, M. (2007). *Experience sampling method: Measuring the quality of everyday life.* London: Sage.

Hevner, K. (1935). Expression in music: A discussion of experimental studies and theories. *Psychological Review, 42,* 186–204.

Izard, C. E. (1977). *The emotions.* New York: Plenum Press.

Izard, C. E. (1993). Four systems for emotion activation: Cognitive and noncognitive processes. *Psychological Review, 100,* 68–90.

Izard, C. E. (2009). Emotion theory and research: Highlights, unanswered questions, and emerging issues. *Annual Review of Psychology, 60,* 1–25.

James, W. (1884). What is an emotion? *Mind, 9,* 188–205.

Juslin, P. N. (1997). Emotional communication in music performance: A functionalist perspective and some data. *Music Perception, 14,* 383–418.

Juslin, P. N. (2009). Emotional responses to music. In S. Hallam, I. Cross, & M. Thaut (eds), *Oxford handbook of music psychology* (pp. 131–140). Oxford: Oxford University Press.

Juslin, P. N., & Laukka, P. (2003). Communication of emotions in vocal expression and music performance: Different channels, same code? *Psychological Bulletin, 129,* 770–814.

Juslin, P. N., & Laukka, P. (2004). Expression, perception, and induction of musical emotions: A review and a questionnaire study of everyday listening. *Journal of New Music Research, 33,* 217–38.

Juslin, P. N., Liljeström, S., Västfjäll, D., Barradas, G., & Silva, A. (2008). An experience sampling study of emotional reactions to music: Listener, music, and situation. *Emotion, 8,* 668–83.

Juslin, P. N., & Scherer, K. R. (2005). Vocal expression of affect. In J. A. Harrigan, R. Rosenthal, & K. R. Scherer (eds), *The new handbook of methods in nonverbal behavior research* (pp. 65–135). Oxford: Oxford University Press.

Juslin, P. N., & Västfjäll, D. (2008). Emotional responses to music: The need to consider underlying mechanisms. *Behavioral and Brain Sciences, 31,* 559–75.

Kastner, M. P., & Crowder, R. G. (1990). Perception of the major/minor distinction: IV. Emotional connotations in young children. *Music Perception, 8*, 189–202.

Kivy, P. (1990). *Music alone: Reflections on a purely musical experience.* Ithaca, NY: Cornell University Press.

Kleinginna, P. R., & Kleinginna, A. M. (1981). A categorized list of emotion definitions, with a suggestion for a consensual definition. *Motivation and Emotion, 5*, 345–71.

Krumhansl, C. L. (1997). An exploratory study of musical emotions and psychophysiology. *Canadian Journal of Experimental Psychology, 51*, 336–52.

Kuhn, T. S. (1962). *The structure of scientific revolutions.* Chicago, IL: University of Chicago Press.

Laukka, P. (2007). Uses of music and psychological well-being among the elderly. *Journal of Happiness Studies, 8*, 215–41.

Lazarus, R. S. (1991). *Emotion and adaptation.* Oxford: Oxford University Press.

Levenson, R. W. (2003). Autonomic specificity and emotion. In R. J. Davidson, K. R. Scherer, & H. H. Goldsmith (eds), *Handbook of affective sciences* (pp. 212–24). Oxford: Oxford University Press.

Lundqvist, L.-O., Carlsson, F., Hilmersson, P., & Juslin, P. N. (2009). Emotional responses to music: Experience, expression, and physiology. *Psychology of Music, 37*, 61–90.

Martin, G. N., Carlson, N. R., & Buskist, W. (2006). *Psychology* (3rd edn). Harlow: Pearson.

Mauss, I. B., Levenson, R. W., McCarter, L., Wilhelm, F. H., and Gross, J. J. (2005). The tie that binds? Coherence among emotion experience, behaviour, and physiology. *Emotion, 5*, 175–90.

Mesquita, B. (2003). Emotions as dynamic cultural phenomena. In R. J. Davidson, K. R. Scherer, & H. H. Goldsmith (eds), *Handbook of affective sciences* (pp. 871–90). Oxford: Oxford University Press.

Meyer, L. B. (1956). *Emotion and meaning in music.* Chicago, IL: Chicago University Press.

North, A. C., Hargreaves, D. J., & Hargreaves, J. J. (2004). The uses of music in everyday life. *Music Perception, 22*, 63–99.

Nyklíček, I., Thayer, J. F., & Van Doornen, L. J. P. (1997). Cardiorespiratory differentiation of musically induced emotions. *Journal of Psychophysiology, 11*, 304–21.

Oatley, K. (1992). *Best laid schemes. The psychology of emotions.* Cambridge, MA: Harvard University Press.

Ortony, A., & Turner, T. J. (1990). What's basic about basic emotions? *Psychological Review, 97*, 315–31.

Osgood, C. E., Suci, G. J., & Tannenbaum, P. H. (1957). *The measurement of meaning.* Urbana, IL: The University of Illinois Press.

Plutchik, R. (1994). *The psychology and biology of emotion.* New York: Harper-Collins.

Power, M., & Dalgleish, T. (1997). *Cognition and emotion. From order to disorder.* Hove, UK: Psychology Press.

Rauscher, F. H., Shaw, G. L., & Hy, K. (1993). Music and spatial task performance. *Nature, 365*, 611.

Rickard, N. S. (2004). Intense emotional responses to music: a test of the physiological arousal hypothesis. *Psychology of Music, 32*, 371–88.

Rosch, R. (1978). Principles of categorization. In E. Rosch & B. B. Loyd (eds), *Cognition and categorization* (pp. 27–48). Hillsdale, NJ: Erlbaum.

Roseman, I. J., Spindel, M. S., & Jose, P. E. (1990). Appraisals of emotion-eliciting events: Testing a theory of discrete emotions. *Journal of Personality and Social Psychology, 59*, 899–915.

Russell, J. A. (1980). A circumplex model of affect. *Journal of Personality and Social Psychology, 39*, 1161–78.

Russell, J. A. (2003). Core affect and the psychological construction of emotion. *Psychological Review*, 110, 145–72.

Saarikallio, S. (2007). *Music as mood regulation in adolescence*. Doctoral dissertation, University of Jyväskylä, Finland.

Scherer, K. R. (1999). Appraisal theories. In T. Dalgleish & M. Power (eds), *Handbook of cognition and emotion* (pp. 637–63). Chichester, UK: Wiley.

Scherer, K. R. (2001). Appraisal considered as a process of multi-level sequential checking. In K. R. Scherer, A. Schorr, & T. Johnstone (eds), *Appraisal processes in emotion: Theory, methods, research* (pp. 92–120). Oxford: Oxford University Press.

Scherer, K. R., & Zentner, M. R. (2001). Emotional effects of music: Production rules. In P. N. Juslin & J. A. Sloboda (eds), *Music and emotion: Theory and research* (pp. 361–92). Oxford: Oxford University Press.

Shaver, P. R., Schwartz, J., Kirson, D., & O'Connor, C. (1987). Emotion knowledge: Further exploration of a prototype approach. *Journal of Personality and Social Psychology*, 52, 1061–86.

Sloboda, J. A. (1986). Cognitive psychology and real music: The psychology of music comes of age. *Psychologica Belgica*, 26, 199–219. (Reprinted in Sloboda, J. A. (2005). *Exploring the musical mind: Cognition, emotion, ability, function* (pp. 97–115). Oxford: Oxford University Press.)

Sloboda, J. A. (1998). Music: where cognition and emotion meet. *The Psychologist*, 12, 450–5. (Reprinted in Sloboda, J. A. (2005). *Exploring the musical mind: Cognition, emotion, ability, function* (pp. 333–44). Oxford: Oxford University Press.)

Sloboda, J. A. (1999/2005). Everyday uses of music: a preliminary study. In S. W. Yi (ed.), *Music, Mind, & Science* (pp. 354–69). Seoul: Seoul National University Press. (Reprinted in Sloboda, J. A. (2005). *Exploring the musical mind: Cognition, emotion, ability, function* (pp. 319–31). Oxford: Oxford University Press.)

Sloboda, J. A., Ivaldi, A., & O'Neill, S. A. (2001). Functions of music in everyday life: An exploratory study using the experience sampling methodology. *Musicae Scientiae*, 5, 9–32.

Sloboda, J. A., Lamont, A., & Greasley, A. (2009). Choosing to hear music. In S. Hallam, I. Cross, & M. Thaut (eds), *Oxford handbook of music psychology* (pp. 431–40). Oxford: Oxford University Press.

Sloboda, J. A., & Lehmann, A. C. (2001). Tracking performance correlates of changes in perceived intensity of emotion during different interpretations of a Chopin piano prelude. *Music Perception*, 19, 87–120.

Steinbeis, N., Koelsch, S., & Sloboda, J. A. (2006). The role of harmonic expectancy violations in musical emotions: Evidence from subjective, physiological, and neural responses. *Journal of Cognitive Neuroscience*, 18, 1380–93.

Thaut, M. H. (1990). Neuropsychological processes in music perception and their relevance in music therapy. In R. F. Unkeler (ed.), *Music therapy in the treatment of adults with mental disorders* (pp. 3–31). New York: Schirmer books.

Thompson, W. F., Graham, P., & Russo, F. A. (2005). Seeing music performance: Visual influences on perception and experience. *Semiotica*, 156, 177–201.

Tomkins, S. (1962). *Affect, imagery, and consciousness: Vol. 1. The positive effects*. New York: Springer.

Van Goethem, A. (2008). Sad, in a nice way. Hear Here. Classic FM/Royal Philharmonic Society. Retrieved from: http://www.classicfm.co.uk/hearhere/Article.asp?id=856556

Västfjäll, D. (2002). A review of the musical mood induction procedure. *Musicae Scientiae*, Special Issue 2001–2002, 173–211.

Wager, T. D., Barrett, L. F., Bliss-Moreau, E., Lindquist, K. A., Duncan, S., Kober, H., Joseph, J., Davidson, M., & Mize, J. (2008). The neuroimaging of emotion. In M. Lewis, J. M. Haviland-Jones, & L. F. Barrett (eds), *Handbook of emotions* (3rd edn) (pp. 249–67). New York: Guilford Press.

Watson, D., & Tellegen, A. (1985). Toward a consensual structure of mood. *Psychological Bulletin*, *98*, 219–35.

Wundt, W. (1897). *Outlines of psychology* (trans. C. H. Judd). Lepzig: Englemann.

Zajonc, R. B. (1994). Emotional expression and temperature modulation. In S. H. M. Van Goozen, N. E. Van de Poll, & J. A. Sergeant (eds), *Emotions: Essays on emotion theory* (pp. 3–27). Hillsdale, NJ: Erlbaum.

Zentner, M. R., Grandjean, D., & Scherer, K. R. (2008). Emotions evoked by the sound of music: Characterization, classification, and measurement. *Emotion*, *8*, 494–521.

TOWARDS A NEUROBIOLOGY OF MUSICAL EMOTIONS

ISABELLE PERETz

THE functioning of the brain is fascinating. It fascinates for the obvious reason that the brain is the commander of all our actions, thoughts, and motivations. By studying its functioning, we hope to obtain crucial information about the biological basis of human cognition and emotion. Neuropsychology is the discipline concerned with these questions. As its name indicates, neuropsychology aims to relate neural mechanisms to mental functions. It is an old discipline, dating back to the discovery by Broca in (1861) that speech was related to the functioning of a small region of the left brain. Following this discovery, the neural correlates of musical abilities were similarly scrutinized (e.g. Bouillaud, 1865). Although the neuropsychological approach to music is a century old, progress has been slow until recently. Recent advances in brain-imaging techniques (see Chapter 12, this volume), as well as the current trend of viewing most human activities from a biological perspective, has intensified research activities in the field.

As a result of this biological trend, neuropsychology has been recently renamed 'cognitive neuroscience'. This change in terminology reflects the intention to include neuropsychology within the vast domain of neuroscience. Because neuroscience covers a large spectrum of discipline—from the physiological study of single neurons in the turtle retina (Sernagor & Grzywacz, 1996) to the brain organization subserving the sense of humour in humans (Shammi & Stuss, 1999)—'cognitive' has qualified the 'neuroscience' term. The qualifier is unfortunate because 'cognitive' usually excludes emotion. Indeed, cognition is often seen as antithetical to emotion. For example, Kivy (1990) in his influential essay on the meaning of music coined the term 'cognitivist' to refer to the position that holds that music simply expresses emotions without inducing them. The opposite position, called 'emotivist', holds that music induces emotions in listeners.

The antagonism between 'cognitivists' and 'emotivists' is not limited to music psychology. It has a long history starting with Descartes's early separation between emotion and reason. Still today, the majority of experimental psychologists are 'cognitivists' by default. They tend to ignore emotions. This neglect partly reflects the information-processing approach that started in the early sixties (e.g. Neisser, 1967), which used the computer as a metaphor for mental functions. According to this approach, the brain is a machine, devoid of emotions.

Recently, however, neuropsychologists (or neuroscientists) have become more concerned with emotions (e.g. Phelps, 2006). Although neuropsychologists continue to distinguish between emotional and cognitive processes, they no longer reject the emotional part as being too obscure or subjective to be studied scientifically. On the contrary, emotions are now studied for their own sake. In their two popular books published in 1994 and 1996 respectively, Damasio and LeDoux contributed greatly to the rapprochement between cognition and emotion in neuropsychology. Reason is no longer seen as the human-specific activity that controls emotional irrationality. As Damasio (1994) showed, emotional processes are an integral part of decision making and are not confined to subcortical brain structures that humans share with other animals. Emotions recruit portions of the frontal lobes, which are the largest and latest brain structures to develop in the human brain. Thus, neuropsychologists are currently studying emotions just as they study any other mental function worthy of inquiry.

The objective of this chapter is to present current knowledge about musical emotions from a neuropsychological perspective. In doing so, I will adopt a biological perspective. Music, and *a fortiori* musical emotions, are generally *not* regarded as biological functions. Rather, music-related functions are considered as a refined product of human culture. Over the last decade, however, research has yielded a considerable amount of data that suggest that music might be part of human nature (Peretz, 2006). The study of musical emotions plays a crucial role in this biological perspective. Indeed, musical emotions are inherent to experiences of music and may account for its ubiquity. Accordingly, understanding the biological origin of musical emotions may shed light on the biological roots of music processing more generally. Here, I will examine the extent to which musical emotions might be biologically determined. Since the evidence points to biological foundations of musical emotions, I will examine the possibility that music is particularly suited (or designed) to invade emotion circuits that have evolved for emotional vocalizations.

5.1 MUSICAL EMOTIONS: UNIVERSALITY AND PREDISPOSITIONS

Musical emotions are often considered to be too personal, elusive, and variable to be studied scientifically. *A fortiori*, emotions could not be subserved by neuroanatomical structures and functions shared by all members of the same species. The work of Paul Ekman on human facial expressions has helped to convince the scientific community that the above view is inadequate (see Peretz, 2001, for a review). In music, the recent focus on 'basic emotions' has provided ample evidence that emotional responses to music can be remarkably invariant across listeners of different ages.

'Basic emotions' refer to emotions like happiness, sadness, anger, and fear. Such basic emotions are today the main focus of neuropsychological studies, because these emotions are assumed to be innate, reflex-like circuits that cause a distinct and recognizable behavioural and physiological pattern (e.g. Panksepp, 1998). Although basic emotions may differ from what most adults experience when listening to music (for example, see Zentner, Grandjean, & Scherer, 2008, for a more nuanced range of musically induced emotions), many researchers believe that music can induce happiness, sadness, and fear. These basic emotions are typically the target of film soundtracks, especially those intended for children. Moreover, these basic emotions are among the easiest to recognize and communicate in music (e.g. Gabrielsson & Juslin, 2003; Juslin & Laukka, 2003). Thus, the present chapter will focus on basic emotions.

If musical communication of basic emotions is biologically prepared, similar emotional intentions should be recognized across music cultures. That is, we should be able to infer the emotions expressed by a musical culture to which we have never been exposed (and which has not yet been 'contaminated' by Western music). Conversely, adults from musically isolated cultures should be able to infer the musical emotions of Western music. Curiously, these predictions are tested rarely. The few published cross-cultural studies are encouraging, in showing that Western listeners can easily recognize joy, sadness, and anger in Hindustani ragas (Balkwill & Thompson, 1999; see also Chapter 27, this volume), and that Japanese listeners are able to recognize joy, anger, and sadness from both Hindustani and Western music. Interestingly, Japanese listeners do not perform systematically better on Japanese than on Hindustani music (Balkwill, Thompson, & Matsunaga, 2004). Similarly, Chinese listeners are able not only to distinguish happy from sad music written following Western conventions, but they also exhibit sensitivity to the same structural features (mode and tempo) as do Westeners (see Table 5.1; Rousseau, Peretz, & Dalla Bella, unpublished data). Thus, these findings point to the existence of some invariance in expressing basic emotions across musical cultures. Although non-Western participants may have assimilated the rules of Western music through exposure, it is remarkable how quickly cues to musical emotions, such as mode, which appear to be so culture-specific, can be internalized by listeners of a different culture. This flexibility is suggestive of an underlying universal bias on which listeners build their own cultural variants and assimilate those of distant cultures.

Remarkable invariance across individuals of different cultures is also evident among members of the same culture. For example, ordinary adult listeners need less than a quarter of a second of music (e.g. one chord or a few notes) to classify musical excerpts as happy or sad (Peretz, Gagnon, & Bouchard, 1998; see Bigand, Vieillard, Madurell, Marozeau, & Dacquet, 2005, for similar findings with slightly longer excerpts—1 second—and more emotions). Moreover and more generally, emotional judgements

Table 5.1 The mean ratings (standard deviation) were provided by 48 Chinese participants (mean age: 21 years), born in China and who emigrated to Canada less than 60 months prior to the testing. They rated whether each musical excerpt sounded happy or sad on a 10-point scale, with 1 indicating very sad and 10 very happy. The original versions were 32 classical musical excerpts (e.g. *Adagio* from Albinoni) that were synthesized and transcribed for piano. These versions were modified so that all tempi were set to a unique median value (tempo change), or were transcribed in the opposite mode (mode change), or contained both the tempo and mode change (tempo + mode change; see Peretz, Gagnon, and Bouchard, 1998 for all the details). As can be seen, listeners' ratings depended on the version, with $F(3,141) = 64.23$, $p<.001$ for the interaction between version and happy/sad tone. The ratings did not differ from those obtained by Western students (Rousseau, Peretz, & Dalla Bella, unpublished data).

	Music	
Version	Happy	Sad
Original	7.9 (0.1)	3.9 (0.1)
Tempo change	7.0 (0.1)	4.5 (0.1)
Mode change	7.3 (0.2)	4.9 (0.1)
Tempo + mode change	6.1 (0.1)	5.4 (0.1)

exhibit a high degree of consistency across listeners of the same culture who vary widely in terms of musical training (e.g. Vieillard et al, 2008). These results indicate that the perception of basic emotions in music is natural and effortless.

The universality of expressions of emotions is necessary but not sufficient for us to conclude that they are biologically determined. Universality could also result from common learning experiences. All infants are exposed to the same situations (e.g. pain, being left alone, or reassured) across cultures. Music is typically used in these contexts. Caregivers around the world sing to their infants, with the intuition (or instinct?) that music has the power to regulate the infant's state (e.g. comforting) or the quality of interaction (e.g. attention getting). Caregivers nicely mirror infants' perceptual abilities by singing more slowly, at a higher pitch, with exaggerated rhythm, and in a more loving or emotionally engaging manner when singing to infants than when singing alone (e.g. Trainor, Clark, Huntley, & Adams, 1997). Exposure to maternal singing, however, cannot account for the observation that two-day-old hearing infants, born from congenitally deaf parents (who sign and do not sing or speak), prefer infant-directed singing to adult-directed singing (Masataka, 1999; see Chapter 23, this volume). In short, responsiveness to infant-directed singing appears to be innate.

Caregivers also speak to infants in a sing-song manner called 'baby-talk' or 'infant-directed' speech. Regardless of the language adults speak, they raise their voice to elicit the infant's attention and talk at a much slower rate. Adults mostly communicate emotions in their infant-directed speech (Trainor, Austin, & Desjardins, 2000) and the communication of these emotions appears to be universal (Bryant & Barrett, 2007). Nevertheless, infants seem to prefer infant-directed singing to infant-directed speech. Nakata and Trehub (2004) exposed six-month-old infants to videotaped performances of their own mothers. The infants showed more sustained attention and engagement to mothers' singing episodes than to their speaking episodes. The observation that emotional communication through singing is powerful for infants, even for hearing newborns of deaf parents, is consistent with the proposal of biological preparedness for music (see Section 5.4 for a plausible neurobiological account of this phenomenon).

Predispositions to respond emotionally to music may account for the fact that young children can easily extract emotion intentions from music. By nine months, infants discriminate happy and sad music (Flom, Gentile, & Pick, 2008). By the age of three years, they show the ability to recognize happiness in elaborate art music of their culture, and by the age of six they show adult-like abilities to identify sadness, fear, and anger in music (Cunningham & Sterling, 1988; Terwogt & van Grinsven, 1988, 1991; but see Dolgin & Adelson, 1990, for later emergence). Furthermore, childhood competence is associated with sensitivity to specific musical features. At five years of age, children are able to discriminate between happy and sad excerpts by relying on tempo differences (fast vs. slow). At six, children show evidence of using both tempo and mode (major vs. minor) as adults do (Dalla Bella, Peretz, Rousseau, & Gosselin, 2001). Although these results suggest that sensitivity to tempo precedes sensitivity to mode, it is remarkable that by the age of six, Western children show full knowledge of the rules that govern the happy–sad character of the music of their culture. This ability remains largely unchanged over the lifespan (Adachi & Trehub, 2000; Dalla Bella, Peretz, Rousseau, & Gosselin, 2001; Gerardi & Gerken, 1995; Gregory, Worrall, & Sarge, 1996; Kastner & Crowder, 1990; Kratus, 1993), until old age, when it declines (Laukka & Juslin, 2007).

Thus, the propensity to respond emotionally to music may be innate. This possibility does not mean that experience plays no role. Infants' musical emotions could emerge from an innate propensity to respond to the emotional tone of the voice, as suggested by the innate bias found in hearing newborns of deaf parents. This innate impulse could, in turn, be shaped by the musical regularities of the culture. Indeed, infants have powerful statistical learning capacities. Two minutes of exposure to tones with variable sequential probabilities of occurrence are sufficient for eight-month-old babies to discover the sequential structure (e.g. Saffran, Johnson, Aslin, & Newport, 1999). In a similar manner, infants may capitalize on the statistical regularities in their auditory emotional environment with relatively little effort. For instance, they may quickly discover that a high pitch level and fast tempi are typically used when a caregiver is happy.

Indeed, among adults, there is robust evidence that emotional responses are modulated by experience. As listeners, we tend to like what we already know (see Bornstein,

1989, for a review). In music, we prefer familiar over unfamiliar music even though we may be unaware of this bias (Peretz, Gaudreau, & Bonnel, 1998). The unconscious affective influence of prior exposure to music may account for a vast array of phenomena, such as the preference for consonance over dissonance (Zentner & Kagan, 1996) and the association of the major and minor modes with happy and sad emotions (Peretz, Gagnon, & Bouchard, 1998).

In sum, with consistency and precociousness, musical emotions might be constrained by innate mechanisms, as are basic tastes (sweet, salt, sour, bitter; Steiner, 1979). The origin of this predisposition remains to be determined. In Section 5.4, I will discuss the possibility that musical emotions owe their precociousness and efficacy to an invasion of the brain circuits that have evolved for emotional responsiveness to vocal expressions.

5.2 MUSICAL EMOTIONS: BRAIN ORGANIZATION

The hypothesis that basic musical emotions exhibit universality and innateness is important from a neuropsychological perspective. In this view, brain organization for these emotions would be expected to recruit neural networks that are fixed not only across members of the same culture but across members of different cultures. Since there is as yet no cross-cultural study of the neural correlates of musical emotions, I will focus here on Western listeners and will examine below the specific brain areas that have been identified to date in the processing of musical emotions. Before doing so, it is important to review briefly the evidence suggestive of a neural pathway for processing musical emotions.

5.2.1 An emotional neural pathway

If basic musical emotions recruit a distinct neural pathway, one should be able to find individuals who cannot respond to music emotionally but are able to perceive and memorize it. Conversely, one would expect to find cases who can respond to music emotionally despite having severe difficulties in perceiving music. Such conditions typically occur after accidental brain damage in adults. Indeed, there are musicians who, after a cerebro-vascular accident, retained their musical skills but complained that they lost interest in music because it sounded 'flat' or emotionless (Griffiths, Warren, Dean, & Howard, 2004; Mazzoni et al, 1993; Mazzuchi, Marchini, Budai, & Parma, 1982). Unfortunately, these reports are anecdotal. The emotional losses have not been assessed.

Similarly, autistic individuals are often described as having superior musical skills but atypical or impaired emotions. This is the case for 'musical savants', whose musical performance has been qualified at times as 'mechanical' (Mottron, Peretz, Belleville, & Rouleau, 1999; Sloboda, Hermelin, & O'Connor, 1985). Nevertheless, musical expressiveness has never been studied experimentally. The only two empirical studies that examined recognition of musical emotions in autism did not report impaired emotions processing (Heaton, Hermelin, & Pring, 1999; Khalfa & Peretz, 2007). In both studies, autistic children and young adults could recognize basic emotions from music as accurately as 'normals' did. It may still be the case that autistic individuals decode musical emotions in a qualitatively anomalous manner. For example, autistic children can recognize and imitate facial expressions as normals do, but no mirror-neuron activity is observed in the inferior frontal gyrus (Dapretto et al, 2006).

There is actually little current evidence that *all* musical emotions can be (1) selectively lost after brain damage or (2) never acquired as a consequence a neurogenetic disorder. Nonetheless, there is clear evidence that *specific* emotions can be lost after brain damage. This is the case for the recognition of 'scary', and to some extent, 'sad', music after damage to the amygdala (Gosselin, Peretz, Johnsen, & Adolphs, 2007; Gosselin et al, 2005), and of the preference for consonance over dissonance after lesion to the parahippocampal gyrus (Gosselin et al, 2006). In both of these instances, perceptual processing of the musical selections was found to be spared. These results support the notion that there is a distinct emotional pathway for music processing, and that this neural pathway may differ according to the emotion considered.

Further support for the existence of a distinct neural pathway for emotions is provided by cases of intact emotions despite severe problems in perception and memory. This is the case for IR, a patient who suffers from long-standing bilateral brain damage to the auditory cortex. Her case is remarkable because 15 years after her brain damage, IR still experiences severe difficulties with music while her language abilities and her general intellectual and memory abilities are normal (Peretz, Belleville, & Fontaine, 1997; Peretz & Gagnon, 1999). Despite her severe musical deficits, she reports that she enjoys music and listens regularly to pre-recorded music. In an experimental study, IR was able to classify melodies as 'happy' and 'sad' in a manner equivalent to normal controls, yet she was impaired in classifying these same melodies on the basis of their familiarity. For example, when presented with the melody of 'Happy birthday' without its lyrics, IR would say 'I don't know that tune but it sounds happy.' CN, another patient with bilateral lesions to the auditory cortex and severe recognition problems for melodies that were once highly familiar to her (Peretz, 1996), made a similarly interesting comment. When listening to the famous *Adagio* of Albinoni taken from her own record collection, CN first said that she had never heard the piece before. Suddenly, she said: 'It makes me feel sad . . . the feeling makes me think of Albinoni's *Adagio*' (Kolinsky, personal communication). In short, both IR and CN were unable to recognize melodies that were highly familiar to them before the brain accident, yet they were able to do so via their emotional responses.

In a follow-up study of IR (Peretz, Gagnon, & Bouchard, 1998), we tested her in a series of experiments using the same set of excerpts taken from the classical repertoire (e.g. Albinoni's *Adagio*). These were selected to convey a 'happy' or 'sad' tone, and they were presented under various transformations and with different task demands. IR was just like normal controls in that she was able to use both the mode and the tempo characteristics to derive the 'happy' or 'sad' tone of the music, and her judgements were immediate. In contrast with her relatively sophisticated emotional processing of the musical excerpts, IR showed impaired performance in her non-emotional assessments. Specifically, she performed well below normal in the discrimination of these musical excerpts in a 'same–different' classification task that was very easy for controls. She also failed to detect most errors purposely inserted on either the pitch or time dimension of the musical excerpts, yet these mistakes were obvious to control subjects. IR was able, however, to use a change of mode (from major to minor and vice versa) to discriminate excerpts. We concluded from these studies with IR and CN that severe deficits in perception and memorization of music can leave emotional judgements of music unimpaired. Such a spectacular isolation of emotional judgements of music suggests the presence of an emotional neural pathway for music. In principle, neural segregation of emotional and non-emotional pathways could be confirmed by functional brain imaging in normal brains. Such a study has not yet been reported.

In summary, brain lesion studies suggest that musical emotions might be subserved by a brain pathway that is separable from that involved in music perception and memory. One attractive possibility, derived from the animal work of LeDoux (1996) and from the theoretical position of Zajonc (1984), is that basic emotions need no cortical mediation. That is, basic emotional responses might function like subcortical reflexes. These emotional responses would be immediate but superficial, because they would not require the additional time taken by elaborate processing of the signal in cortical structures.

5.2.2 Evidence for a subcortical route

There are two plausible levels at which emotion and perception might bifurcate in the processing of music: early on after fast acoustical analysis of the musical input, or later on, after detailed analysis of emotional features. Consider a sudden dissonant chord or crash of cymbals, which may elicit a rapid, reflex-like reaction in the subcortical pathway, in the absence of detailed analysis of the music. This alerting role is probably often exploited in the soundtracks of terror movies. In contrast, the frequent alternation between major and minor keys in Klezmer music is more likely to be mediated cortically.

The subcortical emotional pathway classically reaches the limbic system first (e.g. the amygdala; see Figure 5.1). This system, named '*le grand lobe limbique*' by Broca (1878), corresponds to subcortical structures that appeared early in evolution and are similar across species. The limbic system was designated as the substrate of emotions by Broca a century ago, and later also by Papez (1937). Since then, the concept has gradually developed to include many more regions, both cortical and subcortical (see Damasio, 1994; LeDoux, 1996). In other words, emotions are no longer confined to the functioning of the limbic system, although the limbic system retains a fundamental role.

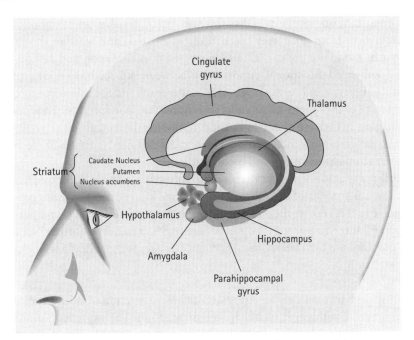

Fig. 5.1 Deep brain structures involved in emotion recognition and represented in a medial inside view of the brain. The limbic lobe includes the hypothalamus, the amygdala, the hippocampus, the thalamus, the cingulate gyrus, and the ventral striatum (which contains the nucleus accumbens).

There is ample evidence that subcortical structures are involved in emotional responses to music (see Figure 5.1 for the localization of these structures). In one early demonstration, Blood and Zatorre (2001) reported cerebral blood flow changes in subcortical neural structures while people experienced musical 'chills' (see also Chapter 21, this volume). They observed increased activation in the ventral striatum (which contains the nucleus accumbens, known to be involved in reward) and *decreased* activation in the amygdala. Similar activation of the nucleus accumbens has been observed while nonmusicians listen to pleasant music (i.e. from recordings) that was either unfamiliar (Brown, Martinez, & Parsons, 2004; Koelsch, Fritz, von Cramon, Müller, & Friederici, 2006) or familiar (Menon & Levitin, 2005; Mitterschiffthaler, Fu, Dalton, Andrew, & Williams, 2007) to the subjects. Some of these regions (especially the nucleus accumbens) have been implicated in response to highly rewarding or motivationally important stimuli (Knutson & Cooper, 2005), including chocolate (Small, Zatorre, Dagher, Evans, & Jones-Gotman, 2001) and drugs of abuse (Breiter et al, 1997). Thus, under certain circumstances, music can access subcortical structures that are associated with primary reinforcers. This neurobiological link between music and the limbic system is not limited to hedonic mechanisms. The amygdala can also be recruited by scary music (Gosselin et al, 2005, 2007). Thus, music may be as effective as food, drug, and facial expressions (Johnson, 2005) in eliciting subcortically mediated affective responses.

One important question is whether this subcortical involvement responds to top-down influences from the cortex (is cortically mediated) and whether the subcortical relay can modulate the cortical processing of music. Menon and Levitin (2005) observed enhanced functional connectivity between subcortical regions (e.g. the nucleus accumbens) and cortical regions (e.g. the insula and the orbitofrontal cortex), but the nature of this connectivity or its direction cannot be specified with functional neuroimaging. In order to obtain indication of whether the subcortical activations precede, are concomitant, or follow cortical mediation, one needs to use other techniques such as intracranial recordings and lesion studies.

Because many emotional responses are fast, automatic, and can be derived from low-level acoustical analysis of the musical input, three kinds of response are potentially informative in this regard: the startle reflex, avoidance of dissonance, and perception of danger. All three responses are optimal at engaging a fast, feed-forward subcortical system that could in turn feed cortical systems. Each response is examined below.

The startle reflex

The acoustical startle reflex is an automatic defensive reaction to an unexpected loud sound. Its neural pathway is relatively well understood. The expression of the reflex itself is controlled at the brain-stem level (Yeomans & Frankland, 1995), but it can be modulated by subcortical structures, notably the amygdala, during exposure to aversive stimuli (Grillon & Baas, 2003). In such cases, the startle reflex is enhanced compared to a neutral situation. The reflex can also be attenuated by pleasant stimuli, as we have shown in the case of pleasant music (Roy et al, 2009). Animal research suggests that lesions to the nucleus accumbens but not lesions of the amygdala can influence pleasure attenuation of the reflex (Koch, Schmid, & Schnitzler, 1996). Presently, however, we do not know whether modulation of the startle reflex via the subcortical structures, such as the nucleus accumbens, precedes or results from cortical analysis of music. Exploration of this issue is currently in progress in our laboratory.

Sensory dissonance

Sensory dissonance can be created by two simultaneous tones one or two semitones apart. This combination creates beating at the level of the basilar membrane in the inner ear. The overlap in vibration patterns compromises the resolution of pitches of different frequency on the basilar membrane, leading to the perception of roughness. Thus, the unpleasant character of dissonant sounds can be computed by the auditory system before it reaches subcortical structures and, hence, before it reaches the auditory cortex where neurons that respond to dissonance are located (Fishman et al, 2001). The functioning of a fast, reflex-like subcortical pathway might rely on these peripheral mechanisms of the auditory system and account for its effect on human behaviour early in development. Newborns and young infants prefer consonant over dissonant tone pairs (Trainor & Heinmiller, 1998) and musical passages (Masataka, 2006; Zentner & Kagan, 1996). This preference for consonance appears innate because even hearing newborns from deaf parents prefer consonance over dissonance (Masataka, 2006).

Support for the involvement of subcortical (or paralimbic) structures in response to dissonance comes from functional neuroimaging and brain lesion studies. Neuroimaging studies have identified the parahippocampal gyrus (Blood, Zatorre, Bermudez, & Evans, 1999) and the amygdala (Ball et al, 2007; Koelsch, Fritz, von Cramon, Müller, & Friederici, 2006) as key brain structures. Interestingly, activity in the right parahippocampal gyrus increases with increasing dissonance (Blood, Zatorre, Bermudez, & Evans, 1999). Lesion data have confirmed the critical involvement of the parahippocampal cortex in evaluating the unpleasantness of dissonance. Substantial resections of the left or right parahippocampal cortex gave highly abnormal judgements to dissonant music, which was judged to be pleasant while controls found it unpleasant. This indifference to dissonance was specific and not due to a perceptual disorder. Moreover, the impairment differed from that induced by amygdala damage alone (Gosselin, Peretz, Johnsen, & Adolphs, 2007; Gosselin et al, 2006). Thus, the current evidence points to the parahippocampal cortex, rather than the amygdala, as being a key structure in the emotional evaluation of dissonance. It remains to be determined, however, if this paralimbic contribution is 'direct' or mediated by cortical analysis. A case like IR, who appears to be deaf to dissonance due to damage to the auditory cortex (Peretz, Gagnon, & Bouchard, 1998), could provide indication in this regard.

To test the importance of the auditory cortex in mediating dissonance judgments, IR was asked to rate the pleasantness of the stimuli used in the neuroimaging study with normals (Blood, Zatorre, Bermudez, & Evans, 1999) and in our prior study (Peretz, Gagnon, & Bouchard, 1998), of which half were manipulated so as to create sensory dissonance. IR was deaf to dissonance: she did not judge the dissonant music as unpleasant as every normal does (Peretz, Blood, Penhune, & Zatorre, 2001). Thus, there was no evidence that IR's intact subcortical pathway could give rise to emotional reactions to dissonance. Rather, the results suggest that emotional responses to dissonance are mediated via an obligatory cortical perceptual relay. Because IR was tested with explicit emotional tasks, it remains possible that the functioning of her intact subcortical pathway was not assessed with appropriate methods. In order to assess a rapid, reflex-like subcortical response to dissonance, one could use functional neuroimaging and see if normal activity can be observed in IR's parahippocampal cortex in response to dissonance. Unfortunately, neuroimaging cannot be used with her due to the presence of metallic clips in her brain. Another, less invasive avenue could be to explore whether conditioning and physiological recordings in response to dissonance can be obtained. If IR were to exhibit evidence of sensitivity to dissonance with such indirect measures, it would be the first demonstration of subcortical emotional responses to music without cortical relay. Future work with intracranial recordings in patients who have depth electrodes implanted in the parahippocampal gyrus should also be informative in this regard.

Scary music

Suspense in music is often created by dissonance (think of *Psycho*, the horror film directed by Alfred Hitchcock), but this is not always the case. In our set of musical clips

composed with the intention of expressing threat (and inspired by real film soundtracks[1]), some of the stimuli were consonant and musically regular. Moreover, the
presence of dissonance, violation of expectancies, and irregularities did not determine
listeners' accuracy in judging the music as scary (Gosselin et al, 2005; Vieillard et al,
2008). This is surprising given the recent finding that auditory uncertainty plays an
important role in activating the amygdala (Herry et al, 2007; Koelsch, Fritz, & Schlaug,
2008). Music might convey anxiety in a variety of ways, which may, in turn, recruit
different perceptual mechanisms.

Nevertheless, our heterogeneous set of 'scary' musical selections was effective in
highlighting the role of the amygdala. Using these stimuli, we found that recognition
of 'scary' music can be impaired by unilateral medial temporal lobe excision (Gosselin
et al, 2005). Patients having sustained such an excision that systematically removes the
amygdala, particularly on the right side of the brain, seemed to have lost the knowledge
of what signals danger from music, as attested by their aberrant choice of 'peacefulness' or 'happiness' as the intended emotion for the scary music. This atypical behaviour did not seem to arise as a consequence of a poor perceptual system. All patients
managed to obtain a fairly high-level performance in an error-detection task that used
the same musical selections. The most likely neural locus underlying this disorder is
the amygdala. Indeed, SM, who has complete bilateral damage relatively restricted
to the amygdala, was selectively impaired in the recognition of 'scary' and 'sad' music.
In contrast, her recognition of 'happy' music was normal. SM's impaired emotional
judgements occurred in an otherwise intact processing system of musical features that
are emotionally relevant (such as mode, tempo, and dissonance). Thus, the amygdala
appears to be *necessary* to perceive musical suspense.

Support for this hypothesis has been obtained recently in two neuroimaging studies, in which increased activity in the amygdala was observed when normal subjects
were viewing films with scary musical soundtracks (Baumgartner, Lutz, Schmidt, &
Jancke, 2006; Eldar, Ganor, Admon, Bleich, & Hendler, 2007). Thus, evidence from
lesion and neuroimaging studies highlights the role of the amygdala as a central hub of
the two emotional routes mentioned earlier, with a fast and coarse reflex-like circuit
that predominantly resides in subcortical structures (Johnson, 2005; LeDoux, 2000),
and a slower, more detailed cortically mediated circuit used for recognition and decision making. In the former, the amygdala assigns affective value to incoming stimuli
directly. In the latter, the amygdala assigns affective values via its connections with the
cortical systems.

It remains to be determined if involvement of the amygdala precedes or follows
a cortical perceptual relay. To this aim, one would need to specify the nature of the
musical features that may express danger from music. The various candidates that we
have tested so far, such as dissonance, rhythmic irregularities, and expectancies, are
elaborate musical features that may require cortical mediation. It remains possible that
the amygdala could be triggered by coarser acoustical features, such as high-spectral

---

[1] The musical selections can be downloaded at the Internet from: www.brams.umontreal.ca/plab/
publications/article/96

sounds, highly dynamic sounds, or highly unpredictable sounds. Thus, future work should aim at defining the nature of the musical characteristics that are quickly and effectively picked up by a subcortical pathway to verify if there is a 'short-cut' from music to emotions. The point is not only theoretically relevant, but clinically important as well. For example, direct access to subcortical structures may account for the fact that patients with Alzheimer dementia continue to respond to music despite the existence of vast and diffuse cortical lesions.

5.2.3 The cortical emotional pathway

Cortical systems are neural structures that are evolutionary relatively recent and particularly developed in the human brain. Another characteristic of these cortical structures is that they exhibit functional specialization within and across the two cerebral hemispheres. For example, it is well established that regions of the left hemisphere of the brain are much more essential for speech than the right side of the brain.

Hemispheric specialization

There is a long-held debate involving two alternative views with respect to emotions. One view is that the right hemisphere is specialized for processing *all* emotions by containing all 'modules' for nonverbal affect computation (e.g. Bowers, Bauer, & Heilman, 1993). This position is known as 'the right hemisphere hypothesis'. The opposing view is 'the valence hypothesis,' which posits that the right hemisphere is more involved in negative emotions while the left hemisphere is more engaged in positive emotions (e.g. Davidson, 1992). The first observations related to the emotional competence of each cerebral hemisphere go back to Jackson (1878), who noticed that emotional language is often preserved in aphasic patients. He attributed the source of the preserved affective utterances to the contribution of the right hemisphere. This dissociation between propositional and affective language has been reported often since then. It is difficult to reconcile, however, with another classical pattern in clinical neurology that identifies each hemisphere with a distinct affective style. A lesion in the right hemisphere often produces indifference (anosognosia) and a tendency to joke. In contrast, an injury in the left hemisphere often leads to depressive-catastrophic states. The former is obviously less comprehensible than the latter as a reaction to the brain accident. The two emotional modes of responding have been associated with differences in 'affective styles' of the cerebral hemispheres. The left and right frontal cortex would be mediating approach and avoidance, respectively (Davidson & Irwin, 1999).

Both hypotheses have been discussed in regard to musical emotions. Support for the valence hypothesis has been obtained in several studies measuring brain electrical activity—the electroencephalogram (EEG)—from scalp electrodes in normal listeners (Altenmuller, Schurmann, Lim, & Parlitz, 2002; Flores-Gutierrez et al, 2007; Schmidt & Trainor, 2001; Tsang, Trainor, Santesso, Tasker, & Schmidt, 2001). Subjects exhibit greater relative left activity to pleasant musical excerpts and greater relative right EEG activity to unpleasant music. Converging results have been obtained from ear asymmetries in normal listeners (Gagnon & Peretz, 2000). Non-musicians were required to classify tonal and atonal melodies as pleasant and unpleasant in one condition. In a non-affective 'control' condition, the same subjects were required to judge if the melodies sounded conventional or not. Listeners exhibited a left-ear superiority effect, taken to reflect the predominance of the right hemisphere, when judging atonal melodies as unpleasant, but they displayed a slight right-ear advantage when judging tonal melodies as pleasant. This pattern of ear-asymmetries was specific to emotional judgements, because a different pattern was obtained when the same melodies had to be classified for 'correctness'.

Nonetheless, the valence account of cerebral asymmetries is not always supported, and results from some studies are more supportive of the right-hemisphere hypothesis. One measured ear asymmetries in normal subjects who were judging major and minor melodies as expressing positive or negative emotions (Bryden, Ley, & Sugarman, 1982). In that study, an overall left-ear (i.e. right-hemisphere) advantage was observed across positive and negative emotional judgements. In another study by Blood, Zatorre, Bermudez, and Evans (1999), the neural structures activated by pleasant, consonant music were found primarily in the right hemisphere. Moreover, reciprocal activations occurring between particular neural structures and the valence of the musical stimulus were found within the same hemisphere.

Although the nature of each hemispheric contribution to the perception of musical emotions remains to be determined, it is plausible that the cortical contribution is related to both the demands of the task and the nature of the perceptual analysis of the input. For example, it is relatively well established that pitch-based mechanisms are more likely to recruit right-hemisphere structures while hemispheric lateralization of time-based mechanisms is less clear (Peretz & Zatorre, 2005). Thus, there is a need to fractionate the processing components involved in each basic musical emotion in order to understand the principles underlying hemispheric differences.

Orbitofrontal cortex and ventromedial prefrontal cortex

As suggested previously, there is solid evidence that various cortical structures are involved in the emotional processing of music. For example, activity in the orbitofrontal cortex (Blood & Zatorre, 2001; Blood, Zatorre, Bermudez, & Evans, 1999; Khalfa, Schon, Anton, & Liegeois-Chauvel, 2005; Menon & Levitin, 2005), the superior temporal cortex, and the anterior cingulate cortex (Blood & Zatorre, 2001; Blood, Zatorre, Bermudez, & Evans, 1999; Mitterschiffthaler, Fu, Dalton, Andrew, & Williams, 2007; Green et al, 2008) has been reported frequently in relation to musical emotions. Among these structures, the orbitofrontal cortex and the ventromedial prefrontal cortex are key in the emotional cortical pathway. The orbitofrontal cortex has robust reciprocal connections with the amygdala, and both areas have strong connections with cortical representations of every sensory modality, so that they form a functional circuit that integrates sensory information.

Among all these brain areas, it is not always easy to determine if the activity is related to emotional or non-emotional processing of the musical structure. In most studies, the musical stimuli vary widely in structure. For example, Mitterschiffthaler et al (2007) selected 'happy' and 'sad' musical excerpts from the classical repertoire. These stimuli, such as *Traviata* from Verdi and the *Adagio* of Albinoni, are polyphonic, complex, familiar to a variable degree, and widely different in acoustical and musical structure. While maximizing the ecological value of the study, the use of real pieces of music may introduce substantial confoundings in terms of acoustical, attentional, musical, and memory differences. All of these acoustical and cognitive differences are likely to recruit largely different and distributed neural networks (Peretz & Zatorre, 2005), thereby making the interpretation of the activated cortical areas difficult.

Yet, it is possible to use brain imaging techniques in the study of emotional responses to musical events in a highly controlled manner. For example, Mizuno and Sugishita (2007) presented musicians with major, minor, and ambiguous isolated chords in the scanner. They found that the inferior frontal gyrus (BA 47), the medial thalamus, and the dorsal anterior cingulate cortex were critically involved in the happy–sad judgements of the major–minor mode distinction. This network of neural activations fits nicely with IR's brain lesions, which largely spared these areas (see above). In Mizuno and Sugishita's study, however, happy–sad judgements were not contrasted with a non-emotional control task, such as asking the subjects to judge the pitch level of the chords (as high or low). Thus, it remains to be determined if these regions are part of the emotional pathway or of the non-emotional cortical pathway.

As yet, no lesion study has attempted to identify focal cortical regions that are part of the cortical emotional pathway in music processing. The paradoxical changes of musical tastes seen in cases of frontotemporal dementia (e.g. Geroldi et al, 2000) support the notion that the orbitofrontal cortex and the ventromedial prefrontal cortex are key brain systems in the emotional cortical circuit subserving musical emotions.

5.3 MUSICAL EMOTIONS: DISCUSSION AND GENERAL REMARKS ON BRAIN ORGANIZATION

The available evidence suggests that the musical input may require cortical mediation in the superior temporal gyri. The perceptual output is then relayed to emotional systems in the limbic and paralimbic structures and in more frontal areas, depending on its valence. This two-stage model suggests that emotion and perception are not taking place along two parallel and independent pathways as some models (LeDoux, 2000; Zajonc, 1984) posit. The cortical and subcortical routes would be serially organized in the case of music.

Each pathway may play a distinct function in emotional responses, with different distributed networks underlying different emotions. Just as cognitive neuroscience has demonstrated the necessity to fractionate global functions, such as face processing or music recognition, into more elementary constituents whose neural substrates can be identified, so too modern research in the neuroscience of emotions suggests fractionation of affective processes. This conclusion highlights what is often not obvious to psychologists. It shows why the study of neural correlates in general, and brain localization in particular, is of importance. Examination of brain correlates can shed light on more general assumptions, by requiring that complex brain functions be decomposed into simpler processes so that components can be localized anatomically and studied in relative isolation. This fractionation into elementary, localized mechanisms can then serve to test current models of emotional functioning or contribute to the development of new models.

From this perspective, brain lesion studies should not be ignored. Though neuroimaging and other brain mapping techniques are of tremendous importance, they have not and cannot replace research with brain-damaged patients. Indeed, brain-mapping techniques cannot disentangle correlation from causation. Emotional processes are distributed across several spatially distinct neural regions that interact in order to implement the function under study. Moreover, the contribution of each component is not fixed but depends on its interactions with other components of the system. 'All of this conspires to make the data that functional imaging studies yield overinclusive' (Adolphs, 2007, p. 426). To causally link a specific neural structure to emotion, we must turn to the effect of brain damage, the 'experiments of nature'. Similarly, intracranial stimulation and newer non-invasive brain stimulation (such as transcranial magnetic stimulation) can causally relate a function and a brain region. In short, all techniques have their strengths and weaknesses, and should be used in combination.

There are a number of issues related to the neural correlates of musical emotions that have not been addressed in this chapter because of insufficient relevant data. This is the case for three of the four basic emotions easily conveyed by music, namely happiness, sadness, and anger. There is as yet no clear indication on how these musical emotions are organized in the brain, although their perceptual determinants are relatively well documented (Chapters 14 and 17, this volume).

Another untackled issue is the possible exploitation of neurochemical correlates of musical emotions. Neurochemicals are neurotransmitters and hormones that alter the response properties of sets of neurons. Music is apparently effective in eliciting such responses, as indicated by the action of the antagonists of endorphins (Goldstein, 1980) and cortisol measures (Khalfa, Dalla Bella, Roy, Peretz, & Lupien, 2003; Suda, Morimoto, Obata, Koizumi, & Maki, 2008; Trehub, 2001; see Chapter 11, this volume). The study of these neurochemicals may provide yet another neuropsychological avenue to a better understanding of the nature and brain organization of musical emotions.

5.4 MUSICAL INVASION OF VOCAL EMOTION CIRCUITS OF THE BRAIN

With limbic mediation, consistency, and precociousness, musical emotions resemble other important classes of emotions, such as facial emotions (Peretz, 2001). As seen above, music recruits key brain regions for processing emotions, such as the striatum, the amygdala, the orbitofrontal cortex, and the anterior cingulate cortex. These emotion circuits have been associated with basic biological functions, such as sex and food. Music can hardly be compared to such basic needs. There seems to be a much larger cultural learning component to musically induced emotions. Thus, one may wonder how the relations between music and these neurobiological substrates should be conceptualized. One possibility is that music is particularly suited (or designed) to invade or co-opt emotion circuits that have evolved for biologically important sounds.

One likely emotional system for neural invasion (or 'neural recycling', to adopt the terminology of Dehaene & Cohen, 2007) is the systems dealing with emotional vocalizations, such as laughs and screams, and prosody. Communication among humans (and animals) is often carried out using acoustical signals, whose affective value might well be genetically transmitted and supported by specialized brain emotion circuits. Musical emotions might invade these evolved circuits for vocal emotions and adjust them for its particularities. If so, the study of musical emotions might benefit from what has been learned about these other emotions. Brain organization for vocal emotions could constrain brain organization for musical emotions.

5.4.1 Vocal emotions: brain organization

In humans, the expression of emotions through the voice can take two different forms. It can be conveyed by the tone of voice in speaking, or by emotional vocalizations such as laughs, cries, and screams. There has been a greater interest in the first category of vocal expressions, which is usually referred to as *affective prosody*. Despite their importance, and in contrast to the large literature on affective prosody, emotional vocalizations have not been extensively studied. Thus, they will be jointly considered here.

A distinct neural pathway

The most remarkable neuropsychological property of the vocal emotional system is its apparent specificity. First, despite the obvious link between facial and vocal expression of emotions, emotional evaluation of the tones of voices is dissociable from the emotional evaluation of faces. Some patients can infer the emotional tone of vocal expressions but not of facial expressions, whereas others show the opposite pattern (e.g. Hornak, Rolls, & Wade, 1996). This dissociation is not due to differences related to the modality of input, because the patient's ability to process other aspects of faces and voices is typically spared. The neural separability of vocal from facial emotions is not trivial, given that they typically signal the same emotion at any given time. Yet the two modes of expressions seem to be subserved by independent neural systems.

Secondly, within the speech signal, the recognition of vocal cues that are emotionally meaningful is dissociable from the recognition of vocal cues that are semantically informative. As mentioned previously, Jackson (1878) was the first to notice the separability of affective prosody from propositional speech. The distinction has been made several times in perception as well. For example, in a dichotic listening study with normal adults, Ley and Bryden (1982) found a left-ear (i.e. right-hemisphere) advantage for the perception of the emotional tone of voice, and a right-ear (i.e. left-hemisphere) superiority for the recognition of the actual semantic content of the words from the same set of sentences. Similarly, there are reports of patients who can no longer understand speech, but who are still able to infer the emotion conveyed by vocal cues (e.g. Barrett, Crucian, Raymer, & Heilman, 1999). These findings show that emotional processing of speech signals can take different routes, one determined by semantic content and one determined by vocal form.

Finally, the tone of the voice is not analysed just for affective purposes. Prosodic cues can provide important person-specific information (e.g. identity, age, and sex) and linguistic, non-semantic information (e.g. differentiating a question from a statement). Once again, the use of these non-affective cues is dissociated from their emotional use. Brain lesions can interfere with the identification of vocal emotions of happiness, sadness, and fear, yet spare the identification of prosodic differences marking questions, exclamations, and assertions in spoken sentences (e.g. Heilman, Bowers, Speedie, & Coslett, 1984). Similarly, functional neuroimaging of neurologically intact brains points to the involvement of distinct neural regions for emotion recognition and for speaker identification (Imaizumi et al, 1997). Together, these findings highlight the fine tuning and specialization of the neural system underlying the emotional interpretation of vocal sounds.

What remains to be determined is to what extent the emotional vocal pathway can be dissociated from the musical one. There are some indications that these may dissociate. For example, Griffiths et al (2004) describe a patient with damage to the left insula and amygdala who experienced a deficit in musical emotions, while retaining normal music perception and voice prosody perception. Unfortunately, as mentioned previously, this report is anecdotal. The emotional losses have not been assessed. To my knowledge, the reverse dissociation—that is, impaired vocal emotions in the presence of normal musical emotions—has not yet been reported. Therefore, it remains possible that the emotional pathway of vocal emotions is shared with (and perhaps invaded by, as discussed below) musical emotions.

Subcortical pathway of vocal emotions

Curiously, evidence for the involvement of the amygdala in vocal emotions is inconsistent. Lesions to the amygdala impair the recognition of vocal expressions of fear sometimes (Scott et al, 1997; Sprengelmeyer et al, 1999), but not at other times (Adolphs & Tranel, 1999; Anderson & Phelps, 1998). In the latter cases, patients with selective bilateral damage to the amygdala show preserved recognition of fearful voices while showing evidence of impaired recognition of fearful faces. One such patient is SM, who showed impaired recognition of both fearful facial expression and scary music (Gosselin et al, 2007). Similarly, neuroimaging data show activation of the amygdala in both visual and auditory fearful expressions in some instances (Dolan, Morris, & de Gelder, 2001; Morris et al, 1996; Phillips et al, 1998), but not in others (Imaizumi et al, 1997; Morris, Scott, & Dolan, 1999; Pourtois, de Gelder, Bol, & Crommelinck, 2005; Royet et al, 2000). When there is evidence of amygdala activation, it may encompass positive (pleasure and laughter) and negative vocal sounds (fear and sadness; Fecteau, Belin, Joanette, & Armony, 2007). The latter finding may be related to two recent findings about the amygdala. First, the amygdala is not a single entity but contains

functionally distinct regions that may respond differentially to positive and negative emotions (Ball et al, 2007). Secondly, the amygdala may act more as a 'relevance
detector' for biologically meaningful events, independently of their valence (Sander,
Grafman, & Zalla, 2003).

Nonetheless, tone of voice is as meaningful and biologically important as facial
expression. Thus, the current inconsistency in engaging the amygdala through the
vocal channel is puzzling. From an evolutionary perspective, one would expect a common pathway. The involvement of subcortical structures in vocal emotions, including
the amygdala but also the basal ganglia, remains poorly understood. In a recent review
of the literature, Schirmer and Kotz (2006) proposed that subcortical mechanisms are
limited to the case of unexpected changes in speaker tone or cases of threat that motivate adjustments to behaviour. In sum, there is so far little support for the notion that
musical emotions invade the subcortical brain circuits devoted to vocal emotions.

Cortical pathway of vocal emotions

At the cortical level, vocal emotions are typically associated with the right hemisphere.
Several recent neuroimaging studies have suggested, however, that decoding emotional
prosody engages both hemispheres (Adolphs, 2002; Schirmer & Kotz, 2006). Studies
in patients with focal brain lesions show that recognition of emotional information
through prosody engages a distributed network of areas, mostly within the right frontal
and parietal lobes. These areas include the temporal cortex, the insula, and the inferior
frontal gyrus (e.g. Schirmer & Kotz, 2006). Some of these findings have been integrated
in a model proposing that regions in the superior temporal sulcus (STS) and superior
temporal gyrus, especially in the right hemisphere, form an emotional 'gestalt', which
is then made accessible for higher-order cognitive processing, possibly taking place in
the orbitofrontal cortex (Schirmer & Kotz, 2006).

Interestingly, some of these brain regions appear to support the processing of
emotional vocalizations in both human and non-human primates. The human right
ventrolateral orbitofrontal cortex responds more to negative than to positive vocalizations of other humans as well as of cats and rhesus monkeys (Belin et al, 2008). This
region is close to areas that are activated in awake macaques when they are presented
with negative and positive monkey vocalizations (Gil-da-Costa et al, 2004). These
results suggest that some of these neural systems for processing vocal emotions are
shared between humans and primates.

5.4.2 Implications of a brain emotion circuit invasion

Although the evidence in support of common brain organization for vocal and musical
emotion is currently scarce, it is theoretically interesting to examine the neurobiological
implications of such an hypothesis:

Availability. As brain circuits dedicated to vocal emotions are invaded by music, their
    prior organization should shape musical emotions early on in infancy. One would
    predict, for example, that the ventral striatum and the amygdala should be tuned

early on by both music (infant-directed singing) and voice (infant-directed speech), depending on the intended emotion. Similarly, processing in the auditory cortex and perhaps in the superior temporal sulcus might respond to emotionally mean- ingful inflections of the voice, pitch level, and tempo in both infant-directed speech and songs. It would be particularly informative to examine whether avoidance of dissonance applies to both musical and vocal sounds. Indeed, the increased ten- sion of the vocal chords in infant cries and distress calls introduces many subhar- monics in the vocal sounds that otherwise are harmonic signals. These distortions in screams sound unpleasant and are effective in triggering a response in others (who will notice it rapidly and will try to stop it; Fitch, Neubauer, & Herzel, 2002). What is needed is a definition of the acoustical correlates of dissonance that can be applied to both musical and vocal sounds (Peretz, 2008).

Reconfigurability. With exposure, the musical invasion scenario might be associated with a re-mapping of the brain emotion circuits via plasticity. An important test of the invasion hypothesis would be to show that there is no creation of domain- specific brain circuits, and that plasticity is expressed by reconfiguring the existing emotional networks. Thus, one might predict different configurations of the same neural circuits to be engaged at different ages. For example, we may expect the neural pathways for musical emotions that are driven by innate mechanisms (e.g. beating and dissonance) to be relatively fixed, whereas musical emotions that are likely driven by (culturally acquired) musical associations (e.g. sadness and mi- nor mode) to be a dynamic process that develops during the first few years of life. Unfortunately, there is as yet no neuroimaging study that has examined musical emotions in infants or during development. Another way to test this prediction is to compare musicians to nonmusicians. For example, Thompson, Schellenberg and Husain (2004) have shown effects of musical lessons on the ability to recognize basic emotions (happy, sad, fearful, or angry) from both speech prosody and tone sequences that mimic this prosody. It would be interesting to see if these effects of musical expertise are due to further specialization of the same brain circuits that are used by non-musicians, or if these effects are due to flexible use of distinct brain circuits.

Efficacy. One interesting possibility is that music invasion of the vocal emotion brain circuitry arises from its efficacy to function as a 'super-stimulus' for the vocal emo- tion system. Juslin and collaborators (Juslin & Laukka, 2003; Juslin & Västfjäll, 2008) have argued that we process music as if it were a *super-expressive voice*. This idea is analogous to what Sperber and Hirschfeld (2004) propose for facial manipulations. Masks, cosmetics, and caricatures may arise from the nature of face coding in the human brain, which allows these cultural artefacts to function as 'su- per-stimuli' for the fusiform face area. In other words, music may aim at the vocal emotional systems just as artistic masks target the face recognition system. Music may exaggerate particular nonverbal vocal features that are effective for bonding. From this perspective, the actual domain of the emotional systems is said to be invaded or co-opted. Music could have stabilized in all cultures because music is so effective at co-opting one or several evolved emotional systems, which have their roots in animal communication. Multiple anchoring in several emotional systems may even contribute to the ubiquity and power of music. As mentioned previously, music appears more effective than stories in attracting infants' attention (Nakata & Trehub, 2004) and in enhancing cognitive recovery after brain damage (Sarkamo et al, 2008).

Clearly, there is a need for comparison between musical and vocal emotions. There are as yet very few studies beyond a meta-analysis of the data obtained in separate experimental settings (Juslin & Laukka, 2003), which indicated that both domains use similar emotional acoustic cues. Partial support for this proposal was provided recently by Ilie and Thompson (2006). They found similar effects on emotional responses by manipulating some acoustical cues such as pitch intensity in both music and speech, but they also found domain-specific effects. Interestingly, music received higher ratings than speech in valence and arousal, suggesting that music may be more engaging than vocal expressions. In sum, there are presently few studies and thus little evidence for the existence of a common channel for conveying emotions through the musical and vocal channels. Future comparisons between domains should not only originate from neuroscience but also from developmental and comparative research, ethnomusicology, and psychology.

5.5 CONCLUSIONS

Although many questions about the neurobiological basis of musical emotions remain unresolved, there is evidence that musical emotions depend on a specialized emotional pathway that recruits various subcortical and cortical structures that may be shared, at least in part, with other biologically important systems. This emotional pathway is not simple. There is not a single, unitary emotional system underlying all emotional responses to music. For instance, most of the neural pathway underlying emotional responses to dissonance has been delineated and involves a complex and distributed system in the brain (Peretz, 2008).

Nevertheless, it is remarkable how much progress has been accomplished over the last decade. As a result, I could not simply update my former review of the field (Peretz, 2001); I had to rewrite it. In this short span of time, research has moved from mere acknowledgment of musical emotions to carefully controlled study in multiple directions. I believe that further major advances will be made by research that involves multiple methods, integrating lesion studies, functional imaging, pharmacology, transcranial magnetic stimulation, psychophysiology, cognitive psychology, comparative psychology, and the emerging fields of behavioural genetics.

The motivation for understanding the biological foundations of musical emotions is currently high in the scientific community. There is increasing awareness of the social and clinical value of music, particularly with respect to its effectiveness in communicating emotions. Today, music plays an even more powerful and unique role in human life than ever, with wide-ranging effects on many aspects of functioning besides its obvious social function. Music has become such a key element in the human behavioural repertoire that it might be considered as a defining human attribute. In fact, music is so highly valued that very few people are willing to acknowledge a lack of emotional responsiveness to music.[2] Much work remains to be done but there is every reason to welcome advances in the biological foundations of musical emotions. We cannot change the way our brain is built, but we can better understand its functioning and adjust musical practices to its biological limitations.

[2] I am grateful to Glenn Schellenberg, Sylvie Hébert, Nathalie Gosselin, Eckart Altenmüller, and two anonymous reviewers for offering insightful comments. The research summarized in this chapter has been supported by research grants from the Natural Sciences and Engineering Research Council of Canada and the Canadian Foundation for Innovation.

Recommended further reading

1. Peretz, I., & Zatorre, R. J. (2005). Brain organization for music processing. *Annual Review of Psychology*, 56, 89–114.
2. Panksepp, J. (1998). *Affective neuroscience*. Oxford: Oxford University Press.
3. Damasio, A. (1994). *Descartes' error: Emotion, reason, and the human brain*. New York: Avon Books.

References

Adachi, M., & Trehub, S. E. (2000). Decoding the expressive intentions in children's songs. *Music Perception*, 18, 213–24.

Adolphs, R. (2002). Neural systems for recognizing emotion. *Current Opinion in Neurobiology*, 12, 169.

Adolphs, R. (2007). Investigating human emotion with lesions and transcranial recording. In J. Allen & J. Coan (eds), *Handbook of emotion elicitation and assessment* (pp. 426–39). New York: Oxford University Press.

Adolphs, R., & Tranel, D. (1999). Intact recognition of emotional prosody following amygdala damage. *Neuropsychologia*, 37, 1285–92.

Altenmuller, E., Schurmann, K., Lim, V. K., & Parlitz, D. (2002). Hits to the left, flops to the right: different emotions during listening to music are reflected in cortical lateralisation patterns. *Neuropsychologia*, 40, 2242–56.

Anderson, A. K., & Phelps, E. A. (1998). Intact recognition of vocal expressions of fear following bilateral lesions of the human amygdala. *Neuroreport*, 9, 3607–13.

Balkwill, L. L., & Thompson, W. F. (1999). A cross-cultural investigation of the perception of emotion in music: Psychophysical and cultural cues. *Music Perception*, 17, 43–64.

Balkwill, L. L., Thompson, W. F., & Matsunaga, R. (2004). Recognition of emotion in Japanese, Western, and Hindustani music by Japanese listeners. *Japanese Psychological Research*, 46, 337–49.

Ball, T., Rahm, B., Eickhoff, S. B., Schulze-Bonhage, A., Speck, O., & Mutschler, I. (2007). Response properties of human amygdala subregions: evidence based on functional MRI combined with probabilistic anatomical maps. *PLoS ONE, 2*, e307.

Barrett, A. M., Crucian, G. P., Raymer, A. M., & Heilman, K. M. (1999). Spared comprehension of emotional prosody in a patient with global aphasia. *Neuropsychiatry, Neuropsychology & Behavioral Neurology, 12*, 117–20.

Baumgartner, T., Lutz, K., Schmidt, C. F., & Jancke, L. (2006). The emotional power of music: How music enhances the feeling of affective pictures. *Brain Research, 1075*, 151–64.

Belin, P., Fecteau, S., Charest, I., Nicastro, N., Hauser, M. D., & Armony, J. L. (2008). Human cerebral response to animal affective vocalizations. *Proceedings in Biological Sciences, 275*, 473–81.

Bigand, E., Vieillard, S., Madurell, F., Marozeau, J., & Dacquet, A. (2005). Multidimensional scaling of emotional responses to music: The effect of musical expertise and of the duration of the excerpts. *Cognition & Emotion, 19*, 1113–39.

Blood, A. J., & Zatorre, R. J. (2001). Intensely pleasurable responses to music correlate with activity in brain regions implicated in reward and emotion. *Proceedings of the National Academy of Sciences, 98*, 11818–23.

Blood, A. J., Zatorre, R. J., Bermudez, P., & Evans, A. C. (1999). Emotional responses to pleasant and unpleasant music correlate with activity in paralimbic brain regions. *Nature Neuroscience, 2*, 382–7.

Bornstein, R. F. (1989). Exposure and affect: Overview and meta-analysis of research, 1968–87. *Psychological Bulletin, 106*, 265–89.

Bouillaud, J. (1865). Sur la faculté du langage articulé. *Bulletin de l'Académie de Médecine, 30*, 752–68.

Bowers, D., Bauer, R. M., & Heilman, K. M. (1993). The nonverbal affect lexicon: Theoretical perspectives from neuropsychological studies of affect perception. *Neuropsychology, 7*, 433–44.

Breiter, H. C., Gollub, R. L., Weisskoff, R. M., Kennedy, D., Makris, N., Berke, J., et al (1997). Acute effects of cocaine on human brain activity. *Neuron, 19*, 591–611.

Broca, P. (1861). Remarques sur le siège de la faculté du langage articulé, suivies d'une observation d'aphémie (Perte de la parole) 'Remarks on the seat of the faculty of articulate language, followed by an observation of aphemia'. *Bulletin de la Société Anatomique, 6*, 330–57.

Broca, P. (1878). Anatomie comparée des circonvolutions cérébrales. *Revue d'Anthopologie, 1*, 385–498.

Brown, S., Martinez, M. J., & Parsons, L. M. (2004). Passive music listening spontaneously engages limbic and paralimbic systems. *NeuroReport, 15*, 2033–7.

Bryant, G. A., & Barrett, H. C. (2007). Recognizing intentions in infant-directed speech: evidence for universals. *Psychological Science, 18*, 746–51.

Bryden, M. P., Ley, R. G., & Sugarman, J. H. (1982). A left-ear advantage for identifying the emotional quality of tonal sequences. *Neuropsychologia, 20*, 83–7.

Cunningham, J. G., & Sterling, R. S. (1988). Developmental change in the understanding of affective meaning in music. *Motivation and Emotion, 12*, 399–413.

Dalla Bella, S., Peretz, I., Rousseau, L., & Gosselin, N. (2001). A developmental study of the affective value of tempo and mode in music. *Cognition, 80*, B1–10.

Damasio, A. (1994). *Descartes' error: Emotion, reason, and the human brain.* New York: Avon Books.

Dapretto, M., Davies, M. S., Pfeifer, J. H., Scott, A. A., Sigman, M., Bookheimer, S. Y., et al (2006). Understanding emotions in others: Mirror neuron dysfunction in children with autism spectrum disorders. *Nature Neuroscience, 9*, 28–30.

Davidson, R. J. (1992). Emotion and affective style. *Psychological Science*, 3, 39–43.

Davidson, R. J., & Irwin, W. (1999). The functional neuroanatomy of emotion and affective style. *Trends in Cognitive Science*, 3, 11–21.

Dehaene, S., & Cohen, L. (2007). Cultural recycling of cortical maps. *Neuron*, 56, 384–98.

Dolan, R. J., Morris, J. S., & de Gelder, B. (2001). Crossmodal binding of fear in voice and face. *Proceeding of the National Academy of Sciences*, 98, 10006–10.

Dolgin, K. G., & Adelson, E. H. (1990). Age changes in the ability to interpret affect in sung and instrumentally-presented melodies. *Psychology of Music*, 18, 87–98.

Eldar, E., Ganor, O., Admon, R., Bleich, A., & Hendler, T. (2007). Feeling the real world: Limbic response to music depends on related content. *Cerebral Cortex*, 17, 2828–40.

Fecteau, S., Belin, P., Joanette, Y., & Armony, J. L. (2007). Amygdala responses to nonlinguistic emotional vocalizations. *Neuroimage*, 36, 480–7.

Fishman, Y. I., Volkov, I. O., Noh, M. D., Garell, P. C., Bakken, H., Arezzo, J. C., et al (2001). Consonance and dissonance of musical chords: Neural correlates in auditory cortex of monkeys and humans. *Journal of Neurophysiology*, 86, 2761–88.

Fitch, W. T., Neubauer, J., & Herzel, H. (2002). Calls out of chaos: the adaptive significance of nonlinear phenomenon in mammalian vocal production. *Animal Behaviour*, 63, 407–18.

Flom, R., Gentile, D., & Pick, A. (2008). Infants' discrimination of happy and sad music. *Infant Behavior and Development*, 31, 716–28.

Flores-Gutierrez, E. O., Diaz, J. L., Barrios, F. A., Favila-Humara, R., Guevara, M. A., del Rio-Portilla, Y., et al (2007). Metabolic and electric brain patterns during pleasant and unpleasant emotions induced by music masterpieces. *International Journal of Psychophysiology*, 65, 69–84.

Gabrielsson, A., & Juslin, P. N. (2003). Emotional expression in music. In R. J. Davidson, H. H. Goldsmith, & K. R. Scherer (eds), *Handbook of affective sciences* (pp. 503–34). New York: Oxford University Press.

Gagnon, L., & Peretz, I. (2000). Laterality effects in processing tonal and atonal melodies with affective and nonaffective task instructions. *Brain & Cognition*, 43, 206–210.

Gerardi, G. M., & Gerken, L. (1995). The development of affective responses to modality and melodic contour. *Music Perception*, 12, 279–90.

Geroldi, C., Metitieri, T., Binetti, G., Zanetti, O., Trabucchi, M., & Frisoni, G. B. (2000). Pop music and frontotemporal dementia. *Neurology*, 55, 1935–6.

Gil-da-Costa, R., Braun, A., Lopes, M., Hauser, M. D., Carson, R. E., Herscovitch, P., et al (2004). Toward an evolutionary perspective on conceptual representation: Species-specific calls activate visual and affective processing systems in the macaque. *Proceedings of the National Academy of Sciences*, 101, 17516–21.

Goldstein, A. (1980). Thrills in response to music and other stimuli. *Physiological Psychology*, 8, 126–9.

Gosselin, N., Peretz, I., Johnsen, E., & Adolphs, R. (2007). Amygdala damage impairs emotion recognition from music. *Neuropsychologia*, 45, 236–44.

Gosselin, N., Peretz, I., Noulhiane, M., Hasboun, D., Beckett, C., Baulac, M., et al (2005). Impaired recognition of scary music following unilateral temporal lobe excision. *Brain*, 128, 628–40.

Gosselin, N., Samson, S., Adolphs, R., Noulhiane, M., Roy, M., Hasboun, D., et al (2006). Emotional responses to unpleasant music correlates with damage to the parahippocampal cortex. *Brain*, 129, 2585–92.

Green, A. C., Baerentsen, K., Stodkilde-Jorgensen, H., Wallentin, M., Roepstorff, A., & Vuust, P. (2008). Music in minor activates limbic structure: a relationship with dissonance? *NeuroReport*, 19, 711–15.

Gregory, A. H., Worrall, L., & Sarge, A. (1996). The development of emotional responses to music in young children. *Motivation and Emotion*, 20, 341–8.

Griffiths, T. D., Warren, J. D., Dean, J. L., & Howard, D. (2004). 'When the feeling's gone': a selective loss of musical emotion. *Journal of Neurology, Neurosurgery & Psychiatry, 75*, 344–5.

Grillon, C., & Baas, J. (2003). A review of the modulation of the startle reflex by affective states and its application in psychiatry. *Clinical neurophysiology, 114*, 1557–79.

Heaton, P., Hermelin, B., & Pring, L. (1999). Can children with autistic spectrum disorders perceive affect in music? An experimental investigation. *Psychological Medicine, 29*, 1405–10.

Heilman, K. M., Bowers, D., Speedie, L., & Coslett, H. B. (1984). Comprehension of affective and nonaffective prosody. *Neurology, 34*, 917–21.

Herry, C., Bach, D. R., Esposito, F., Di Salle, F., Perrig, W. J., Scheffler, K., et al (2007). Processing of temporal unpredictability in human and animal amygdala. *Journal of Neuroscience, 27*, 5958–66.

Hornak, J., Rolls, E. T., & Wade, D. (1996). Face and voice expression identification in patients with emotional and behavioural changes following ventral frontal lobe damage. *Neuropsychologia, 34*, 247–61.

Ilie, G., & Thompson, W. (2006). A comparison of acoustic cues in music and speech for three dimensions of affect. *Music Perception, 23*, 319–29.

Imaizumi, S., Mori, K., Kiritani, S., Kawashima, R., Sugiura, M., Fukuda, H., et al (1997). Vocal identification of speaker and emotion activates different brain regions. *Neuroreport, 8*, 2809–12.

Jackson, J. (1878). On the affections of speech from disease of the brain. *Brain, 1*, 304–330.

Johnson, M. H. (2005). Subcortical face processing. *Nature Review Neuroscience, 6*, 766–74.

Juslin, P. N., & Laukka, P. (2003). Communication of emotions in vocal expression and music performance: Different channels, same code? *Psychological Bulletin, 129*, 770–814.

Juslin, P. N., & Västfjäll, D. (2008). Emotional responses to music: The need to consider underlying mechanisms. *Behavioral and Brain Sciences, 31*, 559–621.

Kastner, M. P., & Crowder, R. G. (1990). Perception of the major/minor distinction: IV. Emotional connotations in young children. *Music Perception, 8*, 189–202.

Khalfa, S., Dalla Bella, S., Roy, M., Peretz, I., & Lupien, S. J. (2003). Effects of relaxing music on salivary cortisol level after psychological stress. *Annals of the New York Academy of Sciences, 999*, 374–6.

Khalfa S., & Peretz, I. (2007). Atypical emotional judgments and skin conductance responses to music and language in autism. In L. B. Zhao (ed.), *Autism research advances* (pp. 101–19). Nova Science Publishers.

Khalfa, S., Schon, D., Anton, J. L., & Liegeois-Chauvel, C. (2005). Brain regions involved in the recognition of happiness and sadness in music. *Neuroreport, 16*, 1981–4.

Kivy, P. (1990). *Music alone. Philosophical reflections on the purely musical experience.* Ithaca: NY: Cornell University Press.

Knutson, B., & Cooper, J. C. (2005). Functional magnetic resonance imaging of reward prediction. *Current Opinion in Neurology, 18*, 411–17.

Koch, M., Schmid, A., & Schnitzler, H. U. (1996). Pleasure-attenuation of startle is disrupted by lesions of the nucleus accumbens. *Neuroreport, 7*, 1442–6.

Koelsch, S., Fritz, T., von Cramon, D. Y., Müller, K., & Friederici, A. D. (2006). Investigating emotion with music: An fMRI study. *Human Brain Mapping, 27*, 239–50.

Koelsch, S., Fritz, T., & Schlaug, G. (2008). Amygdala activity can be modulated by unexpected chord functions during music listening. *NeuroReport, 19*, 1815–19.

Kratus, J. (1993). A developmental study of children's interpretation of emotion in music. *Psychology of Music, 21*, 3–19.

Laukka, P., & Juslin, P. N. (2007). Similar pattern of age-related differences in emotion recognition from speech and music. *Motivation and Emotion, 31*, 182–91.

LeDoux, J. E. (1996). *The emotional brain.* New York: Simon & Schuster.

LeDoux, J. E. (2000). Emotion circuits in the brain. *Annual Review of Neuroscience*, 23, 155–84.

Ley, R. G., & Bryden, M. P. (1982). A dissociation of right and left hemispheric effects for recognizing emotional tone and verbal content. *Brain Cognition*, 1, 3–9.

Masataka, N. (1999). Preference for infant-directed singing in 2-day-old hearing infants of deaf parents. *Developmental Psychology*, 35, 1001–5.

Masataka, N. (2006). Preference for consonance over dissonance by hearing newborns of deaf parents and of hearing parents. *Developmental Science*, 9, 46–50.

Mazzoni, M., Moretti, P., Pardossi, L., Vista, M., Muratorio, A., & Puglioli, M. (1993). A case of music imperception. *Journal of Neurology, Neurosurgery & Psychiatry*, 56, 322.

Mazzuchi, A., Marchini, C., Budai, R., & Parma, M. (1982). A case of receptive amusia with prominent timbre perception defect. *Journal of Neurology, Neurosurgery & Psychiatry*, 45, 644–7.

Menon, V., & Levitin, D. J. (2005). The rewards of music listening: Response and physiological connectivity of the mesolimbic system. *Neuroimage*, 28, 175–84.

Mitterschiffthaler, M. T., Fu, C. H., Dalton, J. A., Andrew, C. M., & Williams, S. C. (2007). A functional MRI study of happy and sad affective states induced by classical music. *Human Brain Mapping*, 28, 1150–62.

Mizuno, T., & Sugishita, M. (2007). Neural correlates underlying perception of tonality-related emotional contents. *Neuroreport*, 18, 1651–5.

Morris, J. S., Frith, C. D., Perrett, D. I., Rowland, D., Young, A. W., Calder, A. J., et al (1996). A differential neural response in the human amygdala to fearful and happy facial expressions. *Nature*, 383, 812–15.

Morris, J. S., Scott, S. K., & Dolan, R. J. (1999). Saying it with feeling: Neural responses to emotional vocalizations. *Neuropsychologia*, 37, 1155–63.

Mottron, L., Peretz, I., Belleville, S., & Rouleau, N. (1999). Absolute pitch in autism: A case study. *Neurocase*, 5, 485–501.

Nakata, T., & Trehub, S. (2004). Infants' responsiveness to maternal speech and singing. *Infant Behavior and Development*, 27, 455–64.

Neisser, U. (1967). *Cognitive psychology*. New York: Appleton-Century-Crofts.

Panksepp, J. (1998). *Affective neuroscience*. New York: Oxford University Press.

Papez, J. (1937). A proposed mechanism for emotion. *Archives of Neurology and Psychiatry*, 38, 725–43.

Peretz, I. (1996). Can we lose memories for music? The case of music agnosia in a nonmusician. *Journal of Cognitive Neurosciences*, 8, 481–96.

Peretz, I. (2001). Listen to the brain: The biological perspective on musical emotions. In P. N. Juslin & J. A. Sloboda (eds), *Music and emotion: Theory and research* (pp. 105–34). Oxford: Oxford University Press.

Peretz, I. (2006). The nature of music from a biological perspective. *Cognition*, 100, 1–32.

Peretz, I. (2008). The need to consider underlying mechanisms: A response from dissonance. *Behavioural and Brain Sciences*, 31, 590–1.

Peretz, I., Belleville, S., & Fontaine, S. (1997). Dissociations between music and language functions after cerebral resection: A new case of amusia without aphasia. *Canadian Journal of Experimental Psychology*, 51, 354–68.

Peretz, I., Blood, A. J., Penhune, V., & Zatorre, R. J. (2001). Cortical deafness to dissonance. *Brain*, 124, 928–40.

Peretz, I., & Gagnon, L. (1999). Dissociation between recognition and emotional judgment for melodies. *Neurocase*, 5, 21–30.

Peretz, I., Gagnon, L., & Bouchard, B. (1998). Music and emotion: Perceptual determinants, immediacy, and isolation after brain damage. *Cognition*, 68, 111–41.

Peretz, I., Gaudreau, D., & Bonnel, A. M. (1998). Exposure effects on music preference and recognition. *Memory and Cognition, 26*, 884–902.

Peretz, I., & Zatorre, R. J. (2005). Brain organization for music processing. *Annual Review of Psychology, 56*, 89–114.

Phelps, E. A. (2006). Emotion and cognition: Insights from studies of the human amygdala. *Annual Review in Psychology, 57*, 27–53.

Phillips, M. L., Young, A. W., Scott, S. K., Calder, A. J., Andrew, C., Giampietro, V., et al (1998). Neural responses to facial and vocal expressions of fear and disgust. *Proceedings of the Royal Society of London Series B—Biological Sciences, 265*, 1809–17.

Pourtois, G., de Gelder, B., Bol, A., & Crommelinck, M. (2005). Perception of facial expressions and voices and of their combination in the human brain. *Cortex, 41*, 49–59.

Roy, M., Mailhot, J.-P., Gosselin, N., Paquette, S., Rainville, P., & Peretz, I. (2009). Modulation of the startle reflex by pleasant and unpleasant music. *International Journal of Psychophysiology, 71*, 37–42.

Royet, J. P., Zald, D., Versace, R., Castes, N., Lavenne, F., Koenig, O., et al (2000). Emotional response to pleasant and unpleasant olfactory, visual, and auditory stimuli: A positron emisson tomography study. *Journal of Neuroscience, 20*, 7752–9.

Saffran, J. R., Johnson, E. K., Aslin, R. N., & Newport, E. L. (1999). Statistical learning of tone sequences by human infants and adults. *Cognition, 70*, 27–52.

Sander, D., Grafman, J., & Zalla, T. (2003). The human amygdala: an evolved system for relevance detection. *Reviews in the Neurosciences, 14*, 303–16.

Sarkamo, T., Tervaniemi, M., Laitinen, S., Forsblom, A., Soinila, S., Mikkonen, M., et al (2008). Music listening enhances cognitive recovery and mood after middle cerebral artery stroke. *Brain, 131*, 866–76.

Schirmer, A., & Kotz, S. A. (2006). Beyond the right hemisphere: brain mechanisms mediating vocal emotional processing. *Trends in Cognitive Sciences, 10*, 24–30.

Schmidt, L. A., & Trainor, L. J. (2001). Frontal brain electrical activity (EEG) distinguishes valence and intensity of musical emotions. *Cognition & Emotion, 15*, 487–500.

Scott, S. K., Young, A. W., Calder, A. J., Hellawell, D. J., Aggleton, J. P., & Johnson, M. (1997). Impaired auditory recognition of fear and anger following bilateral amygdala lesions. *Nature, 385*, 254–7.

Sernagor, E., & Grzywacz, M. (1996). Influence of spontaneous activity and visual experience on developing retinal receptive fields. *Current Biology, 6*, 1503–8.

Shammi, P., & Stuss, D. (1999). Humour appreciation: A role of the right frontal lobe. *Brain, 122*, 657–66.

Sloboda, J. A., Hermelin, B., & O'Connor, N. (1985). An exceptional musical memory. *Music Perception, 3*, 155–70.

Small, D. M., Zatorre, R. J., Dagher, A., Evans, A. C., & Jones-Gotman, M. (2001). Changes in brain activity related to eating chocolate: From pleasure to aversion. *Brain, 124*, 1720–33.

Sperber, D., & Hirschfeld, L. A. (2004). The cognitive foundations of cultural stability and diversity. *Trends in Cognitive Sciences, 8*, 40–6.

Sprengelmeyer, R., Young, A. W., Schroeder, U., Grossenbacher, P. G., Federlein, J., Bütner, T., et al (1999). Knowing to fear. *Proceedings in Biological Sciences The Royal Society London B, 266*, 2451–6.

Steiner, J. E. (1979). Human facial expressions in response to taste and smell stimulation. *Advances in Child Development and Behavior, 13*, 257–95.

Suda, M., Morimoto, K., Obata, A., Koizumi, H., & Maki, A. (2008). Emotional responses to music: Towards scientific perspectives on music therapy. *Neuroreport, 19*, 75–8.

Terwogt, M. M., & van Grinsven, F. (1988). Recognition of emotions in music by children and adults. *Perceptual and Motor Skills, 67*, 697–8.

Terwogt, M. M., & van Grinsven, F. (1991). Musical expression of moodstates. *Psychology of Music*, 19, 99–109.

Thompson, W. F., Schellenberg, E. G., & Husain, G. (2004). Decoding speech prosody: Do music lesson help? *Emotion*, 4, 46–64.

Trainor, L. J., Austin, C. M., & Desjardins, R. N. (2000). Is infant-directed speech prosody a result of the vocal expression of emotion? *Psychological Science*, 11, 188–95.

Trainor, L. J., Clark, E. D., Huntley, A., & Adams, B. A. (1997). The acoustic basis of preferences for infant-directed singing. *Infant Behavior & Development*, 20, 383–96.

Trainor, L. J., & Heinmiller, B. M. (1998). The development of evaluative responses to music: Infants prefer to listen to consonance over dissonance. *Infant Behavior & Development*, 21, 77–88.

Trehub, S. E. (2001). Musical predispositions in infancy. *Annals of the New York Academy of Sciences*, 930, 1–16.

Tsang, C. D., Trainor, L. J., Santesso, D. L., Tasker, S. L., & Schmidt, L. A. (2001). Frontal EEG responses as a function of affective musical features. *Annals of the New York Academy of Sciences*, 930, 439–42.

Vieillard, S., Peretz, I., Gosselin, N., Khalfa, S., Gagnon, L., & Bouchard, B. (2008). Happy, sad, scary and peaceful musical excerpts for research on emotions. *Cognition & Emotion*, 22, 720–52.

Yeomans, J. S., & Frankland, P. W. (1995). The acoustic startle reflex: Neurons and connections. *Brain Research and Brain Research Review*, 21, 301–14.

Zajonc, R. B. (1984). On the primacy of affect. In K. R. Scherer & P. Ekman (eds), *Approaches to emotion* (pp. 259–70). Hillsdale, NJ: Erlbaum.

Zentner M. R., Grandjean D., & Scherer K. R. (2008). Emotions evoked by the sound of music: characterization, classification, and measurement. *Emotion*, 8, 494–521.

Zentner, M. R., & Kagan, J. (1996). Perception of music by infants. *Nature*, 383, 29.

CHAPTER 6

EXPLORING THE HABITUS OF LISTENING

ANTHROPOLOGICAL PERSPECTIVES

JUDITH BECKER

THE study of anthropology is the study of the modes of being human, while the study of ethnomusicology is the study of the modes of music making as a means of cultural expression and as sources of meaning. Both are concerned with human behaviour and the cultural ideologies that inform behaviour; both tend to rely upon ethnographic research and techniques of participant observation, with the results later written and published as a monograph. Within each discipline there are universalists who tend to look for commonalities of behaviour and beliefs, and particularists who are more interested in how we differ one from another, one group from another group. Whatever the difference of perspective, nearly all anthropologists and ethnomusicologists subscribe to the dictum that one must attempt to understand behaviours and belief systems from within; that is, the necessity for making the effort to understand other musics and other styles of emotional expression from the perspective of their owners. This is related to but not the same thing as what is called 'cultural relativism', which is sometimes taken to mean a refusal to make value judgements about beliefs and practices of peoples outside one's own group. A commitment to trying to comprehend the motivations and underlying paradigms of another's actions certainly delays or impedes a 'rush to judgement'. In the case of music and emotion, the ethnographic approach involves both looking closely at the cultural construction of emotion and at the cross-cultural differences in the uses, purposes, and meanings of musical expression.

In this chapter, I will present a theoretical frame for the cross-cultural exploration of music and emotion, provide specific examples, and conclude with a section on the possibility of conjoining humanistic and scientific approaches.

6.1 CULTURALLY INFLECTED LISTENING

Studies on music and emotion conducted by Western scholars and scientists nearly always presume a particular image of musical listeners: silent, still listeners, paying close attention to a piece of music about which they communicate the type of emotion evoked by the piece to an attendant researcher. Communication of the emotion may be immediate in a laboratory setting, or retrospective, recalling the emotion after the musical event.

What is wrong with this image?

Nothing, if the intent is to describe the affective responses to decontextualized performances by middle-class American or European listeners listening to music while seated quietly. The laboratory situation may reflect the habit of many current Western listeners, possibly even more so now than in the past, as so much musical listening takes place attached to headphones rather than at live performances. Silent, still, focused listening is also the habit in some other musical traditions, notably the north Indian Hindustani 'classical' tradition, where one sits quietly, introspectively listening to the gradual developing filigree of the musical structure of a *raga*, played, perhaps, on a sitar. Thoughts and feelings are turned inward. The setting is intimate, conducive to introspection and a distancing from one's fellow listeners.

But if the intent is to delineate something more general about the relationships between musical event and musical affect, the image of an inwardly focused, isolated listener is inadequate. This portrayal of listener and listening presents a set of unexamined ideologies and presuppositions that would not apply for most of the world. The unasked questions include: What constitutes 'listening' to music? What are the appropriate kinds of emotions to feel? What kind of subjectivity is assumed? Who is it that is 'having' the emotions? How is the event framed?

Anthropology and ethnomusicology have contributed to the study of music and emotion an expanded notion of the possible relationships between the musical event and the listener, and the degree to which affective response to musical events is culturally inflected. Performances and listeners find themselves in a relationship in which they define each other through continuous, interactive, ever-evolving musical structures and listener responses. Meaning resides in the mutual relationship established at any given moment in time between particular listeners and musical events. A group of listeners develops a 'community of interpretation' (Fish, 1980), not necessarily uniform, but overlapping in some salient features. When presented with a musical event, this community of interpretation will approach the music with a pre-given set of expectations, a 'forestructure of understandings' (Gergen, 1991, p. 104). Every hearer occupies a position in a cultural field not of his or her own making: Every hearing is situated.

We accumulate our listening habits and expectations largely unawares. Only when confronted with an alternate kind of listening are we likely to reflect upon our own conventionalized mode. Listeners can shift modes in different contexts, such as the ways in which one listens to music at a chamber music recital, or at a rock concert, or a jazz club, or a movie, or at a salsa club (Becker, 1983). Cross-culturally, modes of listening may add features not shared by us, or may not involve features that we take for granted. What is appropriate to say about musical affect, what one does *not* say, what one feels and what one does *not* feel may reveal underlying assumptions surrounding musical listening. What is *not* assumed in one mode (such as bodily movement in Western classical listening) may become central in another mode (such as dancing while listening to a salsa band). To sit quietly focused on musical structure at a salsa concert is as inappropriate as break dancing to a Schubert quintet.

We need a term to express the temporal and spacial situatedness of the hearer that is the aural equivalent of the visual term for modes of seeing; that is, *the gaze*. Frequently a feminist challenge to the dominance of *the male gaze* in literature (Kern, 1996), film (Zizek, 1991, p. 88), painting (Hebdige, 1995), photography (Slater, 1995), television (Morley, 1995), psychoanalysis (Zizek, 1996, p. 90), medicine (O'Neill, 1995), and advertising (Barnard, 1995), the term *gaze* is now used in a wide variety of contexts to exemplify the situatedness of looking, the historical and psychological specificity of any one visual approach, and the complex imbrication of modes of seeing with rhetorical and institutional structures and beliefs (Brennan & Jay, 1996; Gamman & Marshment, 1988; Jenks, 1995). Modes of *looking* imply habits of seeing that change not only across space (Mitchell, 1986), but also at different historical periods within a single culture (Baxandall, 1974; Goldhill, 1996). Similarly, modes of *listening* vary according to the kind of music being played, the expectations of the musical situation, and the kind of subjectivity that a particular culture has fostered in relation to musical events (Cumming, 2000; Johnson, 1995). Even more than modes of looking, modes of listening implicate structures of knowledge and beliefs, and intimate notions of personhood and identity. Listening addresses interiors; listening provides access to what may be hidden from sight.

Styles of audition, of aural perception, of aural awareness, of *listening* in response to musical events directly impinge upon studies of emotion in music. A given community will foster a particular comportment to listening, a comportment not only of attitude, affect, and expectation, but also bodily gesture. Emotional responses to music do not occur spontaneously, nor 'naturally', but rather take place within complex systems of thought and behaviour concerning what music means, what it is for, how it is to be perceived, and what might be appropriate kinds of expressive responses. We need a word like Bourdieu's (1977) *habitus*, coined as an alternative to terms such as 'culture' which seemed too static, and sometimes seemed to imply a rigidity, an all-inclusiveness that obscured individual, idiosyncratic, or innovative modes of thought and behaviour. Still left with the need to refer to the ways in which beliefs and behaviours seem relatively stereotypical within a given society, Bourdieu (1977, p. 72) proposed the term *habitus* to do the theoretical work formerly carried by the word 'culture':

The structures constitutive of a particular type of environment (e.g. the material conditions of existence characteristic of a class condition) produce *habitus*, systems of durable, transposable *dispositions* . . . that is, as principles of the generation and structuring of practices and representations which can be objectively 'regulated' and 'regular' without in any way being the product of obedience to rules, objectively adapted to their goals without presupposing a conscious aiming at ends or an express mastery of the operations necessary to attain them and, being all this, collectively orchestrated without being the product of the orchestrating action of a conductor.

Bourdieu (1977, p. 214, f. 1) goes on to define what he means by *dispositions*:

The word *disposition* seems particularly suited to express what is covered by the concept of habitus defined as a system of dispositions. It expresses first the *result of an organizing action*, with a meaning close to that of words such as structure; it also designates a *way of being*, a *habitual state* (especially of the body) and, in particular, a *predisposition, tendency, propensity*, or *inclination*.

Habitus is an embodied pattern of action and reaction, in which we are not fully conscious of why we do what we do; not totally determined, but a *tendency* to behave in a certain way. Our habitus of listening is tacit, unexamined, seemingly completely 'natural.' We listen in a *particular* way without thinking about it, and without realizing that it even is a particular way of listening. Most of our styles of listening have been learned through unconscious imitation of those who surround us and with whom we continually interact. A habitus of listening suggests not a necessity nor a rule, but an inclination, a disposition to listen with a particular kind of focus, to expect to experience particular kinds of emotion, to move with certain stylized gestures, and to interpret the meaning of the sounds and one's emotional responses to the musical event in somewhat (never totally) predictable ways. Scholars working within the disciplines of anthropology or ethnomusicology typically assume that the stance of the listener is not a given, not *natural*, but necessarily influenced by place, time, the shared context of culture, and the intricate and unreproduceable details of one's personal biography.

The term I have adapted from Bourdieu, habitus of listening, underlines the interrelatedness of the perception of musical emotion and learned interactions with our surroundings. Our perceptions operate within a set of habits gradually established throughout our lives and developed through our continual interaction with the world beyond our bodies, the evolving situation of *being-in-the-world*.

6.2 Emotion as a cultural construct

But recognition of the fact that thought is always culturally patterned and infused with feelings, which themselves reflect a culturally ordered past, suggests that just as thought does not exist in isolation from affective life, so affect is culturally ordered and does not exist apart from thought. (Rosaldo, 1984, p. 137)

This view, while in the ascendancy among cultural anthropologists and ethnomusi-cologists, has not gone unchallenged within the discipline of anthropology:

I can make no sense of a line of thought which claims that 'passions' are culturally defined. From my prejudiced position as a social anthropologist this passage reveals with startling clar-ity the ultimately radical weakness of the basic assumption of cultural anthropology, namely, that not only are cultural systems infinitely variable, but that human individuals are products of their culture rather than of their genetic predisposition.

(Leach, 1981, p. 16)

These two quotations, starkly put and differentiated by nationality, gender, and perspective—the American, female, cultural anthropologist and the British, male, social anthropologist—state baldly the issue at hand: the cultural relativism of emo-tion and thought, or the universality of emotion and thought. (Leach was not a racist, but rather a believer in the commonality of mankind. See also Brown, 1991; Fischer & Manstead, 2000, p. 88; Goodenough, 1970, p. 122; Levi-Strauss, 1962, p. 161; Spiro, 1984; Turner, 1983). These contesting views have elicited penetrating dialogues on both sides of the divide and continue to evoke considerable emotion in their defenders. There are good reasons for these passions: Much is at stake.

Informing our beliefs about the universality or, conversely, the culturally condi-tioned aspects, of music and emotion, the path of Western intellectual history leads in both directions: one direction taken by the sciences that stresses general laws and instances, the other taken by the humanities and cultural anthropology that stresses cases and interpretations (Geertz, 1983a).

One way to understand the divide between the scientific and the cultural approach is to look at its development from the eighteenth-century Enlightenment onwards. One of the great contributions of the Enlightenment was the propagation of the idea (already taught by religion, but little observed by society) that humankind shared a basic natural state, independent of geography, chronology, or personality. ('We hold these truths to be self-evident: that all men are created equal'; Jefferson, 1776/1994). In its day, this doctrine was dazzlingly liberal and liberating. It led, in spite of all the detours to the contrary, to the end (almost) of institutionalized slavery in the Western world. A sentence from a history book of the eighteenth century vividly presents a theatrical metaphor for the belief in the commonality of human life and human nature:

The stage-setting [in different periods of history] is, indeed, altered, the actors change their garb and their appearance; but their inward motions arise from the same desires and passions of men, and produce their effects in the vicissitudes of kingdoms and peoples.

(J. J. Mascou, *Geschichte der Teutschen*, quoted in Lovejoy, 1948, p. 173)

While elegantly simple, and a vast improvement over earlier views concerning 'The Great Chain of Being' (Lovejoy, 1936/1964), this view, in practice, led to the assump-tion that all peoples everywhere thought and felt like educated, male Europeans and Americans. Post-colonial studies (Appadurai, 1996; Bhabha, 1994; Spivak, 1988) and gender studies (McClary, 1991; Solie, 1993) have brought home the bias in such views. We have come to appreciate the nuanced differences of affect with different stage settings, garbs, and appearances. The 'desires and passions of men' have come to be seen as *not* producing identical 'inward motions'. Partly through the cumulative effects of works by cultural anthropologists writing in the 1970s (Geertz, 1973, p. 36; Myers, 1979), the 1980s (Levy, 1984; Lutz, 1986, 1988; Rosaldo, 1984; Shweder & Bourne, 1984), the 1990s and beyond (Harkin, 2003, p. 266; Irvine, 1990; Lutz & Abu-Lughod, 1990; Schieffelin, 1990), scholars who have championed the concept of the cultural construction of emotion, social scientists and psychologists are increasingly sensitive to the cultural component in the categorization of, the interpretation of, and the expression of emotion (Davidson, 1992; Ekman, 1980, p. 90; Ortony et al, 1988, p. 26; Russell, 1991a, 1991b).

If we accept Leach's version of the uniformity of human passions, we condone the silences imposed upon subalterns of all times and places whose feelings were assumed to be isomorphic with those of the persons who controlled the writing of history, and we ignore the developing body of data supporting the cultural inflection of the emotions. If we accept the idea of the social construction of knowledge, of morality, and emotion, we seem to be abandoning the idea of a *human* nature, a bond of mind, emotion, and meaning that enfolds us all, and binds us to one another. We may also be in danger of losing sight of the individual as he or she slips into the constructed conventionality of cultural appearance, behaviour, beliefs, and desires and disappears altogether. Persons may become exemplars, instances of this or that cultural model.

I would like to propose that both approaches have incontrovertible empirical support, and that rather than choose sides, we need to accept the paradox that, in fact, we cannot do without either perspective (Finnegan, 2003; Good, 2004; Hinton, 1999; Needham, 1981; Nettl, 1983, p. 36; Shweder, 1985; Solomon, 1984). Cultural difference in the expression of, the motivation for, and the interpretation of emotion in relation to musical events has been persuasively demonstrated over and over again; for example, in South Africa (Blacking, 1973, p. 68), Liberia (Stone, 1982, p. 79), Brazil (Seeger, 1987, p. 129), New Guinea (Feld, 1982, p. 32), Peru (Turino, 1993, p. 82), South India (Viswanathan & Cormack, 1998, p. 225), Java (Benamou, 2003), Arabic music (Racy, 1998, p. 99), Australian aboriginal music (Magowan, 2007, pp. 70–102), and country music in the United States (Fox, 2004, pp. 152–91). Likewise, the fact that most of us can, with experience and empathy, come to understand differing expressive reactions to different kinds of music as reasonable and coherent demonstrates some level of commonality and universality in relation to both music and emotion. It may be that we come into the world with the full range of human emotional expression available to us (Geertz, 1974, p. 249). Through continual patterns of interaction with (primarily) close family members in the early years, we develop particular patterns of emotional feelings and expressions in relation to the events of our lives. For the most part, habituated responses and actions delimit the range and type of any one person's emotional responses. Yet, it would appear that we can imaginatively enter into a much wider palette of human emotional possibilities. We need to make a Hegelian move and transcend the dichotomy between scientific universalism and humanistic particularity and embrace both as necessary to the study of music and emotion.

6.3 PERSON AS A CULTURAL CONSTRUCT

The 'subjectivity' we are discussing here is the capacity of the speaker to posit himself as 'subject'. It is defined not by the feeling which everyone experiences of being himself (this feeling, to the degree that it can be taken note of, is only a reflection) but as the psychic unity that transcends the totality of the actual experiences it assembles and that makes the permanence of the consciousness.

(Benveniste, 1971, p. 224)

Benveniste has argued that the sense of person is a product of languaging, as have many others, most notably Buddhist philosophers. (The gerund 'languaging' is a form favoured by scholars who wish to differentiate language activity from the structure of language; see Becker, 1995, p. 9; Maturana & Varela, 1987, p. 234; Smith & Ferstman, 1996, p. 52). While the sense of personhood seems inextricably tied to the development of language, one's sense of bodily boundaries, our sense of what (somatically) belongs to us and where our bodies end, seems to escape the linguistic formation of person and takes shape in areas of the brain not directly involved with languaging (Blakeslee & Blakeslee, 2007, pp. 7–27; Damasio, 1999, p. 108; Melzack, 1992). The literature on subjectivity is vast and cannot be dealt with here. Nonetheless, an important aspect of any particular habitus of listening is the way in which the listener thinks of him or herself as a person, how he or she establishes identity in relation to other persons and the phenomenal world:

Nor is the subject isolated in his or her private 'be-ing.' The 'self' is not, as Descarte implied, an ineffable mystery, formed by its own private thoughts existing alone as the reflective spectator on events in the world, skeptical of its own impressions. Rather, 'selfhood' is an intrinsically social, interactive, and mobile experience.

(Cumming, 2000, p. 10)

A classic definition of Western identity is that formulated by Clifford Geertz (1983b, p. 59):

The Western conception of the person as a bounded, unique, more or less integrated motivational cognitive universe, a dynamic center of awareness, emotion, judgement, and action organized into a distinctive whole and set contrastively both against other such wholes and against its social and natural background, is, however incorrigible it may seem to us, a rather peculiar idea within the context of the world's cultures.

Among others, the philosopher Charles Taylor (1989) has written about the development of this style of personhood in the West, from Plato to the present day (see also Gergen, 1991, p. 18):

Our modern notion of the self is related to, one might say constituted by, a certain sense (or perhaps a family of senses) of inwardness . . . The unconscious is for us within, and we think of the depths of the unsaid, the unsayable, the powerful inchoate feelings and affinities and fears which dispute with us the control of our lives, as inner . . . But as strong as this partitioning of the world appears to us, as solid as this localization may seem, and anchored in the very nature of the human agent, it is in large part a feature of our world, the world of modern, Western people. The localization is not a universal one, which human beings recognize as a matter of course, as they do for instance that their heads are above their torsos. Rather it is a function of a historically limited mode of self-interpretation, one which has become dominant in the modern West and which may indeed spread thence to other parts of the globe, but which had a beginning in time and space and may have an end.

(Taylor, 1989, p. 111)

It is almost a truism of contemporary cultural anthropology that the nature of subjectivity, of the sense of self, varies cross-culturally. This is a profoundly anti-intuitive notion, and one that has strong objectors in philosophy from St Augustine (von Campenhausen, 1964, pp. 226–7) to Bertrand Russell (Seckel, 1986, p. 96). As with the issue of 'emotion', to say that subjectivity is culturally constructed seems to deny the basic humanity of mankind. Yet differences seem to remain in how persons think of themselves in relation to other persons, and these differences are often markedly cultural (Fajans, 2006; Schieffelin, 1990; Shweder & Bourne, 1984, p. 191).

6.4 PERSON AND EMOTION IN THE HABITUS OF LISTENING

The particular subjectivity of the listeners described in psychological studies, the pro-to-typical Western, middle-class listener to music, is likely to be some variant of the following: an individual with a strong sense of separateness, of uniqueness from all other persons, an individual whose emotions are felt to be known in their entirety and complexity only to him or herself, whose physical and psychic privacy is treasured, and whose emotional responses to a given piece of music are not felt to be in relation to anything outside his or her own particular self-history and personality: The emotion, for us, belongs to the individual, not to the situation or to relationships. Emotion is the authentic expression of one's being, and is, in some sense, natural and spontaneous. The emotion is interior, may or may not be shared with anyone else, and may be a guide to one's inner essence. Leo Treitler (1993, p. 48) has written about one way in which this style of subjectivity can relate to listening to music:

It is that interaction of the selves of the listener with those in the music—no, better put: the awareness of the self (selves) in the music through its (their) interaction with the listener's self—that interests me here; musical communication as a function of the interaction of identities.

The differing identities of the listening subject and those projected by the music become the focus of interest and affect for Treitler. One common variant of this Western kind of subjectivity while listening to music is to identify with the different identity projected by the music. Listening to music offers the opportunity to temporarily be another kind of person than one's ordinary, everyday self. This interpretation segues into theories concerning one's fantasy life, and seems to be a fruitful approach to the kind of emotion associated with music that one finds, for example, among adolescents (Frith, 1987, p. 143; Shepherd & Giles-David, 1991), and may help to explain their profound identification with the popular music of their times. Musical listening may offer the opportunity of experiencing relief from one's own presentation of everyday self (Goffman, 1959) by trying on another self-presentation (DeNora, 2000, p. 63).

6.4.1 Being a griot

How different is the subjectivity, the habitus of listening, of the community of listeners of the Wolof griots of Senegal as described by Judith Irvine (1990). Among the Wolof, the musical expression of emotion is dialogical and situational, not personal and interior. Griots, low-caste individuals, are believed to be highly expressive, highly excitable, 'volatile and theatrical'. The nobles are believed to be the opposite, composed, 'cool', detached, and somewhat bland in affect. It is the duty of the griots to stimulate the nobles to action, nobles who might otherwise be given over to lethargy. The highly expressive, emotional performances of the griots are intended, in part, to provide the energy to the nobles that they might carry out their governing duties. Irvine relates that a frequent image in Wolof oral poetry and epic narratives involves the playing of an ensemble of drums and iron clappers to awaken the king 'lest his royal duties go unfulfilled' (Irvine, 1990, p. 134). The emotion of the musicians and dancers is contrasted to the lack of emotion of their primary audience, the nobles. Both the emotion of the griots and its absence in the nobles are public, dialogical, and situational, not private and interior. One of the primary manifestations of subjectivity among Europeans and Americans, emotions are not personal attributes for the Wolof griots and nobles in the same way. For us, emotional responses to music are not considered to be assigned by virtue of one's class and profession, but to be an inalienable characteristic of a bounded, inviolate individual. This is not at all to say that Wolof nobles do not feel strong personal emotions, or that a griot is necessarily always highly extroverted and volatile. It is only to say that these are the *dispositions*, the *inclinations* that are likely to be fulfilled more often than not. The key participants in these musical events exhibit a habitus of listening and a type of subjectivity that largely conform to Wolof cultural expectations.

6.4.2 The habitus of listening to the sitar, tambura, and tabla

Earlier, mention was made of the similarity of the habitus of listening of the listener of Hindustani 'classical' music and the Western middle-class listener in terms of physical stillness, focused attention, and inner withdrawal. Furthermore, both traditions would claim that music can *represent* emotion. In his autobiography, Ravi Shankar (1968, pp. 23, 27) describes his own subjectivity as a musician, a style of personhood that seems concordant with what I, or most readers of this essay, might feel of performing musicians:

A *raga* is an aesthetic projection of the artist's inner spirit; it is a representation of his most profound sentiments and sensibilities, set forth through tones and melodies . . . I may play *Raga Malkauns*, whose principal mood [*rasa*] is *veera* [heroic], but I could begin by expressing *shanta* [serenity] and *karuna* [compassion] in the *alap* and develop into *veera* [heroic] and *adbhuta* [astonishment] or even *raudra* [anger] in playing the *jor* or *jhala*.

The inner spirit of the artist, functioning within culturally constructed categories of affect, is made manifest in the outward expressions of his musical presentation. Bringing yet another dimension of similarity to the two listening situations is the fact that emotion (*rasa*) experienced in listening to Hindustani classical music is distanced and impersonal. One can feel the emotion without the troublesome immediacy and consequences of an emotion that compels action (Abhinavagupta in Gnoli, 1968, pp. 82–5; Masson & Patwardhan, 1969, p. 46). June McDaniel (1995, p. 48), writing of *rasa* in the Indian province of Bengal, uses the metaphor of the glass window separating the experiencer from the emotion while still allowing a clear view:

Bhava is a personal emotion; *rasa* is an impersonal or depersonalized emotion, in which the participant is distanced as an observer. Why is a depersonalized emotion considered superior to a personal one? Because the aesthete can experience a wide range of emotions yet be protected from their painful aspects. Emotion is appreciated through a glass window, which keeps out unpleasantness. Though the glass is clear, thus allowing a union of sorts with the observed object, the window is always present, thus maintaining the dualism.

The following description is a Western mirror-image of the classical Indian experience of *rasa*:

When people listen, say, to 'Questi i campi di Tracia' from Monteverdi's *Orfeo* . . . they do not directly perceive the anguish and guilt of the twice-widowed singer. Listeners only hear a *representation* [italics mine] of the way his voice moves under the influence of his emotions. Nevertheless, this can give listeners important insights into a type of emotional response. Monteverdi skillfully displays the contortions through which Orpheus's voice goes. When listeners know how a voice moves under the influence of an affect, they are given (if they are familiar with the conventions of the music, and otherwise qualified) an immediate demonstration of something about the affect. A good performance of this aria immediately demonstrates to a sensitive audience something about what it is like to feel guilt, remorse, and despair.

(Young, 1999, p. 48)

In both the Hindustani and the Western classical listener, an emotion evoked by listening to music can be contemplated with a certain deliberation and calmness. But at some point the congruencies between the habitus of listening of each breaks down. The Western observer may well, as Treitler suggests, be involved with comparing identities, or with constructing a more glamorous self in relation to the music heard, or with contemplating 'what it is like to feel guilt, remorse, and despair'. The Indian, however, may be performing a very different act, a somewhat strenuous religious exercise, a kind of refining of emotional essence, a distillation of his or her emotion that will lead to a transformation of consciousness to a higher level of spirituality. Listening to music for the Hindustani classical music devotee should not be, according to canon, a passive act, but requires the active will and mind of the listener to carry consciousness to a higher plane, closer to the divine (Coomaraswamy, 1957, p. 39). Western references to *inspiration* or *genius*, which at one time perhaps indicated a holy possession, have become largely metaphoric rather than literal expressions of sacred connections between musical performance and musical listening. In Indian classical traditions, the pursuit of emotion, of *rasa*, in relation to listening to music, may be a path to greater awareness, leading one to cosmic insight. Dance, as well, can share in this configuration of emotion as a stepping stone to a higher gnosis. One of India's most revered Bharata Natyam dancers has written the following:

It is here that Bharata Natyam, the ancient and holy art of Indian dance, cuts deeply into the conscious and subconscious levels and revealingly brings to the forefront the fact that it is ultimately and intimately oriented to the nucleus, *atman* [the Universal Self]. It is a revelation not only to the performing artist, but in an equal measure to the audience as well . . . By the inexplicable power born of the union of melody, lyric, rhythm and gesture, the emotions are released from their limited secular locus and are expanded to universal proportions where there is only pure spirit with nothing of the sensual.

(Balasaraswati, 1985, pp. 2–3)

According to the Bengali version of the theory of *rasa*, intense emotions, not milder 'aesthetic emotions', are the appropriate vehicle to lead one to mystical knowledge of life's meaning and purpose. Emotions are compared to water that can best be understood by immersion in an ocean rather than by the delicate feel of a raindrop (McDaniel, 1995, p. 51). What we might call emotional excesses become pregnant possibilities for greater spiritual attainment for an Indian music listener. While the quiet stance and introverted demeanor of the listener in the proto-typical Western case and the Hindustani classical listener is similar, the understanding and interpretation of what is supposed to happen in each case differs. In one case, the listener may be exploring the affective nuances of his or her inner self or identifying with the affective interiors presented by the music; in the other, the listener is trying to bring about a kind of 'sea' change, a different self altogether, one that comes closer to divinity.

6.5 Arousal: a human universal

Particularities relating to the cultural construction of personhood and of emotion may obscure certain physiological constants that are the correlates of listening to music. Arousal, defined in its most narrow sense as stimulation of the autonomic nervous system (ANS), is one of the most important aspects of musical performance and plays into nearly all studies of music and emotion. The heart beats faster, the pulse rises, breathing becomes more shallow, the skin temperature rises, and the pattern of brain waves becomes less regular. All these changes have been observed without any necessary

reference to the affective, interpretive component of arousal. They may occur in relation to sexual activity, to exercise, or as a result of drugs or alcohol, as well as to musical
listening.

In his famous and controversial theory of the emotions, William James claimed
that the physiological component of arousal is primary and precedes the interpretation of the subsequent emotion (James 1890/1950, pp. 442–85). The 'feeling' of anger is
the feeling that results from an angry facial expression, bodily stance, shallow breathing, etc. Anger, the emotion, *is*, according to James, what one *feels* when enacting this
display. Following James, but with much more knowledge of the neurophysiology of
emotion, Damasio suggests that the term 'emotion' should be applied to ANS arousal,
and that 'feeling' that follows 'emotion' should be applied to the complex cognitive,
culturally inflected interpretation of 'emotion' (Damasio, 1999, p. 79). Both the Polish
Grotowski school of acting (Grotowski, 1968) and the Indian Kathakali theatre tradition
(Schechner, 1988, p. 270) seem to support the theories of James and Damasio. Training
a Kathakali actor, or a Western actor of the Grotowski tradition, begins with *mimesis*,
recreating the bodily gestures of an emotion, not with delving into one's memories to
recreate a 'feeling', as in Stanislavsky's school of 'method' acting (Stanislavsky, 1958,
p. 1977).

In any case, it is useful analytically to separate physiological arousal ('emotion' for
James and Damasio) from the more cognitive concept 'feeling'. Unlike feelings that
directly relate to judgements and beliefs learned within a cultural context and that rely
upon linguistic categories that are often incommensurable across languages, arousal
is more clearly a universal response to music listening. Combined with a concentrated
religious focus, musical arousal can contribute to extreme states of emotion.

Happiness is the emotion most frequently associated with music listening, and may
constitute one of the 'universals' of cross-cultural studies of music and emotion. From
the 'polka happiness' of the Polish-American parties of Chicago (Keil, 1987, p. 276),
to the !Kung of the Kalahari desert, 'Being at a dance makes our hearts happy' (Katz,
1982, p. 348), to the Basongye of the Congo who 'make music in order to be happy'
(Merriam, 1964, p. 82), to the extroverted joy of a Pentecostal musical service (Cox,
1995), music has the ability to make people feel good (see also Chapter 4, this volume).
The happiness of listening to music, however one construes happiness, is in part the
simple result of musical arousal. We tend to feel better when we are musically aroused
and excited. The emotion may be attributed to some other aspect of the event such as
the text or our own dancing; nonetheless, the musical stimulation should not be minimized. Music can be a catalyst for a changing state of consciousness.

The following section includes three examples of extreme emotion contextually
situated within a religious ceremony in which music is an essential element; all three
are sites of the author's fieldwork.

6.5.1 Music and ecstasy: the Sufis

The strongest version of happiness in relation to musical listening and an example of
extreme arousal is ecstasy. (See Rouget, 1985, for descriptions of music and trancing in

many time periods and geographical locations.) Usually associated with religious rituals, ecstasy, as extreme joy, almost by definition involves a sense of the sacred, although musical ecstasy can justly be claimed by some attendees at secular musical events such as rock concerts or rave scenes (Sylvan, 2005). The degree to which Muslim Sufi orders have formalized and institutionalized musical ecstasy has seldom been exceeded. The works of the eleventh-century Persian Sufi mystic, al Ghazzali, about music and ecstasy are still basic pedagogical texts for contemporary Sufis in Iran, Afghanistan, Pakistan, and north India.

The heart of man has been so constituted by the Almighty that, like a flint, it contains a hidden fire which is evoked by music and harmony, and renders man beside himself with ecstasy. These harmonies are echoes of that higher world of beauty which we call the world of spirits, they remind man of his relationship to that world, and produce in him an emotion so deep and strange that he himself is powerless to explain it.

(Ghazzali, trans. 1991, p. 57)

Sufi musicians, called *qawwal* in Pakistan and north India, play for religious ceremonies in which the devotees may reach toward a pinnacle of ecstasy that will bring them into close communion with Allah. The *qawwals* move from song to song, eliciting reactions from the devotees such as moaning, sighing, swaying, even rising up and turning in place as a certain text line speaks directly to the spiritual condition of a particular devotee (Qureshi, 1986, p. 119). For a devout Sufi, his ecstasy is a preview, a foretasting of his ultimate union; and though he may weep, he weeps from excess of joy.

Sufi doctrine interprets the music as supportive, as secondary to the all important text, the religious poetry (Qureshi, 1986, p. 83). Yet the question remains: to what degree is the arousal stimulated by the sensual overload of intensifying rhythms and soaring phrases sung over and over again at the top of the *qawwal's* range? (For examples, listen to any of the many CDs of Nusrat Fateh Ali Khan.)

A Sufi habitus of listening at a musical religious ceremony involves a sequence of feeling and action that could be called a 'script' (Russell, 1991a, 1991b). Initially, while sitting quietly and reverently, the listener may hope that he or she will be touched by a particular line of text that seems directly applicable to his or her personal situation. If the lead *qawwal* catches the subtle indications of arousal in a listener, he will begin repeating the verse over and over again. The Sufi script then calls for swaying, weeping, rising up, and finally moving to the center of the room and slowly turning in place (see Figure 6.1). Musical emotion in the listener changes both its form and its intensity as the script progresses. The affect of the script, when fully acted out, is the ultimate joy of a direct and personal intimacy with Allah.

6.5.2 Music and rage: balinese bebuten trancing

In Bali, an exorcist ceremony is performed when misfortune befalls a village in which the negative powers of the divine witch Rangda must be neutralized for the well-being of the community. The elaborate mask of the witch Rangda will be brought from its storage place in the temple, blessed and infused with spirit in a potent ceremony

Fig. 6.1 Dancing Sufis. From the *Divan* (*Book of poems*) of Hafiz (Walters Art Gallery, Baltimore).

conducted by a priest. An exceptionally tall and spiritually strong man will be chosen to undergo the trance of *becoming* the witch. A number of men will volunteer to undergo another kind of trance called *bebuten*, from the root *buta*, which means a creature of base instincts, low on the ladder of sentient beings, often translated as *demon*. These men will confront the witch and ultimately neutralize her power with the help of a magical beast called Barong. *Bebuten* trance is not ecstasy. It is a feeling of rage directed toward the witch Rangda, and may leave the trancer feeling embarrassed later by his behaviour during the trance and with an exhaustion that may last for several days (Eiseman, 1989, p. 153). Yet the trancing is a social obligation that he fulfils voluntarily, surrendering his own comfort for the betterment of his community. He experiences a kind of homicidal rage (or, rather, 'theo-cidal' rage). One experienced trancer (I Wayan Dibia) passionately described his feelings while listening to the music of the gamelan (see Figure 6.2) upon encountering the witch:

When I come up to that tower, when the curtain opens like that, as soon as I step up to approach Rangda, I see a strong fire coming from her eyes! I just—Oh! (slaps his hands together)—I do this! I just jump! I feel myself floating—because of the excitement! . . . Whenever they pick up the music [sings 'jangga jangga jangga'], whenever you sing that song [sings a bit of the gamelan piece that accompanies the trance] people just go crazy! I want to attack Rangda!!!

(I Wayan Dibia, interview, 1996)

Fig. 6.2 Gamelan musicians accompanying a Rangda/Barong ritual (photo by Judith Becker).

Neither the trance, nor the ceremony, nor the pacification of the witch can happen without the gamelan music (Figure 6.3). The habitus of hearing of I Wayan Dibia upon encountering Rangda would have to include a description of not only the gamelan music and the presence of the witch, but a complex of beliefs about the negative forces of the universe, their effects upon human communities, the embodiment of these forces in the divine witch Rangda, and the methods by which she may be contained and controlled. His own emotion, culturally constituted but felt interiorly, is a necessary component of the maintenance of community well-being. His murderous passion has little to do with an interiorized self, with the identity of I Wayan Dibia. His rage, in part musically induced, is in the service of his community. Like the Wolof griots, musical emotion for the trancer in a Balinese Rangda exorcism is public, situational, predictable, and culturally sanctioned.

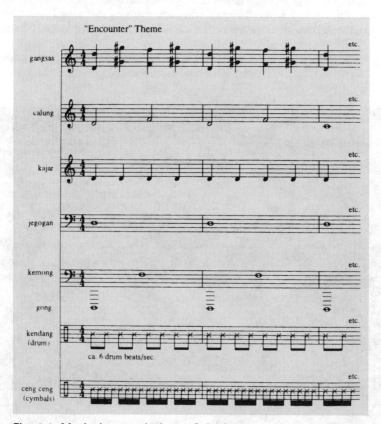

Fig. 6.3 Musical transcriptions of the 'encounter' theme from a Rangda/Barong ritual.

6.5.3 Pentecostal arousal: 'music brought me to Jesus' (Cox, 1995, p. 139)

Pentecostal religions were formally constituted at the beginning of the twentieth century and are now rivalled only by Islam in their spread to all parts of the globe (Cox, 1995, p. 15). Pentecostalism constitutes a faith that is dependent upon music to structure its religious services and to validate its system of beliefs by provoking intense emotional reactions within its most devoted practitioners, leading them to 'testify'. To dance in The Spirit, to be possessed by the Holy Ghost, is demonstration that one is accepted into the congregation of those who will experience the final act of history, the reappearance of Jesus Christ and the establishment of the Kingdom of God on earth (Abell, 1982). Music is the driving force for this emotional apotheosis. From softly played passages underlining a sermon or a prayer, to swinging, driving choruses sustaining a wave of religious emotionalism, music is rarely absent from the hours-long services. Pentecostal musical offerings shape a musical/emotional/religious arc that carries the congregation along with it. A service will begin with quiet, slow, soothing music: 'Music gets people in the attitude of worship. It helps them to forget outside influences and to focus on the Lord' (interview with Jerry Trent, Church of God, Willow Run, Michigan, 1996).

Pentecostal churches may use a wide variety of musical instruments often including piano, electric organ, synthesizer, guitars, and drumset to back up their driving, repetitive gospel hymns. As the music becomes louder, more rhythmic, more repetitive, its driving quality supports, propels, and sustains the hand-waving, hand-clapping, foot-stomping choruses of 'Amen!' as the emotional temperature of the congregation gradually rises. High on the trajectory of the musical arc, worshippers may come forward to the altar to pray, and some may dance or trance. As in the Sufi services, the musical support will continue at a high intensity until all worshippers have worked through their transport and regained their normal composure. Religious ecstasy is always accompanied by great joy as it is a confirmation of the salvation of the worshipper. He or she has become a part of the historical narrative of millenarial Christianity and will join fellow believers and Jesus at the last day. The music never flags as some members are moved to tears, to dance, to quiver and jerk in the uncoordinated gestures of some religious trances. As religious passions subside, so does the music, until every last ecstatic has become quiet—exhausted and joyful. 'And it was terrific,' exclaimed one worshipper at a service marked by intense, sustained, high-energy music, dancing, and trancing; 'and we really *got down* here. I mean we really *had church*' (Cox, 1995, p. 268).

The musical listener at a Pentecostal service is expectant, alert, and waiting for the song leader, the musicians, the singing congregation, and the pastor to transport him or her to the point of experiencing the Holy Spirit in his or her own body. The attitude is one of surrender and openness. No critical irony, no mental busyness, or aesthetic evaluation can be allowed to interfere with a process of holy possession called 'Slain in the Spirit'.

Similar to the Sufi listener and the Balinese *bebuten* trancer, for a Pentecostal listener the habitus of listening involves a scripted sequence of actions, emotions, and interpretations. Within each of these three scripts, musical, behavioural, and emotional events will occur within a certain predictable frame. Simultaneously, each individual event will be unique and non-repeatable. The listeners to a Wolof *griot*, an Indian *sitar* player, a group of *qawwali* singers, a Balinese *bebuten* trancer, or a Pentecostal worshipper have all developed habits of mind and body in response to specific musical events. These habits are acquired throughout their life experiences of interaction with others in similar situations. The emotions are private *and* public, interior *and* exterior, individual *and* communal.

6.6 MUSIC, EMOTION, AND 'BEING': CONJOINING ANTHROPOLOGY, ETHNOMUSICOLOGY, PSYCHOLOGY, AND NEUROPHYSIOLOGY

It seems clear to this author that a common ground needs to be explored between the more humanistic, cultural anthropological approach and the more scientific, cognitive psychological approach (see also Hinton, 1999, and Cross, 2008, for a similar view.) I see the bringing together of the scientific and cultural approaches to the study of music and emotion as one of the great challenges of our fields. While the styles of argument and the criteria for evidence may remain distinct, the conclusions need to be comparable and not incommensurable. Both disciplinary areas may have to modify some of their established scholarly practices in order to communicate effectively across disciplinary boundaries.

6.6.1 Single-brain/-body approaches

For those approaching the study of the emotional effect of musical listening on the brain, the unit of analysis is usually the brain/body of a single listener. From the early studies of music and the brain such as Neher's early work in the 1960s (Neher, 1961, 1962), analysing the brain rhythms of subjects listening to drum beats in a laboratory, to the more recent works of Clynes (1986), Wallin (1991), Blood and Zatorre (2001), Peretz (2001), Menon and Levitin (2005), and many others, musical scholars have adopted the scientific model and studied single brains/bodies in isolation. Studies in music cognition have largely followed the empirical models of cognitive studies in general in their efforts to model the algorithms of single brains processing music (Bangert,

2006; Haueisen & Knosche, 2001; Huron, 2006; Lerdahl & Jackendoff, 1983; Raffman, 1993). Neurophysiologists and psychologists of consciousness likewise follow the dictates of their scientific training, isolating and narrowing the problem as much as possible in order to have some control over the variables. In fact, some of the most exciting advances in the understanding of the mind are coming from scientists and philosophers who have focused on single minds/brains (Churchland, 1986; Dennett, 1991; Edelman, 1992; Janata, 1997; Levitin, 2006; Patel, 2008). The development of technologies such as functional magnetic resonance imaging (fMRI) and positron emission tomography (PET) scanning have reinforced the practice of the study of single minds in the attempt to unravel the mysteries of conscious experience. The choice of a single human brain as the unit of analysis has larger implications as well. The emphasis upon the primacy of the self-contained individual has been a treasured credo of Western intellectual pursuits in all fields for many centuries. Contemporary examples include the cognitive sciences, Piaget's genetic epistemology, and Freudian psychoanalysis.

6.6.2 Supra-individual biological processes

Emotions relating to music are culturally embedded and socially constructed, and can usefully be viewed as being about an individual within a community, rather than being exclusively about internal states. First-person descriptions of music and emotion are rife with tropes of interiority, yet the understanding of how music affects interiors takes place within consensual, shared views of what makes up 'reality', of what music means, and of appropriate emotional reactions to music.

I am suggesting that the scripts of music and emotion, the habitus of listening, can be helpfully understood as a process that is supra-individual, in which the relationship between music and emotion needs to be understood as extending beyond the minds and bodies of single musicians and listeners, as a contextually situated social practice. Musical events set up an aural domain of coordination that envelops all those present.

The neuroscientist Raphael Núñez has developed the idea of 'supra-individual biological processes' as an alternative to the focus on single-brain studies in the neurosciences. He hopes to escape from the dilemmas that he perceives as arising from single-brain studies and to look for a biological account of intersubjectivity (Núñez, 1997, pp. 147-154).

What is a biological process?

The components of a biological process (the participants of the musical event) are dynamically related in a network of ongoing interactions that change the structure of the individuals as well as the structure of their interactions. A biological process has boundaries between itself and the enveloping environment. Further criteria for biological processes are that they are autonomous; that is, that they can specify their own laws, and that they only allow changes to occur dependent upon maintaining the viability of their own structures (Maturana & Varela, 1987, pp. 47–52). Groups of people who are focused on a common event and who share a common history of that event, act, react, and to some extent think in concert, without sacrificing their bounded personal identities.

What is a supra-individual biological process? In Núñez's (1997, p. 155) words:

By supra-individual biological processes I mean those processes relative to life that occur at a level beyond the autonomous beings one is studying . . . The processes intervening in the spread of a cholera epidemic are an example of supra-individual biological processes; the phenomenon is manifested in individuals . . . but it is realized through biological processes that take place beyond the sick individual . . .

Let me further illustrate what I mean by *supra-individual biological* processes with another very simple example: speech accents . . . Although a brain is necessary for a particular speech accent to occur, as an isolated organ it does not determine it. Accents are modes of 'producing noises' during speech whose distinction is made by an observer making reference to collective phenomena (at supra-individual levels). Nonetheless, a speech accent is still a living phenomenon, as it is realized in the ontogeny of some living beings. Accents—although manifested in individuals—have to do with biological processes that are realized at levels that go beyond the individual, and that explain why speech accents are neither randomly distributed among populations nor are they genetically determined.

A linguistic accent can be attributed to a particular individual, but it is not the creation of that individual, but rather, results from historical processes of language imitation and repetition. A person may 'have' an accent, as a person may know how to play a drum, but neither the language accent, nor the knowing of how to play the drum can be attributed solely to an individual. To play the drum correctly or effectively means repeating the sounds in a culturally acceptable manner. Likewise, emotional reactions in musical situations are experienced within individuals, but the musical expressions that trigger those emotions are framed within a historically determined, culturally inflected complex of musical conventions known to musicians and listeners alike. The unit of musicians and listeners can be thought of as 'a community of interpretation' (Fish, 1980), as a single biological process operating within shared musical histories.

6.6.3 Habitus of listening: culture and biology

Núñez is not alone in his appeal for cross-subject brain studies (see also Becker, 2004; Benzon, 2001; Foley, 1997; Freeman, 2000; Maturana & Varela, 1987; Varela, Thompson, & Rosch, 1991). Integrating the insights of phenomenology with those of contemporary biology has brought forth fresh ways to think about human interaction as mutually constituting organisms. The interactions of groups of people in communally shared situations is often called 'communication', invoking the image of something transferred intact from one person's mind to another person's mind, or vaguely referred to as 'bonding' with no explanation of the 'how' by which bonding transpires. Wishing to imply something more fundamentally biological to talk about what are usually referred to as social or cultural phenomena, I am using the term 'structural coupling' developed by Maturana and Varela (1987) to describe a process that encompasses single cell organisms and extends outward to include human social groups, to help imagine what happens when groups of like-minded people are involved in recurrent situations of shared music. Maturana and Varela's usage extends from interactions of single cells to multicellular organisms, to groups of mammals, to human communities. 'Structural coupling' may provide a new perspective on the integration of musical groups, on rhythmic entrainment, and on shared musical emotions.

One begins with the understanding that an organism's first task is to maintain the integrity of its own structure. Or, in the language of Maturana and Varela, organisms are autonomous and autopoietic (self-creating); they will only 'accept' or integrate changes that do not disturb their structural integrity, their internal homeostasis. Most of the activity of our bodies and our brains functions to maintain our physical stability, our internal coherence, our life. For the most part, this activity goes on with no conscious control or conscious awareness. The constant monitoring and adjusting of our internal milieu proceeds whether we are awake or asleep, and regardless of what we may be thinking about at the moment. Damasio (1999) calls this unconscious continual mapping of the body-state the 'proto-self'. Maturana and Varela diagram this self-monitoring activity of all living organisms as a closed circle with arrows going round and round (see Figure 6.4).

If this were all there were to organic life, the result would be total solipsism. But all organisms live within an environment that includes organic and non-organic components with which the organism is necessarily in continual interaction (see Figure 6.5).

The organism, through its continual interaction with the environment, the external milieu, is constantly, inevitably, and subtly changing the environment and just as subtly being changed by it. The organism is not only interacting continuously with the environment that may be inert, but also with other organisms like itself (see Figure 6.6).

Fig. 6.4 Self-monitoring organism (Maturana & Varela, 1987, p. 74).

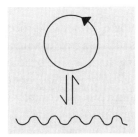

Fig. 6.5 Organism in interaction with external milieu (Maturana & Varela, 1987, p. 74).

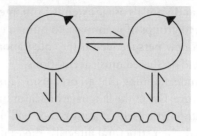

Fig. 6.6 Organisms in interaction with external milieu and each other (Maturana & Varela, 1987, p. 74).

Because of the autonomous nature of the organism, interactions between organisms or interactions between organism and inert environment, called 'perturbations,' never specify what changes may take place in the organism. The organism itself 'determines' which perturbations are 'allowed', how and to what degree a perturbation will be modified. Thus, perturbations never cause the changes in an organism, they can only instigate or trigger change. The organism is 'autopoietic', 'self-creating', and the process of its changes are 'autopoiesis', or 'self-creation'. It is not the environment or the interaction but the organism itself that 'creates' itself.

If interaction between two organisms is recurrent, and if the changes in the two organisms are congruent, if they are similar, then the two organisms become involved in shared ontogenetic change—they change together and become complementary. Over time, cumulative change leads to 'structural coupling' between two organisms as their internal milieu (including human brains and bodies) become linked through repeated interaction, 'co-ontogenies with mutual involvement through their reciprocal structural coupling, each one conserving its adaptation and organization' (Maturana & Varela, 1987, p. 180).

These changes become new domains of knowledge, knowledge gained through interactive behaviours, through doing. Music listeners as well as musicians undergo a learning process, in which they imitate physical and mental gestures that ultimately transform both their inner structures as well as their relations to everything beyond the boundaries of their skins. Music and emotion are part of a larger processual event that includes many other people doing many other things while the whole event unfolds as a unity that has been organized and reorganized over time by small structural changes within the participants.

We are accustomed to thinking of biological processes as extending from a single cell, to multi-cellular organisms such as a tree, to animals, and to a single human being. When groups of people are acting in some kind of accord, we tend to say that the phenomenon is social, or psychological, or political, not biological. If we think of music making and music listening within a process that may also include quiet introspection, or conversely, include preaching, glossolalia, dancing, or the murmuring of mantras, as all part of a biological process that has had a long history of 'structural coupling', or continual self-recreation, we can begin to think of the music, the emotion, and every other aspect of the process as contributing to bringing forth the activities of each other, as bringing forth a world, a reality in which certain emotions and actions are expected and appropriate, and in which the reality brought forth by all is enacted by all (Dreyfus, 1991). A musical event is not just in the minds of the participants, it is in their bodies; like a vocal accent in speaking, emotion in relation to music listening is personally manifested, but exist supra-individually. Each person, musicians and listeners, seem to be acting as self-contained, bounded individuals, and indeed they experience whatever they experience as deeply personal and emotional, but the event as a whole plays itself out in a supra-individual domain: 'I really like a song that you can get into and just *feel* it, and get the crowd to feel it the way you do' (Becky Rollings, country singer, quoted in Fox, 2004, p. 168). Emotion is an enactment, not a representation in the mind. It is a way of *being-in-the-world*, not a way of thinking about the world.

Language, music, and dance become one system of ontogenic coordination of actions. Together, they bring about changes in being and changes in the music event involved. While it is the individual who experiences the emotion, it is the group and its domain of coordinations that triggers the emotion. The changes in the neurophysiology of the listener are not attributable simply to the brain/body of a self-contained individual. They occur through the group processes of recurrent interactions between co-defined individuals in a rhythmic domain of music.

A familiar example of a changed interior, personal consciousness in a musical domain of coordination is the phenomenon of *rhythmic entrainment* (Chapple, 1970, p. 38; Clayton, Sager, & Will, 2005; Condon, 1986; Hall, 1977, p. 61; McNeill, 1995, p. 6; Neher, 1961, 1962; Rider & Eagle, 1986; Vaughn, 1990; Walter & Walter, 1949; Will & Berg, 2007). Bodies and brains synchronize gestures, muscle actions, breathing, and brain waves while enveloped in 'musicking'. (The gerund 'musicking' is preferred for the same reasons as 'languaging.' The activity, the process, the experiencing of music is foregrounded. See Small, 1998.) Many persons, bound together by common aims, may experience revitalization and general good feeling. The situation is communal and individual, music descends upon all alike, while each person's joy is his or her own.

Thinking of the relationship of emotion and music as a biological process with a co-defined, historically enacted ontology, as a group creation in which self-contained individuals have undergone structural changes through their interaction with other self-contained individuals helps to provide an embodied analysis of the relationship of music and emotion and the mysteries of musical affect. The domain of 'musicking' and emotion is intrinsically social, visibly embodied, profoundly cognitive, and biologically consistent with the created domains of many other kinds of living creatures.

This type of analysis is aided by technologies such as film and video. One needs to be able to see everything at once, and to have the opportunity to replay the event. Regula Qureshi's skilful score-like transcriptions of the multiple events at a Sufi religious ceremony demonstrate one method of researching music and emotion that does not focus on individual emotions, but on individual emotions within the context of many other individual emotions (Qureshi, 1986, pp. 143–86). One can study her scores and literally *see* how the musicians interact with the congregants, and one can imagine how the emotions of one listener may have stimulated the emotions of another, leading to the ultimate reaction, an enactment of trancing and ecstatic union with Allah (see Figure 6.7).

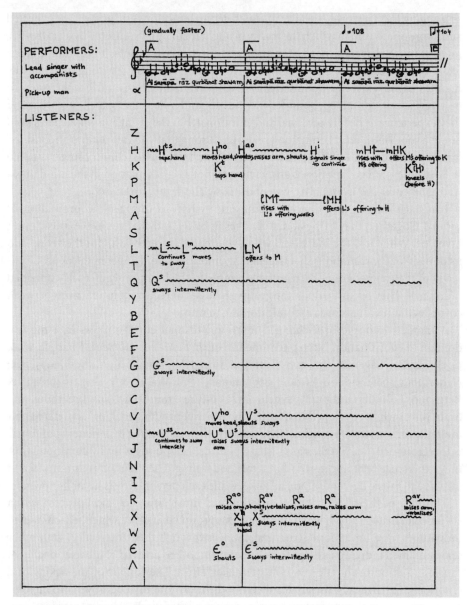

Fig. 6.7 Transcription (excerpt) of music/participant interactions in a north Indian Sufi ritual (from Qureshi, 1986, p. 171).

6.6.4 What is gained by claiming that these processes are biological?

We may claim that special modes of conscious experience such as emotional responses to music listening, an habitus of listening, emerges as a phenotypic feature of humankind, as a biological development in the evolution of the species, emerging from both genetic and environmental influences. Emotion and music, viewed as evolving together in the interaction of each individual with performances throughout his or her life, dissolves intractable dichotomies concerning nature versus culture, and scientific universalism versus cultural particularism.

This embodied understanding, including dispositions in the habitus, is tacit knowledge and hence one can only be subsidiarily aware of it; this accounts for why so much of the habitus is preconscious and unable to be reflected on or modified. This conservatism leads to the practices generated by the dispositions of the habitus being transmitted from generation to generation, in other words they are potentially *cultural practices*. Culture in this view is that transgenerational domain of practices through which human organisms in a social system communicate with each other. These practices may be verbal or non-verbal, but they must be communicative in the sense that they occur as part of ongoing histories of social structural coupling and contribute to the viability of continued coupling . . . Culture, then, consists of the things people do to communicate in ongoing transgenerational histories of social interaction.

(Foley, 1997, p. 14)

For those of us who want to use the word 'culture' but are inhibited by all the recent attacks upon the term relating to essentialism, historical stasis, and reified, abstracted psychology, culture can be restored as a more precise, more useful term. Culture (redefined) can be understood as a supra-individual biological phenomenon, a transgenerational history of social interactions that become embodied in the individual and transmitted through future actions.

No habitus of listening is entirely stable nor entirely fluid. As interactions change, so do the interiors of those who are interacting. We may have developed a habitus of listening that inclines us to introspectively contemplate the colorful fluidity of changing emotional states in response to Bach's *Musical Offering*, but if it would not disturb the viability of our own structures, we could learn to dance ecstatically in The Spirit with the Pentecostals.

Recommended further reading

1. Racy, A. J. (2003). *Making music in the Arab world: the culture and artistry of tarab.* Cambridge, UK: Cambridge University Press.
2. Wong, D. (2004). *Speak it louder: Asian Americans making music.* New York: Routledge.
3. Koen, B. (2009). *Beyond the roof of the world: Music, prayer, and healing in the Pamir mountains.* Oxford: Oxford University Press.

References

Abell, T. D. (1982). *Better felt than said: The Holiness-Pentecostal experience in southern Appalachia.* Waco, TX: Markham Press.

Appadurai, A. (1996). *Modernity at large: Cultural dimensions of globalization.* Minneapolis, MN: University of Minnesota Press.

Balasaraswati, T. (1985). The art of bharata natyam: a personal statement. In B. T.Jones (ed.), *Dance as cultural heritage, 2, Dance Research Annual XV* (pp. 1–7). New York: Congress on Research in Dance.

Bangert, M. (2006). Brain activation during piano playing. In E. Altenmüller & J. Kesselring (eds), *Music, motor control and the brain* (pp. 173–188). Oxford: Oxford University Press.

Barnard, M. (1995). Advertising: The rhetorical imperative. In C. Jenks (ed.), *Visual culture* (pp. 26–41). London: Routledge.

Baxandall, M. (1974). *Painting and experience in fifteenth century Italy: A primer in the social history of pictorial style.* New York: Oxford University Press.

Becker, A. L. (1995). *Beyond translation: Essays toward a modern philology.* Ann Arbor, MI: University of Michigan Press.

Becker, A. L. (1999). A short, familiar essay on person. *Language Sciences, 21,* 229–36.

Becker, J. (1983). 'Aesthetics' in Late 20th Century Scholarship. *The World of Music, 25,* 65–80.

Becker, J. (2004). *Deep listeners: Music, emotion, and trancing.* Bloomington, IN: Indiana University Press.

Benamou, M. (2003). Comparing musical affect: Java and the West. *World of Music, 45,* 57–76.

Benveniste, E. (1971). Subjectivity in language. In *Problems in general linguistics* (trans. M. E. Meek) (pp. 223–30). Coral Gables, FL: University of Miami Press.

Benzon, W. L. (2001). *Beethoven's anvil: Music in mind and culture.* New York: Basic Books.

Bhabha, H. K. (1994). *The location of culture.* London: Routledge.

Blacking, J. (1973). *How musical is man?* Seattle, WA: University of Washington Press.

Blakeslee, S., & Blakeslee, M. (2007). *The body has a mind of its own: How body maps in your brain help you do (almost) everything better.* New York: Random House.

Blood, A. J., & Zatorre, R. J. (2001). Intensely pleasurable responses to music correlate with activity in brain regions implicated in reward and emotion. *Proceedings of the National Academy of Science, 98,* 11818–23.

Bourdieu, P. (1977). *Outline of a theory of practice* (trans. R. Nice). Cambridge, UK: Cambridge University Press.

Brennan, T., & Jay, M. (eds) (1996). *Vision in context: Historical and contemporary perspectives on sight.* London: Routledge.

Brown, D. E. (1991). *Human universals.* Philadelphia, PA: Temple University Press.

Chapple, E. D. (1970). *Culture and biological man: Explorations in behavioral anthropology.* New York: Rinehart & Winston.

Clayton, M., Sager, R., & Will, U. (2005). In time with the music: the concept of entrainment and its significance for ethnomusicology. *European Meetings in Ethnomusicology, 11,* 3–75.

Clynes, M. (1986). When time is music. In J. Evans & M. Clynes (eds), *Rhythm in psychological, linguistic and musical processes* (pp. 169–224). Springfield, IL: C. C. Thomas.

Churchland, P. S. (1986). *Neurophilosophy: Toward a unified science of the mind-brain.* Cambridge, MA: MIT Press.

Condon, W. S. (1986). Communication: Rhythm and structure. In J. Evans & M. Clynes (eds), *Rhythm in psychological, linguistic and musical processes* (pp. 55–77). Springfield, IL: C.C. Thomas.

Coomaraswamy, A. K. (1957). *The dance of Shiva.* New York: The Noonday Press.

Cox, H. (1995). *Fire from heaven: The rise of Pentecostal spirituality and the reshaping of religion in the twenty-first century.* Reading, MA: Addison-Wesley.

Cross, I. (2008). Musicality and the human capacity for culture. *Musicae Scientiae, Speical Issue: Narrative in Music and Interaction,* 147–67.

Cumming, N. (2000). *The sonic self: Musical subjectivity and signification.* Bloomington, IN: Indiana University Press.

Damasio, A. R. (1999). *The feeling of what happens: Body and emotion in the making of consciousness.* New York: Harcourt Brace & Co.

Davidson, R. J. (1992). Prolegomenon to the structure of emotion: Gleanings from neuro-psychology. *Cognition & Emotion,* 6, 245–68.

Dennett, D. (1991). *Consciousness explained.* Boston, MA: Little, Brown & Co.

DeNora, T. (2000). *Music in everyday life.* Cambridge, UK: Cambridge University Press.

Dreyfus, H. L. (1991). *Being-in-the-world: A commentary on Heidegger's Being and Time, Division I.* Cambridge, MA: MIT Press.

Edelman, G. (1992). *Bright air, brilliant fire: On the matter of the mind.* New York: Basic Books.

Eiseman, F. B., Jr. (1989). *Bali: Sekala and niskala. Vol.1: Essays on religion, ritual, and art.* Berkeley, CA: Periplus Editions.

Ekman, P. (1980). Biological and cultural contributions to body and facial movement in the expression of emotions. In A. Rorty (ed.), *Explaining emotions* (pp. 73–101). Berkeley, CA: University of California Press.

Fajans, J. (2006). Autonomy and relatedness: Emotion and the tension between individuality and sociality. *Critique of Anthropology,* 26, 103–19.

Feld, S. (1982). *Sound and sentiment: Birds, weeping, poetics, and song in Kaluli expression.* Philadelphia, PA: University of Pennsylvania Press.

Finnegan, R. (2003). Music, experience, and the anthropology of emotion. In M. Clayton, T. Herbert, & R. Middleton (eds), *The cultural study of music: A critical introduction* (pp. 181–92). Routledge: London.

Fischer, A. H., & Manstead, A. S. R. (2000). The relation between gender and emotions in different cultures. In A. H. Fischer (ed.), *Gender and emotion: Social and psychological perspectives* (pp. 71–94). Cambridge, UK: Cambridge University Press.

Fish, S. (1980). *Is there a text in this class? The authority of interpreting communities.* Cambridge, MA: Harvard University Press.

Foley, W. A. (1997). *Anthropological linguistics: An introduction.* Oxford: Blackwell.

Fox, A. A. (2004). *Real country: Music and language in working-class culture.* Durham and London: Duke University Press.

Freeman, W. (2000). A neurobiological role of music in social bonding. In N. L. Wallin, B. Merker, & S. Brown (eds), *The origins of music* (pp. 411–24). Cambridge, MA: MIT Press.

Frith, S. (1987). Towards an aesthetic of popular music. In R. Leppert & S. McClary (eds), *Music and society: The politics of composition, performance and reception* (pp. 133–49). Cambridge, UK: Cambridge University Press.

Gamman, L., & Marshment, M. (eds) (1988). *The female gaze: Women as viewers of popular culture.* London: The Women's Press.

Ghazzali, A. H. M. (1991). *The alchemy of happiness* (trans. Claud Field and Rev. E. Daniel). London: M. E. Sharpe.

Geertz, C. (1973). The impact of the concept of culture on the concept of man. In *The interpretation of cultures* (pp. 33–54). New York: Basic Books.

Geertz, C. (1983a). Blurred genres: The refiguration of social thought. In *Local knowledge: Further essays in interpretive anthropology* (pp. 19–35). New York: Basic Books.

Geertz, C. (1983b). 'Native's point of view': Anthropological understanding. In *Local knowledge: Further essays in interpretive anthropology* (pp. 55–70). New York: Basic Books.

Geertz, H. (1974). The vocabulary of emotion: A study of Javanese socialization processes. In R. A. LeVine (ed.), *Culture and personality: Contemporary readings* (pp. 249–64). Chicago, IL: Aldine.

Gergen, K. J. (1991). *The saturated self: Dilemmas of identity in contemporary life.* New York: Basic Books.

Gnoli, R. (1968). *The aesthetic experience according to Abhinava Gupta.* Varanasi, India: Chowkhamba Publications.

Good, B. J. (2004). Rethinking 'emotions' in Southeast Asia. *Ethnos, 69,* 529–33.

Goffman, E. (1959). *The presentation of self in everyday life.* Garden City, NY: Doubleday/ Anchor Books.

Goldhill, S. (1996). Refracting classical vision: Changing cultures of viewing. In T. Brennan & M. Jay (eds), *Vision in context: Historical and contemporary perspectives on sight* (pp. 17–28). London: Routledge.

Goodenough, W. H. (1970). *Description and comparison in cultural anthropology.* Chicago, IL: Aldine.

Grotowski, J. (1968). *Towards a poor theatre.* New York: Simon and Schuster.

Hall, E. (1977). *Beyond culture.* Garden City, NY: Anchor Books.

Harkin, M. E. (2003). Feeling and thinking in memory and forgetting: Toward an ethnohistory of the emotions. *Ethnohistory, 50,* 261–84.

Haueisen, J., & Knosche, T. R. (2001). Involuntary motor activity in pianists evoked by music perception. *Journal of Cognitive Neuroscience, 13,* 786–92.

Hebdige, D. (1995). Fabulous confusion! Pop before pop? In C. Jenks (ed.), *Visual culture* (pp. 96–122). London: Routledge.

Hinton, A. L. (1999). Introduction: Developing a biocultural approach to the emotions. In A. L. Hinton (ed.), *Biocultural approaches to the emotions* (pp. 1–37). Cambridge, UK: Cambridge University Press.

Huron, D. (2006). *Sweet anticipation: Music and the psychology of expectation.* Cambridge, MA: MIT Press.

Irvine, J. T. (1990). Registering affect: heteroglossia in the linguistic expression of emotion. In C. Lutz, & L. Abu-Lughod (eds), *Language and the politics of emotion* (pp. 126–61). Cambridge, UK: Cambridge University Press.

James, W. (1890/1950). *The principles of psychology, Vol. 2.* New York: Dover Publications.

Janata, P. (1997). *Electrophysiological studies of auditory contexts.* Dissertation Abstracts International. Section B: The Sciences and Engineering, University of Oregon, USA.

Jefferson, T. (1994). *Declaration of independence and the constitution of the United States of America: the texts.* Washington, DC: National Defense Press. (Originally published 1776)

Jenks, C. (ed.) (1995). *Visual culture.* London: Routledge.

Johnson, J. H. (1995). *Listening in Paris.* Berkeley, CA: University of California Press.

Katz, R. (1982). Accepting 'Boiling energy': The experience of !Kia healing among the !Kung. *Ethos, 19,* 348.

Keil, C. (1987). Participatory discrepancies and the power of music. *Cultural Anthropology, 2,* 275–83.

Kern, S. (1996). *Eyes of love: The gaze in English and French painting and novels, 1840–1900.* London: Reaktion Books.

Leach, E. (1981). A poetics of power. *New Republic, 184,* 14.

Lerdahl, F., & Jackendoff, R. (1983). *A generative theory of tonal music.* Cambridge, MA: MIT Press.

Levi-Strauss, C. (1962). *The savage mind.* London: Wiedenfeld & Nicholson.

Levitin, D. J. (2006). *This is your brain on music: The science of a human obsession.* New York: Dutton.

Levy, R. I. (1984). Emotion, knowing, and culture. In R. Shweder & R. LeVine (eds), *Culture theory: Essays on mind, self, and emotion* (pp. 214–37). Cambridge, UK: Cambridge University Press.

Lovejoy, A. O. (1948). *Essays in the history of ideas*. Baltimore, MD: The John Hopkins Press.

Lovejoy, A. O. (1964). *The great chain of being: a study of the history of an idea*. Cambridge, MA: Harvard University Press. (Originally published 1936)

Lutz, C. A. (1986). Emotion, thought, and estrangement: Emotion as a cultural category. *Cultural Anthropology*, 1, 287–309.

Lutz, C. A. (1988). *Unnatural emotions: Everyday sentiments on a Micronesian atoll and their challenge to Western theory*. Chicago, IL: University of Chicago Press.

Lutz, C. A., & Abu-Lughod, L. (1990). Introduction: emotion, discourse, and the politics of everyday life. In C. A.Lutz & L. Abu-Lughod (eds), *Language and the politics of emotion* (pp. 1–23). Cambridge, UK: Cambridge University Press.

Magowan, F. (2007). *Melodies of mourning: Music and emotion in Northern Australia*. Santa Fe, NM: School for Advanced Research Press.

Masson, J. L., & Patwardhan, M. V. (1969). *Santarasa*. Poona, India: Bhandarkar Oriental Research Institute.

Maturana, H., & Varela, F. J. (1987). *The tree of knowledge: The biological roots of human understanding*. Boston: New Science Library.

McClary, S. (1991). *Feminine endings: Music, gender, and sexuality*. Minneapolis, MN: University of Minnesota Press.

McDaniel, J. (1995). Emotion in Bengali religious thought: Substance and metaphor. In J. Marks & R. T. Ames (eds), *Emotions in Asian thought: A dialogue in comparative philosophy* (pp. 39–63). Albany, NY: State University of New York Press.

McNeill, W. H. (1995). *Keeping together in time: Dance and drill in human history*. Cambridge, MA: Harvard University Press.

Menon, V., & Levitin, D. J. (2005). The rewards of music listening: Response and physiological connectivity of the mesolimbic system. *NeuroImage*, 28, 175–84.

Melzack, R. (1992). Phantom limbs. *Scientific American*, 266, 120–126.

Merriam, A. P. (1964). *The anthropology of music*. Evanston, IL: Northwestern University Press.

Mitchell, W. J. T. (1986). *Iconology: Image, text, ideology*. Chicago, IL: University of Chicago Press.

Morley, D. (1995). Television: Not so much a visual medium, more a visible object. In C. Jenks (ed.), *Visual culture* (pp. 170–89). London: Routledge.

Myers, F. R. (1979). Emotions and the self: A theory of personhood and political order among Pintupi aborigines. *Ethos*, 7, 343–70.

Needham, R. (1981). Inner states as universals. In *Circumstantial deliveries* (pp. 53–71). Berkeley, CA: University of California Press.

Neher, A. (1961). Auditory driving observed with scalp electrodes in normal subjects. *Electroencephalography and Clinical Neurophysiology*, 13, 449–51.

Neher, A. (1962). A physiological explanation of unusual behavior in ceremonies involving drums. *Human Biology*, 34, 151–60.

Nettl, B. (1983). *The study of ethnomusicology: Twenty-nine issues and concepts*. Chicago, IL: University of Illinois Press.

Núñez, R. E. (1997). Eating soup with chopsticks: Dogmas, difficulties and alternatives in the study of conscious experience. *Journal of Consciousness Studies*, 4, 143–66.

Núñez, R., & Freeman, W. (eds) (1999). *Reclaiming cognition: The primacy of action, intention and emotion*. Bowling Green, OH: Imprint Academic.

O'Neill, J. (1995). Foucault's optics: The (in)vision of mortality and modernity. In C. Jenks (ed.), *Visual culture* (pp. 190–201). London: Routledge.

Ortony, A., Clore, G. L., & Collins, A. (1988). *The cognitive structure of emotions*. Cambridge, UK: Cambridge University Press.

Patel, A. D. (2008). *Music, language, and the brain*. Oxford: Oxford University Press.

Peretz, I. (2001). Listen to the brain: A biological perspective on musical emotions. In P. N. Juslin & J. A. Sloboda (eds), *Music and emotion: Theory and research* (pp. 105–34). Oxford: Oxford University Press.

Qureshi, R. B. (1986). *Sufi music of India and Pakistan: Sound, context and meaning in qawwali*. Cambridge, UK: Cambridge University Press.

Racy, A. J. (1998). Improvisation, ecstasy, and performance dynamics in Arabic music. In B. Nettl & M. Russell (eds), *In the course of performance: Studies in the world of musical improvisation* (pp. 95–112). Chicago, IL: University of Chicago Press.

Raffman, D. (1993). *Language, music, and mind*. Cambridge, MA: MIT Press.

Rider, M. S., & Eagle, C. T., Jr. (1986). Rhythmic entrainment as a mechanism for learning in music therapy. In J. Evans & M. Clynes (eds), *Rhythm in psychological, linguistic and musical processes* (pp. 225–48). Springfield, IL: C. C. Thomas.

Rosaldo, M. Z. (1984). Toward an anthropology of self and feeling. In R. Shweder & R. LeVine (eds), *Culture theory: Essays on mind, self, and emotion* (pp. 137–57). Cambridge, UK: Cambridge University Press.

Rouget, G. (1985). *Music and trance: A theory of the relations between music and possession* (trans. B. Beibuyck). Chicago, IL: The University of Chicago Press.

Russell, J. A. (1991a). Culture and the categorization of emotions. *Psychological Bulletin, 110,* 326–450.

Russell, J. A. (1991b). In defense of a prototype approach to emotion concepts. *Journal of Personality and Social Psychology, 60,* 37–47.

Schechner, R. (1988). *Performance theory*. London: Routledge.

Schieffelin, B. (1990). *The give and take of everyday life: Language and socialization of Kaluli children*. Cambridge, UK: Cambridge University Press.

Seckel, A. (ed.) (1986). *Bertrand Russell on God and religion*. Buffalo, NY: Prometheus Books.

Seeger, A. (1987). *Why Suya sing: A musical anthropology of an Amazonian people*. Cambridge, UK: Cambridge University Press.

Shankar, R. (1968). *My music, my life*. New Delhi, India: Vikas Publications.

Shepherd, J., & Giles-David, J. (1991). Music, text and subjectivity. In *Music as social text* (pp. 174–85). Cambridge, MA: Polity Press.

Shweder, R. A. (1985). Menstrual pollution, soul loss, and the comparative study of emotions. In A. Kleinman & B. Good (eds), *Culture and depression: studies in the anthropology and cross-cultural psychiatry of affect and disorder* (pp. 182–215). Berkeley, CA: University of California Press.

Shweder, R. A. (1979). Rethinking culture and personality theory. *Ethos, 7,* 279–311.

Shweder, R. A., & Bourne, E. J. (1984). Does the concept of the person vary cross-culturally? In R. Shweder & R. Levine (eds), *Culture theory: Essays on mind, self, and emotion* (pp. 158–99). Cambridge, UK: Cambridge University Press.

Slater, D. (1995). Photography and modern vision: The spectacle of 'natural magic'. In C. Jenks (ed.), *Visual culture* (pp. 218–37). London: Routledge.

Small, C. (1998). *Musicking: The meanings of performing and listening*. London: Wesleyan University Press.

Smith, J. C., & Ferstman, C. (1996). Knowledge and the languaging body. In J. Smith (ed.), *The castration of Oedipus: Feminism, psychoanalysis, and the will to power* (pp. 52–79). New York: New York University Press.

Solie, R. A. (1993). *Musicology and difference: Gender and sexuality in music scholarship*. Berkeley, CA: University of California Press.

Solomon, R. C. (1984). The Jamesian theory of emotion in anthropology. In R. Shweder & R. LeVine (eds), *Culture theory: Essays on mind, self, and emotion* (pp. 238–54). Cambridge, UK: Cambridge University Press.

Spiro, M. E. (1984). Some reflections on cultural determinism and relativism with special reference to emotion and reason. In R. Shweder & R. LeVine (eds), *Culture theory: Essays on mind, self, and emotion* (pp.323–46). Cambridge, MA: Cambridge University Press.

Spivak, G. C. (1988). *In other worlds: Essays in cultural politics*. New York: Routledge.

Stanislavsky, K. (1977). *An actor prepares* (trans. E. R. Hapgood). New York: Theatre Arts Books. (Originally published 1936)

Stanislavsky, K. (1958). *Stanslavski's legacy: A collection of comments on a variety of aspects of an actor's art and life* (ed. and trans. E. R. Hapgood). New York: Theatre Arts Books.

Stone, R. (1982). *Let the inside be sweet: The interpretation of music event among the Kpelle of Liberia*. Bloomington, IN: Indiana University Press.

Sylvan, R. (2005). *Trance formation: The spiritual and religious dimensions of global rave culture*. London: Routledge.

Taylor, C. (1989). *Sources of the self: The making of the modern identity*. Cambridge, MA: Harvard University Press.

Treitler, L. (1993). Reflections on the communication of affect and idea through music. In S. Feder, R. Karmel, & G. Pollock (eds), *Psychoanalytic explorations in music, second series* (pp. 43–62). Madison, CT: International Universities Press.

Turino, T. (1993). *Moving away from silence: Music of the Peruvian altiplano and the experience of urban migration*. Chicago, IL: University of Chicago Press.

Turner, V. (1983). Body, brain, and culture. *Zygon, 18*, 221–45.

Varela, F. J., Thompson, E., & Rosch, E. (1991). *The embodied mind: Cognitive science and human experience*. Cambridge, MA: MIT Press.

Vaughn, K. (1990). Exploring emotion in sub-structural aspects of Karelian lament: Application of time series analysis to digitalized melody. *Yearbook for Traditional Music, 22*, 106–22.

Viswanathan, T., & Cormack, J. (1998). Melodic improvisation in Karnatak music: The manifestation of raga. In B. Nettl & M. Russell (eds), *In the course of performance: Studies in the world of musical improvisation* (pp. 219–33). Chicago, IL: University of Chicago Press.

von Campenhausen, H. (1964). *The fathers of the Latin church* (trans. M. Hoffman). London: Adam & Charles Black.

Wallin, N. L. (1991). *Biomusicology: Neurophysiological, neuropsychological, and evolutionary perspectives on the origins and purposes of music*. Stuyvesant, NY: Pendragon Press.

Walter, V. J., & Walter, W. G. (1949). The central effects of rhythmic sensory stimulation. *Electroencephalography and Clinical Neurophysiology, 1*, 57–86.

Will, U., & Berg, E. (2007). Brain wave synchronization and entrainment to periodic acoustic stimuli. *Neuroscience Letters, 424*, 55–60.

Young, J. O. (1999). The cognitive value of music. *The Journal of Aesthetics and Art Criticism, 57*, 1–54.

Zizek, S. (1991). *Looking Awry: An introduction to Jacques Lacan through popular culture*. Cambridge, MA: MIT Press.

Zizek, S. (1996). 'I hear you with my eyes'; or, the invisible master. In R. Saleci & S. Zizek (eds), *Gaze and voice as love objects* (pp. 90–126). London: Duke University Press.

CHAPTER 7

....

EMOTION
AS SOCIAL
EMERGENCE

PERSPECTIVES FROM
MUSIC SOCIOLOGY

....

TIA DENORA

7.1 THE SOCIOLOGICAL APPROACH

....

SOCIOLOGY considers the interactive relations between forms of social organization and forms of action and experience. While it is appreciative of anthropological approaches and cross-cultural variation, its primary focus is not on the 'what' of societies and social order (e.g. different cultural patterns and customs) but the 'how' of social order, the practices and mechanisms that stabilize and destabilize groups, communities and larger, more diffuse clusters of social actors. In this sense, sociology as a discipline can be applied to any collective, past or present, and to any part of the globe.

Traditionally, sociology's core subject matter has been the study of social action, by which is usually meant, to paraphrase Max Weber (1978, vol 1, p. 4), conduct meaningfully oriented in its course and outcome. As I describe below, the emphasis on meaning has led to a rationalist bias within sociology, a focus on rule following and rule application, meaning, and verbal communication. Until relatively recently, the result was a diminished emphasis on embodied phenomena and the non- or pre-cognitive realm in relation to action (Acord & DeNora, 2008). Over the past ten years—and especially since the last edition of this volume—sociology has experienced a so-called cultural turn in which emotion, mood, and embodiment are now of central concern, providing both foundation and medium of action and cognition (Jackson & Scott, 2007; Witz et al, 2003; Barbalet, 1998; Collins, 1993, 2004). The aim of this chapter is to describe these developments and their implications for music and the study of emotion, sociologically conceived.

Sociology has always been an inclusive discipline, one open to interdisciplinary dialogue and debate. Nonetheless, it is also possible to specify concern shared by virtually all sociologists with action, inter-subjectivity, taste, the production of culture and knowledge, institutions, organizations and their conventions, and the implications of all these things for the social lives and life chances of individuals. More deeply, sociologists are concerned with what Durkheim described as the social *sui generis*, that is, as a subject matter irreducible to individuals and as a type of phenomenon that emerges from social interaction and simultaneously conditions that action.

The key themes for the sociological study of emotion revolve around the question of how culture may be said to inform or 'get into' emotional experience. These themes include: (1) a focus on emotion as informally learned, modelled, and achieved in interaction with often tacit reference to cultural resources, (2) a focus on the mutually constituted, two-way relation between embodied experience, emotion, feeling, and cultural forms, which is to say a focus on emergence as described above, and (3) a focus on the social distribution of emotion along various social lines, such as by class, gender, age, geographic and, in recent literature, according to more fluidly formed identities. Thus, the sociology of emotion goes to the heart of the question of how personal and subjective experience can be said to be socially mediated and connects with philosophical perspectives that emphasize the extended character of both mind and emotional experience (Clark & Chalmers, 1998; Colombetti, 2008). Using music as a prism from which to examine each of these themes is useful: it concentrates attention on the mechanisms by which culture comes to inform emotional experience.

In what follows, I begin by considering the status of the emotions within sociology's paradigms. From there, I move to a discussion of music's position within sociology and focus in particular on the changing conception of music's link to social life that has emerged within sociology of music over the past decade. I then survey classic work (and more recent classics) in the sociology of music as it illuminates music as a 'device' for the constitution of subjectivity and emotion in a range of settings. Throughout these discussions, my aim is to demonstrate how new approaches within the sociology of music help to illuminate a congenital feature of sociology writ large, namely, the concern with social experience and social action, their sources and structures.

7.2 THE REDISCOVERY OF EMOTION WITHIN SOCIOLOGY

There has been a long-standing interest within sociological theory in the emotions. One strand has developed out of Tönnies' (1957) concepts of *Gemeinschaft* and *Gessellschaft*.

Tönnies used these terms to distinguish between social bonds built upon communal, emotional, traditional, and personal grounds versus those produced via rational and administrative procedures. The distinction, and with it a concern with the 'feeling' bases of social organization, has persisted and has established itself across a range of sociological perspectives. Max Weber's concern with the affective action (Weber, 1978, vol. 1, pp. 24–8), Vilfredo Pareto's discussion of sentiments and non-logical action (Pareto, 1963, p. 161), the 'Human Relations Management' of Elton Mayo (Mayo, 1933; Witkin, 1995), Charles Horton Cooley's 'looking-glass self' and its focus on emotion as the outcome of imaginative cooperation with external images (Cooley, 1902/1983), and Randall Collins's treatment of emotion in relation to rational choice theory (Collins, 1993) have all highlighted emotion's role in relation to action and social structure.

And yet, despite this interest (and despite the formation of a thriving section on Sociology of the Emotions within the American Sociological Association), the affective dimension of human social being was, throughout the 1980s, mostly relegated to sociology's periphery. Particularly in the United States, where the discipline was dominated by rational actor models, and an attendant preoccupation with rule following, choice, and free will, the sociology of emotions was typically viewed as an offshoot of 'micro'-sociology, and thus disconnected from structuralist and 'macro' concerns. Within sociology's dominant disciplinary frameworks, phenomena such as revolution and war, diplomacy, occupations, social and class rivalry, political and economic activity, organizational and institutional behaviour, the rise and fall of social movements, and the exercise of social control were all portrayed as if they took place in passionless corridors, executed by agents who possessed reason but who did not *feel*.

Over the past decade, more sensitive sociological portraits of action have begun to emerge. With them, the status of the emotions as a topic has been elevated. From a number of sub-disciplinary directions has come a new concern with the 'feeling' component of social action. This emphasis can be seen in current approaches to the sociological study of social and political movements and the emerging focus on the affective character of identification with a movement (Melucci, 1996a, 1996b) and 'structures of feeling' as these are entered into, adopted and adapted in the course of identity politics and movement activity (Hetherington, 1998). This emotion renaissance is also evident in new work on political affiliation, for example, on the processes by which citizens transfer feelings of 'belonging' from nations to global entities (Berezin, 1999). It has been further fuelled by a rapidly growing sociology of the body (Featherstone, Hepworth, & Turner, 1991; Turner, 1984) and embodied experience (Bourdieu, 1998; Delamont & Stephens, 2008; Shilling, 2008; Wacquant, 2006; Williams, 1996, 1998).

Thus, sociology is now much more closely affiliated with concerns and topics traditionally lodged within the purview of social psychology. But this trend toward motivation and emotion has simultaneously been linked to sociology's abiding concern with, as described above, the social *sui generis*. This concern takes empirical specification via the study of emotions as they take shape in relation to social contexts—situations, occasions, institutions and organizations—and with the hitherto 'macro' sociological terrain of collective and institutional action. The result is that sociology is now less separated into macro versus micro approaches and increasingly likely to focus on experience as the fulcrum between personal and organizational realms. As Alberto Melucci (1996b, p. 1) expressed it:

Each and every day we make ritual gestures, we move to the rhythm of external and personal cadences, we cultivate our memories, we plan for the future. And everyone else does likewise. Daily experiences are only fragments in the life of an individual, far removed from the collective events more visible to us, and distant from the great changes sweeping through our culture. Yet almost everything that is important for social life unfolds within this minute web of times, spaces, gestures, and relations. It is through this web that our sense of what we are doing is created, and in it lie dormant those energies that unleash sensational events.

The playing out of social change, politics, social movements, and relations of production are experienced and renewed from within this 'web', as Melucci calls it; it is from within the matrix of 'times, spaces, gestures and relations' that these 'larger' things are realized. Put differently, the drama of social life is performed on the stage of the quotidian; it is on the platform of the mundane and the sensual that the specificity of social experience is rendered and patterns are renewed. It is important to note here that the term 'mundane' in this context by no means refers to a part of social life. By contrast, all realms, even those normally sequestered as 'sacred' can be understood to be pragmatically crafted, to take shape expressly through the activities that generate faith and extraordinary experience (Hennion, 2007).

   It is from within this framework and its emphasis on pragmatic action that the sociology of music can be seen to interact with the broader sociological focus on emotion. Having undergone significant transformation in the past decade, socio-music studies have moved from preoccupations with music's production to concerns with how it is consumed and what it 'does' in social life. In this regard, developments within the sociology of music merge with developments in the sociology of the arts more widely (Bowler, 1994). Recent developments within the field have examined connections between musical consumption and musical experience as a means for producing and sustaining social ordering in 'real time', which is viewable and/or theorizable in naturally occurring action, over the life course, and with reference to organizational and collective spheres of action. These developments have helped to return the sociology of music to the systematic concerns laid out early on in the area by figures such as Max Weber (1921/1958), T. W. Adorno (1967, 1973, 1976, 1999), and Alfred Schutz (1964), who is of particular interest because of his focus on music's relation to, and ability to configure, 'inner time' (pp. 172, 174). They have helped to renew the sociology of music's emphasis on fundamental questions concerning music's role as an active ingredient of social formation, its traditional and common-sense role as the medium par excellence of emotion construction. In short, there is now a place at the top of sociology's table for the study of music.

   Such a project involves considerable sweep: it encompasses matters that are usually desegregated—a focus on systems of music production and distribution, on organizational ecology and management, and on subjective experience as it is configured in relation to musical media.

7.3 MUSIC AND SOCIAL STRUCTURES—THE MOVEMENT TOWARD CONCEPTUAL SYMMETRY

From the 1970s to fairly recently, the sociology of music and the sociology of culture more broadly have been concerned with how music is *produced*, with its occupational politics and distribution systems, and with semiotic readings of musical forms. The emphasis was upon music as an object shaped by social relations. What was suppressed was any symmetrical attempt to conceive of music as a potentially dynamic medium, or to consider what music may 'do' in, to, and for the social relations in which it is embedded. Thus, only one half of the equation was present, albeit a crucial half, focusing on how musical works take shape in ways that are enabled and constrained by their cultures and worlds of production. As a result, apart from some notable exceptions discussed below, the matter of musical experience, and music's links to emotion, passion, and energy, to the phenomenological and existential features of social life, were all uncharted waters within sociology's paradigm. Even when sociologists considered music consumption, the focus was directed less to the matter of musical experience than to the ways in which tastes, musical values, and listening practices served as symbolic boundaries for status groups and status differences (Bourdieu, 1984; Bryson, 1996; DeNora, 1995; DiMaggio, 1982; Lamont, 1992; Peterson & Simkus, 1992; DiMaggio & Useem, 1978).

As Peter Martin (1995, p. 1) has observed, music is ubiquitous in modern societies, yet the significance of music's ubiquity often goes unnoticed within social sciences. In recent years, music's ubiquity has been examined as a topic in its own right (Bosci & Kasabian, forthcoming), bringing with it a much sharper focus on the question of what music can 'do'. Within music sociology, it is now possible to conceptualize music as a device for the constitution of emotive action in and across a range of social settings. This concern with *emotion construction* (through musical practice) offers an avenue into sociology's new concerns with the non-cognitive bases of agency (i.e. organized action, feeling, being, and awareness) and also bypasses the conventional barriers between macro and micro analytical levels as discussed above. It also highlights what medical sociologist Mildred Blaxter terms 'sociobiologic translations' (Blaxter, 2003, p. 74), that is, the processes by which perceptions are translated into biological signals that may exacerbate or ameliorate seemingly physiological conditions such as disease and illness. Here, recent work in the sociology of everyday musicking (i.e. music-linked activity in its broadest sense; Small, 1998) has, as will be described below, considerably enriched our understanding of the interplay between cultural activity, emotional experience, the subjective experience of health and illness and—most intriguingly— clinically assessed changes in health states. In the remainder of this chapter, I will discuss work that exemplifies these themes. I begin, in the next section, with reference to two, originally distinct, strands within the discipline that can be understood to provide the bedrock for more recent work: Adorno's theory of music as a medium of social organization and more overtly empirical and ethnographic studies of music and lifestyle practice as propounded by Paul Willis in the 1970s.

7.4 MUSIC AND SUBJECTIVITY—SOCIOLOGY'S CLASSIC MODELS

For Theodor Adorno, music was inextricably connected to habits of mind, to social structural organization, and to modes of subjectivity. For example, he viewed the music of Arnold Schoenberg as able to foster critical consciousness because its material organization went against the grain of musical convention and cliché. Conversely, in the age of 'total administration', music was also a medium that 'trains the unconscious for conditioned reflexes' (Adorno, 1976, p. 53). Jazz, Tin Pan Alley, and nearly every other popular music genre was linked, in Adorno's view, to forms of regression and infantile dependency (Adorno, 1990).

Adorno's work explores the idea that music interiorizes and is able to instigate forms of social organization in and through the ways that it works on and configures its subject-recipient. Put bluntly, Adorno conceived of music as active, indeed formative of consciousness. In this regard, his work makes some of the strongest claims on behalf of music's power in any discipline. But because Adorno provided no machinery for conceptualizing music's power empirically, his work is also frustrating: it never operationalizes the claim that music 'trains' the unconscious, nor points the way toward how these matters might be observed at the grounded level of musical practice. Adorno's work remained in the safe haven of theory and semiotic 'readings' of (primarily art-music) works. It ventured but little into the realm of empirical analysis and the sphere of music consumption (indeed, Adorno's comments on music reception delineate a hierarchy of listener types). In its refusal to go out and look at the world, Adorno's work suffers at times from parochialism (e.g. his views on jazz, his unilateral condemnation of popular culture, and his tendency to prescribe musical taste; see DeNora, 2003).

During the 1970s, more empirically oriented work on 'music and society' provided an alternative to Adorno's hypothetical approach. The originally British tradition of cultural studies, ethnographically conceived, was directed at exploring connections between music and lived experience—identity creation, feeling, and the social constitution of embodied action and its parameters. Moreover, these explicitly ethnographic works may be read, with hindsight, to have presaged current developments.

Within the classic studies of young people and their intimate involvement with music, in books such as Paul Willis's *Profane Culture* (1978), and Simon Frith's early monographs, *Sound Effects* (1981) and *The Sociology of Rock* (1978), music's social presence was illuminated in ways that address all three of the core themes in the sociological study of emotion as listed above, and which are now considered in turn:

Theme one, informal learning and tacit reference to cultural resources: Rereading these works with their characteristic focus on the experience of music, it is possible to see music providing a resource in and through which agency, identity, and peer culture are produced in ways that are shaped by and in turn shape peer-group culture. Indeed, these studies can be seen to be compatible with Adorno's concern with music's link, and ability to instigate, social being. But this time, the mechanism that linked music to social structure was specified in a manner that made it easier to observe: it focused on how music was actually consumed and used within the peer group, and on how being part of a sub- or idio-culture entailed being socialized into the forms of feeling emblematic there, understood in terms of the processes by which these forms were achieved, in situated action.

Theme two, emotion and culture as mutually referencing and emergent phenomena: The study by Willis (1978) showed how music was appropriated by actors as a resource for emotional experience. Though Willis does not put it this way, music *afforded* emotional experience (DeNora, 2000, 2003; Clarke, 2005). Affordance, importantly for sociology, is by no means stimulus. The sense in which the concept of affordance is used within sociology (Anderson & Sharrock, 1993; DeNora, 2000, p. 40) diverges somewhat from Gibson's (1966) original and pioneering usage: in sociology, particularly sociologies influenced by and contributing to actor network approaches, objects do not inherently provide affordances but rather their affordances are constituted through the ways they mesh with many other features of a setting and actions directed to them. In sociology, the concept of affordances becomes relational, or, in other words, objects and their affordances emerge from the networks within which they are approached, both physically and conceptually. With regard to music, affordances for emotional experience emerge from the interactions between actors, materials (musical and other), and conventions of use.

For example, in his report on the culture of the 'bikeboys', Willis noted that the boys' preferred songs were fast-paced and characterized by a strong beat, a pulsating rhythm. Willis showed how the boys established connections between music and social life and how they chose music that allowed them to orient to it in ways that were emotionally transformative. This is to say that the structural similarities—homologies—between music and social behaviour that could be perceived (e.g. fast music, rising excitement) were forged through the bikeboys' music-consumption practices and the meanings they attributed to their chosen music.

In other words, Willis demystified how music 'works' in relation to emotional experience. His focus was directed at the question of how particular actors make connections or, as Stuart Hall (1980, 1986) later put it, 'articulations' between music and social phenomena and how this process of linking music with forms of social life is part of actors' ongoing constitution of their life worlds and themselves. Although he never described his project as such, Willis's work on the bikeboys and on music's role as part of 'profane culture' more widely served to establish no less than an interactionist version of Adorno's original vision, which is an approach to the question of music's link to subjectivity, to cognitive style, and to actors' ontological orientations. Key here, however, was that Willis's approach captured music's social impact as it was achieved by the ways in which actors themselves made 'articulations' or links between forms of music and forms of social life. It drew upon the basic interactionist tenet within sociology that agents attach connotations to things and orient to social circumstances on the basis of perceived meanings. And it illuminated, through ethnographic description, the way in which social forms of organization are made through reference to aesthetic materials. This focus on the social process of world making (and the role of cultural media in this process) signalled an important shift in focus from aesthetic objects and their 'content' (static) to the cultural practices in and through which aesthetic materials were appropriated and used (dynamic) to produce social life. It simultaneously served to justify the need for 'symmetrical' conceptualizations of the relationship between music and social structure. In other words, music is a medium of environment making, and that making includes, as I describe in the next theme, making forms of difference between agents in the world.

Theme three, the social distribution of emotion: It is important to note that Willis was speaking of bike *boys*. Here is where we see music's link to emotional experience, and to models of how to be an emotional agent, as characterized by various (cross-cutting, often fluid) social distributions, in this case, to a particular form of young masculinity (explicitly contrasted in his book with the 'head' culture of a different group). In this case, the bike boys' music, as Willis (1978) noted, did not leave its recipients 'just sit[ting] there moping all night' (p. 69). On the contrary, it invited—and provided an exemplar of—movement. As one of the boys put it, 'If you hear a fast record you've got to get up and do something, I think. If you can't dance any more, or if the dance is over, you've just got to go for a burn-up [motorcycle ride]' (p. 73).

Willis's work was thus pioneering in its demonstration of how music does much more than 'depict' or embody values. It portrayed music as active and dynamic, as constitutive not merely of 'values' but constitutive of trajectories and styles of conduct. As one of the boys observed, 'You can hear the beat in your head, don't you . . . you go with the beat, don't you?' (p. 72). This insight was germane to more recent developments in the field for it points to the ways in which music, as it is heard or imagined, may serve to organize or 'configure' its users. Willis showed, for example, how music was implicated in the temporal structure of the bikeboys' evening, how it took them from—or provided the fulcrum for—one state (sitting around) to another (dancing as the music plays) to another (riding as the music plays in memory). Viewed in this way, music can be conceived of as a kind of aesthetic technology, an instrument of social ordering.

Similar points have been made with regard to the emergence of new categories of emotional stances as exhibited in musical performance. DeNora (2004, 2006) has described how the embodied requirements of Beethoven's concertos in early nineteenth-century Vienna affected patterns of pianistic decorum in ways that came to be understood as masculine modes of performance, and that this inadvertently excluded women from performing Beethoven's more 'heroic' concerto works. (Women were increasingly cast as performers/keepers of the Mozartian flame, the earlier and less physical style.) The figure of the soloist at the keyboard implied by these works was one both in accord with and able to advance then-emerging romantic notions of the sublime and of the 'master' of music—an agent characterized increasingly by demonstrative physical prowess, and a particular type of performer who was not only increasingly male but a particular variety of male—dashing, brooding, seen in profile. The concerto provided, as it were, an object lesson that broadcast delineated meanings (Green, 1997) about specifically male forms of emotional and embodied agency at the piano but also outside the concert hall, and simultaneously offered new forms of emotional experience for listeners (male and female) who could now, in the presence of the sublime music and the master/virtuoso, surrender themselves to music's powers. As a cultural form, in other words, music models categories of emotion, which in turn provide candidate forms of experience for recipients, which then impact back on musical forms.

Thinking about culture as it is appropriated, gets into action, and comes to configure agents in particular ways is a topic that has been explored in detail by ethnographically oriented music sociologists. Sarah Cohen, for instance, was one of the first to call for a renewal of an ethnography of musical practice in her insistence that 'focus upon people and their musical practices and processes rather than upon structures, texts or products illuminates the ways in which music is used and the important role that it plays in everyday life and in society generally' (Cohen, 1993, p. 127). Similarly, Georgina Born (1995) argued, in her ethnography of IRCAM (Institut de Recherche et Coordination Acoustique/Musique), that it is necessary to focus on 'the actual uses of technologies [she could just as well have said 'musics'], which are often depicted in idealized, unproblematic, and normative ways' (p. 15). In common with all instruments and technological devices, then, music needs to be understood in terms of its (non-verbal) capacities for enabling and constraining its user(s). Within current sociology, this focus has been directed at how individuals come to appropriate musical forms, and how musical forms feature within social settings as organizing materials of action. How, then, can this idea be developed and how can music's structuring powers be illuminated at the level of social experience? In the remaining sections of this chapter, I present two more examples of recent work concerned with music's role as a resource for the constitution of emotional experience. This discussion should be read in conjunction with the chapter by Sloboda and O'Neill (2001) on everyday listening to music and with Sloboda's chapter on music in everyday life (Chapter 18, this volume), where issues concerning ecological validity are directly addressed.

7.5 MUSIC AND EMOTION WORK—PRODUCING FEELING IN DAILY LIFE

One of the most promising trends in current music sociology has been the focus on how music may be used—with varying degrees of conscious awareness by and on behalf of actors as a resource—to construct self-identity and to create and maintain a variety of feeling states. This work clearly connects with pioneering efforts within music psychology (Sloboda, 1999/2005; see also Chapter 18, this volume) and ethnomusicology (Crafts, Cavicci, & Keil, 1993). But it also speaks to an explicitly sociological concern with the aesthetic organization of scenes and settings (including those not normally deemed 'aesthetic', such as the workplace), and with the social distribution of emotion and conventional notions concerning feeling structures within particular social settings (e.g. matters such as who is entitled to feel what type of emotion, where, when, and how).

The distinctively sociological quality of this concern is its focus on how individuals are produced or produce themselves as social agents with attendant styles of feeling and emotionally laden postures. Thus, from within sociology, emotions are regarded as 'socially constituted' so that the study of music reception and consumption connects with recent discussions within sociology of 'aesthetic reflexivity' (Lash & Urry, 1994, Ch. 4) and 'aesthetic agency' (DeNora, 1997, 2000; Witkin & DeNora, 1997). These terms highlight the consumption of aesthetic media as a means for self-interpretation and self-constitution, for the doing, being, and feeling that are the matrix of social experience. They simultaneously call for an overtly ethnographic turn in the study of aesthetic reception, and thus interact with developments in the sociology of media and the plastic arts (Radway, 1988; Press, 1994; Tota, 1997, 1999).

7.5.1 Music as a technology of emotion construction

Two studies conducted in the late 1990s help introduce these points. The first focuses upon music consumption in France (Gomart & Hennion, 1999; Hennion & Maisonneuve, 1998), the second on England and the USA (DeNora, 1999, 2000). Both draw on roughly 50 in-depth interviews, and both have concentrated on music's role in relation to the achieved character of feeling, to the ways in which actors' adoption of emotional stances, subject positions, and states are simultaneously the objects of actors' cultural practices in specific settings. In this regard, these works have begun to pave the way for a new sociology of music and emotions, one that connects an ethnomethodological focus (on the procedures and practical activities in and through which social ordering is accomplished in situ and in particular social contexts: Garfinkel, 1967; Heritage, 1984; Law, 1994; Law & Hassard, 1999) with a focus on emotions in terms of how they are crafted and experienced within social situations.

In a piece that compares the love of music with the love of taking drugs, and which draws upon in-depth interviews with music lovers and drug addicts, Gomart and Hennion (1999) examine actors as they engage in 'techniques of preparation' that produce forms of attachment, so as to illuminate the mechanisms that produce 'dispositions'. In so doing, they shift the focus of their particular theoretical persuasion, 'actor network theory', from action to the study of interaction between people and things, and with this shift they make a concomitant move away from the overly general category of 'action' to the more specific concept of 'event'. They highlight 'what occurs' when, as part of the musical—or narcotic—experience, the self is 'abandoned' or given over to sensation or emotion. They are interested in no less than an ethnographic sociology of the production of passion.

With regard to the music lovers, Gomart and Hennion (1999) delineate the various practices involved in preparing for aesthetic experience. For example, they describe how their interviewees describe becoming 'ready in one's head' for the ear to hear and the body to respond (p. 232) or how they employ particular listening strategies and rhythms so as to be ready to respond in preferred or expected ways. This process is akin to 'tuning in' or attempting to produce, through fine-tuning practices, a signal's power and clarity. Listeners, they suggest, like drug users, 'meticulously *establish conditions*: active work must be done in order to be moved' (p. 227 [emphasis in original]). Listeners are by no means simply 'affected' by music but are rather active in constructing their 'passivity' to music—their ability to be 'moved'. The music 'user' is thus deeply implicated as a producer of his or her own emotional response, and is one who:

... strives tentatively to fulfil those conditions which will let him be seized and taken over by a potentially exogenous force. 'Passivity' then is not a moment of inaction—not a lack of will of the user who suddenly fails to be a full subject. Rather passivity adds to action, potentializes action.

(Gomart & Hennion, 1999, p. 243)

Gomart and Hennion were attuned to the question of how 'events' of musical passion and emotional response—the being 'taken over' by music—is reflexively accomplished by music lovers. Similarly, DeNora's (2000) study deals with music's role in the day-to-day lives of American and British women as they used music to regulate, enhance, and change qualities and levels of emotion.

Nearly all the women in DeNora's study spoke explicitly about music's role as an ordering device at the 'personal' level, as a means for creating, enhancing, sustaining, and changing subjective, cognitive, bodily, and self-conceptual states. Levels of musical training not withstanding, the respondents exhibited considerable awareness about the music they 'needed' to hear in different situations and at different times, drawing upon elaborate repertoires of musical programming practice, and were sharply aware of how to mobilize music to arrive at, enhance, and alter aspects of themselves and their self-concepts. Part of their criteria for the 'right' music was how well it 'fit[ted]' or was suitable for the purpose or situation they wished to achieve, or for achieving a particular emotional state (see the discussion of 'fit' in Sloboda & O'Neill, 2001, and in Chapters 18 and 32, this volume). For example, as one respondent, Lucy, put it describing how she came to take time out to listen to some of the Schubert *Impromptus*:

... I was feeling very 'stressed' this morning 'cause we're in the throes of moving house and it's, you know, we're not, we haven't sold our house yet, and it's moving, you know, and, um, so I actively decided to put on Schubert's *Impromptus* because they were my father's favourite— you might want to come along to that again, because Schubert's *Impromptus* have a long history with my life—and I thought, my husband had just gone off to work and I thought well, about half an hour before I come up here [to her place of paid work], I'll just listen to them. So, the speakers are [she gestures] there and there on either side of what used to be the fireplace and I sit in a rocking chair facing them, so I get the sound in between the speakers, and I just sat there and listened [sighs, gentle laughter].

Q. [gentle laughter]

A. But I needed it. It was only ten minutes or so, you know, I didn't listen to them all. I just listened to the bits I wanted to listen to.

(Quoted in DeNora, 2000, p. 16)

Here, the music's powers to instigate emotion (the relational character of music's affordances) are activated by Lucy herself and in relation to a range of practices and objects (see Figure 7.1). The *Impromptus* are, for Lucy, powerful on many levels. Their character as physical sound structures and their relation to a body of musical-stylistic convention is interpolated with, for Lucy, equally important biographical connotations and with a history of use. The music she chooses calms her not only because it embodies musical calm, but because it restores to Lucy a sense of her own identity. First, for Lucy, the works are associated with comfort; they are bound up with a complex of childhood memories and associations. Her late father, to whom she was close, used to play the piano after dinner and these works, wafting up the stairs, were ones Lucy used to hear as she was falling asleep. Second, the material culture of listening is also an accomplice, in this example, of music's power to shift Lucy's mood on the morning she describes. Lucy's listening is conducted in a quiet room. She sits in a rocking chair placed between the speakers, and so is almost nestled in the, as she perceives it, calm and nurturing music. (The vocabulary of nurturing is Lucy's. As she puts it, music, 'soothes me', 'I retreat into music when I can't bear the rest of the world, you know,' 'You can go into [music] and have it around you or be in it.')

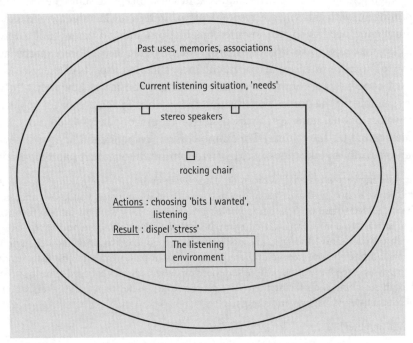

Fig. 7.1 10–15 minutes spent with music: 'Lucy' and Schubert's *Impromptus*.

7.5.2 Tacit practice and emotional work

This example typifies the kind of practical knowledge respondents exhibited repeatedly in their accounts of often tacit music practices. Through these practices, respondents produced themselves as coherent social and socially disciplined beings. As in the French data reported by Gomart and Hennion, the British and American respondents here routinely engaged in various practices of 'tuning in', of producing a musical event that would be capable of 'moving' them, and this production of passivity in the face of music, and its subsequent emotional 'effects' was achieved through an assemblage of musical practices: the choice of specific recordings, volume levels, material cultural and temporal environments of listening (e.g. choosing to listen in bed, in a rocking chair, in the bath in the evening, the morning, while preparing to go out), and the pairing and compiling of musical works, memories, previous and current contexts of hearing such that the respondents could often be conceived as—and spoke of themselves as—disc jockeys to themselves.

In both the French and the British/American studies, music can be seen as a medium or device for achieving 'emotional work'. First coined by Arlie Hochschild (1983) to describe practices within the workplace where workers were required to produce not only material goods or services but also to produce themselves as types of emotional agents acting under the organizational cultural auspices, the concept of emotional work bears strong resemblance to Cooley's conception of emotion constitution in his discussion of looking-glass self. The concept of emotional work has since been adopted more widely within sociology, where emotion is conceived as a 'bodily co-operation with an image, a thought, a memory—a co-operation of which the individual is aware' (Hochschild, 1979, p. 551, quoted in Williams, 1996, p. 129). Respondents described how they used music both routinely and in exceptional circumstances to regulate moods and energy levels, to enhance and maintain desired states of feeling and bodily energy (e.g. relaxation, excitement) and to diminish or modify undesirable emotional states (e.g. stress, fatigue).

For example, in their own words, the British and American women interviewed by DeNora described how music's specific properties such as rhythms, gestures, harmonies, and styles provided them with referents or representations of 'where' they wish to 'be' or 'go', emotionally, physically, and so on:

> Like with my R&B, um, most of the time I listen to it when I'm, you know, trying to relax. I'm gonna sleep, sometimes I'll throw on a few tracks to wake me up, nice 'n' slow and then I'll throw on something else. And then, sometimes, you know, if I'm not really not in that relaxed mood, I'm like, you know, 'I don't wanna listen to that' and I'll throw something fast on, or, something fast is playing and I'm like 'That's too chaotic for me right now, I have to put something slow on.
>
> (Latoya, New York City, quoted in DeNora, 2000, p. 49)

Respondents made, in other words, articulations between musical works, styles, and materials on the one hand and desired modes of agency on the other, and then used music to presage, inspire, elaborate, or remind them of those modes of agency and their associated emotional forms. When respondents chose music as part of this care of self, they often engaged in self-conscious articulation work, thinking ahead about the music that might 'work' for them. And their articulations were made on the basis of what they perceived the music to afford. This perception is in turn shaped by a range of matters. Among these are previous associations respondents have made between particular musical materials and other things (biographical, situational), their under-standings of the emotional implications of conventional musical devices, genres, and styles, and their perceived parallels (articulations/homologies) between musical mate-rials/processes and social or physical materials/processes.

George Gittoes's 2004 documentary film *Soundtrack to war* makes similar points about soldiers' use of music in battle (see Chapter 26, this volume). There, soldiers appropriated music that provided sonic features which, for them, 'fit[ted]' their work tasks and helped them psych themselves up in occupationally appropriate ways (in Hochschild's terms, a 'bodily cooperation with' an image of their role). Gittoes shows us how, in other words, music was one of the materials to which soldiers turned as they prepared to engage in destruction.

Of course, interview data is abstracted from the actual flow on ongoing musical con-duct and the usual provisory warnings apply in terms of how interviews may generate little more than accounts and self-presentations. However, the point of the in-depth, semi-structured ethnographic interview is to lead the respondent into discussion of actual happenings and practices (e.g. 'Do you have a radio alarm clock? What channel is it set to? When was the last time you listened to X, Y, Z? Can you tell me about that?). From there it is possible to begin to contextualize respondents' accounts in terms of the more concrete features that they report. Interviews are mediated; however, they provide a more naturalistic form of data than do surveys or experiments, permitting better glimpses into the processes by which articulations/connections between music and action (and emotional experience) take shape.

Simultaneously, we need to think about how to approach the topic of music as an 'equal partner' in the constitution of emotion in action. In addition to chapters 14 and 17 in this volume, this question has been explored, music-analytically, by Richard Middleton (1990), who provides a useful bridge between sociology's focus on the articulations actors forge between music and feeling and music-ontological questions about the role of music's temporal, rhythmic, and harmonic structures in condition-ing appropriation and response. Middleton discusses what he refers to as 'exosemantic correspondences' between music and spatial or emotional structures/forms (e.g. slow and quiet: 'relaxed'; minor mode: 'depressed') and develops semiotic concepts of 'pri-mary' and 'secondary' signification (pp. 220–32). The former refers to music's internal references and relationships, its arrangement of structural elements, and to the ways in which its relationships become terms in which to map, frame, and configure (in this case) emotions: '. . . as this note is to that note, as tonic is to dominant, as ascent is to descent, as accent is to weak beat (and so on), so X is to Y' (p. 223). The latter refers to music's connotative level, its ability to invoke or symbolize images, emotions, and ideas. It is, as Middleton emphasizes repeatedly, crucial to examine the specificity of musical structures in terms of how they lend themselves to, afford, and come to be appropriated as embodying various emotional states and styles. Adhering to this point, new sociologies of musical practice and emotional work recognize the importance of music's material specificity in relation to emotions and their production in social settings.

At the same time, music's capacity to engender emotion is by no means preordained. A characteristic of the perspectives on music and emotions discussed so far is their circumvention of, on the one hand, essentialist conceptions of subjectivity (as if feeling arises from internal processes) and, on the other, the notion that music is a 'cause' of emotional states. By contrast, these 'subject–object' dichotomies are bypassed by considering music as part of—a resource for—the reflexive constitution or working up of emotional states or events. Here, music is not conceived as a 'stimulus', nor does it, pace Langer (1942) merely 'resonate' with some pre-existing subjective or mental state to which it exists in parallel. Indeed, this view, of which Langer is an exponent, has been subject to criticism from within sociology by Shepherd and Wicke (1997, pp. 12–14) who, though they endorse the idea that homologies exist or are forged between emotions and musical structures, suggest that the insights from musicology on the ways in which music's structures symbolize emotional structures do not 'stretch to an explanation of the mechanisms through which musical processes and processes of subjectivity are involved with one another' (p. 13). In contrast with musicological conceptions that confine analytical focus to, for the most part, the musical 'object' (though in recent musicological work this focus often gives way to a concern with musical ecology; e.g. Clarke, 2005), sociologists tend to conceive of music as providing a *resource* for emotional states and their achievement. Neither a cause nor parallel of emotional states, music is conceived within sociology as providing a candidate simulacrum or contrast structure against which feeling may be formulated. To speak of music in this way is to speak of it as a material against which 'how one feels' may be identified, elaborated, and made into an object of knowledge. One may, for example, say in reference to a musical example, '*This* is how I feel,' and thereby grow tense or relax as the music does, when the music does, or in ways that are modelled, often without conscious awareness, on the music. It is here, then, that music's vital, and indeed, moral, dimension—as declaimed by classic philosophers such as Plato ('in music that the guardians will build their guardhouse'; 1966, p. 72) and Aristotle ('What we have said makes it clear that music possesses the power of producing an effect on the character of the soul [by which I read aesthetic inclination for action]'; 1980, p. 24) can be seen: musical structures and representations are drawn, by actors themselves, into the vortex of feeling production; they literally 'get into' action and subjectivity.

In short, recent studies of music in relation to the achievement of emotional states and events point to music's use in real social settings as a device that actors employ for entraining and structuring feeling trajectories. Music can be a resource to which agents turn so as to regulate themselves as aesthetic agents, as feeling, thinking, and acting beings in their day-to-day lives. Achieving this regulation requires a high degree of practical reflexivity. And the respondents in both the French and the English/American case studies show how actors often perceive their 'need' for this regulation and know that the techniques of auto-emotion work. These techniques may be found inadvertently (e.g. something is tried once and 'works' and so is later repeated and so becomes part of an individual repertoire), or they may be suggested through culture and the media (and so be, at least initially, imitative), or they may be handed down by associates (and so exist as part of group or family culture) or initially encountered in a social setting—all of these technique locations were mentioned by respondents. The natural history of the processes through which feeling states are identified and 'expressed' (i.e. enacted to self or other over time) is, moreover, a topic to be developed as it concerns the question of how aesthetic agency is configured in actual interactions, as passion is choreographed and entrained. Holding on to this focus, but widening it from the individual experience of culture (and the social regulation of subjectivity in and through reference to cultural materials) to music's role in relation to the organization of collective action and its emotional component is but the next step within this programme. In the remainder of this chapter, I survey classic and recent work devoted to music's regulatory role in relation to emotional conduct between two actors engaged in intimate conduct, to self-care and health promotion, and between groups of actors, using the case of social movement activity.

7.6 MUSIC AND EMOTIONS IN CLOSE INTERACTION

Studies of gender and musical taste have long directed their focus to music's connections to love and to courtship. Shepherd and Giles-Davis (1991), for example, have reported on the consumption and use of music by a small number of middle-class English-speaking teenage girls in Montreal, showing how music provides a kind of template for the formation of sexuality and emotional state. More recently, focus has shifted to the question of how music is actually used during intimate occasions, and how it may draw bodies into temporal trajectories (rhythms, pulses, corporeal grammars, movement styles, and feeling grammars). Here, music is viewed as a non-verbal accomplice for particular intimate action forms (DeNora, 1997), such that 'who puts what on the record player' as a prelude or backdrop for intimacy is overtly conceived as a question of love's real-time construction and its politics.

Many of the interviewees in DeNora's study (in particular the two younger age groups) described, through a rich series of examples from their daily lives, how they sought to structure both the grammar and style of intimate interaction through musical means and also to reproduce feeling styles and forms by using music that had served as the soundtrack on prior intimate occasions. The typical category for this activity was the concept of 'background' or 'mood' music, and the interviewees were unanimous on one point: the music should not be fast paced, loud, or jolting. To the contrary, respondents spoke of how they valued the temporal structures and embodied practices

commensurate with a slow pace, with leisured intimate activity. Their responses overlapped with what has already been observed in relation to gender and musical taste
(Peterson & Simkus, 1992; Bryson, 1996). 'Setting is very important,' as one respondent
put it, because getting the music 'right' is simultaneously a way of trying to make the
action 'right', not merely in the embodied and technical sense, but as a way of prospec-
tively calling out forms of emotional and embodied agency that are comfortable and
preferable, that 'feel' right in emotional and embodied terms. (Such agency, of course,
includes specific material practices, e.g. a 'light' touch, an 'unhurried' approach . . . and
the music can be perceived as providing 'primary significations' of these things and
hence employed as a model or blueprint for action):

Melinda: I think, last night, it was really funny, it was like 'mood setting' in a way. Cause, like,
he had *Enya* on, and like, as people call that, 'chick music' [i.e. 'women's' music that young
men may choose to play when entertaining women because they think it is what women pre-
fer] . . . and he was trying to produce a relaxed atmosphere and um, I think in a way it does
promote physical, or just intimacy in general because it's just like, certain music's more calming and, I remember like I think *Stigma* or *Hyper* came on and we were like, 'No no no, we
don't want that!' and we like tried to get this piece, like I had him play the *First Night* soundtrack, which I love, and there's like, a love song I, there, that's so beautiful, but everything else
is like, 'bu bu de bah' [she sings here a triplet followed by a whole note the interval of a fifth
higher than the triplet figure] and I'm like, 'No, no, this is not good,' but I do, I think it was
just very, it's very calming, very intimacy . . .

Q. So it's part of what creates an intimate atmosphere?

Melinda: Yeah, definitely. I think it's, setting is very important, and like music is a very big
part of that.

(Quoted in DeNora, 2000, p. 112)

7.7 EVERYDAY MUSICAL ACTIVITY AND EVERYDAY HEALTH PRACTICE

The care of self has been a prominent theme in nearly all of the studies considered so
far, either explicitly or, more often, implicitly. Yet, until recently, apart from some
notable exceptions (Batt-Rawden, 2006, 2007b; DeNora, 2000; Gouk, 2000; Pavlicevic
& Ansdell, 2004; Stige, 2003; Trythall, 2005; see also Chapter 30, this volume), music's
role as an everyday health technology outside the medical/therapeutic arena has been
little studied.

One study recently completed by Batt-Rawden (2007a) conducted repeated ethnographic interviews with 22 people suffering or in recovery from chronic illness (eight
times per respondent over a year). The project focused on how individuals were using
and could learn to use music so as to regulate their emotions in ways that helped

them manage and cope with their conditions. A wide range of 'uses' emerged from Batt-Rawden's interview data. Participants described how music helped them cope with a range of tasks, problems, and symptoms—for example, as a substitute for sleeping tablets or pain medication, as a motivational device to 'move' out of low moods or depression, as a model or exemplar of where they hoped to be, in terms of health, in the future, as a reminder of how they 'could' be or how they were when they were 'at their best', as a way of representing and working through various problems and sorrows, and as a medium through which they forestalled social isolation and connected with others.

Batt-Rawden's research was explicitly action-oriented. This is to say that she was not simply attempting to discover or observe impartially what her respondents did with music. Rather, the use of repeated interviews provided her participants with informal training, helping them to expand their repertoires of music use by talking with them about how music was and might be used so as to promote health. In this respect, she was not merely seeking data—as an interviewer—but was functioning also as a kind of conductor of health-music practice, a pedagogue in how to use music to prompt imagination and modify bodily states and thus, also, to some extent, a lay 'musical carer'. The action research feature of her study was thus devoted to eliciting and encouraging narratives about how the music 'worked'. These narratives in turn helped to frame the music, further empowering it for the task of self-healthcare via emotion management.

7.8 Music and collective action— striving and contention

Another area in which music sociology has highlighted music as a model for the constitution of emotion is social movement activity (see also Chapter 26, this volume). There scholars have sought to draw together the sociology of emotions and the sociology of collective action. Taking inspiration from anthropologist Victor Turner's (1981) concern with 'action paradigms' (i.e. cultural materials such as narratives and imagery that may be used in ways that 'emplot' courses of action), Ron Eyerman and Andrew Jamison (1998, p. 23) have attempted to specify how music may be understood to play an organizing role in the structure of collective action:

To the categories of action discussed by sociologists we wish to add the concept of exemplary action. As represented or articulated in the cognitive praxis of social movements, exemplary action can be thought of as a specification of the symbolic action discussed by Melucci and others. The exemplary action of cognitive praxis is symbolic in several senses; but it is also 'more' than merely symbolic. As real cultural representations—art, literature, songs—it is artefactual and material, as well. What we are attempting to capture with the term is the exemplary use of music and art in social movements, the various ways in which songs and singers can serve a function akin to the exemplary works that Thomas Kuhn characterized as being central to scientific revolutions: the paradigm-constituting entities that serve to realign scientific thinking and that represent ideal examples of fundamentally innovative scientific work (Kuhn 1970). The difference between culture and science, however, is that the exemplary action of music and art is lived as well as thought: it is cognitive, but it also draws on more emotive aspects of human consciousness.

As with the examples of individual feeling work discussed by DeNora (1999, 2000) and Hennion (Gomart & Hennion, 1999; Hennion & Masisonneuve, 1998), Eyerman and Jameson describe how music may serve, within the context of social movement activity, as a pre-scriptive device of agency. Within music's structures, its perceived connotations, its sensual parameters (dynamics, sound envelopes, harmonies, textures, colours, etc.), actors may 'find' or compose themselves as agents with particular capacities for social action. For example, Eyerman and Jameson (1998) describe how Todd Gitlin, a president of the Students for a Democratic Society (SDS) in the 1960s, described the SDS's identification with the music of Bob Dylan: 'We followed his career as if he were singing our song; we got in the habit of asking where he was taking us next' (p. 116). Of course, this example is anecdotal and thus primarily heuristic, since Eyerman and Jamieson were less concerned with empirically specifying the validity of the example than they were with making an innovative conceptual move in favour of music as exemplar. (Subsequent work (Bergh, 2007) has been devoted to reinvestigating retrospective accounts, controlling for the situation and time of interview and interviewer effects.) Nonetheless, Eyerman and Jamieson help us to consider what Robert Witkin (1974) calls a 'holding form'—a set of motifs that proceed, and serve as a reference point for, lines of feeling and lines of conduct over time. Viewed as such, music plays a role that is similar to that of memory artefacts, as discussed by Urry (1996) and Radley (1990): musical motifs are oriented to for the ways they encapsulate and provide a container for what might otherwise pass as momentary impulse to act, or a momentary identification of some kind. Holding forms thus provide a touchstone to which actors may return as they engage in collective expressive activity. They are the templates within which agency takes shape and to which actors may refer to renew themselves as types of agents and emotional agents.

   In recent studies of the role of applied music listening in situations of conflict resolution, the collective shaping of emotion has been highlighted, both insofar as music is employed as a common ground and thus neutral territory (Bergh, 2007, 2008) and as a means for transforming emotional dynamics between adversarial groups (Jordanger et al, 2006). This focus has also included a very sober investigation of some of the mythic powers attached to music as a sometimes assumed 'golden' force within worlds riven by conflict. Most promisingly, new work on music and conflict resolution promises to illuminate the actual conditions and mechanisms under which music affords resolution, and to distinguish between fantasy and wishful thinking on the one hand, and actual operations on the other, thus reminding us that, despite its reputation as a 'universal language', music's powers operate typically via grassroots appropriations of music, which themselves require unpacking if music is to become an effective resource in the conflict-resolution 'toolkit' (Bergh, 2007, 2008).

Seen in this light, research on collective behaviour and emotional work highlights a fundamental topic within sociology: it provides a way of exploring how social reality, and with it forms and relations of feeling, are produced in and within specific social milieux. Critical then is the issue that held Adorno and that concerns music's role in modern societies, the matter of how the aesthetic environments that come to afford agency's production are themselves produced. And so the study of consumption returns full circle to the study of production and dissemination as complementary enterprises. Especially with regard to the public spaces where agency is produced, music's role here has grown massively over the past three decades. And if music on occasion provides a device of social ordering, if—in and through its manner of appropriation—it is a potential resource against which holding forms, templates, and parameters of action and experience are forged, if it can be seen to have 'effects' upon bodies, hearts, and minds, *then* the matter of music in the social space is, as I have discussed above, an aesthetic-political matter. This is why matters of musical taste have, throughout history and across culture, often been contentious.

7.9 CONCLUSION

It seems fair to characterize music sociology as involved in two projects with regard to the emotions. The first is to produce portraits of music 'in action', that is, documentaries of actors' musical practices and of the role these practices play in the production of emotion in specific social settings, using research methods such as in-depth interviews, narrative analysis, video analysis, and participant observation that are able to capture naturally occurring data. The second is to use these ethnographic reports to generate grounded hypotheses of how music functions in social life, what it does and how it is reflexively implicated in the creation and recreation of social realms, events, and states.

With regard to this second aim, current work on music as a dynamic medium in social life has highlighted music's role as providing a structure or container for feeling, one whose specific properties contribute to the shape and quality of feeling as it is articulated and sustained within and between individuals as part of the fabrication of ongoing social existence. In short, music offers a resource for the practical constitution of entities we know as 'selves' and also for states we refer to as 'intersubjective'. It is also a resource for the prospective structuring of action and a material that actors may employ as a referent or template as they elaborate and fill in, to themselves and to others, the modes of agency and subjective stances and identities that are structure in action.

Since the first edition of this volume, music sociology has significantly advanced our understanding of how music provides conditions of emotional experience, in particular by linking the sociology of musically mediated emotion to applied contexts such as health, conflict resolution, the history of consciousness and subjectivity, and work. It is concerned with specifying these matters at the level of action where actors interact with and appropriate musical forms as part of their interactive crafting of experience in ways that lead to forms of social differentiation. It is also concerned to consider emotions as phenomena that emerge in relation to materials and environments external to the individual but acted and operated upon by individuals as part of all their activities in ways that structure their subjective experience.

Future directions will no doubt include a continued focus on affordances and on the tacit practices by which musical forms are incorporated into emotional experience, and they will push music sociology's perhaps strongest claims to ecological validity and to a focus on the collective and relational character of emotional experience. In particular, music sociology is equipped conceptually and methodologically to highlight the processes by which musical-emotional experience is crafted in interactive settings where actors and materials come together. It also highlights how emotional experience is conditioned by these settings, and by the patterns of musical production, distribution, and consumption within social worlds. There have, in the past few years, been important methodological advances for this exploration that link sociology to ecologically oriented forms of social psychology. These include experience sampling (Sloboda & O'Neill, 2001; Chapters 18 and 22, this volume), conceptual schemes for participant observation such as the musical event (DeNora, 2003), action/participatory research techniques (Batt-Rawden, 2007). These methodological advances have in turn been harnessed to areas of applied research, most notably studies in the recent areas of community music therapy and community music. Future work will no doubt drive socio-musical study of emotion further into interdisciplinary terrain, as exemplified by the chapters in this volume.

RECOMMENDED FURTHER READING

1. DeNora, T. (2003). *After Adorno: Rethinking music sociology*. Cambridge, UK: Cambridge University Press.
2. Hennion, A. (2007). Those things that hold us together: Taste and sociology. *Cultural Sociology 1*, 97–114.

REFERENCES

Acord, S. K., & DeNora, T. (2008). Culture and the arts: From art worlds to arts-in-action. *Annals of the American Academy of Political and Social Science, 619*, 223–37.

Adorno, T. W. (1967). *Prisms* (trans. S. & S. Weber). London: Neville Spearman.

Adorno, T. W. (1973). *Philosophy of modern music* (trans. W. Blomster). New York: Seabury.

Adorno, T. W. (1976). *Introduction to the sociology of music* (trans. E. B. Ashby). New York: Seabury.

Adorno T. W. (1990). On popular music. In S. Frith, & A. Goodwin (eds), *On record: Rock, pop and the written word* (pp. 301–14). London: Routledge. (Originally published 1949)

Adorno, T. W. (1999). *Sound figures.* Stanford, CA: Stanford University Press.

Anderson, R., & Sharrock, W. (1993). Can organizations afford knowledge? *Computer Supported Cooperative Work*, 1, 143–61.

Aristotle. (1980). *The politics.* Oxford: Oxford University Press.

Barbalet, J. (1998). *Emotion, social theory and social structure.* Cambridge, UK: Cambridge University Press.

Batt-Rawden. K. (2006). Music—a strategy to promote health in rehabilitation? An evaluation of participation in a 'music and health promotion project'. *International Journal of Rehabilitation Research*, 29, 171–3.

Batt-Rawden, K. (2007a). *Music and health promotion: The role and significance of music and musicking in everyday life for the long term ill.* Doctoral dissertation, University of Exeter, UK.

Batt-Rawden, K. (2007b). Music as a transfer of faith. *Journal of Research in Nursing*, 12, 87–99.

Berezin, M. (1999). *Emotions unbound: Feeling political incorporation in the new Europe.* Paper presented at special session on Emotions and Macrosociology, American Sociological Association, August 1999.

Bergh, A. (2007). I'd like to teach the world to sing: Music and conflict transformation. *Musicae Scientiae, Special Issue 2007 (Music Matters)*, 141–57.

Bergh, A. (2008). Everlasting love: The sustainability of top-down vs bottom-up approaches to music and conflict transformation. In S. Kagan & V. Kirchberg (eds), *Sustainability: A new frontier for the arts and cultures* (pp. 351–82). Bad Homburg, Germany: VAS-Verlag.

Blaxter, M. (2004). *Health: Key concepts.* Cambridge, UK: Polity.

Born, G. (1995). *Rationalizing culture: IRCAM, Boulez, and the institutionalization of the musical avant-garde.* Berkeley, CA: University of California Press.

Bourdieu, P. (1984). *Distinction: A social critique of the judgement of taste* (trans. R. Nice). Cambridge, UK: Polity Press.

Bourdieu, P. (1998). *La domination masculine.* Paris, France: Seuil.

Bowler, A. (1994). Methodological dilemmas in the sociology of art. In D. Crane (ed.), *The sociology of culture* (pp. 247–66). Oxford: Blackwell.

Bryson, B. (1996). 'Anything but heavy metal': Symbolic exclusion and musical dislikes. *American Sociological Review*, 61, 884–99.

Clark, A., & Chalmers, A. (1998). The extended mind. *Analysis*, 58, 10–23.

Clarke, E. F. (2005). *Ways of listening: An ecological approach to perception of musical meaning.* Oxford: Oxford University Press.

Cohen, S. (1993). Ethnography and popular music studies. *Popular Music*, 12, 123–38.

Collins, R. (2004). *Ritual interaction chains.* Princeton, NJ: Princeton University Press.

Collins, R. (1993). Emotional energy as the common denominator of rational choice. *Rationality and Society*, 5, 203–30.

Colombetti, G. (2008). *How language interacts with affect.* Paper presented at the Fifth Central and Eastern European Conference on Phenomenology (Corporeity and Affectivity), Prague, September 2008.

Cooley, C. H. (1983). *Human nature and the social order.* New Brunswick, NJ: Transaction. (Originally published 1902)

Crafts, S., Cavicchi, D., & Keil, C. (1993). *My music.* Hanover, NH: Wesleyan University Press.

Delamont, S., & Stephens, N. (2008). Up on the roof: the embodied habitus of disporic capoiera. *Cultural Sociology*, 2, 57–74.

DeNora, T. (1995). *Beethoven and the construction of genius: musical politics in Vienna 1792–1803.* Berkeley, CA: University of California Press.

DeNora, T. (1997). Music and erotic agency—sonic resources and social-sexual action. *Body & Society, 3,* 43–65.

DeNora, T. (1999). Music as a technology of the self. *Poetics: Journal of Empirical Research on Literature, the Media and the Arts, 26,* 1–26.

DeNora, T. (2000). *Music in everyday life.* Cambridge, UK: Cambridge University Press.

DeNora, T. (2003). *After Adorno: Rethinking music sociology.* Cambridge, UK: Cambridge University Press.

DeNora, T. (2004). Embodiment and opportunity: Performing gender in Beethoven's Vienna. In W. Weber (ed.), *The musician as entrepreneur and opportunist, 1600–1900* (pp. 185–97). Bloomington, IN: Indiana University Press.

DeNora, T. (2006). Music as agency in Beethoven's Vienna. In R. Eyerman & L. McCormick (eds), *Myth, meaning and performance: Toward a new cultural sociology of the arts* (pp. 103–20). New York: Paradigm Press.

DiMaggio, P. (1982). Cultural entrepreneurship in nineteenth-century Boston: The creation of an organizational base for high culture in America. Parts 1 and 2. *Media, Culture and Society, 4,* 35–50, 303–22.

Eyerman, R., & Jamieson, A. (1998). *Music and social movements: Mobilizing tradition in the 20th century.* Cambridge, UK: Cambridge University Press.

Featherstone, M., Hepworth, M., & Turner, B. S. (eds) (1991). *The body: Social process and cultural theory.* London: Sage.

Frith, S. (1978). *The sociology of rock.* London: Constable.

Frith, S. (1981). *Sound effects: Youth, leisure, and the politics of rock 'n' roll.* New York: Pantheon.

Garfinkel, H. (1967). *Studies in ethnomethodology.* Cambridge, UK: Polity.

Gibson, J. J. (1966). *The senses considered as perceptual systems.* Boston, MA: Houghton Mifflin.

Gomart, E., & Hennion, A. (1999). A sociology of attachment: music amateurs, drug users. In J. Law & J. Hazzart (eds), *Actor network theory and after* (pp. 220–47). Oxford: Blackwell.

Gouk, P. (ed.). (2000). *Musical healing in cultural contexts.* Aldershot, UK: Ashgate.

Green, L. (1997). *Music, gender, education.* Cambridge, UK: Cambridge University Press.

Hall, S. (1986). On postmodernism and articulation: An interview with Stuart Hall. *Journal of Communication Inquiry, 10,* 45–60.

Hall, S. (1980). Recent developments in theories of language and ideology: A critical note. In S. Hall, D. Hobson, A. Lowe, & P. Willis (eds), *Culture, media, language: Working papers in cultural studies 1972–79* (pp. 157–62). London: Hutchinson.

Hennion, A. (2007). Those things that hold us together: Taste and sociology. *Cultural Sociology, 1,* 97–114.

Hennion, A., & Maisonneuve, S. with Gomart, E. (1998). *Figures de l'amateur: Formes, objects et pratiques de l'amour de la musique aujourd'hui.* Paris: Ministere de la culture.

Heritage, J. (1984). *Garfinkel and ethnomethodology.* Cambridge, UK: Polity.

Hetherington, K. (1998). *Expressions of identity: Space, performance, politics.* London: Sage.

Hochschild, A. (1979). Emotion work, feeling rules and social structure. *American Journal of Sociology, 85,* 551–75.

Hochschild, A. (1983). *The managed heart.* Berkeley, CA: University of California Press.

Jackson, S., & Scott, S. (2007). Faking it like a woman: Towards an interpretive theorization of sexual pleasure. *Body & Society, 13,* 95–116.

Jordanger, V., Popov, A., Aas Rustad, S., & Vitvitsky, A. (2006). *The North Caucasus Dialogue Project: Report on the IPC Two Years Project 2004–6.* Retrieved from: http://buildingpeaces.org/filer/TheIPCtwoyearproject2004-2006.pdf

Lamont, M. (1992). *Money, morals, and manners.* Chicago, IL: University of Chicago Press.

Langer, S. (1942). *Philosophy in a new key.* Cambridge, MA: Harvard University Press.

Lash, S., & Urry, J. (1994). *Economies of signs and space.* London: Sage.

Law, J. (1994). *Organizing modernity.* Cambridge, UK: Polity.

Law, J., & Hassard, J. (1999). *Actor network theory and after.* Oxford: Blackwell.

Martin, P. (1995). *Sounds and society: Themes in the sociology of music.* Manchester, UK: Manchester University Press.

Mayo, E. (1933). *The human problems of an industrialized civilization.* Harvard University Graduate School of Business, USA.

Melucci, Λ. (1996a). *Challenging codes: Collective action in the information age.* Cambridge, UK: Cambridge University Press.

Melucci, A. (1996b). *The playing self: Person and meaning in the planetary society.* Cambridge, UK: Cambridge University Press.

Middleton, R. (1990). *Studying popular music.* Milton Keynes, UK: Open University Press.

Pareto, W. (1963). *Treatise on general sociology.* New York: Dover.

Pavlicevic, M., & Ansdell, G. (2004). *Community music therapy.* London: Jessica Kingsley.

Peterson, R., & Simkus, A. (1992). How musical tastes mark occupational status groups. In M. Lamont & M. Fournier (eds), *Cultivating differences: Symbolic boundaries and the making of inequality* (pp. 152–86). Chicago, IL: University of Chicago Press.

Plato (1966). *The republic* (ed. and trans. by I. A. Richards). Cambridge, UK: Cambridge Univeristy Press.

Press, A. (1994). The sociology of cultural reception: notes toward an emerging paradigm. In D. Crane (ed.), *The sociology of culture* (pp. 221–46). Oxford: Blackwell.

Radley, A. (1990). Artefacts, memory and a sense of the past. In D. Middleton & D. Edwards (eds), *Collective remembering.* London: Sage.

Radway, J. (1988). Reception study: ethnography and the problems of dispersed audiences and nomadic subjects. *Cultural Studies, 2,* 359–76.

Schutz, A. (1964). *Making music together. Collected Papers. Vol 2.* The Hague, The Netherlands: Martinus Nijhoff.

Shepherd, J., & Giles-Davies, J. (1991). Music, text and subjectivity. In *Music as social text* (pp. 174–87). Cambridge, UK: Polity Press.

Shepherd, J., & Wicke, P. (1997). *Music and cultural theory.* Cambridge, UK: Polity.

Shilling, C. (2008). *Changing bodies.* London: Sage.

Sloboda, J. A. (1999). Everyday uses of music: a preliminary study. In S.W. Yi (ed.), *Music, Mind, & Science* (pp. 354–69). Seoul: Seoul National University Press. (Reprinted in Sloboda, J. A. (2005). *Exploring the musical mind: Cognition, emotion, ability, function* (pp. 319–31). Oxford: Oxford University Press.)

Sloboda, J. A., & O'Neill, S. A. (2001). Emotions in everyday listening to music. In P. N. Juslin & J. A. Sloboda (eds), *Music and emotion: theory and research* (pp. 413–29). Oxford: Oxford University Press.

Small, C. (1998). *Musicking.* Hanover, NH: Wesleyan University Press.

Stige, B. (2003). *Elaborations towards a notion of community music therapy.* Unpublished doctoral dissertation, Faculty of Arts, University of Oslo, Norway.

Tönnies, F. (1957). *Community and society.* New York: Harper. (Originally published 1887)

Tota, A. L. (1997). *Etnografia dell'arte: Per una sociologia dei contesti artistici.* Rome, Italy: Logica University Press.

Tota, A. L. (1999). *Sociologie dell'arte: Dal museo tradizionale all'arte multimediale.* Rome, Italy: Carocci.

Trythall, S. (2005). Live music in hospitals: A new 'alternative' therapy. *Journal of the Royal Society for the Promotion of Health, 126*, 113–4.

Turner, B. S. (1984). *The body and society*. Oxford: Blackwell.

Turner, V. (1981). Social dramas and stories about them. In W. J. T. Mitchell (ed.), *On narrative* (pp. 137–64). Chicago, IL: University of Chicago Press.

Urry, J. (1996). How societies remember the past. In S. Macdonald & G. Fyfe (eds), *Theorizing museums: Representing identity and diversity in a changing world* (pp. 45–68). Oxford: Blackwell.

Wacquant, L. (2006). *Body and soul: Notebooks of an apprentice boxer*. Oxford: Oxford University Press.

Weber, M. (1958). *The rational and social foundations of music*. Carbondale, IL: Southern Illinois University Press. (Originally published 1921)

Weber, M. (1978). *Economy and society* (eds G. Roth, & C. Wittich, trans. E. Fischoff et al) Berkeley, CA: University of California Press.

Williams, S. J. (1996). The 'emotional' body. *Body & Society, 2*, 125–39.

Williams, S. J. (1998). Modernity and the emotions: Reflections on the (ir)rational. *Sociology, 32*, 747–69.

Willis, P. (1978). *Profane culture*. London: Routledge.

Witkin, R. W. (1974). *The intelligence of feeling*. London: Heineman.

Witkin, R. W. (1995). *Art and social structure*. Cambridge, UK: Polity Press.

Witkin, R. W., & DeNora, T. (1997). Aesthetic materials and aesthetic action. *Culture: The Newsletter of the American Sociological Association*, October.

Witz, A., Warhurst, C., & Nickson, D. (2003). The labour of aesthetics and the aesthetics of organization. *Organization, 10*, 33–54.

PART III

MEASUREMENT

CHAPTER 8

....

SELF-REPORT MEASURES AND MODELS

....

MARCEL ZENTNER AND TUOMAS EEROLA

8.1 INTRODUCTION

....

SCIENCE strives for objectivity. However, by their very nature, experienced emotions are subjective phenomena. This could give the impression that the topic of the current chapter—subjectively felt or perceived musical emotions—is not suited for scientific study. Undoubtedly, this is how many people feel about emotional responses to music. They are seen as diffuse reactions that differ from individual to individual, from moment to moment, and that therefore elude scientific examination. As we shall see in this chapter, psychology provides an armamentarium of self-report methods and instruments, by means of which subjectively experienced states such as emotions and moods can be assessed with some reliability (Section 8.2). These well-established self-report instruments have been consistently applied to the study of musical emotions over the last 25 years.

Self-report instruments are typically derived from a theory or model of emotion. Because measures and models of emotion are inextricably linked, the focus of the current chapter extends from measures of emotion to models of emotions and their adequacy in accounting for emotional responses to music. Specifically, as we will show in Sections 8.3 and 8.4, most instruments are derived from one of two models of emotion: the discrete (or basic) emotion theory or the dimensional model of emotion.

In these sections, we trace the progress that has been achieved in the study of music and emotion using these assessment tools. Section 8.5 raises some questions about the almost exclusive reliance on categorical and dimensional approaches to emotion in the study of music and emotion. In this section, we review emotion approaches that are more specifically designed to assess emotions to music. In Section 8.6, we examine questions of differential validity of the measurement approaches reviewed in Sections 8.3 to 8.5. In the final section (8.7), we address general problems and considerations and conclude with some general remarks about the place and value of self-report measures in the study of musical emotions. Before going into the heart of this chapter, we start by providing two important definitional clarifications and distinctions.

(a) *Emotion.* As of today, there is no agreement on what an emotion is (Frijda, 2007; Scherer, 2005). In a recent survey, 33 internationally known experts in emotion responded to a request to give a definition of an emotion. As was to be expected, there was no consensus (Izard, 2007, p. 271). Still, there is some consensus with regard to the view that emotions have more than one psychological or behavioural manifestation: in addition to subjective feeling, they also contain action tendencies, physiological arousal, cognitive appraisals, and expressive motor behaviour (Niedenthal, Krauth-Gruber, & Ric, 2006, pp. 6–8; and Chapter 4, this volume). Self-reports typically provide information about the *subjectively experienced* component of an emotion. This subjectively experienced, consciously accessible part of the emotion is usually referred to as *feeling.*

(b) *Perceived and felt emotion.* It is generally recognized that there are two types of emotional experience in relation to music. Many classical studies in the area have examined listeners' judgements of emotional characteristics of the music. In these studies, listeners were instructed to describe the music in emotional terms (e.g. this music is sad) or what the music may be expressive of (e.g. this music expresses sadness). In the current chapter, we refer to this kind of musical emotion as *perceived* emotion. More recently, investigators have become increasingly interested in examining how music makes listeners feel. We refer to the latter as *felt* emotion. This distinction is not only conceptually plausible, there is also mounting evidence to suggest these two modes of emotional responses can be empirically differentiated (e.g. Evans & Schubert, 2008; Kallinen & Ravaja, 2006; Zentner, Grandjean, & Scherer, 2008).

8.2 SPECTRUM OF SELF-REPORT METHODOLOGIES

In this section, we describe different kinds of self-report methods and instruments that have been used in the study of music and emotion, starting from closed-response formats and working our way towards the more open ones. For convenience, the types of self-report instruments are outlined in Table 8.1.

Table 8.1 Types of self-report instruments and methods

Instrument	Example
Likert Scales	Likert ratings of emotion concepts
Adjective checklist	Selection of appropriate adjectives
Visual Analogue Scales	Continuous rating scales without intermediate steps
Continuous response versions of self-report instruments	Continuous evaluations of emotion concepts using a computer interface (see Chapter 9)
Non-verbal evaluation tasks	Arrangement of emotional stimuli according to their similarity without use of verbal labels
Experience sampling method	Structured report of ongoing activities related to emotion and their causes at times prompted by a pager (e.g. cell phone)
Diary study	Detailed daily report of the central emotional episodes and their causes and effects
Free / phenomenological report / narrative method	Description of the personal experience. The actual format and focus may vary greatly (retrospective reports over a lifetime of experiences, writing about the recent important emotional episodes, etc.)

8.2.1 Standard self-report instruments

Standardized mood/emotion scales are among the most widely used self-report methods to examine perceived and felt emotion to music. Examples include the *Differential Emotion Scale* (DES, Izard et al, 1993) and the *Positive and Negative Affect Schedule* (PANAS, Watson, Clark, & Tellegen, 1988, also PANAS-X, Watson & Clark, 1994). The DES contains 30 emotion words, 3 for each of 10 basic emotions. In the PANAS-X, participants are requested to rate 60 words that characterize emotion or feeling (e.g. inspired, calm, distressed) on a response scale that includes 'very slightly', 'a little', 'moderately', 'quite a bit', and 'extremely'. The *Profile of Mood States* (POMS, McNair, Lorr, & Droppleman, 1981) is another commonly used instrument for assessing mood featuring 65 adjectives that are rated on a 5-point scale. Similar to standard Likert rating scales are adjective checklists, such as the *Activation–Deactivation Adjective Check List* (Thayer, 1986). In this method, sets of adjectives that tap the emotions of interest are presented to the participants in a scrambled order. The participants tick the terms that correspond to the emotion they feel, and the researcher computes an aggregate sum of the adjectives for each target emotion. Finally, the *Affect Intensity Measure* (AIM, Larsen & Diener, 1987) is a questionnaire that seeks to quantify the intensity of an individual's experiences of emotion. Table 8.2 provides an overview of some widely used self-report instruments in the study of music and emotion.

Table 8.2 A selection of standard mood and emotion self-report instruments

Instrument	Concepts	Reference
Activation–Deactivation Adjective Checklist	Activation	Thayer (1986)
Affect Grid	Simultaneous rating of pleasure and arousal	Russell, Weiss, & Mendelsohn (1989)
Affect Intensity Measure (AIM)	Intensity of experienced emotion	Larsen & Diener (1987)
Differential Emotion Scale (DES)	Basic emotions	Izard et al (1993)
Geneva Emotional Music Scales (GEMS)	Nine music-relevant dimensions of emotional experience	Zentner et al (2008)
Multiple Affect Checklist Revised (MAACL-R)	Positive and negative mood, sensation seeking, anxiety	Lubin et al (1986)
Positive and Negative Affect Schedule (PANAS, PANAS-X)	Joviality, self-assurance, attentiveness, etc.	Watson et al (1988)
Profile of Mood States (POMS)	Mood (positive/negative)	McNair, Lorr, & Droppleman (1981)
UWIST Mood Adjective Checklist	Energetic arousal, tense arousal, hedonic tone/displeasure-pleasure	Matthews, Jones, & Chamberlain (1990)

The intensity of perceived or experienced emotions may sometimes appear to be more continuous than is implied by discrete steps, such as 'none', 'slightly', 'moderately', and 'extremely'—especially when ratings need to be adjusted continually as in the continuous self-report methodology (see below). The *Visual Analogue Scale* (VAS) captures intensity of feeling by avoiding discrete jumps. Commonly it is a horizontal line, 100 mm in length, anchored by word descriptors at each end (e.g. 'not at all joyful', 'extremely joyful'). The subject marks the point on the line that they feel represents their perception of their current state. The VAS score is determined by measuring in millimetres from the left-hand end of the line to the point that the patient marks. Today the VAS can be easily administered in computerized form. There are also other ways in which the VAS can be presented, including vertical lines and lines with extra descriptors. Ahearn (1997) provides an informative discussion of the benefits and shortcomings of different versions of VAS.

In some cases, pictorial versions of rating scales are used to avoid semantic misunderstandings or when participants are not able to read (e.g. children). For example, the *Self-Assessment Manikin* scales (SAM, Bradley & Lang, 1994) assess experienced pleasure and arousal based on iconic images of human characters with caricatural facial expressions of affect. Alternatively, photographs or drawings of facial expressions may be used if basic emotions are studied. Examples from developmental studies of music and emotion (Dalla Bella et al, 2001; Nawrot, 2003) are shown in Figure 8.1.

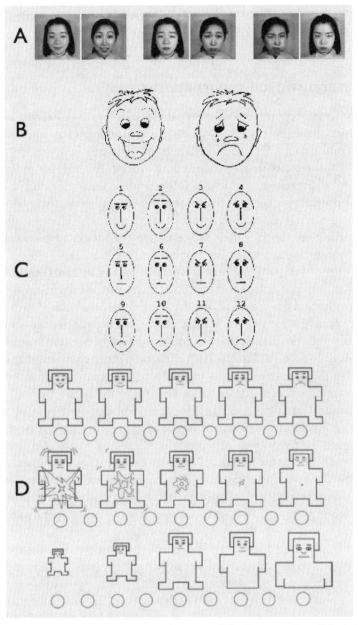

Fig. 8.1 A selection of visual response formats: (A) photographs of facial expressions representing basic emotions (happiness, sadness, and anger) from Lyons et al, 1998, (B) drawn illustrations of a happy and sad face from Dalla Bella et al, 2001, (C) stylized faces displaying variant expressions of basic emotions, including ambiguous versions of these (faces 3, 4, 5, 6, 8, and 10; see Bouhuys, Bloem, & Groothuis, 1995) and (D) The Self-Assessment Manikin (Bradley & Lang, 1994), displaying three sets of iconic images of a human representing three dimensions (pleasure, arousal, and dominance), each having a 9-point rating scale underneath the images.

In most such cases, the method of selection is called *forced choice*, as the participant has to choose one category of emotion out of the few available ones.

8.2.2 Naturalistic self-report approaches

There are other self-report methods that enable researchers to gather data in naturalistic settings and that allow situational variables and meanings of an emotional episode to be taken into account. One such method is the *experience sampling method* (ESM), in which the participants are paged at random times during the day and report their emotions and all the relevant contextual information at the moment of paging. Juslin et al (2008) provide evidence for the value of this technique to study felt emotional responses to music in everyday life. A variant of this method is known as *diary studies*, in which participants describe their daily emotion episodes in a typical diary fashion (Oatley & Duncan, 1992; in music, see Sloboda & O'Neill, 2001).

The experience-sampling method is typically used in listeners' natural environments, but conventional self-report instruments can also be used to assess emotion in music's most natural environment, the live concert performance. However, because rating more than just a few emotion words during a live performance would overtax the listeners' goodwill, one can also present a longer list of emotion terms and simply ask the auditor to scan the list quickly, to tick only those emotions that were experienced (as in the adjective checklist methodology), or indicate whether the chosen emotions were experienced somewhat or a lot (as in the Likert method). The non-chosen terms are then simply coded as o (see Zentner et al, 2008). Vaitl et al (1993) demonstrated that an emotion assessment can be brought into a performance setting by having listeners rate emotional arousal whilst listening to selected 'leitmotifs' of Wagner's operas during the Bayreuth Festival in the late 1980s. McAdams et al (2004) extended this idea by asking a large number of concert-goers ($N = 110$) to continuously rate the felt 'emotional force' (collapsing negative and positive emotions into one rating) at a concert premiere. The work in question was a contemporary composition, *The Angel of Death* by Roger Reynolds, which contained interesting textures and structural cues and was studied separately in detail by the same group (LaLitte et al, 2004). The experiment was actually carried out in two separate cities (Paris and La Jolla), where the audience responses were captured using small responses boxes specifically made for the occasion. The results from both premieres demonstrated that meaningful mean ratings of 'emotional force' were obtained, which were related to the musical structure, although much variability in the ratings was related to the levels of musical expertise of the participants.

To collect data in a live performance situation, technical considerations (e.g. over 100 easy-to-use continuous response devices) and design and instruction issues have to be dealt with. The results of both studies above suggest that self-reports may be successfully taken into realistic performance contexts, and that listeners are able to report at least one aspect of the emotional experience at a given time. The task of evaluating the emotional experience constantly throughout the performance might overtax listeners' attentional and perceptive capacities. However, these potentially emotion-attenuating circumstances might be outweighed by the emotion-enhancing power of the natural environment; that is, the visual cues from the performers and the unique sense of sharing a cultural experience with other audience members.

8.2.3 Issues of response format and language

Whereas most of the previously discussed instruments contain a predetermined selection of emotion or mood terms, it is also possible to collect free verbal responses that relate to music. The most influential use of this technique was made by Gabrielsson in his research on Strong Experiences in Music (SEM, Gabrielsson & Lindström Wik, 2003; Chapter 20, this volume). Gabrielsson and his colleagues obtained hundreds of reports in which people freely described their strongest experiences in connection with music. From a careful content analysis of these narratives (the approach is often called the 'narrative' or 'phenomenological' method) that were provided by both musicians and non-musicians, Gabrielsson and collaborators derived a set of categories that reflect the basic components of these unique musical experiences. Free descriptions of emotion-like reactions, which form the category 'emotion', show appreciable overlap with findings obtained by the use of predetermined response formats (Laukka, 2007; Zentner et al, 2008). In a different context, Juslin (1997b) collected judgements of perceived emotion by using both free and structured reports ('the parallel enrichment procedure') and found a substantial degree of overlap.

The open-ended (e.g. free descriptions, diary studies) and closed-response formats (e.g. adjective checklists, rating scales, forced-choice tasks) have different methodological and conceptual advantages and disadvantages. For purposes of discovery, to unveil the range of possible responses to music-emotional and other-open-ended formats are an indispensable tool. However, there are also some limitations to this approach. First, free descriptions are not easily amenable to systematic data treatment and analysis. Although computer programs using dictionary lookup systems can be used to score the free responses and place them into a limited list of emotion typologies, this may not turn out to be a relevant form of analysis for many questions (see Gabrielsson's SEM approach). Second, listeners may often lack interest or the necessary vocabulary to provide accurate verbalizations of their emotional experiences. This may lead to significant under-reporting.

The advantage of closed-response formats lies in the ease of quantification of the responses, provided that interval or ordinal scales have been used. However, in using a closed set of descriptors, one might miss out on important aspects of the phenomenon and merely learn more about the initial choices of words and scales. Relatedly, the predetermined choices might influence the participant to respond along the provided categories. Finally, the interpretation of the terms provided by the researcher might vary considerably across people, though this drawback is common to all methodologies relying on verbal reports. To maximize the advantages and minimize the disadvantages, one can use both approaches in combination (Juslin et al, 2008; Zentner et al, 2008).

On a more technical level, it is important to note that the type of response format may have a strong effect on participants' ratings (Schimmack et al, 2002). Symmetrical response formats are often interpreted as bipolar scales and asymmetrical as unipolar. For example, a 5-point Likert scale of happiness using a symmetric format (i.e. implied bipolarity) suggests that low ratings represent high sadness, the middle category response is neutral in terms of sadness/happiness, and the highest category denotes high happiness. If the same scale is used in terms of amount of happiness (in unipolar fashion), the lowest options indicate absence of happiness, the middle option moderate happiness, and the highest options strong happiness. This has significant consequences if the researcher wants to conclude that, for example, pleasantness and unpleasantness are mutually exclusive categories. Fortunately, most standard instruments use unipolar scales (e.g. 'How happy did you feel?' on a Likert scale range 1–5), which are less prone to interpretation errors.

It is also important to bear in mind that the terms are not easy to translate. The emotion vocabularies are known to vary across cultures, although certain emotion concepts (those, for instance, representing basic emotions) can be found in most cultures (Russell, 1991). However, the finer details of emotions in terms of their causes (appraisals) and states vary considerably (Wierzbicka, 1999). It is not only the language that might pose problems, but also cultural traditions themselves might affect self-report. However, several self-report studies of emotion recognition have been carried out across cultures that have partly replicated the findings of the American or Central European researchers in a variety of cultures (e.g. Almagor & Ben-Porath, 1989; Scherer, Banse, & Wallbott, 2001; Scherer & Wallbott, 1994).

Because of the difficulties that are sometimes involved in verbal reports of emotions, it is particularly important to point out that self-report methods do not necessarily have to use verbal labels of any kind. For example, Bigand et al (2005) asked participants to organize a set of musical examples in terms of their similarity. The results, summarized in Section 8.5 of this chapter and discussed in Section 8.8, are not dependent on any verbal descriptions. Such methods could also be taken into the context of everyday emotions by looking, for example, at the individuals' electronic playlists on a personal music device or computer, which are often organized in terms of moods.

8.2.4 Retrospective vs. real-time assessment

Another demarcation line in the self-rating methodology is whether the ratings are collected post-performance or continuously. Because this issue is extensively treated in Chapter 9, our comments will be brief. Most studies have adopted the post-performance approach, in which a single retrospective rating is provided after stimulus exposure. As we all know, music unfolds in time, and affective experiences also change as the music progresses. To capture the moment-by-moment fluctuations in the affective experience, researchers have developed continuous self-report measures. The paradigm, pioneered by Nielsen (1983), has recently been extended and refined, for example, by Schubert (see Chapter 9, this volume), who has collected valence and arousal data simultaneously, using a two-dimensional visual computer interface (see also Nagel et al, 2007, for a similar approach). Others have collected ratings for various emotional dimensions in separate sessions (Krumhansl, 1997; Luck et al, 2006). The simultaneous approach can be criticized because of the heavy cognitive load it exerts on participants.[1] Post-performance ratings are certainly simpler to collect and analyse, but these average ratings of experienced emotion are sometimes difficult to interpret. For example, the paradigm comparing ratings of pain in real time and retrospectively has shown that pain memories are best predicted by peak and end experiences, rather than by an average of all responses over time (Kahneman et al, 1993).

8.3 MEASURES AND FINDINGS RELATING TO THE BASIC EMOTION MODEL

With few exceptions, the self-report instruments just described reflect two current models of emotion: either the basic emotion theory (also referred to as discrete or categorical emotion theory) or the dimensional model of emotion (e.g. the affective circumplex). In this and the following section, we briefly characterize each model (see also Chapter 4, this volume) and describe music studies that have used the basic emotion or dimensional emotion frameworks. We will also compare studies from both traditions, describe their respective frequencies, and pinpoint their advantages and disadvantages.

Basic emotion theory posits that all emotions can be derived from a limited set of universal and innate basic emotions, which typically include fear, anger, disgust, sadness, and happiness (Ekman, 1992; Panksepp, 1998), but also may include emotions such as shame, embarrassment, contempt, and guilt (Ekman, 1999; for an overview, see Ortony & Turner, 1990). Each basic emotion category may be explained functionally in terms of goal-relevant events that have been shaped by evolution (Johnson-Laird & Oatley, 1992). Although the actual number of categories and the labels for those categories have been debated, the categorical emotion model has amassed supporting evidence from cross-cultural, developmental, neural, and physiological studies spanning four decades (e.g. Panksepp, 1992).

In studies of emotions aroused by music using self-report, about a third of the studies have utilized the categorical emotion model, mirroring its popularity in the psychology of emotion (Table 8.3). The popularity in music may stem from the fact

---

[1] For example, when M.Z. and his colleagues in Geneva created an interface for the continuous measurement of music-induced emotion in the late 1990s, they first provided a computerized emotion wheel that featured several domains of emotion at once. The listeners' task was to 'navigate' this multiple emotion map according to changes in feeling tone. However, participants were overwhelmed by the requested 'quadruple-tasking'—listening, monitoring feeling, choosing among several emotion categories, and moving the mouse to the appropriate place. From this experience, we believe that continuous measurement of emotion should ideally be reduced to ratings of one emotion at a time.

Table 8.3 Summary of methodological and conceptual approaches to music and emotions in journal articles during the last two decades[2]

	No. of studies (F/P)[a]	Example studies (Felt)	Example studies (Perceived)
Methodological approach			
Self-report	89 (32/58)	Gfeller et al (1991), Juslin & Laukka (2004), Konečni et al (2008)	Juslin (1997b), Schubert (2003), Ritossa & Rickard (2004)
Neurological	26 (11/8)	Blood & Zatorre (2001), Koelsch et al (2006)	Peretz et al (2001), Gosselin et al (2005)
Theoretical	19 (7/2)	London (2001), Sloboda (2001), Scherer (2004)	Scherer (1995)
Physiological	24 (17/3)	Krumhansl (1997), Gomez & Danuser (2004), Witvliet & Vrana (2007)	Khalfa et al (2008b)
Individual differences	16 (5/7)	Kallinen & Ravaja (2004), Nater et al (2006)	Rawlings & Leow (2008)
Clinical	12 (1/10)	Khalfa et al (2008a)	Nielzen et al (1993), Dellacherie et al (2008)
Developmental	6 (–/6)		Terwogt & Van Grinsven (1991), Dalla Bella et al (2001), Nawrot (2003)
Conceptualization of emotions			
Dimensional	61 (28/33)	McFarland & Kennison (1989), Leman et al (2005), Grewe et al (2007)	Gagnon & Peretz (2000), Ilie & Thompson (2006)
Categorical	50 (13/34)	Krumhansl (1997), Kreutz et al (2002), Baumgartner et al (2006)	Juslin (1997a), Resnicow et al (2004), Kallinen (2005)
Other (intensity, tension, etc.)	31 (13/14)	Thaut & Davis (1993), Bigand et al (2005)	Brittin & Duke (1997), Frego (1999)
Domain-specific	11 (3/8)	Dibben (2004), Zentner et al (2008)	Gfeller et al (1991), Bartel (1992)

[a] F = focus on felt emotions, P = focus on perceived emotions (both may be indicated by a single study or, in some cases, the focus cannot be reliably assessed from the report).

[2] The frequential summary provided in Table 8.3 is based on an analysis of studies published since 1985 in refereed journals or proceedings (excluding book chapters). A total of 160 papers were annotated in terms of the approach, conceptual framework for emotions, and whether the emphasis was clearly on perceived or felt emotions. The individual-differences approach includes studies relating to personality and expertise that moderate music-induced emotions. The *dimensional* framework for emotions includes all studies that employ valence, arousal/activity, or another clearly dimensional concept. Studies within the *categorical* framework for emotions include variants of the basic emotions, even if only a limited number of categories have been used (e.g. happy and sad).

that categories lend themselves easily to be used in recognition paradigms, common in developmental studies (e.g. Adachi & Trehub, 1998; Dalla Bella et al, 2001; Nawrot, 2003) and in production-recognition studies (e.g. Gabrielsson & Juslin, 1996; Juslin, 1997a; Laukka & Gabrielsson, 2000). Similarly, when unique response profiles to music-induced emotions are sought, emotion categories are favoured both in physiological (e.g. Baumgartner et al, 2006; Etzel et al, 2006; Gomez & Danuser, 2004) and neurological studies (e.g. Gosselin et al, 2005; Peretz et al, 1998). Sometimes, traditional emotion categories have been modified by replacing musically inappropriate categories such as disgust and surprise with more fitting categories such as tenderness or peacefulness (e.g. Balkwill & Thompson, 1999; Gabrielsson & Juslin, 1996; Vieillard et al, 2007).

The ratings of emotion categories can be gathered by asking listeners to choose between the emotion categories ('forced-choice paradigm', e.g. Kallinen, 2005), using photographs of facial expressions from Ekman's studies (Ekman & Friesen, 1975) or using drawings of faces intended for children (Dalla Bella et al, 2001, see Figure 8.1). A more common approach is to invite listeners to rate how much the music evokes or expresses each emotion category (e.g. Dibben, 2004; Juslin, 2000; Resnicow et al, 2004). Although a continuum between certain emotion categories, such as happy and sad, has also been rated using a single scale ranging from happy to sad (e.g. Dalla Bella et al, 2001; Gagnon & Peretz, 2003), the strength of the categorical self-report paradigm is that it may provide insights regarding complex emotional processes such as 'conflicting emotions', for instance music simultaneously evoking happy and sad emotion (Hunter et al, 2008).

Studies from the discrete emotion tradition have more often focused on perceived emotions (production-recognition and developmental studies) than on felt emotions, although the physiological studies have naturally emphasized the latter. For instance, a landmark study by Krumhansl (1997) explored to what degree various physiological (including cardiac, vascular, electrodermal, and respiratory) measures could discriminate emotional responses between two musical excerpts representing sad, fear, and happy categories (six excerpts in total). In the first part of the experiment, a pool of participants rated the four target emotions using continuous ratings (10 participants per emotion). They also rated each excerpt in terms of 13 adjective scales (angry, afraid, amused, anxious, contemptuous, contented, disgusted, embarrassed, happy, interested, relieved, sad, and surprised) to establish that the chosen musical excerpts conveyed the appointed emotions. In the second part of the study, 38 new participants were fitted with the measurement devices and listened to the excerpts with appropriate silence conditions. The time-series values obtained from the continuous ratings correlated significantly—but weakly—with several physiological measures from the second group of participants.

The *other* framework includes emotional intensity, preference, similarity, tension, or some other construct related to affect in general. The *domain-specific* framework refers to studies that employ the emotion model specifically constructed for music. As a portion of studies utilizes several approaches and frameworks and concentrates on both felt and perceived emotions, these studies contribute to several categories in the table.

The main focus of the study, however, was to discriminate the physiological reactions during the excerpts from each other and from the baseline measures using averaged data. This discrimination was largely successful, and the largest changes in all physiological measures occurred during the sad excerpts, whilst the happy excerpts mainly displayed changes in the respiration measures.

However, these category-specific physiological signatures were not identical to the ones obtained in emotion research in general, although certain similarities have been observed in the results obtained with suppressed emotions (Gross & Levenson, 1993). When compared with the physiological findings of other music-related studies (Etzel et al, 2006; Rickard, 2004; Chapter 11, this volume) the pattern is still fragmentary. This leads to a more critical issue regarding the categorical view of emotions in general, namely the claim that the categories are innate, reflex-like modules that involve unique behavioural, neural, and physiological patterns (e.g. Panksepp, 1998). Although a wealth of evidence has been accumulated about the specificities of the physiological signature concerning basic emotions (reviewed in Levenson, 2003), the debate has been fuelled by the lack of consistent evidence over a range of measures (see critical meta-analyses in Barrett & Wager, 2006; Cacioppo, Berntson, Larsen, Poehlmann, & Ito, 2000). Also, the disagreement about the exact number and labelling of emotion categories suggests that these may be based on linguistic and cultural taxonomies, rather than on emotions themselves. We will next look at the alternative, which avoids categorization by outlining various dimensions that characterize emotional experiences.

8.4 MEASURES AND FINDINGS RELATING TO DIMENSIONAL EMOTION MODELS

The main alternative to categorical models is a dimensional approach, most notably the *circumplex model* (Russell, 1980; Figure 4.1 in Chapter 4, this volume). This model proposes that emotions represent a mixture of two core dimensions, *valence* and *arousal*, representing pleasure–displeasure and activation–deactivation continuums that are orthogonally situated in the affective space. This model has received support in large studies of self-reported emotions (e.g. Barrett & Russell, 1999), cross-cultural comparison (Russell, 1983), and psychometric studies (reviewed in Posner et al, 2005), and has thus been used in a large number of emotion studies in psychology.

Influential variants of the two-dimensional models have also been offered. Watson and Tellegen (1985) rotated the circumplex model by 45° relative to valence and arousal, thus obtaining a *Positive Affective* (PA) dimension, which combines positive valence and high arousal, and a *Negative Affective* (NA) dimension, which combines negative valence and high arousal (later known as Positive and Negative Affect Schedule, PANAS, Watson et al, 1988). Thayer (1989) reorganized the arousal dimension into *energetic arousal* (EA) and *tense arousal* (TA) on the basis of separate psychobiological

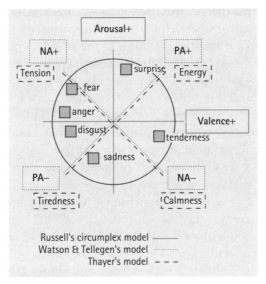

Fig. 8.2 Integrated illustration of two-dimensional models of emotions with the most common basic emotions attached.

systems that are responsible for energy (readiness for vigorous action) and tension (preparatory-emergency system). These main formulations of the affective circumplex are visualized in Figure 8.2.

If the categorical model was the focus of attention in about a third of the music and emotion studies during the last two decades (see Table 8.3), valence–arousal has been the subject of another third of the studies (e.g. Gomez & Danuser, 2004; Schubert, 1999; Witvliet & Vrana, 2007). Typically in these studies, participants are asked to rate valence and arousal independently on bipolar scales (negative valence to positive valence and low arousal to high arousal). On a theoretical basis, unipolar intensity scales (e.g. from 'not at all' to 'maximum' in arousal) may be preferred, because the opposite ends of the dimensions might theoretically be independent of each other (Watson & Tellegen, 1999). However, such constructs have rarely been used in music-related research, and even then have been converted into bipolar scales without adverse effects on the data (Ilie & Thompson, 2006). In addition, the emotion categories are occasionally implicitly present in self-report studies using dimensional rating scales, either in terms of of stimuli that represent basic emotion categories (e.g. Gosselin, Peretz, Johnsen, & Adolphs, 2007), or because the veritable terminology used in the rating scales has explicitly referred to discrete emotion terms, for instance specifying the bipolar extreme of valence as happy (e.g. Baumgartner et al, 2006).

Many of the studies using valence and arousal have concluded that the two-dimensional model is not able to account for all the variance in music-mediated emotions (Bigand et al, 2005; Collier, 2007; Ilie & Thompson, 2006; Leman et al, 2005; Nyklicek, Thayer, & Van Doornen, 1997). Indeed, emotion research in general has noted that the two-dimensional models place emotions commonly regarded as distant in close proximity in the affective space; for instance, anger and fear are both negatively valenced and highly active (Scherer, Johnstone, & Klasmeyer, 2003).

The other drawback is that the alignment of the axes does not necessarily correspond with the underlying physiological system that is driving the affective experience, although Thayer's (1989) (re)formulation is clearly an attempt to capture this. Three approaches to overcome this problem have been offered. The first is to simply add a dimension to the model, the second is to postulate a hybrid theory combining both dimensions and emotion categories (Christie & Friedman, 2004; Russell, 2003), and the third is to represent emotion categories as prototypes that vary in their typicality (Fehr & Russell, 1984; see Chapter 4, this volume). In music and emotion research, several additional dimensions have been proposed over the years (potency, intensity, dominance, solemnity, interest; see Gabrielsson & Juslin, 2003; Leman et al, 2005).

Perhaps the most convincing *three-dimensional model* has been obtained by combining Russell's circumplex model with Thayer's variant. The resulting model with *valence, energy arousal,* and *tension arousal* dimensions has received support in reanalyses of affect data (Schimmack & Grob, 2000; Schimmack & Rainer, 2002), which have demonstrated that three dimensions cannot be reduced onto a two-dimensional space. The underlying reason is that the two activation dimensions are related to different physiological systems (Watson, Wiese, Vaidya, & Tellegen, 1999), which can be separately manipulated. For example, a study on the influence of experimentally induced hypoglycaemia showed that energetic arousal and tense arousal could change in opposite directions (Gold, Deary, MacLeod, Thompson, & Frier, 1995). In music, this model has not yet been fully employed (Eerola & Vuoskoski, 2009; Ilie & Thompson, 2006), but it is tempting because of its emphasis on tension, a particularly appropriate concept for music, which has generated a great deal of empirical and theoretical attention even without the possible link with emotions (Lerdahl & Krumhansl, 2007).

The categorical and dimensional models can coexist by postulating that the core affects and the underlying mechanism are best described by a dimensional model, but the conscious interpretation of these is categorical and influenced by the conceptual categories people have for emotions. This scheme, illustrated in Figure 8.3 and known as the Conceptual Act Model (Barrett, 2006), provides an attractive compromise between the two positions. Moreover, this notion might offer insights into possible music-specific emotions by making the distinction between affect mechanisms and culturally influenced interpretations.

Because issues of verbalization are a matter of concern in verbal reports of emotion, studies without any references to emotion categories or dimensions are especially interesting in this respect if they provide consistent findings with existing models without any verbal labels. Bigand et al (2005) used free and pair-wise similarity rating tasks to arrange 27 musical examples according to their perceived emotional similarity, where the participants (both musicians and non-musicians) were asked to focus on their own emotional experiences. The resulting distances could be mapped into a three-dimensional space in which the X-axis corresponded roughly to valence and the Y-axis to arousal. The first two axes also correlated highly with independently obtained

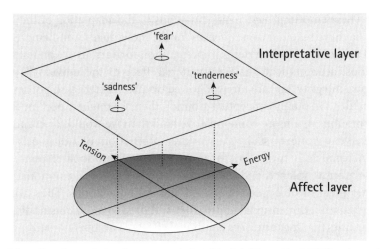

Fig. 8.3 Visualization of the Conceptual Act Model (Barrett, 2006), where the core affect level is shown at the bottom, and the conscious, labelled, interpretation at the top.

ratings of arousal and valence for these same excerpts. The Z-axis could not be fully explained, although the authors suggest connections to gestures and body postures.

Vieillard et al (2007) have obtained similar results with 56 specifically composed music excerpts using an emotion-similarity rating task. Interestingly, the resulting mapping could not be easily explained in terms of orthogonal valence and arousal dimensions, but rather was best explained in terms of tension and energy dimensions (resembling Thayer's formulation of the two-dimensional model).

8.5 MEASURES AND FINDINGS RELATING TO DOMAIN-SPECIFIC APPROACHES

By relying almost exclusively on measures from categorical and dimensional models of emotion, researchers apply instruments from non-musical areas of emotion research to the study of musical emotions. This practice capitalizes on the assumption that musical emotions and other emotions are identical. Though emotions elicited in music and non-musical contexts do overlap to a certain degree, it is nonetheless important to emphasize that general models of emotion were not devised to capture musical emotions.

Specifically, discrete or basic emotion theory focuses on a small set of evolutionary continuous emotions, in particular anger, fear, happiness, sadness, disgust, shame, and guilt. These emotions have major functions in the adaptation of the individual to events that have material consequences for the individual's well-being. Such emotions tend to mobilize body systems in preparation for various action tendencies. In contrast, musical events do not have any material effects on the individual's physical or psychological integrity, and are rarely followed by direct, external responses of a goal-oriented nature. On purely conceptual grounds, then, we might expect musical events to evoke emotions of a more contemplative kind than we would for events in extra-musical everyday contexts, such as an insult, a promotion, or a diagnosis of cancer. Dimensional models, in turn, allow for an assessment of emotional responses to music in terms of arousal, valence, and tension gradations. However, emotional responses to any other event or object can be parsed into such gradations. Thus, while all are descriptively useful, dimensional approaches add little to an understanding of those emotive qualities that make music's emotional effects so uniquely rewarding.

The general notion that emotions generated by music may have special characteristics compared with day-to-day emotions, or with emotions generated by other arts, attracted several nineteenth-century scholars. In *The Power of Sound*, Gurney (1880) stated, 'The prime characteristic of Music, the alpha and omega of its essential effect [is] its perpetual production in us of an excitement of a very intense kind, which yet cannot be defined under any known head of emotion' (p. 120). An influential attempt to develop a domain-specific classification of emotions was undertaken by Hevner (1936). She developed the *adjective clock*, a circle consisting of eight clusters with 6–11 supposedly acquainted adjectives in each cluster (see Chapter 14, this volume). It was called a clock because adjacent clusters were supposed to deviate slightly by cumulative steps until reaching a contrast in the opposite position, for instance, Cluster A 'happiness' versus Cluster F 'sadness' (see Figure 8.4 with an updated version of the Hevner circle from Schubert, 2003).

In the following decades, several authors (e.g. Campbell, 1942; Farnsworth, 1954; Watson, 1942) further elaborated this taxonomy. However, in his 1964 review article, Rigg noted that 'discrepancies in the use of terms are not sufficiently serious to prevent a comparison of the results of various research workers' (p. 429) and that 'to those who may view this field as one capable of yielding only nebulous results, it may come as a surprise to find general agreement' (p. 429). This amounted to a judgement in defence of Hevner's original conception.

In the early seventies, Wedin (1972) proposed that emotions to music can be accounted for by three bipolar emotion factors: 'gaiety versus gloom', 'tension versus relaxation', and 'solemnity versus triviality'. The possibility that musically induced emotions might be poorly captured by canonical emotion labels has prompted a few researchers to rely on emotional descriptors that seem musically more plausible (e.g. Batel, 1976). Although these approaches may be more valid phenomenologically, they have been eclectic in nature, with the choice of emotion labels depending on the authors' particular views of musically induced emotions, rather than on a systematic, empirically founded taxonomy of music-relevant emotion terms (Scherer, 2004).

Drawing on the work summarized by Rigg (1964), Asmus (1985) first compiled a list of music-relevant affect terms. After applying factorial analyses to the felt emotion

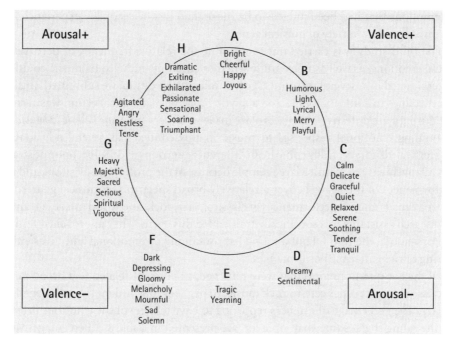

Fig. 8.4 Representation of Hevner's adjective clock (with updated terminology from Schubert, 2003).

ratings of three excerpts of music, he concluded that musical feelings could be described along nine dimensions of affect. In the subsequent two decades, attempts to develop comprehensive taxonomies of music-induced emotion faded, and were replaced by investigations focusing on more specific aspects of emotional responses to music, such as 'thrills' (e.g. Guhn, Hamm, & Zentner, 2007; Konečni, Wanic, & Brown, 2007; Panksepp, 1995), strong experiences with music (Gabrielsson, 2001, 2006), and uses of music in everyday life (Juslin & Laukka, 2004; Laukka, 2007; Sloboda & O'Neill, 2001).

Previous research on the characterization and classification of emotions induced or expressed by music had little impact on subsequent attempts to study musically induced emotions, as a result of several limitations. Among these limitations were a failure to distinguish felt from perceived emotion, vague criteria for selection of affect terms, lack of methodological rigour, and the absence of contextualization of the musical emotions within the broader context of emotion research. In a recent study, Zentner, Grandjean, and Scherer (2008) reconsidered a domain-specific approach to musical emotions by (a) trying to avoid some of the conceptual or methodological pitfalls that undermined the validity of previous domain-specific models and (b) contextualizing their findings on musically induced emotions within other current models of emotion. Four interrelated studies were carried out for this purpose. The initial two studies were devoted to a compilation of music-relevant emotion terms. This work led to a list of

66 emotions that had been judged to be more than just occasionally experienced or perceived across a variety of musical genres.

The third study was carried out to examine the relative frequency of occurrence of the emotions, as well as to examine whether emotions induced by music could be differentiated into several sub-units. To examine this question, we submitted musical affect ratings to confirmatory factor-analytic procedures. Data collection was carried out during a music festival that takes place in Geneva every June, *the Fête de la Musique*. Examining emotional responses to music in this context has several advantages. The festival visitors typically come from different age groups and socioeconomic strata, it is relatively easy to recruit a large sample because of the profusion of visitors, and the performances of the festival cover a relatively broad spectrum of musical genres. To cover a broad range of performances of classical, jazz, rock, and world music, a team of 10 research assistants was specifically trained for this event. They approached festival visitors, asking them to fill out a rating list containing 66 emotional adjectives either during or right after the performances.

Of the 801 questionnaires that were returned, 72 per cent related to a broad range of classical music, 11 per cent to rock music, 10 per cent to world music, and 7 per cent to jazz. The percentage of listeners reporting to have felt any of the emotions printed on the rating sheet 'somewhat' or 'a lot' are presented in Table 8.4. Percentages were calculated for the entire sample and for each genre of music separately. Because classical music was over-represented as a result of the festival's emphasis on classical music, we used the average across the five within-genre percentages as a criterion for elimination. The relative frequencies of reported emotions in the music festival study are of note, because they closely match the reports of felt emotions from two Swedish samples of adults (Juslin & Laukka, 2004) and elderly people (Laukka, 2007; see also Chapter 22, this volume). Specifically, feeling moved, nostalgic, relaxed, enchanted, and tender were all among the most frequently reported emotions. 'Admiring', a frequently reported state in the Swedish studies, was the term most often added in the free-response spaces of the current study. These consistencies across studies are noteworthy considering the differences in samples of listeners, in music-listening contexts, and most likely also in music excerpts.

The second aim of this study was to take a closer look at the structure underlying ratings of musical affect. On the basis of a series of confirmatory factor analyses, the authors found that a model featuring nine emotion factors best fitted the data. The nine categories with the respective marker terms are reproduced in Table 8.5. This model presents some distinctive features in comparison with mainstream emotion models, such as the basic emotion model. In contrast to the latter, most of its emotions are positive. Furthermore, the domain-specific model contains emotion categories such as wonder, nostalgia, and transcendence, which are not a central part of any current model of emotion. Although some of the current emotion components seem similar to emotion components from other emotion models, similarities in the general factor labels may obscure subtle differences in meaning. For instance, we found

Table 8.4 Percentage of listeners that reported having felt each affect state somewhat or a lot

Affective state	% Yes	Affective state	% Yes
Relaxed	44.6	Spiritual feeling	15.3
Happy	41.5	Affectionate	13.8
Joyful	39.0	Exciting	13.7
Dreamy	37.1	Feeling of transcendence	13.7
Stimulated	35.4	Mellowed	12.4
Dancing (bouncy)	33.5	Disinhibited	12.3
Enchanted	32.8	Caressing	12.0
Nostalgic	32.1	Shivers (thrills)	11.2
Allured	31.0	Electrified	11.2
Touched	30.9	Agitated	10.6
Free	30.7	Fiery	10.4
Calm	28.0	Sad	10.2
Sentimental	27.5	Triumphant	10.1
Energetic	27.4	Voluptuous	9.6
Filled with wonder	26.5	Goose bumps	9.1
Amused	23.6	Solemn	8.3
Passionate	23.4	Languorous	7.8
Animated	22.6	Heroic	7.2
Melancholic	22.5	Impatient	6.8
Light	22.5	Serious	6.6
Moved	21.9	Irritated	6.6
Inspired	21.6	Proud	6.4
Dazzled	21.3	Revolted	6.3
Serene	21.3	Annoyed	6.2
Tender	19.8	Nervous	5.5
Euphoric	19.7	Tense	5.2
Meditative	18.4	Bittersweet	4.7
Floating	18.3	Indifferent	4.6
Sweet	18.2	Aggressive	4.2
Soothed	17.8	Anxious	3.4
In love	17.8	Sorrowful	3.4
Sensual	17.5	Depressed	2.7
Strong	15.3	Angry	2.4

Adapted from Zentner et al, 2008 (Table 2)

Table 8.5 The Geneva Emotional Music Scales (GEMS), derived from confirmatory factor analyses of ratings of emotions evoked by various genres of music

Musical emotion factors with characteristic feeling terms
Wonder
Filled with wonder, amazed, allured, dazzled, admiring, moved
Transcendence
Inspired, feeling of transcendence, feeling of spirituality, overwhelmed, thrills
Tenderness
In love, sensual, affectionate, tender, mellowed
Nostalgia
Nostalgic, melancholic, dreamy, sentimental
Peacefulness
Calm, relaxed, serene, soothed, meditative
Power
Energetic, triumphant, fiery, strong, heroic
Joyful activation
Stimulated, joyful, animated, feel like dancing, amused
Tension
Agitated, nervous, tense, impatient, irritated
Sadness
Sad, sorrowful (blue)

Adapted from Zentner et al, 2008 (Appendix A)[3]

that musically induced joy implies an action tendency to dance, which is unlike the common meaning of joy. Similarly, 'musical' sadness may not be quite the same as the basic emotion sadness, because aversive aspects of sadness, such as feeling gloomy, depressed, or unhappy, were only very rarely reported in response to music (see also Laukka, 2007).

Although the previous considerations offer an explanation for the relative scarcity of negative emotional responses and the presence of refined positive emotional responses to music, they do not account for the specific kinds of positive emotions identified in the current research. One possibility relates to the functions of music in both daily life and evolutionary history. One of the striking findings across studies in this area is the

---

[3] The full, short, and ultra-short versions of the GEMS (GEMS-45, GEMS-25, GEMS-9) are available from the first author on request.

prominence that nostalgia occupies in the spectrum of music-induced feelings. This puzzling finding can be better understood in light of the functions that music serves in daily life. For example, one of the most frequently mentioned functions of music in daily life is as a reminder of a valued past event (Sloboda & O'Neill, 2001; North, Hargreaves, & Hargreaves, 2004). These findings not only suggest a link between functions of music and music-related emotion, but they also point to the mediating roles of memory and imagery in musical emotion induction (e.g. Juslin & Västfjäll, 2008; Konečni et al, 2008).

Also prominent in the list of musically induced emotions is love, especially as it appears in two different, though complementary, ways. Whereas the tenderness component in our classification relates to feelings of love, affection, and tenderness, wonder relates to the arresting qualities of music: feeling enchanted, charmed, dazzled, or amazed. Although largely ignored in today's research on music and emotion, the wonder-related feelings are perhaps the most potent emotions generated by music, the most rewarding ones, those that 'hook' people to music. It is therefore not surprising that, when music made its first appearance in Western literature 2,800 years ago, its effects were primarily described in terms of their potential for seduction. As will be remembered, in the *Odyssey* seamen who sailed near the Sirens were lured by their ravishing music and voices to shipwreck on the rocky coasts in the vicinity of the Isle of Capri. Only by having his sailors plug their ears with beeswax and tying him to the mast could Ulysses and his sailors resist the musical temptations of the Sirens.

Feelings of attraction and seduction were also central to Darwin's (1871) evolutionary views on the emotions induced by music. In *The Descent of Man*, Darwin observed that the sounds that some species produce during the mating season seem musical in that they resemble short melodic phrases or songs. Whereas the 'distal' function is the propagation of the species, Darwin proposed that the 'proximal' function of these musical vocal utterances is to call, charm, and excite the opposite sex (1871, p. 880). Current evolutionary theories of the origins of musically induced passions have expanded these views, including the notion that emotive vocal utterances were also used to express triumph over mating rivals and as a means of territorial defence. Hence, the emergence of a power factor in the current model could also be related to evolutionary mechanisms. Although these views are speculative and unlikely to provide a complete answer to the kinds of emotions felt in response to music, they attract increasing interest and may ultimately provide valuable insights regarding the differentiation of musically induced emotion (e.g. Levitin, 2006; Miller, 2000; Vitouch & Ladinig, 2009).

Awe, though an emotion that is sometimes cited in the context of music and other arts (e.g. Haidt & Keltner, 2003; Konečni, 2005), seems to be lacking in the current classification. However, this absence may simply be due to the lack of a French term for awe (as the present study was carried out in a francophone city). In substantive terms, transcendence (e.g. feeling overwhelmed, inspired) and wonder (e.g. feeling moved, admiring) seem both related to the English awe. Of interest is that the current musical emotion factors do not include a direct equivalent for happiness in a general sense. Rather, musically induced happiness either takes the form of bliss or enchantment—as in wonder—or takes the form of joy combined with a curious, yet universal 'affordance' of music, its tendency to trigger movement—as in joyful activation (see Zentner & Eerola, 2009).

Peacefulness and tension turned out to be further important classificatory units of musically induced affect. Peacefulness and relaxation seem an obvious affective consequence of the prototypical mental state of the music listener—one in which there is a certain detachment from the 'real' world with its physical and psychological threats. The calming effects of music on emotional as well as physiological arousal have been put to use since the Middle Ages. In Fez, Morocco, an asylum for the mentally ill had been built in the thirteenth century, and musico-therapy figured prominently among the various treatments. Today, there is growing research evidence for the usefulness of music as a relaxant in medical settings (see Chapters 29 and 30, this volume).

The factor tension lends itself to two possible interpretations. In the influential writings by Meyer (1956), surprise, tension, and relief were the principal musical emotions, because harmonic, rhythmic, and melodic progressions create expectations that are fulfilled or violated (see Huron, 2006, and Chapter 21, this volume, for modern elaborations). However, like other researchers (Juslin & Laukka, 2004; Laukka, 2007), we did not find surprise to be among the more common musical emotions. This inconsistency may be linked to a listener's musical expertise. Thus, an unexpected shift in tonal key or melody, while evoking surprise in a music expert, may induce a thrill or a delightful sense of amazement in the non-expert auditor.

A second meaning of tension relates to irritation. We believe that in rare cases, irritation or anger can be driven by the inherent properties of music, for example, when it contains an inordinate amount of successive sharp, unresolved dissonances. Although Arnold Schönberg (1984) believed dissonance aversion to be a pure product of acculturation, it has been observed in young infants and it is probably universal (e.g. Masataka, 2006; Zentner & Kagan, 1996). However, more typically, irritation and anger arise when people are exposed to music they dislike, fail to understand, or even abhor. A good case in point is heavy metal music, which is generally thought of as a prototyp'e of aggression-inducing music. However, heavy metal music does not evoke anger in people who identify with it; only listeners who do not like heavy metal show elevated levels of anger when listening to it (Gowensmith & Bloom, 1997).

The general absence of fear in the spectrum of musically induced emotions will surprise some readers. However, when people refer to the fear-inducing capacities of music, they usually think of soundtracks in thrillers. Because in the thriller or horror movie, the content of the narrative and the music are hopelessly confounded, it is impossible to know whether the music acts as producer, as amplifier, or as neither. In addition, the wide diffusion of sounds accompanying thrillers may easily have led to fearful reactions occurring, not because of the sounds themselves, but because of a learned association. Hence, although fear and anger reactions to music may occasionally be driven by the inherent qualities of the music, more typically these emotions may arise from conditioning (fear) and from violation of certain tastes or attitudes (anger).

8.6 WHICH EMOTION MODEL ACCOUNTS BEST FOR EMOTIONAL RESPONSES TO MUSIC?

In their study, Zentner et al (2008) also compared the differential validity of their nine-dimensional framework vis-à-vis the basic emotion and dimensional emotion models discussed in Sections 8.3 and 8.4 of this chapter. To evaluate comparative validity, they used three criteria: (a) whether listeners would choose emotion terms provided by the domain-specific model, the basic emotion, or the dimensional emotion model most often when describing their affective reactions to music; (b) whether the domain-specific model would provide higher agreement across listeners than the other two models; and (c) whether ratings based on the domain-specific model would provide a sharper discrimination of music excerpts than ratings based on the other two models.

To examine these questions, Zentner et al asked listeners to rate emotions induced by experimenter-selected music excerpts at the university and by additional, but freely chosen, music excerpts at their homes. Participants received a rating form, labelled the 'comparative emotion model checklist', representing the basic emotion model, the dimensional model, and the domain-specific model (GEMS). Overall, listeners clearly preferred to describe what they felt with the terms representative of GEMS, rather than the terms representative of the discrete or the dimensional model. Second, the GEMS tended to enhance agreement across listeners in ratings of music excerpts relative to the checklists of the two alternative models. Finally, the most powerful discrimination of musical excerpts was obtained from the ratings of emotion terms provided by the GEMS (Zentner et al, 2008).

Although these findings appear to recommend the domain-specific model as a model of choice in the study of music-evoked emotions, some caveats have to be kept in mind. The Geneva study was about the feeling terms characteristic of each model, rather than about the models in toto. Thus, an appropriately cautious conclusion is that the clusters of interrelated feeling attributes characterizing the domain-specific model have greater relevance to music than do the emotion components characteristic of the alternative models tested. Furthermore, the authors also addressed the question of whether the better performance of the domain-specific model generalized to the case of *perceived* musical emotion. Comparing the fit of the musical emotion model and the basic emotion model to ratings of induced and perceived emotion, they found that the musical emotion model performed better for ratings of induced emotions than perceived emotion. Conversely, the basic emotion model performed better in the case of ratings of perceived compared to induced emotions. Thus, although the findings suggested that terms derived from the basic emotion and dimensional models do not account well for musically induced emotions, they also suggested that this outcome may not generalize to perceived emotions. One possible explanation for this outcome is that music may express emotions by symbolically mimicking a broad range of human expressive behaviour, including negative behaviours. However, the perceptions of negative emotional characteristics do not readily translate into felt negative emotion, because the listener in most music-listening contexts is safely removed from threats, dangers, or the possibility of losses. Still, Collier (2007) found that accounting for perceived emotions in music also requires multiple dimensions that clearly go beyond those of the dimensional models reviewed earlier. Thus, what kind of model provides the best fit for perceived musical emotions remains unclear.

8.7 PROBLEMS AND CONSIDERATIONS IN THE USE OF SELF-REPORT

Before concluding, it is important to take a look at the place, value, and limitations of self-report measures in the study of musical emotions more generally. There are four important limitations to self-report methodology, though not all of them are equally relevant when it comes to assessing emotions to music: (a) demand characteristics, (b) self-presentation biases, (c) limited awareness of one's emotions, and (d) difficulties in the verbalization of emotion perception or experience (see also Chapter 10, this volume). *Demand characteristics* are cues that convey the experimental hypothesis to the subject and therefore may induce hypothesis-consistent behaviour. There are several practices that can be used to reduce the effects of demand characteristics, such as the use of a 'cover story' that conceals the purpose of the experiment.

Self-presentation biases refer to individuals' tendency to feel uneasy about reporting states that may be seen as undesirable. This is clearly a problem when individuals are asked about matters that relate to issues of self-esteem and social desirability. Although most felt or perceived emotions in music are unlikely to fall into this class of socially undesirable states, cultural differences due to language and customary norms in expressing appropriate emotions may sometimes present a problem in verbal reports of emotions to music.

Limitations in the awareness of one's emotions are a potential problem in the study of emotion, including emotions to music. However, if one is primarily interested in the study of *feeling*, which is by definition the *subjectively experienced component of an emotion*, that is, the consciously accessible part of the emotion, the problem does not arise. Rather, what is at stake is the value of self-reported feelings in the study of emotions more generally. Indeed, many investigators believe that, to be informative or even interpretable, self-report data must be 'backed' by other emotion-relevant information, such as behavioural, physiological, or cognitive evidence. This belief is due to the widespread notion that it is the combined elicitation of various emotion components that represents the true signature of an emotion.

One serious problem with the idea of specific components (e.g. cognitive appraisals, feelings, physiological arousal, action tendencies, and expressive motor behaviour) being coordinated, or even synchronized, during an emotion is that coherence in various emotion components may be the exception rather than the rule (Niedenthal et al, 2006). Because emotion components are not activated simultaneously in many cases, one is left to wonder which component should be relied upon when deciding on the presence (or absence) of an emotion. An alternative to the notion of synchronization is to look at the various emotion components being elicited by different objects or events (Ellsworth & Scherer, 2003). In the case of musical events, and aesthetic events more generally, feeling may well be the most obvious emotion component to study.

For an appreciation of this view, it is useful to return to the distinction between 'coarse' and 'refined' emotions, introduced by William James and recently particularized by Frijda and Sundararajan (2007). Refined emotions are typically elicited in situations where individuals suspend goals whose violation or achievement would be critical to their physical or psychological integrity. Thus, when individuals find themselves in a state of mind that is detached from pragmatic, self-related concerns, emotions lose their urgency, but may nonetheless retain their inner structure and action tendencies. Refined emotions 'are more felt than acted upon and thus do not obviously manifest themselves in overt behaviours like attack, embrace, or flight; may not show pronounced physiological upset; are often about complex events or subtle event aspects; and are not done justice by common emotion labels' (Frijda & Sundararajan, 2007, p. 227). To the extent that these kinds of states are experienced in aesthetic contexts, we suggest a distinction between *aesthetic* and *utilitarian* emotions (Scherer & Zentner, 2008; Zentner et al, 2008). Thus, it makes no sense to downplay the emotional significance of music-induced feelings, should these feelings fail to be consistently followed by those overt actions or physiological patterning that is characteristic of coarse or utilitarian emotions, such as basic emotions.

Difficulties in the verbalization of musical emotions represent the most serious limitation of verbal reports. Clearly, our emotional responses to music may sometimes be difficult, and occasionally impossible, to verbalize (Chapter 20, this volume). It needs to be acknowledged that verbal reports of feeling are, at best, approximations or circumscriptions of the inner experience of a listener; they are not direct mirror images of this experience. This limitation of self-report methods is beyond doubt, but it also needs to be put in perspective.

First of all, verbal reports and self-reports are not the same thing. As mentioned in Section 8.2, participants can make similarity judgements of music without using any verbal label. Consider an experiment in which the stimulus material consists of 20 excerpts of music, of which 5 have been previously found to induce verbally reported nostalgia, 5 joy, 5 tenderness, and 5 peacefulness. Participants can be required to listen to all the pieces and then to group those that evoked similar emotional experiences together. Cluster analysis or multi-dimensional scaling can be used to examine whether the non-verbal groupings fit the original classification based on verbal reports. Such methodology could also be applied to data obtained in naturally occurring environments, for example, by looking at individuals' electronic playlists on their personal music devices, which are often organized in terms of their emotional effects. This procedure, which offers the possibility to cross-validate verbal classifications of emotional music with non-verbal ones, should be used more frequently in the future.

A second issue is that, although verbal formulations of experienced feelings are mere circumscriptions, the latter can be more or less accurate. Indeed, individuals differ in their capacity to describe their own emotional experiences (Barrett, 2004). While at one end we may have someone with little interest in music, a limited capacity for introspection, and a limited working vocabulary, at the other end we may have a highly perceptive writer with a complete mastery of language and a lifelong passion for music. The former may be lost when it comes to verbalizing emotional effects of music, whereas the latter may produce extremely accurate verbal descriptions of such effects. Thomas Mann's characterizations of Beethoven's last piano sonata in *Doktor Faustus*, which contain several references to emotion, have earned him lasting admiration because of the precision with which he characterized a musical experience (Schiff, 2006). No less impressive are Marcel Proust's circumscriptions of musical experiences, such as this beautiful characterization of music-evoked wonder:

'But then at a certain moment, without being able to distinguish any clear outline, or to give a name to what was pleasing him, suddenly enraptured, he had tried to grasp the phrase or harmony—he did not know which—that had just been played and that had opened and expanded his soul, as the fragrance of certain roses, wafted upon the moist air of evening, has the power of dilating one's nostrils' (Proust, 1913/1996, p, 250).

The main point here is that the rich and complex emotions evoked by music can be captured only by a commensurately rich and complex emotion vocabulary. The aim of the GEMS is to provide such a vocabulary.

Third, verbal self-reports of musical emotions have their limitations, but do other methods offer better alternatives? Emotions that belong to James's 'coarse' category, such as anger in response to an insult or fear in an encounter with a thief at night, are revealed through channels other than the experiential one, such as facial expressions, action tendencies, and physiological upset. But because emotional responses to music are not usually followed by overt expressions or actions, the subjective experiential dimension will often be the only one activated. Therefore, a systematic study of self-reported felt or perceived emotion is a viable method to map out the territory of musical emotions in our view. Once this has been achieved, a more detailed understanding of music-generated emotions will almost certainly be achieved by using additional measures.

Consider nostalgia, an emotion whose importance to music would probably never have been discovered without cumulative evidence from self-report data. Because nostalgia typically involves memories of past events, an obvious question of interest here is whether brain areas related to mnemonic activity, such as the hippocampus, are being activated during musically induced nostalgia (Juslin & Västfjäll, 2008). We consider these questions, which are treated in more detail in Chapters 11 and 12 of this volume, of great importance. As a consequence, we are both currently involved in collaborations with neuroscientists, hoping to identify some of the neurobiological correlates of musical emotions (e.g. Trost, Zentner, & Vuillmeumier, 2009). What remains tricky in our view is that, at the moment, it is much easier to obtain a fine-grained differentiation of musical emotions at the experiential level than at the neurobiological level. The day that a neuroscientist can confidently tell whether a listener experienced a brief period of amazement, a momentary surge of tenderness, or a pang of nostalgia, just by looking at the listener's brain activation profiles, may not be very near (Kagan, 2009).

A final critique, most typically voiced by musicians, is that music possesses a power that goes beyond words. Thus, attempts to understand musical experiences by the means of language are doomed to failure. In his most recent book, Daniel Barenboim declares at the outset: 'I firmly believe that it is impossible to speak about music' (Barenboim, 2008, p. 5). One of us (M.Z.) vividly remembers a televised interview with the great twentieth-century conductor Sergiu Celibidache, in which he proclaimed that the term 'music' as such should be abolished. Thus, whenever his interviewer nonetheless used the word music by mistake or habit, the maestro would scold him for not respecting his veto of the word.

The notion that words should not be used to describe music is somewhat reminiscent of the ban on creating pictorial images of Jesus in the heyday of Byzantine iconoclasm. For iconoclasts, the only real religious image had to be an exact likeness of the prototype, which they considered impossible. But such a view, which is comparable to the rejection of words as means of 'depicting' music and its meanings, confounds the value of the subjective experience with the value of its objectification through a process of rational inquiry. There can be little doubt that the primordial affective experience of music can neither be replaced nor fully captured by words. However, thinking about this experience and achieving an understanding of it, as partial as they might remain, are possible. And they are important as documented in the current book and other publications on the enhancing effects of music (Zentner, 2009). In the end, the purpose of science is not to replace the unique subjective experience of the world's natural and cultural phenomena. Rather, it is to describe, understand, and explain such phenomena by an array of methods and procedures that include equations, models, and verbal statements. To criticize researchers because their concepts of music cannot render the unique experience of listening to a piece of music is a bit like criticizing physicists because their formulas for the sun's declination are strangely removed from the experience of a beautiful sunset.

RECOMMENDED FURTHER READING

1. Bigand, E., Vieillard, S., Madurell, F., Marozeau, J., & Dacquet, A. (2005). Multidimensional scaling of emotional responses to music: The effect of musical expertise and of the duration of the excerpts. *Cognition & Emotion, 19,* 1113–39.
2. Juslin, P. N., Liljeström, S., Västfjäll, D., Barradas, G., & Silva, A. (2008). An experience sampling study of emotional reactions to music: Listener, music, and situation. *Emotion, 8,* 668–83.
3. Zentner, M. R., Grandjean, D., & Scherer, K. R. (2008). Emotions evoked by the sound of music: Characterization, classification, and measurement. *Emotion, 8,* 494–521.

References

Adachi, M., & Trehub, S. E. (1998). Children's expression of emotion in song. *Psychology of Music, 26,* 133–53.

Ahearn, E. (1997). The use of visual analog scales in mood disorders: A critical review. *Journal of Psychiatric Research, 31,* 569–79.

Almagor, M., & Ben-Porath, Y. S. (1989). The two-factor model of self-reported mood: A cross-cultural replication. *Journal of Personality Assessment, 53,* 10–21.

Asmus, E. (1985). The development of a multidimensional instrument for the measurement of affective responses to music. *Psychology of Music, 13,* 19–30.

Balkwill, L.-L., & Thompson, W. F. (1999). A cross-cultural investigation of the perception of emotion in music: psychophysical and cultural cues. *Music Perception, 17,* 43–64.

Barrett, L. F. (2004). Feelings or words? Understanding the content in self-report ratings of experienced emotion. *Journal of Personality and Social Psychology, 87,* 266–81.

Barrett, L. F. (2006). Emotions as natural kinds? *Perspectives on Psychological Science, 1,* 28–58.

Barrett, L. F., & Russell, J. A. (1999). Structure of current affect. *Current Directions in Psychological Science, 8,* 10–14.

Barrett, L. F., & Wager, T. (2006). The structure of emotion: Evidence from the neuroimaging of emotion. *Current Directions in Psychological Science, 15,* 79–85.

Bartel, L. R. (1992). The development of the cognitive-affective response test-music. *Psychomusicology, 11,* 15–26.

Batel, G. (1976). *Komponenten musikalischen Erlebens. Eine experimentalpsychologische Untersuchung.* [Components of musical experience: An experimental investigation]. Göttingen, Germany: Göttinger Musikwissenschaftliche Arbeiten.

Baumgartner, T., Esslen, M., & Jancke, L. (2006). From emotion perception to emotion experience: Emotions evoked by pictures and classical music. *International Journal of Psychophysiology, 60,* 34–43.

Bigand, E., Vieillard, S., Madurell, F., Marozeau, J., & Dacquet, A. (2005). Multidimensional scaling of emotional responses to music: The effect of musical expertise and of the duration of the excerpts. *Cognition & Emotion, 19,* 1113–39.

Blood, A. J., & Zatorre, R. J. (2001). Intensely pleasurable responses to music correlate with activity in brain regions implicated in reward and emotion. *Proceedings of the National Academy of Sciences, 98,* 11818–23.

Bouhuys, A. L., Bloem, G. M., & Groothuis, T. G. G. (1995). Induction of depressed and elated mood by music influences the perception of facial emotional expressions in healthy subjects. *Journal of Affective Disorders, 33,* 215–26.

Bradley, M. M., & Lang, P. J. (1994), Measuring emotion: The self-assessment manikin and the semantic differential. *Journal of Behavioral Therapy and Experimental Psychiatry, 25,* 49–59.

Brittin, R. V., & Duke, R. A. (1997). Continuous versus summative evaluations of musical intensity: A comparison of two methods for measuring overall effect. *Journal of Research in Music Education, 45,* 245–58.

Cacioppo, J. T., Berntson, G. G., Larsen, J. T., Poehlmann, K. M., & Ito, T. A. (2000). The psychophysiology of emotion. In R. Lewis & J. M. Haviland-Jones (eds), *The handbook of emotion* (2nd edn, p. 173–91). New York: Guilford Press.

Campbell, I. G. (1942). Basal emotional patterns expressible in music. *American Journal of Psychology, 55,* 1–17.

Christie, I. C., & Friedman, B. H. (2004). Autonomic specificity of discrete emotion and dimensions of affective space: a multivariate approach. *International Journal of Psychophysiology, 51,* 143–53.

Collier, G. L. (2007). Beyond valence and activity in the emotional connotations of music. *Psychology of Music, 35*, 110–31.

Dalla Bella, S., Peretz, I., Rousseau, L., & Gosselin, N. (2001). A developmental study of the affective value of tempo and mode in music. *Cognition, 80*, B1–10.

Darwin, C. (1871). *The descent of man, and selection in relation to sex (2 vols.)*. London: John Murray.

Dellacherie, D., Ehrlé, N., & Samson, S. (2008). Is the neutral condition relevant to study musical emotion in patients? *Music Perception, 25*, 285–94.

Dibben, N. (2004). The role of peripheral feedback in emotional experience with music. *Music Perception, 22*, 79–115.

Eerola, T., & Vuoskoski, J. (in press). A comparison of the discrete and dimensional models of emotion in music. *Psychology of Music.*

Ekman, P. (1992). An argument for basic emotions. *Cognition & Emotion, 6*, 169–200.

Ekman, P. (1999). Basic emotions. In T. Dalgleish & M. J. Power (eds), *Handbook of cognition and emotion* (p. 301–20). New York: John Wiley.

Ekman, P., & Friesen, W. V. (1975). *Unmasking the face: A guide to recognizing emotions from facial expressions.* Englewood Cliffs, NJ: Prentice-Hall.

Ellsworth, P. C., & Scherer, K. R. (2003). Appraisal processes in emotion. In R. J. Davidson, K. R. Scherer, & H. H. Goldsmith (eds), *Handbook of affective sciences* (pp. 572–95). Oxford: Oxford University Press.

Etzel, J. A., Johnsen, E. L., Dickerson, J., Tranel, D., & Adolphs, R. (2006). Cardiovascular and respiratory responses during musical mood induction. *International Journal of Psychophysiology, 61*, 57–69.

Evans, P., & Schubert, E. (2008). Relationships between expressed and felt emotions in music. *Musicae Scientiae, 12*, 75–99.

Farnsworth, P. R. (1954). A study of the Hevner adjective list. *Journal of Aesthetics and Art Criticism, 13*, 97–103.

Fehr, B., & Russell, J. A. (1984). Concept of emotion viewed from a prototype perspective. *Journal of Experimental Psychology: General, 113*, 464–86.

Frego, R. J. D. (1999). Effects of aural and visual conditions on response to perceived artistic tension in music and dance. *Journal of Research in Music Education, 47*, 31–43.

Frijda, N. H. (2007). What might an emotion be? Comments on the comments. *Social Science Information, 46*, 433–43.

Frijda, N. H., & Sundararajan, L. (2007). Emotion refinement: A theory inspired by Chinese poetics. *Perspectives on Psychological Science, 2*, 227–41.

Gabrielsson, A. (1973). Adjective ratings and dimension analysis of auditory rhythm patterns. *Scandinavian Journal of Psychology, 14*, 244–60.

Gabrielsson, A. (2001). Emotions in strong experiences with music. In P. N. Juslin & J. A. Sloboda (eds), *Music and emotion: Theory and research* (pp. 431–49). Oxford: Oxford University Press.

Gabrielsson, A. (2002). Emotion perceived and emotion felt. *Musicae Scientiae, Special issue 2001–2002*, 123–47.

Gabrielsson, A. (2006). Strong experiences elicited by music—What music? In P. Locher, C. Martindale, & L. Dorfman (eds), *New directions in aesthetics, creativity, and the arts* (pp. 251–67). New York: Baywood Press.

Gabrielsson, A., & Juslin, P. N. (1996). Emotional expression in music performance: Between the performer's intention and the listener's experience. *Psychology of Music, 24*, 68–91.

Gabrielsson, A., & Juslin, P. N. (2003). Emotional expression in music. In R. J. Davidson, K. R. Scherer, & H. H. Goldsmith (eds), *Handbook of affective sciences* (pp. 503–534). Oxford: Oxford University Press.

Gabrielsson, A., & Lindström Wik, S. (2003). Strong experiences related to music: A descriptive system. *Musicae Scientiae, 7,* 157–217.

Gagnon, L., & Peretz, I. (2000). Laterality effects in processing tonal and atonal melodies with affective and nonaffective task instructions. *Brain Cognition, 43,* 206–10.

Gagnon, L., & Peretz, I. (2003). Mode and tempo relative contributions to 'happy-sad' judgments in equitone melodies. *Cognition & Emotion, 17,* 25–40.

Gfeller, K., Asmus, E. P., & Eckert, M. (1991). An investigation of emotional response to music and text. *Psychology of Music, 19,* 128–41.

Gold, A., Deary, I., MacLeod, K., Thomson, K., & Frier, B. (1995). Cognitive function during insulin-induced hypoglycemia in humans: short-term cerebral adaptation does not occur. *Psychopharmacology, 119,* 325–33.

Gomez, P., & Danuser, B. (2004). Affective and physiological responses to environmental noises and music. *International Journal of Psychophysiology, 53,* 91–103.

Gosselin, N., Peretz, I., Johnsen, E., & Adolphs, R. (2007). Amygdala damage impairs emotion recognition from music. *Neuropsychologia, 45,* 236–44.

Gosselin, N., Peretz, I., Noulhiane, M., Hasboun, D., Beckett, C., Baulac, M., & Samson, S. (2005). Impaired recognition of scary music following unilateral temporal lobe excision. *Brain, 128,* 628–40.

Gowensmith, W. N., & Bloom, L. J. (1997). The effects of heavy metal music on arousal and anger. *Journal of Music Therapy, 1,* 33–45.

Grewe, O., Nagel, F., Kopiez, R., & Altenmüller, E. (2007). Emotions over time: synchronicity and development of subjective, physiological, and facial affective reactions to music. *Emotion, 7,* 774–88.

Gross, J. J., & Levenson, R. W. (1993). Emotion suppression: Physiological, self-report, and expressive behavior. *Journal of Personality and Social Psychology, 64,* 970–86.

Guhn, M., Hamm, A., & Zentner, M. R. (2007). Physiological and musico-acoustic correlates of the chill response. *Music Perception, 24,* 473–83.

Gurney, E. (1880). *The power of sound.* London: Smith, Elder & Co.

Haidt, J., & Keltner, D. (2003). Approaching awe, a moral, spiritual, and aesthetic emotion. *Cognition & Emotion, 17,* 297–314.

Hevner, K. (1936). Experimental studies of the elements of expression in music. *American Journal of Psychology, 48,* 248–68.

Hunter, P. G., Schellenberg, E. G., & Schimmack, U. (2008). Mixed affective responses to music with conflicting cues. *Cognition & Emotion, 22,* 327.

Huron, D. (2006). *Sweet anticipation. Music and the psychology of expectation.* Cambridge, MA: MIT Press.

Ilie, G., & Thompson, W. F. (2006). A comparison of acoustic cues in music and speech for three dimensions of affect. *Music Perception, 23,* 319–29.

Izard, C. E. (2007). Basic emotions, natural kinds, emotion schemas, and a new paradigm. *Perspectives on Psychological Science, 2,* 260–80.

Izard, C. E., Libero, D., Putnam, P., & Haynes, O. (1993). Stability of emotion experiences and their relations to personality traits. *Journal of Personality and Social Psychology, 64,* 847–60.

Johnson-Laird, P. N., & Oatley, K. (1992). Basic emotions, rationality, and folk theory. *Cognition & Emotion, 6,* 201–23.

Juslin, P. N. (1997a). Emotional communication in music performance: A functionalist perspective and some data. *Music Perception, 14,* 383–418.

Juslin, P. N. (1997b). Can results from studies of perceived expression in musical performances be generalized across response formats? *Psychomusicology, 16,* 77–101.

Juslin, P. N. (2000). Cue utilization in communication of emotion in music performance: relating performance to perception. *Journal of Experimental Psychology: Human Perception and Performance, 26,* 1797–1813.

Juslin, P. N., & Laukka, P. (2004). Expression, perception, and induction of musical emotions: A review and a questionnaire study of everyday listening. *Journal of New Music Research, 33,* 217–38.

Juslin, P. N., Liljeström, S., Västfjäll, D., Barradas, G., & Silva, A. (2008). An experience sampling study of emotional reactions to music: Listener, music, and situation. *Emotion, 8,* 668–83.

Juslin, P. N., & Västfjäll, D. (2008). Emotional responses to music: The need to consider underlying mechanisms. *Behavioral and Brain Sciences, 31,* 559–75.

Kagan, J. (2009). *The three cultures. Natural sciences, social sciences, and the humanities in the 21st century.* Cambridge, UK: Cambridge University Press.

Kahneman, D., Fredrickson, D. L., Schreiber, C. A., & Redelmeier, D. A. (1993). When more pain is preferred to less: Adding a better end. *Psychological Science, 4,* 401–5.

Kallinen, K. (2005). Emotional ratings of music excerpts in the western art music repertoire and their self-organization in the Kohonen neural network. *Psychology of Music, 33,* 373–93.

Kallinen, K., & Ravaja, N. (2004). Emotion-related effects of speech rate and rising vs. falling background music melody during audio news: the moderating influence of personality. *Personality and Individual Differences, 37,* 275–88.

Kallinen, K., & Ravaja, N. (2006). Emotion perceived and emotion felt: Same and different. *Musicae Scientiae, 10,* 191–213.

Khalfa, S., Delbe, C., Bigand, E., Reynaud, E., Chauvel, P., & Liégeois-Chauvel, C. (2008a). Positive and negative music recognition reveals a specialization of mesio-temporal structures in epileptic patients. *Music Perception, 25,* 295–302.

Khalfa, S., Roy, M., Rainville, P., Dalla Bella, S., & Peretz, I. (2008b). Role of tempo entrainment in psychophysiological differentiation of happy and sad music? *International Journal of Psychophysiology, 68,* 17–26.

Koelsch, S., Fritz, T., von Cramon, D. Y., Muller, K., & Friederici, A. D. (2006). Investigating emotion with music: an FMRI study. *Human Brain Mapping, 27,* 239–50.

Konečni, V. J. (2005). The aesthetic trinity: Awe, being moved, thrills. *Bulletin of Psychology and the Arts, 5,* 27–44.

Konečni, V. J., Brown, A., & Wanic, R. A. (2008). Comparative effects of music and recalled life events on emotional state. *Psychology of Music, 3,* 1–20.

Konečni, V. J., Wanic, R. A., & Brown, A. (2007). Emotional and aesthetic antecedents and consequences of music-induced thrills. *American Journal of Psychology, 120,* 619–44.

Kreutz, G., Bongard, S., & Von Jussis, J. (2002). Cardiovascular responses to music listening: The effects of musical expertise and emotional expression. *Musicae Scientiae, 6,* 257–78.

Krumhansl, C. L. (1997). An exploratory study of musical emotions and psychophysiology. *Canadian Journal of Experimental Psychology, 51,* 336–52.

Lalitte, P., Bigand, E., Poulin-Charronnat, B., McAdams, S., Delbe, C., & D'Adamo, D. (2004). The perceptual structure of thematic materials in The Angel of Death. *Music Perception, 22,* 265–96.

Larsen, R. J., & Diener, E. (1987). Affect intensity as an individual difference characteristic: A review. *Journal of Research in Personality, 21,* 1–39.

Laukka, P. (2007). Uses of music and psychological well-being among the elderly. *Journal of Happiness Studies, 8,* 215–41.

Laukka, P., & Gabrielsson, A. (2000). Emotional expression in drumming performance. *Psychology of Music, 28,* 181–9.

Leman, M., Vermeulen, V., De Voogdt, L., Moelants, D., & Lesaffre, M. (2005). Prediction of musical affect using a combination of acoustic structural cues. *Journal of New Music Research*, *34*, 39–67.

Lerdahl, F., & Krumhansl, C. L. (2007). Modeling tonal tension. *Music Perception*, *24*, 329–66.

Levenson, R. W. (2003). Autonomic specificity and emotion. In R. J. Davidson, K. R. Scherer, & H. H. Goldsmith (eds), *Handbook of affective sciences* (pp. 212–24). Oxford: Oxford University Press.

Levitin, D. (2006). *This is your brain on music. The science of an obsession*. New York: Dutton/Penguin.

London, J. (2002). Some theories of emotion in music and their implications for research in music psychology. *Musicae Scientiae, Special Issue 2001–2002*, 23–36.

Lubin, B., Zuckerman, M., Hanson, P., Armstrong, T., Rink, C., & Seever, M. (1986). Reliability and validity of the Multiple Affect Adjective Check List-Revised. *Journal of Psychopathology and Behavioral Assessment*, *8*, 103–17.

Luck, G., Riikkilä, K., Lartillot, O., Erkkilä, J., Toiviainen, P., Mäkelä, A., et al (2006). Exploring relationships between level of mental retardation and features of music therapy improvisations: A computational approach. *Nordic Journal of Music Therapy*, *15*, 30–48.

Lyons, M. J., Akamatsu, S., Kamachi, M., & Gyoba, J. (1998). Coding facial expressions with gabor wavelets. In *Proceedings of the Third IEEE International Conference on Automatic Face and Gesture Recognition, April 1998* (pp. 200–5). Nara, Japan: IEEE Computer Society.

Masataka, N. (2006). Preference for consonance and dissonance by hearing newborns of deaf parents and of hearing parents. *Developmental Science*, *9*, 46–50.

Matthews, G., Jones, D. M., & Chamberlain, A. G. (1990), Refining the measurement of mood: the UWIST Mood Adjective Checklist. *British Journal of Psychology*, *81*, 17–42.

McAdams, S., Vines, B., Vieillard, S., Smith, B., & Reynolds, R. (2004). Influences of large-scale form on continuous ratings in response to a contemporary piece in a live concert setting. *Music Perception*, *22*, 297–350.

McFarland, R. A., & Kennison, R. (1989). Handedness affects emotional valence asymmetry. *Perceptual and Motor Skills*, *68*, 435–41.

McNair, D. M., Lorr, M., & Droppleman, L. F. (1981). *Manual for the profile of mood states*. San Diego, CA: Educational and Industrial Testing Service.

Meyer, L. B. (1956). *Emotion and meaning in music*. Chicago, IL: Chicago University Press.

Miller, G. (2000). Evolution of human music through sexual selection. In N. L. Wallin, B. Merker, & S. Brown (eds), *The origins of music* (pp. 329–60). Cambridge, MA: MIT Press.

Nagel, F., Kopiez, R., Grewe, O., & Altenmüller, E. (2007). EMuJoy: Software for the continous measurement of perceived emotion in music. *Behavior Research Methods*, *39*, 283–90.

Nater, U. M., Abbruzzese, E., Krebs, M., & Ehlert, U. (2006). Sex differences in emotional and psychophysiological responses to musical stimuli. *International Journal of Psychophysiology*, *62*, 300–8.

Nawrot, E. S. (2003). The perception of emotional expression in music: Evidence from infants, children and adults. *Psychology of Music*, *31*, 75–92.

Niedenthal, P. M., Krauth-Gruber, S., & Ric, F. (2006). *Psychology of emotion. Interpersonal, experiential, and cognitive approaches*. New York: Psychology Press.

Nielsen, F. V. (1983). *Oplevelse af musikask spanding (experience of musical tension)*. Copenhagen, Denmark: Akademisk Forlag.

Nielzén, S., Olsson, O., & Öhman, R. (1993). On perception of complex sound in schizophrenia and mania. *Psychopathology*, *26*, 13–23.

North, A. C., Hargreaves, D. J., & Hargreaves, J. J. (2004) Uses of music in everyday life. *Music Perception*, *22*, 41–77.

Nyklícek, I., Thayer, J. F., & Van Doornen, L. J. P. (1997). Cardiorespiratory differentiation of musically-induced emotions. *Journal of Psychophysiology*, 11, 304–21.

Oatley, K., & Duncan, E. (1992). Incidents of emotion in daily life. *International Review of Studies on Emotion*, 2, 249–93.

Ortony, A., & Turner, T. J. (1990). What's basic about basic emotions? *Psychological Review*, 97, 315–31.

Panksepp, J. (1992). A critical role for 'affective neuroscience' in resolving what is basic about basic emotions. *Psychological Review*, 99, 554–60.

Panksepp, J. (1995). The emotional sources of 'chills' induced by music. *Music Perception*, 13, 171–207.

Panksepp, J. (1998). *Affective neuroscience: the foundations of human and animal emotions*. Oxford: Oxford University Press.

Peretz, I., Blood, A. J., Penhune, V., & Zatorre, R. (2001). Cortical deafness to dissonance. *Brain*, 124, 928–40.

Peretz, I., Gagnon, L., & Bouchard, B. (1998). Music and emotion: perceptual determinants, immediacy, and isolation after brain damage. *Cognition*, 68, 111–41.

Posner, J., Russell, J. A., & Peterson, B. S. (2005). The circumplex model of affect: An integrative approach to affective neuroscience, cognitive development, and psychopathology. *Development and Psychopathology*, 17, 715–34.

Proust, M. (1996). *In search of lost time: Vol. 1. Swann's way* (S. Moncrieff & T. Kilmartin, trans). London: Vintage Books. (Original work published 1913 by Grasset).

Rawlings, D., & Leow, S. H. (2008). Investigating the role of psychoticism and sensation seeking in predicting emotional reactions to music. *Psychology of Music*, 36, 269–87.

Resnicow, J. E., Salovey, P., & Repp, B. H. (2004). Is recognition of emotion in music performance an aspect of emotional intelligence? *Music Perception*, 22, 145–58.

Rickard, N. (2004). Intense emotional responses to music: a test of the physiological arousal hypothesis. *Psychology of Music*, 32, 371–88.

Rigg, M. G. (1964). The mood effects of music: A comparison of data from earlier investigations. *Journal of Psychology*, 58, 427–38.

Ritossa, D. A., & Rickard, N. S. (2004). The relative utility of 'pleasantness' and 'liking' dimensions in predicting the emotions expressed by music. *Psychology of Music*, 32, 5–22.

Russell, J. A. (1980). A circumplex model of affect. *Journal of Personality and Social Psychology*, 39, 1161–78.

Russell, J. A. (1983). Pancultural aspects of human conceptual organization of emotions. *Journal of Personality and Social Psychology*, 45, 1281–8.

Russell, J. A. (1991). Culture and the categorization of emotions. *Psychological Bulletin*, 110, 426–50.

Russell, J. A. (2003). Core affect and the psychological construction of emotion. *Psychological Review*, 110, 145–72.

Russell, J., Weiss, A., & Mendelsohn, G. (1989). Affect grid: A single-item scale of pleasure and arousal. *Journal of Personality and Social Psychology*, 57, 493–502.

Scherer, K. R. (1995). Expression of emotion in voice and music. *Journal of Voice*, 9, 235–48.

Scherer, K. R. (2004). Which emotions can be induced by music? What are the underlying mechanisms? And how can we measure them? *Journal of New Music Research*, 33, 239–51.

Scherer, K. R. (2005). What are emotions? And how can they be measured? *Social Science Information*, 44, 693–727.

Scherer, K. R., Banse, R., & Wallbott, H. (2001). Emotion inferences from vocal expression correlate across languages and cultures. *Journal of Cross-Cultural Psychology*, 32, 76–92.

Scherer, K. R., Johnstone, T., & Klasmeyer, G. (2003). Vocal expression of emotion. In R. J. Davidson, K. R. Scherer, & H. H. Goldsmith (eds), *Handbook of affective sciences* (pp 433–56). Oxford: Oxford University Press.

Scherer, K. R., & Wallbott, H. G. (1994). Evidence for universality and cultural variation of differential emotion response patterning. *Journal of Personality and Social Psychology, 66,* 310–28.

Scherer, K. R., & Zentner, M. R. (2008). Music evoked emotions are different—more often aesthetic than utilitarian. *Behavioral and Brain Sciences, 31,* 595–6.

Schiff, A. (2006). Lectures-recitals on the 32 Beethoven piano sonatas at Wigmore Hall. *The Guardian online* [http://music.guardian.co.uk/classical/page/0,,1943867,00.html].

Schimmack, U., Bockenholt, U., & Reisenzein, R. (2002). Response styles in affect ratings: Making a mountain out of a molehill. *Journal of Personality Assessment, 78,* 461–83.

Schimmack, U., & Grob, A. (2000). Dimensional models of core affect: A quantitative comparison by means of structural equation modeling. *European Journal of Personality, 14,* 325–45.

Schimmack, U., & Rainer, R. (2002). Experiencing activation: Energetic arousal and tense arousal are not mixtures of valence and activation. *Emotion, 2,* 412–17.

Schönberg, A. (1984). *Style and idea.* Berkeley, CA: University of California Press.

Schubert, E. (1999). Measuring emotion continuously: Validity and reliability of the two-dimensional emotion-space. *Australian Journal of Psychology, 51,* 154–65.

Schubert, E. (2003). Update of Hevner's adjective checklist. *Perceptual and Motor Skills, 96,* 1117–22.

Sloboda, J. A. (2002). The 'sound of music' versus the 'essence of music': Dilemmas for music-emotion researchers: Commentary. *Musicae Scientiae, Special Issue 2001–2,* 237–55.

Sloboda, J. A., & O'Neill, S. A. (2001). Emotions in everyday listening to music. In P. N. Juslin & J. A. Sloboda (eds), *Music and emotion: Theory and research* (pp. 415–30). Oxford: Oxford University Press.

Terwogt, M. M., & Van Grinsven, F. (1991). Musical expression of moodstates. *Psychology of Music, 19,* 99–109.

Thaut, M. H., & Davis, W. B. (1993). The influence of subject-selected versus experimenter-chosen music on affect, anxiety, and relaxation. *Journal of Music Therapy, 30,* 210–23.

Thayer, R. (1986). Activation-Deactivation Adjective Check List: Current overview and structural analysis. *Psychological Reports, 58,* 607–14.

Thayer, R. E. (1989). *The biopsychology of mood and arousal.* Oxford: Oxford University Press.

Trost, W., Zentner, M. R., & Vuilleumier, P. (2009). *The neural correlates of musical emotions.* Poster presented at the ESCOM Conference, August 2009, Jyväskylä, Finland.

Vaitl, D., Vehrs, W., & Sternagel, S. (1993). Prompts—Leitmotif—Emotion: Play it again, Richard Wagner. In N. Birnbaumer & A. Öhman (eds), *The structure of emotion: Psychophysiological, cognitive, and clinical aspects* (pp. 169–89). Seattle, WA: Hogrefe & Huber.

Vieillard, S., Peretz, I., Gosselin, N., Khalfa, S., Gagnon, L., & Bouchard, B. (2007). Happy, sad, scary and peaceful musical excerpts for research on emotions. *Cognition & Emotion, 2,* 720–52.

Vitouch, O., & Ladinig (eds), (2009). Music and evolution. *Musicae Scientiae, Special Issue.*

Watson, D., & Clark, L. (1994). *The PANAS-X: Manual for the Positive and Negative Affect Schedule—Expanded Form.* Unpublished manuscript, University of Iowa.

Watson, D., Clark, L. A., & Tellegen, A. (1988). Development and validation of brief measures of positive and negative affect: The PANAS scales. *Journal of Personality and Social Psychology, 54,* 1063–70.

Watson, D., & Tellegen, A. (1985). Toward a consensual structure of mood. *Psychological Bulletin, 98,* 219–35.

Watson, D., & Tellegen, A. (1999). Issues in the dimensional structure of affect: Effects of descriptors, measurement error, and response formats: Comment on Russell and Carroll (1999). *Psychological Bulletin, 125,* 601–10.

Watson, D., Wiese, D., Vaidya, J., & Tellegen, A. (1999). The two general activation systems of affect: Structural findings, evolutionary considerations, and psychobiological evidence. *Journal of Personality and Social Psychology, 76,* 820–38.

Watson, K. B. (1942). The nature and measurement of musical meanings. *Psychological Monographs, 54,* 1–43.

Wedin, L. (1972). A multidimensional study of perceptual-emotional qualities in music. *Scandinavian Journal of Psychology, 13,* 241–57.

Wierzbicka, A. (1999). *Emotions across languages and cultures.* Cambridge, UK: Cambridge University Press.

Witvliet, C. V. O., & Vrana, S. R. (2007). Play it again Sam: Repeated exposure to emotionally evocative music polarises liking and smiling responses, and influences other affective reports, facial EMG, and heart rate. *Cognition & Emotion, 21,* 1–23.

Zentner, M. (2009). Augmenting cognition with music. *Frontiers of Neuroscience, 3,* 98–99.

Zentner, M., & Eerola, T. (2009). *Music-induced movement in infants: Rhythmicity, synchronization, and positive affect.* Manuscript submitted for publication.

Zentner, M. R., Grandjean, D., & Scherer, K. R. (2008). Emotions evoked by the sound of music: Characterization, classification, and measurement. *Emotion, 8,* 494–521.

Zentner, M. R., & Kagan, J. (1996). Perception of music by infants. *Nature, 383,* 29.

CHAPTER 9

CONTINUOUS SELF-REPORT METHODS

EMERY SCHUBERT

9.1 INTRODUCTION

AN undeniable, fundamental property of music is that it requires time to exist. Any definition of music must include this property, even if by implication. For example, the well-worn definition of music being 'organized sound' does not explicitly mention time dependence, but sound requires the projection of energy through space and time as an absolute minimum. Emotion also requires time to unfold, but this is not mandatory to its definition, since an emotion can be detected in a static image or object such as a photograph. However, given the intricate connection between music and emotion, it stands to reason that emotions occurring in response to unfolding music should also be time dependent.

While this may be obvious, it is true too that, of all the research in music perception and cognition, only a small fraction has focused on the fundamental nature of time in music and the emotion it produces. In the last 80 years, there has been the implicit assumption that music emotion can be understood by collecting (emotional) responses or assessments after a musical stimulus has been sounded, the so-called 'post-performance' response (e.g. Sloboda & Lehmann, 2001). Since the first important English-language experiments on the topic (Heinlein, 1928; Hevner, 1935; Rigg, 1937; Sherman, 1928), the reasons for such an approach can be identified as pragmatism and tradition. Collecting self-report responses continuously requires careful synchronization of each response with the time in the music at which the response occurred.

Frequent sampling of responses over time can produce large sets of data, too. Apart from a few ingenious solutions, this methodology needed significant computational power, something that would not be widespread until the 1990s. As researchers began to explore this time-dependent mode of data collection, they were faced with the problem of how to interpret the huge data sets accumulated. Indeed, there are now several methods of data collection and analysis of continuous emotional responses to music, many of them quite recent developments. In this chapter, I will discuss some of these (measurement and analysis methods) after defining continuous response. I will conclude by briefly discussing some of the current issues in continuous-response method in connection with emotion and music, and speculate on some future directions and challenges.

9.2 WHAT IS CONTINUOUS RESPONSE?

'Continuous response' is a problematic and perhaps unfortunate expression for the method and phenomena under investigation. 'Continuous' has two quite different meanings to different readers: continuous in time, and continuous in an orthogonal dimension, such as loudness or sadness. An example of the latter is a type of measurement where an ordered set of possible responses are related, such as that found on a rating scale. Such a rating-scale response is not bound to unfolding time, although most of the methods for recording continuous cognitive responses happen to use these 'continuous' rating scales. The 'continuous response' discussed in this chapter refers to the time dimension: responses are collected without interruption. Strictly speaking, digital devices, such as computers, do not collect data continuously. They collect data in incrementing, discrete samples. The sampling rate used may be so high that the illusion of continuous response can be produced.

Yet even this interpretation of the term 'continuous' does not provide an unambiguous definition of what 'continuous response' refers to. The time series analysis literature provides a clearer picture for a time-series—which is what continuous responses produce—'a sequence of observations taken sequentially in time' (Box, Jenkins, & Reinsel, 1994, p. 1). Sometimes the term 'time-varying' is used (e.g. Vines, Krumhansl, Wanderley, & Levitin, 2006), but this too has an ambiguity through the implication that the response is varying, denying the possibility that a response value may not be varying at all as a piece of music unfolds in time.

The term 'continuous' is more correct when referring to the response process of a human who, having a biological rather than a digital processor, might be imagined to have a continuous (i.e. uninterrupted) response. Yet this too has a drawback, because we cannot be certain that the listener is always responding 'on-task'. The task might be too complex or tiring to allow a good indication of the cognitive response(s) under investigation throughout the entire listening period. Nevertheless, the expression 'continuous response' has infiltrated the literature and established itself as the ubiquitous term for this method of enquiry. It should always be taken to mean 'time-dependent response'.

This chapter will examine the literature on continuous-response measurements of emotion to music. It will further limit the scope to self-report measures (see also Chapter 8, this volume), rather than physiological and observational methods.

9.3 MEASUREMENT: HOW ARE THE DATA COLLECTED?

9.3.1 Sampling rate and response latency

With emotional scale response interfaces, the participant is typically moving a slider or two in real time as the music unfolds. When a computer display interface is used by a participant, a footpedal, joystick, or mouse is used to move the cursor, and the cursor position is recorded along with the time at which the movement was made. Because computers are digital devices, they cannot record the mouse movements in a strictly analogue form. The slider representing an emotional scale has its values digitized (usually according to a defined scale, limited by the pixel resolution of the computer display, the programming parameters, or by the interface used), and the number of times the value is 'read' by the computer is also digitized. The time dimension digitization is referred to as the sampling rate and is expressed either as number of samples per second (a frequency) or as the time elapsed between a sample (sampling period). The sampling period is directly related to the rate. For example, one sample every 0.25 seconds is the same as 1/0.25 or 4 Hz (Hz is the standard unit for frequency).

The required sampling rate can be determined by addressing two questions: what is the optimum sampling frequency, and what is the highest sampling rate that we might expect to record? With the advent of fast computers with large memory capacity and efficient programs, the problem of sampling rate can be resolved by adopting the highest available. A very fast sampling period might be 1 millisecond (a sample every one thousandth of a second, which is 1000 Hz). However, these data need to be stored and analysed, and the large masses of data this sampling rate produces may create unnecessary redundancy. This led Schubert (2001) to recommend a sampling rate of 2 Hz, because self-reported arousal responses to loudness lagged the causal musical event by around three seconds, but could sometimes occur with a lag of one second. The 2 Hz suggestion comes from the application of Nyquist's sampling theorem, which states that the sampling rate should be twice the highest expected frequency.

A sampling rate of around 2 Hz is a bit dated these days given that higher sampling rates can easily be obtained on modern computers. In fact Nagel et al (2007) are critical of the 2 Hz rate, arguing that it is possible for participants to react emotionally to music quite rapidly, irrespective of the response delay ('lag structure') between music and emotion. In line with this criticism, evidence suggests that emotional responses to music can be made in less than one second (Bigand, Filipic, & Lalitte, 2005), and this is supported by the 'startle' outliers found in the Schubert and Dunsmuir (1999) analysis of arousal response to loudness, where sudden bursts of loudness produce a fast arousal response, compared with more gradual shifts in loudness, which lead arousal response by 2 to 4 seconds (see also Krumhansl, 1996; Schubert, 2004; Smith & Cuddy, 2003; who report these general, typical longer delays). Luck (2008) argued that 'lag structure' might also be determined by the number of dimensions that the participant must respond to simultaneously. The recommendation, therefore, is to select a comfortably (from the processors and storage perspective) high sampling rate, and that it be at least 2 Hz, and then down-sample to an appropriate sampling rate at the analysis stage.

Down-sampling refers to the extraction of a lower sampling rate after the samples have been collected. It is possible to resample something that has been recorded at 4 Hz down to 2 Hz without corrupting the data. However, it is not as simple to go the other way around (to 'up-sample'): If a sampling rate of 2 Hz is used, it is not possible to obtain a 4 Hz sampling rate without using some interpolation procedure that potentially introduces artefacts (because the missing sample may not have corresponded to the interpolated value). Thus, a higher initial (i.e. when response data are being collected) sampling rate is generally preferable.

The consensus emerging for the upper sampling rate is around 20 to 30 samples per second (Nagel et al, 2007; Schubert, 2007b). These rates happen to be in the order of samples used in high-quality digitized motion pictures, and therefore lend themselves to ensuring a firm synchronization between the location of a piece of music or multimedia, and the time at which the response occurred. For example, Schubert's (2007b) *Real Time Cognitive Response Recorder* reads code from the stimulus file in frames per second, which translates to a sampling rate of 30 Hz. This high sampling rate is stored internally and the experimenter can then export the response file at a sampling rate of 30 Hz or less. Tests demonstrated that for older computers a sampling rate of 30 Hz is hard to achieve, and that 2 to 5 Hz was an appropriate, realistic range. However, recently higher sampling rates are becoming routine and relatively inexpensive to achieve.

To summarize, sampling rate is not just a matter of adopting the fastest possible rate. Collecting data on personal computers will be affected by the non data-collection tasks that the processor is required to do, and the current evidence suggests that self-reported emotional responses do not change quickly enough to require very high sampling rates. Two to 30 Hz seems to encompass the present consensus of typical sampling rates.

9.3.2 What emotions should be measured?

Collecting emotional response continuously, in real time, produces an interesting problem. If emotions themselves are so complex, how can they be measured at all, and especially in real time in response to music, where the music acts in such a way as to change emotion, sometimes several times throughout the piece? To answer this question we need to understand the structure of emotion. There is still some contro-versy over the theoretical definition of the structure of emotion (Barrett, Mesquita, Ochsner, & Gross, 2007; Barrett & Wager, 2006). The two main theories are (1) emo-tions as a collection of discrete, separate entities (such as happiness, sadness, and anger) and (2) emotions as lying on various continua of underlying emotional dimensions—for example, happiness and sadness lying at roughly opposite ends of a 'valence' con-tinuum (see Chapter 4, this volume). Each theory, emotions as discrete and emotions as interrelated, have implications on how to measure emotion continuously.

Discrete models suggest that a selection of discrete emotions (e.g. happy, sad, peace-ful, angry) should be available to the listener so that they may indicate which emotion or emotions the music is expressing or evoking as it unfolds. This method has two pioneers: Kate Hevner and Seiichiro Namba. In the 1930s, Hevner published the adjec-tive checklist, which arranged a series of emotion-laden adjectives in a circular form grouped by similarity of meaning (see Hevner, 1936; Schubert, 2003; see also Figure 14.1 in Chapter 14, this volume). Hevner also produced a study where responses were recorded as a piece of music unfolded. While she did not have the technology to collect responses at close, regular time intervals, she obtained responses to a piece of music in different sections of the piece, making her study perhaps the first, albeit crude, continu-ous self-report emotion in music study (Hevner, 1936; see Schubert, 2001). Technology for rapid data collection was one problem in this study, but so was the relatively large number of adjectives that the listener had to choose from, a burden on the cognitive load of the listener (Pass, Renkl, & Sweller, 2004). The Namba study (Namba, Kuwano, Hatoh, & Kato, 1991) addressed some of these issues by using a smaller number of adjec-tives, and using selected keys on a computer keyboard representing each adjective, so that key strokes could be recorded as a piece of music unfolded. While important in the development of continuous-response methods, these discrete emotion-based approaches realized as checklist-type responses have never really gained popularity amongst the research community because of the advantages of applying rating scales.

This does not mean that discrete emotions cannot be used in continuous-response tasks. Rather, it means that it is advisable to use a small number of emotions to make the continuous-response task feasible. So, rating one discrete emotion at a time is feasi-ble, and can produce more information if presented as a scale (e.g. amount or intensity of 'sadness', 'happiness', 'anger', etc.). Nevertheless, the dimensional theoretical stance has been viewed (perhaps inaccurately) as having some advantage over the use of dis-crete emotions. One should bear in mind, however, that it is not the structural model of emotion that is most significant here (dimensional vs. categorical), but simply the number of responses an individual can make while listening to a piece of music.

The dimensional approach to emotion has been heavily influenced by the circumplex structure proposed by James Russell (1980, 1989), where there are two main dimensions underlying the structure of emotion: *valence* (distinguishing emotions such as happy from sad) and *arousal* (distinguishing emotions such as excited from sleepy). Further, Russell's model can be presented on a two-dimensional Cartesian plane, with valence and arousal as perpendicular axes (X and Y respectively, for example; see Figure 9.1). This means that a significant and meaningful emotion can be reported with a single point in space (Russell, Weiss, & Mendelsohn, 1989), making this combination of two rating scales an excellent interface for continuous emotional response.

Since the 1980s, single rating scale response approaches have been obtained in music-emotion studies, in particular the work of Geringer, Madsen, Frederickson, and colleagues (for a review, see Geringer, Madsen, & Gregory, 2004). They used scales such as 'tension' (Fredrickson, 2001), 'musical intensity' (Duke & Colprit, 2001), and 'aesthetic response' (Madsen & Coggiola, 2001), which were recorded on a dial or slider connected to a computer and moved by the participant as the music unfolded.

The distinction between categorical and dimensional data collections can become blurred when categorical emotions are used as unipolar scales, recording the intensity or presence of a specific emotion. It can create confusion about whether a categorical model is being applied or a dimensional one, and in fact for the purposes of data collection, the distinction is more or less arbitrary. For example, Krumhansl (1997) collected continuous responses along several emotion labels that may be thought of as categories. One group of participants rated the amount of sadness experienced using a slider. Fear, happiness, and tension were also rated on separate passes (listenings). Krumhansl's study demonstrates how the distinction between categorical and dimensional models might be arbitrary. For example, the happiness and tension ratings might produce reasonably similar responses to the 2DES described below. In a theoretical sense the rating scales derive from a categorical model, because an indication of an amount of a specific emotion is requested. Dimensional models will generate scales that are more typically attuning to an emotion along a scale of emotions that are labelled with antonyms at the ends of the scale (happy–sad, aroused–sleepy, and so forth). Hence, dimensional models are rated as bipolar scales, while categorical models are rated as unipolar scales. An extreme example is Hevner's adjective checklist (already described), where an adjective is checked by the participant if thought to be a description of the mood of the music. This is akin to a unipolar scale with two levels (present if checked and absent if unchecked).

9.3.3 Response collection interfaces

Several interfaces have been used to automatically collect continuous self-report emotional response data (see Ruef & Levenson, 2007, for examples used in the non-music domain; for collection of continuous responses to music involving non-affective aspects, see for example Thompson, Williamon, & Valentine, 2007). *The Continuous Response Digital Interface* (CRDI) (Geringer et al, 2004; Gregory, 1989) was devised in the 1980s, and consists of a dial or slider on a box that the participant can use to indicate the amount of emotion (as discussed above) in the music. The slider data is then transmitted to a computer for storage and analysis. *EmotionSpace Lab* (Schubert, 1996, 1999) was a software package that featured the *Two-Dimensional Emotion-Space* (2DES), a two-dimensional emotion-space based on Russell's model and tailor-made for collecting emotional responses to words, pictures, and music. Responses to music were collected continuously. The interface required only the existing computer display and a mouse. Since it was devised in 1996, the two-dimensional approach has been a fairly common way of collecting continuous emotional responses (e.g. Cowie

& Cornelius, 2003; Cowie et al, 2001; Geringer et al, 2004; Nagel et al, 2007; Schubert, 2007b; Stevens, Glass, Schubert, Chen, & Winskel, 2007; Stevens et al, 2009). *RTCRR* ('arty-car', Schubert, 2007b) is a freely available program that supersedes *EmotionSpace Lab* by providing greater flexibility, for example in labelling the axes and allowing various sampling rates (up to 30Hz). *EMuJoy* (Nagel et al, 2007) is a considerably improved version of *EmotionSpace Lab*, with faster sampling rate (50 ms sampling period), cross-platform capability, and operation over the web. It is also freely available. Two-dimensional versions of the CRDI have also been developed (Madsen, 1997).

Since the work of Cowie and colleagues (Cowie et al, 2000; McMahon, Cowie, & André, 2004), which produced the *Feeltrace* program, the moving worm rather than a lone cursor has become a common method of providing feedback to the participant about their location in the emotion-space. Screen shots of four programs using such feedback in two-dimensional space are shown in Figure 9.1. The most sophisticated form of the worm is *EMuJoy*, which provides a schematic face at the current time point indicating the part of the emotion space the participant is in, for example a happy face in the top right quadrant (see Figure 9.1A).

While dominant, rating scales and checklists are not the only input modes for collecting continuous responses. For example, button presses can be used to indicate the presence of some emotional event (e.g. 'when the music causes something to happen to you', Waterman, 1996, p. 56), and a participant can make a mark on a sound recording or on a musical score to indicate that they had a particular emotional response at that point (e.g. Sloboda, 1991). These 'place marker' approaches usually require additional analysis to tease out the detail of the point or region of music indicated by the participant. But the number of place markers and their location can provide interesting information in themselves.

One novel approach for collecting emotional responses from the participant is the *sentograph* developed by Manfred Clynes (1973, 1989; see also Chapter 14, this volume), although this device claims to access more subconscious, rather than self-report, effects. Another is the recording and analysis of a laser pointer wiggled around on a screen by the listener as a piece of music unfolds (Camurri, Castellano, Ricchetti, & Volpe, 2006) which, like the sentograph, was not strictly accessing self-report emotions: 'Our purpose was to find an adequate way to obtain measures of the emotional engagement, that were halfway between conscious (e.g. mouse, slider, haptic interfaces to communicate the experienced emotion) and unconscious (physiological measures: e.g. skin conductance, heart rate, breath rate, blood pressure)' (p. 269).

9.4 HOW ARE THE DATA ANALYSED?

One of the major challenges of continuous-response methods is to determine how to analyse the data. While this depends on the research questions, it is quite often instructive to plot the continuous responses on a time chart, with time on the X-axis and the

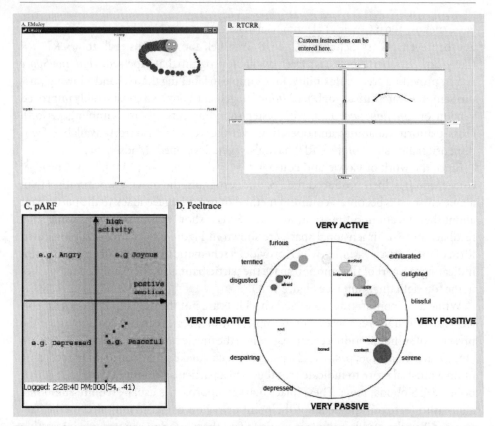

Fig. 9.1 Sample display of four continuous-response collection interfaces using two-dimensional emotion-spaces. (A) EMuJoy (Nagel et al, 2007); (B) RTCRR (Schubert, 2007b); (C) pARF (Stevens et al, 2009); (D) Feeltrace (McMahon et al, 2004). Each version provides a sample of the layout of the emotion-space used, and different ways the position feedback worm is displayed. EMuJoy (A) uses a schematic facial expression representing the location in the emotion space at the head of the worm (e.g. a happy, excited face in the top right quadrant). Feeltrace (D) changes cursor colour to provide additional feedback about location in emotion space. RTCRR (B) and pARF (C) use a trail of dots or lines only.

emotional response scale on the Y-axis. If a data set from more than one dimension is collected, plotting each dimension separately, but so that they can be aligned for comparison, can be informative. Such plots can immediately provide a visual overview of the responses unfolding in time. However, this is at best a starting point for analysis. There are complexities in time series data—that arise because the data are by definition time dependent—that may need to be considered before plausible conclusions can be drawn.

A time series plot on its own provides information about the presence of undulations, unusual patterns, and so forth. However, a meaningful analysis needs to be comparative in some way. For example, was there an expected pattern in the profile? Do the profiles of other listeners to the same piece of music produce a similar pattern? What exactly are the bounds of a so-called 'similar' pattern across two or more times series plots? Do the musical features provide any explanation for the shape of the profile? Is it possible and worthwhile to apply some kind of more in-depth statistical analytic technique?

If emotional responses to the same piece from several participants are gathered, is it better to examine plots of individual responses or to use some central tendency measure? Plotting numerous individual responses of the emotion scale values provides an indication of how much agreement or disagreement there is in different parts of the piece. However, with too few participants the relationships may seem random, and with many participants the variability in responses may seem too large. A sample-by-sample central tendency measure can be helpful, and although the mean is commonly used, the median is also appropriate because it is less susceptible to outliers, and makes fewer assumptions about the nature of the distribution. But any measure of central tendency alone can be misleading and only provides a description of the data that is susceptible to subjective interpretations and premature conclusions. In general, a balance between examining individual responses at one analytic extreme and trying to digest all individual responses plotted together is advisable.

Analytic techniques can be classified as descriptive or inferential. Descriptive techniques rely largely on visual inspection or observation of sample-by-sample means (or other central tendency measure). Inferential approaches use statistical techniques and models to provide quantifiable values of error probability (e.g. the probability of concluding that there is a difference between two sets of means when there actually is no difference). Inferential methods can be thought of as lying along a continuum of sophistication. A relatively simple method of inferring information from a time-series is the second-order standard deviation threshold (see Section 9.4.7). At the other end of the spectrum, we have highly sophisticated analytic methods such as the Autoregressive Integrated Moving Average (ARIMA, discussed in Section 9.4.7) model (Bowerman, O'Connell, & Koechler, 2005; Box et al, 1994) and the recent employment of functional data analysis (Levitin, Nuzzo, Vines, & Ramsay, 2007; Ramsay & Silverman, 2002).

9.4.1 Descriptive approaches

Visual descriptive techniques involve 'eyeballing' time series graphs and making assertions about the unfolding patterns. For example, Fredrickson and Coggiola (2003) asked 40 music majors and 30 non-music majors to rate the tension ('that they heard') as one of two performances of 'St Louis Blues' by W. C. Handy unfolded, one performance sung by Nat King Cole and the other sung by Ella Fitzgerald. The *CRDI* converted responses to a tension scale from 0 to 255. Each participant group was further divided into two subgroups, so that the order of presentation could be counterbalanced: Group A heard Cole, then Fitzgerald; Group B Fitzgerald, then Cole. By plotting the sample-by-sample average, the time series profile (or 'footprint', to use

Fredrickson and Coggiola's terminology) emerged, allowing comparison of four plots per piece—the two counterbalanced music major groups and the two counterbalanced non-music major groups.

Similarities in the undulations of the four profiles could easily be identified. There was a general rising trend, with several local maxima ('bumps') and minima ('dips') occurring until around the 120th second of the piece, then climbing more slowly or plateauing (still with local maxima and minima) until the end of the piece. And slight differences in absolute mean tension ratings could also be seen. The group of music majors that heard the Nat King Cole version first tended to give lower tension ratings than the group that heard the Fitzgerald version first (see Figure 9.2). Comparing different groups allows identification of the profiles that appeared to be 'significant'. For example, the Fitzgerald profiles showed a clustering together of the non-music major responses and another clustering of the music major groups, particularly in the early parts of the piece. Having a single time series plot on its own would make it hard to know what effect different experimental and demographic conditions might have on the participants' responses, and whether any particular undulations were meaningful. Comparing groups helps to alleviate this problem.

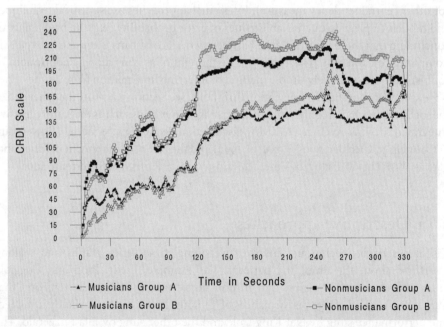

Fig. 9.2 Mean perceived tension responses to 'St Louis Blues' performed by Ella Fitzgerald, demonstrating how comparison of mean profiles can provide a frame of reference for comparing groups of participants. From Frederickson and Coggiola (2003, p. 266). Copyright © 2003 by MENC: The National Association for Music Education. Reprinted with permission.

9.4.2 Inferential approaches

Another method, which still relies on visual inspection of the mean response profiles, is to superimpose the time series plot with a sample-by-sample measure of the spread of scores, such as the standard deviation, standard error, or semi-interquartile values. For example, if this were conducted in the Fredrickson and Caggiola study discussed above, it would be possible to make a testable assertion of the point at which the mean scores break away from each other, as appears to happen at around the 250th second (see Figure 9.2). A significance criterion, such as one time-series being more than two standard errors away from the other at any given point in time, could be used to determine when the responses of one participant group differs from another in a manner more objective than just 'eyeballing' the mean time-series.

However, the more parameters we introduce, the more complex the analytic story becomes. Some measures of spread have statistical (parametric) implications. For example, if a score in a series falls within one standard error of another mean at a given point in time, we may conclude that the two means are not significantly different; or more specifically, we may be 68 per cent confident that the means come from the same population. But this approach is problematic because it makes the assumption that the data under investigation come from a normally distributed population. In time series data, this may not always be the case. One reason is because data at different time points are correlated. Take the point in Figure 9.2 for the music major group A at $t = 120$. The value is relatively close to the value at $t = 121$. And this is self-evidently the case for all pairs of emotion ratings on any one profile at adjacent time points. When a rating scale is used for collecting responses, it is physically impossible to jump from one end of the scale to the other without passing through all the intermediate points, regardless of how quickly the response movement is made. In fact, the nature of many time-series is that they exhibit this 'serial correlation' (i.e. they do not fluctuate randomly from time point to time point), and this can violate the assumptions made in tests found in more conventional experimental studies in which the data are parametric. It is as though there is an additional inertial or gravitational-like force pulling data points toward the points that have recently unfolded. Therefore, care needs to be taken if applying any parametric methods to time series data.

9.4.3 Reliability and the second-order deviation threshold

Examining the spread of scores is also useful for investigating whether a sample-by-sample averaged time-series provides a reliable indication of the population distribution mean at a given point in time. A time series plot of the responses made by several participants to the same piece of music can, therefore, reveal periods of high agreement in some sections, and periods of greater variation (disagreement) in other periods. The variation in spread is referred to as heteroskedasticity, and its identification is of interest in time series data. Several non-visual methods are available for identifying when the spread of scores in a time-series varies considerably (Dufour, Khalaf, Bernard, & Genest, 2004; Engle, 1995, 2001).

Schubert (2007d) suggested a method using only mean and standard deviation (SD) calculations, and plotting these to allow a graphical identification of 'reliable' parts of the time-series. This method was referred to as the second-order standard deviation threshold. The principle underlying this method is, first, to evaluate the sample-by-sample ('vertical') deviation scores (where each deviation score is the difference, at a particular sampled time point, between the rating score for an individual participant and the mean rating score over all participants), and then to determine when variability in these deviation scores falls below a threshold (the 'reliable' region for rater judgements). One can imagine that at some sampled time points the deviation scores may vary somewhat more compared to the deviation scores at other sampled time points in the response profile, whether due to random fluctuations or disagreement in raters' subjective emotional evaluation. Low variability in deviation scores suggests better agreement in, and hence reliability of, rater judgement over those points in time.

When can we conclude that the inter-rater variability is 'small enough', in other words, that the rater judgements are reliable? Schubert calculated the SD of the sample by sample (or 'vertical') deviation scores (across raters) at each sampled time point. He then calculated the mean and the SD (across sampled time points) of these standard deviations. This 'second-order' SD was used to determine a threshold of 'significance', in the sense that variability among a set of rater judgements lower than the threshold was 'significantly' small (i.e. the raters' ratings were reliable). Hence the descriptor 'second-order standard deviation threshold' was used to describe the method.

The second-order standard deviation (calculated across sampled time points) may be thought of as a 'horizontal' standard deviation, because the time axis generally appears horizontally on time series plots. It may be calculated over the entire duration of the piece, or over sections where there is a clear homogeneity in the response pattern that is distinct from the response pattern over other regions of the piece. In other words, a time window of interest needs to be selected over which the standard deviation series is selected.

To identify significant rater reliability at a particular sampled time point, we focus on vertical standard deviation scores that are small. In particular, if the vertical standard deviation score at that sampled time point falls below a threshold value given by the mean of the vertical SD scores of the chosen time window minus some small multiple of the horizontal SD, we conclude that the variability among rater judgements is 'significantly' small at that time point; that is, the rater judgements are reliable. This can be represented by the formula:

$$Threshold = \bar{X} - k\bar{\sigma} \qquad\qquad 9.1$$

where $\bar{X}$ is the mean of the vertical SDs, and $\bar{\sigma}$ is the horizontal (second order) *SD*, and k is a small number. For example, suppose we define the threshold as mean minus one horizontal *SD* unit (i.e. $k = 1$). Suppose further that the mean of the vertical *SDs* ($\bar{X}$) is 30 emotional units and the horizontal SD ($\bar{\sigma}$) is 10 emotional units. Then, if at a particular point in the piece the vertical *SD* is 18 units, we will conclude that rater judgements are reliable at this particular point because 18 is smaller than the threshold value 20 (= 30–10). Adjusting the threshold value by using a multiple of 0.5 horizontal *SD* units (i.e. $k = 0.5$) will cause the threshold to rise to 25 (=30–5). This would bring larger vertical SD scores within the range of significance, and hence provide a less conservative assessment of 'significant' points than in the previous example.

A drawback of this method is that it is likely always to define some vertical SD values as 'significant'. For this reason, it is more accurately described as a way of producing a ranking of significance. Further, the use of mean and standard deviation statistics was a deliberate simplification made by Schubert (2007d), susceptible to invalid assumptions about the distribution inferred by the mean and standard deviation when applied to time series data. The use of semi-interquartile range instead of standard deviation, and the use of median instead of mean in the above, and then applying non-parametric statistical analyses (Sprent, 1993) provides a more statistically robust alternative to the identification of reliable regions along the time-series, because using semi-interquartile and median statistics makes fewer assumptions about the nature of the data.

9.4.4 Comparing magnitude of response across different parts of the same time series

More conventional methods have been used to address the different question of when a mean response is different in one part of a piece compared to another. Sloboda and Lehmann (2001) examined the amount of 'emotionality' in Chopin's *Prelude Op. 28, No. 4*, as perceived by 28 musicians. The piece was divided *a priori* into four sections, and the mean of each segment was compared using Repeated Measures Analysis of Variance, which demonstrated that emotionality scores were different across all adjacent section pairs.

9.4.5 Comparing two or more time-series

When responses are collected in two different conditions in response to the same performance, for example using participants with different demographics, or to examine differences across the time series profile responses amongst the performed items (like the responses shown in Figure 9.2), researchers may wish to determine which sections are significantly different across the groups. McAdams et al (2004) used running F tests at each time sample of data to compare the 'emotional force' of two performances of the same piece (one performed in Paris and the other in La Jolla). These 'functional F tests' produced an additional time series of F values which, when falling below a predetermined threshold, would be considered statistically significant. They mention the problems caused by multiple comparisons, but neither this paper nor Schubert (2007d) provide explicit solutions. Rather, the approach has been that, if multiple comparisons and violations of assumptions must be made, the significance threshold should be adjusted.

In another analysis in the same artice, McAdams et al compared versions of the same section of music in different positions and performances. The difference of the mean for each combination was compared using single sample *t* tests. The test determined whether the difference was significantly non-zero, with a footnote indicating that the high significance found for all the tests reported (all with $p < .0001$) should be interpreted with caution due to the possible effects of serial correlation. However, even when some adjustments were made, the results were still highly significant. They described how the autocorrelation function can be used to ascertain regions where serial correlation diminishes. For the section of the piece they were examining (*Angel of Death* by Roger Reynolds), they found that serial correlation was quite low after 60 seconds, requiring a relatively small adjustment in degrees of freedom to compensate for serial correlation.

9.4.6 Autocorrelation diagnostics

Autocorrelation is an important tool for assessing the behaviour of a time-series. It consists of a series of repeated steps. First, the time-series is duplicated and the two series are correlated. This correlation coefficient is plotted at an X-axis value of 0 corresponding to 'zero lag'. It should be obvious that this will produce a correlation coefficient of exactly 1 (because the series is correlated with itself). Next, one of the series is shifted across one time unit and the correlation coefficient is calculated. This time the correlation is likely to be less than 1, and is plotted at the X-axis value of 1 (corresponding to the one time unit shift; for an example, see the bar at time lag 1 in the top right plot of Figure 9.3). The process is repeated until a stream of correlation coefficients is plotted (the series of bars in the same figure).

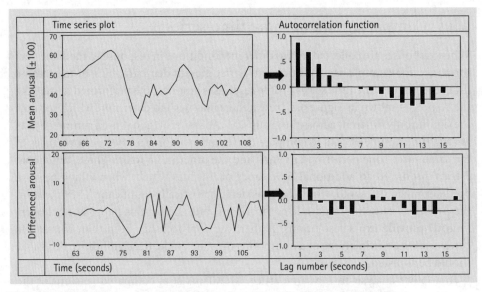

Fig. 9.3 **Diagnosing serial correlation using autocorrelation functions.**

The shape of the plot provides many insights into the nature of the time series. For example, if from lag 1 the correlation coefficients drop to small values, and oscillate about 0 randomly, the time series exhibits no serial correlation, meaning that the series can be treated using traditional parametric-based statistical approaches. Statistical tests can be used that provide a confidence interval within which these correlations are no longer significant (Bowerman et al, 2005). However, a slow decay in the 'auto-correlogram' across consecutive lags indicates the presence of serial correlation and perhaps the presence of a general trend in the data, and repeating oscillatory patterns may be indicative of cyclical patterns in the series, as shown in the top right panel of Figure 9.3.

9.4.7 Time series analysis and ARIMA-based models

Time series analysis may be broken up into families of analytic techniques. One family, which I will refer to as the *traditional time series* (TTS) approach, includes methods described by Box and Jenkins in the 1970s (Box et al, 1994), where the aim is to remove or model out the deterministic (or systematic) components of the series, such as trends (gradual rises and falls in the series) as well as the components in the stochastic residual (the time-series remaining when the deterministic components are taken out). For example, a residual time series may look 'random' to the naked eye, but may still contain various time series processes as it unfolds (Gottman, 1981).

There are three theoretical processes that Box and Jenkins's models aim to identify and model out: the moving average (MA, which is a function of random fluctuations but also some simple combination of the previous error terms of the residual), the integral (I, which can be modelled out by examining the difference in values between consecutive points of a series) and the autoregression (AR, where the residual is a combination of random fluctuations but also some simple combination of the residual values that occurred earlier in time). These three processes, which are not necessarily independent of one another, are sometimes referred to as the family of ARIMA models.

By modelling any or all of these processes out of a time-series (should they be identified), the residual (remaining) series will end up being a set of random fluctuations that satisfy the statistical assumptions of the model. The autocorrelation function (described above) is then used to examine the success of the model. In addition, a partial autocorrelation assessment of the model can be used to examine correlations while holding the effect of intervening correlations constant. Both autocorrelogram and partial autocorrelogram are used together to help identify the processes underlying the time-series (for accessible introductions to ARIMA models, see Bowerman et al, 2005; Gottman, 1981).

An example of an application of time series analysis of this kind was the modelling out of integral and autoregression components reported by Schubert (2004). Emotional responses to five pieces of Western art music were collected from 67 participants using the *2DES* provided in *EmotionSpace Lab* (described in Section 9.3.3;

a fragment of responses to one of these pieces is presented in Figure 9.3). The sample-by-sample mean emotional response was represented as a function of musical features; that is, musical features were regressed onto emotional response—emotional response being arousal or valence. Because the emotion time-series and the musical feature time-series (tempo, loudness, and so forth) all contained serial correlation (identifiable through inspection and autocorrelograms; see top panes of Figure 9.3), the 'integral' component of each series was modelled out by a 'difference transformation', which involved subtracting the value at one point in time from the time value of the previous sampled point in time, to produce a new 'differenced' series (see bottom panes of Figure 9.3 for an example). Differencing can be interpreted as meaning 'change in' response or musical feature, which Schubert argued was a simple and intuitive concept and therefore a psychologically meaningful transformation, not just a mathematical one.

Several models of emotional arousal or valence, each as a function of musical features, with the integrated and autoregressive components modelled out, were then reported. Schubert proposed that the autoregressive component is, in part, representing the short-term memory of the listener. The resulting model was diagnosed as successful, because the residuals were not serially correlated. Here 'residual' is the value left over when the model-predicted value (emotional arousal in this case) is subtracted from the actual (emotional arousal) data point. An assumption of regression modelling is that the residual will consist of random, uncorrelated fluctuations. Without treating the data with difference transformations and extracting other serial processes, this assumption will frequently be violated. Schubert's model demonstrated how the assumptions could be satisfied.

A similar approach was applied by Korhonen et al (2006), using a technique called 'system identification', which produced emotion-predicting models using 17 input variables, including those used by Schubert and several others generated by audio feature extraction programs such as *PsySound* (Cabrera, 1999) and *MARSYAS* (Tzanetakis & Cook, 2000). Korhonen's approach embellished the modelling of emotion as a function of musical features in two ways. First, his models generally better explained the variation in emotional response than Schubert's model, perhaps in part due to the larger number of explanatory variables. Second, he generated a single model, which was then used to predict emotional response of an entire excerpt. Schubert produced one model per piece, because not enough variables were included to allow generalization across pieces.

This raises interesting questions about whether more input variables are useful because they cover more of the vast gamut of musical features that can be used to define a musical signal, or whether the variables we use in conventional parlance (such as tempo, articulation, melodic pitch, and harmony) already correlate to such an extent that they will impair the viability of the model. This effect is referred to as collinearity and can be controlled to some extent. Hence, Korhonen's approach may be further refined in the future to produce improved predictions of emotional response as a function of musical features. An important corollary of this research is that it is providing a framework for explaining how and when musical features produce emotional responses in typical listeners using various kinds of statistical modelling.

9.4.8 Functional data analysis

Another family of time series techniques is *Functional Data Analysis* (FDA, see Levitin, Nuzzo, Vines, & Ramsay, 2007), which distinguishes itself from TTS models by using smooth, mathematical curves fitted to sets of time series data rather than the data themselves. It is easy to determine the derivative (rate of change) of such curves. 'The resulting functional objects are considered to approximate the smooth continuous process underlying the recorded data samples' (McAdams et al, 2004, p. 312).

The process has the advantage of reducing the extraneous high-frequency noise that can be introduced when differencing unsmoothed data. Differencing or differentiating experimental data inevitably has this problem. Even a small amount of random noise on two successive data produces a large proportional error in their difference and gives rise to high-frequency noise in the result. However, in FDA the joins between the functions must also be smooth to reduce the chance of such artefactual high frequencies being introduced anyway, and this is generally hard to do.

One study applying FDA to emotional response was reported by McAdams et al (2004) in analysing, among other things, 'emotional force' responses to a work by Roger Reynolds (already mentioned), in which responses to different performances (same work at different times, and with the position of segments of the work moved) were investigated. McAdams et al fitted smooth functions over lengths of 3 to 4 seconds of the responses in such a way that each fragment joined together (p. 312). In that study, the FDA method was used mostly to demonstrate how continuous emotion response could be represented by FDA and when differences between two versions occurred. Another interesting application of FDA to emotion in music was described in a study by Vines et al (2005). They plotted affective 'velocity' against 'acceleration' to produce phase-plane plots. Musical velocity was thought of, here, as the rate of change of emotional tension with time.

9.5 SOME INSIGHTS

Collection of continuous emotional responses to music has led to some novel understandings of how music elicits emotional responses that would be difficult to obtain without using time-dependent approaches. One of the most important issues that is observed using continuous response is 'lag structure'. Here, we are interested in the coupling between musical features and consequent emotional responses (Sloboda, 2005, Ch. 8), and we are interested not just in whether an emotional response can be linked to the temporal unfolding of musical events, but also the time dependence of the relationship. This is referred to as 'lag structure', and continuous-response methods have verified that an emotional response is not made—or at least not reported—immediately following the musical feature that is its putative cause. Responses can take in the order of seconds, which might reflect perceptual processing, as well as the time to produce computer mouse movements.

In this respect, most is understood about the relationship between emotional arousal and the variations in loudness that manipulate it (Schubert, 2004), where arousal responses follow the path of loudness with a delay of 2 to 4 seconds. This 'lag structure' is altered by several factors. For example, loud sudden bursts of sound reduce the response lag (Schubert & Dunsmuir, 1999), and the beginning and ending of a piece may have special 'orienting effects'. For example, Schubert (2008) found that participants may require several seconds of music to pass before they start making reliable responses. The length of the delay seems to be related to the musical features. Schubert speculated that fast or loud music required less initial orientation time.

Margulis (2007) used continuous ratings of a tension-measuring joystick to examine how participants perceive silences in music. The continuous-response approach allowed tension responses to be compared between silent and non-silent passages, while enabling 'ecologically plausible' musical situations. The findings demonstrated that, for example, silence before musical closure produces greater tension than silence immediately after musical closure.

These findings provide quantifiable results that post-performance measures cannot, and that are difficult to demonstrate through more speculative, rationalist means found in, for example, musicology. Given that continuous self-report is a new and burgeoning field, there are many more concrete applications of continuous response awaiting. Many of them are suffering growing pains, as new problems are discovered and require solutions. The next section, therefore, describes some other developments that are more or less peculiar to continuous emotional response research, with identification of some current and potential stumbling blocks.

9.6 SOME DILEMMAS AND POSSIBLE FUTURE DIRECTIONS

9.6.1 Interfaces based on dimensional models of emotion

Dimensionally based response collection has received some important challenges in recent years. The arousal dimension has been reported as comprising two subdimensions—activity arousal and tension arousal, allowing distinction between emotions such as fear and anger (fear has lower activity than anger) (Ilie & Thompson, 2006; Schimmack & Grob, 2000; see Chapter 8, this volume). However, some studies in music-emotion response have indicated that the so-called arousal dimension produces responses quite similar to many other emotion scales, such as 'emotional strength', 'aesthetic response' (Schubert, 2001), 'musical tension', and 'musical affect'

(Krumhansl, 1996; Krumhansl & Schenck, 1997; Vines et al, 2005; Vines, Wanderley, Krumhansl, Nuzzo, & Levitin, 2003). These are each expressions that could be clumped together to mean roughly the same thing, or to produce similar responses, although McAdams et al (2004) argue that such clumping together into a generic arousal-like dimension is simplistic.

Schubert (2007a) attempted to use 'dominance'—a possible third dimension according to Russell (1977) and Plutchik (1962), and similar to 'potency' reported by Osgood et al (1957; see also Laukka, Juslin, & Bresin, 2005; Scherer, Dan, & Flykt, 2006), which might help to distinguish certain emotions (such as anger-dominant and fear-submissive)—to find that the dominance scale produced little distinction in response. On the one hand, arousal is too broad a dimension to be useful as a response scale (because there is more than one kind of 'arousal'), on the other hand it only taps into part of a generalized response anyway (because arousal seems to be similar to emotional strength, aspects of tension, activity, and so forth). Further research will determine which interpretation of arousal will persevere. But the research interest will also help to decide the level of refinement required. A general measure of the construct associated with arousal, activity, or just emotion in general can be obtained by any of these labels. But a refined analysis that distinguishes subtle nuances and clear outliers in response would require the smaller conceptual subdivisions of arousal, such as activity-arousal versus tension-arousal.

To summarize, the published literature on continuous emotional response reflects a strong preference for dimensional response devices over selections from lists of discrete emotion terms. The rating-scales approaches can be further divided into single scale ratings (e.g. Krumhansl, 1997; Madsen, Brittin, & Capperella-Sheldon, 1993) or two-dimensional approaches (e.g. Cowie et al, 2000; Madsen, 1997; Nagel et al, 2007; Schubert, 1996). No study has used a three-dimensional interface, although it should be possible using a device such as a three-dimensional computer mouse, or a haptic surface, in combination with training.

Nevertheless, there is some warranted concern in the research community that gathering responses along two or more scales in the same pass may place excessive cognitive load on the participant, and lead to degradation of responses. Luck et al (2008) expressed concern that responding to more than one dimension simultaneously may lead to an inflated 'lag structure'—longer delay between musical feature and associated emotional response—than might occur when a single rating scale is used. However, no study has yet explicitly demonstrated what degradations occur when one, two, or three emotion dimensions are rated simultaneously (see Schubert, 1999), nor the effects of training and experience with such tasks. The current evidence suggests that, since results appear to be on the whole meaningful and reasonably consistent, two-dimensional recording on a single pass need not be treated with such suspicion, especially given the gains in efficiency of data collection. For example, recording emotional valence responses and emotional activity response on two passes (two listenings) may produce very similar results as the *2DES* format, but take twice as long.

9.6.2 FDA versus traditional times-series

As stated earlier, the main difference between FDA and other time series approaches is that FDA converts collections of sampled points into functional units, while TTS methods leave the values as samples prior to further processing. It was also mentioned that FDA has advantages in being easily differentiable, making it appropriate to apply to phase-plane charts, for example. And the computationally expensive function fitting exercise is fairly easy to justify with fast computers. However, it is yet to be shown exactly what analytic advantages FDA will hold over traditional time series analytic techniques for music-emotion research. Some of the apparent advantages of FDA can be equalled or simulated with TTS techniques. For example, the smoothing of data in FDA through the use of polynomial and other 'continuous' functions can be achieved in TTS by applying a moving average transformation to the raw data.

Also, it is not clear what advantages 'functional F tests' have over running F tests that could be conducted on smoothed, sampled data. It is even possible to produce phase-plane charts using sample data, by simply plotting the first- and second-order differences of the smoothed, original series (corresponding to the first derivative and second derivative functions in FDA) and fitting these with a smooth curve. Further work comparing the two approaches will clarify whether there are any more than cosmetic differences between the approaches. FDA has the advantage for applications that require continuous functions, such as calculus. TTS techniques have a historical advantage, but like FDA applications to emotion in music, are still developing.

9.6.3 Comparing different performances of the same piece

Some research questions may require comparison of emotional responses to one performance of a piece to those of a different performance of the same piece. Unless the performer is strictly constrained, it is unlikely that the two performances will be of identical length, and it is unlikely that the temporal expressive deviations will be executed identically in each. So, to produce a direct comparison of the two, it may be necessary to stretch or shrink the time line of one performance to match that of the other. A simple visual approach is one that can be executed on many plotting and spreadsheet programs, where the time axis of one plot is stretched to match the time axis of the other, and then the two can be observed beside each other with time axes aligned or superimposed. Quantitatively, this involves adjusting the time values of one series using the ratio of its duration to the duration of the comparison piece. This approach will work in pieces that do not change in expressive content in terms of tempo, such as much popular dance music.

However, Western art music can have numerous expressive performance variation requirements within a piece (Clarke & Windsor, 2000; Friberg, 2006; Juslin, Friberg, & Bresin, 2002; Widmer, 2002), as well as sections with explicit requirements for change in tempo that will not be identically executed by all performers. To address this more complex scaling problem, McAdams et al (2004) describe the method of temporal alignment called registration, where landmarks in the piece are identified (e.g. a change in tempo or a new section), and the time points between these landmarks are adjusted by linear dilation—adjusting each sample point in one performance by a factor that will ensure the data arrive together at the next landmark, like the graphical stretching approach described above, but done over smaller sections of the performance (see also Levitin et al, 2007). This is a practical approach to allowing comparison of responses to different performances.

Each of these methods is linear, and therefore may not be able to capture the variation in the rate of change that might be found in some sections of a performance, particularly in the case of different performances of a ritardando or accelerando (e.g. Friberg & Sundberg, 1999; Honing, 2003; Schulze, Cordes, & Vorberg, 2005). With a view to this problem, the technique of dynamic time warping provides a promising solution (Dixon & Widmer, 2005).

9.6.4 The relationship between continuous and post-performance response

Continuous-response methods allow insight into the time-point-to-time-point fluctuations in response as a piece of music unfolds. Schubert (2001) asked that if these fluctuations are not of primary interest, why not just collect post-performance response? It is generally simpler to collect post-performance data (for both participant and researcher), and to store and analyse it, in comparison to continuous response. For example, a researcher may collect responses continuously, take the average of the scores across time points, and report this average as a summary of the response.

The question 'If that is all that is going to be reported why not just collect post-performance data?' has an answer emerging in the literature that 'It matters because they are not the same thing.' Duke and Colprit (2001) compared post-performance responses with averaged continuous-response data, and found that post-performance ratings (in this case 'musical intensity') were higher than the averaged continuous-response data. This is consistent with the human continuous-response literature, for example in pain studies where the memory of the event was best predicted by the 'peak' (wherever it occurred) and 'end' experiences, rather than the average of the responses over time (Kahneman, Fredrickson, Schreiber, & Redelmeier, 1993; Redelmeier, Katz, & Kahneman, 2003; Schreiber & Kahneman, 2000). Rozin, Rozin, and Goldberg (2004) obtained similar results to a variety of musical excerpts when comparing continuous emotional intensity ratings with the post-performance, or 'remembered', emotion intensity. They reported that:

The peak value of momentary intensity and the end value both significantly influence listeners' retrospective judgements of music . . . [and] the moment-to-moment context also shapes remembered affect. A momentary intensity that is much greater than the previous momentary intensity greatly influences determinations of remembered intensity. (p. 34)

This phenomenon is sometimes referred to as 'duration neglect', and has an implication that the post-performance experience is information poor. Many of the emotional experiences during the piece are potentially lost or forgotten. This non-linearity between continuous response and post-performance or 'summative' response (to use Duke and Colprit's terminology) is an area that will provide interesting further research into not only emotional response to music, but also the role of memory in music-emotion experience. It is another one of the essential contributions that continuous-response research is making. For example, it may inform composers about more efficient ways to compose, capitalizing on the high impact of certain parts of a piece, but also emphasizing the need for contrast.

From a more philosophical perspective, it raises questions on what the phenomenological differences are between the emotions expressed in a 70-minute Mahler symphony versus a 25-minute Sibelius symphony, and versus a three-minute pop song. If each happens to produce equivalent recency effects, similar peak experience intensity, and so forth, such that they produce equivalent post-performance ratings, is there an inefficiency in the Mahler? Rozin et al (2004) exemplify this with the results of two versions of 'When I Am Laid in Earth' from *Dido and Aeneas*, in which a long version and a short version were rated as statistically the same. They concluded that 'the longer version did not add to participants' memories of intensity' (p. 25).

Of course, the 'Mahler inefficiency' argument is an artefactual one. Continuous-response studies are generally limited to highly reductionist measures, which have not been able to encapsulate the full depth of the musical experience. What is important here is that technology is moving forward and beginning to provide scientific insights into the deep and complex world of aesthetic experience and meaning. It cannot be claimed that such problems have been solved, but rather that new puzzles, such as 'duration neglect', can be discovered, debated, and perhaps eventually explained adequately.

9.6.5 Felt versus perceived emotion

In self-report data collection paradigms, the distinction between felt (induced) emotions in response to music and emotion thought to be expressed (perceived emotion) by the music can be investigated by changing the wording of the task to be performed by the participant (e.g. 'How does the piece make you feel?' versus 'What is the music trying to convey?'). However, the situation becomes complicated when certain emotions are not found to be expressible by music (Gabrielsson, 2002) and when physiological responses (Chapter 11, this volume) are seen as an 'implicit' measure of felt emotional response (see also Chapter 10, this volume).

The only study cited that has compared felt and perceived emotions continuously was conducted by Krumhansl (1997). In the study, 40 college students had physiological measures taken while judging the emotion expressed by musical items intended to express emotions of sadness, fear, and happiness. There was strong evidence that different emotions that the music portrayed—sadness, happiness, and fear—produced different physiological responses in the listeners. The felt emotions were therefore associated with physiological change, which does not lend itself to direct comparison with perceived emotions, because a physiological scale measures a variable directly from the human body, such as blood pressure, heart rate, and skin conductance, without being mediated by language. No studies have been cited that specifically compare continuous self-report of felt emotions with continuous self-report of perceived emotions on semantically identical scales, to the same music, and by the same participants. Researchers to date have either specified that they want participants to think about the emotion that the music is expressing (e.g. Korhonen et al, 2006; Luck et al, 2008; Schubert, 2004; Toiviainen & Krumhansl, 2003) or how the music makes the listener feel (e.g. Grewe, Nagel, Kopiez, & Altenmüller, 2005, 2007; McAdams et al, 2004; Waterman, 1996).

In the future, direct comparisons of felt and perceived emotions will be made using the same self-report scales for both emotional 'loci' (felt and perceived), to see if the results are similar to those found in post-performance paradigms (e.g. Dibben, 2004; Evans & Schubert, 2008; Schubert, 2007c). Because perceived and felt emotions are not always the same (Evans & Schubert, 2008; Gabrielsson, 2002; see also Chapters 4, 8, and 22, this volume), continuous-response measures should provide new insights into whether there are any time points within a piece where the two locus conditions deviate from one another, and whether these are tied to particular musical characteristics or not. Given that this is a new field using traditional approaches, and lacking in application of well-grounded theory, such studies are likely to be exploratory.

9.6.6 Dealing with serial correlation

As suggested throughout this chapter, a fundamental distinction between time series data and data used in post-performance experiments is that time series data points have a dependency on other points that have occurred or are about to occur. This serial correlation is an important concept that needs to be understood by researchers moving from parametric statistical models to time-series, particularly when trying to extract generalizable patterns from empirical data, such as predicting emotional responses based on information about unfolding musical features (Schubert, 2004).

For example, reporting correlation coefficients between two time-series will generally produce inflated results. Schubert (2002) recommended a difference transformation of the time-series to produce a more plausible correlation analysis. Using non-parametric correlation analysis, such as the Spearman rank correlation, is suggested as another possible solution, Vines et al (2006) describe the method of *averaged parametric correlation* (APC), where effects of serial correlation are reduced by breaking the continuous response into sections exhibiting some kind of distinction that are at least two seconds apart, and usually based on phrase boundaries in the music. Similarly, Luck et al (2008) used downsampling to reduce the effects of serial correlation. That is, instead of using each response data point (sampled at 2 Hz), they used every 12th data point, an effective sampling period of six seconds. This longer period allows more of the typical kinds of serial correlation found in such data to dissipate.

These time thresholds were determined empirically and seem to provide a minimum time period after which the effect of first-order serial correlation may not be so strong, certainly compared to the serial correlation that will be present in much shorter time spans—imagine the logical extreme of two consecutive samples made 0.25 seconds apart. The participant will have had little time to move the response slider (or other interface) even if a fast response was required, hence a necessary serial correlation over short time periods. Vines and colleagues compared the APC and Spearman correlations for responses to two musical performances. On the whole, APC and Spearman methods produced fairly similar coefficients, with Spearman correlations tending to be slightly lower in value. Only six comparisons could be made in the study, and so further work is required to determine whether one method has the edge over the other.

9.6.7 Time domain or frequency domain

Not discussed in this chapter are the frequency-domain approaches to studying time series data, such as Fourier transformation and wavelet analysis, as they have not been cited in application to continuous self-reports of emotional response to music. It could be that the time-domain approach, the domain of analysis described in this chapter, provides sufficient analytic resources that have not yet been exploited, or that researchers in the area are not feeling adventurous enough. Frequency domain may have some advantages in computation and interpretation compared to time-domain approaches, such as easy identification of cyclical patterns in the music signal and the emotional response, and in identifying how energy in such a music-emotion system is distributed (for an introduction to these approaches, see Graps, 1995). It is true, too, that the two domains can be shown to be equivalent, so while there is no specific need to use one or the other, the issue is moot. Recall the example earlier in this chapter (Section 9.4.8), when the discussion of high-frequency noise artefacts (a frequency-domain variable) was explained in terms of time domain. It may be that working in the time domain is conceptually simpler for some.

9.7 SUMMARY AND CONCLUSIONS

This chapter has introduced the basic principles of continuous response and analysis of emotion in music. Continuous response is an important part of the researcher's 'tool kit' because it enables measurement of the necessary, fundamental time-dependent properties of music, and acknowledges the potential for emotions to vary in response to the unfolding musical stimulus. While methods of studying emotion in music continuously have been slow to move, in the last few years we have seen a flurry of continuous-response collection devices, some of which are freely available, and we have moved to a point where previously pertinent questions such as sampling rate are no longer so crucial because of the head room allowed by fast computers.

New applications of analytic techniques have also continued to enter the area. We are now seeing different and sophisticated modelling techniques being adapted from traditional time series approaches, such as autoregression models and the emerging methods of functional data analysis. These now complement the more commonly found descriptive, visual inspection of time-chart approaches, and promise a new level and depth of understanding of the nature of continuous emotional response to music.

Although much of this chapter describes progress and developments that are quite new compared to the review conducted some nine years ago (Schubert, 2001), we are still at the tip of the iceberg—but the tip is getting bigger. Given that there are fairly distinct differences between continuous and post-performance self-reports, and given routine access to fast computers, it may one day become the norm for most researchers of music emotion to record and analyse responses continuously and meaningfully, as is the case today with post-performance experimental designs and parametric statistics. From this perspective, a major challenge is to find continuous-response methods and software solutions that are packaged in such a way as to entice researchers not yet specialized but who are sufficiently fascinated and have the drive to discover how and why emotion in music works.

Many publications using continuous-response methods for collecting emotional responses to music are still exploratory. There are two important research areas that have emerged which are peculiar to or dependent on the method. One is our ability to investigate 'lag structure'—the delay between an emotional response and its causal musical antecedent. This is research that was not possible and would be very difficult without continuous-response technology. The other is the relationship between continuous responses and post-performance response. This research has produced interesting debates about the equivalence or otherwise of the two ways of 'experiencing' or analysing music. In Western culture, the reliving and recalling of a musical experience after the event (from the perspective of social interaction, or the report of the music critic) produces profound philosophical questions about the nature of the musical experience in the light of the discoveries presented by continuous self-report methods.

But it would be a mistake to conclude that continuous-response methods are the only way forward with regard to questions about emotion in music. Researchers are advised to try to match the requirements of the research question with the efficiency and appropriateness of the tools available. For some research questions, other methods may be more appropriate. However, exploration with these devices should be encouraged. For example, modelling emotions as a function of musical features could be done most efficiently (from an experimental design perspective) using post-performance paradigms, as evidenced in the large amount of knowledge on the topic from such approaches (e.g. see Chapters 14 and 17, this volume). However, it was a continuous-response study that was the first to identify the critical importance of fluctuations in loudness upon emotional arousal (Schubert, 2004), a finding rarely emphasized in post-performance-based studies before that time. While not denying the current poverty of substantive theory-driven work that is adopted in research on continuous response to emotion in music, by the same token, the perhaps more risky, exploratory study should always have a role to play.

A frequently cited weakness of self-report continuous-response research is that it tends to use response formats that collect slider information representing one or two concepts; it is therefore overly reductionist, and requires a lot of effort by the participant compared with post-performance measures, where the participant is free to listen without interference from the incessant response task and therefore able to focus on a more detailed, meaningful response when the music is finished. My response to this, to some extent valid, criticism is twofold. First, as we have seen, we cannot assume that a post-performance response will be identical to a continuous response. Second, the richness and new angles afforded by examining the time course of such responses outweigh this negative aspect. It is more a matter of whether the research community can embrace a new, imperfect path to discovering aspects of the neglected, yet essential, time course of responses to music.[1]

[1] I am grateful to the anonymous reviewers and the editors for their helpful comments on the draft of this chapter. I am also deeply indebted to my friends and colleagues, Eric Sowey, Joe Wolfe, Roger Dean, and Alfonso Egan for their incisive and collegial comments and for continuing to support me. This work was also supported by the Australian Research Council through a Discovery Project Grant DP0452290.

RECOMMENDED FURTHER READING

1. Levitin, D. J., Nuzzo, R. L., Vines, B. W., & Ramsay, J. O. (2007). Introduction to functional data analysis. *Canadian Psychology, 48*, 135–55.
2. Schubert, E., & Dunsmuir, W. (1999). Regression modelling continuous data in music psychology. In S. W. Yi (ed.), *Music, mind, and science* (pp. 298–352). Seoul, South Korea: Seoul National University.
3. Schubert, E. (2001). Continuous measurement of self-report emotional response to music. In P. N. Juslin & J. A. Sloboda (eds), *Music and emotion: Theory and research* (pp. 393–414). Oxford: Oxford University Press.

REFERENCES

Barrett, L. F., Mesquita, B., Ochsner, K. N., & Gross, J. J. (2007). The experience of emotion. *Annual Review of Psychology, 58*, 373–403.

Barrett, L. F., & Wager, T. D. (2006). The structure of emotion: Evidence from neuroimaging studies. *Current Directions in Psychological Science, 15*, 79–83.

Bigand, E., Filipic, S., & Lalitte, P. (2005). The time course of emotional responses to music. *Annals of the New York Academy of Sciences, 1060*, 429–37.

Bowerman, B. L., O'Connell, R. T., & Koechler, A. B. (2005). *Forecasting, time series, and regression: An applied approach* (4th edn). Belmont, CA: Thompson Brooks/Cole.

Box, G. E. P., Jenkins, G. M., & Reinsel, G. C. (1994). *Time series analysis: Forecasting and control* (3rd edn). Englewood Cliffs, NJ: Prentice-Hall.

Cabrera, D. (1999). PsySound: A computer program for the psychoacoustical analysis of music. Retrieved from: http://www.mikropol.net/

Camurri, A., Castellano, G., Ricchetti, M., & Volpe, G. (2006). Subject interfaces: Measuring bodily activation during an emotional experience of music. *Gesture in Human–Computer Interaction and Simulation, 3881,* 268–79.

Clarke, E. F., & Windsor, W. L. (2000). Real and simulated expression: A listening study. *Music Perception, 17,* 277–313.

Clynes, M. (1973). Sentics: Biocybernetics of emotion communication. *Annals of the New York Academy of Sciences, 220,* 55–131.

Clynes, M. (1989). Methodology in sentographic measurement of motor expression of emotion: Two-dimensional freedom of gesture essential. *Perceptual and Motor Skills, 68,* 779–83.

Cowie, R., & Cornelius, R. R. (2003). Describing the emotional states that are expressed in speech. *Speech Communication, 40,* 5–32.

Cowie, R., Douglas-Cowie, E., Savvidou, S., McMahon, E., Sawey, M., & Schroeder, M. (2000). FEELTRACE: an instrument for recording perceived emotion in real time. In R. Cowie, E. Douglas-Cowie, & M. Schroeder (eds), *Speech and emotion: Proceedings of the ISCA workshop* (pp. 19–24). Newcastle, UK: Co. Down.

Cowie, R., Douglas-Cowie, E., Tsapatsoulis, N., Votsis, G., Kollias, S., Fellenz, W., et al (2001). Emotion recognition in human–computer interaction. *IEEE Signal Processing Magazine, 18,* 32–80.

Dibben, N. (2004). The role of peripheral feedback in emotional experience with music. *Music Perception, 22,* 79–115.

Dixon, S., & Widmer, G. (2005). MATCH: A music alignment tool chest. *Proceedings of the 6th International Conference on Music Information Retrieval* (pp. 492–7). London: ISMIR.

Dufour, J.-M., Khalaf, L., Bernard, J.-T., & Genest, I. (2004). Simulation-based finite-sample tests for heteroskedasticity and ARCH effects. *Journal of Econometrics, 122,* 317–47.

Duke, R. A., & Colprit, E. J. (2001). Summarizing listener perceptions over time. *Journal of Research in Music Education, 49,* 330–42.

Engle, R. F. (2001). GARCH 101: The use of ARCH/GARCH model in applied economics. *Journal of Economic Perspectives, 15,* 157–68.

Engle, R. F. (ed.). (1995). *ARCH: Selected readings.* Oxford: Oxford University Press.

Evans, P., & Schubert, E. (2008). Relationships between expressed and felt emotions in music. *Musicae Scientiae, 12,* 75–99.

Fredrickson, W. E. (2001). The effect of performance medium on perception of musical tension. *Bulletin of the Council for Research in Music Education, 148,* 60–64.

Fredrickson, W. E., & Coggiola, J. C. (2003). A comparison of music majors' and nonmajors' perceptions of tension for two selections of jazz music. *Journal of Research in Music Education, 51,* 259–70.

Friberg, A. (2006). pDM: An expressive sequencer with real-time control of the KTH music-performance rules. *Computer Music Journal, 30,* 37–48.

Friberg, A., & Sundberg, J. (1999). Does music performance allude to locomotion? A model of final ritardandi derived from measurements of stopping runners. *Journal of the Acoustical Society of America, 105,* 1469–84.

Gabrielsson, A. (2002). Emotion perceived and emotion felt: Same or different? *Musicae Scientiae, Special Issue 2001–2002,* 123–47.

Geringer, J. M., Madsen, C. K., & Gregory, D. (2004). A fifteen-year history of the Continuous Response Digital Interface: Issues relating to validity and reliability. *Bulletin of the Council for Research in Music Education, 160,* 1–15.

Gottman, J. M. (1981). *Time series analysis: A comprehensive introduction for social scientists.* Cambridge, UK: Cambridge University Press.

Graps, A. (1995). An introduction to wavelets. *IEEE Computational Science and Engineering, 2,* 50–61.

Gregory, D. (1989). Using computers to measure continuous music responses. *Psychomusicology, 8,* 127–34.

Grewe, O., Nagel, F., Kopiez, R., & Altenmüller, E. (2005). How does music arouse 'chills'? Investigating strong emotions, combining psychological, physiological, and psychoacoustical methods. *Annals of the New York Academy of Sciences, 1060,* 446–9.

Grewe, O., Nagel, F., Kopiez, R., & Altenmüller, E. (2007). Listening to music as a re-creative process: Physiological, psychological, and psychoacoustical correlates of chills and strong emotions. *Music Perception, 24,* 297–314.

Heinlein, C. P. (1928). The affective character of the major and minor modes in music. *Journal of Comparative Psychology, 8,* 101–42.

Hevner, K. (1935). Expression in music: a discussion of experimental studies and theories. *Psychological Review, 42,* 187–204.

Hevner, K. (1936). Experimental studies of the elements of expression in music. *American Journal of Psychology, 48,* 246–68.

Honing, H. (2003). The final ritard: on music, motion, and kinematic models. *Computer Music Journal, 27,* 66–72.

Ilie, G., & Thompson, W. F. (2006). A comparison of acoustic cues in music and speech for three dimensions of affect. *Music Perception, 23,* 319–29.

Juslin, P. N., Friberg, A., & Bresin, R. (2002). Toward a computational model of expression in music performance: The GERM model. *Musicae Scientiae, Special Issue 2001–2,* 63–122.

Kahneman, D., Fredrickson, B. L., Schreiber, C. A., & Redelmeier, D. A. (1993). When more pain is preferred to less—Adding a better end. *Psychological Science, 4,* 401–5.

Korhonen, M. D., Clausi, D. A., & Jernigan, M. E. (2006). Modeling emotional content of music using system identification. *IEEE Transactions on Systems Man and Cybernetics Part B—Cybernetics, 36,* 588–99.

Krumhansl, C. L. (1996). A perceptual analysis of Mozart's piano sonata K. 282: Segmentation, tension, and musical ideas. *Music Perception, 13,* 401–32.

Krumhansl, C. L. (1997). An exploratory study of musical emotions and psychophysiology. *Canadian Journal of Experimental Psychology, 51,* 336–52.

Krumhansl, C. L., & Schenck, D. L. (1997). Can dance reflect the structural and expressive qualities of music? A perceptual experiment on Balanchine's choreography of Mozart's Divertimento no. 15. *Musicae Scientiae, 1,* 63–85.

Laukka, P., Juslin, P. N., & Bresin, R. (2005). A dimensional approach to vocal expression of emotion. *Cognition & Emotion, 19,* 633–53.

Levitin, D. J., Nuzzo, R. L., Vines, B. W., & Ramsay, J. O. (2007). Introduction to functional data analysis. *Canadian Psychology, 48,* 135–55.

Luck, G., Toiviainen, P., Erkkila, J., Lartillot, O., Riikkila, K., Makela, A., et al (2008). Modelling the relationships between emotional responses to, and musical content of, music therapy improvisations. *Psychology of Music, 36,* 25–45.

Madsen, C. K. (1997). Emotional response to music as measured by the two-dimensional CRDI. *Journal Of Music Therapy, 34,* 187–99.

Madsen, C. K., Brittin, R. V., & Capperella-Sheldon, D. A. (1993). An empirical-method for measuring the aesthetic experience to music. *Journal of Research in Music Education, 41,* 57–69.

Madsen, C. K., & Coggiola, J. C. (2001). The effect of manipulating a CRDI dial on the focus of attention of musicans/nonmusicans and perceived aesthetic response. *Bulletin of the Council for Research in Music Education*, *149*, 13–22.

Margulis, E. H. (2007). Silences in music are musical not silent: An exploratory study of context effects on the experience of musical pauses. *Music Perception*, *24*, 485–506.

McAdams, S., Vines, B. W., Vieillard, S., Smith, B. K., & Reynolds, R. (2004). Influences of large-scale form on continuous ratings in response to a contemporary piece in a live concert setting. *Music Perception*, *22*, 297–350.

McMahon, E., Cowie, R., & André, E. (2004*). Describing the feelings that music communicates*: *A dimensional approach*. Belfast: Queen's University.

Nagel, F., Kopiez, R., Grewe, O., & Altenmüller, E. (2007). EMuJoy: Software for continuous measurement of perceived emotions in music. *Behavior Research Methods*, *39*, 283–90.

Namba, S., Kuwano, S., Hatoh, T., & Kato, M. (1991). Assessment of musical performance by using the method of continuous judgment by selected description. *Music Perception*, *8*, 251–75.

Osgood, C. E., Suci, G. J., & Tannenbaum, P. H. (1957). *The measurement of meaning*. Urbana, IL: University of Illinois Press.

Pass, F., Renkl, A., & Sweller, J. (2004). Cognitive load theory: Instructional implications of the interaction between information structures and cognitive architecture. *Instructional Science*, *32*, 1–8.

Plutchik, R. (1962). *The emotions: Facts, theories and a new model*. New York: Random House.

Ramsay, J. O., & Silverman, B. W. (2002). *Applied functional data analysis*: *Methods and case studies*. New York: Springer.

Redelmeier, D. A., Katz, J., & Kahneman, D. (2003). Memories of colonoscopy: a randomized trial. *Pain*, *104*, 187–94.

Rigg, M. (1937). An experiment to determine how accurately college students can interpret the intended meanings of musical compositions. *Journal of Experimental Psychology*, *21*, 223–9.

Rozin, A., Rozin, P., & Goldberg, E. (2004). The feeling of music past: How listeners remember musical affect. *Music Perception*, *22*, 15–39.

Ruef, A. M., & Levenson, R. W. (2007). Continuous measurement of emotion: The affect rating dial. In J. A. Coan & J. J. B. Allen (eds), *Handbook of emotion elicitation and assessment*. Oxford: Oxford University Press.

Russell, J. A. (1980). A circumplex model of affect. *Journal of Social Psychology*, *39*, 1161–78.

Russell, J. A. (1989). Measures of emotion. In R. Plutchik & H. Kellerman (eds), *Emotion*: *Theory, research, and experience* (Vol. 4, pp. 81–111). New York: Academic Press.

Russell, J. A., & Mehrabian, A. (1977). Evidence for a 3-factor theory of emotions. *Journal of Research in Personality*, *11*, 273–94.

Russell, J. A., Weiss, A., & Mendelsohn, G. A. (1989). Affect grid: a single-item scale of pleasure and arousal. *Journal of Personality and Social Psychology*, *57*, 493–502.

Scherer, K. R., Dan, E. S., & Flykt, A. (2006). What determines a feeling's position in affective space? A case for appraisal. *Cognition & Emotion*, *20*, 92–113.

Schimmack, U., & Grob, A. (2000). Dimensional models of core affect: A quantitative comparison by means of structural equation modeling. *European Journal of Personality*, *14*, 325–45.

Schreiber, C. A., & Kahneman, D. (2000). Determinants of the remembered utility of aversive sounds. *Journal of Experimental Psychology*: *General*, *129*, 27–42.

Schubert, E. (1996). Continuous response to music using a two dimensional emotion space. In B. Pennycook & E. Costa-Giomi (eds), *Proceedings of the Fourth International Conference of Music Perception and Cognition* (pp. 263–8). McGill University, Montreal, Canada.

Schubert, E. (1999). Measuring emotion continuously: Validity and reliability of the two-dimensional emotion-space. *Australian Journal of Psychology*, 51, 154–65.

Schubert, E. (2001). Continuous measurement of self-report emotional response to music. In P. N. Juslin & J. A. Sloboda (eds), *Music and emotion: Theory and research* (pp. 393–414). Oxford: Oxford University Press.

Schubert, E. (2002). Correlation analysis of continuous emotional response to music: Correcting for the effects of serial correlation. *Musicae Scientiae, Special Issue 2001–2*, 213–36.

Schubert, E. (2003). Update of Hevner's adjective checklist. *Perceptual and Motor Skills*, 96, 1117–22.

Schubert, E. (2004). Modeling perceived emotion with continuous musical features. *Music Perception*, 21, 561–85.

Schubert, E. (2007a). Locus of emotion: The effect of task order and age on emotion perceived and emotion felt in response to music. *Journal of Music Therapy*, 44, 344–68.

Schubert, E. (2007b). Real time cognitive response recording. In E. Schubert, K. Buckley, R. Eliott, B. Koboroff, J. Chen, & C. Stevens (eds), *Proceedings of the Inaugural International Conference on Music Communication Science* (pp. 139–42). Sydney, Australia: ARC Research Network in Human Communication Science (HCSNet), University of Western Sydney.

Schubert, E. (2007c). The influence of emotion, locus of emotion and familiarity upon preference in music. *Psychology of Music*, 35, 499–515.

Schubert, E. (2007d). When is an event in a time series significant? In E. Schubert, K. Buckley, R. Eliott, B. Koboroff, J. Chen, & C. Stevens (eds), *Proceedings of the Inaugural International Conference on Music Communication Science* (pp. 135–8). Sydney, Australia: ARC Research Network in Human Communication Science (HCSNet), University of Western Sydney.

Schubert, E. (2008). *Orientation effect in continuous emotional response tasks*. Paper presented at the 10th International Conference on Music Perception and Cognition, Sapporo, Japan, August 2008.

Schubert, E., & Dunsmuir, W. (1999). Regression modelling continuous data in music psychology. In S. W. Yi (ed.), *Music, mind, and science* (pp. 298–352). Seoul, South Korea: Seoul National University.

Schulze, H.-H., Cordes, A., & Vorberg, D. (2005). Keeping synchrony while tempo changes: Accelerando and ritardando. *Music Perception*, 22, 461–77.

Sherman, M. (1928). Emotional character of the singing voice. *Journal of Experimental Psychology*, 11, 495–7.

Sloboda, J. A. (1991). Music structure and emotional response: Some empirical findings. *Psychology of Music*, 19, 110–20.

Sloboda, J. A. (2005). *Exploring the musical mind: Cognition, emotion, ability, function*. Oxford: Oxford University Press.

Sloboda, J. A., & Lehmann, A. C. (2001). Tracking performance correlates of changes in perceived intensity of emotion during different interpretations of a Chopin piano prelude. *Music Perception*, 19, 87–120.

Sprent, P. (1993). *Applied nonparametric statistical methods* (2nd edn). London: Chapman & Hall.

Stevens, C., Glass, R., Schubert, E., Chen, J., & Winskel, H. (2007). Methods for measuring audience reactions. In E. Schubert, K. Buckley, R. Eliott, B. Koboroff, J. Chen, & C. Stevens (eds), *Proceedings of the Inaugural International Conference on Music Communication Science* (pp. 155–158). Sydney, Australia: ARC Research Network in Human Communication Science (HCSNet), University of Western Sydney.

Stevens, C., Schubert, E., Haszard Morris, R., Frear, M., Chen, J., Healey, S., et al (2009). *The portable Audience Response Facility (pARF): PDAs that record real-time and instantaneous data during live or recorded performance*. Manuscript submitted for publication.

Thompson, S., Williamon, A., & Valentine, E. (2007). Time-dependent characteristics of performance evaluation. *Music Perception*, *25*, 13–29.

Toiviainen, P., & Krumhansl, C. L. (2003). Measuring and modeling real-time responses to music: The dynamics of tonality induction. *Perception*, *32*, 741–66.

Tzanetakis, G., & Cook, P. (2000). MARSYAS: A framework for audio analysis. *Organised Sound*, *4*, 169–75.

Vines, B. W., Krumhansl, C. L., Wanderley, M. M., & Levitin, D. J. (2006). Cross-modal interactions in the perception of musical performance. *Cognition*, *101*, 80–113.

Vines, B. W., Nuzzo, R. L., & Levitin, D. J. (2005). Analyzing temporal dynamics in music: Differential calculus, physics, and functional data analysis techniques. *Music Perception*, *23*, 137–52.

Vines, B. W., Wanderley, M. M., Krumhansl, C. L., Nuzzo, R. L., & Levitin, D. J. (2003). Performance gestures of musicians: What structural and emotional information do they convey? *Gesture-Based Communication in Human–Computer Interaction*, *2915*, 468–78.

Waterman, M. (1996). Emotional responses to music: Implicit and explicit effects in listeners and performers. *Psychology of Music*, *24*, 53–67.

Widmer, G. (2002). Machine discoveries: A few simple, robust local expression principles. *Journal of New Music Research*, *31*, 37–50.

CHAPTER 10

INDIRECT PERCEPTUAL, COGNITIVE, AND BEHAVIOURAL MEASURES

DANIEL VÄSTFJÄLL

'I hesitate it is impossible to measure the feelings of the human heart.'

William Stanley Jevons, *The theory of political economy* (1871/1888)

AFFECT is central to our everyday life, and there is little doubt that we experience affect in relation to various external stimuli, including music. Throughout the history of scientific psychology, there have been doubts about how we should measure affect, echoing Sir William Jevons's concern that it is a difficult, if not impossible, endeavour to capture the feelings of the human heart. However, recent development and refinement in data collection methods in areas such as social, personality, and emotion psychology now provide us with a battery of affect measures, including self-report measures, psychophysiological measures, brain measures, and behavioural measures (Chapters 8-12, this volume).

The aim of this chapter is to review a number of perceptual, cognitive, and behavioural (indirect) measures of affect that may help us understand musical emotions. The chapter is organized as follows. First, the problems and limitations of self-report are described. Two main problems, demand characteristics and limited access to one own's internal processes, are discussed. Following this, the logic of indirect measures of affect is outlined, along with a set of definitions. This section also features a conceptual model of affective responding, which aims to facilitate distinctions and integration between different classes of indirect measures. The subsequent section describes seven classes of indirect measures and provides detailed examples of each class. It is the intention that the reader should get an understanding of the basics of each measure, along with ideas of how to implement them in their own research on music and emotion. Many of the reviewed measures are from non-musical domains, but, whenever possible, a description is provided that will enable use in a musical context. The chapter ends with a brief summary and conclusions.

10.1 Problems with self-reports of affect

Many students of affect assert that 'multi-method approaches' are needed to understand affective responses (Lang, 1995; see also Chapter 4, this volume). Nonetheless, the golden standard in most studies of affective phenomena is to rely solely on self-reports. An earlier review of empirical studies using music to induce affect showed that self-report was by far the most widely used method to assess the affect induced by music (Västfjäll, 2002). There are good reasons for this reliance on self-reports. Self-reports are relatively easy and cheap to administer and interpret. But self-reports of affect also have some serious drawbacks that question the validity, and sometimes the veracity, of the responses. Among these, perhaps the two most important limitations are (1) demand characteristics and (2) limited accessibility and knowledge about internal processes.

10.1.1 Demand characteristics and strategic responding

Studies using self-report often rely on multiple assessments within a single exposure. A representative example is a study by Lenton and Martin (1991), which asked participants to report their affect both prior to and after the music, so that a change score could be calculated for each participant. In another study, participants were asked to report their affective reactions to the music on four or more occasions for the same musical piece (Albersnagel, 1988). Specific methods aiming to induce affect with music (e.g. the music and contemplation induction method; see Eich, Ng, Macaulay, Percy, & Grebneva, 2007) ask participants to rate their affect every fifth minute, and the induction procedure continues until participants reach a predetermined scale criterion (e.g. a specific scale value). The use of multiple self-report assessments within the same listening session and procedures that continue until the participant reports a specific scale value is subject to a serious experimental bias: demand characteristics. *Demand characteristics* can be defined as the total sum of cues that convey an experimental hypothesis to the participant and therefore become significant determinants of the participant's behaviour (Orne, 1962). Another, related, problem is that of *self-presentation bias* and *strategic responding*. It has been found that people are unwilling to accurately report their internal states when doing so may reveal that the person is experiencing something undesirable or socially unacceptable (Bradburn, Sudman, & Warsink, 2004). In such cases, people are likely to respond strategically in ways that are self-enhancing and that they believe are socially accepted.

Studies of musical emotion that utilize multiple assessments and scale criteria are vulnerable to these types of threats to validity. A major problem is that the participant can fairly easily guess the research hypothesis and adjust his or her ratings to this. Various attempts to overcome this threat to validity have been offered. Some studies used deception and cover stories to hide the true purpose of the study (e.g. Pignatiello et al, 1986). In these studies, participants were told that 'questions concerning the music would later be asked' and that they thus should attend carefully to the music. Siemer (2001) used a different cover story, telling participants that they were participating in two different experiments, one on 'music appreciation' that is unrelated to a second experiment (where an affect-sensitive task is used). In other studies, participants have simply been asked to rate the extent to which their experienced affect is 'genuine' (Eich et al, 2007), or have been probed about the real purpose of the study (Terezis, 1993).

The problems of self-presentation bias and demand characteristics persist in spite of such precautions. Lack of awareness of demand in a post-experimental questionnaire does not mean that they did not respond to demand during the experiment (Buchwald, Strack, & Coyne, 1981), and self-presentation biases are rarely accessible to conscious experience.

10.1.2 Limited access to internal process

Limited access to internal processes is another major disadvantage of self-reports. For participants to accurately and truthfully report their experiences, a first premise is that they have access to that same experience. In the case of musical emotions, individuals must access their subjective experience of affect (i.e. feeling) and transform it into scale values. In domains other than affect (e.g. cognitive psychology), it has long been known that participants sometimes have very limited access to their own mental processes (Nisbett & Wilson, 1977; Wilson & Brekke, 1994). Historically, affect research has put subjective experience at a premium, starting with William James's (1890/1950) proposal that that the subjective experience of affect is brought about by observing one's own physiological reactions. Today, however, subjective experience of affect is no longer the 'crown jewel' of the affect chain, and some researchers have begun to talk about 'unconscious affect' and 'preattentive affective behavior' (Winkielman & Berridge, 2004, Öhman & Mineka, 2001). Further, the full chain of affect is separated from the subjective sense of affect—or feeling (Damasio, 1994).

If affect may exist without conscious experience, it follows that self-report measures will not be able to capture all aspects of affect. Some limited empirical evidence in the musical domain points to this. Martin and Metha (1997) used a standard self-report measure to assess the effects of music on affective experience, and found no differences between 'positive', 'negative', and 'neutral' affect conditions. They did, however, find an effect of the manipulation on their dependent measure (an affect-sensitive task). This finding suggests that various 'indirect' measures that are sensitive to changes in affect may sometimes be a better alternative than self-report.

10.2 THE LOGIC OF INDIRECT MEASURES

Indirect measures circumvent many of the problems associated with self-reports. The rationale behind indirect measures is that the subjective experience of affect is only one component of the 'affect chain' (Carver, 2001). Often, but not always, the subjective experience of affect will co-vary with other psychological processes. Many of the major affect theories postulate that for affect to be experienced, accompanying changes (preceding or as a consequence of the experienced state, depending on the theory) in physiology (including motor control), information processing, expression, behaviour, and regulatory strategies occur (Lazarus, 1991). For example, negative affect tends to slow down motor movement, bias information processing in favour of negative information, and lead to attempts to recover from the negative feeling state. Positive affect tends to energize the person, favour broad information processing, and motivate behaviour to maintain positive affect. Indirect measures capitalize on these processes. Rather than directly assessing the subjective experience, indirect measures focus on capturing the effects of an experienced affective state on motor performance, information processing, behaviour, and affect regulation.

Figure 10.1 outlines the conceptual framework guiding the present analysis. Our focus here is that music elicits affect (as addressed in numerous other chapters in this book). The elicited affect can be a specific emotion with accompanying changes in appraisal tendencies and physiology (Scherer, 2001) or diffuse, valenced 'core affect' with more general effects on behaviour (Russell, 2003). Both types of affect will have consequences for motor behaviour, cognitive processes (e.g. information processing and memory), and implicit (e.g. behavioural tendency) or explicit (i.e. overt action) behaviour.

Affect has many different effects on cognition. In general, two main effects on cognitive processes can be distinguished. First, affect may influence the content of people's thoughts. For instance, participants who experience diffuse positive affect may think positive thoughts and recall positive memories more often, while participants who experience negative affect recall negative memories more often, or are biased towards greater negativity (Forgas, 1995). This effect has been known as *mood congruence* (Bower, 1981; Wright & Bower, 1992). Second, other research has shown that positive and negative affect might influence *processing styles* (Luce, Bettman, & Payne, 1997).

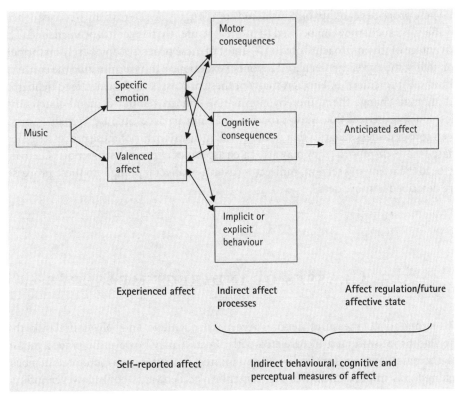

Fig. 10.1 Schematic illustration of the relationship between musically induced emotion and indirect perceptual, cognitive and behavioural measures.

For instance, happy individuals tend to process information in a less elaborated and systematic manner than do people in a negative affect (Isen, 2000). However, other research has shown that positive affect leads to more holistic and broader information processing (Clore & Huntsinger, 2007).

Once an affect is elicited, various attempts to regulate this state will take place (Gross, 2007). Affect regulation will be elicited with the aim to change, enhance, or attenuate the current affect. Important here is that the anticipated affect, the predicted end result of affect regulation, is guiding behaviour (Baumeister et al, 2007; Västfjäll, Gärling, & Kleiner, 2001). For example, happy individuals may avoid negative events and outcomes, and even process information systematically, if doing so helps them to maintain their positive affect. Sad individuals may seek positive experience to 'repair' their negative affect (but see also Västfjäll & Gärling, 2006, for an analysis of why individuals may sometimes prefer negative affect). Fredrickson and Levenson (1998) showed that attaining positive affect speeds physiological recovery from negative affect. Similarly, Taylor (1991) reviewed findings suggesting that negative events induce affective and physiological responses to which the organism mobilizes behavioural, phenomenological, and physiological resources in order to minimize the impact of the event.

These processes can thus be considered components or determinants/consequences of affect. As such, they can be used to indirectly infer that affect has been elicited. The advantage of this approach is obvious—most of these processes do not rely on the person telling the experimenter about his or her experience, thus minimizing the concerns about self-presentation. Further, many of these processes are insensitive to deliberate attempts to change them, thereby eliminating concerns about demand characteristics. Finally, the fact that these processes may not be accessible for verbalization or even consciousness suggests that not only will measurements of these processes be less biased than self-reports, they may also catch aspects of affect that self-reports fail to tap into. In the following section, indirect measures of affect tapping into these processes are described in more detail.

10.3 CLASSES OF INDIRECT MEASURES

The term 'indirect measures' denotes perceptual, cognitive, and behavioural tasks that tap into processes that are correlated with affect. It may however be argued that *all* psychological measures are 'indirect', and indirect measures have therefore often been referred to as 'implicit' measures (e.g. Wittenbrink & Schwarz, 2007). However, indirect measures are measures that do not directly ask people about their affect—the affective states are inferred from behaviour (Campbell, 1950). Indirect measures can be based on, but are not limited to, processes that are unavailable for introspective access. Implicit measures, on the other hand, further assume that the measures produce 'measurement outcomes that reflect the to-be-measured construct by virtue of processes that are uncontrolled, unintentional, goal independent, purely stimulus driven, autonomous, unconscious, efficient, or fast' (De Houwer & Moors, 2007, pp. 188–9). Clearly, many of the components outlined above do not meet these criteria, and the term indirect measures will therefore be used throughout the remainder of this chapter to refer to any kind of measurement that does not rely on explicit self-reports. Most implicit measures have been developed in social psychological research to reveal implicit attitudes (Wittenbrink & Schwarz, 2007). Since implicit measures capture constructs that are not available for explicit reports, correlations between explicit and implicit measures are often low in this research (Fazio & Olsen, 2003). For affective phenomena, however, the type of affect-sensitive tasks used often show a high correlation with self-reports (Mayer & Brewer, 1985; Kuykendall et al, 1988), which suggests that the measured affect process co-varies with subjective experience. As mentioned earlier, however, there are instances where a low correlation between an indirect and a direct measure of emotion is to be expected (e.g. 'unconscious affect'; see Winkielman & Berridge, 2004).

In the following, perceptual, cognitive, and behavioural that have been shown to correlate with affective experience will be reviewed. The tasks do not include physiological measures or facial or body expressions (Mauss & Robinson, 2009; see also Chapter 11, this volume), even though such methods are often used to triangulate

Table 10.1 Classes of indirect measures and examples of measures used in studies of musical emotions

Indirect measure	Description
Psycho-motor	Measures motor retardation as a function of experienced affect
	Example: counting numbers backwards
Perceptual	Systematic biases in perception as a consequence of affect
	Example: judgement of distance
Information processing	Measures affect-induced attention and affect-congruent processing of information such as elevated threat in fear
	Example: reaction times responding to threat vs. non-threat words
Memory	Affect-congruent biases in memory recall and recognition
	Example: recall of autobiographical memories
Evaluative misattribution	Transfer of currently experienced affect to unrelated evaluative judgement task
	Example: judgement of affectively neutral target
Behaviour	Affect-driven behaviour
	Example: consumption of goods
Affect regulation	Deliberate strategies employed to change currently experienced affects
	Example: incentive to take part in social activities

affective experience through self-report, behaviour, and physiology (Bradley & Lang, 2000). The focus is instead on the following seven classes of measures: (1) psycho-motor, (2) perceptual, (3) information processing, (4) memory, (5) evaluative misattribution, (6) behaviour, and (7) affect regulation. Table 10.1 offers a description of the main classes. For an indirect measure to be useful, it needs to be reliable, valid, sensitive, and relatively easy to administer. When possible, the various classes of indirect measures will be evaluated on how they fare against these criteria.

10.4 EXAMPLES OF INDIRECT MEASURES

10.4.1 Psycho-motor measures

An early view of how affect might influence human behaviour focused on psycho-motor retardation (Johnson, 1937). Affect was thought of mainly in terms of arousal, where the experience of affect would lead to significant changes in speed and precision of motor performance (Velten, 1968). Specifically, negative affect was expected to decrease both speed and precision relative to positive emotions on the assumption that they are associated with higher arousal (Clark, 1983). Psychomotor tasks thus rely on after-effects of emotion on behaviour that tend to occur implicitly and automatically. Psychomotor tasks have mainly been used in studies of general valenced affect, several of them including music as the eliciting stimulus.

Building on the early work by Johnson (1937), Clark (1983) used a measure of the time it takes to count from 1 to 10 as a measure of affect. It was predicted that negative affect would be associated with slower counting than positive affect. To time counting, Clark and Teasdale (1985) recorded participants' voices. Today, audio editors and other software are readily available, but Clark and Teasdale had to use a polygraph to obtain a visual speech print from which duration of counting could be measured. From this, they did indeed find that the music that was supposed to induce negative affect was associated with longer count times than the music that was intended to induce positive affect. Following Clark and Teasdale's initial findings, several researchers have replicated this finding using music, and extended the method to include several variations such as paced and fast counting (Clark et al, 2001; Wood et al, 1990). The counting task is relatively simple and easy to administer. A clear advantage is that it requires minimal instructions: 'Count backwards from 10.' The only equipment requirement is that the experimenter can record, store, and analyse the time patterns of participants' countings in order to find the fine time resolution needed.

A similar task is based on writing numbers. Participants are asked to write down numbers in descending order from 100, and are given one minute to do so (Velten, 1968). The numbers written down are seen as an index of motor speed. Two studies have found that this measure can discriminate between positive and negative affect induced by music (Clark, 1983; Kenealy, 1988), but other studies have not been able to replicate this (Parrott, 1991; Parrott & Sabini, 1990). Clark (1983) noted that all of the studies that showed a significant effect with this measure used analyses that took into account individuals' pre-induction writing speed, while almost all of the studies that failed to find an effect used analyses that did *not* take into account individuals' pre-induction scores. A study by Pignatiello et al (1986) supports the notion that between-individual variance must be eliminated before this measure is used. In one experiment, Pignatiello et al used only post-induction scores as a between-groups variable and failed to find any reliable difference between negative and positive affect. However, in another experiment when a pre-measure was included and used as a covariate in the subsequent analysis, a significant effect between the positive and negative conditions was obtained. It appears that the writing task is a robust method once between-subjects variance is minimized by including a pre-measure, and change scores rather than 'raw' scores are used. Obvious advantages of this method include its simplicity, the low cost, and the possibility of using it several times.

A theoretical concern with these and other methods relying on arousal to slow down motor performance is the assumption that negative affect is associated with more intense arousal than positive affect. However, Robinson et al (2004) have shown that the arousal component is mainly linked to defensive reflexes. Positive affect is often, but not always, linked to appetitive reflexes. Robinson et al showed that it is possible to disentangle the arousal component from the valence component, thus allowing for high arousal positive affect to be assessed also using this method.

Related methods that capitalize on the fact that negative affect (activation of defensive reflexes) tends to consume cognitive and attentional resources are the *word association speed task* and the *decision time task*. These methods predict that people experiencing negative affect will take longer time to produce single-word associates to stimulus words or make decisions than participants experiencing positive affect. Kenealy (1988) found exactly this result for music intended to induce negative vs. positive affect in the listener. While these measures are relatively easy to implement, more recent studies have shown that not only the speed with which participants can produce responses, but also more cognitive dimensions, such as the unusualness of the words produced, are influenced by the valence of the induced affect (Isen, 2000).

Other research has used more general speed of processing measures (similar to those used in gerontology to assess decline in cognitive abilities with age). Unfortunately, very few studies have used this type of measure in relation to music. One example is a study that used a procedure that presents participants with a coding scheme, in which the numbers correspond to a certain symbol (*symbol–number test*). The participant is asked to fill out 72 empty boxes using this coding scheme. While previous research has demonstrated that sad participants are slower than happy participants on this task, Wood et al (1990) failed to find any effect of music that was intended to make the participant feel either sad or happy (but see a later study by Green et al, 2003).

10.4.2 Perceptual measures

Perceptual measures rely on changes in the impression of physical reality concurrently with a change in affective experience (Clore & Huntsinger, 2007). This class includes any measure that has linked affect to biases in estimation of various physical properties or interpretation of information. These processes tend to occur often in real life, and seem to be automatic and resistant to volitional control (Clore & Huntsinger, 2007). Unfortunately, only a few studies have focused on musically induced emotions and perceptual biases.

A rare example, however, is a recent study by Riener (2007). In several experiments, music intended to make participants sad while standing at the bottom of a steep hill led the participants to overestimate the incline of the hill, compared with participants in a control condition. Along a similar line, Kenealy (1988) used a procedure in which participants were asked to estimate a specified distance by placing their hands that distance apart. Participants listening to music intended to make them feel sad estimated a significantly smaller distance than did participants listening to music intended to make them feel happy. The major difference between Riener's study and Kenealy's study is that, in the former, negative affect led to an overestimation of a potentially strenuous task, whereas in the latter, negative affect led to underestimation of a physical feature.

Both findings are in line with the literature on 'affect-congruent effects' (for an over-view, see Schwarz & Strack, 1999, and the section on evaluative misattribution below).

Bouhuys et al (1995) studied the effects of music on perception of facial expressions. They found that participants experiencing negative affect after listening to music per-ceived more sadness and less happiness in facial expressions than did participants experiencing positive affect (see also Kern, 2007).

Overall, it appears that affect biases perception in systematic and predictable ways. However, the empirical studies, and thus the developed methods and materials, are scarce, therefore it is difficult to assess the usefulness of perceptual measures as indirect measures of musical emotion.

10.4.3 Cognitive measures

Indirect measures relying on changes in information processing as a consequence of experienced affect is by far the biggest class. Two major branches within this class have either focused on attentional measures (Mathews & MacLeod, 1994) or evaluative responding measures (Wittenbrink & Schwarz, 2007). Both types of measures seem to rely on automatic responses that are resistant to deliberate attempts to modulate the responses. Unfortunately, since the development of these measures is relatively new, few studies have used music to induce affect. These measures will nonetheless be reviewed here, since they have been shown to be reliable and sensitive measures of affect-induced changes in processing (Mathews & MacLeod, 1994).

Attention biases associated with affect can be assessed with indirect measures rely-ing on reaction times. A basic assumption is that people in certain affective states that signal danger (e.g. anxiety, fear) will have a heightened sensitivity to environmental information. Increased perceptual vigilance has been shown in numerous experimen-tal studies: anxious people are particularly prone to bias their attention towards threat-ening information (Mathews & MacLeod, 1994; Mogg & Bradley, 1998). Two tasks have become particularly popular: the *dot probe task* and the *emotional Stroop task* (Mathews & MacLeod, 1985).

The dot probe task requires a computer to administer the task. Participants are briefly presented with two words on a screen (of which one is typically threatening), followed by a dot probe appearing in the location of one of the preceding words. The logic behind this task is that participants experiencing a negative affect will be quicker at detecting dot probes when they replace a threat word than when they replace a neutral word.

The emotional Stroop task is also best performed in a controlled computer environ-ment, but can also be done in a modified paper-and-pencil version (Vargas et al, 2007). The test presents participants with words in different colours, and participants are instructed to name the colour but ignore the meaning of the word. Building on a simi-lar logic as the dot probe task, participants experiencing a negative affect are expected to be slower at naming the colour of threatening words than at doing so for neutral words (Mathews & MacLeod, 1985).

The *Implicit Association Test* (IAT; Greenwald, McGhee, & Schwartz, 1998) measures strength of associations between concepts by comparing response times on two combined discrimination tasks. Participants are required to sort stimuli representing four concepts using just two responses, each assigned to two of the four concepts. The basic assumption of the IAT is that if two concepts are highly associated, the sorting task will be easier (i.e. faster) if the two associated concepts share the same response key than if they have different response keys. One example of the IAT procedure is as follows. The participant's task is to categorize pleasant versus unpleasant words and to classify items (e.g. *my* or *they*) into 'self' and 'other' categories. An IAT measure of implicit self-esteem is computed as the difference in mean categorization latency when self and pleasant share the same response key, compared with when self and unpleasant share the same response key. The IAT effect thus measures how much easier it is for the participant to categorize self items with pleasant items than it is to categorize self items with unpleasant items (Egloff & Schmuckle, 2002).

While the IAT was originally intended to measure attitudes (which researchers construe as both affective and cognitive), recent research has attempted to develop indirect measures of affect using the IAT methodology. For instance, Egloff and Schmuckle (2002) developed the *IAT-anxiety* by combining the self and other categories of classification of items with anxiety and calmness categories. Like the standard IAT, the anxiety version comprises five blocks presented on a computer screen. In each block, a series of words is presented sequentially, and participants are asked to categorize each word as quickly as possible into one of two categories. Blocks 1 and 2 are practice trials where participants are asked to sort either anxiety-inducing or self-related words. Block 3 is a critical trial: participants categorize items into two combined categories, each including the attribute and the target concept that were assigned to the same key in the preceding two blocks (e.g. self-anxiety for the left key, and other-calmness for the right key). Block 4 is a reversal of the attribute dimensions (i.e. other is now combined with anxiety). Block 5 repeats block 3 with a reversal of the keys. Implicit anxiety is then computed as the difference in response latency between self-anxiety and self-calmness. A longer latency for the self-anxiety categorization than for the self-calmness categorization (and thus a larger difference) is expected for participants who are experiencing anxiety. A recent version of the IAT measuring happiness has also been proposed (Walker & Schimmack, 2007). In the *IAT-happiness*, in block 3, responses to *me* and *happy* words are paired on the same mouse button, and responses to *not me* and *sad* words are paired on the same button. In block 5, the button assignments in block 3 are reversed.

The IAT measure is very popular in attitude research since it seems reliable, yields large effect sizes, and is relatively easy to administer. While several recent adaptations have made it more relevant to affect research, existing versions mainly tap into chronic or dispositional affect, such as trait anxiety or happiness. It is possible that the IAT can be used to assess more temporary affective states, because it is developed using the same type of rationale as the emotional Stroop and other tasks. In fact, some recent affective priming tasks borrowing from the IAT and other evaluative responding measures suggest that this is the case.

Genell et al (2007) developed a method where participants were asked to judge the valence of target stimuli (either affectively laden words as in the emotional Stroop task, or smiley faces) as quickly as possible. Targets were paired with auditory stimulation (noise, sounds, or music) intended to make the participant experience either negative or positive affect. Participants experiencing negative affect responded faster to negative targets, while participants experiencing positive affect responded faster to positive targets. This affect-congruent effect is consistent with the affective priming literature: affect activates affect-congruent material in memory, resulting in affect-congruent judgement (Bower, 1981).

A second approach predicts the opposite causal flow, where subliminal priming induces some form of unconscious affect (Winkielman, Zajonc, & Schwarz, 1997). In a recent study by Sollenberger et al (2003), it was demonstrated that the affective tone of musical chords may influence the evaluation of target words. In one experiment, participants heard either consonant chords with three tones or dissonant chords with four tones as primes, and then saw a positive or a negative word as target. Even participants who were unaware of the hypothesis of the experiment evaluated the target words faster if the words were preceded by a similarly valenced chord (e.g. consonant–holiday) than if they were preceded by an incongruent chord (e.g. dissonant–humour).

10.4.4 Memory measures

Musical emotion is strongly linked to episodic memories (Juslin & Västfjäll, 2008; Chapter 22, this volume). This fact has been used in a number of studies that used memory recall or recognition as an index of affective experience (e.g. Balch et al, 1999; Parrott, 1991). For instance, Clark and Teasdale (1985) investigated the effects of music on the recall of positive and negative words. Music that elicited negative affect in the participants led to more negative than positive words being recalled, while the reverse was found for music that elicited positive affect. Similar results have been obtained for autobiographical memories (Parrott & Sabini, 1990) and affectively neutral stories (Västfjäll, 2002). Balch et al (1999) found that material learned in a positively valenced affective state induced by music was better recalled in the same affective state than in a negatively valenced state (see also de l'Etoile, 2002; Eich & Metcalfe, 1989; Eich et al, 2007). Thus, affective memory is a very consistent indirect measure of affect. It seems that it can be used to assess generally valenced affect, and it is possible that emotions with specific appraisal tendencies may also evoke more specific memories.

10.4.5 Evaluative misattribution measures

Since the beginning of psychology, ambiguous material has been used to make inferences about internal processes. Most famous is the Rorschach inkblot test. Rorschach and other tests have been called 'projective tests', because the interpretation of the ambiguous information is thought to be a projection of the person's feelings and thoughts (interestingly often believed to be 'implicit' or unavailable to the person him- or herself). Music has been used to bias the interpretation of projective tests. Several studies using the *Thematic Apperception Test* (TAT) have found that music that elicits negative vs. positive affect can bias the interpretation of pictorial ambiguous stimuli in an affect-congruent manner (Carlton & Macdonald, 2004), including studies that validated that affect was experienced using physiological measures (Linnet & Västfjäll, 2005). The TAT methodology is relatively simple. Participants are shown pictures and are asked to write a short story on what they think is happening in each picture. Participants are asked to report the background story to the scene, rather than just a physical description of the picture. The written descriptions are collected and coded. Figure 10.2 shows an example of a picture and its associated coding scheme.

The TAT and other projective tests have been severely criticized for low validity and even for failing to capture underlying psychological states. Though projective tests may be questioned as measures of personality, it appears that the robust affect-biasing effect on perception of ambiguous information can be captured effectively using these measures.

Fig. 10.2 Example of TAT picture and coding scheme from Murray (1938).
Scoring Guide (1 = very negative, 5 = very positive)
1. Holding onto man for evil purposes. Triangular jealousy.
2. Abandonment. Negative attitude. Infidelity.
3. Argument (more pos or neg depending on other traits).
4. One intending to defend the other. Love.
5. Happy, frivolous behaviour. Advancing other's cause.

The finding that affect biases interpretation of projective tests is found more generally in studies of how people make judgements and decisions. A persistent finding in the judgement literature is that currently experienced affect is misattributed in reaction to an unrelated target. A classic study by Schwarz and Clore (1983) showed that the affect induced by sunny versus cloudy weather systematically influenced well-being ratings (with higher well-being during sunny days: i.e. an affect-congruent effect). A similar effect can be seen for arousal where unrelated physiological arousal (elicited by walking a high bridge or doing physical exercise) can bias the judgement of a target.

The robust evaluative misattribution findings can be used to infer the affective impact of music. For instance, Gorn et al (2001) showed that arousal and pleasantness induced by music had different effects on evaluations of advertisements. In their first study, music was used to induce positive versus negative affects that were similar in arousal levels. Following this procedure, participants were exposed to an ad that either had a positive affective tone or was ambiguous in its affective tone. Positive affect increased the positive evaluation of the ad, whereas negative affect increased negative evaluations of the ad. However, this effect occurred only when the ad had an ambiguous affective tone. Therefore, Gorn et al's second study used a target ad that had a clear positive or negative affective tone, and the valence and arousal dimensions of the affect were manipulated independently. In this case, arousal seemed to have a stronger impact. Specifically, ad evaluations were more polarized in the direction of the ad's affective tone under high arousal than under low arousal.

The mechanism underlying these findings is that when asked to make an evaluative judgement, individuals seek information to determine how they should make this judgement. People tend use whatever information is available to them at the time of making the decision (Clore & Huntsinger, 2007). In absence of other relevant or more salient information, people will use their affective reactions to the target to evaluate the object (Pham, 1998). People in positive affect tend to evaluate objects more favourably than participants in negative affect (mood congruence; Schwarz & Clore, 1983; but see Andrade, 2005, for a discussion about mood-incongruent effects also). It should be noted that the influence of unrelated affective reactions is greatest when the target is neutral, ambiguous, or carries little evaluative meaning. If the target carries affect itself, the effect of the unrelated affect is likely to diminish.

In a recent study, affective priming and evaluative misattribution were joined into a single indirect measure (Payne et al, 2005). In this procedure, people are asked to make evaluative judgements in an ambiguous judgement situation. An attitude object is used as a prime that can give rise to either negative or positive affect (e.g. George W. Bush). After the prime, participants are presented with a target that is ambiguous in how it should be evaluated (an abstract symbol). Participants are explicitly instructed to avoid expressing any influence of the prime in their judgement, and to evaluate only the symbol. However, since individuals misattribute their reactions from the attitude object to the target, the prime will systematically bias evaluations of the target. One important point here is that people incorrectly attribute their incidental affective reactions as a reaction to the target. This misattribution can be corrected or changed by introducing information that questions the diagnostic value of the affective reaction for the judgement. For instance, in the Schwarz and Clore (1983) study, participants were given a simple reminder about the cause (i.e. sunny vs. cloudy weather) of their affect, which resulted in that affect no longer influencing the judgements of well-being. Importantly though, it was the diagnostic value of the affective reaction for the judgement task, not the affective reaction itself, that was affected by this manipulation.

While evaluative misattribution is strongest for neutral and meaningless stimuli, it also occurs for some other types of judgements. Judgements of likelihood and subjective probability estimates of future events have also been shown to be responsive to induced affect, in that participants experiencing negative affect are more pessimistic than participants experiencing positive affect (Mayer & Bremer, 1985). Teasdale and Spencer (1984) explored the effects of music on such estimates. Participants listening to music intended to make them feel sad gave lower estimates of the probability of future successes, and lower estimates of the number of past successes, than participants listening to music intended to make them feel happy (see also replication of this effect in studies by Stöber, 1997, and Clark et al, 2001).

10.4.6 Behavioural measures

Real everyday behaviour is the ultimate indirect measure of affect. Several studies have tried to link affect to behaviour in one way or the other. Examples include eating behaviour (Heatherton et al, 1998; Willner et al, 1998), creative behaviour (Adaman & Blaney, 1995), aggressive behaviour/challenge (Durand & Mapstone, 1998), helping (North, Tarrant, & Hargreaves, 2004), and consumption (Bruner, 1990; Gardner, 1985; North & Hargreaves, 1997). A fundamental problem with behaviour as a measure of affect is that it is often not reliable or predictable, in that the same affective state might cause different behaviours both within the same person across situations and between people. Indeed, affective behaviour is one of the most difficult components of the affect chain to capture. This assertion might appear strange given that ample research has shown strong links between specific emotions (e.g. fear) and behaviour (e.g. flee) (Lazarus, 1991). Izard and Ackerman (2002) even noted that 'emotion-behavior relations begin to develop early and remain stable over time' (p. 254). However, the relationship between a given emotion and a specific behaviour is not one-to-one. Take the example of anger. Anger may in certain situations lead to approach behaviour (e.g. retaliate), in others to avoidance. Baumeister et al (2007) suggested that affect, rather than being the direct cause of behaviour, often indirectly through feedback and anticipation guides behaviour. This appears to hold especially true as we move from more reflex-like (e.g. startle response preparing the body to flee) to more cognitive, planned, and goal-oriented behaviour (e.g. buying clothes when feeling sad). The very same affect-eliciting event may therefore result in different behaviours. At the heart of the variability of behaviour following an affect-eliciting event is the notion of affect regulation.

10.4.7 Affect regulation measures

When experiencing affect, people will adapt their behaviour to maintain or change the response. Overall, people appear to prefer (and thus want to maintain) positive feelings and to dislike (and thus want to change) negative feelings (Västfjäll & Gärling, 2006). To maintain a positive feeling or 'repair' a negative feeling, people anticipate how different behaviours will make them feel (Baumeister et al, 2007). When feeling sad, people may want to reward themselves by eating sweet foods or consuming luxury goods (Gross, 2007). When feeling happy, people may choose not to think about the book chapter that they promised to write. Regardless of what people choose to do, they do it because they think that it will influence how they feel. The same holds true for musically induced feelings (e.g. Chen et al, 2007; Saarikallio & Erkkilä, 2007).

The conceptual model in Figure 10.1 outlines anticipation (the process of imagining possible future behaviours and the affect associated with them) as key for affect regulation and affective behaviour after an affect-eliciting event. It may be argued that understanding idiosyncratic affect regulation attempts is essential to use behaviour as an indirect measure of affect. For example, a study by Alpert and Alpert (1988) found that music intended to make participants happy indeed made the participants happier as indexed by self-reports, but music intended to make participants sad produced the highest purchase intentions. These seemingly contradictory findings can be understood from the affect regulation perspective. According to the evaluative misattribution perspective (see Section 10.4.5), happy participants should be more prone to purchase products, since they misattribute their positive affect to the target product. However, according to the affect regulation perspective, sad participants have more to gain by purchasing products (given their naïve theory that buying something will decrease their negative affect) than happy participants who already experience positive affect. This line of reasoning applies to several of the affective behaviours used as a measure of musical emotion (e.g. helping can either increase or decrease when you compare happy versus sad participants; North et al, 2004).

Affect regulation in itself can be used as an indirect measure. Researchers have tried to develop self-report scales to capture affect regulation attempts. Clark (1983) showed that 'incentives ratings' may be used, since loss of incentive is often a feature of negative affect. In an attempt to measure incentives, Clark and Teasdale (1985) asked participants, given the chance at the moment of rating, how much they would like to engage in each of eight positive activities: 'Right now, how much would you like to: (1) sit at home in your favorite couch reading a book, (2) have coffee with old friends, (3) go out shopping, (4) go to a party, (5) take a long, hot bath, (6) listen to your favorite record with your best friends, (7) take some physical exercise for yourself, and (8) go for a meal with some new and interesting people. Clark and Teasdale found that participants listening to music intended to make them feel sad gave lower incentive ratings than did participants listening to music intended to make them feel happy (see also Wood et al, 1990). Actual affect regulation can be studied in real life or laboratory using real-life situations (for an overview, see Gross, 2007).

10.5 CONCLUDING REMARKS

This chapter aimed to review different indirect measures of musical emotions. While not exhaustive in its scope, the review provided popular examples of seven different classes of indirect measures, primarily used in domains other than music research. It was possible to identify at least one study using music as the affect-inducing stimulus in each of the classes, but the music and emotion research field has by no means utilized indirect measures to the extent that it could.

This review has shown that indirect measures are reliable and often relatively easy to administer. The fact that there exist different classes, which tap into different aspects of the affect chain, makes it possible for researchers to use measures that are tailored to a specific research question. Most importantly, this chapter has shown that measures other than verbal self-report may be used to infer musical emotion. These measures are less reactive to demand characteristics and strategic responding than are self-reports. Furthermore, these measures may capture aspects of affect that is not evident to listeners when they report their feelings.

However, there are also certain drawbacks to indirect measures. The most important drawback is that using indirect measures alone to infer that affective processes have taken place may be close to impossible, and in many cases a circular argument would be the end result. Moreover, many of the paradigms such as motor retardation or reaction time could indicate differences even in the absence of affect. Thus, just as brain imaging (Chapter 12, this volume) must rely on self-reports to validate that blood flow changes are related to affective experience, indirect measures must rely on other indices of affect to conclude that a difference in, say, counting times is evidence of affect. Relatively little is known about how affect influences various associated components such as information processing and behaviour. It may therefore be premature to rely only on indirect perceptual, cognitive and behavioural measures in the study of musical emotion. The ideal would be to use a 'triangulation approach', where indirect measures such as those reviewed here are used together with physiological and self-report measures.

The reviewed measures could in some cases be applied in their current form in the study of musical emotions, but it is also my hope that this review will stimulate further thinking and development of new indirect measures of musical emotion. As is evident from this review, the need for validation of existing measures in the musical domain and development of novel measures is great. Certain measures such as the IAT are in their current form time consuming and may not be an ideal measure of musical emotion. For the study of music and emotion, aspects such as timing, participant burden, and interference of a dual task on music listening itself must be considered. Novel methods inspired by existing indirect measures, but applied to musical settings, can hopefully be developed in the near future.

This chapter also outlined a conceptual model of affective responses with the hope of better clarifying how different components (and thus different indirect measures) could interact. When using indirect measures, a model of how affect regulation goals, anticipation, and behaviour interact is needed to guide predictions. Even if affective behaviours are complex, understanding how music is related to affective experience will ultimately also demand an understanding of every component of the affect chain. Indirect perceptual, cognitive, and behavioural measures, as some of many affect measures, can help us reach this goal faster.[1]

[1] I would like to thank Patrik Juslin for our discussions on the topic of measurement of musical emotions, which helped shape the ideas presented in this chapter. The preparation of this chapter was supported by grants from the Swedish Research Council.

RECOMMENDED FURTHER READING

1. Eich, E., Ng, J. T. W., Macaulay, D., Percy, A. D., & Grebneva, I. (2007). Combining music with thought to change mood. In J. A. Coan & J. J. B. Allen (eds.), *Handbook of emotion elicitation and assessment* (pp. 124–36). Oxford: Oxford University Press.
2. Wittenbrink, B., & Schwarz, N. (2007). *Implicit measures of attitudes*. New York: Guilford Press.
3. Västfjäll, D. (2002). A review of the musical mood induction procedure. *Musicae Scientiae, Special Issue 2001–2*, 173–211.

REFERENCES

Adaman, J. E., & Blaney, P. H. (1995). The effects of musical mood induction on creativity. *Journal of Creative Behavior*, 29, 95–108.

Albersnagel, F. A. (1988). Velten and musical mood induction procedures: A comparison with accessibility in thought associations. *Behaviour Research and Therapy*, 26, 79–96.

Alpert, J. I., & Alpert, M. J. (1988). Background music as an influence in consumer mood and advertising responses. In T. K. Srull (ed.), *Advances in consumer research, Vol. 16* (pp. 485–91). Honolulu, HI: Association for consumer research.

Andrade, E. B. (2005). Behavioral consequences of affect: Combining evaluative and regulatory mechanisms. *Journal of Consumer Research*, 32, 355–62.

Balch, W. R., & Lewis, B. S. (1996). Music-dependent memory: The roles of tempo change and mood mediation. *Journal of Experimental Psychology: Learning, Memory, and Cognition*, 22, 1354–63.

Balch, W. R., Myers, D. M., & Papotto, C. (1999). Dimensions of mood in mood-dependent memory. *Journal of Experimental Psychology: Learning, Memory, and Cognition*, 25, 70–83.

Baumeister, R. F., Vohs, K. D., DeWall, C. N., & Zhang, L. (2007). How emotion shapes behavior: Feedback, anticipation, and reflection, rather than direct causation. *Personality and Social Psychology Review*, 11, 167–203.

Birch, C. D., Stewart, S. H., Wall, A., McKee, S. A., Eisnor, S. J., & Theakston, J. A. (2004). Mood-induced increases in alcohol expectancy strength in internally motivated drinkers. *Psychology of Addictive Behaviors*, 18, 231–8.

Bouhuys, A. L., Bloem, G. M., & Groothuis, G. G. T. (1995). Induction of depressed and elated mood by music influences the perception of facial emotional expressions in healthy subjects, *Journal of Affective Disorders*, *33*, 215–26.

Bower, G. H. (1981). Mood and memory. *American Psychologist*, *36*, 129–48.

Bradburn, N., Sudman, S., & Wansing, B. (2004). *Asking questions* (2nd edn). San Francisco, CA: Jossy-Bass.

Bradley, M. M., & Lang, P. J. (2000). Measuring emotion: Behavior, feeling and physiology. In R. Lane & L. Nadel (eds), *Cognitive neuroscience of emotion* (pp. 242–76). Oxford: Oxford University Press.

Bruner II, G. C. (1990). Music, mood and marketing. *Journal of Marketing*, *54*, 94–104.

Buchwald, A. M., Strack, S., & Coyne, C. (1981). Demand characteristics and the Velten mood induction procedure. *Journal of Consulting and Clinical Psychology*, *49*, 478–9.

Campbell, D. T. (1950). The indirect assessment of social attitudes. *Psychological Bulletin*, *47*, 15–38.

Carlton, L., & MacDonald, R. A. R. (2004). An investigation of the effects of music on thematic apperception test (TAT) interpretations *Musicae Scientiae, Special Issue 2003–4*, 9–31.

Carter, F. A., Wilson, J. S., Lawson, R. H., & Bulik, C. M. (1995). Mood induction procedure: Importance of individualising music. *Behaviour Change*, *12*, 159–61.

Carver, C. S. (2001). Affect and the functional bases of behavior: On the dimensional structure of affective experience. *Personality and Social Psychology Review*, *5*, 345–56.

Chen, L., Zhou, S., & Bryant, J. (2007). Temporal changes in mood repair through music consumption: Effects of mood, mood salience, and individual differences. *Media Psychology*, *9*, 695–713.

Clark, D. M. (1983). On the induction of depressed mood in the laboratory: Evaluation and comparison of the Velten and musical procedures. *Advances in Behaviour Research and Therapy*, *5*, 27–49.

Clark, D. M., & Teasdale, J. D. (1985). Constraints on the effect of mood on memory. *Journal of Personality and Social Psychology*, *48*, 1595–1608.

Clark, L., Iversen, S. D., & Goodwin, G. M. (2001). The influence of positive and negative mood states on risk taking, verbal fluency, and salivary cortisol. *Journal of Affective Disorders*, *63*, 179–87.

Clore, G. L., & Huntsinger, J. R. (2007). How emotions inform judgment and regulate thought. *Trends in Cognitive Science*, *11*, 393–9.

Damasio, A. R. (1994). *Descartes' error: Emotion, reason, and the human brain*. New York: Avon.

De Houwer, J., & Moors, A. (2007). How to define and examine the implicitness of implicit measures. In B. Wittenbrink & N. Schwarz, (eds), *Implicit measures of attitudes* (pp. 179–94). New York: Guilford Press.

de l'Etoile, S. K. (2002). The effect of musical mood induction procedure on mood state-dependent word retrieval. *Journal of Music Therapy*, *39*, 145–60.

Durand, V. M., & Mapstone, E. (1998). Influence of 'mood-inducing' music on challenging behavior. *American Journal on Mental Retardation*, *102*, 367–78.

Eich, J. E., & Metcalfe, J. (1989). Mood-dependent memory for internal versus external events. *Journal of Experimental Psychology: Learning, Memory, and Cognition*, *15*, 433–55.

Eich, J. E. Joycelin, T. W., Ng, D., Macaulay, D., Percy, A. D., & Grebneva, I. (2007). Combining music with thought to change mood. In J. A. Coan & J. J. B. Allen (eds), *Handbook of emotion elicitation and assessment* (pp. 124–36). Oxford: Oxford University Press.

Egloff, B., & Schmuckle, S. C. (2002). Predictive validity of an implicit association test for assessing anxiety. *Journal of Personality and Social Psychology*, *83*, 1441–55.

Fazio, R. H., & Olson, M. A. (2003). Implicit measures in social cognition research: Their meaning and use. *Annual Review of Psychology, 54,* 297–327.

Forgas, J. P. (1995). Mood and judgment: The affect infusion model (AIM). *Psychological Bulletin, 117,* 39–66.

Fredrickson, B. L., & Levenson, R. W. (1998). Positive emotions speed recovery from the cardiovascular sequlae of negative emotions. *Cognition & Emotion, 12,* 191–220.

Gardner, M. P. (1985). Mood states and consumer behavior: A critical review. *Journal of Consumer Research, 12,* 281–300.

Genell, A., Bergman, P., Tajadura, A., & Västfjäll, D. (2007). An emotional reaction time task sensitive to auditory valence. *Report 2:07, Division of Applied Acoustics, Chalmers University of Technology, Sweden.*

Gorn, G., Pham, M. T., & Sin, L. Y. (2001). When arousal influences ad evaluation and valence does not (and vice versa). *Journal of Consumer Psychology, 11,* 43–55.

Green, J. D., Sedikides, C., Saltzberg, J. A., Wood, J. V., & Forzano, L. B. (2003). Happy mood decreases self-focused attention. *British Journal of Social Psychology, 42,* 147–57.

Greenwald, A. G., McGhee, D. E., & Schwartz, J. L. K. (1998). Measuring individual differences in implicit cognition: The Implicit Association Test. *Journal of Personality and Social Psychology, 74,* 1464–80.

Gross, J. (Ed.) (2007). *Handbook of emotion regulation.* New York: Guilford Press.

Heatherton, T. F., Striepe, M., & Wittenberg, L. (1998). Emotional distress and disinhibited eating: the role of the self. *Personality and Social Psychology Bulletin, 24,* 301–13.

Isen, A. M. (2000). Positive affect and decision making. In M. Lewis & J. M. Haviland-Jones (eds), *Handbook of emotions* (2nd edn, pp. 417–35). New York: Guilford Press.

James, W. (1890/1950). *The principles of psychology, Vol. 2.* New York: Dover.

Johnson, W. B. (1937). Euphoric and depressed moods in normal subjects. *Character and Personality, 6,* 79–98.

Juslin, P. N., & Västfjäll, D. (2008). Emotional responses to music: The need to consider underlying mechanisms. *Behavioral and Brain Sciences, 31,* 559–75.

Linnet, M., & Västfjäll, D. (2005). *Musically induced emotion, physiology, and the interpretation of ambiguous stimuli.* Unpublished manuscript.

Kern, N. L. (2007). Musical mood induction as it affects the projection of emotion onto ambiguous facial stimuli. *Dissertation Abstracts International. Section B: The Sciences and Engineering, 67,* 10–B.

Kenealy, P. (1988). Validation of a music mood induction procedure: Some preliminary findings. *Cognition & Emotion, 2,* 41–8.

Kuyekendall, D., Keating, J. P., & Wagaman, J. (1988). Assessing affective states: A new methodology for some old problems. *Cognitive Therapy and Research, 12,* 279–94.

Lang, P. J. (1995). The emotion probe: Studies of motivation and attention. *American Psychologist, 50,* 372–85.

Lazarus, R. S. (1991). *Emotion and adaptation.* Oxford: Oxford University Press.

Lenton, S. R., & Martin, P. R. (1991). The contribution of music vs. instructions in the musical mood induction procedure. *Behaviour Research and Therapy, 29,* 623–5.

Lewis, L. M., Dember, W. N., Schefft, B. K., & Radenhausen, R. A. (1995). Can experimentally induced mood affect optimism and pessimism scores? *Current Psychology: Developmental, Learning, Personality, Social, 14,* 29–41.

Luce, M., Bettman, J., & Payne, J. W. (1997). Choice processing in emotionally difficult decisions. *Journal of Experimental Psychology: Learning, Memory, and Cognition, 23,* 384–405.

Martin, M. A., & Metha, A. (1997). Recall of early childhood memories through musical mood induction. *The Arts in Psychotherapy, 24,* 447–54.

Mathews, A., & Bradley, B. (1983). Mood and the self-reference bias in recall. *Behavior Research and Therapy*, *21*, 233–9.

Mathews, A., & MacLeod, C. (1985). Selective processing of threat cues in anxiety states. *Behavior and Research Therapy*, *23*, 563–9.

Mathews, A., & MacLeod, C. (1994). Cognitive approaches to emotion and emotional disorders. *Annual Review of Psychology*, *45*, 25–50.

Mauss, I. B., & Robinson, M. D. (2009). Measures of emotion: A review. *Cognition & Emotion*, *23*, 209–37.

Mayer, J. D., & Bremer, D. (1985). Assessing mood with affect-sensitive tasks. *Journal of Personality Assessment*, *49*, 95–9.

Mayer, J. D., Gayle, M., Meehan, M. E., & Haarman, A. K. (1990). Towards better specification of the mood-congruency effect in recall. *Journal of Experimental Social Psychology*, *26*, 465–80.

McFarland, R. A. (1984). Effects of music upon emotional content of TAT stories. *The Journal of Psychology*, *116*, 227–34.

Mogg, K., & Bradley, B. P. (1998). A cognitive-motivational analysis of anxiety. *Behavior Research and Therapy*, *36*, 809–48.

Murray, H. A. (1938). *Thematic apperception test*. Cambridge, MA: Harvard University Press.

Nisbett, R. E., & Wilson, T. D. (1977). Telling more than we can know: Verbal reports on mental processes. *Psychological Review*, *84*, 231–59.

North, A. C., & Hargreaves, D. J. (1997). Music and consumer behavior. In D. J. Hargreaves & A. C. North (eds), *The social psychology of music* (pp. 268–89). Oxford: Oxford University Press.

North, A. C., Tarrant, M., & Hargreaves, D. J. (2004). The effects of music on helping behavior: A field study. *Environment and Behavior*, *36*, 266–75.

Orne, M. T. (1962). On the social psychology of the psychological experiment with particular reference to demand characteristics and their implications. *American Psychologist*, *17*, 776–83.

Öhman, A., & Mineka, S. (2001). Fears, phobias, and preparedness: Towards an evolved module of fear and fear learning. *Psychological Review*, *108*, 483–522.

Parrott, W. G. (1991). Mood induction and instructions to sustain moods: A test of the subject compliance hypothesis of mood congruent memory. *Cognition & Emotion*, *5*, 41–52.

Parrott, W. G., & Sabini, J. (1990). Mood and memory under natural conditions: Evidence for mood incongruent recall. *Journal of Personality and Social Psychology*, *59*, 321–36.

Payne, B. K., Cheng, C. M., Govorun, O., & Stewart, B. D. (2005). An inkblot for attitudes: affect misattribution as implicit measurement. *Journal of Personality and Social Psychology*, *89*, 277–93.

Pham, M. T. (1998). Representativeness, relevance, and the use of feelings in decision making. *Journal of Consumer Research*, *25*, 144–59.

Pignatiello, M. F., Camp, C. J., & Rasar, L. A. (1986). Musical mood induction: An alternative to the Velten technique. *Journal of Abnormal Psychology*, *94*, 51–63.

Pignatiello, M. F., Camp, C. J., Elder, S. T., & Rasar, L. A (1989). A psychophysiological comparison of the Velten and musical mood induction techniques. *Journal of Music Therapy*, *26*, 140–54.

Polivy, J., & Doyle, C. (1980). Laboratory induction of mood states through the reading of self-referent mood states: Affective changes or demand characteristics. *Journal of Abnormal Psychology*, *89*, 286–90.

Robinson, M. D., Storbeck, J., Meier, J. P., & Kirkeby, P. S. (2004). Look out! That could be dangerous. Valence-arousal interactions in evaluative processing. *Personality and Social Psychology Bulletin*, *30*, 1472–84.

Rogowski, J. P. (1991). Comparison of the effects of musical and cognitive mood induction pro-cedures on self-report and behavioral mood measures. *Dissertation Abstracts International,* 52, 4961.

Russell, J. A. (2003). Core affect and the psychological construction of emotion. *Psychological Review,* 110, 145–72.

Schwarz, N., & Strack, F. (1999). Reports of subjective well-being: Judgmental processes and their methodological implications. In D. Kahneman, E. Diener, & N. Schwarz (eds), *Well-being: The foundation of hedonic psychology* (pp. 61–84). New York: Russell Sage Foundation.

Scherer, K. R. (2001). Appraisal considered as a process of multilevel sequential checking. In K. R. Scherer, A. Schorr, & T. Johnstone (eds), *Appraisal processes in emotion: Theory, methods, research* (pp. 92–120). Oxford: Oxford University Press.

Schwarz, N., & Clore, G. L. (1983). Mood, misattribution and judgments of well-being: Informative and directive functions of affective states. *Journal of Personality and Social Psychology,* 45, 513–23.

Siemer, M. (2001). Mood-specific effects on appraisal and emotion judgments. *Cognition & Emotion,* 15, 453–85.

Sollberger, B., Reber, R., & Eckstein, D. (2003). Musical chords as affective priming context in a word-evaluation task. *Music Perception,* 20, 263–82.

Stöber, J. (1997). Trait anxiety and pessimistic appraisal of risk and chance. *Personality and Individual Differences,* 22, 465–76.

Sutherland, G., Newman, B., & Rachman, S. (1982). Experimental investigations of the relations between mood and intrusive, unwanted cognitions. *British Journal of Medical Psychology,* 55, 127–38.

Sutton, L. J., Teasdale, D., & Broadbent, D. E. (1982). Negative self-schema: The effects of induced depressed mood. *British Journal of Clinical Psychology,* 27, 188–90.

Taylor, S. E. (1991). Asymmetrical effects of positive and negative events: The mobilization–minimization hypothesis. *Psychological Bulletin,* 110, 67–85.

Teasdale, J. D., & Fogarty, J. S. (1979). Differential effects of induced mood on retrieval of pleasant and unpleasant events from episodic memory. *Journal of Abnormal Psychology,* 88, 248–57.

Teasdale, J. D., & Spencer, P. (1984). Induced mood and estimates of past success. *British Journal of Clinical Psychology,* 23, 149–52.

Terezis, H. C. (1993). Variables influencing cognitive and affective reactions to a musical mood induction procedure. *Dissertation Abstracts International. Section B: The Sciences and Engineering,* 55, 1654.

Vargas. P. T., Sekaquaptewa, D., & von Hippel, W. (2007). Armed only with paper and pencil: 'low-tech' measures of implicit attitudes. In B. Wittenbrink & N. Schwarz (eds), *Implicit measures of attitudes* (pp. 103–24). New York: Guilford Press.

Västfjäll, D. (2002). A review of the musical mood induction procedure. *Musicae Scientiae,* Special Issue 2001–2002, 173–211.

Västfjäll, D., & Gärling, T. (2006). Preference for negative emotion. *Emotion,* 6, 326–9.

Västfjäll, D., Gärling, T., & Kleiner, M. (2001). How do I like feeling this way? A core affect account of preferences for current mood. *Journal of Happiness Studies,* 2, 337–54.

Velten, E. (1968). A laboratory task for induction of mood states. *Behavior Research and Therapy,* 6, 473–82.

Walker, S., & Schimmak, U. (in press). Validity of a happiness Implicit Association Test as a measure of subjective well-being. *Journal of Personality.*

Wenzlaff, R. M., Wegner, D. M., & Klein, S. B. (1991). The role of thought suppression in the bonding of thought and mood. *Journal of Personality and Social Psychology, 60*, 500–8.

Willner, P., Benton, D., Brown, E., Survjit, C., Gareth, D., Morgan, J., & Morgan, M. (1998). 'Depression' increases 'craving' for sweet rewards in animal and human models of depression and craving. *Psychopharmacology, 136*, 272–83.

Wilson, T. D., & Brekke, N. (1994). Mental contamination and mental correction: Unwanted influences on judgments and evaluations. *Psychological Bulletin, 116*, 117–42.

Winkielman, P., & Berridge, K. C. (2004) Unconscious emotion. *Current Directions in Psychological Sciences, 13*, 120–3

Winkielman, P., Zajonc, R. B., & Schwarz, N. (1997). Subliminal affective priming resists attributional interventions. *Cognition & Emotion, 11*, 433–65.

Wittenbrink, B., & Schwarz, N. (2007). *Implicit measures of attitudes*. New York: Guilford Press.

Wright, W. F., & Bower, G. H. (1992). Mood effect on subjective probability assessment. *Organizational Behavior and Human Decision Processes, 22*, 276–91.

Wood, J. V., Saltzberg, J. A., & Goldsamt, L. A. (1990). Does affect induce self-focused attention? *Journal of Personality and Social Psychology, 58*, 899–908.

CHAPTER 11

PSYCHO-PHYSIOLOGICAL MEASURES

DONALD A. HODGES

IMAGINE you have observed the following scenarios:

Jason has been waiting impatiently for hours with his buddies, along with several thousand others; he has endured a warm-up act and another wait. Finally, to the roar of the crowd, his favourite rock group bounds on stage and slams into its mega-hit, accompanied by flashing lights, smoke bombs, and wildly gyrating dancers. Jason is caught up in the frenzy that surrounds him.

Mary is sitting quietly in the corner of a darkened room. Her mother is approaching death and a music therapist has come to aid in the transition. As the hospice-trained musician begins to strum on a guitar and sing one of her mother's favourite hymns, Mary weeps silently.

Allison clutches her programme as she breathlessly awaits the arrival of one of the era's greatest pianists. Finally, the lights in the concert hall dim, the artist confidently strides onstage, bows briefly, and immediately launches into the Bach *Chromatic Fantasy and Fugue*. Allison is instantly transported.

It is easy to imagine that strong emotional responses accompany each of these music-listening situations, and further that these emotional responses include a host of concomitant psychophysiological responses as well. Juslin and Västfjäll (2008, p. 561) define emotions as:

Relatively intense affective responses that usually involve a number of sub-components—subjective feeling, physiological arousal, expression, action tendency, and regulation—which are more or less 'synchronized'. Emotions focus on specific objects, and last minutes to a few hours.

Granted that psychophysiological activity is an important ingredient of emotions, making specific connections between the two is not easy (Etzel et al, 2006). Stemmler (2003) also acknowledges that linkages between the two are exceedingly complex and difficult to interpret. The purpose of this chapter is to examine these relationships.

Psychophysiology concerns relationships between physiology and behaviour, where behaviour is broadly construed to include such activities as sleep, problem solving, reactions to stress, learning, attention, memory, information processing, sensation, perception, and emotional responses (Andreassi, 2007). Psychophysiological responses include what are commonly referred to as 'physiological responses'—covert changes in such things as heart rate, blood pressure, or skin conductivity—as well as more overt, expressive responses such as crying, facial expressions, and body movements. Although brain activations might also be included, this topic is discussed in a separate chapter (Chapter 12, this volume).

Gradually, music psychologists have developed a clearer understanding of distinctions between *perceived* expressions of emotions (cognitivist position) and *induced* or felt emotions (emotivist position; Kivy 1989, 1990). The cognitivist position is that the listener can perceive expressions of emotions in the music, without necessarily feeling that emotion. The emotivist position is that music induces emotions in listeners—they actually experience feelings such as elation or grief. While there is some correspondence between emotions perceived and emotions felt, there are also demonstrable differences (Juslin & Laukka, 2004; Kallinen & Ravaja, 2006; Schubert, 2007). Because psychophysiological responses may be absent in situations where emotional expressions are perceived but not felt, a major concern of this chapter is with the role that psychophysiological responses play in induced musical emotions.

In focusing on psychophysiological processes, a number of questions arise: How many and what kinds of such responses to music are there? How can they be measured? How is psychophysiological activity connected to musical emotions? Is it possible to experience changes in psychophysiological responses without having an emotional response? How can one untangle responses to music from the accompanying personal, social, and contextual variables? Thus, while it is quite clear from the scenarios described at the outset, from our own, personal experiences, and from research that emotional responses to music include psychophysiological activity, relationships between the two are considerably murkier.

11.1 A BRIEF OVERVIEW OF THE LITERATURE

As long ago as the ancient Greeks, and probably much earlier, there was awareness of the effects of music on the body. Perhaps the earliest recorded attempt to determine the effects of music on the body in a modern, scientific way was a study by the Frenchman Grétry. In 1741 he felt his own pulse as he listened to music at varying tempos, and

Table 11.1 Reviews of related literature concerning physiological responses to music

Author(s)	Year	Title
Diserens	1926	The influence of music on behaviour
Schoen	1927	The effects of music
Diserens & Fine	1939	A psychology of music
Schoen	1940	The psychology of music
Lundin	1967	An objective psychology of music (2nd edn)
Farnsworth	1969	The social psychology of music (2nd edn)
Dainow	1977	Physical and motor responses to music
Hodges	1980	Physiological responses to music
Standley	1995	Music as a therapeutic intervention in medical and dental treatment: research and clinical applications
Bartlett	1996	Physiological responses to music and sound stimuli
Scherer & Zentner	2001	Emotional effects of music: production rules
Radocy & Boyle	2003	Psychological foundations of musical behaviour (4th edn)
Hodges	2009	Bodily responses to music

noticed that his pulse sped up or slowed down according to the pace of the music (cited in Diserens, 1926). More than 150 years later, Warthin (1894) reported heart rate changes when he played music to hypnotized patients. Since these early attempts, the literature has been expanded considerably, and from time-to-time, reviews of pertinent literature have appeared, as shown in Table 11.1.

Attention paid to the various types of psychophysiological responses varies enormously. As can be seen in Table 11.2, heart or pulse rate has been the most frequently studied response, and most likely this represents the relative ease with which this response can be measured. Other responses, such as blood oxygen saturation, have received scant attention. The number of studies on each topic does not tell the entire story. Another consideration is the time frame in which studies on a given topic appear. For example, heart rate studies began at least with the aforementioned eighteenth-century study, while studies of biochemical responses to music have only recently been possible.

11.2 PSYCHOPHYSIOLOGICAL PROCESSES

....

Before considering specific research studies, it may be useful to consider a brief overview of the biology of the peripheral nervous system. The central nervous system

Table 11.2 Frequency of published reports on psychophysiological responses to music

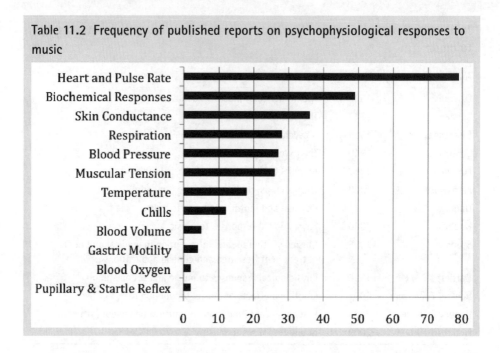

(i.e. the brain and spinal cord) sends signals to, and receives signals from, the peripheral nervous system. The peripheral nervous system itself is further divided into the autonomic and somatic nervous systems (Larsen et al, 2008).

The autonomic nervous system (ANS) is primarily responsible for maintaining homeostasis; that is, to keep a relatively stable internal environment in spite of external changes (Jänig, 2003). The ANS regulates a wide variety of cardiovascular, gastrointestinal, electrodermal, respitory, endocrine, and exocrine organs (Levenson, 2003). The ANS contains both the sympathetic division (prepares the body for fight or flight responses) and the parasympathetic division (works to conserve energy) (Bloom, Lazerson, & Hofstadter, 1985; LeDoux, 1986, 1994). The sympathetic division energizes the body by increasing heart rate, blood pressure, and tension in voluntary muscles, stimulating the secretion of adrenalin and a variety of neurotransmitters, and stimulating the conversion of glycogen for energy, along with decreased blood flow to internal organs and extremities (Andreassi, 2007). The parasympathetic nervous system returns bodily actions to a state of rest and restoration by slowing down the heart rate and stimulating peristalsis (digestion) and the secretion of saliva. Although the two divisions may seem to be contradictory, they work in tandem as the ANS regulates a complicated series of chemical reactions. The historical view of the ANS was one of 'mass discharge'; however, recent evidence indicates that the ANS can respond with a wide variety of patterns of peripheral activity. The somatic nervous system innervates the skeletal muscles, including those of the face. Extensive research in psychophysiology has demonstrated that autonomic and somatic processes are intimately associated with emotional responses (Larsen et al, 2008).

11.2.1 Measuring psychophysiological responses

A wide variety of monitoring devices and techniques has been used in measuring psychophysiological responses to music. In Table 11.3, examples of these devices and techniques, along with one or more recent sources that provide additional details, are

Table 11.3 Measurement of psychophysiological responses

Psychophysiological response	Measurement	Source
Heart or pulse rate	ECG: electrocardiogram; F1000 polygraph instrumentation system; Biovew series IV, sensor electrodes	Bernardi, Porta, & Sleight, 2006; Blood & Zatorre, 2001; Rickard, 2004
Skin conductance	F1000 polygraph instrumentation system; Bioview series IV, sensor electrodes	Blood & Zatorre, 2001; Rickard, 2004
Blood pressure	Applanation tonometry for radial artery, TCD: trancranial Doppler probe for mid-cerebral artery	Bernardi, Porta, & Sleight, 2006
Biochemical responses	Biochemical analysis of saliva samples, blood samples, urine samples	Beck et al, 2000; Rickard, 2004
Respiration	Inductive plethysmography; F1000 polygraph instrumentation system	Bernardi, Porta, & Sleight, 2006; Blood & Zatorre, 2001
Temperature	F1000 polygraph instrumentation system; Omega OL-729 Thermistor probe; Bioview series IV, sensor electrodes	Blood & Zatorre, 2001; Craig, 2005; Rickard, 2004
Blood volume	FPA: finger pulse amplitude	Krumhansl, 1997
Gastric motility	EGG: electrogastrogram	Chen et al, 2005
Blood–oxygen saturation	Ohmeda Biox 3700 pulse oximeter	Cassidy & Standley, 1995
Muscular tension	EMG: electromyography	Rickard, 2004
Zygomaticus activity	Facial EMG	Witvliet & Vrana, 2007
Facial expressions and head movements	Facial coding systems	Cohn, Ambador, & Ekman, 2007; Levenson, 2007
Chills	Raised index finger; 'chills intensity' rating scale (0–10); button push	Blood & Zatorre, 2001; Craig, 2005; Guhn, Hamm, & Zentner, 2007
Piloerection	Observation of forearm	Craig, 2005
Startle reflex	EMG: electromyography	Mathieu et al, 2009
Expressions of anxiety or arousal	Spielberger State Trait Anxiety Inventory	Rickard, 2004

given for each psychophysiological response variable. For anyone interested in setting up a lab, Curtin, Lozano, and Allen (2007) provide a detailed description of equipment, software, materials, and room set-up for a state-of-the-art psychophysiological laboratory.

Extremely succinct reviews of the literature are presented in the following sections under the various physiological responses measured. Generally, studies can be categorized into those that report 'increased', 'decreased', or 'unchanged' responses to music listening. A cataloguing of published literature has been done to emphasize the contradictory nature of the findings. For example, there are 54 studies in support of the notion that music can influence heart rate and 26 studies that found no change in heart rate. Beyond this simplistic categorization scheme lies an enormous complexity. Comments in these review sections are kept to a minimum, and issues dealing with general principles involving psychophysiological responses are dealt with in subsequent sections.

Several other points to note are that the literature cited is restricted to published studies and to those utilizing music, as opposed to non-musical sounds. For a review that includes both unpublished studies and non-musical stimuli, readers should consult Bartlett (1996). In terminology usage, music with high arousal potential is often referred to as stimulative by music therapists (Gaston, 1951), and is characterized by music that emphasizes rhythm rather than melody or harmony and is faster, louder, and more staccato than average, with wide pitch ranges and abrupt, unpredictable changes. Conversely, music with low arousal potential, or sedative music, emphasizes melody and harmony more than rhythm, and is slower, softer, and more legato, with narrow pitch ranges and gradual, predictable changes.

Whenever a large number of studies are reported they are presented in tabular form for ease in reading. The extensive listings under Heart or Pulse rate and Skin conductivity are organized chronologically to indicate the timeline of this research. Otherwise, citations are reported in normal fashion. A final point is that what follows in Sections 11.2.2 to 11.2.14 are listings of studies in univariate fashion; that is, focusing on only one variable. Readers may note that several authors appear under more than one heading because they studied multiple response types. Multivariate approaches are discussed in Section 11.3.1.

11.2.2 The effects of music on heart or pulse rate

Heart rate, sometimes referred to as pulse rate, is based on the number of beats per minute, and is recorded with an electrocardiogram (Andreassi, 2007). Heart rate is associated with emotional responses, among other things (e.g. mental activity, motor performance). At least 54 published studies, presented in Table 11.4, provided data in support of the notion that listening to music can cause changes in heart rate; although the vast majority of these studies measured heart rate only, a few included additional cardiac variables such as pre-ejection period, inter-beat-interval, and cardiac output (Krumhansl, 1997; Nyklíček, Thayer, & Van Doornen, 1997).

Table 11.4 Chronological listing of studies with meaningful changes in heart rate

Author(s)	Date	Author(s)	Date	Author(s)	Date
Shepard	1906	Bonny	1983	Iwanaga & Moroki	1999
Weld	1912	Updike & Charles	1987	McNamara & Ballard	1999
Hyde & Scalapino	1918	Zimmerman et al	1988	Savan	1999
Coleman	1920	Geden et al	1989	Blood & Zatorre	2001
Hyde	1927	Guzzetta	1989	Knight & Rickard	2001
Ellis & Brighouse	1952	Thierbach	1989	Thayer & Faith	2001
Shatin	1957	Barker	1991	Rickard	2004
Kagan & Lewis	1965	Edwards et al	1991	Ellis & Simons	2005
Brackbill et al	1966	Pignatiello et al	1991	Nater et al	2005
Graham & Clifton	1966	Rider et al	1991	Baumgartner et al	2006
Lewis	1971	Standley	1991	Bernardi et al	2006
DeJong et al	1973	Lorch et al	1994	Etzel et al	2006
Hunter	1974	Cassidy & Standley	1995	Gomez & Danuser	2007
Landreth & Landreth	1974	Miluk-Kolasa et al	1995	Guhn et al	2007
Harrer & Harrer	1977	Iwanaga et al	1996	Sammler et al	2007
Wilson & Aiken	1977	Krumhansl	1997	Yamamoto et al	2007
Barger	1979	Nyklíček et al	1997	Khalfa et al	2008
Loscin	1981	Witvliet et al	1998	Lundqvist et al	2009

In general, high arousal or stimulative music tends to cause an increase in heart rate or pulse rate, while sedative music tends to cause a decrease. However, some researchers have found that any music, whether stimulative or sedative, tends to increase heart rate (Ellis & Brighouse, 1952; Krumhansl, 1997; Rickard, 2004; Shatin, 1957; Weld, 1912). Iwanaga et al (1996) found that heart rate decreased during sedative music, but did not change to stimulative music. McNamara and Ballard (1999) found that men who preferred arousing music had lower resting heart rates, but women who preferred arousing music had higher resting heart rates. Twenty-six studies reported that music caused no changes in heart rate (Table 11.5).

Few studies have been conducted on the effects of performing music on heart rate. Harrer and Harrer (1977) found that peak heart rate for the conductor Herbert von Karajan occurred during the most emotional passages, rather than those that required more physical exertion. Furthermore, his heart rate was higher while conducting than while flying his jet plane. Haider and Groll-Knapp (1981) monitored heart rate in 24 members of the Vienna Symphony during rehearsals and performances. Heart rate was higher during performances than rehearsals and peaked at 151 beats per minute. The style of music being performed had an effect on heart rate, with tempo being the most influential factor. A number of studies have also shown that high school and university

Table 11.5 Chronological listing of studies with no meaningful changes in heart rate

Author(s)	Date	Author(s)	Date	Author(s)	Date
Weld	1912	Wilson & Aiken	1977	Standley	1991
Hyde & Scalapino	1918	Barger	1979	Davis	1992
Hyde	1927	Davis-Rollans & Cunningham	1987	Pujol	1994
Trenes	1937	Zimmerman et al	1988	Iwanaga et al	1996
Johnson & Trawick	1938	Geden et al	1989	Gendolla & Krüsken	2001
Ellis & Brighouse	1952	Davis & Thaut	1989	Gupta & Gupta	2005
Shatin	1957	Barker	1991	Gomez & Danuser	2004
Zimny & Weidenfeller	1963	Madsen et al	1991	Mathieu et al	2009
Coutts	1965	Menegazzi	1991		

student musicians experience increased heart rates before or during performances in front of audiences or judges (Abel & Larkin, 1990; Abrams & Manstead, 1981; Brotons, 1994; Hunsaker, 1994; LeBlanc et al, 1997).

11.2.3 The effects of music on biochemical processes

Psychoneuroimmunolgy is an interdisciplinary convergence of the behavioural sciences, the neurosciences, endocrinology, and immunology (Ader, 2007). Behavioural experiences affect the mind/brain, which in turn alters the immune function (Conti, 2000). Considerable activity of late has focused on biochemical changes in blood, urine, or saliva as a result of listening to music. The majority of published reports presented in Table 11.6 indicate meaningful changes in biochemicals in response to music listening or musical experiences; however, the nature of these changes is highly varied.

This cursory review gives some indication of the enormous complexity of hormonal responses to music. It is a line of investigation still in its infancy, and yet one of enormous potential. Already there are direct applications in music medicine (Pratt & Spintge, 1995; Spintge & Droh, 1987, 1992a, 1992b), where music is used to control pain and anxiety, and to reduce drug dosages (Conrad et al, 2007; see also Chapter 30, this volume). Much more work needs to be done, however, to understand relationships among music, biochemicals, and emotions.

11.2.4 The effects of music on skin conductance

Skin conductance response is a measurement of electrodermal activity or electrical resistance of the skin (Andreassi, 2007). Changes in skin conductance reflect mental

Table 11.6 The effects of music on biochemicals

Adrenocorticotropic hormone (ACTH)

> Increased: Gerra et al, 1998.

> Decreased: Möckel et al, 1994; Oyama et al, 1987b.

> Did not change: Evers & Suhr, 2000.

Beta-endorphins

> Increased: Gerra et al, 1998; Goldstein, 1980.

> Decreased: McKinney et al, 1997b.

Blood glucose

> Decreased: After being raised due to pre-surgical stress, blood glucose decreased to below baseline during music listening (Miluk-Kolasa, Matejek, & Stupnicki, 1996).

Cortisol

> Increased: Beck et al, 2000; Gerra et al, 1998; VanderArk & Ely, 1992, 1993.

> Decreased: Bartlett et al, 1993; Beck et al, 2000; Enk et al, 2008; Kreutz et al, 2004; Leardi et al, 2007; McKinney et al, 1997a; Möckel et al, 1994; Tsao et al, 1991.

> Increased in music majors but decreased in non-music majors: VanderArk & Ely, 1992, 1993.

> Did not change: Clark et al, 2001; Oyama et al, 1987a; Rickard, 2004; Rider, Floyd & Kirkpatrick, 1985; Stefano et al, 2004; Yamamoto et al, 2007.

> A psychological stressor caused a sharp increase in salivary cortisol which decreased more rapidly in those who listened to relaxing music than in those who recovered in silence (Khalfa et al, 2003) or which did not increase during music listening (Knight & Rickard, 2001).

Dehydroepiandrosterone

> Did not change: Conrad et al, 2007

Dopamine

> Activations in mesolimbic structures (e.g. nucleus accumbens, ventral tegmental area, hypothalamus, and insula) involved in reward processing have been found in response to music listening (Blood & Zatorre, 2001; Brown et al, 2004; Menon & Levitin, 2005), providing indications of dopamine release. Hirokawa & Ohira (2003) found no change in dopamine after listening to music.

Epinephrine

> Increased: Kumar et al, 1999; VanderArk & Ely, 1992, 1993.

> Decreased: Conrad et al, 2007

> Did not change: Gerra et al, 1998; Hirokawa & Ohira, 2003

Genetic stress hormone markers

> Reversal in 19 of 45 genetic stress hormone markers was demonstrated in participants in a recreational music-making program (Bittman et al, 2005)

Growth Hormone

> Increased: Conrad et al, 2007; Gerra et al, 1998.

Interleukin-1

> Increased: Bartlett et al, 1993.

Table 11.6 The effects of music on biochemicals (continued)

Interleukin-6

    Decreased: Conrad et al, 2007.

Interleukin-10

    Decreased: Wachi et al, 2007.

Melatonin

    Increased: Kumar et al, 1999.

Mu-opiate receptor expression

    Increased: Stefano et al, 2004

Natural killer cells

    Increased after one hour of recreational music making: Wachi et al, 2007.

    Did not change: Hirokawa & Ohira, 2003.

Neutrophils and lymphocytes

    Decreased: Rider & Achtherberg, 1989.

Norepinephrine

    Increased: Gerra et al, 1998; Kumar et al, 1999; VanderArk & Ely, 1992, 1993.

    Did not change: Hirokawa & Ohira, 2003.

Oxytocin

    Freeman (1995) suggested that oxytocin is released when mothers sing lullabies to infants, but no published research studies have been identified to support this contention.

Prolactin

    Did not change: Gerra et al, 1998; Evers & Suhr, 2000; Kumar et al, 1999.

Secretory immunoglobulin A (SIgA)

    Increased: Beck et al, 2000; Charnetski & Brennan, 1998; Enk et al, 2008; Knight & Rickard, 2001; Kreutz et al, 2004; Lane, 1991; McCraty et al, 1996; Rider et al, 1991, 1998; Rider & Weldin, 1990; Tsao et al, 1991.

    Decreased: Miluk-Lolasa et al, 1994.

    Did not change: Hirokawa & Ohira, 2003; Oyama et al, 1987a; Rider et al, 1985.

Serotonin

    Increased to pleasant music, decreased to unpleasant music: Evers & Suhr 2000.

    Did not change: Kumar et al, 1999.

Testosterone

    Testosterone decreased in males for each of six different musical styles and increased in females (Fukui, 2001).

T lymphocytes ($CD4^+$, $CD8^+$, $CXD16^+$)

    Did not change: Hirokawa & Ohira, 2003.

Table 11.7 Chronological listing of studies with meaningful changes in skin conductance

Author(s)	Date	Author(s)	Date	Author(s)	Date
Wechsler	1925	Harrer & Harrer	1977	Craig	2005
Davis	1934	Wilson & Aiken	1977	Ellis & Simons	2005
Phares	1934	Edwards et al	1991	Baumgartner et al	2006
Dreher	1948	VanderArk & Ely	1992	Grewe et al	2007a
Henkin	1957	VanderArk & Ely	1993	Grewe et al	2007b
Shrift	1957	Vaitl et al	1993	Gomez & Danuser	2007
Winold	1959	Nater et al	1995	Guhn et al	2007a
Weidenfeller & Zimny	1962	Krumhansl	1997	Guhn et al	2007b
Zimny & Weidenfeller	1963	Witvliet et al	1998	Yamamoto et al	2007
Ries	1969	Khalfa et al	2002	Khalfa et al	2008
DeJong et al	1973	Gomez & Danuser	2004	Lundqvist et al	2009
Peretti & Swenson	1974	Rickard	2004	Mathieu et al	2009

activity, usually of an affective nature (Venables, 1987). Under arousal conditions, resistance decreases, and skin conductance increases. Significant changes in skin conductance in response to music listening were found in the studies presented in Table 11.7. However, in six studies, listening to music brought about no meaningful changes in skin conductance (Blood & Zatorre, 2001; Davis, 1934; DeJong et al, 1973; Jellison, 1975; Keller & Seraganian, 1984; Ries, 1969).

11.2.5   The effects of music on respiration

Respiration or breathing rate is measured by a respiratory inductive plethysmograph (Sackner et al, 1989). Respiration is strongly linked to emotional responses. Respiration or breathing rate increased in 19 studies: Baumgartner et al (2006), Blood & Zatorre (2001), Cassidy and Standley (1995), DeJong et al (1973), Ellis and Brighouse (1952), Foster and Gamble (1906), Gomez and Danuser (2004, 2007), Haas et al (1986), Iwanaga and Moroki (1999), Kneutgen (1974), Krumhansl (1997), Lorch et al (1994), Nyklíček, Thayer, and Van Doornen (1997), Pignatiello et al (1989), Ries (1969), Thayer and Faith (2001), Vaitl et al (1993), and Wilson and Aiken (1977). Respiration rates decreased in participants who listened to low-tempo music following a high-stress task (Yamamoto, Naga, & Shimizu, 2007). Musical preferences correlated with increases in respiration (Ries, 1969), but respiration did not change as a result of listening to music in four studies (Davis, 1992; Davis-Rollans & Cunningham, 1987; Foster & Gamble, 1906; Weld, 1912). In one study, listening to stimulative music did not change respiration, but listening to sedative music caused a decrease (Iwanaga et al, 1996). Breathing rates entrained with musical rhythm in four studies (Etzel et al, 2006; Haas et al, 1986; Khalfa et al, 2008; Kneutgen, 1974).[1]

11.2.6 The effects of music on blood pressure

Blood pressure is a general index of cardiac health and is measured by a sphygmomanometer (Adreassi, 2007). Readings are given for both systolic blood pressure, the point of maximal pressure exerted by circulating blood, and diastolic blood pressure, the point of minimal pressure. Blood pressure has been linked to emotional responses in numerous studies.

In seven studies, blood pressure increased when participants listened to stimulative music (Bernardi et al, 2006; Hyde, 1927; Hyde & Scalapino, 1918; Khalfa et al, 2008; Krumhansl, 1997; Nyklíček, Thayer, & Van Doornen, 1997; Pignatiello et al, 1989). Blood pressure decreased as well, most often in response to sedative music, though sometimes to stimulative music (Hyde & Scalapino, 1918; Khalfa et al, 2008; Knight & Rickard, 2001; Lorch et al, 1994; Miluk-Kolasa, Matejek, & Stupnicki, 1996; Savan, 1999). Self-selected music lowered blood pressure (Geden et al, 1989; Oyama et al, 1987a, 1987b; Schuster, 1985; Updike & Charles, 1987). Men who preferred arousing music had lower resting blood pressure, while women who preferred arousing music had higher resting blood pressure (McNamara & Ballard, 1999). Contradicting these results were studies in which listening to music did not change blood pressure (Bonny, 1983; Gupta & Gupta, 2005; Jellison, 1975; Pignatiello et al, 1989; Strauser, 1997; Sunderman, 1946); this included music that was self-selected (Geden et al, 1989; Schuster, 1985; Zimmerman et al, 1988). Blood pressure increased in music students who were about to be evaluated on their musical performances (Abel & Larkin, 1990).

11.2.7 The effects of music on muscular tension

Surface electromyography (EMG) is a means of measuring muscle tension via electrodes placed on the skin over the muscle group of interest (Andreassi, 2007). Researchers have been interested in whether listening to music changes muscle tension, and overwhelmingly findings support the notion that it does so: Blood and Zatorre (2001), Davis and Thaut (1989), Hunter (1974), Rickard (2004), Rider (1985), Rider et al (1991), Safranek et al (1982), Scartelli (1982, 1984), Scartelli and Borling (1986), Sears (1958), and Thaut, Schleiffers, and Davis (1991). Only Davis and Thaut (1989) and Scartelli (1984) reported no changes in EMG while listening to music. Music listeners squeezed harder on a pair of tongs as tension in the music increased (Nielsen, 1983, 1987; cited in Gabrielsson &

---

[1] Respiration entrainment occurs when breathing rate corresponds to characteristics of the music, most often tempo or rhythm. For example, a faster tempo could be correlated with a faster breathing rate (see Chapter 22, this volume, for further discussion of entrainment).

Lindström, 2001; see Chapter 14, this volume). Sedative music decreased tension more quickly than stimulative music increased tension (Sears, 1958). Harrer and Harrer (1977) and Wilson and Davey (2002) found that subjects' ankles moved in foot tapping responses to music. Music listening increased postural stability (Carrick et al, 2007).

Facial expressions are among the more obvious indicators of emotions. Objective measurements of facial expressions are made through electromyography by placing electrodes on the smile muscles (zygomaticus), frown muscles of the eyebrow (corrugator), and muscles under the eyes (orbicularis oculi) (Andreassi, 2007). Researchers found that 'happy' music elicited increased smile muscle activity compared to 'sad' music (Lundqvist et al, 2009; Witvliet et al, 1998). Listeners smiled most during arousing music with positive affect and least during arousing music with negative affect (Witvliet & Vrana, 2007). This was demonstrated in zygomaticus, corrugator, and orbicularis oculi EMG readings. Ellis and Simons (2005) found that corrugator EMG increased during negative music and zygomaticus increased during positive music. Mathieu et al (2009) found that corrugator muscle activity was higher during unpleasant music, but that zygomaticus muscle activity did not change between pleasant and unpleasant music. Thayer and Faith (2001) and Kfalfa et al (2008) demonstrated through facial EMG that music elicited discrete emotions such as happiness, sadness, agitation, and serenity.

In addition to EMG, there are also subjective methods to evaluate expressive facial gestures, such as coding systems used to analyse videotapes. Levenson (2007) identified several coding systems, including the Facial Action Coding System (FACS). Coders using FACS can view videotapes in slow motion and stop-time (frame-by-frame analysis) to categorize fine-grained, discrete facial expressions into action units (Cohn, Ambadar, & Ekman, 2007). FACS includes nine action units in the upper face and 18 in the lower face, along with nine eye positions and movements, five miscellaneous action units, nine action descriptors, nine gross behaviours, and five visibility codes. To avoid the subjectivity of human observers and the invasiveness of using EMG electrodes placed on the face, recent work has been initiated in the use of automated facial image analysis using computer vision (Cohn & Kanade, 2007). Unfortunately, facial coding methodologies have not yet been applied to an analysis of the music listener's face.

11.2.8 The effects of music on finger, peripheral skin, or body temperature

Skin temperature is related to blood flow in skin tissue and is measured by a plethysmograph (Andreassi, 2007). Skin temperature is a reflection of vasoconstriction/vasodilation and has been linked to emotional states. However, temperature responses to emotions elicited by music are inconsistent.

Skin temperature changes in response to music listening were reported in a majority of the studies published: Baumgartner et al (2006), Davis and Thaut (1989), Guzzetta (1989), Kibler and Rider (1983), Krumhansl (1997), Lundqvist et al (2009), McFarland (1985), McFarland and Kadish (1991), Miluk-Kolasa, Matejek, and Stupnicki (1996),

Nater et al (2005), Peach (1984), Rickard (2004), Savan (1999), Standley (1991), and Zimmerman et al (1988). However, there was very little consistency in the results. Temperature increased to sedative music (Kibler & Rider, 1983; Peach, 1984), to stimulative music (Lundqvist et al, 2009; Standley, 1991), or to any music (Rickard, 2004; Zimmerman et al, 1988), though decreased in other cases (Krumhansl, 1997; Nater et al, 2005; Savan, 1999), or caused no change (Blood & Zatorre, 2001; Craig, 2005; Guzzetta, 1989; Kibler & Rider, 1983; Rider et al, 1991; Zimmerman et al, 1988).

11.2.9 The effects of music on chills

A number of investigators have grouped a variety of expressive responses together under the heading of 'chills' (sometimes called 'thrills'). These responses include such things as crying, lump in the throat, shivering, a prickly feeling on the back of the neck, tingling along the spine or in the extremities, and goosebumps (pilo-motor reflex) (Konečni, 2005). Findings have consistently supported the notion that music listeners experience chills. In fact, 75–96 per cent of those interviewed reported having chills to music (Goldstein, 1980; Sloboda, 1991) and do so reliably (Konečni, Wanic, & Brown, 2007; Waterman, 1996).

Guhn, Hamm, and Zentner (2007) found that musical passages that elicited the greatest number of chills also elicited the greatest increase in heart rate and skin conductance. Skin conductance was higher for those who experienced chills than those who did not, but there was no difference in heart rate (even though both groups did experience an increase). These results confirm previous findings of Craig (2005), Grewe et al (2007b), Panksepp (1995), and Rickard (2004). However, they contradict the results of Blood and Zatorre (2001) in that these authors did not find an increase in skin conductance during chills. They did find increases and decreases in blood flow to different brain areas, along with increases in heart rate, respiration, and forearm muscular tension. Grewe et al (2007b) and Sloboda (1991) found that chills were related to distinct musical events, such as a sudden change in dynamics. In writing about their strongest experiences with music, participants commonly mentioned tears, both independently and in connection with chills (Gabrielsson, 2001; Chapter 20, this volume; for a discussion of chills/thrills, see Chapter 21, this volume).

11.2.10 The effects of music on blood volume

Blood volume is the amount of blood present in particular body tissue (e.g. hand or arm) and is measured by a plethysmograph (Andreassi, 2007). Blood volume changes have been linked to sexual responses and to an orienting response in reaction to novel stimuli, but are not so clearly responsive to emotions. Perhaps this explains the lack of consistency in the effects of music on blood volume. Davis and Thaut (1989) and Krumhansl (1997) found significant, meaningful changes in blood volume in response to music listening, but Jellison (1975), Nater et al (2005), and Pignatiello et al (1989) did not.

11.2.11 The effects of music on gastric motility

Gastric motility (peristalsis) refers to stomach contractions that move food along the alimentary canal. Gastric slow waves are measured by electrogastrography (Rothstein, Alavi, & Reynolds, 1993). Very limited work has been done on the effect of music listening on gastric motility. Although Chen et al (2005, 2008), Demling et al (1970), and Wilson (1957) found supporting evidence that music affected gastric motility, results were conflicting, depending on whether particpants were in a fasting or fed state and whether the music was high or low arousing.

11.2.12 The effects of music on blood-oxygen saturation

Blood-oxygen saturation refers to the amount of oxygen present in the blood and is measured by an oximeter (Hill & Stoneham, 2000). Music had a positive effect on blood-oxygen saturation levels in low birthweight infants (Cassidy & Standley, 1995), and changes in musical stimuli brought about changes in oxygen saturation levels (Lovett Doust & Schneider, 1952).

11.2.13 The effects of music on pupillary reflex and startle eye blink reflex

Slaughter (1954) used a subjective, observational methodology to determine that music had a significant effect on pupillary reflex, with dilation occurring during stimulative music and constriction during sedative music. Modern technology allows for more sophisticated measurements of pupillary reflex (Andreassi, 2007), but no studies have been identified in relation to music. Mathieu et al (2009) found that startle eye blink reflex was larger and faster for unpleasant compared to pleasant music.

11.2.14 The effects of music on body movements

Many action units utilized by Cohn, Ambadar, and Ekman (2007), such as head movements forward, back, and side to side, seem to be particularly suited to musical responsiveness. Our brains and bodies seem to be wired to respond to sound and to rhythmic sounds in particular (Koepchen et al, 1992; Scherer & Zentner, 2001). Todd (1995, 1999) proposed two models that offer a possible explanation for why music listeners respond with body movements. The vestibulomotor mechanism involves connections between the vestibulo-spinal-tract and myogenic (i.e. muscle generated) responses. For example, myogenic vestibularly evoked potentials to auditory stimuli have been measured in neck muscles. They can occur in response to auditory stimuli such as music and might explain reflexive muscle responses such as head bobbing.

The audio-visuo-motor mechanism connects auditory or visual representations of temporal information to motor representations of the musculoskeletal system (Baumann et al 2007; Brown, 2006; Thaut, 2003). These representations are linked by the cerebellum, and come together in sensory-guided actions. A major principle of sensory-motor theory is that sensations of motion may be experienced, even if the musculoskeletal system does not move. Thus, even passive listening to music may elicit a sense of motion. The vestibulomotor mechanism is low-level, direct, and reflexive, while the audio-visuo-motor mechanism is high-level, indirect, and a product of learning. Working together they may account for why music listening often elicits bodily responses such as head nodding, toe tapping, and body swaying. Unfortunately, investigations of head and body movements have not been pursued in terms of psychophysiological responses in typical music listening experiences. Only one study (Grewe et al, 2007a) has examined this issue. Self-reports of a desire for movement were significantly higher for a highly rhythmic dance tune than for other musical pieces.

11.3 Discussion

Sections 11.2.2–11.2.14 include 158 published articles concerning psychophysiological responses to music. Of these, 108 studies included measurements of psychophysiological responses without considering emotions. Of the 50 studies that included emotions, 17 dealt with stress or anxiety, mostly in medical or musical performance settings. The remaining 39 studies considered relationships among various psychophysiological and emotional responses. Thus, only a relatively small amount of the literature, approximately 25 per cent, connects psychophsyiological responses to music with emotions. Fortunately, however, the trend has increased since 2000, as 23 of these 39 articles have been published in the past eight years. The numbers in this discussion should be taken as approximations rather than exact numbers due to inconsistent use of terminology. What some authors refer to as emotions may actually be moods, feelings, anxiety, and so on (see Konečni, 2008).

The 119 studies not specifically concerned with emotions have firmly established the notion that there are numerous bodily responses to music. This has been most useful in the fields of music therapy and music medicine (see Chapters 29 and 30, this volume). However, the following discussion concentrates on the remaining 39 studies identified as most closely linking psychophysiological responses to emotions; these are marked with an asterisk (*) in the reference list.

11.3.1 Multivariate approaches in the search for emotion-specific patterns

The previous review sections presented a variety of psychophsyiological measurements in isolation. While this provides information about music's effects on each variable, it does not accurately reflect a recent trend toward multivariate approaches. A multivariate approach involves monitoring a variety of psychophysiological variables in an attempt to identify patterns among the responses. For example, Nyklíček, Thayer, and Van Doornen (1997) found that, although most univariate variables could not differentiate between emotions, a multivariate approach did lead to significant differentiation.

A major issue is whether there are emotion-specific patterns of psychophysiological activity. Among the numerous theories that have been proposed (see Strongman, 1996, who identifies 14 theories of emotion), three major theories have come to dominate current thinking and research on this issue (Larsen et al, 2008). (1) Different patterns of somatovisceral activity produce different emotions (James, 1884). (2) Different emotions produce different patterns of somatovisceral activity (Cannon, 1927). (3) Undifferentiated somatovisceral activity can produce distinct and differentiated emotions depending on situational context (Schacter & Singer, 1962). Levenson (2003a) frames the discussion by polarizing two extreme viewpoints: (a) every emotion is autonomically unique and (b) every emotion is autonomically the same. He cites research findings that lead to the rejection of both extremes.

Some researchers (e.g. Ekman, Levenson, & Friesen, 1983; Levenson, 1992) have produced evidence to support the notion that there are emotion-specific patterns of autonomic responses. Others, however, stated that such findings were inconclusive and ambiguous (e.g. Zajonc & McIntosh, 1992). In an attempt to resolve this issue, Cacioppo et al (2000) conducted a meta-analysis of all published studies using two or more discrete emotions and two or more autonomic measures. Meta-analysis indicated that 'even a limited set of discrete emotions such as happy, sad, fear, anger, and disgust cannot be fully differentiated by visceral activity alone' (p. 183). Negative emotions are, however, associated with stronger autonomic responses than are positive emotions. Cumulative evidence for emotion-specific patterns remains inconclusive. One reason for this may be the type and intensity of emotion (Mauss et al, 2005). Certain emotions (e.g. surprise or anxiety) may have more cognitive involvement. Further, coherence (synchronization) among response systems may be greater as the intensity of the emotion increases.

Multivariate approaches have been used more commonly in the past decade in music research. For example, Krumhansl (1997) conducted a landmark study in which 11 physiological variables (heart rate, blood pressure, skin conductance, and temperature) and emotional responses were monitored on a second-by-second basis. She found evidence for emotion-specific patterns: music expressing sadness produced the largest changes in heart rate, blood pressure, skin conductance, and temperature; respiration changed more for happy excerpts.

Nyklíček et al (1997) measured 16 cardiorespiratory variables, and found clear evidence for physiological differentiation of emotions. Gomez and Danuser (2007) explored relationships among structural features of music, physiological measures (respiration, skin conductance, and heart rate), and emotions (self-reports of valence and arousal). They found important interrelationships among all three; for example, rhythmic articulation was among the structural features of music that best differentiated between high and low arousal and positive and negative valence, and best correlated with physiological measures. Guhn et al (2007) found that the highest number of chills occurred in music with similar structural characteristics, which coincided with distinct patterns of heart rate and skin conductance increases.

According to Juslin and Laukka (2004), 'emotion is inferred on the basis of three kinds of evidence: (a) self-report, (b) behaviour (e.g. facial expressions), and (c) physiological reaction' (p. 222). A study involving all three forms of evidence was conducted by Khalfa et al (2008), who found that participant judgments of 'happy' and 'sad' music were significantly differentiated by facial EMG (zygomaticus activity), blood pressure, and skin conductance. Similarly, Witvliet and Vrana (2007) found emotion effects across a range of self-report, autonomic (heart rate), and somatic (facial EMG) measures. Finally, Lundqvist et al (2009) found coherence among experiential (self-rated emotion), expressive (facial EMG), and physiological components of an emotional response system. 'Happy' music generated more zygomaticus activity, greater skin conductance, and lower temperature than 'sad' music. In sum, though the issue is not entirely settled, there is mounting evidence that multivariate approaches may lead to the discovery of distinct patterns of psychophysiological activity that can differentiate among various emotions.

11.3.2 The role of psychophysiological processes in induced emotions

As indicated previously, the literature is somewhat divided between those who support a cognitivist position and those who support an emotivist position. Considering the role of psychophysiological responses in this debate, there is some support for a cognitivist view. Grewe et al (2007a), for example, combined physiological arousal (skin conductance), motor response (facial muscle activity), and subjective feeling (self-report of affective reactions) in both overall and second-by-second reactions to seven different musical pieces. They found that most of the subjective feelings were not accompanied by significant physiological or motor responses. They could not find 'any affective events that regularly occurred across all three components' (p. 786) in response to the music. According to them, the notion that distinct musical patterns may induce emotions should be questioned.

Konečni, Brown, and Wanic (2008, p. 292) concur and state the following:

The physiological record alone does not equal the presence of emotional experience. . . In our view, music can add to the physiological substrate of genuine emotions, but not cause the emotions themselves.

Following an extensive review of pertinent studies, including many cited immediately below in support of an emotivist position, Konečni (2008) contends that psychophysiological responses may occur in the presence of music without necessarily leading to emotional responses. In a similar review of research evidence, Scherer and Zentner (2001) state that 'we are far from being able to provide a clear answer to the question of how music can actually produce emotional states' (p. 382). Scherer (2004) further contends that 'listening to music is unlikely to evoke a limited number of neuromotor programs resulting in highly emotion-specific facial expressions or physiological response patterns' (p. 246).

In contrast, a larger number of empirical studies that incorporated measurements of psychophysiological responses support an emotivist position. Krumhansl (1997) found that 'the physiological effects of music observed generally support the emotivist view of musical emotions' (p. 336). Rickard (2004) demonstrated that emotionally powerful music elicited greater increases in skin conductance and number of chills. She, too, called this support for an emotivist position. In analysing nearly 400 written responses describing the strongest, most intense musical encounter that participants had experienced, Gabrielsson (2001) found that physiological and behavioural responses were frequent components of reported emotional reactions. Sloboda (1991) obtained similar results. Lundqvist et al (2009) found support for an emotivist position by demonstrating that induced emotions, which included physiological responses, matched emotions expressed in the music. Gomez and Danuser (2007) found similarities in relations obtained between musical structure and perceived emotion, and between musical structure and experienced emotions, which also included physiological reactions. Other researchers who found changes in psychophysiological variables related to induced emotional responses include Baumgartner et al (2006), Guhn, Hamm, and Zentner (2007), Khalfa et al (2008), Mathieu et al (2009), Nater et al (2006), Nyklíček, Thayer, and Van Doornen (1997), Thayer and Faith (2001), Witvliet and Vrana (2007), and Witvliet et al (1998).

In sum, it appears that more researchers favour an emotivist position than a cognitivist one. Clearly, though, the issue is not settled. One of the central issues to be resolved is what constitutes an induced emotion. In their critiques of much of the literature cited here in support of an emotivist position, both Konečni (2008) and Scherer (2004) based much of their rejection of the findings on the grounds that researchers have not adequately distinguished between emotion and mood, and have not dealt with serious methodological shortcomings. However, Juslin and Västfjäll (2008) have proposed a new theoretical framework that they see as a means of guiding research to resolve the disagreements on this issue. Their model combines cognitive appraisal with six psychological induction mechanisms: (a) brain stem reflexes, (b) evaluative conditioning, (c) emotional contagion, (d) visual imagery, (e) episodic memory, and (f) musical expectancy (Chapter 22, this volume). Ideally, this framework, and perhaps others to come, will lead to experiments that significantly improve our understanding of this issue.

11.4 TOPICS FOR FUTURE RESEARCH

Significant progress has been made on the role of psychophysiological processes in music emotions in recent years. Perhaps the factor most responsible for this progress is the increasing use of multivariate approaches that include not only a variety of somatovisceral measurements but also assessments of felt emotions as well. Below are five selected topics that researchers have indicated are critical for increased understanding of this field.

11.4.1 Integrated approaches

As an extension of the multivariate approaches discussed in 11.3.1, Levenson (2003a) feels that the study of psychophysiological activity in emotions should be broadened to include an integrative approach that demonstrates how various response systems are coordinated; these should include facial activity, subjective emotional experiences, autonomic responses, brain activity, and neurohormonal activity. By way of example, only a limited number of studies have included brain activations: Blood and Zatorre (2001) combined brain imaging with subjective reports of chills and measurements of heart rate, respiration, muscle tension, skin conductance, and skin temperature. Sammler et al (2007) incorporated brain wave, muscle tension, and heart rate data, along with valence of perceived emotions. In a series of studies, Thayer and Faith (2001) measured cardiovascular, respiratory, muscle tension, and brain wave activity while examining emotional valence and arousal. Rather than using a different set of variables for each study, it would be helpful if researchers would follow a systematic paradigm. There is need for a model similar to the aforementioned theoretical framework proposed by Juslin and Västfjäll (2008) for the study of mechanisms that induce musical emotions.

11.4.2 Timing issues

Levenson (2003a) argues that emotions do not typically occur in isolation; often there are emotion 'blends' as one emotion overlaps another, or emotion sequences as one emotion transitions into another. Related to this is the need for longer musical excerpts and ongoing, moment-to-moment data collection (Gomez & Danuser, 2007). Table 11.8 presents a sample of studies that utilized brief musical excerpts focusing on a single emotion.

Table 11.8 Brevity of unimodal musical stimuli

Author/date	Stimuli	Length
Gomez & Danuser, 2007	16 excerpts: each consistent in tempo, mode, etc.	30 sec. each
Krumhansl, 1997	6 excerpts: 2 each for *happy, sad,* and *fear*	3 min. each
Nyklíček et al, 1996	12 excerpts: 3 each for *happy, sad, serene,* and *agitated*	65–230 seconds each
Witvliet & Vrana, 2007	12 excerpts: 3 each from the four quadrants of valence X arousal space	26 seconds

As music unfolds over time, it is important to capture the ways psychophsyiological activity changes during the course of the listening experience. Using longer musical examples (e.g. an entire movement) and collecting moment-by-moment data will also provide information about how somatovisceral activity might reflect shifting emotions over time.

11.4.3 Naturalistic settings

For obvious reasons, most experiments are conducted in laboratories. Although several experiments have been conducted on performers in natural settings (see Section 11.2.2), little work has been done with music listeners. Vaitl, Vehrs, and Sternagel (1993) monitored skin conductance, respiration, and emotional arousal continuously throughout a performance of Wagner's *Die Meistersinger von Nürnberg* at the Bayreuth Festival. Physiological responses did vary with different leitmotifs and their musical features, though there was only a weak correspondence between physiological measurements and emotional arousal ratings. More recently, progress has been made in ambulatory assessment that allows for a variety of psychophysiological processes to be monitored in naturalistic settings (Fahrenberg, 2001). Dyer (2006) reported on an experiment involving a conductor, five members of a symphony orchestra, and 15 audience members who were wired to record heart rate, muscle tension, respiration, and skin conductance during a performance. Unfortunately, the results of this study have not yet been published.

Participants in laboratory experiments may suppress overt responses to the music. This is probably exacerbated when classical music is used as a stimulus, since concert etiquette requires a minimum of body movements. Krumhansl (1997) found that the effects of music on physiological measures in her investigation were similar to non-music research involving suppressed emotion conditions. She states that such suppression of overt responses during music listening may affect physiological responses. Exploring psychophysiological responses in naturalistic settings, including an extension into everyday listening (e.g. Juslin & Laukka, 2004; Chapter 18, this volume), may provide answers to these issues and is an area that needs greatly increased attention. An added layer of complexity, and one yet unexplored, is the effects of situational contexts (e.g. as in the opening scenarios) on musical emotions.

11.4.4 Structural features of music

Although considerable work has been done on relationships between musical structures (e.g. melodic properties, major–minor mode, etc.) and perceived emotions (see Chapter 14, this volume), much less work has been done on relationships between musical structures and induced emotions (Juslin 2009), and even less on connections with psychophysiological variables. Sloboda (1991) asked music listeners to identify specific points in the music when they had a physical response. Of the 165 participants, 10 were unable to specify or to comply, 46 indicated a whole piece or movement, and

52 indicated a section of a piece or a movement. Only 57 (35 per cent) were able to pinpoint the moment to a theme, phrase, motive, measure, chord, or moment. Only two respondents of these 57 were non-performers, indicating that considerable musical experience may be necessary to pinpoint physical response to specific places in the music. Gomez and Danuser (2007), Guhn et al (2007), and Rickard (2004) have also made connections between somatovisceral activity and musical elements, but much more needs to be done in this regard.

11.4.5 Personal variables

Very limited work has been done on personal variables. For example, Lundqvist et al (2009) did not find gender differences in psychophysiological variables, whereas McFarland and Kadish (1991), McNamara and Ballard (1999), and Nater et al (2006) did. Rickard (2004) found that personality factors were correlated with psychophysiological variables (e.g. extraversion correlated positively with heart rate, agreeableness correlated positively with skin conductance, conscientiousness and internal locus of control correlated negatively with salivary cortisol). Obviously, the influence of personal variables on psychophysiological acitivity is in need of considerably more study (Levenson, 2003a; Witvliet & Vrana, 2007).

Emotional responses to music are undoubtedly at the core of why human beings value music so highly. Psychophysiological processes are an integral part of these emotional reactions. Clarifying the role that psychophysiology plays in musical emotions is fraught with numerous theoretical and methodological problems. However, progress is being made and will undoubtedly continue.

RECOMMENDED FURTHER READING

1. Bartlett, D. (1996). Physiological responses to music and sound stimuli. In D. Hodges (ed.), *Handbook of music psychology* (2nd edn, pp. 343–85). San Antonio, TX: IMR Press.
2. Andreassi, J. (2007). *Psychophysiology: Human behavior & physiological response* (5th edn). Mahwah, NJ: Erlbaum.
3. Curtin, J., Lozano, D., & Allen, J. (2007). The psychophysiological laboratory. In J. A. Coan & J. B Allen (eds), *Handbook of emotion elicitation and assessment* (pp. 398–425). Oxford: Oxford University Press.

REFERENCES

Note. Studies identified as most closely linking psychophysiological responses to emotions are indicated with an asterisk (*).

Abel, J., & Larkin, K. (1990). Anticipation of performance among musicians: Physiological arousal, confidence, and state anxiety. *Psychology of Music, 18*, 171–82.

Abrams, D., & Manstead, A. (1981). A test of theories of social facilitation using a musical task. *British Journal of Social Psychology*, 20, 271–8.

Ader, R. (ed.). (2007). *Psychoneuroimmunology* (4th edn). New York: Elsevier.

Andreassi, J. (2007). *Psychophysiology: Human behavior & physiological response* (5th edn). Mahwah, NJ: Erlbaum.

Barger, D. (1979). The effects of music and verbal suggestion on heart rate and self-reports. *Journal of Music Therapy*, 16, 158–71.

Barker, L. (1991). The use of music and relaxation techniques to reduce pain of burn patients during daily debridement. In C. Maranto (ed.), *Applications of music in medicine* (pp. 124–40). Washington, DC: National Association for Music Therapy.

Bartlett, D. (1996). Physiological responses to music and sound stimuli. In D. Hodges (ed.), *Handbook of music psychology* (2nd edn, pp. 343–385). San Antonio, TX: IMR Press.

Bartlett, D., Kaufman, D., & Smeltekop, R. (1993). The effects of music listening and perceived sensory experiences on the immune system as measured by interleukin-1 and cortisol. *Journal of Music Therapy*, 30, 194–209.

*Baumgartner, T., Esslen, M., & Jäncke, L. (2006). From emotion perception to emotion experience: Emotions evoked by pictures and classical music. *International Journal of Psychophysiology*, 60, 34–43.

Baumann, S., Koeneke, S., Schmidt, C., Meyer, M., Lutz, K., & Jäncke, L. (2007). A network for audio-motor coordination in skilled pianists and non-musicians. *Brain Research*, 1161, 65–78.

Beck, R., Cesario, T., Yousefi, A., & Enamoto, H. (2000). Choral singing, performance perception, and immune system changes in salivary immunoglobulin A and cortisol. *Music Perception*, 18, 87–106.

Bernardi, L., Porta, C., & Sleight, P. (2006). Cardiovascular, cerebrovascular, and respiratory changes induced by different types of music in musicians and non-musicians: The importance of silence. *Heart*, 92, 445–52.

Bittman, B., Berk, L., Shannon, M., Sharaf, M., Westengard, J., Guegler, K., & Ruff, D. (2005). Recreational music making modulates the human stress response: A preliminary individualized gene expression strategy. *Medical Science Monitor*, 11, BR231–40.

*Blood, A., & Zatorre, R. (2001). Intensely pleasurable responses to music correlate with activity in brain regions implicated in reward and emotion. *Proceedings of the National Academy of Sciences*, 98, 11818–23.

Bloom, F., Lazerson, A., & Hofstadter, L. (1985). *Brain, mind, and behavior*. New York: Freeman.

Bonny, H. (1983). Music listening for intensive coronary care units: A pilot project. *Music Therapy*, 3, 4–16.

Brackbill, Y., Adams, G., Crowell, D., & Gray, M. (1966). Arousal level in neonates and preschool children under continuous auditory stimulation. *Journal of Experimental Child Psychology*, 4, 178–88.

Brotons, M. (1994). Effects of performing conditions on music performance anxiety and performance quality. *Journal of Music Therapy*, 31, 63–81.

Brown, S., Martinez, M., & Parsons, L. (2004). Passive music listening spontaneously engages limbic and paralimbic systems. *NeuroReport*, 15, 2033–7.

Brown, S., Martinez, M., & Parsons, L. (2006). The neural basis of human dance. *Cerebral Cortex*, 16, 1157–67.

Cacioppo, J., Berntson, G., Larsen, J., Poehlmann, K., & Ito, T. (2000). The psychophysiology of emotion. In M. Lewis & J. K. Haviland-Jones (eds) *The handbook of emotions* (2nd edn, pp. 173–191). New York: Guilford Press.

Canon, W. (1927). The James-Lange theory of emotions: A critical examination and an alternative theory. *American Journal of Psychology*, 39, 106–124.

Carrick, F., Oggero, E., & Pagnacco, G. (2007). Posturographic changes associated with music listening. *The Journal of Alternative and Complementary Medicine, 13*, 519–26.

Cassidy, J., & Standley, J. (1995). The effect of music listening on physiological responses of premature infants in the NICU. *Journal of Music Therapy, 32*, 208–27.

Charnetski, C., & Brennan, F. Jr. (1998). Effect of music and auditory stimuli on secretory immunoglobulin A (IgA). *Perceptual and Motor Skills, 87*, 1163–70.

Chen, D., Xu, X., Zhao, Q., Yin, J., Sallam, H., & Chen, J. (2008). Effects of audio stimulation on gastric myoelectrical activity and sympathovagal balance in healthy adolescents and adults. *Journal of Gastroenterology and Hepatology, 23*, 141–9.

Chen, D., Xu, X., Wang, Z., & Chen, J. (2005). Alteration of gastric myoelectrical and autonomic activities with audio stimulation in healthy humans. *Scandinavian Journal of Gastroenterology, 40*, 814–21.

Clark, L., Iversen, S., & Goodwin, G. (2001). The influence of positive and negative mood states on risk taking, verbal fluency, and salivary cortisol. *Journal of Affective Disorders, 63*, 179–87.

Cohn, J., Ambador, Z., & Ekman, P. (2007). Observer-based measurement of facial expression with the Facial Action Coding System. In J. A. Coan & J. B Allen (eds), *Handbook of emotion elicitation and assessment* (pp. 203–21). Oxford: Oxford University Press.

Cohn, J., & Kanade, T. (2007). Use of automated facial image analysis for measurement of emotion expression. In J. A. Coan & J. B Allen (eds), *Handbook of emotion elicitation and assessment* (pp. 222–38). Oxford: Oxford University Press.

Coleman, W. (1920). On the correlation of the rate of heart beat, breathing, bodily movement, and sensory stimuli. *Journal of Physiology, 54*, 213–7.

Conti, A. (2000). Oncology in neuroimmunomodulation: What progress has been made? *Annals of the New York Academy of Sciences, 917*, 68–83.

Conrad, C., Niess, H., Jauch, K-W., Bruns, C., Hartl, W., & Welker, L. (2007). Overture for growth hormone: Requiem for interleukin-6? *Critical Care Medicine, 35*, 2709–13.

Coutts, C. (1965). Effects of music on pulse rates and work output of short duration. *Research Quarterly, 36*, 17–21.

*Craig, D. (2005). An exploratory study of physiological changes during 'chills' induced by music. *Musicae Scientiae, 9*, 273–85.

Curtin, J., Lozano, D., & Allen, J. (2007). The psychophysiological laboratory. In J. A. Coan & J. B Allen (eds), *Handbook of emotion elicitation and assessment* (pp. 398–425). Oxford: Oxford University Press.

Dainow, E. (1977). Physical effects and motor responses to music. *Journal of Research in Music Education, 25*, 211–21.

Davis, C. (1992). The effects of music and basic relaxation instruction on pain and anxiety of women undergoing in-office gynecological procedures. *Journal of Music Therapy, 29*, 202–16.

Davis, R. (1934). Modification of the galvanic reflex by daily repetition of a stimulus. *Journal of Experimental Psychology, 17*, 504–35.

Davis, W., & Thaut, M. (1989). The influence of preferred relaxing music on measures of state anxiety, relaxation, and physiological responses. *Journal of Music Therapy, 26*, 168–87.

Davis-Rollans, C., & Cunningham, S. (1987). Physiologic responses of coronary care patients to selected music. *Heart Lung, 16*, 370–8.

DeJong, M., van Mourik, K., & Schellekiens, H. (1973). A physiological approach to aesthetic preference—music. *Psychotherapy and Psychosomatics, 22*, 46–51.

Demling, L., Tzschoppe, M., & Classen, M. (1970). The effect of various types of music on the secretory function of the stomach. *Digestive Diseases and Sciences, 15*, 15–20.

Diserens, C. (1926). *The influence of music on behavior.* Princeton, NJ: Princeton University Press.

Diserens, C., & Fine, H. (1939). *A psychology of music*. Cincinnati, OH: Authors.

Dreher, R. (1948). The relationship between verbal reports and galvanic skin responses to music. *American Psychologist*, 3, 275–6.

Dyer, R. (2006). A new kind of experimental music. *Boston Globe*, April 16.

Edwards, M., Eagle, C., Pennebaker, J., & Tunks, T. (1991). Relationships among elements of music and physiological responses of listeners. In C. Maranto (ed.), *Applications of music in medicine* (pp. 41–57). Washington, DC: National Association for Music Therapy.

Ekman, P., Levenson, R., & Friesen, W. (1983). Autonomic nervous system activity distinguishes among emotions. *Science*, 221, 1200–10.

Ellis, D., & Brighouse, G. (1952). Effects of music on respiration and heart rate. *American Journal of Psychology*, 65, 39–47.

*Ellis, R., & Simons, F. (2005). The impact of music on subjective and physiological measures of emotion while viewing films. *Psychomusicology*, 19, 15–40.

Enk, R., Franzke, P., Offermanns, K., Hohenadel, M., Boehlig, A., Nitsche, I., Kalda, T., Sack, U., & Koelsch, S. (2008). Music and the immune system. *International Journal of Psychophysiology*, 69, 207–41.

*Etzel, J., Johnsen, E., Dickerson, J., Tranel, D., & Adolphs, R. (2006). Cardiovascular and respiratory responses during musical mood induction. *International Journal of Pscyhophysiology*, 61, 57–69.

Evers, S., & Suhr, B. (2000). Changes of the neurotransmitter serotonin but not of hormones during short time music perception. *European Archives of Psychiatry and Clinical Neuroscience*, 250, 144–7.

Fahrenberg, J. (2001). Origins and developments of ambulatory monitoring and assessment. In J. Fahrenberg & M. Myrtek (eds), *Progress in ambulatory assessment. Computer-assisted psychological and psychophysiological methods in monitoring and field Studies*. Seattle, WA: Hogrefe and Huber.

Farnsworth, P. (1969). *The social psychology of music* (2nd edn). Ames, IA: Iowa State University Press.

Foster, E., & Gamble, E. (1906). The effect of music on thoracic breathing. *American Journal of Psychology*, 17, 406–14.

Freeman, W. (1995). *Societies of brains: A study in the neuroscience of love and hate*. Hillsdale, NJ: Erlbaum.

Fukui, H. (2001). Music and testosterone: A new hypothesis for the origin and function of music. *Annals of the New York Academy of Sciences*, 999, 448–51.

*Gabrielsson, A. (2001). Emotions in strong experiences with music. In P. N. Juslin & J. A. Sloboda (eds), *Music and emotion: Theory and research* (pp. 431–49). Oxford: Oxford University Press.

Gabrielsson, A., & Lindström, E. (2001). The influence of musical structure on emotional expression. In P. N Juslin & J. A. Sloboda (eds), *Music and emotion: Theory and research* (pp. 223–48). Oxford: Oxford University Press.

Gaston, E. (1951). Dynamic music factors in mood change. *Music Educators Journal*, 37, 42–4.

Geden, E., Lower, M., Beattie, S., & Beck, N. (1989). Effects of music and imagery on physiologic and self-report of analogued labor pain. *Nursing Research*, 38, 37–41.

*Gendolla, G., & Krüsken, J. (2001). Mood state and cardiovascular response in active coping with an affect-regulative challenge. *International Journal of Psychophysiology*, 41, 169–80.

*Gerra, G., Zaimovic, A., Franchini, D., Palladino, M., Guicastro, G., Reali, N., Maestri, D., Caccavari, R., Delsignore, R., & Brambilla, F. (1998). Neuroendocrine responses of healthy volunteers to 'techno-music': relationships with personality traits and emotional state. *International Journal of Psychophysiology*, 28, 99–111.

*Goldstein, A. (1980). Thrills in response to music and other stimuli. *Physiological Psychology*, 3, 126–9.

*Gomez, P., & Danuser, B. (2007). Relationships between musical structure and psychophysiological measures of emotion. *Emotion*, 7, 377–87.

*Gomez, P., & Danuser, B. (2004). Affective and physiological responses to environmental noises and music. *International Journal of Psychophysiology*, 53, 91–103.

Graham, R., & Clifton, R. (1966). Heart-rate change as a component of the orienting response. *Psychological Bulletin*, 65, 305–20.

*Grewe, O., Nagel, F., Kopiez, R., & Altenmüller, E. (2007a). Emotions over time: Synchronicity and development of subjective, physiological, and facial affective relations to music. *Emotion*, 7, 774–88.

*Grewe, O., Nagel, F., Kopiez, R., & Altenmüller, E. (2007b). Listening to music as a re-creative process: Physiological, psychological, and psychoacoustical correlates of chills and strong emotions. *Music Perception*, 24, 297–14.

*Guhn, M., Hamm, A., & Zentner, M. R. (2007). Physiological and music-acoustic correlates of the chill response. *Music Perception*, 24, 473–83.

Gupta, U., & Gupta, B. (2005). Psychophysiological responsivity to Indian instrumental music. *Psychology of Music*, 33, 363–72.

Guzzetta, C. (1989). Effects of relaxation and music therapy on patients in a coronary care unit with presumptive acute myocardial infarction. *Heart Lung*, 18, 609–16.

Haas, F., Distenfeld, S., & Axen, K. (1986). Effects of perceived musical rhythm on respiratory patterns. *Journal of Applied Physiology*, 61, 1185–91.

Haider, M., & Groll-Knapp, E. (1981). Psychophysiological investigations into the stress experienced by musicians in a symphony orchestra. In M. Piperek (ed.), *Stress and music* (pp. 15–34). Vienna, Austria: Wilhelm Braumüller.

*Harrer, G., & Harrer, H. (1977). Music, emotion, and autonomic function. In M. Critchley & R. Henson (eds), *Music and the brain* (pp. 202–16). London: William Heinemann Medical Books.

Henkin, R. (1957). The prediction of behavior response patterns to music. *Journal of Psychology*, 44, 111–27.

Hill, E., & Stoneham, M. (2000). Practical applications of pulse oximetry. *Update in Anaesthesia*, 11, 1–2.

Hirokawa, E., & Ohira, H. (2003). The effects of music listening after a stressful task on immune functions, neuroendocrine responses, and emotional states in college students. *Journal of Music Therapy*, 40, 189–211.

Hodges, D. (1980). Physiological responses to music. In D. Hodges (ed.), *Handbook of music psychology* (pp. 392–400). Lawrence, KS: National Association for Music Therapy.

Hodges, D. (2009). Bodily responses to music. In S. Hallam, I. Cross, & M. Thaut (eds), *Oxford handbook of music psychology* (pp. 121–30). Oxford: Oxford University Press.

Hunsaker, L. (1994). Heart rate and rhythm responses during trumpet playing. *Medical Problems of Perform Artists*, 9, 69–72.

Hunter, H. (1974). An investigation of psychological and physiological changes apparently elicited by musical stimuli. *Psychology of Music*, 2, 53–68.

Hyde, I. (1927). Effects of music upon electrocardiograms and blood pressure. In M. Schoen (ed.), *The effects of music* (pp. 184–98). New York: Harcourt, Brace.

Hyde, I., & Scalapino, W. (1918). Influence of music upon electrocardiograms and blood pressure. *American Journal of Physiology*, 46, 35–8.

Iwanaga, M., Ikeda, M., & Iwaki, T. (1996). The effects of repetitive exposure to music on subjective and physiological responses. *Journal of Music Therapy*, 33, 219–30.

*Iwanaga, M., & Moroki, Y. (1999). Subjective and physiological responses to music stimuli controlled over activity and preference. *Journal of Music Therapy, 36,* 26–38.

James, W. (1884). What is an emotion? *Mind, 9,* 199–205.

Jänig, W. (2003). The autonomic nervous system and its coordination by the brain. In R. J. Davidson, K. R. Scherer, & H. H Goldsmith (eds), *Handbook of affective sciences* (pp. 135–86). Oxford: Oxford University Press.

Jellison, J. (1975). The effect of music on autonomic stress responses and verbal reports. In C. K. Madsen, R. Greer, & C. H. Madsen (eds), *Research in music behavior: Modifying music behavior in the classroom* (pp. 206–19). New York: Teachers College Press.

Johnson, D., & Trawick, M. (1938). Influence of rhythmic sensory stimuli upon the heart rate. *Journal of Psychology, 6,* 303–10.

Juslin, P. N. (2009). Emotional responses to music. In S. Hallam, I. Cross, & M. Thaut (eds), *Oxford handbook of music psychology* (pp. 131–40). Oxford: Oxford University Press.

Juslin, P. N., & Laukka, P. (2004). Expression, perception, and induction of musical emotions: A review and a questionnaire study of everyday listening. *Journal of New Music Research, 33,* 217–38.

Juslin, P. N., & Västfjäll, D. (2008). Emotional responses to music: The need to consider underlying mechanisms. *Behavioral and Brain Sciences, 31,* 559–75.

Kagan, J., & Lewis, M. (1965). Studies of attention in the human infant. *Merrill-Palmer Quarterly, 11,* 95–127.

Kallinen, K., & Ravaja, N. (2006). Emotion perceived and emotion felt: Same and different. *Musicæ Scientiæ, 10,* 191–213.

Keller, S., & Seraganian, P. (1984). Physical fitness level and autonomic reactivity to psychosocial stress. *Journal of Psychosomatic Research, 28,* 279–87.

Khalfa, S., Dalla Bella, S., Roy, M., Peretz, I., & Lupien, S. (2003). Effects of relaxing music on salivary cortisol level after psychological stress. *Annals of the New York Academy of Sciences, 999,* 374–6.

*Khalfa, S., Peretz, I., Blondin, J., & Manon, R. (2002). Event-related skin conductance responses to musical emotions in humans. *Neuroscience Letters, 328,* 145–9.

*Khalfa, S., Roy, M., Rainville, P., Dalla Bella, S., & Peretz, I. (2008). Role of tempo entrainment in psychophysiological differentiation of happy and sad music? *International Journal of Psychophysiology, 68,* 17–26.

Knight, W., & Rickard, N. (2001). Relaxing music prevents stress-induced increases in subjective anxiety, systolic blood pressure, and heart rate in healthy males and females. *Journal of Music Therapy, 38,* 254–72.

Kibler, V., & Rider, M. (1983). The effect of progressive muscle relaxation and music on stress as measured by finger temperature response. *Journal of Clinical Psychology, 39,* 213–5.

Kivy, P. (1989). *Sound sentiment: An essay on the musical emotions.* Philadelphia, PA: Temple University Press.

Kivy, P. (1990). *Music alone: Philosohical reflections on the purely musical experience.* Ithaca, NY: Cornell University Press.

Koepchen, H., Droh, R., Spintge, R., Abel, H-H., Klüssenorf, D., & Koralewski, E. (1992). Physiological rhythmicity and music in medicine. In R Spintge & R Droh (eds), *MusicMedicine* (pp. 39–70). St. Louis, MI: MMB Music.

Konečni, V. (2005). The aesthetic trinity: Awe, being moved, thrills. *Bulletin of Psychology and the Arts, 5,* 27–44.

Konečni, V. (2008). Does music induce emotion? A theoretical and methodological analysis. *Psychology of Aesthetics, Creativity, and the Arts, 2,* 115–29.

*Konečni, V., Brown, A., & Wanic, R. (2008). Comparative effects of music and recalled life-events on emotional state. *Psychology of Music, 36,* 289–308.

*Konečni, V., Wanic, R., & Brown, A. (2007). Emotional and aesthetic antecedents and conse-quences of music-induced thrills. *American Journal of Psychology, 120,* 619–43.

Kneutgen, J. (1974). Eine Musikform und ihre biologische Funktion: Uber die Wirkungsweise der Weigenlieder. *Psychological Abstracts, 45,* 6016.

*Kreutz, G., Bongard, S., Rohrmann, S., Hodapp, V., & Grebe, D. (2004). Effects of choir singing or listening on secretory immunoglobulin A, cortisol, and emotional state. *Journal of Behavioral Medicine, 27,* 623–35.

*Krumhansl, C. (1997). An exploratory study of musical emotions and psychophysiology. *Canadian Journal of Experimental Psychology, 51,* 336–52.

Kumar, A., Tims, F., Cruess, D., Mintzer, M. et al (1999). Music therapy increases serum melatonin levels in patients with Alzheimer's disease. *Alternative Therapies in Health and Medicine, 5,* 49–57.

Landreth, J., & Landreth, H. (1974). Effects of music on physiological response. *Journal of Research in Music Education, 22,* 4–12.

Lane, L. (1991). The effect of a single music therapy session on hospitalized children as mea-sured by salivary immunoglobulin A, speech pause time, and a patient opinion Likert scale. *Pediatric Research, 29,* 11A.

Larsen, J., Berntson, G., Poehlmann, K., Ito, T., & Cacioppo, J. (2008). The psychophysiology of emotion. In M. Lewis, J. M. Haviland-Jones, & L. F. Barrett (eds), *Handbook of emotions* (3rd edn, pp. 180–95). New York: Guilford Press.

Leardi, S., Pietroletti, R., Angeloni, G., Necozione, S., Ranalletta, G., & Del Gusto, B. (2007). Randomized clinical trial examining the effect of music therapy in stress response to day surgery. *British Journal of Surgery, 94,* 943–7.

LeBlanc, A., Jin, Y., Obert, M., & Siivola, C. (1997). Effect of audience on music performance anxiety. *Journal of Research in Music Education, 45,* 480–96.

LeDoux, J. E. (1986). The neurobiology of emotion. In J. E. LeDoux & W. Hirst (eds), *Mind and brain* (pp. 301–354). Cambridge, UK: Cambridge University Press.

LeDoux, J. E. (1994). Emotion, memory, and the brain. *Scientific American, 270,* 50–57.

Levenson, R. (1992). Autonomic nervous system differences among emotions. *Psychological Science, 3,* 23–7.

Levenson, R. (2003a). Autonomic specificity and emotion. In R. J. Davidson, K. R. Scherer, & H. H. Goldsmith (eds), *Handbook of affective sciences* (pp. 212–24). Oxford: Oxford University Press.

Levenson, R. (2003b). Blood, sweat, and fears: The autonomic architecture of emotions. *Annals of the New York Academy of Sciences, 1000,* 348–66.

Levenson, R. (2007). Emotion elicitation with neurological patients. In J. A. Coan & J. B. Allen (eds), *Handbook of emotion elicitation and assessment* (pp. 158–68). Oxford: Oxford University Press.

Lewis, M. (1971). A developmental study of the cardiac response to stimulus onset and offset during the first year of life. *Psychophysiology, 8,* 689–98.

Lorch, C., Lorch, V., Diefendorf, A., & Earl, P. (1994). Effect of stimulative and sedative music on systolic blood pressure, heart rate, and respiratory rate in premature infants. *Journal of Music Therapy, 31,* 105–18.

Loscin, R. (1981). The effect of music on the pain of selected postoperative patients. *Journal of Advanced Nursing, 6,* 19–25.

Lovett Doust, J., & Schneider, R. (1952). Studies on the physiology of awareness: The effect of rhythmic sensory bombardment on emotions, blood oxygen saturation, and the levels of consciousness. *Journal of Mental Science, 98,* 640–53.

Lundin, R. (1967). *An objective psychology of music* (2nd edn). New York: Ronald Press.

*Lundqvist, L.-O., Carlsson, F., Hilmersson, P., & Juslin, P. N. (2009). Emotional responses to music: Experience, expression, and physiology. *Psychology of Music, 37*, 61–90.

Madsen, C., Standley, J., & Gregory, D. (1991). The effect of a vibrotactile device, somatron, on physiological and psychological responses: Musicians versus nonmusicians. *Journal of Music Therapy, 28*, 14–22.

Mathieu, R., Mailhot, J., Gosselin, N., Paquette, S., & Peretz, I. (2009). Modulation of the startle reflex by pleasant and unpleasant music. *International Journal of Psychophysiology, 71*, 37–42.

Maier, S., Watkins, L., & Fleshner, M. (1994). Psychoneuroimmunology: The interface between behavior, brain, and immunity. *American Psychologist, 49*, 1004–17.

Mauss, I., Levenson, R., McCarter, L., Wilhelm, F., & Gross, J. (2005). The tie that binds? Coherence among emotion experience, behavior, and physiology. *Emotion, 5*, 175–90.

*McCraty, R., Atkinson, M., Rein, G., & Watkins, A. (1996). Music enhances the effect of positive emotional states on salivary IgA. *Stress Medicine, 12*, 167–75.

*McFarland, R. (1985). Relationship of skin temperature changes to the emotions accompanying music. *Biofeedback and Self-regulation, 10*, 255–67.

McFarland, R., & Kadish, R. (1991). Sex differences in finger temperature response to music. *International Journal of Psychophysiology, 11*, 295–8.

McKinney, C., Antoni, M., Kumar, M., Tims, F., & McCabe, P. (1997a). Effects of Guided Imagery and Music (GIM) therapy on mood and cortisol in healthy adults. *Health Psychology, 16*, 390–400.

McKinney, C., Tims, F., Kumar, A., & Kumar, M. (1997b). The effect of selected classical music and spontaneous imagery on plasma beta-endorphin. *Journal of Behavioral Medicine, 20*, 85–99.

McNamara, L., & Ballard, M. (1999). Resting arousal, sensation seeking, and music preference. *Genetic, Social & General Psychology Monographs, 125*, 229–51.

Menegazzi, J. (1991). A randomized, controlled trial of the use of music during laceration repair. *Emergency Medical Abstracts, 20*, 348.

Menon, V., & Levitin, D. (2005). The rewards of music listening: Response and physiological connectivity of the mesolimbic system. *NeuroImage, 28*, 175–84.

Miluk-Kolasa, B., Matejek, M., & Stupnicki, R. (1996). The effects of music listening on changes in selected physiological parameters in adult pre-surgical patients. *Journal of Music Therapy, 33*, 208–18.

Miluk-Kolasa, B., Obminski, Z., Stupnicki, R., & Golec, L. (1994). Effects of music treatment on salivary cortisol in patients exposed to pre-surgical stress. *Experimental and Clinical Endocrinology, 102*, 118–120.

Möckel, M., Röcker, L., Störk, T., Vollert, J., Danne, O., Eichstädt, H., Müller, R., & Hochrein, H. (1994). Immediate physiological responses of healthy volunteers to different types of music: Cardiovascular, hormonal and mental changes. *European Journal of Applied Physiology, 68*, 451–9.

*Nater, U., Abbruzzese, E., Krebs, M., & Ehlert, U. (2006). Sex differences in emotional and psychophysiological responses to musical stimuli. *International Journal of Psychophysiology, 62*, 300–8.

Nater, U., Krebs, M., & Ehlert, U. (2005). Sensation seeking, music preference, and psychophysiological reactivity to music. *Musicæ Scientiæ, 9*, 239–54.

*Nyklíček, I., Thayer, J., & Van Doornen, L. (1997). Cardiorespiratory differentiation of musically-induced emotions. *Journal of Psychophysiology, 11*, 304–21.

Oyama, T., Sato, Y., Kudo, T., Spintge, R., & Droh, R. (1987a). Effect of anxiolytic music on endocrine function in surgical patients. In R. Spintge & R. Droh (eds), *Music in medicine* (pp. 169–74). Berlin, Germany: Springer-Verlag.

Oyama, T., Hatano, K., Sato, Y., Kudo, M., Spintge, R., & Droh, R. (1987b). Endocrine effect of anxiolytic music in dental patients. In R. Spintge & R. Droh (eds), *Music in medicine* (pp. 223–6). Berlin, Germany: Springer-Verlag.

Panksepp, J. (1995). The emotional sources of 'chills' induced by music. *Music Perception, 13,* 171–207.

Peach, S. (1984). Some implications for the clinical use of music facilitated imagery. *Journal of Music Therapy, 21,* 27–34.

Peretti, P., & Swenson, K. (1974). Effects of music on anxiety as determined by physiological skin responses. *Journal of Research in Music Education, 22,* 278–83.

Phares, M. (1934). Analysis of music appreciation by means of psychogalvanic reflex technique. *Journal of Experimental Psychology, 17,* 119–40.

*Pignatiello, M., Camp, C., Elder, S., & Rasar, L. (1989). A psychophysiological comparison of the Velten and musical mood induction techniques. *Journal of Music Therapy, 26,* 140–54.

Pratt, R., & Spintge, R. (eds). (1995). *MusicMedicine 2.* St. Louis, MI: MMB.

Pujol, K. (1994). The effect of vibrotactile stimulation, instrumentation, and precomposed melodies on physiological and behavioral responses of profoundly retarded children and adults. *Journal of Music Therapy, 31,* 186–205.

Radocy, R., & Boyle, J. (2003). *Psychological foundations of musical behavior* (4th edn). Springfield, IL: Charles C. Thomas.

*Rickard, N. (2004). Intense emotional responses to music: a test of the physiological arousal hypothesis. *Psychology of Music, 32,* 371–88.

Rider, M. (1985). Entrainment mechanisms are involved in pain reduction, muscle relaxation, and music-mediated imagery. *Journal of Music Therapy, 22,* 183–192.

Rider, M., & Achterberg, J. (1989). Effect of music-assisted imagery on neutrophils and lymphocytes. *Biofeedback and Self-Regulation, 14,* 247–57.

Rider, M., Floyd, J., & Kirkpatrick, J. (1985). The effect of music, imagery, and relaxation on adrenal corticosteroids and the re-entrainment of circadian rhythms. *Journal of Music Therapy, 22,* 46–58.

Rider, M., Mickey, C., Weldin, C., & Hawkinson, R. (1991). The effects of toning, listening, and singing on psychophysiological responses. In C. Maranto (ed.), *Applications of music in medicine* (pp. 73–84). Washington, DC: National Association for Music Therapy.

Rider, M., & Weldin, C. (1990). Imagery, improvisation and immunity. *The Arts in Psychotherapy, 17,* 211–6.

*Ries, H. (1969). GSR and breathing amplitude related to emotional reactions to music. *Psychonomic Science, 14,* 62.

Rothstein, R., Alavi, A., & Reynolds, J. (1993). Electrogastrography in patients with gastroparesis and effect of long-term cisapride. *Digestive Diseases and Sciences, 38,* 1518–24.

Sackner, M., Watson, H., Belsito, A., Feinerman, D., Suarez, M., Gonzalez, G., Bizousky, F., & Krieger, B. (1989). Calibration of respiratory inductive plethysomograph during natural breathing. *Journal of Applied Physiology, 66,* 410–20.

Safranek, M., Koshland, G., & Raymond, G. (1982). Effect of auditory rhythm on muscle activity. *Physical Therapy, 62,* 161–8.

*Sammler, D., Grigutsch, M., Fritz, T., & Koelsch, S. (2007). Music and emotion: Electrophysiological correlates of the processing of pleasant and unpleasant music. *Psychophysiology, 44,* 293–304.

Savan, A. (1999). The effect of background music on learning. *Psychology of Music, 27,* 138–46.

Scartelli, J. (1982). The effect of sedative music on electromyographic biofeedback-assisted relaxation training of spastic cerebral palsied adults. *Journal of Music Therapy, 19,* 210–18.

Scartelli, J. (1984). The effect of EMG biofeedback and sedative music, EMG biofeedback only, and sedative music only on frontalis muscle relaxation ability. *Journal of Music Therapy*, *21*, 67–78.

Scartelli, J., & Borling, J. (1986). The effects of sequenced versus simultaneous EMG biofeedback and sedative music on frontalis relaxation training. *Journal of Music Therapy*, *23*, 157–65.

Schacter, S., & Singer, J. (1962). Cognitive, social, and physiological determinants of emotional state. *Psychological Review*, *69*, 379–99.

Scherer, K. R. (2004). Which emotions can be induced by music? What are the underlying mechanisms? And how can we measure them? *Journal of New Music Research*, *33*, 239–51.

Scherer, K. R., & Zentner, M. R. (2001). Emotional effects of music: Production rules. In P. N. Juslin & J. A. Sloboda (eds), *Music and emotion: Theory and research* (pp. 361–92). Oxford: Oxford University Press.

Schoen, M. (ed.). (1927). *The effects of music*. New York: Harcourt, Brace, & Company.

Schoen, M. (1940). *The psychology of music*. New York: Ronald Press.

Schubert, E. (2007). Locus of emotion: The effect of task order and age on emotion perceived and emotion felt in response to music. *Journal of Music Therapy*, *44*, 344–68.

Schuster, B. (1985). The effect of music listening on blood pressure fluctuations in adult hemodialysis patients. *Journal of Music Therapy*, *22*, 146–53.

Sears, W. (1958). The effect of music on muscle tonus. In E. Gaston (ed.), *Music therapy* (pp. 199–205). Lawrence, KS: Allen Press.

Shaver, P., Schwartz, J., Kirson, D., & O'Connor, C. (1997). Emotion knowledge: Further exploration of a prototype approach. *Journal of Personality and Social Psychology*, *52*, 1061–86.

Shatin, L. (1957). The influence of rhythmic drumbeat stimuli upon the pulse rate and general activity of long-term schizophrenics. *Journal of Mental Science*, *103*, 172–88.

Shepard, J. (1906). Organic changes and feeling. *American Journal of Psychology*, *17*, 521–84.

Shrift, D. (1957). The galvanic skin response to two contrasting types of music. In E. Gaston (ed.), *Music therapy* (pp. 235–9). Lawrence, KS: Allen Press.

Slaughter, F. (1954). The effect of stimulative and sedative types of music on normal and abnormal subjects as indicated by pupillary reflexes. In M. Bing (ed.), *Music therapy* (pp. 246–8). Lawrence, KS: Allen Press.

*Sloboda, J. A. (1991). Music structure and emotional response: Some empirical findings. *Psychology of Music*, *19*, 110–120.

Spintge, R., & Droh, R. (eds). (1987). *Music in medicine*. Berlin, Germany: Springer-Verlag.

Spintge, R., & Droh, R. (eds). (1992a). *MusicMedicine*. St. Louis, MI: MMB.

Spintge, R., & Droh, R. (1992b). Toward a research standard in music medicine/music therapy: A proposal for a multimodal approach. In R. Spintge & R. Droh (eds), *MusicMedicine* (pp. 345–9). St. Louis, MI: MMB Music.

Standley, J. (1991). The effect of vibrotactile and auditory stimuli on perception of comfort, heart rate, and peripheral finger temperature. *Journal of Music Therapy*, *28*, 120–34.

Standley, J. (1995). Music as a therapeutic intervention in medical and dental treatment: Research and clinical applications. In T. Wigram, B. Saperston, & R. West (eds), *The art & science of music therapy* (pp. 3–22). Newark, NJ: Harwood Academic Publishers.

Stefano, G., Zhu, W., Cadet, P., Salamon, E., & Monatione, K. (2004). Music alters constitutively expressed opiate and cytokine processes in listeners. *Medical Science Monitor*, *10*, MS18–27.

Stemmler, G. (2003). Introduction: Autonomic psychophysiology. In R. J. Davidson, K. R. Scherer, & H. H. Goldsmith (eds), *Handbook of affective sciences* (pp. 131–4). Oxford: Oxford University Press.

Strauser, J. (1997). The effects of music versus silence on measures of state anxiety, perceived relaxation, and physiological responses of patients receiving chiropractic interventions. *Journal of Music Therapy, 34,* 88–105.

Strongman, K. (1996). *The psychology of emotion* (4th edn). New York: Wiley.

Sunderman, L. (1946). A study of some physiological differences between musicians and non-musicians, 1: Blood pressure. *Journal of Social Psychology, 23,* 205–15.

Thaut, M. (2003). Neural basis of rhythmic timing networks in the human brain. *Annals of the New York Academy of Sciences, 999,* 364–73.

Thaut, M., Schleiffers, S., & Davis, W. (1991). Analysis of EMG activity in biceps and triceps muscle in an upper extremity gross motor task under the influence of auditory rhythm. *Journal of Music Therapy, 28,* 4–88.

*Thayer, J., & Faith, M. (2001). A dynamic systems model of musically induced emotions. *Annals of the New York Academy of Sciences, 999,* 452–6.

Thierbach, H. (1989). Physiological and psychological aspects of the experience of music— report on two experimental studies. *International Journal of Psychophysiology, 7,* 412–3.

Todd, N. (1995). The kinematics of musical expression. *Journal of the Acoustical Society of America, 97,* 1940–9.

Todd, N. (1999). Motion in music: A neurobiological perspective. *Music Perception, 17,* 115–26.

Trenes, N. (1937). Study of the effects of music on cancer patients. *Hospital Social Service, 16,* 131.

Tsao, C., Gordon, T., Maranto, C., Lerman, C., & Murasko, D. (1991). The effects of music and directed biological imagery on immune response S-IgA. In C. Maranto (ed.), *Applications of music in medicine* (pp. 85–121). Washington, DC: National Association for Music Therapy.

Updike, P., & Charles, D. (1987). Music Rx: Physiological and emotional responses to taped music programs of preoperative patients awaiting plastic surgery. *Annals of Plastic Surgery, 19,* 29–33.

*Vaitl, D., Vehrs, W., & Sternagel, S. (1993). Prompts–leitmotif—emotion: Play it again, Richard Wagner. In N. Birbaumer & A. Öhman (eds), *The structure of emotion: Psychophysiological, cognitive, and clinical Aspects* (pp. 169–89). Seattle, WA: Hogrefe & Hüber.

VanderArk, S., & Ely, D. (1992). Biochemical and galvanic skin responses to music stimuli by college students in biology and music. *Perceptual and Motor Skills, 74,* 1079–90.

VanderArk, S., & Ely, D. (1993). Cortisol, biochemical and galvanic skin responses to music stimuli of different preference values by college students in biology and music. *Perceptual and Motor Skills, 77,* 227–34.

Venables, P. (1987). Electrodermal activity. In R. Gregory (ed.), *The Oxford companion to the mind* (pp. 213–4). Oxford: Oxford University Press.

Wachi, M., Koyama, M., Utsuyama, M., Bittman, B., Kitagawa, M., & Hirokawa, K. (2007). Recreational music-making modulates natural killer cell activity, cytokines, and mood states in corporate employees. *Medical Science Monitor, 13,* CR57–70.

Warthin, A. (1894). Some physiologic effects of music in hypnotized subjects. *Medical News, 65,* 89.

*Waterman, M. (1996). Emotional responses to music: Implicit and explicit effects in listeners and performers. *Psychology of Music, 24,* 53–67.

*Wechsler, D. (1925). The measurement of emotional reactions: Researches on the psychogalvanic reflex. *Archives of Psychology, 76,* 1–181.

Weidenfeller, E., & Zimny, G. (1962). Effects of music upon GSR of depressives and schizophrenics. *Journal of Abnormal and Social Psychology, 64,* 307–12.

Weld, H. (1912). An experimental study of musical enjoyment. *American Journal of Psychology, 23,* 245–308.

Wilson, V. (1957). Variations in gastric motility due to musical stimuli. In E. Gaston (ed.), *Music therapy* (pp. 243–9). Lawrence, KS: Allen Press.

*Wilson, C., & Aiken, L. (1977). The effect of intensity levels upon physiological and subjective affective response to rock music. *Journal of Music Therapy*, *14*, 60–76.

Wilson, E., & Davey, N. (2002). Musical beat influences corticospinal drive to ankle flexor and extensor muscles in man. *International Journal of Psychophysiology*, *44*, 177–84.

Winold, A. (1959). The effect of changes in harmonic tension on the galvanic skin responses. In E. Schneider (ed.), *Music therapy* (pp. 188–92). Lawrence, KS: Allen Press.

*Witvliet, C., & Vrana, S. (2007). Play it again Sam: Repeated exposure to emotionally evocative music polarizes liking and smiling responses, and influences other affects reports, facial EMG, and heart rate. *Cognition & Emotion*, *21*, 3–25.

*Witvliet, C., Vrana, S., & Webb-Talmadge, N. (1998). In the mood: Emotion and facial expressions during and after instrumental music, and during an emotional inhibition task. *Psychophysiology Supplement*, S88.

Yamamoto, M., Naga, S., & Shimizu, J. (2007). Positive musical effects of two types of negative stressful conditions. *Psychology of Music*, *35*, 249–75.

Zajonc, R., & McIntosh, D. (1992). Emotions research: Some promising questions and some questionable promises. *Psychological Science*, *3*, 70–74.

Zimmerman, L., Pierson, M., & Marker, J. (1988). Effects of music on patient anxiety in coronary care units. *Heart Lung*, *17*, 560–6.

Zimny, G., & Weidenfeller, E. (1962). Effects of music upon GSR of children. *Child Development*, *33*, 891–6.

Zimny, G., & Weidenfeller, E. (1963). Effects of music on GSR and heart rate. *American Journal of Psychology*, *76*, 311–4.

CHAPTER 12

FUNCTIONAL NEUROIMAGING

STEFAN KOELSCH,
WALTER A. SIEBEL, AND
THOMAS FRITZ

FUNCTIONAL neuroimaging broadly refers to methods used to visualize neural activity in the brain in relation to a specific experimental variable (e.g. an emotion). With regard to the investigation of emotion with music, the most widely used functional neuroimaging techniques are *functional magnetic resonance imaging* (fMRI) and *positron emission tomography* (PET). (These methods are described in Section 12.12.)

Using music to investigate the neural correlates of emotion has several advantages: (1) Music can evoke stronger emotions than many other stimuli. (2) Music can evoke different positive emotions, such as the experience of 'tender happy' emotions, reward-related experiences of 'fun', or extremely pleasurable experiences such as 'chills'. (3) Both listening to music and making music can evoke emotions, enabling investigators to study interactions between emotion and action. (4) With regard to human evolution, music is originally a social activity. Therefore, music is particularly suited to study interactions between emotion and social factors. (5) Music can evoke emotions over a relatively long time period (in the range of minutes, or even longer), enabling investigations into the time course of emotional processes. It is for such reasons that functional neuroimaging studies with music can extend our views on the neural correlates of emotion. In fact, we believe that the understanding of human emotions remains incomplete unless we have a thorough knowledge about the neural correlates of emotions as evoked by music.

It was only about ten years ago that neuroscientists began to use functional neuroimaging to investigate the neural substrates of emotion with music. The first part of this chapter provides a review of functional neuroimaging studies of emotion and music.

This part illustrates how music may be used for research on emotion, and how music studies have contributed to a better understanding of the neural correlates of emotion. For example, we explain that the amygdala has different subregions with different functional properties that relate to emotion, and that each of these subregions has specific anatomical and functional connections to other structures of the brain. We also present evidence from music studies showing that the amygdala is not only involved in negative, but also in positive emotions.

We then describe and discuss the functional significance of a number of brain structures crucially involved in emotional processing (summarized in Table 12.1). For the neuroscientifically untrained, these sections aim to help the development of experimental hypotheses when preparing a study, and to aid in the interpretation of functional imaging data. For the expert, we offer new ideas and hypotheses about the functional significance of some limbic and paralimbic structures. These hypotheses are supposed to open new perspectives on emotional processing and its physiological correlates.

We then devote a section to musical emotions, emphasizing (1) that music is capable of evoking 'real' and 'basic' emotions, (2) that music can evoke even more than just those basic emotions, and (3) that if an emotion can never be evoked by music, then it is not an emotion at all. Thus, we do not make any essential difference between 'musical' and other emotions. We use the term 'musical emotions' simply to make clear that an emotion has occurred as an effect of music listening or making music (see also Table 1.2, Chapter 1, this volume).

Finally, we discuss some methodological aspects. Some of these are intended for the neuroscientifically untrained as an introduction to the techniques in functional brain imaging, but some also inform experts about novel methodological issues. These issues include the interleaved silent steady state imaging technique as a promising scanning paradigm for auditory experiments, or the problem that subject selection may be more crucial in emotion research than in other areas of functional neuroimaging.

12.1 FUNCTIONAL NEUROIMAGING STUDIES ON EMOTION WITH MUSIC

The first functional neuroimaging study on music and emotion was published by Anne Blood and colleagues (Blood et al, 1999). Using PET, they investigated the emotional dimension of pleasantness vs. unpleasantness with sequences of harmonized melodies. The stimuli varied in their degree of (permanent) dissonance, and were perceived as less or more unpleasant (stimuli with the highest degree of permanent dissonance were rated as the most unpleasant). Stimuli were presented under computerized control without musical expression. Thus, this paradigm was able to evoke unpleasantness, but was hardly able to evoke pleasant emotional reactions, even when stimuli were mainly consonant. This was perhaps the reason why the results did not reveal activations of central limbic structures such as the amygdala—to the disappointment of some researchers, because no evidence was obtained for the assumption that music can modulate activity in core structures of emotional processing. Thus, the results did not provide any reason to reject the hypothesis that music cannot evoke 'real' emotions. Nevertheless, variations in pleasantness–unpleasantness affected activity in the medial subcallosal cingulate cortex, as well as in a number of paralimbic structures: Increasing unpleasantness correlated with activations of the (right) parahippocampal gyrus, while decreasing unpleasantness of the stimuli correlated with activations of frontopolar and orbitofrontal cortex (for anatomical illustrations, see Figure 12.1).

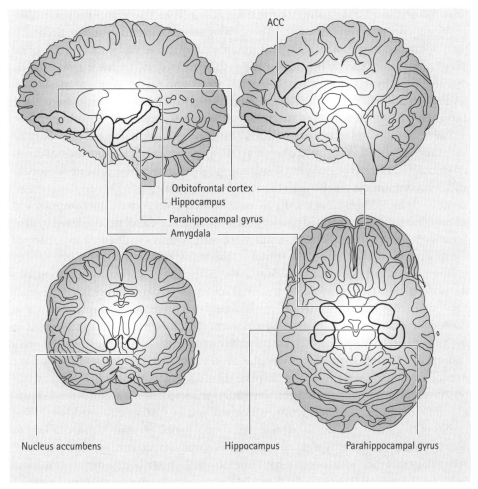

Fig. 12.1 Sagittal views (top row), coronal view (bottom left), and axial view (view from bottom) of a human brain.

Soon after this study, Blood and Zatorre (2001) conducted another PET experiment using naturalistic music to study emotion. Changes in *regional cerebral blood flow* (rCBF) were measured during 'chills' when participants were presented with a piece of their own favourite music (using normal CD recordings; as a control condition, participants listened to the favourite piece of another subject). Increasing chill intensity correlated with increases in rCBF in brain regions thought to be involved in reward and emotion, including the insula, orbitofrontal cortex, the ventral medial prefrontal cortex, and the ventral striatum. Also correlated with increasing chill intensity were decreases in rCBF in the amygdala and the hippocampus (see Figure 12.1). Thus, in this study, activity changes were observed in central structures of the limbic system (e.g. amygdala and hippocampus). This was the first study to show modulation of amygdala activity with music (for studies showing amygdala activity elicited by the emotional processing of non-verbal vocal expressions, see, e.g. Morris et al, 1999; Phillips et al, 1998; Sander & Scheich, 2001). This finding was important for two reasons: Firstly, it provided evidence for the assumption that music can evoke 'real' emotions, because the activity of core structures of emotion processing was modulated by music. Secondly, the finding that amygdala activity was modulated by music was important, because affective disorders, such as depression and pathologic anxiety, are related to amygdala dysfunction (Drevets et al, 2002; Stein et al, 2007), and the influence of music perception on amygdala activity strengthens the empirical basis for music-therapeutic approaches for the treatment of affective disorders (see Chapter 29, this volume).

The findings of limbic activations during listening to music have been corroborated with fMRI. An fMRI study by Koelsch et al (2006) used pleasant and unpleasant musical stimuli (similar to the study by Blood et al, 1999; for further studies using consonant and dissonant stimuli, see also Ball et al, 2007; Sammler et al, 2007). However, in contrast to the study by Blood et al (1999), the pleasant musical excerpts were not computerized sounds, but natural, performed music (joyful instrumental dance tunes, played by professional musicians). Unpleasant stimuli were permanently dissonant counterparts of the original musical excerpts. The stimuli of this study were thus not only intended to induce unpleasantness, but also pleasantness (particularly happiness) in response to the joyful music. The use of identical stimuli across participants allowed the investigation of emotion independently of listeners' personal preferences. Unpleasant music elicited increases in *blood-oxygen-level dependent* (BOLD, see Section 12.12.1) signals in the amygdala, the hippocampus, the parahippocampal gyrus, and the temporal poles (a decrease of BOLD signal was observed in these structures in response to the pleasant music). During the presentation of the pleasant music, an increase of BOLD signal was observed in the ventral striatum and the insula (and in cortical structures not belonging to limbic or paralimbic circuits, which will not be further discussed here). The results of this study thus demonstrated that simply joyful, pleasant music can lead to activity changes in the amygdala and the hippocampus (i.e. in core areas of the limbic system), even if individuals do not have intense 'chill' or 'thrill' experiences (the same holds for the ventral striatum, which will be discussed in Section 12.7 of this chapter).

Activity changes in the amygdala in response to music were also reported in another recent fMRI study (Ball et al, 2007). The study used original (mainly consonant) piano pieces as pleasant stimuli, and electronically manipulated, permanently dissonant versions of these stimuli as unpleasant stimuli (similarly to the study by Koelsch et al, 2006). Interestingly, signal changes in the amygdala in response to both consonant and dissonant musical stimuli were positive in a central region of the amygdala (also referred to as laterobasal group by the authors), and negative in a dorsal region of the amygdala (also referred to as centromedial group by the authors). This shows that different subregions of the amygdala show different response properties to auditory stimulation. (This issue will be described in more detail in Section 12.2.) Curiously, no signal difference was found in the amygdala between the consonant and the dissonant music conditions, although participants clearly rated the consonant pieces as more pleasant, perhaps because the consonant pieces were not all happy dance tunes (as in the study by Koelsch et al, 2006), or perhaps due to the selection of participants (see Section 12.12.6).

Another interesting fMRI study by Eldar et al (2007) showed that activity changes in response to music in both the amygdala and the hippocampus can be strongly increased when the music is presented simultaneously with film clips (film clips were neutral scenes from commercials; positive music was also taken from commercials, and negative music mainly from soundtracks of horror movies). Interestingly, the combined conditions—positive music with neutral film, as well as negative music with neutral film—were not rated as more positive or negative than when music was presented alone. (Note that film clips played without music were rated as neutral.) Nevertheless, activity changes in the amygdala were considerably larger for the combined (film and music) presentation than for the presentation of film clips alone, or music alone. Analogue response properties were observed in areas of the ventro-lateral frontal cortex for both positive and negative, and in the hippocampus for negative, music combined with the film clips. Notably, emotional music on its own did not elicit a differential response in these regions. Perhaps the combination of emotional music with neutral film clips stimulated fantasies about positive or negative things that might happen next, increasing the overall emotional activity. However, if merely neutral film clips (when presented with music) have such a strong influence on limbic brain activity, we can imagine how much stronger this influence would be if the visual information of a film clip (or of an opera scene) also has a strong positive or negative emotional content.

Similarly, an fMRI study by Baumgartner et al (2006) showed that emotional responses to negative (fearful or sad) pictures were considerably stronger when pictures were presented together with fearful or sad music. Correspondingly, brain activations were stronger during the combined presentation of pictures and music than during the presentation of pictures alone. For example, activation of the amygdala was only observed in the combined condition, but not in the condition where only pictures were presented. The combined presentation also elicited stronger activation in the hippocampus, the parahippocampal gyrus, and the temporal poles. The network comprising amygdala, hippocampus, parahippocampal gyrus, and temporal poles has also been observed in studies by Koelsch et al (2006) and Fritz and Koelsch (2005, see also below) for emotions induced by music. This suggests that these structures play a consistent role in the emotional processing of music, perhaps along with the pre-genual cingulate cortex (which—like hippocampus, parahippocampal gyrus, and temporal pole—is also mono-synaptically connected with the amygdala).

Finally, a recent study showed that the amygdala can also be activated by unexpected (i.e. music-syntactically irregular) chord functions (Koelsch et al, 2008), indicating that activity of the amygdala can be modulated even by fairly abstract musical features. Notably, involvement of the amygdala in the emotional processing of music has not only been reported in functional neuroimaging studies, but also in a lesion study by Gosselin et al (2005), in which patients with medial temporal lobe resections that included the amygdala showed impaired recognition of fearful music (see also Chapter 5, this volume). With regard to the induction of emotion, Griffiths et al (2004) reported that a patient with a lesion of the left amygdala and the left insula showed a selective loss of intensely pleasurable experiences, and of vegetative responses, during music listening. The patient lost the capability to experience 'chills' in response to musical pieces that had elicited 'chills' in him before the brain lesion.

Functional neuroimaging studies using major and minor music to investigate 'happiness and sadness' (Khalfa et al, 2005; Mitterschiffthaler et al, 2007), 'musical beauty' (Suzuki et al, 2008), or 'liking' (Green et al, 2008) have not yet yielded a consistent picture, except perhaps activation of the anterior fronto-median cortex for the contrast minor-major music in the studies by both Green et al (2008) and Khalfa et al (2005; the latter study referred to that region as orbitofrontal cortex). Problems in comparing these studies include: (a) different participant populations (only males in the study by Suzuki et al, 2008; eight males and five females in the study by Khalfa et al, 2005; no information about gender of participants was provided in the study by Green et al, 2008), (b) interpretation of unsystematic effects (in the PET study by Suzuki et al, 2008, rCBF in a supposedly striatal region decreased during 'beautiful major', increased during 'beautiful minor', but increased during 'ugly major', and decreased during 'ugly minor' music), (c) use of 'true performances' (Khalfa et al, 2005; Mitterschiffthaler et al, 2007) on the one hand, and use of melodies (Green et al, 2008) and chords (Mizuno & Sugishita, 2007; Suzuki et al, 2008) played without musical expression on the other, and (d) different tasks: Participants were asked 'how well they liked it' (Green et al, 2008), to 'rate the beauty of the chord sequence' (Suzuki et al, 2008), to rate 'their mood state . . . from sad . . . to happy' (Mitterschiffthaler et al, 2007), or to 'judge the emotion represented in the music . . . from sad to happy' (Khalfa et al, 2005).

Moreover, whereas some studies aimed to match major and minor stimuli in tempo, timbre, etc. (Green et al, 2008; Mizuno & Sugishita, 2007; Suzuki et al, 2008), 'happy' and 'sad' stimuli in the studies by Khalfa et al (2005) and Mitterschiffthaler et al (2007) differed considerably in their acoustic and musical properties (e.g. 'happy' excerpts were faster than 'sad' excerpts in both studies). Thus, future studies are needed to tell us more about the neural correlates of happiness and sadness, how major and minor tonal features might contribute to emotional effects related to happiness and sadness, and how such effects are related to music preference and cultural experience.

12.2 DIFFERENT SUB-REGIONS OF THE AMYGDALA AND CONNECTED NETWORKS

The amygdala is not a single nucleus, but is composed of several distinct groups of cells. These are usually referred to as the lateral, basal, and accessory basal nuclei (which are often collectively termed the basolateral amygdala), as well as of several surrounding structures, including the central, medial, and cortical nuclei. These surrounding structures, together with the basolateral amygdala, are often referred to as 'the amygdala', although the amygdala is clearly not a functional unity (Ball et al, 2007; Davis & Whalen, 2001; Fritz & Koelsch, 2005).

A recent fMRI study investigated the role of the amygdala in the processing of both pleasant and unpleasant stimuli (unpublished data by SK and TF; see also Fritz & Koelsch, 2005). Short pleasant music excerpts and their manipulated unpleasant counterparts (similar to the studies by Blood et al, 1999, and Koelsch et al, 2006) were used to investigate the initial brain response to pleasant and unpleasant music. Importantly, separate anatomical regions of the amygdala were shown to be selectively involved in the perception of stimuli with positive and negative valence: A correlation of BOLD signal with decreasing valence showed an activation of a central aspect of the amygdala (presumably lateral or basal nuclei), whereas a correlation of BOLD signal with increasing valence revealed activations in a dorsal aspect of the amygdala (including the substantia innominata). Importantly, a functional connectivity analysis (see Section 12.12.2) with seed voxels in these dorsal and central aspects of the amygdala revealed two different networks displaying BOLD synchronicities with the respective amygdala regions: The central aspect of the amygdala (involved in processing of stimuli with negative emotional valence) was functionally connected to the temporal pole, the hippocampus, and the parahippocampal gyrus. The coordinates of these activations were virtually identical to our previous study using a similar experimental paradigm (Koelsch et al, 2006). Notably, the dorsal aspect of the amygdala (involved in processing stimuli with positive emotional valence) was functionally connected with the ventral striatum and the orbitofrontal cortex (these connections parallel the anatomical connections among the amygdala and those regions; Nieuwenhuys et al, 2007; see also Figure 12.2). That is, there are presumably at least two networks of emotional processing in which different aspects of the amygdala are involved: one for a processing of stimuli with positive, and one for a processing of stimuli with negative emotional valence. This notion is supported by the findings of differential responses of the amygdala to music in the study from Ball et al (2007, see above), in which an increase of BOLD signal in response to music was measured in the central amygdala, whereas a decrease of BOLD signal was measured in the dorsal amygdala (independent of the valence of the music).

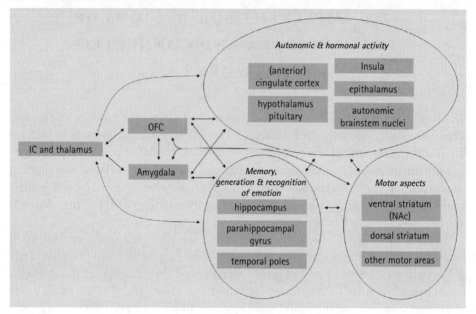

Fig. 12.2 Overview of connections between limbic and paralimbic structures (IC: inferior colliculus, OFC: orbitofrontal cortex, NAc: nucleus accumbens).

12.3 THE INVOLVEMENT OF THE AMYGDALA IN POSITIVE EMOTIONS

The corroborated finding that activity in the amygdala can be modulated by music listening (Ball et al, 2007; Baumgartner et al, 2006; Blood & Zatorre, 2001; Eldar et al, 2007; Koelsch et al, 2006) has important implications for music-therapeutic interventions, such as down-regulation of fear-related amygdala activity in patients with anxiety disorders, or modulation of amygdala activity related to pleasantness in patients with depression. In addition, these findings have important theoretical implications: Firstly, because the amygdala is a core structure of emotional processing, the findings indicate that music is capable of inducing 'real' emotions, similar to emotion induction by faces, pain stimuli, or vocalizations. Secondly, certain regions of the amygdala can be *deactivated* by pleasant music (Blood & Zatorre, 2001; Koelsch et al, 2006), whereas other regions can be activated by positive music (Eldar et al, 2007; Fritz & Koelsch, 2005). This shows that activity changes within the amygdala are related not only to unpleasant, but also to pleasant, emotion (see also Davis & Whalen, 2001; Zald, 2003). Thus, the notion that the amygdala is only a 'fear centre' in the brain is wrong. A number of studies suggest that the amygdala is involved in the generation of fear in response to external as well as internal fear-inducing stimuli, but the amygdala also plays a role in emotions that we perceive as pleasant. This further means that we have to be careful about the notion that it is only the experience of cortical inhibition of the 'reptile brain' that gives us pleasure during music listening (Huron, 2006), and instead recognize that the amygdala is also actively involved in the experience that something is beautiful, aesthetic, and pleasurable (see also Table 12.1).

Table 12.1 Overview of limbic and paralimbic structures, as well as their putative function, and previous functional neuroimaging studies on music and emotion that reported activation of a respective structure

Structure	Function	Study
Inferior colliculus and thalamus	Detection of auditory signals of danger.	Nieuwenhuys et al (2007); Koelsch & Siebel (2005)
Orbitofrontal cortex (BA 47, 11)	Control of emotional behaviour, imbuement of stimuli with emotional valence, generation of 'moral emotions' such as guilt, regret, shame, bad consciousness. The OFC appears to contain knowledge about social norms and roles. Activation of the OFC in functional imaging experiments (in which subjects are required to lie still during the presentation of musical stimuli) might reflect that participants wanted to move (e.g. dance, tap) during the presentation of the music, but that they had to control this impetus to fulfil the requirements of the experimental setting.	Blood et al (1999); Blood & Zatorre (2001); Tillmann et al (2006); Koelsch et al (2005); Fritz et al (2008); Rolls & Grabenhorst (2008)
Amygdala	Initiation of emotional, autonomic, and hormonal responses. Presumably termination of positive emotions in the face of danger.	Blood & Zatorre (2001); Koelsch et al (2006, 2007); Baumgartner et al (2006); Ball et al (2007); Eldar et al (2007); Fritz et al (2008)
Hippocampus	Memory formation and probably generation of (positive) emotions.	Blood & Zatorre (2001); Brown et al (2004); Koelsch et al (2006, 2007); Baumgartner et al (2006); Eldar et al (2008); Fritz et al (2008)
Parahippocampal gyrus	Memory for emotional experiences and recognition of emotion.	Blood et al (1999); Koelsch et al (2006); Baumgartner et al (2006); Fritz et al (2008)

Table 12.1 Overview of limbic and paralimbic structures (continued)

Structure	Function	Study
Temporal poles	Emotional memory retrieval, perhaps also multisensory integration.	Koelsch et al (2006); Baumgartner et al (2006); Fritz et al (2008)
Anterior cingulate cortex	Regulation of autonomic and emotional responses, modulation of motivation and attention, interface between emotion and cognition, probably synchronization of biological subsystems (cognitive appraisal, vegetative modulation, motor activity, motivation, and monitoring).	Blood & Zatorre (2001)
Hypothalamus	Hormonal regulation with autonomic effects.	
Insula	Autonomic regulation and integration of visceral and somatosensory information with autonomic activity.	Blood & Zatorre (2001); Koelsch et al (2006); Baumgartner et al (2006); Fritz et al (2008)
Ventral striatum (NAc)	Invigoration, selection and direction of behaviour in response to incentive stimuli.	Blood & Zatorre (2001); Brown et al (2004); Levitin & Menon (2005); Koelsch et al (2006); Baumgartner et al (2006); Fritz et al (2008)

12.4 HIPPOCAMPUS

The involvement of the hippocampus is a striking concordance of several studies on music and emotion (Baumgartner et al, 2006; Blood & Zatorre, 2001; Eldar et al, 2007; Fritz & Koelsch, 2005; Koelsch et al, 2006). The hippocampus undoubtedly plays an important role for learning and memory (e.g. Brown & Aggleton, 2001; Eichenbaum, 2000; Greicius et al, 2003). However, too many researchers tend to ignore the fact that the hippocampus is also important for emotional processing. In the following, we provide some facts to illustrate this importance.

The hippocampus has dense reciprocal connections with structures involved in the regulation of behaviors essential for survival (such as ingestive, reproductive, and defensive behaviors), and in the regulation of autonomic, hormonal, and immune system activity (Nieuwenhuys et al, 2007). Such structures include the amygdala, hypothalamus, thalamic nuclei, the septal-diagonal band complex, the cingulate gyrus, the insula, and autonomic centers in the brain stem. Efferent connections include (among many other structures) the nucleus accumbens, caudate nucleus, and putamen

(Nieuwenhuys et al, 2007). The functional significance of these connections puts the hippocampus, along with the amygdala and the orbitofrontal cortex, in a key position for emotional processing, and renders a 'pure' memory function of the hippocampus unlikely.

Another indication that the hippocampus is related to emotional processing is the fact that the hippocampus is unique in that (a) hippocampal neurogenesis is reduced in response to emotional stressors, and (b) hippocampal neurons may even be destroyed by severe emotional stress (for a review, see Warner-Schmidt & Duman, 2006). In animals, mild chronic stress related to helplessness and behavioural despair can lead to loss of hippocampal neurons and related hippocampal atrophy. Studies with humans have shown a relation between depression and decreased hippocampal volume (Sapolsky, 2001; Warner-Schmidt & Duman, 2006), and revealed that the hippocampus can be damaged by suffering, witnessing, or executing extreme violence. For example, both childhood sexual abuse and post-traumatic stress disorder can lead to hippocampal volume reduction (Bremner, 1999; Stein et al, 1997). The loss of hippocampal volume after traumatization or during depression appears to be partly due to both a down-regulation of neurogenesis in the hippocampus and death of hippocampal neurons (Warner-Schmidt & Duman, 2006). Notably, due to the power of music to evoke happiness and to ameliorate stress and anxiety, it is conceivable that music therapy with depressed patients has positive effects on the up-regulation of neurogenesis in the hippocampus.

Specific information about the involvement of the hippocampus in the processing of different emotions is not yet available. One hypothesis endorsed here is that the hippocampus is a critical structure for the generation of soft, or tender, positive emotions (Siebel, 1994; see also Koelsch et al, 2007). Such positive emotions can be described, for instance, as loving, warm, and joyful (as opposed to, e.g. aggressive, hostile, anxious, manic, or depressive affect). This hypothesis is supported by the finding that activity changes in the hippocampus (and the amygdala) in response to pleasant and unpleasant music are blunted in individuals with reduced capability of producing tender positive emotions (Koelsch et al, 2007; see also Section 12.12.6). Moreover, as described above, the hippocampus is unique in its sensitivity to emotional stressors (because only hippocampal neurons can be destroyed by severe, chronic emotional stress). This suggests a particular association between the hippocampus and tender emotions.

Notably, due to its particular sensitivity to emotional stressors, inhibition of neural pathways projecting to the hippocampus during the perception of unpleasant stimuli could represent a sensitive neural mechanism that serves to prevent potential damage to hippocampal neurons. In other words, it is possible that activity changes observed in the amygdala and the hippocampus during the presentation of an unpleasant (or threatening) stimulus are not due to the generation of fear (or other unpleasant emotions), but rather due to inhibitory processes activated to prevent the hippocampus from traumatization during the exposure to potentially harmful stimuli. It is thus possible that, in the studies by Koelsch et al (2006, 2007), Baumgartner et al (2006), and Eldar et al (2007), the signal increase ('activation') of the amygdala and the hippocampus during the unpleasant music actually reflects inhibitory processes that are automatically initiated in response to aversive stimuli in order to protect hippocampal neurons from potential damage. These issues remain to be explored in future research.

12.5 Parahippocampal gyrus

The parahippocampal gyrus plays an important role for encoding and storage of memories of emotional events (e.g. Kilpatrick & Cahill, 2003; Rugg & Yonelinas, 2003). We assume that this also holds for emotional events related to music, and that the parahippocampal gyrus thus may enable us to remember the emotions of previously experienced music (or sounds), and thus to recognize musical emotions (see also evaluative conditioning and episodic memory, two mechanisms through which music listening might evoke emotions; Juslin & Västfjäll, 2008; Chapter 22, this volume).

A number of functional imaging studies on music and emotion reported an involvement of the parahippocampal gyrus in networks responsive to unpleasant music, and a comparison of these studies reveals striking similarities in the coordinates of the local maxima of activity within the parahippocampal gyrus (Blood et al, 1999: 25, –28, –21; Koelsch et al, 2006: –25, –26, –11 / 22, –26, –13; Fritz & Koelsch, 2005: –20, –30, –9, in response to unpleasant stimuli; ter Haar et al, 2007: –23, –29, –9, correlated with sounds of increasing dissonance; coordinates refer to stereotactic space). In addition, a lesion study by Gosselin et al (2006) reported that patients with lesions of the (left or right) parahippocampal gyrus did not rate dissonant music excerpts as unpleasant as did control participants. Activity changes due to unpleasant music were more pronounced in the right parahippocampal gyrus in the study by Blood et al (1999), and stronger in the left (though with lower statistical threshold also present in the right) parahippocampal gyrus in the study by Koelsch et al (2006; see also Fritz & Koelsch, 2005). The causes of these hemispheric weightings remain to be specified. However, the consistency of the coordinates listed above suggests that the parahippocampal gyrus plays a particular role in the processing of auditory stimuli with different degrees of consonance/dissonance, and therefore presumably also with different degrees of acoustic roughness (which is an acoustic feature that is evolutionarily perhaps more relevant than consonance/dissonance).

12.6 A network comprising hippocampus, parahippocampal gyrus, and temporal poles

So far, three functional imaging studies on music and emotion have reported an involvement of the hippocampus, the parahippocampal gyrus, and the temporal poles (Baumgartner et al, 2006; Fritz & Koelsch, 2005; Koelsch et al, 2006). The latter study in particular showed a functional connectivity between (a central aspect of) the amygdala, and the hippocampus, the parahippocampal gyrus, and the temporal poles. Thus, it appears that the 'memory network' comprising the hippocampus, parahippocampal gyrus, and temporal poles is also crucially involved in emotional processing. Within this network, the hippocampus is presumably involved in memory formation and generation of (supposedly positive) emotions; the parahippocampal gyrus in storing emotional memories and recognition of emotion; and the temporal poles perhaps in the retrieval of emotional memories. The network comprising these structures is functionally connected with the amygdala, presumably with the basolateral amygdala.

12.7 THE (VENTRAL) STRIATUM AND MUSIC LISTENING

Another structure that Blood and Zatorre (2001) already reported to be involved in intensely pleasurable responses to music is the ventral striatum—presumably the nucleus accumbens, NAc, which is part of the ventral striatum. The NAc is innervated by dopaminergic brainstem neurons (located mainly in the ventral tegmental area of the midbrain) and appears to play a role in invigorating, and perhaps even selecting and directing, behaviour in response to incentive stimuli (Nicola, 2007). For example, when our ancestors strolled through the woods looking for food, it was not sufficient to see berries hanging from a bush and then go past the bush (without grabbing them), it was also necessary to move towards the bush, to grab the berries, etc. The ventral striatum appears to play an important role in directing our behaviour towards incentive stimuli, as well as in motivating and rewarding such behaviour.

The NAc is considered a 'limbic motor interface' (Mogenson et al, 1980; Nieuwenhuys et al, 2007), because (1) the NAc receives input from limbic structures such as amygdala and hippocampus, (2) injecting dopamine in the NAc causes an increase in locomotion, and (3) the NAc projects to the basal ganglia, which play an important role for the learning, selection, and execution of actions. Notably, the ventral striatum (together with the NAc and perhaps the ventral insular cortex) exhibits greater activity for immediate rewards, whereas the dorsal striatum (and perhaps the dorsal insular cortex) exhibits greater activity for future rewards (Tanaka et al, 2004; see also Graybiel, 2005).

Importantly, activity in the NAc correlates with experiences of pleasure (Kilpatrick et al, 2000), for instance during the process of obtaining a goal, or when an unexpected reachable incentive is encountered. Moreover, activity in the NAc has been shown to correlate with self-reported positive emotion elicited by a reward cue (Knutson et al, 2001). More detailed information about the functional significance of the NAc for different emotions is not currently available. However, it is important to differentiate the feelings related to the activation of the 'reward circuit' (from the lateral hypothalamus via the medial forebrain bundle to the mesolimbic dopamine pathway involving the ventral tegmental area with projection to the NAc) from the tender feelings that involve activity of the hippocampus (Siebel, in press). Feelings arising from activity of the former circuit (involving the NAc) might perhaps best be referred to as *fun*, whereas *happiness* might require activity involving the hippocampus (see also Siebel, in press).

Activation of 'fun centres' such as the ventral striatum in response to pleasant music was observed in the fMRI studies by Menon and Levitin (2005) and Koelsch et al (2006). In the former study, the ventral striatum and the ventral tegmental area (VTA) were activated in response to normal musical pieces contrasted with scrambled, unpleasant counterparts of those pieces. Using PET, Brown et al (2004) showed activation of the ventral striatum during listening to two unfamiliar, pleasant pieces contrasted with a resting condition (pleasant music also activated the subcallosal cingulate cortex, the anterior insula, and the posterior part of the hippocampus). The findings of activation of the ventral striatum across different studies offer some assurance that this brain area can be activated by music.

Importantly, results from the reviewed studies suggest that music not only can be fun, it can also make people happy. We believe that this is one of the great powers of music, and that this power needs to be explored in the future, to provide more systematic, more widespread, and more theoretically grounded applications of music in education and therapy.

12.8 THE ROLE OF ACC AND INSULAR CORTEX IN THE EMOTIONAL PROCESSING OF MUSIC

Emotional activity is always associated with modulation of vegetative (also referred to as autonomic) activity, as well as—correspondingly—with modulation of endocrine (hormonal) activity (see Chapter 11, this volume). Vegetative activity includes, for example, modulation of heart rate, heart rate variability, sweat production, pupil response, congestion, breathing rate, and fast regulation of blood pressure. Hormonal effects have, in turn, effects on immune system function, particularly when they are related to a reduction of stress, depression, or anxiety (Koelsch & Siebel, 2005). These are important aspects in relation to music, because better knowledge about the emotional effects of music on vegetative, hormonal, and immune system activity will pave the way for stronger involvement of music therapy in the treatment of diseases related to endocrine, vegetative, or immune system dysfunction.

Changes in vegetative activity have been reported to be associated with activity changes in the anterior cingulate cortex (ACC; see Figure 12.1) and the insular cortex (Critchley, 2005; Critchley et al, 2000). Thus, interpretation of functional imaging data on emotion should take into account the possibility that activations in these structures are not related to emotional processing per se, but to vegetative effects of emotional processing (but see also below). It is even conceivable that—without any apparent emotional effects—changes in the ACC and the insula can simply be induced by different musical tempos or different loudness levels, which modify the vegetative activity (e.g. the heart beat, breathing rate, electrodermal activity, or blood pressure) of listeners (see also Bernardi et al, 2006).

The ACC has also been implicated in motivational processes, error monitoring, motor programming, performance monitoring (particularly with regards to the rostral cingulate zone, RCZ), and immediate adjustments of actions to achieve a goal (also RCZ). The rostral cingulate motor area in particular (also referred to as RCZ) has a specific role in error detection (e.g. Bush et al, 2000; Devinsky et al, 1995; Ridderinkhof et al, 2004; Ullsperger & von Cramon, 2003). With regard to the different functions in which the ACC is involved, we propose here that the ACC is involved in what Scherer (2000) has referred to as the 'synchronization of biological subsystems'. In fact, Scherer even defines an emotion as a synchronization of biological subsystems that comprise cognitive appraisal, physiological arousal, motor expression, motivational processes, and monitoring processes.

Although we do not entirely concur with Scherer's definition of emotion (mainly because, in our view, synchronization of these subsystems can also occur as an effect of emotional processes, instead of being the emotion itself), we agree that a synchronization of subsystems is an important aspect of emotional experience. Such synchronization is likely to occur as an effect of every emotional instance, and may be indispensable for subjective emotional experiences (usually referred to as 'feelings'). The ACC is in a unique position to accomplish such synchronization, due to its involvement in cognition, vegetative modulation, motor activity, motivation, and monitoring. Thus, it is likely that emotional processes activate areas within the ACC due to its involvement in the synchronization of biological subsystems, which is a substantial, perhaps indispensable, aspect of emotion. However, note that activity within the ACC is not always related to emotional processes.

The insula is also involved in vegetative regulation, but is in addition a visceral sensory, somatosensory, visceral motor, and motor association area (Augustine, 1996; Mega et al, 1997). The insula has main connections with the cingulate cortex, orbitofrontal cortex (OFC), second somatosensory area, retroinsular area of the parietal cortex, temporal poles, superior temporal sulcus (STS), amygdala, hippocampus, and parahippocampal gyrus, as well as with the frontal operculum and lateral premotor cortex (PMC). Particularly the anterior insula, which has subcortical, limbic, and brain stem connections, appears to play a specific role in the integration of visceral and somatosensory information with vegetative activity (see also Flynn et al, 1999). Thus, it appears that one important function of the anterior insula is the adjustment, or regulation, of the intensity of vegetative activity to an appropriate level according to somatosensory, visceral sensory, and vegetative information. In concert with the ACC, which may prevent emotions from going 'overboard', the insula prevents vegetative activity from going 'overboard', but also from being blunted, or from instantly ebbing away.

The posterior insula is functionally linked to somatomotor systems, and has a particular role in somatosensory, vestibular, and motor integration. The part of the insula lying in between the anterior and posterior insula represents an anatomical and functional transition between these regions. Intra-insular projections are predominantly directed from anterior to more posterior regions, suggesting that the posterior insula also serves as an integrative heteromodal association area for information received by all five senses (e.g. Augustine, 1996; Flynn et al, 1999). Notably, the insula also plays a role when vegetative activity is modulated by interoceptive awareness (Critchley et al, 2004), and activity of the anterior insula has also been associated in previous fMRI studies with modulation of (pre)motor activity (e.g. Koelsch et al, 2006; Sander & Scheich, 2001; Wildgruber et al, 2004; see also Molnar-Szakacs & Overy, 2006).

12.9 TIME COURSE OF EMOTION

The intensity of an emotion usually changes over time (even if the emotion itself may be the same). Intuitively, it seems plausible that aversive sounds elicit quick emotional responses (although long durations of such sounds might even increase the degree of unpleasantness), and that especially tender emotions might take a while to unfold. To date, little is known about the time course of emotional processing and the underlying neural mechanisms.

One of the few psychophysiological studies that have investigated the time course of emotion was conducted by Krumhansl (1997). In this study, several physiological measures (including cardiac, vascular, electrodermal, and respiratory functions) were recorded while listeners heard musical excerpts (each ~ 3 min) chosen to represent one of three emotions (sadness, fear, happiness). Significant correlations were found between most of the recorded physiological responses and time (measured in one-second intervals from the beginning of the presentation of each musical excerpt). The strongest physiological effects for each emotion type tended to increase over time, suggesting that the intensity of an emotional experience is likely to increase over time during the perception of a musical excerpt. In studies measuring changes in heart rate and breathing rate to music, we found that these two physiological parameters mainly change within the first 20 seconds of a musical excerpt, and then remain relatively stable (Enk & Koelsch, 2007; see also Lundqvist et al, 2009). Recent studies have also shown physiological changes related to emotional valence and arousal as elicited by music over time (Grewe et al, 2007a, 2007b; for a review, see Chapter 11, this volume).

Activity changes over time due to emotional processing were also observed in a previous fMRI study (Koelsch et al, 2006). In that study, the (pleasant and unpleasant) musical excerpts had a duration of about 1 min, and data were not only modelled for the entire excerpts, but also separately for the first 30 sec and for the remaining 30 sec to investigate possible differences in brain activity over time. When looking at activation differences between the first 30 sec and the remaining 30 sec, activations of the amygdala, parahippocampal gyrus, temporal poles, insula, and ventral striatum were stronger during the second block of the musical excerpts, presumably because the intensity of listeners' emotional experiences increased during the perception of both the pleasant and the unpleasant musical excerpts. These findings support the notion of a canonical activation and deactivation of the different neural correlates of emotional processing.

Information about the temporal order in which neural structures of emotional processing become active, or inactive, remains to be specified. Note that music is an ideal stimulus to investigate this, because music always unfolds over time (see also the study by Blood & Zatorre, 2001, in which musical stimuli selected to evoke 'chills' had durations of about 90 sec). New studies of emotional processing with music should more often conduct investigations of the activity of the structures involved in emotional processing over time (e.g. by doing split-half analyses of the data). Information about activity changes over time of the structures implicated in emotion (such as information about how activity in one structure affects activity in another) would provide important insight into the functional significance of these structures.

12.10 MUSICAL EXPECTATIONS AND EMOTIONAL RESPONSES

The studies reviewed so far used experimental paradigms employing 'pleasant', 'unpleasant', 'scary', 'happy', 'sad', or 'peaceful' tunes. However, there are also other musical features that elicit emotional responses, namely music-syntactically (e.g. harmonically) irregular chords. Meyer (1956) proposed a theory of musical emotions on the basis of fulfilled or suspended musical expectations (see Chapter 21, this volume). He proposed that the confirmation or violation of such musical expectations produces emotions in the listener. In accordance with this proposal, Sloboda (1991) found that specific musical structures were associated with specific psycho-physiological reactions (shivers, for example, were often evoked by new or unexpected harmonies).

A recent study by Steinbeis et al (2006) tested the hypothesis that emotional responses can be evoked by unexpected chords. In this study, physiological measures including EEG, electrodermal activity (EDA), and heart rate were recorded while subjects listened to three versions of Bach chorales. One version was the original version composed by Bach with a harmonic sequence that ended on an irregular chord function (e.g. a submediant). The same chord was also rendered expected (using a tonic chord), and very unexpected (a Neapolitan sixth chord). The EDA to these three different chord types showed clear differences between the expected and the unexpected (as well as between expected and very unexpected) chords. Because the EDA reflects activity of the sympathetic nervous system, and because this system is intimately linked to emotional experiences, these data clearly corroborate the assumption that unexpected harmonies elicit emotional responses. The findings from this study were later replicated in another study (Koelsch et al, 2008), which also obtained behavioural data showing that irregular chords were perceived by listeners as surprising and less pleasant than regular chords.

Corroborating these findings, functional imaging experiments using chord sequences with unexpected harmonies (originally designed to investigate music-syntactic processing; Koelsch et al, 2005, Tillmann et al, 2006) showed activations of the amygdala (Koelsch et al, 2008), as well as of orbital frontal (Tillmann et al, 2006), and orbital fronto-lateral cortex (Koelsch et al, 2005) in response to the unexpected chords. The orbital fronto-lateral cortex (OFLC), comprising the lateral part of the orbital gyrus as well as the medial part of the inferior frontal gyrus, is a paralimbic structure that plays an important role in emotional processing: The OFLC has been implicated in the evaluation of the emotional significance of sensory stimuli, and is considered a gateway for pre-processed sensory information into the medial orbito-frontal paralimbic division (which is also involved in emotional processing; see Mega et al, 1997; Rolls & Grabenhorst, 2008). As mentioned above, the violation of musical expectancies has been regarded as an important aspect of generating emotions when listening to music (Meyer, 1956; see Chapter 21, this volume), and 'breaches of expectations' have been shown to activate the lateral OFC (Nobre et al, 1999). Moreover, the perception of irregular chord functions has been shown to lead to an increase of perceived tension (Bigand et al, 1996), and perception of tension has also been linked to emotional experience during music listening (Krumhansl, 1997).

Similar OFC activations have also been reported by Levitin and Menon (2003) in response to normal music contrasted with scrambled music, and it is likely that this activation is due to differences in the emotional valence of the natural music on the one hand, and of the scrambled music (which sounds rather unpleasant) on the other. When tested with a specific regional hypothesis, the data obtained in the study by Koelsch et al (2005) also showed bilateral activations of the amygdala in response to the unexpected chords, substantiating the assumption that unexpected, or irregular, chords elicit emotional responses (Koelsch et al, 2008).

The above findings show that unexpected musical events do not only elicit responses related to the processing of the structure of the music, but also emotional responses. (This presumably also holds for unexpected words in sentences, and any other stimulus which is perceived as more or less expected.) Thus, research using stimuli that are systematically more or less expected should ideally assess the valence and arousal experience of the listener (even if an experiment is not originally designed to investigate emotion), so that these variables can potentially be used to explain variance in the data.

12.11 COMMENTS ON THE CONCEPT OF 'MUSICAL EMOTIONS'

Some researchers advocate that music can evoke a wide spectrum of 'real' emotions, whereas others advocate that emotions evoked by music are artificial (and not real). For example, Zentner, Grandjean, and Scherer (2008, p. 496) state that 'musical antecedents do not usually have any obvious material effect on the individual's well-being and are infrequently followed by direct external responses of a goal-oriented nature' and thus reject the notion that music makes listeners happy, sad, angry, or fearful. Similarly, Scherer (2004, p. 244) writes that 'music is unlikely to produce basic emotions', Noy (1993, p. 126) states that 'the emotions evoked by music are not identical with the emotions aroused by everyday, interpersonal activity', and Konečni (2003, p. 333) claims that 'instrumental music cannot directly induce genuine emotions in listeners'. However, the assumption that music cannot induce basic emotions conflicts with the induction of happiness through music listening in many individuals (see Section 12.11.1).

Some argue that music cannot induce basic emotions related to survival functions because music does ostensibly not have material effects on the individual's well-being (e.g. Kivy, 1990; Scherer, 2004; Zentner et al, 2008). In Section 12.11.2, we will offer several arguments that speak against this notion. Another classical argument against the assumption that music can evoke basic emotions is that music cannot evoke real (or 'everyday') sadness, because in 'real' life, sadness tends to be experienced as an aversive state (connected, for example, to the loss of a loved one), which most people try to avoid. By contrast, some individuals do not turn off the radio when sad music is played. Arguments for the notion that music can actually evoke 'real' sadness are presented in Section 12.11.3.

The fact that music does usually not evoke all basic emotions equally often does not mean that music is not capable of evoking these emotions (e.g. music usually evokes happiness more often than disgust). Moreover, even if music does not evoke a basic emotion in an individual with the same intensity as a particular 'real life' situation, the underlying brain circuits are nevertheless presumably the same (whether I am strongly or moderately happy, the emotion is still happiness).

12.11.1 Music and 'real' emotions

Juslin and Västfjäll (2008, p. 561) suggested that music can evoke 'a wide range of both basic and complex emotions in listeners via several psychological mechanisms that emotions to music share with other emotions' (see also Chapter 22, this volume). We would like to add here that simply listening to music can evoke changes in the three major reaction components of an emotion: It elicits changes in autonomic and endocrine activity (physiological arousal), is experienced as pleasant, happy, sad, etc. (subjective feeling), and usually has effects on an individual's motor expression (e.g. smiling, dancing, foot tapping, clapping, or even just premotor activity). In addition, the fact that music can modulate activity in all limbic and paralimbic structures (including core structures of emotional processing, such as the amygdala) shows that music can indeed evoke real emotions.

12.11.2 Music and 'basic' emotions

Many individuals experience the elicitation of happiness through music listening (for many, this is actually a frequent motivation for listening to music). It has also been shown that music can elicit surprise (Koelsch et al, 2008; see also Meyer, 1956), and some subjects in an earlier study (Koelsch et al, 2006) reported to us that the permanently, highly dissonant stimuli used in that study evoked a feeling of disgust and vertigo. Most people get quite angry when they have to listen to music that they utterly dislike, and music is sometimes even used to stimulate anger and aggression in listeners (e.g. the 'hate music' of neo-Nazis; Becker et al, 2006; Chapter 26, this volume; and partly also military music). Music-evoked sadness is dealt with in the next section.

12.11.3 'Everyday' and music-evoked sadness

Some people like to 'play' with sadness, because they experience true sadness during music listening (or during performing music) and enjoy the relief when they become aware that, in reality, nothing bad has happened. This relief may then be perceived as fun, and presumably activates reward circuits in the brain (similar to when surviving a potentially aversive activity; see also Section 12.7). However, this game only works if 'real' neural activity is elicited which is indistinguishable from 'everyday' sadness. Obviously, there might be different patterns of motor-expression, cognition, and neurophysiology while listening to sad music compared with when being sad because of a loss. However, such difference between the sadness experienced during music listening and the 'day-to-day' sadness by no means rules out that a sadness circuit in the brain is active in both cases, and thus that sadness can be evoked by listening to music.

12.11.4 Music and survival functions

Regenerative effects of music (e.g. beneficial hormonal and immunological effects; for a review, see Koelsch & Siebel, 2005) *are* material effects for the individual. Moreover, social functions of music such as communication, cooperation, group cohesion, and social cognition are all functions that were critical for the survival of the human species, and that are vital for the well-being of an individual. Therefore, the pleasure in practising these social functions is indeed related to survival functions and to functions that are of vital importance for the individual.

12.11.5 All 'real' emotions can be evoked by music

As soon as the brain defines a situation as 'real', it is real in its consequences for the brain, including emotional processes (see also Roediger & McDermott, 1995, for studies on false memories). That is, as soon as the brain gets involved in a situation that evokes an emotion, this emotion is real in its consequences. Similar to our notion that music can evoke basic emotions, we also advocate that none of the emotions that can be evoked by music is artificial (in the sense that they can *only* be elicited by music). Therefore, we use the term 'musical emotion' and 'emotion' interchangeably, and support the view that if there is any emotion that music cannot evoke, then it is not an emotion at all. We would like to mention that it has been argued that an emotion is only induced when an event is appraised as having the capacity to influence the goals of the perceiver somehow (e.g. Scherer, 1999); however, if this does not apply to all emotions evoked by music, then this means, in our view, that the given definition of emotion is too narrow.

12.12 METHODOLOGICAL ISSUES

12.12.1 Functional imaging methods: fMRI and PET

In fMRI, time series of Magnetic Resonance (MR) images are recorded. The image intensity therein is a representation of the chemical environment of hydrogen isotopes in the brain (particularly in water and fat). These isotopes are subjected to a strong magnetic field, and excited by suitable radiowave pulses. MR images mainly reflect brain structure, but also contain small contributions from blood flow (on the order of 2 per cent of maximum intensity), which is a delayed function of brain cell activity: If neurons are active, their metabolic rate, including the consumption of oxygen, will increase. This causes changes in the local metabolite composition, which in turn modulates blood vessel diameters, so that an over-compensation of oxygenated blood concentration (and a higher local cerebral blood volume) in the milieu of the preceding nerve cell activity is established. The peak of this hemodynamic response usually has a latency of around 4-5 seconds. Oxygenated blood has a higher ratio of oxyhemoglobin (i.e. hemoglobin carrying oxygen) to deoxyhemoglobin (i.e. hemoglobin that has dispensed its oxygen), than deoxygenated blood. Importantly, oxyhemoglobin and deoxyhemoglobin have different magnetic properties—oxyhemoglobin is diamagnetic and exerts little influence on the local magnetic field, whereas deoxyhemoglobin is paramagnetic and causes signal loss in the corresponding volume elements of the image. This *blood-oxygen-level dependent* (BOLD) image contrast is most commonly measured with functional MRI, and provides an indirect measure of preceding neural activity in the brain (for a more comprehensive explanation of the principles of fMRI, see Faro, 2006).

Unlike PET (or Computed Tomography, a method commonly employed for structural imaging), fMRI does not employ radioactive substances or ionizing radiation and is therefore regarded as a very safe procedure, if safety precautions are strictly followed. These include the stipulation that individuals with ferromagnetic metal implants and cardiac pacemakers are prevented from having MRI scans (due to the high magnetic field), and that no ferromagnetic metals are brought into the scanner room, especially not while an individual is scanned. (The magnetic forces of the scanner can easily turn ferromagnetic objects into projectiles.)

Image acquisition relies on supplementary magnetic fields to encode spatial information, which is achieved by means of dedicated magnetic gradient coils. Their rapid switching requires strong electric currents, which interact with the main magnetic field. The resulting minute vibrations of the coil materials propagate into the surrounding air, in which they are audible as loud noise. The sound intensity of such noise can reach up to 130 dB, which can damage the hair cells in the inner ear. Hence, the appropriate use of ear protection is mandatory during fMRI. Both the loud scanner and the requirement for ear protection make it challenging to perform experiments with auditory stimulation in the fMRI scanner. Section 12.13 of this chapter will deal with some techniques to overcome such problems.

Another functional imaging technique is PET. Although fMRI is used more widely now as a functional neuroimaging technique, PET was actually used before fMRI in neuroscience. As mentioned above, activity of nerve cells correlates with the regional flow of blood, and this regional cerebral blood flow (rCBF) can also be measured using a radioactive tracer, which decays by emitting a positron (e.g. oxygen-15, O-15). Thus, after injection of such a tracer, areas with increased brain activity are associated with areas of high radioactivity. When the radioisotope emits a positron, the positron encounters and annihilates with an electron (the antimatter counterpart of a positron), producing a pair of annihilation (gamma) photons moving in opposite directions. These two photons are detected by the scanning device, and registered when they reach the detector at the same time (i.e. within a few nanoseconds). Because most gamma photons are emitted at almost 180 degrees to each other, it is possible to localize the source of a pair of gamma photons that reach the detector at the same time. O-15 has a short half-life (of around two minutes), hence this tracer must be injected directly before the beginning of an experimental block (for a more comprehensive explanation of the principles of PET, see Phelps, 2006).

Besides the obvious disadvantage of using radioactive substances, PET has also a lower spatial resolution than fMRI. However, PET has also important advantages compared with fMRI: Firstly, PET is practically silent. Secondly, tracers can be used that distribute in tissues by partially following the metabolic pathways of their natural analogues, or that bind with specificity in the tissues containing a particular receptor protein. Hence, PET can be used to trace the biological pathways of specific compounds, or the distribution of compounds (e.g. dopamine) in response to an experimental stimulus.

12.12.2 Analysis of functional imaging data

Functional imaging data can be analysed in numerous ways. In commonly applied statistical analyses, the time course of BOLD response is correlated with an independent variable, which may for example relate to different tasks, or a difference in perceived pleasantness of the stimulus categories, or different subject groups. One way to detect correlations between brain responses and a variation of an experimental parameter is to statistically assess the difference between the averaged pattern of the BOLD response of two experimental conditions (i.e. to 'contrast' the two conditions against each other). A reliably detected difference is then assumed to pertain to differential cognitive processing during the two conditions. For example, images acquired during pleasant music can be contrasted with those acquired during unpleasant music. The statistical parametric map (SPM) of the contrast indicates whether differences in BOLD response between the contrasted conditions are significant.

To investigate correlations between spatially remote neurophysiological events, *connectivity analyses* can be applied. In this correlational approach (often labelled functional connectivity), the time course of BOLD signal in one region (often referred to as 'seed-region') is correlated with the time course of BOLD signals in all other voxels of the brain. This provides a measure for BOLD response synchrony, and it is assumed that brain structures showing such synchrony are functionally connected with each other. Functional connectivity analyses have been developed to investigate functional networks in the brain. Note, however, that functional connectivity does not provide information about anatomical connections, only about BOLD time-course synchrony. A third method for the analysis of fMRI data is the *psycho-physiological interaction analysis* (PPI). PPI allows for a comparison of functional connectivity between experimental conditions (Friston et al, 1997). This is relevant because the BOLD synchrony between brain regions may differ between different experimental conditions.

Unlike functional connectivity analyses, effective connectivity analyses aim to investigate directional influences of one neuronal system on another. Such methods comprise *dynamic causal modelling* (DCM), *Granger causality mapping* (GCM), and *structural equation modelling* (SEM), methods which will not be described further in this chapter (for detailed explanations, see Friston et al, 2003; Goebel et al, 2003; McIntosh & Gonzalez-Lima, 1994). Finally, one further method for the analysis of BOLD signals is the *pattern classification analysis*, which can be applied in an attempt to read out psychological states from fMRI data. For this kind of analysis, pattern recognition algorithms are trained through the pairing of a psychological variable and patterns of BOLD response (for details, see Haynes & Rees, 2005).

12.12.3 Sparse temporal sampling vs. continuous scanning

In the fMRI scanner, the loud scanner noise makes it difficult to perform experiments with auditory stimulation. One possibility to make the musical stimulus more audible in the fMRI is to apply a sparse temporal scanning design (Gaab et al, 2003, 2007; Hall et al, 1999), in which functional MR images are not acquired continuously, but with a pause of a few seconds between two image acquisitions, so that an auditory stimulus can be presented in the pause between two acquisitions. The pause between two acquisitions can vary between experiments, from about four to up to 14 seconds (depending, e.g. on how long the stimuli are). When activations within the auditory cortex are the focus of the investigation, then a sparse temporal sampling design is indispensable (e.g. Gaab et al, 2007). In fMRI experiments on emotion, participants might find the loudness related to continuous scanning distressing, particularly in experiments using devices operating at or above 3 T (Tesla). Therefore, 1.5 T devices (which are not as loud as 3 T devices) are, for example, better suited when a high signal-to-noise-ratio and minimized distress for participants are more important than high spatial resolution.

12.12.4 Interleaved silent steady state imaging

Another option is *interleaved silent steady state* (ISSS) imaging (Schwarzbauer et al, 2006; ISSS is only an option if the required sequences can be made available for the MR scanner used for the experiment). The ISSS imaging design is also a sparse temporal sampling design, but here several images (not just one) are acquired after a 'silence' period of no scanning. Importantly, the images are acquired more rapidly than usual, and the T1-related signal decay during the silence periods is avoided by maintaining a steady state (longitudinal) magnetization with a train of relatively silent slice-selective excitation pulses during the silence period, resulting in a better signal-to-noise ratio of the fMRI images acquired after the presentation of the stimulus. However, maintaining the steady state magnetization also produces noise (although it is considerably less loud than the EPI noise), and the ISSS design is intended for stimuli that do not exceed a duration of a few seconds. For such stimuli, this scanning protocol is very useful. Whether this scanning protocol is suited for block designs with block durations of several tens of seconds remains to be investigated.

12.12.5 'Activation of' vs. 'activity changes within' limbic and paralimbic structures

One has to be careful about the limitations, and thus also the interpretation, of fMRI and PET data. Signal changes in the amygdala, and in other limbic and paralimbic structures, do not necessarily originate from excitatory (post-)synaptic activity. It is equally plausible that such changes are the result of *inhibitory* synaptic processes (Buxton, 2002; Lauritzen, 2008; Shibasaki, 2008). The word 'activation' is associated with excitatory, rather than inhibitory, processes. However, changes in BOLD signal or rCBF, for example in the amygdala, do not tell us whether these changes are related to excitatory or inhibitory processes within the amygdala. Therefore, we have to be careful about simply speaking of 'activation of the amygdala'. The more accurate terminology is 'activity changes within the amygdala'.

This is an important distinction, because an activity change in a part of the amygdala (or other regions such as hippocampus, temporal poles, or parahippocampal gyrus) in response to a fear-inducing stimulus might reflect three different things. Firstly, it might simply reflect inhibition (or down-regulation) of processes related to positive emotions: The emergence of a negative emotion usually also means decrease of a positive emotion, and it is possible that only the decrease of positive, but not the emergence of negative, emotion is actually reflected in the BOLD or rCBF signals. Secondly, the signal change might actually reflect activation of a fear network. Thirdly, due to restricted spatial resolution, it might reflect both of the above. However, with the measurement techniques usually employed with PET and fMRI, we cannot say which of the three possibilities the data reflect, and we should be aware of the different possibilities.

It is also important to be aware that, in an experimental setup, participants realize that the experiment does not only consist of unpleasant, but also of pleasant stimuli.

Therefore, it is possible that the expectation of, or preparation for, a pleasant stimulus during the perception of an unpleasant stimulus (which will soon be followed by a pleasant stimulus) is reflected in activity changes in the limbic and paralimbic brain regions. In other words, it is possible that activity in a brain structure is mistakenly taken as the cause of an unpleasant emotional experience simply because such activity occurs at the same time as the stimulus evoking unpleasantness is presented. Experimenters should know that this is not always a valid conclusion. Unfortunately, random ordering of different stimulus conditions does not entirely circumvent this problem, because participants are still aware during unpleasant stimuli that they will eventually again be presented with a pleasant stimulus. Finally, experimenters should also be aware that it is possible that fear levels induced by the PET or fMRI environment (which is perceived as scary by many individuals) are reduced by pleasant music, and that this reduction of fear might be reflected in a decrease of amygdala activity during listening to pleasant music.

12.12.6 Subject selection

Almost everybody is capable of experiencing negative emotions. However, converging evidence suggests that some individuals have a strongly reduced capability of experiencing soft, positive emotions (Koelsch et al, 2007), such as (tender) joy and happiness (not to be confused with ecstatic, or manic affect). When conducting experiments on tender positive emotions, investigators should either exclude the individuals with reduced tender positive emotionality, or introduce this personality trait as an additional variable in the data analysis to explain the variance. One possibility is to use personality questionnaires, such as the revised version of the Toronto Alexithymia Scale (Bagby et al, 1994; subjects should score inside the 1 SD range above *and below* (!) the mean on each of the three subscales), or parts of the NEO PI-R (Costa & McCrae, 1992; subjects should score normal on the facets positive emotion, warmth, and tender-mindedness). However, it is recommended to also obtain physiological measures of emotionality. With regard to this, a relatively simple but reliable technique has recently been described by Koelsch et al (2007). This technique makes use of amplitude relations of a short resting electroencephalogram. Such amplitude relations are influenced by vegetative parameters associated with the emotional personality of an individual, and they can be measured and evaluated within about 10–15 minutes. Such measures should ideally be used in combination with personality questionnaires.

12.13 OUTLOOK

The different neural circuits that mediate different emotions are still poorly understood. Future studies should aim at specifying the neural signatures of different emotions, with a particular emphasis on thorough discrimination between different positive and different negative emotions, and on different mechanisms (whether conscious or unconscious) evoking or regulating positive and negative emotions (see also Juslin & Västfjäll, 2008; Chapter 22, this volume). Such mechanisms can, for example, be investigated using musical preferences, or the manipulation of such preferences, as independent experimental variables.

A difficulty in the research on emotion is that language is used to describe emotions (by both experimenters and subjects); that is, language is used to refer to phenomena with specific neural signatures that still remain to be specified. This is particularly critical because different individuals often refer to different emotions using the same word. For example, when two individuals speak of emotions such as happiness, joy, fun, or love, they may not actually refer to the same phenomena. Perhaps, music might turn out to be better suited for the labelling of emotions than language. For example, although the Rejouissance from Bach's *Fourth Orchestral Suite* and Elvis's 'Blue Suede Shoes' are usually both perceived as positive and pleasant (unless an individual has some negative association with these pieces), the characters of the emotions evoked by these two pieces are quite different, and words are—at least at present—not as well suited to describe these characters as the pieces themselves.

With regard to clinical applications, it would be useful to have more insight into the neural correlates of the anxiety-reducing effects of music listening. Similarly, we need more knowledge about the neural correlates of the emotional effects used in music therapy for the treatment of patients. Notably, this does not only pertain to patients with affective disorders (such as Depression), but also—due to the effects of emotions on the autonomic, endocrine, and immune system—to patients with diseases related to dysfunctions of these systems (such as autoimmune diseases). Such knowledge would help to develop more systematic, widespread, and evidence-based applications, which make use of the powerful effects of music on emotions to improve human health.[1]

---

[1] We thank Daniel Mietchen and Karsten Müller for editing the sections on functional neuroimaging techniques and methods.

RECOMMENDED FURTHER READING

1. Eldar, E., Ganor, O., Admon, R., Bleich, A., & Hendler, T. (2007). Feeling the real world: limbic response to music depends on related content. *Cerebral Cortex, 17,* 2828–40.
2. Ball, T., Rahm, B., Eickhoff, S. B., Schulze-Bonhage, A., Speck, O., & Mutschler, I. (2007). Response properties of human amygdala subregions: evidence based on functional MRI combined with probabilistic anatomical maps. *PLoS ONE, 2,* e307.
3. Blood, A., & Zatorre, R. J. (2001). Intensely pleasurable responses to music correlate with activity in brain regions implicated in reward and emotion. *Proceedings of the National Academy of Sciences, 98,* 11818–23.

References

Augustine, J. R. (1996). Circuitry and functional aspects of the insular lobe in primates including humans. *Brain Research Reviews*, *22*, 229–44.

Bagby, R. M., Parker, J. D., & Taylor, G. J. (1994). The twenty-item Toronto Alexithymia Scale—I. Item selection and cross-validation of the factor structure. *Journal of Psychosomatic Research*, *38*, 23–32.

Ball, T., Rahm, B., Eickhoff, S. B., Schulze-Bonhage, A., Speck, O., & Mutschler, I. (2007). Response properties of human amygdala subregions: evidence based on functional MRI combined with probabilistic anatomical maps. *PLoS ONE*, *2*, e307.

Baumgartner, T., Lutz, K., Schmidt, C. F., & Jäncke, L. (2006). The emotional power of music: how music enhances the feeling of affective pictures. *Brain Research*, *1075*, 151–64.

Becker, P. J., Byers, B. D., Jipson, A. J., & Messner, B. A. (2006). *The hardest hate: A sociological analysis of hate music*. Paper presented at the Annual Meeting of the American Society of Criminology (ASC), Los Angeles Convention Center, Los Angeles, CA. Retrieved from http://www.allacademic.com/meta/p126659_index.html

Bernardi, L., Porta, C., & Sleight, P. (2006). Cardiovascular, cerebrovascular, and respiratory changes induced by different types of music in musicians and non-musicians: the importance of silence. *Heart*, *92*, 445–52.

Bigand, E., Parncutt, R., & Lerdahl, F. (1996). Perception of musical tension in short chord sequences: The influence of harmonic function, sensory dissonance, horizontal motion, and musical training. *Perception & Psychophysics*, *58*, 125–41.

Blood, A. J., Zatorre, R. J., Bermudez, P., & Evans, A. C. (1999). Emotional responses to pleasant and unpleasant music correlate with activity in paralimbic brain regions. *Nature Neuroscience*, *2*, 382–7.

Blood, A., & Zatorre, R. J. (2001). Intensely pleasurable responses to music correlate with activity in brain regions implicated in reward and emotion. *Proceedings of the National Academy of Sciences*, *98*, 11818–23.

Bremner, J. D. (1999). Does stress damage the brain? *Biological Psychiatry*, *45*, 797–805.

Brown, M. W., & Aggleton, J. P. (2001). Recognition memory: what are the roles of the perirhinal cortex and hippocampus? *Nature Reviews Neuroscience*, *2*, 51–61.

Brown, S., Martinez, M., & Parsons, L. M. (2004). Passive music listening spontaneously engages limbic and paralimbic systems. *NeuroReport*, *15*, 2033–7.

Bush G., Luu, P., & Posner, M. I. (2000). Cognitive and emotional influences in anterior cingulate cortex. *Trends in Cognitive Sciences*, *4*, 215–22.

Buxton, R. B. (2002). *An introduction to functional magnetic resonance imaging: Principles and techniques*. Cambridge, UK: Cambridge University Press.

Costa, P. T., Jr., & McCrae, R. R. (1992). *NEO PI-R professional manual*. Odessa, FL: Psychological Assessment Resources.

Critchley, H. D., Corfield, D. R., Chandler, M. P., Mathias, C. J., & Dolan, R. J. (2000). Cerebral correlates of autonomic cardiovascular arousal: a functional neuroimaging investigation in humans. *Journal of Physiology*, *523*, 259–70.

Critchley, H. D., Wiens, S., Rotshtein, P., Öhman, A., & Dolan, R. J. (2004). Neural systems supporting interoceptive awareness. *Nature Neuroscience*, *7*, 189–95.

Critchley, H. D. (2005). Neural mechanisms of autonomic, affective, and cognitive integration. *Journal of Comparative Neurology*, *493*, 154–66.

Davis, M., & Whalen, P. J. (2001). The amygdala: vigilance and emotion. *Molecular Psychiatry*, *6*, 13–34.

Devinsky, O., Morrell, M. J., & Vogt, B. A. (1995). Contributions of anterior cingulate cortex to behaviour. *Brain*, *118*, 279–306.

Drevets, W. C., Price, J. L., Bardgett, M. E., Reich, T., Todd, R. D., & Raichle, M. E. (2002) Glucose metabolism in the amygdala in depression: relationship to diagnostic subtype and plasma cortisol levels. *Pharmacology Biochemistry and Behavior*, *71*, 431–47.

Eichenbaum, H. (2000). A cortical-hippocampal system for declarative memory. *Nature Reviews Neuroscience*, *1*, 41–50.

Eldar, E., Ganor, O., Admon, R., Bleich, A., & Hendler, T. (2007). Feeling the real world: limbic response to music depends on related content. *Cerebral Cortex*, *17*, 2828–40.

Enk, R., & Koelsch, S. (2007). *Physiological effects of pleasant and unpleasant music.* Poster presented at Evolution of Emotional Communication: From Sounds in Nonhuman Mammals to Speech and Music in Man, Hannover, Germany, September 2007.

Faro, S. H. (ed.). (2006). *Functional MRI: Basic principles and clinical applications*. New York: Springer.

Flynn, F. G., Benson, D. F., & Ardila, A. (1999). Anatomy of the insula functional and clinical correlates. *Aphasiology*, *13*, 55–78.

Fritz, T., & Koelsch, S. (2005). Initial response to pleasant and unpleasant music: An fMRI study. *NeuroImage*, *26*, Suppl.: T-AM 271.

Friston, K. J., Buechel, C., Fink, G. R., Morris, J., Rolls, E., & Dolan, R. J. (1997). Psychophysiological and modulatory interactions in neuroimaging. *Neuroimage*, *6*, 218–29.

Friston, K. J., Harisson, L., & Penny, W. (2003). Dynamic causal modelling. *Neuroimage*, *19*, 1273–1302.

Gaab, N., Gaser, C., Zaehle, T., Jancke, L., & Schlaug, G. (2003). Functional anatomy of pitch memory—an fMRI study with sparse temporal sampling. *NeuroImage*, *19*, 1417–26.

Gaab, N., Gabrieli, J. D., & Glover, G. H. (2007). Assessing the influence of scanner background noise on auditory processing. I: an fMRI study comparing three experimental designs with varying degrees of scanner noise. *Human Brain Mapping*, *28*, 703–20.

Goebel, R., Roebroeck, A., Kim, D. S., & Formisano, E. (2003). Investigating directed cortical interactions in time-resolved fMRI data using vector autoregressive modeling and Granger causality mapping. *Magnetic Resononance Imaging*, *21*, 1251–61.

Gosselin, N., Peretz, I., Noulhiane, M., Hasboun, D., Beckett, C., Baulac, M., & Samson, S. (2005). Impaired recognition of scary music following unilateral temporal lobe excision. *Brain*, *128*, 628–40.

Gosselin, N., Samson, S., Adolphs, R., Noulhiane, M., Roy, M., Hasboun, D., Baulac, M., & Peretz, I. (2006). Emotional responses to unpleasant music correlates with damage to the parahippocampal cortex. *Brain*, *129*, 2585–92.

Graybiel, A. M. (2005). The basal ganglia: learning new tricks and loving it. *Current Opinion in Neurobiology*, *15*, 638–44.

Green, A. C., Baerentsen, K. B., Stødkilde-Jørgensen, H., Wallentin, M., Roepstorff, A., & Vuust, P. (2008). Music in minor activates limbic structures: a relationship with dissonance? *NeuroReport*, *19*, 711–15.

Greicius, M., Krasnow, B., Boyett-Anderson, J., Eliez, S., Schatzberg, A., Reiss, A., & Menon, V. (2003). Regional analysis of hippocampal activation during memory encoding and retrieval: fMRI study. *Hippocampus*, *13*, 164–74.

Grewe, O., Nagel, F., Kopiez, R., & Altenmüller, E. (2007a). Listening to music as a re-creative process: Physiological, psychological, and psychoacoustical correlates of chills and strong emotions. *Music Perception*, *24*, 297–314.

Grewe, O., Nagel, F., Kopiez, R., & Altenmüller, E. (2007b). Emotions over time: Synchronicity and development of subjective, physiological, and facial affective reactions to music. *Emotion*, *7*, 774–88.

Griffiths, T. D., Warren, J. D., Dean, J. L., & Howard, D. (2004). 'When the feeling's gone': a selective loss of musical emotion. *Journal of Neurology, Neurosurgery, and Psychiatry*, *75*, 344–5.

Hall, D. A., Haggard, M. P., Akeroyd, M. A., Palmer, A. R., Summerfield, A. Q., Elliott, M. R., Gurney, E. M., & Bowtell, R. W. (1999). 'Sparse' temporal sampling in auditory fMRI. *Human Brain Mapping*, *7*, 213–23.

Haynes, J. D., & Rees, G. (2005). Predicting the orientation of invisible stimuli from activity in human primary visual cortex. *Nature Neuroscience*, *8*, 686–91.

Huron, D. (2006). *Sweet anticipation: Music and the psychology of expectation*. Cambridge, MA: MIT Press.

Juslin, P. N., & Västfjäll, D. (2008). Emotional responses to music: The need to consider underlying mechanisms. *Behavioral and Brain Sciences*, *31*, 559–75.

Khalfa, S., Schon, D., Anton, J. L., & Liégeois-Chauvel, C. (2005) Brain regions involved in the recognition of happiness and sadness in music. *NeuroReport*, *16*, 1981–4.

Kilpatrick, M. R., Rooney, M. B., Michael, D. J., & Wightman, R. M. (2000). Extracellular dopamine dynamics in rat caudate-putamen during experimenter-delivered and intracranial self-stimulation. *Neuroscience*, *96*, 697–706.

Kilpatrick, L., & Cahill, L. (2003). Amygdala modulation of parahippocampal and frontal regions during emotionally influenced memory storage. *NeuroImage*, *20*, 2091–9.

Kivy, P. (1990). *Music alone: Philosophical reflections on a purely musical experience*. Ithaca, NY: Cornell University Press.

Knutson, B., Adams, C. M., Fong, G. W., & Hommer, D. (2001). Anticipation of increasing monetary reward selectively recruits nucleus accumbens. *Journal of Neuroscience*, *21*, RC159.

Koelsch, S., Gunter, T. C., Friederici, A. D., & Schröger, E. (2000). Brain indices of music processing: 'Non-musicians' are musical. *Journal of Cognitive Neuroscience*, *12*, 520–41.

Koelsch, S., & Siebel, W. (2005). Towards a neural basis of music perception. *Trends in Cognitive Sciences*, *9*, 578–84.

Koelsch, S., Fritz, T., von Cramon, D. Y., Müller, K., & Friederici, A. D. (2006). Investigating emotion with music: An fMRI study. *Human Brain Mapping*, *27*, 239–50.

Koelsch, S., Fritz, T., Schulze, K., Alsop, D., & Schlaug, G. (2005). Adults and children processing music: An fMRI study. *NeuroImage*, *25*, 1068–76.

Koelsch, S., Remppis, A., Sammler, D., Jentschke, S., Mietchen, D., Fritz, T., Bonnemeier, H., & Siebel, W. A. (2007). A cardiac signature of emotionality. *European Journal of Neuroscience*, *26*, 3328–38.

Koelsch, S., Kilches, S., Steinbeis, N., & Schelinksi, S. (2008). Effects of unexpected chords and of performer's expression on brain responses and electrodermal activity. *PLoS ONE 3*, e2631. doi:10.1371/journal.pone.0002631

Koelsch, S., Fritz, T., & Schlaug, G. (2008). Amygdala activity can be modulated by unexpected chord functions during music listening. *NeuroReport*, *19*, 1815–9.

Konečni, V. J. (2003). Review of P. N. Juslin and J. A. Sloboda (eds), 'Music and Emotion: Theory and Research.' *Music Perception*, *20*, 332–41.

Krumhansl, C. L. (1997). An exploratory study of musical emotions and psychophysiology. *Canadian Journal of Experimental Psychology*, *51*, 336–53.

Lauritzen, M. (2008). On the neural basis of fMRI signals. *Clinical Neurophysiology*, *119*, 729–30.

Levitin, D. J., & Menon, V. (2003). Musical structure is processed in 'language' areas of the brain: a possible role for Brodmann area 47 in temporal coherence. *NeuroImage*, *20*, 2142–52.

Lundqvist, L.-O., Carlsson, F., Hilmersson, P., & Juslin, P. N. (2009). Emotional responses to music: Experience, expression, and physiology. *Psychology of Music, 37*, 61–90.

McIntosh, A. R., & Gonzalez-Lima, F. (1994). Structural equation modeling and its application to network analysis in functional brain imaging. *Human Brain Mapping, 2*, 2–22.

Mega, M. S., Cummings, J. L., Salloway, S., & Malloy, P. (1997). The limbic system: An anatomic, phylogenetic, and clinical perspective. In S. Salloway, P. Malloy, & J. L. Cummings (eds), *The neuropsychiatry of limbic and subcortical disorders* (pp. 3–18). Washington, DC: American Psychiatric Press.

Menon, V., & Levitin, D. J. (2005). The rewards of music listening: Response and physiological connectivity of the mesolimbic system. *NeuroImage, 28*, 175–84.

Meyer, L. B. (1956). *Emotion and meaning in music.* Chicago, IL: Chicago University Press.

Mitterschiffthaler, M. T., Fu, C. H., Dalton, J. A., Andrew, C. M., & Williams, S. C. (2007). A functional MRI study of happy and sad affective states induced by classical music. *Human Brain Mapping, 28*, 1150–62.

Mizuno, T., & Sugishita, M. (2007). Neural correlates underlying perception of tonality-related emotional contents. *NeuroReport, 18*, 1651–5.

Mogenson, G. J., Jones, D. L., & Yim, C. Y. (1980). From motivation to action: functional interface between the limbic system and the motor system. *Progress in Neurobiology, 14*, 69–97.

Molnar-Szakacs, I., & Overy, K. (2006). Music and mirror neurons: from motion to 'e'motion. *Social Cognitive and Affective Neuroscience, 1*, 235–41.

Morris, J., Scott, S., & Dolan, R. (1999): Saying it with feeling: neural responses to emotional vocalizations. *Neuropsychologia, 37*, 1155–63.

Nicola, S. M. (2007). The nucleus accumbens as part of a basal ganglia action selection circuit. *Psychopharmacology, 191*, 521–50.

Nieuwenhuys, R., Voogd, J., & van Huijzen, C. (2007). *The human central nervous system: A synopsis and atlas* (4th edn). Berlin, Germany: Springer.

Nobre, A. C., Coull, J. T., Frith, C. D., & Mesulam, M. M. (1999). Orbitofrontal cortex is activated during breaches of expectations in tasks of visual attention. *Nature Neuroscience, 2*, 11–12.

Noy, P. (1993). How music conveys emotion. In S. Feder, R. L. Karmel, & G. H. Pollock (eds), *Psychoanalytic explorations in music* (2nd edn, pp. 125–49). Madison, CT: International Universities Press.

Phelps, M. E. (2006). *PET: physics, instrumentation, and scanners.* New York: Springer.

Phillips, M. L., Young, A. W., Scott, S. K., Calder, A. J., Andrew, C., Giampietro, V., Williams, S. C. R., Bullmore, E., Brammer, M., & Gray, J. A. (1998). Neural responses to facial and vocal expressions of fear and disgust. *Proceedings of the Royal Society of London, Series B, 265*, 1809–17.

Ridderinkhof, K. R., Ullsperger, M., Crone, E. A., & Nieuwenhuys, S. (2004). The role of the medial frontal cortex in cognitive control. *Science, 306*, 443–7.

Roediger, H. L., & McDermott, K. B. (1995). Creating false memories: Remembering words not presented in lists. *Journal of Experimental Psychology: Learning, Memory, and Cognition, 21*, 803–14.

Rolls, E. T., & Grabenhorst, F. (2008). The orbitofrontal cortex and beyond: From affect to decision-making. *Progress in Neurobiology, 86*, 216–44.

Rugg, M. D., & Yonelinas, A. P. (2003). Human recognition memory: a cognitive neuroscience perspective. *Trends in Cognitive Sciences, 7*, 313–19.

Sammler, D., Grigutsch, M., Fritz, T., & Koelsch, S. (2007). Music and emotion: electrophysiological correlates of the processing of pleasant and unpleasant music. *Psychophysiology, 44*, 293–304.

Sander, K., & Scheich, H. (2001). Auditory perception of laughing and crying activates human amygdala regardless of attentional state. *Cognitive Brain Research*, 12, 181–98.

Sapolsky, R. (2001). Depression, antidepressants, and the shrinking hippocampus. *Proceedings of the National Academy of Sciences*, 98, 12320–2.

Scherer, K. R. (1999). Appraisal theories. In T. Dalgleish & M. Power (eds), *Handbook of cognition and emotion* (pp. 637–63). Chichester, UK: Wiley.

Scherer, K. R. (2000). Emotions as episodes of subsystem synchronization driven by nonlinear appraisal processes. In M. D. Lewis & I. Granic (eds), *Emotion, development, and self-organization: Dynamic systems approaches to emotional development* (pp. 70–99). Cambridge, UK: Cambridge University Press.

Scherer, K. R. (2004). Which emotions can be induced by music? What are the underlying mechanisms? And how can we measure them? *Journal of New Music Research*, 33, 239–51.

Schwarzbauer, C., Davis, M. H., Rodd, J. M., & Johnsrude, I. (2006). Interleaved silent steady state (ISSS) imaging: a new sparse imaging method applied to auditory fMRI. *NeuroImage*, 29, 774–82.

Shibasaki, H. (2008). Human brain mapping: Hemodynamic response and electrophysiology. *Clinical Neurophysiology*, 119, 731–43.

Siebel, W. A. (1994). *Human interaction*. Langwedel, Germany: Glaser.

Siebel, W. A. (in press). Thalamic balance can be misunderstood as happiness. *Interdis— Journal for Interdisciplinary Research*.

Sloboda, J. A. (1991). Music structure and emotional response: Some empirical findings. *Psychology of Music*, 19, 110–20.

Stein, M. B., Koverola, C., Hanna, C., Torchia, M. G., & McClarty, B. (1997). Hippocampal volume in women victimized by childhood sexual abuse. *Psychological Medicine*, 27, 951–9.

Stein, M. B., Simmons, A. N., Feinstein, J. S., & Paulus, M. P. (2007). Increased amygdala and insula activation during emotion processing in anxiety-prone subjects. *American Journal of Psychiatry*, 164, 318–27.

Steinbeis, N., Koelsch, S., & Sloboda, J. A. (2006). The role of musical structure in emotion: Investigating neural, physiological, and subjective emotional responses to harmonic expectancy violations. *Journal of Cognitive Neuroscience*, 18, 1380–93.

Suzuki, M., Okamura, N., Kawachi, Y., Tashiro, M., Arao, H., Hoshishiba, T., Gyoba, J., & Yanai, K. (2008). Discrete cortical regions associated with the musical beauty of major and minor chords. *Cognitive, Affective, & Behavioral Neuroscience*, 8, 126–31.

Tanaka, S. C., Doya, K., Okada, G., Ueda, K., Okamoto, Y., & Yamawaki, S. (2004). Prediction of immediate and future rewards differentially recruits cortico-basal ganglia loops. *Nature Neuroscience*, 7, 887–93.

Ter Haar, S., Mietchen, D., Koelsch, S., & Fritz, T. (2007). *Auditory perception of acoustic roughness and frequency sweeps*. Poster presented at Evolution of Emotional Communication: From Sounds in Nonhuman Mammals to Speech and Music in Man, Hannover, Germany, September 2007.

Tillmann, B., Koelsch, S., Escoffier, N., Bigand, E., Lalitte, P., Friederici, A. D., & von Cramon, D. Y. (2006). Cognitive priming in sung and instrumental music: activation of inferior frontal cortex. *NeuroImage*, 31, 1771–82.

Ullsperger, M., & von Cramon, D. Y. (2003). Error monitoring using external feedback: specific roles of the habenular complex, the reward system, and the cingulate motor area revealed by functional magnetic resonance imaging. *Journal of Neuroscience*, 23, 4308–14.

Warner-Schmidt, J. L., & Duman, R. S. (2006). Hippocampal neurogenesis: opposing effects of stress and antidepressant treatment. *Hippocampus*, 16, 239–49.

Wildgruber, D., Hertrich, I., Riecker, A., Erb, M., Anders, S., Grodd, W., & Ackermann, H. (2004). Distinct frontal regions subserve evaluation of linguistic and emotional aspects of speech intonation. *Cerebral Cortex, 14*, 1384–9.

Zald, D. H. (2003). The human amygdala and the emotional evaluation of sensory stimuli. *Brain Research Reviews, 41*, 88–123.

Zentner, M., Grandjean, D., & Scherer, K. R. (2008). Emotions evoked by the sound of music: characterization, classification, and measurement. *Emotion, 8*, 494–521.

PART IV

MUSIC MAKING

CHAPTER 13

EMOTION AND COMPOSITION IN CLASSICAL MUSIC

HISTORIOMETRIC PERSPECTIVES

DEAN KEITH SIMONTON

THE compositions that constitute the classical music tradition of the Western world probably have many different functions. Yet among those functions is probably some kind of emotional expression or communication. That is, when aficionados of classical music attend a concert or turn on their stereo, they usually expect to be 'moved'. Furthermore, listeners often believe that these emotional reactions are what the composer intended—that the work is a vehicle for emotional communication. As Beethoven once put it, 'Coming from the heart, may it go to the heart' (Scherman & Biancolli, 1972, p. 951). What makes these expectations somewhat surprising is the fact that classical music constitutes a fairly abstract form of aesthetic expression. Indeed, the concert halls are often dominated by purely instrumental forms—such as the symphony, concerto, quartet, and sonata—in which not a single word or programme gives any clue what the piece is actually about. Moreover, looking at a music score does not help render a classical composition any less abstract. On the contrary, musical notation is far more precise, rarified, and refined than can be found in any other form of artistic expression. Superficially at least, a score has more in common with a mathematical proof than with a painting, poem, or sculpture. This mathematical abstraction even holds for vocal forms, such as opera, oratorio, cantata, and song, where the words to be sung occupy a relatively small space on the page relative to all those meticulously placed symbols indicating pitch, duration, rhythm, dynamics, and other essential features of a composition. No wonder Claude Debussy could claim that 'Music is the arithmetic of sounds as optics is the geometry of light' (*Who Said What When*, 1991, p. 252).

These observations thus lead to the following question: how do the abstractions of classical music evoke emotional reactions? There are many useful routes to addressing this issue. One option is to engage in a detailed musicological analysis, such as Leonard Meyer (1956) did in his classic book, *Emotion and meaning in music*. Alternatively, one can conduct a laboratory experiment in which the emotional responses of listeners are assessed directly. An example is Krumhansl's (1997) psychophysiological study of the reactions of college students to musical excerpts from the classical repertoire (see also Kallinen, 2005; Kallinen & Ravaja, 2006). These musicological and experimental inquires have contributed a great deal to our understanding of the emotional impact of classical music. Yet they by no means exhaust the available methodological approaches.

Here, in fact, I adopt a distinctive analytical strategy that is far less common than either musicological analysis or laboratory experiments. This approach entails the historiometric study of the composers and compositions that define the classical repertoire. By *historiometrics* I mean the adaptation of psychometric methods to examine data about historic individuals (Simonton, 1990, 1999b; cf. Woods, 1909, 1911). In the case of classical composers, these data can include both (a) biographical information about their lives and (b) content-analytical information about their works. In a series of articles published since 1977, I have been using this specific technique to study creativity and aesthetics in classical music (e.g. Simonton, 1977b, 1991, 1995, 2007). This research was part of a broader series of studies devoted to understanding the psychology of creative genius. Although this research programme was not directed specifically at investigating emotional expression in music, some of the empirical results might possibly shed a little light on how this phenomenon operates, at least within the classical music tradition.

I begin by describing an objective and quantitative measure of a composition's melodic originality. I then show that scores on this computerized measure have certain aesthetic consequences, consequences apparently consistent with the assumption that the measure gauges something of a composition's 'arousal potential'. These content-analytical scores are next shown to relate to the composer's biography in a manner seemingly compatible with the same assumption. I then conclude with a general evaluation about what this research programme may possibly suggest about music and emotion.

13.1 MELODIC ORIGINALITY

The original impetus for this research came from an unexpected direction: the issue of musical style. Those with lots of performing or listening experience with classical music eventually learn to identify the distinctive styles of particular composers. Not only does Beethoven's music sound different in comparison to that of Monteverdi, Handel, Tchaikovsky, or Bartók, but it is even recognizably different from fellow composers of the Classical Period, such as Haydn and Mozart. But what makes one composer noticeably different from another, even when they both are composing in the same period style? To answer this question, Paisley (1964) developed an idea taken from those art critics who try to identify the creators of certain unsigned Renaissance paintings. What the critics learn to look for are certain 'minor encoding habits', such as the way a particular painter depicts ears, hands, or stones. Because these objects are rather secondary in importance relative to the composition as a whole, they will often be executed in a mechanical, almost mindless manner. Minor encoding habits have also proven useful in identifying the unknown author of various literary texts (Holsti, 1969). These habits include favorite function words, such as preferred prepositions and conjunctions. Paisley wished to determine whether classical composers betrayed their identity through analogous coding habits.

Paisley's (1964) specific solution was to perform a content analysis of the melodies or themes that make up almost any musical composition. Taking the first four notes of each theme, he then determined which combinations of notes were the most common for particular composers. Paisley found that different composers had distinctive ways of constructing their thematic material, and that these coding habits could be used to predict the identity of the composer of anonymous test samples. Using this technique, Beethoven's work could be easily distinguished from that of other classical composers, including the works of Haydn and Mozart.

If composers can reveal their identity from just the first four notes of their melodies, what else can be learned from the content analysis of their melodic ideas? I decided to develop Paisley's approach to an objective and quantified assessment of an important property of music, namely its melodic originality.

13.1.1 Computerized measurement: two-note transition probabilities

The first task was to obtain a large and representative sample of classical composers. The sampling began with all those whose music could be found in a two-volume dictionary of musical themes (Barlow & Morgenstern, 1948, 1950). This dictionary included all of the classical music that was recorded as of the middle of the twentieth century. After deleting anonymous compositions and other problematic works, the sample consisted of 15,618 themes by 479 composers (Simonton, 1980b). This could hardly be called a 'sample' at all, given its size. In fact, according to one study based on performance data, only 100 composers account for 94 per cent of the music that has any place whatsoever in the standard repertoire of classical music (Moles 1958/1968; see also Simonton, 1991). So the sample was exhaustive when it came to major composers. In addition, the sample was fairly exhaustive when it came to the principal compositions by the tradition's major figures. For instance, among the 15,618 themes were those coming from *all* of

Beethoven's symphonies, concertos, string quartets, and piano sonatas (for complete listing, see Barlow & Morgenstern, 1948, 1950).

Following Paisley (1964), the thematic dictionaries that generated the sample also provided the foundation for the content analysis. For each theme, the dictionaries give the beginning notes, all transposed to a C tonic. In other words, all melodies in the major mode had been transposed into C Major, and all those in the minor mode had been transposed into C Minor. Although Paisley accomplished a lot with only the first four notes, I decided to use the first *six* notes of each of the 15,618 melodies. These data were all entered into a huge machine-readable data file. The next step was to have a computer calculate the two-note transition probabilities. That is, the first six notes contain five two-note transitions (first to second, second to third, etc.). The partial results of this computerized content analysis are shown in Table 13.1 (for a more complete table, see Simonton, 1984, Table 1).

Clearly, some two-note transitions are far more common than others. On the one hand, the dominant-dominant (GG), tonic-tonic (CC), and dominant-tonic (GC) together account for about 17 per cent of all two-note combinations. On the other hand, combinations involving sharps and flats are much more rare—all occurring less than 2 per cent of the time. Moreover, those that do appear, namely Eb and Ab, are not chromatic, but rather are representative of the minor mode. Truly chromatic notes (i.e. those that depart from either the major or the minor mode) are even more improbable, only F# occurring with any frequency whatsoever.

It should be pointed out that the probabilities presented in Table 13.1 were averaged across all five two-note transitions. Slightly different results obtain when the two-note probabilities are calculated separately for each of the five transitions. For instance, two-note combinations involving the tonic and dominant decline in frequency from the first to the sixth note. Thus, over 11 per cent of the time, the first transition contains the dominant-dominant (GG) pairing, but this figure decreases to less than 5 per cent by

Table 13.1 Two-note transition probabilities from the first six notes of 15,618 classical themes

$p \geq .06$: GG (.067)

$p \geq .05$: CC (.053)

$p \geq .04$: GC (.049) and CD (.044)

$p \geq .03$: CB (.032), CG (.032), GF (.031), EE (.030), ED (.030), and DC (.030).

$p \geq .02$: GE (.029), GA (.029), EF (.028), EG (.026), DE (.024), BC (.023), CE (.022), FG (.021), FE (.021), GA (.021), and AG (2.0).

$p \geq .01$: EbD (.018), EC (.016), DEb (.014), AB (.012), BA (.011), AbG (.011), and DD (.011).

Note: Probabilities given in parentheses are averaged across the first five two-note transitions (extracted from the more complete listing in Simonton, 1984).

the fifth transition. In contrast, those transitions that involve other notes of the scale increase in frequency. Apparently, when composers first begin constructing a melody, they usually start by defining the theme's key with the most definitive notes of the scale before incorporating the other notes of the diatonic scale, such as the mediant, subdominant, and leading tone.

These latter, transition-specific probabilities were then used to construct a quantitative measure of melodic originality (Simonton, 1980b). For each of the 15,618 themes, the probability of each of its five transitions were calculated, and then an average taken. The result is a number that represents the mean percentage of times a particular theme's five two-note transitions appear in the entire repertoire. To illustrate, the second movement of Haydn's Symphony No. 94 (the 'Surprise') opens with an extremely simple theme that begins CCEEGG. All of the component two-note transitions are extremely commonplace: The average transition probability is .040. A similar degree of predictability is found in the main theme of the concluding movement of Beethoven's 'Waldstein' Sonata, which begins GGEDGC, yielding a mean transition probability of .041. By comparison, the opening theme of the Introduction to Mozart's 'Dissonant' Quartet commences with AGF#GABb, or a mean probability of .005. The theme that initiates Liszt's Faust Symphony is even more unlikely: AbGBEbF#Bb, yielding an average two-note probability of less than .001 (for more examples, see Simonton, 1984, Table 3). In any case, given these numbers, a measure of each theme's melodic originality can be defined as one minus the mean probability (i.e. $1—\Sigma\, p_i/5$). The higher this number, the higher the assigned score for melodic originality.

This computerized measure may seem very crude. To begin with, the measure concentrates solely on the melody, thereby completely ignoring instrumentation, counterpoint, harmony, formal structure, and text (if any). The implicit assumption being made is that 'melody is the main thing', to quote Haydn (Landowska, 1964, p. 336). But even with respect to melody alone, the computer-generated score ignores the theme's key, its rhythmic structure, and many other significant features (see Chapter 14, this volume). Instead, the measure concentrates on the relationships between consecutive pitches. Nevertheless, it turns out that this objective and quantitative score is not only perfectly reliable—the reliability coefficient is necessarily unity—but in addition it enjoys enough validity for research purposes.

13.1.2 Measure validation

The melodic originality measure was validated several ways. One very direct validation involved the comparison of the measure based on two-note transition probabilities with an alternative measure based on three-note transition probabilities (see Table 2 in Simonton, 1984). These two measures correlate so highly that they yield practically the same results (Simonton, 1980a). Perhaps this should not be too surprising, given that the most likely three-note transitions tend to be made up of the most common two-note transitions (e.g. GGG and CCC). In addition, originality scores based on the probabilities specific to each consecutive two-note transition produce almost the same outcomes as those based upon probabilities that are averaged across all transitions for all 15,618 themes (Simonton, 1984). Hence, this gauge of melodic originality is not contingent on the particular operational definition adopted.

Another route to measure validation was to see if melodic originality correlates with other characteristics of the composition in a manner consistent with expectation. These correlations can be grouped into two categories: general correlates with other characteristics of the composition and those correlates that may more specifically link the measure with emotional expressiveness (Simonton, 1994).

General correlations with compositional characteristics

The melodic originality of the themes in a composition is associated with other aspects of that composition. These linkages suggest that the computer content analysis has captured something that has musical significance. In particular, consider the following four empirical findings:

First, originality is higher for those themes that are also more metrically complex (Simonton, 1987). By metric complexity, I mean melodies in less common meters, such as 3/2 or 9/8 rather than 2/4 or 4/4 time. Thus, as the two-note transitions become more unpredictable, the beats that contain the corresponding pitches become less simple. This hints that the originality measure might indirectly encompass more compositional effects than just melody alone.

Second, originality is higher for themes from instrumental works than those from vocal works (Simonton, 1980b). Part of this relation may reflect the superior flexibility of most musical instruments relative to the human voice (e.g. the virtuoso violin versus a coloratura soprano). But another part may be ascribed to the fact that in vocal compositions, the text has part of the responsibility for communicating content (including any emotional expression).

Third, originality is higher for themes from chamber compositions than those from orchestral compositions, the latter in turn having more original themes than those from theatrical works, such as ballet (Simonton, 1980b). In chamber compositions, such as sonatas and quartets, largely the thematic material carries the burden of maintaining listener interest. As the instrumental resources increase, as in symphonies, tone poems, and overtures, the opportunities rendered by orchestration can assume more importance in maintaining such appeal and attention. In theatrical compositions, extra-musical stimulation becomes prominent as well, such as costumes, sets, and choreography. This renders melodic originality even less necessary.

Fourth, originality is higher in the outer movements of multi-movement compositions than in the inner movements (Simonton, 1987). For instance, symphonies and quartets will most often contain four movements: the first usually in sonata-allegro form, the second a slow movement in song or theme-variation form, a third a minuet (or scherzo) and trio, and a fourth that is in sonata-allegro, rondo, or variation form. The first movement contains the themes with the highest melodic originality, followed by the last movement. The middle movement or movements features the themes with the lowest melodic originality. Evidently, once the composer has gotten the listener's attention, originality can relax momentarily, until the intensity picks up again in the work's conclusion.

Specific correlations with emotional expression and impact

Although the melodic originality measure was not designed to tap the emotional content of a composition, two empirical findings suggest that some connection might exist: First, originality is higher for themes in minor keys than for those in major keys (Simonton, 1987). As is apparent from Table 13.1, transitions containing the notes that define the minor mode have lower probabilities than those from the major mode, which gives minor-key themes their higher originality scores. This fits the subjective experiences of many music listeners, who tend to find themes in the minor more exotic, strange, or unusual in some way (Meyer, 1956). That impression reflects the greater unpredictability of melodies that necessarily flow by less predictable transition probabilities. Perhaps as a consequence, composers frequently choose the minor mode for emotionally expressive compositions. Representative examples include Chopin's F Minor Fantasia, Mozart's G Minor String Quintet, Rachmaninoff's C Minor Piano Concerto No. 2, or Tchaikovsky's B Minor 'Pathétique' Symphony. 'The minor mode is not only associated with intense feeling in general but with the delineation of sadness, suffering, and anguish in particular', observed Meyer (1956, p. 297). Later in this chapter, Meyer's assertion will receive some historiometric support.

Second, scores on the melodic originality measure can be directly compared with the subjective experiences of human listeners. Melodies that score higher in melodic originality should sound more unpredictable, interesting, or complex than melodies that score much lower. Anyone familiar with the themes mentioned earlier should agree that this is the case. The Haydn theme sounds very much like a simple nursery tune ('Twinkle, Twinkle, Little Star', in its English version), whereas the Mozart theme was so incomprehensible to Mozart's contemporaries (including Haydn) that the quartet that it opens has been known as the 'dissonant' ever since. More importantly, one experimental investigation found that the originality scores correspond with subjective assessments of a theme's arousal potential (Martindale & Uemura, 1983). The originality scores were calculated using the two-note transition probabilities for themes by 252 composers, with one theme per composer. Naïve listeners then made an independent assessment of arousal potential of each theme after listening to recordings made by a professional violinist. Those themes that scored higher on the objective measure of melodic originality tended to be those that also scored higher on the subjective measure of arousal potential. In other words, melodic originality predicts whether a theme will be perceived as exciting, stimulating, or arousing. Admittedly, the correlation was only .21 ($p < .001$), but this coefficient was probably attenuated by two factors. The first factor is that the transition probabilities were based on only 252 themes rather than 15,618. The second attenuating factor is that the variance in melodic originality would probably be truncated, given that only 252 themes by 252 composers were examined instead of 15,618 themes by 479 composers. If this correlation is then taken as the lower bound for the true correlation, it seems reasonable to conclude that, within the entire classical repertoire, those themes that contain more original two-note transition probabilities will be more likely to evoke emotional reactions in listeners.[1]

13.2 AESTHETIC CONSEQUENCES

If the hypothesized linkage between melodic originality and arousal potential has some justification, then the content-analytical measure should bear a theoretically meaningful association with (a) a composition's aesthetic impact on listeners and (b) changes in aesthetic style within a composer's career and within the history of classical music. The reasons for these expectations will become clear below.

13.2.1 Compositional impact

Research in experimental aesthetics (Chapter 19, this volume) has suggested that the aesthetic success of any work of art is partly a function of its capacity to evoke emotional arousal (e.g. Berlyne, 1971, 1974). The arousal potential of a given work is associated with such things as the complexity, novelty, surprisingness, and ambiguity of the aesthetic stimulus. The more complex, novel, surprising, or ambiguous the stimulus, the higher the magnitude of arousal elicited. However, the functional relation between arousal potential and aesthetic impact is not linear, but rather curvilinear. That is, the relation is described by what has been called the Wundt curve (Berlyne, 1971). The most successful works are those that evoke an optimal level of arousal. In contrast, compositions with low arousal potential will prove to be predictable, commonplace, or obvious—and hence boring. And compositions that provoke excessive arousal will induce a state of stress, anxiety, or even fear (e.g. the notorious debut of Stravinsky's *Rite of Spring*). A number of investigations in experimental aesthetics have in fact found curvilinear inverted-U relations between measures of arousal potential and aesthetic preferences (e.g. Kammann, 1966; Steck & Machotka, 1975; Vitz, 1964; see also Chapter 19, this volume).

However, most of these experimental studies have used artificial 'art-like' stimuli, which were rated by college students in somewhat unnatural laboratory conditions (Berlyne, 1974). This may help to explain why the results are not always consistent with theoretical expectation (e.g. Martindale & Moore, 1989). Therefore, it behooves us to

---

[1] Tuomas Eerola (personal communication, 26 March 1999) informed me that he had found a correlation of .93 between the melodic originality measure and an alternative measure of melodic complexity derived from research on music perception (cf. Eerola, Himberg, Toiviainen, & Louhivuori, 2006). This constitutes another independent validation of the computer-generated scores.

ask whether the same Wundt curve can be found under more natural circumstances. In particular, is the aesthetic success of real compositions in the classical repertoire partially determined by the melodic originality of the themes those compositions contain? If this content-analytical measure can really be taken as an approximate gauge of a theme's arousal potential, then scores should predict a composition's aesthetic impact. This is, in fact, the case for both objective and subjective indicators.

The *objective ratings* were based on the actual success of the composition in the classical repertoire (Simonton, 1980a, 1980b, 1983). That is, these ratings gauged the frequency that a musical product is likely to be heard in the concert hall, opera house, and recording studio (for a psychometric assessment of such indicators, see Simonton,

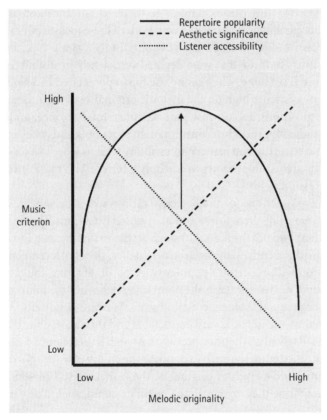

Fig. 13.1 The graph summarizes the empirical results regarding how a theme's melodic originality (as computed from two-note transition probabilities) is associated with three musical criteria: objective repertoire popularity (a composite measure of the performance and recording frequency of the composition which contains the theme) and subjective assessments of its aesthetic significance and listener accessibility (according to Halsey, 1976). The arrow indicates the explanatory hypothesis that the peak of the curvilinear function might reside where the product of aesthetic significance and listener accessibility may be maximized.

1998a). The relationship between this objective measure and melodic originality is neither linear positive nor linear negative, but rather curvilinear. In particular, the relationship is best described as an inverted backward-J curve, as shown in Fig 13.1 (Simonton, 1980b). The most popular works are those that have moderate levels of melodic originality, whereas the most unpopular works are those with the highest levels of melodic originality—the pieces with low melodic originality having more middling popularity. This curvilinear function demonstrates that the Wundt curve provides an adequate description of what happens in the real world of music listening. At least this function holds for the 15,618 themes that define the classical repertoire. The same function has also been shown to hold for the 593 themes that Beethoven contributed to the classical repertoire (Simonton, 1987).[2]

The *subjective ratings* were taken from Halsey (1976), who rated thousands of classical compositions on two dimensions, namely aesthetic significance and listener accessibility. Melodic originality was correlated with both of these measures, albeit in opposite directions, as also indicated in Figure 13.1 (Simonton, 1986a). Aesthetically significant compositions are those that were deemed sufficiently profound that they could withstand repeated listening. They cannot be fully appreciated in a single, superficial hearing. Such pieces score high on the melodic originality of their thematic material. Accessible compositions, in contrast, can be understood at once, and thereby lend themselves to music appreciation courses taught at schools and colleges. Not surprisingly, works that score high on listener accessibility tend to score low on melodic originality. Highly unpredictable themes would only interfere with making an immediately favorable impression.

Notice that the functions for the objective ratings were curvilinear, whereas those for the subjective ratings were linear and in opposed directions. Do these results contradict each other? I do not think so. Although aesthetic significance and listener accessibility correlate differently with melodic originality, they both correlate in the same positive direction with repertoire popularity. Accordingly, one could argue that the peak of the Wundt curve represents the point that maximizes the joint contribution of aesthetic significance and listener accessibility to repertoire popularity. At low levels of melodic originality, the music is very predictable and thus accessible, but the music is also considered of trivial aesthetic importance. At high levels of melodic originality, the aesthetic significance is not so much in doubt as the ability of listeners to appreciate the composition. At middle levels of originality, the works are still reasonably accessible while at the same time they are above the norm in significance. The vertical arrow in

---

[2] Here, as in the rest of this chapter, I am more precisely speaking of *repertoire* melodic originality; that is, the unpredictability of the sequence of pitches when compared with the entire standard repertoire of classical music. Another kind of originality has been defined, namely *Zeitgeist* melodic originality (Simonton, 1980b). In this case, originality is gauged according to whether a particular theme's construction fits the stylistic norms at the time the work was composed. This distinction is crucial, because the two kinds of melodic originality do not correlate the same way with other variables. For example, the popularity of a composition is a U-shaped function of its Zeitgeist melodic originality (Simonton, 1980b). The most successful works are those that depart (in either direction) from the level of repertoire melodic originality most typical of the day.

Figure 13.1 represents the hypothesis that the highest popularity is to be found where the product of aesthetic significance and listener accessibility is maximal.

Interestingly, because low melodic originality is preferred over high melodic originality in terms of repertoire popularity, aesthetic significance appears to have less weight than listener accessibility. On the whole, at least with respect to emotional arousal, listeners would rather be quietly entertained than anxiously provoked.

13.2.2 Stylistic transformations

If the relation between aesthetic impact and melodic originality is mediated by the emotional arousal that highly original compositions evoke, then this relation could be moderated by another basic psychological process: *habituation*. With repetition, the response to an arousing stimulus will often diminish (Berlyne, 1971). As a consequence, over time it may require increasingly higher levels of melodic originality in order to elicit the same optimal level of arousal in music listeners (Martindale, 1990; for literary illustrations, see Kamman, 1966; Simonton, 2004). According to trend analyses of all 15,618 themes by 479 composers, this upward movement manifests itself in two ways (Simonton, 1997).

First, composers tend to steadily increase their use of melodic originality as their careers progress (Simonton, 1980b). Originality is lowest at the beginning of the career, but at once begins to increase. The only exception to this upward growth occurs at around the 56th year of life, where originality tends to reach a peak. After this, a modest decline sets in. Beethoven enthusiasts may find the peak at 56 the most intriguing. Beethoven died at that age, which means that he should have been publishing his most original work then, if his career followed the same pattern as 478 other classical composers. A hearing of his Late Quartets suggests that this was indeed the case.

Second, there exists an overall tendency for melodic originality to increase from the Renaissance to the twentieth century (Simonton, 1980b). This upward trend suggests that each generation of composers feels compelled to produce work that overcomes habituation to a given level of originality, just as predicted by Martindale's (1990) theory of stylistic change. However, just as an exception to the general positive trend was found for composer's careers, so are curious departures found across the history of the classic music tradition. Specifically, superimposed over the positive linear trend are cyclical fluctuations. Melodies in the Renaissance were highly predictable, but by the time of Monteverdi and Gesualdo, originality had reached a maximum point, with a degree of chromaticism that was to be unmatched for nearly three centuries. After that, themes became more predictable again, albeit not so predictable as during the Renaissance. The trough occurred during the time of the Classical Period—Haydn, Mozart, and Beethoven—when thematic material would be constructed from basic chords (e.g. the opening of Beethoven's *Eroica* Symphony). With the advent of the Romantic Period, melodic originality increased, most notably with the chromaticism of Chopin, Brahms, and Wagner (e.g. the famous Prelude to *Tristan und Isolde)*. This trend reached a new height about the time of the First World War. It was this peak that witnessed the emergence of the atonal and serial music of Arnold Schoenberg, such as his *Pierrot Lunaire*. Then, melodic originality saw another decline, although again not going as low as the two previous lows. The music of Aaron Copland and Sergei Prokofiev is indicative of this retrogression.

The superimposed oscillation would seem to contradict the basic proposition that arousal potential has tended to increase over time. Yet, if this cyclical pattern is examined more closely, it becomes evident that the momentary declines in melodic originality tend to come during those periods in which composers acquire new ways to increase the arousal potential of their works besides increasing the novelty, complexity, surprisingness, and ambiguity of the thematic material. Rather than augment the magnitude of chromaticism, for example, the composer may have access to novel forms, rhythms, and orchestration. In partial support for this conjecture, not only is melodic originality lower in those forms giving the composer greater resources (as noted earlier), but also the relation between melodic originality and repertoire popularity is moderated by the size of the work (Simonton, 1980b). The larger the form in which the composer writes, the weaker is the relation between originality and the composition's impact.

In any event, once alternative techniques for evoking emotional reactions become fully incorporated in the repertoire, the composers must again resort to melodic originality as a primary means to overcome the pressures produced by jaded tastes. Furthermore, it is essential to recognize that as the history of classical music unfolds, the troughs in originality get less deep and the crests become more elevated. Hence, the musical history of melodic originality never really repeats itself.

13.3 BIOGRAPHICAL ANTECEDENTS

For a chapter that purports to deal with music and emotion, the results so far may seem a bit cold. Granted, the objective and quantified indicator of melodic originality may indeed correspond with a theme's capacity to stimulate arousal—and that stimulation may shape a composition's aesthetic impact. But emotion in music is often seen as entailing much more than the simple activation of the human sympathetic nervous system. Emotion is also seen as a form of expression, as a means of communicating feelings between a creative artist and an audience. Yet so far we have treated melodic originality as some compositional quality that a composer must manipulate in order to keep listeners from falling asleep—or from running out of the concert hall in disgust or terror.

Fortunately, research using the computerized measure has provided ample reason for believing that melodic originality may reflect the emotional state of the composer at the time of a work's composition. For example, the composer's use of melodic originality is noticeably altered when a composition is created during traumatic political events, such as international war (Simonton, 1986, 1987; see also Brook, 1969; Cerulo, 1984). In particular, compositions penned during times of warfare exhibit much greater variation in melodic originality, extremely unpredictable and extremely predictable themes being found in the same work. It is almost as if such highly stressful events polarize emotional reactions, inspiring vast mood swings between resignation and despair, hope and fear. Shostakovitch's notable (and notorious) *Leningrad Symphony* provides a graphic auditory illustration of the magnitude of this polarization of trite and profound.

More significant, however, is the impact of highly personal events in the life of the composer. Below I treat two potential instances of this personal connection: biographical stress and late-life effects.

13.3.1 Biographical stress

Of special interest to any emotional-expression hypothesis is the relation between the amount of stress occurring in a composer's personal life and the amount of melodic originality appearing in work created during the same period. If 'music sounds the way emotions feel' (Pratt, 1954, p. 296, italics removed), and if stressful events provoke strong emotions, some correspondence between the two should be found. Moreover, the measure of melodic originality would seem to capture some of the attributes of music that contribute to its emotional expressiveness. An excellent example is chromaticism, or the use of notes beside those that define the theme's key. Chromatic notes are often used to express feelings, the unpredictability of the melodic line reflecting the turmoil of our internal emotional state (Meyer, 1956). Indeed, this usage is not even confined to the classical music tradition, as the expressive use of chromatic 'blue notes' in blues and jazz illustrates (La Rue, 1970).

To test the hypothesized linkage between life stress and melodic originality, I took advantage of an earlier data set that had been compiled for a different purpose (Simonton, 1977a). The careers of classical composers were scrutinized to determine the factors that affect a composer's output across the lifespan. The particular composers were the ten most eminent according to a large survey of musicologists (Farnsworth, 1969), namely Bach, Handel, Haydn, Mozart, Beethoven, Schubert, Chopin, Wagner, Brahms, and Debussy. Among the potential predictors of compositional productivity was the occurrence of stressful or traumatic events in the composer's life. To obtain a measure of these events, a chronology of such events was first compiled from the extensive biographies available for these illustrious contributors to the classical repertoire. The next step was to convert these raw facts into a quantitative measure of the degree of stress experienced by each composer during consecutive periods of his life. This conversion was achieved by adapting the Social Readjustment Rating Scale, which has proven its utility in research on psychosomatic illnesses (Holmes & Holmes, 1970; Holmes & Rahe, 1967; see also Simonton, 1998b). Table 13.2 shows some of the biographical events and the weights they were each assigned in the resulting tabulations.

Given these previously calculated assessments, it was a relatively simple matter to estimate the relation between a theme's melodic originality and the amount of stress the composer had experienced during the period of composition (tabulated in cumulative

Table 13.2 Biographical stress coding scheme designed for ten classical composers

Legal difficulties: litigation or lawsuit (30); detention in jail or exile to avoid arrest (63).

Economic problems: major loan (20); trouble with creditors (30); aversive change in financial state or business readjustment (38).

Educational changes: change in schools (20); begin or terminate formal schooling (26).

Vocational changes or problems: job change (20); trouble with employer or superior (23); change in responsibilities at work (29); begin or end work but not fired or retired (36); retirement (45); fired from work (47).

Mobility: city or town of permanent residence changed (30 per move); nation of permanent residence changed (40 per move).

Interpersonal problems: duels, fights, and other physical confrontations (10); argument with friend (10); disappointed or unrequited love (15); onset or termination of a reciprocated love affair (30); death of a close friend (37).

Family problems: gain of a new family member, including adoption (39); change in health or behaviour of family member (44); death of close family member, except children under three (63).

Marital difficulties: marital reconciliation (45); marriage (50); marital separation (65); divorce (73); death of spouse, unless separated (100).

Note: The points assigned to each life-change stress are given in parentheses.

five-year periods). The association was found to be positive, even after introducing controls for other confounding factors, such as the composer's age at the time a work was conceived (Simonton, 1980a). This finding was replicated and extended in a second study that concentrated just on the career of Beethoven (Simonton, 1987). Besides replicating the positive association between stress and originality, this investigation tabulated a measure of the life-span fluctuations in Beethoven's physical health (cf. Porter & Suedfeld, 1981; Simonton, 1998b). This latter measure was also found to correspond to the melodic originality found in Beethoven's compositions. When the composer was experiencing robust health, originality tended to be relatively low, whereas when the composer's health failed, originality was likely to be high. Given that physical illness can be considered a major source of life stress, this finding reinforces what was found for biographical stress. The thematic material found in a composer's works may indeed communicate to the listener something of the composer's underlying emotional life at the time of their composition.

13.3.2 Late-life effects

Biographical stress and physical illness serve to heighten levels of melodic originality. Yet sometimes certain life events can operate in a contrary manner. This contrast is found in a study conducted of what was called the 'swan-song phenomenon' (Simonton,

1989). There has been much speculation about whether artistic creators exhibit a 'late-life' or 'old-age' style (e.g. Arnheim, 1986; Munsterberg, 1983), and even some empirical evidence suggests that these speculations have captured a grain of truth (Lindauer, 1993, 2003). Analogous speculations have been advanced regarding supposed last-work effects in classical music (Einstein, 1956). So, do late-life compositions exhibit any consistent stylistic shifts? This question was addressed by examining melodic originality in 1,919 works by 172 classical composers, and a striking developmental pattern was identified (Simonton, 1989). In the years immediately preceding death, a composer's compositions exhibit rapidly declining levels of melodic originality. In other words, the thematic material becomes much more predictable. Significantly, this effect survived statistical control for the composer's age. Hence, the decline is a consequence of the proximity of death rather than old age. Composers who died young, such as Mozart and Schubert, could thus display the same swan-song effects as those who died at relatively advanced ages, like Vaughan Williams and Stravinsky.

But what is the psychological basis for this swan-song phenomenon? One possibility is to dismiss this effect as an example of the mental deterioration that too often occurs towards the end of any person's life (e.g. Suedfeld & Piedrahita, 1984). Consistent with this interpretation, not only do the melodies tend to be less original in last works, but in addition the works themselves are of shorter duration, on the average (Simonton, 1989). Even so, this negative interpretation does not seem very compatible with other empirical results: the closer to the composer's death a work appears, the more frequently it is performed in the classical repertoire and the higher the rating it receives in aesthetic significance. Hence, swan songs may be shorter and have more simple melodies, but they are also more successful in terms of popular and critical appraisal!

Given the sum total of these findings, it seems more likely that the lower melodic originality in late works is deliberate rather than negligent. If high originality is associated with highly emotional states, then low originality may reveal low levels of emotionality. For a composer who may feel that the end is quickly and inevitably approaching—as perhaps indicated by terminal illnesses or the frailties of old age—that low-arousal state may hint that he has resigned himself to his fate. That resignation, that acceptance then takes the form of powerful and expressive swan songs that communicate the most with the least. This communication of internal peace can itself be considered a form of emotional expression. To get a direct sense of that feeling, we need only listen to the final chorale of Bach's *The Art of the Fugue*, Mozart's *Ave Verum Corpus*, Brahms's Four Serious Songs, or Richard Strauss's Four Last Songs.

13.4 CONCLUSION

The research just reviewed has many limitations, two of which are especially critical here. First, none of these studies was specifically dedicated to scrutinizing the relation between music and emotion. Instead, their primary purpose was to comprehend more

generally the creativity of music composers and the aesthetic impact of their compositions. In only one investigation was emotional impact directly assessed, and then only
in the rather stripped-down form of 'arousal potential' (Martindale & Uemura, 1983).
The more differentiated emotional states seen in other investigations, such as happiness
and sadness, have no direct representation in this historiometric literature (cf. Kallinen,
2005; Krumhansl, 1997). Furthermore, emotional reactions were mostly introduced as
intervening variables to predict or explain the empirical relations between observed
variables. Thus, the positive association between biographical stress and melodic originality was predicted under the assumptions that (a) stress produces emotional states
and (b) such emotional states influence the composer's melodic creativity (e.g. the use
of chromaticism). Likewise, the expected curvilinear relation between melodic originality and repertoire popularity was directly based on Berlyne's (1971) optimal-arousal
model of the relation between collative variation and aesthetic preference—and the
Wundt curve that it theoretically predicts.

Fortunately, none of the empirical findings contradicted the twofold supposition
that melodic originality both influenced listeners' emotional response and reflected
the composer's emotional state. In addition, a strong agreement exists between many
of these findings and what Meyer (1956) argued on the basis of a detailed, sophisticated
analysis of a select number of representative musical scores (e.g. the relation between
emotion and the violation of melodic expectations). Nonetheless, to make a stronger
case for this supposition, these historiometric results should be tied more closely with
findings from laboratory experiments. For instance, I have previously suggested using
the two-note transition probabilities to construct artificial musical stimuli (Simonton,
1984). Experiments can then gauge whether these stimuli influence both physiological responses and subjective feelings of participants (e.g. as in Krumhansl, 1997). This
extension would introduce the experimental controls so obviously lacking in historiometric inquiries.

The second limitation concerns the fact that the correlations between melodic originality and other significant factors are far from perfect. At no time can we say that even
a quarter of the variance is accounted for by any one relationship, and more often the
effects hover around one or two percent. Yet we should not expect it to be otherwise.
Musical creativity, like other forms of creative behavior, is a complex, multi-determined
phenomenon (Simonton, 1999a). It probably would take hundreds of variables to fully
describe what happens when a composer puts notes on a piece of paper—or when a
listener emotionally responds to their performance. In addition, it must be reiterated
that the computerized assessment of melodic originality remains only a crude approximation. Composers have a great deal more in their expressive tool kit than the choice of
pitches (Chapter 14, this volume). It certainly makes a difference in emotional impact
whether the tempo is adagio or presto, the rhythm regular or syncopated, the dynamics pianissimo or fortissimo, the melody line played on a violin or tuba. Indeed, when
the current scheme is compared with various alternative content-analytical measures,
its simplicity becomes quite obvious (see, e.g. Cerulo, 1988, 1989; Eerola, Himberg,
Toiviainen, & Louhivuori, 2006). A certain price has been paid to quantify efficiently
and objectively so many themes and their corresponding compositions.

All that admitted, the fact remains that the discovered relationships, whatever their limitations, hold for all of the works that dominate the classical repertoire. Certainly, 15,618 themes by 479 composers constitute a far more representative sample than seen in any other investigation, whether musicological or experimental. Therefore, it may be worthwhile to lend serious consideration to the results that connect the computer-generated melodic originality with a provocative array of variables. Scores on this content-analytical attribute have been empirically linked with various characteristics of classical works, including their key, rhythm, medium, form, and compositional structure. Even more pertinent here is the fact that melodic originality seems to bear some connection with a theme's emotional expressiveness. This latter consequence, however modest, has implications for understanding (a) how compositions vary in their repertoire popularity, listener accessibility, and aesthetic significance, and (b) how melodic originality changes during the development of a composer's career and during the evolution of musical history. At the same time, the melodic originality granted particular themes appears to have some foundation in the life experiences prevailing at the time the works were created by the composer. Stressful and even traumatic events tend to intensify the level of melodic originality in concomitant compositions.

All of these empirical relationships imply that melodic originality, at least to some degree, forms part of the music composer's tools for expressing emotion. It seems most likely that more sophisticated methods of assessing the expressive qualities of music will reinforce rather than contradict this conclusion.

Recommended further reading

1. Kozbelt, A., & Burger-Pianko, Z. (2007). Words, music, and other measures: Predicting the repertoire popularity of 597 Schubert lieder. *Psychology of Aesthetics, Creativity, and the Arts, 1,* 191–203.
2. Simonton, D. K. (in press). Creative genius in classical music: Biographical influences on composition and eminence. *The Psychologist.*
3. Simonton, D. K. (in press). The decline and fall of musical art: What happened to classical composers? *Empirical Studies of the Arts.*

References

Arnheim, R. (1986). *New essays on the psychology of art.* Berkeley, CA: University of California Press.

Barlow, H., & Morgenstern, S. (1948). *A dictionary of musical themes.* New York: Crown.

Barlow, H., & Morgenstern, S. (1950). *A dictionary of vocal themes.* New York: Crown.

Berlyne, D. (1971). *Aesthetics and psychobiology.* New York: Appleton-Century-Crofts.

Berlyne, D. E. (ed.). (1974). *Studies in the new experimental aesthetics.* Washington, DC: Hemisphere.

Brook, B. S. (1969). Style and content analysis in music: The simplified 'Plaine and Easie Code'. In G. Gerbner, O. R. Holsti, K. Krippendorff, W. J. Paisley, & P. J. Stone (eds), *The analysis of communication content* (pp. 287–96). New York: Wiley.

Cerulo, K. A. (1984). Social disruption and its effects on music: An empirical analysis. *Social Forces, 62,* 885–904.

Cerulo, K. A. (1988). Analyzing cultural products: A new method of measurement. *Social Science Research, 17,* 317–52.

Cerulo, K. A. (1989). Variations in musical syntax: Patterns of measurement. *Communication Research, 16,* 204–35.

Eerola, T., Himberg, T., Toiviainen, P., & Louhivuori, J. (2006). Perceived complexity of Western and African folk melodies by Western and African listeners. *Psychology of Music, 34,* 337–71.

Einstein, A. (1956). *Essays on music.* New York: Norton.

Farnsworth, P. R. (1969). *The social psychology of music* (2nd edn). Ames, IA: Iowa State University Press.

Halsey, R. S. (1976). *Classical music recordings for home and library.* Chicago, IL: American Library Association.

Holmes, T. S., & Holmes, T. H. (1970). Short-term intrusions into the life style routine. *Journal of Psychosomatic Research, 14,* 121–32.

Holmes, T. S., & Rahe, R. H. (1967). The social readjustment rating scale. *Journal of Psychosomatic Research, 11,* 213–8.

Holsti, O. R. (1969). *Content analysis for the social sciences and humanities.* Reading, MA: Addison-Wesley.

Kammann, R. (1966). Verbal complexity and preferences in poetry. *Journal of Verbal Learning and Verbal Behavior, 5,* 536–40.

Kallinen, K. (2005). Emotional ratings of music excerpts in the Western art music repertoire and their self-organization in the Kohonen neural network. *Psychology of Music, 33,* 373–93.

Kallinen, K., & Ravaja, N. (2006). Emotion perceived and emotion felt: Same and different. *Musicae Scientiae, 10,* 191–213.

Krumhansl, C. L. (1997). An exploratory study of musical emotions and psychophysiology. *Canadian Journal of Experimental Psychology, 51,* 336–52.

La Rue, J. (1970). *Guidelines for style analysis.* New York: Norton.

Landowska, W. (1964). *Landowska on music* (D. Restout, ed. & trans.). New York: Stein & Day.

Lindauer, M. S. (1993). The old-age style and its artists. *Empirical Studies and the Arts, 11,* 135–46.

Lindauer, M. S. (2003). *Aging, creativity, and art: A positive perspective on late-life development.* New York: Kluwer Academic/Plenum Publishers.

Martindale, C. (1990). *The clockwork muse: The predictability of artistic styles.* New York: Basic Books.

Martindale, C., & Moore, K. (1989). Relationship of musical preference to collative, ecological, and psychophysical variables. *Music Perception, 6,* 431–46.

Martindale, C., & Uemura, A. (1983). Stylistic evolution in European music. *Leonardo, 16,* 225–8.

Meyer, L. B. (1956). *Emotion and meaning in music.* Chicago, IL: Chicago University Press.

Moles, A. (1968). *Information theory and esthetic perception* (J. E. Cohen, trans.). Urbana, IL: University of Illinois Press. (Originally published 1958)

Munsterberg, H. (1983). *The crown of life: Artistic creativity in old age*. San Diego, CA: Harcourt-Brace-Jovanovich.

Paisley, W. J. (1964). Identifying the unknown communicator in painting, literature and music: The significance of minor encoding habits. *Journal of Communication*, 14, 219–37.

Porter, C. A., & Suedfeld, P. (1981). Integrative complexity in the correspondence of literary figures: Effects of personal and societal stress. *Journal of Personality and Social Psychology*, 40, 321–30.

Pratt, C. C. (1954). The design of music. *Journal of Aesthetics and Art Criticism*, 12, 289–300.

Schermann, T. K., & Biancolli, L. (eds). (1972). *The Beethoven companion*. Garden City, NY: Doubleday.

Simonton, D. K. (1977a). Creative productivity, age, and stress: A biographical time-series analysis of 10 classical composers. *Journal of Personality and Social Psychology*, 35, 791–804.

Simonton, D. K. (1977b). Eminence, creativity, and geographic marginality: A recursive structural equation model. *Journal of Personality and Social Psychology*, 35, 805–16.

Simonton, D. K. (1980a). Thematic fame and melodic originality in classical music: A multi-variate computer-content analysis. *Journal of Personality*, 48, 206–19.

Simonton, D. K. (1980b). Thematic fame, melodic originality, and musical Zeitgeist: A bio-graphical and transhistorical content analysis. *Journal of Personality and Social Psychology*, 38, 972–83.

Simonton, D. K. (1983). Esthetics, biography, and history in musical creativity. In *Documentary report of the Ann Arbor Symposium* (Session 3, pp. 41–48). Reston, VA: Music Educators National Conference.

Simonton, D. K. (1984). Melodic structure and note transition probabilities: A content analysis of 15,618 classical themes. *Psychology of Music*, 12, 3–16.

Simonton, D. K. (1986). Aesthetic success in classical music: A computer analysis of 1,935 compositions. *Empirical Studies of the Arts*, 4, 1–17.

Simonton, D. K. (1987). Musical aesthetics and creativity in Beethoven: A computer analysis of 105 compositions. *Empirical Studies of the Arts*, 5, 87–104.

Simonton, D. K. (1989). The swan-song phenomenon: Last-works effects for 172 classical composers. *Psychology and Aging*, 4, 42–7.

Simonton, D. K. (1990). *Psychology, science, and history: An introduction to historiometry*. New Haven, CT: Yale University Press.

Simonton, D. K. (1991). Emergence and realization of genius: The lives and works of 120 classical composers. *Journal of Personality and Social Psychology*, 61, 829–40.

Simonton, D. K. (1994). Computer content analysis of melodic structure: Classical composers and their compositions. *Psychology of Music*, 22, 31–43.

Simonton, D. K. (1995). Drawing inferences from symphonic programmes: Musical attributes versus listener attributions. *Music Perception*, 12, 307–22.

Simonton, D. K. (1997). Products, persons, and periods: Historiometric analyses of compo-sitional creativity. In D. J Hargreaves & A. C. North (eds), *The social psychology of music* (pp. 107–22). Oxford: Oxford University Press.

Simonton, D. K. (1998a). Fickle fashion versus immortal fame: Transhistorical assessments of creative products in the opera house. *Journal of Personality and Social Psychology*, 75, 198–210.

Simonton, D. K. (1998b). Mad King George: The impact of personal and political stress on mental and physical health. *Journal of Personality*, 66, 443–66.

Simonton, D. K. (1999a). *Origins of genius: Darwinian perspectives on creativity*. New York: Oxford University Press.

Simonton, D. K. (1999b). Significant samples: The psychological study of eminent individuals. *Psychological Methods, 4,* 425–51.

Simonton, D. K. (2004). Thematic content and political context in Shakespeare's dramatic output, with implications for authorship and chronology controversies. *Empirical Studies of the Arts, 22,* 201–13.

Simonton, D. K. (2007). Cinema composers: Career trajectories for creative productivity in film music. *Psychology of Aesthetics, Creativity, and the Arts, 1,* 160–9.

Steck, L., & Machotka, P. (1975). Preference for musical complexity: Effects of context. *Journal of Experimental Psychology: Human Perception and Performance, 104,* 170–4.

Suedfeld, P., & Piedrahita, L. E. (1984). Intimations of mortality: Integrative simplification as a predictor of death. *Journal of Personality and Social Psychology, 47,* 848–52.

Vitz, P. C. (1964). Preferences for rates of information presented by sequences of tones. *Journal of Experimental Psychology, 68,* 176–83.

Who said what when: A chronological dictionary of quotations. (1991). New York: Hippocrene Books.

Woods, F. A. (1909). A new name for a new science. *Science, 30,* 703–4.

Woods, F. A. (1911). Historiometry as an exact science. *Science, 33,* 568–74.

CHAPTER 14

THE ROLE OF STRUCTURE IN THE MUSICAL EXPRESSION OF EMOTIONS

ALF GABRIELSSON AND ERIK LINDSTRÖM

14.1 INTRODUCTION

THE expressive qualities of music have been a matter of discussion by philosophers and music theorists ever since Antiquity. It has been proposed that music may express, reflect, or represent events/situations ('programme music'), motion, dynamic forces, human character, personality, social conditions, religious faith, and—above all— emotions (Gabrielsson, 2005, 2009).

Empirical research on emotional expression started about one hundred years ago, and has successively increased in scope up till now. Generally, this research aims at finding out, on the one hand, which emotions can be reliably expressed in music (reviewed in Gabrielsson & Juslin, 2003), and, on the other hand, which factors in musical structure contribute to the perceived emotional expression (this chapter). These factors are usually represented by designations in the conventional musical notation, such as tempo markings, dynamic markings, pitch, intervals, mode, melody, rhythm, harmony, and various formal properties (e.g. repetition, variation, transposition). Composers use these factors in order to achieve intended expressions: 'A composer . . . knows the forms of emotions and can handle them, "compose" them' (Langer, 1957, p. 222). Whether these expressions reflect the composer's own feelings or not probably varies among composers and on different occasions. Tchaikovsky, usually considered a very 'emotional' composer, took a clear standpoint on this matter: 'Those who imagine that a creative artist can . . . express his feelings at the moment when he is *moved*, make the greatest mistake. Emotions, sad or joyful, can be expressed only *retrospectively* . . . a work composed in the happiest surroundings may be touched with dark and gloomy colors' (cited in Fisk, 1997, p. 157). For further discussion of these questions, see Davies (1994, Chapters 4–6; see also Chapters 2, 3, and 13, this volume).

The purpose of this chapter is to review empirical research on how different factors in the composed musical structure influence the perceived emotional expression.[1] Most of this research deals with Western classical music. However, because listeners usually judge perceived expression of composed music as realized in performance, there is a confounding of the properties of the composed structure and the properties of the performance. As a rule, performance involves various modifications of the notated structure, such as variations of tempo, note timing, articulation, and intonation (for reviews, see Gabrielsson, 1999, 2003). Perceived expression is thus dependent both on factors in the composed structure and factors in the performance. Although it is sometimes difficult to distinguish between these factors in published reports, the focus of the present review is on the effects of the composed structure; performance aspects are treated by Juslin and Timmers (Chapter 17, this volume).

Furthermore, listeners' perception of emotional expression—for instance, to perceive a piece of music as 'happy'—should be distinguished from listeners' own emotional reactions, for instance, to feel happy. (Listeners' emotional reactions are treated in Section V of this volume.) The border between these two alternatives is sometimes blurred, and the relationship between them may vary (Evans & Schubert, 2008; Gabrielsson, 2002; Gomez & Danuser, 2007; Juslin & Laukka, 2004; Kallinen & Ravaja, 2006; Konečni et al, 2008).

There are more than 100 studies of the relationship between musical structure and emotional expression, featuring a variety of methods. We first review the methodological approaches that have been used in these studies (Section 14.2). The findings from these studies are then summarized separately for each structural factor in Section 14.3. Finally, Section 14.4 provides an overall summary and some implications for future research.

---

[1] This chapter is a revised and updated version of Gabrielsson and Lindström (2001). We are grateful for suggestions made by three anonymous reviewers.

14.2 DIFFERENT METHODOLOGICAL APPROACHES

14.2.1 General methods

Stimuli

Stimuli were usually recordings of selected pieces of music or synthesized tone stimuli. However, before the common use of modern sound recording, the pieces were performed live by one or more musicians (e.g. Downey, 1897; Gilman, 1891; Hevner, 1935a; Rigg, 1937).

Reporting the perceived expression

Subjects reported the perceived expression by means of;

(a) free phenomenological description (e.g. Huber, 1923; Tagg, 2006) or free choice of descriptive terms (Imberty, 1979);

(b) choice among descriptive terms provided by the investigator (e.g. Gundlach, 1935; Hevner, 1935a; Wedin, 1972b);

(c) combination of free description and choice among descriptive terms (Rigg, 1937);

(d) ratings of how well selected descriptive terms applied to the music in question (e.g. Gabrielsson, 1973; Nielzén & Cesarec, 1982; Tillman & Bigand, 1996; Wedin, 1969); Collier (2007, Experiment 1) used ranking of emotion words;

(e) non-verbal methods, for instance, pressing a pair of tongs to indicate the perceived tension (Nielsen, 1983, 1987), finger pressure on a so-called sentograph (see Section 14.2.2) to study expression of different emotions (Clynes & Nettheim, 1982; de Vries, 1991); or

(f) various technical or computerized devices to allow continuous recording of perceived tension (e.g. Fredrickson, 2000; Krumhansl, 1996; Madsen & Fredrickson, 1993) or perception of various emotions (Krumhansl, 1997; Schubert, 2004).

Free descriptions were usually subjected to content analysis. Listeners' choices among descriptive terms were analysed regarding frequency of each chosen term and regarding inter-subject agreement. Ratings were usually analysed by multivariate techniques (factor analysis, cluster analysis, correspondence analysis, multi-dimensional scaling) in order to find a limited number of fundamental, descriptive dimensions. Continuous and/or non-verbal recordings of perceived expression were studied in relation to selected properties of the musical structure.

Analysis of structure-emotion relationships

The relationship between the composed structure and perceived expression was studied by:

(a) analysing the musical score in relation to perceived expression (e.g. Costa, Fine, & Ricci Bitti, 2004; Gundlach, 1935; Imberty, 1979; Krumhansl, 1996; Nielsen, 1983; Thompson & Robitaille, 1992);

(b) having musical experts judge the selected pieces with regard to structural proper-
     ties (e.g. Kleinen, 1968; Watson, 1942; Wedin, 1972c);
(c) using various devices for measuring the acoustical properties of the music (e.g.
     Schubert, 2004); or
(d) using systematic manipulation of musical stimuli and noting the effects on per-
     ceived expression (e.g. Hevner, 1937; Rigg, 1939; Juslin, 1997; Ilie & Thompson,
     2006).

Experimental control vs. ecological validity

The above alternatives concerning stimuli, responses, and analysis methods have been
combined in different ways that affect the possibility of clear conclusions. There is no
single best alternative. Studying emotional expression using real music (Section 14.2.2)
means good ecological validity, but conclusions regarding the effects of separate structural factors can only be tentative since they are usually confounded in musical contexts. An alternative that allows more definite conclusions is to systematically vary one or
more structural factors (e.g. mode, pitch level) in short sound sequences without musical
context (Section 14.2.3); then, however, the ecological validity is limited. A compromise
between these two approaches is to use systematic manipulation of various factors within
a musical context (Section 14.2.4), for instance, to systematically vary tempo, mode, or
melodic direction in real pieces of music and thus try to combine the advantages of the
before-mentioned strategies. However, some types of manipulation may result in musically unnatural stimuli, thus jeopardizing the ecological validity.

14.2.2 Studying emotional expression using real music

Free descriptions, choice among descriptive terms

The earliest reported empirical investigations on musical expression may be those by
Gilman (1891, 1892) and Downey (1897). Their subjects listened to performances on
piano, or piano and violin, of classical music and gave free phenomenological reports
of the perceived expression. A variety of emotions was reported and some tentative
relationships were noted, for instance, descending thirds in an aria by Handel to
indicate sadness.

Gundlach (1935) presented 40 musical phrases from different classical compositions
to listeners, who were asked to judge 'what mood or attitude the composer has suc-
ceeded in expressing' (p. 628) by choosing one or more out of 17 descriptive terms.
Gundlach concluded that speed was the most important factor for perceived expression, followed by rhythm, interval distribution, orchestral range, loudness, mean pitch,
and melodic range.

Rigg (1937) used 20 short phrases played on the piano and supposed to express joy,
lamentation, longing, or love. Listeners answered the question 'What emotion is suggested to you by each passage?' either by giving free descriptions or by choosing among
the above emotion terms plus anger, fear, and disgust. Rigg discussed advantages and

disadvantages of these procedures. With free descriptions, responses may be scattered, but coherence in listeners' responses would be of more significance than if they merely checked terms in a list. With choice among descriptive terms, responses may be easier to treat, but will partly be a product of the given terms. Expression of joy was convincingly indicated by the listeners, and some musical characteristics of the joy excerpts were rapid tempo, major mode, simple harmony, staccato notes, and forte dynamics.

Watson (1942) had 20 musical experts mark which out of 15 selected adjectives were appropriate for each of 30 musical examples. They also judged the examples regarding pitch (low–high), loudness (soft–loud), tempo (slow–fast), sound (pretty–ugly), dynamics (no quick changes in loudness–very many changes), and rhythm (regular–irregular), thus enabling a study of the relationships between these factors and perceived expression. For instance, high pitch and fast tempo tended to express happiness and excitement, low pitch and slow tempo sadness, high loudness excitement, and small dynamic range dignity, sadness, and peacefulness.

Tagg (2006) presented ten title themes for film or television to listeners who were asked to write down what they thought might be happening on the screen along with each tune ('free induction'). The results were reduced to single concepts, 'visual-verbal associations' (VVA), which were classified into various categories. Certain tunes elicited impressions of male or female figures/characters, and some 60 VVAs were listed for 'male' and 'female' tunes. Among them were a number of emotional descriptors, many more for female (love, sad, melancholy, loneliness, calm, pastoral, tragic, beautiful, crying, nostalgia, sentimental, caressing, dark, kissing, ecstatic, harmonious) than for male (excitement, tough, cruel, hard, rebellious, bad) tunes. The latter descriptors reflect higher arousal and potency than the former; practically all descriptors for female tunes reflect low arousal. In comparison with male tunes, female tunes were slower, more legato, had longer phrases, no repeated notes, static bass line, rare offbeats/syncopation, no brass or percussion, and the tonal idiom was classical/romantic compared to rock and jazz in male tunes.

Ratings and multivariate analysis techniques

In studies by Kleinen (1968), Wedin (1969, 1972a), Gabrielsson (1973, Experiments 4-5), and Nielzén and Cesarec (1981, 1982), subjects judged selected pieces of music using a large number of rating scales. The judgements were subjected to factor analysis, and the resulting factors were given similar interpretations in all studies: tension–energy, gaiety–gloom, and solemnity–triviality (Wedin, 1969, 1972a); intensity–softness, pleasantness–unpleasantness, and solemnity–triviality (Wedin, 1972b, 1972c, using multi-dimensional scaling); tension–relaxation, gaiety–gloom, and attraction–repulsion (Nielzén & Cesarec, 1981); gay/vital–dull, excited–calm (Gabrielsson, 1973); '*Heiterkeit–Ernst*' (cheerful–serious) and '*Robustheit–Zartheit*' (strong/powerful–soft/tender; Kleinen, 1968).

Musical experts rated the respective pieces of music with regard to structural properties. For example, Wedin (1972c) used five-point scales for rating intensity (pp–ff), pitch (bass–treble), rhythm (outstanding–vague), tempo (fast–slow), rhythmic articulation (firm–fluent, staccato–legato), harmony (dissonant–consonant, complex–simple), tonality (atonal–tonal), modality (major–minor), melody (melodious–unmelodious), type of music (serious–popular), and style (date of composition).

Imberty (1979) had 80 non-musical subjects freely choose any adjectives that came to their mind while listening to excerpts from Debussy's *Préludes* for piano. Out of a total of 1,063 adjectives, 172 were retained for analysis by correspondence analysis, which provided a joint representation of the musical excerpts and the adjectives on a number of dimensions. The first two dimensions were *Les schèmes de tension et de détente* (tension vs. relaxation) and *Les schèmes de résonances émotionelles* (positive vs. negative emotions). Imberty went on to construct indices for formal complexity and *dynamisme géneral* by combining variables like note duration, *intervalle métrique* (duration between two accented notes), density of notes per time unit, loudness, accents, syncopations, and certain characteristics of melodic, harmonic, and rhythmic motives. Using these indices, he claimed that (a) low complexity combined with average dynamism means formal integration and expression of positive emotions, (b) high formal complexity combined with low dynamism means formal disintegration and expression of melancholy and depression, and (c) high formal complexity combined with high dynamism means formal disintegration and expression of anxiety and aggressiveness.

Collier (2007, Experiment 1) used ranking of emotion words for ten pieces of music. The following correspondence analysis showed two dimensions, valence and activity/arousal; activity was related to tempo. When ranking was restricted to emotion words within single quadrants of the valence-arousal (or 'circumplex') model (Russell, 1980; see Figure 4.1 in Chapter 4, this volume), there were indications of some subtler dimensions beyond activity and valence; however, data were still very tentative, and nothing was said about possible underlying structural properties. Collier (2007, Experiment 2) also had listeners make free selections among a large set of emotion words to fit each of the ten pieces. Cluster analysis revealed a basic distinction between activity and valence at the highest level and up to nine separate clusters with more subtle distinctions; most of them were similar to the clusters found by Wedin (1972c).

Bigand, Vieillard, Madurell, Marozeau, and Dacquet (2005) used multi-dimensional scaling and cluster analysis to analyse listeners' emotional responses (emotions felt) to 27 excerpts from classical music; however, they indicated that listeners' responses may just as well reflect perceived emotional expression or a mixture of emotion perceived and emotion felt. The analyses revealed the common valence and arousal dimensions and a third dimension related to different melodic gestures that may link perceived emotions with body postures and gesture. The same dimensions appeared even when the duration of the music excerpts was limited to one second, and the results were highly similar for musicians and non-musicians.

The above studies show similar results converging on two main dimensions: valence (pleasantness–unpleasantness, gaiety–gloom) and activity/arousal (tension–relaxation, excited–calm), in accordance with the valence-arousal model of emotions (Russell, 1980). There are also indications of a potency dimension (Kleinen, 1968; cf. Osgood, Suci, & Tannenbaum, 1957) and a dimension reflecting stylistic differences between classical and popular music: solemnity vs. triviality (Wedin, 1969, 1972b). A further proposal involves a distinction between energy arousal (awake–tired) and tension arousal (tense–relaxed); see Ilie and Thompson (2006) in Section 14.2.4 (see also Chapter 8, this volume, for a discussion of various dimensional models).

Continuous recording of emotional expression

As type and intensity of emotional expression usually vary in classical music, researchers may want to use a technique for continuous recording of perceived expression (see also Chapter 9, this volume). Nielsen (1983, 1987) pioneered in developing such a technique for continuous recording of perceived tension. While listening to the music, his subjects continuously pressed a pair of tongs in proportion to the perceived tension—the more tension, the harder the press, and vice versa. The pressures were registered on a polygraph, and showed 'pressure curves' with waves of heightened tension alternating with periods of relaxation. Tension peaks were mainly associated with high intensity (fortissimo), but increased tension could also be related to ascending melody, increased note density, dissonance, harmonic complexity, rhythmic complexity, and formal properties like repetition of various units, condensation of musical material, sequential development, and pauses. Nielsen pointed out that tension may be regarded both as a component of musical structure—alternations between tension and release—and as emotional expression.

Another response device (the Continuous Response Digital Interface, CRDI) was used by Madsen and Fredrickson (1993), Fredrickson (1997, 1999, 2000), and Fredrickson and Coggiola (2003). These studies demonstrated similarities in perceived tension by subjects of different age and musical training. Krumhansl (1996) asked subjects to adjust a slider on a computer display to indicate perceived tension while listening to a Piano Sonata by Mozart. Tension was influenced by melodic contour, note density, dynamics, harmony, and tonality. Tension peaks followed by rapid decrease occurred at the end of large-scale sections, and judgements of new musical ideas co-occurred with low tension levels. Lerdahl and Krumhansl (2007) tested Lerdahl's theory of tonal tension using both continuous recording of tension and a 'stop-tension' procedure in which subjects indicated the perceived tension for single tones in successively longer sequences.

Margulis (2007) studied perceived tension during rests in music. Subjects listened to 20 excerpts of classical instrumental music, each of which contained a rest somewhere, and moved a slider to indicate perceived tension during the excerpt. Tension during rests was lower and decreased faster when the rest followed a resolving tonic pitch/chord, than when it came after an unresolved predominant chord. These results were replicated in another experiment with constructed musical excerpts.

Other studies included more emotions. Namba, Kuwano, Hatoh, and Kato (1991) had subjects use keys on a computer keyboard to continuously indicate perceived emotion—each key represented one out of 15 emotion adjectives—during listening to the Promenade in Moussorgsky's *Pictures at an Exhibition*. Madsen (1997, 1998) and Schubert (1999) designed procedures in accordance with the valence-arousal model (Russell, 1980). Listeners faced a computer screen displaying a coordinate system with valence (negative–positive) along the horizontal axis and arousal/activation (low–high) along the vertical axis and were asked to successively move the mouse cursor to a position that corresponded to the perceived expression. By comparing the successive positions of the cursor in the 'emotion space' with various features of the corresponding musical structure (e.g. melodic contour, tempo, loudness, texture, spectral centroid), one may study the relationships between structural properties and perceived expression. However, there are still several problems with regard to adequate treatment and interpretation of data (Schubert, 2001, 2002, 2004; Vines, Nuzzo, & Levitin, 2005; see Chapter 9, this volume).

Non-verbal responses

The above methods for studying tension were mainly non-verbal, but use of non-verbal responses to indicate other emotional expression is rare. Clynes (1977) introduced the *sentograph*—a device for recording the pressure exerted by a finger upon a small disk—to study how subjects expressed different emotions. He discovered different pressure patterns (sentograms) with regard to duration and dynamics for different emotions (joy, grief, anger, hate, reverence, love, sex; depicted in Clynes, 1977, p. 29 onwards), and then tried to trace corresponding patterns in music (Clynes & Walker, 1982).

de Vries (1991) had 30 subjects use a sentograph while listening to ten pieces of music, and found that sentograms were different for different pieces, and that there were similarities between the sentograms for pieces with a certain emotional expression (e.g. anger, grief, joy, love) and Clynes's sentograms for the corresponding emotions. Some evidence in the same direction was found in Gabrielsson (1995) and Gabrielsson and Lindström (1995). (Another non-verbal response—drawing to describe musical intervals—is described in Section 14.2.3.)

Specially composed music

Thompson and Robitaille (1992) asked composers to compose short monophonic melodies to express joy, sorrow, excitement, dullness, anger, and peace. Their scores were transformed to sounding music using a sampled grand piano sound. In general, listeners perceived the intended expressions. Analysis of the scores showed that joyful melodies were strongly tonal and rhythmically varied. Sad melodies were slow with implied minor or chromatic harmony. Melodies for excitement were fast, contained intervallic leaps and high pitches. Dull melodies were tonal in stepwise motion. Angry melodies were rhythmically complex and with implied chromatic harmony or atonality, and melodies for peacefulness were tonal, slow, and often involved stepwise motion leading to melodic leaps.

14.2.3 Manipulation of structural factors without musical context

Intervals

A distinction must be made between harmonic (simultaneous) intervals (e.g. two-tone chords, bichords) and melodic (successive) intervals. Costa, Ricci Bitti, and Bonfiglioli (2000) used all 12 equal-tempered harmonic intervals (organ sound) contained in an octave, one set in a low register (geometric mean 185 Hz), another in a high register (geometric mean 1,510 Hz) and had listeners rate them on 30 bipolar scales, reflecting 'emotional evaluation', 'activity', and 'potency'. High register bichords were rated higher in 'activity' (e.g. more unstable, restless, tense) and 'potency' (stronger) than low register bichords, and low register bichords were evaluated more negatively than high register bichords. Dissonant bichords were judged as more negative, more active, and stronger than consonant bichords; minor bichords as more dull and weak than major bichords. Females showed greater polarisation of scores, and judged bichords as more active and tense than males. Difference in musical experience had no effect. Generally, intervals differed more in emotional evaluation and activity than in potency.

Maher (1980), using 14 different harmonic intervals in just-intonation with triangular wave forms in two sets, one high-pitched (geometric mean frequency 500 Hz) and one low-pitched (250 Hz), obtained some similar results. High-pitched intervals were rated as more happy and powerful than low-pitched intervals. Minor and major second, minor and major seventh, and minor ninth were rated as most displeasing.

Maher and Berlyne (1982) investigated perception of 12 melodic intervals, sine-wave intervals in tempered intonation, rising and falling, with common 500 Hz geometric mean frequency. Larger intervals were judged as more 'powerful' than smaller ones; the minor second was considered the most 'melancholic' interval, whereas the octave, fourth, fifth, major sixth, and minor seventh were most 'carefree'.

Smith and Williams (1999) had South African children listen to six ascending intervals performed on a flute and represent them in drawings. The primary distinction was between consonance and dissonance, the former associated with home, family, and stability, the latter with unpleasant events. Major seventh and augmented fourth tended to be associated with danger and violence, perfect fifth with activity, perfect fourth with being desolate and old. The octave was perceived as positive and strong, major third as neutral with no particular meaning. The children's responses were influenced by level of schooling, race, and living environment.

Huber (1923) presented short pitch patterns to musical listeners who were asked to freely describe perceived expression. The reports were classified into (a) mood impressions; (b) impressions of human character, for instance 'an elderly man'; (c) emotionally coloured announcements, such as a call, question, or request; (d) impressions of movement; and (e) various inner images. Referring to Huber, Langer (1957, p. 231) remarked that 'the entire study shows effectively how many factors of possible expressive virtue are involved even in the simplest musical structure'.

Mode

Heinlein (1928) investigated listeners' perception of major and minor chords in all keys, at different intensities and pitch levels. Subjects described the perceived expression, choosing among adjectives such as bright, happy, joyful (supposed to reflect major mode), melancholy, sad, and soothing (minor mode). None of the 30 subjects got all responses 'correct': there were sad-type responses to major chords and happy-type responses to minor chords. Loud chords and chords at high pitch level evoked more happy-type responses than soft chords and chords at low pitch level, irrespective of mode. However, Crowder (1984) showed in a re-analysis of Heinlein's data that all but one of the 30 listeners in fact gave more happy-type responses to major chords than to minor chords. Crowder (1985) found the major-happy and minor-sad associations in young adults who listened to sine-wave triads in three tonalities and two inversions of each chord.

Rhythm and tempo

Motte-Haber (1968) presented ten rhythm patterns—differing in meter, sound event density, and homogeneity—using three different metronomic tempos (ratios 1:2:4). Listeners rated the patterns on a large number of bipolar scales (i.e., 'Polaritätsprofile'). Metronomically rapid rhythms were rated happier ('fröhlicher') than slow rhythms. Happiness ratings were strongly correlated with ratings of *subjective* tempo, which was related not only to metronomic tempo but also to sound event density and other rhythm characteristics that interacted with the metronomic tempo. Similar relations appeared in Gabrielsson (1973, Experiments 1–3), using other rhythm patterns.

Melodic properties

Gabriel (1978) investigated perceived expression of 16 short tone sequences ('basic terms'), which music theorist Deryck Cooke (1959) claimed to recur with the same expression in Western music from late Middle Ages up to the twentieth century. For instance, an ascending major triad (1–3–5), with possible insertions of the intervening notes (2 or 4), was said to express 'an outgoing, active, assertion of joy' (Cooke, 1959, p. 115). Its counterpart in minor would be 'expressive of an outgoing feeling of pain—an assertion of sorrow, a complaint, a protest against misfortune' (Cooke, 1959, p. 122). Gabriel generated the 16 basic terms using sinusoidals, constant tempo, and uniform rhythm, and had listeners judge whether Cooke's characteristics were adequate. The result was mainly negative. However, this experiment has in its turn been criticized regarding the choice of stimuli, lack of context, and use of musically untrained listeners (Cazden, 1979; Gabriel, 1979; Nettheim, 1979; Sloboda, 1985, pp. 60-64; Kaminska & Woolf, 2000; for a discussion of Cooke's theory, see Chapter 3, this volume).

    Kaminska and Woolf (2000) derived four bipolar dimensions (finality–continuation, joy–sorrow, outburst–constancy, assertiveness–submissiveness) from Cooke's descriptive terms and asked listeners to rate Cooke's 16 basic terms on these dimensions. Results showed that melodic lines could convey emotional meaning in a consistent way, although usually not in accordance with Cooke's detailed description; his theory was supported only with respect to the emotions of sorrow and joy.

Synthesized tone sequences

Scherer and Oshinsky (1977) investigated the relative importance of several factors by systematic manipulation of synthesized eight-tone sequences. Manipulated variables were amplitude variation (small–large), pitch level (high–low), pitch contour (up–down), pitch variation (small–large), rhythm (even–uneven), tonality (major, minor, atonal), tempo (slow–fast), envelope (round–sharp), and filtration cut-off level (intermediate–high). Psychology students rated the stimuli on three bipolar scales: pleasantness–unpleasantness, activity–passivity, and potency–weakness, and also indicated whether each sequence expressed any or more of the following emotions: happiness, sadness, anger, fear, boredom, surprise, and disgust. Multiple regression analysis was used to estimate the predictive strength of each acoustic parameter on each emotion dimension. Most of the results can be found in Table 14.2 (in Section 14.3). As seen there, each acoustic variable was associated with several emotions, listed in decreasing order of associative strength, and in some cases even with seemingly 'opposite' emotions (e.g. low pitch associated with boredom, pleasantness, and sadness).

14.2.4 Manipulation of structural factors in musical context

Manipulation of several factors

The earliest investigations with systematic manipulations of various factors in real music are those by Hevner (1935a, 1935b, 1936, 1937). She arranged a large number of emotion terms in eight clusters in a circular configuration, an 'adjective circle' (see Figure 14.1). The terms within each cluster were supposed to be close in meaning, and adjacent clusters would deviate slightly by cumulative steps until reaching a contrast in the opposite position. Inspection of Figure 14.1 suggests an implicit dimensionality similar to that described previously in Section 14.2.2; in other words, valence (happiness–sadness, cluster 6–cluster 2) and activity/arousal (exciting/vigorous–serene/dreamy, clusters 7/8–clusters 4/3). The circular configuration is reminiscent of the 'circumplex' model by Russell (1980), and could be one of the earliest indications of this conception (Remington, Fabrigar, & Visser, 2000; for an updated version of Hevner's adjective checklist, see Schubert, 2003). Listeners were instructed to mark as many of these terms as they found appropriate for each piece of music. Hevner selected short pieces of tonal music, but besides the original version she also constructed a variant that differed from the original in (a) mode, a piece in major mode was also played in minor mode (Hevner, 1935a); (b) melodic direction (ascending vs. descending), harmony (simple consonant harmonies vs. complex dissonant harmonies), and rhythm (firm vs. flowing; that is, a firm beat with a chord on every beat vs. a flowing motion in which the chords were broken up; Hevner, 1936); and (c) tempo (fast vs. slow) and pitch level (one octave or more apart; Hevner, 1937).

All versions were performed by an experienced pianist, and listeners were hundreds of students, most of then without musical training. The joint conclusions of several experiments were that the variables with the largest effects on listeners' judgements were tempo and mode, followed by pitch level, harmony, and rhythm. In contrast, melodic direction had little if any effect (Hevner, 1937). Table 14.1 shows the relative weights of each musical factor for each emotion cluster; for instance, minor mode, low pitch, and slow tempo were most important, in that order, for the sad–heavy cluster, whereas major mode, fast tempo, and simple harmony were most important for the happy–bright cluster.

Hevner (1935b, 1937) noted the difficulties of manipulating real pieces of music and still having the manipulated versions sound musically acceptable (cf. Behne, 1972; Peretz, Gagnon, & Bouchard, 1998, p. 118, footnote). She emphasized the necessity of

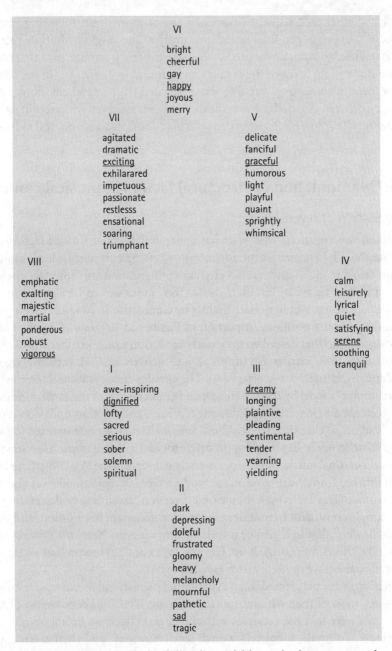

Fig. 14.1 Hevner's adjective circle. Adjectives within each cluster appear in alphabetical order. Adjectives used by Hevner (1936, 1937) to represent the respective clusters are underlined (adapted from Farnsworth 1954, p. 98).

using pieces with similar emotional expression throughout, and remarked that the results should only be interpreted in a relative and contextual sense. For instance, although happiness was usually associated with major mode, a piece in minor mode

Table 14.1 Hevner's summary of results from six experiments

Musical factor	dignified–solemn	sad–heavy	dreamy–sentimental	serene–gentle	graceful–sparkling	happy–bright	exciting–elated	vigorous–majestic
Mode	minor 4	minor 20	minor 12	major 3	major 21	major 24	–	–
Tempo	slow 14	slow 12	slow 16	slow 20	fast 6	fast 20	fast 21	fast 6
Pitch	low 10	low 19	high 6	high 8	high 16	high 6	low 9	low 13
Rhythm	firm 18	firm 3	flowing 9	flowing 2	flowing 8	flowing 10	firm 2	firm 10
Harmony	simple 3	complex 7	simple 4	simple 10	simple 12	simple 16	complex 14	complex 8
Melody	ascend 4	–	–	ascend 3	descend 3	–	descend 7	descend 8

Note: The numbers indicate the relative weight of each musical factor (left column) for each emotion cluster. (Adapted from Hevner, 1937, p. 626)

may sound happy due to other factors, such as tempo and rhythm. She warned against drawing too far-reaching conclusions since the results may be dependent on the selected pieces and, above all, since emotional expression usually results from several musical factors in complex interplay. These arguments should be carefully considered by any researcher of emotional expression in music.

Rigg (1939) composed five four-bar phrases supposed to represent two emotion categories: pleasant/happy or sad/serious. They were systematically manipulated regarding tempo, mode, articulation (legato, staccato), pitch level, loudness, rhythm (iambic, trochaic), and certain intervals in a large number of variations. Listeners described the perceived expression by choosing first among the above-mentioned alternatives and then among sub-categories within each of them (e.g. hopeful longing, sorrowful longing). In a subsequent experiment (Rigg, 1940a), the same phrases were transposed up or down an octave, to the dominant (a fifth upwards or a fourth down-wards), a second down, and a minor second up. Shifts an octave upward made the phrase happier or less sorrowful, and vice versa. There were lesser effects of the dominant transposition, and practically no effect of the smallest transpositions. Finally, Rigg (1940b) had the same five phrases played by a pianist at six different tempos, from 60 to 160 bpm (beat = quarter-note), and found that the higher tempo, the more pleasant/happy and the less serious/sad judgements were given. However, one of the phrases, supposed to express lamentation, still sounded sad even at the highest tempo, and for another one, supposed to express sorrowful longing, there was roughly the same number of happy and sad responses at the highest tempo. Both these phrases were in minor mode and had descending minor or major seconds in the upper voice. Rigg (1964) reviewed the results obtained by Gundlach (1935), Hevner (1935a, 1936, 1937), Rigg (1937, 1939, 1940a, 1940b), and Watson (1942).

Juslin (1997, Experiment 2) used synthesized versions of 'Nobody knows the trouble I've seen', manipulating tempo (slow, medium, fast), sound level (low, medium, high), frequency spectrum (soft, bright, sharp), articulation (legato, staccato), and tone attack (slow, fast). Students rated these versions on six adjective scales: happy, sad, angry, fearful, tender, and expressive. Multiple regression analyses showed that the variance accounted for (R^2) by the manipulated factors was typically .78–.88, except for fearful (.55) and expressive (.46). Sharp spectrum (higher partials amplified) and high sound level were the most important predictors for angry; fast tempo for happy; slow tempo for sad; slow tempo, soft spectrum (higher partials attenuated), and legato articulation for tender; low sound level and staccato articulation for fearful; and legato articulation for expressive.

Peretz, Gagnon, and Bouchard (1998, Experiment 2) manipulated tempo and mode in synthesized versions of 32 excerpts of classical music, and found that these factors affected both normal listeners' and one brain-injured listener's perception of happiness and sadness in similar ways. Moreover, exposition shorter than a second was enough for reliable recognition of these expressions. In a follow-up study, Gagnon and Peretz (2003) constructed short tone sequences, manipulated their tempo and mode in various combinations, and had them judged by nonmusicians. Tempo proved to be more important than mode in influencing happy–sad judgements.

Kamenetsky, Hill, and Trehub (1997) compared listeners' ratings of emotional expression in synthesized versions of two baroque and two romantic keyboard pieces. The 'original' version with variations in both tempo and dynamics was rated as most expressive. Removing tempo variations but keeping variations in dynamics reduced expressiveness only marginally, whereas removing variation in dynamics but keeping tempo variations reduced perceived expressiveness significantly.

Schellenberg, Krysciak and Campbell (2000) selected melodies judged as representative of expression of three emotions: happy, sad, and scary. Each melody was manipulated in three different ways: (a) original pitches retained, but individual tone durations set to the same duration; (b) original tone durations retained, but all pitches set to the same pitch (the median pitch); and (c) all tones having uniform pitch and duration. Ratings were influenced more by differences in pitch than by differences in rhythm. Whenever rhythm influenced ratings, it interacted with pitch. However, effects of pitch and rhythm varied across melodies, suggesting the influence by still other factors, such as meter, note density, pitch range, melodic contour, and rhythm pattern.

Costa, Fine, and Ricci Bitti (2004) investigated interval distribution, mode, and tonal strength of melodies as predictors of perceived emotion in 51 musical excerpts. The melodies were analysed regarding interval occurrence and direction (ascending, descending). Unisons and seconds accounted for 62 per cent of all intervals, intervals from unisons up to and including fifths accounted for 85 per cent; descending seconds were more common than ascending seconds, but otherwise there were no significant differences in occurrence of ascending and descending intervals. Almost half of the melodies (47 per cent) were in minor mode, 39 per cent in major mode, and 14 per cent were atonal. Listeners rated the melodies using ten bipolar scales reflecting valence, activity, potency, and aesthetic judgement. Regression analyses showed that mode was the only significant predictor of valence. Happiness and serenity were associated with major mode. Activity (dynamism, instability) was expressed by melodies with a greater occurrence of minor seconds, tritones, and intervals larger than the octave. Potency (vigour, power) was associated with more frequent occurrences of unisons and octaves. Pleasant and agreeable melodies had clear tonality, greater occurrence of perfect fourths and minor sevenths and no or less tritones. As pointed out, however, beyond the relative occurrence of different intervals one should also study in which order the different intervals appear in the melody, further their position in relation to accented or unaccented beats in different rhythmic patterns, and still other factors.

Ilie and Thompson (2006) manipulated intensity/sound level, rate/tempo, and pitch height in phrases from eight pieces of classical music and in spoken text. Listeners judged the stimuli on bipolar scales for valence, energy arousal, and tension arousal. A distinction was thus made between energy arousal (awake–tired), and tension arousal (tense–relaxed), in accordance with Schimmack and Grob (2000). Higher intensity increased perceived energy arousal and tension arousal, and lower intensity increased valence, for both music and speech. Fast rate/tempo increased perceived energy arousal and tension arousal for music and energy arousal for speech, and slow rate increased valence for speech. Higher pitch level increased tension arousal for music and both valence and energy arousal for speech, and lower pitch level increased valence for music. Some effects were thus similar for both music and speech, others differed.

Lindström (2006) hypothesized that listeners' perception of structure and emotion would be affected by different accent structures. If important notes in a given mode (e.g. tonic, dominant, major third in major mode, minor third in minor mode) appear in accented position(s), this may increase the perceived stability as well as the perceived emotion (e.g. happiness in major mode, sadness in minor mode); if they appear in other positions, this may decrease perceived stability and emotion. Different accent structures were obtained by constructing 72 versions of *Frère Jacques*, varying in mode (major–minor), melodic direction and contour, rhythm (duration ratios between successive notes), and latent harmonic progressions. Listeners' ratings of all versions revealed both main effects of these factors as well as many complex interactions, which usually could be interpreted with reference to different accent structures in accordance with the hypothesis. Supplementing multiple regression analyses showed that accent structure was a significant predictor alongside mode, harmonic progression, and rhythm, whereas there were little or no contribution by melodic direction and contour.

Balkwill and Thompson (1999) asked two professional Hindustani musicians to perform a short *alap* (improvised opening section) from any *raga* they would choose to convey each of four emotions: joy, sadness, anger, and peace. Canadian students demonstrated successful recognition of the intended emotions, except for peace and some confusion between joy and anger and between sadness and peace. Judgements by four experts on Hindustani music showed a similar pattern. On the whole, then, Western listeners were sensitive to intended emotions in Hindustani music. Joy was associated with faster tempo and less melodic and rhythmic complexity; sadness with slower tempo and melodic and rhythmic complexity; anger with the timbre of stringed instruments; and peace with slow tempo, flute timbre, and less melodic and rhythmic complexity.

Tempo

Behne (1972) presented ten pieces of recorded music at three different tempos. With decreased tempo of the pieces, music students rated them as more serious ('*ernst*') and complaining ('*klagend*'). In another experiment, six eight-bar versions of a theme were composed to represent three different basic tempi (slow, midway, rapid) and two levels of harmonic complexity (simple, complex). Each version was then performed at five different tempi by a woodwind trio and rated by 30 subjects. The (complex) results were discussed in relation to conceived tempo, performed tempo, and to melodic and harmonic information density. Hevner's (1935b, 1937) observation that it is difficult to manipulate different factors independently of another in real music was confirmed: the two levels of harmonic complexity were not equivalent across the different tempi.

A developmental study (Dalla Bella, Peretz, Rousseau, & Goselin, 2001) indicated that sensitivity to tempo change emerges earlier than sensitivity to different modes (cf. Dalla Bella et al, in the next paragraph on mode and key).

Mode, key

Kastner and Crowder (1990) presented 12 short melodies, in major or minor mode, to 38 children from preschool and elementary school. For each presentation they were asked to choose among four pictures of faces: happy, contented, sad, and angry. All children, even the youngest (three years), showed a reliable positive–major and negative–minor association. It was not perfect, but significantly different from chance performance. In similar studies by Gerardi and Gerken (1995), Gregory, Worrall, and Sarge (1996), and Dalla Bella et al (2001), the happy–major and sad–minor association was found in children aged six to eight years, and in young adults but not in children aged three to five years. Thus, in all four studies the happy–major and sad–minor association was present in older children, whereas the results for younger children are inconclusive.

Hill, Kamenetsky, and Trehub (1996) studied which of two alternatives—salvation or condemnation—adults associated with a setting either in Ionian mode or in Phrygian mode of an early seventeenth-century melody, variously known as '*Herzlich tut mich verlangen*' (promise of salvation, reward) or '*Ach Herr, mich armen Sünder*' (fear of condemnation, punishment), both in settings by J. S. Bach. Adults as well as children judged the Ionian mode as more suitable for the 'salvation/reward' alternative and the Phrygian mode as more suitable for the 'condemnation/punishment' alternative. The fact that the Ionian mode is identical to the major mode may have contributed to its association with the 'salvation/reward' alternative.

Powell and Dibben (2005) reviewed historical and contemporary opinions on the existence of associations between certain keys and certain moods. They presented music students with two pieces of music with widely different moods, either in their original key or transposed one semitone up. The students were asked to identify the key of the respective versions of each piece and to indicate the associated moods. Most of the students had pre-conceptions of key-mood relationships in accordance with a 'sharp–flat principle'; that is, sharp keys are considered happy, bright and cheerful, flat keys mellow, romantic, sad and warm, in agreement with the mood preconceptions of eighteenth- and nineteenth-century music theorists. However, the total number of correct identification of keys was no better than would have been achieved by chance, and the moods indicated for the different versions showed no consistent differences; there was rather a considerable amount of mood agreement regardless of key shifts.

Musical form

Konečni and his co-workers (Gotlieb & Konečni, 1985; Karno & Konečni, 1992; Konečni, 1984; Konečni & Karno, 1994) demonstrated that changing the order of movements in Beethoven sonatas and string quartets, randomizing the order of variations in Bach's *Goldberg Variations*, or rearranging the order of different parts in sonata form as in the first movement of Mozart's Symphony in G minor K. 550, had little or no effects on university students' ratings on various hedonic (e.g. beautiful, pleasing) or emotion-related (e.g. exciting, emotional) scales.

Tillman and Bigand (1996) chunked three pieces by Bach, Mozart, and Schoenberg into (musically adequate) segments of about six seconds, and then played these either in original or in backward order to university students, who rated them on emotion-related scales. There were significant differences among the *pieces* in all scales but only two significant differences between the two *versions* (original vs. backward) of each piece. They concluded that for these subjects, musical expressiveness was mainly influenced by local structures within the chunks, not by global musical structure.

14.3 EFFECTS OF SEPARATE MUSICAL FACTORS

Most results from the studies reviewed above are summarized in Table 14.2. The first column contains different structural factors in alphabetical order, the second different levels within each factor, and the third column the corresponding emotional expression according to different studies. Authors' names are abbreviated to the initial two letters of the (first) author and publication year to the two last digits (e.g. He36 = Hevner, 1936); papers after 2000 have complete-year designation (e.g. Li2006 = Lindström, 2006). Studies are grouped into (A) early studies using choice among descriptive terms, (B) studies based on multivariate analyses, and (C) later experimental studies, thus offering alternative bases for interpretation of the results. As a rule, emotions are listed in decreasing order of association with the corresponding factor. Following Rigg (1964), results of the early studies (A) are described in terms of Hevner's clusters designated by Roman numbers and the adjective that Hevner used as label for each cluster (Hevner, 1936, p. 265).

14.3.1 Tempo, note density

Among factors affecting emotional expression in music, tempo is usually considered the most important (e.g. Gagnon & Peretz, 2003; Gundlach, 1935; Hevner, 1937; Juslin, 1997; Rigg, 1964; Scherer & Oshinsky, 1977). The studies listed under Tempo in Table 14.2

Table 14.2 Summary of results from reviewed studies

Factor	Levels	Emotional expression
Amplitude envelope	Round	(C) Disgust, sadness, fear, boredom, potency (Sc77), tenderness, fear, sadness (Ju97)
	Sharp	(C) Pleasantness, happiness, surprise, activity (Sc77), anger (Ju97)
Articulation	Staccato	(A) VI: Gaiety; VII: agitation (Ri39) (B) Intensity/energy/activity (We72c), gaiety (Ni82) (C) Fear, anger (Ju97)
	Legato	(A) I: Solemn; II: melancholoy, lamentation; III: longing (Ri39) (B) Softness (We72c) (C) Tenderness, sadness (Ju97)
Harmony	Simple/Consonant	(A) VI: Happy (He36, Wa42), joy (Ri39); V: graceful; IV: serene; III: dreamy (He36); I: dignified (He36, Wa42), serious (Wa42), solemn (Ri39); VIII: majestic (Wa42) (B) Gaiety, pleasantness (We72c), attraction (Ni82) (C) Tenderness (Li2006)
	Complex/Dissonant	(A) VII: Exciting (He36,Wa42), agitation (Ri39); VIII: vigorous (He36); II: sad (He36, Wa42) (B) Gloom, unpleasantness (We72c), tension (Ni82, Kr96) (C) Tension (Ni83, Kr96), fear (Kr97), anger (Li2006)
Intervals	Harmonic: Consonant Dissonant High-pitched Low-pitched	(C) Pleasant, 'non-active' (Co2000) (C) Displeasing (Ma80), unpleasant, 'active', strong (Co2000) (C) Happy, powerful (Ma80), 'activity', potency (Co2000) (C) Sad, less powerful (Ma80, Co2000)
	Melodic: Large Minor 2nd Perfect 4th, perfect 5th, major 6th, minor 7th, octave	(C) Powerful (Ma82) (C) Melancholy (Ma82) (C) Carefree (Ma82)
	Perfect 5th Octave	(C) Activity (Sm99) (C) Positive/Strong (Sm99)
Loudness	Loud	(A) VII: Excitement (Wa42), triumphant (Gu35); VI: joy (Ri39) (B) Gaiety (Ni82), intensity (We72), strength/power (Kl68), tension (Ni83, Kr96) (C) Anger (Ju97), energy arousal and tension arousal (Ilie2006)
	Soft	(A) II: Melancholy (Gu35); V: delicate (Gu35); IV: peaceful (Wa42) (B) Softness (Kl68, We72c), tenderness (Kl68), solemnity (We72c) (C) Fear, tenderness, sadness (Ju97), lower intensity, increased valence (Ilie2006)
Loudness variation	Large Small	(C) Fear (Sc77) (C) Happiness, pleasantness, activity (Sc77)
	Rapid changes	(A) V: Playful, amusing; III: pleading (Wa42) (C) Fear (Kr97)
	Few/No changes	(A) II: Sad; IV: peaceful; I: dignified, serious; VI: happy (Wa42)

Factor	Levels	Emotional expression
Melodic (pitch) range	Wide	(A) V: Whimsical; VI: glad; VII: uneasy (Gu35) (C) Fear (Kr97), Joy (Ba99), Scary (Sch2000)
	Narrow	(A) I: Dignified; II: melancholy; III: sentimental; IV: tranquil; V: delicate; VII: triumphant (Gu35) (C) Sadness (Ba99)
Melodic direction	Ascending	(A) I: Dignified; IV: serene (He36) (C) Tension (Ni83, Kr96), happiness (Ge95)
	Descending	(A) VII: Exciting; V: graceful; VIII: vigorous (He36) (C) Sadness (Ge95)
Pitch contour	Up	(C) Fear, surprise, anger, potency (Sc77), happiness (Co2001)
	Down	(C) Sadness, boredom, pleasantness (Sc77)
Melodic motion	Stepwise motion	(C) Dull melodies (Th92)
	Intervallic leaps	(C) Excitement (Th92)
	Stepwise + leaps	(C) Peacefulness (Th92)
Distribution of intervals in melodies	Minor seconds, tritones, intervals larger than the octave	(C) Activity, dynamism (Co2004)
	Unisons and octaves	(C) Potency, power, vigour (Co2004)
	Perfect fourths and minor sevenths, no or less tritones	(C) Pleasantness, agreeableness (Co2004)
Mode	Major	(A) VI: Happy (He36), joy (Ri39); V: graceful (He36); IV: serene (He36); I: solemn (Ri39) (B) Happiness (Kl68, We72c), attraction (Ni82) (C) Happiness (Sc77, Cr85, Kr97, Pe98, Gag2003, Co2004, Li2006), serenity (Co2004), tenderness (Li2006)
	Minor	(A) II: Sad (He36); lamentation (Ri39); III: dreamy; I: dignified (He36); VII: agitation (Ri39) (B) Sadness (Kl68, We72c), tension (Ni82) (C) Sadness(Cr85, Kr97, Pe98, Gag2003, Li2006), disgust, anger (Sc77)
Pause/Rest	After tonal closure	(C) Less tension
	After no tonal closure	Higher tension than after tonal closure (Ma2007)
Pitch level	High	(A) V: Graceful; IV: serene; VI: happy (He37), joy (Ri40); III: dreamy (He37), sentimental (Gu35), pleading (Wa42); VII: triumph (Ri39), exciting (Wa42) (B) Gaiety (Kl68, We72c) (C) Surprise, potency, anger, fear, activity (Sc77), happiness (Co2001), increased tension arousal (Ilie2006)
	Low	(A) II: Sad (He37, Wa42), melancholy (Gu35), lamentation (Ri40); VIII: vigorous (He37); I: dignified (He37), serious (Wa42), solemn (Ri40); VII: exciting (He37), agitation (Ri40); IV: tranquil (Gu35)

Table 14.2 Summary of results from reviewed studies (continued)

Factor	Levels	Emotional expression
		(B) Serious (Kl68), sadness, solemnity (We72c)
		(C) Boredom, pleasantness, sadness (Sc77), increased valence (Ilie2006)
Pitch variation	Large	(C) Happiness, pleasantness, activity, surprise (Sc77)
	Small	(C) Disgust, anger, fear, boredom (Sc77)
Rhythm	Regular/Smooth	(A) VI: Happiness (Wa42), glad (Gu35);
		I: serious, dignified, IV: peaceful, (Wa42); VIII: majestic (Wa42); V: Flippant(Gu35)
	Irregular/Rough	(A) V: Amusing (Wa42); VII: uneasy (Gu35)
	Complex	(C) Angry melodies (Th92), anger (Li2006)
	Varied	(C) Joyful melodies (Th92)
	Firm	(A) I: Dignified; VIII: vigorous; II: sad; VII: exciting (He36)
		(C) Sad (We72c)
	Flowing/Fluent	(A) VI: Happy; III: dreamy; V: graceful; IV: serene (He36)
		(C) Gaiety (We72c)
Tempo	Fast	(A) VII: Exciting (He37, Wa42), uneasy (Gu35) agitation, triumph (Ri40b); VI: happy, (He37, Wa42), glad (Gu35), gaiety, joy, (Ri40b); V: graceful (He37), mischievous (Wa42), whimsical, flippant (Gu35); VIII: vigorous (He37)
		(B) Happiness, pleasantness (Kl68, Mo68, We72c, Ga73, Ni82)
		(C) Activity, surprise, happiness, pleasantness, potency, fear; anger (Sc77), happiness, anger (Ju97), happiness (Th 92, Kr97, Pe98, Co2001, Gag2003), joy (Ba99), excitement (Th92), energy arousal and tension arousal (Ilie2006), activity (Co2007)
	Slow	(A) IV: Serene (He37), tranquil (Gu35); III: dreamy (He37), longing (Ri40b), sentimental (Gu35); I: dignified (He37), serious (Wa42), dignified (Gu35), solemn (Ri40b); II: sad (He37; Wa42), lamentation (Ri40b); VIII: excited (Gu35)
		(B) Sadness (Kl68, Be72, We72a, Ni82), solemnity (We72c)
		(C) Sadness, boredom, disgust (Sc77), sadness, tenderness (Ju97), sadness (Th92, Kr97, Pe98, Ba99, Gag2003), peace (Ba99)
Timbre	Few harmonics	(C) Pleasantness, boredom, happiness, sadness (Sc77)
	Many harmonics	(C) Potency, anger, disgust, fear, activity, surprise (Sc77)
	Soft	(C) Tenderness, sadness (Ju97)
	Sharp	(C) Anger (Ju97)
Tonality	Tonal	(C) In joyful, dull, peaceful melodies (Th92), pleasantness (Co2004)
	Atonal	(C) In angry melodies (Th92)
	Chromatic	(C) In sad and angry melodies (Th92)

Factor	Levels	Emotional expression
Musical form	Low complexity + average dynamism	(C) Relaxation/less tension (Ni83), joy, peace (Ba99) (B) Positive emotions (Im 79)
	High complexity (melodic/ harmonic/ rhythmic)	(C) Tension (Ni83, Kr96), sadness (Ba99)
	+ low dynamism	(B) Melancholy and depression (Im79)
	+ high dynamism	(B) Anxiety and aggressiveness (Im79)
	Repetition, condensation, sequential development etc.	(C) Increased tension (Ni83)
	End of large-scale sections	(C) Tension peaks followed by rapid decrease (Kr96)
	New musical ideas	(C) Low tension (Kr96)
	Disruption of global form	(C) Little effect (Ko84, Go85, Ka92, Ko94, Ti96)

Note: Left two columns indicate structural factor and levels within each factor, right column the associated emotional expression. Within each factor studies are grouped into (A) early studies using choice among descriptive terms, (B) studies based on multivariate analyses, and (C) later experimental studies. Authors' names are abbreviated to the initial two letters of the (first) author, publication year to the two last digits (e.g., He36 = Hevner, 1936); papers after 2000 have a complete year designation (e.g. Li2006 = Lindström, 2006). See text for further explanation.

indicate that fast tempo may be associated with various expressions of activity/excitement, happiness/joy/pleasantness, potency, surprise, flippancy/whimsicality, anger, uneasiness, and fear. Slow tempo may be associated with various expressions of calmness/serenity, peace, sadness, dignity/solemnity, tenderness, longing, boredom, and disgust. Both fast and slow tempo may thus be associated with many different expressions. Which expression is perceived in each case is dependent on the context; that is, presence and level of other structural factors. For instance, although faster tempo tends to increase perceived happiness, other factors may overrule this tendency, such as minor mode and descending seconds (e.g. Rigg, 1940; see Section 14.2.4). In terms of the valence-arousal model, fast tempo is generally associated with high(er) activation, slow tempo with low(er) activation, while both of them may be associated with either positive or negative valence.

The term tempo may not always have the same meaning, as discussed in Behne (1972), Gabrielsson (1986, 1988, 1999), and Motte-Haber (1968). Usually tempo refers to perceived pulse rate. However, sometimes the pulse may be felt at, say, half or double pace. Perceived speed may also be influenced by note density, the number of notes per unit of time (e.g. per second), as well as density of melodic or harmonic changes. Note density is usually higher in expressions of happiness, anger, and fear than in expression of sadness; see, for instance, the melodies used by Schellenberg et al (2000). Tempo and note density may sometimes be additive—fast tempo combined with high note density results in still higher activation, slow tempo combined with low note density results in still lower activation—sometimes present an ambiguous picture, such as when high note density appears in combination with slow tempo (Gabrielsson 1986, 1988).

14.3.2 Mode, key

Major mode may be associated with happiness/joy, minor mode with sadness, at least from six to eight years of age. Major mode may also be associated with expressions as graceful, serene, and solemn; minor mode also with expressions as dreamy, dignified, tension, disgust, and anger. What expression is perceived depends on the context. For instance, loud chords and high-pitched chords may suggest more happiness than soft chords and low-pitched chords, irrespective of mode. Moreover, major mode is not a necessary condition for perceived happiness; a piece in minor mode in fast tempo may very well sound happy, like the last movement, *Badinerie*, in J. S. Bach's *Second Suite for Orchestra*; see Figure 14.2. The theme in B minor with its forward-driving rhythm pattern is usually played in rapid tempo and can hardly be associated with sadness— the title itself suggests happiness (French: *badinerie*, joke). However, if the same theme would be transferred to B major, it would sound even happier (cf. Hevner, 1935b, p. 202). Using scales as stimuli, Collier and Hubbard (2001a) claimed that pitch height and direction of pitch movement (contour) may be more important than mode for expression of happiness.

While differences between fast and slow tempo are mainly associated with difference in activation, differences between major and minor mode are mainly associated with difference in valence, positive or negative. The common belief that certain keys in music are associated with certain moods has no empirical support (cf. Powell & Dibben, 2005, in Section 14.2.4).

Fig. 14.2 Beginning of 'Badinerie', in J. S. Bach's *Second Suite for Orchestra*.

14.3.3 Loudness (intensity)

Loud music may be associated with various expressions of intensity/power, excitement, tension, anger, and joy; soft music with softness, peace, tenderness, sadness,
solemnity, and fear. On the whole, loud music seems to be associated with high activation and potency, soft music with low activation and maybe submissiveness.

Large variations of intensity/loudness may suggest fear, small variations happiness
or activity. Rapid changes in intensity may be associated with playfulness, pleading
or fear, few or no changes with sadness, peace, and dignity (see also Chapter 17, this
volume).

14.3.4 Timbre

Tones with many higher harmonics may suggest potency, anger, disgust, fear, activity, or
surprise, thus usually high activation. Tones with few, low harmonics may be associated
with pleasantness, boredom, happiness, or sadness, and tones with suppressed higher
harmonics may suggest tenderness and sadness, thus usually low(er) activation.

There is no systematic research on how the timbre of different musical instruments
may influence perceived emotional expression. However, Behrens and Green (1993)
found sadness to be best expressed by singing voice or by violin, anger by timpani,
and fear by violin. With Hindustani music judged by Western listeners, Balkwill and
Thompson (1999) found stringed instruments to be associated with expression of
anger, flute with expression of peace.

14.3.5 Pitch

High pitch may be associated with expressions like happy, graceful, serene, dreamy,
and exciting, further with surprise, potency, anger, fear, and activity. Low pitch may
suggest sadness, dignity/solemnity, vigour, and excitement, further boredom and
pleasantness (such an apparent 'contradiction' may depend on the musical context).
Large pitch variation may be associated with happiness, pleasantness, activity, or surprise; small pitch variation with disgust, anger, fear, or boredom.

14.3.6 Intervals

For harmonic intervals, results concerning consonance and dissonance are similar to
the corresponding results under Harmony (see Section 14.3.8) and concerning high and
low pitch level similar to the corresponding results under Pitch (see Section 14.3.5).

Regarding melodic intervals, some results are that large intervals are perceived as
more powerful than small ones, the octave is positive and strong, and the minor second
is the most sad interval.

14.3.7 Melody

Melodic range

Wide melodic range may be associated with joy, whimsicality, uneasiness, and fear; narrow range with expressions like sad, dignified, sentimental, tranquil, delicate, and triumphant.

Melodic direction (pitch contour)

Ascending melody may be associated with dignity, serenity, tension, and happiness (but not for children; see Gerardi & Gerken, 1995), further with fear, surprise, anger, and potency. Descending melody may be associated with expressions like exciting, graceful, vigorous, and sadness (especially when combined with minor mode; Gerardi & Gerken, 1995), further with boredom and pleasantness.

However, according to Gundlach (1935), Hevner (1937), and Rigg (1939, 1964), melodic direction has no or little importance for emotional expression. Lindström (2006) found little or no general effect of melodic direction and contour, but these factors entered into several interactions with other factors (e.g. rhythm) in judgements of happiness–sadness.

Melodic motion

Stepwise motion may suggest dullness, intervallic leaps excitement; melodies for peacefulness often involve stepwise motion leading to melodic leaps (Thompson & Robitaille, 1992). Activity (dynamism, instability) may be expressed by melodies with a greater occurrence of minor seconds, tritones, and intervals larger than the octave; pleasantness by melodies with clear tonality, greater occurrence of perfect fourths and minor sevenths, and no or few tritones; potency (vigour and power) by a greater occurrence of unisons and octaves (Costa et al, 2004). It should be noted that the above results usually do not consider in what specific order the different intervals appear in the melody.

14.3.8 Harmony

Simple, consonant harmony may be associated with expressions like happy/gay, relaxed, graceful, serene, dreamy, dignified, serious, and majestic; complex and dissonant harmony with excitement, tension, vigour, anger, sadness, and unpleasantness.

14.3.9 Tonality

Melodies composed to sound joyful, dull, and peaceful were tonal, while angry melodies could be atonal. Sad and angry melodies included chromatic harmony (Thompson & Robitaille, 1992).

14.3.10 Rhythm

Regular/smooth rhythm may be perceived as expressing happiness, dignity, majesty, and peace; irregular/rough rhythm may express amusement, uneasiness, and anger; varied rhythm may express joy. Firm rhythm may be associated with expressions of sadness, dignity, and vigour, and flowing/fluent rhythm with expressions like happy/ gay, graceful, dreamy, and serene. Terminology varies among authors, which makes comparisons difficult.

14.3.11 Articulation

Staccato may be associated with gaiety, energy, activity, fear, and anger; legato with sadness, tenderness, solemnity, and softness. Articulation is usually discussed more in connection with performance (Chapter 17, this volume).

14.3.12 Amplitude envelope

This refers to the type of attack and decay of tones. Sharp envelope (rapid attack and decay) may be associated with anger, happiness, surprise, and activity; and round envelope with tenderness, sadness, fear, disgust, boredom, and potency. Shaping of amplitude envelope is usually discussed more in connection with performance (Chapter 17, this volume).

14.3.13 Pauses/rests

Perception of rests is dependent on musical context. Rests following tonal closure were identified more quickly and perceived as less tense than silences following music lacking such closure (Margulis, 2007).

14.3.14 Musical form

The influence of various aspects of musical form has been little studied. High complexity (melodic/harmonic/rhythmic) may be associated with tension or sadness; and low complexity with relaxation, joy, or peace. High complexity combined with low dynamism may express melancholy and depression; high complexity combined with high dynamism may express anxiety and aggressiveness; and low complexity and average dynamism may be associated with positive emotions (Imberty, 1979). Repetition, condensation, sequential development, and pauses may suggest increased tension. Disruption of global form (e.g. changing the order of sections or movements in a musical work) may have little effect on (unknowing) listeners' perception of expression.

14.3.15 Expression as a function of many factors

It is evident that each structural factor may influence many different emotional expressions. This means, conversely, that emotional expression in music is rarely or never exclusively determined by a single factor, but is a function of many factors. A systematic exposition of how different emotional expressions are influenced by various structural features is given in the extensive Table 26.2 in Gabrielsson and Juslin (2003).

How different factors are combined to achieve a certain expression is a complex question. Generally, factors may work independently of each other, that is, in an additive way, or interact in different ways. Several studies identified interactions 'post hoc'; for instance, mode x tempo (Rigg, 1940b), intensity x pitch height and pitch height x tempo regarding valence (Ilie & Thompson, 2006), scale direction x tempo regarding happiness (Collier & Hubbard, 2001b), and triple interaction rhythm x contour x melodic progression in ratings of happiness (Lindström, 2006); see also comments on possible interactions in Schubert (2004). However, there are only a few studies that deliberately planned to study the presence (or not) of specific interactions (e.g. Langner & Goebl, 2003; Makris & Mullet, 2003; Schellenberg et al, 2000; Webster & Weir, 2005). Webster and Weir identified several two- and three-way interactive effects of mode, texture, and tempo, furthermore interactions including gender and musical experience; however, it is not quite clear if these involved perceived emotion or felt emotion or both.

On the other hand, some results indicate that listeners are able to perceive the 'correct' expression even in excerpts lasting only one second or less (Bigand et al, 2005; Peretz et al, 1998). It also seems that, on the whole, perceived emotional expression in music is not, or only marginally, influenced by differences in gender or musical experience (e.g. Bigand et al, 2005; Fredrickson 1999, 2000; Gagnon & Peretz, 2003; Makris & Mullet, 2003; Robazza, Macaluso, & D'Urso, 1994; Wedin, 1969). However, some gender differences were reported by Costa et al (2000) regarding expression of bichords, Webster and Weir (2005) regarding the effect of mode on happy-sad ratings, Kamenetsky et al (1997; women may find music more emotionally expressive than men), and Tagg (2006) regarding male and female tunes.

14.4 EXPRESSION OF EMOTION: SUMMARY AND IMPLICATIONS

The above review shows a complex picture. Results seem most clear-cut regarding effects of tempo/speed, intensity/loudness, and timbre/spectrum: Increase in any of them results in higher activation, decrease in lower activation (by increase in timbre is meant more higher harmonics). Tempo and loudness, in particular, seem to reign over

most other factors, and generally the activation dimension seems more salient and easier to judge than the valence dimension (Gomez & Danuser, 2007; Leman, Vermeulen,
De Voogdt, Moelants, & Lesaffre, 2005; Schubert, 2004). Results regarding pitch seem
more ambiguous than those of loudness or tempo; for instance, while the effects of
fast tempo and/or high loudness are associated with high activation, high pitch may be
associated with both high and low activation, and the same is true for low pitch.

The most distinct results thus concern effects of basic variables in human audition
(loudness, timbre) and motion (tempo/speed). With regard to more typical 'musical'
variables, results are less clear and more dependent on the context; that is, presence
and level of other factors. The typical major–happy and minor–sad associations may
be modified due to influence of tempo and pitch height (Section 14.3.2) and do not
appear until the age of six to eight years. The expression of melodic intervals is little
investigated, and probably depends very much on in what tempo, in what direction
(up, down), and in what rhythmic and melodic pattern the interval appears. Studies
of melody are so far limited to melodic range and direction, while different kinds of
melodic motion—that is, the specific sequence of pitches/intervals in a melody and
their rhythmic structure—remain to be investigated. Research on harmony has
focused on the effects of consonance and dissonance, while there is practically nothing
on how different kinds of chords, harmonic progressions, or implied harmony may
affect expression.

Moreover, most factors are studied only regarding two 'extreme' levels—fast or
slow tempo, high or low pitch, loud or soft sound, ascending or descending melody,
legato or staccato articulation. Intermediate levels are usually neglected, probably on
the implicit assumption that their effects may be inferred from results at the extreme
levels. Nor are the effects of transitions from one level to another investigated, such as
crescendo or diminuendo, accelerando or ritardando, glissando, diatonicism to chromaticism, thin to thick texture, or various combinations of these factors. Practically
any piece of art music demonstrates the composer's use of such changes—abrupt or
gradual—for expressive purposes.

Many such changes can be considered as vitality affects in the sense introduced by
Daniel Stern (1985). Vitality affects refer to qualities 'captured by dynamic, kinetic
terms such as "surging", "fading away", "fleeting", "explosive", "crescendo", "decre-
scendo", "bursting", "drawn out" and so on' (p. 54), and 'abstract dance and music are
examples par excellence of the expressiveness of vitality affects' (p. 56). Gestalt psychologist Wolfgang Köhler found musical dynamic concepts as crescendo or diminuendo,
accelerando or ritardando useful to describe perceptual and emotional processes (cited
in Langer, 1957, p. 226), and Susanne Langer's views on music as expressing 'patters
of motion and rest, of tension and release, of agreement and disagreement, preparation, fulfilment, excitation, sudden change' (Langer, 1957 p. 228), 'growth and attenuation, flowing and stowing, conflict and resolution' (Langer, 1953 p. 27) come close
to Stern's concept. However, vitality affects have so far got little attention in research
on music and emotion with the notable exception of Imberty (1997, 2005, Ch. 6). It
is a challenge for continued research to refine the concept of vitality affects in relation to music—Imberty (2005) conceives them as *vecteurs dynamiques*—and develop

suitable methods to study them. As they refer to changes over time, some kind of continuous recording is necessary (Section 14.2.2); progress may also be favoured by free verbal description of perceived expression, especially during exploratory stages.

Recently, questions about musical structure and emotion have also attracted interest from researchers in other areas, such as information technology and computer science. Facing the vast music libraries that can be accessed through the Internet, there is a need to sort this mass of music into different categories, making it easier for users to find the type of music they want. Various sorting principles have been tried (see MacDorman, Ough, & Ho, 2007), such as sorting by conventional musical genres, or by acoustic similarity, or by type of emotion, which is the alternative of interest here. The goal is to achieve automatic prediction of emotion from a combination of acoustic structural cues. Leman et al (2005) compiled a database of 60 musical audio excerpts, representing many different musical genres, and explored different ways of achieving such prediction of perceived emotion, focusing on dimensions representing valence and activity. Many of the specific results were similar to those reviewed earlier in this chapter, and it was concluded that emotion attribution could partly be predicted using a combination of acoustic structural cues. So far, however, judgements of structural content by musicologists worked better than use of acoustical cues.

This type of investigation is rapidly increasing and offers many interesting possibilities for emotion research, not least the use of a much larger musical material and more musical genres than classical music, which has dominated so far. One could invite people who listen to music on the Internet to give their free descriptions of music that they find particularly expressive. This could provide a large, diversified, and ecologically valid material for analysis and various follow-up studies. Generally, free descriptions should be used more frequently in studies of musical expression, since many of music's characteristics are so variable, multi-faceted, and subtle that they can hardly be captured by having listeners choose among given adjectives or use simple rating scales. Results from studies of strong experiences with music (Chapter 20, this volume) show convincingly that free verbal descriptions can provide much more insight into people's experiences than more 'formal' methods such as questionnaires or ratings (which can be used as well).

The same study also demonstrated that choice of particularly 'strong' examples of a phenomenon provides a more comprehensive picture of the phenomenon than what can be expected from 'average' or 'mild' examples. With regard to perceived emotional expression, it may thus be preferable to use music with particularly strong and varying expressions as in, say, parts of Romantic operas or programme music, in which also the composer's expressive intentions are clear from the libretto or the written programme. (In passing it may be remarked that the influence of text/lyrics on emotional expression, in lieder, romances and many tunes in popular music, is so far a neglected area of research.)

Emotional expression in music is a central topic in music psychology. In order to further advance research in this area, we have pointed out several gaps in research that should be filled, and furthermore suggested that one should focus on vitality affects, extend the use of free verbal descriptions, examine particularly expressive music from many different genres, and take advantage of the facilities offered by the Internet.

RECOMMENDED FURTHER READING

1. Gabrielsson, A., & Juslin, P. N. (2003). Emotional expression in music. In R. J. Davidson, K. R. Scherer, & H. H. Goldsmith, (eds), *Handbook of affective sciences* (pp. 503–34). Oxford: Oxford University Press.
2. Gabrielsson, A. (2009). The relationship between musical structure and perceived expression. In S. Hallam, I. Cross, & M. Thaut (eds), *Oxford handbook of music psychology* (pp. 141–50). Oxford: Oxford University Press.
3. Imberty, M. (2005). *La musique creuse le temps. De Wagner à Boulez: Musique, psychologie, psychanalyse*. Paris, France: L'Harmattan.

REFERENCES

Balkwill, L. L., & Thompson, W. F. (1999). A cross-cultural investigation of the perception of emotion in music: Psychophysical and cultural cues. *Music Perception, 17*, 43–64.

Behne, K. E. (1972). *Der Einfluss des Tempos auf die Beurteilung von Musik* [The influence of tempo on judgement of music]. Köln, Germany: Arno Volk Verlag.

Behrens, G. A., & Green, S. B. (1993). The ability to identify emotional content of solo improvisations performed vocally and on three different instruments. *Psychology of Music, 21*, 20–33.

Bigand, E., Vieillard, S., Madurell, F., Marozeau, J., & Dacquet, A. (2005). Multidimensional scaling of emotional responses to music: The effect of musical expertise and of the duration of the excerpts. *Cognition & Emotion, 19*, 1113–39.

Cazden, N. (1979). Can verbal meanings inhere in fragments of melody? *Psychology of Music, 7*, 34–8.

Clynes, M. (1977). *Sentics: The touch of emotions*. New York: Anchor Press/Doubleday.

Clynes, M., & Nettheim, N. (1982). The living quality of music: Neurobiologic patterns of communicating feeling. In M. Clynes (ed.), *Music, mind, and brain: The neuropsychology of music* (pp. 47–82). New York: Plenum Press.

Clynes, M., & Walker, J. (1982). Neurobiologic functions of rhythm, time, and pulse in music. In M. Clynes (ed.), *Music, mind, and brain. The neuropsychology of music* (pp 171–216). New York: Plenum Press.

Collier, G. L. (2007). Beyond valence and activity in the emotional connotations of music. *Psychology of Music, 35*, 110–31.

Collier, G. L., & Hubbard, T. L. (2001a). Musical scales and evaluations of happiness and awkwardness: Effects of pitch, direction, and scale mode. *American Journal of Psychology, 114*, 355–75.

Collier, G. L., & Hubbard, T. L. (2001b). Judgements of happiness, brightness, speed and tempo change of auditory stimuli varying in pitch and tempo. *Psychomusicology, 17*, 36–55.

Cooke, D. (1959). *The language of music*. London: Oxford University Press.

Costa, M., Ricci Bitti, P. E., & Bonfiglioli, L. (2000). Psychological connotations of harmonic musical intervals. *Psychology of Music, 28*, 4–22.

Costa, M., Fine, P., & Ricci Bitti, P. E. (2004). Interval distribution, mode, and tonal strength of melodies as predictors of perceived emotion. *Music Perception, 22*, 1–14.

Crowder, R. G. (1984). Perception of the major/minor distinction: I. Historical and theoretical foundations. *Psychomusicology, 4*, 3–12.

Crowder, R. G. (1985). Perception of the major/minor distinction: III. Hedonic, musical, and affective discriminations. *Bulletin of the Psychonomic Society, 23*, 314–16.

Dalla Bella, S., Peretz, I., Rousseau, L., & Goselin, N. (2001). A developmental study of the affective value of tempo and mode in music. *Cognition, 80*, B1–B10.

Davies, S. (1994). *Musical meaning and expression*. Ithaca, NY: Cornell University Press.

Downey, J. E. (1897). A musical experiment. *American Journal of Psychology, 9*, 63–9.

Evans, P., & Schubert, E. (2008). Relationships between expressed and felt emotions in music. *Musicae Scientiae, 12*, 75–99.

Farnsworth, P. R. (1954). A study of the Hevner adjective list. *Journal of Aesthetics and Art Criticism, 13*, 97–103.

Fisk, J. (ed.). (1997). *Composers on music*. Boston, MA: Northeastern University Press.

Fredrickson, W. E. (1997). Elementary, middle, and high school student perceptions of tension in music. *Journal of Research in Music Education, 45*, 626–35.

Fredrickson, W. E. (1999). Effect of musical performance on perception of tension in Gustav Holst's First Suite in E-flat. *Journal of Research in Music Education, 47*, 44–52.

Fredrickson, W. E. (2000). Perception of tension in music: Musicians versus nonmusicians. *Journal of Music Therapy, 37*, 40–50.

Fredrickson, W. E., & Coggiola, J. C. (2003). A comparison of music majors' and nonmajors' perceptions of tension for two selections of jazz music. *Journal of Research in Music Education, 51*, 259–70.

Gabriel, C. (1978). An experimental study of Deryck Cooke's theory of music and meaning. *Psychology of Music, 6*, 13–20.

Gabriel, C. (1979). A note on comments by Nettheim and Cazden. *Psychology of Music, 7*, 39–40.

Gabrielsson, A. (1973). Adjective ratings and dimension analysis of auditory rhythm patterns. *Scandinavian Journal of Psychology, 14*, 244–60.

Gabrielsson, A. (1986). Rhythm in music. In J. R. Evans & M. Clynes (eds), *Rhythm in psychological, linguistic and musical processes* (pp. 131–67). Springfield, IL: Charles C. Thomas.

Gabrielsson, A. (1988). Timing in music performance and its relations to music experience. In J. A. Sloboda (ed.), *Generative processes in music: The psychology of performance, improvisation, and composition* (pp. 27–51). Oxford: Clarendon Press.

Gabrielsson, A. (1995). Expressive intention and performance. In R. Steinberg (ed.), *Music and the mind machine* (pp. 35–47). Heidelberg, Germany: Springer.

Gabrielsson, A. (1999). The performance of music. In D. Deutsch (ed.), *The psychology of music* (2nd edn, pp. 501–602). San Diego, CA: Academic Press.

Gabrielsson, A. (2002). Emotion perceived and emotion felt: same or different? *Musicae Scientiae, Special Issue 2001–2002*, 123–47.

Gabrielsson, A. (2003). Music performance research at the millennium. *Psychology of Music, 31*, 221–72.

Gabrielsson, A. (2005). Aspekte expressiver Gestaltung musikalischer Aufführungen. In T. S. Stoffer, & R. Oerter (eds), *Enzyklopädie der Psychologie. Musikpsychologie Bd 1. Allgemeine Musikpsychologie: Allgemeinpsychologische Grundlagen musikalischen Handels* (pp. 843–75). Göttingen, Germany: Hogrefe.

Gabrielsson, A. (2009). The relationship between musical structure and perceived expression. In S. Hallam, I. Cross, & M. Thaut (eds), *Oxford handbook of music psychology* (pp. 141–50). Oxford: Oxford University Press.

Gabrielsson, A., & Juslin, P. N. (2003). Emotional expression in music. In R. J. Davidson, K. R. Scherer, & H. H. Goldsmith, (eds), *Handbook of affective sciences* (pp. 503–34). Oxford: Oxford University Press.

Gabrielsson, A., & Lindström, E. (1995). Emotional expression in synthesizer and sentograph performance. *Psychomusicology, 14,* 94–116.

Gabrielsson, A., & Lindström, E. (2001). The influence of musical structure on emotional expression. In P. N. Juslin & J. A. Sloboda (eds), *Music and emotion: Theory and research* (pp. 223–48). Oxford: Oxford University Press.

Gagnon, L, & Peretz, I. (2003). Mode and tempo relative contributions to happy–sad judgements in equitone melodies. *Cognition & Emotion, 17,* 25–40.

Gerardi, G. M., & Gerken, L. (1995). The development of affective responses to modality and melodic contour. *Music Perception, 12,* 279–90.

Gilman, B. I. (1891). Report on an experimental test of musical expressiveness. *American Journal of Psychology, 4,* 558–76.

Gilman, B. I. (1892). Report of an experimental test of musical expressiveness (continued). *American Journal of Psychology, 5,* 42–73.

Gomez, P., & Danuser, B. (2007). Relationships between musical structure and psychophysiological measures of emotion. *Emotion, 7,* 377–87.

Gotlieb, H., & Konečni, V. J. (1985). The effects of instrumentation, playing style, and structure in the Goldberg Variations by Johann Sebastian Bach. *Music Perception, 3,* 87–102.

Gregory, A. H., Worrall, L., & Sarge, A. (1996). The development of emotional responses to music in young children. *Motivation and Emotion, 20,* 341–8.

Gundlach, R. H. (1935). Factors determining the characterization of musical phrases. *American Journal of Psychology, 47,* 624–44.

Heinlein, C. P. (1928). The affective character of the major and minor modes in music. *Journal of Comparative Psychology, 8,* 101–42.

Hevner, K. (1935a). The affective character of the major and minor modes in music. *American Journal of Psychology, 47,* 103–18.

Hevner, K. (1935b). Expression in music: A discussion of experimental studies and theories. *Psychological Review, 47,* 186–204.

Hevner, K. (1936). Experimental studies of the elements of expression in music. *American Journal of Psychology, 48,* 246–68.

Hevner, K. (1937). The affective value of pitch and tempo in music. *American Journal of Psychology, 49,* 621–30.

Hill, D. S., Kamenetsky, S. B., & Trehub, S. E. (1996). Relations among text, mode, and medium: Historical and empirical perspectives. *Music Perception, 14,* 3–21.

Huber, K. (1923). *Der Ausdruck musikalischer Elementarmotive.* Leipzig, Germany: Johann Ambrosius Barth.

Ilie, G., & Thompson, W. F. (2006). A comparison of acoustic cues in music and speech for three dimensions of affect. *Music Perception, 23,* 319–29.

Imberty, M. (1979). *Entendre la musique.* Paris, France: Dunod.

Imberty, M. (1997). Can one seriously speak of narrativity in music? In A. Gabrielsson (ed.), *Proceedings of the Third Triennial ESCOM conference, Uppsala, 7–12 June 1997* (pp. 13–22; French original text, pp. 23–32). Uppsala: Sweden: Department of Psychology.

Imberty, M. (2005). *La musique creuse le temps. De Wagner à Boulez: Musique, psychologie, psychanalyse.* Paris, France: L'Harmattan.

Juslin, P. N. (1997). Perceived emotional expression in synthesized performances of a short melody: Capturing the listener's judgment policy. *Musicae Scientiae*, 1, 225–56.

Juslin, P. N., & Laukka, P. (2004). Expression, perception, and induction of musical emotions: A review and a questionnaire study of everyday listening. *Journal of New Music Research*, 33, 217–38.

Kallinen, K., & Ravaja, N. (2006). Emotion perceived and emotion felt: Same and different. *Musicae Scientiae*, 10, 191–213.

Kamenetsky, S. B., Hill, D. S., & Trehub, S. E. (1997). Effect of tempo and dynamics on the perception of emotion in music. *Psychology of Music*, 25, 149–60.

Kaminska, Z., & Woolf, J. (2000). Melodic line and emotion: Cooke's theory revisited. *Psychology of Music*, 28, 133–53.

Karno, M., & Konečni, V. J. (1992). The effects of structural interventions in the first movement of Mozart's Symphony in G minor K. 550 on aesthetic preference. *Music Perception*, 10, 63–72.

Kastner, M. P., & Crowder, R. G. (1990). Perception of the major/minor distinction: IV. Emotional connotations in young children. *Music Perception*, 8, 189–202.

Kleinen, G. (1968). *Experimentelle Studien zum musikalischen Ausdruck* [Experimental studies on musical expression]. Hamburg, Germany: Universität Hamburg.

Konečni, V. J. (1984). Elusive effects of artists' 'messages'. In W. R. Crozier & A. J. Chapman (eds), *Cognitive processes in the perception of art* (pp. 71–93). Amsterdam, The Netherlands: North-Holland.

Konečni, V. J., & Karno, M. (1994). Empirical investigations of the hedonic and emotional effects of musical structure. *Musikpsychologie. Jahrbuch der Deutschen Gesellschaft für Musikpsychologie*, 11, 119–37.

Konečni, V. J., Brown, A., & Wanic, R. A. (2008). Comparative effects of music and recalled life-events on emotional state. *Psychology of Music*, 36, 289–308.

Krumhansl, C. L. (1996). A perceptual analysis of Mozart's Piano Sonata K. 282: Segmentation, tension, and musical ideas. *Music Perception*, 13, 401–32.

Krumhansl, C. L. (1997). An exploratory study of musical emotions and psychophysiology. *Canadian Journal of Experimental Psychology*, 51, 336–52.

Langer, S. K. (1953). *Feeling and form*. London: Routledge.

Langer, S. K. (1957). *Philosophy in a new key* (3rd edn). Cambridge, MA: Harvard University Press.

Langner J., & Goebl W. (2003). Visualizing expressive performance in tempo-loudness space. *Computer Music Journal*, 27, 69–83.

Leman, M., Vermeulen, V., De Voogdt, L., Moelants, D., & Lesaffre, M. (2005). Prediction of musical affect using a combination of acoustic structural cues. *Journal of New Music Research*, 34, 39–67.

Lerdahl, F., & Krumhansl, C. L. (2007). Modeling musical tension. *Music Perception*, 24, 329–66.

Lindström, E. (2006). Impact of melodic organization on perceived structure and emotional expression in music. *Musicae Scientiae*, 10, 85–117.

MacDorman, K. F., Ough, S., & Ho, C-C. (2007). Automatic emotion prediction of song excerpts: Index construction, algorithm design, and empirical comparison. *Journal of New Music Research*, 36, 283–301.

Madsen, C. K. (1997). Emotional responses to music. *Psychomusicology*, 16, 59–67.

Madsen, C. K. (1998). Emotion versus tension in Haydn's Symphony No. 104 as measured by the two-dimensional continuous response digital interface. *Journal of Research in Music Education*, 46, 546–54.

Madsen, C. K., & Fredrickson, W. E. (1993). The experience of musical tension: A replication of Nielsen's research using the continuous response digital interface. *Journal of Music Therapy, 30*, 46–63.

Maher, T. F. (1980). A rigorous test of the proposition that musical intervals have different psychological effects. *American Journal of Psychology, 93*, 309–27.

Maher, T. F., & Berlyne, D. E. (1982). Verbal and exploratory responses to melodic musical intervals. *Psychology of Music, 10*, 11–27.

Makris, I., & Mullet, E. (2003). Judging the pleasantness of contour-rhythm-pitch-timbre musical combinations. *American Journal of Psychology, 116*, 581–611.

Margulis, E. H. (2007). Silences in music are musical not silent: An exploratory study of context effects on the experience of musical pauses. *Music Perception, 24*, 485–506.

Motte-Haber, H. de la (1968). *Ein Beitrag zur Klassifikation musikalischer Rhythmen* [A contribution to the classification of musical rhythms]. Köln, Germany: Arno Volk Verlag.

Namba, S., Kuwano, S., Hatoh, T., & Kato, M. (1991). Assessment of musical performance by using the method of continuous judgment by selected description. *Music Perception, 8*, 251–76.

Nettheim, N. (1979). Comment on a paper by Gabriel on Cooke's theory. *Psychology of Music, 7*, 32–3.

Nielsen, F. V. (1983). *Oplevelse av musikalsk spænding [Experience of musical tension]*. Copenhagen, Denmark: Akademisk Forlag. (Includes summary in English)

Nielsen, F. V. (1987). Musical 'tension' and related concepts. In T. A. Sebeok & J. Umiker-Sebeok (eds), *The semiotic web '86. An international yearbook* (pp. 491–513). Berlin, Germany: Mouton de Gruyter.

Nielzén, S., & Cesarec, Z. (1981). On the perception of emotional meaning in music. *Psychology of Music, 9*, 17–31.

Nielzén, S., & Cesarec, Z. (1982). Emotional experience of music as a function of musical structure. *Psychology of Music, 10*, 7–17.

Osgood, C. E., Suci, G. J., & Tannenbaum, P. H. (1957). *The measurement of meaning*. Urbana, IL: University of Illinois Press.

Peretz, I., Gagnon, L., & Bouchard, B. (1998). Music and emotion: perceptual determinants, immediacy, and isolation after brain damage. *Cognition, 68*, 111–41.

Powell, J., & Dibben, N. (2005). Key-mood association: A self perpetuating myth. *Musicae Scientiae, 9*, 289–311.

Remington, N. A., Fabrigar, L. R., & Visser, P. S. (2000). Reexamining the circumplex model of affect. *Journal of Personality and Social Psychology, 79*, 286–300.

Rigg, M. G. (1937). Musical expression: An investigation of the theories of Erich Sorantin. *Journal of Experimental Psychology, 21*, 442–55.

Rigg, M. G. (1939). What features of a musical phrase have emotional suggestiveness? *Publications of the Social Science Research Council of the Oklahoma Agricultural and Mechanical College, No. 1.*

Rigg, M. G. (1940a). The effect of register and tonality upon musical mood. *Journal of Musicology, 2*, 49–61.

Rigg, M. G. (1940b). Speed as a determiner of musical mood. *Journal of Experimental Psychology, 27*, 566–71.

Rigg, M. G. (1964). The mood effects of music: A comparison of data from four investigators. *Journal of Psychology, 58*, 427–38.

Robazza, C., Macaluso, C., & D'Urso, V. (1994). Emotional reactions to music by gender, age, and expertise. *Perceptual and Motor Skills, 79*, 939–44.

Russell, J. A. (1980). A circumplex model of affect. *Journal of Personality and Social Psychology*, 39, 1161–78.

Schellenberg, E. G., Krysciak, A. M., & Campbell, R. J. (2000). Perceiving emotion in melody: Interactive effects of pitch and rhythm. *Music Perception*, 18, 155–71.

Scherer, K. R., & Oshinsky, J. S. (1977). Cue utilisation in emotion attribution from auditory stimuli. *Motivation and Emotion*, 1, 331–46.

Schimmack, U., & Grob, A. (2000). Dimensional models of core affect: A quantitative comparison by means of structural equation modeling. *European Journal of Personality*, 14, 325–45.

Schubert, E. (1999). *Measurement and time series analysis of emotion in music*. Unpublished doctoral dissertation, University of South Wales, Sydney, Australia.

Schubert, E. (2001). Continuous measurement of self-report emotional response to music. In P. N. Juslin & J. A. Sloboda (eds), *Music and emotion: Theory and research* (pp. 393–414). Oxford: Oxford University Press.

Schubert, E. (2002). Correlation analysis of continuous emotional response to music: Correcting for the effects of serial correlation. *Musicae Scientiae, Special Issue 2001–2*, 213–36.

Schubert, E. (2003). Update of the Hevner adjective checklist. *Perceptual and Motor Skills*, 96, 1117–22.

Schubert, E. (2004). Modeling perceived emotion with continuous musical features. *Music Perception*, 21, 561–85.

Sloboda, J. A. (1985). *The musical mind. The cognitive psychology of music*. Oxford: Clarendon Press.

Smith, L. D., & Williams, R. N. (1999). Children's artistic responses to musical intervals. *American Journal of Psychology*, 112, 383–410.

Stern, D. N. (1985). *The interpersonal world of the infant. A view from psychoanalysis and developmental psychology*. New York: Basic Books.

Tagg, P. (2006). Music, moving images, semiotics, and the democratic right to know. In S. Brown & U.Volgsten (eds), *Music and manipulation. On the social uses and social control of music* (pp. 163–186). New York: Berghahn Books.

Thompson, W. F., & Robitaille, B. (1992). Can composers express emotions through music? *Empirical Studies of the Arts*, 10, 79–89.

Tillman, B., & Bigand, E. (1996). Does formal musical structure affect perception of musical expressiveness? *Psychology of Music*, 24, 1–17.

Vines, B. W., Nuzzo, R. L., & Levitin, D. J. (2005). Analyzing temporal dynamics in music: Differential calculus, physics, and functional data analysis techniques. *Music Perception*, 23, 137–52.

deVries, B (1991). Assessment of the affective response to music with Clynes's sentograph. *Psychology of Music*, 19, 46–64.

Watson, K. B. (1942). The nature and measurement of musical meanings. *Psychological Monographs*, 54, 1–43.

Webster, G. D., & Weir, C. G. (2005). Emotional responses to music: Interactive effects of mode, texture, and tempo. *Motivation and Emotion*, 29, 19–39.

Wedin, L. (1969). Dimension analysis of emotional expression in music. *Swedish Journal of Musicology*, 51, 119–40.

Wedin, L. (1972a). Evaluation of a three-dimensional model of emotional expression in music. *Reports from the Psychological Laboratories, University of Stockholm, No. 349*.

Wedin, L. (1972b). Multidimensional scaling of emotional expression in music. *Swedish Journal of Musicology*, 54, 1–17.

Wedin, L. (1972c). Multidimensional study of perceptual-emotional qualities in music. *Scandinavian Journal of Psychology*, 13, 241–57.

....

CHAPTER 15

EMOTION AND MOTIVATION IN THE LIVES OF PERFORMERS

....

ROBERT H. WOODY AND GARY E. MCPHERSON

15.1 INTRODUCTION

....

IN his authoritative book *The Art of Piano Playing*, Heinrich Neuhaus (1973, p. 29) asserted:

Whoever is moved by music to the depths of his soul, and works on his instrument like one possessed, who loves music and his instrument with passion, will acquire virtuoso technique; he will be able to recreate the artistic image of the composition; he will be a performer.

Because music is often regarded as the 'language of the emotions' (Mithen, 2006, p. 24), it makes sense within this book to explore emotion in the lives of performers—those musicians who are charged with the responsibility of communicating composed or improvised music to listeners, and of doing so in the fashion described by Neuhaus above; that is, in ways that bring to life an aural experience that can be deeply emotive for themselves and for those of us who are the recipients of their efforts. Such emotional responses during the act of performing and perceiving music seem especially important given the amount of time and effort musicians invest into refining their craft, and the difficulty many have reaching the level described by Neuhaus.

The chapter begins with sections dealing with the role of emotions in everyday life and the intrinsic and emotional rewards offered by music. We then turn our attention to a number of specific aspects of emotion and music performance: the role of practice and gaining expertise, the generation of expressive performance, and the off-stage emotional issues of performers. The key messages we wish to convey are that emotions play an important part in the lives of performers, and that any explanation of the art of music performance must involve more than a description of mere technical accomplishment. In our view, a more complete account of the art of performance would include an explanation of the emotional climate in which the musician works and performs, and the array of emotions inferred in the quote cited above. The elements of this explanation and the research into these mechanisms form the basis of this chapter.

15.2 PURSUING A LIFE OF MUSICAL PERFORMANCE

Music can be one of the most personally rewarding and satisfying pastimes or careers in which a person can be actively engaged. Some of us are informed connoisseurs, while others have had a passing or periodic infatuation with music. Those of us who participate actively can do so as amateurs or as professionals. Whether one engages in music for love or for money (or both!), there is widespread agreement that music is basic to our human design and a species-wide behaviour that involves a considerable emotional component (Welch & Adams, 2003). Throughout our lives, the intrinsic appeal of music is evident in the attention infants give to music and the rhythmic movements and vocalizations they make early in life, why children engage in music informally as part of their daily play activities, how music shapes our identity during adolescence, the role of music in adult lives, and why so many choose to be involved with music more intensively by learning to play an instrument or seeking opportunities to sing with others.

15.2.1 Choosing and sustaining musical involvement

As with any domain, motivation for engaging in music involves much more than just a feeling of wanting to do it. Musicians who complain that they are 'not motivated to practise' may really be saying that it does not sound enjoyable to them, or that it does not match the mood they are in at that particular moment. Yet they may still decide to practise in spite of this feeling, knowing they may feel a sense of accomplishment or satisfaction with themselves afterward. Obviously, there are reasons for behaviour other than an immediate emotional reward. Yet the connection between motivation and emotion is strong (Lewis & Sullivan, 2005; Welch & Adams, 2003). People's feelings about themselves and others affect their beliefs and perceptions about the activities they choose to undertake, and are an inescapable source of their motivation. This is particularly important in a domain such as music, where personal feelings have such a powerful effect on one's overall sense of well-being and social identity (McPherson & McCormick, 2006).

Emotional and aesthetic rewards of music making

The capacity of music to evoke emotions is no doubt a primary reason—perhaps *the main reason*—that people listen to music. Because listening to music always precedes performing it in a musician's development, it is likely the two activities share underlying motives. Based on his research, Persson (2001) asserted that musicians pursue performance primarily from a *hedonic* motive; that is 'a means to generate positive emotional experiences mostly for one's own satisfaction' (p. 277). If hearing a beautiful melody is pleasing, it seems that being able to perform it oneself can be an even more powerful experience.

Some emotional reactions to music can be extremely powerful and influential in a person's life. Humanistic psychologist Abraham Maslow coined the term 'peak experiences' to describe intensely emotional experiences (Maslow, 1968). Maslow and others who extended his work devoted specific attention to the power of music to evoke states of ecstasy in people (Panzarella, 1980). More recent work by Sloboda (1990, 1991, 1998) and Gabrielsson (Chapter 20, this volume) has provided insight into the nature of these experiences with music. When young children have peak experiences with music, it serves as a motivational 'hook' to further their engagement with music. Participants in Sloboda's (1990) study reported having such experiences as young as seven years old, often describing them as significant in determining the course of their musical lives from that point on.

Emotional peak experiences can result from active participation in a musical experience, but can also come from the perspective of an observer and still be highly motivating toward performance. Interestingly, Sloboda found that the context of the experience (e.g. physical setting, social dynamics) is as important as, if not more so than, the musical content itself. A good example can be seen in classical guitarist Andrés Segovia's childhood account of seeing a strolling flamenco guitar player:

At the first flourish, more noise than music burst from the strings and, as if it had happened yesterday, I remember my fright at this explosion of sounds . . . rearing from the impact, I fell over backward. However, when he scratched out some of those variations he said were *soleares*, I felt them inside of me as if they had penetrated through every pore of my body.

(Segovia, 1976, p. 3)

Once young people begin pursuing increased music participation for themselves, they soon discover the emotional rewards of performance. Music making, whether alone or with others, has the potential to be an absorbing experience. A self-rewarding feeling of *flow* can be attained when people are so engaged in an activity that they lose self-consciousness, feel a merging of awareness and action, and even lose track of time (Csikszentmihalyi, 1990; see also Chapter 20, this volume). Achieving flow depends on a balance between a person's skill level and the challenge presented in a task. If one's skill exceeds the challenge, the result is boredom; if the challenge exceeds one's skill, feelings of anxiety result. Either case leads to diminished motivation and emotional engagement for pursuing the activity. Music making offers the potential for flow to people of all ages. For example, Custodero (2002) found that musical flow experiences in early childhood tend to occur with active multi-sensory involvement, presented in a socially playful or game-like context. Flow experiences are also important in older music students' emotional well-being and securing their commitment to future musical involvement (Fritz & Avsec, 2007; O'Neill, 1999; Chapter 28, this volume).

Performing for an audience seems to offer particularly heightened emotional rewards beyond those of music making (Bailey & Davidson, 2005). These may explain why a person seeks to make music the focus of a career, as opposed to following the path of a music enthusiast or amateur, although it is undoubtedly true also that playing music for the sheer love of it can add a dimension to one's life that is deeply satisfying: the kind of 'loving play' that Booth (1999) distinguishes as the mark of a true performer whose engagement with music adds value to the quality of life lived while doing it.

While some have argued that decisions about becoming a performer typically occur as a result of social praise blended with a degree of exhibitionist impulses (e.g. Persson, 2001), and that these factors are often more pronounced in solo rather than ensemble participation (Davidson, 2002), as we will see in sections to follow, a deep connection with music both emotionally and intellectually provides the foundation from which an individual may choose to embark on an active, lifelong involvement with music.

Emotional connection with others

Much research has documented the motivational role of other people in musicians' development. Adults contribute much in the way of resources to music students, such as parents paying for an instrument and lessons, and teachers offering instruction and performance opportunities (Davidson, Howe, Moore, & Sloboda, 1996; Davidson, Sloboda, & Howe, 1996; Davidson, Sloboda, Moore, & Howe, 1998). Of course, these people are also key contributors of emotional support. Young students are more likely to continue in music if they have a parent who not only monitors their practice, but also helps them cope with the emotional difficulties that come with learning an instrument (McPherson, 2009; McPherson & Davidson, 2002). These attributes are also important in a child's connection with his or her early teachers, given evidence that high-achieving music students tend to describe their first teachers as warm, encouraging, and fun to be with (Davidson et al, 1998).

Usually when young musicians enter adolescence, they begin looking to their peers more and more. The social influence of musical peers lasts well into adulthood. Membership in a music group, be it a school ensemble or a peer-organized 'garage band', can provide a sense of belonging needed for a musician's identity development. The lives of some young people may be so occupied with music that they find it difficult to relate to non-musical peers (Burland & Davidson, 2002; Davidson et al, 1996). The simple camaraderie experienced in a music group may be no different than that found on teams and clubs organized around other activities. However, the act of group music making may be unique in its opportunity for introspection and catharsis, perhaps adding to the emotional connection members feels with one another (Bailey & Davidson, 2002, 2005).

Of course, relationships between co-performers take time to develop and are not always marked by positive feelings. The social processes of a group are largely determined by the roles assumed by members. Larger ensembles with a designated leader, say a teacher or conductor, may not face as many interpersonal challenges during rehearsal, but still have the potential for conflict among members competing for status within the group. This is particularly evident when musical comparisons are made during the process of auditioning for a chair or stand placement in an ensemble. Smaller groups with no official authority structure undergo a 'working out' of roles as they address issues of musical coordination (timing, intonation) and performer idiosyncrasies. Successful cohesive groups tend to show characteristics of both individual leadership and democratic process (Allsup, 2003; Ford & Davidson, 2003). Members who do not like their roles with a particular group, or who do not feel valued by the others, are likely to end their involvement. The moods of individual musicians do affect a group's overall dynamic and the musical progress it will make (King, 2006). Even in a large ensemble led by a conductor, a positive group mood can be a prerequisite to enhancing ensemble performance quality (Boerner & Von Streit, 2007).

To summarize, musicians develop very close relationships with others as members of a group. The personal connections they feel with each other can add to the music-induced emotions experienced in their group activities (see Bakker, 2005, for a study of how flow experiences cross over from music teachers to their students). Group emotional experiences can be most intense during moments of performance. For example, Sawyer (2006) offered an account of the *group flow* phenomenon that occurs as jazz performers interact with one another around elements of structure and improvisation. Drawing largely from Berliner (1994), Sawyer quotes musicians who compare the 'emotional empathy' of group performance to 'lovemaking', a 'high', and 'ecstasy' (pp. 158–9). It is also noteworthy that musicians' chief mechanisms for communicating with each other during performance, eye contact and bodily gesture, are primary and natural ways that human beings express emotion (Bastien & Hostager, 1988; Poggi, 2002; Williamon & Davidson, 2002).

Nowhere are these attributes more evident than in the role of a conductor (Price & Byo, 2002). For example, one of the most famous conductors of the Berlin Philharmonic Orchestra, Wilhelm Furtwängler, has been described as a 'formidable magician, a man capable of setting an entire ensemble of musicians on fire, sending them into a state of ecstasy' (Eschenbach, no date). Such reflections highlight the level of emotional engagement demanded during rehearsals and performances of high-quality music, plus also the intense relationships that develop between members of professional ensembles whose careers depend on achieving a consistent level of excellence of a type and intensity that are rare in other disciplines.

Dropout and burnout

Unfortunately, the emotional effects of music participation are not always positive. Just as some children have peak experiences that launch them into a lifetime of music making, others experience traumatic events centred on music involvement. These may produce feelings of anxiety and humiliation, which essentially preclude any future active participation in music (Sloboda, 1990). Even barring any such extreme episode, a young person's choice whether to continue in music is influenced by many factors. Among these, people's perceptions of themselves (e.g. their abilities and temperament) and their beliefs about the nature and value of music, are informed by the emotions they experience while engaging in music (Austin et al, 2006).

Sadly, children whose musical involvement yields feelings of boredom, guilt, or shame will probably discontinue it before attaining any appreciable level of performing ability. In contrast, relatively high-achieving students may ultimately end their music involvement without the proper emotional elements in their development. Research by Moore, Burland, and Davidson (2003) suggests that young musicians who do not enjoy positive social contact with musical peers are susceptible to 'burnout'. Instead of connecting with and drawing emotional support from peers, some students find themselves part of a 'conservatory culture' characterized by heavy criticism and competition among musicians (Kingsbury, 1988). Such an atmosphere can detract from students' intrinsic enjoyment of music, including their capacity to experience musical flow or other heightened states of emotional engagement (O'Neill, 1999).

15.2.2 Emotional motivation to practise

The positive socio-emotional effects of music making can be so rewarding that people are able to attain a level of music performance competency primarily through group activities. Many popular (or vernacular) musicians acquire their skills outside any formal context whatsoever. Green (2001) detailed the learning processes of these performers, pointing out the differences between them and the practice normally carried out by formally trained musicians. The sessions of popular musicians tended to include songs and 'riffs' (i.e. short repetitive phrases) that they wanted to learn (as opposed to exercises and literature assigned by teachers), and were often undertaken in a group setting with peers instead of isolated individual practice sessions. Despite investing much time and effort in this learning process, vernacular musicians are resistant to calling it 'practice', perhaps because they perceive it as voluntary, enjoyable, and what they love to do.

In contrast, a majority of formally trained 'classical' musicians acquire their skills through participation in school-based ensembles (as in the United States), or through the tutelage of a one-to-one private instructor (as in the United Kingdom and most parts of Europe). One negative consequence of formal training is that so few students, especially in the beginning stages of development, experience their musical practice as an enjoyable activity, and certainly not in the way that Green's sample of popular musicians described in her study. For example, in the beginning stages of learning an instrument, students typically spend most of their practice time simply playing through pieces from beginning to end, without any real evidence that they are either emotionally committed to improving their performance or intellectually curious about the pieces they are learning (McPherson & Davidson, 2006; McPherson & Renwick, 2001). Some suggest that this is because they have not developed appropriate internal representations of the piece they are learning and may even be unaware they are making mistakes (Barrry & Hallam, 2002). Others such as Bamberger (2006) suggest that young learners are often unable to focus on 'structurally meaningful entities such as motives, figures, and phrases' (Bamberger, 1996, p. 42) or on the intimate ways of knowing (figures, felt paths, context, and function) which allow them to experience heightened feelings of emotional engagement as they learn to play. Either way, it seems a pity that the music education profession is so poorly equipped with knowledge that explains more precisely how some students become intellectually curious and emotionally engaged in the repertoire they are studying, in contrast to others who display neither of these attributes during their practice.

Renwick and McPherson (2002) provide a description of a highly efficient practice session of the type that is rarely seen in young music learners. Their analyses of videotapes of a young clarinetist's practice shows quite convincingly how little this musician (Clarissa) was emotionally engaged when practising literature assigned by her teacher, in distinct contrast to her efforts to learn a piece that she wanted to learn herself, and where the efficiency of her practice was markedly superior. During her practice of teacher-assigned repertoire, Clarissa showed little if any emotional engagement in the pieces she was learning. However, for the piece she was driven to learn herself, Clarissa was able to scaffold herself to a much higher level of functioning, as evidenced in the more varied strategies (e.g. silent fingerings, thinking, singing) she employed while practising. Most of all, the young learner's body language was more positive in this session, and she looked and sounded quite different from when she was learning her teacher-assigned repertoire.

The desire to learn by seeking to master new challenges of the type described above is considered an integral part of intrinsic motivation in *self-determination theory* (Deci & Ryan, 1985; Ryan & Deci, 2000). Applying this theory to music suggests that musicians' practising often begins as an extrinsically motivated activity (e.g. when another musician demonstrates or provides an exemplary model of the piece and how it should be played), before evolving into an intrinsically motivated desire. As people invest themselves more in something, they go beyond the initial level of *external regulation* (i.e. pure extrinsic motivation) to reach *introjected regulation*. Here, developing musicians are in part led to practice as they link it with the emotional rewards of social approval or the avoidance of personal feelings of guilt. Further internalization occurs in approaching the next level, *identified regulation*, in which 'behaviour is guided by a conscious valuing of the activity, such as when a committed young musician practises technical exercises that are far from being inherently pleasurable, but valued for their beneficial effect on technique' (Austin, Renwick, & McPherson, 2007, p. 225). At the final level of *integrated regulation*, a musician's performance activities have become such a significant part of his or her identity that practising becomes more or less second nature.

On the road to reaching high levels of intrinsic motivation, three basic psychological needs—competence, autonomy, relatedness—come into play (Deci & Ryan, 2000; McPherson, 2009). First, when musicians perceive themselves as competent, they are more likely to engage in music at a higher level and utilize the skills and strategies they possess, in addition to persisting when they confront difficulties. Second, people have a basic need to feel autonomous, and to make independent choices about their own learning and level of engagement. As shown in the case study of the young learner described above, autonomy is related to musicians' level of intellectual curiosity and emotional engagement while they are learning and performing. Finally, people have a deep desire to feel related to others. High levels of intrinsic motivation occur when the emotional climate of the musical environment is supportive, caring, and non-threatening.

The findings outlined above have contrasted both 'formal' and 'informal' aspects of practice. In formal learning settings such as individual tuition on an instrument, both seem to be important. For example, Sloboda and Davidson (1996), in their study involving 257 school-aged students, found that high-achieving musicians tended to do significantly greater amounts of 'formal' practice, such as scales, pieces, and technical exercises, than their less successful peers. In this study, high achievers were also likely to report more 'informal' practice, such as playing their favourite pieces by ear or improvising. These 'informal' ways of practising seem to enable higher-achieving students to find the right balance between freedom and discipline in their practice (see also McPherson & Davidson, 2006; McPherson & McCormick, 1999).

To summarize then, although practice may not always be considered an enjoyable or aesthetically pleasing activity, it still offers indirect emotional reward. In the best scenario, musicians learn to see practice as a puzzle to be solved, or a challenge to be taken on. They may thrive on the prospect of learning something new and discovering the means of accomplishing it, especially in situations where they possess a strong desire to learn the piece themselves. Additionally, one's self-monitoring in practice does not end at detecting errors, but further involves devising strategies to correct them. Whereas some music students may be deterred from practice because of the temporary performance failures encountered, others seek the emotional rewards of overcoming the challenges presented.

Dweck (2000) described these two contrasting motivational patterns as *helpless-oriented* and *mastery-oriented*. Students with a helpless orientation tend to experience more negative emotions when faced with musical problems, and as a result are more likely to eventually give up on their musical pursuits (O'Neill, 1997; O'Neill & Sloboda, 1997). In contrast, a mastery-oriented musician shows a pattern of persistence and can even enjoy the challenge posed by learning a new skill. This suggests *not* that successful musicians must live without emotional reinforcement, but rather that in some situations they need to learn to appreciate delayed gratification.

15.3 EMOTIONS IN GENERATING PERFORMANCE

The emotional aspects of music can be considerably different with a public performance, as opposed to performing in an informal setting. As detailed above, musicians can draw emotional rewards from the simple act of engaging in an artistic or aesthetic endeavour. They can also enjoy the social rewards of collaborating with other musicians or informally interacting with people in a musical way. Public performance, however, introduces the potential for more intense experiences for performers. The added emotions can make performance an even more satisfying activity for musicians, or become a distracting force that undermines their enjoyment of music making.

Successful performers learn to manage their emotions before and during performances. First and foremost, they are able to mentally and physically execute the music on their instrument or voice. Not only do they want to eliminate negative emotions that will interfere (e.g. performance anxiety), but they will also need to find an emotional state for themselves that actually enhances their performance (Williamon, 2004). Especially in a public performance, musicians' moods and emotional states can affect how well they can focus on a performance task at hand, recall what they have practised, and physically execute the motor skills needed (recall the discussion of *flow* in section 15.2.1). Beyond this, performers need to also consider the experience of the audience, and communicate their own emotional intentions into a performance that will evoke an emotional response from listeners. In this regard, newly emerging evidence is starting to define the types of brain activation of performers during solo memorized (Parsons, Sergent, Hodges, & Fox, 2005) and improvised performances (Brown et al, 2008), to reveal more precisely the extent to which performers who give the appearance of being engaged emotionally in music are in fact actually emotionally committed. Such research has the potential to shape future thinking about the process of musical performance and how performers can project more vivid interpretations of the music they are performing for their audience.

15.3.1 Preparing for a performance

There are numerous factors that determine a musician's mental preparations for public performance, as well as the mindset possessed upon entering the stage. Some factors relate to musicians' general beliefs about music and their basic enjoyment of singing or playing their instruments. Added to this, however, are other social and self-image factors. People's attitudes about themselves and others can greatly affect how they feel when putting themselves 'on display'. In some cases, the emotions surrounding a performance are marked by fear and worry, such that a musician who otherwise loves music and enjoys making it will avoid doing it before an audience. Kenny (Chapter 16, this volume) explores this phenomenon in depth, specifically identifying how musicians' negative emotions contribute to performance anxiety and how addressing them is involved in treatment.

The presence of an audience introduces yet another emotional factor in a performer's music making. As suggested earlier, most people initially pursue music performance for hedonic (i.e. emotionally self-satisfying) motives, and their involvement is further reinforced by emotional connections with other musicians. Public performance requires musicians to consider the emotions of the audience and the task of affecting them through music. This can, of course, divert performers' attention from what they can control to what they cannot. In large part, successful management of emotions prior to performance hinges on musicians being able to focus their attention on the musical tasks at hand.

The prospect of an upcoming public performance can be exciting. For many musicians, the very thought of it acts as a 'call to action' to their autonomic nervous systems, resulting in physiological arousal. In the case of performance anxiety, the autonomic arousal constitutes a 'fight or flight' defence mechanism, reflecting a musician's perception of a performance situation as a threat. But not all physiological arousal is detrimental to performance. There is a level of optimal arousal that enhances the performance quality (Lehmann, Sloboda, & Woody, 2007; Wilson & Roland, 2002; see also Chapter 16, this volume). The mental and physical demands of music performance require some degree of physiological readiness, although the exact level can vary greatly according to the nature of the performance task.

Autonomic arousal is obviously involved in the experience of emotion (see Chapter 11, this volume). Although musicians may notice the physical symptoms (e.g. racing heartbeat, muscle tension) mostly right before and during a performance, the cognitive symptoms can manifest themselves days or weeks beforehand. These have the potential to interfere with musicians' emotional well-being during performance preparations, not to mention their ability to focus on expressive musical aspects during practice. Because over-arousal is a common pre-performance issue for musicians, Connolly and Williamon (2004) recommended that relaxation exercises be a part of mental skills development. They additionally documented the benefits of mental rehearsal and visualization techniques in music performance training. The ultimate purpose of such approaches is to enable a musician to 'guide oneself consistently into a calm, focused, flexible, goal-oriented state of mind' (p. 241).

This suggests that during performance preparations, musicians' emotional energies should be focused on the emotions involved in the music making, as opposed to the emotions surrounding the performance and its consequences. This is not always easy for musicians to do, after enjoying the applause and praise following previous performance successes. Whether a performer's focus is on the musical task or the socio-emotional rewards of success relates to goal orientation toward performance (Maehr, Pintrich, & Linnenbrink, 2002). People whose goals are *task involved* see practice sessions as opportunities to build toward self-set standards; they see performances as special 'check points' or demonstrations of the new skills they wanted to acquire. In contrast, musicians with *ego-involved* goals see their skill development as a contributor to their social status; keeping in mind that they (and their musical skills) are being judged by others, they see performances as opportunities for positive recognition or embarrassment. Of course, most musicians' performance goals are neither *purely* task nor ego involved. It is simply human for people to care about what others think of them. The use of these categories, however, may prompt musicians to examine the focus of their attention during performance preparations. While neither goal orientation promises to deliver a more successful public performance, each seems to offer a different emotional experience for the musicians involved.

Other research suggests that ego involvement—at least some form of it—is a constructive part of the emotional experiences of performers. A belief in one's musical ability is considered a key ingredient to performance success. *Self-efficacy* is the 'conviction that one can successfully execute the behavior required to produce the outcome' (Bandura, 1997, p. 79). Research in music education has shown self-efficacy to be highly predictive of performance achievement (McCormick & McPherson, 2003; McPherson & McCormick, 2006). For a performer, as compared to say an amateur musician, the ultimate task is not just making music, but doing it for an audience. They believe not only in their ability to play or sing well, but in their ability to do it 'in the spotlight'. In many cases, performers actively seek opportunities to do this, largely because of the great emotional rewards of public performance. To describe this performer mentality, Davidson (2002) drew upon her own experiences as a solo classical singer, explaining, 'I feel positive about going on stage and presenting myself to an audience. I do it for the challenge and the thrill of the situation, coupled with a love of music' (p. 98). So whether performers are driven to express a musical message that is important to them (task-involved goal), or impress others with their skills (ego-involved), they must have utmost confidence in their own abilities and want to share these with an audience.

In the moments prior to taking the stage, performers can experience a great deal of physiological arousal that, if left unchecked, can undermine the confidence built over the course of their preparations. To deal with this, some musicians develop pre-performance routines that allow them to arrive at an ideal mental and emotional state at concert's start (Partington, 1995). Perhaps several days in advance, performers begin paying closer attention to their physical health (e.g. nutrition, sleep) and increasing their use of relaxation and visualization techniques. In the minutes just before performance, it is common for musicians to try to create a mood that is fitting to express the music they are about to play.

15.3.2 Approaches to expressivity

Eliminating negative emotions and other hindrances to performance is only half the battle. Most would agree that a performer's ultimate goal is to produce music that engenders an emotional response from listeners. Musicians face the task of infusing the pitches and rhythms of their music performance with expressive qualities that communicate their own feelings or emotional ideas (see Chapter 17, this volume). Additionally, those in the Western classical tradition are expected to understand and realize in their performance (i.e. 'be true to') the expressive intentions of the composer. Of course, any musical message or performer feelings will not be received by the audience unless they are manifested as acoustic properties and, in the case of a live performance, visual cues. As described below, musicians go about doing this in a variety of ways.

Self-induced felt emotion

Many musicians strive to make their performances expressive through no strategic or technical means, but by focusing on their own felt emotion while performing

(Laukka, 2004; Lindström, Juslin, Bresin, & Williamon, 2003). In what Persson (2001) called *mood induction*, a performer may consciously recall specific personal memories in order to experience emotions (while performing) appropriate for the music. It is a common belief among many musicians that a performance is not truly expressive unless the performers themselves actually *feel* the emotions they intend to communicate in their music. Classical composer C.P. E. Bach asserted, 'A musician cannot move others unless he too is moved' (Bach, 1778/1985, as cited in Persson, 2001). Within this approach to expressivity, not only is performer-felt emotion required, it is solely sufficient for producing an expressive performance. Musicians may object to attention to acoustic sound properties or advanced planning of expressive devices (e.g. crescendos, ritardandos) for fear of their performances sounding contrived or uninspired. The college musicians in a study by Woody (2000) talked of learning to 'feel the music' and 'use your soul', in order to avoid 'simulating' expressivity by merely manipulating elements like tempo and dynamics (see also Lindström et al, 2003).

When musicians simply focus their mental energies on 'mustering up' felt emotions, how does that affect their performance? First, there is the possibility that their performance actually is *not* affected, that their *expectations* bias their perception (Repp, 1992; Woody, 2002b). In other words, because they intend to be expressive, they believe they hear it in their performances. It is also possible that the expressive features in their performances are automatically applied conventions of 'musicality', rather than the result of felt emotion (Woody, 2003). Expressive conventions such as 'tapering the phrase' are so ingrained in advanced musicians that they perform them unintentionally (and in fact, are often unable to suppress them).

This is not to say, however, that emotion-induced musical expression is merely a myth. Clearly, emotion affects psychological and physical functioning, which in turn can shape musical behaviour and sound. In everyday life, human beings naturally— and in some cases universally—express emotions in their facial countenance, body carriage, and voice usage. Important examples are the mother–child interactions during the first months after birth, which possess a music-like rhythmic and melodic quality. Malloch (2000) describes these interactions as *communicative musicality*, because they entail 'dance-like' gestures involving vocalizations, facial expressions, and bodily movements. In a similar vein, Trehub and Trainor (1998) describe how mothers will sing play songs to create a unique performance style that projects positive feelings to their infant (see also Chapter 23, this volume).

In musical performances, physical manifestations can affect production aspects of music performance, which include (depending on musical instrument) stroke technique, embouchure, breath support, and vocalization. An obvious example is the jazz musician whose vocalizing includes moans and sighs as she 'sings the blues'. In fact, it is likely that the acoustic cues of musical expression are generally informed by human vocal expression of emotion (Juslin, 1997; Juslin & Laukka, 2003; see Chapter 17, this volume). Of course, live performance also allows an audience to see musicians' facial and bodily demonstrations of felt emotion. A wealth of research by Jane Davidson and colleagues shows that such physical gestures tend to coincide with performers' intentions for musical expression, and that these visual cues may in some instances be more communicative to audience members than the sound properties (e.g. Davidson, 1993, 2005; Davidson & Correia, 2002).

It is unlikely, however, that any performer relies solely on felt emotion in generating musical expression. There is a developmental process by which young musicians acquire the skill of translating their own emotional experience into expressive sound cues that would be perceived by listeners. Based on their review of research at the time, Sloboda and Davidson (1996) proposed that performers develop their emotional 'intuition' through a process of expressive trial and error. In trying out a variety of interpretations of, say, a particular melody, a musician monitors his or her own emotional reaction to the sound. This kind of emotional monitoring also often takes place as a music student works closely with a teacher and hears expert performance models provided. Research shows that one-to-one private instruction is a primary means by which music students acquire expressive performance skills (Woody, 2000, 2003), and that aural modeling is a popular approach used therein (Laukka, 2004; Lindström et al, 2003). Within this context students learn to link emotional terminology with producible sound possibilities on their instruments. During the process, music students' well-developed emotional reactivity may aid their building a repertoire of musical expressions of emotions. Instead of having to remember vast amounts of aural performance information, they can abstract it into more manageable 'extramusical templates' based on familiar emotional expressions or gestures (Sloboda, 1996). For example, it may be easier for a performer to memorize an image of an ocean wave swelling and crashing on the shore, as opposed to the equivalent timing and loudness qualities of an accelerando–crescendo combination.

Imagery and metaphor

Musicians often bring to mind imagery in order to evoke emotions for performance. Using what Persson (2001) calls *visualization*, a performer might conjure up a powerful visual image (e.g. a frightened child), or imagine being involved in an emotional scenario (e.g. hearing of a loved one's death). Many music teachers are firm advocates of this approach, and regularly offer instruction to students in the form of metaphors and imagery examples (e.g. Karlsson & Juslin, 2008; Lindström et al, 2003; Woody, 2000). While most experienced musicians seem to be able to accommodate this approach (Sheldon, 2004; Woody, 2006b), it is not without the potential for problems. If a teacher's imagery examples are perceived as too vague or unfamiliar, misunderstandings result (Karlsson & Juslin, 2008). At worst, teachers risk confusing and discouraging students if they are unable to relate to the imagery offered (Persson, 1996).

This calls to question exactly what happens in the mind of musicians when presented with an imagery example. Woody (2006a) provided imagery examples to college instrumentalists, who then reported their thoughts while working up expressive performances. At issue was whether the musician used an 'intuitive' felt-emotion approach, or utilized a cognitive strategy of translating the imagery into an explicit plan for the sound properties of performance. The results showed that both broad approaches were used. For example, one imagery example in the study (offered for a Schubert melody) was 'Bouncy and happy; rustic, as if you're a happy peasant, with no cares or worries, strolling along, singing a song'. One participant, identified as using a felt-emotion approach, prepared his performance only by thinking 'Light, free . . . happy thoughts', and further personalized the image, reporting, 'I'm reminded of walking out of the gymnasium after receiving my diploma from high school' (p. 131). In contrast, a different musician reported thinking, '. . . a bouncy feel, but making a line out of it. I put a crescendo through the first four eighth notes, slurred the first two sixteenth notes to give them something' (p. 131).

Most interesting in the study was the finding that a purely felt-emotion approach tended to be used by the least and most experienced musicians. Those musicians in the middle range of experience tended to use the cognitive translation process. Their explicit attention to sound properties such as loudness, tempo, and articulation may represent a 'bridge' between the naïve use of felt emotion (which may or may not result in perceptible expressivity) and the most advanced musicians' use of the approach, which has essentially automatized the cognitive translation process. In other words, experienced musicians develop a repertoire of performance-directed emotions. By mentally dwelling on an imagery example and the evoked emotion, they have access to appropriate expressive performance devices stored in memory. This theory brings to mind Sloboda's (1996) notion of 'extramusical templates' mentioned above.

In all likelihood, a felt-emotion approach to performance occurs in conjunction with other approaches to expressivity. As musicians develop, they hear many imagery examples, experience emotional responses to expert aural models, and learn conventions for expressive properties like loudness, tempo, and articulation. Through all these sources, a musician's own emotional reactivity may be key. In a discussion of how aural modeling and mental imagery interact, Davidson (1989) suggested that a 'metaphor creates an affective state within which the performer can attempt to match the model' (p. 95). The *mood congruency* theory of memory indicates that cognitive function is affected by emotional experience. Specifically, information encoded while in a particular mood is most readily recalled and conveyed later while in the same mood (Waterman, 1996). Houston and Haddock (2007) found that that memory for music is enhanced by being in a mood (positive versus negative) that matches the valence of music being worked with (major versus minor). Thus, if musicians have a memory of a performance that evoked an emotional response in them, such as of a teacher or admired professional performer, they are best able to bring that model to mind (in order to guide their own performance) if they put themselves in the right mood (see also Woody, 2000).

15.4 PERSONAL FACTORS AND PERFORMER EMOTION

Given the uniqueness of a performing musician's activities, one might wonder if it takes a particular kind of person to succeed as a performer. Given the integral role of emotion in music performance, one might also wonder about the types of emotional

problems musicians typically encounter as a result of their lifestyle. These two facets
are discussed below.

15.4.1 Personality traits

Many research studies have examined the personality traits of musicians, and based
on their results, it is safe to say there is no single 'performer personality'. It is possible, however, to identify some connections and tendencies within the personalities of
musicians. Kemp (1996) offered the most comprehensive look at this topic, and is the
main source of what follows in this section.

There is some evidence that musicians have an anxious disposition in general. This
trait anxiety, probably the product of both biological and environmental factors, may be
especially common among classical musicians. There are two correlates of trait anxiety
that provide insight into musicians of this type. First, *perfectionism* is a characteristic
defined by unrealistically high expectations. This is not the admirable quality of having high performance standards, but an irrational concern about minor mistakes and
inconsistencies. It is easy to see how some musicians may take on this attribute, given the
amount of time spent in rehearsals and individual practice, where a primary activity is the
identification of errors. Second, musicians tend to score high in measures of *neuroticism*,
or emotional instability. In some respect, this trait also makes sense for musicians, who
often rely on a great breadth of felt emotions to guide their performance expressivity.
Neuroticism is often manifested in mood swings and strained personal relationships.

The trait anxiety of classical musicians bears similarity to social anxiety (Chapter 16,
this volume). This is related to their tendency for higher levels of introversion. Introverts
naturally keep their feelings to themselves, and tend to be independent and self-
sufficient. Considering the hours of isolated practice expected of classical performers,
this could be viewed as an adaptive trait. Even the expressive performance conventions in
classical music are relatively reserved (compared to other styles), dealing with nuances of
sound and formal stage etiquette. In contrast, popular musicians tend to be extroverted,
and more comfortable in social environments. This too would be facilitative of their performing style, marked by demonstrative musical effects and physical movements.

Musicians also tend to score high in measures of sensitivity, imagination, and intuition.
Taken together, these characteristics help performers tap into the symbolic and emotional
aspects of music. This general quality is particularly interesting when combined with the
introversion of many classical musicians. The result is that 'musicians often conceal the
very thing that motivates them most highly, thus obscuring their raison d'être and rendering them somewhat enigmatic to others, particularly of another type' (Kemp, 1996, p. 84).

15.4.2 Emotional problems

While the emotional intensity of musicians can contribute to performance, it can also
make them susceptible to problems in their personal lives. Research has shown that

some musicians experience high levels of occupational stress. The distinctive challenges and conditions of a music career can make it especially difficult for them to detach themselves from their work (Spahn, Strukely, & Lehmann, 2004). It is possible to identify a number of common sources of stress (James, 2000; Sternbach, 1995; Wills & Cooper, 1988). Perhaps foremost is the general employment insecurity and financial strain that some performers face. As an outgrowth, they may struggle to find time for practice while balancing the demands of work and personal commitments. Difficulties with marriage and family relationships can result, which themselves amount to additional sources of stress. Time-related stressors also include the late hours of some performance 'gigs', the extended rehearsals that sometimes precede them, and the time spent travelling to and from. As mentioned earlier, some rehearsal environments are marked by much musical criticism and interpersonal conflicts with co-performers.

Stress can be particularly problematic for musicians as it can physically impair their performance. Emotional stress is usually manifested in the body as excessive muscle tension, which presents an added danger to instrumentalists already at risk of overuse injuries. It can also be an aggravating factor in musicians' development of focal dystonia, a condition of involuntary muscular contraction and incoordination (Jabusch & Altenmüller, 2004). Such problems can lead to a vicious circle, as physical impediments to performance cause additional stress. Moreover, sometimes the only solution is a complete stoppage of performing (including practice), a course of action that many musicians are unable or unwilling to take.

The most serious emotional problems experienced by musicians are mood disorders. While it is difficult to establish whether musicians are at greater risk of these, it has been suggested that careers in the arts, as opposed to other more regulated professions, are more inclusive of emotionally unstable people (Ludwig, 1995). The most common mood disorder is *depression*, which is characterized by extended periods of overwhelming sadness. Although there has not been a great deal of research on the incidence of depression among musicians, surveys studies suggest that approximately 20 per cent of musicians suffer from depression (Brodsky, 1995; Raeburn, 2000). Substance abuse is a frequent symptom of depression, and may be a unique problem for musicians. Drug and alcohol use may actually be valued within some musicians' social environments and readily available where they perform. Although the exact prevalence of abuse is unclear, some believe the problem is widespread among certain populations of musicians (Chesky & Hipple, 1999; Raeburn, 2000).

The rarer *bipolar disorder* involves alternations between heightened moods, called manic episodes, and periods of major depression (this disorder was previously referred to as 'manic-depression' among mental health professions). In manic episodes, people experience intense feelings of euphoria, and sometimes a frenetic drive to plan and accomplish grandiose things. A number of eminent composers and music performers have been identified as bipolar, producing much debate about a relationship between 'genius and madness', such as in the case of Robert Schumann whose emotional problems have been documented and discussed at considerable length (Slater & Meyer, 1959; Weisberg, 1994). Another example is Gustav Mahler, who rather famously consulted with Sigmund Freud about his own psychological problems. Research has focused on the question of whether the elevated mood of bipolar disorder coincides with increased creative productivity among artists (including musicians). For example, Jamison (1993) presented biographical and scientific evidence of a 'vastly disproportionate rate' of mood disorders among artists, compared to the general population (p. 5). It is unlikely, however, that extreme moods or a hypersensitivity to emotion facilitates artistic creativity. Instead, mood elevation may be conducive to several psychological factors of creativity, such as an ability to generate many and varied ideas, an openness to new approaches, and stronger self-confidence and persistence (Kinney & Richards, 2007).

Clearly, the life of a performing musician can be emotionally demanding. The work-related and personal stressors may be exacerbated by the prominent role of felt emotion in a performer's day-to-day activities. It is unclear to what extent musicians avail themselves of proper resources for dealing with emotional problems. In a study of health problems among conservatoire students, Williamon and Thompson (2006) found that these musicians most often consulted their instrumental teachers for psychological (and physical health-related) advice, over medical practitioners. It is likely that most musicians would benefit from increased awareness of potential mental health risks and strategies for prevention (Sataloff, Brandfonbrener, & Lederman, 1998).

15.5 CONCLUSION

We began our chapter with a quote by Neuhaus describing the intense emotional commitment required for performance at the highest levels, which we then used to frame this survey of emotion in the lives of performers. Overall, we organized the content of the chapter in terms of the emotions involved during the act of making music, as compared to the emotional reactions that performers experience during everyday life and in their communication with others more generally.

For young, developing musicians, there is clear evidence that the emotional climate in which learning takes place is of critical importance. In formal contexts, early teachers tend to be more successful when they provide a learning environment that is warm and encouraging, and emotionally supportive. Likewise, in early through to advanced stages of development, we know also that learners are best placed to progress if their practice balances playing to improve with playing for pleasure. This feature is a distinguishing characteristic of highly skilled musicians who have typically learned to 'focus more on the pleasurable aspects of practice (e.g. phrasing, dynamics, expressiveness, etc.) and less on the taxing requirements of skill acquisition that challenge less experienced players' (Williamon & Valentine, 1998, p. 327).

Musicians whose performances focus on informal contexts such as pop groups or jazz ensembles often develop very close bonds with their peers that can add to the music-induced emotions they experience individually and collectively. We cited examples of the group flow that occurs in jazz ensembles, but that would be typical also of all other types of ensembles, where the emotional empathy within the group's performance can be as intense to them as making love and feeling high. Importantly also, we showed that the primary and most natural ways that humans express emotion is through eye contact and bodily gestures, which are features of all performance, be it solo or ensemble. All of this can go wrong however, when musicians do not like their roles within the group or do not feel valued by others. Many successful ensembles become stale and eventually break up because the emotional climate in which they perform is fraught with negative in-fighting within the group that ultimately impacts on the level of commitment and time individual members are willing to invest in continuing their participation.

In all forms of musical exposure and interaction, two ingredients seem especially important to explaining the intense and deeply personal ways in which music shapes performers' lives: intellectual curiosity and emotional engagement. When these two ingredients are blended together, we see powerful examples of efficient and effective musical practice and performance, such as our examples of children whose practice is highly efficient (e.g. Clarissa, reported earlier), and also in the many descriptions of expert musicians we have described throughout this chapter.

At the uppermost extremities, something very special happens in the life of the most outstanding performers, something that Michael Tilson Thomas (2008) expressed eloquently in his reflection on fellow conductor Leonard Bernstein:

His conception of a performance was that it should reveal the emotional states that the composer had experienced as the work was created. For him, that meant being totally emotionally
and physically involved. It was compulsive! He felt he wasn't really doing his best unless he
was swaying on the precipice of his endurance. Whether he was conducting Mahler or playing a Haydn trio it was the same; oceans of sweat, fluttering eyes, hyper-reactive athleticism.
He'd get a bemused far-away look that seemed to gaze off beyond the horizon into the spirit
of the music itself. It was extreme, but he'd been like this for such a long time no one noticed
anything strange about it. It's what they expected. But, make no mistake. None of this was
put on. It was his authentic essential experience of music and of life. It couldn't be otherwise.
Whatever he had to do to achieve it, maintain it, he did. The public loved it, understanding it
was all part of the supreme sacrifice of himself he was making for them.

All of the above helps frame an understanding of the role emotions—both positive and negative—play in the lives of performers. In closing however, it would be remiss of us not to emphasize how little research there is on this topic, and how much more needs to be done to provide real evidence of the range of factors, situations, and contexts in which emotions either hinder or enhance music making. Unlike other areas of music, the research base on this topic is not extensive, and there is much we need to do in order to extend current knowledge. In our opinion, many fruitful options remain to be explored, such as parallels in other areas of the performing arts where similar discussions attempt to understand the role of emotion in the lives of actors and danc-ers. Noice and Noice (2006) for example, suggest that the 'affect of an actor during performance is highly complex and includes feelings of both the actor-as-character and actor-as-actor' (p. 495). They describe how many actors report using emotional events outside the theatre 'to feed into and color their performances' (p. 495), and use the example of the 'avowedly technical "anti-method" actor', Laurence Olivier, whom they quote as stating that acting is 'an emotional problem. You've got to feel it, a great test for the imagination' (p. 495).

In a similar manner to the studies on actors described by Noice and Noice, our profession's finest musicians do not always give emotionally moving performances every time they appear on stage, and such fluctuations are not easily attributed to training, experience, motivation or practice, but are part of the 'mystery of artistic endeavour' (p. 501). Explaining these mysteries in the performing arts will not only entail a great deal more research, but also require distinctly different interdisciplinary approaches than researchers have incorporated into their research to date. We look forward to following the discussions about this topic as they evolve further during the years ahead.

Recommended further reading

1. Austin, J., Renwick, J., & McPherson, G. E. (2006). Developing motivation. In G. E McPherson (ed.), *The child as musician: A handbook of musical development* (pp. 213–238). Oxford: Oxford University Press.
2. Williamon, A. (ed.). (2004). *Musical excellence: Strategies and techniques to enhance performance.* Oxford, UK: Oxford University Press. (See in particular chapters 1, 4, and 12.)
3. Woody, R. H. (2006). Musicians' cognitive processing of imagery-based instructions for expressive performance. *Journal of Research in Music Education, 54,* 125–137.

References

Allsup, R. E. (2003). Mutual learning and democratic action in instrumental music education. *Journal of Research in Music Education, 51,* 24–37.

Austin, J., Renwick, J., & McPherson, G. E. (2006). Developing motivation. In G. E. McPherson (ed.), *The child as musician: A handbook of musical development* (pp. 213–38). Oxford: Oxford University Press.

Bach, C. P. E. (1985). *Essay on the true art of playing keyboard instruments* (W. J. Mitchell, ed. and trans.). London: Eulenburg Books. (Originally published 1778)

Bailey, B. A., & Davidson, J. W. (2005). Effects of group singing and performance for marginalized and middle-class singers. *Psychology of Music, 33,* 269–303.

Bakker, A. B. (2005). Flow among music teachers and their students: The crossover of peak experiences. *Journal of Vocational Behavior, 66,* 26–44.

Bandura, A. (1997). *Self-efficacy: The exercise of control.* New York: W. H Freeman and Company.

Barry, N., & Hallam, S. (2001). Practice. In R. Parncutt & G. E. McPherson (eds), *The science and psychology of music performance: Creative strategies for teaching and learning* (pp. 151–66). Oxford: Oxford University Press.

Bastien, D. T., & Hostager, T.J. (1988). Jazz as a process of organizational innovation. *Communication Research, 15,* 582–602.

Berliner, P. (1994). *Thinking in jazz: The infinite art of improvisation*. Chicago. IL: University of Chicago Press.

Boerner, S., & Von Streit, C. F. (2007). Promoting orchestral performance: The interplay between musicians' mood and a conductor's leadership style. *Psychology of Music, 35,* 132–43.

Booth, W. (1999). *For the love of it: Amateuring and its rivals*. Chicago, IL: The University of Chicago Press.

Brodsky, M. (1995). Blues musicians' access to health care. *Medical Problems of Performing Artists, 10,* 18–23.

Brown, S., Martinez, M. J., & Parsons, L. M. (2006). Music and language side by side in the brain: A PET study of generating melodies and sentences. *European Journal of Neuroscience, 23,* 2791–2803.

Burland, K, & Davidson, J. W. (2002). Training the talented. *Music Education Research, 4,* 121–40.

Chesky, K., & Hipple, J. (1999). Musicians' perceptions of widespread drug use among musicians. *Medical Problems of Performing Artists, 14,* 187–95.

Connolly, C., & Williamon, A. (2004). Mental skills training. In A. Williamon (ed.), *Musical excellence: Strategies and techniques to enhance performance* (pp. 221–45). Oxford: Oxford University Press.

Custodero, L. A. (2002). Seeking challenge, finding skill: Flow experience and music education. *Arts Education Policy Review, 103,* 3–9.

Davidson, J. W. (1993). Visual perception of performance manner in the movements of solo musicians. *Psychology of Music, 21,* 103–13.

Davidson, J. W. (2002). The solo performer's identity. In R. MacDonald, D. J. Hargreaves, & D. Miell (eds), *Musical identities* (pp. 97–113). Oxford: Oxford University Press.

Davidson, J. W. (2005). Bodily communication in musical performance. In D. Miell, R. MacDonald, & D. J. Hargreaves (eds), *Musical communication* (pp. 215–37). Oxford: Oxford University Press.

Davidson, J. W., & Correia, J. S. (2002). In R. Parncutt & G. E. McPherson (eds), *The science and psychology of music performance: Creative strategies for teaching and learning* (pp. 237–50). Oxford: Oxford University Press.

Davidson, J. W., Howe, M. J. A., Moore, D. G., & Sloboda, J. A. (1996). The role of parental influences in the development of musical performance. *British Journal of Developmental Psychology, 14,* 399–412.

Davidson, J. W., Sloboda, J. A., & Howe, M. J. A. (1996). The role of parents and teachers in the success and failure of instrumental learners. *Bulletin of the Council for Research in Music Education, 127,* 40–44.

Davidson, J. W., Sloboda, J. A., Moore, D. G., & Howe, M. J. A. (1998). Characteristics of music teachers and the progress of young instrumentalists. *Journal of Research in Music Education, 46,* 141–60.

Davidson, L. (1989). Observing a yang ch'in lesson: Learning by modeling and metaphor. *Journal of Aesthetic Education, 23,* 85–99.

Deci, E. L, & Ryan, R. M. (1985). *Intrinsic motivation and self-determination in human behavior*. New York: Plenum.

Deci, E. L., & Ryan, R. M. (2000). The 'what' and 'why' of goal pursuits: Human needs and the self-determination of behavior. *Psychological Inquiry, 11,* 227–68.

Dweck, C. S. (2000). *Self-theories: Their role in motivation, personality and development*. Philadelphia, PA: Psychology Press.

Eschenbach, C. (no date). Biography and photos. Retrieved from Christoph Eschenbach's web page: http://www.christoph-eschenbach.com/index.php?lid=en&cid=2.2&pid=2

Ford, L., & Davidson, J. W. (2003). An investigation of members' roles in wind quintets. *Psychology of Music*, *31*, 53–74.

Fritz, B. S., & Avsec, A. (2007). The experience of flow and subjective well-being of music students. *Horizons of Psychology*, *16*, 5–17.

Green, L. (2001). *How popular musicians learn: A way ahead for music education*. Aldershot, UK: Ashgate.

Hallam, S. (1997). Approaches to instrumental music practice of experts and novices. In H. Jørgensen & A. C. Lehmann (eds), *Does practice make perfect? Current theory and research on instrumental music practice* (pp. 89–107). Oslo, Norway: Norges musikkhøgskole.

Houston, D., & Haddock, G. (2007). On auditing auditory information: The influence of mood on memory for music. *Psychology of Music*, *35*, 201–12.

Jabusch, H., & Altenmüller, E. (2004). Anxiety as an aggravating factor during onset of focal dystonia in musicians. *Medical Problems of Performing Artists*, *19*, 75–81.

James, I. M. (2000). Survey of orchestras. In R. Tubiana & P. C. Amadio (eds), *Medical problems of the instrumentalist musician* (pp. 195–201). London: Martin Dunitz.

Jamison, K. R. (1993). *Touched with fire: Manic depressive illness and the artistic temperament*. New York: Simon and Schuster.

Jørgensen, H. (2004). Strategies for individual practice. In A. Williamon (ed.), *Musical excellence: Strategies and techniques to enhance performance* (pp. 85–104). Oxford: Oxford University Press.

Juslin, P. N. (1997). Emotional communication in music performance: A functionalist perspective and some data. *Music Perception*, *14*, 383–418.

Juslin, P. N., & Laukka, P. (2003). Communication of emotions in vocal expression and music performance: Different channels, same code? *Psychological Bulletin*, *129*, 770–814.

Karlsson, J., & Juslin, P. N. (2008). Musical expression: An observational study of instrumental teaching. *Psychology of Music*, *36*, 309–34.

Kemp, A. E. (1996). *The musical temperament: Psychology and personality of musicians*. Oxford: Oxford University Press.

King, E. C. (2006). The roles of student musicians in quartet rehearsals. *Psychology of Music*, *34*, 262–82.

Kinney, D. K., & Richards, R. L. (2007). Artistic creativity and affective disorders: Are they connected? In C. Martindale, P. Locher, & V. M. Petrov (eds), *Evolutionary and neurocognitive approaches to aesthetics, creativity and the arts* (pp. 225–37). Amityville, NY: Baywood Publishing Company.

Laukka, P. (2004). Instrumental music teachers' views on expressivity: A report from music conservatoires. *Music Education Research*, *6*, 45–56.

Lehmann, A. C., Sloboda, J. A., & Woody, R. H. (2007). *Psychology for musicians: Understanding and acquiring the skills*. Oxford: Oxford University Press.

Lewis, M., & Sullivan, M. W. (2005). The development of self-conscious emotions. In A. J. Elliot & C. S. Dweck (eds), *Handbook of competence and motivation* (pp. 185–201). New York: Guilford Press.

Limb, C. J., & Braun, A. R. (2008). Substrates of spontaneous musical performance: An fMRI study of jazz improvisation. *PLoS One*, *3*, 1–9, e1679.

Lindström, E., Juslin, P. N., Bresin, R., & Williamon, A. (2003). 'Expressivity comes from within your soul': A questionnaire study of music students' perspectives on expressivity. *Research Studies in Music Education*, *20*, 23–47.

Ludwig, A. M. (1995). *The price of greatness: Resolving the creativity and madness controversy*. New York: Guilford.

Maehr, M. L., Pintrich, P. R., & Linnenbrink, E. A. (2002). Motivation and achievement. In R. Colwell & C. Richardson (eds), *The new handbook of research on music teaching and learning* (pp. 348–72). Oxford: Oxford University Press.

Malloch, S. (2000). Mothers and infants and communicative musicality. *Musicæ Scientiæ, Special Issue 1999–2000*, 29–57.

Maslow, A. H. (1968). *Toward a psychology of being* (2nd edn). New York: Van Nostrand Reinhold.

McCormick, J., & McPherson, G. E. (2003). The role of self-efficacy in a musical performance examination: An exploratory structural equation analysis. *Psychology of Music, 31*, 37–51.

McPherson, G. E. (2009). The role of parents in children's musical development. *Psychology of Music, 37*, 91–110.

McPherson, G. E., & Davidson, J. W. (2002). Musical practice: Mother and child interactions during the first year of learning an instrument. *Music Education Research, 4*, 141–56.

McPherson, G. E., & McCormick, J. (2006). Self-efficacy and music performance. *Psychology of Music, 34*, 322–66.

McPherson, G. E., & Renwick, J. M. (2001). A longitudinal study of self-regulation in children's musical practice. *Music Education Research, 3*, 169–86.

Mithen, S. (2006). *The singing neanderthals: The origins of music, language, mind, and body.* Cambridge, MA: Harvard University Press.

Neuhaus, H. (1973). *The art of piano playing* (K. A. Leibovitch, trans.). London: Barrie & Jenkins.

Noice, H., & Noice, T. (2006). Artistic performance: Acting, ballet, and contemporary dance. In K. A. Ericsson, N. Charness, P. J. Feltovich, & R. R. Hoffman (eds), *The Cambridge handbook of expertise and expert performance* (pp. 489–503). Cambridge, UK: Cambridge University Press.

O'Neill, S. A. (1997). The role of practice in children's early musical performance achievement. In H. Jørgensen & A. C. Lehmann (eds), *Does practice make perfect: Current theory and research on instrumental music practice* (pp. 53–70). Oslo, Norway: Norges musikkhøgskole.

O'Neill, S. A. (1999). Flow theory and the development of musical performance skills. *Bulletin of the Council for Research in Music Education, 141*, 129–34.

O'Neill, S. A., & Sloboda, J. A. (1997). The effects of failure on children's ability to perform a musical test. *Psychology of Music, 25*, 18–34.

Panzarella, R. (1980). The phenomenology of aesthetic peak experiences. *Journal of Humanistic Psychology, 20*, 69–85.

Parsons, L. M., Sergent, J., Hodges, D. A., & Fox, P. T. (2005). Brain basis of piano performance. *Neuropsychologia, 43*, 199–215.

Persson, R. S. (2001). The subjective world of the performer. In P. N. Juslin & J. A. Sloboda (eds), *Music and emotion: Theory and research* (pp. 275–89). Oxford: Oxford University Press.

Persson, R. (1996). Brilliant performers as teachers: A case study of commonsense teaching in a conservatoire setting. *International Journal of Music Education, 28*, 25–36.

Poggi, I. (2002). The lexicon of the conductor's face. In P. McKevitt, S. O. Nualláin, & C. Mulvihill (eds), *Language, vision and music: Selected papers form the 8th International Workshop on the Cognitive Science of Natural Language Processing, Galway, Ireland 1999* (pp. 271–84). Amsterdam, The Netherlands: John Benjamins.

Price, H., & Byo, J. M. (2002). Rehearsing and conducting. In R. Parncutt & G. E. McPherson (eds), *The science and psychology of music performance: Creative strategies for teaching and learning* (pp. 335–52). Oxford: Oxford University Press.

Raeburn, S. (2000). Psychological issues and treatment strategies in popular musicians: A review: Part 2. *Medical Problems of Performing Artists, 15*, 6–17.

Renwick, J. M., & McPherson, G. E. (2002). Interest and choice: Student-selected repertoire and its effect on practising behaviour. *British Journal of Music Education*, 19, 173–88.

Repp, B. H. (1992). A constraint on the expressive timing of a melodic gesture: Evidence from performance and aesthetic judgment. *Music Perception*, 10, 221–42.

Ryan, R. M., & Deci, E. L. (2000). Self-determination theory and the facilitation of intrinsic motivation, social development, and well-being. *American Psychologist*, 55, 68–78.

Sawyer, R. K. (2006). Group creativity: Musical performance and collaboration. *Psychology of Music*, 34, 148–65.

Sataloff, R. T., Brandfonbrener, A. G., & Lederman, R. J. (1998). *Performing arts medicine* (2nd edn). San Diego, CA: Singular.

Segovia, A. (1976). *Andrés Segovia: an autobiography of the years 1893–1920* (W. F. O'Brien, trans.). New York: Macmillan.

Shavinina, L. V. (in press). When child prodigies, unique representations, and the extracognitive combine: Toward a cognitive-developmental theory of giftedness. In L. V. Shavinina (ed.), *The international handbook on giftedness*. Amsterdam, The Netherlands: Springer Science & Business Media.

Sheldon, D. A. (2004). Listeners' identification of musical expression through figurative language and musical terminology. *Journal of Research in Music Education*, 52, 357–68.

Slater, E., & Meyer, A. (1959). Contributions to a pathography of the musicians: Robert Schumann. *Confinia Psychiatrica*, 2, 65–94.

Sloboda, J. A. (1998). Does music mean anything? *Musicae Scientiae*, 2, 21–31.

Sloboda, J. A. (1990). Music as language. In F. R. Wilson & F. L. Roehmann (eds), *Music and child development: The biology of music making* (pp. 28–43). St. Louis, MO: MMB Music.

Sloboda, J. A. (1991). Music structure and emotional response: Some empirical findings. *Psychology of Music*, 19, 110–20.

Sloboda, J. A. (1996). The acquisition of musical performance expertise: Deconstructing the 'talent' account of individual differences in musical expressivity. In K. A. Ericsson (ed.), *The road to excellence: The acquisition of expert performance in the arts and sciences, sports and games* (pp. 107–26). Mahwah, NJ: Erlbaum.

Sloboda, J. A., & Davidson, J. W. (1996). The young performing musician. In I. Deliège & J. A. Sloboda (eds), *Musical beginnings: Origins and development of musical competence* (pp. 171–90). Oxford: Oxford University Press.

Smiley, P. A., & Dweck, C. S. (1994). Individual differences in achievement goals among young children. *Child Development*, 65, 1723–43.

Spahn, C., Strukely, S., & Lehmann, A. (2004). Health conditions, attitudes toward study, and attitudes toward health at the beginning of university study: Music students in comparison with other student populations. *Medical Problems of Performing Musicians*, 19, 26–33.

Sternbach, D. J. (1995). Musicians: A neglected working population in crisis. In S. L. Sauter & L R. Murphy (eds), *Organizational risk factors for job stress* (pp. 283–302). Washington, DC: American Psychological Association.

Tilson Thomas, M. (2008). *Being Leonard Bernstein*. Retrieved September 21, 2008 from http://michaeltilsonthomas.com/press/

Trehub, S. E., & Trainor, L. (1998). Singing to infants: Lullabies and play songs. In C. Rovee-Collier, L. P. Lipsitt, & H. Hayne (eds), *Advances in Infancy Research: Vol. 12* (pp. 43–77). Stamford, CT: Ablex.

Trehub, S. E. (2006). Infants as musical connoisseurs. In G. E. McPherson (ed.), *The child as musician: A handbook of musical development* (pp. 33–50). Oxford: Oxford University Press.

Vandervert, L. R. (2007). Cognitive functions of the cerebellum explain how Ericsson's deliberate practice produces giftedness. *High Ability Studies*, 18, 89–92.

Vandervert, L. R., & Liu, H. (in press). How working memory and the cognitive cerebellum collaboratively produce the child prodigy. In L. V. Shavinina (ed.), *The international handbook of giftedness*. Amsterdam, The Netherlands: Springer Science & Business Media.

Weisberg, R. W. (1994). Genius and madness? A quasi-experimental test of the hypothesis that manic-depression increases creativity. *Psychological Science, 5*, 361–7.

Welch, G., & Adam, P. (2003). *How is music learning celebrated and developed? A professional user review of UK and related international research undertaken by the British Educational Research Association*. Southwell, UK: British Educational Research Association.

Williamon, A. (2004). A guide to enhancing musical performance. In A. Williamon (ed.), *Musical excellence: Strategies and techniques to enhance performance* (pp. 3–18). Oxford: Oxford University Press.

Williamon, A., & Davidson, J. W. (2002). Exploring co-performer communication. *Musicae Scientiae, 6*, 53–72.

Williamon, A., & Thompson, S. (2006). Awareness and incidence of health problems among conservatoire students. *Psychology of Music, 34*, 411–30.

Williamon, A., & Valentine, E. (1998). 'Practice makes perfect': The effects of piece and ability level on performance preparation. In S. W. Yi (ed.), *Proceedings of the 5th International Conference on Music Perception and Cognition, August, 1998* (pp. 323–8). Seoul, South Korea: Seoul National University.

Wills, G., & Cooper, C. L. (1988). *Pressure sensitive: Popular musicians under stress*. London: Sage.

Wilson, G. D., & Roland, D. (2002). Performance anxiety. In R. Parncutt & G. E. McPherson (ed.), *The science and psychology of music: Creative strategies for teaching and learning* (pp. 47–61). Oxford: Oxford University Press.

Winner, E. (1996). *Gifted children: Myths and realities*. New York: Basic Books.

Woody, R. H. (2000). Learning expressivity in music performance: An exploratory study. *Research Studies in Music Education, 14*, 14–23.

Woody, R. H. (2002a). Emotion, imagery and metaphor in the acquisition of musical performance skill. *Music Education Research, 4*, 213–24.

Woody, R. H. (2002b). The relationship between musicians' expectations and their perception of expressive features in an aural model. *Research Studies in Music Education, 18*, 53–61.

Woody, R. H. (2003). Explaining expressive performance: Component cognitive skills in an aural modeling task. *Journal of Research in Music Education, 51*, 51–63.

Woody, R. H. (2006a). Musician's cognitive processing of imagery-based instructions for expressive performance. *Journal of Research in Music Education, 54*, 125–37.

Woody, R. H. (2006b). The effect of various instructional conditions on expressive music performance. *Journal of Research in Music Education, 54*, 21–36.

CHAPTER 16

THE ROLE OF NEGATIVE EMOTIONS IN PERFORMANCE ANXIETY

DIANNA T. KENNY

Most of the research on anxiety in general (Beck & Clark, 1997; Mandler, 1984; Spielberger, 1985) and music performance anxiety in particular (Kenny, 2005, 2006) has emphasised the etiological role of faulty cognitions in both adult (Papageorgi, Hallam, & Welch, 2007) and adolescent musicians (Kenny & Osborne, 2006; Osborne, Kenny, & Cooksey, 2007). Cognitive and cognitive-behavioural therapies, focused on modifying faulty cognitions and the consequent problematic behaviours to which they give rise, have been developed in the past three decades (Butler, Chapman, Forman, & Beck, 2006; Kenny, 2005; Lazarus & Abramovitz, 2004; Turkington, Dudley, Warman, & Beck, 2006) and are widely considered to be the treatment of choice for both the anxiety disorders in general (Rodebaugh, Holaway, & Heimberg, 2004) and for performance anxiety in particular (Kenny, 2005). Empirical work to date indicates that combinations of cognitive and behavioural approaches show the best outcomes for these conditions, although sufferers are rarely 'cured' (Kenny, 2005; Kenny, Osborne, & Cooksey, 2007). There are few texts in which explicit discussion regarding the role of the *emotions* in the aetiology and maintenance of music performance anxiety (MPA) occurs, or whether emotions should be specifically targeted in treatment.

The aim of this chapter, therefore, is to elucidate the role of (negative) emotions, with a primary focus on anxiety, in music making, their role in the experience of music performance anxiety, and how theorizing in this area may be enhanced by affording emotions a central role in our conceptualization of music performance anxiety. Prior to embarking on this challenge, we need to understand the relationship between emotion, cognition, and anxiety.

16.1 EMOTION, COGNITION, AND ANXIETY

Once viewed as separate disciplines, recent formulations of cognition and emotion now acknowledge that 'the neural circuitry of emotion and cognition interact from early perception to decision making and reasoning' (Phelps, 2006, p. 28). Originating in a neurobiological system, emotion is a multi-component process, including our subjective experience of affect (i.e. feeling states such as happiness, anger, and surprise), a set of expressive behaviours (i.e. innate patterns of responding such as facial expression and bodily postures), and cognitive appraisal (i.e. how events are perceived and interpreted may determine the type and intensity of the emotional response) (Barlow, 2002; Lazarus, 1984, 1991a).

Cognitive appraisal is a complex process that in a music performance context involves assessment of the demands of the performance, the personal resources that can be accessed to meet the demands, the possible consequences of the performance, and the meaning of those consequences to the musician (Smith, Maragos, & van Dyke, 2000). In the two illustrations in Figure 16.1, the cognitive appraisal of the task was such that performance demands were (subjectively) minimized, hence requiring very few personal resources. The conductor and percussionist would experience very low performance anxiety until, perhaps, they were confronted with the consequences of their performance by their fellow musicians and their likely expulsion from their ensembles!

Early theories asserted that anxiety was primarily a cognitive process in which danger is exaggerated, misperceived, or misinterpreted (see e.g. Beck & Clark, 1997; Mandler, 1984; Spielberger, 1985). These theories state that anxiety is experienced primarily as a result of distorted cognitions that arise from faulty information processing that triggers inappropriate motor, physiological, and affective responses. More recent formulations of anxiety and the anxiety disorders give primacy to emotion: 'Common to the anxiety disorders is the *emotion of anxiety* [author's emphasis] and associated cognitions related to present and future threat of harm, physiological arousal when confronted with anxiety-relevant stimuli and behavioural tendencies to escape from or avoid anxiety triggers and to prevent anticipated harm' (p. 1788) (Cahill & Foa, 2006).

Izard (1993) has attempted an integrative theory of emotion involving four subsystems—neurobiological, motor/behavioural, physiological/motivational, and cognitive. These four systems combine with environmental contingences, learning, and

Fig. 16.1 Minimized demands in music performance situations.

individual characteristics to produce emotional experience. Thus, anxiety is defined as a complex (learned) emotion in which fear is combined with other emotions such as anger, shame, guilt, and excitement (Izard, 1977). The 'development of an anxious personality results from the interaction of learning with basic emotions, resulting in stable *affective-cognitive structures that are trait-like*' [author's emphasis] (Izard & Blumberg, 1985, cited in Barlow, 2002, p. 42).

Anxious apprehension, the perception that one cannot predict, nor have control over possible future threats and their consequences, is fundamental to the experience of anxiety. Anxious apprehension is a future-oriented mood state that is accompanied by a feeling of helplessness and a shift in the focus of attention to oneself, in which the negative affective state and negative cognitions about one's inability to cope are prominent. Physiological arousal, in the form of generalized autonomic reactivity and hyper vigilance, prepares the person to deal with the (perceived) threat (Barlow, 2002). Negative self-evaluative focus and disruption of attention to the task result in performance impairment, which in turn increases arousal and accompanying negative affective and cognitive states. Anxious apprehension is both an emotional and cognitive process. Highly anxious people engage in a number of related cognitive activities such as hyper vigilance for threat-related stimuli (Eysenck, 1991), reduced cue utilization with narrowing of attention to mood-congruent cues (Easterbrook, 1959), attentional bias to threat-relevant stimuli and self-evaluative concerns (Puliafico & Kendall, 2006), (implicit) memory bias (i.e. showing better memory and more neural activity for words describing threatening bodily sensations) (Pauli et al, 1997), and interpretive bias (i.e. anxious people are more likely to interpret ambiguous material as threatening) (Clarke et al, 1997).

In this chapter, I will explore the emotion-based theories of the anxiety disorders, and propose a modified theory of the aetiology of music performance anxiety derived from the emotion-based theory of the aetiology of social phobia. Before embarking on this exposition, I will recapitulate briefly the epidemiological, phenomenological, and definitional commonalities and differences between the anxiety disorders, in particular social phobia and music performance anxiety, to lay the foundation for extrapolating theory from the former to the latter.

16.2 EPIDEMIOLOGY OF THE ANXIETY DISORDERS AND MUSIC PERFORMANCE ANXIETY

Anxiety disorders are the most frequently occurring mental health problems in both adults (Kessler et al, 2005) and children and adolescents (Cartwright-Hatton, McNicol, & Doubleday, 2006). About 29 per cent of the adult population report an anxiety disorder, a specific phobia (12.5 per cent), or a social phobia (also called social anxiety disorder) (12.1 per cent) over their lifetime (Kessler et al, 2005). Women are 85 per cent more likely to develop all forms of anxiety disorders than men (Ginsberg, 2004). The same gender bias is evident in children, with prevalence rates higher for girls than boys (Ford et al, 2003). Approximately one-third of people with an anxiety disorder also have a mood disorder (i.e. dysthymia or major depression) (Brown et al, 2001).

Powell (2004) estimated that approximately 2 per cent of the US population suffers from debilitating performance anxiety (including public speaking, test taking, 'stage fright' in performing artists and athletes, and writer's block). About one-third of these have other comorbid conditions, including another anxiety disorder (usually generalized anxiety disorder or social anxiety) (Sanderson, di Nardo, Rapee, & Barlow, 1990) or depression (Kessler, Strang, Wittchen, Stein, & Walters, 1999).

Researchers continue to rely on estimates of the prevalence of music performance anxiety from studies of professional orchestral musicians conducted between ten and 20 years ago. Estimates of severe and persistent music performance anxiety range from 15 to 25 per cent (Fishbein, Middlestadt, Ottati, Strauss, & Ellis, 1988; James, 1997; van Kemenade et al, 1995), although a significantly greater proportion (59 per cent) reported intermittent or less severe forms of performance anxiety that were nonetheless severe enough to impair performance and/or well-being (van Kemenade et al, 1995). James's (1997) review of 56 orchestras in five continents indicated that 70 per cent of orchestral musicians reported performance-impairing anxiety, with 16 per cent experiencing anxiety of this severity more than once a week. Almost all professional orchestral musicians (96 per cent) report occupational stress (Bartel & Thompson, 1994).

Adult, adolescent, and child musicians all report music performance anxiety. They present the same cognitive concerns and describe similar patterns of physiological arousal regarding their music performance (Ryan, 1998, 2003). Similar percentages of child and adolescent orchestral musicians (75 per cent), compared with adult orchestral musicians (Britsch, 2005), report music performance anxiety. Severity and frequency of music performance anxiety in adolescents appear to be unrelated to years of training or level of skill attainment as assessed by musical grade (Rae & McCambridge, 2004).

Music performance anxiety occurs in both solo and ensemble performers in both singers and instrumentalists. (For a more detailed coverage of the distribution of music performance anxiety among sub groups of performing musicians, see Kenny, 2006). The key point is that the phenomenology of music performance anxiety and other anxiety disorders is similar and the gender bias for females occurs in both conditions. Further, there is a consistently strong association between trait anxiety and music performance anxiety in both adult (Kenny, Davis, & Oates, 2004) and adolescent college students (McCoy, 1999). Trait anxiety (Osborne & Kenny, 2005) and neuroticism (Rae & McCambridge, 2004; Smith & Rickard, 2004) are significant predictors of music performance anxiety in high school music students.

16.3 Is music performance anxiety a social phobia?

Before we can decide whether music performance anxiety is a social phobia, we need to identify the defining features of the condition. The oft quoted definition of music performance anxiety as 'the experience of persisting, distressful *apprehension* and/or actual impairment of performance skills in a public context, *to a degree unwarranted given the individual's musical aptitude, training, and level of preparation*' [author's emphasis] (Salmon, 1990, p. 3) needs critical analysis. There are a number of components to this definition. Firstly, it correctly refers to 'distressful apprehension', akin to Barlow's anxious apprehension, which may or may not be accompanied by performance impairment. However, the definition becomes problematic when it states that a diagnosis of music performance anxiety only applies if the apprehension is not consistent with musical aptitude, training, and preparation. Research shows that musicians of all ages, levels of aptitude, training, experience, and preparation report music performance anxiety (Brotons, 1994; Cox & Kenardy, 1993; Kenny, 2009; Tamborrino, 2001; Simon & Martens, 1979; Wesner et al, 1990; Wolfe, 1989). Secondly, the definition appears to reserve the diagnosis for accomplished musicians (however defined at each level of musical development), who have had sufficient training and practice for their performance. It further implies that if there were little musical aptitude, insufficient training, or inadequate preparation, whatever apprehension is felt by musicians in these circumstances cannot be described as music performance anxiety. However, these factors are causally implicated in some, but not all, cases of music performance anxiety. Clearly, the field is in need of a new definition. I will return to this issue later in the chapter.

The literature on music performance anxiety shows that many researchers use the terms 'stage fright', 'performance anxiety', and 'music performance anxiety' interchangeably (Brodsky, 1996; Papageorgi et al, 2007; Salmon, 1990). The term 'music performance anxiety' is preferred to stage fright, because fright refers to the sudden, intense fear or alarm felt on stage that leads to performance breakdown (Senyshyn, 1999), a relatively rare event (Hardy & Parfitt, 1991). The field needs to develop more rigour, and to make the distinction between fear and anxiety (discussed above and elsewhere in this chapter) as for the anxiety disorders.

At the time of writing, I could find no longitudinal studies of the developmental trajectory of music performance anxiety, nor any detailed theoretical discussion of the aetiology of the condition, which, given the absence of prospective studies, can only at this stage be speculative. Although performance anxiety can significantly impair a performer's occupational functioning, prior to 1994, the condition had not been classified in the classificatory systems of psychological or psychiatric disorders. In DSM-IV (APA, 1994) and DSM-IV-TR (APA, 2000), performance anxiety is only briefly discussed in a section on differential diagnosis in social phobia:

Performance anxiety, stage fright, and shyness in social situations that involve unfamiliar people are common and should not be diagnosed as Social Phobia unless the anxiety or avoidance leads to clinically significant impairment or marked distress. Children commonly exhibit social anxiety, particularly when interacting with unfamiliar adults. A diagnosis of Social Phobia should not be made in children unless the social anxiety is also evident in peer settings and persists for at least 6 months.

(DSM-IV-TR, 300.23, APA, 2000)

Social phobia is defined as:

A marked and persistent fear of one or more social or performance situations in which the person is exposed to unfamiliar people or to possible scrutiny by others. The individual fears that he or she will act in a way (or show anxiety symptoms) that will be humiliating or embarrassing.

(DSM-IV-TR, 300.23, APA, 2000)

Humans and primates appear to be biologically prepared to associate fear with angry facial expressions (Öhman, 1986). Social phobia, in which there is an exaggerated fear of being watched or judged, may have its origins in this biological predisposition, which no doubt has survival value for some species. Some researchers argue that performance anxiety may be a subcategory of social phobia (Hook & Valentine, 2002; Turner, Johnson, Beidel, Heiser, & Lydiard, 2003). The classification of social phobia into *generalized* (i.e. anxiety is experienced about interpersonal interactions generally), *non-generalized* (i.e. anxiety is experienced in settings in which the individual is being scrutinized) and *specific* (i.e. anxiety is reserved for a very few performance situations) subtypes (Turner, Johnson, Beidel, Heiser, & Lydiard, 2003) may assist in the clarification of music performance anxiety as a form of the specific social phobia subtype.

There is evidence of significant comorbidity between social phobia and other anxiety disorders and musical performance anxiety. Clark and Agras (1991), for example, found that 95 per cent of a sample of college and adult musicians with high music performance anxiety qualified for a diagnosis of social phobia. Similarly, Kessler et al (1994) reported that approximately one-third of musicians presenting with severe performance anxiety had comorbid generalized anxiety disorder. Other evidence from child and adolescent musicians, in whom heightened performance anxiety was found in those showing probable and possible diagnoses of social phobia (Osborne & Kenny, 2005), strengthens the claim that these two conditions may share common roots. These studies also suggest that MPA should not be considered in isolation. Careful diagnostic assessment is needed to identify those with comorbid conditions, since comorbidity indicates a more serious course of illness (Kessler et al, 1999). However, comorbidity studies beg the question: If music performance anxiety is a social phobia, how can someone diagnosed with music performance anxiety have a comorbid social phobia? Perhaps the differential diagnosis is between a specific social phobia, where the condition is manifested only in music performance, and other more generalized manifestations of social phobia that are consistent with the DSM-IV-TR.

In a book that is generally considered the authoritative text on the anxiety disorders (Barlow, 2002), performance anxiety is treated as a (specific) social phobia. The chapter on social phobia (social anxiety disorder) opens with an account of the severe music performance anxiety of Donny Osmond (a famous pop singer), thereby conflating the two conditions. In a subsequent paper entitled *Etiology and treatment of social anxiety*, Bitran and Barlow (2004) reproduce a figure presented in Barlow (2002) as a model of the aetiology of social phobia, but rename it as a model of social phobia and performance anxiety. Any subsequent definition of music performance anxiety must resolve these diagnostic issues.

While there are some similarities between social phobia, in particular the specific social phobia subtype, and music performance anxiety, other factors distinguish social phobics from those with focal performance anxiety. Those with performance anxiety are more likely to have higher expectations of themselves (Abbott & Rapee, 2004); greater fear of their own evaluation of their performance, as opposed to fear of the scrutiny of others in social phobia (Stoebert & Eismann, in press), though the latter is also present in music performance anxiety; a higher degree of post-event rumination (Abbott & Rapee, 2004); and a continued commitment to the feared performance situation, as opposed to avoidance of the feared situation in social phobia (Powell, 2004). Further, although performing music is described as a social event involving evaluation akin to situations feared by people with social phobia (Antony & Swinson, 2000), in social phobia, the feared task is not usually cognitively or physically demanding and is usually already in the behavioural repertoire; that is, social anxiety is not generally associated with social or behavioural skills deficits (Hofmann, Gerlach, Wender, & Roth, 1997).

Many of the core symptoms of social anxiety, such as eating food in a restaurant, engaging in social interactions at parties or at work, signing one's name on a document in a bank, or for men, urinating in a public toilet, are not complex cognitive or motor tasks that need hours of practice to perform. Musical and sports performances, on the other hand, require complex skill acquisition, intensive practice, mental and physical rehearsal, coordination, and great demands on cognitive capacity and memory. Ericsson, Krampe, and Tesch-Römer (1993) estimated that a 22-year-old violinist making her concert debut will have practised for about 15,000 hours to perfect her art. Thus, musical performance makes multiple simultaneous demands on the cognitive (Kenny & Osborne, 2006), attentional (Erickson, Drevets, & Schulkin, 2003), affective (Kenny, 2005), conative, kinaesthetic (Altenmueller, Gruhn, Liebert, & Parlitz, 2000), and motor systems (Kenny & Ackermann, 2009). Performance anxiety may also be associated with failure of task mastery (Wilson, 2002) or attempts to perform tasks that exceed the capacity of the performer (Fehm & Schmidt, 2006)—circumstances rarely present in social phobia, except, to some extent, for the more performance-based tasks, such as public speaking.

Unlike social anxiety, which requires minimal arousal to perform simple social tasks competently, Mor et al (1995) showed that performance anxiety can have both facilitating and debilitating functions, and that these functions are negatively correlated. Facilitative (functional) anxiety readies the performer for the challenge ahead by directing preparatory arousal into effective task-oriented action; in debilitating anxiety, preparatory arousal is appraised negatively as anxious apprehension, and attention is directed away from the task to self-focused negative affects and cognitions. Optimal arousal in music performance is dependent on trait anxiety (Kenny et al, 2004), state anxiety (Martens et al, 1990), music performance anxiety (Kenny & Osborne, 2006; van Kemenade et al, 1995), personality characteristics (Peterson, 2000; Seligman, 1991), cognitive capacity (Libkuman, Stabler, & Otani, 2004), cognitions (Sternbach, 1995), physiological arousal (McNally, 2002), task complexity (Tassi, Bonnefond, Hoeft, Eschenlauer, & Muzet, 2003), task mastery, including motor skill (Kokotsaki & Davidson, 2003; Sparrow & Newell, 1998), situational factors (Ackermann & Adams, 2004; Brotons, 1994; Horvath, 2002), and availability of working memory resources (Libkuman et al, 2004). Few would argue that most tasks feared by people with social phobia are so multi-determined.

In social phobia, the audience is often imaginary (or arises, in psychoanalytic terms, as a projected aspect of oneself). Objectively, the socially phobic individual may fear that everyone is watching and judging them, when the reality may be that the person has not been noticed in the feared social setting. Of course, in one sense, the audience is always both real and imagined; there is always the internalized audience of one's original audience—one's parents and what they represent to the individual. For the artistic or sports performer, the audience is real in the sense that they are objectively physically present during the performance, and performers are usually correct in their assessment that these people are watching and judging them (Brotons, 1994). This is not to say that people with social phobia have a less serious condition. My purpose in making these distinctions is to highlight the differences between social phobia and music performance anxiety, and to point out that although they share some characteristics, the conditions are not the same and hence may need different or adjunctive theoretical conceptualizations, management, and intervention. In particular, aspects of the feared stimulus, the music performance, must form an integral part of the theoretical formulation and treatment of music performance anxiety.

Finally, aspiring and professional musicians are highly invested in their identities as musicians, and find it difficult to disentangle their self-esteem (i.e. the view that one has value) from their musical self-efficacy (i.e. the belief that one can perform well on one's instrument) (Kemp, 1996). This high investment makes musicians and other high-level performers such as elite athletes, actors, and dancers more vulnerable to anxiety, because of the perception that if they fail as performing artists, they also fail as people (Chesky & Hipple, 1997).

The lack of a clear definition of music performance anxiety, and the failure to make explicit the criteria that distinguish music performance anxiety from other anxiety disorders, including its close relative, specific social phobia, is a theoretical impediment to the field, compromises identification of those who need treatment, and hinders development of appropriate treatments. Hence, I tentatively offer a new definition of music performance anxiety that is more consistent with current knowledge of the condition and aligns with research on the anxiety disorders in general and social phobia in particular:

Music performance anxiety is the experience of marked and persistent anxious apprehension related to musical performance that has arisen through specific anxiety-conditioning experiences. It is manifested through combinations of affective, cognitive, somatic and behavioural symptoms and may occur in a range of performance settings, but is usually more severe in settings involving high ego investment and evaluative threat. It may be focal (i.e. focused only on music performance), or occur comorbidly with other anxiety disorders, in particular social phobia. It affects musicians across the lifespan and is at least partially independent of years of training, practice, and level of musical accomplishment. It may or may not impair the quality of the musical performance.

16.4 EMOTION-BASED THEORIES OF ANXIETY

The vast literature on the aetiology of the anxiety disorders can profitably be used to build on the research in music performance anxiety to extrapolate potential aetiological factors and to produce a theory that can be subjected to empirical verification. Prior to embarking on this endeavour, it should be noted that theorizing about music performance anxiety lags far behind the anxiety disorders, and that the extrapolations presented here are intended as a stimulus for progressing research in this important but neglected area of anxiety management.

A number of theorists have proposed emotion-based theories of anxiety development. Lang (1979), for example, argued that anxiety is manifested in an individual whose *fear structure* is activated by a specific experience or event. A fear structure contains information, learnt and stored from past experiences, that alerts the person to (perceived) danger. Lazarus (1984, 1991a) contends that an affective stimulus alone cannot trigger emotion but has to be at least minimally processed before it can do so. The concept of cognitive appraisal is the central feature of Lazarus's theory. Cognitive appraisal, which is influenced by biological variability, temperament, learning experiences, and sociocultural factors, determines the emotional response (e.g. anxiety, anger, guilt, or shame) to given situations. Appraisal involves an assessment of *goal relevance* (whether anything is at stake), *goal congruence* (whether the encounter is appraised as harmful—or threatening if it is future harm—or beneficial), and *goal content* (the type of ego involvement required). Secondary appraisal involves the determination of the capacity to cope with the situation. The goal content of anxiety involves future threat associated with uncertainty about outcomes and consequences and hence is accompanied by a feeling of powerlessness (Lazarus, 1991b, 2000). The threat is goal incongruent (i.e. the encounter is perceived as harmful) and under such circumstances, avoidance or escape are the preferred coping strategies.

Kenny (2000) proposed a developmental theory of coping that included an assessment of the quality of attachment, determined by the quality of parenting and by the presence and quality of compensatory relationships and/or experiences that were available to the child at critical periods in development. Object relations (i.e. internal working models of one's experience of primary emotional relationships, which become a template for evaluating other relationships) and available resources, both material and personal, determine the way in which life experiences are appraised, and these factors underpin the coping repertoire of the child. From this repertoire, emotional and behavioural attempts to cope with challenges emerge, and the outcome of this coping behaviour is either resilience (positive coping under conditions of risk) or vulnerability (maladaptive coping, including the development of psychopathology). A family environment characterized by limited opportunity for personal control is associated with the development of anxiety (Chorpita, Brown, & Barlow, 1998). Building a positive learning history in childhood by providing opportunities to cope adaptively with challenges should immunize children against the development of anxiety in response to subsequent negative learning episodes (Barlow, 2002; Field, 2006).

Foa and Kozak (1986) distinguished between normal (i.e. reality-based) and pathological fear structures. Emotional processing of the fear is required to alter the fear structure and reduce anxiety. For this to occur, the fear structure must be activated by direct exposure or through symbolic means (imagination). In this way, the fear will gradually reduce as will the emotional engagement in the feared stimulus or situation, through a process called habituation. Exposure procedures underlie most current treatments for anxiety (Powell, 2004). Repeated and prolonged exposure to the feared situation promotes re-evaluation (corrective or fear-disconfirming information) of the meaning and consequences of the feared situation, as well as a reduction in emotional and physiological arousal. While this theory has been shown to be effective in the treatment of many forms of anxiety, including specific phobias, post traumatic stress disorder, and agoraphobia, in the case of performance anxiety, repeated exposure to the feared situation (music performance) in the absence of the development of skills and strategies to ensure success is likely to have a deleterious effect on the performer, with potentially devastating consequences.

Barlow (2000) has also proposed an elegant emotion-based model of anxiety development that owes much to Lazarus, whose relevance to understanding performance anxiety has been discussed in detail elsewhere (see Kenny & Osborne, 2006; Kenny, 2006). The key points will be summarized here as a preamble to the introduction of a modified theory of the aetiology of music performance anxiety. Barlow proposed a two-stage process—a biological vulnerability and a generalized psychological vulnerability based on early experiences—for the development of anxious apprehension. These vulnerabilities, in the absence of conditioning experiences, are unlikely to lead to the development of an anxiety disorder. Conditioning history is therefore a necessary component in anxiety disorder aetiology (Field, 2006). A third stage, in which specific environmental experiences become conditioned in specific situations is necessary for the development of non-generalized and specific (social) phobias, and by extension, music performance anxiety.

A salient example from my case book demonstrates this phenomenon for the development of music performance anxiety. A young oboe player completed his undergraduate and postgraduate oboe performance studies with distinction at a prestigious music school. He denied any experience of music performance anxiety, even in highly challenging environments such as his final senior recital. After graduation, he began attending auditions to obtain a place in a national or international orchestra. He recounted that as many as 30 oboe players would present for audition for one position. The audition was an impersonal affair, with performances often conducted behind a screen to prevent the introduction of bias into the assessment process. Musicians were given five to ten minutes to demonstrate their prowess, after which they were dismissed without comment. No feedback is given following unsuccessful auditions, so musicians cannot learn from previous performances how to improve subsequent performances, except from their own critical appraisal of their performance, which may or may not have been accurate with respect to the reasons for the adjudicators' selection or non-selection. After many unsuccessful auditions, this musician reported the development of severe music performance anxiety, expressed as anticipatory worry and dread, expectation of failure, and dry mouth (particularly problematic for wind players), accompanied by feelings of hopelessness and depression. Although remaining committed to the audition process, he described a loss of self-efficacy and decreased preparedness to invest the practice time necessary for a successful audition. Fortunately, his anxiety remained focused on the audition situation and did not generalize to other performance opportunities that came his way, including achieving several temporary contracts with prestigious national orchestras.

This case example illustrates a number of key components of the emotion-based theory of anxiety development. The critical feature of this account is the sense of uncontrollability and unpredictability in a specific situation, in this case, the audition, and the subsequent reporting of negative affect—anxiety, hopelessness, and depression. While unpredictability leads to anxiety, uncontrollability results in depression, although there is overlap between these two concepts and their consequences (Mineka & Zinbarg, 1996). Physiological arousal in the form of dry mouth added to the feeling of uncontrollability (wind players need to be well hydrated to perform), along with situational cues that evoke anxious responding (e.g. the coldness of the adjudicators, the impersonal and dehumanizing assessment procedures, and the lack of feedback), attentional shift whereby the focus is directed away from the performance task to a self-focus, and fear of negative evaluation and failure. The process is as follows: 'Situational cues associated with negative affect result in a shift from an external to an internal focus of attention directed to somatic sensations, as well as the affective and self-evaluative components of the context, which result in further increases in arousal and anxiety' (Barlow, 2002, p. 84). The audition example indicates the specificity of the situation in some cases of music performance anxiety. In this case, the audition process was objectively extremely aversive, fostering by its nature all the precursors to anxious apprehension and vulnerability to the development of a clinically significant anxiety disorder in a highly gifted, previously confident performer.

Below is an account from an advanced tertiary music student that illustrates other key dimensions of Barlow's emotion-based theory of anxiety:

I suffer from music performance anxiety. I only get it just before or on the day before a concert. I don't tend to think about it the week before. I don't sweat or get shaky or anything like that. *I am just so worried about what people think if it goes wrong.* Once I go out there *I concentrate so hard to relax and it goes the other way* and then I end up being really casual about it and probably not concentrating enough. It got a lot worse once I started more serious music, when I left school at 18 and probably when I was performing at the academy because it was actual fellow musicians in the audience whereas before it had just been parents and friends. That was when I first started to think 'Oh God!' I don't know why it has turned out this way—*I've been lucky and never really had a bad experience.* Even if I made mistakes I wasn't really that worried about it. But now, before a concert, it's a complete nightmare. *I don't think there is anything I can do with it so I just leave it at that.* I go through my normal routine that I would any other day. *Before the concert I just wander round feeling nervous.* The biggest fear is making a mistake and other people noticing it. *I get really pissed off when I make any mistake,* especially in orchestral playing. It is not as bad playing in gigs and stuff especially when nobody knows you and people are not really listening.

(Male clarinettist, aged 22, italics added)

There are a number of interesting features in this account. Firstly, this young musician experiences a strong sense of uncontrollability and unpredictability in his concert performances. Although they are a 'complete nightmare', he does not think that he can do anything about the anxiety and just 'leaves it at that'. He denies excessive physiological arousal and states that he has never had a bad experience (i.e. he does not remember any aversive music performance experiences) that could have conditioned his present fear of performing. Note that he describes himself as 'lucky' not to have had such experiences, thus further demonstrating his overall sense of uncontrollability. This attribution of 'luck' as responsible for positive outcomes demonstrates an external locus of control (Seligman, 1991) (i.e. the belief that one has no control over events in one's life). Only when he became 'serious' (i.e. personally invested) about music did he succumb to performance anxiety; that is, he began to conflate his self-esteem with his musical self-efficacy.

In our experience working with young musicians, this is not an unusual (self-reported) trajectory (Osborne & Kenny, 2008), which is probably related to the development of self-reflective function and the capacity for self-evaluation (self-criticism) that emerges in middle to late adolescence (Jackson & Lurie, 2006). The changing nature of the performance setting and the (perceived) increased demands from the audience ('before it was parents and friends', now it is 'fellow musicians') also plays a role in his anxious responding. He displays the typical fear of negative evaluation and excessively high (perfectionistic) expectations of his performance ('I get really pissed off if I make *any* mistake'). He also reports pervasive negative affect ('I just wander round feeling nervous'), attentional shift away from the task ('I concentrate so hard to relax and it goes the other way'), and situationally specific anxiety (anxiety occurs in orchestral playing but not 'in gigs because nobody knows you and people are not really listening').

Compare the above account with this account from a female pianist:

Everybody says that performance anxiety or having nerves before a performance is a good thing. Teachers and everybody say that. I suppose a little bit is OK but not the extent to which I feel it. I always experience it before I go on—there is always that *incredible fear and tension and worry that something will go wrong* and *if it does I get a massive panic attack*. I fall apart and then I just panic completely. Before I go on, *I get awful cramps in my stomach* . . . like really bad period pain cramp . . . it's so awful I had to go to the doctor about it. It has always affected me like that and I need to go to the toilet all the time. *Every single time I know it is going to happen.*

(Female pianist, aged 20 years, italics added)

Unlike our male clarinettist who denied somatic symptoms, for this pianist the level of physiological arousal was extremely aversive and dominated the account of her experience. This young woman no doubt suffers from neurobiological hyper reactivity that triggers 'false alarms' (Barlow, 2002; and see below) in even mildly anxiety-provoking situations. However, there is still a strong emotional component: 'incredible fear and tension and worry that something will go wrong', which will trigger a 'panic attack' during which she 'falls apart'. It is interesting that she describes her experience as panic, because there is a strong association between internal (cardiovascular, physiological, etc.) cues and false alarms in panic disorder (Dworkin, 1993), compared with specific phobias in which the focus is on external cues, as in the case of the student at audition. This young woman may in fact have a comorbid panic disorder for which a differential diagnosis would be necessary. The conditioning of her response to the performance setting is very well established: 'Every single time I know it is going to happen'. Her commitment to the feared situation is compelling—she continues to perform despite this very disturbing account of her performance experience.

Research with child musicians demonstrates similar phenomena. For example, Osborne and Kenny (2006), using a retrospective recall method, explored the reports of young musicians' worst performance experiences with their scores on measures of trait anxiety and music performance anxiety. Here is one example of an account from a 13-year-old pianist sitting for a music exam: 'I had practised until perfect and remembered scales beforehand. I walked in and got very nervous. I played three pieces OK but scales were terrible. I forgot the notes and fingering totally . . . I came out crying and felt like a failure.' Music students who reported a negative music performance experience scored significantly higher on the scale used to measure music performance anxiety (MPAI-A) (Osborne, Kenny, & Holsomback, 2005) than those who did not report such an experience. Trait anxiety was also higher in the group recalling a worst performance. There was a positive linear association between trait anxiety and music performance anxiety, though caution is needed in the interpretation of these findings. It is possible that those young musicians who recalled a worst performance experience and/or provided the most detail in the recalled event (hence receiving higher anxiety scores for their account), may have been those with a greater propensity to experience anxiety because of their higher biological and/or psychological vulnerability (i.e. that pre-dated their worst experience). It is possible that low-anxious young performers may also have had similar 'worst performance' experiences, but did not recall them or did not recall them in vivid detail because they did not appraise them in such a negative way as the highly anxious musicians, and hence the experience was not salient enough to be stored in long-term memory. However, the key point here is that there appears to be a universality in the phenomenology of the experience of music performance anxiety across the lifespan.

How can we explain these extreme reactions to musical performance in otherwise highly intelligent, musically gifted, and socially competent young musicians? These accounts present vivid examples of *emotional learning*, the process whereby a stimulus (in this case, music performance) acquires emotional properties. These acquired emotional reactions are conditioned fear responses (Phelps, 2006). In humans, the fear response can be elicited automatically if we are confronted by a real and present danger that threatens our well-being. Fear triggers automatic emergency physiological reactions that were famously described by Cannon (1929) as 'fight or flight' responses that aimed at readying us to deal with the threat. Barlow (2002) refers to these responses as 'true alarms' (p. 219). 'False alarms' (p. 220) are fear responses that occur in the absence of a real or present danger, and are a defining characteristic of panic disorders and phobias—and, it seems, of music performance anxiety. In my experience, many accounts of severe music performance anxiety contain very strong words associated with fear and panic, as the accounts given here show.

What triggers false alarms? This is a complex question, since it is likely that they are multi-determined. Barlow suggests that individuals who experience false alarms may have heightened neurobiological hyper reactivity, which triggers basic emotions such as fear or defensive reactions such as panic attacks. Recent research has identified different roles for different neural substrates in fear conditioning. For example, the amygdala is involved in the physiological response to conditioned fear (Gazzaniga, Irvy, & Magnun, 2002), whereas the hippocampus is involved in the associative learning (conditioning) component, particularly if the context is important for learning (Squire & Zola-Morgan, 1991; for a detailed review, see Phelps, 2006). This hyper reactivity interacts with psychological triggers and is expressed as anxiety. Initially, false alarms appear uncued and unexpected; however, with prompting, 80 per cent of people with panic disorder can recall a negative life event that preceded their first panic (Doctor, 1982). Sensitivity to anxiety appears to be normally distributed throughout the population, indicating that it is a dimensional rather than a categorical construct (Reiss, Peterson, Gursky, & McNally, 1986). Almost all the anxiety disorders are characterized by chronic hyper arousal (Nash & Potokar, 2004). High anxiety sensitivity appears to be a risk factor for false alarms and subsequent development of panic attacks, particularly in individuals with high negative affect (Hayward et al, 2000). High anxiety sensitivity constitutes the first component (i.e. biological vulnerability) and negative affect the second component (i.e. psychological vulnerability) of the three-factor emotion-based theory of anxiety proposed by Barlow (2000).

Another possible explanation for the triggering of false of alarms is that false alarms mimic the panic and distress evident in children who have experienced separation from their mothers, a phenomenon known as separation anxiety (Bowlby, 1973). The evidence for this proposition is not strong (Hayward, Killen, Kraemer, & Taylor, 2000). A more plausible explanation comes from the work of Ehlers (1993), who showed that people with panic attacks report observing more panic behaviours in their parents than people with other anxiety disorders and people with no anxiety disorder. Many people who develop anxiety disorders report early learning experiences as children whereby their caregivers focused anxious attention on bodily sensations and communicated their beliefs regarding the danger surrounding these symptoms and sensations (Chambless, Caputo, Gright, & Gallagher, 1984).

This research points to several possible learning processes whereby false alarms may be conditioned in vulnerable individuals: respondent (or classical) conditioning, observational (vicarious) learning or modelling, and information/verbal instruction (Rachman, 1991) or instructed fear (Olsson & Phelps, 2004). In classical or 'Pavlovian' (Pavlov, 1927) conditioning, a neutral stimulus that is present during a fear-arousing experience (called the unconditioned stimulus—UCS) may acquire the capacity to elicit the fear response in the absence of the original fear-arousing experience. The neutral experience thus becomes a conditioned stimulus (CS) for fear through its paired association with the UCS. Fear in this circumstance is called conditioned fear because the neutral stimulus would not have elicited fear without its pairing with the UCS; that is, without undergoing conditioning. The strength of the relationship between the CS and the conditioned response (CR) depends on the number of pairings that have occurred between the UCS and the CR and the intensity of the fear invoked by the UCS. Internal somatic sensations may become conditioned stimuli (Gosch, Flannery-Schroeder, Mauro, & Compton, 2006), particularly in those who have heightened neurobiological hyper reactivity and/ or learning experiences that teaches them to be anxious about their somatic sensations. Some specific phobias are apparently acquired in this way. A person may experience a false alarm of such intensity that learning in the situation in which the person experiences the false alarm takes place. Subsequently, the person comes to experience anxiety in the situation that was the location of the first false alarm. Anxiety then arises in anticipation of the occurrence of another false alarm in the conditioning situation (Barlow, 2002).

Other factors such as temperament, context, past experience, cognition (Field, 2006), and the evaluation of the unconditioned stimulus itself (Dadds et al, 2001) all play a part in (fear) conditioning experiences. Although fear is conditioned in this way, it is avoidance learning (i.e. learning to avoid the feared stimulus; Mowrer, 1947) that maintains the fear. Emotional conditioning, including fear conditioning, does not require conscious awareness of the temporal association between the UCS, UCR, and CR (LeDoux, 1996).

Classical conditioning models are not sufficient to account for all observed phenomena in fear and anxiety conditioning. Miller and Dollard (1941) were the first behaviourists to note the importance of imitation in learning. Bandura (1969) later elaborated this idea, demonstrating that we can learn by observing others (observational learning), and what we learn depends on the importance we attach to the behaviour and the significance of the model to the observer. Such learning can occur even when neither the observer nor the model is rewarded for the behaviour. Because parents are very significant models for their children, social learning theory (Bandura, 1977) helps us to understand how children acquire complex ideals, characteristics, and ways of relating to others. Children identify with and imitate their parents' behaviour. This process is so powerful that children will often repeat in their adult lives the behaviours and relationships of their parents (Taubman-Ben-Ari, Mikulincer, & Gillath, 2005; Sinclair, Dunn, & Lowery, 2005). Parents of socially anxious children are themselves often socially anxious, and interact with their children in ways that encourage the development of anxious apprehension in social situations, by discussing the potential threat in particular social situations and reinforcing their children's socially anxious behaviours, such as avoidance of situations feared by their parents (Barrett, Rapee, Dadds, & Ryan, 1996). One critical element in vicarious learning of anxious or phobic responding is the strength of the fear response in the model, enhanced by a phenomenon called 'emotional contagion' (see Chapter 22, this volume) in which the observer reacts with the same intensity to a situation as the model even in the absence of any overt threat (Mineka, 1987). Some fear responses can be symbolically acquired; that is, emotional reactions attach to stimuli in the absence of aversive stimuli; they can be conditioned via a paradigm known as 'instructed fear' in which verbal instructions that there will be an aversive consequence in a given situation are sufficient to condition an emotional response to that stimulus (Öst, 1985).

Another learning paradigm that could condition false alarms is operant conditioning. In operant conditioning, the person must make a response; that is, operate on his environment in some way. If the response is followed by a reward, called positive reinforcement, then that response is more likely to occur again in a similar situation. However, if the response is punished or ignored, the occurrence of the response becomes less likely in the future. A third consequence of responding, that of preventing an unpleasant event from occurring, is called negative reinforcement. This consequence also increases the probability of the response re-occurring in the future (Skinner, 1961). This form of conditioning appears to be associated with true rather than false alarms and to be more common in people with non-generalized or specific social phobia, who exhibit fear responses compared with those with the generalized subtype who are more likely to exhibit anxiety (Barlow, 2002). The former group are more likely to attribute their fear of the social/performance situation to panic, whereas the latter group are more likely to attribute their anxiety to fear of negative evaluation (Heimberg, Holt, Schneier, Spitzer, & Liebowitz, 1993). It should be noted that the shared feature underlying all relatively recent models of conditioning is the concept of *reciprocal determinism*, the view that genetic and biological predisposition, internal emotional and cognitive processes, life experiences, environmental events, and behaviour are interdependent and influence each other (Bandura, 1978).

16.5 AN EMOTIONAL-BASED THEORETICAL MODEL OF MUSIC PERFORMANCE ANXIETY

Based on the foregoing discussion, I propose a conceptually modified model for the aetiology and maintenance of MPA based on Barlow's model of the development of social phobia, as follows. In MPA, the stressful event is almost always described as a performance situation with an evaluative component such as a recital, concert, examination, audition, or eisteddfod. It may or may not involve an audience other than the examiner or adjudicator. The performance can be solo, orchestral, or choral (Kenny, Davis, & Oats, 2004).

Figure 16.2 shows a schematic representation of the pathways to and from music performance anxiety. The shaded area indicates the basic conditioning process for the development of anxious apprehension and hence generalized social phobia, or if a specific psychological vulnerability is present, a non-generalized social phobia. When anxious apprehension becomes focused on a complex music performance, multiple factors, outlined earlier, need to be addressed in order to reduce the level of apprehension and before the experience of too many alarms in the performance setting start to condition the anxiety response to performing. Finally, the model emphasizes the iterative and mutually causal nature of the relationship between false and true alarms, a relationship that has not been discussed in the model for social phobia.

In this model, both false and true alarms are the panic-like negative emotions and other forms of reactivity that have been conditioned in response to direct experience, stress, or conditioning in those with generalized biological and psychological vulnerability. These early experiences establish the propensity for anxious apprehension in performance situations. A number of outcomes of a performance become possible at this point. Repeated successful performances may eventually reduce the amount of anxious apprehension experienced before performances so that MPA does not develop. However, if the performance is impaired or is perceived to be impaired, the negative emotions and self-evaluation that follow may compound the anxious apprehension and trigger further alarms, which in turn increase the risk of impaired performance, in a vicious circle until the performance setting itself triggers conditioned alarms, even before the performance has taken place. Many performance settings, such as the audition process for orchestral musicians described above, are genuinely

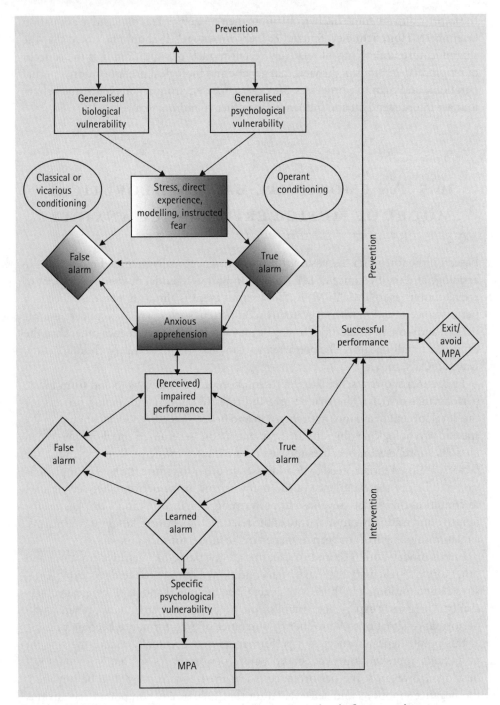

Fig. 16.2 Model of the development, maintenance, and exit from music performance anxiety.

threatening, unpredictable, and uncontrollable, and may provide very little chance of success despite adequate preparation and task mastery. In these circumstances, performance is followed by actual negative consequences, such as non-selection at audition. If this sequence is repeated, the negative consequences will heighten antici-patory apprehension prior to subsequent performances. In MPA, true alarms and false alarms may become mutually recursive, such that successive performance impairments or successive exposures to genuinely threatening performance experiences increase subsequent true alarms, which in turn, increase the probability of subsequent perfor-mance impairments because of the interference effects of alarms on performance.

The model also attempts to account for those musicians who report intense feel-ings of music performance anxiety, but do not experience performance impairment or breakdown. A false alarm involves the experiencing of cognitive, emotional, and/or somatic anticipatory responses (physiological arousal and/or dread and worry) about a performance that is not subsequently impaired in performers who have not pre-viously experienced performance impairment. However, these aversive anticipatory responses are contiguously associated with the performance situation, and have been triggered by combinations of the biological and psychological vulnerabilities described in Barlow's theory. I would tentatively hypothesize that this subgroup of musicians may have comorbid anxiety disorders or be generally more vulnerable to the develop-ment of anxiety disorders than those whose MPA has been conditioned by true alarms in genuinely highly stressful performance settings.

Successful performances, despite their success, may still evoke alarm reactions, which, if repeated, become learned alarm responses triggered by the performance context. This, combined with the specific psychological vulnerability required for the develop-ment of a specific phobia, will thus become strongly associated with the performance situation, despite a lack of negative consequences, which under other circumstances would be extinguished because no aversive outcomes accrued. Hence, both classical and operant conditioning combine to produce learned alarms that, if not extinguished by appropriate interventions and performance outcomes, are likely to develop into music performance anxiety. It is possible, in certain individuals with particularly strong biological and/or psychological vulnerabilities, that no further impaired performances are needed to progress to MPA, since the learned alarm has become fully conditioned to the performance situation, as in our female pianist described earlier.

One feature of MPA that is not seen in other social phobias is the tendency of musi-cians to remain in the aversive situation, rather than engaging in avoidance or escape behaviours. One explanation is the strong personal investment in performing that musi-cians demonstrate, such that the approach gradient (the desire to remain in the field) remains stronger than the avoidance gradient (the desire to leave the field) (Dollard & Miller, 1950), even in situations that musicians describe as extremely aversive. If negative emotions become overwhelming and efforts to control them are unsuccessful, musicians may eventually leave the field (of music performance), and some may do so even if they have not experienced any serious performance breakdowns.

Given the known precursors to the development of the specific social/performance anxieties, it would be prudent to assess young musicians for generalized biological and psychological vulnerability and to implement preventive strategies early in their musical training. Education of parents and teachers in the aetiology of these disorders and their prevention would also be useful. Possible interventions for those already suffering from the condition are described in Kenny (in press).

16.6 SUMMARY, CONCLUSIONS AND FUTURE DIRECTIONS

In this chapter, I have attempted to provide a model for the development of music performance anxiety based on the emotion theories of anxiety, in particular specific social phobia. Single approaches rarely account for all the observations in behavioural manifestations of emotional disorders; however, there has been a neglect of the role of emotions in music performance anxiety, and this chapter attempts to redress that imbalance.

I have also proposed a new definition for music performance anxiety that is more consistent with the empirical evidence available about the development and phenomenology of this condition. Future research will need to verify the claims made in this chapter and justify the emphases given in this new definition.

The account presented here indicates that there may be subtypes of music performance anxiety, with different aetiologies, developmental trajectories, and clinical presentations. Music performance anxiety may form part of a more generalized anxiety disorder, be comorbid with other more specific anxiety disorders such as (specific) social phobia, or be genuinely focal and restricted only to the music performance setting. The proposed model attempts to account for the multi-determined aetiological pathways to music performance anxiety, its different presentations, and its maintenance. Empirical tests of both the theory and the model are now needed. To date, there have been no prospective, longitudinal studies of the development of music performance anxiety. Such studies are now required to further advance our understanding of this complex phenomenon.

RECOMMENDED FURTHER READING

1. Langendörfer, F., Hodapp, V., Kreutz, G., & Stephan Bongard, S. (2006). Personality and performance: Anxiety among professional orchestra musicians. *Individual Differences, 27,* 162–71.
2. Williamon, A. (ed.). (2004). *Musical Excellence: Strategies and techniques to enhance performance.* Oxford: Oxford University Press.
3. Kenny, D. T. (in press). Treatment of music performance anxiety. In A. Williamon (ed.), *International handbook of musicians' health and wellbeing.* Oxford: Oxford University Press.

References

Abbott, M. J., & Rapee, R. M. (2004). Post-event rumination and negative self-appraisal in social phobia before and after treatment. *Journal of Abnormal Psychology, 113*, 136–44.

Abel, J. L., & Larkin, K. T. (1990). Anticipation of performance among musicians: Physiological arousal, confidence, and state-anxiety. *Psychology of Music, 18*, 171–82.

Ackermann, B. J., & Adams, R. (2004). Inter-observer reliability of general practice physiotherapists in rating aspects of the movement patterns of skilled violinists. *Medical Problems of Performing Artists, 19*, 3–11.

Altenmueller, E., Gruhn, W., Liebert, G., & Parlitz, D. (2000). The impact of music education on brain networks: evidence from EEG studies. *International Journal of Music Education, 35*, 47–53.

American Psychiatric Association. (1994). *Diagnostic and Statistical Manual of Mental Disorders* (4th edn). Washington, DC: American Psychiatric Association.

American Psychiatric Association. (2000). *Diagnostic and Statistical Manual of Mental Disorders -TR* (4th edn). Washington, DC: American Psychiatric Association.

Antony, M. M., & Swinson, R. P. (2000). Social phobia. In M. M. Antony & R. P. Swinson (eds), *Phobic disorders and panic in adults: A guide to assessment and treatment* (pp. 49–77). Washington, DC: American Psychological Association.

Bandura, A. (1969). *Principles of behavior modification*. Oxford: Holt, Rinehart, & Winston.

Bandura, A. (1977). *Social learning theory*. Oxford: Prentice-Hall.

Bandura, A. (1978). The self system in reciprocal determinism. *American Psychologist, 33*, 344–58.

Barlow, H. (2000). Unravelling the mysteries of anxiety and its disorders from the perspective of emotion theory. *American Psychologist, 55*, 1245–63.

Barlow, D. H. (2002). *Anxiety and its disorders. The nature and treatment of anxiety and panic.* New York: Guildford Press.

Barrett, P. M., Rapee, R. M., Dadds, M. M., & Ryan, S. M. (1996). Family enhancement of cognitive style in anxious and aggressive children. *Journal of Abnormal Child Psychology, 24*, 187–203.

Bartel, L. R., & Thompson, E. G. (1994). Coping with performance stress: A study of professional orchestral musicians in Canada. *The Quarterly Journal of Music Teaching and Learning, 5*, 70–8.

Beck, A. T., & Clark, D. A. (1997). An information processing model of anxiety: Automatic and strategic processes. *Behaviour Research and Therapy, 35*, 40–58.

Bitran, S., & Barlow, D. H. (2004). Etiology and treatment of social anxiety: A commentary. *Journal of Clinical Psychology, 60*, 881–6.

Bowlby, J. (1973). *Attachment and loss. Volume 2: Separation: anxiety and anger*. New York: Basic Books.

Britsch, L. (2005). Investigating performance-related problems of young musicians. *Medical Problems of Performing Artists, 20*, 40–7.

Brodsky, W. (1996). Music performance anxiety reconceptualised: A critique of current research practice and findings. *Medical Problems of Performing Artists, 11*, 88–98.

Brotons, M. (1994). Effects of performing conditions on music performance anxiety and performance quality. *Journal of Music Therapy, 31*, 63–81.

Brown, T. A., Campbell, L. A., Lehman, C. L., Grisham, J. R., & Mancill, R. B. (2001). Current and lifetime cormorbidity of the DSM-IV anxiety and mood disorders in a large clinical sample. *Journal of Abnormal Psychology, 110*, 585–99.

Butler, A. C., Chapman, J. E., Forman, E. M., & Beck, A. T. (2006). The empirical status of cognitive-behavioral therapy: A review of meta-analyses. *Clinical Psychology Review, 26*, 17–31.

Cannon, W. B. (1929). *Bodily changes in pain, hunger, fear and rage* (2nd edn). New York: Appleton-Century-Crofts.

Cartwright-Hatton, S., McNicol, K., & Doubleday, E. (2006). Anxiety in a neglected population: Prevalence of anxiety disorders in pre-adolescent children. *Clinical Psychology Review*, 26, 817–33.

Chambless, D. L., Caputo, G. C., Bright, P., & Gallagher, R. (1984). Assessment of fear of fear in agoraphobics: The Body Sensations Questionnaire and the Agoraphobic Cognitions Questionnaire. *Journal of Consulting and Clinical Psychology*, 52, 1090–7.

Chesky, K. S., & Hippel, J. (1997). Performance anxiety, alcohol-related problems, and social/emotional difficulties of college students: A comparative study between lower-division music and non-music majors. *Medical Problems of Performing Artists*, 12, 126–32.

Chorpita, B. F., Brown, T. A., & Barlow, D. H. (1998). Perceived control as a mediator of family environment in etiological models of childhood anxiety. *Behavior Therapy*, 29, 457–76.

Clark, D. B., & Agras, W. S. (1991). The assessment and treatment of performance anxiety in musicians. *American Journal of Psychiatry*, 148, 598–605.

Clark, D. M., Salkovskis, P. M., Öst, L.-G., Breitholtz, E., Koehler, K. A., Westling, B. E., Jeavons, A., & Gelder, M. (1997). Misinterpretation of body sensations in panic disorder. *Journal of Consulting and Clinical Psychology*, 65, 203–13.

Cox, B. J., & Kenardy, J. (1993). Performance anxiety, social phobia, and setting effects in instrumental music students. *Journal of Anxiety Disorders*, 7, 49–60.

Craske, M. G., & Craig, K. D. (1984). Musical performance anxiety: The three-systems model and self-efficacy theory. *Behavior Research and Therapy*, 22, 267–80.

Dadds, M. R., Davey, G. C. L., & Field, A. P. (2001). Developmental aspects of conditioning processes in anxiety disorders. In M. W. Vasey & M. R. Dadds (eds), *The developmental psychopathology of anxiety* (pp. 205–30). Oxford: Oxford University Press.

Doctor, R. M. (1982). Major results of a large-scale pre-treatment survey of agoraphobics. In R. L. DuPont (ed.), *Phobia: A comprehensive summary of modern treatments*. New York: Brunner/Mazel.

Dollard, J., & Miller, N. E. (1950). *Personality and psychotherapy: An analysis in terms of learning, thinking, and culture*. New York: McGraw-Hill.

Dworkin, B. R. (1993). *Learning and physiological regulation*. Chicago, IL: University of Chicago Press.

Easterbrook, J. A. (1959). The effect of emotion on cue utilization and the organization of behavior. *Psychological Review*, 66, 183–201.

Ehlers, A. (1993). Somatic symptoms and panic attacks: A retrospective study of learning experiences. *Behaviour Research and Therapy*, 31, 269–78.

Ericsson, K. A., Krampe, R. T., & Tesch-Römer, C. (1993). The role of deliberate practice in the acquisition of expert performance. *Psychological Review*, 100, 363–406.

Erickson, K., Drevets, W., & Schulkin, J. (2003). Glucocorticoid regulation of diverse cognitive functions in normal and pathological emotional states. *Neuroscience and Biobehavioral Reviews*, 27, 233–46.

Eysenck, M. W. (1991). Anxiety and attention. In R. Schwarzer & R. A. Wicklund (eds), *Anxiety and self-focused attention* (pp. 125–31). Chur, Switzerland: Harwood.

Fehm, L., & Schmidt, K. (2006). Performance anxiety in gifted adolescent musicians. *Journal of Anxiety Disorders*, 20, 98–109.

Field, A. P. (2006). Is conditioning a useful framework for understanding the development and treatment of phobias? *Clinical Psychology Review*, 26, 857–75.

Fishbein, M., Middlestadt, S. E., Ottati, V., Strauss, S., & Ellis, A. (1988). Medical problems among ICSOM musicians: Overview of a national survey. *Medical Problems of Performing Artists*, 3, 1–8.

Foa, E. B., & Kozak, M. (1986). Emotional processing of fear: Exposure to corrective informa-tion. *Psychological Bulletin*, *99*, 20–35.

Ford, T., Goodman, R., & Meltzer, H. (2003). The British Child and Adolescent Mental Health Survey 1999: The prevalence of DSM-IV disorders. *Journal of the American Academy of Child and Adolescent Psychiatry*, *42*, 1203–11.

Fredrikson, M., & Gunnarsson, R. (1992). Psychobiology of stage fright: The effect of public performance on neuroendocrine, cardiovascular and subjective ratings. *Biological Psychology*, *33*, 51–62.

Friedman, H. S., & Silver, R. C. (eds). (2007). *Foundations of health psychology*. Oxford: Oxford University Press.

Gazzaniga, M. S., Irvy, R., & Magnun, G. R. (2002). *Cognitive neuroscience: The biology of the mind* (2nd edn). New York: Norton.

Ginsberg, D. L. (2004). Women and anxiety disorders: Implications for diagnosis and treatment. *CNS Spectrums*, *9*, 1–16.

Gosch, E. A., Flannery-Schroeder, E., Mauro, C. F., & Compton, S. N. (2006). Principles of cognitive-behavioral therapy for anxiety disorders in children. *Journal of Cognitive Psychotherapy*, *20*, 247–62.

Hardy, L., & Parfitt, G. (1991). A catastrophe model of anxiety and performance. *British Journal of Psychology*, *82*, 163–78.

Hayward, C., Killen, J. D., Kraemer, H. C., & Taylor, C. B. (2000). Predictors of panic attacks in adolescents. *Journal of the American Academy of Child and Adolescent Psychiatry*, *39*, 1–8.

Heimberg, R. G., Holt, C. S., Schneier, F. R., Spitzer, R. L., & Liebowitz, M. R. (1993). The issue of subtypes in the diagnosis of social phobia. *Journal of Anxiety Disorders*, *7*, 249–69.

Hofmann, S. G., Gerlach, A., Wender, A., & Roth, W. T. (1997). Speech disturbances and gaze behaviour during public speaking in subtypes of social phobia. *Journal of Anxiety Disorders*, *11*, 573–85.

Hook, J. N., & Valentiner, D. P. (2002). Are specific and generalized social phobias qualita-tively distinct? *Clinical Psychology: Science and Practice*, *9*, 379–95.

Horvath, J. (2002). *Playing (less) hurt*. Kearney, NE: Morris.

Izard, C. E. (1977). *Human emotions*. New York: Plenum Press.

Izard, C. E. (1993). Four systems for emotion activation: Cognitive and noncognitive processes. *Psychological Review*, *100*, 68–90.

Izard, C. E., & Blumberg, M. A. (1985). Emotion theory and the role of emotions in anxiety in children and adults. In A. H. Tuma & J. D. Maser (eds), *Anxiety and the anxiety disorders* (pp. 681–706). Hillsdale, NJ: Erlbaum.

Jackson, B., & Lurie, S. (2006). Adolescent depression: Challenges and opportunities. A review and current recommendations for clinical practice. *Advances in Pediatrics*, *53*, 111–63.

James, I. (1997). *Federation Internationale des Musiciens 1997 survey of 56 orchestras*. Paris, France: International Federation of Musicians.

Kemp, A. E. (1996). *The musical temperament: Psychology and personality of musicians*. Oxford: Oxford University Press.

Kenny, D. T. (2000). Psychological foundations of stress and coping: A developmental per-spective. In D. T. Kenny, J. G. Carlson, F. J. McGuigan, & J. L. Sheppard (eds), *Stress and health: Research and clinical applications* (pp. 73–104). Amsterdam, The Netherlands: Gordon Breach Science/Harwood.

Kenny, D. T. (2005). A systematic review of treatment for music performance anxiety. *Anxiety, Stress and Coping*, *18*, 183–208.

Kenny, D. T. (2006). Music performance anxiety: Origins, phenomenology, assessment and treatment. *Context: A Journal of Music Research, Special Issue: Renegotiating Musicology*, *31*, 51–64.

Kenny, D. T. (in press). Treatment of music performance anxiety. In A. Williamon (ed.), *International handbook of musicians' health and wellbeing*. Oxford: Oxford University Press.

Kenny, D. T., & Ackermann, B. (2009). Optimising physical and mental health in performing musicians. In S. Hallam, I. Cross, & M. Thaut (eds), *Oxford handbook of music psychology*. Oxford: Oxford University Press.

Kenny, D. T., Davis, P. J., & Oates, J. (2004). Music performance anxiety and occupational stress amongst opera chorus artists and their relationship with state and trait anxiety and perfectionism. *Journal of Anxiety Disorders, 18*, 757–77.

Kenny, D. T., & Osborne, M. S. (2006). Music performance anxiety: New insights from young musicians. In W. F. Thompson (ed.), *Advances in Cognitive Psychology, 2*, 103–112.

Kessler, R. C., Chiu, W. T., Demler, O., & Walters, E. E. (2005). Prevalence, severity, and comorbidity of 12-month DSM-IV disorders in the National Comorbidity Survey Replication. *Archives of General Psychiatry, 62*, 617–27.

Kessler, R. C., McGonagle, K. A., Zhao, S., Nelson, C. B., Hughes, M., Eshleman, S., et al (1994). Lifetime and 12-month prevalence of DSM-III-R psychiatric disorders in the United States. *Archives of General Psychiatry, 51*, 8–19.

Kessler, R. C., Stang, H. U., Wittchen, H.-U., Stein, M., & Walters, E. E. (1999). Lifetime co-morbidities between social phobia and mood disorders in the US National Comorbidity Survey. *Psychological Medicine, 29*, 555–67.

King, N. J., Ollendick, T. H., & Murphy, G. C. (1997). Assessment of childhood phobias. *Clinical Psychology Review, 17*, 667–87.

Kokotsaki, D., & Davidson, J. W. (2003). Investigating musical performance anxiety among music college singing students: A quantitative analysis. *Music Education Research, 5*, 45–59.

Lang, P. J. (1979). A bio-informational theory of emotional imagery. *Psychophysiology, 16*, 495–512.

Lazarus, R. S. (1984). On the primacy of cognition. *American Psychologist, 39*, 124–9.

Lazarus, R. S. (1991a). Cognition and motivation in emotion. *American Psychologist, 46*, 352–67.

Lazarus, R. S. (1991b). Progress on a cognitive-motivational-relational theory of emotion. *American Psychologist, 46*, 819–34.

Lazarus, R. S. (2000). How emotions influence performance in competitive sports. *The Sport Psychologist, 14*, 229–52.

Lazarus, A. A., & Abramovitz, A. (2004). A multimodal behavioral approach to performance anxiety. *Journal of Clinical Psychology, 60*, 831–40.

LeDoux, J. E. (1996). *The emotional brain*. New York: Simon & Schuster.

Libkuman, T. M., Stabler, C. L., & Otani, H. (2004). Arousal, valence, and memory for detail. *Memory, 12*, 237–47.

Mandler, G. (1984). *Mind and body: Psychology of emotion and stress*. New York: Norton.

Martens, R., Burton, D., Vealey, R., Bump, L., & Smith, D. (1990). The Development of the competitive state anxiety inventory-2 (CSAI-2). In R. Martens, R. S. Vealey, & D. Burton (eds), *Competitive anxiety in sport* (pp. 117–90). Champaign, IL: Human Kinetics.

Martens, R., Vealey, R., & Burton, D. (1990). *Competitive anxiety in sport*. Champaign, IL: Human Kinetics Books.

McNally, I. M. (2002). Contrasting concepts of competitive state-anxiety in sport: Multidimensional anxiety and catastrophe theories. *Athletic Insight: Online Journal of Sport Psychology, 4*, NP.

Miller, N. E., & Dollard, J. (1941). *Social learning and imitation*. New Haven, CT: Yale University Press.

Mineka, S. (1987). A primate model of phobic fears. In H. Eysenck & I. Martin (eds), *Theoretical foundations of behavior therapy* (pp. 81–111). New York: Plenum Press.

Mineka, S., & Zinbarg, R. (1996). Conditioning and ethological models of anxiety disorders: Stress in dynamic-context anxiety models. In D. A. Hope (ed.), *Nebraska symposium on motivation. Volume 43: Perspectives on anxiety, panic and fear.* Lincoln, NE: University of Nebraska Press.

Mor, S., Day, H. I., Flett, G. L., & Hewitt, P. L. (1995). Perfectionism, control, and components of performance anxiety in professional artists. *Cognitive Therapy and Research, 19,* 207–25.

Mowrer, O. H. (1947). On the dual nature of learning: A reinterpretation of 'conditioning' and 'problem solving'. *Harvard Educational Review, 17,* 102–48.

Mulcahy, D., Keegan, J., Fingret, A., Wright, C., Park, A., Sparrow, J. et al (1990). Circadian variation of heart rate is affected by environment: A study of continuous electrocardiographic monitoring in members of a symphony orchestra. *British Heart Journal, 64,* 388–92.

Nash, J., & Potokar, J. (2004). Anxiety disorders. *Medicine, 32,* 17–21.

Öhman, A. (1986). Face the beast and fear the face: Animal and social fears as prototypes for evolutionary analyses of emotion. *Psychophysiology, 23,* 123–54.

Ollendick, T. H. (1995). Cognitive-behavioral treatment of panic disorder with agoraphobia in adolescents: A multiple baseline design analysis. *Behavior Therapy, 26,* 517–31.

Olsson, A., & Phelps, E. A. (2004). Learned fear of 'unseen' faces after Pavlovian, observational, and instructed fear. *Psychological Science, 15,* 822–8.

Osborne, M. S., & Kenny, D. T. (2005). Development and validation of a music performance anxiety inventory for gifted adolescent musicians. *Journal of Anxiety Disorders, 19,* 725–51.

Osborne, M. S., & Kenny, D. T. (2008). The role of sensitizing experiences in music performance anxiety in adolescent musicians. *Psychology of Music, 36,* 447–462.

Osborne, M. S., Kenny, D. T., & Holsomback, R. (2005). Assessment of music performance anxiety in late childhood: A validation study of the Music Performance Anxiety Inventory for Adolescents (MPAI-A). *International Journal of Stress Management, 12,* 312–30.

Osborne, M. S., Kenny D. T., & Cooksey, J. (2007). Impact of a cognitive-behavioural treatment program on music performance anxiety in secondary school music students: A pilot study. *Musicae Scientiae, Special Issue 2007,* 53–84.

Öst, L.-G. (1985). Mode of acquisition of phobias. *Acta Universitatis Uppsaliensis (Abstracts of Uppsala Dissertations from the Faculty of Medicine), 529,* 1–45.

Ostwald, P. F. (1994). Historical perspectives on the treatment of performing and creative artists. *Medical Problems of Performing Artists, 9,* 113–18.

Ostwald, P. F., Baron, B. C., Byl, N. M., et al (1994). Performing arts medicine. *Western Journal of Medicine, 160,* 48–52.

Papageorgi, I., Hallam, S., & Welch, G. F. (2007). A conceptual framework for understanding musical performance. *Research Studies in Music Education, 28,* 83–107.

Puliafico, A. C., & Kendall, P. C. (2006). Threat-related attentional bias in anxious youth: A review. *Clinical Child and Family Psychology Review, 9,* 162–80.

Pauli, P., Dengler, W., Wiedmann, G., Montoya, P., Flor, H., Birbaumer, N., & Buchkremer, G. (1997). Behavioral and neurophysiological evidence for altered processing of anxiety-related words in panic disorder. *Journal of Abnormal Psychology, 106,* 213–20.

Pavlov, I. P. (1927). *Conditioned reflexes: An investigation of the physiological activity of the cerebral cortex* (trans. and ed. G. V. Anrep). London: Oxford University Press.

Peterson, C. (2000). The future of optimism. *American Psychologist, 55,* 44–55.

Phelps, E. A. (2006). Emotion and cognition: Insights from studies of the human amygdala. *Annual Review of Psychology, 57,* 27–53.

Powell, D. H. (2004). Behavioral treatment of debilitating test anxiety among medical students. *Journal of Clinical Psychology, 60,* 853–65.

Rachman, S. J. (1991). Neo-conditioning and the classical theory of fear acquisition. *Clinical Psychology Review, 11,* 155–73.

Reiss, S., Peterson., R. A., Gursky, D. M., & McNally, R. J. (1986). Anxiety sensitivity, anxiety frequency, and the predction of fearfulness. *Behavior Research and Therapy, 24,* 1–8.

Rae, G., & McCambridge, K. (2004). Correlates of performance anxiety in practical music exams. *Psychology of Music, 32,* 432–9.

Rodebaugh, T. L., Holaway, R. M., & Heimberg, R. G. (2004). The treatment of social anxiety disorder. *Clinical Psychology Review, 24,* 883–908.

Ryan, C. A. (1998). Exploring musical performance anxiety in children. *Medical Problems of Performing Artists, 13,* 83–8.

Ryan, C. A. (2003). A study of the differential responses of male and female children to musical performance anxiety. *Dissertation Abstracts International Section A: Humanities and Social Sciences, 63 (7-A),* 2487.

Salmon, P. (1990). A psychological perspective on musical performance anxiety: A review of the literature. *Medical Problems of Performing Artists, 5,* 2–11.

Sanderson, W. C., DiNardo, P. A., Rapee, R. M., & Barlow, D. H. (1990). Syndrome comorbidity in patients diagnosed with a DSM-III-R anxicty disorder. *Journal of Abnormal Psychology, 99,* 308–12.

Seligman, M. E. P. (1991). *Learned optimism: How to change your mind and your life.* New York: Pocket Books.

Senyshyn, Y. (1999). Perspectives on performance and anxiety and their implications for creative teaching. *Canadian Journal of Education, 24,* 30–41.

Simon, J. A., & Martens, R. (1979). Children's activity in sport and nonsport evaluative activities. *Journal of Sport Psychology, 1,* 160–9.

Sinclair, S., Dunn, E., & Lowery, B. (2005). The relationship between parental racial attitudes and children's implicit prejudice. *Journal of Experimental Social Psychology, 41,* 283–9.

Skinner, B. F. (1961). *Reinforcement today.* East Norwalk, CT: Appleton-Century-Crofts.

Smith, A. M., Maragos, A., & van Dyke, A. (2000). Psychology of the musician. In R. Tubiana & P. Camadio (eds), *Medical problems of the instrumentalist musician* (pp. 135–70). London: Martin Dunitz.

Smith, A. J., & Rickard, N. S. (2004). Prediction of music performance anxiety via personality and trait anxiety in young musicians. *Australian Journal of Music Education, 1,* 3–12.

Sparrow, W. A., & Newell, K. M. (1998). Metabolic energy expenditure and the regulation of movement economy. *Psychonomic Bulletin and Review, 5,* 173–96.

Spielberger, C. D. (1985). Anxiety, cognition, and affect: A state–trait perspective. In A. H. Tuma & J. D. Maser (eds), *Anxiety and the anxiety disorders* (pp. 171–82). Hillsdale, NJ: Erlbaum.

Squire, L. R., & Zola-Morgan, S. (1991). The medial temporal lobe memory system. *Science, 253,* 1380–6.

Steptoe, A. (1998). Psychophysiological bases of disease. In D. W. Johnston & M. Johnston (eds), *Comprehensive clinical psychology. Volume 8: Health psychology* (pp. 39–78). New York: Elsevier.

Steptoe, A. (2001). Negative emotions in music making: The problem of performance anxiety. In P. N. Juslin & J. A. Sloboda (eds), *Music and emotion: Theory and research* (pp. 291–307). Oxford: Oxford University Press.

Sternbach, D. J. (1995). Musicians: a neglected working population in crisis. In S. L Sauter & L. R. Murphy (eds), *Organizational risk factors for job stress* (pp. 283–302). Washington, DC: American Psychological Association.

Stoebert, J., & Eismann, U. (in press). Perfectionism in young musicians: Relations with motivation, effort, achievement and distress. *Personality and Individual Differences*.

Tamborrino, R. A. (2001). An examination of performance anxiety associated with solo performance of college-level music majors. *Dissertation Abstracts International*, *62 (5-A)*, 1636.

Tassi, P., Bonnefond, A., Hoeft, A., Eschenlauer, R., & Muzet, A. (2003). Arousal and vigilance: Do they differ? Study in a sleep inertia paradigm. *Sleep Research Online*, *5*, 83–7. Retrieved from http://www.sro.org/2003/Tassi/83/

Taubman-Ben-Ari, O., Mikulincer, M., & Gillath, O. (2005). From parents to children—similarity in parents and offspring driving styles. *Transportation Research Part F: Traffic Psychology and Behaviour*, *8*, 19–29.

Turkington, D., Dudley, R., Warman, D. M., & Beck, A. T. (2006). Cognitive-behavioral therapy for schizophrenia: A review. *Focus*, *4*, 223–33.

Turner, S. M., Johnson, M. R., Beidel, D. C., Heiser, N. A., & Lydiard, R. B. (2003). The social thoughts and beliefs scale: a new inventory for assessing cognitions in social phobia. *Psychological Assessment*, *15*, 384–91.

van Kemenade, J. F., van Son, M. J., & van Heesch, N. C. (1995). Performance anxiety among professional musicians in symphonic orchestras: a self-report study. *Psychological Reports*, *77*, 555–62.

Wesner, R. B., Noyes, R., Jr., & Davis, T. L. (1990). The occurrence of performance anxiety among musicians. *Journal of Affective Disorders*, *18*, 177–85.

Wolfe, M. L. (1989). Correlates of adaptive and maladaptive musical performance anxiety. *Medical Problems of Performing Artists*, *4*, 49–56.

CHAPTER 17

EXPRESSION AND COMMUNICATION OF EMOTION IN MUSIC PERFORMANCE

PATRIK N. JUSLIN AND RENEE TIMMERS

17.1 INTRODUCTION

Music researchers frequently regard music in terms of works, and regard these works in terms of scores. Yet in an important sense, music exists only in the moment of its performance, and performances of the same work may differ considerably. Repp (1998) found that commercial recordings of the same piece by different pianists can differ in tempo by up to a factor of two. Such findings suggest that performers play a crucial role in shaping how listeners experience music. Performers bring pieces of music to life, thus increasing the chances that listeners will perceive the music as expressive of emotions (among other things). The precise nature of this process has been elusive, and it is only in the previous decade that researchers have started to investigate more systematically how emotional expression in performance is achieved.

The aim of this chapter is to provide an up-to-date review of theory and research on how music performers express and communicate emotions to listeners through their performances.[1] The main focus is on music-psychological studies of *expression* and *perception* of emotions in Western music performances, though towards the end we also briefly discuss how a performer might contribute to the *induction* of felt emotions in listeners.

17.1.1 Performance expression: a working definition

There is still no universally accepted definition of the concept of *expression*. In the previous literature on music performance (Gabrielsson, 1999, 2003), the term has been used to refer to both (a) the relationships among a performer's interpretation of a specific piece of music and measurable small-scale variations in timing, dynamics, vibrato, and articulation that make up the 'microstructure' of the performance, and (b) the relationships among such variations in the performance and the listener's perception of the performance. To fully understand expression, however, it is important to study both production and perception of expression in a combined fashion; that is, expressive variations in performance should be related to both the performer's intention and the listener's perception (Gabrielsson & Juslin, 1996).

Expression has often been treated as a homogeneous category, of which there is more or less (Marchand, 1975). However, a careful review of the literature suggests that performance expression is better conceived of as a *multi-dimensional* phenomenon that can be decomposed into subcomponents that make distinct contributions to the aesthetic impact of a performance. The exact nature of these components of expression is still being discussed, although drawing on previous research, it has been suggested that expression in a performance derives from five main sources, collectively referred to as the GERMS model (Juslin, 2003):

- *Generative rules (G)* that mark the structure in a musical manner (Clarke, 1988). By means of variations in such parameters as timing, dynamics, and articulation, a performer is able to highlight group boundaries, metrical accents, and harmonic structure.
- *Emotional expression (E)* that serves to communicate emotions to listeners (Juslin, 1997a). By manipulating features of the performance such as tempo or loudness, a performer might (explicitly or implicitly) attempt to render the performance with an emotional character that appears suitable for the piece in question.
- *Random fluctuations (R)* that reflect human limitations in motor precision (Gilden, 2001). It has been shown in several studies that when expert musicians try to play perfectly even time intervals, they still show small, involuntary fluctuations in timing.
- *Motion principles (M)* that hold that tempo changes should follow natural patterns of human movement or 'biological motion' in order to obtain a pleasing shape (Shove & Repp, 1995).

---

[1] This a thoroughly revised version of a previous overview of the field (Juslin, 2001).

- *Stylistic unexpectedness (S)* that reflects a performer's deliberate attempts to 'deviate' from stylistic expectations regarding performance conventions, to add tension and unpredictability to the performance (Meyer, 1956, p. 206).

In a good performance, all components merge seamlessly together, though for particular purposes (e.g. research, teaching), it may be useful to consider them separately. The reasons for this are that the components have different origins, show different characteristics, and are processed by partly different regions of the brain (Juslin, 2003). Table 17.1 presents some of the hypothesized characteristics of each component (see also Juslin, Friberg, & Bresin, 2002).

17.1.2 Expression and communication of emotions

In this chapter, we focus on *emotional* expression (for a working definition of emotions, see Chapter 1, this volume), whilst acknowledging that the other components are also important. In one sense, the term 'emotional expression' is slightly misleading: it is only sometimes that performers are truly expressing their own emotions during the performance—perhaps because optimal performance requires a type of psychological state (e.g. relaxed concentration) that is incompatible with strong emotions (Connolly & Williamon, 2004). What is usually presented in a music performance is not the emotion itself, but rather its *expressive form*—derived from other forms of non-verbal communication. Still, the term 'emotional expression' is now widely established, and has been used in both cases where the expression is 'spontaneous' (genuinely felt) and cases where it is 'symbolic' (portrayed).

The notion of 'expression' does not require that there is a correspondence between what the listener perceives in a performance and what the performer intends to express. In contrast, the concept of 'communication' requires that there is both a performer's intention to express a specific emotion and recognition of this emotion by a listener. The listener may, additionally, come to experience or *feel* the emotion in question—but this is not required for it to qualify as a case of communication.[2] Note also that the term 'communication' can be used regardless of whether the transmitted emotions are genuinely felt or simply 'portrayed' by the performer in a more symbolic manner, since music's potential to convey referential information is separate from the issue of whether the music is the result of felt emotion or a sending intention or both.

Regarding music as communication of emotions is not uncontroversial (for a discussion, see Juslin, 2005), though it is reasonable to assume that many performers are concerned about whether their musical interpretation is perceived by the audience the

---

[2] As discussed later in this chapter (see Section 17.4), a performer might also want to 'move' the listener through his or her performance. Hence, a performer may both intend to express (or portray) an emotion that is recognized by the listener and influence the emotion felt by the listener. Unlike Trehub et al in Chapter 23 (this volume) we do not regard these possibilities as mutually exclusive. On the contrary, it is known from research in non-verbal communication of affect that people do both (Juslin & Scherer, 2005, p. 82).

Table 17.1 Summary of hypotheses for five components of performance expression according to the GERMS model (adapted from Juslin, 2003)

Characteristic	Component				
	G	E	R	M	S
Origin of pattern	Generative transformations of the musical structure	Emotion-specific patterns of acoustic cues deriving from vocal expression	Internal timekeeper and motor delay variance reflecting human limitations	Biological motion; distinct patterns of movement typical of human beings	Deviations from expected performance conventions
Nature of pattern	Local expressive features related to the structural interpretation	Mainly overall levels of multiple uncertain, partly redundant cues that are compensatory	Semi-random patterns, (1/f noise and white noise); very small in magnitude, irregular	Dynamic, non-compensatory patterns; smooth and global	Local features, not predictable from the music structure
Salient brain regions in pattern processing	Left hemisphere, areas adjacent to Broca's area	Right inferior frontal regions, basal ganglia, mirror neurons in pre-motor regions	Left hemisphere, motor areas, the cerebellum	Left hemisphere, STS (the superior temporal sulcus)	Anterior cingulate cortex
Perceptual effects	Clarifies the structure; enhances the inherent expression of a piece	Expresses emotions (primarily in broad emotion categories)	Generates a 'living' and natural quality	Yields expressive form that is similar to human gestures	Heightens tension and unpredictability
Knowledge dependence	Medium	Low	None	Low	High
Aesthetic contribution	Beauty, Order, Coherence	Recognition, Arousal, Personal expression	Unevenness, Novelty	Balance, Unity, Recognition	Originality, Arousal
Under voluntary control	Yes, partly	Yes	No	Yes, partly	Yes

way that they intended it: 'unless you think of what the music carries, you will not convey it to the audience' (Menuhin, 1996, p. 406). A performer might, for instance, wish to highlight an emotional character in the piece. The degree to which performer and listeners agree about the resulting expression could pragmatically be seen as a measure of whether the communication was successful or not.

The importance of emotion and communication in music performance is highlighted in survey studies and in-depth interviews with performers and listeners. In a study featuring 145 listeners (17–74 years old), the majority of the participants reported experiencing that music communicates emotions, as revealed by their own free responses to an open-ended question, and 76 per cent of them responded that music expresses emotions 'often' (Juslin & Laukka, 2004). Similarly, a study by Lindström, Juslin, Bresin, and Williamon (2003), featuring 135 expert musicians from well-known music conservatoires in England, Italy and Sweden revealed that the majority of the musicians defined expression in performance in terms of 'communicating emotions' and 'playing with feeling', as indicated by their own free responses. Furthermore, 83 per cent of the musicians claimed that they try to express specific emotions in their performance 'always' or 'often'. Minassian, Gayford, and Sloboda (2003) conducted a questionnaire study featuring 53 high-level classical performers, and investigated which factors were statistically associated with an 'optimal' performance. Performances judged as optimal tended to be those where the performer (a) had a clear intention to communicate (usually an emotional message), (b) was emotionally engaged with the music, and (c) believed the message had been received by the audience. Interview studies with popular musicians confirm the importance of emotion, feeling, expression, and communication (Boyd & George-Warren, 1992, pp. 103–8; see also Chapter 15, this volume).

Although these results suggest considerable agreement among musicians concerning the importance of expressing emotions in musical performances, opinions of individual musicians differ. They range from strong opponents to 'emotion in performance' in general to outspoken proponents of the need to experience feelings to successfully portray emotions in performance (Jarosy & Fiedler, 1936). Intentions to express emotions in the performance may certainly be more common in certain musical styles (e.g. opera, blues, baroque) than in others (e.g. serial music), and they may also be more common among certain performers (Figure 17.1) than among others. Still, they occur frequently enough to be of legitimate interest to artists and researchers alike. Hence, expression and communication of emotion in music performance has attracted a fair amount of empirical research, as reviewed in the following.

17.2 EMPIRICAL RESEARCH

Historical treatises written by both music performers and composers provide a rich source of information about performers' views on expression, and often feature

Fig. 17.1 Expressive performance: blues guitarist B. B. King in concert. King (1996) explained his relationship to the guitar: 'If I was feeling lonely, I'd pick up the guitar; feel like talking, pick up the guitar; if something's bugging me, just grab the guitar and play out the anger; happy, horny, mad or sad, the guitar was right there. It was incredible luxury to have this instrument to stroke whenever the passion overcame me' (p. 41). 'I started experimenting with sounds that expressed my emotions, whether happy or sad, bouncy or bluesy. I was looking for ways to let my guitar sing' (p. 123). (Photographs by Steve Berman.)

detailed descriptions or prescriptions about performance practices to enhance emotional expression (Bach, 1778/1985; Buelow, 1983; Mattheson, 1739). Topics addressed include interpretative choices with regard to tempo, rubato, vibrato, ornamentation, phrasing, and the structural interpretation of figural patterns. Instead of repeating these prescriptions, which have not been scientifically evaluated in most cases, we will review modern music-psychological studies of how performers express emotions. We shall begin by reviewing the most well-developed line of research, based on the so-called standard paradigm, before considering alternative paradigms and future directions in the domain.

17.2.1 The standard paradigm

Although the perceived expression of a piece depends *both* on the composed structure and on its realization in performance, one may, in principle at least, separate the two aspects for research purposes. In fact, such a distinction has formed the basis of a series of studies in the 1990s of how performers communicate emotions to listeners. However, the roots of this research can be found in the 1930s, when Seashore famously suggested that 'deviation from the exact . . . is the medium for the creation of the beautiful—for the conveying of emotion' (quoted in H. G. Seashore, 1937, p. 155). Seashore did not provide any theory to explain *how* such deviations convey emotions to a listener, as noted by Meyer (1956). However, Seashore did suggest a paradigm suitable for studying this problem: he referred to a study by Fairbanks (1940), where actors were required to express various emotions in speech sequences that were later analysed acoustically. Seashore concluded that 'we can exactly parallel this experiment in the field of music' (Seashore, 1947, p. 176). Strangely, Seashore's plea went unheard, and he did not publish any study of that sort himself. By the late eighties, only two studies on this topic had been published (i.e. Kotlyar & Morozov, 1976; Senju & Ohgushi, 1987). After this modest beginning, however, there was a virtual explosion of studies in the early 1990s. Most of these studies used the paradigm Seashore had suggested 40 years earlier.

The *standard paradigm*, a term borrowed from studies of vocal expression, means that performers are asked to play melodies with the aim of expressing different emotions selected by the researcher. The resulting performances are first recorded, and then evaluated in listening tests to study whether listeners can recognize the intended expressions. The performances are commonly presented in an experimental set-up in which participants systematically judge the performances in random order. Listeners' judgements are measured in terms of *forced choice* (Juslin, 1997b, Experiment 1), *adjective ratings* (Juslin, 1997a), *free labelling* (Juslin, 1997c), or *continuous response* (Sloboda & Lehmann, 2001; for an overview of continuous response methods, see Chapter 9, this volume). Furthermore, each performance is analysed in detail to explore what acoustic means the performers used to achieve each emotional expression. The assumption is that, because the melody remains the same in different emotional expressions, any effects that appear in listeners' judgements or in acoustic measures should mainly be the result of the performer's expressive intention. To have performers play the same piece with different expressions might appear 'unnatural' from a musical point of view. However, this design is required to secure the internal validity of the experiment: if different emotions are expressed by different melodies, it is really impossible to know whether the obtained effects on listener judgements and performance measures are due to the melody, the performance, or some interaction among the two. Indeed, the standard paradigm has proved to be fruitful in a number of ways, as demonstrated below.

17.2.2 Accuracy of communication

The primary issue is whether music performers are able to communicate emotions to listeners at all. In a pioneering study, Kotlyar and Morozov (1976) asked ten opera singers to perform phrases from various pieces of music in such a way that they would communicate *joy*, *anger*, *sorrow* and *fear* to listeners. Musically trained listeners were asked to judge the expression of each performance. The results showed that the listeners were highly successful at recognizing the intended expression. Since then, several studies have confirmed that performers are able to communicate emotions to listeners (e.g. Behrens & Green, 1993; Gabrielsson & Juslin, 1996; Gabrielsson & Lindström, 1995; Juslin, 1997a, 1997c, 2000; Juslin & Madison, 1999; Ohgushi & Hattori, 1996; Sundberg, Iwarsson, & Hagegård, 1995).

Juslin and Laukka (2003) reviewed 41 studies of emotional expression in performance. The studies covered a wide range of musical styles such as classical music, folk music, Indian *ragas*, jazz, pop, rock, children's songs, and free improvisations. The most common style was classical music (17 studies = 41 per cent). The number of emotions studied ranged from three to nine ($M = 4.98$) and very frequently included the five emotions *happiness, sadness, anger, fear,* and *love/tenderness*. Twelve musical instruments and twelve nationalities were included. Most studies used professional performers, and their performances were typically monophonic to facilitate acoustic measurements. A meta-analysis of communication accuracy, as measured in a subset of 29 studies, suggested that professional performers could communicate the above emotions to listeners with an accuracy nearly as high as in facial and vocal expression of emotions. The overall decoding accuracy was equivalent to a raw score of proportion correct of $p_c = .70$ in a forced-choice task with five response alternatives. Across studies, *sadness* and *anger* were the two emotions communicated with the highest level of accuracy—and this pattern was obtained for both musical and vocal expression.

One objection to the above findings could be that the accuracy is boosted because of the response formats used. In most studies, the listeners made their judgements by means of forced choice or adjective ratings—methods that offer only a limited number of response options. To address this problem, Juslin (1997c) explored the generalizability of decoding accuracy across different response formats, using a *parallel enrichment procedure* (see Rosenthal, 1982). That is, quantitative data from forced-choice judgements of music performances were augmented by qualitative data from free labelling of the same performances. Results indicated that successful communication was possible regardless of the response format, although free labelling yielded larger variability in listeners' responses—as could be expected.

17.2.3 Code description

Like most psychological processes, the expressive strategies used by music performers are not always available to conscious introspection. Hence, researchers must capture the strategies by means of acoustic measurements, commonly carried out using computer software. Table 17.2 presents a summary of the most important acoustic parameters and also explains how they are measured. In the following, we refer to these parameters as *cues* (i.e. bits of information) that together make up the *code* (i.e. the particular combination of cue values) used to express each emotion. Studies have shown that the performer's expressive intention might affect numerous cues in the performance. Acoustic analyses have been simplified by the development of some fairly advanced software packages for digital sound analysis. One of the more frequently used

Table 17.2 Definition and measurement of the primary acoustic cues in emotional expression in music performance

Acoustic cues	Perceived correlate	Definition and measurement
Pitch		
Fundamental frequency (F0)	Pitch	Acoustically, F0 is defined as the lowest periodic cycle component of the acoustic waveform. One can distinguish between the macro pitch level of particular musical pieces, and the micro intonation of the performance. The former is often given in the unit of the semitone, the latter is given in terms of deviations from the notated macro pitch (e.g. in cents).
F0 contour	Intonation contour	Sequence of F0 values. In music, intonation refers to the manner in which the performer approaches and/or maintains the prescribed pitch of notes, in terms of deviations from precise pitch.
Vibrato	Vibrato	Periodic changes in the pitch (or loudness) of a tone. Depth and rate of vibrato can be measured manually from the F0 trace (or amplitude envelope).
Intensity		
Intensity	Loudness	Intensity is a measure of the energy in the acoustic signal. Usually measured from the amplitude of the acoustic waveform. The standard unit used to quantify intensity is a logarithmic transformation of the amplitude called the decibel (dB).
Attack	Rapidity of tone onsets	Attack refers to the rise time or rate of rise of the amplitude of individual notes. Usually measured from the acoustic waveform.
Temporal features		
Tempo	Velocity of music	The mean tempo of a performance is obtained by dividing the total duration of the performance until the onset of its final note by the number of beats, and then calculating the number of beats per minute (bpm).
Articulation	Proportion of sound to silence in successive notes	The mean articulation of a performance is typically obtained by measuring two durations for each tone—the duration from the onset of a tone until the onset of the next tone (d_{ii}), and the duration from the onset of a tone until its offset (d_{io}). These durations are used to calculate the d_{io}/d_{ii} ratio (the articulation) of each tone. These values are averaged across the performance and expressed as a percentage. A value around 100% refers to *legato* articulation; a value of c. 70% or lower refers to staccato articulation.
Timing	Tempo and rhythm variation	Timing variations are usually described as 'deviations' from the nominal values of a musical notation. Overall measures of the amount of deviations in a performance may be obtained by calculating the number of notes whose deviation is less than a given percent of the note value. Another index of timing changes concerns so-called durational contrasts between 'long' and 'short' notes in rhythm patterns. Contrasts may be played with 'sharp' durational contrasts (close to or larger than the nominal ratio) or with 'soft' durational contrasts (a reduced ratio).

Table 17.2 Definition and measurement of the primary acoustic cues in emotional expression in music performance (continued)

Acoustic cues	Perceived correlate	Definition and measurement
Timbre		
High-frequency energy	Timbre	Refers to the relative proportion of total acoustic energy above versus below a certain cut-off frequency in the frequency spectrum of the performance. In music performance, timbre is in part a characteristic of the specific instrument. However, different techniques of playing may also influence the timbre of many instruments, such as the guitar.
The singer's formant	Timbre	The singer's formant refers to a strong resonance around 2500–3000 Hz, and adds brilliance and carrying power to the voice. It is attributed to a lowered larynx and widened pharynx, which form an additional resonance cavity (see p. 597).

program packages is the *PRAAT* software, developed by Boersma and Weenink (1999), which can be freely downloaded for research purposes at: http://www.fon.hum.uva.nl/praat/. Though the program was intended for analysis of emotion in speech (Juslin & Scherer, 2005), it offers excellent possibilities for analysing (most of) the acoustic cues used in music performance. In addition, researchers have recently developed algorithms for an automatic analysis of acoustic cues (Friberg, Schoonderwaldt, & Juslin, 2007), which could help to speed up the complicated and time-consuming process of manually analysing cues.

A description of the code established in studies so far is presented in Figure 17.2. Included are the emotions that have been studied most thoroughly: *happiness, sadness, anger, fear,* and *love/tenderness.* These emotions represent a natural point of departure since they are regarded as 'typical' emotions by lay people (Shaver, Schwartz, Kirson, & O'Connor, 1987), have been postulated as *basic emotions* by researchers (Plutchik, 1994, Chapter 3), occur in expression marks of musical scores (festoso, dolente, furioso, timoroso, teneramente), and figure prominently in both performance treatises (Hudson, 1994) and sleeve notes to music CDs. Figure 17.2 combines categorical and dimensional approaches to emotions in music to illustrate that the code allows performers to communicate both graded signals (e.g. level of activity) and categorical signals (e.g. sadness). Each basic emotion is located at an approximate point in the two-dimensional emotional space constituted by *valence* and *activity level.* The placement of each emotion was largely based on the findings from a study where participants rated the valence and activity of 400 emotion terms (Whissell, 1989; see also Russell, 1980).

As seen in Figure 17.2, the acoustic cues include tempo, sound level, timing, intonation, articulation, timbre, vibrato, tone attacks, tone decays, and pauses. Both the mean level of a cue and its variability throughout the performance may be important for the communicative process. For example, *sadness* expressions are associated with

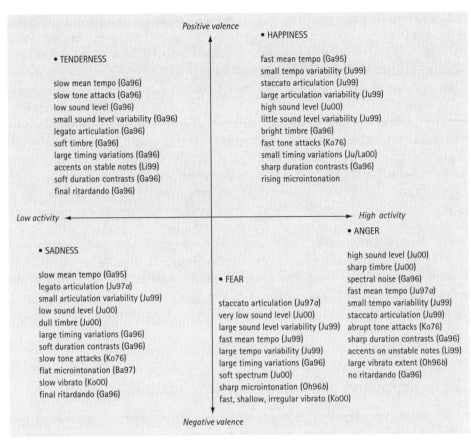

Positive valence

• HAPPINESS

• TENDERNESS

slow mean tempo (Ga96)
slow tone attacks (Ga96)
low sound level (Ga96)
small sound level variability (Ga96)
legato articulation (Ga96)
soft timbre (Ga96)
large timing variations (Ga96)
accents on stable notes (Li99)
soft duration contrasts (Ga96)
final ritardando (Ga96)

fast mean tempo (Ga95)
small tempo variability (Ju99)
staccato articulation (Ju99)
large articulation variability (Ju99)
high sound level (Ju00)
little sound level variability (Ju99)
bright timbre (Ga96)
fast tone attacks (Ko76)
small timing variations (Ju/La00)
sharp duration contrasts (Ga96)
rising microintonation

Low activity ◄———————————————————► *High activity*

• ANGER

• SADNESS

slow mean tempo (Ga95)
legato articulation (Ju97*a*)
small articulation variability (Ju99)
low sound level (Ju00)
dull timbre (Ju00)
large timing variations (Ga96)
soft duration contrasts (Ga96)
slow tone attacks (Ko76)
flat microintonation (Ba97)
slow vibrato (Ko00)
final ritardando (Ga96)

• FEAR

staccato articulation (Ju97*a*)
very low sound level (Ju00)
large sound level variability (Ju99)
fast mean tempo (Ju99)
large tempo variability (Ju99)
large timing variations (Ga96)
soft spectrum (Ju00)
sharp microintonation (Oh96*b*)
fast, shallow, irregular vibrato (Ko00)

high sound level (Ju00)
sharp timbre (Ju00)
spectral noise (Ga96)
fast mean tempo (Ju97*a*)
small tempo variability (Ju99)
staccato articulation (Ju99)
abrupt tone attacks (Ko76)
sharp duration contrasts (Ga96)
accents on unstable notes (Li99)
large vibrato extent (Oh96*b*)
no ritardando (Ga96)

Negative valence

Fig. 17.2 Summary of cue utilization in performers' communication of emotion in music. (One representative study is cited for each cue. Authors' names are abbreviated to the initial two letters of the first author (and the second author if needed for clarity), and the publication year of the last two digits, e.g. Ko76 = Kotlyar & Morozov, 1976).

slow tempo, low sound level, legato articulation, small articulation variability, slow tone attacks, and soft timbre, whereas *happiness* expressions are associated with fast tempo, high sound level, staccato articulation, large articulation variability, fast tone attacks, and bright timbre. Figure 17.2 is limited to a few seemingly 'static' emotion categories, but it is easy to imagine how the emotional expression might be gradually changed along the two dimensions during the course of a performance. In particular, continuously varying levels of activity or emotion intensity can easily be conveyed by means of global and local performance cues (Sloboda & Lehmann, 2001; Timmers, 2007b, Timmers, 2007c). Some of the expressive cues in Figure 17.2 (e.g. tempo) are perhaps common knowledge to most performers, whereas others (e.g. duration contrasts) are less obvious. The exact number of cues available depends on the instrument used. Moreover, the cue utilization is not completely consistent across performers, instruments, or pieces of music (Juslin, 2000), because performers have to adapt the code to different aspects of the performance context.

Research to date has primarily focused on the expression of a set of basic emotions. The basic emotions represent important 'anchor points' in the emotion space (see Figure 17.2), but do not exhaust the expressive possibilities available to the performer. Further complexity may be derived through qualifications of basic emotions. Thus, for example, two recent studies have indicated that performers can successfully communicate different levels of emotion intensity (weak vs. strong) of the same emotion to their listeners (Laukka & Juslin, 2007; Timmers & Ashley, 2007). One can also speculate whether 'secondary' or 'complex' emotions might be conveyed to some degree. Many researchers believe that such emotions constitute 'mixtures' of more basic emotions. For example, it has been proposed that *pride* involves a combination of *happiness* and *anger* (Plutchik, 1994, p. 61). Judging from Figure 17.2, the expression of *pride* would then presumably involve some kind of compromise among the patterns of cues used to communicate *happiness* and *anger*—but perhaps with a lower activity level (Whissell, 1989). Few studies have investigated more complex emotions (see Juslin et al, 2004, Table 13.2, for an example of results for complex emotions), but preliminary evidence suggests that complex emotions are difficult to communicate reliably to listeners (e.g. Gabrielsson & Juslin, 1996)—at least without additional context. Further research on complex emotions is urgently needed to clarify the boundaries of the communicative process.

17.2.4 Expressive patterns and ornamentation

Most studies of emotional expression involving the standard paradigm have concentrated on 'overall' cues that are applied in much the same manner and to the same extent throughout a musical passage (see Figure 17.2), and, indeed, experiments suggest that 'overall' levels of cues such as mean tempo explain considerably more variance in listeners' emotion judgements than does variability (Madison, 2000). Nevertheless, subtle patterns of changes or irregularities in tempo and dynamics may also suggest specific emotions. Listening tests featuring systematic, re-synthesized manipulations of real performances indicate that such patterns may be used by listeners to decode the emotional expression (Juslin & Madison, 1999). Figure 17.3 presents two examples of expressive patterns of articulation in a *sad* and a *happy* performance respectively by a professional guitar player. Note that, besides overall differences in articulation, there are also differences in the specific patterns of articulation.

What is it in the patterns that conveys the relevant information? One clue comes from a study by Lindström (1999). He found that performers emphasized different notes of a melody depending on the intended expression. For example, if a specific note in the melodic structure was regarded as especially 'happy' by the performer, then the performer emphasized this note in *happiness* expressions, but de-emphasized it in *sadness* expressions. The note emphasis was achieved by means of accents in timing, dynamics, and articulation. Leech-Wilkinson (2006a) has observed how preferences for specific means of emphasis—or 'expressive gestures'—have changed over time, in response to the wider context: 'a prominent note in a score that in 1910 was emphasized

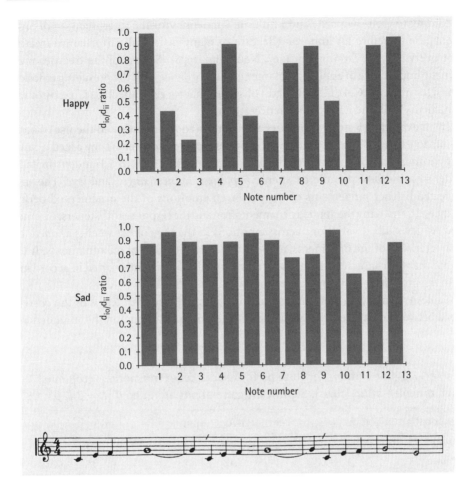

Fig. 17.3 Articulation patterns for happy and sad performances of 'When the Saints' on the electric guitar (unpublished data from Juslin 1997a). The duration from the onset of a tone until the onset of the next tone (d_{io}) and the duration from the onset of a tone until its offset (d_{ii}) were used to calculate the d_{io}/d_{ii} ratio, i.e. the articulation. Articulation close to 1.0 may be referred to as legato, whereas articulation below 0.7 may be referred to as staccato.

by sliding up to it from the note below, in 1950 might have been emphasized by vibrating on it, and in 1990 by increasing and decreasing its amplitude' (p. 60). However, the function of the gesture remains the same: it signals the importance of a specific note in the musical structure. Which note is deemed important depends on the performer's interpretation.

Another structure-related means of expressing emotions in a musical performance is the use of *ornamentation*. Ornaments are notes that embellish a melodic line and can be added or omitted without influencing the underlying melodic structure. Especially in baroque music, it was common practice for performers to embellish the music according to their own taste and intuition. Guidelines for the interpretation of ornaments are therefore an important feature of many historical performance treatises (for overviews, see Donington, 1963; Neumann, 1978). Several of the treatises mention the importance of applying ornaments in accordance with the prevailing emotion. Thus, for instance, C. P. E. Bach (1752) observed that for each affect, be it happy or sad, ornaments 'will lend a fitting assistance' (p. 79).

In an exploratory study, Timmers and Ashley (2007) investigated the use of ornaments to express different emotions by present-day performers. They asked a flutist and violinist to ornament three musical fragments taken from a Handel sonata, in order to communicate mild or intense *happiness, sadness, anger,* and *love.* They also collected listener judgements of the perceived emotions of the ornamented performances. In analysing the applied ornamentation and the responses of listeners, Timmers and Ashley studied variations across emotions in the type of ornaments applied, the characteristics of the ornaments, and the structural position of the ornaments. It was found that the characteristics of the ornaments were consistently varied in accordance with the intended emotional expression.

Tables 17.3 and 17.4 show an overview of the main results in terms of the correlations between measured characteristics of the ornamentation and the intended and

Table 17.3 Correlations for flute performances between emotions (columns) and ornamentation (rows). Significant correlations are in bold (N = 24, p <.05)

Emotion*	i–H	i–L	i–S	i–A	r–H	r–L	r–S	r–A
Single	−.09	−.02	**.59**	−.48	−.42	**.53**	**.70**	**−.62**
Double	−.27	−.03	.11	.18	.13	−.01	.07	.03
Trill	.17	.13	**−.60**	.30	.30	−.44	**−.66**	**.54**
Turn	.41	−.35	−.10	.05	.10	−.19	−.16	.12
Mordent	.05	−.23	−.12	.29	−.05	−.31	−.21	.39
Slide	.00	**.55**	−.17	−.38	.14	.32	−.05	−.17
Arpeggio	.08	−.11	−.42	**.45**	.22	**−.50**	**−.55**	**.41**
Substitute	.08	.04	−.28	.17	.08	−.26	−.19	.04
Complexity	.07	.01	**−.55**	**.46**	.41	**−.49**	**−.68**	**.62**
Density	−.25	.42	−.27	.10	**.56**	.08	−.27	−.05
On-timing	−.41	−.28	**.48**	.21	−.22	−.07	.35	.09
Duration	−.32	.17	**.61**	−.46	−.25	**.57**	**.64**	−.48
Direction	.18	.25	.02	−.45	.00	**.55**	.25	**−.59**
Harmony	−.02	.20	**−.55**	.38	−.36	−.45	**−.56**	.52
Meter	−.42	−.32	**.79**	−.05	−.47	−.20	**.62**	.21
Form pos	−.03	−.17	**.41**	−.22	−.19	.18	.33	−.14
Bar pos	.28	−.29	.04	−.04	.03	−.11	−.17	.05

* Emotions are intended (i–H, i–L, i–S, i–A) or rated (r–H, r–L, r–S, r–A).
(From Timmers & Ashley, 2007)

Table 17.4 Correlations for violin performances between emotions (columns) and ornamentation (rows). Significant correlations are in bold (*N* = 24, *p* <.05)

Emotion*	i-H	i-L	i-S	i-A	r-H	r-L	r-S	r-A
Single app.	−.28	**.43**	.11	−.26	−.39	.18	.26	−.14
Double app.	.39	−.23	**−.58**	**.43**	.23	−.37	**−.48**	.36
Trill	**.64**	−.11	−.29	−.25	.34	.12	−.08	−.16
Turn	−.19	.11	−.19	.27	**.53**	−.07	−.27	.22
Mordent	.01	−.09	−.11	.19	.35	−.06	−.23	.14
Slide	.19	−.19	−.19	.19	.14	−.18	−.18	.24
Arpeggio	.08	−.13	.03	.02	−.15	−.04	−.19	.02
Substitute	−.24	−.08	**.55**	−.23	−.27	.16	**.48**	−.29
Complexity	.19	−.26	**−.47**	**.54**	**.57**	−.34	**−.53**	**.44**
Density	.12	−.04	**−.53**	**.45**	.16	**−.42**	**−.67**	**.54**
On-timing	.04	.19	.32	**−.55**	−.10	**.39**	**.46**	**−.41**
Duration	.11	−.26	.21	−.06	.05	−.08	.09	−.02
Direction	−.08	−.02	−.03	.13	.12	−.09	.08	.04
Harmony	.03	.28	−.17	−.13	.04	.08	−.01	.09
Meter	−.09	.23	**.46**	**−.60**	−.14	**.42**	**.51**	**−.47**
Form pos	**.45**	−.18	−.25	−.02	.27	−.02	.04	−.10
Bar pos	−.10	−.27	.29	.08	.07	−.11	.01	.02

* *Emotions are intended (i-H, i-L, i-S, i-A) or rated (r-H, r-L, r-S, r-A).*
(From Timmers & Ashley, 2007)

rated emotions, respectively. The top rows show the relative frequency of application of particular ornaments. The types of ornament distinguished were *single appoggiatura* consisting of one note, *double appoggiatura* consisting of two notes, *trills* (a rapid alternation of two notes), *turn* (the main note is ornamented by the note above and the note below the main note in this order: upper, main, lower, main note), *mordent* (the ornament follows the main note and returns to the main note: main, upper, main note), *slide* (interpolation of a leap by stepwise intervals), *arpeggio* (broken chords or large intervals), and *substitute* (the ornamental note replaces the main note).

The second set of rows in the tables shows the characteristics of the ornaments. Thus, the ornaments were either *simple*, consisting of one note, or *complex*, consisting of more than one note. The number of ornamental notes per ornament was counted ('density'). The ornaments were either timed *on the beat*, in which case the main note was displaced (delayed), or *before the beat*, in which case the main note was performed at its original metrical position (referred to as 'on-timing' in tables). The ornaments were either *short* in duration, taking less than half of the original duration of the main note, or *long*, taking half or more than half of the duration of the main note. The ornaments also *ascended* or *descended* to the main note (coded by using the interval between the first ornament and the main note). Finally, each ornamental note had a *harmonic* relationship with the root of the chord of the main note (dissonant vs. consonant—averaged across the notes).

The third set of rows indicates the structural position of the ornaments. Every ornamental note has a specific position within the *metrical* hierarchy; the metrical position of the different notes was averaged. Ornaments also occur at a particular position within the *musical fragment* (start, middle or end) and at a particular position within the *bar* (first or second half).

Tables 17.3 and 17.4 suggest that performers used most complex ornaments for *angry* performances, and least complex ornaments for *sad* performances. The simple ornaments in *sad* performances were frequently long and timed on the beat. Correspondingly, many single appoggiaturas were used in *sad* performances, but few in *angry* performances. Although the performers used distinct strategies to convey the emotions, the communication accuracy was nonetheless fairly high—with the exception of *happiness*. It should be noted that many of the above codings are approximate, and further improvements of the methodology are needed to understand the role of ornaments in communication of emotions.

17.2.5 Verifying code descriptions: synthesis

Performance analyses have shown that music performers may use a number of cues to express particular emotions. However, these analyses do not prove that listeners actually *use* the same cues in their judgements. Thus, to test the validity of hypotheses about expressive cues derived from performance analyses, it is necessary to conduct listening experiments using *synthesized* performances. There are at least two different approaches to synthesis of emotional expression in musical performance, which can answer different types of questions. Based on a distinction introduced by Egon Brunswik (1956), they can be called *representative design* and *systematic design* (Juslin, 1997b).

Representative design means that one tries to recreate the emotional expressions of real music performances by programming a computer to perform in accordance with the emotion-specific patterns of acoustic cues obtained in previous studies (Figure 17.2). Ideally, the patterns used to synthesize the emotional expression should be representative of real performances in the sense that they display similar statistical characteristics (e.g. cue intercorrelations, means, and standard deviations). Preliminary studies have shown that one can program a computer to communicate emotions with the same level of accuracy as a human performer (Juslin, 1997b, Experiment 1; see also Bresin & Friberg, 2000). Synthesized performances may be regarded as 'computational models' that demonstrate the validity of proposed hypotheses, by showing that they really 'work' with respect to listeners. However, such synthesized performances do not sound as musically satisfying as human performances do, maybe because they lack other expressive features (such as marking of structure, biological motion and random fluctuations) that are also important (Juslin et al, 2002). A representative design is useful when comparing the decoding accuracy of real and synthesized performances, although it cannot prove that the implementation of an individual cue is correct, or even that listeners are using the cue.

To be able to unambiguously attribute variance in a listener's judgements of emotions to individual acoustic cues, one has to use a systematic design, or, more specifically, a *factorial design* (i.e. an experimental design featuring all combinations of the respective factor levels). Such a design removes all intercorrelations among cues and makes it possible to ascertain the causal effects of individual cues. Note that only some of the cues listed in Figure 17.2 (i.e. mean tempo, mean sound level, mean articulation, tone attack and timbre) and none of the ornament cues have been tested in this way (see e.g, Juslin, 1997b, Experiment 2). The same reasoning applies to any experiment that attempts to establish causal relationships with dimensions, such as arousal and valence—the acoustic cues must be manipulated independently.

Lack of independent manipulation of cues might explain why many of the early studies of emotional expression in music concluded—unjustifiably—that there are strong interactions among the musical factors. Note that the occurrence of a fast tempo in a piece of music rated by listeners as 'sad' is not necessarily evidence of a cue interaction: the 'happy' effect of the fast tempo may simply have been overridden by a large number of other additive cues, which suggested a 'sad' piece; the piece might have been rated as even more 'sad', had there been a slow tempo also. Indeed, interactions can only be established in experiments using a factorial design, and such studies are still rare (e.g. Juslin, 1997b, Experiment 2; Scherer & Oshinsky, 1977). Evidence so far suggests that there are certain interactions, but that the main effects of cues explain most of the variance (Juslin & Lindström, 2009). Tempo, sound level, and timbre are the performance cues that appear to have the greatest impact on listeners' judgements of the emotional expression (if the cues are allowed to vary freely).

17.3 A THEORETICAL APPROACH: THE FUNCTIONALIST PERSPECTIVE

That music performers are able to communicate emotions to listeners is something that really requires an explanation. What is it that makes this process possible? What is the origin of the code used by performers and listeners? The only theoretical framework aimed specifically at performance aspects has been presented by Juslin (1997a; 1998). It is called the *functionalist perspective* because it assumes that many of the present characteristics of the communicative process can be understood by considering the functions that the non-verbal communication of emotions has served throughout evolution.

17.3.1 Functionalist origins of the code

Juslin (1997a, 1998, 2001) has proposed that the code used in emotional expression in music performance reflects two main factors. The first (primary) factor is innate programmes for vocal expression of basic emotions. According to this hypothesis partly inspired by Herbert Spencer (1857), the origin of the 'expressive code' is to be sought in involuntary and emotion-specific physiological changes associated with emotional reactions, which strongly influence different aspects of voice production (for a review of the relationships among emotion, physiology, and voice, see Juslin & Scherer, 2005). This notion was later named 'Spencer's law' by Juslin and Laukka (2003). It is further assumed that encoding and decoding of emotions proceed largely in terms of a limited number of basic emotion categories (Ekman, 1999; Izard, 2007; Johnson Laird & Oatley, 1992; Plutchik, 1994) that provide decoders with maximum information and discriminability. To be useful as guides to action, emotion expressions are quickly decoded in terms of just a few emotion categories related to essential life problems, such as danger (*fear*), competition (*anger*), loss (*sadness*), cooperation (*happiness*), and caregiving (*love*). One may speculate that the origins of music may be found in ceremonies of the distant past that related vocal expressions to singing: vocal expressions of basic emotions such as *happiness*, *sadness*, *anger*, and *love* probably became gradually meshed with vocal music that accompanied related cultural activities such as festivities, funerals, wars, and caregiving. The implication for music performance is that basic emotions will be *privileged* in terms of their biological preparedness for effective communication. This is not to deny that more precise emotional contents may be communicated to listeners in some cases (e.g. through context or musical conventions). (It is important to note also that this hypothesis about basic emotions concerns *only* expression and perception of emotions in music. The emotions typically *evoked* by music in listeners include a much wider range of human emotions, including many complex emotions; Juslin & Laukka, 2004; Chapter 22, this volume.)

The second factor that shapes emotional expression in performance is social learning of various forms. This is a lifelong process beginning with the early interaction between mother and infant (in fact, the 'imprinting' process could begin even prior to birth; see e.g. Parncutt, 2006). For example, when mothers talk to their infants, if they want to calm the child, they reduce the tempo and intensity of their speech, and talk with slowly falling pitch contours. If they want to express disapproval toward some unfavourable activity, they employ brief, sharp, and staccato-like contours (Papoušek, 1996). Even in the first months of life, infants are able to differentiate vocal affect expressions in infant-directed speech, and to respond adequately to their categorical emotional messages (Papoušek, Bornstein, Nuzzo, Papoušek, & Symmes, 1990). Although the code used by mothers seems to be universal, the unique expressive style of the mother modulates the expressive style of the infant—shaping its expressive skills. This modulation of expressive skills continues throughout life, as one accumulates experience and learns links between cues and extra-musical aspects such as movement (e.g. in terms of the 'extramusical templates' proposed by Sloboda, 1996). Expressive skills also develop as a result of musical training. Skilled performers of different times adapt the expressive code to their own performing style, yet show strong consistencies in their strategies for expressing different emotions (Timmers, 2007a).

Consistent with the notion that emotional expression in music performance is primarily based on a general, innate code for vocal expression of basic emotions that has served crucial functions throughout evolution is evidence that:

- there are strong similarities in the cues used to express basic emotions in vocal expression and music performance (Juslin & Laukka, 2003, Table 7)
- basic emotions in vocal expression are perceived categorically (Laukka, 2005)
- basic emotions are easier to communicate than other emotions (Gabrielsson & Juslin, 1996)
- decoding of basic emotions in music is very quick (Peretz, Gagnon, & Bouchard, 1998)
- decoding of basic emotions in music does not require musical training (Juslin, 1997a)
- expression of basic emotions in music does not require musical training (Yamasaki, 2002)
- even children (3–4 years old) are able to decode basic emotions in music with better than chance accuracy (Cunningham & Sterling, 1988)
- even children are be able to use voice-related cues to express basic emotions in their songs (Adachi & Trehub, 1998)
- the ability to decode basic emotions in music performances is correlated with measures of emotional intelligence (Resnicow, Salovey, & Repp, 2004)
- there are cross-cultural similarities in cue utilization for cues that are shared between vocal expression and music performance (Balkwill & Thompson, 1999)
- decoding of basic emotions in music performances involves many of the same brain regions as perception of basic emotions in vocal expression (Nair, Large, Steinberg, & Kelso, 2002).

17.3.2 Capturing the functional relationships: the lens model

Studies of communication of emotions in music performance present some puzzling findings, which can only be explained if the nature of the communication process is explored in greater detail. For instance, how can the communicative process usually be successful despite the fact that different instruments offer different cues and that there are so wide individual differences among performers in expressive style? One way of capturing the crucial characteristics of the communicative process is to conceptualize it in terms of a variant of Egon Brunswik's (1956) *lens model*, as first suggested and implemented by Juslin (1995, 2000).[3]

---

[3] Brunswik's (1956) lens model was originally a model of visual perception, but was subsequently used mainly in studies of cognitive judgement (for further discussion, see Juslin & Bänziger, 2009). However, Brunswik did actually also apply the model to social perception (e.g. the perception of facial expressions of emotion).

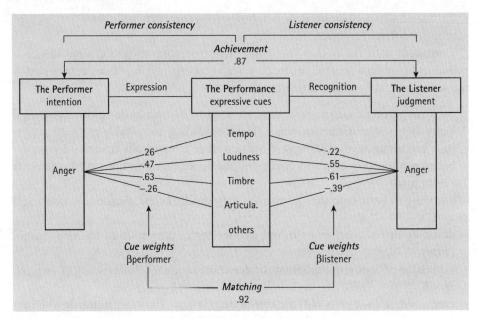

Fig. 17.4 Modified lens model of communication of emotions in musical performance (adapted from Juslin, 1995).

The modified lens model (Figure 17.4) shows how the performer 'encodes' (i.e. expresses) emotions by means of a set of acoustic cues (e.g. variations of tempo, sound level, or timbre) that are 'probabilistic' (i.e. uncertain) and partly redundant. The emotions are 'decoded' (i.e. recognized) by the listener, who utilizes these same cues to infer the expression. The cues are probabilistic because they are not perfectly reliable indicators of the intended expression. For example, a fast tempo is not a perfectly reliable indicator of *happiness* expressions, because a fast tempo occurs also in *anger* expressions. Thus, relationships among cues and emotions are merely correlational— they do not have a one-to-one mapping. Consequently, performers and listeners have to *combine* many cues for reliable communication to occur. This is not a simple matter of 'pattern matching' however, since cues contribute in an additive fashion to listeners' judgements—each expressive cue is neither necessary, nor sufficient, but the larger the number of cues used, the more reliable the communication. Redundancy among the cues reflects how sounds are produced on musical instruments. For example, a harder string attack will produce a tone that is both louder and sharper in timbre. The correlational and partly redundant nature of the cues can be nicely captured by conducting multiple regression analyses of both sides of the lens—performer and listener (see Juslin, 2000, for examples).

There are a number of indices in the lens model that are important in understanding the communicative process:

Achievement (r_a) refers to the relationship between the performer's expressive intention (e.g. intending to express sadness) and the listener's judgement (e.g. perceiving sadness). It is a measure of how well the performer succeeds in communicating a given emotion to listeners.

Cue weight ($\beta_1, \beta_2, \beta_3 \ldots$) refers to the strength of the relationship between an individual cue (e.g. tempo), on the one hand, and a performer's intentions or listeners' judgements, on the other. Cue weights indicate how individual cues are actually used by performers and listeners, respectively (e.g. that the performer is using a slow tempo to express sadness).

Matching (G) refers to the degree of similarity between the performer's and the listeners' use of acoustic cues, respectively. For effective communication to occur, the performer's use of cues (i.e. his or her cue weights) must be reasonably matched to the listeners' use of cues.

Consistency (R_e, R_s) refers to the degree of consistency with which the performer and listeners, respectively, are able to use the cues. Other things equal, the communication will be more effective if the cues are used consistently.

17.3.3 The lens model equation

As demonstrated by Juslin (2000), regression models of music performers and listeners can be mathematically related to each other by means of the *Lens Model Equation* (LME). The LME was originally presented in an influential article by Hursch, Hammond, and Hursch (1964) in the context of studies of cognitive judgement. The aim in these studies was to relate the judge's 'cognitive system' to a statistical description of the judgement task (Cooksey, 1996). However, the LME can also be used to describe music performance.

The LME (Equation 17.1) embodies the fact that the communication accuracy, or achievement (r_a), is a function of two additive components. The first component is usually called the *linear* component, because it represents that component of the achievement which can be attributed to the linear regression models of the performer and the listener. The linear component shows that achievement is a function of *performer consistency* (R_e), *listener consistency* (R_s), and *matching* (G). Performer consistency refers to the multiple correlation of the performer model (i.e. performer's intention and cues) and listener consistency refers to the multiple correlation of the listener model (i.e. listener's judgement and cues). Both these indices reflect the degree to which the regression models fit the cue utilization and are usually interpreted as measures of consistency of the cue utilization. If $R = 1.0$, then the cue utilization is perfectly consistent. Matching (G) is a measure of the extent to which the cue weights of performers and listeners are similar to each other – that is, whether they use the same code. This index is obtained by correlating the predicted values of the performer's regression model with the predicted values of the listener's regression model. The resulting correlation is conceptually interpreted as the extent to which the performer's cue weights and the listener's cue weights would agree if both regression models were perfect (i.e. $R_e = R_s = 1.0$).

$$r_a = G R_e R_s + C \sqrt{(1-R_e^2)} \sqrt{(1-R_s^2)} \qquad 17.1$$

If the communication under study is unsuccessful, we might ask whether this is because (a) the performer uses a different code from that of the listeners (indicated by a low G value), (b) the performer is applying the code inconsistently (indicated by a low R_e value), or (c) the listeners apply their code inconsistently (indicated by a low R_s value). These three factors set the upper limit of achievement (Hursch et al, 1964). By analysing each of them separately, it becomes possible to see how the communicative process can be improved (Juslin, 1998).

The second component of the LME is typically called the *unmodelled* component of the communicative process. It includes both unsystematic and systematic variance not accounted for by the linear component. This includes effects of inconsistent cue utilization, order effects, distractions, memory intrusions, omission of relevant cues, or 'configural cue utilization' (i.e. the use of specific patterns of cue values). $(1-R^2_e)$ and $(1-R^2_s)$ refer to the residual variance of the regression models of performers and listeners, respectively. C, or *unmodelled matching*, represents the correlation between the residuals of the performer's model and the residuals of the listener's model. If C is high it may indicate (a) a common reliance on acoustic cues in the performance not included in the regression models, (b) chance agreement between the random model errors, (c) cue interactions common to both models, or (d) nonlinear cue function forms common to both models (e.g. Cooksey, 1996). However, studies indicate that the unmodelled matching of the cue utilization is fairly small in music performance (Juslin & Madison, 1999), which means that most of the variance is explained by the additive combination of the cues.

17.3.4 Implications and findings

Although the lens model may appear simple, it has a crucial implication for research on communication: if the cues are redundant to some extent, more than one way of using the cues may lead to a similarly high level of decoding accuracy, because different cues may substitute for one another—so-called *vicarious functioning*. Hence, Brunswik's lens model may explain why there is accurate communication of emotions, even when the cues are used inconsistently across different performers or pieces of music. Multiple cues that are partly redundant yield a robust communicative system that is forgiving toward deviations from optimal cue utilization. Therefore, researchers should not expect acoustic cues in expressive performances to conform exactly to the patterns shown in Figure 17.2: the communicative system is so robust that perfect consistency is not required. This robustness comes with a price, however. The redundancy of the cues means that the same information is conveyed by several cues. This limits the amount of information that can be transmitted through the channel, which is another reason why basic emotion categories may be easier to convey to listeners than complex emotions.

The beauty of the redundant nature of the communication system is that performers can convey emotions reliably without compromising their personal playing styles. This is another characteristic that can be understood from a functionalistic perspective: in Brunswik's (1956) own words, the system aims at 'smallness of error at the expense of the highest frequency of precision' (p. 146). Such a system involves 'compromise and falling short of precision, but also the relative infrequency of drastic error' (p. 145). It is easy to see how a communication system with this characteristic might have survival value—ultimately, it is more important to avoid making serious mistakes (e.g. mistaking anger for joy) than to have the ability to make subtle discriminations among states (e.g. reliably detecting all the different kinds of joy).[4]

Analyses based on the lens model paradigm have generated a number of findings. First, linear regression models provide a good fit to the cue utilization, explaining c. 70–80 per cent of the variance in performance and judgement (Juslin, 1997b, 2000). Second, achievement appears to depend primarily on the extent to which the cue utilization of the performer is matched to the cue utilization of the listener, at least as regards professional performers. Amateur performers may also differ with regard to the consistency of their cue utilization (Juslin & Laukka, 2000). Third, cue utilization is more consistent across different pieces of music than across different performers. Finally, two performers can communicate equally well despite certain differences in their cue utilization (Juslin, 2000)—as predicted by the lens model.

17.3.5 The expanded lens model

The 'original' version of the lens model was limited to performance cues (Juslin, 1995), but listeners' perception of emotions could also be affected by an interplay between composer and performer cues. Hence, we have suggested an *expanded lens model* (Juslin & Lindström, 2003; see Figure 17.5), in which both composer cues and performance cues are included to make it possible to explore their relative contributions. Furthermore, important interactions between performer and composition cues are included as separate predictors in the regression models. An experimental study based on this framework, using synthesized and systematically varied pieces of music, showed that about 75–85 per cent of the variance in listeners' emotion ratings could be explained by a linear combination of the main effects alone. The results also indicated that interactions between different composer and performer cues made small—but not negligible—contributions to predictive power. (For a discussion of various composer cues associated with the musical structure, see Gabrielsson & Juslin, 2003; and Chapter 14, this volume.)

---

[4] However, as noted earlier, performers do seem to be able to communicate different levels of emotion intensity to listeners. This may reflect the functional importance of being able to judge the 'urgency' of a situation, as reflected in the emotional expressions of one's fellow beings.

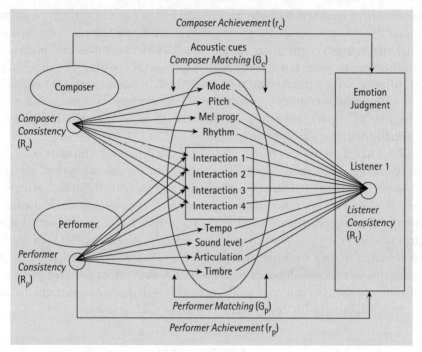

Fig. 17.5 Extended lens model of communication of emotions in music (from Juslin & Lindström, 2003),

17.4 MUSIC PERFORMANCE AND FELT EMOTIONS

17.4.1 Felt emotion in listeners

The research reviewed so far in this chapter has concerned expression and perception of emotions, but for most performers the goal is to go even further: to be able to actually 'move' and induce emotions in the listeners (e.g. Menuhin, 1996, p. 413). Surprisingly, this aspect of music performance has hardly been investigated, although preliminary estimates indicate that performance features can be important determinants of emotional reactions to music (Scherer, Zentner, & Schacht, 2002). In particular, modulation of dynamics may play an important role in influencing listeners emotionally (Nagel et al, 2008; Timmers et al, 2006). Still, we know little about exactly *how* various aspects of the performance influence emotions. Chapter 22 in this volume outlines seven psychological mechanisms through which music, in general, might evoke emotions in listeners, based on the framework presented by Juslin and Västfjäll (2008). An interesting question is which of these seven mechanisms are especially relevant in relation to performance.

One induction mechanism that would seem to be especially relevant to the performer's contribution is *emotional contagion*. This refers to a process whereby emotion is induced by music because the listener perceives the emotional expression of the music and then 'mimics' this expression, which leads to the induction of the same emotion (Juslin, 2001)—for instance, music expressing sadness making you sad (Lundqvist, Carlsson, Hilmersson, & Juslin, 2009). That many features of expression in performance are similar to vocal expression of emotions (Juslin & Laukka, 2003, Table 7) suggests that we get aroused by the 'voice-like' features of music performances. Juslin (2004) argued that what makes a specific music performance on, say, the violin, so moving, is the fact that it sounds a lot like the human voice, whereas at the same time it goes well *beyond* what the human voice could do (e.g. in terms of tempo, pitch range, and timbre). Consequently, one may speculate that musical instruments are sometimes processed by an independent brain module as a kind of 'super-expressive' voice (e.g. Juslin, 2004). One can predict that the instruments that resemble the human voice most closely (e.g. the violin, the cello) will be most effective in evoking emotions in listeners via contagion (for further discussion of emotional contagion, see Chapter 22, this volume).

Emotions may also be induced when *musical expectations* are violated in some way. It is easy to imagine this happening with respect to a music performance. Hence, Meyer (1956) proposed that expressive variations in a musical performance may serve an aesthetic function by 'delaying an expected resolution', or simply 'creating psychological tension' (p. 206; see also Huron, 2006). Juslin (2001) noted that such effects can be achieved in different ways: for instance, a performer can enhance listeners' emotional responses to the music by emphasizing certain notes that are of particular 'significance' in the music composition (Lindström, 1999), thereby enhancing violations of musical expectations that are already inherent in the structure. However, a performer could also induce emotions in listeners by performing in a manner that deviates from performance conventions with regard to the shaping of a particular structure.

Cognitive appraisal is widely regarded as the default mechanism for emotion induction in everyday life. The notion of appraisal theory is that emotions arise and are distinguished on the basis of the individual's subjective evaluation of an event on dimensions, such as novelty, urgency, goal congruence, coping potential, and norm compatibility (Juslin & Scherer, 2005). How can a music performer be implicated in a cognitive appraisal? Sloboda (1999) suggested the case of virtuosity as a source of emotion. For instance, we may marvel with amazement or awe at the exceptional speed with which a pianist is able to play a difficult passage. Similarly, an aesthetic evaluation of the performance could induce emotions. Support for this notion was found in a study by Timmers (2007c) where listeners' ratings of their 'emotional engagement' correlated with their ratings of the quality of the music performances heard. Unfortunately we lack a proper theory of how musical quality is aesthetically evaluated by listeners.[5]

---

[5] For further discussion of the relationship between musical emotions and aesthetic responses, see Chapter 22, this volume.

17.4.2 Felt emotion in performers

Music performers try to 'move' their listeners by means of expressive performances. In doing so, should they strive to *feel* themselves the emotions they wish to portray or communicate in their music performances? This issue is often discussed by music performers (Chapter 15, this volume). Like in the world of acting, there are different 'approaches' to how to best achieve a convincing expression. Many music students and teachers believe that an emotion *must* be felt by the performer to be communicated well (Laukka, 2004; Lindström et al, 2003). However, felt emotion provides no guarantee that an emotion will be successfully conveyed to listeners. Thus, Tomes (2003) admitted to have had 'the experience of feeling particularly moved when recording certain passages, and finding that nothing special has found its way on to the disc'. In fact, strong emotional involvement may lead to muscle tension, with detrimental effects on the performance (Gellrich, 1991). As pointed out by the performer Daniel Barenboim, 'Your task is to convey the emotion, not to experience it.' What counts is the *sound* that reaches the listener, not what the performer is feeling. Thus, a crucial goal for music education may be to increase music students' aural awareness and knowledge with regard to emotional expression. Empirical research may be useful in this regard.

17.5 Emotional expression in music education

Although most music performers consider expression and emotion important, many sources suggest that these issues are slightly neglected in music education (Chapter 28, this volume). In principle, there is a range of teaching strategies that may be used to teach expression (see Chapters 15 and 28, this volume), but we have little systematic knowledge so far about how emotional expressivity is actually addressed in teaching. Karlsson and Juslin (2008) recently explored instrumental teaching in its natural context, with a focus on expression and emotion. Lessons featuring five music teachers and 12 students were videofilmed, transcribed, content analysed, and coded into categories of feedback and language use. Results suggested that the focus of teaching was mainly on technique and on the score. Lessons were dominated by talk—mainly by the teacher. The most common strategy was 'outcome feedback' (i.e. the teacher offers information on whether the performance is good or bad, although no information about why), followed by verbal instruction. Modelling and especially metaphors were less frequently used, contrary to finding that music students prefer the use of metaphors (see Lindström et al, 2003). Emotional expression was rarely addressed explicitly in terms of specific cues that can be used to achieve particular emotional expressions, thus confirming Elliott's (2005) intuition that, 'contrary to what most non-musicians might assume, music teachers seldom think about whether or how sonic-musical patterns may be expressive of specific emotions' (p. 94).

We hope that the research reviewed in this chapter may help to 'demystify' expression and contribute to more systematic approaches to teaching expression. Research has revealed that explicit instruction is beneficial to learning expression (e.g. Johnson, 1998; Juslin et al, 2006; Woody, 1999). A research-based approach was proposed by

Juslin (1998), in terms of *cognitive feedback*. The idea is to allow a performer to compare a regression model of his or her way of communicating specific emotions with an optimal regression model based on how listeners judge the emotions. This strategy, based on the lens model framework (Juslin, 2000), was first tested with favourable results in a pilot study by Juslin and Laukka (2000). However, it required time-consuming manual measurements of acoustic cues, and it was thus suggested that the whole procedure should instead be handled automatically by computer software.

Applications of computer feedback for various aspects of music performance have been available for a long time (for a review, see Webster, 2002). However, none of the applications has focused on expression of emotions. Therefore an inter-disciplinary project at the Uppsala University, *Feedback-learning of Musical Expressivity* (*Feel-ME*), recently created and tested a new computer program that automatically analyses music performances and offers specific feedback to musicians in order to enhance their communication of emotions in performances. The *Feel-ME* program was evaluated in an experimental study in which 36 semi-professional jazz/rock guitar players were randomly assigned to one of three conditions: (1) feedback from the computer program, (2) feedback from music teachers, and (3) repetition without feedback. Performance measures revealed the greatest improvement in communication accuracy for the program, and usability measures showed that the program was evaluated positively. Yet, when the performers were asked whether they would consider using the program in the future, 75 per cent of them responded negatively (Juslin et al, 2006).

How can the apparent reluctance to embrace this new technology be explained? Karlsson, Liljeström, and Juslin (2009) explored possible reasons behind the negative impressions. Eighty guitarists performed a piece of music to convey various emotions, received feedback on their performances, and judged the quality of the feedback they received on rating scales. A 2 x 2 between-subjects factorial design manipulated (a) the performers' beliefs concerning whether the feedback was produced by a teacher or a computer program (*feedback delivery*) and (b) the feedback contents in terms of whether they were really produced by a teacher or a computer program (*feedback production*). Results revealed significant main effects of both production and delivery, but no interaction between the two. That is, the mere belief that the feedback derived from a teacher yielded higher-quality ratings, but so also did feedback that did indeed derive from a teacher. While both types of feedback were rated as equally easy to understand, feedback from teachers was rated as more detailed. Additional analyses revealed that teacher-produced feedback was appreciated because it offered encouragement, examples, and explanations. These findings suggest ways of improving the *Feel-ME* program in further work so that computer-assisted teaching may serve as a complement to 'traditional' teaching.

17.6 FUTURE RESEARCH DIRECTIONS

As shown by the present review, researchers have made much progress in understanding how music performers are able to communicate emotions via music performances.

However, there are several limitations that need to be addressed in future research. One limitation is that most studies have focused on Western music (however, see Balkwill & Thompson, 1999; Clayton, 2005). Hence, it remains to be seen how much of the current findings will generalize to other musical cultures. Even within the current culture, more research is required to examine more style-specific aspects of music that contribute to the expression (e.g. ornamentation, gesture; Leech-Wilkinson, 2006a; Timmers, 2007b). Another crucial future direction is to study more closely how the different aspects of expression (e.g. structure marking, emotional expression, motion) interact with one another (e.g. Juslin et al, 2002). So far, the components have been studied either separately, or as an indivisible whole. Closer collaboration among performance researchers within different 'sub-specialties' represents a promising avenue towards a deeper understanding of performance expression in all its complexity. One further topic that currently receives increasing attention is the influence of other perceptual channels. While most studies of expression in music performance have focused only on auditory features, it also seems that visual features of the performer can make important contributions to the perceived expression of the music in live settings (see Dahl & Friberg, 2007; Thompson, Graham, & Russo, 2005). Further, much current work concerns applications of findings in music education (Juslin et al, 2006), therapy (Bunt & Pavlicevic, 2001), the gaming industry (Livingstone & Brown, 2005), ringtones for mobile phones (Bresin & Friberg, 2001), and automatic decoding of emotion in music (e.g. Friberg, Schoonderwaldt, Juslin, & Bresin, 2002), which might be used in content-based music searches on the Internet (Wieczorkowska et al, 2005). The latter examples reflect increasing work on musical emotions in computer science (van de Laar, 2006), which has to a large extent replicated previous studies in music psychology using multivariate techniques.

One important issue for future research is to consider alternative forms of coding in the expression of emotions. The emotion-specific patterns of acoustic cues shown in Figure 17.2 are all examples of 'iconic' sources of perceived emotions (Dowling & Harwood, 1986; Sloboda & Juslin, 2001); that is, they represent emotions through their *structural similarity* with other phenomena that express emotions (e.g. emotions in speech). This is probably the most potent source of perceived emotions in music. However, music performances may also be perceived as expressive of specific emotions through conditioned responses (what Dowling & Harwood, 1986, referred to as 'index', and Sloboda & Juslin, 2001, referred to as 'associative sources'). In other words, a performance of music may be perceived as expressive of a specific emotion simply because something in the manner of performance has been repeatedly (and arbitrarily) paired with other meaningful stimuli or events in the past.[6] In addition, the perceived emotion in a performance may be influenced by 'internal' sources of emotion (Sloboda & Juslin, 2001)—features of the performance that enhance the interaction of different parts within the musical structure itself ('symbol', in the Dowling & Harwood

---

[6] We suspect that such conditioned responses may often have a tendency to induce *felt* emotion also, as discussed further in Chapter 22, this volume, making it particularly difficult to separate perception and induction.

terminology). Although Meyer's (1956) theory focused primarily on how the thwarting of musical expectations might *induce* emotions in listeners, it seems likely that the internal play of the musical structure can also influence the *perceived* emotions (e.g. the emotional intensity; see Sloboda & Lehmann, 2001; Timmers & Ashley 2007, for preliminary examples). Hence it would be interesting to investigate in future research how such 'associative' and 'internal' sources may add to and modulate the emotional expression produced by the 'iconic' sources discussed in previous sections.

Most of what we know about emotional expression in music performance derives from studies based on the standard paradigm and computer synthesis. Such systematic experiments are required to draw strong conclusions about causal effects of acoustic cues. However, there is no denying that such paradigms involve fairly artificial settings. Thus, such research should be complemented by investigations that have a greater ecological validity. This could involve analyses of commercial recordings of music performances (Leech-Wilkinson, 2006a, 2006b; Rapoport, 1996; Siegwart & Scherer, 1995; Timmers, 2007a); observing performers from the preparation of a piece to concert performance (Clarke, Cook, Harrison, & Thomas, 2005); or using surveys to study listeners' reactions to performances at live concerts (Thompson, 2006). Such research has only begun, but promises to widen the scope of investigation considerably.

One important goal for studies based on commercial recordings may be to demonstrate how the processes described in this chapter occur in more realistic settings. Leech-Wilkinson (2006a), for instance, offered a number of examples of expressive gestures used by singers to express basic emotions such as *fear, sadness, anger, love*, and *disgust* in Schubert Lieder. He also provided examples of how the expressive style might change in response to the changing moods of the times (Leech-Wilkinson, 2006b). Although recordings of musical performances do not capture all features of a performance (e.g. visual features, the social context), they are nonetheless highly relevant, considering that music is seldom consumed through live concerts these days—even among young and musically interested people (Juslin, Liljeström, Västfjäll, Silva, & Barradas, 2008).

When exploring performances in real-world settings, interactions with other expressive aspects than emotion become more pronounced. Performers must negotiate between different performance goals and different communicative intentions. As implied by the GERMS model (Juslin, 2003), a performer must be able to modify acoustic parameters for many different and sometimes opposing purposes. This may include, for example, a differential use of tempo and dynamics for structural and emotional demarcation (Timmers et al, 2006). On the other hand, sometimes different performance goals may overlap and reinforce each other; for instance, the communication of emotions may be assisted by the communication of certain motion patterns (Timmers, 2007b)—which may in turn be enhanced by the performer's movements during the performance (Davidson, 2005).

A promising direction for future research might be to investigate in close collaboration with musicians how they actually approach emotional expression in preparing a performance. How do they select sub-areas of the 'emotional space' (see Figure 17.2) from the wider space of possible performances? What kind of expression do they strive for? How do expressive aims differ for performers working in different musical traditions? How does a performer achieve an optimal balance between the demands of performance practice and the demands related to expression? What is the creative input of the individual performer in shaping the expression? We would welcome systematic research on all of these issues.

17.7 CONCLUDING REMARKS

This chapter has shown how music performers may communicate basic emotions to listeners by using a number of probabilistic but partly redundant cues in the performance. The relative importance of the performance for the expression differs depending on the performer, genre, and piece—ranging all the way from the faithful rendition of a piece of avant-garde music to the improvised solo of a slow blues. The vicarious functioning of cues allows a performer to simultaneously convey emotions to listeners in a universally accessible manner and develop a personal expression. Hence, this communicative system constitutes the happy marriage of the general and the individual, of the biological and the cultural. The system is fairly robust, but has a limited information capacity, ultimately leaving it to the listeners to specify the precise meaning of the music. The phylogenetic origin of this communicative system can explain its powerful impact and also why many performers regard emotions as 'the essence' of musical communication. The subtle nuances of music might seem a distant cry from the evolutionary framework of basic emotions that was presented in this chapter. Still, it could be argued that, ultimately, the real force of music's expressiveness—if not its uttermost subtlety—resides in such roots. It appears plausible that music has developed from a means of communication of emotions to an art form in its own right. Even so, when music performances are at their most *powerful*, they do not stray very far from the origin in terms of non-verbal communication of emotions. Hence, the music performance that touches us the most does not necessarily come from someone who plays and sings with the grace of a god, but from someone 'bold enough to act as a messenger of the heart' (Schumacher, 1995, p. 314).

RECOMMENDED FURTHER READING

1. Gabrielsson, A. (2003). Music performance research at the millennium. *Psychology of Music*, 31, 221–72.
2. Juslin, P. N., & Laukka, P. (2003). Communication of emotions in vocal expression and music performance: Different channels, same code? *Psychological Bulletin*, 129, 770–814.

REFERENCES

Adachi, M., & Trehub, S. E. (1998). Children's expression of emotion in song. *Psychology of Music, 26,* 133–53.

Bach, C. P. E. (1778/1985). *Essay on the true art of playing keyboard instruments* (W. J. Mitchell, trans.). London: Eulenburg Books.

Baroni, M., Caterina, R., Regazzi, F., & Zanarini, G. (1997). Emotional aspects of singing voice. In A. Gabrielsson (ed.), *Proceedings of the Third Triennial ESCOM conference* (pp. 484–9). Uppsala, Sweden: Department of Psychology, Uppsala University.

Balkwill, L-L, & Thompson, W. F. (1999). A cross-cultural investigation of the perception of emotion in music: Psychophysical and cultural cues. *Music Perception, 17,* 43–64.

Behrens, G. A., & Green, S. B. (1993). The ability to identify emotional content of solo improvisations performed vocally and on three different instruments. *Psychology of Music, 21,* 20–33.

Boersma, P., & Weenink, D. (1999). *Praat 3.8.24.* Computer software, Institute of Phonetic Sciences, University of Amsterdam, Amsterdam, The Netherlands.

Boyd, J., & George-Warren, H. (1992). *Musicians in tune: Seventy-five contemporary musicians discuss the creative process.* New York: Fireside.

Bresin, R., & Friberg, A. (2000). Emotional coloring of computer-controlled music performance. *Computer Music Journal, 24,* 44–62.

Bresin, R., & Friberg, A. (2001). Expressive musical icons. In J. Hiipakka, N. Zakarov, & T. Takala (eds), *Proceedings of the International Conference on Auditory Display (ICAD) 2001* (pp. 141–143). Espoo, Finland: ICAD.

Brunswik, E. (1956). *Perception and the representative design of experiments.* Berkeley, CA: University of California Press.

Buelow, G. J. (1983). Johann Mattheson and the invention of the Affektenlehre. In G. J. Buelow & H. J. Marx (eds), *New Mattheson studies* (pp. 393–407). Cambridge, UK: Cambridge University Press.

Bunt, L., & Pavlicevic, M. (2001). Music and emotion: Perspectives from music therapy. In P. N. Juslin & J. A. Sloboda (eds), *Music and emotion: Theory and research* (pp. 181–201). Oxford: Oxford University Press.

Clarke, E. F. (1988). Generative principles in music performance. In J. A. Sloboda (ed.), *Generative processes in music: The psychology of performance, improvisation, and composition* (pp. 1–26). Oxford: Clarendon Press.

Clarke, E. F., Cook, N., Harrison, B., & Thomas, P. (2005). Interpretation and performance in Bryn Harrison's *être-temps. Musicae Scientiae, 9,* 31–74.

Clayton, M. (2005). Communication in Indian Raga performance. In D. Miell, D. J. Hargreaves, & R. MacDonald (eds), *Musical communication* (pp. 361–81). Oxford: Oxford University Press.

Connolly, C., & Williamon, A. (2004). Mental skills training. In A. Williamon (ed.), *Musical excellence: Strategies and techniques to enhance performance* (pp. 220–45). Oxford: Oxford University Press.

Cooksey, R. W. (1996). *Judgment analysis.* New York: Academic Press.

Cunningham, J. G., & Sterling, R. S. (1988). Developmental changes in the understanding of affective meaning in music. *Motivation and Emotion, 12,* 399–413.

Dahl, S., & Friberg, A. (2007). Visual perception of expressiveness in musicians' body movements. *Music Perception, 24,* 433–54.

Davidson, J. W. (2005). Bodily communication in musical performance. In D. Miell, R. MacDonald, & D. J. Hargreaves (eds), *Musical communication* (pp. 215–37). Oxford: Oxford University Press.

Donington, R. (1963). *The interpretation of early music*. London: Faber and Faber.

Dowling W. J., & Harwood, D. L. (1986). *Music cognition*. New York: Academic Press.

Ekman, P. (1999). Basic emotions. In T. Dalgleish & M. Power (eds), *Handbook of cognition and emotion* (pp. 45–60). Sussex, UK: John Wiley & Sons.

Elliott, D. J. (2005). Musical understanding, musical works, and emotional expression: Implications for music education. *Educational Philosophy and Theory, 37*, 93–103.

Fairbanks, G. (1940). Recent experimental investigation of vocal pitch in voice. *Journal of the Acoustical Society of America, 11*, 457–66.

Friberg, A., Schoonderwaldt, E., & Juslin, P. N. (2007). CUEX: An algorithm for automatic extraction of expressive tone parameters in music performance from acoustic signals. *Acta Acustica United with Acustica, 93*, 411–20.

Friberg, A., Schoonderwaldt, E., Juslin, P. N., & Bresin, R. (2002). Automatic real-time extraction of musical expression. In *Proceedings of the International Computer Music Conference, Göteborg, September 2002* (pp. 365–7). San Francisco, CA: International Computer Music Association.

Gabrielsson, A. (1999). The performance of music. In D. Deutsch (ed.), *The psychology of music* (2nd edn). (pp. 501–602). San Diego, CA: Academic Press.

Gabrielsson, A. (2003). Music performance research at the millennium. *Psychology of Music, 31*, 221–72.

Gabrielsson, A., & Juslin, P. N. (1996). Emotional expression in music performance: Between the performer's intention and the listener's experience. *Psychology of Music, 24*, 68–91.

Gabrielsson, A., & Juslin, P. N. (2003). Emotional expression in music. In R. J. Davidson, K. R. Scherer, & H. H. Goldsmith (eds), *Handbook of affective sciences* (pp. 503–34). Oxford: Oxford University Press.

Gabrielsson, A., & Lindström, E. (1995). Emotional expression in synthesizer and sentograph performance. *Psychomusicology, 14*, 94–116.

Gellrich, M. (1991). Concentration and tension. *British Journal of Music Education, 8*, 167–79.

Gilden, D. L. (2001). Cognitive emissions of 1/f noise. *Psychological Review, 108*, 33–56.

Hudson, R. (1994). *Stolen time. The history of tempo rubato*. Oxford: Clarendon Press.

Huron, D. (2006). *Sweet anticipation. Music and the psychology of expectation*. Cambridge, MA: MIT Press.

Hursch, C. J., Hammond, K. R., & Hursch, J. L. (1964). Some methodological considerations in multiple-cue probability studies. *Psychological Review, 71*, 42–60.

Izard, C. E. (2007). Basic emotions, natural kinds, emotion schemas, and a new paradigm. *Perspectives on Psychological Science, 2*, 260–80.

Jarosy, A., & Fiedler, H. E. (1936). Emotion in performance. *Music & Letters, XVII*, 54–8.

Johnson, C. M. (1998). Effect of instruction in appropriate rubato usage on the onset timings and perceived musicianship of musical performances. *Journal of Research in Music Education, 46*, 436–45.

Johnson-Laird, P. N., & Oatley, K. (1992). Basic emotions, rationality, and folk theory. *Cognition & Emotion, 6*, 201–23.

Juslin, P. N. (1995). Emotional communication in music viewed through a Brunswikian lens. In G. Kleinen (ed.), *Music and expression: Proceedings of the Conference of DGM and ESCOM, Bremen, 1995* (pp. 21–5). Bremen, Germany: University of Bremen.

Juslin, P. N. (1997a). Emotional communication in music performance: A functionalist perspective and some data. *Music Perception, 14*, 383–418.

Juslin, P. N. (1997b). Perceived emotional expression in synthesized performances of a short melody: Capturing the listener's judgment policy. *Musicæ Scientiae*, 1, 225–56.

Juslin, P. N. (1997c). Can results from studies of perceived expression in musical performances be generalized across response formats? *Psychomusicology*, 16, 77–101.

Juslin, P. N. (1998). A functionalist perspective on emotional communication in music performance. *Comprehensive Summaries of Uppsala Dissertations from the Faculty of Social Sciences 78*. Uppsala, Sweden: Uppsala University Library.

Juslin, P. N. (2000). Cue utilization in communication of emotion in music performance: Relating performance to perception. *Journal of Experimental Psychology: Human Perception and Performance*, 26, 1797–1813.

Juslin, P. N. (2001). Communicating emotion in music performance: A review and a theoretical framework. In P. N. Juslin & J. A. Sloboda (eds), *Music and emotion: Theory and research* (pp. 309–37). Oxford: Oxford University Press.

Juslin, P. N. (2003). Five facets of musical expression: A psychologist's perspective on music performance. *Psychology of Music*, 31, 273–302.

Juslin, P. N. (2004). Vocal expression and musical expression: Parallels and contrasts. In A. Kappas (ed.), *ISRE 2000: Proceedings of the 11th Meeting of the International Society for Research on Emotions, Quebec City, August 2000* (pp. 281–4). Amsterdam, The Netherlands: ISRE publications.

Juslin, P. N. (2005). From mimesis to catharsis: Expression, perception, and induction of emotion in music. In D. Miell, R. MacDonald, & D. J. Hargreaves (eds), *Musical communication* (pp. 85–115). Oxford: Oxford University Press.

Juslin, P. N., & Bänziger, T. (2009). Brunswikian lens model. In D. Sander & K. R. Scherer (eds), *Oxford companion to emotion and the affective sciences* (pp. 80–81). Oxford: Oxford University Press.

Juslin, P. N., Friberg, A., & Bresin, R. (2002). Toward a computational model of expression in music performance: The GERM model. *Musicæ Scientiae, Special Issue 2001–2*, 63–122.

Juslin, P. N., Friberg, A., Schoonderwaldt, E., & Karlsson, J. (2004). Feedback-learning of musical expressivity. In A. Williamon (ed.), *Musical excellence: Strategies and techniques for enhancing performance* (pp. 247–70). Oxford: Oxford University press.

Juslin, P. N., Karlsson, J., Lindström, E., Friberg, A., & Schoonderwaldt, E. (2006). Play it again with feeling: Computer feedback in musical communication of emotions. *Journal of Experimental Psychology: Applied*, 12, 79–95.

Juslin, P. N., & Laukka, P. (2000). Improving emotional communication in music performance through cognitive feedback. *Musicae Scientiae*, 4, 151–83.

Juslin, P. N., & Laukka, P. (2003). Communication of emotions in vocal expression and music performance: Different channels, same code? *Psychological Bulletin*, 129, 770–814.

Juslin, P. N., & Laukka, P. (2004). Expression, perception, and induction of musical emotions: A review and a questionnaire study of everyday listening. *Journal of New Music Research*, 33, 217–38.

Juslin, P. N., Liljeström, S., Västfjäll, D., Barradas, G., & Silva, A. (2008). An experience sampling study of emotional reactions to music: Listener, music, and situation. *Emotion*, 8, 668–83.

Juslin, P. N., & Lindström, E. (2003). *Musical expression of emotions: Modeling composed and performed features.* Paper presented at Fifth Conference of the European Society for the Cognitive Sciences of Music (ESCOM), Hanover, Germany, September 2003.

Juslin, P. N., & Lindström, E. (2009). *Musical expression of emotions: Modeling listeners' judgments of composed and performed features.* Manuscript submitted for publication.

Juslin, P. N., & Madison, G. (1999). The role of timing patterns in recognition of emotional expression from musical performance. *Music Perception*, 17, 197–221.

Juslin, P. N., & Persson, R. S. (2002). Emotional communication. In R. Parncutt & G. E. McPherson (eds), *The science and psychology of music performance. Creative strategies for teaching and learning* (pp. 219–36). Oxford: Oxford University Press.

Juslin, P. N., & Scherer, K. R. (2005). Vocal expression of affect. In J. A. Harrigan, R. Rosenthal, & K. R. Scherer (eds), *The new handbook of methods in nonverbal behavior research* (pp. 65–135). Oxford: Oxford University Press.

Juslin, P. N., & Sloboda, J. A. (eds). (2001). *Music and emotion: Theory and research*. Oxford: Oxford University Press.

Juslin, P. N., & Västfjäll, D. (2008). Emotional responses to music: The need to consider underlying mechanisms. *Behavioral and Brain Sciences, 31,* 559–75.

Karlsson, J., & Juslin, P. N. (2008). Musical expression: An observational study of instrumental teaching. *Psychology of Music, 36,* 309–34.

Karlsson, J., Liljeström, S., & Juslin, P. N. (2009). Teaching musical expression: Effects of production and delivery of feedback by teacher vs. computer on rated feedback quality. *Music Education Research, 11,* 175–91.

Konishi, T., Imaizumi, S., & Niimi, S. (2000). Vibrato and emotion in singing voice (abstract). In C. Woods, G. Luck, R. Brochard, F. Seddon, & J. A. Sloboda (eds), *Proceedings of the Sixth International Conference on Music Perception and Cognition, August 2000* (CD-rom). Keele University, UK.

Kotlyar, G. M., & Morozov, V. P. (1976). Acoustic correlates of the emotional content of vocalized speech. *Soviet Physics. Acoustics, 22,* 370–6.

Laukka, P. (2004). Instrumental music teachers' views on expressivity: A report from music conservatoires. *Music Education Research, 6,* 45–56.

Laukka, P. (2005). Categorical perception of vocal emotion expressions. *Emotion, 5,* 277–95.

Laukka, P., & Juslin, P. N. (2007). Similar pattern of age-related differences in emotion recognition from speech and music. *Motivation and Emotion, 31,* 182–191.

Leech-Wilkinson, D. (2006a). Expressive gestures in Schubert singing on record. *Nordic Journal of Aesthetics, 33,* 51–70.

Leech-Wilkinson, D. (2006b). Portamento and musical meaning. *Journal of New Music Research, 25,* 233–61.

Lindström, E. (1999). *Expression in music: Interaction between performance and melodic structure.* Paper presented at the Meeting of the Society for Music Perception and Cognition, Evanston, USA, August 1999.

Lindström, E., Juslin, P. N., Bresin, R., & Williamon, A. (2003). 'Expressivity comes from within your soul': a questionnaire study of music students' perspectives on expressivity. *Research Studies in Music Education, 20,* 23–47.

Livingstone, S. R., & Brown, A. R. (2005). Dynamic response: real-time adaption for music emotion. In Y. Pisan (ed.), *Proceedings of the Second Australasian Conference on Interactive Entertainment* (pp. 105–111). Sydney, Australia: Creativity & Cognition Studios Press.

Lundqvist, L.-O., Carlsson, F., Hilmersson, P., & Juslin, P. N. (2009). Emotional responses to music: Experience, expression, and physiology. *Psychology of Music, 37,* 61–90.

Madison, G. (2000). Properties of expressive variability patterns in music performance. *Journal of New Music Research, 29,* 335–56.

Marchand, D. J. (1975). A study of two approaches to developing expressive performance. *Journal of Research in Music Education, 23,* 14–22.

Mattheson, J. (1739). *Der volkommene Capellmeister.* (Facsimile edition 1954, Bärenreiter Verlag, Kassel and Basel.)

Menuhin, Y. (1996). *Unfinished journey.* London: Methuen.

Meyer, L. B. (1956). *Emotion and meaning in music.* Chicago, IL: Chicago University Press.

Minassian, C., Gayford, C., & Sloboda, J. A. (2003). *Optimal experience in musical performance: a survey of young musicians*. Paper presented at the Meeting of the Society for Education, Music, and Psychology Research, London, March 2003.

Nagel, F., Kopiez, R., Grewe, O., & Altenmüller, E. (2008). Psychoacoustical correlates of musically induced chills. *Musicae Scientiae, 12*, 103–15.

Nair, D. G., Large, E. W., Steinberg, F., & Kelso, J. A. S. (2002). Perceiving emotion in expressive piano performance: A functional MRI study. In K. Stevens, D. Burnham, G. McPherson, E. Schubert, & J. Renwick (eds), *Proceedings of the 7th International Conference on Music Perception and Cognition, July 2002* (CD rom). Adelaide, Australia: Causal Productions.

Neumann, F. (1978). *Ornamentation in Baroque and post-Baroque music: with special emphasis on J. S. Bach*. Princeton, NJ: Princeton University Press.

Ohgushi, K., & Hattori, M. (1996). *Acoustic correlates of the emotional expression in vocal performance*. Paper presented at the Third Joint Meeting of the Acoustical Society of America and the Acoustical Society of Japan, Honolulu, Hawaii, December 1996.

Papoušek, M. (1996). Intuitive parenting: A hidden source of musical stimulation in infancy. In I. Deliége & J. A. Sloboda (eds), *Musical beginnings: Origins and development of musical competence* (pp. 89–112). Oxford: Oxford University Press.

Papoušek, M., Bornstein, M. H., Nuzzo, C., Papoušek, H., & Symmes, D. (1990). Infant responses to prototypical melodic contours in parental speech. *Infant Behavior and Development, 13*, 539–45.

Parncutt, R. (2006). Prenatal development. In G. E. McPherson (ed.), *The child as musician* (pp. 1–31). Oxford: Oxford University Press.

Peretz, I., Gagnon, L., & Bouchard, B. (1998). Music and emotion: Perceptual determinants, immediacy, and isolation after brain damage. *Cognition, 68*, 111–41.

Persson, R. S. (1993). *The subjectivity of musical performance: An exploratory music-psychological real world enquiry into the determinants and education of musical reality*. Unpublished doctoral dissertation, University of Huddersfield, UK.

Plutchik, R. (1994). *The psychology and biology of emotion*. New York: Harper-Collins College Publishers.

Rapoport, E. (1996). Emotional expression code in opera and lied singing. *Journal of New Music Research, 25*, 109–49.

Repp, B. H. (1998). A microcosm of musical expression I: Quantitative analysis of pianists' timing in the initial measures of Chopin's Etude in E major. *Journal of the Acoustical Society of America, 102*, 1085–99.

Resnicow, J. E., Salovey, P., & Repp, B. H. (2004). Is recognition of emotion in music performance an aspect of emotional intelligence? *Music Perception, 22*, 145–58.

Rosenthal, R. (1982). Judgment studies. In K. R. Scherer & P. Ekman (eds), *Handbook of methods in nonverbal behavior research* (pp. 287–361). Cambridge, UK: Cambridge University Press.

Russell, J. A. (1980). A circumplex model of affect. *Journal of Personality and Social Psychology, 39*, 1161–78.

Scherer, K. R., & Oshinsky, J. S. (1977). Cue utilisation in emotion attribution from auditory stimuli. *Motivation and Emotion, 1*, 331–46.

Scherer, K. R., Zentner, M. R., & Schacht, A. (2002). Emotional states generated by music: An exploratory study of music experts. *Musicae Scientiae, Special Issue 2001–2*, 149–71.

Schumacher, M. (1995). *Crossroads. The life and music of Eric Clapton*. New York: Hyperion.

Seashore, C. E. (1947). *In search of beauty in music. A scientific approach to musical aesthetics*. Westport, CT: Grenwood Press.

Seashore, H. G. (1937). An objective analysis of artistic singing. In C. E. Seashore (ed.), *Objective analysis of musical performance: University of Iowa studies in the psychology of music. Vol. 4* (pp. 12–157). Iowa City, IA: University of Iowa.

Senju, M., & Ohgushi, K. (1987). How are the player's ideas conveyed to the audience? *Music Perception, 4,* 311–24.

Shaver, P., Schwartz, J., Kirson, D., & O'Connor, C. (1987). Emotion knowledge: Further explorations of a prototype approach. *Journal of Personality and Social Psychology, 52,* 1061–86.

Shove, P., & Repp, B. H. (1995). Musical motion and performance: Theoretical and empirical perspectives. In J. Rink (ed.), *The practice of performance: Studies in musical interpretation* (pp. 55–83). Cambridge, UK: Cambridge University Press.

Siegwart, H., & Scherer, K. R. (1995). Acoustic concomitants of emotional expression in operatic singing: The case of Lucia in Ardi gli incensi. *Journal of Voice, 9,* 249–60.

Sloboda, J. A. (1996). The acquisition of musical performance expertise: Deconstructing the 'talent' account of individual differences in musical expressivity. In K. A. Ericsson (ed.), *The road to excellence* (pp. 107–26). Mahwah, NJ: Erlbaum.

Sloboda, J. A. (1999). Music performance and emotion: Issues and developments. In S. W. Yi (ed.), *Music, mind, and science* (pp. 220–38). Seoul, South Korea: Seoul National University Press.

Sloboda, J. A., & Juslin, P. N. (2001). Psychological perspectives on music and emotion. In P. N. Juslin & J. A. Sloboda (eds), *Music and emotion: Theory and research* (pp. 71–104). Oxford: Oxford University Press.

Sloboda, J. A., & Lehmann, A. C. (2001). Tracking performance correlates of changes in perceived intensity of emotion during different interpretations of a Chopin piano prelude. *Music Perception, 19,* 87–120.

Spencer, H. (1857). The origin and function of music. *Fraser's Magazine, 56,* 396–408.

Sundberg, J., Iwarsson, J., & Hagegård, H. (1995). A singer's expression of emotions in sung performance. In O. Fujimura & M. Hirano (eds), *Vocal fold physiology: Voice quality control* (pp. 217–29). San Diego, CA: Singular Press.

Thompson, S. (2006). Audience responses to a live orchestral concert. *Musicae Scientiae, 10,* 215–44.

Thompson, W. F., Graham, P., & Russo, F. A. (2005). Seeing music performance: Visual influences on perception and experience. *Semiotica, 156,* 203–27.

Timmers, R. (2007a). Vocal expression in recorded performances of Schubert songs. *Musicae Scientiae, 11,* 237–68.

Timmers, R. (2007b). Communication of (e)motion: Two case studies. *Orbis Musicae, 14,* 116–40.

Timmers, R. (2007c). Perception of music performance in historical and modern commercial recordings. *Journal of the Acoustical Society of America, 122,* 2872–80.

Timmers, R., & Ashley, R. (2007). Emotional ornamentation in performances of a Handel sonata. *Music Perception, 25,* 117–34.

Timmers, R., Marolt, M., Camurri, A., & Volpe, G. (2006). Listeners' emotional engagement with performances of a Scriabin etude: An explorative case study. *Psychology of Music, 34,* 481–510.

Tomes, S. (2003). Emotional rescues. *The Guardian, Saturday November 22,* retrieved from: http://www.guardian.co.uk/music/2003/nov/22/classicalmusicandopera1

van de Laar, B. (2006). Emotion detection in music: a survey. In *Proceedings of the Fifth Twente Student Conference on Information Technology* (1:700). Enschede, The Netherlands: Twente University Press.

Webster, P. R. (2002). Computer-based technology and music teaching and learning. In R. Colwell & C. Richardson (eds), *The new handbook of research on music teaching and learning* (pp. 416–39). Oxford: Oxford University Press.

Wieczorkowska, A., Synak, P., Lewis, R., & Zbigniew, W. R. (2005). Extracting emotions from music data. *Lecture Notes in Computer Science, 3488,* 456–65.

Whissell, C. M. (1989). The dictionary of affect in language. In R. Plutchik & H. Kellerman (eds), *Emotion: Theory, research, and experience: Volume 4. The measurement of emotions* (pp. 113–31). New York: Academic Press.

Woody, R. H. (1999). The relationship between explicit planning and expressive performance of dynamic variations in an aural modeling task. *Journal of Research in Music Education*, *47*, 331–42.

Yamasaki, T. (2002). Emotional communication in improvised performance by musically untrained players. In T. Kato (ed.), *Proceedings of the 17th International Congress of the International Association of Empirical Aesthetics* (pp. 521–4). Osaka: IAEA.

PART V

MUSIC LISTENING

CHAPTER 18

MUSIC IN EVERYDAY LIFE

THE ROLE OF EMOTIONS

JOHN A. SLOBODA

18.1 Scope and purpose

THE term 'music in everyday life' has been prevalent in the research literature for about a decade. The only book to be so far published with this precise title is DeNora (2000), although other terms, such as 'music in daily life' have preceded it (e.g. Crafts, Cavicchi, & Keil, 1993). Earliest treatments were predominantly found within sociology and media studies, with increasing attention by psychologists in more recent years.

Although this is a new topic of study, it is a fast-growing one within music psychology. This can be illustrated by the relative coverage of the topic in two comprehensive reviews of the discipline published in the last decade. There is only the briefest of mentions of the topic in the specially commissioned multi-authored entry on 'psychology of music' in *The new Grove dictionary of music and musicians* (Sadie, 2001). Yet only a few years later, 'music in everyday life' was considered so central that it was assigned a six-chapter section to itself within the nine-section structure of the *Oxford handbook of music psychology* (Hallam, Cross, & Thaut, 2009).

The purpose of this chapter is not to document every type of activity that falls under the rubric of music in everyday life. For that, the reader is referred to Sloboda, Lamont, and Greasley (2009) and related chapters in Hallam et al (2009). Rather the current purpose is to extract and try to systematize some key issues relating to emotion as it impinges on, and interacts with, music in everyday life.

In the book (Juslin & Sloboda, 2001) from which the current volume developed, Sloboda and O'Neill (2001) contributed a chapter using primarily their own work to illustrate some key issues regarding emotions in everyday listening to music. That strategy was appropriate to what was then a very young field. The current chapter adopts a different strategy, drawing on the considerably larger body of research literature that has emerged since 2000 to formalize ten key propositions which aim to reflect what the research has suggested to us about emotion in everyday music. While these propositions are rooted in published empirical findings, they deliberately push beyond published formulations as a stimulus to future research.

In her introduction, DeNora (2000, p. xi) specifies her domain and intent as:

> . . . to document some of the many uses to which music is and can be put, and to describe a range of strategies through which music is mobilized as a resource for producing the scenes, routines, assumptions and occasions that constitute 'social life'.

'Social life' is a catch-all category, since it can be argued that all uses of music, even the most solitary, are elements of social life. Nothing is left out. Like most researchers in the field, DeNora's work tends to define 'everyday' implicitly, through the actual examples of music use and experience that are studied. This chapter considers more explicitly some of the dimensions along which one might assess whether or not a musical event counts as 'everyday'. A test of whether such dimensions are useful is whether they can be used to exclude anything. If they cannot, then the term 'everyday' is really not very useful. I hope that the result of this exercise may be a little more clarity about a term which is often used in the literature, but sometimes without a great deal of precision. Without that clarity it is hard to assess what the distinctive role of emotions, if any, might be in such experiences.

I have found ten dimensions on which everyday music has been distinguished (whether explicitly or otherwise) from the 'non-everyday'. I describe each of these dimensions in turn, drawing out potential implications for emotion of each dimension. These implications will act as working hypotheses against which to organize and evaluate the empirical research literature.

18.2 TEN PROPOSITIONS ABOUT EMOTION IN EVERYDAY MUSIC

18.2.1 Frequency of occurrence

Everyday music is the kind of musical experience that is prone to happen often, and could plausibly happen every day. This gives it a strong cultural specificity. Musicians' everyday experiences will be very different from those of non-musicians, Nigerian everyday experience will be different from Swedish. Frequency could also relate to the number of people for whom a set of experiences is typical. More people in Western cultures hear music on radio than on player piano (pianola), therefore listening to the radio is arguably more 'everyday' than listening to player piano. However, 100 years ago, many homes and meeting places had pianolas—so at that time pianolas were 'everyday'. Now most people have to go to a museum to hear one.

Implications for emotion. In general emotions are strongest when events are unexpected and surprising (Sonnemans & Frijda, 1995). Frequent events tend not to be very surprising, so they tend to elicit weaker emotions.

Proposition 1: everyday emotions to music tend to be of low intensity rather than high intensity

Research evaluation. Proposition 1 is not to be confused with a different but superficially similar claim that emotions involving music in everyday life are trivial or unimportant. On the contrary, because everyday life is the 'ground' for our existence, small emotional differences from day to day can have enormous cumulative effects. Rather, the claim is that music has its typical effect by shifting mild emotion by small steps rather than pushing people to strong extremes of elation, despair or fury. A typical emotional result might be that it helps a boring task to be less boring, or a sad mood to tip to a contented one. Such modest outcomes can have significant effects on life—they can improve both cognitive and social functioning (e.g. Thompson, 1991).

One indication that low-intensity emotions are typical for the everyday comes from North, Hargreaves, and Hargreaves (2004) where they found that participants selected 'helped create or accentuate an emotion' from a list of potential functions to describe only 20 per cent of all occurrences of self-selected music listening. This does not mean that there were no emotional effects in the other 80 per cent of cases, but it does suggest that these effects were small, and possibly bound up in a broader judgement of outcome (such as 'it helped pass the time'). A more direct piece of evidence comes from a recent experience-sampling study by Juslin, Liljeström, Västfjäll, Barradas, and Silva (2008) where they asked respondents to explicitly identify whether a specific episode of exposure to music in daily life affected the way they felt. On 36 per cent of occasions respondents specifically asserted that the music did not affect them emotionally.

Similarly, Sloboda, O'Neill, and Ivaldi (2001) carried out a study where participants self-rated change in affect after everyday instances of musical exposure on a series of seven-point scales (e.g. very happy, quite happy, somewhat happy, neutral, somewhat sad, quite sad, very sad). The modal change was one scale point (mean = 1.3). It was very common for a person to shift from neutral to somewhat happy, for instance, but there were no instances where the shift was from one end of the scale to the other.

18.2.2 Ordinariness versus specialness of the context or the experience

Everyday life tends to exclude the protected or 'specialist' environments in which music takes on a 'heavier' social or cultural weight than normal. Special environments could include a concert, a wedding, a rave, or a funeral. Perhaps the everyday also excludes the transcendental and the 'peak' (see Chapter 20, this volume; see also Whaley, Sloboda, & Gabrielsson, 2009)—these could be seen as 'special' experiences, even if they do not occur in special contexts. In contrast, everyday experiences tend to be rather mundane and insignificant, concerned with the unexciting business of managing home, food, cleaning, getting to and from work, shopping, and so on (North et al, 2004). These experiences blur into one another; it is hard to distinguish one ordinary day from another for most people (Stein, Ornstein, Tversky, & Brainerd, 1996).

Implications for emotion. Memory for emotions tends to be greatest when the emotion is intense, or when the event of which the emotion is part has a high personal significance (Levene, 1997, Levene & Safer, 2002).

Proposition 2: everyday musical emotions are rather unmemorable on average

Research evaluation. If we assume that music exposure is generally likely to have some emotional impact on a listener, we can take answers to questions such as 'How often do you feel emotions in response to music?' as some measure of the memorability of music-related emotions. Laukka (2007), in a questionnaire study with 500 participants aged 65 and over, found that 55 per cent of respondents responded 'sometimes' or less frequently (where sometimes was defined as 33–66 per cent of listening time). Therefore, there were significant numbers of participants who could not recall experiencing any particular emotion to the majority of musical episodes in their life.

Why might this be? One potential line of explanation is that music is generally only one part of a composite experience, which involves concurrent non-musical aspects as well. Memorability may thus be affected by what is going on alongside the music. In general, listening to music as the main activity (or for its own sake) is rather rare in everyday life. North et al (2004) found that only 12 per cent of episodes of hearing music were classified as 'at home deliberately listening to music'. In Sloboda, O'Neill, and Ivaldi's study, the proportion was even less (2 per cent of episodes were classified as listening to music as the 'main activity'). The non-musical activities found most frequently to accompany music were, in North et al, driving (12 per cent), 'at home doing an intellectual demanding task' (12 per cent), and 'at home doing housework' (7 per cent); while in Sloboda et al they were maintenance (washing, getting dressed, cooking, eating at home, housework, shopping—30 per cent) and travel (leaving home, driving, walking, going home—23 per cent). These are kinds of activity that take place on many days if not every day, and whose emotional significance can be expected to be, on average, low. If routine activities are not very memorable, then the music that accompanies them may generally also be forgotten, along with the emotions they may have engendered.

We do, of course, need to take cognizance of the fact that some proportion of musical experiences in everyday life do elicit strong and memorable emotions. Perhaps the most widely cited category of such strong experiences come from hearing music which has become associated with an emotionally charged past event. Familiar music can be a trigger to strong emotional memories of earlier times in life, close relationships, love, and loss (Baumgartner, 1992). Indeed, 'memory of valued past events' was one of the most cited categories of musical function in the free written responses provided by the participants in Sloboda's (1999/2005) study. But the existence of a small number of emotionally memorable music experiences need not invalidate the general conclusion that the majority of everyday musical experiences are unmemorable.

18.2.3 Location of occurrence

Everyday music tends to refer to music in the home, the street, shops, pubs, restaurants, and other public places characterized by the freedom to move through them at will and without a special 'appointment'. Workplaces are included, and public transport—but generally not concert halls. There are some environments where the use of music tends to be restricted, or controlled by professionals, such as hospitals and schools. This makes them sit both sides of the divide. We might view the CDs and MP3s that students swap with one another in the playground to be everyday, but not the specific pedagogical use of musical materials by a teacher in a music lesson. Similarly, the music playing in the hospital canteen might be everyday, while the music used by an anaesthetist to assist pre-operative relaxation may not be. Music in film is an interesting case. Is it 'everyday' when you hear it at home on the TV, and 'non-everyday' when you go and see the same film in a cinema? This may be a matter of degree: if you organize to watch a film at home 'seriously', you will turn off your phone, lower the lights, not stop halfway through to do something else—in other words, you will turn the everyday into the 'special' and will make your home into a temporary movie theatre, thus transforming the everyday into the special.

Implications for emotion. The locations involved provide significant opportunities for distraction and flux in experience, with transitions to and from different settings and activities.

Proposition 3: everyday musical emotions are short lived and multiple, rather than integrated or sustained

Research evaluation. A variety of studies, using experience sampling and other time-sensitive monitoring methods have indicated that many people are exposed to a significant number of separate and potentially unconnected musical stimuli in the course of a day. For instance, the non-musician participants studied by Sloboda et al (2001) reported hearing music four times a day on average. Among a self-selected sample of 222 respondents in a radio survey carried out for the BBC (for further information, see: http://www.bbc.co.uk/radio4/arts/frontrow/reith_diary.shtml), the average number of times music was heard was 11 times per day.

Since the range of contexts and types of music can be very broad, ranging from self-chosen music at home or in transport, to music encountered in shops and other public places, the potential for fragmentation and variety must be great. Unfortunately, none of the studies published to date has looked at the temporal succession of events within individuals on a day-by-day or hour-by-hour basis, although such data could clearly be extracted and analysed from several of the studies.

18.2.4 Circumstance of exposure: the role of choice

Much everyday music is unchosen—people come across it as they go around their daily routine (e.g. in shops or malls). Other music is chosen, and this relates to the technology available (CD player, hi-fi, iPod, etc.). This range of circumstances brings the issue of choice to centre stage. People in everyday life need constantly to negotiate situations of greater or lesser choice, and some of their emotional reactions may derive directly from the way they handle choice (or the lack of it). In general, the everyday has a character where choice is always open to subversion, simply because of the rather uncontrolled and 'open' nature of the everyday domain, where whatever you are doing is always prone to interruption or interference from other surrounding activities. Special music environments are generally ones where control is increased, and efforts are made to reduce interruption or interference to a practical minimum. That is what makes them 'non-everyday'.

Implications for emotion. Lack of choice tends to generate negative emotions as a response to the thwarting of goals or values.

Proposition 4: everyday musical emotions include a significant proportion of negative emotions such as irritation, disapproval, and dislike

One of the repeated findings of the literature is that, overall, people are surprisingly tolerant of music that they have not chosen, and are often positively disposed towards it. This suggests an overall positive attitude to music among people who hear it, and may also indicate that those who choose music for playing in public places are often doing so with an informed intention to increase the positivity or enjoyment of the public (i.e. they accurately judge the music that the majority of people will appreciate).

For instance, in the North et al (2004) study with 346 UK participants aged 18–78, the most frequently chosen response for music that participants had not chosen to hear was 'it helped to create the right atmosphere' (32 per cent) followed closely by 'I enjoyed it' (29 per cent). Similarly, in the Sloboda et al study (2001), positive mood changes as a result of music significantly outnumbered negative mood changes, and this was true even when the music was not chosen, although the mean degree of change was less in such cases.

On the other hand, most studies indicate a number of cases where the emotional reactions are not positive. In the North et al study, around 27 per cent of the responses to unchosen music were negative (e.g. 'it annoyed me', 'it hindered my attempts to do what I was trying to do'). Negative reactions were most typical when the participant was trying to undertake demanding intellectual work. Presumably the music broke their concentration.

A small but vocal minority experiences very extreme negative emotions to music in public places, to such an extent that they have made their dislike of it into a campaigning issue. There is an organization called 'Pipedown' dedicated to banning all music in public places (see DeNora, 2003, and http://www.pipedown.info/). Sloboda (1999/2005) analysed written responses from a self-selected UK sample to the open question 'please could you tell us all about you and music' and discovered that the demographic group most likely to volunteer strong negative reactions to music in public places were males over the age of 40. It was hypothesized that men of this age, being at the height of their earning power and associated social status, would be most used to being able to exercise control and choice in their lives, and therefore most negatively emotionally affected when such choice was thwarted.

It should not be assumed that all chosen music elicits positive emotions. Sometimes people choose music to encourage or augment negative emotions such as grief or anger. However, it would be safe to suggest that the frequency of negative emotions to chosen music is considerably lower than to that of unchosen music—a suggestion supported by the findings of Sloboda et al (2001) that chosen music is on average associated with significantly greater levels of positive emotional change than unchosen music.

18.2.5 Nature of transmission

Most music in industrialized cultures is now recorded music. Many cultures are characterized by a paucity of live music. In the ESM study of Juslin et al (2008), only 7 per cent of the musical emotion episodes during a two-week period involved live music. Live music is increasingly heard only in specialized controlled (and thus non-everyday) environments. Probably the only serious example of live everyday music would be the street musician (busker). The consequence of the domination of recorded music is that the origins and mode of production of the music are de-emphasized or hidden. It is easy, even typical, for a listener not to know anything about the composer, performer, or mediator of the music experience. The archetype of this is the 'hidden' background music found in shops, airports, and malls. You do not know who made the music, or who decided to impose it on the situation, or why, and you do not have easy means of finding out. This is rarely the case in 'non-everyday music', where the choice of the music is explained and articulated (e.g. through programme notes) and where the identity of those who produced the music is a central aspect of what it is that listeners are expected to know.

Implications for emotion. Everyday emotions to music are less likely to contain those 'social' emotions that rely on in-depth knowledge about the person producing the music (e.g. admiration, envy, empathy).

Proposition 5: everyday emotions in music are more self-referring (e.g. cheerful, anxious) than other-referring (e.g. proud of, approving of)

Research evaluation. Juslin and Laukka (2004) provide a list of felt emotions to music, in order of frequency of occurrence (reproduced here in Table 18.1). The first other-referring emotion ('admiration') appears seventeenth in the list. 'Happy', 'relaxed', and 'calm' are the three most cited emotions. A similar pattern was shown in Laukka (2007; see also Chapter 22, this volume).

Table 18.1 Relative frequency of felt emotions in response to music, as estimated by listeners in a questionnaire study by Juslin and Laukka (2004)

1. Happy	23. Empathic
2. Relaxed	24. Proud
3. Calm	25. Spiritual
4. Moved	26. Curious
5. Nostalgic	27. Relieved
6. Pleasurable	28. Bored
7. Loving	29. Indifferent
8. Sad	30. Frustrated
9. Longing	31. Tense
10. Tender	32. Disappointed
11. Amused	33. Surprised
12. Hopeful	34. Honored
13. Enchanted	35. Regretful
14. Expectant	36. Contemptuous
15. Solemn	37. Confused
16. Interested	38. Anxious
17. Admiring	39. Afraid
18. Angry	40. Jealous
19. Ecstatic	41. Disgusted
20. Lonely	42. Guilty
21. Content	43. Shameful
22. Desiring	44. Humiliated

Note: the emotions are listed from the most commonly experienced to the least commonly experienced.

18.2.6   Centrality of music to the experience, and the salience of the context

'Special' contexts for music engagement are those that tend to focus maximum attention on the music itself, and minimize other concerns. Music comes centre stage, and the aim is almost to make the context fade away into the background (Small, 1998). Everyday uses of music tend to be characterized by a much stronger role for the context or the accompanying activity. If you use music while engaging in some activity, such as exercising or working, you are not, thereby, elevating the music above the non-musical activity. The non-musical task still 'drives' the situation, in that the non-musical goals remain to be achieved. Even if music is used to distract consciousness from a boring or routine task, the user still needs to maintain whatever level of attention and control is needed to complete the task.

Implications for emotion. With a strong 'balance of attention' outside the music, emotions are likely to be less dependent on the music itself than in specialized musical settings. This could also mean that such emotions are going to show even more inter-individual variation than in more controlled settings (because the meaning of the context, or the music–context interaction, is more likely to be different for different people).

Proposition 6: everyday emotion to music reflects and is influenced by the personal emotional meaning of the non-musical context

Research evaluation. The non-musical context can impact on emotional response in at least two separate ways. The first source of influence is the current non-musical context, both internal and external: what is actually going on (including what has recently happened and what may happen in the immediate future) at the time the music is heard. But a second, and sometimes strong, source of influence is through memories of non-musical contexts that are triggered by, and associated with, the musical piece itself. So, when a person hears a particular piece of music, it may remind them of a time in their life when this piece was central, or it may remind them of a significant person or relationship (Schulkind, Hennis, & Rubin, 1999). Or it may simply remind them of some general cultural association (e.g. organ music signifies churches, classical music signifies high culture and privilege, etc.)

It could be argued that this second source of non-musical influence, which one might call 'personal and cultural associations' is not specific to everyday music. These same associations are also present and operating in the special and non-everyday exposure to music of the concert hall or the 'attentive absorption' in music. Although this is true, the emotional outcomes may be quite different. One aspect of emotional response is the generation of action tendencies (Frijda, 1986). In the context of the everyday, these action tendencies can be immediately translated into actions, which can 'cash in' the emotional energy in some way. So, for instance, if I hear a piece of music in a shop that has negative emotional connotations for me, I can often choose to walk out of the shop, thus removing myself from the source of unwanted emotions (cf. Sloboda 1999/2005). Or, if a piece of Mediterranean music reminds me of a pleasant holiday, I may be more inclined to pick up and buy a bottle of Italian wine (North, Hargreaves, & McKendrick, 1999). In the context of the concert hall, these same emotional tendencies cannot lead to action. In general, specialized music-listening contexts are ones that suppress or defer action tendencies, and that encourage the emotional effects to be noticed, savoured, held, and fed back and integrated into the attentional response to the unfolding musical event. Of course, the contrast is not complete. If concert music rouses enough non-musical associations, one can often find that one's attention is taken away from the music onto non-musical problem solving or rumination. In effect, one can 'walk away from the concert' inside one's head (e.g. Flowers & O'Neill, 2005).

But as a generalization, the specialist music environment is one that suppresses, dampens, or defers action tendencies, whereas the everyday environment is one that enables and facilitates the conversion of action tendencies into immediate action. Some support for this notion comes from Krumhansl's (1997) study, where music listeners in a decontextualized laboratory environment showed psychophysiological responses similar to those typically found in contexts where emotional responses are suppressed.

The impact of non-musical information on the emotional impact of music has been studied in a variety of ways. For instance, Thompson, Graham, and Russo (2005) showed that the same musical stimulus is rated as more happy when accompanied by visual exposure to a smiling face than to a sad face. Evidence of effects of non-musical context on emotions felt to music has been provided by Cantor and Zillman (1973), Dibben (2004), and Konečni, Wanic, and Brown (2007), using factorial experimental designs.

18.2.7 Nature of the music

Is some music by its very nature 'everyday'? Could an advertising jingle, a chart song, or the signature tune for a TV show be 'everyday music', while a symphony or an opera is not? It is possible that this distinction is partly a distinction between 'high' and 'low' culture, between art music versus vernacular music (DiMaggio, 1987). It is art music that is likely to be presented in specialized non-everyday contexts, to allow a fuller and more contemplative attention to it, whereas vernacular music is designed to rub along with anything else that is happening in the marketplace of experience. It is possible that some negative emotions are due to the evaluation of this kind of mismatch (e.g. people experiencing the playing of art music in elevators as some kind of cultural transgression, as described in Barenboim, 2006). On the other hand, any simplistic identification of the popular with the everyday needs to be avoided. Popular music is, for many people, the locus of serious 'connoisseurship' that is every bit as specialist as the attending given by some listeners to classical music (Frith, 1996).

In general, art music tends towards length and complexity (a symphony can last an hour, an opera can last three hours), whereas vernacular music tends to brevity and simplicity (the standard popular track or song lasts three minutes; musical 'signatures' such as theme-tunes can last for much less time than this—a few seconds, e.g. the 'start up' tune on Microsoft Windows, which lasts around three seconds). These are by no means rigid distinctions. Classical art music can be made more 'everyday' by cutting it up into shorter segments (as happens on some 'populist' classical music radio stations—probably in part explaining the ferocious hostility to this practice expressed by some classical music aficionados). On the other side, there are some examples of what might be broadly termed popular music because of some shared stylistic features, which are long, complex, or both (such as the contemporary sub-genre math rock, or the work of musicians such as Mike Oldfield). But in a sense these are exceptions that confirm the rule, and what makes them interesting and controversial is precisely that they do not conform to the norm.

Implications for emotion. One of the functions of vernacular culture is to provide easily recognized symbols, and these symbols can have a clear emotional element, because they may need to get across their symbolic meaning in noisy and diverse situations. This suggests that the more subtle, aesthetically tinged emotions may have lesser import.

Proposition 7: everyday emotional responses to music prioritize basic rather than complex emotions

Research evaluation. For obvious reasons, musical experiences in everyday life will tend to be more short lived than in specialized music-listening contexts. Everyday experience is full of 'snatched moments' where we might overhear a few seconds of a musical piece, as we move past a particular location.

There is considerable evidence that very short musical extracts (even as short as one second) are capable of communicating clear emotional signals, about which there is little inter-rater disagreement (e.g. Bigand, Filipic, & Lalitte, 2005; Watt & Ash, 1998). This suggests that such emotions may be 'read off' the musical surface, rather than through deep structural analysis. Similarly, such surface characteristics might directly influence brain pathways to change emotional state, without any need for close attention to musical symbols (see Chapter 5, this volume).

Everyday music might be considered to be that music whose emotional message is primarily designed to be one that can be read off the surface. Those musical forms that are primarily designed for everyday use (e.g. signature themes for TV programmes) need to be designed for instant recognition and instant response in complex social environments where there are competing attentional demands. Art music also has 'surface', and therefore it is possible, if one's attention is not fully on it, to respond to it entirely in terms of its surface characteristics. It is exactly in such everyday situations as overhearing a snatch of art music in an elevator that such 'surface hearing' is most likely.

Obviously, people experience complex emotions in everyday life. What is being suggested here is that the complexity is more likely to be sourced through the non-musical aspects of the situation than through the musical. If a piece of music reminds me of a person with whom I have a problematic and unresolved relationship, I may well experience complex emotions, but these emotions are not engendered by a nuanced engagement with the musical elements, but a nuanced engagement with cognitions about the person that the music reminds me of. For instance, nostalgic rumination on past events and relationships is one key function of music noted in a variety of studies (e.g. Sloboda, 1999/2005).

Within the set of basic emotions, it is also possible to question whether each basic emotion is as likely to occur as any other. There is evidence that music engenders some basic emotions more easily than others. For instance, Zentner, Grandjean, and Scherer (2008) found that people were 16 times more likely to report feeling happy to music than they were to report feeling angry (p. 504, Table 2).

18.2.8 Method of investigation

The term 'everyday' is sometimes used to refer to research strategy, and the prioritizing of 'ecological validity'. Everyday research studies are those that tend to involve field rather than laboratory situations, and often involve self-report and other 'rich' interpretative user-driven forms of data (see Chapter 8, this volume, for a more detailed discussion of self-report). This means that the researcher often is unable, or unwilling, to impose control methodologies (e.g. factorial experimental design) on a situation, thus limiting the degree of rigorous theory testing possible (see Chapter 25, this volume, for a defence of experimental approaches). Another feature of the every-day methodology is that intrusive measurement techniques (e.g. psychophysiological monitoring; Chapter 11, this volume) are not generally used in this work (although there is no reason in principle why not—miniaturization of means of recording heart rate, skin conductance, and other relevant physiological measures means that partici-pants in research may carry monitoring equipment in their pockets as they go about their everyday lives; e.g. Steptoe, Cropley, & Joekes, 2000).

Implications for emotion. Preferred methods for assessing emotional response are post hoc and interview or questionnaire based.

Proposition 8: everyday emotions to music are elicited by retrospective self-report

Research evaluation. Two factors are responsible for restricting almost all data gathering on everyday emotions to self-report. The first of these is technical: music researchers have in general not found ways to directly observe or record physiological aspects of emotional response whilst leaving participants complete freedom to go about their daily affairs. There is no reason why future research should not remedy this. The sec-ond of these is more substantive—and relates to the difficulty of identifying emotion from physiological or observational data without the self-report of the participant as an interpretational guide. You cannot tell which emotion a person is feeling just from physiological measures alone (Scherer & Zentner, 2001).

The wish to leave participants maximum freedom has also restricted the amount of work using experimental paradigms, which means, in particular, that causal infer-ences are hard to make. However, some researchers have found means of imposing some experimental control on situations that still leave the participants the freedom of manoeuvre typical of everyday situations. These means include simulation studies, where key elements of the real-life situation are recreated in the laboratory (e.g. studies of driving behaviour with driving simulators; Brodsky, 2002). They also include stud-ies in real-life situations where the experimenter exerts some degree of control (e.g. altering the musical background in real-life settings such as shops, canteens, on-hold music, and gyms; see North & Hargreaves, 2009). In such situations, elements of the stimulus fall under experimenter control, but there are no prescriptions for participant behaviour additional to those already present in the real-life situation. These types of methods would seem readily adaptable to the experimental study of everyday emotional responses to music.

The main dimensions on which studies of everyday emotions vary relate to (a) the tools used to elicit self-report (free versus categorical), and (b) the time delay between event and response. In free response, respondents are asked to describe their emotional reactions in their own words (e.g. Batt-Rawden & DeNora, 2005; DeNora, 2000; Sloboda, 1999/2005; see also Chapter 22, this volume). In categorized response, respondents are asked to tick or rate researcher-specified categories and dimensions (e.g. Juslin & Laukka, 2004; North et al, 2004; Sloboda et al, 2001). Both alternatives have advantages and present problems. Free response encourages respondents to think more deeply about their experience, and is more motivating. However when individuals are left free to choose their own words, then differences in vocabulary and culture make it difficult to compare data across individuals, let alone across studies (Scherer, Wranik, Sangsue, Tran, & Scherer, 2004). Forced-choice judgements provide advantages for the researcher in terms of analytic ease and cross-individual comparisons. However, when individuals select emotion labels from a predetermined list, the danger is that the word chosen does not reflect their true response so much as a 'nearest fit' or some judgement of what would seem the 'appropriate' label to pick (as a result of perceived emotional character of the music, rather than their own experience; or as a result of demand characteristics of the study, see Chapter 10, this volume).

The main threat to the validity and reliability of data gathered in everyday situations is the vulnerability of self-reports to bias (see Ericsson & Simon, 1980). When relating to emotion, these biases are likely to include forgetting or conflating of routine and low-intensity experiences, and processes of reinterpretation of high-intensity experience in the light of post-experience events and current psychological state (Levine & Safer, 2002). Such biases are likely to be least pronounced where data is gathered as close in time to the event concerned as possible. The most 'proximal' is some form of participant observation where the researcher is actually in the presence of the research participant (e.g. accompanying them on a shopping trip, or eliciting concurrent commentary; e.g. De Nora, 2000).

Next in proximity come *experience-sampling methodologies* (ESM), when participants are contacted electronically (e.g. mobile phone) while going about their daily lives and asked to report on a concurrent or recent event (North et al, 2004; Juslin et al, 2008). This typically reduces average delay between event and report to a few hours at most, and minutes at best. This method was pioneered by Cziksentmihalyi and colleagues (e.g. Csikszentmihalyi & Lefevre, 1989) and introduced to music study by Sloboda, O'Neill, and Ivaldi (2001). A recent review of the research applications of ESM is given by Hektner, Schmidt, and Csikzentmihalyi (2007).

It remains the case, however, that a very substantial part of the literature on this topic derives from 'one time' encounters with participants, through questionnaires or interviews that integrate memory-based material over a significant time span, which can vary from the immediately preceding time span (e.g. 'Can you tell me about yesterday?'—DeNora, 2000) through targeted distant times (e.g. 'the first 10 years of life'—Sloboda, 1989/2005), to more unspecific generalized approaches ('Tell me about the role of music in your life'—Hays & Minichiello, 2005; Sloboda, 1999/2005). In expanding the time span in this way, research can quite significantly limit reliability, validity, and precision of the data so collected.

Although careful methodological decisions can raise the reliability and validity of the data collected on emotional responses to everyday musical experiences, it is difficult to test strong causal theories about the relationship of music to emotion through such work, since there is little or no opportunity for a researcher to manipulate independent variables in a controlled fashion. This does not mean that research into everyday music is free of serious attempts at generalization. Far from it, as I hope the material reviewed in this chapter shows. What it does mean is that the work of testing theories of specific psychological mechanisms through which emotions are engendered remains at a quite preliminary stage (see Juslin & Västfjäll, 2008, for a critical evaluation of this area).

18.2.9 Intellectual stance of writer/researcher

In general, 'music in everyday life' seems to be an emblem for an anti-elitist approach, which wishes to explore the full range of ways in which people engage with music in their lives, rather than starting from some premise of how people 'should' engage with music. Such an approach takes particular care not to start from the views of musicians and musical elites (composers, performers, critics, broadcasters). Rather, it starts from the point of view of the consumer. It also reflects an approach that places as much interest in activities where music plays a minor or supporting role, as those where music is the 'main act'.

Implications for emotion. The everyday approach sits somewhat lightly to any a priori attempt to predict emotional response from the nature of the musical materials. It will take emotion to arise from a materials-listener-context complex in which the composer/performer and the musical work have no privileged position.

Proposition 9: everyday emotions to music are listener focused rather than focused on the musical work

Research evaluation. When a music-emotion researcher engages with a participant, it is very hard to avoid giving the impression to the participant that you are particularly interested in their responses *to* the music. So questions such as 'How did the music make you feel?', and 'What is it about this music that you like?' are the stock in trade of the music-emotion researcher. There is, for that reason, a strong reason to believe that respondents will try, wherever possible, to reference their emotional responses to the musical object, and privilege such response over others.

In a laboratory study of music listening, Waterman (1996) classified free verbal descriptions of moments in deliberate focused music listening when the participants 'felt something'. Only two of the 13 classifications were not pointing to characteristics of the musical work. These two were sensual/physical reactions (e.g. 'I felt a lump in my throat') and association (e.g. 'It reminded me of when …'). Even among non-musically trained respondents, only some 17 per cent of responses fell into these two categories. The remaining 83 per cent referenced the content of the stimulus in some way (e.g. 'I noticed the change in mood', 'I felt it because it got louder', 'The music is cheap').

However, like the vast majority of research situations, the Waterman experiment was designed to make music 'centre stage' in the participant's awareness, recreating in the laboratory that 'special' and 'non-everyday' context of the concert hall where hushed and reverent attention is being given to the music and where one monitors self-consciously the effect that the music is having on the self. Everyday uses of music are not generally like this. They are only like this in those somewhat rare situations when the listener's attention is predominantly on the music and his or her reactions to it, and not on the external context (or non-musical cognitions, memories, associations).

Those of us who research and write about music tend to do so because music is of deep interest to us—our own experience of it is rich, complex, and necessarily quite explicit. We may forget that there are some people, possibly many people, for whom talking and thinking precisely about their musical experiences may be a rare and unpractised activity. Even when asked to focus their attention on specific music-listening experiences by a researcher, they may have rather little authentic to say! In a recent study by Greasley and Lamont (2006), participants of different reported levels of engagement with music were intensively interviewed about their uses of and reactions to music in their everyday lives. According to the authors, less engaged participants often found it more difficult to articulate why they liked music ('It's got me annoyed now, 'cause I can't explain why I like it, but I just do . . . there's very few songs I could explain why I like it').

In the study by Sloboda (1999/2005), participants were asked to write in their own words about 'music and you'. It was very clear that the 'you' half of the pair received much more elaboration than the 'music' half. Few people talked about specific pieces, or their understanding of musical content and style. Many responses were notable for failing to reference a single style of music (e.g. pop, classical), far less an individual piece. But all respondents wrote, sometimes at great length, about the contexts in which they listened to music, and the personal functions that music listening fulfilled. A typical statement offered was: 'On arrival home from work, music lifts the stress of work: it has an immediate healing effect.' The implication of this statement is that the person concerned had long ago settled the issue of *what* music to listen to on arrival home from work. Everything was set up, and he or she could simply enjoy the habitual effects of this, much as the effects of a warm bath, without too much focused cognition on the what and how.

On the other hand, there is some evidence that encouraging people to focus on their emotional responses can actually help to bring music's function into explicit awareness for participants, thus enhancing their ability to reflect on and discuss it, and possibly use it more strategically in their everyday lives in the future (e.g. Batt-Rawden & DeNora, 2005; see Chapter 7, this volume). But even then, it is possible that the greater reflexivity achieved relates not so much to a more detailed attention to the musical content as to a more detailed attention to one's own psychological states.

Is there any way of researching everyday emotional impact of music without telling participants that this is what you are researching? It is hard to see how unless one embeds this in a wider study of everyday emotions, where music just happens to crop up as one of a whole variety of external stimuli: or where the emotional response is measured through non-verbal means (e.g. physiological monitoring). There remain significant challenges ahead for music researchers that have by and large not been addressed in the methodological approaches outlined in Section III of this handbook, where most of the approaches involve high levels of researcher-induced attention to the details of the musical experience.

18.2.10 Contextual specificity of judgement obtained

There are many studies that ask people about their music preferences (see Konečni, 1982; and Chapters 24 and 25, this volume). These would appear to tap the enduring emotional value of particular pieces of music. However, where these preferences are generalized ('I like style x more than y'), these seem to take the studies out of the realm of everyday life to some Platonic sphere of comparative aesthetic values. Studies of preference only become 'everyday' when preferences are linked to contexts (e.g. 'I like style x to work to, exercise to, wake up to in the morning'). Indeed, it could be argued that there is always a cultural 'frame' for comparisons between different pieces of music; it is simply that in some contexts this frame is implicit and unstated. The everyday approach is to assume that music is functional for the individual's goal achievement. There may be no such thing as 'listening to music for its own sake' even when that listening is solitary and self-referring. There is always a social or cultural outcome, even if only in the imagination. If this is the correct way to look at music engagement, then it should be possible, through sufficient probing or deconstruction, to uncover a specific functional explanation behind any statement of generalized liking or preference. Such general statements will simply be shorthand for an emotional orientation towards a piece of music, or a genre, which reflects the emotional outcomes of previous specific encounters with that music that achieved specific functional outcomes for that person.

Implications for emotion: The functional approach highlights emotions relevant to goal achievement (including mood regulation), rather than emotions relating to enduring traits or attitudes.

Proposition 10: everyday emotions to music arise from transient aspects of goal achievement with which the music becomes associated, rather than from stable evaluative attitudes to the music

Research evaluation. Sloboda et al (2009) reviewed research studies on music listening by choice (as opposed to involuntary exposure). They organized their review by the functional niche that the music is chosen to be part of. They identified five main everyday niches in the research literature. These are (a) travel (e.g. driving a car, walking, using public transport); (b) physical work (everyday routines like washing, cleaning, cooking, and other forms of manual labour); (c) brain work (e.g. private study, reading, writing, and other forms of thinking); (d) body work (e.g. exercise, yoga, relaxation, pain management); and (e) emotional work (e.g. mood management, reminiscence, presentation of identity).

In reviewing the research literature, Sloboda et al identified four recurring functions of self-chosen music use. *Distraction* is a way of engaging unallocated attention and reducing boredom (as evidenced in studies on pain management—e.g. Mitchell, MacDonald, Knussen, & Serpell, 2007). *Energizing* is a means of maintaining arousal and task attention (as evidenced by research on driving—e.g. Cummings, Koepsell, Moffat, & Rivara, 2001). In *entrainment*, the task movements are timed to coincide with the rhythmic pulses of the music, giving the task or activity elements of a dance (shown to be a significant factor in choice of music to accompany physical exercise— e.g. Belcher & DeNora, 1999). Finally, *meaning enhancement* is where the music draws out and adds to the significance of the task or activity in some way (as in the use of music to enhance personal reminiscence—e.g. Greasley & Lamont, 2006). A related classificatory scheme has been applied to music use in adolescents by Saarikallio and Erkkila (2007).

In many of the functional niches for self-chosen music, emotions are not the primary intended functional outcome. Rather, outcomes such as task completion are primary (e.g. getting the housework done). However, emotions and affective states in general can be secondary or intermediate outcomes. If I find housework boring and demotivating, then I may be able to get through the housework more successfully if I use music to help me feel more cheerful. There is little research evidence on how these 'secondary' emotions work.

However, the fifth functional niche identified by Sloboda et al (mood management, reminiscence, presentation of identity) is more directly concerned with the achievement of desired emotional outcomes as a primary goal. Evidence for deliberate and self-conscious use of music to manage (or regulate) mood comes from a range of qualitative studies, where respondents are asked to explain their music use in an intensive way (e.g. Batt Rawden & DeNora, 2005; DeNora, 2000; Sloboda, 1999/2005). There is clear evidence that the ability to use music in this way is subject to individual differences. Women generally give more detailed and articulate accounts of their regulatory strategies than men (North, Hargreaves, & O'Neill, 2000), and people who have a low level of engagement with music (as evidenced by their self-rated subjective importance of music-listening) appear less aware of the range of emotional functions that music can fulfil than more engaged listeners (Greasley & Lamont, 2006). There is evidence that self-aware use of music for mood regulation can be enhanced through therapeutic or educational intervention (Batt-Rawden & DeNora, 2005), although the conditions under which this may best take place have not yet been systematically investigated.

There also exists a broader general psychological literature on mood regulation, which studies the use made by people of a variety of strategies and tactics to create, maintain, enhance, or change a mood or emotion in an intended direction (Parkinson, Totterdell, Briner, & Richards, 1996). Music is only one of many devices by which people attempt to regulate their mood (they also include eating, exercise, watching TV, etc.). The detailed research on everyday uses of music is by and large not closely informed by the wider literature on mood regulation, and as a result there is little comparative analysis of the specific characteristics and potentials of music as opposed to other available (and effective) mood-regulation tactics (Van-Goethem, 2008).

The line of argument being pursued is that everyday emotions to music rarely if ever arise out of a decontextualized aesthetic relationship to the music as object.

In other words, it is difficult to find instances in everyday music listening where you can convincingly account for an emotional response purely on the basis that the listener *likes* the music in question, regardless of any psychological outcomes that the music might be allowing the listener to achieve. One well-researched factor in accounting for emotional attachments to music is identity: that specific pieces or genres of music reflect and communicate, to the listener and to those in his or her social world, something about who he or she is, and about values (see, for instance, MacDonald, Hargeaves, & Miell, 2002). In this context, a strong positive emotional response to a particular piece of identity-confirming music may arise from a sense of pride, belonging, resistance against a common foe, personal honour or value, which the identity confers, and that the music reminds the listener of. For that reason, the same piece of music should always simultaneously be capable of engendering emotions deriving from exclusion, alienation, indifference, or disaffection in those whose identity is not associated with the music in question.

18.3 CONCLUDING REMARKS

Table 18.2 summarizes the issues that this chapter has reviewed. The dimensions on which everyday music has been characterized fall into three main groups. The first group (propositions 1–3) concern general qualities of the emotional experience. The second group (propositions 4–7) concern the specific emotional content, and the third group (propositions 8–10) concern the context in which the emotions are experienced and researched. In each case, everyday music has been contrasted, either implicitly or

Table 18.2 Summary of emotions in hearing music

Theme	Topic	Everyday	Non-everyday
Quality	1. intensity	low	high
	2. memorability	low	high
	3. integration	low	high
Content	4. valence	higher negativity	lower negativity
	5. reference	self	other
	6. focus	external to music	internal to music
	7. level	basic	complex
Context	8. elicitation	mainly self-report	broad range of methods
	9. referent	listener	producer
	10. attitude	goal achievement	aesthetic

explicitly, to the 'non-everyday' or 'special' reception of music, of which the experiences of an attentive and informed audience of a classical symphony concert might be considered a paradigm. The table summarizes these constrasts in the columns headed 'Everyday' and 'Non-everyday'.

In relation to quality of the experience, everyday experiences are low on intensity, memorability, and integration; whereas the non-everyday experiences are, on average, higher in all these respects. In relation to content, everyday experiences involve basic-level self-referential emotions, with a focus on factors external to the music, and a significant proportion of negative reactions; whereas non-everyday experiences tend towards more complex, broadly positive, and other-referenced emotions drawing on the music itself. The context for everyday experience is one focused on the goal achievement of the listener as elicited through discourse; whereas the non-everyday context focuses on aesthetic reactions to the work and those who produced it, as elicited through a range of behavioural and psychophysiological measures.

For most of its short life, the psychological study of emotional responses to music has focused primarily on the non-everyday. Its methods, theories, and base assumptions have been deeply influenced by this orientation. Historians and sociologists of the subject can profitably analyse why this might have come about—in relation to the institutions, professions, and key individuals which have shaped the discipline. But in general, there seems to be a strong cultural tendency to elevate the aesthetic discourse of music over the practical, which runs more strongly for music than for some other domains.

It is instructive, for instance, to compare the way we think about the consumption of music to way we think about the consumption of food. Both music and food have practical and aesthetic components. As for music, some people interested in food ('gourmets') are willing to pay substantial sums of money to go to 'special' non-everyday places, where food is prepared and served with great thought and care, and everything is done to ensure that full attention is placed on the textural, sensual, and structural properties of the meal. This is a perfectly valid way of consuming food, and one which merits close study. It undoubtedly brings with it a set of emotional responses that are distinctive and interesting. But it would be very strange if food psychologists were to act in ways that implied that they thought that the gourmet experience was the most central or paradigmatic mode of food consumption, and the one which merited central study, relegating the study of everyday food consumption to the margins.

Maybe the difference between food and music is the issue of necessity. If we don't eat we die, and therefore the mundane, goal-oriented (and survival-oriented) aspects of food consumption are clearly central to any psychological consideration of it. Music is not a necessity for individual survival, and so, although it may be recruited for goal-oriented activities, there is nothing to require this. People who want to 'reserve' music for the aesthetic domain are free to do so, and this somewhat elitist impulse seems to have dominated the scholarly study of music.

It is my belief that the role of psychological investigation is to describe and explain what is there, in all its rich complexity. Everyday music listening probably comprises the vast bulk of 'what is there' within contemporary music experience. Describing and explaining the special is important too, as it helps us to understand the potentials and limits of human capacity. But unless our examination of the ordinary and the exceptional interact and cross-fertilize each other, then an integrated understanding will be hard to achieve.

RECOMMENDED FURTHER READING

1. DeNora, T. (2000). *Music in everyday life.* Cambridge, UK: Cambridge University Press.
2. Hallam, S., Cross, I., & Thaut, M. (eds). (2009). *Oxford handbook of music psychology.* Oxford: Oxford University Press. (Chapters 40–5)

REFERENCES

Barenboim, D. (2006). *The neglected sense.* 2nd BBC Reith Lecture. Retrieved from: http://www.bbc.co.uk/radio4/reith2006/lecture2.shtml

Batt-Rawden, K., & DeNora, T. (2005). Music and informal learning in everyday life. *Music Education Research, 7,* 289–304.

Baumgartner, H. (1992), Remembrance of things past: music, autobiographical memory and emotion. *Advances in Consumer Research, 19,* 613–20.

Belcher, S., & DeNora, T. (1999). Music is part of the equipment that makes your body hard! *eXercise, 5,* 4–5.

Bigand, E., Filipic, S., & Lalitte, P. (2005). The time course of emotional response to music. *Annals of the New York Academy of Science, 1060,* 429–37.

Brodsky, W. (2002). The effects of music tempo on simulated driving performance and vehicular control. *Transportation Research Part F, 4,* 219–41.

Cantor, J. R., & Zillman, D. (1973). The effect of affective state and emotional arousal on music appreciation. *Journal of General Psychology, 89,* 97–108.

Clarke, E. F., Cross, I., Deutsch, D., Drake, C., Gabrielsson, A., Hargreaves, D. J., Kemp, A. E., McAdams, S., North, A., O'Neill, S. A., Parncutt, R., Sloboda, J. A., Trehub, S. E., & Zatorre, R. (2001). Psychology of music. In S. Sadie (ed.), *The new Grove dictionary of music and musicians* (2nd edn, Vol. 20, pp. 527–62). London: Macmillan.

Crafts, S. D., Cavicchi, D., Keil, C., & the Music in Daily Life Project (1993). *My music.* Hanover, NH: Wesleyan University Press.

Csikszentmihalyi, M., & Lefevre, J. (1989). Optimal experience in work and leisure. *Journal of Personality and Social Psychology, 56,* 815–22.

Cummings, R., Kopesell, T. D., Moffat, J. M., & Rivara, F. P. (2001). Drowsiness, countermeasures to drowsiness, and the risk of a motor vehicle crash. *Injury Prevention, 7,* 194–99.

DeNora, T. (2000). *Music in everyday life.* Cambridge, UK: Cambridge University Press.

DeNora, T. (2003). The sociology of music listening in everyday life. In R. Kopiez, A. C. Lehmann, I. Wolther, & C. Wolf (eds), *Proceeding of the Fifth Triennial ESCOM Conference.* Hanover, Germany: Hanover University of Music & Drama. (CD rom)

Dibben, N. J. (2004). The role of peripheral feedback in emotional experience with music. *Music Perception, 22,* 79–115.

DiMaggio, P. (1987). Classification in art. *American Sociological Review, 52,* 440–55.

Ericsson, K. A., & Simon, H. A. (1980). Verbal reports as data, *Psychological Review, 87,* 215–51.

Flowers, P. J., & O'Neill, A. M. (2005). Self-reported distractions of middle school students in listening to music and prose. *Journal of Research in Music Education*, *53*, 308–21.

Frijda, N. H. (1986). *The emotions*. Cambridge, UK: Cambridge University Press.

Frith, S. (1996). *Performing rites: on the value of popular music*. Cambridge, MA: Harvard University Press.

Greasley, A. E., & Lamont, A. (2006). Music preference in adulthood: Why do we like the music we do? In M. Baroni, A. R. Adessi, R. Caterina, & M. Costa (eds), *Proceedings of the 9th International Conference on Music Perception and Cognition* (pp. 960–6). Bologna, Italy: University of Bologna.

Hallam, S., Cross, I., & Thaut, M. (eds). (2009). *Oxford handbook of music psychology*. Oxford: Oxford University Press.

Hays, T., & Minichiello, V. (2005). The meaning of music in the lives of older people: a qualitative study. *Psychology of Music*, *33*, 437–51.

Hektner, J. M., Schmidt, J. A., & Csikszentmihalyi, M. (2007). *Experience Sampling Method: Measuring the quality of everyday life*. London: Sage.

Juslin, P. N., & Laukka, P. (2004). Expression, perception and induction of musical emotions: a review and a questionnaire study of everyday listening. *Journal of New Music Research*, *33*, 217–38.

Juslin, P. N., Liljeström, S., Västfjäll, D., Barradas, G., & Silva, A. (2008). An experience sampling study of emotional reactions to music: Listener, music, and situation. *Emotion*, *8*, 668–83.

Juslin, P. N., & Västfjäll, D. (2008). Emotional responses to music: The need to consider underlying mechanisms. *Behavioral and Brain Sciences*, *31*, 559–75.

Konečni, V. (1982). Social interaction and musical preference. In D. Deutsch (ed.), *The psychology of music* (pp. 497–516). New York: Academic Press.

Konečni, V. J., Wanic, R. A., & Brown, A. (2007). Emotional and aesthetic antecedents and consequences of music-induced thrills. *American Journal of Psychology*, *120*, 619–43.

Krumhansl, C. L. (1997). An exploratory study of musical emotions and psychophysiology. *Canadian Journal of Experimental Psychology*, *51*, 336–52.

Laukka, P. (2007). Uses of music and psychological well-being among the elderly. *Journal of Happiness Studies*, *8*, 215–41.

Levene, L. (1997). Reconstructing memory for emotions. *Journal of Experimental Psychology: General*, *126*, 165–77.

Levine, L., & Safer, M. J. (2002). Sources of bias in memory for emotions. *Current Directions in Psychological Science*, *11*, 169–73.

MacDonald, R., Hargreaves, D. J., & Miell, D. (eds). (2002). *Musical identities*. Oxford: Oxford University Press.

Mitchell, L. A., MacDonald, R., Knussen, C., & Serpell, M. G. (2007). A survey investigation of the effects of music listening on chronic pain. *Psychology of Music*, *35*, 39–59.

North, A. C., & Hargreaves, D. J. (2009). Music and consumer behaviour. In S. Hallam, I. Cross, & M. Thaut (eds), *Oxford handbook of music psychology* (pp. 481–90). Oxford: Oxford University Press.

North, A. C., Hargreaves, D. J., & Hargreaves, J. J. (2004). Uses of music in everyday life. *Music Perception*, *22*, 41–77.

North, A. C., Hargreaves, D. J., & McKendrick, J. (1999). The effect of music on in-store wine selections. *Journal of Applied Psychology*, *84*, 271–6.

North, A. C., Hargreaves, D. J., & O'Neill, S. A. (2000). The importance of music to adolescents. *British Journal of Educational Psychology*, *70*, 255–72.

Parkinson, B., Totterdell, P., Briner, R. B., & Richards, J. M. (1996). *Changing moods: The psychology of mood regulation*. London: Longman.

Saarikallio, S., & Erkkila, J. (2007). The role of music in adolescents' mood regulation. *Psychology of Music*, 35, 88–109.

Scherer, K. R., Wranik, T., Sangsue, J., Tran, V., & Scherer, U. (2004). Emotions in everyday life: Probability of occurence, risk factors, appraisal and reaction patterns. *Social Science Information*, 43, 499–570.

Scherer, K. R., & Zentner, M. R. (2001). Emotional effects of music: Production rules. In P. N. Juslin & J. A. Sloboda (eds), *Music and emotion: Theory and research* (pp. 361–92). Oxford: Oxford University Press.

Schulkind, M. D., Hennis, L. K., & Rubin, D. C. (1999). Music, emotion, and authobiographical memory; They're playing your song. *Memory & Cognition*, 27, 948–55.

Sloboda, J. A. (1989/2005). Music as a language. In F. Wilson & F. Roehmann (eds), *Music and child development: Proceedings of the 1987 Biology of Music Making Conference* (pp. 28–43). St. Louis, MO: MMB Music. (Reprinted in Sloboda, J. A. (2005). *Exploring the musical mind: Cognition, emotion, ability, function* (pp. 175–190). Oxford: Oxford University Press.)

Sloboda, J. A. (1999/2005). Everyday uses of music: a preliminary study. In S. W. Yi (ed.), *Music, Mind, & Science* (pp. 354–369). Seoul: Seoul National University Press. (Reprinted in Sloboda, J. A. (2005). *Exploring the musical mind: Cognition, emotion, ability, function* (pp. 319–31). Oxford: Oxford University Press.)

Sloboda, J. A., & O'Neill, S. A. (2001). Emotions in everyday listening to music. In P. N. Juslin & J. A. Sloboda (eds), *Music and emotion: Theory and research* (pp. 415–30). Oxford: Oxford University Press.

Sloboda, J. A., O'Neill, S. A., & Ivaldi, A. (2001). Functions of music in everyday life: an exploratory study using the Experience Sampling Methodology. *Musicae Scientiae*, 5, 9–32.

Sloboda, J. A., Lamont, A. M., & Greasley, A. E. (2009). Choosing to hear music: motivation, process, and effect. In S. Hallam, I. Cross, & M. Thaut (eds), *Oxford handbook of music psychology* (pp. 431–40). Oxford: Oxford University Press.

Small, C. (1998). *Musicking: the meaning of performing and listening*. Hanover, NH: Wesleyan University Press.

Sonnemans, J., & Frijda, N. H. (1995). The determinants of subjective emotional intensity. *Cognition & Emotion*, 9, 483–506.

Stein, N. L., Ornstein, P., Tversky, B., & Brainerd, C. (1996). *Memory for everyday and emotional events*. Mahwah, NJ: Erlbaum.

Steptoe, A., Cropley, M., & Joekes, K. (2000). Task demands and the pressures of everyday life: associations between cardiovascular reactivity and work blood pressure and heart rate. *Health Psychology*, 19, 46–54.

Thompson, R. A. (1991). Emotional regulation and emotional development. *Educational Psychology Review*, 3, 269–307.

Thompson, W. F., Graham, P., & Russo, F. A. (2005). Seeing music performance: visual influences on perception and experience. *Semiotica*, 156, 177–201.

Van-Goethem, A. (2008). *Mood regulation and music*. Paper presented at the Music, Health, and Happiness conference, Royal Northern College of Music, UK, November 2008.

Watt, R. J., & Ash, R. L. (1998). A psychological investigation into meaning in music. *Musicae Scientiae*, 2, 33–53.

Whaley, J., Sloboda, J. A., & Gabrielsson, A. (2009). Peak experiences in music. In S. Hallam, I. Cross, & M. Thaut (eds), *Oxford handbook of music psychology* (pp. 452–61). Oxford: Oxford University Press.

Zentner, M. R., Grandjean, D., & Scherer, K. R. (2008). Emotions evoked by the sound of music: characterization, classification and measurement. *Emotion*, 8, 494–521.

CHAPTER 19

EXPERIMENTAL AESTHETICS AND LIKING FOR MUSIC

DAVID J. HARGREAVES AND ADRIAN C. NORTH

19.1 INTRODUCTION

THE study of aesthetics, involving the creation and appreciation of art and beauty, has been approached in two distinct ways. 'Speculative aesthetics' is concerned with high-level, abstract questions such as the meaning and nature of art, and is dealt with in the disciplines of philosophy, art history, and art criticism. 'Empirical aesthetics', on the other hand, is the scientific study of the nature of appreciation. Adherents of these two approaches may well differ about the suitability of the scientific approach, about what constitutes a work of art and is therefore worthy of investigation, and even about what constitutes an 'aesthetic response'. In this chapter, we focus explicitly on the second approach: our central concern is to review the wide range of empirical studies that have been conducted from various theoretical points of view on the aesthetic response to music.

Empirical aesthetics started very clearly with the publication of Gustav Theodor Fechner's *Vorschule der Äesthetik* in 1876. This shows that experimental aesthetics is one of the oldest topics in experimental psychology, which itself was in its early stages at that time. Fechner characterized his approach as 'aesthetics from below', by which he meant that his starting point was the response to simple shapes, colours, sounds, geometrical forms, and so on. He considered that an understanding of these basic principles would eventually lead to an 'aesthetics from above'; that is, to an understanding of the broader aesthetic questions. He used this approach in attempting to test the notion of the 'aesthetic mean', according to which beauty is associated with the absence of extremes. The most pleasing sounds might be those which are neither too strong nor too weak, for example. His respondents were presented with different-shaped rectangles in order to test the 'golden section' hypothesis that the ratio of 0.62 between the lengths of the longer and shorter sides may have unique aesthetic properties.

The results from studies in this tradition over the next few decades were generally inconclusive, and other areas of early research along related lines, for example those that attempted to identify characteristic individual styles of aesthetic appreciation, or 'apperceptive types', similarly failed to fulfil their promise (e.g. Binet, 1903). However, the field of experimental aesthetics gained new maturity in the work of Daniel Berlyne (e.g. Berlyne, 1974) in the mid 1960s. Berlyne developed what became known as the 'new experimental aesthetics', to which we shall return later in this chapter.

Since the 1960s and 1970s, the field of music psychology has grown very rapidly in a number of new directions (e.g. Hargreaves, Miell, & MacDonald, 2002). The early emphasis on psychometrics, psychoacoustics, and cognitive psychology became seen as having an over-emphasis on the minutiae of musical behaviour and experience, as frequently using artificial experimental paradigms based in the laboratory rather than in real life, and as having a limited range of participants. This is particularly true of experimental aesthetics: most studies in this tradition have dealt with musical elements such as tones, intervals, and scales, rather than with real-life experiences of music. In the last two decades or so, this approach, though no less important, is no longer as central within music psychology, and the discipline as a whole has diversified into several sub-disciplines. Alongside the contemporary cognitive psychology of music (e.g. Deliège & Sloboda, 1997), whose scope has broadened to include a much wider range of phenomena, we can identify the developmental psychology of music (e.g. Hargreaves, 1986; McPherson, 2006) and the social psychology of music (e.g. North & Hargreaves, 2008). In the latter book, we stress the importance of the real-life applications of music psychology, and outline several areas in which this is being done.

In this chapter, we draw on experimental aesthetics to a considerable extent. But we also take on board the social and developmental perspectives by adopting a much broader approach to the role of social and cultural factors in aesthetic responses to music, and have particular interest in how these responses develop across the lifespan. We begin by sketching the broad scope of the field, and looking at some definitions that have been proposed of different aspects of responses to music, and briefly outline some of the main methodological approaches. We then present a conceptual framework for the study of music listening that has been developed by Hargreaves, Miell, and MacDonald (2005), which we call the 'reciprocal feedback' response model. This has at its heart the interaction between the musical stimuli (the traditional province of experimental aesthetics), the situation in which listening takes place (which is usually ignored in most experimental aesthetic studies), and the characteristics of the listener. This model forms the basis of the organization of the rest of the chapter, which looks in turn at different aspects of the music, of the listening situation, and of the listener.

19.2 DEFINITIONS AND METHODS

The terms 'aesthetic response' and 'affective response' are sometimes used interchangeably in the literature, and sometimes not. Some observers, such as perhaps the critic, see the former as intense, subjective, and personal—as existing at a high intellectual level, and as requiring a fairly sophisticated level of knowledge and experience, such as might occur when a sophisticated connoisseur experiences a sublime work of art. 'Affective responses', on the other hand, are those that involve moods and emotions, and are generally regarded as being more superficial. The term 'appreciation' can be thought of as encompassing both of these; it provides a general description of the response to music that includes both 'aesthetic' and 'affective' components. Many researchers in experimental aesthetics implicitly take this latter view, referring to more or less any reaction that any person might have to any work of art, defined in the broadest possible terms. Our own principal interest has been in trying to account for everyday likes and dislikes in music rather than rarified reactions.

On a more pragmatic level, one notable aspect of the literature on liking for music, and particularly that on experimental aesthetics, is that it has developed in parallel to, rather than in conjunction with, that concerning more fine-grained emotional responses to music. At present, there exists a literature on liking for music and, in effect, a largely separate literature on specific emotional responses to music. One of the tasks that we attempted to accomplish in our recent book, *The social and applied psychology of music* (North & Hargreaves, 2008), was to propose an explicit means of forging links between the two fields. What is interesting about this in the context of the present chapter is that we proposed that the concept that may establish a bridgehead between liking for and emotional reactions to music is that of physiological arousal. As we will see shortly, physiological arousal, as defined by researchers within the new experimental aesthetics, has enjoyed some success as a predictor of musical preference; and some more recent work (e.g. North & Hargreaves, 1997) has applied liking for music and arousal induced by music to fine-grained emotional reactions, such as the extent to which a given piece of music may be experienced as, for example, exciting, relaxing, boring, or unsettling. In short, the literature on experimental aesthetics may have the, as yet largely untapped, potential to also explain emotional reactions.

Another feature of our own approach to the subject (reviewed in more detail in North & Hargreaves, 2008) has also been to use 'real' music, 'real' people, and 'real' contexts as much as possible. Since statistics on CD sales, radio station listening figures, and Internet downloads make it clear that these are dominated by pop music, and also show that classical music represents a minority interest among the general population, our own focus has been on pop music, despite the predominance of classical music in the development of Western music as a whole, and in a great deal of psychological research that uses real musical stimuli. Any representative view of music psychology should be based on the widest possible range of listeners and musical forms, and the term 'preference' is accordingly used in a neutral sense to refer to a person's *liking* for one piece of music as compared with another. 'Musical taste' is similarly used to refer to the *overall* patterning of an individual's preferences, in whatever genre they might be.

We can distinguish between two main methodological approaches to research on responses to music, which might be called 'experimental' and 'naturalistic' approaches (cf. Sluckin, Hargreaves, & Colman, 1983). The former approach uses stimuli such as electronically generated wave forms, intervals or tone sequences played under laboratory conditions; participants' responses are assessed by means of standardized rating scales, questionnaires, and the like. The naturalistic approach, on the other hand, uses 'real' music that is played under conditions that are designed to be as lifelike as possible; and responses can include a much wider variety of methods. These have been comprehensively reviewed by Abeles and Chung (1996), and there is no need to repeat this here. Suffice it to say that they categorize the main approaches as *verbal reports* (including open-ended techniques such as interviews, narratives, or diaries) and *physiological measures* such as heart rate, respiration rate, galvanic skin response, electroencephalograms, and blood pressure. In some of our own research, which is conducted in real-life listening situations such as shops, restaurants, or the workplace, response measures have included waiting times, sales figures, or productivity ratings.

19.3 THE RECIPROCAL FEEDBACK MODEL OF RESPONSES TO MUSIC

Hargreaves, Miell, and MacDonald (2005) proposed a 'reciprocal feedback' model of musical response, which is shown in Figure 19.1. This describes some of many specific aspects of what we see as the three main determinants of a specific *response* to a given musical stimulus: the *music*, the *listening situation*, and the *listener*. This three-fold description forms the basis of the organization of this chapter, as we said earlier, and although we will provide a much more detailed review of the research in each of the three main areas, it is nevertheless useful to provide a brief preview of the main contents of the model here.

Responses to music are many and varied, as the previous section makes clear, and Figure 19.1 includes just three of the main areas of psychological investigation. The five *physiological* measures listed above are often associated with the arousal level of the autonomic nervous system, and we shall see later that arousal forms the basis of one of the most prominent approaches to aesthetic responses to music, namely that of Daniel Berlyne. The box lists two behavioural manifestations of arousal level, namely listeners' level of engagement with the music, and the extent to which they actively control their listening as distinct from responding passively. Contemporary listeners take active control of the genres, styles, artists, and pieces they hear on their radios, iPods, or CD players, and they do so in order to manage their mood states; in doing so they are likely to be highly engaged. When exposed to the 'piped music' in a supermarket or

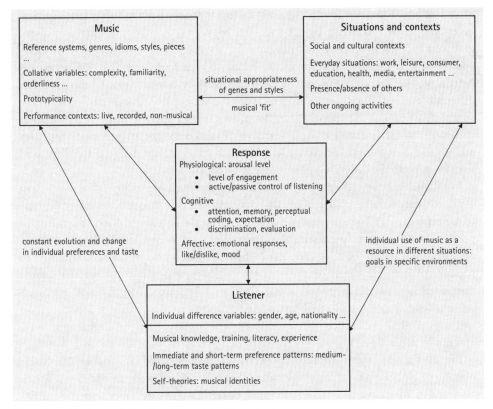

Fig. 19.1 Reciprocal feedback model of musical response.

restaurant, on the other hand, their level of engagement may be so low that they are not even aware of its existence.

The cognitive psychology of music, which deals with the internalized rules, strategies, and operations that people employ in creating and responding to music, has generated a number of its own specific measures of response, which are operationalized in terms of aspects of musical attention, memory, perceptual coding, and expectation. These are usually, though not always, employed within experimental rather than in naturalistic studies, and typically involve listeners' responses to tones, intervals, scales, melody, harmony, and other aspects of musical structure. Aesthetic responses to music usually have both *cognitive* and *affective* aspects: although they are partly dependent on listeners' cognitive discriminations and evaluations of different stimuli, the affective components are their main determinant, involving emotional responses and their effects on mood, which form an important part of musical likes and dislikes. The contents of this handbook clearly illustrate the importance of research on the emotional effects of music in the last decade, which has grown very rapidly in the few years that have elapsed since the publication of Juslin and Sloboda's (2001) original volume.

The *music* itself can be analysed in many different ways, and it is impossible to provide anything like a comprehensive account here; but for the purposes of the model we have listed just four of the main factors that have been to subject of empirical investigation. Musicologists before and since Meyer's (1956, 1967) seminal work have grappled with the problem of defining musical style, and musicologists as well as psychologists have conducted empirical research on style and genre (e.g. Hargreaves & North, 1999). The box lists some of the terms used by Nattiez (1990), who proposes different levels of musical style ranging from the very culture specific through to the completely non culture specific: thus, he moves from a specific work by a particular composer, to a style during one phase in the life of a composer, to intermediate genres and idioms, to systems of reference within which styles are defined (e.g. tonality), and then through to the universals of music (e.g. pitch, rhythm).

We shall deal later in the chapter with the extensive body of psychological research in experimental aesthetics, particularly that deriving from the theoretical work of Berlyne (e.g. Berlyne, 1971). In brief, Berlyne suggested that the listener 'collates' the different properties of a given musical stimulus, such as its complexity, familiarity, or orderliness, and that these 'collative variables', which are listed next in the box, combine to produce predictable effects on the level of activity, or arousal, of the listener's autonomic nervous system. We shall also see later that Berlyne's arousal-based approach was challenged in the 1980s by Martindale's group (e.g. Martindale & Moore, 1988), who argued that preference is determined by the *prototypicality* of different stimuli, and not by arousal.

Finally, the *performance contexts* in which music can be heard vary widely. The development of global digital technology means that live, broadcast, or recorded music can be heard in an almost infinitely wide range of settings. The development and miniaturization of high-capacity digital portable players such as the iPod mean that listeners carry their entire music collections with them wherever they go, and research by Sloboda, O'Neill, and Ivaldi (2001) and North, Hargreaves, and Hargreaves (2004) has clearly demonstrated the ubiquity of music listening in the everyday lives of many people in the UK at least. It is clear that this interaction between aspects of the music, and extra-musical aspects of the situations in which it is heard, are of great importance in explaining aesthetic responses to music.

This takes us on to the situations and contexts within which music is heard: the link between the 'music' and 'situations and contexts' boxes in Figure 19.1 shows that different genres and styles are seen as appropriate or inappropriate to varying degrees in particular listening situations. Situations and contexts can vary in many respects, of course, and some of the key aspects of this are shown in the figure. We have drawn elsewhere on Doise's (1986) four 'levels of analysis' in social psychology, namely the intraindividual, interindividual/ situational, socio-positional, and ideological (Hargreaves & North, 1997; North & Hargreaves, 2008). Our main focus here is on the third of these, which considers relationships between individuals with reference to differences in their social position, such as their group membership (e.g. the particular music that is associated with a sports club or a school), or with reference to larger social institutions, such as political movements or national charity campaigns.

Research in the social psychology of music is beginning to show how these specific social and institutional contexts exert a powerful influence on the responses to music within them, and we have undertaken many of these studies ourselves (see North

& Hargreaves, 2008). These studies have taken place in everyday settings including restaurants, bars, banks, shops, computer assembly plants, exercise and relaxation clubs, and on-hold telephones, and have shown some of the influences on behaviour, including: consumer product choice and shopping; work efficiency; time perception in waiting in queues; the speed of eating and drinking; moods and emotional states; and so on. These behavioural effects have also been clearly shown to be influenced by other features of the immediate situation, including the presence or absence of others and/or simultaneous engagement in other ongoing activities (North, Hargreaves, & Hargreaves, 2004).

We suggest that people now use music as a resource in order to achieve certain psychological states in different everyday situations, and this is shown in the reciprocal feedback relationship between 'situations and contexts' and 'the listener' shown in Figure 19.1. We shall return later in this chapter to the issue of what we have called 'arousal-state goals', which are specific to particular environments. We shall also return to look in more depth at those factors that are listed in the 'listener' box, which include 'individual difference' factors such as age, gender, and personality above the horizontal line in Figure 19.1. Below this line are other individual factors that are more specifically related to music, including musical training, knowledge, and experience. The relationship between musical preferences and tastes, which we defined in Section 19.2, are closely interrelated. Most people have immediate, short-term reactions to particular pieces in particular situations, and these reveal distinctive patterns of preference; over time and across situations, these accumulate and combine to form medium-term and longer-term taste patterns, which are fairly stable (see also Chapter 24, this volume). The long-term development of these patterns can become an important part of individuals' self-concepts, which gives rise to the notion of 'musical identities' (Hargreaves, Miell, & MacDonald, 2002).

Although these medium- and long-term patterns are fairly stable, they continually develop and change as listeners hear new pieces and styles: this is shown in Figure 19.1 as a reciprocal feedback relationship between the music and the listener. Individuals' initial responses to new music are based on their long-term taste patterns, but these responses themselves feed back into the system and change the longer-term patterns, such that the preference or identity system is in a constant state of evolution and change.

19.4 THE MUSIC: STRUCTURAL FACTORS AND SITUATIONAL INFLUENCES

19.4.1 The new experimental aesthetics

As we explained earlier, the research that followed Fechner's (1876) pioneering studies of 'aesthetics from below' were generally inconclusive, and interest in experimental aesthetics declined until the mid 1960s, when Daniel Berlyne's work led to a distinct revival of interest with a new focus. Berlyne's 'new experimental aesthetics' adopted a neo-behaviouristic, psychobiological approach, with an emphasis on the role of *arousal* in the ascending reticular activating system (ARAS), which is responsible for the degree of physiological arousal we experience. This is the major determinant of aesthetic response, according to Berlyne, along with what he called the 'collative properties' of stimuli, which exist alongside their 'psychophysical' (intrinsic physical) properties, and their 'ecological' properties (their signal value or 'meaningfulness'). Art objects were seen to produce pleasure by manipulating the level of arousal of the observer, and to do so by properties such as their complexity, familiarity, and surprisingness. The observer 'collates' information from these different properties, and the resulting level of arousal determines the likelihood of further exploration of that stimulus.

Berlyne's (1971) theory, which dominated research efforts for three decades, states that preference for artistic stimuli such as music is related to their 'arousal potential', which is determined by their collative properties. Music with an intermediate degree of arousal potential is liked most, and this degree of liking gradually decreases towards the extremes of arousal potential: this is expressed as an 'inverted-U' relationship between preference and stimulus arousal potential (see Figure 19.2). This was clearly related to the well-known Wundt curve (Wundt, 1874) as well as to the arguments of Fechner, Plato, and Aristotle.

The theory was supported by the results of a number of laboratory studies carried out between the 1960s and early 1980s, which provided evidence of an inverted-U relationship between liking for pieces of music and their complexity. For example, Vitz (1966) found an inverted-U relationship between the information content of tone sequences, and subjects' ratings of their pleasantness, and Crozier (1974) and Simon and Wohlwill (1968) found similar results following similar lines of investigation. McMullen's (1974)

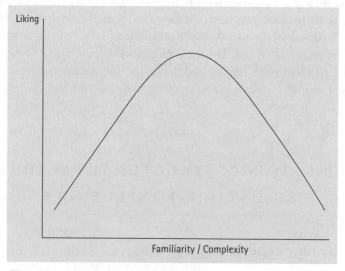

Fig. 19.2 The inverted–U relationship between liking for music and its arousal-evoking qualities.

school-age subjects preferred melodies of intermediate complexity, defined in terms of their informational redundancy and of the number of pitches from which they were constructed, to those of high or low complexity, and McMullen and Arnold (1976) found that preference for rhythmic sequences was an inverted-U function of their redundancy. Heyduk's (1975) 'optimal complexity' model was supported by his results from subjects' preference ratings of four piano compositions that were specially constructed to represent different levels of objective complexity, and Steck and Machotka (1975) found further evidence to support the optimal complexity model. They also suggested that complexity preferences are relative, not absolute, since the shapes of the preference curves for sounds of varying complexities were determined by the overall stimulus range, rather than by the absolute complexity levels of the stimuli.

In these studies, objectively determined stimulus complexity is seen as the main determinant of arousal potential, although other studies sought to demonstrate an inverted-U relationship between liking and familiarity (see Hargreaves, 1986). The evidence for this version of the inverted-U is less clear, and findings that are inconsistent with the theory have sometimes been explained by their failure to include a full range of stimulus familiarity. We will not repeat details of these findings and arguments here, since they are reviewed extensively elsewhere (see reviews by Hargreaves, 1986, and Finnäs, 1989). From the social psychological point of view, our own primary interest has been in whether an inverted-U relationship between liking for music and its arousal potential can be demonstrated in everyday music listening circumstances.

Three naturalistic studies of the relationship between *familiarity* and musical preference produced evidence in support of the inverted-U curve. These used the 'repeated exposure' paradigm, which was frequently employed in research based on Zajonc's (1968) 'mere exposure' hypothesis, which held that 'mere repeated exposure of the individual to a stimulus is a sufficient condition for the enhancement of his attitude toward it' (p. 1). The more you hear or see something, in other words, the more you like it. This of course ran counter to Berlyne's view, which exerted far more influence on the course of subsequent research. Broadcasters and recording companies have a keen commercial interest in the effects of repeatedly playing pop songs and advertising jingles, for example, on audience reaction, and these three studies were in this tradition. Erdelyi (1940) found an inverted-U relationship between the extent of the 'plugging' of 20 records on the radio and sales of the sheet music for those records, which suggests that as plugging increased listeners' familiarity with the records, so the popularity of the latter rose and then fell. For 18 of those 20 songs, he found that variations in 'plugging systematically precedes sales' (p. 500) by about two weeks, which shows that the plugging seems to *cause* changes in the popularity of the music, as Berlyne's theory predicts.

Direct predictions about the effects of repetition on liking can be made from Berlyne's inverted-U theory if we draw a distinction between objective and subjective complexity: the latter is the listener's *perception* of the complexity of the music rather than an objective property. If the initial level of subjective complexity of a piece of music falls below a listener's optimum level, as in the case of a sophisticated critic listening to a very simple melody, repetition should have the effect of shifting liking further down the descending part of the inverted-U curve; that is, it should decrease liking still further. If the initial subjective complexity level is higher than the optimum for the listener, however (e.g. in the case of a child or non-musician listening to a highly complex piece), repetition should serve to shift liking further up the ascending part of the curve; that is, liking should show an increase. Hargreaves (1986) carried out a systematic review of ten studies of the effects of repetition that provided evidence for and against the theory, and found that about half of them supported the inverted-U hypothesis, whilst the other half showed a positive monotonic 'mere exposure' relationship between familiarity and liking, to which we referred above. This 50–50 split in support for the competing theories could be explained as a result of differences between the experimental designs, procedures, and samples in the various studies; Hargreaves concluded that the inverted-U curve is the most general form of the relationship between liking and subjective complexity, and that mere exposure effects are represented by the rising part of the curve.

Eerola's (1997) studies of the objective complexity of the 12 UK albums by The Beatles used computerized techniques to score each of the songs and to calculate an overall complexity score for each album, and compared that figure with the number of weeks that the album stayed in the chart after its release. The results supported the idea of an inverted-U relationship between liking, complexity, and familiarity. Albums of lower complexity 'peaked early' in the charts, but then failed to sustain this early level of sales. *Please Please Me*, for example, showed high sales figures when first released, and in the following weeks and months, but has not received as much critical acclaim in subsequent decades. More complex albums such as *Abbey Road*, on the other hand, which took longer to peak when first released, have received higher levels of continued sales and critical acclaim since their release. In terms of the inverted-U curve, the less complex albums have peaked early and then tailed off in popularity, whereas the more complex ones have peaked much later and then not tailed off to the same extent.

19.4.2 Preference for prototypes

The notion of cognitive 'schemes' or 'schemata' were proposed long ago by Piaget (1950), and were more formally proposed in cognitive psychology in the 1970s and 1980s. Piaget used these terms to refer to internally stored abstract mental operations such as mathematical concepts in children, as well as to visual images of real objects, and cognitive psychologists (e.g. Schank & Abelson, 1988) developed the idea of 'scripts' to refer to stored knowledge about typical sequences of actions (e.g. 'going to a restaurant'), and 'frames' to refer to common sets of similar visual stimuli (e.g. 'an office'). The basic idea is that people classify stimuli and plan their actions by matching them against these abstract schemas, scripts, or frames; and furthermore that there exist idealized versions or 'prototypes' of these concepts (e.g. Posner & Keele, 1968). Our everyday experiences are classified by comparing them with prototypes for those kinds of experience, and repeated exposure to exemplars of particular categories of stimuli or action gives rise to learning more about the prototypes.

Colin Martindale proposed a rival approach to challenge Berlyne's arousal-based theories in the 1980s, which was based on the idea that people's aesthetic likes and dislikes are based on *preference for prototypes*. This was based on the idea of neural networks. Martindale and Moore (1988) conceived of the mind as comprising inter-connected cognitive units, each of which holds the representation of a different object. Units coding more prototypical stimuli are activated more frequently, because these stimuli are experienced more frequently than those coding atypical stimuli. This leads to the proposal that 'aesthetic preference is hypothetically a positive function of the degree to which the mental representation of a stimulus is activated. Because more typical stimuli are coded by mental representations capable of greater activation, preference should be positively related to prototypicality' (p. 661). Martindale con-sidered that the prototypicality of real-life artistic objects may be a stronger determi-nant of preference than their arousal-evoking qualities, and this contrasts directly with Berlyne's (1971) approach.

Most of the research conducted to test this approach has investigated whether preference increases with prototypicality: typical instances of any category should be preferred because they give rise to a stronger activation of the relevant cognitive repre-sentations than atypical instances. Moore and Martindale (1983), for example, found that the colour typicality of random polygons accounted for 79 per cent of the variance in people's preferences for them, whereas complexity accounted for only 1 per cent. Martindale, Moore, and Borkum (1990) also carried out a series of studies of people's preferences for polygons, line drawings, and paintings, and found that variations on the typicality of these stimuli explained more of the variance in people's preference for them than did complexity. Investigating people's liking for themes in classical music, Martindale and Moore (1989) found that 51 per cent of the variance was accounted for by typicality measures, whereas complexity accounted for only 4 per cent of that variance. Similar results from other studies of preferences for stimuli such as furniture designs and cubist paintings were reported by other investigators including Whitfield and Slatter (1979) and Hekkert and van Wieringen (1990). Martindale, Moore, and West (1988) concluded that these results suggest that 'collative variables are probably a good deal less important in determining preference than Berlyne thought them to be. Furthermore, they probably determine preference via mechanisms different than those proposed by Berlyne' (p. 94).

However, we have argued elsewhere (North & Hargreaves, 2000a) that Berlyne's arousal-based approach and the preference for prototypes model may be compatible in certain respects when closer attention is paid to the nature of the variables under consideration, and we make four main points in advancing this proposal. The first is that assessments of the relative contribution of prototypicality and arousal-mediating variables to likes and dislikes is bound to reflect the extent to which the art works vary in terms of those variables. In a set of musical pieces with very varied levels of com-plexity, for example, complexity is likely to be a significant determinant of preference, whereas if the variation in complexity is low, other factors are likely to assume greater significance. Secondly, it is possible that the concept of prototypicality itself may actu-ally incorporate some of Berlyne's collative variables. For example, modern jazz fans typically experience music with high levels of complexity; new-age music fans typically experience music with low levels of complexity; and rock music or modern-day dance music fans typically experience fast-tempo music. In other words, an individual's prototypes of 'music' as a whole, as a result of their listening history, are dependent on factors that are crucial to Berlyne's theory. Berlynian factors contribute to prototypicality, such that the two are not so independent as they might appear.

A third point follows from this, namely that the extent to which particular musical pieces are considered unpredictable or erratic—that is, the extent to which they depart from prototypes—are dependent on the cultural expectations concerning how that piece might progress. A piece of Japanese traditional music might seem very strange or unpredictable to Western ears, but appear fairly conventional to a Japanese listener who is familiar with the genre. In other words, collative variables can only really be defined in relation to specific musical cultures; that is, to those with which the listeners are typically familiar, and for which they have existing cognitive representations. Complexity has to be defined relative to prototypes that are individually and culturally specific.

Fourthly, as a corollary, we might add that Berlyne's notion of ecological variables can also account for the meaningfulness of a piece of music to an individual in the same way as prototypicality: although his favoured explanation of this relationship was psychobiological rather than cognitive, both theories can account for the effects of the meaningfulness of a piece of music or liking for it. Our conclusion is that Berlyne's theory and the preference for prototypes model may be compatible in certain operational respects, and that *both* can still be useful.

19.5 THE SITUATION: SOCIAL AND CULTURAL INFLUENCES

It should be clear from the early sections of this chapter that the traditional methodological approach of studies in experimental aesthetics, such as those outlined in the previous section, has some obvious limitations. We have rehearsed these arguments in detail elsewhere (e.g. Hargreaves & North, 1997), and indeed a good deal of our own research since then has been designed to overcome these limitations. When (typically) undergraduate students respond to specially composed music under laboratory conditions, the sounds they hear are unlikely to be typical of their real-life listening experiences, and are themselves unlikely to reflect the tastes and preferences of the population as a whole. Thirdly, and most significantly, people listen to music in a wide variety of listening situations in everyday life, such that the laboratory is untypical and likely to be artificial. We hear music in cars, restaurants, in the workplace, on answerphones, in the media, while doing housework, and indeed in most settings in which it is possible to either be within range of a loudspeaker or wear a pair of earphones. Our own research has been devoted to exploring the ways in which these real-life settings influence musical behaviour and experience (North & Hargreaves, 2008), and although the classic laboratory-based approach in experimental aesthetics is typically unable to resolve these issues, we and others have nevertheless attempted to broaden the application of the experimental approach in various ways. In this section, we review some of Vladimir Konečni's research that has been carried out in the context of experimental aesthetics—research that has adopted both arousal- and typicality-based approaches to explaining why musical preferences vary from one place to another; and research investigating how musical preferences can be influenced by the opinions of others in the immediate environment.

19.5.1 Konečni's arousal-based approach

Vladimir Konečni and his associates at the University of California at San Diego carried out an important body of research in the 1980s that was the first to deal with music psychologists' failure at the time to take adequate account of the social context of music listening, and which also adopted an experimental framework that was grounded in Berlyne's (1971) arousal-based approach. The work and more recent advances upon it is reviewed by Konečni himself (see Chapter 25, this volume), and so we will deliberately limit our coverage here. Konečni (1982, pp. 500–1) proposed a theoretical model, which draws together the social environment, the listener's emotional state, and musical preference:

The model assumes that music, and aesthetic stimuli in general . . . are simply another aspect of a person's acoustic (or visual) environment and that they are chosen largely for the purpose of mood- and emotion-optimization. The model regards a person as being engaged in a constant exchange with the social and nonsocial environment, of which the acoustic stimuli are a part. The social behavior of others . . . is assumed to have a profound effect on a person's emotional states, which, in turn, affect aesthetic choices, including the choice of music, that a person will make in a given situation. The degree of enjoyment of the chosen piece presumably varies as a function of the concurrent social and nonsocial micro-environmental conditions . . . Listening to music is further assumed to produce changes in the listener's emotional state and thereby affect his or her behavior toward others in the situation. Since social behavior is by definition interactive, it is safe to assume that the behavior directed toward the listener by others will also change, leading to a further modification in the listener's emotional state, and possibly to different subsequent musical choices. The model thus contains a feedback-loop feature representing the ongoing nature of a person's interaction with the social and musical environment—a series of aesthetic episodes mediated by changes in emotional state and mood.

Konečni and his colleagues operationalized the model by conducting experimental manipulations of the social situation in a variety of ways, thereby producing different emotional states in their listeners, and then assessing their liking for different pieces of music under these conditions. At the beginning of Konečni, Crozier, and Doob's (1976) study, for example, some of the participants were repeatedly insulted by an accomplice of the experimenter, posing as another participant, which had already been found to reliably induce anger, in terms of both physiological measures and subjective reports. The participants then chose on each of 50 trials to listen to ten-second episodes of either one of two different types of computer-generated melody, by pressing one of two buttons. These melodies were either of low or high objective complexity. The participants were divided into three groups: those in the 'annoy-wait' group were insulted, then waited alone in a room with nothing to do, and then listened to the melodies. They showed a strong preference for the simple melodies, choosing to listen to them on approximately 70 per cent of the trials. Participants in the 'no annoy-wait' group, who were not insulted and who also waited, showed no such preference. Participants in the third 'annoy-shock' group were insulted in the same way as the 'annoy-wait' group, but were then given the chance to retaliate against the accomplice by delivering a fixed number of what they thought were electric shocks. Like the 'no annoy-wait' group, these subjects showed no pronounced preference for either type of melody. Konečni et al concluded from these results that the angry state of the 'annoy-wait' group represented a high level of arousal, which was not present in the 'no annoy-wait' subjects, and that they chose the simple rather than the complex melodies in order to minimize any further increases in arousal. They also suggested that the retaliatory aggression of the 'annoy-shock' group served to 'let off steam'; that is, to bring the level of arousal back down to normal, such that their preferences once again resembled those of the 'no annoy-wait' group. Overall, 'The findings . . . show that a socially induced change in a listener's emotional state may strongly affect that person's aesthetic choice' (Konečni, 1982, p. 503).

Konečni and Sargent-Pollock (1976) reached similar conclusions, finding that when participants carried out complex mental tasks while listening to music, they tended to choose to listen to simple rather than complex melodies. We also found some support for this notion in a study (North & Hargreaves, 1999) in which participants were asked to complete five laps of a computer motor-racing game whilst listening to either a loud, fast (i.e. high arousal) or slow, quiet (i.e. low arousal) version of the same piece of music. The task was made even more difficult in some conditions by asking participants to count backwards in intervals of three. We found that lap times were slowest when participants heard the high-arousal music and were counting backwards, and quickest when they heard the low-arousal music and did not have to count backwards. This supports Konečni's arguments, in that the music and the backwards counting task were presumably competing for information-processing resources, and that this was influenced by arousal level.

These findings confirm Konečni's idea that we are engaged in a constant exchange with the social and nonsocial environment, of which the acoustic stimuli are a part, and can explain several aspects of everyday musical experiences. For example, we are quite likely to turn down the volume on the car radio when we come into heavy traffic, presumably to reduce the cognitive/arousal load imposed by the music in order to release more attentional capacity for dealing with the difficult traffic conditions. Conversely, we may well turn up the car radio volume on long journeys when the roads are quiet, so as to increase our arousal as a means of reducing the boredom of the drive (and perhaps also the possibility of falling asleep). We should acknowledge that there are some obvious criticisms that can be made of Konečni's research. The experimental paradigms are based on those used in studies of authority and obedience, and apart from the well-known problems concerning the ethical aspects of these paradigms, it could also be argued that the laboratory-based conditions were artificial and contrived, even though the intention was to model naturalistic music listening.

A second and probably more important issue is that the theoretical model adopted in these early studies may not provide a fully adequate explanation of how the listening situation itself mediates musical preferences. Whilst Konečni's theoretical model is based on the idea of arousal *moderation*—that people try to choose musical stimuli so as to reduce high arousal levels or to increase low levels—this provides an incomplete picture, as there are some situations in which people choose to *polarize* their levels of arousal still further rather than to moderate it. We follow up this idea of *arousal-state goals* in the next section. In concluding this one, however, there be no doubt that Konečni's bold, imaginative studies were important, pioneering steps towards the investigation of the role of social, emotional, and cognitive factors in music listening.

19.5.2 Arousal-state goals

One of the ideas contained within our 'reciprocal feedback' model of responses to music, discussed in Section 19.4, is that people use music as a resource in order to achieve certain psychological states in different everyday situations; and furthermore, that different arousal states are considered appropriate for different environments. This is shown in the reciprocal feedback relationship between 'situations and contexts' and 'the listener' in Figure 19.1. The notion of arousal-state goals is based on this—that certain pieces or genres of music are appropriate in particular listening situations to varying degrees, and that this can often be linked to levels of arousal, which in turn influence liking.

In one of our own studies, for example (North & Hargreaves, 1996), we found that the music seen as appropriate by participants in aerobics classes, which typically involve high levels of physical arousal, gave rise to different levels of ratings of liking and complexity from that appropriate for yoga classes, which involve lower levels of arousal. In other words, people choose what is normatively seen as situationally appropriate music to moderate their arousal states, so as to match particular listening situations.

We investigated this in two further studies (North & Hargreaves, 2000b), the first of which was based on Konečni's research. Participants were asked either to ride an exercise bike, in order to produce high arousal, or to lie down on a quilt and relax, to produce low arousal. They were then asked to listen to one of two pieces of music: either a loud, fast piece (i.e. high arousal) or a slow, quiet version of the same piece (i.e. low arousal). We found that participants preferred the version that would serve to moderate the arousal level resulting from their earlier activity: those who rode the exercise bike preferred the slow, quiet version of the music, whereas people in the relaxation group preferred the loud, fast version. This confirms Konečni's view that listeners tend to choose music that is likely to moderate their arousal level. In the second study, the participants were asked to choose between the two types of music *while* they either rode the exercise bike or relaxed on the quilt, and this produced the opposite result to that of the first experiment: participants on the exercise bike preferred the loud, fast version, whereas those who were relaxing preferred the slow, quiet version. Our explanation of both of these results is in terms of arousal-based goals. In the second study, the goal of the participants on the exercise bike was to achieve a high level of arousal, whereas that of those on the quilt was to achieve a low level, and so they chose the music that they did in order to polarize their arousal levels, so as to achieve these goals. In contrast, participants in the first study had already finished either exercising or relaxing before listening to the music, so that they wanted to moderate their levels of arousal rather than to polarize it—they chose arousal-moderating music in order to achieve this goal.

The notion that music can be used to achieve arousal-based goals is likely to be widely applicable to many different everyday life situations, but very little research has investigated this (though see Chapter 7, this volume). The notion has the potential to explain a good deal of people's anecdotal experiences of the ways in which they use music in everyday life. After a stressful, hard-working week, the office worker wants to 'wind down', and may do so by playing relaxing, low-arousal music, whereas those hosting a lively party may want to create an exciting, uninhibited atmosphere and play loud, fast, and arousing music. When driving a car in heavy traffic, we may well want to reduce our stress levels and play slow, calming music, or indeed to turn it off altogether, whereas long-distance journeys on very quiet motorways may well induce the driver to play loud, fast music to heighten arousal so as to reduce boredom and maybe also to stay awake. Further research along these lines would have some obvious practical applications.

19.5.3   Conformity: compliance and prestige

In this section, we review research on how aesthetic responses to music can be influenced by other social influences in the immediate environment. One of us (Hargreaves, 1986) reviewed this literature well over 20 years ago, suggesting that 'a small body of empirical research has accumulated which has experimentally investigated . . . *prestige* effects upon aesthetic reactions to works in different art forms . . . some other studies have approached the related question of the effects of *propaganda* about different artists and art works on reactions to them. The two influences are combined and/ or indistinguishable in many of the experiments, and so I shall consider them both together' (p. 194). Hargreaves also reviewed three studies on *conformity* effects on musical preferences. The results from all three types of study led to the clear conclusion that these social influences exert a very powerful influence on people's responses to music.

The field of study has not advanced a great deal in the intervening years, and so we do not propose to revisit it in any detail. A useful reconceptualization of this field as a whole might be to view all of these studies as involving *conformity* in one form or another. This term represents the general effects of various social influences on the individual listener. Conformity can then be seen as taking two distinct forms (Levine & Russo, 1987), namely *compliance* and *prestige*. The former arise from individuals' desire to conform with the opinions of valued social groups, so as to confer increased status with those groups, whereas the latter is based on particular information which is available about the music in question. The latter is especially important when very little is known, such that conformity effects are at their most powerful; and these are the conditions under which propaganda can be used, to refer back to the earlier term.

We can still only find four studies of compliance in musical judgements in the research literature. Radocy's (1975) study was very clearly modelled on Asch's famous study of small group effects on people's judgements of the relative lengths of lines, in which naïve participants made clearly erroneous judgements of the lengths in order to conform with the apparent judgements of other members in the group, which were in fact faked. Radocy played a so-called 'standard' tone to his participants before playing them three 'comparison' tones, one of which was the same pitch or loudness as the standard. The task was to say which of the three options was the same as the standard tone. Before responding, each participant first heard the answers of four other participants who were actually confederates of Radocy, and who had all been instructed to all give the same incorrect answer on certain critical trials. The naïve participants complied with the incorrect judgement of the confederates on 30 per cent of the pitch questions, and 49 per cent of the volume questions. These results are particularly powerful in that the participants were all music students who would have been very skilled and practised at tasks such as these.

The other three studies deal more directly with musical preferences as such. Inglefield's (1968) study with ninth graders used a similar methodology to Radocy's Asch-type task, but used scores on a music-preference inventory as the dependent variable. He found that compliance was greatest for preferences for jazz, and also that it was higher for participants who scored highly on measures of 'other-directedness', need for social approval, and dependency. Crowther (1985) asked each of his participants to listen to one of four types of music, two of which were expected to be liked by them (disco and rock 'n' roll), and two which were expected to be disliked (heavy metal and reggae). Whilst listening, all participants could see a panel of lights that supposedly showed what other participants were listening to, and Crowther programmed this panel to show (falsely) that the majority of participants were listening to the disliked music. Under these conditions, the participants actually did start listening to the disliked music, and demonstrated what Crowther called *minority* influences on musical preference: the minority influence of the other participants' apparent preferences could apparently override the majority influence of normative musical tastes for that group. Furman and Duke (1988), also using a very similar methodology to Radocy (1975), found no evidence of compliance in the preferences of music and non-music major students concerning pop music, though the preferences of non-music majors were subject to compliance effects when orchestral music was used.

The second type of conformity that we identified at the start of this section is based on particular information that is available about the music in question, a good deal of which involves 'prestige effects'. These are likely to occur when listeners have little knowledge of the music, and so their responses are more likely to be influenced by information from other sources. Hargreaves's (1986) review of 7 studies led to the conclusion that 'All but one of the studies summarized . . . found social influences to have a significant effect on aesthetic judgements, and it may be that these are more powerful in the case of music than in other art forms' (p. 198). These included Rigg's (1948) study, carried out just before the outbreak of the Second World War, in which participants were played pieces of music including those by Wagner, and told that Wagner was one of Hitler's favourite composers. Alpert (1982) found that approval of classical music by a music teacher and a disc jockey increased classical music preferences and listening among fifth-grade school pupils, and Fiese (1990) found that false attributions of musical pieces to Beethoven and Strauss influenced music students' judgements of the quality of the pieces. Similar findings are reported in more detail in the studies reviewed by Hargreaves, one of which (Geiger, 1950) is particularly noteworthy in that it provides evidence for prestige effects occurring in the 'real world' context of audience listening figures for identical radio programmes described as featuring either 'popular gramophone music' or 'classical music'.

In spite of the apparent consistency of the results of these studies with music, Crozier and Chapman's (1981) review of this literature across all art forms led them to conclude that prestige effects across the arts as a whole are sometimes small, unstable, and difficult to replicate. Weaknesses in the design of many of the studies may mean that prestige effects are often artefacts of particular experimental procedures and conditions. These include the features of particular musical pieces or excerpts (e.g. their degree of familiarity to the listeners); the particular ways in which different art works are described or labelled; the stability or reliability of any prestige effects that are obtained given variations in the procedure of studies; and the effects of individual differences in susceptibility to prestige effects, such as might result from specific training or experience. Finally, very little attention has been paid to *how* prestige effects might be explained. Crozier and Chapman (1981) suggested that providing information about an art work can not only change the perceiver's of that work, but may also affect the way it is perceived. This is an interesting theoretical challenge which remains unaddressed.

19.6 THE LISTENER: INDIVIDUAL DIFFERENCES IN RESPONSE

In this final section, we focus on the third of the main boxes in Figure 19.1, which deals with the effect of listener characteristics on the aesthetic response to music. The research literature in this area is scattered and diverse, dealing with a wide range of different personal variables, as well as with a wide range of styles and genres of music. Some of these studies go back many years, and have emerged sporadically over the last few decades. Some of these early studies were based on psychometric tests, and some have simultaneously considered the effects of several different demographic and personal variables. We shall devote most of our attention in this section to studies of the effects of age. The literature on the other areas of individual difference (social class, gender, personality, and musical training) does not yield many clear or consistent conclusions of general theoretical significance, and so we shall attempt no more than a very brief summary of these.

19.6.1 Age: the development of aesthetic responses to music across the lifespan

An increasing body of evidence shows not only that young infants respond to music, but that their responses could be clearly described in certain respects as being 'aesthetic' (see reviews by Parncutt, 2006, and Trehub, 2006). The title of Trehub's (2006) wide-ranging chapter, for example, is 'Infants as musical connoisseurs'. Trehub claims that 'their precocious music listening skills, excellent memory for music, highly musical environment, and intense interest in expressive musical performances compensate for their obvious ignorance of musical conventions' (p. 33), and feels that being a discerning listener, in the sense of having keen perceptual skills, may be more important that translating this ability into making comparative judgements about individual pieces and works.

There is also evidence that the origins of musical behaviour occur even earlier, in the foetus. A series of studies by Peter Hepper and Sara Shahidullah suggest that the foetus can respond to music in the mother's womb. Hepper (1991), for example, showed that newborns who had heard a popular TV soap opera theme tune (from *Neighbours*) during gestation showed changes in heart rate, movement, and other aspects of their behaviour when they heard the same theme a few days after birth; and that foetuses between 29 and 37 weeks of gestational age showed changes in their movements when played a tune to which they had already been exposed during pregnancy. Shahidullah and Hepper (1994) also showed that foetuses at 35 weeks were better able to distinguish between different pure tone frequencies than those at 27 weeks, which suggests that musical listening abilities are developing over this prenatal period.

It seems that the foetus is in some way able to recognize music heard earlier, and that the behavioural effects are specific to particular pieces of music, rather than to music in general. They seem to be able to distinguish between notes of different pitch, and these discrimination abilities may develop with age in the womb. Although these foetal responses are not equivalent to the aesthetic responses made by children and adults, they nevertheless have some of the essential qualities of Trehub's view of 'infant musical connoisseurship' described above (see also Chapter 23, this volume). We may well need to rethink our view of what constitutes an aesthetic response to music, and to consider that this begins to develop well before the ages that have largely been investigated in the literature.

As we shall see below, this literature has generally suggested that children are only able to identify and reliably distinguish between different musical styles by the age of 6 or so, though Marshall and Hargreaves (2007) recently demonstrated that pre-schoolers can do so if the conditions of assessment are appropriate. The investigation of 'musical style sensitivity' in the early years has been difficult, because typical test procedures have relied heavily on verbal instructions, and have demanded levels of concentration, attention, and memory span that are beyond most pre-schoolers. Generally speaking, we need to approach the literature on the development of 'aesthetic responses to music'—which has largely been interpreted as 'musical preference and taste'—by making a clear distinction between the capabilities that appear to be involved in making a particular preference decision, and the actual content of that decision. The former allows for Trehub's notion of infants as 'musical connoisseurs', and also applies to the small body of research that has built up on the development of what has become known as 'musical style sensitivity'(i.e. the ability to distinguish between exemplars of different musical styles in the culture), which is also variously known in the literature as stylistic discrimination, knowledge, liking, tolerance, or competence (see discussion by Hargreaves & North, 1999).

A pioneering study in this area was carried out by Gardner (1973), who showed that children older than 11 years were better able than 6- to 11-year-olds to discriminate between excerpts drawn from different styles of classical music ('baroque', 'classical', 'romantic', and 'modern'), for example, but that the 11-year-olds were able to do this best overall. The tendency to use such 'stylistic labels' was only apparent amongst the 14-year-olds in this study. Castell (1982) repeated Gardner's study, including pop and jazz music alongside classical pieces, and by using instructions that were embedded in a plausible story rather than being administered neutrally, she found that all of her 8- to 9-year-olds and 10- to 11-year-olds were much better on the task with pop than with classical styles, and that her younger participants performed better with the pop music styles than did her 10- to 11-year-olds.

Several subsequent cross-sectional studies have also been carried out, which have used different age groups, musical styles, and task procedures (e.g. Hargreaves & North, 1999). From this we can conclude that although some age-related changes in stylistic discrimination and knowledge do seem to be identifiable, their manifestation is strongly dependent on cultural and social factors. It may well be, as we suggested in our own study in this area (Hargreaves & North, 1999), that there exist consistent age-related changes in the cognitive components of musical style perception, but that their emotional or affective components are much more variable.

This takes us on to the more extensive body of research on 'musical preference and taste'; that is, on the *content* of the musical preferences of different age groups. This literature has been reviewed by Finnäs (1989) and LeBlanc (1991), and more recently by Hargreaves, North, and Tarrant (2006). LeBlanc's (1991) review dealt with the effects of 'maturation/aging' on music listening preference, and our own review updated and tabulated the different studies, which is reproduced here as Table 19.1. This table summarizes the main features of most of the studies reviewed by LeBlanc, and also includes some that have been conducted more recently. LeBlanc summarized his review by drawing on the concept of 'open-earedness', a term that was first employed by Hargreaves (1982) and Castell (1982), in explaining the overall pattern of these results. This term was originally used as a shorthand way of suggesting that younger children were more readily able to listen to and maybe also enjoy unconventional or unusual (e.g. 'avant garde', aleatory or electronic) musical forms, as they may 'show less evidence of acculturation to normative standards of "good taste" than older children' (Hargreaves, 1982, p. 51). LeBlanc operationalized 'open-earedness' as 'listener tolerance' for a range of musical styles, which was operationalized in turn in terms of preference. His model of the course of maturational changes in musical preference was formulated in the form of four hypotheses as follows: that '(a) younger children are more open-eared, (b) open-earedness declines as the child enters adolescence, (c) there is a partial rebound of open-earedness as the listener matures from adolescence to young adulthood, and (d) open-earedness declines as the listener matures to old age' (p. 2).

A closer look at Table 19.1 shows that, with one or two exceptions, LeBlanc's hypotheses receive general support. The decline in open-earedness that occurs in later childhood and its subsequent 'rebound' seems to occur at about the age of 10–11 years, and is seen in terms of the strong expression of preferences for a narrow range of pop styles, and an equally strong general dislike for all other styles. After this, there appears to be a general decline in liking for popular music styles across the rest of the lifespan, and a corresponding general increase in more 'serious' styles—although this is not universally true (e.g. for contemporary art music). Hargreaves and Castell's (1987) study suggests that these effects may be influenced by the familiarity and complexity of the music, and several of the studies suggest that age and musical training are associated with preference for more 'serious' music, but the results of these studies do not lead to any clear theoretical explanations of age effects. The idea that some musical styles may be considered as somehow more or less 'serious' than others is also highly dubious, and we have argued against it elsewhere (e.g. Hargreaves, 1986). In the post-modern age, the idea that broad styles or genres can be characterized as such makes no sense, because the works that collectively define a style range widely in their 'seriousness' or in other characteristics such as their 'quality'; because such judgements need to be made *within* the aesthetic standards of the style itself rather than between styles; and because those styles themselves are changing and evolving more rapidly than ever in today's rapidly globalizing world.

LeBlanc, Sims, Siivola, and Obert (1993) tested this model by asking 2,262 listeners aged between 6 and 91 years to express their preferences for 30-second recordings of 'art music', trad jazz, and rock, and their results confirmed that there was a 'dip' in preference in adolescence, followed by an increase towards adulthood, and a final decline in old age. One severe limitation of LeBlanc et al's study is that musical styles were operationalized in terms of specific pieces: it is quite possible that their participants were responding to artefactual features of those pieces, rather than to the style they were supposed to represent. Hargreaves and North's (1999a) study dealt with the issue by asking people from five age groups across the lifespan to nominate as many different types of rock and pop music, classical music, and jazz as they could, and also to rate their liking for each of these types using a 0-10 scale. They found, as expected, that liking for pop music was higher for younger people than for older people, and that the reverse was true for classical music and jazz. However, the average rating over all

Table 19.1 Summary of empirical studies of age differences in stylistic preference (from Hargreaves, North, & Tarrant, 2006)

	Participants	Music	Results
Rubin-Rabson (1940)	70 adults 20–70 yrs	24 art music orchestral works 1750–1925: 'classic', 'transitional', 'modern' periods	'classic' and 'modern' preference > with age
Fisher (1951)	251 grades 6, 9, 10, and college students	art music of differing levels of formality	grade 6 preferred Gould (least formal) > Haydn (most), college students vice versa
Keston & Pinto (1955)	202 college students at three age levels	'serious classical', 'popular classical', 'dinner', 'popular'	r = 0.38 between age and preference for 'good' music
Rogers (1957)	635 grades 4, 7, 9, 12	'seriously classical', 'popular classical', 'dinner', 'popular'	preference for classical > with age, diversity of preferences > between grades 4–12
Baumann (1960)	1410 12–20 yrs	range of styles within 'art music', 'popular', 'traditional'	popular preference > with age, classical preference < with age
Taylor (1969)	800 8–11 yrs	paired excerpts of art music by composers from six historical periods	preference for 20C composers > with age, for later baroque composers < with age
Meadows (1970)	982 grades 7–college students	30 excepts from ten 'popular' and 'art music' styles	art music preference < with age
Greer et al (1974)	134 grades K–6	'top 20' 'rock' and 'non-rock' styles, operant listening task	older Ps preferred 'rock', becoming significant at grade 2
Bragg & Crozier (1974)	12 at each of 8–9, 14–15, 20+ yrs	random electronic stimuli at six complexity levels: studies I, II, III with different preference tasks	I older Ps preferred more complex on verbal rating scale task: II no age effect on paired comparison task: III no age effect on untimed task
Eisenstein (1979)	64 grades 2–6	Webern tone rows	younger Ps listened for longer than older
Geringer (1982)	40 grades 5/6, college music and non-music majors	popular and art music, operant listening task	college music majors preferred art music, other two groups preferred popular
May (1985)	577 grades 1–3	24 pieces representing nine generic styles including art music, popular music, non-Western music	overall preference > with age, decline for 'rock' and 'country' styles less than for other styles

	Participants	Music	Results
Hargreaves & Castell (1987)	96, 16 in each of grades K, 2, 4, 6, 9, college	familiar/unfamiliar real melodies, near/far approximations to music	preference for approximations > with age; preference for real melodies suggest inverted-U preference function with age
Haack (1988)	108 25–54 yrs	pop song titles 1945–82: selection of 'top 10 of all time'	preference for music popular in mid 20s
LeBlanc et al (1988)	926 grades 3, 5, 7, 9, 10, 11, 12, college	24 trad jazz pieces at different tempo levels	preferences summed over tempo levels: U-shaped curve with age
Le Blanc et al (1993)	2262 6–91 yrs	'art music', trad jazz, rock	preference > in adolescence, < in adulthood, > in old age
Hargreaves et al (1995)	278 grades 7, 11	ratings of 12 style category labels	overall liking > with age, especially for 'serious' styles
North & Hargreaves (1995)	275 9–78 yrs	nominations of 30 most eminent pop artists 1955–94	general preference for artists from late adolescence/early adulthood: Beatles/Elvis nominated by all
Hargreaves & North (1999)	275 9–78 yrs	ratings of liking for self-nominated styles	liking for rock/pop styles > with age, for classical < with age: 'cross over' in middle age?
Gembris & Schellenberg (2003)	591 grades K–6	popular, classical, avant garde, ethnic	overall preference > with age: grade 1 most positive, grade 6 most negative, overall preference for pop

three styles together was very similar for all the age groups, which suggests that when people have choice over the music to which they choose to listen, liking for music does not necessarily dip during adolescence, nor show any other age-related patterns. It may simply be that different age groups have their own specific musical preferences.

Further insight into this conclusion is provided by one of our earlier studies of age effects on judgements of musical *eminence*. North and Hargreaves (1995) asked participants in five age groups (9–10, 14–15, 18–24, 25–49, and 50+ years) to choose up to 30 pop groups and artists, from a list of 200, 'who in your own personal opinion have performed music that deserves to be called to the attention of others'. All of these groups and singers had had a number-1 single in the UK record charts over several decades; 50 had had their first number 1 between 1955 and 1964, 50 between 1965 and 1974, 50 between 1975 and 1984, and 50 between 1985 and 1994. The results were very clear: all participants showed a strong tendency to select as eminent those artists who had their first UK number-1 single when the participants were themselves late adolescents/young adults, and this was consistently so across the whole age range in the study.

Another clear finding was that certain artists—two in particular (The Beatles and Elvis Presley)—seemed to transcend this pattern, and received high eminence ratings from listeners of all ages.

It seems, in conclusion, that people's specific musical likes and dislikes in late adolescence and early adulthood exert a strong influence on the patterns of taste that they develop later in life, and may even act as a kind of 'blueprint' or 'critical period' for those later developments. But we must be very cautious in drawing such conclusions from studies that are almost entirely based on cross-sectional operationalizations of age effects. Expressed preferences for specific artists, musicians, styles, or genres are inevitably grounded in their particular cultural and temporal contexts, and cross-sectional studies cannot throw any light on the changes over time of different age cohorts of listeners. This would require complementary longitudinal evidence as well, ideally with much more detailed information about the psychological *functions* of specific musical preferences at different ages. We must be cautious in drawing any general conclusions about the lifespan development of aesthetic responses to music in the absence of this kind of evidence.

19.6.2 Other individual differences in aesthetic responses to music

As we said above, the research literature on other individual difference factors, of which the main ones are social class, gender, personality, and musical training, is scattered and diverse, and gives rise to few clear or consistent general conclusions. So, we shall attempt no more here than to summarize some of the main directions that have been pursued in these four areas, which we have covered in more detail elsewhere (North & Hargreaves, 2008; see also Hargreaves, 1986).

Sociologists working in the 1960s and 1970s were interested in the role of social class in differentiating musical preferences, and probably the most influential theoretical approach was that of Bourdieu (1971, 1984), who argued that the sociology of art should address the relationship between a piece of art, its producer, and the various institutions in the 'field of production' in which cultural goods are created (e.g. conservatories, learned societies, etc.). These institutions 'legitimize' or endorse certain works and not others, such that individual listeners' own preferences are based on their membership of those bodies that constitute those institutions. Thus, the professional classes attend 'highbrow' musical events such as opera, whereas working classes correspondingly consume 'lowbrow' music designed and marketed for the masses. This leads to the argument that social background determines musical taste, and indeed sociological research has provided some support for this idea by classifying fans of certain musical styles into so-called 'taste publics' (see e.g. Gans, 1974; Fox & Wince, 1975; and reviews by Hargreaves, 1986, and Shepherd, 2003). The empirical research in this field does generally support the view that 'people from higher socioeconomic groups are more likely to prefer "serious" music than are those from lower groups' (Hargreaves, 1986,

p. 193), though it is important to point out that the main studies in this field were carried out well over two decades ago, and that a good many of them were based on college students.

There are several reasons why this kind of conclusion may now be invalid. First, the notion of a particular style as such being somehow more or less 'serious' than another has already been challenged in this chapter. Second, the notion of defining a 'taste public' or a 'taste culture' is much more difficult and perhaps impossible in the post-modern age, in which 'patterns of legitimation' are constantly changing, such that what was perceived as 'low culture' can come to be perceived as legitimized 'high culture'. Thirdly, as we have already seen, what constitute the major styles and genres of pop music are subject to continual and increasingly rapid change, and it may also be that the social and cultural identities of *individuals* are just as important as those of the social groups and taste publics of which they are a part.

We pursued this line of argument in our own investigations of differences in the socio-economic status of 2,062 fans of 19 different musical styles (North & Hargreaves 2007a, 2007b, 2007c). In summary, our conclusions were that fans of 'high art' music such as opera and classical music, in comparison to other groups, had higher incomes, were better educated, spent the most money per month on food, were most likely to drink wine, smoked and drank alcohol least, and had more conservative lifestyles and beliefs. Although this is a very oversimplified account of our results, and there were many exceptions that indicate more complex interactions between preference and life-style, we must nevertheless conclude that Bourdieu's view of social class and musical taste is broadly supported.

The results of the small literature on gender effects in musical preference are much less clear-cut, and most studies that have been carried out have dealt with either atti-tudes towards music as a whole, or preference for specific styles and pieces. As far as the first of these is concerned, a consistent finding is that girls generally have more positive attitudes towards music than do boys (e.g. Crowther & Durkin, 1982; Eccles, Wigfield, Harold, & Blumenfeld, 1993). Hargreaves, Comber, and Colley's (1995) study of 278 British school pupils from the 11- to 12-year-old and 15- to 16-year-old age groups, for example, found that girls expressed liking for a wider range of styles than did boys, and especially for 'serious' styles such as jazz, classical, and opera, although this might be better expressed as a lower level of disliking than as a positive effect.

Other data on gender differences in preferences for different pieces and styles is inconclusive. Abeles and Chung's (1996) review led them to conclude that there were no such consistent differences for short-term preferences between individual pieces, whereas there may be such differences for longer-term liking for musical styles. Women may prefer 'softer' musical styles such as mainstream pop, whereas males tend to pre-fer 'harder' styles such as rock, for example (see e.g. Appleton, 1970; Baumann, 1960; Christenson & Peterson, 1988; Skipper, 1975). This idea may be reflected in more recent styles such as the aggressive styles of rap and heavy rock, which tend to be preferred by males (see e.g. Robinson, Weaver, & Zillmann, 1996).

Anthony Kemp (1996), in his pioneering and extensive studies of various aspects of the relationships between personality factors and musical behaviour, included a

review of studies that have investigated the personality correlates of musical preferences, and of the different listening styles people adopt, and found very few clear-cut
relationships. This research and the limited amount of work that has been carried out
subsequently are reviewed in Chapter 24 (this volume) and by North and Hargreaves
(2008). The lack of consistent conclusions relative to other areas of music psychology
may be partly because of the causal nature of any such relationships, and of the specific
role that music plays in individuals' lives. Two contrasting views are that liking for a
piece or style may *reflect* particular aspects of a person's personality; the other, opposing, alternative is that people listen to particular pieces in order to *compensate* for that
aspect of their personality. For example, the putative relationship between extroversion–
introversion and liking for music with different arousal-inducing properties may occur
because people want music either to *reflect* or to *compensate for* their personality style
by lowering or increasing arousal (Eysenck & Eysenck, 1975).

The evidence seems to suggest that the former is the case: musical preferences seem
to *reflect* rather than to *compensate for* different aspects of fans' personality. For example, 'sensation seeking' (the need for varied, novel, and complex experiences, and the
willingness to take risks accordingly; see Zuckerman, 1979) has been shown to be associated with preference for arousing music, in particular heavy rock (e.g. Arnett, 1991,
1992; Stratton & Zalanowski, 1997). Correspondingly, other studies suggest that fans of
classical music score more highly on measures of conservatism. This raises the question
of the relationship between antisocial behaviour and preference for certain 'problem
music' styles such as rap and hip-hop. Are fans of these styles more likely to become
involved in acts of rebelliousness? There is some evidence to support this view. Hansen
and Hansen (1991) found that heavy metal fans were higher on questionnaire measures
of 'Machiavellianism' and 'machismo' and lower on measures of need for cognition
than were non-fans, for example, and that punk fans were less accepting of authority than were non-fans. Rentfrow and Gosling (2003) found that liking for 'intense
and rebellious' music was associated with openness to new experiences, athleticism,
self-perceived intelligence, and verbal ability.

This leads on the vexed question of the role of 'problem music' styles such as hip-hop
in promoting antisocial and criminal behaviour in young people, including speculation in the media that it could have played a significant role in some of the horrifying
murders that occurred amongst secondary school children in the UK in 2007. This
emphasizes the importance of research in this field, but is beyond our scope here. The
topic is reviewed in depth for the first time from a psychological perspective by North
and Hargreaves (2008).

Finally, the effects of musical training and ability on musical preference seem to
be similar. In general, the very limited research literature suggests that people with
high levels of musical training and/or musical ability prefer more complex music than
do people with low levels of training and/or ability. Rubin-Rabson (1940) found that
level of musical training was positively correlated with preference for what they at the
time called 'modern' music, Fay and Middleton (1941) found that people who preferred 'swing' music were 'decidedly inferior in their sense of pitch, rhythm and time'
to those who preferred classical music, and Hargreaves, Messerschmidt, and Rubert

(1980) found that participants with musical training gave higher overall liking ratings to the music used in the research than did 'untrained' participants, and that this effect was more pronounced for pieces of classical music than for pop.

19.7 CONCLUSION

We have seen in this chapter that experimental aesthetics can do much to explain musical preferences. But what is also clear from the above is that concepts such as arousal cannot capture every aspect of musical preference. Work on preference for prototypes has attempted to explain the specific extent to which arousal has explanatory power, but we have already seen evidence on how individual differences and social psychological factors, such as the listening situation and conformity, to name just two that are reviewed here, also play an important role. Furthermore, music industry factors (see Chapter 32, this volume, and North & Hargreaves, 2008, for a more detailed coverage) undoubtedly mediate the link between the arousal-evoking characteristics of the music we are exposed to and that which we actually purchase and listen to. What this points to is a clear need to employ the concepts derived from experimental aesthetics in a much more 'heads up' manner, which recognizes the range of factors that they interact with in specific everyday contexts and within a broader musical culture. Much of the work by Simonton (1997) has made valuable headway in this respect, and Martindale's (1990) notion of *The Clockwork Muse* again acknowledges the importance of the broader cultural context in which any particular piece of music is composed. We hope and expect that future work in experimental aesthetics will not 'throw the baby out with the bathwater' by turning its back on notions such as arousal and typicality, but will instead investigate the extent to which theories relating to these developed under lab conditions must necessarily be adapted to explain actual everyday music listening.

This wide-ranging chapter has revealed some of the scope and potential of empirical studies of aesthetic responses to music, and has shown how much the field has changed in character and emphasis since the early days of experimental aesthetics. It is clearly vital that empirical studies should possess ecological validity, which necessarily means taking account of the real-life contexts within which music listening occurs. This means that the nature of the listening situation must form an integral consideration in the design of any study, and this aspect is formalized in our 'reciprocal feedback' model of musical response. We also feel that it is vital for empirical studies to be predicated on specific theoretical models, or general theoretical approaches, if our knowledge and understanding are to develop. Responses to music fulfil specific functions for individuals in specific situations, who have specific practical goals. A deeper understanding of these functions will lead to practical applications as well as to further theoretical advance.

RECOMMENDED FURTHER READING

1. Berlyne, D. E. (1971). *Aesthetics and psychobiology*. New York: Appleton-Century-Crofts.
2. Martindale, C., & Moore, K, (1988). Priming, prototypicality, and preference. *Journal of Experimental Psychology: Human Perception and Performance, 14*, 661–70.
3. North, A. C., & Hargreaves, D. J. (2008). *The social and applied psychology of music*. Oxford: Oxford University Press.

REFERENCES

Abeles, H., & Chung, J. W. (1996). Responses to music. In D. A. Hodges (ed.), *Handbook of music psychology* (2nd edn, pp. 285–342). San Antonio, TX: IMR Press.
Alpert, J. (1982). The effect of disc-jockey, peer, and music teacher approval of music on music selection and preference. *Journal of Research in Music Education, 30*, 173–86.
Appleton, C. R. (1970). *The comparative preferential response of black and white college students to black and white folk and popular musical styles*. Ph.D. Dissertation, New York University, USA.
Arnett, J. (1991). Heavy metal music and reckless behavior among adolescents. *Journal of Youth and Adolescence, 20*, 573–92.
Arnett, J. (1992). The soundtrack of recklessness: musical preferences and reckless behaviour among adolescents. *Journal of Adolescent Research, 7*, 313–31.
Baumann, V. H. (1960). Teen-age music preferences. *Journal of Research in Music Education, 8*, 75–84.
Berlyne, D. E. (1971). *Aesthetics and psychobiology*. New York: Appleton-Century-Crofts.
Berlyne, D. E. (1974). The new experimental aesthetics. In D. E. Berlyne (ed.), *Studies in the new experimental aesthetics: steps toward an objective psychology of aesthetic appreciation* (pp. 1–25). New York: Halsted Press.
Binet, A. (1903). *L'étude expérimentale de l'intelligence*. Paris, France: Schleicher.
Bourdieu, P. (1971). Intellectual field and creative project. In M. F. D. Young (ed.), *Knowledge and control* (pp. 161–188). London: Collier-Macmillan.
Bourdieu, P. (1984). *Distinction: a social critique of the judgement of taste*. London: Routledge.
Castell, K. C. (1982). Children's sensitivity to stylistic differences in 'classical' and 'popular' music. *Psychology of Music, Special Issue*, 22–5.
Christenson, P. G., & Peterson, J. B. (1988). Genre and gender in the structure of music preferences. *Communication Research, 15*, 282–301.
Crowther, R. D. (1985). A social psychological approach to adolescents' musical preferences. *Psychology of Music, 13*, 64.
Crowther, R. D., & Durkin, K. (1982). Sex- and age-related differences in the musical behaviour, interests and attitudes towards music of 232 secondary school students. *Educational Studies, 20*, 13–18.
Crozier, J. B. (1974). Verbal and exploratory responses to sound sequences varying in uncertainty level. In D. E. Berlyne (ed.), *Studies in the new experimental aesthetics* (pp. 27–90). New York: Wiley.
Crozier, W. R., & Chapman, A. J. (1981). Aesthetic preferences, prestige, and social class. In D. O'Hare (ed.), *Psychology and the arts* (pp. 242–78). Brighton, UK: Harvester.
Deliege, I., & Sloboda, J. A. (eds). (1997). *Perception and cognition of music*. Hove, UK: Psychology Press.

Doise, W. (1986). *Levels of explanation in social psychology*. Cambridge, UK: Cambridge University Press.

Eccles, J., Wigfield, A., Harold, R. D., & Blumenfeld, P. (1993). Age and gender differences in children's self- and task perceptions during elementary school. *Child Development, 64*, 830–47.

Erdelyi, M. (1940). The relation between 'radio plugs' and sheet sales of popular music. *Journal of Applied Psychology, 24*, 696–702.

Eerola, T. (1997). The rise and fall of the experimental style of the Beatles: the life span of stylistic periods in music. In A. Gabrielsson (ed.), *Proceedings of the Third Triennial ESCOM Conference* (pp. 377–81). Uppsala, Sweden: Department of Psychology, Uppsala University.

Eysenck H. J., & Eysenck S. B. G. (1975). *Manual of the Eysenck Personality Questionnaire*. London: Hodder and Stoughton.

Fay, P. J., & Middleton, W. C. (1941). Relationship between musical talent and preferences for different types of music. *Journal of Educational Psychology, 32*, 573–83.

Fechner, G. T. (1876). *Vorschule der ästhetik*. Leipzig, Germany: Breitkopf and Hartel.

Fiese, R. K. (1990). The effects of non-musical cues on the rankings of music scores by undergraduate conducting students based on judgements of quality. *Journal of Band Research, 25*, 13–21.

Finnäs, L. (1989). A comparison between young people's privately and publicly expressed musical preferences. *Psychology of Music, 17*, 132–45.

Fox, W. S., & Wince, M. H. (1975). Musical taste cultures and taste publics. *Youth and Society, 7*, 198–224.

Furman, C. E., & Duke, R. A. (1988). Effect of majority consensus on preferences for recorded orchestral and popular music. *Journal of Research in Music Education, 36*, 220–31.

Gans, H. J. (1974). *Popular culture and high culture: an analysis and evaluation of taste*. New York: Basic Books.

Gardner, H. (1973). *The arts and human development*. New York: John Wiley.

Geiger, T. (1950). A radio test of musical taste. *Public Opinion Quarterly, 14*, 453–60.

Hansen, C. H., & Hansen, R. D. (1991). Constructing personality and social reality through music: individual differences among fans of punk and heavy metal music. *Journal of Broadcasting and Electronic Media, 35*, 335–50.

Hargreaves, D. J. (1982). The development of aesthetic reactions to music. *Psychology of Music, Special Issue*, 51–4.

Hargreaves, D. J. (1986). *The developmental psychology of music*. Cambridge, UK: Cambridge University Press.

Hargreaves, D. J., & Castell, K. C. (1987). Development of liking for familiar and unfamiliar melodies. *Council for Research in Music Education Bulletin, 91*, 665–9.

Hargreaves, D. J., & North, A. C. (1999). Developing concepts of musical style. *Musicae Scientiae, 3*, 193–216.

Hargreaves, D. J., & North, A. C. (eds). (1997). *The social psychology of music*. Oxford: Oxford University Press.

Hargreaves, D. J., Comber, C., & Colley, A. (1995). Effects of age, gender, and training on musical preferences of British secondary school students. *Journal of Research in Music Education, 43*, 242–50.

Hargreaves, D. J., Messerschmidt, P., & Rubert, C. (1980). Musical preference and evaluation. *Psychology of Music, 8*, 13–18.

Hargreaves, D. J., Miell, D. E., & MacDonald, R. A. R. (2002). What are musical identities, and why are they important? In R. A. R. MacDonald, D. J. Hargreaves, & D. E. Miell (eds), *Musical identities* (pp. 1–20). Oxford: Oxford University Press.

Hargreaves, D. J., Miell, D. E., MacDonald, R. A. R. (2005). How do people communicate using music? In D. E. Miell, R. A. R. MacDonald, & D. J. Hargreaves (eds), *Musical communication* (pp. 1–25). Oxford: Oxford University Press.

Hargreaves, D. J., North, A. C., & Tarrant, M. (2006). The development of musical preference and taste in childhood and adolescence. In G. E. McPherson (ed.), *The child as musician: a handbook of musical development* (pp. 135–54). Oxford: Oxford University Press.

Hekkert, P., & van Wieringen, P. C. W. (1990). Complexity and prototypicality as determinants of the appraisal of cubist paintings. *British Journal of Psychology, 81*, 483–95.

Hepper, P. G. (1991). An examination of fetal learning before and after birth. *Irish Journal of Psychology, 12*, 95–107.

Heyduk, R. G. (1975). Rated preference for musical composition as it relates to complexity and exposure frequency. *Perception and Psychophysics, 17*, 84–91.

Inglefield, H. G. (1968). *The relationship of selected personality variables to conformity behaviour reflected in the musical preferences of adolescents when exposed to peer group leader influences.* Unpublished doctoral dissertation, Ohio State University, USA.

Juslin, P. N., & Sloboda, J. A. (eds). (2001). *Music and emotion: Theory and research.* Oxford: Oxford University Press.

Kemp, A. E. (1996). *The musical temperament: psychology and personality of musicians.* Oxford: Oxford University Press.

Konečni, V. J. (1982). Social interaction and musical preference. In D. Deutsch (ed.), *The psychology of music* (pp. 497–516). New York: Academic Press.

Konečni, V. J., & Sargent-Pollock, D. (1976). Choice between melodies differing in complexity under divided-attention conditions. *Journal of Experimental Psychology: Human Perception and Performance, 2*, 347–56.

Konečni, V. J., Crozier, J. B., & Doob, A. N. (1976). Anger and expression of aggression: effects on aesthetic preference. *Scientific Aesthetics/Sciences de l'Art, 1*, 47–55.

LeBlanc, A. (1991). *Effect of maturation/aging on music listening preference: a review of the literature.* Paper presented at the Ninth National Symposium on Research in Music Behavior, Canon Beach, Oregon, USA.

LeBlanc, A., Sims, W. L. Siivola, C., & Obert, M. (1993). *Music style preferences of different-age listeners.* Paper presented at the Tenth National Symposium on Research in Music Behavior, University of Alabama, Tuscaloosa, Alabama, USA.

Levine, J. M., & Russo, E. M. (1987). Majority and minority influence. In C. Hendrick (ed.), *Review of personality and social psychology, Vol. 8* (pp. 13–54). London: Sage.

Marshall, N., & Hargreaves, D. J. (2007). Musical style discrimination in the early years. *Journal of Early Childhood Research, 5*, 32–46.

Martindale, C. (1990). *The clockwork muse: the predictability of artistic change.* New York: Basic Books.

Martindale, C., & Moore, K. (1988). Priming, prototypicality, and preference. *Journal of Experimental Psychology: Human Perception and Performance, 14*, 661–70.

Martindale, C., & Moore, K. (1989). Relationship of musical preference to collative, ecological, and psychophysical variables. *Music Perception, 6*, 431–55.

Martindale, C., Moore, K., & West, A. (1988). Relationship of preference judgements to typicality, novelty, and mere exposure. *Empirical Studies of the Arts, 6*, 79–96.

Martindale, C., Moore, K., & Borkum, J. (1990). Aesthetic preference: anomalous findings for Berlyne's psychobiological theory. *American Journal of Psychology, 103*, 53–80.

McMullen, P. T. (1974). Influence of number of different pitches and melodic redundancy on preference responses. *Journal of Research in Music Education, 22*, 198–204.

McMullen, P. T., & Arnold, M. J. (1976). Preference and interest as a function of distributional redundancy in rhythmic sequences. *Journal of Research in Music Education, 24,* 22–31.

McPherson, G. E. (ed.). (2006). *The child as musician: a handbook of musical development.* Oxford: Oxford University Press.

Meyer, L. B. (1956). *Emotion and meaning in music.* Chicago, IL: Chicago University Press.

Meyer, L. B. (1967). *Music, the arts, and ideas.* Chicago, IL: University of Chicago Press.

Moore, K., & Martindale, C. (1983). *Preference for shapes varying in color, color typicality, size, and complexity.* Paper presented at the International Conference on Psychology and the Arts, Cardiff, UK.

Nattiez, J.-J. (1990). *Music and discourse: toward a semiology of music* (trans. C. Abbate). Princeton, NJ: Princeton University Press.

North, A. C., & Hargreaves, D. J. (1995). Eminence in pop music. *Popular Music and Society, 19,* 41–66.

North, A. C., & Hargreaves, D. J. (1996). Responses to music in aerobic exercise and yogic relaxation classes. *British Journal of Psychology, 87,* 535–47.

North, A. C., & Hargreaves, D. J. (1997). Liking, arousal potential, and the emotions expressed by music. *Scandinavian Journal of Psychology, 38,* 45–53.

North, A. C., & Hargreaves, D. J. (1999). Music and driving game performance. *Scandinavian Journal of Psychology, 40,* 285–92.

North, A. C., & Hargreaves, D. J. (2000a). Collative variables versus prototypicality. *Empirical Studies of the Arts, 18,* 13–17.

North, A. C., & Hargreaves, D. J. (2000b). Musical preference during and after relaxation and exercise. *American Journal of Psychology, 113,* 43–67.

North, A. C., & Hargreaves, D. J. (2007a). Lifestyle correlates of musical preference: 1. Relationships, living arrangements, beliefs, and crime. *Psychology of Music, 35,* 58–87.

North, A. C., & Hargreaves, D. J. (2007b). Lifestyle correlates of musical preference: 2. Media, leisure time, and music. *Psychology of Music, 35,* 179–200.

North, A. C., & Hargreaves, D. J. (2007c). Lifestyle correlates of musical preference: 3. Travel, money, education, employment, and health. *Psychology of Music, 35,* 473–97.

North, A. C., & Hargreaves, D. J. (2008). *The social and applied psychology of music.* Oxford: Oxford University Press.

North, A. C., Hargreaves, D. J., & Hargreaves, J. J. (2004). The uses of music in everyday life. *Music Perception, 22,* 63–99.

Parncutt, R. (2006). Prenatal development. In G. E. McPherson (ed.), *The child as musician: a handbook of musical development* (pp. 1–31). Oxford: Oxford University Press.

Piaget, J. (1950). *Introduction à l'Épistémologie Génétique.* Paris, France: Presses Universitaires de France.

Posner, M. I., & Keele, S. W. (1968). On the genesis of abstract ideas. *Journal of Experimental Psychology, 77,* 353–63.

Radocy, R. E. (1975). A naïve minority of one and deliberate majority mismatches of tonal stimuli. *Journal of Research in Music Education, 23,* 120–33.

Rentfrow, P. J., & Gosling, S. D. (2003). The do re mi's of everyday life: the structure and personality correlates of musical preference. *Journal of Personality and Social Psychology, 84,* 1236–56.

Rigg, M. G. (1948). Favorable versus unfavorable propaganda in the enjoyment of music. *Journal of Experimental Psychology, 38,* 78–81.

Robinson, T. O., Weaver, J. B., & Zillmann, D. (1996). Exploring the relation between personality and the appreciation of rock music. *Psychological Reports, 78,* 259–69.

Rubin-Rabson, G. (1940). The influence of age, intelligence and training on reactions to classical and modern music. *Journal of General Psychology, 22,* 413–29.

Schank, R. C., & Abelson, R. P. (1988). In A. M. Collins & E. E. Smith (eds), *Readings in cognitive science: a perspective from psychology and artificial intelligence* (pp. 190–223). San Mateo, CA: Morgan Kaufmann.

Shahidullah, S., & Hepper, P. G. (1994). Frequency discrimination by the fetus. *Early Human Development, 36,* 13–26.

Shepherd, J. (2003). Music and social categories. In M. Clayton, T. Herbert, & R. Middleton (eds), *The cultural study of music: a critical introduction* (pp. 69–79). London: Routledge.

Simon, C. R., & Wohlwill, J. F. (1968). An experimental study of the role of expectation and variation in music. *Journal of Research in Music Education, 16,* 227–38.

Simonton, D. K. (1997). Products, persons, and periods: historiometric analyses of compositional creativity. In D. J. Hargreaves & A. C. North (eds), *The social psychology of music* (pp. 109–22). Oxford: Oxford University Press.

Skipper, J. K. (1975). Musical tastes of Canadian and American college students: an examination of the massification and Americanization theses. *Canadian Journal of Sociology, 1,* 49–59.

Sloboda, J. A., O'Neill, S. A., & Ivaldi, A. (2001). Functions of music in everyday life: an exploratory study using the experience sampling method. *Musicae Scientiae, 5,* 9–32.

Sluckin, W., Hargreaves, D. J., & Colman, A. M. (1983). Novelty and human aesthetic preferences. In J. Archer & L. Birke (eds), *Exploration in animals and humans* (pp. 245–69). London: Van Nostrand Reinhold.

Steck, L., & Machotka, P. (1975). Preference for musical complexity: effects of context. *Journal of Experimental Psychology: Human Perception and Performance, 104,* 170–4.

Stratton, V. N., & Zalanowski, A. H. (1997). The relationship between characteristic moods and most commonly listened to types of music. *Journal of Music Therapy, 34,* 129–40.

Trehub, S. E. (2006). Infants as musical connoisseurs. In G. E. McPherson (ed.), *The child as musician: a handbook of musical development* (pp. 33–49). Oxford: Oxford University Press.

Vitz, P. C. (1966). Affect as a function of stimulus variation. *Journal of Experimental Psychology, 71,* 74–9.

Whitfield, T. W. A., & Slatter, P. E. (1979). The effects of categorization and prototypicality on aesthetic choice in a furniture selection task. *British Journal of Psychology, 70,* 65–75.

Wundt, W. M. (1874). *Grundzuge der physiologischen psychologie.* Leipzig, Germany: Engelmann.

Zajonc, R. B. (1968). Attitudinal effects of mere exposure. *Journal of Personality and Social Psychology, 9,* 1–27.

Zuckerman, M. (1979). *Sensation seeking: beyond the optimal level of arousal.* Hillsdale, NJ: Erlbaum.

CHAPTER 20

....

STRONG
EXPERIENCES
WITH MUSIC

....

ALF GABRIELSSON

WHILE perception of musical expression has been given considerable attention in empirical music psychology (cf. overviews by Gabrielsson & Juslin, 2003; Gabrielsson & Lindström, 2001; Chapters 14 and 17, this volume), there is much less research concerning the experience of music—how we react to music. There are several plausible reasons for this neglect. Music experience is a complex phenomenon, and is influenced by a variety of interacting factors. Different individuals react differently, and reactions to the same music may vary on different occasions. Many people find it extremely difficult to describe their experience; it seems to elude common vocabulary.

Music psychology, then, has few answers to the question that most people interested in music consider the most relevant: how are we affected by music? Disappointment with this state of affairs was the basic motivation for the *Strong Experiences with Music* (SEM) project described below. William James (1902/1985) stated that 'we learn most about a thing when we view it . . . in its most exaggerated form' (p. 39). Following James, we decided to focus on strong experiences of music, because they could be expected to provide the most comprehensive picture of how we may be affected. The project started at the very end of the 1980s (Gabrielsson, 1989), went on with some intermissions during the 1990s, and continued for some years into the new millennium.

The purpose of the project, and of this chapter, is to describe what reactions may occur in particularly strong experiences with music, to explore which factors can elicit such reactions, and to consider what consequences the experience may have for the individual. This chapter includes a review of earlier research on strong experiences (Section 20.1), followed by a description of the SEM project (20.2), the associated analysis of reactions (20.3), the music in SEM (20.4), influencing factors (20.5), and a concluding discussion (20.6).

20.1 EARLIER RESEARCH ON STRONG EXPERIENCES

In empirical psychology, the best-known analysis of strong experiences was furnished by Abraham Maslow, one of the founders of humanistic psychology. Maslow coined the term *peak experience*, which he originally associated with self-actualization, the highest level in his well-known hierarchy of needs (Maslow, 1954, Chapter 5). To explore such experiences, Maslow asked people to describe 'the most wonderful experience of your life; happiest moments, ecstatic moments, moments of rapture, perhaps from being in love, or from listening to music, or suddenly "being hit" by a book or a painting, or from some great creative moment' (Maslow, 1968, p. 71). Surveying the contents of these descriptions, he found several characteristics of generalized peak experience, such as total attention on the object in question, complete absorption, disorientation in time and space, transcendence of ego, and identification or even fusion of the perceiver and the perceived. Peak experience is good and desirable; there is a complete loss of fear, anxiety, inhibition, defence, and control. Moreover, 'the emotional reaction in the peak experience has a special flavour of wonder, of awe, of reverence, of humility and surrender before the experience as before something great' (Maslow, 1968, pp. 87–8), even a fear of being overwhelmed by more than what one can bear. The experience may occasionally be described as sacred.

Maslow found that 'the two easiest ways of getting peak experiences . . . are through music and through sex' (Maslow, 1976, p. 169). Regarding music, he found peak experiences reported solely from classical music, 'the great classics' (p. 170). He claimed that music and art can do the same as psychotherapy, and that 'music and rhythm and dancing are excellent ways of moving toward the discovering of identity' (p. 171).

However, Maslow did not publish any of the reports that he had obtained from his subjects. He just mentioned that no one subject reported all of the above characteristics of peak experience; these characteristics represent an addition of all partial responses in order to 'make a "perfect" composite syndrome' (Maslow, 1968, p. 71).

As an extension of Maslow's investigations, Panzarella (1980) gathered reports on an 'intense joyous experience of listening to music or looking at visual art' (p. 71) from a sample of 103 persons, 51 describing musical experiences and 52 visual art experiences. Content analysis followed by factor analysis revealed four major factors of the experience: (a) *renewal ecstasy*, an altered perception of the world. 'The world is better, more beautiful than had been thought before' (p. 73); (b) *motor-sensory ecstasy*, physical responses (changes in heart rate, breathing, posture, or locomotion, presence of shivers, chills, etc.) and quasi-physical responses (e.g. feeling 'high', 'floating'); (c) *withdrawal ecstasy*, loss of contact with both the physical and social environment; and (d) *fusion-emotional ecstasy*, merging with the aesthetic object. Motor-sensory ecstasy and fusion-emotional ecstasy were more pronounced in music reports than in visual art reports, renewal ecstasy more pronounced in visual art reports, and withdrawal ecstasy was about equally common in music reports and visual art reports. The musical pieces usually belonged to classical music, but there were some examples of folk songs and rock 'n' roll. A few reports with classical music were cited.

Laski (1961) asked 63 individuals whether they had known an experience of 'transcendent ecstasy', and further analysed texts from selected literary sources and from books on religious experience. Triggers of such experiences included nature, sexual love, childbirth, religion, art, science, creative work, 'beauty', and others. The contents of the descriptions were classified into four broad categories: (a) feelings of loss of something (e.g. loss of time, place, sense, self); (b) feelings of gain of something (e.g. gain of timelessness, release, satisfaction, joy, salvation, perfection, new knowledge); (c) feelings of ineffability (e.g. the experience is indescribable, eludes verbal communication); and (d) quasi-physical feelings (e.g. light and/or heat words, improvement words, pain words, calm and peace words). Classical music was the most frequently mentioned trigger among the arts.

The concept of 'peak' has also been used in connection with performance. Peak performance means some kind of superior behaviour, better than ordinary behaviour; the person's achievement surpasses what would usually be predicted or expected (Privette & Landsman, 1983, p. 195). As a musical example the authors cited a saxophone player who during a concert performance felt that everything that he had practised earlier just came out quite naturally without any effort whatsoever. The piece sounded exactly as it should be played. The concept of *flow* (Csikszentmihalyi, 1990) has a similar meaning. It refers to a state of intense but yet effortless involvement in an activity, the experience of which is 'so enjoyable that people will do it . . . for the sheer sake of doing it' (p. 4). With regard to music, flow may involve mastering a difficult piece in a fully concentrated but seemingly effortless involvement, a phenomenon often reported by musicians as the most happy moments in their activities (e.g. Boyd & George-Warren, 1992). The relationships between the concepts of peak experience, peak performance, and flow were discussed by Privette (1983) and Privette and Bundrick (1987); see also Whaley, Sloboda, and Gabrielsson (2009).

While there are practically no later studies intended to study musical peak experiences including all or most of Maslow's characteristics for such experiences, there are some studies focusing on especially strong emotional experiences with music. Scherer, Zentner, and Schacht (2001–2) had 98 musical experts attending a conference complete a questionnaire on their reactions to a piece of music that had produced a strong emotional state in them. The responses were coded into a number of categories: physiological symptoms (increased heart rate, shivers, goose bumps, etc.); expressive behaviour (eye symptoms, i.e. tears); motivation/action tendencies (e.g. urge to move, feel energized, focused attention); and subjective feeling, divided into specific feeling, unspecific feeling, basic emotions, arousal/calm, valence, and ambivalent feelings. There were more pieces of non-classical music than of classical music that had elicited the strong emotional response. Among influencing factors, musical factors—musical structure, acoustic features, interpretation, technical quality—were judged more important than personal factors (mood, affective involvement, personality) and context factors. But most important were 'other factors' added by the participants themselves. These other factors varied enormously across the participants. Hence, it was assumed that 'whether an emotional reaction occurs or not may be determined, to a large extent, by factors that are very specific for each individual' (p. 160).

Lowis (1998) had subjects listen to classical music including five pieces of 'gentle' music (e.g. 'Nimrod' from *Enigma Variations* by Elgar) and nine pieces of 'up-beat' music (e.g. ending of *The Firebird* by Stravinsky), and use a button device to indicate 'a moment of particularly deep and profound pleasure or joy . . . the sort that produces a tingle in the spine' (p. 212). Roughly two-thirds of the subjects pressed the button at least once. The 'up-beat' music generated significantly more responses than the 'gentle' music. Significant correlations were found between frequency of button pressings and ratings for the following feelings evoked by the music: joy, love/tenderness, longing, sadness, reverence/spirituality, action, and memory/thoughtfulness.

Other studies focused on physical aspects of strong experiences, especially responses alternately called thrills, chills, or shivers. From answers to a questionnaire, Goldstein (1980) concluded that thrills may be elicited by a large variety of stimuli; most frequently mentioned were musical passages, indicated by 96 per cent of the respondents. Subjects in Sloboda's (1991) study reported physical responses located to a specific theme, phrase, motif, bar, chord, or moment in pieces of classical music; tears were provoked by melodic appoggiaturas, shivers by sudden changes in harmony, and a racing heart either by syncopation or by a prominent event occurring earlier than expected. Panksepp (1995) found that chills peaked at intense and dramatic crescendos. Sadness and chills occurred together more clearly than happiness and chills, and this relationship was more evident in women. Chills occurred more frequently for pieces brought by the subjects themselves than for other pieces, which suggested effects of conditioning. For a more detailed review of these pioneering studies and more recent studies on thrills/chills, see Chapter 21 (this volume). On the whole, however, results concerning thrills/chills in relation to musical variables are still tentative. Moreover, individuals vary greatly both in the number of reported chills (some report no chills at all) and/or regarding when chills occur during the course of a musical piece. Chills are only cursorily mentioned by Maslow and Panzarella, and in our own study thrills/chills were reported by only about 10 per cent of the participants (see Section 20.3.2). Konečni, Wanic, and Brown (2007), after having investigated various emotional and aesthetic antecedents and consequences of music-induced thrills, concluded that thrills may accompany profound aesthetic experiences but are themselves of limited psychological significance.

Most studies cited in the latter part of this section deal with separate aspects—physical or emotional—of strong experiences with music. The early studies by Maslow, Panzarella, and Laski were far more comprehensive, and identified many more aspects. However, the number of subjects was relatively small, about 50 in Panzarella's study, while it is unclear how many were in Maslow's study. The background and the circumstances around the experience were usually not reported. Moreover, we found it doubtful that strong experiences with music are always positive—as implied by Maslow's definition of peak experiences—or that they are limited to classical music. Considerations such as these and a general dissatisfaction with the scant research on the experience of music led us to initiate the SEM project.

20.2 THE SEM PROJECT

The primary purpose of the SEM project was to obtain a comprehensive and detailed description of the components—physical, behavioural, perceptual, cognitive, emotional, social, and others—contained in strong experiences related to music. We also wanted to explore the 'causes' of such experiences; that is, what factors in the music, the person, and the situation may contribute to the strong experience. Furthermore, we were interested in what consequences the experience may have had for the person in question.

Rather than speaking about peak experience in strict adherence to Maslow's (1968) terminology and criteria, we preferred to adopt a more general view of the phenomena under investigation and to refer to them as strong experiences. Furthermore, unlike Maslow we did not provide any hints or examples of such experiences to our subjects, but only asked them to report any strong experiences related to music.

The very beginning of the project was briefly reported in Gabrielsson (1989). A sketch of a descriptive system for SEM first appeared in Gabrielsson and Lindström (1993). It was successively further elaborated in Gabrielsson and Lindström (2000), Gabrielsson (2001), and, especially, in Gabrielsson and Lindström Wik (2003) and Gabrielsson (2008). Examples of therapeutic effects of SEM were given in Gabrielsson and Lindström (1995), old people's remembrance of SEM in Gabrielsson (2002), and description of the different types of music in SEM in Gabrielsson (2006, 2008).

20.2.1 Data collection

Briefly, subjects were asked to describe 'the strongest, most intense experience of music that you have ever had. Please, describe your experience and reactions in as much detail as you can'. Supplementary questions concerned whether or not this was the first time one had listened to the music in question, and if the same strong experience had recurred when one heard the same music on later occasions; how the respondent felt before and after the experience, and what the experience had meant in a long-term perspective; how often such strong experiences occurred, and if similar strong experiences occurred in situations other than with music; and if the respondent had any idea about what caused the strong experience. The reports were obtained by means of interviews (about 10 per cent) and as written reports.

Most participants (n = 522) also answered a questionnaire containing either 98 or 74 statements concerning reactions in strong experiences of music. The task was to judge how well one's own experience agreed with each of the statements, using a scale extending from 0 ('no agreement at all') to 10 ('perfect agreement'). Ratings were analysed in terms of conventional descriptive statistics followed by factor analysis in order to find some fundamental dimensions underlying the ratings. For further description of the methods and results of the questionnaire, see Gabrielsson and Lindström Wik (2003).

20.2.2 Subjects

Participation in the project was basically on a voluntary basis. Attempts were made to collect reports from both women and men, from people of different ages, with different occupations, and different musical preferences. An initial study comprised musicians and music students with preferences for classical music. It was followed by studies focusing on fans of jazz, rock music, and folk music. Further studies included high school students, choir singers, elderly people, and persons who reported strong experiences related to dance and to visual art. Advertisements in mass media resulted in hundreds of reports from persons with widely varying background and preferences. For details, see Gabrielsson and Lindström Wik (2003) and Gabrielsson (2008).

In all, 953 persons provided SEM reports. About 250 of them provided two or more reports. The total number of reports is 1,354. The majority of participants were women (62 per cent). Ages of the participants ranged from 13 to 91 years with fairly equal distribution (116–176 persons) across successive 10-year intervals (10–19, 20–29 . . . 60–69 years). Furthermore, some 80 persons were older than 70 years.

A little more than half of the participants (56 per cent) described themselves as amateur musicians, a fifth (20 per cent) as professional musicians, and about a quarter (24 per cent) did not perform music themselves. There was wide variation with regard to education and occupation. Musical preferences were spread across most genres: classical music, opera, musical, folk music, jazz, pop/rock, melodies/tunes, religious music, and still others. As could be expected, preferences differed greatly between different age groups: the older the participants, the more preference for classical music; the younger, the more preference for pop/rock.

Altogether, the participants represent a broad cross-section of gender, age, education, occupation, musical experience, and musical preferences. It is thus reasonable to assume that their SEM reports are fairly representative of the population of possible strong experiences related to music in the given cultural context.

20.2.3 Analysis

SEM reports were subjected to content analysis, gathering all reactions mentioned and successively exploring different ways of sorting them into a limited number of fundamental categories. This work was conducted independently by the author and one or two of his co-workers. After the necessarily tentative analysis of the earliest reports, the consensus between the analysts gradually increased and is now very high, provided that one is familiar with all the details in the SEM descriptive system (see Table 20.1 and the more complete presentation in Gabrielsson & Lindström Wik, 2003, Appendix). As human experiences and reactions are hard to fit into truly exhaustive and mutually exclusive categories, there is some overlapping between different categories. Therefore, I now prefer to talk about a descriptive system rather than a classification.

20.2.4 Some general results and an example

The length and detail of the reports vary widely, from only a few sentences up to ten pages or more. Each report represents a unique case with regard to contents of the experience and influencing factors.

The reported experiences extend across almost 100 years, from 1908 to 2004. About 13 per cent of them occurred before 1950, 42 per cent occurred before 1980. Thus, more than half of the experiences occurred after 1980, of which a large part comes from the youngest participants. Counted in relation to the participants' age, almost half of all experiences occurred within the previous ten years of their life, about 75 per cent within the last 30 years. About 25 per cent thus date back in time more than 30 years, and about 6 per cent more than 60 years.

Here follows a somewhat abbreviated report of a strong experience. It came from a young woman and illustrates many different aspects of SEM. The numbers within parentheses refer to the corresponding items in the SEM descriptive system (see Table 20.1) and may be neglected for the moment.

I looked forward curiously (4.1) to my first meeting with a band playing Finnish tango. It was in a pub crowded with people (3.2). There was no stage so the band was standing at the same level as all the others and this gave another kind of community between musicians and audience (7.4). The band started and let their instruments whirl in fervent dramatic tango rhythms (4.7). Even then I was filled by a special feeling that the music began to take command of my body (2.3; 4.2). I was charged in a way (2.3). A tremendous feeling of harmony (5.2) which made me really enjoy the music (5.2), and I found it difficult to stand still (2.2).

But it was not until the second half of the performance that the mystery and the power (4.7) really gripped me (4.3). I was filled by an enormous warmth and heat (2.1). I really swallowed all the notes that were streaming out in the air, not a single note, effect or sequence missed my hungry ears (3.7). The music became so distinct (3.7). I was captivated by each of the instruments and what they had to offer me (3.7; 4.3). Nothing else existed (4.1)!

I was dancing, whirling (2.2) and really gave myself up to the music and the rhythms (4.4), overjoyed (5.2)—laughing (2.2). Tears came into my eyes (2.1)—however strange that may seem—and it was as a further sign, some kind of liberation. The music set me free from my sober everyday life (7.1). Now I could let my body parts dance as freely as they wanted (2.2)—just let them follow the rhythms and totally lose control (4.3).

The music danced around like a whirlwind (4.7) in the narrow room and all the dramatic sentiment that it conveyed (4.7) reflected my own situation in life (7.3)—but in a new way that I liked (5.2). I went hand in hand with the music (4.4). Afterwards I remained standing flushed with joy (5.2), as if intoxicated (5.2), and it was a real kick for me (7.1). I felt religious (6.3)—and the music was my god.

Before I was in a very bad state. Depressed (5.3). It was during the most critical time ever in my life. I found it hard to get on with people and had to really exert myself to be able to get to grips with things. Afterwards I was bouncy, giggling (2.2), lively and filled with deep joy (5.2). It was really about a life-kick (7.1). There was also a kind of religious feeling. It was so bewildering that it almost felt as a salvation (6.3). It was as if I was selected to take part in such an experience when I needed it the most (7.3). I was filled by zest for life and suddenly had quite another view of the grey tomorrow (6.1, 7.1).

This event became a kind of turning point in my life (6.1; 7.1). During the period after the experience it was very important. It helped to loosen all knots that I had within me so that instead of going even further into my depression I started to climb out of it (5.4; 7.1).

20.3 DESCRIPTIVE SYSTEM FOR SEM

The descriptive system (SEM-DS) comprises seven basic categories: (1) General Characteristics, (2) Physical Reactions and Behaviours, (3) Perception, (4) Cognition, (5) Feelings/Emotion, (6) Existential and Transcendental aspects, and (7) Personal and Social aspects. Each of these contains a number of sub-categories, as seen in Table 20.1. They are briefly exemplified and discussed below.

20.3.1 General characteristics

This category has two subcategories:

(a) *Unique experience.* SEM is described as a unique, fantastic, incredible, unforgettable experience.

(b) *Hard-to-describe experience, words insufficient.* Many participants state that it was difficult or even impossible to describe their SEM in verbal terms.

20.3.2 Physical reactions and behaviours

This category includes three subcategories:

(a) *Physiological reactions.* The most common physiological reaction was tears, described by 24 per cent of the participants, more in women (28 per cent) than in men (18 per cent). The next most common were thrills (chills, shivers: 10 per cent), and piloerection (goose bumps: 5 per cent). These reactions seem to appear when one is moved (taken, captivated) by the music and/or in situations

Table 20.1 SEM descriptive system (abbreviated)

1. *General characteristics*
1.1 Unique, fantastic, incredible, unforgettable experience
1.2 Hard-to-describe experience, words insufficient

2. *Physical reactions, behaviours*
2.1 Physiological reactions
2.2 Behaviours, actions
2.3 Quasi-physical reactions

3. *Perception*
3.1 Auditory
3.2 Visual
3.3 Tactile
3.4 Kinaesthetic
3.5 Other senses
3.6 Synaesthetic
3.7 Intensified perception, multimodal perception
3.8 Musical perception–cognition

4. *Cognition*
4.1 Changed attitude
4.2 Changed experience of situation, body and mind, time and space, part and whole
4.3 Loss of control
4.4 Changed relation/attitude to the music
4.5 Associations, memories, thoughts
4.6 Imagery
4.7 Musical cognition–emotion

5. *Feelings/emotions*
5.1 Intense/powerful feelings
5.2 Positive feelings
5.3 Negative feelings
5.4 Different feelings (mixed, conflicting, changed)

6. *Existential and transcendental aspects*
6.1 Existence
6.2 Transcendence
6.3 Religious experience

7. *Personal and social aspects*
7.1 New insights, possibilities, needs
7.2 Music: new insights, possibilities, needs
7.3 Confirmation of identity, self-actualization
7.4 Community/communication

Note: For a more complete version of the SEM descriptive system, see Appendix in Gabrielsson and Lindström Wik (2003).

in which one is especially receptive or expectant. They were usually connected to positive feelings; however, tears occasionally also appeared in connection with negative feelings such as anxiety, sorrow, and despair.

Other physiological reactions reported to a lesser extent were muscle tension or relaxation, warmth (perspiration), palpitation of the heart, changed breathing, trembling/quivers, various reactions in the chest and stomach, lump in the throat, dizziness, and pain. Most of the physiological reactions reflect activation of the sympathetic nervous system; however, tears involve the parasympathetic system (see Chapter 11, this volume).

(b) *Behaviours, actions*. There were essentially two different kinds of behaviours. On the one hand, activities such as jumping, dancing, clapping hands, shouting, singing along, and the like were reported by 11 per cent of the participants, and were typical of audience reactions at rock/pop concerts. On the other hand, the opposite reaction—to become motionless, quiet, and interrupt any activity—was described by 9 per cent of the participants, and occurred mostly in connection with classical music.

A special reaction was the desire to conceal any visible reaction that may reveal one's strong feelings; one should 'behave'. Another special reaction was the inability to speak, sing, or play because one was overwhelmed, sometimes to the extent that one could not stand the situation and had to get away from it. Some participants reported that, after a strong experience at a concert, they tried to avoid other people in order to be alone with their thoughts and feelings.

(c) *Quasi-physical reactions*. Examples of quasi-physical reactions, reported by about 9 per cent of the respondents, were feeling light or weightless, feeling as being lifted from the ground, or feeling as floating/soaring. Other reactions were that the body felt as if as filled with music ('the whole body is music'), or feeling as if charged, ruled, or being carried away ('kidnapped') by the music. The most spectacular examples of quasi-physical reactions were out-of-body experiences. There were about ten reports in which the person suddenly was looking at her-/himself from outside (e.g. musicians watching their own performance).

20.3.3 Perception

Perception of music involves many sense modalities, mainly auditory, tactile, and visual.

Auditory

Certain aspects of SEM may be described as mainly auditory in nature (rather than purely musical), such as noticing a special timbre, a special loudness, or special acoustical conditions such as the reverberation, direction and diffusion of sounds. To feel totally surrounded/enclosed by sounds/music was described as a very strong experience.

Tactile

Loud music may evoke tactile sensations in different parts of the body; for instance: 'I feel how the bass comes in from the ground via the soles of my feet, continues up through my calves, thighs, the spine and I am filled by the music.'

Visual

Visual impressions of the performers (their appearance, devotion, communication, charisma), the stage setting, the audience and its reactions were reported by about half of all participants. It was not uncommon to report the experience in visual terms; for example: 'That was the best concert I have ever seen.'

Other senses, synaesthetic perception

There were occasional examples of impressions in other sense modalities (e.g. smell) and of synaesthetic perception, for example, colour impressions in connection with certain instruments, composers, or pieces of music. Other possibly synaesthetic phenomena were impressions of a special light surrounding or filling the person ('I was sitting in a huge light-globe, filled of music'; 'I felt as if filled with a strong light, as if I was fluorescent').

Intensified perception, multimodal perception

Respondents also described a kind of intensified perception. One perceives the music more intensely than usual, and pays attention to every detail: 'This piece engraved itself into my consciousness, tone by tone.' This type of experience borders on cognitive aspects (Section 20.3.4). Respondents also emphasized the importance of multimodal perception; that is, the combination of simultaneous auditory, tactile, and visual impressions.

Musical perception-cognition

This category contains statements about perceived 'objective/technical' qualities of the music or the performance (see also Musical cognition-emotion in Section 20.3.4 below).

20.3.4 Cognition

Cognitive aspects of strong experiences may be partitioned in the following, partly overlapping, aspects.

Changed/special attitude: expectancy, receptivity, absorption

About 30 per cent of the participants reported that they felt expectant, curious, open and receptive, 'hungry for music'. On the other hand, there were also respondents who were 'neutral', and a few even had negative expectations.

Whatever the case, the music suddenly or gradually demanded full attention. One is totally absorbed by the music, nothing else matters. There are no thoughts, no analyses, just presence, the here and now. Reactions such as these were reported by about 20 per cent of the respondents. For performers, absorption meant total focus on the performance in order to achieve one's utmost.

Changed experience of situation, body-mind, time-space, part-whole

Absorption may assume many forms. It may be felt as a special mood/atmosphere, especially in a situation with live music. The world around disappears, one dwells in one's own world, inaccessible to others. Time stands still, does not exist; the whole experience regardless of its length is contained in a single 'now'. One may lose consciousness of the body, and the ego may feel dissolved or merged in something greater. Everything is unreal, like a dream, 'it can't be true'. One wants this state to last forever, and it is a disappointment to return to 'reality' afterwards. Everything seems to fit together, all impressions are concordant—the music, people, time, place, atmosphere, the surroundings, etc. Suddenly everything feels simple, natural, and self-evident. Some form of the above reactions was described by about 35 per cent of the participants.

Loss of control

Strong experiences mean a loss of control, surrender to the experience: one is surprised, amazed, touched, taken, even hit, shaken, shocked, spellbound, totally overwhelmed. The music goes straight through all cognitive barriers into one's innermost being. It may even become unbearable ('I can't stand it any more, please stop').

Reactions like these were found in reports from 42 per cent of the respondents. Many of them obviously involved emotional aspects, and other researchers might rather put them under Feelings/emotion below. While acknowledging the emotional aspects, I still prefer to put them under Cognition as they clearly represent a different way of processing the music.

Changed/special relation to the music

Reactions such as absorption and loss of control usually also imply a special relation to the music. One feels enclosed by, embedded in, drawn into the music, merges with the music, identifies oneself with the music, feels at one with the music. It is as if the music addresses oneself, one understands what it says, it seems genuine, true, natural, self-evident, as if it were timeless. Such reactions were reported by about 20 per cent of the participants.

Performers feel as if they surpass their usual competence, everything works, it feels as if 'someone else is playing me'. Such experiences represent peaks in musicians' lives and provide strong motivation to continue performing music.

Associations, memories, thoughts

About 12 per cent of the respondents reported various associations and memories linked to the music. They were highly idiosyncratic and concerned specific people, specific events, situations, or other music. Many (27 per cent) contributed thoughts and reflections about the music, such as whether or not they recognized the music, and what in the music may have elicited the strong reaction. There were also reflections on the importance of music, in general or with regard to special music, and on possible reasons why people have different musical preferences.

Imagery

The music may evoke various inner images, such as of nature, people, situations, and events, dreams of another environment, another life, something different and better. Listeners may imagine that they themselves are standing on the stage performing the music. Inner images were reported by about 10 per cent of the participants.

Sometimes SEM may be elicited by 'inner music'; that is, imagined music. There were about ten reports of such experiences. Music is 'heard', it just comes for no obvious reason and 'sounds' as clear and distinct as live music. Some respondents realized that it was 'only' imagined music, but for others the experience was so vivid that they were surprised to learn that there was in fact no sounding music present at all.

There were also a few reports by composers, who reported strong experiences while composing, especially on certain occasions when they, after a long period of futile attempts, suddenly got the idea of how the music should be worked out. It was like a flash, a kind of creative ecstasy—suddenly everything seemed obvious, as if the music composed itself.

Musical cognition-emotion

This category contains statements about the music or the performance in 'subjective/ emotional' terms, for instance regarding the perceived emotional expression of the music (cf. Musical perception-cognition in Section 20.3.3 above).

20.3.5 Feelings/emotion

The SEM reports contained a large variety of feelings that we have sorted into four groups: Intense feelings, Positive feelings, Negative feelings, and Different (mixed, conflicting, changed) feelings.

Intense/powerful feelings

About 15 per cent of the subjects reported intense/powerful feelings in general: 'I had to close my eyes, it was such an enormous emotional experience'; 'An emotional charge that was about to blow us up'; 'Overwhelming waves of feelings that were thrown forth as reaction to the music'. It is thus the intensity and power of the evoked feelings that were emphasized, without mentioning any specific feeling.

Positive feelings

As could be expected, this is the largest group. Some kind of positive feelings were reported by 72 per cent of the respondents. Number and percentage of subjects reporting different positive feelings are shown in Table 20.2 in an approximate order from low to high arousal; feelings that are close in meaning are put together (e.g. peace, calm, harmony, stillness).

The by far most frequently mentioned feelings were joy, happiness, enjoyment, delight, sweetness, and beauty. They were often mentioned together in different combinations. (While beauty is usually thought of as a perceived quality of the music, it is clear that the respondents also used beauty as synonymous with enjoyment.) The next most frequently mentioned feelings were, on the one hand, low arousal feelings such as peace, calm, harmony, and stillness; and on the other hand high arousal feelings such as elation, excitement, tension, euphoria, intoxication, rapture, and ecstasy. Contentment, satisfaction, and gratitude were also frequently mentioned. The remaining feelings were reported less frequently, some of them rarely (humility, insignificance, solemnity, patriotism).

Table 20.2 Number and percentage of subjects reporting different positive feelings/emotions, ordered (approximately) from low to high arousal

Feeling/emotion	Number	%
Peace, calm, harmony, stillness	106	11.1
Safety, warmth	44	4.6
Humility, insignificance	9	0.9
Wonder, admiration, reverence, respect	31	3.3
Solemnity, patriotism	19	2.0
Contentment, satisfaction, gratitude	86	9.0
Enjoyment, delight, sweetness, beauty	260	27.3
Joy, happiness, bliss	370	38.8
Elation, excitement, tension	92	9.7
Love, sexual feelings	39	4.1
Perfection, everything fits	32	3.4
Feeling proud, powerful	31	3.3
Euphoria, as if intoxicated, rapture, ecstasy	80	8.4

Negative feelings

Negative feelings are by definition excluded from Maslow's concept of peak experience. However, some kind of negative feelings were reported by 23 per cent of our respondents. Most of these feelings were not particularly 'serious', and were usually not caused by the music itself but depended on associated circumstances, such as unhappy love, illness, loss of friends or parents, attempted suicide, or intolerant others. Number and percentage of subjects reporting different negative feelings/emotions are shown in Table 20.3.

The most frequently mentioned negative feelings were melancholy, unhappiness, and sadness, and feeling tired, faint, exhausted, and 'empty'. The latter feelings usually appeared just after the music had finished; the listeners had got such a strong experience that they felt 'totally gone'. Musicians who had invested all their energy in the performance felt exhausted (but may have felt happy as well).

The next most frequently mentioned negative feelings were confusion, nervousness, tension, and worry. Nervousness was mentioned especially by musicians just before their performance. The remaining feelings were reported less frequently, some of them rarely—for example, embarrassment/shame, which usually depended on the inability to conceal one's strong reactions in front of other people, and feeling lonely, abandoned, small or insignificant. To feel small/insignificant was also mentioned under Positive feelings. When feeling small/insignificant appears here under Negative feelings, this is because these feelings were mentioned in connection with expressions of feeling lonely and abandoned. When they are put under Positive feelings, they have

Table 20.3 Number and percentage of subjects reporting different negative feelings/emotions ordered (approximately) from low to high arousal

Feeling/emotion	Number	%
Feel tired, faint, exhausted, 'empty'	80	8.4
Feel lonely, abandoned, small, insignificant	6	0.6
Longing	9	0.9
Melancholy, unhappiness, sadness	82	8.6
Confusion, nervousness, tension, worry	52	5.5
Frustration, disappointment	14	1.5
Embarrassment, shame	14	1.5
Discomfort, (psychic) pain, envy, jealousy	30	3.1
Anxiety, fear, dread, despair	36	3.8
Anger, rage, hate	8	0.8
Shock, horror, terror, chaos, panic, unbearable	18	1.9

appeared in connection with the expression of humility, which is rather more positive than negative.

As mentioned above, only a minor part of the negative feelings were caused by the music itself. Musical elements eliciting negative feelings were usually a loud sound level, sharp/shrill timbre, and frequent dissonances (for examples, see Gabrielsson, 2008).

Different feelings (mixed, conflicting, changed)

Feelings may change during the course of the music. Different feelings follow each other, positive and negative feelings are mixed, negative feelings are replaced by positive feelings, etc. Some kind of mixed feelings were reported by 13 per cent of the subjects, changed feelings by 11 per cent.

Music associated with broken love may evoke bittersweet feelings as well as music associated with pleasant events in the past that may never appear again. Musicians' nervousness before a performance may successively be replaced by feelings of trust in one's ability, perhaps ending in happiness, even euphoria: 'we made it'. Afterwards they may feel tired and happy at the same time. There were several examples of how music may act as a therapeutic agent, turning negative feelings into positive ones. Still other examples of change from negative to positive feelings were found in reports of strong experiences of music during funerals.

Using music to affect one's mood

Many respondents reported that their SEM made them use the same music in the future to affect their mood, either by listening or performing the music or simply by imagining the music or the situation in which SEM occurred. The experience thus becomes a resource for the future. In fact, although we did not specifically ask for this, about 10 per cent of the respondents spontaneously reported that they use music to affect their mood. They have a selection of musical pieces designed for different situations, such as when tired after long work, when driving the car, when preparing for an examination, to get in the mood for a party, and the like. This is similar to findings in reports of the use of music in everyday life (DeNora, 2000; Juslin & Laukka, 2004; Laukka, 2007; North, Hargreaves, & O'Neill, 2000; Saarikallio, & Erkkilä, 2007; Öblad, 2000; see also Chapters 7 and 18, this volume).

20.3.6 Existential and transcendental aspects

Many SEM reports touched on questions of life, existence, and transcendental experiences.

Existential aspects

SEM may include reflections on the meaning of life and existence. The music may be felt as a mirror of life, its greatness as well as its transiency, its different phases, and its mixture of feelings: 'pain, sorrow, passion, joy—yes, everything, life, death, to exist as a human being'. It may lead to changed views of oneself, of other people, and of existence in general, and may give rise to action. Some respondents reported that just a few minutes of music radically changed their whole life.

SEM may also convey a sense of special presence in life, an intense feeling of living, just here, just now. On such rare occasions, the only thing that matters is simply to 'just be', to let all worries and 'musts' sink away and to enjoy the privilege of existing and receiving what the world and life may offer.

A variant of this are experiences described as 'ultimate', 'unrivalled', even 'sacred', moments in life, experiences of such strength and character that one cannot expect to experience them ever again—'it can't be better than this', 'now I can pass away happy'.

Some version of the above existential aspects was found in about 8 per cent of the respondents. The majority (about three-quarters) of these reports concerned the meaning of life/existence and changed views of oneself, of other people, and of existence in general.

Transcendental aspects

Experiences of transcendence have been sorted into five somewhat overlapping groups:

(a) Experiences characterized as extrasensory, magical, mysterious, occult, extraterrestrial, heavenly, or spiritual. The latter terms (heavenly, spiritual) may also refer to religious experiences, but are placed here when it is clear from the context that they don't refer to religious experiences; for instance: 'It was a spiritual experience without having anything to do with religion.'

(b) Experiences described as ecstasy or trance. These terms are used interchangeably by the respondents as well as by experts (see comments in Gabrielsson and Lindström Wik, 2003).

(c) 'Out-of-body' experiences or similar experiences, also earlier mentioned under Quasi-physical reactions.
(d) Cosmic experiences: experiences of infinity, timelessness, and eternity, or the experience of merging with something greater; merging with the universe.
(e) A neighbouring group of experiences of other worlds, other forms of existence.

Some version of the above transcendental aspects was found in close to 15 per cent of the respondents, about 5 per cent each for alternatives (a), (b), and (d + e). There were about ten reports of out-of-body experiences.

Religious experiences

Religious experiences may be considered a special class of transcendent experiences with the special characteristic that they involve a relation to a higher power, a god. Reports with religious contents have been sorted into five somewhat overlapping groups:

(a) Experiences of very general or vague religious character; for instance: 'I felt religious' or 'It was a religious experience.'
(b) Experiences including visions of heaven, an afterlife, paradise, or eternity.
(c) Experiences of special spiritual peace, a holy atmosphere, and/or a Christian community.
(d) Experiences of religious communication, either that the music conveys a religious message, or that one seeks contact with God through prayers or songs of praise.
(e) The strongest and most detailed reports of religious experiences appeared in descriptions of salvation and meetings with the divine—God, Jesus Christ, or the Holy Spirit.

Some kind of religious experiences in SEM was reported by about 11 per cent of the participants. Alternative (d), experiences of religious communication, was the most frequent, about twice as frequent as each of the other alternatives.

20.3.7 Personal and social aspects

Many respondents reported that SEM had important consequences for their personal development and quality of life.

New insights, possibilities, needs

SEM may provide new insights, open new possibilities, and arouse certain needs as exemplified in the following (partly overlapping) aspects, reported by 41 per cent of the respondents:

(a) The experience may provide new insights into oneself, into others, and into life in general. Latent thoughts and feelings may become apparent; it feels as if one is reaching one's innermost being.
(b) The experience makes the person feel free/liberated, inspired, refreshed, reborn, lifted, enriched, matured as a human being.

(c) The experience is described as an inner cleansing, release of pent-up feelings, catharsis, a healing experience.

(d) The experience may provide consolation, hope, relaxation, relief, power/energy, courage, a kick.

(e) The experience may make the person more open/unreserved. Usual defences and control mechanisms disappear, one feels ready to face new experiences without prejudices.

New insights, possibilities, and needs concerning music

Almost half of the participants (44 per cent) commented on consequences regarding their attitude and relationship to music:

(a) Most comments indicate that the person developed interest in a certain piece of music, a certain musical genre, or a certain composer or artist. One takes every possibility to listen to the music again, buy records, new sound equipment, attend concerts, etc.

(b) One gets increased interest and curiosity concerning music in general, a new view of what music can mean and how it can be used.

(c) The experience evokes a wish to learn how to perform music or to continue performing music more than ever before.

(d) About ten participants were inspired to compose music or write lyrics to songs.

(e) For about ten respondents, the experience resulted in a decision to choose music as a profession. Five of these respondents were still children at the time of the SEM, four were teenagers.

(f) One wants other people to realize what fantastic experiences may be brought about by music. About 30 participants thus wanted to tell other people about their SEM, perform music to them, inspire them to listen to music, encourage them to perform themselves, etc.

(g) As noted earlier, many respondents were inspired to use music to affect their mood or even to use music as a form of therapy for themselves.

In general, then, SEM provided a strong motivation to continue the relationship with music, in listening and/or performance (cf. Manturzewska, 1990; Sloboda, 2005, pp. 175–189).

Confirmation, self-actualization

To feel confirmed—accepted, understood, valued, needed, chosen—is a fundamental need for everyone. Music may be felt to reflect and confirm one's own person and/or make the listener feel chosen to receive the music. Moreover, performing music is a way of being seen and noticed, and may open new possibilities of expressing oneself. About 15 per cent of the participants commented on these questions:

(a) Most comments (about half) reported that the experience provided some kind of confirmation and increased self-confidence. Common examples are musicians whose performance was praised by the audience.

(b) Other comments reported that the music seemed to reflect one's personality, one's thoughts and feelings. One is not alone, 'there are others who think and feel in the same way as I do'.
(c) Still other comments indicated that the person feels especially chosen to receive the music, the music is directed just toward oneself. There may be many people around, but 'they played solely for me'.

Community, communication

There were frequent comments on music's ability to generate community and communication. Four aspects may be distinguished:

(a) Community among listeners (e.g. among listeners attending the same concert).
(b) Community among performers, either described by performers themselves or as observed by people watching the performers.
(c) Feeling of community/communication between listeners and performers was a strong component in many reports.
(d) A few respondents described a kind of boundless community, community with the whole of mankind.

Such comments were given by 18 per cent of the participants, with about equal distribution across alternatives (a), (b), and (c).

20.3.8 Some supplemental results

Most SEM (81 per cent) occurred during listening to music. The remaining ones (19 per cent) occurred during one's own performance of music or, in a few cases, while composing music. Most SEM (73 per cent) occurred with live music, the remaining 27 per cent with reproduced music (records, radio, television, etc.). The largest share of live music included folk music, religious music, and scenic (e.g. opera) music, whereas pop music had the largest share of reproduced music. More than half of the participants (54 per cent) had heard the music some time(s) earlier. This figure was higher (67 per cent) for the youngest participants (< 30 years) but lower (41 per cent) for the oldest participants (> 60 years). Most respondents did not get the same strong experience when they heard/played the same music again. Some respondents said that 'it was still a strong experience but not as much as then', others declared that 'this time there was no strong experience at all'. On the whole, SEM is not a frequent phenomenon. Most participants said that SEM may occur about once a year or less. Some respondents even reported that this was their only SEM so far.

There were no large differences between musicians' and non-musicians' descriptions of listening experiences. Musicians tend to use a few more technical terms, and their own experiences as musicians may be hinted at, but the basic features of the experience are very similar for both groups. In fact, some professionals pointed out that their usual analysis of the music and the performance seemed irrelevant in SEM—as one of them said: 'I just listened to the music.' More details and discussion of these results are given in Gabrielsson (2008).

20.3.9 SEM in performers

As pointed out above (Section 20.3.8), most SEM occurred while listening to music. This was true even for the participants who were musicians themselves. For professional musicians, listening experiences comprised 71 per cent of the cases, while 29 per cent occurred in connection with their own performance.

There are some aspects typical for SEM during one's own performance. Performers may feel that they suddenly 'understand' the music completely, are at one with the music. A young pianist, practising one of Bach's preludes and fugues, felt as if she was charged with Bach's spirit, and the music became self-evident. A singer practising Schumann's '*Mondnacht*' was suddenly 'within the song', as if he were standing in the moonlight, not performing the song but living in it; each tone meant something special and he understood everything.

Many performers report intense feelings in interaction with other performers, not least in improvisation. The opportunity to play together with more advanced musicians is highly rewarding, and inspires to further practice. Another important factor is audience response. Positive feedback from the audience inspires performers to still higher achievement, which increases audience feedback still more, and so forth.

Some performers' SEM occurred in situations in which they initially felt extremely nervous, but then successfully overcame their performance anxiety, resulting in extreme happiness and increased self-confidence. Others described performances in which they were overwhelmed by the expression in the music, and were unable to perform adequately, just simulated performing.

Maybe the strongest experiences occur in what many musicians call 'magic moments' when everything works. There are no problems whatsoever; it is as if somebody else takes care of the performance—'somebody is playing me', 'the music plays itself'—one feels as if one is a listener rather than a performer. Such experiences are real 'peaks', they compensate for all the hours spent in laborious practice, and provide strong motivation to continue performing.

Many reports include SEM while singing in a choir. The voice gets support and resonance from others, and it sounds better and louder than otherwise. One is part of something greater, sharing the expression and power that the choir may achieve. It may act as confirmation and may increase self-confidence, in combination with collective pride in the choir's achievements. Moreover, choir singing often generates close social relationships.

20.4 NOTE ON MUSIC IN SEM

Detailed description of what music appeared in the participants' SEM is given in Gabrielsson (2006, 2008). Some key findings are briefly summarized here.

About 1,300 examples of music were mentioned. While earlier studies (by Maslow, Panzarella, Laski) indicated that strong experiences were almost exclusively triggered by classical music, the present investigation indicates a much more diversified distribution, encompassing 16 categories as follows (numbers in parentheses indicate percentage of the total distribution):

Classical, non religious, music (30.6 per cent)
Religious music, mostly classical (15.6 per cent)
Scenic music (opera, operetta, musical; 6.6 per cent)
Folk music (5.7 per cent)
Jazz music (6.1 per cent)
Rock music (6.6 per cent)
Pop music (3.5 per cent)
Songs, tunes, hits, etc. (9.7 per cent)
Entertainment music (1.6)
Mixed genres (in popular music; 3.0 per cent)
Dance music (1.2 per cent)
Improvisation (0.7 per cent)
Certain artists (mostly classical; 3.2 per cent)
Music from other cultures (0.5 per cent)
Certain instruments (2.6 per cent)
Others, unspecified (2.8 per cent).

Using a still simpler division, one may say that 'classical' music (the first three categories plus Certain artists) occupies a little more than half of the total number, while 'non-classical' music (Folk music, Jazz, Rock, Pop, Songs/tunes, Mixed genres, Entertainment music, and Dance music) accounts for about 37 per cent. However, there are marked differences related to the participants' gender and age. Women have a higher representation of classical genres than men, whereas men have a higher representation of jazz and rock music than women. The older the participants, the more classical music; the younger the participants, the more pop, rock, and mixed genres. The largest difference is between older women (> 60 years) and younger men (< 30 years). For older women, classical music appears in 74.4 per cent of the cases compared to 29.6 per cent for younger men. On the other hand, common categories of 'popular' music (jazz, rock, pop and mixed genres) appear in 51.1 per cent of the cases for younger men, but only in 1.2 per cent for older women.

With regard to the participants' age at the time of SEM, 35.3 per cent of SEM occurred before 20 years of age, and 62.7 per cent before 30 years of age. These high values partly reflect the fact that almost a third of the participants were less than 30 years old. Detailed lists of composers, artists, and pieces of music are provided in Gabrielsson (2006), and, especially, Gabrielsson (2008). The latter reference also explores some relationships between musical genres and SEM reactions.

20.5 INFLUENCING FACTORS

Any experience of music depends on the interplay between three overall factors: the music, the person, and the situation. It is an illusion to believe that SEM depends solely on musical factors. The same piece of music may be experienced differently by different persons, and differently in different situations. It seems that there has to be a unique coincidence of 'the right music for the right person in the right situation' to elicit SEM. The following paragraphs provide a condensed review of influencing factors abstracted from Gabrielsson (2008).

20.5.1 Musical factors

Participants' opinions on what features in the music contributed to SEM revealed a variety of factors, extending from the impact of a single tone or chord to the piece as a whole. SEM may be related to, for instance, the timbre of an instrument or voice, intonation (perfect or special), sound level (loud or soft), dynamics, tempo, mode, rhythmic/melodic motives, harmonic progressions, themes, phrases, movements, text/lyrics, and various formal aspects—all these in specific ways in each individual case. Many respondents simply referred to the emotional expression of the music. Others referred to the qualities of the performance, such as the performers' skill and personal expression, their appearance, engagement, and charisma.

20.5.2 Personal factors

Many respondents emphasized that the reason for their SEM must be sought in themselves, and suggested a number of possible factors such as physical and mental condition (e.g. feeling well, relaxed, tired, depressed, ill), attitudes and expectations in relation to the music (e.g. open, curious, expectant, reserved, 'suspicious'), earlier experience (or not) of the same or similar pieces of music, and musical knowledge in general. Many also indicated that SEM occurred because they had reached a certain age or maturity: 'the time was ripe for such an experience'. Furthermore, many referred to heightened sensitivity during teenage years. Some suggested that they may have been longing for music that would reflect their thoughts and feelings, and thus serve as confirmation. Performers may have been eager to demonstrate their skill, to express themselves and gain appreciation and confirmation. Several respondents referred to characteristics of their personality (e.g. introvert–extrovert, optimistic–pessimistic), or to the influence of cultural, political, and religious attitudes. Last but not least, the music may have been associated with emotionally significant persons or events (e.g. love relationships, important other persons, exotic places, war, and death).

20.5.3 Situational factors, physical and social

It seems that SEM may occur in any place or at any time. In this study, the most common places were at home, in churches, concert halls, assembly halls, and outdoors, but there were many other places mentioned as well, even such as hospitals, hotels, shops, workrooms, and military camps.

The acoustical conditions may be very influential, such as good diffusion of sound and appropriate reverberation. To feel surrounded by the music was mentioned as an important aspect. Visual impressions were generally important as well, especially regarding the appearance of performers and audience (if any).

Instances of SEM extended over almost 100 years, from 1908 to 2004, and the respondents were affected by what music was heard or performed at different times during this epoch in Sweden. Other time aspects concerned SEM during different seasons of the year and different times of day or night, the latter often associated with how awake or tired the respondent felt. Some reports indicated that the borderland between wakefulness and sleep may be favourable for intense experiences. Music on the radio during the night has brought relief and support to persons in difficult situations.

There were three possible social situations represented in the reports (the respective percentages appear in parentheses): being alone (19 per cent), together with acquaintances (68 per cent), or together with unknown people (12 per cent). In most cases, then, SEM occurred in the presence of other people. Their attitudes and reactions may enhance one's own reaction; for example, one subject remarked that 'if I were there quite alone listening to the artist, it wouldn't be the same thing at all'. On the other hand, the presence of others may restrict one's reactions, for instance, conceal any visible reaction that may reveal one's strong feelings. In solitude, however, one can let one's feelings and reactions come out uninhibited.

20.5.4 Interplay of music, person, and situation

It is obvious that reactions in SEM depend on the interaction between musical, personal, and situational factors (the latter two are sometimes indistinguishable). Their influence varies from case to case, but none of them can ever be excluded. Even in reports where musical factors appear to be strong determinants, there are usually influences from other factors as well. In many cases, personal and/or situational factors are more important than the music—for instance, if a piece of music is associated with war, with happy or unhappy love, with beautiful nature, with certain ceremonies, etc. Scherer et al (2002) likewise found a highly varying mixture of influencing factors (see Section 20.1).

20.6 DISCUSSION

Reactions in SEM are of many different kinds: physical, quasi-physical, perceptual, cognitive, and emotional. They may also involve existential, transcendental, and religious aspects, and have important personal and social consequences. The SEM Descriptive System (SEM-DS) is an attempt to represent this multitude of reactions in a condensed form. It should be noted, however, that it represents accumulated evidence from some

950 respondents. Any single SEM report does not contain more than a fraction of the complete system. Yet each report represents a unique music experience that ought to be read in its whole in order to grasp the background and essence of the experience. Some 50 reports have been translated into English and published in Gabrielsson (2001, 2002), Gabrielsson and Lindström (1993, 1995), and Gabrielsson & Lindström Wik (2000, 2003). More than 500 reports appear in the most complete presentation of the project (Gabrielsson, 2008).

SEM-DS is no 'final' description. It is a proposal, subject to continuous modification and refinement. Many of its different aspects agree with the criteria for peak experiences proposed by Maslow (1968, 1976), and with results presented in Panzarella (1980), Laski (1961), Privette and Landsman (1983), and Scherer et al (2002).However, SEM-DS is far more complete and based upon a much larger number of respondents and reports than in previous work.

The present reports vary much with regard to what aspects are emphasized. Focus may be on any aspect(s) in SEM-DS, such as perceptual aspects (e.g. timbre, intensified perception), cognitive aspects (e.g. loss of control, changed relation to music, imagery), feelings/emotions (mostly positive, sometimes negative), existential aspects (e.g. meaning of life), transcendental aspects (e.g. cosmic experience, experience of other worlds), religious aspects (e.g. meeting the divine), personal aspects (e.g. new insights, confirmation of identity), or various combinations of different aspects. SEM-DS offers a convenient way of comparing different kinds of strong experiences, and can be used for comparisons with results from investigations on music in daily life (see references at the very end of Section 20.3.5).

Feelings/emotions are the most frequently reported components in our SEM reports. There are, however, reports in which feelings/emotions are not mentioned at all. This does not necessarily mean that they were absent, but rather that the respondent's focus was on other aspects. Furthermore, feelings/emotions are frequently interwoven with cognitive or perceptual-cognitive aspects. Most of the aspects listed under Cognition (Table 20.1) have emotional connotations. For example, changed experience of body and mind, or of time and space undoubtedly include feelings, although it may be hard to tell precisely which ones. There are likewise feelings involved in other cognition categories, such as loss of control, changed relation to the music, associations/memories, and imagery. Experiences of existential and transcendental character also involve strong feelings, not to mention religious experiences. Many personal aspects reported as consequences of the experience are described in terms of feelings, for instance feeling liberated, inspired, relieved, uplifted, or feeling confirmed in one's identity. Generally, our respondents' reports of their experiences often defy common technical terminology and classification in psychology—at least until we arrive at more precise definitions of central concepts such as perception, cognition, and emotion and their internal relationships.

In the account of feelings/emotions (Section 20.3.5) positive and negative feelings were tentatively ordered with regard to activation level, in accordance with the valence-arousal or 'circumplex' model (Russell, 1980). This model is appropriate for surveying a large number of feelings/emotions in a condensed way, and offers a convenient alternative for the present descriptive purposes. However, this should not be understood as taking a stand in the discussion regarding different theories on emotion. In fact, retrospective accounts of feelings/emotions can hardly be unambiguously used as arguments for any of the competing theories of emotion. Further comments on these questions, as well as on the validity of retrospective reports and autobiographical memories, are given in Gabrielsson (2001) and Gabrielsson and Lindström Wik (2003).

Strong experiences are, of course, not unique to music. Our participants indicated that they had strong experiences in many other contexts, for instance in nature, love, religion, literature, art, theatre, film, sex, and others (Gabrielsson, 2008). Best known are numerous examples of mystical experience investigated in the psychology of religion (e.g. Geels, 1991; James, 1902/1985; Stace, 1960), which show many reactions similar to those reported in peak experience (Maslow, 1968), ecstasy (Laski, 1961), and SEM. A survey of related empirical studies on religious experience is given in Lindström Wik (2001). Becker (2004) surveyed trance experience in different cultures, especially religious institutionalized trancing. She used the term 'deep listeners', that is, 'persons who are profoundly moved, perhaps even to tears, by simply listening to a piece of music' (p. 2), and regarded deep listening as 'a kind of secular trancing, divorced from religious practice but often carrying religious sentiments such as feelings of transcendence or a sense of communion with a power beyond oneself' (p. 2; see also Chapter 6, this volume).

Strong experiences with music are sometimes seen as examples of aesthetic experience (e.g. Panzarella, 1980). However, this concept is notoriously hard to define (see also Chapter 22, this volume), and none of our participants referred to aesthetic experience. Konečni (2005, 2008) regards aesthetic experience as a trinity of awe, being moved, and thrills, with aesthetic awe as the central component. Furthermore, music may become sublime and induce aesthetic awe 'only when it is performed in vast architectural spaces with superb acoustics' (Konečni, 2008, p. 124), for instance in European mediaeval cathedrals. There are a few experiences in our material that approach this condition. However, whether or not one accepts Konečni's definition, or any other definition of aesthetic experience, it would only apply to a minority of the experiences in our collection of SEM reports.

Strong experiences, whatever the domain, are not a common topic in mainstream psychology, nor in music psychology. They are a relatively rare phenomenon, but may be of profound importance for the individual, as reported both in this chapter (e.g. Section 20.3.7) and in previous studies (Section 20.1). It is urgent, therefore, that they be given much more attention in psychology than hitherto, using a variety of approaches. Experimental procedures may be used to find out what features in the musical structure are related to different aspects of SEM (cf. Sloboda, 1991, and similar studies in Section 20.1). However, strong experiences may depend as much on personal and situational factors that lie outside experimental control. Continued research on strong experiences should apply a flexible interplay between naturalistic and experimental approaches in order to combine their respective advantages and compensate for their respective drawbacks. It is my conviction that free phenomenological report is an indispensable component in this work.[1]

[1] My sincere thanks to Siv Lindström Wik and other co-workers for many years of continuous analysis and discussion of the SEM material. This research was supported by The Bank of Sweden Tercentenary Foundation and The Royal Swedish Academy of Music.

RECOMMENDED FURTHER READING

1. Becker, J. (2004). *Deep listeners. Music, emotion and trancing.* Bloomington, IN: Indiana University Press.
2. Whaley, J., Sloboda, J. A., & Gabrielsson, A. (2009). Peak experiences in music. In S. Hallam, I. Cross, & M. Thaut (eds), *Oxford handbook of music psychology* (pp. 452–61). Oxford: Oxford University Press.
3. Rouget, G. (1985). *Music and trance. A theory of the relations between music and possession.* Chicago, IL: Chicago University Press.

REFERENCES

Becker, J. (2004). *Deep listeners. Music, emotion and trancing.* Bloomington, IN: Indiana University Press.

Boyd, J., & George-Warren, H. (1992). *Musicians in tune.* New York: Simon & Schuster.

Csikszentmihalyi, M. (1990). *Flow. The psychology of optimal experience.* New York: Harper & Row.

DeNora, T. (2000). *Music in everyday life.* Cambridge, UK: Cambridge University Press.

Gabrielsson, A. (1989). Intense emotional experiences of music. In *Proceedings of the First International Conference on Music Perception and Cognition* (pp. 371–6). Kyoto, Japan: The Japanese Society of Music Perception and Cognition.

Gabrielsson, A. (2001). Emotions in strong experiences with music. In P. N. Juslin & J. A. Sloboda (eds), *Music and emotion: Theory and research* (pp. 431–49). Oxford: Oxford University Press.

Gabrielsson, A. (2002). Old people's remembrance of strong experiences related to music. *Psychomusicology, 18,* 103–22.

Gabrielsson, A. (2006). Strong experiences elicited by music—What music? In P. Locher, C. Martindale, & L. Dorfman (eds), *New directions in aesthetics, creativity, and the psychology of art* (pp. 251–67). Amityville, NY: Baywood.

Gabrielsson, A. (2008). *Starka musikupplevelser—Musik är mycket mer är mycket mer än bara musik [Strong experiences with music—Music is much more than just music].* Hedemora, Sweden: Gidlunds.

Gabrielsson, A., & Juslin, P. N. (2003). Emotional expression in music. In R. J. Davidson, K. R. Scherer, & H. H. Goldsmith (eds), *Handbook of affective sciences* (pp. 503–34). Oxford: Oxford University Press.

Gabrielsson, A., & Lindström, E. (2001). The influence of musical structure on emotional expression. In P. N. Juslin & J. A. Sloboda (eds), *Music and emotion: Theory and research* (pp. 223–48). Oxford: Oxford University Press.

Gabrielsson, A., & Lindström, S. (1993). On strong experiences of music. *Musikpsychologie. Jahrbuch der Deutschen Gesellschaft für Musikpsychologie, 10,* 118–39.

Gabrielsson, A., & Lindström, S. (1995). Can strong experiences of music have therapeutic implications? In R. Steinberg (ed.), *Music and the mind machine. The psychophysiology and psychopathology of the sense of music* (pp. 195–202). New York: Springer.

Gabrielsson, A., & Lindström Wik, S. (2000). Strong experiences of and with music. In D. Greer (ed.), *Musicology and sister disciplines: Past, present and future* (pp 100–8). Oxford: Oxford University Press.

Gabrielsson, A., & Lindström Wik, S. (2003). Strong experiences related to music: A descriptive system. *Musicae Scientiae, 7*, 157–217.

Geels, A. (1991). *Att möta Gud i kaos. Religiösa visioner i dagens Sverige [Meeting God in chaos. Religious visions in Sweden of today]*. Stockholm, Sweden: Norstedts.

Goldstein, A. (1980). Thrills in response to music and other stimuli. *Physiological Psychology, 8*, 126–9.

James, W. (1902/1985). *The varieties of religious experience*. Harmondsworth, UK: Penguin Books.

Juslin, P. N., & Laukka, P. (2004). Expression, perception, and induction of musical emotions: A review and a questionnaire study of everyday listening. *Journal of New Music Research, 33*, 217–38.

Konečni, V. J. (2005). The aesthetic trinity: Awe, being moved, thrills. *Bulletin of Psychology and the Arts, 5*, 27–44.

Konečni, V. J. (2008). Does music induce emotion? A theoretical and methodological analysis. *Psychology of Aesthetics, Creativity, and the Arts, 2*, 115–29.

Konečni, V. J., Wanic, R. A., & Brown, A. (2007). Emotional and aesthetic antecedents and consequences of music-induced thrills. *American Journal of Psychology, 120*, 619–43.

Laski, M. (1961). *Ecstasy. A study of some secular and religious experiences*. London: Cresset.

Laukka, P. (2007). Uses of music and psychological well-being among the elderly. *Journal of Happiness Studies, 8*, 215–41.

Lindström Wik, S. (2001). *Strong experiences related to music and their connection to religious experience*. Licentiate thesis, Department of Psychology, Uppsala University.

Lowis, M. J. (1998). Music and peak experiences: An empirical study. *The Mankind Quarterly, 39*, 203–24.

Manturzewska, M. (1990). A biographical study of the life-span development of professional musicians. *Psychology of Music, 18*, 112–39.

Maslow, A. H. (1954). *Motivation and personality*. New York: Harper.

Maslow, A. H. (1968). *Toward a psychology of being* (2nd edn). New York: Van Nostrand Reinhold.

Maslow, A. H. (1976). *The farther reaches of human nature*. New York: Penguin Books.

North, A. C., Hargreaves, D. J., & O'Neill, S. A. (2000). The importance of music to adolescents. *British Journal of Educational Psychology, 70*, 255–72.

Öblad, C. (2000). *Att använda musik—om bilen som konsertlokal (Using music—The car as concert hall)*. Publications from Department of Musicology, Gothenburg University, no. 63.

Panzarella, R. (1980). The phenomenology of aesthetic peak experiences. *Journal of Humanistic Psychology, 20*, 69–85.

Panksepp, J. (1995). The emotional sources of 'chills' induced by music. *Music Perception, 13*, 171–207.

Privette, G. (1983). Peak experience, peak performance, and flow: A comparative analysis of positive human experiences. *Journal of Personality and Social Psychology, 45*, 1361–8.

Privette, G., & Bundrick, C. M. (1987). Measurement of experience: Construct and content validity of the experience questionnaire. *Perceptual and Motor Skills, 65*, 315–32.

Privette, G., & Landsman, T. (1983). Factor analysis of peak performance: the full use of potential. *Journal of Personality and Social Psychology, 44*, 195–200.

Russell, J. A. (1980). A circumplex model of affect. *Journal of Personality and Social Psychology, 39*, 1161–78.

Saarikallio, S., & Erkkilä, J. (2007). The role of music in adolescents' mood regulation. *Psychology of Music, 35*, 88–109.

Scherer, K. R., Zentner, M. R., & Schacht, A. (2002). Emotional states generated by music: an exploratory study of music experts. *Musicae Scientiae, Special issue 2001–2*, 149–71.

Sloboda, J. A. (1991). Music structure and emotional response: Some empirical findings. *Psychology of Music, 19*, 110–20.

Sloboda, J. A. (2005). *Exploring the musical mind: Cognition, emotion, ability, function.* Oxford: Oxford University Press.

Stace, W. T. (1960). *Mysticism and philosophy.* New York: Lippincott.

Whaley, J., Sloboda, J. A., & Gabrielsson, A. (2009). Peak experiences in music. In S. Hallam, I. Cross, & M. Thaut (eds), *The Oxford handbook of music psychology* (pp. 452–61) Oxford: Oxford University Press.

CHAPTER 21

MUSICAL EXPECTANCY AND THRILLS

DAVID HURON AND ELIZABETH HELLMUTH MARGULIS

21.1 INTRODUCTION

IN the history of scholarship pertaining to music and emotion, the phenomenon of *expectation* has occupied a central and perhaps privileged position. The traditional emphasis on expectation may be traced in part to some of the unique properties of music compared with other arts. Commentators have suggested that in many arts, emotions are evoked through stylized depictions or representations of common emotional displays (e.g. Aiken, 1998). In arts such as portraiture, sculpture, drama, film, mime, and dance, human body language and facial expressions may evoke, portray, or suggest particular affective states. While music sometimes contains representational elements, philosophers and music commentators have long recognized that music is not a representational art in the way that painting or sculpture can be.

Nevertheless, throughout history, music has frequently been described as the most 'emotional' of the arts. Next to conversation with a close friend, music is the most commonly sought catalyst when people want to change moods (Thayer, 1996). Whether people seek joyful animation or sad nostalgia, music is often the art of choice.

Paradoxically, music achieves its affective power through seemingly abstract tone sequences, largely devoid of representational content. What accounts for music's success in evoking emotions when its capabilities for representing the natural world seem so constrained?

A possible answer to this question begins with the recognition that music consists of a sequence of sound events that unfold in time.[1] The foremost dimension available to musicians is the temporal dimension. While other elements of music may play important emotional roles, a number of scholars have understood that the psychology of time plays a paramount role in musical experience (Jones, 1976). Temporally rooted phenomena such as anticipation, surprise, and delay underlie important aspects of musically evoked affect.

The idea that time is a central element in emotion contrasts starkly with mainstream research in the psychology of emotion. Until recently, emotion research has been unduly consumed with facial expression. The psychology of emotion's preoccupation with visual stimuli has been accompanied by a corresponding neglect of the role of time. But time permits a listener to engage with a stimulus in an active, predictive way, allowing for dynamic fluctuations in affective responses.

In this chapter, we provide an overview of contemporary and historical research on music and expectation. We describe some of the functional biology involved in prospective cognition, review common experimental methods used in expectation research, summarize some of the pertinent neuroanatomy and physiology, discuss some of the mechanisms by which expectations are thought to be acquired, and identify some of the affective consequences of expectation. In addition, we summarize some of the main theories of musical expectation, including theories by Meyer, Narmour, Margulis, and Huron. The chapter ends with an extended discussion of the phenomenon of music-induced *frisson*—the 'chills' or 'thrills' characterized by a sensation of the hair standing up on the back of one's neck, accompanied by sensations of coldness and pleasure.

21.2 BIOLOGICAL ORIGINS

A number of authors (Hawkins & Blakeslee, 2004; Huron, 2006; Raichle et al, 2000; Suddendorf, 2005) have drawn attention to the biological importance of expectation. The ability to foretell the future confers obvious survival benefits even when the predicted future is just seconds away. The mental aptitude to form expectations is widely assumed to be a product of evolution by natural selection. That is, our predictive faculties arose through efforts over millions of years to produce organisms capable of clairvoyance and prophecy.

The adaptive value of accurate expectation is evident in the speed of behavioural responses. Innumerable reaction-time studies have shown that people respond to stimuli more quickly when the stimulus is more predictable (e.g. Aarden, 2002;

---

[1] These issues have been explored in relation to other temporal art forms, such as film. See, for example, Aumont et al (2002).

Bharucha & Stoeckig, 1986; Bigand & Pineau, 1997; Margulis & Levine, 2006; Tillman, Bigand, & Pineau, 1998). For example, when asked to indicate whether pitches go up or down, listeners are faster to respond when the melodic contours conform to their expectations (Aarden, 2003). In general, anticipating events buys an organism additional time—time to prepare.

21.3 THE NATURE OF MUSICAL EXPECTATIONS

Prediction is so important for survival that evolution appears to have created more than one predictive mechanism. One way that organisms prepare for the future is by mentally enacting different future scenarios through the process of *imagination* (Wilson & Gilbert, 2005). Imagining future scenarios is not limited to humans. In running a maze, the brain areas associated with different spatial trajectories are activated when a mouse pauses to consider its options (Johnson & Redish, 2007). That is, the neural regions associated with different pathways are active, suggesting that the stationary mouse is imagining different routes.

Other predictive mechanisms are more automatic and require no active contemplation. When listening to a familiar playlist of songs, for example, listeners typically anticipate the beginning of the next song in the playlist as the current song ends. This familiar experience occurs even when the relationship between successive songs is entirely arbitrary. That is, listeners can learn to anticipate future sounds, even when there is no musical principle or structural relationship connecting the two events.

21.3.1 Statistical learning

More formal demonstrations of this effect have been made by Jenny Saffran, Richard Aslin, and their collaborators. In a classic experiment, Saffran et al (1999) constructed small musical 'vocabularies' consisting of six three-note 'figures'. Using these figures, they then constructed long tone sequences in which the six figures were played repeated in random order. The tone sequences were constrained so that the same figure was never presented twice in succession. They then exposed eight-month old infants to this isochronous tone sequence for up to 20 minutes. Infants heard a steady stream of pitches with no grouping cues to indicate that the sequences had been constructed out of three-note figures. Following this exposure phase, the infants heard pairs of three-note figures. Using a head-turning paradigm, Saffran and her colleagues demonstrated that the infants had abstracted the three-note figures from the original vocabulary used to construct the tone sequences. Experimental controls allowed Saffran and her colleagues to conclude that the infant responses had nothing to do with the structure of the figures and related only to their familiarity.

Over the past decade, a considerable volume of experimental research has accumulated supporting this phenomenon of statistical learning. Listeners learn to anticipate sequences of sounds merely through exposure; they anticipate most strongly the sound sequences to which they have been most frequently exposed.

These learned expectations are limited to prospective rather than retrospective relationships between stimuli. For example, listening to the beginning of one song does not typically help a listener recall the end of the previous song on a familiar playlist. That is, expectations move forward in time. From a biological perspective, this limitation makes sense, since the goal of expectation is to prepare an organism for the future, not the past.

Statistical learning is evident in many aspects of music listening. In Western music, duple and quadruple meters are more commonplace than triple meters. Consistent with this, Brochard et al (2003) have shown that listeners exhibit a binary meter bias. Similarly, nearly three-quarters of Western music is in the major mode. Consistent with this, Huron (2006) has noted that listeners assume unfamiliar works to be in major keys.

In many ways, the statistical nature of these automatic expectations should not be surprising. When predicting future events, a straightforward strategy is to predict the recurrence of the most common past event, including the most common contingencies (X typically occurs in context Y). Notice that if expectations arise from commonly occurring sound patterns, then the main factor influencing expectation is the listener's sonic environment. Because listeners have different listening backgrounds, predictability must be listener specific. Nevertheless, since listeners in a given culture are exposed to broadly similar acoustical environments, they will probably acquire broadly similar expectations. Since musicians cannot afford to tailor musical works for a specific individual listener, only the culturally shared forms of predictability are available in the musician's psychological tool kit.

21.3.2 Mental representations for expectation

The mental representation for prospective knowledge remains an open area of research. In describing expectation-related knowledge, researchers have appealed to a variety of concepts, including *paradigms*, *scripts*, and *heuristic rules*. Whatever the nature of prospective knowledge, experimental evidence suggests that the knowledge listeners have of future events represents imperfect approximations of objective patterns.

An example of such an imperfect approximation can be found in the phenomenon Leonard Meyer famously referred to as 'gap fill'—what von Hippel referred to as 'post-skip reversal'. Post-skip reversal is the notion that listeners expect a large interval to be followed by a change of direction. This pattern can be observed in music all around the world. The majority of large melodic leaps are indeed followed by a change of direction. However, this pattern is known to be an artefact of a well-known statistical behaviour, *regression to the mean*. If we encounter a tall person on the street, the next person we encounter is likely to be shorter. But the presence of the tall person did not *cause* a shorter person to appear. The operative principle is that most people are of average height. Similarly, high pitches are likely to be followed by pitches closer to the average pitch. Since large melodic intervals will tend to move a melody away from the central pitch region, large melodic intervals will tend to be followed by a change of direction. However, the large interval does not *cause* this reversal. Instead, the operative principle is that most pitches in a melody are of average pitch height. Using large samples of music from five continents and spanning six centuries, Von Hippel and Huron (2000) provided a formal statistical demonstration of regression to the mean in the case of music. There is no objective tendency for large intervals to be followed by a change of direction apart from regression to the mean.

However, subsequent experiments carried out by von Hippel (2002) and by Aarden (2003) showed that Western-enculturated listeners expect post-skip reversal rather than regression to the mean. Listeners with musical training do not expect ensuing pitches to be closer to the average pitch. Instead, they expect large leaps to be followed by a change of direction. For this particular pitch pattern, listeners have acquired an expectation that is an imperfect approximation of the pattern evident in real music. Meyer's notion of 'gap fill' is an appropriate description of listener psychology, but an erroneous description of objective musical organization: 'gap fill' exists in listeners' heads, not in musical scores. Other examples of such imperfect heuristic expectations are documented in Huron (2006).

21.3.3 Memory

In recent years, psychologists have become more cognizant of the importance of predictive brain mechanisms. Hawkins and Blakeslee (2004) emphasize that 'prediction is not just one of the things your brain does, it's the primary thing . . . the cortex is an organ of prediction' (p. 89). Suddendorf (2006) characterizes the capacity to anticipate the future as a transformative step in human evolution. Raichle and Gusnard (2005) suggest that anticipation is a primary component of the *default mode*, the pattern of neural activity that occurs when the mind is not engaged in any particular task (Bar et al, 2007).

The concept of the predictive brain has transformed thinking in many areas of psychology, notably core research in memory. For much of the past century, memory has been conceived of as a sort of storage system akin to a library—something like a repository of past experiences. Yet in recent decades, researchers have recognized that the adaptive purpose of memory must be prospective rather than retrospective. From a biological perspective, memory would be useless unless it helped future behaviours to be more adaptive (Huron, 2006).

The role of memory in prospective cognition is evident, for example, in the process of imagination (mentioned earlier). Recent research has shown that memory provides the database for simulating future scenarios. For example, patients suffering from amnesia due to hippocampal damage show specific impairments when imagining scenarios such as a day at the beach or a shopping trip (Hassabis, Kumaran, Vann, & Maguire, 2007). In contemplating the future, remembered events are woven together to create plausible future storylines. Addis, Wong, and Schacter (2007) argue, for example, that 'future thinking' is 'an important, if not the primary, function of episodic memory' (p. 1374).

The idea that the biological function of memory must be prospective rather than retrospective suggests that the classic distinctions between various forms of memory (e.g. semantic memory, episodic memory, working memory, etc.) are better thought of as different forms of expectation. This idea was first advanced for music by Jamshed Bharucha (1994), who distinguished schematic from veridical expectations and linked them to long-term and episodic memory respectively.

Bharucha suggested that knowledge of how a particular musical work goes is a different sort of knowledge from knowledge of how music in general goes. Both types of knowledge are omnipresent in listening. That is, when anticipating the unfolding of events in a musical work, our expectations are informed not just by (possible) familiarity with the work, but by familiarity with a musical language. These independent parallel processes help to explain a classic problem in musical expectation, sometimes referred to as *Wittgenstein's puzzle* (Dowling & Harwood, 1986): How is it possible that a deceptive cadence can continue to sound deceptive even though a listener's familiarity with the work means that the deception is entirely expected? According to Bharucha's view, schematic expectations (reflecting how music in general goes) remain surprised, even though veridical expectations (reflecting how this work goes) remain unsurprised.

Further conceptual developments can be expected as psychologists reinterpret the huge memory literature in light of the prospective functioning of memory. All memory research will need to be reinterpreted in terms of the question 'How does this memory phenomenon assist an organism by creating future adaptive behaviours?'

21.4 AFFECTIVE CONSEQUENCES OF EXPECTATION

In tandem with this reconception of memory, there has been a parallel reconception of emotion and motivation systems. In the past, affective neuroscientists focused on the pleasures associated with achieving particular desirable outcomes (such as food, warmth, companionship, etc.). The hormone and neurotransmitter dopamine, for example, has long been viewed as the brain's principal reward system,[2] and until recently was thought

---

[2] An alternative theory attributes dopamine release to increases in arousal and motivation (see Horvitz, 2000).

to reward particular outcomes. However, researchers now regard the hedonic effects of dopamine as linked to the experience of seeking/expectation rather than to the pleasure of consumption/satiety (e.g. Panksepp, 1998). For example, dopamine is released as the moment approaches when an animal receives a reward (e.g. food, water, sex, play object). But when the reward is received or consumption begins, dopamine levels drop. When the dopamine system is destroyed, an animal may die of hunger, even when food is plentiful, and even though eating the food will be pleasurable—simply because the animal is not motivated to eat (Panksepp, 1998). The dopamine deficiency characteristic of Parkinson's disease robs individuals of their will.

Dopamine appears to reward *wanting* or *expectation*, not consummation. The role of dopamine is apparent in the effects of exogenous drugs (like cocaine) that emulate the effect of endogenous dopamine. These drugs do not simply result in a blissful stupor. Instead, they cause users to feel a strong sense of pleasurable engagement—of energy, focus, purpose, drive, zest, or concentration. The positive feelings evoked by consumption involve different hedonic systems.

Like a driver seeking a filling station, the feeling of wanting must occur well before the fuel is actually needed. (If organisms got hungry only when glucose levels approached 'empty', then more animals would die of hunger.) In short, all feelings of want, desire, anticipation, drive, or interest (such as feelings like hunger or curiosity) are future-oriented affects intended to promote specific future-adapative outcomes. The most important brain rewards are not those that reward the acquisition of particular resources, but those that reward striving for those resources.

21.5 PREDICTION EFFECT

Another example of reinterpreting the emotional literature in light of prospective brain operations can be found in the so-called 'mere exposure effect' (Moreland & Zajonc, 1977). In 1903, Max Meyer demonstrated that listeners show increased liking for a musical work as they become increasingly familiar with it. Throughout the twentieth century, a large volume of research accrued consistent with a preference for familiar stimuli (for a review, see Bornstein, 1989).

However, Huron (2006) argues that the empirical research has been misinterpreted. Huron proposed that accurate prediction is so essential for survival that brains must have special structures that motivate (reward) accurate prediction. Rather than a preference for familiarity, he argues that the experimental evidence is more consistent with a 'prediction effect', where the rewards for accurate prediction are misattributed to expected stimuli. Listeners prefer familiar stimuli not because they are familiar, but because they are predictable. In Huron (2006), this suggestion is used to explain many music-related feelings, such as the increased satisfaction associated with ending on a cadential tonic rather than the leading tone.

21.6 EXPERIMENTAL METHODS IN
EXPECTATION RESEARCH

Expectations can take various forms and trigger various consequences. Accordingly, the methodologies used to investigate them vary widely. Broadly speaking, investigators can take an explicit or implicit approach in collecting data. Explicit approaches require the listener to directly report his or her expectations; implicit approaches uncover them more obliquely. Implicit approaches are generally preferred because they minimize demand characteristics—in which the behaviour of experimental participants is influenced by their own hypotheses about the purpose of the experiment (see Chapter 10, this volume).

21.6.1 Explicit approaches

One type of explicit approach involves asking participants to perform continuations after hearing an initial musical fragment or prime. Carlsen (1981) and Lake (1987) asked participants to sing continuations following melodic primes. Schmuckler (1989) asked pianists to perform continuations on a keyboard, and Larson (2002) asked music theorists to notate melodic continuations to a given antecedent. Performed completion tasks rely on musically sophisticated participants, and so the results may not be generalizable to a wider population. Performed completion tasks may also introduce production constraints (such as range limitations in the voice) that are not necessarily related to expectations. However, performed completion tasks have the benefit of allowing participants to respond with indefinitely long continuations. Since many other research methods artificially limit responses to a single consequent tone, performed continuations can provide valuable information about the scope of musical expectations.

Another explicit approach builds on the probe-tone methodology pioneered by Roger Shepard and Carol Krumhansl (1979). In probe-tone experiments, participants hear many repetitions of the same contextual passage, each one followed by a different probe. Listeners rate how well the probe fits the preceding context (e.g. Cuddy & Lunney, 1995; Krumhansl & Kessler, 1982; Schellenberg, 1996; Schmuckler, 1989). An advantage of probe-tone experiments is that they allow investigators to collect data about many potential continuations. However, since the probe-tone methodology involves stopping or interrupting the musical flow, it has been suggested that the responses are confounded with judgements about the suitability of a tone for terminating a phrase.

A third explicit approach, the betting paradigm, was used by von Hippel, Huron, and Harnish (1998). Participants heard antecedent passages and were invited to bet on the likeliest continuations. This methodology allows the subjective probabilities for different continuations to be assessed, but proceeds slowly (on average participants took three minutes to place their bets for each melodic note) and thus places high demands on the attention and stamina of participants.

21.6.2 Implicit approaches

An early implicit approach involved participants listening to tones presented alongside a continuous loud noise, and indicating whether or not they heard a tone (Greenberg & Larkin, 1968). Listeners were better able to detect a tone if it was expected. A series of subsequent studies used reaction time to illuminate expectations inaccessible to explicit report; listeners respond faster to expected continuations. Bharucha and Stoeckig (1986), Bigand and Pineau (1997), and Tillman, Bigand, and Pineau (1998) show this effect for harmonic sequences, and Aarden (2002) and Margulis and Levine (2006) adapt this approach to the study of melodies.

Perhaps the most commonly used implicit approach for the study of expectation involves event-related potentials (ERPs). ERPs entail measurement of electromagnetic activity produced by large collections of neurons, as measured on the scalp (for a review, see Besson, 1997). Different ERP features are known to be associated with various behavioural outcomes. For example, surprising events such as a musically incongruous out-of-key ending evoke distinctive ERPs (Besson & Macar, 1987; Verleger, 1990). These responses differ depending on the extent of a listener's prior musical training (Besson & Faïta, 1995; Koelsch, Schmidt, & Kansok, 2002). Useful ERP data can be collected even when listeners ignore the music and concentrate on another task (Koelsch, Schroger, & Gunter, 2002). Schön and Besson (2005) used ERPs to provide important evidence for the potential modularity of some aspects of music processing. They examined ERPs in musicians as they listened to music while viewing the score. Incongruous events elicited a late positive component (LPC) even when they were notated in the score, and thus known in advance to the listener. This finding is consistent with the idea that musical processing may involve some degree of informational encapsulation—the ear does not always know what the eye sees.

Other implicit methods include metabolic measurements, such as heart rate and skin conductance. Steinbeis, Koelsch, and Sloboda (2006), for example, found electrodermal activity and heart rate changes at moments that were harmonically unexpected. Additionally, head-turning paradigms have been used to study expectations in infants and non-human animals (cf. Weiss, Zelazo & Swain, 1988).

21.7 THEORETICAL APPROACHES TO EXPECTATION IN MUSIC

The subject of musical expectation has attracted sustained interest from both experimental psychologists and music theorists. Nearly all psychologists working in the field of music cognition have carried out experiments that bear directly on the issue of expectation. This includes work by Mireille Besson, Jamshed Bharucha, Emmanuel Bigand, Lola Cuddy, Irène Deliège, Peter Desain, Diana Deutsch, Jay Dowling, Alf Gabrielsson, Andrew Gregory, Mari Reiss Jones, Patrik Juslin, Carol Krumhansl,

Dirk-Jan Povel, Glenn Schellenberg, Mark Schmuckler, John Sloboda, Johan Sundberg, Barbara Tillmann, among others. A smattering of physiologically oriented research has also been carried out, most notably studies by Petr Janata and Jaak Panksepp. Similarly, many music scholars have addressed issues of expectation, including Bret Aarden, Zohar Eitan, Robert Gjerdingen, Paul von Hippel, Henkjan Honing, Steve Larson, Fred Lerdahl, Justin London, Elizabeth West Marvin, Dirk Moelants, Yuet-Hon Ng, Bob Snyder, and David Temperley. However, the most comprehensive theoretical attempts to account for the role of expectation in musical experience are found in the work of Leonard Meyer (1956), Eugene Narmour (1990, 1992), Elizabeth Margulis (2005, 2007), and David Huron (2006), to which we now turn.

21.7.1 Meyer's emotion and meaning

Leonard B. Meyer ignited contemporary interest in expectation as a core component of musically evoked emotion. In *Emotion and meaning in music* (1956), Meyer looked to John Dewey's (1894) 'conflict theory of emotions' (as modified by MacCurdy, 1925), which suggested that affect arises from the inhibition of tendency. As an example of this effect, Meyer contrasted the relatively unemotional scenario of a person searching for and finding a cigarette in his pocket, compared with the relatively emotion-laden scenario of a person searching for and failing to find the same cigarette.

Although many mid-century music theorists were interested in the psychology of the listener, few scholars dared to embrace a psychological approach to analysis. In order to analyse music from the perspective of the listener, a scholar would have to wrestle with the variability of human responses, and the whole enterprise seemed destined to collapse in the chaos of multiple meanings. Since musical scores rarely change, the study of musical scores held a much stronger allure.

By focusing narrowly on expectation, and by positing an idealized competent listener, Meyer was able to avoid many of the difficulties raised by psychologically inspired analysis. Moreover, in Dewey's theory, Meyer found a way to analyse listener responses in a systematic way: 'granted listeners who have developed reaction patterns appropriate to the work in question, the structure of the affective response to a piece of music can be studied by examining the music itself . . . the study of the affective content of a particular work . . . can be made without continual and explicit reference to the responses of the listener or critic. That is, subjective content can be discussed objectively' (1956, p. 32).

Given norms that listeners had abstracted from prior exposure to the relevant style or genre, certain musical events could be understood to imply other ones, or to produce a tendency to continue to them. When that tendency was inhibited, affect could arise. This view allowed musical affect, a notoriously subjective phenomenon, to be investigated in relation to musical structure, rather than in relation to the idiosyncratic propensities of individual listeners.

A classic example is found in the *deceptive cadence*, a harmonic progression in which the normal dominant-to-tonic resolution is replaced by a dominant-to-submediant progression. (The tonic and submediant chords share two pitches in common, so the difference between the two progressions involves a seemingly modest change of shifting one tone by one step.) In the deceptive cadence, the 'felt urgency' (Meyer, 1956, p. 61) for resolution to the tonic is denied with dramatic psychological results. Another classic example appears in rondos at points where thematic return is expected; considerable tension can arise simply by delaying the theme's reoccurrence.

Throughout analytic discourse, expectations are most often mentioned when they are violated (Margulis, 2007). But in addition to the affect triggered by violations, Meyer postulates a different type of response—'apprehension and anxiety' (1956, p. 26)—that is thought to arise out of uncertainty. Uncertainty can be understood as the absence of clear expectations (most commonly experienced when listening to music in an unfamiliar style or genre), or the stimulation of multiple, mutually exclusive expectations (for example, an event that hovers ambiguously between several possible interpretations). Thus, expectations can contribute to affect both in the case that they are denied, and in the case that they fail to be clearly established. The default, unvalenced scenario, then, would be one in which expectations are clearly established and fulfilled. According to Meyer's conception, such banal music would be rare, since composers are typically interested in moving listeners. Most works would entail a mixed choreography of expectations fulfilled and expectations thwarted.

Meyer's work coincided with the introduction of a new mathematical tool, *information theory*. Devised at the Bell Telephone Laboratories by Claude Shannon, information theory provides a generalized method for characterizing the quantity of information in any message. It does so by measuring the predictability of successive symbols. When a symbol (such as a musical note) is virtually certain, it carries little information. Conversely, high uncertainty is associated with high information. Shannon himself recognized the applicability of his theory to music, and Meyer (1957) saw the link between Shannon's theory and his own ideas about musical implications.

Beginning in the late 1950s, a number of music scholars further explored the applicability of information theory to music (cf. Youngblood, 1958; Krahenbuehl & Coons, 1959; for more recent accounts, see Knopoff & Hutchinson, 1981; and Snyder, 1990), often using the theory to understand characteristics of musical styles. The psychoaesthetics movement in the 1970s (Berlyne, 1971; see also Chapter 19, this volume) sought to connect information theory to musical experience in the tradition of Meyer, and several recent studies have pursued this line of inquiry, looking at how information theory and other probabilistic approaches to music might underlie cognitive and affective processing (Huron, 2006; Margulis & Beatty, 2008; Temperley, 2007).

In assessing Meyer's contribution, it is appropriate to emphasize the novel and pioneering spirit of his work. Although ordinary listeners were captivated by possible relationships between music and emotion, the intellectual milieu of mid-century American scholarship was remarkably hostile to the study of musical emotion. On the one hand, American psychology was dominated by a severe form of behaviourism that regarded emotions as occult qualities beyond the realm of legitimate psychological research. On the other hand, American musicology was dominated by a reaction against the excesses of nineteenth-century (romantic) scholarly writing in which authors indulged in effusive emotional descriptions whose introspective flights of fancy tainted the entire subject of musical emotion.

From our current vantage point, Meyer might be faulted for having relied too heavily on Gestalt principles, whose woolly formulations have received sustained criticism by perceptual psychologists. However, Meyer was far ahead of his time in integrating cognitive and affective aspects of mental functioning. In drawing attention to the importance of expectation, Meyer anticipated the conclusions of cognitive neuroscience by half a century. Meyer was a lone voice, largely out of step with mainstream currents in both musicology and psychology, whose work was nevertheless philosophically erudite and musically sophisticated. He single-handedly carved out an important area of scholarship. His legacy—usefully dubbed the 'Penn School' by David Butler—has included such psychologically informed theorists as Robert Gjerdingen, Eugene Narmour, and Justin London.

21.7.2 Narmour's Implication-Realization theory

In some ways, Eugene Narmour's Implication-Realization theory might be regarded as a generalization and deep explication of Meyer's notion of 'gap fill'. However, Narmour's monumental work (1990, 1992) goes beyond Meyer's nascent ideas to build a more embracing theory of the cognition of melody. Unfortunately, limitations of space permit only a bare outline of the theory.

The Implication-Realization theory is based on two overarching principles: that similarity implies further similarity, and differentiation implies further differentiation. Narmour regards these principles as applicable in all musical parameters, including pitch intervals, melodic contour, dynamics, rhythm, and (forthcoming) harmony. Applying the principles to *intervallic motion* (the size of successive melodic intervals) and *registral direction* (the contour—up, down, or lateral—of these intervals), Narmour creates a taxonomy of melodic figures, each with its own implicative content. For example, process (P) signifies a small melodic interval followed by another small melodic interval in the same direction; the similarity in both domains (small interval to small interval, the preservation of direction) yields an implication for further similarity: continuation to another small interval in the same direction. Reversal (R), however, signifies a large melodic interval followed by a small interval in the opposite direction. It represents differentiation in both domains (large interval to small interval, a change of direction). In addition, the reversal creates closure—a point after the fulfilment of strong implications at which further implications are suppressed. Both bottom-up perceptual principles and top-down stylistic constraints play roles in the theory.

Narmour's theory attempts to characterize the fluctuating sense of goal-directedness in melodies, explaining where melodies seem strongly implicative, and where they seem less so. The theory emphasizes note-to-note connections over more background, hierarchic ones. Margulis (2005), building on Narmour's theory, has used Lerdahl and Jackendoff's (1983) time-span reduction to add a hierarchic account. Narmour hypothesizes a variety of possible affective responses to implication, including *cognitive exhilaration* when subconscious inferences are validated, *cognitive irony* when they are proved only partly right, and *cognitive shock* when the inferences prove incorrect (where the qualifier 'cognitive' is meant to distinguish these aesthetically induced states from their everyday counterparts).

Of the many contributions made by Narmour, it is important to draw attention to his revolutionary attitude toward empirical testing. In the past, music theorists typically offered interpretations of musical phenomena with little interest in testing their ideas. If a particular theory was inherently unfalsifiable, music theorists tended to view this as a strength of the theory rather than a weakness. Following a trend begun by Lerdahl, Narmour has been a strong advocate for holding up theoretical claims to the light of empirical tests. Although not himself an experimentalist, his books typically end with a litany of empirically testable claims that derive from his theorizing, and an invitation to experimental psychologists to separate the defensible from the indefensible. The happy consequence of this attitude has been an explosion in experimentation, with a predictable mix of success and failure (Cuddy & Lunney, 1995; Krumhansl, 1995; Schellenberg, 1996). In promoting empirical engagement, Narmour has raised the bar for music theorizing.

21.7.3 Margulis's theory

Margulis (2005), building on Lerdahl's notions about the relationship between attraction and tension (Lerdahl, 2001; Lerdahl & Jackendoff, 1983; Lerdahl & Krumhansl, 2007), proposes three types of musical tension that arise from specific circumstances within a model of deeply schematic melodic expectations—expectations that influence listeners' experience, but are not themselves directly accessible. The model produces quantitative predictions about the expectedness of notes within melodies, and proposes a relationship between these predictions and experiences of musical tension. The model assumes that tension is not a unitary, all-or-nothing phenomenon, but rather a differentiated one, admitting of multiple distinctive types. Surprise-tension is thought to arise when events occur that were not predictable beforehand, and registers phenomenologically as an experience of intensity and dynamism, motivating closer attention from the listener. Denial-tension is thought to occur when an unexpected event occurs in place of an alternative, highly expected event, and registers phenomenologically as an impression of intentionality or will in the music. Expectancy-tension is thought to occur when an event generates a particularly strong expectation for a subsequent one, and registers phenomenologically as an impression of forward-directedness in the melody. All of these impressions are fleeting, subtle, distinctly musical, and, this model argues, consequences of expectations formed dynamically as music transpires. Margulis's model builds on the work of Lerdahl and Narmour, adds a hierarchic component, forms quantitative predictions, and makes explicit a proposed relationship between expectation and tension.

21.7.4 Huron's ITPRA theory

Compared with other theories of expectation, Huron's (2006) account places greater emphasis on biology and enculturation. He emphasizes the adaptive advantage of forming accurate expectations, and suggests that expectation-related emotions are intended to 'reinforce accurate prediction, promote appropriate event-readiness, and increase the likelihood of future positive outcomes' (p. 4). At the same time, Huron's theory emphasizes the role of cultural environment and statistical learning as the source of listener expectancies.

The core of Huron's theory is an analysis of the timecourse of expected/unexpected events (see Figure 21.1). Huron proposes that responses to future events can be usefully divided into five components dubbed *Imagination, Tension, Prediction, Reaction,* and *Appraisal* (ITPRA for short). The five components can be grouped into *pre-outcome* and *post-outcome* phases. In the *pre-outcome* phase, an individual might consciously *imagine* different possible outcomes and vicariously experience some of the feelings that would be expected for each outcome. For example, the act of imagining being reunited with a loved one may evoke anticipatory feelings that act as the motivation to embark on a long journey. Independent of the emotions evoked by imagining outcomes, the pre-outcome phase also entails a tension component: As an anticipated event approaches, arousal and attention states are fine tuned so that ensuing behaviours are optimized. Expecting to catch a ball requires a different mental and corporal state from expecting a phone call, or expecting a sought word to come to mind. These preparations are accompanied by distinctive feelings, associated with muscle tone, respiration, rumination, etc.

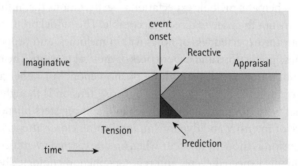

Fig. 21.1 Illustration of the time course for Huron's ITPRA theory of expectation. Feeling states are first activated by imagining different outcomes (I). As an anticipated event approaches, physiological arousal typically increases, often leading to a feeling of increasing tension (T). Once the event has happened, some feelings are immediately evoked related to whether one's predictions were borne out (P). In addition, a fast reaction response is activated based on a very cursory and conservative assessment of the situation (R). Finally, feeling states are evoked that represent a less hasty appraisal of the outcome (A) (from Huron, 2006).

After an event has occurred (*post-outcome* phase), three distinct processes are initiated. The accuracy of an individual's prediction is assessed (*prediction response*). Positive feelings are evoked when the outcome is expected, and negative feelings are evoked when the outcome is surprising. The purpose of the prediction response is to reinforce accurate prediction. At the same time, a 'quick and dirty' *reaction response* is generated. Reaction responses (such as the startle reflex) are defensive in function. These short-lived responses tend to assume a worst-case scenario, and so most of these responses prove to be overreactions that are quickly extinguished. Finally, the *appraisal response* represents a more leisurely assessment of the situation that takes into account complex social and situational factors. Appraisal responses (which originate in the cortex but are not necessarily conscious) commonly inhibit reaction responses (which originate in subcortical structures). Because *reaction* responses involve fewer synaptic connections, they are considerably faster than *appraisal* responses. These fast and slow responses reflect the neurological embodiment of two usually contradictory goals: (1) the need to respond as *quickly* as possible to dangerous circumstances, and (2) the need to judge as *accurately* as possible the value of some event or situation.

Huron suggests that for a given sound event (like the onset of a chord), the listener's overall feeling state is a dynamic mixture of the feelings generated by the *imagination*, *tension*, *prediction*, *reaction*, and *appraisal* responses. These responses may all be positively valenced, or they may all be negatively valenced. But most experiences involve a complex mix of positively and negatively valenced responses.

21.8 MUSICAL EXAMPLES

Scholars have suggested that many psychological effects arise from the phenomenon of expectation, including delay, anticipatory tension, premonition, deception, humor, garden-path phenomena, and others (e.g. Huron, 2006; Margulis, 2005; Meyer, 1956; Narmour, 1990, 1992; Temperley, 2007). The analytic literature provides many musical examples of these purported effects. However, limited space precludes illustrating all of the suggested effects. Here we briefly describe two examples of musical surprise.

Figure 21.2 shows the well-known opening to Sergey Prokofiev's *Peter and the Wolf*. The upbeat tempo, wide leaps, dotted rhythms, major-key harmony, and use of staccato all contribute to a happy, carefree feeling. At the third measure, however, Prokofiev abruptly shifts to a lowered submediant harmony. This harmonic surprise is accompanied by an unorthodox melody that oscillates between E flat and B natural—a rare use of the augmented fifth interval. The B natural clashes with the C of the accompanying harmony. Above the melody, some of the transitional probabilities for successive scale tones are shown (expressed in bits). For major key melodies, typical transitional probabilities lie in the range of three to five bits (Huron, 2006). In this context, the E flat/B natural alternation jumps out. The probability of the seventh scale tone being followed

Fig. 21.2 The opening to Sergey Prokofiev's *Peter and the Wolf.*

by the lowered third scale tone is just .00004. Compared with the melodic intervals in the first two measures, the intervals of the third measure are strikingly improbable. For many listeners, the pitches sound 'wrong', as though Prokofiev had mistakenly written B4 rather than C5. In fact, music theorists refer to such transgressions as 'wrong-note' harmonies or 'wrong-note' melodies (Rifkin, 2000).

Prokofiev's 'wrong notes' display a number of characteristic properties. The notes typically involve semitone displacements from tonally appropriate notes. Often the pitches are flat by a half step. The 'wrong notes' are commonly approached and left by melodic leaps. As in the above example, Prokofiev tends to immediately repeat the wrong-note sequence—as if to say 'Yes, I really intended that pitch.'

Prokofiev's 'wrong notes' are probably not unrelated to his penchant for neo-classical writing. In choosing to write music with conventional tonal and phrase structures, Prokofiev makes his 'wrong notes' more obvious to listeners accustomed to the musical language of the classical period. Prokofiev's conventional classical style provides the schematic backdrop for his 'wrong notes'. The psychological effect of Prokofiev's music has been variously described as 'quirky', 'weird', and 'impertinent'. By repeating these improbable patterns, Prokofiev assures listeners that the notes are clearly intentional. It is not inappropriate for listeners to interpret 'intended wrongness' as a symptom of 'impertinence'.

Recall earlier, Bharucha's distinction between generalized (schematic) expectations and work-specific (veridical) expectations. Like the deceptive cadence, frequent exposure to Prokofiev's music will significantly attenuate the sense of surprise, although veridical familiarity will fail to extinguish the schematic surprises. Familiarity will lessen, but not eliminate, the sense of oddity.

If Bharucha's schematic/veridical distinction holds merit, then we ought to be able to observe musical passages that exhibit the reverse scenario—a veridical surprise accompanied by a schematic non-surprise. Figure 21.3 shows such a passage (discussed in Huron, 2006). The passage is from the Adagio movement of Peter Schickele's *Quodlibet for Small Orchestra* (1959). Schickele is a musical humorist, better known as PDQ Bach. In the live Vanguard recording of this work, the passage evokes sustained and appreciative laughter.

The passage is a modified quotation from the second movement of Beethoven's Fifth Symphony (also shown in Figure 21.3). The two passages are identical until the

Fig. 21.3 Passage from the Adagio movement of Peter Schickele's *Quodlibet for Small Orchestra* (A), which is a modified quotation from the second movement of Beethoven's fifth symphony (B).

beginning of the fourth measure: Where Beethoven follows the B flat with an E natural, Schickele follows the B flat with an A flat (see marked intervals). In the original, Beethoven's theme branches into a new key area, but Schickele simply brings the phrase to a stereotypic close. Schickele's version is surprising only to listeners familiar with the original Beethoven, and this familiarity is essential to the musical humour. In fact, Schickele's version is much more consistent with the norms of Western classical music. In most musical humour, gags involve doing something absurdly improbable. But in this situation, Schickele achieves a humorous effect by substituting a musically banal passage for a musically adventurous one. Schematic and veridical expectations can be surprised independently.

In the two examples described above, we have seen how surprise might lead to feelings such as oddity or levity. But these examples only hint at the range of psychological effects evoked by choreographing listener expectations.

21.9 FRISSON—THRILLS FROM CHILLS

A musically induced affect that shows close links to musical surprise is the phenomenon of frisson (e.g. Sloboda, 1991; Gabrielsson & Lindström, 1993, 2003). Frisson can be described as a pleasant tingling feeling associated with the flexing of hair follicles, resulting in gooseflesh (technically called piloerection) accompanied by a cold sensation, and sometimes producing a shiver. Dimpled skin is evident in the region of the back of the neck and upper spine, often including the shoulders, scalp and cheeks, and sometimes extending to the entire back, belly, groin, arms, chest, or legs (Panksepp, 1995). The experience may last from less than a second to more than ten seconds. Longer responses usually involve one or more 'waves' of spreading gooseflesh. Grewe,

Nagel, Kopiez, and Altenmüller (2007) note that the occurrence of such 'shivers' is significantly correlated with judgements of the pleasantness of music works. Some reports mention that the response may be accompanied by smiling, laughing, weeping, lump-in-throat, sighing, breath-holding, or heart palpitation. For the purposes of this chapter, we will focus exclusively on the prototypical response involving topical (skin-related) sensations.

Researchers have proposed a number of different labels for this response, including *thrills* (e.g. Goldstein, 1980; Konečni et al, 2007), *chills* (e.g. Grewe et al, 2007; Guhn et al, 2007), and *frisson* (Huron, 2006; Sloboda, 1991). Bernatzky has suggested the term *skin orgasm* (see also Panksepp, 1995); however, this term has gained few adherents. In the interests of precision, we will follow Sloboda's suggestion and use the term *frisson*. Listeners can find music 'thrilling' without necessarily experiencing gooseflesh. The term 'chills' is best reserved for the phenomenological feeling of coldness, which, like piloerection, may be considered a characteristic symptom of the frisson response.

Apart from music, gooseflesh (piloerection) can be evoked in many other situations. Gooseflesh can occur when experiencing fear (such as hearing an unknown sound while walking alone in a dark alley), when viewing disgusting photographs, during orgasm, or in response to fingernails scratching a blackboard (Halpern et al, 1986). Of course, gooseflesh is a common response when we are cold, but paradoxically, it can also arise when immersing ourselves in a hot bath. Gooseflesh can also be evoked by physical contact with another person, when experiencing a sudden insight (such as an unexpected solution to a problem), while observing an inspiring moment in a competitive sport, or when experiencing great natural beauty, such as viewing a large canyon (Goldstein, 1980). Notice that the experience of gooseflesh can be either pleasant or unpleasant. The term 'frisson', however, applies only to the pleasure-inducing form. Simply put, frisson might be defined as 'pleasurable piloerection' or 'enjoyable gooseflesh'.

21.9.1 Individual differences

Not everyone experiences music-induced frisson. Goldstein (1980) carried out a survey of employees in a business unconnected to music, in which he achieved a 100 per cent return rate. Of these, 47 per cent reported never having experienced a music-induced 'thrill'. Similarly, Grewe et al (2007) found only 55 per cent of participants reported music-induced 'chills'. Konečni et al (2007) were able to induce 'thrills' in only 35 per cent of participants. By contrast, 90 per cent of the music students included in Goldstein's (1980) study reported having experienced music-induced 'thrills'. It appears that only about half of the general population may be familiar with the experience. The capacity to experience music-induced frisson may encourage certain people to pursue a career in music.

Panksepp (1995) and others have observed that music-induced frisson is more likely to be reported by female listeners than by male listeners. In addition to gender differences, personality differences have been observed by Grewe et al (2007). As measured using the Sensation Seeking Scale (Litle & Zuckerman, 1986), 'chill responders' are less adventurous or thrill seeking. That is, reactive listeners are less likely to enjoy physical risk taking, such as skydiving or riding rollercoasters. One might say these listeners are 'more sensitive' or 'thin-skinned'. Grewe and his colleagues also found that the more reactive listeners have greater familiarity with classical music, identify more with the music they prefer, and are more likely to listen to music in concentrated (rather than background) situations. In short, susceptibility to music-induced frisson is correlated with musical interest.

Listeners who experience music-induced frisson are typically able to point to particular moments in a work when the frisson is evoked (Sloboda, 1991). This specificity has encouraged researchers to search for musical features that might be responsible for the frisson. These efforts have been confounded, however, by poor inter-listener consistency (e.g. Blood & Zatorre, 2001). Early on, investigators discovered that musical works that evoke frisson for the experimenter commonly fail to evoke frisson in other listeners. Asking participants to bring their own frisson-inducing music reinforced this discovery: when participant-selected music is employed as stimuli, listeners inevitably experience more frisson in response to their own music than to music brought by other participants (e.g. Konečni et al, 2007). Moreover, when different listeners experienced frisson in the same work, the points of frisson can differ.

This effect led some researchers to conclude that familiarity may be a key to music-induced frisson. However, this observation is confounded by the reliance on participant-selected music: if asked to bring a piece of music 'that causes you to shiver', participants are likely to choose pieces that they particularly love, and well-loved pieces are apt to be highly familiar. Consider a gustatory parallel. If asked to bring a dish of your favourite food to a pot-luck dinner, what is the likelihood that you will encounter a dish brought by someone else that you prefer over your own contribution? If people attending a pot-luck dinner tended to prefer their own culinary offering to those of others, one would not be justified in claiming that familiarity is the most important aspect of taste.

Guhn, Hamm, and Zentner (2007) addressed this possible confound by measuring the familiarity of different works *not* selected by the participants. They found a correlation of zero between the frequency of frisson responses and familiarity. This suggests that listeners become familiar with works that a priori cause them to experience frisson, not that frisson arises due to increasing familiarity.

21.9.2 Causes of frisson

In light of the high proportion of non-responders, and given the high individual variability between responders, the best efforts to identify potential causes of frisson have involved careful pre-selection of experimental participants. When participants were selected according to high self-reports for musical sensitivity, Guhn et al (2007) were able to show a high degree of inter-subjective consistency in the location of frisson responses as determined by self-report and skin conductance measures. In addition,

Guhn et al found that heart rate responses are also highly correlated between such participants. Even when a participant doesn't exhibit a frisson response, heart rates are still highest at moments when frisson responses are evoked for other participants. This suggests that sympathetic arousal may be a necessary, though not sufficient, component of frisson.

Among researchers, there is considerable agreement about acoustical and musical correlates of frisson (Blood & Zatorre, 2001; Craig, 2005; Grewe, et al 2007; Guhn, et al 2007; Panksepp, 1995, 1998; Rickard, 2004; Sloboda, 1991). The most important acoustic correlate is a rapid large change of loudness, especially a large increase in loudness (subito forte). A less robust acoustic correlate appears to be the broadening of the frequency range (i.e. the addition of low bass and/or high treble). Musical correlates include the entry of one or more instruments or voices; the return of a melody, theme, or motive; an abrupt change of tempo or rhythm; a new or unprepared harmony; abrupt modulation; or a sudden change of texture. Music deemed 'sad' (e.g. slow tempo, quiet dynamic, minor key) is roughly twice as likely to evoke frisson as 'happy' music (Panksepp, 1995).

Notice that two common elements can be found in this list of features. First, adjectives such as abrupt, rapid, sudden, new, and unprepared suggest that the precipitating musical events may be surprising or unexpected. A second common theme is high energy, such as increased loudness or the addition of sound sources. Notice also that slow, quiet passages (such as are commonly found in sad music) provide an especially contrasting background against which unexpectedly energetic events may be highlighted.

21.9.3 Examples

Figures 21.4 and 21.5 illustrate some of these frisson-inducing properties. Figure 21.4 shows a passage from Pink Floyd's 'The Final Cut' that, as reported by Panksepp (1995), displayed a high probability of evoking frisson responses. The most obvious feature of this passage is the dramatic increase in loudness. The initial phrase is sung in nearly a whispered voice, whereas the subsequent phrase is sung in a shouting voice.

Figure 21.5 shows a more complicated frisson-inducing passage identified by one of the respondents to Sloboda's (1991) survey. The passage, from Schoenberg's

Fig. 21.4 Vocal melody from Pink Floyd's 'The Final Cut'. One of the frisson-inducing passages reported in Panksepp (1995).

Fig. 21.5 Piano reduction of bars 225–230 from Schoenberg's *Verklärte Nacht,* a passage identified by one of Sloboda's (1991) respondents as reliably evoking a frisson response.

Verklärte Nacht, exhibits a subito forte dynamic contrast. In addition, harmonic and rhythmic surprises coincide with the onset of the D-major chord at the beginning of measure 229. In the key of G minor, the D-major chord is the dominant; a progression from E-flat major (VI) to V would be a relatively common progression. However, in approaching this passage, there is no hint of G minor, and the E-flat chord is minor rather than major. Consequently, for Western-enculturated listeners, the D-major chord would be harmonically unexpected. The advent of this chord also involves an element of temporal surprise. Prior to measure 229, chord onsets systematically avoid the downbeat, so the sense of meter is significantly eroded. Although the D-major chord occurs on the downbeat, this moment is no longer expected for most listeners. In short, the frisson-inducing moment coincides with a combination of temporal surprise, harmonic surprise, and abrupt increase in loudness.

21.9.4 Physiological correlates

Apart from behavioural studies, the frisson response has also attracted physiological studies, including observations of skin conductance, heart rate, neurochemical changes, and hemodynamic changes. Gooseflesh or piloerection is positively correlated with heart rate, although peak heart rate is not a good predictor of frisson responses (Guhn et al, 2007). Frisson is more strongly correlated with increases in skin conductance response (Craig, 2005; Guhn et al, 2007; Rickard, 2004; see also Chapter 11, this volume).

Neurochemical changes associated with frisson were investigated by Goldstein (1980). Goldstein administered naloxone, an opiate receptor antagonist, to healthy volunteers. Naloxone is able to block or significantly attenuate the positive feelings that normally accompany the release of endogeneous opioids such as endorphins. Goldstein used a double-blind protocol in which members of a control group were injected with an inert saline solution. Of the 10 volunteers who received naloxone, three reported a significant reduction in music-induced 'thrills' to participant-selected music. Goldstein's study implies two conclusions. First, the results are consistent with the view that music-induced frisson can lead to the release of endogenous opiates (such as endorphins), commonly associated with the experience of pleasure. At the same time, the results seem equivocal: only three of ten volunteers showed any effect. Since only about half of the population experience music-induced frisson, the mixed results might be attributable to the considerable individual variation in frisson responsiveness.

Neurohemodynamic changes associated with frisson have been investigated by Blood and Zatorre (2001), who carried out PET scans of volunteers listening to participant-selected music. They found that frisson responses coincided with increased blood flow in the nucleus accumbens, the left ventral tegmental area, the dorsomedial midbrain, the insula, thalamus, anterior cingulate, the supplementary motor area and bilateral cerebellum. Decreased blood flow was observed in the amygdala, left hippocampus, and the posterior cortex. This hemodynamic pattern has been found by other researchers to be characteristic of euphoric or pleasurable experiences (Breiter et al, 1997; see also Chapter 12, this volume). In addition, increased activity in the thalamus and anterior cingulate are associated with increased attention.

21.9.5 Theories of music-induced frisson

Two theories have been proposed that attempt to account for the origin of music-induced frisson: Panksepp's *Separation Distress* theory and Huron's *Contrastive Valence* theory. Both theories rely on evolutionary arguments linking affective experience to physiological changes.

Panksepp's Separation Distress theory

Panksepp (1995, 1998) has proposed a theory of music-induced frisson whose foundation is the reactiveness of caregivers to the distress calls of offspring. Few experiences are more traumatic than the separation of mother and child, ewe and lamb, or hen and chick. When visual contact fails, offspring typically rely on distress calls as a way of signalling their location. In order for the distress call to be effective, caregivers must be responsive. Given the biological importance of nurturing and protecting offspring, one would expect distress calls to have a powerful motivating (i.e. emotional) effect on caregivers.

While providing food and protection are the foremost tasks of any parent, the most common behaviour simply involves reassuring offspring of the parent's presence. For most animals, physical contact (so-called 'comfort touch') provides such reassurance. The contact between caregiver and offspring typically results in a mutual increase in skin temperature. In human language, social comfort is often described using thermal metaphors, such as 'warm personality' or 'cold shoulder'. When a caregiver perceives a distress call, Panksepp suggests that feelings of coldness or chill may provide increased motivation for social reunion. Panksepp and Bernatzky (2002) have suggested that frisson-inducing musical passages exhibit acoustic properties similar to the separation calls of young animals.

Inspired by Panksepp's theory, Beeman (2005) has assembled various analyses related to the acoustics of human infant cries. Note that human hearing is not equally sensitive at all frequencies. Due to resonances in the pinna and ear canal, the threshold of hearing is much more sensitive in the region 1–6 kHz. Within this region, sensitivity is most acute in a narrow region between 3 and 4 Hz (Fletcher & Munson, 1933). Beeman notes that human infant cries show an energy peak in this region. Other research has established that the sound of a crying baby is highly distressing for adult listeners (Drummond et al, 1999; Lester, 1978; Lester et al, 1992). Apart from the presumed cognitive motivations, there are straightforward sensory reasons why a crying baby attracts our attention.

Infant cries are not the only sounds that show a high energy peak in the ear's most sensitive region. The adult human scream also displays a disproportionate amount of energy in the broad 1–6 kHz region where human hearing is best. This is true of screams produced by both males and females. A human scream is the sound humans can hear at the greatest distance. Beeman (2005) also notes that this auditory sensitivity is exploited by professional singers. Sundberg (1972, 1987) discovered that operatic singers are able to concentrate acoustic energy in the so-called *singer's formant*. In one study, for example, Sundberg measured the spectral resonances in recordings by the famous Swedish tenor, Jussi Björling, and found an especially strong resonance in the region around 3 kHz (Sundberg, 1972, 1977). Similarly, Johnstone and Scherer (1995) measured the spectral resonances in recordings of the Slovakian soprano, Edita Gruberová, and found high energy peaks between 2.9 and 4.1 kHz. The singer's formant is variously described by vocal teachers as 'acoustic ping' or *squillo*. As pointed out by Beeman (2005), production of the singer's formant is one of the principal aims of professional operatic training.

Of course, many listeners report that they dislike the sound of the Western operatic voice. People who hate opera often say that the singers sound 'hysterical' or overwrought. Professional writers tend to be reserved when criticizing opera, but amateurs writing on the web are more frank. In the words of one web writer: 'I don't like opera because people scream all the time' (www.pencollectors.com/projects.htm, 2007/12/16). For these listeners, it is possible that the acoustic similarity between operatic *squillo* and screaming is just too close.

Panksepp notes that not everyone is equally responsive to distress calls. A crying baby may evoke strong nurturing instincts in its parents, but strangers are more likely to find the sound annoying. The strongest nurturing emotions are evoked when an adult has *bonded* with its offspring. A key factor in bonding is familiarity, and Panksepp suggests that familiarity with a given musical work has an effect similar to parental bonding. As a result, he suggests that music-induced frisson is more likely to arise with familiar music (1995, p. 202).

By way of summary, Panksepp's theory suggests that the emotional power of the frisson response lies in the receptiveness and sensitivity of the auditory system to infant distress calls. Since the principal caregivers in most species are mothers, females would be expected to be more attentive to separation distress calls, and so would be expected to be more reactive to music-induced frisson.

Huron's Contrastive Valence theory

Although Panksepp's separation distress theory appears to provide a good account of music-induced frisson, difficulties arise in trying to extend the theory to other forms of frisson. Apart from music, pleasant piloerection can arise when immersing ourselves in a hot bath, when a potential lover first touches our hand, when experiencing a sudden insight, or when riding a rollercoaster. Unpleasant piloerection can arise when experiencing fear or when we are cold. When exposed to disgusting photographs, the ensuing piloerection may be described by viewers as 'making my skin crawl'. Huron's (2006) theory of expectation attempts to place music-induced frisson within a larger account of pleasant and unpleasant piloerection.

Gooseflesh is a thermoregulatory response: raised hair provides a good insulator—although the response is less effective in relatively hairless humans. Piloerection is also used in aggression displays and as a response, when afraid, to discourage attack by others. Throughout the animal kingdom, a common response to fear is to attempt to appear larger. When threatened, for example, a cat will arch its back and make its hair stand on end. Although principally intended to regulate temperature, fear-induced piloerection appears to be an *exaptation*—a pre-existing physiological response that is 'borrowed' for other purposes.

In the ITPRA theory, a distinction is made between the *reaction* and *appraisal* post-outcome responses. The fast reactive response is restricted to the brain stem, whereas the slow appraisal response also involves the neocortex (LeDoux, 1996). Because brain-stem pathways involve fewer synaptic connections, they respond much faster than cortical pathways. This neuroanatomical difference is reflected functionally in the two responses. Reaction responses (such as the startle reflex) are defensive in function; these fast-onset responses tend to assume a worst-case scenario, and so most of these responses prove to be overreactions. The appraisal response represents a more leisurely (and accurate) assessment of situations. Reaction responses are especially sensitive to cues suggesting danger. Appropriate acoustic cues include loud sounds (indicating high energy), and sounds that resemble human alarm signals (such as screams). As noted earlier, another potent fear-inducing situation arises from surprise. Although it is possible to be 'pleasantly surprised' (see below), the failure to anticipate an outcome means that the individual is not prepared for the future.

A classic illustration of the effect can be observed in a surprise party. When a person is unexpectedly surprised by her friends, the first response is one of terror: the eyelids are retracted and the jaw drops, resulting in a classic 'terror' expression. But within half a second, fear is replaced by happy celebration as the individual recognizes her friends and the positive social meaning of the event. A quick defensive reaction response is followed by a slower (inhibitory) cognitive appraisal.

Feeling states appear to be strongly influenced by contrast. If we initially feel bad and then feel good, the good feeling tends to be stronger than if the good experience occurred without the preceding bad feeling. Conversely, if we initially feel good and then feel bad, the bad feeling tends to feel worse (e.g. McGraw, 1999). This 'contrastive valence' may account for the difference between pleasant and unpleasant piloerection. When we feel cold, the experience is simply unpleasant, so the resulting shivers are felt as bad. However, when descending into a warm bath, the quick negative reaction to the rapid change of skin temperature is dismissed by the slower appraisal that judges the temperature to be welcome. When we are unexpectedly touched by a stranger, our reaction is wholly negative. But when the unexpected touch comes from a prospective lover, the initial shock of surprise is quickly displaced by a highly positive appraisal with a memorably large contrast in feelings from bad to good. Wrestling with a difficult problem, an unexpected moment of insight replaces a period of stressful rumination with a sudden feeling of achievement. The terror of riding a rollercoaster is held at bay by the cortical conviction that 'I'm not going to die'. Hearing a loud, scream-like, or unexpected, sound, sets off reactive alarm bells. But a cortical appraisal inevitably concludes that 'it's just music'. According to Huron (2006), frisson arises when an initial negative response is superseded by a neutral or positive appraisal. Fear, panic, or anger may all lead to piloerection. But the ensuing cortical processes form their own judgements about the situation. When the appraisal response concurs with the reaction response, the sense of fear, panic, or anger is amplified. But when the appraisal response contradicts the reaction response, the cortex belatedly inhibits the fast subcortical responses and contrastive valence transforms the negative feelings into something positive.

   Notice that the evoking of frisson depends on the individual's susceptibility to experiencing fear. 'Thick-skinned' individuals who are less responsive to fear would be less likely to experience fear-induced piloerection, and so less likely to experience frisson. Since males commonly score higher on measures of sensation-seeking, they are less susceptible to fear, and so may be less likely to experience frisson than females.

   An important question raised by this theory is how frisson might be reliably evoked when a given listener hears a passage repeatedly. If piloerection is a response to fear or panic, won't musical familiarity ultimately dull the response? Although repeated stimulation normally leads to 'habituation', an exception occurs in the case of defensive responses, such as pain. Because the function of fast responses is primarily defensive, these responses must always be ready, even in a world full of false alarms. In order for defensive responses to remain effective, they must be resistant to habituation or unlearning. The principal way that biology deals with false alarms is not by desensitizing defensive reflexes, but by adding inhibitory circuits that suppress inappropriate defensive behaviours after they have already begun. While slower than the reaction responses, appraisal circuits often begin the process of inhibition within about 500 milliseconds. As a result, fast reaction responses are typically short lived and rarely reach conscious awareness. Our brains and bodies engage in frequent skirmishes with ghostly dangers while we remain blissfully unaware. It is this resistance to habituation and unlearning that allows the music to retain its hair-raising power.

   Neurological tests of this theory are scant. Consistent with the theory, Blood and Zatorre (2001) observed a marked decrease in amygdala activity in response to musically induced frisson. However, due to the poor temporal resolution of PET, the conjecture that decreased amygdala activity is preceded by a short burst of activity remains untested.

This summary provides a cursory introduction to Huron (2006), whose theory includes two other strong affective states: laughter and awe. While large violations of expectation may produce pleasurable gooseflesh (frisson), they can also lead to outbursts of laughter, or to the expansive breath-holding characteristic of awe. In Huron's theory, all three originate as negatively valenced affects that are transformed through contrastive valence into positive experiences.

21.10 CONCLUSION

The feeling of shivers running up and down one's spine is widely reported as one of the most memorable and pleasurable experiences induced by music. Not all listeners experience musical frisson, however. Its rarity notwithstanding, frisson is readily observed. Craig (2005) has noted that gooseflesh can be directly observed on the forearm of listeners. Consequently, frisson provides an especially fruitful phenomenon for the study of music and emotion. We anticipate that frisson will continue to be an attractive topic of research in the field of music and emotion.

Since Meyer's (1956) pioneering work in the 1950s, considerable progress has been made in understanding the psychology of expectation. The theoretical literature is rich with speculations concerning plausible expectation-related affects, including different forms of tension, surprise, deception, premonition, anticipation, relief, humour, and other phenomena. In this chapter, we have addressed in detail only the phenomenon of frisson. As the empirical research continues to progress, we anticipate that detailed theories will emerge concerning the role expectation plays in auditory experience, including many aspects of musical emotions.

RECOMMENDED FURTHER READING

1. Huron, D. (2006). *Sweet anticipation: Music and the psychology of expectation*. Cambridge, MA: MIT Press.
2. Meyer, L. B. (1956). *Emotion and meaning in music*. Chicago, IL: Chicago University Press.

REFERENCES

Aarden, B. (2003). *Dynamic melodic expectancy*. Ph.D. dissertation, School of Music, Ohio State University, USA.

Aarden, B. (2002). Expectancy vs. retrospective perception: Reconsidering the effects of schema and continuation judgments on measures of melodic expectancy. In C. Stevens,

D. Burnham, G. McPherson, E. Schuberg, & J. Renwick (eds), *Proceedings of the 7th International Conference on Music Perception and Cognition* (pp. 469–472). Adelaide, Australia: Causal Productions.

Addis, D. R., Wong, A. T., & Schacter, D. L. (2007). Remembering the past and imagining the future: Common and distinct neural substrates during event construction and elaboration. *Neuropsychologia, 45*, 1363–77.

Aiken, N. E. (1998). *The biological origins of art*. Westport, CT: Praeger.

Aumont, J., Bergala, A., Marie, M., & Vernet, M. (2002). *Aesthetics of film* (trans. R. Neupert). Austin, TX: University of Texas Press.

Bar, M., Aminoff, E., Mason, M., & Fenske, M. (2007). The units of thought. *Hippocampus, 17*, 420–8.

Beeman, W. O. (2005). Making grown men weep. In A. Hobart & B. Kapferer (eds), *Aesthetics and performance: The art of rite* (pp. 23–42). New York: Berghahn Books.

Berlyne, D. E. (1971). *Aesthetics and psychobiology*. New York: Appleton-Century-Crofts.

Besson, M. (1997). Eletrophysicological studies of music processing. In I. Deliège & J. A. Sloboda (eds), *Perception and cognition of music* (pp. 217–50). Hove, UK: Psychology Press.

Besson, M., & Faïta, F. (1995). An event-related potential (ERP) study of musical expectancy: Comparison of musicians with nonmusicians. *Journal of Experimental Psychology: Human Perception and Performance, 21*, 1278–96.

Besson, M., & Macar, F. (1987). An event-related potential analysis of incongruity in music and other non-linguistic contexts.*Psychophysiology, 24*, 14–25.

Bharucha, J. (1994). Tonality and expectation. In R. Aiello (ed.), *Musical perceptions* (pp. 213–239). Oxford: Oxford University Press.

Bharucha, J., & Stoeckig, K. (1986). Reaction time and musical expectancy: priming of chords. *Journal of Experimental Psychology: Human Perception and Performance, 12*, 403–10.

Bigand, E., & Pineau, M. (1997). Global context effects on musical expectancy. *Perception & Psychophysics, 59*, 1098–1107.

Blood, A. J., & Zatorre, R. J. (2001). Intensely pleasurable responses to music correlate with activity in brain regions implicated in reward and emotion. *Proceedings of the National Academy of Sciences, 98*, 11818–23.

Bornstein, R. F. (1989). Exposure and affect: Overview and meta-analysis of research, 1968–87. *Psychological Bulletin, 106*, 265–89.

Breiter, H. C., Gollub, R. L., Weisskoff, R. M., Kennedy, D. N.,Makris, N., Berke, J. D., Goodman, J. M., Kantor, H. L.,Gastfriend, D. R., Riorden, J. P., Mathew, R. T., Rosen, B. R., & Hyman, S. E. (1997). Acute effects of cocaine on human brain activity and emotion. *Neuron, 19*, 591–611.

Brochard, R., Abecasis, D., Potter, D., Ragot, R., & Drake, C. (2003). The 'tick tock' of our internal clock: Direct brain evidence of subjective accents in isochronous sequences. *Psychological Science, 14*, 362–6.

Carlsen, J. C. (1981). Some factors which influence melodic expectancy. *Psychomusicology, 1*, 12–29.

Cloninger, R. C., Przybeck, T. R., Svrakic, D. M., & Wetzel, R. D. (1999). *Das Temperament-und Charakter-Inventar. [The temperament and character inventory]* (trans. J. E. Richter, M. Eisemann, G. Richter, R. C. Cloninger). Frankfurt, Germany: Swets & Zeitlinger. (Originally published 1994)

Craig, D. G. (2005). An exploratory study of physiological changes during 'chills' induced by music. *Musicae Scientiae, 9*, 273–87.

Cuddy, L. L., & Lunney, C. A. (1995). Expectancies generated by melodic intervals: Perceptual judgments of melodic continuity. *Perception & Psychophysics, 57*, 451–62.

Dewey, J. (1894). The theory of emotion. *Psychological Review, 1*, 553–69.

Dowling, W. J., & Harwood, D. L. (1986). *Music cognition.* San Diego, CA: Academic Press.

Drummond, J., Letourneau, N., Neufeld, S., Harvey, H., Elliott, R., & Reilly, S. (1999). Infant crying and parent-infant interaction: Theory and measurement. *Infant Mental Health Journal, 20*, 452–65.

Fletcher, H., & Munson, W. A. (1933). Loudness, its definition, measurement, and calculation. *Journal of the Acoustical Society of America, 5*, 82–108.

Gabrielsson, A., & Lindström, S. (1993). On strong experiences of music. *Musikpsychologie: Jahrbuch der Deutschen Gesellschaft für Musikpsychologie, 10*, 118–39.

Gabrielsson, A., & Lindström Wik, S. (2003). Strong experiences related to music: A descriptive system. *Musicae Scientiae, 7*, 157–217.

Greenberg, G. Z., & Larkin, W. D. (1968). Frequency-response characteristic of auditory observers detecting signals of a single frequency in noise: The probe-signal method. *Journal of the Acoustical Society of America, 44*, 1513–23.

Grewe, O., Nagel, F., Kopiez, R., & Altenmüller, E. (2007). Listening to music as a re-creative process: Physiological, psychological, and psychoacoustical correlates of chills and strong emotions. *Music Perception, 24*, 297–314.

Guhn, M., Hamm, A., & Zentner, M. R. (2007). Physiological and musico-acoustic correlates of the chill response. *Music Perception, 24*, 473–83.

Halpern, D. L., Blake, R., & Hillenbrand, J. (1986). Psychoacoustics of a chilling sound. *Perceptual Psychophysics, 39*, 77–80.

Hassabis D., Kumaran, D., Vann, S. D., & Maguire, E. A. (2007). Patients with hippocampal amnesia cannot imagine new experiences. *Proceedings of the National Academy of Sciences, 104*, 1726–31.

Hawkins, J., & Blakeslee, S. (2004). *On intelligence.* New York: Times Books.

Horvitz, J. C. (2000). Mesolimbocortical and nigrostriatal dopamine responsesto salient non-reward events. *Neuroscience, 96*, 651–6.

Huron, D. (2006). *Sweet anticipation: Music and the psychology of expectation.* Cambridge, MA: MIT Press.

Johnson, A., & Redish, A. D. (2007). Neural ensembles in CA3 transiently encode paths forward of the animal at a decision point. *Journal of Neuroscience, 27*, 12176–89.

Johnstone, I. T., & Scherer, K. R. (1995). Spectral measurement of voice quality in opera singers: The case of Gruberova. *Proceedings of the XIIIth International Congress of Phonetic Sciences, 1*, 218–21.

Jones, M. R. (1976). Time, our lost dimension: Toward a new theory of perception, attention, and memory. *Psychological Review, 83*, 323–55.

Koelsch, S., Schroger, E., & Gunter, T. C. (2002). Music matters: Preattentive musicality of the human brain. *Psychophysiology, 39*, 38–48.

Koelsch, S., Schmidt, B.-H., & Kansok, J. (2002). Effects of musical expertise on the early right anterior negativity: An event-related brain potential study. *Psychophysiology, 39*, 657–63.

Konečni, V. J., Wanic, R. A., & Brown, A. (2007). Emotional and aesthetic antecedents and consequences of music-induced thrills. *American Journal of Psychology, 120*, 619–43.

Knopoff, L., & Hutchinson, W. (1981). Information theory for musical continua. *Journal of Music Theory, 25*, 17–44.

Krahenbuehl, D., & Coons, E. (1959). Information as a measure of experience in music. *Journal of Aesthetics and Art Criticism, 17*, 510–22.

Krumhansl, C. L., & Shepard, R. N. (1979). Quantification of the hierarchy of tonal functions within a diatonic context. *Journal of Experimental Psychology: Human Perception and Performance, 5*, 579–94.

Lake, W. (1987). *Melodic perception and cognition: The influence of tonality.* Unpublished doctoral dissertation, University of Michigan, Ann Arbor, USA.

Larson, S. (2002). Musical forces, melodic expectation, and jazz melody. *Music Perception,* 19, 351–85.

LeDoux, J. E. (1996). *The emotional brain.* New York: Simon & Schuster.

Lerdahl, F. (2001). *Tonal pitch space.* Oxford: Oxford University Press.

Lerdahl, F., & Jackendoff, R. (1983). *A generative theory of tonal music.* Cambridge, MA: MIT Press.

Lerdahl, F., & Krumhansl, C. L. (2007). Modeling tonal tension. *Music Perception,* 24, 329–66.

Lester, B. M. (1978). The organization of crying in the neonate. *Journal of Pediatric Psychology,* 3, 122–30.

Lester, B. M., Boukydis, C. F. Z., Garcia-Coll, C. T., Hole, W., & Peucker, M. (1992). Infantile colic: Acoustic cry characteristics, maternal perception of cry, and temperament. *Infant Behavior and Development,* 15, 15–26.

Litle, P., & Zuckerman, M. (1986). Sensation seeking and music preferences. *Personality and Individual Differences,* 7, 575–7.

MacCurdy, J. T. (1925). *The psychology of emotion.* New York: Harcourt Brace.

Margulis, E. H. (2007). Surprise and listening ahead: Analytic engagements with musical tendencies. *Music Theory Spectrum,* 29, 197–218.

Margulis, E. H. (2005). A model of melodic expectation. *Music Perception,* 22, 663–714.

Margulis, E. H., & Beatty, A. P. (2008). Musical style, psychoaesthetics, and prospects for entropy as an analytic tool. *Computer Music Journal,* 32, 64–78.

Margulis, E. H., & Levine, W. H. (2006). Timbre priming effects and expectation in melody. *Journal of New Music Research,* 35, 175–82.

McGraw, A. P. (1999). *Expectations and emotions in sports.* Master's thesis. Ohio State University, USA.

Meyer, L. B. (1956). *Emotion and meaning in music.* Chicago, IL: Chicago University Press.

Meyer, L. B. (1957). Meaning in music and information theory. *Journal of Aesthetics and Art Criticism,* 15, 412–24.

Meyer, M. (1903). Experimental studies in the psychology of music. *American Journal of Psychology,* 14, 456–75.

Moreland, R. L., & Zajonc, R. B. (1977). Is stimulus recognition a necessary condition for the occurrence of exposure effects? *Journal of Personality and Social Psychology,* 35, 191–9.

Narmour, E. (1990). *The analysis and cognition of basic melodic structures.* Chicago, IL: University of Chicago Press.

Narmour, E. (1992). *The analysis and cognition of melodic complexity.* Chicago, IL: University of Chicago Press

Panksepp, J. (1995). The emotional sources of 'chills' induced by music. *Music Perception,* 13, 171–207.

Panksepp, J. (1998). *Affective neuroscience: The foundations of human and animal emotions.* Oxford: Oxford University Press.

Panksepp, J., & Bernatzky, G. (2002). Emotional sounds and the brain: The neuro-affective foundations of musical appreciation. *Behavioral Processes,* 60, 133–55.

Raichle, M. E., & Gusnard, D. A. (2005). Intrinsic brain activity sets the stage for expression of motivated behavior. *Journal of Comparative Neurology,* 493, 167–76.

Raichle, M. E., MacLeod, A. M., Snyder, A. E., Powers, W. J., Gusnard, D. A., & Shulman, G. L. (2001). A default mode of brain function. *Proceedings of the National Academy of Sciences,* 98, 676–82.

Rickard, N. S. (2004). Intense emotional responses to music: A test of the physiological arousal hypothesis. *Psychology of Music, 32,* 371–88.

Rifkin, D. (2000). *Tonal coherence in Prokofiev's music: A study of the interrelationships of structure, motives, and design.* Ph.D. Dissertation, Eastman School of Music, USA.

Saffran, J. R., Johnson, E. K., Aslin, R. N., & Newport, E. L. (1999). Statistical learning of tone sequences by human infants and adults. *Cognition, 70,* 27–52.

Schellenberg, E. G. (1996). Expectancy in melody: Tests of the implication-realization model. *Cognition, 58,* 75–125.

Schmuckler, M. (1989). Expectation in music: Investigation of melodic and harmonic processes. *Music Perception, 7,* 109–50.

Schön D., & Besson M. (2005). Visually induced auditory expectancy in music reading: a behavioural and electrophysicological study. *Journal of Cognitive Neuroscience, 17,* 693–704.

Shannon, C. E. (1948). A mathematical theory of communication. *Bell Systems Technical Journal, 27,* 379–423.

Sloboda, J. A. (1991). Music structure and emotional response: Some empirical findings. *Psychology of Music, 19,* 110–20.

Snyder, J. L. (1990). Entropy as a measure of musical style: The influence of a priori assumptions. *Music Theory Spectrum, 12,* 121–60.

Steinbeis, N., Koelsch, S., & Sloboda, J. A. (2006). The role of harmonic expectancy violations in musical emotions: evidence from subjective, physiological and neural responses. *Journal of Cognitive Neuroscience, 18,* 1380–93.

Suddendorf, T. (2006). Foresight and evolution of the human mind. *Science, 312,* 1006–7.

Sundberg, J. (1972). An articulatory interpretation of the 'singing formant'. *Speech Transmission Laboratory/Quarterly Progress Status Report, Stockholm, 1,* 45–53.

Sundberg, J. (1977). The acoustics of the singing voice. *Scientific American, 236,* 82–91.

Sundberg, J. (1987). *The science of the singing voice.* DeKalb, IL: Northern Illinois University Press.

Temperley, D. (2007). *Music and probability.* Cambridge, MA: MIT Press.

Thayer, R. E. (1996). *The origin of everyday moods: Managing energy, tension, and stress.* Oxford: Oxford University Press.

Tillmann, B., Bigand, E., & Pineau, M. (1998). Effects of global and local contexts on harmonic expectancy. *Music Perception, 16,* 99–118.

Verleger, R. (1990). P3-evoking wrong notes: Unexpected, awaited, or arousing? *International Journal of Neuroscience, 55,* 171–9.

von Hippel, P. (2002). Melodic-expectation rules as learned heuristics. In C. Stevens, D. Burnham, G. McPherson, E. Schubert, & J. Renwick (eds), *Proceedings of the 7th International Conference on Music Perception and Cognition* (pp. 315–317). Adelaide, Australia: Causal Productions.

von Hippel, P., & Huron, D. (2000). Why do skips precede reversals? The effect of tessitura on melodic structure. *Music Perception, 18,* 59–85.

von Hippel, P., Huron, D., & Harnish, D. (1998). *Melodic expectation for a Balinese melody: A comparison of Balinese and American musicians.* Unpublished manuscript.

Weiss, M. J., Zelazo, P. R., & Swain, I. U. (1988). Newborn response to auditory stimulus discrepancy. *Child Development, 59,* 530–41.

Wilson, T. D., & Gilbert, D. T. (2005). Affective forecasting: Knowing what to want. *Current Directions in Psychological Science, 14,* 131–4.

Youngblood, J. E. (1958). Style as information. *Journal of Music Theory, 2,* 24–35.

CHAPTER 22

HOW DOES MUSIC EVOKE EMOTIONS?

EXPLORING THE UNDERLYING MECHANISMS

PATRIK N. JUSLIN,
SIMON LILJESTRÖM,
DANIEL VÄSTFJÄLL, AND
LARS-OLOV LUNDQVIST

Of all the problems concerning musical emotions discussed by the philosophers since ancient Greece (Budd, 1985), none is perhaps more intriguing than the question of *how* music evokes emotions (Dowling & Harwood, 1986). Besides being important in itself, the question also has far-reaching implications for other issues currently debated in the field (Which emotions does music evoke? Which areas of the brain are involved in musical emotions? What is the relation between perceived and felt emotions?). Indeed, we suggest that the issue is even at the core of arguments about whether music may evoke emotions at all. To see why, consider the fact that in everyday life an emotion is usually induced when an event or object is appraised as having the capacity to influence the goals of the perceiver somehow (Scherer, 1999). Because music does not seem to have such goal implications,[1] it appears more difficult to explain why music

---

[1] To avoid confusion, we emphasize that there is a distinction between *using* music to achieve a goal (e.g. to relax) and a goal being involved in the actual *emotion induction* (i.e. the psychological process that evokes the affective response).

should evoke emotions—especially emotions of the 'garden variety'. Kivy (1990) argued that:

> the lack of an explanation in ordinary, 'folkpsychological' terms for the purported arousal of the garden-variety emotions seems convincing if not, perhaps, absolutely conclusive evidence that no such arousal takes place. (p. 152)

> Music provides neither the objects nor, therefore, the belief-opportunities that would make it possible for musical works to arouse such emotions as anger, sadness, joy . . . (p. 165)

> *If* music arouses such emotions . . . some special explanation is required. (p. 149)

Considering that studies have suggested that listeners *do* experience the 'garden variety' emotions to music (see Section 22.2), it would seem important to intensify the search for such 'special explanations'. That is, we should consider mechanisms other than cognitive appraisal that can account for these emotions.

As explained further below, we will use the term 'psychological mechanism' broadly in this chapter to refer to any information processing that may lead to the induction of emotions through listening to music. As noted in Chapter 4 (this volume), postulating mechanisms that can explain how music induces emotions in listeners is an essential aspect of a psychological approach. Still, a search of the literature reveals that very few articles have actually proposed or tested any theory about mechanisms (Juslin & Västfjäll, 2008a, p. 560). In fact, apart from Meyer's (1956) and Berlyne's (1971) books, most theories focus on the expressive properties of music that allow listeners to *perceive* emotion in music (Clynes, 1977; Cooke, 1959; Juslin, 2001; Langer, 1957). Studies of emotional *reactions* to music have mostly been untheoretical in nature. In particular, musical emotions have been studied without respect to how they were evoked, which has contributed to confusion and controversy in the field. It has also prevented researchers from explaining individual differences—for instance, why the same piece of music can evoke different emotions in different listeners.

The aim of this chapter is to present a research project devoted specifically to studying the underlying mechanisms responsible for induction of emotion through music listening. In the following, we present a research strategy, a novel theoretical framework and preliminary findings from our ongoing studies that explore underlying mechanisms. We also discuss the implications of this work for other issues in the field of musical emotions. The early parts of the chapter review findings about the *prevalence* of musical emotions, because a first step in developing a framework is to know what phenomena the framework is supposed to explain.[2] The latter parts of the chapter present a unified theoretical framework that can explain these prevalence findings in terms of seven distinct mechanisms, besides cognitive appraisal. This will illustrate the role of psychological theory in telling researchers where to look for 'clues' in their quest to unravel the mystery of emotional responses to music.

---

[2] The term *prevalence*, borrowed from epidemiology, refers to the proportion or relative frequency of occurrence of a phenomenon—such as particular emotions—in the population of interest.

22.1 A NEW APPROACH TO AN OLD PROBLEM: THE AMUSE PROJECT

There are few long-term research programmes dedicated to musical emotions, though one such programme is the Appraisal in Music and Emotion (AMUSE) project at the Uppsala University (http://www.psyk.uu.se/hemsidor/musicpsy2/). The aim of this project is to develop a model that can explain and even predict listeners' emotional reactions to music. The primary issues addressed are:

- What psychological mechanisms underlie the induction of emotions through music listening?
- What factors in the listener, the music, and the situation influence the emotions?
- How may individual differences among listeners be explained in terms of these mechanisms and causal factors?
- How well can emotional responses to music be predicted in different situations?

To address these issues, the AMUSE project involves a research strategy consisting of a close interplay between field studies (questionnaire studies, experience-sampling studies) and experimental studies (e.g. Juslin & Västfjäll, 2008a; see Figure 22.1). Instead of advocating only field studies (Chapter 7, this volume) or experimental studies (Chapter 25, this volume), it can be argued that both types of studies have obvious strengths as well as weaknesses. Laboratory experiments do not capture all relevant aspects, and the artificial settings raise concerns about the generalizability of results. Field studies, on the other hand, could jeopardize the validity of causal inferences. Hence, the best solution may be to apply a multi-method approach.

Field studies that enable researchers to capture listeners' musical emotions in the natural environment might generate hypotheses about possible causal factors and relationships. These variables and relationships may then be formalized in a preliminary

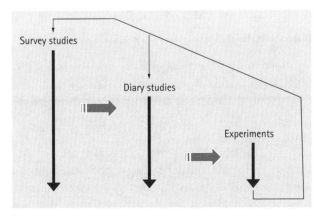

Fig. 22.1 Method triangulation in the AMUSE project.

model, which is evaluated in experiments. These experiments may suggest the need for further knowledge about specific variables, to be addressed in further field studies. By combining the various methods, one can eventually arrive at principles that hold regardless of the method of data collection. Further, one can achieve the goal of a representative sampling of participants (survey studies), situations (diary studies) and musical stimuli (experiments), respectively.

22.2 QUESTIONNAIRE STUDIES: MAPPING THE TERRAIN

A natural point of departure in attempting to explain emotional reactions to music is to collect a large number of verbal self-reports of emotional experiences that have involved music. The goal is to obtain an ecologically representative sample (cf. Brunswik, 1956) of music listeners and their musical events, reflecting the total range of emotional responses that may occur, and the variables that may influence these responses. (This type of information cannot be obtained by experimental methods.) It is well known that precisely who participates in an investigation may have a profound effect on what results are obtained, and college students are known to be unrepresentative of the general population in many ways (e.g. Vissner et al, 2000). Adequate sampling of participants is particularly important when it comes to estimating prevalence. By featuring a listener sample that reflects the full heterogeneity of the population, a survey study can help us to discover background variables that explain individual differences in prevalence. Moreover, results from questionnaires may provide information about causal factors that need to be addressed in subsequent experience-sampling studies (Section 22.3).

22.2.1 What needs to be explained: prevalence of musical emotions

An important requirement for a theory of musical emotion is that it can account for the kinds of affective states usually evoked by music. The question of which emotions music evokes is commonly debated, but rarely investigated empirically, even though this aspect can probably be reliably self-reported by participants. As pointed out by Griffiths (1997), people are rarely mistaken about how they feel. The wide range of different emotions reported in Gabrielsson's (2001, Table 19.1) study of strong experiences with music shows that in principle, and depending on the context, music can evoke just about any emotion felt in other realms of human life. But given the rarity and probably also extreme nature of such peak experiences, a more interesting question is perhaps which emotions music usually induces in listeners. This question has been addressed in a handful of survey studies that have offered preliminary evidence of prevalence.

The findings largely suggest that *happiness, calm, love, sadness, excitement,* and *nostalgia* are frequent emotions to music whereas *fear, shame,* and *jealousy* are not (Juslin & Laukka, 2004, Table 4; Sloboda, 1992, Table 1; Wells & Hakanen, 1991, Table 1; Zentner et al, 2008, Table 2). However, none of these studies used a representative sample of participants. Thus, it was considered important in the present project to investigate the prevalence of emotions to music using a more representative sample.

A survey approach focuses on self-reports of emotion. One can distinguish two general kinds of emotional self-report based on a distinction in memory research (Robinson & Clore, 2002; Tulving, 1984). Self-reports of emotion episodes that are relatively close in time to the report (e.g. How did you feel an hour ago? How did you feel last evening?) involve judgements based on *episodic memory.* Episodic knowledge is experiential in nature and is usually rich in information about the time and place of the recalled episode. One's ability to retrieve episodic information declines over time, but *emotional* events tend to be better remembered than non-emotional events (e.g. Reisberg & Heuer, 2004). Self-reports of emotions involving aggregated estimates (e.g. How frequently do you feel like this, generally?), on the other hand, involve judgements based on *semantic memory.* Semantic knowledge is abstract and frequency-based, although it is also prone to certain retrospective biases because it may be influenced by erroneous beliefs (Robinson & Clore, 2002). For example, if someone asks you 'How often do you experience happiness at concerts?' you may tend to overestimate this frequency based on folk theory (e.g. the belief that the emotion 'happiness' is typical of what people feel at music concerts). In our questionnaire research, we have used both semantic and episodic estimates, by asking both about emotions *in general* and about the most *recent* emotion episode.

In a recent survey study—based on a randomized and statistically representative sample of the Swedish population—706 participants reported their most recent emotional experience of music (Juslin et al, 2009). The participants described their feelings using their own words, rather than using a pre-selected list. Eighty-four per cent of the episodes referred to *positive* as opposed to *negative* affective states, and 8 per cent referred to 'general' (positive or negative) affect, rather than to specific emotions. Of the 92 per cent of the episodes that referred to specific emotions, 11 per cent featured 'mixed' or 'combined' emotions (e.g. both anger and sadness), whereas the remaining 89 per cent involved 'pure' or 'single' emotions. Because participants commonly used closely related synonyms (e.g. joyful, elated) in their responses, it was decided to sort similar emotion terms into common emotion categories, or 'emotion families' (Ekman, 1992), which is customary in studies that use open-ended responses. Figure 22.2 shows the ten most frequently reported categories of emotion. As seen there, the most frequently reported emotion category was *happy-elated,* which accounted for over 50 per cent of the musical episodes. This was followed by *sad-melancholic, calm-content,* and *nostalgic-longing.* Notably, the ten emotion categories featured both 'basic' (e.g. happiness, sadness) and 'complex' (e.g. nostalgia, pride) emotions. Furthermore, only two of the emotion categories (i.e. *sad-melancholic, angry-irritated*) were clearly negative in valence. In general, these findings suggest that listening to music primarily involves single occurrences of specific emotions that are positively valenced.

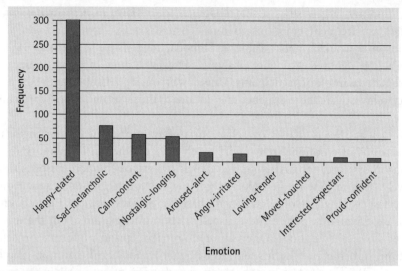

Fig. 22.2 Prevalence of freely reported emotions to music from a randomized and statistically representative sample of the Swedish population (*N* = 706) (from Juslin et al, 2009).

Some scholars have claimed that listeners' emotional reactions to music mainly consist of the state of 'being moved'—for instance by the sheer beauty of the music (see Kivy, 1990). This notion is not supported by the present results: only ten of 706 listeners mentioned 'being moved' in their response. One likely explanation is that the expression 'being moved' simply refers to being emotionally affected, without specifying the precise affective state (Robinson, 2005). Hence when asked to describe what they felt, most participants reported more specific affective states. It should further be noted that affective states such as *wonder* and *chills* were rare in listeners' responses, as previously suggested by Huron (2006).

The above study also featured semantic estimates of prevalence. (The results were quite similar to those from Juslin and Laukka, 2004, shown in Chapter 18, this volume, Table 18.1.) Semantic and episodic estimates of prevalence produced largely similar findings, although the emotion *sadness* appeared to be more frequent, judging from episodic data, than from semantic data.[3] One possible explanation is that the participants display a kind of *positivity bias* in their semantic estimates, such that they underestimate the degree to which they experience negative emotions like sadness to music in everyday life. This bias may not be present in the reports of the most *recent* experience of a musical emotion, because these rely on episodic memory.

---

[3] It can further be noted that some states that were rated as quite frequent in the semantic data (e.g. 'moved') did rarely occur in the musical episodes, where listeners could report their feelings using their own words.

Overall, the survey studies of prevalence of musical emotions to date show quite similar results (see also Chapter 8, this volume). However, all these studies share two problems. First, they rely on aggregated and/or retrospective self-reports that may not be reliable. Second, they do not directly *compare* musical with non-musical emotions as they occur in real-life contexts. These issues have been addressed in our experience-sampling studies (Section 22.3 below).

22.2.2 Possible causal influences on musical emotions

In the questionnaire study outlined earlier (Juslin et al, 2009), we also made a first attempt to explore causes of musical emotions. As explained above, the participants reported their latest emotional experience with music. In this context they were asked what they believed 'caused' their emotion. We used an open-ended response format and the responses were coded by two independent coders ('mean inter-coder agreement', Cohen's κ = .91) into the following seven categories: 'musical factors' (45 per cent; e.g. 'good song', 'the singing voice', 'a fast tempo', 'the melody', 'the excellent performance'), 'situation factors' (27 per cent; e.g. 'my father's funeral', 'the weather', 'the social atmosphere'), 'memory factors' (24 per cent; e.g. 'nostalgic recognition', 'sad memory'), 'lyrics' (10 per cent; e.g. 'the words', 'the message of the lyrics', 'the truthfulness of the words'), 'pre-existing mood' (9 per cent; e.g. 'loneliness', 'being in love'), 'other factors' (4 per cent; rare responses that did not fit into the above categories) and 'non-causal response' (4 per cent; responses that were irrelevant to the cause of the emotion).[4] Overall, these results suggest that factors in the listener, music, and situation are all important in the process. One problem concerning the goal to capture *mechanisms* was that, overall, the participants did not appear to spontaneously focus on a 'mechanistic' level—with the exception of memories—and were inclined to simply report external variables. These results suggest that open-ended responses are not optimal for investigating underlying mechanisms: participants need probing in order to focus on possible mechanisms (Section 22.3.2).

A more positive result, however, was that musical emotions could be *predicted* to some degree based on information about the precise circumstances of the situation where the music occurred. Fifteen predictors were featured in a discriminant analysis, five for each of the main factors (listener, music, situation). The analysis focused on predicting three frequent and pure emotion categories in the present sample of musical episodes: *happy-elated*, *sad-melancholic*, and *nostalgic-longing*. It was found that these emotions could be predicted with an overall hit ratio of 66 per cent correct—compared to a hit ratio of 33 per cent that would be expected by chance alone. Variables that made significant and unique contributions to predictive power featured 'musical causes', 'situational causes', 'gender', 'emotional stability', and 'work versus leisure'.

---

[4] Numbers show the percentage of episodes in which the participant mentioned each type of causal factor. The categories are not mutually exclusive, and since several episodes featured more than one factor (e.g. musical factors + lyrics), the sum of percentages > 100.

This success, though modest, in predicting three common emotions in musical episodes shows that such emotions are not 'too subjective' or 'too varied' to be modelled successfully, in principle—there are quite systematic relationships among musical emotions and a range of predictors.

22.3 EXPERIENCE-SAMPLING STUDIES: CAPTURING MUSICAL EMOTIONS IN THE FIELD

If the goal is to investigate experiences of music in their natural environment, question-naire studies represent only a first approximation. Ideally one would like to follow par-ticipants in their daily lives to obtain self-reports about their music experiences as these occur naturally. This can be achieved through experience-sampling studies (Conner Christensen et al, 2003; Reis & Gable, 2000). The *Experience-Sampling Methodology* (ESM) means that subjects are provided with small palmtop computers that they carry with them at all waking hours during a week or so. During the week, the palmtop emits sound signals at certain predetermined or—preferably—randomized intervals. Each time the participant hears the sound signal, he or she should immediately respond to various questions administered by the palmtop about his or her latest musical experi-ence. Multiple-choice questions, open-ended questions, and rating scales may be used to describe the nature of each experience, whereas targeted questions may probe the participant concerning whether particular psychological mechanisms were involved in the emotion episode (e.g. Did the music evoke a memory from the past? Did the music influence any of your current goals? Did the music evoke visual imagery?).

One obvious advantage of ESM studies is that they enable the investigation of musi-cal events as they unfold in their natural and spontaneous context. Another advantage is that they render possible repeated measurements over time, so that one may obtain a better sense of whether a phenomenon occurs in particular recurrent patterns—for instance, on certain days of the week. Information may also be obtained about the events that preceded the relevant experiences and that may play an important causal role, and about the consequences of the experience. Even in such cases where frequency estimates (e.g. the prevalence of particular emotions) are desired, this method may produce more reliable results than the common aggregated, retrospective, and cognitively biased esti-mates obtained in questionnaires (Ready, Weinberger, & Jones, 2007).

22.3.1 ESM estimates of prevalence of musical emotions

To correctly estimate the prevalence of specific emotions, it may be necessary to capture the emotions as they spontaneously occur. The ESM is useful for this aim. Sloboda, O'Neill, and Ivaldi (2001) pioneered the use of the ESM in music, and concluded that the ESM is a robust method to study music listening in everyday life (see also Chapter 18, this volume). However, that study did not aim to report prevalence of specific emotions. A more recent ESM study of musical emotions in everyday life by Juslin et al (2008) provided estimates of occurrence of 14 emotional states in response to music as well as to other stimuli during a two-week period. The listener sample consisted of 32 college students (aged 20–31 years), of whom 44 per cent played a musical instrument and 31 per cent had some formal music education. These participants carried a palmtop computer that emitted a sound signal seven times per day at random intervals for two weeks. When signalled, participants were required to complete a questionnaire on the palmtop. Results revealed that music occurred in 37 per cent of the random episodes, and in 64 per cent of the music episodes the participants reported that the music influenced their feelings. Emotional reactions to music were most frequent in the evening and during weekends.

The participants reported their felt emotion by choosing from a fixed list of 14 emotion terms (the use of only 14 categories was due to software limitations). Selecting 14 terms from the several hundreds of terms available is no easy task, but the goal was to include both terms that are representative of the two dominant conceptualizations of emotion (i.e. categories and dimensions) and terms that could be particularly relevant with respect to music. Hence, the 13 emotion terms included the 'basic' emotions typical of discrete emotion theories, such as *happiness, surprise, interest, anger,* and *fear* (Izard, 1977), covered all four quadrants of the circumplex model in terms of valence and arousal (Russell, 1980) and featured more music-related terms, such as *pleasure, nostalgia,* and *expectancy* (Figure 22.3). In addition, the participant could select the alternative 'other emotion', if none of the provided emotion terms was found suitable. The response alternatives thus included the emotions reported most frequently in the above survey study (Juslin et al, 2009), but also included other emotions, in order not to prejudge the issue of which emotions music might evoke.[5]

Figure 22.4 presents the prevalence (per cent) of emotions caused by music and emotions caused by other stimuli respectively. As can be seen, emotions such as *calm-contentment, happiness-elation,* and *interest-expectancy* were common in general, whereas emotions such as *disgust-contempt* were not so common. A comparison of musical with non-musical emotion episodes revealed that *happiness-elation* and *nostalgia-longing* were significantly more frequent ($p < .05$) in episodes with musical emotions, whereas *anger-irritation, boredom-indifference,* and *anxiety-fear* were all significantly more frequent in episodes with non-musical emotions. The remaining differences were not significant. In only 3 per cent of the musical emotion episodes did a listener select the 'other emotion' option, indicating that the emotion terms provided covered listeners' responses reasonably well. Further, individual prevalence of emotions to music was correlated with 'Big Five' personality characteristics, as measured by the NEO-PI-R, notably Extroversion and Openness.

[5] In a sense, this response format represents a compromise among the three response paradigms discussed in Chapter 8 (this volume).

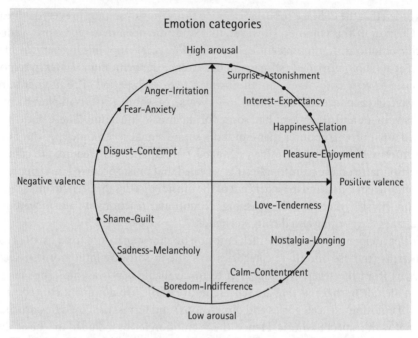

Fig. 22.3 Approximate positions in the circumplex model of the 13 emotion terms used as response alternatives in the experience-sampling study by Juslin et al (2008).

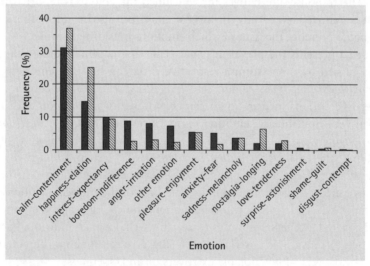

Fig. 22.4 Relative frequency (in per cent) of specific emotions in non-musical emotion episodes (dark bars) and musical emotion episodes (striped bars) in everyday life during a two-week period. From Juslin et al (2008).

However, it must be noted that the prevalence of specific musical emotions varied a lot depending on the situation; for example, some emotions such as *happiness-elation*, *pleasure-enjoyment*, and *anger-irritation* occurred frequently in 'social' settings, whereas others such as *calm-contentment*, *nostalgia-longing*, and *sadness-melancholy* occurred frequently in more 'solitary' settings. This highlights the need to use representative samples of situations in order to obtain valid estimates of the prevalence of specific musical emotions. Experimental studies, or studies that look at a single setting, are likely to produce biased estimates.[6]

Although difficulties involved in translating emotion experiences into verbal labels must be kept in mind, the results from both this and the above studies suggest that music can evoke a range of both basic and complex emotions as well as 'mixed' emotions (Gabrielsson, 2001). Music listeners can experience anything from mere arousal, 'thrills' and 'basic' emotions like happiness and sadness to more 'complex' emotions, such as nostalgia and pride. This, then, is what any satisfactory theory of musical emotions must be able to explain.

22.3.2 ESM data on possible mechanisms

The findings of the survey study by Juslin et al (2009) suggested that open-ended responses may not be optimal for exploring underlying mechanisms—participants need help in order to focus on possible mechanisms. A more theory-based approach to causes of musical emotions was adopted in our ESM study (Juslin et al, 2008). Listeners were asked what they believed 'caused' their emotion in each episode. However, rather than respond freely—with the risk that the answers would not address any of the possible mechanisms—they could choose from ten alternatives based on previous research and, especially, the framework proposed by Juslin and Västfjäll (2008a). Based on a synthesis of the literature, Juslin and Västfjäll proposed seven mechanisms (explained further in Section 22.4.1 below) through which music might induce emotions:

(1) *Brain stem response*, related to 'pre-wired' attention responses to simple acoustic characteristics of the music (e.g. loudness, speed);

(2) *Evaluative conditioning*, related to a regular pairing of a music stimulus and other positive or negative stimulus;

(3) *Emotional contagion*, related to an internal 'mimicry' of the perceived emotional expression of the music;

(4) *Visual imagery*, related to visual images of an emotional nature conjured up by the listener while listening to the music;

(5) *Episodic memory*, related to specific memories from the listener's past evoked by the music;

---

[6] One reason may be that different situations tend to involve different mechanisms, which in turn tend to evoke different emotions (see Section 22.5.2).

(6) *Music expectancy*, related to the gradual unfolding of the musical structure and how unexpected continuations may evoke emotions in the listener, and

(7) *Cognitive appraisal*, related to an evaluation of the music on various dimensions in relation to current goals or plans of the individual.

The participants in the study could choose any of these mechanisms, each one carefully explained in a booklet, and the alternatives also included 'lyrics', 'other', and 'I don't know', so that participants would not feel forced to select one of the mechanisms.

Figure 22.5 shows the results. Firstly, all of the included underlying mechanisms occurred in at least some episodes. Secondly, the most commonly self-reported causes were *emotional contagion, brain stem response,* and *episodic memory*. Together, these accounted for 71 per cent of the episodes. Thirdly, the least commonly reported cause was *cognitive appraisal*—indicating that music rarely has implications for goals in life, and hence suggesting that appraisal theory has a limited explanatory value in regard to music. Finally, the options *other* and *I don't know* were seldom chosen (4 per cent and 3 per cent of the episodes respectively), suggesting that the response alternatives provided were considered appropriate in most musical emotion episodes.

Previous studies have revealed that the listener's degree of choice of music is important for the induction of emotions in music listening (Harrer & Harrer, 1977; Sloboda et al, 2001). Table 22.1 shows the relative frequencies (in per cent) of responses regarding choice of music as a function of self-reported cause of the emotion (i.e. the psychological mechanism). As can be seen, a high proportion of self-chosen music occurred in musical emotion episodes evoked by *episodic memory*, whereas considerably lower proportions of choice occurred for emotion episodes evoked by *musical expectancy* and

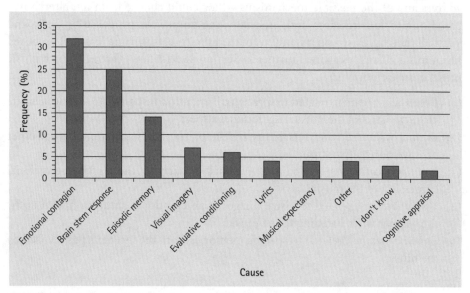

Fig. 22.5 Relative frequency (in per cent) of self–reported causes of 573 musical emotion episodes (based on data in Juslin et al, 2008).

Table 22.1 Relative frequencies (in per cent) of responses with regard to choice of music as a function of self-reported mechanism evoking the emotion (re-analysed data from Juslin et al, 2008)

Mechanism	Choice	
	Yes	No
Episodic memory	74	26
Emotional contagion	66	34
Brain stem response	62	38
Visual imagery	73	27
Musical expectancy	54	46
Evaluative conditioning	22	78
Cognitive appraisal	60	40
Lyrics	72	28

evaluative conditioning. These results imply that, whether subjects in listening experiments are able to choose the music themselves or not may influence which mechanisms are activated, which, in turn, may influence which emotions are evoked. In the ESM study, *nostalgia-longing* reactions often occurred with *episodic memory*, rather than with *visual imagery*, whereas the opposite pattern was true of *pleasure-enjoyment* responses.

The above study is the first to explore mechanisms underlying musical emotions in daily life. The results provide at least tentative estimates of the frequency of occurrence for various mechanisms. Clearly, however, these results must be interpreted with caution. This study was based only on self-reports, and as with all self-reports, the participants report only what they can, or are willing to, report. The participants may sometimes have been unaware of the 'true' causes of their emotions. Furthermore, psychological mechanisms that are 'implicit' in nature (conditioning) are likely to be under-reported, relative to mechanisms that are more 'salient' in conscious experience (episodic memory). Consequently, it is important also to conduct studies of mechanisms in more controlled laboratory settings where stronger conclusions about causal relations can be drawn (Section 22.4). On the other hand, field studies are required, because if there are several mechanisms that might induce musical emotions, and their importance varies depending on the situation, only by sampling a wide variety of real-life situations can we hope to capture all relevant mechanisms and estimate their importance in real-world contexts.

The results from ESM studies may be analysed by means of Hierarchical Linear Models (Raudenbush & Bryk, 2002). This allows a researcher to simultaneously analyse ESM data on the level of a listener's repeated musical emotion episodes over time (level 1) and on the level of the listener (level 2), featuring, for instance, personality measures. HLM is thus suitable for modelling the complex interactions between the listener,

Table 22.2 Summary of fixed effects for a two-level hierarchical linear model predicting the occurrence of *pleasure-enjoyment* in music listeners' emotion episodes in everyday life during a period of two weeks (see text for further explanation)

	Coefficient	Odds ratio	Conf. interval	d.f.	t
Predictor					
Intercept	-3.687	0.025	0.012 - 0.054	29	-9.830**
Neuroticism	0.020	1.020	1.002 - 1.039	29	2.212*
Others present	1.770	5.869	2.102 - 16.388	507	3.381**
Activity	2.034	7.647	0.825 - 70.848	507	1.793[†]
Vis.Imagery	1.378	3.967	1.267 - 12.427	507	2.368*

[†]p <.10; *p <.05; **p <.01

the music, and the situation. Equation 22.1 presents an example of a relatively simple, two-level model based on the data from the above ESM study by Juslin et al (2008):

$$\eta = \beta_{00} + \beta_{01}*NEURO + \beta_{10}*PRESENT + \beta_{20}*ACTIVITY + \beta_{30}*VISIMAGE + \gamma_{0}$$

$$22.1$$

The occurrence of *pleasure-enjoyment* (coded dichotomously, 0/1) during a musical emotion episode at a particular point in time is predicted by the level-1 predictors *other people present* (alone vs. with other people), *activity* (leisure vs. work), and *visual imagery* (activated vs. not activated), as well as the level-2 predictor *neuroticism* (individual test score from NEO-PI-R). Table 22.2 shows the results. As seen there, all predictors except *activity* contributed uniquely and significantly to the prediction of *pleasure-enjoyment*. More specifically, the experience of *pleasure-enjoyment* was positively correlated with a neurotic personality, being the sole person in the situation, and experiencing music-induced visual imagery.

22.4 EXPERIMENTS: TESTING CAUSAL RELATIONSHIPS

Field studies do not enable researchers to draw definitive conclusions with respect to causal relationships—due to insufficient experimental control. Therefore, it is necessary to conduct experiments in the laboratory where factors that seem important on the basis of field studies are manipulated in a systematic (albeit necessarily simplified) manner. Another reason why field studies are not sufficient is that participants can only report psychological processes of which they are consciously aware, whereas unconscious (or 'implicit') processes on 'lower' levels (e.g. conditioning) can only be studied using indirect methods that are easier to apply in a laboratory. As part of our experimental approach to underlying mechanisms of musical emotions, we have developed a new framework that can guide experimental studies. Before discussing such experiments, we outline the framework and its theoretical predictions.

22.4.1 A unified theoretical framework: BRECVEM

Although some researchers have acknowledged that there may be more than one mechanism that can evoke emotions in music listening (e.g. Berlyne, 1971; Dowling & Harwood, 1986; Meyer, 1956; Robinson, 2005; Scherer & Zentner, 2001; Sloboda & Juslin, 2001), there has been no attempt to develop an integrated theoretical framework featuring a set of hypotheses concerning the nature of each mechanism.

As noted previously, we use the term *psychological mechanism* to refer to any kind of information processing that may lead to the induction of emotions through listening to music. What all the mechanisms discussed below have in common is that they can become activated by taking music as their 'object'. We adhere to the notion that a defining feature of emotions is that they involve intentional objects: they are 'about' something (Frijda, 1999, p. 191). For example, we are sad about the death of a loved one. The same, we propose, is true of musical emotions (although importantly, the listener need not be *consciously aware* of the 'object' of the emotion, as revealed in the classic experiment by Öhman & Soares, 1994, where subjects with spider phobia showed physiological fear reactions to masked and undetected pictures of spiders). This is one of the reasons why music listeners' affective states should be referred to as emotions proper, rather than moods.[7] Therefore, we agree with Kivy (1990) that 'clearly, the object must be *the music*—or, when we refine things a bit, various features of the music' (p. 159). However, we differ from Kivy in that we think that music features many different kinds of information that can evoke an emotional response—not only 'beauty'. As noted by Patel (2008), humans are unparalleled in their ability to make sense out of sound, including music.

Most scholars who have written about possible mechanisms have limited themselves to one or a few mechanisms (Berlyne, 1971; Meyer, 1956). Thus, for example, Levinson (1997) suggested that there are two parallel mechanisms, the *sensory* and the *perceptual-imaginative* routes (pp. 27–8). Other researchers have argued that a *cognitive*

---

[7] There are, in fact, several reasons why listeners' responses should be 'emotions' rather than 'moods' (see the working definitions in Chapter 1, this volume). Besides the fact that the underlying mechanisms focus on an object (the music or more specifically certain information in the music processed in relation to individual and situational factors), the experienced states last for a limited duration (Juslin et al, 2009; Panksepp & Bernatsky, 2002; Västfjäll, 2002, p. 192); they have a fairly strong intensity (Juslin et al, 2008); and involve autonomic responses (e.g. Krumhansl, 1997; see also Chapter 11, this volume). These features are usually believed to be associated with 'emotions', rather than 'moods' (Beedie, Terry, & Lane, 2005).

appraisal approach may be most suitable to explain emotions to music (e.g. Waterman, 1996).

In contrast, Juslin and Västfjäll (2008a), building on the pioneering research by Berlyne (1971) and Meyer (1956) as well as on more recent research, presented a framework featuring six psychological mechanisms—in addition to cognitive appraisal—through which music may evoke emotions, singularly or in combination. In this chapter, we provide a revised version of this framework, featuring an additional mechanism (suggested in several commentaries on the original version; Juslin & Västfjäll, 2008b, p. 605). Thus, the current framwork features seven mechanisms: *Brain stem reflexes, Rhythmic entrainment, Evaluative conditioning, Contagion, Visual imagery, Episodic memory* and *Musical expectancy*; these may be collectively referred to as the BRECVEM model.

Juslin and Västfjäll (2008) argue that one may think of these mechanisms as based on a number of distinct 'brain functions', which have developed gradually and in a particular order during the evolutionary process, from simple sensations to syntactical processing (Gärdenfors, 2003). The mechanisms are seen as 'information-processing devices' at different levels of the brain that utilize different means to track significant aspects of the environment, and that may lead to conflicting outputs under some circumstances. All mechanisms take the music as their 'object', treating the music (rightly or wrongly) as if it features information that, in some way, warrants an emotional response. All of the mechanisms have their origins outside the musical domain, and in that sense there is no such thing as 'a purely musical experience' (Kivy, 1990).

Also implicit in the model is the fact that all emotions to music require mediation, in terms of information processing. Hence, it is not meaningful to make a distinction between 'mediated' and 'unmediated' musical emotions. (Induction of emotions without any kind of information processing would be magical indeed!) Since each mechanism depends on brain functions with unique evolutionary origins, each mechanism is expected to have some unique characteristics, which one should be able to demonstrate, for instance, in carefully designed experiments.

Below, we first outline each mechanism. Then, we present an updated set of hypotheses based on Juslin and Västfjäll (2008a) that may help researchers to distinguish the mechanisms theoretically and empirically. We emphasize that our mechanism descriptions and hypotheses are only preliminary. (For a more detailed discussion, see Juslin and Västfjäll, 2008a, 2008b.)

Brain stem reflex refers to a process whereby an emotion is induced by music because one or more fundamental acoustical characteristics of the music are taken by the brain stem to signal a potentially important and urgent event. All other things being equal, sounds that are sudden, loud, dissonant, or that feature fast temporal patterns, induce arousal in the listener. Such responses reflect the impact of simple auditory sensations (i.e. music as *sound* in the most basic sense). The perceptual system is constantly scanning the immediate environment in order to discover potentially important changes or events. Sounds that meet certain criteria will thus induce an increased activation of the central nervous system in the early stages of auditory processing. The precise physiological processes underlying such brain stem responses are not completely understood, although evidence suggests that they occur in close connection with the reticular formation of the brain stem and the intralaminar nuclei of the thalamus, which receive inputs from the auditory system. The brainstem is an ancient structure of the brain that sub-serves a number of sensory and motor functions including, but not limited to, auditory perception and the mediation and control of attention, emotional arousal, heart rate, breathing, and movement (Joseph, 2000). It may thus influence physiological processes related to emotions such that the listener's arousal level increases or decreases (Berlyne, 1971).

Rhythmic entrainment refers to a process whereby an emotion is induced by a piece of music because the powerful, external rhythm of the music interacts with an internal body rhythm of the listener such as heart rate, such that the latter rhythm adjusts towards and eventually 'locks in' to a common periodicity. The adjusted heart rate may then spread to other components of emotion (e.g. feeling) through proprioceptive feedback, thereby producing increased arousal in the listener.[8] There are two components required in entrainment (see Clayton et al, 2005). First, there must be (at least) two autonomous rhythmic processes or *oscillators*. (Autonomy means that they should both be able to oscillate, even if they are separated—which excludes resonance from the notion of entrainment.) Second, the two oscillators must interact in some way.[9] Entrainment is found throughout nature. It occurs in some way or another in all animal species, and humans appear to have an innate propensity to entrain (Clayton et al, 2005). The cooperative and oscillatory activities of brain neurons may form part of the basis for timing in sensory–motor coordination and metre perception (Jones, 2009). Clayton (2009) has proposed that entrainment is particularly noticeable in activities where rhythmic coordination will make physical work more efficient. Entrainment has not been systematically studied with respect to musical emotion. Kneutgen (1970) found that when soothing lullabies were played for infants, their breathing rhythms became synchronized with the musical rhythm. Further, Landreth and Landreth (1974) found changes in heart rate to be directly related to changes in tempo. Harrer and Harrer (1977) reported that music listeners tended to synchronize either their heart rate or their respiration to the music, and that one could 'drive' the pulse with appropriate music. The entrainment-inducing properties of music that produce affect presumably depend on the music having a marked pulse—and preferably one that is relatively close to the 'natural' heart rate or respiration of the listener. Oscillators do not synchronize instantaneously, and the period takes longer to adjust than the phase (Clayton et al, 2005, p. 9, p. 15). This means that entrainment is a slower induction process than, say, a brain stem reflex.

---

[8] The phenomenon of entrainment was discovered in 1665 by the scientist Huygens, who observed that two pendulum clocks with close but unsynchronized periods would 'phase-lock' their strokes. Since then, entrainment has been studied in several disciplines—such as physics, mathematics, biology, and the social sciences.

[9] Entrainment thus defined excludes some broader uses of the term in which it seems to denote almost any form of synchronization. Critical in establishing genuine entrainment is to identify disturbances—perturbations and transitions—in the synchronization process (Clayton et al, 2005).

Evaluative conditioning (EC) refers to a process whereby an emotion is induced by a piece of music simply because this stimulus has often been paired with other positive or negative stimuli (De Houwer, Thomas, & Baeyens, 2001). For example, a particular piece of music may have occurred repeatedly together in time with a specific event that always makes you happy, such as meeting one of your friends. Over time, through repeated pairings, the music itself will eventually evoke happiness even in the absence of the friendly interaction. There are few studies of EC with music (but see Blair & Shimp, 1992), though EC has a number of features that are interesting in regard to music. Firstly, EC can occur even if the participant is unaware of the contingency of the two stimuli. In fact, it has been found that EC can be both established and induce emotions without awareness (e.g. Martin et al, 1984). Secondly, EC appears to be fairly resistant to extinction, compared with classical conditioning. Music often occurs in situations where music listening is not the main activity (Sloboda, O'Neill, & Ivaldi, 2001) and where subtle conditioning processes outside awareness could easily occur. Thus, it appears plausible that EC could account for many of our responses to music in everyday life—including those that involve the mere exposure effect (Zajonc, 2001). This can be regarded as a form of EC if one assumes that the absence of aversive events constitutes the unconditioned stimulus. That is, stimuli that we have encountered repeatedly, without suffering any negative consequences, will eventually produce positively valenced responses.

Emotional *contagion* refers to a process whereby an emotion is induced by a piece of music because the listener perceives the emotional expression of the music and then 'mimics' this expression internally (Juslin, 2001). Emotional contagion has mostly been studied regarding facial expression (Hatfield, Cacioppo, & Rapson, 1994), but Neumann and Strack (2000) also found evidence of contagion from emotional speech. Because music may often feature sound patterns similar to those that occur in emotional speech (Juslin & Laukka, 2003; and Chapter 17, this volume), it has been proposed that we get aroused by voice-like aspects of music via a process in which a neural 'module' responds quickly and automatically to certain stimulus features, which leads us to mimic the perceived emotion internally (Juslin, 2001). While the notion of emotional contagion via music admittedly remains somewhat speculative, a recent fMRI study by Koelsch et al (2006) found that music listening activated brain areas related to a circuitry serving the formation of pre-motor representations for vocal sound production (no singing was observed among the participants). Koelsch et al concluded that this could reflect a mirror-function mechanism, similar to the so-called 'mirror neurons' proposed as a possible explanation of emotional contagion via other non-verbal channels (Preston & de Waal, 2002).

Visual imagery refers to a process whereby an emotion is induced in a listener because he or she conjures up visual images (e.g. of a beautiful landscape) while listening to the music. The emotions experienced are the result of an interaction between the music and these images. The precise nature of this process remains to be described, but listeners appear to conceptualize the musical structure through a metaphorical non-verbal mapping between the music and 'image schemata' grounded in bodily experience (see Lakoff & Johnson, 1980); for instance, hearing melodic movement as 'upward'. Listeners might respond to mental images in much the same way as they would to the corresponding stimuli in the 'real' world: for instance, reacting with positive emotions to a beautiful nature scene. Mental imagery in relation to music has mostly been explored in the context of music therapy (Toomey, 1996–7). Helen Bonny developed a method, *Guided Imagery and Music* (GIM), where a 'traveller' is invited to 'share' his or her images as they are experienced in real time during a programmed musical sequence (Bonny & Savary, 1973). Characteristic of visual imagery as an induction mechanism is that the listener is able to influence the process to a considerable extent. Although images might come into the mind unbidden, often a listener may conjure up, manipulate, and dismiss images at will.

Episodic memory refers to a process whereby an emotion is induced in a listener because the music evokes a personal memory of a specific event in the listener's life (Baumgartner, 1992). This has been referred to as the 'Darling, they are playing our tune' phenomenon (see Davies, 1978). When the memory is evoked, so also is the emotion associated with the memory. Such emotions may be intense—perhaps because the physiological response patterns to the original events are stored in memory along with the experiential contents. Many listeners use music to remind them of valued past events, suggesting that music may serve an important 'nostalgic' function in everyday life. Music plays a very prominent role in adolescents' lives in regard to the development of a self-identity (e.g. Saarikallio, 2007). Hence, one could expect episodic memories associated with music to be particularly emotionally vivid and frequent with regard to music from young adulthood, as indeed seems to be the case. Schulkind, Hennis, and Rubin (1999) found that older adults preferred and knew more about, as well as had stronger reactions to, music popular during their youth than to music popular later in life. Studies have revealed that episodic memories often evoke musical emotions (Janata, Tomic, & Rakowski, 2007; Juslin et al, 2008, 2009).

Musical expectancy refers to a process whereby an emotion is induced in a listener because a specific feature of the music violates, delays, or confirms the listener's expectations about the continuation of the music (Meyer, 1956; see also Narmour, 1992). For instance, the sequential progression of E–F# sets up the expectation that the music will continue with G#. If this does not happen, listeners familiar with the musical idiom may become surprised. The expectations are based on the listener's previous experiences of the same style of music. Although Meyer's theory is highly regarded, it has not stimulated much research on emotions (but see Sloboda, 1991), perhaps because the theory is difficult to test. For instance, a musical piece may evoke several different musical expectations at different levels of the music, and these expectations may also be different for different listeners. However, support for Meyer's theory was found by Steinbeis, Koelsch, and Sloboda (2006), who used subjective and physiological measures to capture emotional responses to unexpected events in music. Recent work on expectancy in music has produced some sophisticated models (Chapter 21, this volume) that may be used to further explore the characteristics of this mechanism.

22.4.2 Theoretical predictions

Only a few of the above mechanisms have been investigated in regard to music, but one thing is clear: there is no single mechanism that can account for all instances of musical emotion. A crucial goal for future research is to develop a process model of the induction process, though given the large number of mechanisms, such an endeavour is a formidable undertaking. A first step could be to specify the precise characteristics of each mechanism. Hence, by synthesizing theory and findings from several different domains outside music, Juslin and Västfjäll (2008a) were able to provide the first set of hypotheses that may help researchers to distinguish among the various mechanisms. Table 22.3 presents an updated version of these hypotheses featuring the added mechanism *rhythmic entrainment*.

The hypotheses can be divided into two subgroups: the first subgroup concerns the nature of the psychological mechanism as such.

Survival value of brain function describes the most important benefit that each brain function brought to those organisms that possessed this brain function. Visual imagery, for example, allowed an organism to 'simulate' important events internally, by means of self-conjured images in the absence of direct sensory input, which meant that overt and potentially dangerous action plans could be tested and evaluated before they were implemented in the external world.

Information focus specifies broadly the type of information that each mechanism is processing. For instance, evaluative conditioning focuses on covariation between events.

Ontogenetic development concerns the approximate time in the development when respective mechanism might begin to have a noticeable effect on musical emotions. Brain stem reflexes to music could be functional even prior to birth, whereas responses involving musical expectancy may not develop fully until between the ages of 5 and 11.

Key brain regions describes those regions of the brain that have been most consistently associated with each mechanism in neuroimaging studies.[10] Notably, musical emotions can be expected to involve three kinds of brain regions: (1) regions usually involved when music is perceived, such as the primary auditory cortex; (2) regions usually involved in the conscious experience of emotions regardless of the exact cause of the emotion (e.g. the rostral anterior cingulate and the medial prefrontal cortex; Lane, 2000, pp. 356–358; PAG, Panksepp, 1998); and (3) regions involved in emotional information processing that partly differ depending on the mechanism inducing the emotion. Thus, although musical emotions involve several brain regions (Chapters 5 and 12, this volume), the hypotheses in Table 22.3 focus on the last type of regions—those that might help researchers to *discriminate* among mechanisms.

Cultural impact and learning refers to the relative extent to which each mechanism is influenced differently by music that differs from one culture to another. For example, brain stem reflexes reflect primarily 'hard-wired' reactions to simple features that are not affected much by learning, whereas musical expectancy reflects learned schemata

---

[10] Note that these hypotheses were mostly developed based on imaging studies of each mechanism in non-musical contexts (see Juslin & Västfjäll, 2008a, Table 4).

Table 22.3 Hypotheses for seven psychological mechanisms through which music might induce emotions in listeners

	Survival value of brain function	Information focus	Ontogenetic development
Mechanism			
Brain stem reflex	Focusing attention on potentially important changes or events in the close environment	Extreme or rapidly changing basic acoustic characteristics	Prior to birth
Rhythmic entrainment	Facilitating motor coordination in physical work tasks	Periodic pulses in rhythms, especially around 2Hz	Prior to birth (perception only)
Evaluative conditioning	Being able to associate objects or events with positive and negative outcomes	Covariation between events	Prior to birth
Contagion	Enhancing group cohesion and social interaction, e.g. between mother and infant	Emotional motor expression	First year
Visual imagery	Permitting internal simulations of events that substitute for overt and risky actions	Self-conjured visual images	Pre-school years
Episodic memory	Allowing conscious recollections of previous events and binding the self to reality	Personal events in particular places and at particular times	3–4 years
Musical expectancy	Facilitating symbolic language with a complex semantics	Syntactic information	5–11 years

	Key brain regions	Cultural impact/learning
Mechanism		
Brain stem reflex	Reticular formation in the brain stem, the intralaminar nuclei of the thalamus, the inferior colliculus	Low
Rhythmic entrainment	Networks of multiple oscillators in the cerebellum and the sensorimotor regions	Low
Evaluative conditioning	The lateral nucleus of the amygdala, the interpositus nucleus of the cerebellum	High
Contagion	'Mirror neurons' in the pre-motor regions, right inferior frontal regions, the basal ganglia	Low
Visual imagery	Spatially mapped regions of the occipital cortex, the visual association cortex, and (for image generation) left temporo-occipital regions	High

(Continued)

Table 22.3 Hypotheses for seven psychological mechanisms through which music might induce emotions in listeners (continued)

	Key brain regions	Cultural impact/learning	
Mechanism			
Episodic memory	The medial temporal lobe, especially the hippocampus, and the right anterior prefrontal cortex (applies to memory retrieval)	High	
Musical expectancy	The left perisylvian cortex, 'Broca's area', the dorsal region of the anterior cingulate cortex	High	
	Induced affect	**Induction speed**	**Degree of volitional influence**
Mechanism			
Brain stem reflex	General arousal, unpleasantness vs. pleasantness	High	Low
Rhythmic entrainment	General arousal, pleasant feelings of communion	Low	Low
Evaluative conditioning	Basic emotions	High	Low
Contagion	Basic emotions	High	Low
Visual imagery	All possible emotions	Low	High
Episodic memory	All possible emotions, although especially nostalgia	Low	Medium
Musical expectancy	Surprise, awe, pleasure, 'thrills', disappointment, hope, anxiety	Low	Low
	Availability to consciousness	**Modularity**	**Dependence on musical structure**
Mechanism			
Brain stem reflex	Low	High	Medium
Rhythmic entrainment	Low	High	Medium
Evaluative conditioning	Low	High	Low
Emotional contagion	Low	High	Medium
Visual imagery	High	Low	Medium
Episodic memory	High	Low	Low
Musical expectancy	Medium	Medium	High

about specific styles of music that differ from one culture to another and that make listeners from different cultures react differently to the same piece of music.

A second group of characteristics (see Table 22.3) concerns the nature of the emotion induction process associated with each mechanism. *Induced affect* specifies which affective states might be expected to be induced, depending on the mechanism. For example, whereas emotional contagion might be expected to induce only 'basic' emotions, which have more or less distinct non-verbal expressions, imagery might be expected to induce all possible human emotions. Each mechanism has a tendency to evoke certain emotions rather than others, but between them, the mechanisms can account for a wide range of different emotions to music.

Induction speed refers to how much time each mechanism requires, in relation to other mechanisms, for an emotion to occur in a specific situation. For example, brain stem reflexes can induce emotions very quickly (in less than a second), whereas musical expectancy can be expected to require more time (a number of seconds), since some of the musical structure has to unfold in order for any musical expectation to occur that can be confirmed or violated.

Degree of volitional influence refers to the extent to which the listener him- or herself could actively influence the induction process (e.g. through focus of attention, active recall, self-activation). For instance, emotional reactions that involve evaluative conditioning might be involuntary and automatic, whereas reactions that involve visual imagery may be strongly influenced by the way a listener actively chooses to entertain some inner images and themes rather than others.

Availability to consciousness is the extent to which at least *some* aspects of the induction process are available to the listener's consciousness, so that the listener may be able to explain his or her response. For example, if a piece of music evokes an episodic memory, the listener will have a conscious recollection of the previous event and some inkling of the reasons (e.g. the appraisal) that made this event evoke the emotion that is now re-experienced. Conversely, evaluative conditioning responses to music can be both learned and aroused outside conscious awareness. Therefore, a listener that experiences a musical emotion via this mechanism might be completely unable to explain any aspect of the induction process.

Modularity refers to the extent to which the induction process of each mechanism may function as an independent and information-encapsulated 'module' that may be activated in parallel with other psychological processes. Thus, for example, emotional contagion may be described as highly 'modular', because it may be activated independently of other processes, and is not influenced by the information of other modules (e.g. we respond to the expressive characteristics of the music *as if* they came from a human being expressing emotions through the voice, even if we know, at some cognitive level, that the music is not really a voice).

Dependence on musical structure refers to the extent to which the induction depends on the precise structure or style of the music heard. At one extreme, the structure of the music is not important as such—it mainly functions as a 'retrieval cue'. This is the case for evaluative conditioning and episodic memory. At the other extreme, the precise unfolding pattern of the musical structure strongly determines the nature of the induced response. This is the case for musical expectancy.

A similar set of hypotheses for the *cognitive appraisal* mechanism does not exist so far, but could probably be developed based on one of the available theories (e.g. Scherer, 1999). Although we believe that this mechanism is less important in regard to music (see the results reported in Section 22.3.2.), music might occasionally lead to induction of emotions through some of the common appraisal dimensions; for example, a person might be trying to sleep at night, but is prevented from doing so by the disturbing sounds from a neighbour playing loud music on his or her stereo. In this case, the music becomes an object of the person's irritation because it blocks the person's goal—to fall asleep. For this regular type of emotion, we need no 'special explanation' of the type discussed by Kivy (1990): Traditional theories of emotion will suffice to provide a plausible explanation. However, as indicated by the findings outlined earlier, most musical emotions appear to be evoked by mechanisms other than appraisal.

22.4.3 Ongoing experiments

Experiments may test the different psychological mechanisms that have been proposed in the literature (see Section 22.4.2), along with selected individual and situational variables, which have proved to be important in field studies. One can use multiple measures to establish with certainty that a listener is experiencing a particular emotion, such as verbal self-report, facial expressions (as revealed by EMG measures), traditional physiological measures (particularly finger temperature, galvanic skin response, pulse, and respiration), and influences on the voice that may reflect emotion (see Juslin & Scherer, 2005). Use of more sophisticated multivariate techniques can help researchers to actually discriminate among specific emotions on the basis of psychophysiological indices (e.g. Rainville, Bechara, Naqvi, & Damasio, 2006; Nyklíček, Thayer, & Van Doornen, 1997; Chapter 11, this volume). Indirect measures that might reveal different emotions may also be used—including word association, decision time, and distance judgements (Västfjäll, 2002; Chapter 10, this volume). The use of a broad range of measures in studies of responses to art was advocated by Berlyne (1971, p. 7) several years ago, but so far, few researchers have followed this advice. This may be partly due to practical and economic considerations, but may also reflect a certain laziness—it is easier to rely only on self-report. It can be argued, however, that use of multiple emotion measures could help to resolve ongoing debates about whether music really evokes emotion. Scherer and Zentner (2001) proposed the rather conservative criterion that an emotion to music should involve a synchronized response of all or most organismic subsystems (components).

A first preliminary experiment, aiming to resolve the debate between 'cognitivists' and 'emotivists' (Chapter 4, this volume), was presented by Lundqvist, Carlsson, Hilmersson and Juslin (2009). The study measured self-reported feeling, facial muscle activity and autonomic activity in 32 participants while they listened to popular music pieces composed with either a happy or a sad emotional expression, in order to create conditions beneficial for an emotional contagion response (Section 22.4.1). The results revealed a synchronized manifestation in the experiential, expressive, and physiological components of the emotion system, supporting the emotivist position. More specifically, 'happy' music generated more zygomatic facial muscle activity, greater skin conductance, lower finger temperature, more felt happiness, and less felt sadness than 'sad' music. The finding that the emotion induced in the listener was the same as the emotion expressed in the music is consistent with the idea that music may evoke emotions via emotional contagion, since the study used specially composed music to which the listeners had no previous associations.

Further experimental studies are currently under way in the project. A major problem is how to handle the large individual differences among listeners in musical emotions (Sloboda, 1996). Appraisal theory highlights that psychological stimuli obtain their emotional meaning through the subjective evaluation that individuals make in their appraisal (see Scherer, 1999), and the same is true of most of the alternative mechanisms discussed earlier. For instance, the mechanisms *evaluative conditioning*, *episodic memory*, and *musical expectancy* all depend on the listener's previous experience (or 'learning history'). This complicates research endavours because a given piece of music may not actually be the 'same' stimulus for different listeners.

One way to handle this issue is to first set up a large sample of individuals which will serve as a 'pool' of participants. Within this pool, the participants are tested through the use of a carefully constructed questionnaire regarding background variables, music preferences, listening habits, favourite pieces of music, experience of various styles of music, personality characteristics etc. From this information, one may create suitable sub-groups of participants with certain characteristics in relation to experimental stimuli, who are randomly assigned to various conditions in order to manipulate, for instance, the familiarity with the music or trait empathy. Much work needs to be devoted to the design of clever experiments that allow one to manipulate and clearly separate different mechanisms that underlie emotions. To facilitate such experiments, it is necessary to create standard paradigms that can reliably evoke specific emotions in listeners through each of the seven mechanisms discussed earlier.

Possible stimuli and procedures for activating certain mechanisms can already be found in the literature (see Juslin & Västfjäll, 2008a, p. 574, for some examples) although they need further testing and refinement. To test the hypotheses in Table 22.3, we need not only to be able to activate each mechanism. To separate the effect of specific mechanisms, we should also be able to suppress or eliminate particular mechanisms in individual cases. This could be done in two principal ways. First, one could systematically manipulate musical stimuli in such a way as to withhold or eliminate information required for a specific mechanism to be activated (*the principle of information impoverishment*). Musical structures are easy to manipulate and there are sophisticated techniques in acoustics that enable researchers to standardize a stimulus with regard to certain acoustic features, while leaving others intact. Secondly, one could design the procedure in such a manner that it will prevent the type of information processing required for a particular mechanism to be activated (*the principle of interference*). This could be done in a number of ways. One approach could be to force listeners to allocate the 'cognitive resources' needed for a specific mechanism to a task instead; for instance, one could use an experimental task that recruits attentional resources to such an extent that visual imagery, also dependent on these resources, will be made impossible. Another possibility could be to use a neurochemical interference strategy; for example, it has been shown that blocking of a specific class of amino acid receptors (NMDA) in the lateral amygdala can interfere with the acquisition of evaluative conditioning (Miserendino et al, 1990). Still another form of interference involves the use of *transcranial magnetic stimulation* (Pascual-Leone et al, 2002). By disrupting brain activity at crucial times and locations, one might prevent a specific mechanism from becoming activated by a musical stimulus (Juslin & Västfjäll, 2008a).

However, for obvious reasons, not all future studies can rely on such advanced methods. Experimental studies are painfully inadequate when it comes to investigating many important aspects of music such as the emotional uses and functions of music, the prevalence of musical emotions, or the situational factors that affect musical emotions in the real world. Such studies will have to continue to rely on various forms of self-report of spontaneously occurring music events. A crucial goal for future research could be to develop a set of diagnostic questions that may help researchers to indirectly determine which mechanism caused a particular emotion in a self-report context. (This might also encompass more questions about the particular acoustic characteristics of the stimulus in each episode, though we stress that it will be difficult to find direct links between acoustic parameters and emotions.) Figure 22.6 presents an example of what diagnostic questions for distinguishing mechanisms 'post hoc' could look like; such questions could help a researcher to determine the cause of an emotional reaction to music in such cases where it is not practically feasible to manipulate or control for the underlying mechanism, and where one must instead gradually include or exclude possible causes of the response. We note that such diagnostic questions must be carefully tested and refined before systematic use.

22.5 IMPLICATIONS AND DIRECTIONS FOR FUTURE RESEARCH

One implication of the new framework is that it can resolve many disagreements in the field: specifically, apparent contradictions of different approaches may be reconciled by observing that they focus on different mechanisms. Hence, the framework can help to resolve previous disagreements about which emotions music can induce, how early musical emotions develop, whether listeners are active or passive in the causal process, how much time it takes to induce an emotion through music, and whether emotions to music are innate or learned responses—it all depends on the mechanism concerned (see Table 22.3).

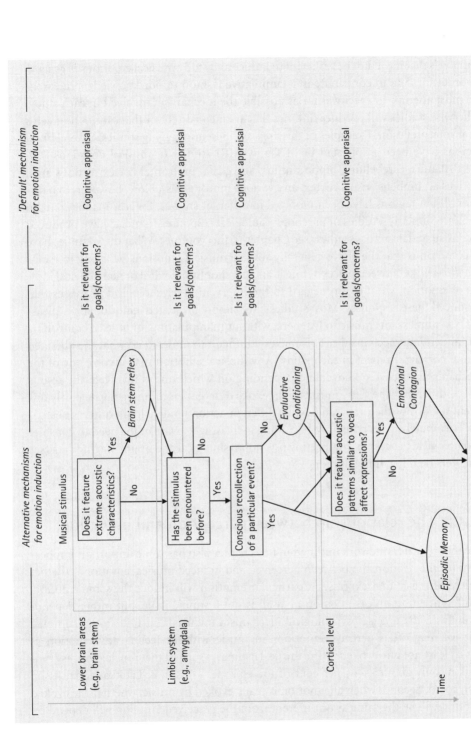

Fig. 22.6 Examples of diagnostic questions for distinguishing underlying mechanisms 'post hoc'.

22.5.1 All emotions are not created equal

Perhaps the most important implication of the framework for future research in this domain is that it will not be sufficient to induce and study musical emotions *in general*. In order for data to contribute in a cumulative fashion to our knowledge, researchers must attempt to specify as far as possible the mechanism involved in each study; otherwise studies will produce findings that are inconsistent or that cannot be given a clear interpretation. Examples of this are seen in neuroimaging studies. Several brain regions have been implicated in PET and fMRI studies of musical emotions (e.g. the thalamus, cerebellum, hippocampus, amygdala, prefrontal cortex, Broca's area, nucleus accumbens, visual cortex, and various motor areas). Note, however, that different brain regions have been reported in different studies, for reasons that remain unclear. Similarly, studies of psychophysiological responses to music have produced inconsistent data across studies (see Chapter 11, this volume). What these studies have in common is that they have generally studied musical emotions by trying to establish *direct* links between pieces of music and psychophysiological or neurological indices of emotion, without any regard to the intervening psychological processes that produced these responses. Most studies have simply presented 'emotional' or 'pleasant' vs. 'unpleasant' music to listeners, without manipulating, or at least controlling for, underlying mechanisms. This makes it difficult to understand what the obtained neural correlates reflect in each study. Any musical emotion may involve any of the mechanisms discussed above, and depending on which one is involved, the results will be different. The same music might evoke different emotions, activate partly different regions of the brain, and evoke different action tendencies in different listeners. Fortunately, researchers are becoming increasingly aware of the need to consider psychological process in interpreting psychophysiological and brain imaging data (see Chapters 11 and 12, this volume).

22.5.2 The relationship between perception and induction

The theoretical framework outlined in this chapter also has some important implications for the relationship between perceived and induced musical emotion. Whether a piece of music that expresses a particular emotion will induce the same emotion, a different emotion, or no emotion at all is not a simple issue, but rather depends strongly on the precise psychological mechanism involved. First, it should be noted that we may often perceive emotions in music without feeling any emotion at all—at least not one evoked by the music. (Estimates suggest that music induces emotions in only about 55–65 per cent of the episodes—Juslin & Laukka, 2004; Juslin et al, 2008). Second, when an emotion is really evoked by music, whether the evoked emotion will be the same as or different from the perceived emotion will depend on the precise mechanism involved. Emotional contagion, for instance, will by definition involve the same emotion, whereas this may not necessarily be the case for episodic memory—a 'happy' piece may well remind us of a sad memory from the past, which makes us sad.

A few laboratory studies recently compared perception and induction of emotion using music mostly unfamiliar to listeners, and these studies found that emotions evoked tended to be similar to emotions perceived (Kallinen & Ravaja, 2006; Schubert, 2007). This is the kind of pattern we would expect if emotional contagion is involved, but not if episodic memory or musical expectancy is involved. Unfortunately, it is rarely realized that the context will affect the results. The artificial laboratory environment will create conditions that permit only some mechanisms and emotions to occur. In real life, musical emotions can be evoked by different mechanisms in different situations, and different mechanisms may induce different emotions; for example, in the ESM study by Juslin et al (2008) discussed above, *nostalgia-longing* was related to episodic memory, whereas *interest-expectancy* was not. Only by sampling a variety of situations can we hope to capture all relevant mechanisms and thereby achieve an accurate understanding of the relationship between perception and induction of emotion in music.

22.5.3 Implications for health research and music therapy

Real-world research has shown that music is often intentionally used by listeners to regulate their moods and emotions, and that positive emotions tend to dominate in the reactions. The latter result has stimulated interest in effects of music on physical health and subjective well-being. It has been increasingly recognized that music could have positive health effects (e.g. Khalfa et al, 2003; Pelletier, 2004; see also Chapter 30, this volume). We suggest that many of these effects are mediated by the emotions that the music evokes—which in turn influence biochemical substances like cortisol, oxytocin, dopamine and serotonin. An interdisciplinary project in Sweden currently explores psychological and neurobiological mechanisms through which music can influence physical health and subjective well-being, with the aim to develop new and more individualized health interventions (Helsing, Västfjäll, Juslin, & Hartig, 2009).

The development of such interventions will obviously benefit from a better understanding of the underlying mechanisms. The framework outlined earlier can hopefully contribute to more hypothesis-driven approaches to exploring mechanisms affecting emotion and stress. It might also contribute to music therapy practice, by illuminating the processes that underlie different therapy techniques such as the 'iso principle' or Guided Imagery with Music (for a discussion of implications for music therapy, see Juslin, in press). It has already been recognized by many therapists that there are no simple links between music and response—'musical selections that are relaxing and meditative to one client can be disruptive and annoying to another' (Guzzetta, 1991, p. 159). Mechanisms are key in understanding this issue, and several of the mechanisms in the present model can be seen at work in music therapy practice (Chapter 29, this volume).

22.6 EMOTION AND AESTHETIC RESPONSE

In this final section, we offer some comments on the complex relationship between emotion and aesthetic response—particularly in relation to the theoretical framework outlined earlier. The notion of 'aesthetic emotions' has occurred repeatedly in the literature, and it is possible to discern at least two different uses of the term. First, some scholars use this term simply to refer to *all* emotional responses to 'art objects' (music, theatre, painting, literature)—without implying that the emotions themselves are of a special kind. We argue against the use of this term in regard to emotional reactions to music: since it does not actually exclude anything, it does not add anything useful to our understanding. (In fact, the term can lead to confusion by suggesting that the emotions really *are* special, contrary to what the author intended.)

Second, some scholars use the term 'aesthetic emotion' to suggest that there is indeed a 'special' kind of emotion that is 'unique' to art. For example, Zentner et al (2008; Chapter 8, this volume) proposed a distinction between 'utilitarian' and 'aesthetic' emotions: 'utilitarian' emotions are triggered by a need to adapt to specific situations that are of central significance to the individual's goals, whereas 'aesthetic' emotions are triggered in situations that have no obvious material effect on the individual's well-being and rarely lead to specific goal-oriented responses. Though such a distinction may appear straightforward, we find it problematic upon reflection.

First, the distinction bears a striking resemblence to the one made previously, between appraisal-based emotions (which involve evaluations in relation to goals and action-oriented coping) and emotions evoked by other mechanisms (which do not involve goals). Appraisal-based emotions may lead to goal-oriented action responses even with music (e.g. getting the neighbours to turn off that loud music!), whereas non-appraisal emotions (mostly) do not. The mistake is to assume that the latter kind of emotions are unique to *music*, or art more generally. (Most) musical emotions differ from (most) non-musical emotions in that they do not depend on cognitive appraisals, and this aspect may indeed affect their characteristics to some extent. However, the critical feature is the underlying *mechanism*, and not the music (as 'art object'), because non-musical emotions may *also* be evoked through mechanisms other than appraisal (e.g. conditioning, contagion, episodic memory).

Second, the distinction between 'utilitarian' and 'aesthetic' emotions seems to involve the flawed assumption that the mechanisms that evoke emotions from music somehow *know* which stimuli are 'art objects' and which are not. This is clearly not the case: most mechanisms simply respond to a specific kind of information in the object (considered in relation to, and influenced by, various individual and situational variables)—whether this resides in music or some other stimulus. (If the mechanisms really were 'aware' that the object was 'just' music, they would presumably not respond to it in the first place![11]) Furthermore, whether the given emotion is 'utilitarian' or not

---

[11] It has been noted that emotions to music are different from non-musical emotions in that they do not lead to immediate 'goal-directed' or 'adaptive' behaviour (e.g. Zentner et al, 2008). However,

is something that can only really be evaluated 'post hoc', when the consequences have been evaluated. A musically induced emotion may well be utilitarian, if it leads to a highly desirable outcome in the life of the emotion-experiencing listener.

Finally, we object to the notion of 'aesthetic emotions'. Neill (2003) suggests that 'the character of aesthetic emotion and its difference from garden-variety emotion is more than a little mysterious' in that 'there appear to be plenty of people for whom introspection reveals no such distinction in feeling' (p. 424). Furthermore, we submit that the term is problematic because the concepts of 'emotion' and 'aesthetic response' should not be equated with each other. To understand why, we must consider the notion of 'aesthetic response' more closely.

Philosophers have discussed this time-honoured problem within the field of *aesthetics*, the branch of philosophy devoted to conceptual and theoretical inquiry into art and aesthetic experience (Levenson, 2003, p. 3)—although without reaching a consensus that might guide research. Part of the problem is defining 'art', with some scholars noting that the concept of art is inherently open and so resistant to definition. Despite the problems of definition, which are not unlike those relating to emotion in psychology (see Chapter 4, this volume), common conceptions of 'aesthetic experience' emphasize its focus on an object's *aesthetic properties*, its form and content. Hence, according to Levenson (2003) 'it is widely agreed that aesthetic properties are *perceptual* properties relevant to the *aesthetic value* of the object that possesses them' (p. 6, italics added). Such properties might involve such aspects as the beauty, balance, sublimity, power, wittiness or expressivity of the object. Thus, an aesthetic response to music involves some kind of evaluation of the music as an object of 'art', some aspects of which are more sensory/perceptual and others which are more cognitive/reflective (including judgements of the genre, skill, or medium used—all based on knowledge of art).

Psychologists have tended to avoid studying aesthetic response to music. In the field of 'new empirical aesthetics', psychologists have rather focused on more mundane aspects such as preference (Chapters 19 and 24, this volume). Konečni (1979), however, proposed that an aesthetic response is an intense personal experience which involves emotional, cognitive, and social components. We agree that cognitive (which can regarded as including also perceptual) aspects are *required* for an aesthetic response to occur; and furthermore that social aspects are unavoidable because aesthetic and stylistic norms and values change over time in society. The picture is more complex when it comes to the role of emotion, however: We will propose here that although an

---

the same is probably true of most non-musical emotions in everyday life as well—it is simply not the case that every time we experience an emotion, we immediately carry out some action. We often experience emotions without any urgent need to act—for instance when a memory is evoked, when we catch the happy emotion of a smiling stranger, or when we are engaged in visual imagery. Only some emotions prompt 'direct action', whether they are musical or not. Further, even emotions that evoke action tendencies are usually regulated. In many emotional episodes, acting on the emotional impulse is not appropriate. Thus, many of the seemingly 'obvious' differences among musical and non-musical emotions do not hold up when examined closer. The reason for this is that musical emotions are evoked by general mechanisms that did not evolve specifically to respond to music, and that thus do not respect any distinction of the kind mentioned previously (with the possible exception of the appraisal mechanism, which is more 'realistic' and less 'modular' in its response, but also less frequent in musical contexts, as shown earlier).

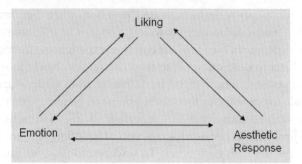

Fig. 22.7 Relationships among emotion, liking, and aesthetic response.

emotion may sometimes occur with an aesthetic response, it is not a *required* feature for a listener's response to qualify as 'aesthetic'.

Figure 22.7 illustrates how we conceive of the relations between the phenomena *emotion*, *preference (liking)*, and *aesthetic response* (for precise working definitions of preference and emotion, see Chapter 1, this volume). The primary aspect is that each phenomenon can occur in separation from the others even if they do occur together sometimes; that is, they are partly independent but frequently mutually influencing phenomena. The independence is observable in several ways.

First, as the foregoing sections should have made clear, it is perfectly possible for music to evoke an emotion in a listener, without the listener experiencing anything like an 'aesthetic response'. For instance, a piece of music may subconsciously evoke sadness in a listener who does not even attend to the sounds, simply because the music has repeatedly been paired with sadness-evoking stimuli in the past (i.e. *evaluative conditioning*). The mechanisms described in Section 22.4 can all evoke an emotion independently of any aesthetic evaluation.

Second, researchers in the affective sciences distinguish 'liking' from 'emotion' in that the former is an example of 'preference': a long-lasting affective state of a low intensity. It is perfectly possible to 'like' a piece of music heard on the radio without the music inducing an emotional response (with a synchronized reaction in experience, physiology, and expression). We may simply prefer the piece heard at the moment, over a piece heard earlier. Further, this liking response need not involve an evaluation of the piece's quality as an art object, because the music in question (e.g. a pop song) may not be considered 'art' and hence does not invite an 'aesthetic attitude'.

Finally, despite the frequently occurring term 'aesthetic emotion', an aesthetic response may well occur without either emotion or liking. In fact, it has repeatedly been argued that an aesthetic response is—or should be—a 'detached' or 'distanced' consideration of an art object that does *not* let emotions 'get in the way'. Thus, we can evaluate an art object (including a piece of music), without necessarily experiencing any emotional response. Members of a jury in a piano performance contest repeatedly make evaluations of the aesthetic merit of different interpretations, but the circumstances may not be optimal for evoking emotions. Of course, if we do value an art object very highly, chances are that we cannot avoid being 'moved' by the object! (Aesthetic evaluations can activate psychological mechanisms.) However, if emotions to music were typically dependent on an aesthetic evaluation, then emotions such as 'wonder' and 'awe' should be frequent responses to music in everyday life. This is, as we saw earlier in this chapter, not the case. 'Wonder', 'awe', and 'chills' are very rare responses (Huron, 2006), which seem to occur mainly in 'peak' experiences (Chapter 20, this volume).

Despite the fact that emotion, liking, and aesthetic response may occur independently of each other in many real-life contexts, they can also influence each other in complicated ways. Obviously, we tend to like music that we regard as aesthetically valuable and that manages to evoke emotions in us, but the causal influence may work in different ways: We may judge the music as aesthetically valuable *because* it managed to induce an emotion. Or we may respond with an emotion because of how highly we value the music (e.g. its beauty) aesthetically. We may react with an emotion because we happened to come across a piece of music that we like. Hence, one can easily envisage the causal arrow moving in different directions (see Figure 22.7).

Most of these processes have not yet been empirically investigated. We argue, however, that realizing that emotion, preference, and aesthetic response are partly independent processes may benefit further exploration of these issues, something which is urgently needed. In music, emotions may co-occur with aesthetic evaluations (being activated independently—in parallel) or may follow partly as a result of an aesthetic judgement. Unfortunately we still lack a proper psychological theory of how music is aesthetically evaluated. Perhaps evolutionary aesthetics (to reveal innate perceptual preferences) and musicological analyses (to uncover the evolution of stylistic norms over time) might be helpful in developing such a theory. Nevertheless, most emotions to music in everyday life do not seem to involve an aesthetic judgement (as defined here), and whereas aesthetic ideals change considerably over time, the basic operation of the emotion induction mechanisms are consistent over time. Hence, the two need to be analysed separately to some extent.

In sum, the notion of 'aesthetic emotions' obscures more than it illuminates, and only makes us look for answers in the wrong direction.[12] Key to make progress is to explore how general emotion-inducing mechanisms can be 'recruited' by musical events in everyday life. Psychological theory plays a key role in this endeavour. Kivy (1990) admits that, 'we are in the need of "psychology", right from the start'—although adding, 'that is what bothers me' (p. 150). Whatever concerns one might harbour with respect to the psychological approach, the fact remains that a neglect of psychological mechanisms will lead to erroneous assumptions, inconsistent findings and unnecessary controversy regarding musical emotions. Thus, it will seriously detract from our understanding of how music evokes emotions.

---

[12] This does not mean that we believe that there is nothing special or unique about music experience as a whole (as defined in Table 20.1, Chapter 20, this volume). Rather, the claim is that this 'uniqueness' does not reside in the *mechanisms* activated or the *emotions* aroused, but rather in other aspects of the music experience (Juslin & Västfjäll, 2008b).

Musical emotions tell a story about who we are, both as individuals (in terms of our life experiences, memories, and preferences) and as a species (in terms of our innate dispositions to utilize sounds as sources of information, in our inferences about possible danger, affective states of other individuals, and future events). Exploring how various musical emotions come about through the interaction of multiple psychological mechanisms is an exciting endeavour that has just begun.

RECOMMENDED FURTHER READING

1. Berlyne, D. E. (1971). *Aesthetics and psychobiology*. New York: Appleton Century Crofts.
2. Juslin, P. N., & Västfjäll, D. (2008a). Emotional responses to music: The need to consider underlying mechanisms. *Behavioral and Brain Sciences, 31*, 559–575.

REFERENCES

Baumgartner, H. (1992). Remembrance of things past: Music, autobiographical memory, and emotion. *Advances in Consumer Research, 19*, 613–20.

Beedie, C. J., Terry, P. C., & Lane, A. M. (2005). Distinctions between emotion and mood. *Cognition & Emotion, 19*, 847–78.

Berlyne, D. E. (1971). *Aesthetics and psychobiology*. New York: Appleton Century Crofts.

Blair, M. E., & Shimp, T. A. (1992). Consequences of an unpleasant experience with music: A second-order negative conditioning perspective. *Journal of Advertising, 21*, 35–43.

Blood, A. J., & Zatorre, R. J. (2001). Intensely pleasurable responses to music correlate with activity in brain regions implicated in reward and emotion. *Proceedings of National Academy of Sciences, 98*, 11818–23.

Bonny, H. L., & Savery, L. M. (1973). *Music and your mind*. New York: Station Hill.

Brunswik, E. (1956). Perception and the representative design of psychological experiments. Berkeley, CA: University of California Press.

Budd, M. (1985). *Music and the emotions. The philosophical theories*. London: Routledge.

Clayton, M. (2009). The social and personal functions of music in cross-cultural perspective. In S. Hallam, I. Cross, & M. Thaut (eds), *Oxford handbook of music psychology* (pp. 35–44). Oxford: Oxford University Press.

Clayton, M., Sager, R., & Will, U. (2005). In time with the music: the concept of entrainment and its significance for ethnomusicology. *European Meetings in Ethnomusicology, 11*, 3–75.

Clynes, M. (1977). *Sentics: The touch of emotions*. New York: Doubleday.

Conner Christensen, T., Barrett, L. F., Bliss-Moreau, E., Lebo, K., & Kaschub, C. (2003). A practical guide to experience-sampling procedures. *Journal of Happiness Studies, 4*, 53–78.

Cooke, D. (1959). *The language of music*. London: Oxford University Press.

Davies, J. B. (1978). *The psychology of music*. London: Hutchinson.

De Houwer, J., Thomas, S., & Baeyens, F. (2001). Associative learning of likes and dislikes: A review of 25 years of research on human evaluative conditioning. *Psychological Bulletin, 127*, 853–69.

DeNora, T. (2000). *Music in everyday life*. Cambridge: Cambridge University Press.

Dowling W. J., & Harwood, D. L. (1986). *Music cognition*. New York: Academic Press.

Ekman, P. (1992). An argument for basic emotions. *Cognition & Emotion*, 6, 169–200.

Frijda, N. H. (1999). Emotions and hedonic experience. In D. Kahneman, E. Diener, & N. Schwarz (eds), *Well-being: The foundations of hedonic psychology* (pp. 190–210). New York: Sage.

Gabrielsson, A. (2001). Emotions in strong experiences with music. In P. N. Juslin & J. A. Sloboda (eds), *Music and emotion: Theory and research* (pp. 431–49). Oxford: Oxford University Press.

Gärdenfors, P. (2003). *How homo became sapiens: On the evolution of thinking*. Oxford: Oxford University Press.

Griffiths, P. (1997). *What emotions really are*. Chicago, IL: University of Chicago Press.

Guzzetta, C. E. (1991). Music therapy: Nursing the music of the soul. In. D. Campbell (ed.), *Music physician for times to come* (pp. 146–66). Wheaton, IL: Quest Books.

Harrer, G., & Harrer, H. (1977). Music, emotion, and autonomic function. In M. Critchley & R. A. Henson (eds), *Music and the brain. Studies in the neurology of music* (pp. 202–16). London: William Heinemann medical books.

Hatfield, E., Cacioppo, J. T., & Rapson, R. L. (1994). *Emotional contagion*. Cambridge, UK: Cambridge University Press.

Helsing, M., Västfjäll, D., Juslin, P. N, & Hartig, T. (2009). *Perceived stress, health, and everyday music listening*. Manuscript submitted for publication.

Huron, D. (2006). *Sweet anticipation: Music and the psychology of expectation*. Cambridge, MA: MIT Press.

Izard, C. E. (1977). *Human emotions*. New York: Plenum Press.

Janata, P., Tomic, S. T., & Rakowski, S. K. (2007). Characterization of music-evoked autobiographical memories. *Memory*, 15, 845–60.

Jones, M. R. (2009). Musical time. In S. Hallam, I. Cross, & M. Thaut (eds), *Oxford handbook of music psychology* (pp. 81–92). Oxford: Oxford University Press.

Joseph, R. (2000). *Neuropsychiatry, neuropsychology, clinical neuroscience*. New York: Academic Press.

Juslin, P. N. (2001). Communicating emotion in music performance: A review and a theoretical framework. In P. N. Juslin & J. A. Sloboda (eds), *Music and emotion: Theory and research* (pp. 309–337). Oxford: Oxford University Press.

Juslin, P. N. (2009). Emotional responses to music. In S. Hallam, I. Cross, & M. Thaut (eds), *Oxford handbook of music psychology* (pp. 131–40). Oxford: Oxford University Press.

Juslin, P. N. (in press). Sound of music: Seven ways in which the brain can evoke emotions from sound. In F. Mossberg (ed.), *Sound, man, and emotion (Report No. 7 from the Sound Environment Centre)*. Lund, Sweden: Sound Environment Centre.

Juslin, P. N., & Laukka, P. (2003). Communication of emotions in vocal expression and music performance: Different channels, same code? *Psychological Bulletin*, 129, 770–814.

Juslin, P. N., & Laukka, P. (2004). Expression, perception, and induction of musical emotions: A review and a questionnaire study of everyday listening. *Journal of New Music Research*, 33, 217–38.

Juslin, P. N., Laukka, P., Liljeström, S., Västfjäll, D., & Lundqvist, L.-O. (2009). *A nationally representative survey study of emotional reactions to music: Prevalence and causal influences*. Manuscript submitted for publication.

Juslin, P. N., Liljeström, S., Västfjäll, D., Barradas, G., & Silva, A. (2008). An experience sampling study of emotional reactions to music: Listener, music, and situation. *Emotion*, 8, 668–83.

Juslin, P. N., & Scherer, K. R. (2005). Vocal expression of affect. In J. A. Harrigan, R. Rosenthal, & K. R. Scherer (eds), *The new handbook of methods in nonverbal behavior research* (pp. 65–135). New York: Oxford University Press.

Juslin, P. N., & Sloboda, J. A. (eds). (2001). *Music and emotion: Theory and research*. Oxford: Oxford University Press.

Juslin, P. N., & Västfjäll, D. (2008a). Emotional responses to music: The need to consider underlying mechanisms. *Behavioral and Brain Sciences*, *31*, 559–75.

Juslin, P. N., & Västfjäll, D. (2008b). All emotions are not created equal: Reaching beyond the traditional disputes. *Behavioral and Brain Sciences*, *31*, 600–21.

Kallinen, K., & Ravaja, N. (2006). Emotion perceived and emotion felt: Same and different. *Musicae Scientiae*, *10*, 191–213.

Khalfa, S., Dalla Bella, S., Roy, M., Peretz, I., & Lupien, S. J. (2003). Effects of relaxing music on salivary cortisol level after psychological stress. *Annals of the New York Academy of Science*, *999*, 374–6.

Kivy, P. (1990). *Music alone: Reflections on a purely musical experience*. Ithaca, NY: Cornell University Press.

Kneutgen, J. (1970). Eine Musikform und ihre biologische Funktion. Ueber die Wirkungsweise der Wiegenlieder. *Zeitschrift für Experimentelle und Angewandte Psychologie*, *17*, 245–65.

Koelsch, S., Fritz, T., von Cramon, D. Y., Müller, K., & Friederici, A. D. (2006). Investigating emotion with music: An fMRI study. *Human Brain Mapping*, *27*, 239–50.

Konečni, V. J. (1979). Determinants of aesthetic preference and effects of exposure to aesthetic stimuli: Social, emotional, and cognitive factors. In B. A. Maher (ed.), *Progress in experimental personality research* (Vol. 9, pp. 149–97). New York: Academic Press.

Krumhansl, C. L. (1997). An exploratory study of musical emotions and psychophysiology. *Canadian Journal of Experimental Psychology*, *51*, 336–52.

Lakoff, G., & Johnson, M. (1980). *Metaphors we live by*. Chicago, IL: University of Chicago Press.

Landreth, J. E., & Landreth, F. (1974). Effects of music on physiological response. *Journal of Research in Music Education*, *22*, 4–12.

Lane, R. D. (2000). Neural correlates of conscious emotional experience. In R. D. Lane & L. Nadel (ed.), *Cognitive neuroscience of emotion* (pp. 345–70). Oxford: Oxford University Press.

Langer, S. K. (1957). *Philosophy in a new key*. (3rd edn). Cambridge, MA: Harvard University Press.

Levenson, J. (1997). Emotion in response to art. In M. Hjort & S. Laver (eds), *Emotion and the arts* (pp. 20–34). Oxford: Oxford University Press.

Levenson, J. (2003). Philosophical aesthetics: an overview. In J. Levenson (ed.), *Oxford handbook of aesthetics* (pp. 3–24). Oxford: Oxford University Press.

Lundqvist, L.-O., Carlsson, F., Hilmersson, P., & Juslin, P. N. (2009). Emotional responses to music: Experience, expression, and physiology. *Psychology of Music*, *37*, 61–90.

Martin, D. G., Stambrook, M., Tataryn, D. J., & Beihl, H. (1984). Conditioning in the unattended left ear. *International Journal of Neuroscience*, *23*, 95–102.

Meyer, L. B. (1956). *Emotion and meaning in music*. Chicago, IL: Chicago University Press.

Miserendino, M. J. D., Sananes, C. B., Melia, K. R., & Davis, M. (1990). Blocking of acquisition but not expression of conditioned fear-potentiated startle by NMDA antagonists in the amygdala. *Nature*, *345*, 716–8.

Narmour, E. (1992). *The analysis and cognition of melodic complexity: The Implication-Realization Model*. Chicago, IL: University of Chicago Press.

Neill, A. (2003). Art and emotion. In J. Levenson (ed.), *Oxford handbook of aesthetics* (pp. 421–35). Oxford: Oxford University Press.

Neumann, R., & Strack, F. (2000). Mood contagion: The automatic transfer of mood between persons. *Journal of Personality and Social Psychology*, *79*, 211–23.

Nyklíček, I., Thayer, J. F., & Van Doornen, L. J. P. (1997). Cardiorespiratory differentiation of musically-induced emotions. *Journal of Psychophysiology*, *11*, 304–21.

Öhman, A., & Soares, J. J. F. (1994). Unconscious anxiety: Phobic responses to masked stimuli. *Journal of Abnormal Psychology*, *103*, 231–40.

Panksepp, J. (1998). *Affective neuroscience*. New York: Oxford University Press.

Panksepp, J., & Bernatzky, G. (2002). Emotional sounds and the brain: The neuro-affective foundations of musical appreciation. *Behavioural Processes*, *60*, 133–55.

Pascual-Leone, A., Davey, N. J., Rothwell, J., Wassermann, E. M., & Puri, B. K. (eds). (2002). *Handbook of transcranial magnetic stimulation*. Oxford: Oxford University Press.

Patel, A. D. (2008). *Music, language, and brain*. Oxford: Oxford University Press.

Pelletier, C. L. (2004). The effect of music on decreasing arousal due to stress: a meta-analysis. *Journal of Music Therapy*, *41*, 192–214.

Preston, S. D., & de Waal, F. B. M. (2002). Empathy: its ultimate and proximate basis. *Behavioral and Brain Sciences*, *25*, 1–72.

Rainville, P., Bechara, A., Naqvi, N., & Damasio, A. R. (2006). Basic emotions are associated with distinct patterns of cardiovascular reactivity. *International Journal of Psychophysiology*, *61*, 5–18.

Raudenbush, S. W., & Bryk, A. S. (2002). *Hierarchical linear models: Applications and data analysis methods* (2nd edn). London: Sage.

Ready, R. E., Weinberger, M. I., & Jones, K. M. (2007). How happy have you felt lately? Two diary studies of emotion recall in older and younger adults. *Cognition & Emotion*, *21*, 728–57.

Reis, H. T., & Gable, S. L. (2000). Event-sampling and other methods for studying everyday experience. In H. T. Reis & C. M. Judd (eds), *Handbook of research methods in social and personality psychology* (pp. 190–222). Cambridge, UK: Cambridge University Press.

Reisberg, D., & Heuer, F. (2004). Memory for emotional events. In D. Reisberg & P. Hertel (eds), *Memory and emotion* (pp. 3–41). Oxford: Oxford University Press.

Robinson, J. (2005). *Deeper than reason: Emotion and its role in literature, music, and art*. Oxford: Oxford University Press.

Robinson, M. D., & Clore, G. L. (2002). Episodic and semantic knowledge in emotional self-report: Evidence for two judgment processes. *Journal of Personality and Social Psychology*, *83*, 198–215.

Russell, J. A. (1980). A circumplex model of affect. *Journal of Personality and Social Psychology*, *39*, 1161–78.

Saarikallio, S. (2007). *Music as mood regulation in adolescence*. Doctoral dissertation, University of Jyväskylä, Finland.

Scherer, K. R. (1999). Appraisal theories. In T. Dalgleish & M. Power (eds), *Handbook of cognition and emotion* (pp. 637–63). Chichester, UK: Wiley.

Scherer, K. R., & Zentner, M. R. (2001). Emotional effects of music: Production rules. In P. N. Juslin & J. A. Sloboda (eds), *Music and emotion: Theory and research* (pp. 361–92). Oxford: Oxford University Press.

Schubert, E. (2007). The influence of emotion, locus of emotion, and familiarity upon preference in music. *Psychology of Music*, *35*, 499–515.

Schulkind, M. D., Hennis, L. K., & Rubin, D. C. (1999). Music, emotion, and autobiographical memory: They are playing our song. *Memory & Cognition*, *27*, 948–55.

Sloboda, J. A. (1991). Music structure and emotional response: Some empirical findings. *Psychology of Music*, *19*, 110–120.

Sloboda, J. A. (1992). Empirical studies of emotional response to music. In M. Riess-Jones & S. Holleran (eds), *Cognitive bases of musical communication* (pp. 33–46). Washington, DC: American Psychological Association.

Sloboda, J. A. (1996). Emotional responses to music: a review. In K. Riederer & T. Lahti (eds), *Proceedings of the Nordic Acoustical Meeting (NAM96)* (pp. 385–92). Helsinki, Finland: The Acoustical Society of Finland.

Sloboda, J. A., O'Neill, S. A., & Ivaldi, A. (2001). Functions of music in everyday life: an exploratory study using the Experience Sampling Method. *Musicae Scientiae*, 5, 9–32.

Steinbeis, N., Koelsch, S., & Sloboda, J. A. (2006). The role of harmonic expectancy violations in musical emotions: Evidence from subjective, physiological, and neural responses. *Journal of Cognitive Neuroscience*, 18, 1380–93.

Toomey, L. (1996–7). Literature review: The Bonny Method of Guided Imagery and Music. *Journal of the Association for Music and Imagery*, 5, 75–103.

Tulving, E. (1983). *Elements of episodic memory*. Oxford, UK: Oxford University Press.

Vissner, P. S., Krosnick, J. A., & Lavrakas, P. J. (2000). Survey research. In In H. T. Reis & C. M. Judd (eds), *Handbook of research methods in social and personality psychology* (pp. 223–52). Cambridge, UK: Cambridge University Press.

Västfjäll, D. (2002). A review of the musical mood induction procedure. *Musicae Scientiae*, Special Issue 2001–2, 173–211.

Waterman, M. (1996). Emotional responses to music: Implicit and explicit effects in listeners and performers. *Psychology of Music*, 24, 53–67.

Wells, A., & Hakanen, E. A. (1991). The emotional uses of popular music by adolescents. *Journalism Quarterly*, 68, 445–54.

Zajonc, R. B. (2001). Mere exposure: a gateway to the subliminal. *Current Directions in Psychological Science*, 6, 224–8.

Zentner, M. R., Grandjean, D., Scherer, K. R. (2008). Emotions evoked by the sound of music: Characterization, classification, and measurement. *Emotion*, 8, 494–521.

PART VI

DEVELOPMENT, PERSONALITY, AND SOCIAL FACTORS

PERSPECTIVES ON MUSIC AND AFFECT IN THE EARLY YEARS

SANDRA E. TREHUB,
ERIN E. HANNON, AND
ADENA SCHACHNER

23.1 PREAMBLE

THE study of music and emotion presents enormous challenges from a developmental perspective. For example, the dominant method for studying the perception of emotion in music requires listeners to assign emotion labels to musical excerpts, usually from a limited set of alternatives (e.g. happy, sad, angry, fearful). Obviously, this approach, which depends on mastery of the emotion lexicon, musical conventions, and emotional displays, is inappropriate for very young listeners. Our goal in the present chapter is to explore the emotional ramifications of music for those whose abilities, interpretations, and response patterns differ dramatically from those of adults, notably infants and young children. As a result, we limit our coverage to periods in which conventional emotional interpretations or responses to music are absent or incomplete—infants, primarily, and young children, secondarily. In our view, insight into the affective musical cues in the infant's musical environment and infants' responses to such cues can illuminate early perceptual and learning biases that provide a foundation for subsequent musical development.

We conceive of music as a form of communication, one that originates in vocal affect. Moreover, we endorse Bachorowski and Owren's (2003) view that the principal function of affective vocal signals is to influence listeners' affect, attitudes, and behaviour in ways that are favourable to the signaller, such influences having shaped the signalling process over evolutionary time. We acknowledge, as they do, that some affective responses are a direct consequence of signal acoustics (e.g. amplitude, variability), with others being indirect consequences of experience (e.g. familiarity, prior associations). From this perspective, composers and performers attempt, implicitly or explicitly, to modulate listener affect by capitalizing on domain-general cues (e.g. tempo, amplitude), culture-specific cues (e.g. shared customs and history), music-specific cues (e.g. major/minor mode, harmony), or specific knowledge of the intended audience. We take issue with the view that musical performances convey discrete emotional messages that can be described by conventional emotional labels (Juslin & Laukka, 2003). Instead, we contend that the affective intentions of performers are more general and the responses more variable, reflecting listeners' musical experiences as well as their life experiences.

In the pages that follow, we begin by describing musical elements in the infants' environment, which arise primarily from mothers' (or primary caregivers') speech and singing. We outline differences in these modes of expression, their consequences for infants, and possible links to the origins of music. We also consider infants' responsiveness to aspects of non-vocal music that have affective consequences for adults.

Our consideration of maternal speech to pre-verbal infants may seem unusual to those who view music through the narrow lens of music as practised in contemporary mainstream cultures. We aim, instead, for an approach to music and emotion that has developmental, historical, and cross-cultural resonance. The prevailing wisdom is that music making and music listening in the distant past were ubiquitous, with the forms of such music being tied to specific contexts and functions. Accordingly, we include the structured vocal tones of melodious maternal speech to avoid value judgements grounded in music as we know it today. Judgements of musical status are subjective and highly variable both across cultures (e.g. designating some music as primitive) and within cultures, as evidenced by reactions to hip-hop, post-industrial music, and the infamous 4'33" by John Cage.

After describing the music available to infants and their responsiveness to it, we summarize evidence of children's gradual acquisition of conventional interpretations and expressions of emotion in music. Initially, children rely largely on expressive cues shared by speech and music (e.g. tempo, loudness, pitch level). Later, they add music-specific cues to their interpretive and expressive repertoire. Children's intense interest in music and their sensitivity to its emotional connotations, even in the context of social, cognitive, or sensory disabilities, lend credence to the centrality of music in childhood.

23.2 MUSIC AND CAREGIVING

The musical experiences of infants are largely intimate ones, involving vocal behaviours on the part of the principal caregiver that are aimed at affect regulation and interpersonal attunement. In early infancy, arousal is labile, positive affect is infrequent, and the limited self-soothing repertoire (e.g. sucking) is ineffectual for high arousal levels. In general, caregivers respond sensitively, not only to alleviate distress but also to promote infant attention and positive affect (Thompson, 1994). They do so by combining stylized vocalization, touch, movement, and visual gestures in unique ways.

23.2.1 Musical conversations with infants

The ubiquity of speech to pre-verbal infants may seem odd until one reflects on the irrelevance of *what* is said and the significance of *how* it is said. The surface features of infant-directed (ID) speech contrast markedly with those of adult-directed (AD) speech in ways that make the former sound much more musical than the latter (Fernald, 1991; Trehub & Trainor, 1998). Prototypical ID speech is distinguished by its elevated pitch, increased pitch range, distinctive pitch contours, slow tempo, rhythmicity, and repetitiveness, which have been documented in numerous languages and cultures (e.g. Fernald et al, 1989). These features apply primarily to playful rather than soothing ID vocalizations, which are characterized by low pitch, falling pitch contours, and very slow tempo. Aspects of the ID speech style are also evident in women's emotionally charged utterances to familiar adults (Trainor, Austin, & Desjardins, 2000) and pets (e.g. Burnham, Kitamura, & Vollmer-Conna, 2002), highlighting acoustic correlates of the speaker's arousal level and social regulatory goals.

ID speech occurs in a pseudo-conversational context. Mothers pose frequent questions with rising pitch contours, an acoustic form that succeeds in attracting infant attention and heightening arousal (Fernald, 1991). Coos, gurgles, and smiles are treated as credible infant turns, and the conversation proceeds so long as the infant shows signs of continuing engagement. There are notable cross-cultural differences. In contrast to American mothers, who often promote infant excitement and exuberance—positive affect coupled with high arousal—Japanese mothers rely on falling pitch contours in their quest for calm, contented infants—positive affect coupled with low arousal (Morikawa, Shand, & Kosawa, 1988).

23.2.2 Unique melodies in maternal speech

Universal melodies are thought to figure prominently in spoken social regulatory messages to infants (Bryant & Barrett, 2007). In line with linguistic conventions, the term *melody* is typically used to describe intonation or pitch contours. Musical conventions, by contrast, dictate more precise criteria, including specific intervals and rhythms.

Because verbal content is irrelevant to pre-verbal infants, it is not surprising that mothers often repeat the same stereotyped utterances on different occasions (e.g. *How's my big girl? Do you want me to change your diaper?*). Detailed comparisons of such repeated utterances (i.e. identical verbal content) reveal that they are rhythmically similar, but substantially different in their pitch level and tempo (Bergeson & Trehub, 2002). If maternal speech is largely about form rather than content, it may be more fruitful to focus on melodic repetitions. Indeed, mothers use a small set of stable melodies or interval sequences in their repeated interactions with infants, with the component intervals being unrelated to conventional musical intervals (Bergeson & Trehub, 2007). Although some common pitch contours (e.g. rising) are evident across mothers, their component intervals differ across mothers. In other words, each mother seems to use unique or *signature* tunes that are likely to promote maternal voice recognition and infant attachment. Perhaps it is not surprising, then, that infants distinguish their mother's voice from a stranger's voice only when the vocal renditions are normally intonated (Mehler, Bertoncini, Barriere, & Jassik-Gerschenfeld, 1978).

23.2.3 The impact of musical speech

Infants are in no position to state their preferences, but they can show them in experiments designed specifically for that purpose. In typical preference procedures, one auditory pattern continues to play so long as infants look at a display in one location, and a contrasting auditory pattern plays so long as they look at the same display in another location. Because infants' visual attention controls the duration of exposure to each pattern, the distribution of attention over time reflects their attention or preference for one pattern over the other.

In this manner, infants have demonstrated their preference for ID over AD speech (e.g. Fernald, 1985; Werker, Pegg, & McLeod, 1994), for approving over disapproving ID utterances (Papoušek, Bornstein, Nuzzo, Papoušek, & Symmes, 1990), and for affectively positive AD utterances over affectively neutral ID or AD utterances (e.g. Singh, Morgan, & Best, 2002). The implication is that positive affect underlies infants' enhanced attention to ID speech. Because the ID or affectively positive speech in these experiments was higher in pitch, greater in pitch range, louder, and more variable, the preference could be attributable to greater acoustic salience. A stronger test of the preference for speech with positive affect would necessitate the separation of positive affect or other expressive cues from acoustic variability.

In the early days of life, natural speech samples seem to be necessary for a demonstrable ID preference (Cooper & Aslin, 1994). By 4 months of age, however, the isolated pitch contours of ID speech are preferred to those of AD speech (Fernald & Kuhl, 1987). As infants begin to understand the verbal content of speech, their preference for ID prosody wanes (Hayashi, Tamekawa, & Kiritani, 2001; Newman & Hussain, 2006), but does not disappear.

The characteristic vocal affect of ID speech seems to have favourable consequences on perception and memory. For example, 7-month-old infants more readily extract regularities from syllable sequences spoken with ID prosody than with AD prosody (Thiessen, Hill, & Saffran, 2005). Muted affect in the speech of depressed mothers results in diminished learning in early infancy (Kaplan, Bachorowski, Smoski, & Hudenko, 2002). Positive vocal affect also has social consequences. After 5-month-olds are exposed to audiovisual samples of two women using ID or AD speech, they prefer a photograph of the ID speaker to one of the AD speaker (Schachner & Hannon, 2008). Enhanced learning in the context of ID speech may be mediated by arousal or mood, just as preferred music enhances children's and adults' performance in various domains (Schellenberg & Hallam, 2005; Schellenberg, Nakata, Hunter, & Tamoto, 2007; Thompson, Schellenberg, & Hussain, 2001).

In short, the affectively charged utterances of maternal speech influence infants in ways that are favourable to the speaker, which is consistent with Bachorowski and Owren's (2003) functional account of vocal affect. Maternal utterances fulfil caregiving goals by capturing and maintaining infant attention or soothing and comforting infants, as required. Aside from intuitive adjustments to accommodate infants' perceptual needs and preferences, mothers generate unique speech melodies that differentiate their utterances from those of others, with the likely consequence of enhanced infant attachment.

23.2.4 Maternal songs

Singing is another means by which mothers and other caregivers across cultures regulate infant affect. For soothing and inducing sleep, they use lullabies, moving rhythmically and synchronously as they sing. In general, lullabies are characterized by slow tempo, melodic, rhythmic, and syllabic repetition, and smooth, falling pitch contours (Unyk, Trehub, Trainor, & Schellenberg, 1992). Collectively, these features generate a distinctive quality that enables adult listeners to differentiate unfamiliar foreign lullabies from non-lullabies, even when the songs are matched on culture and tempo (Trehub, Unyk, & Trainor, 1993a). Cultures that idealize calm, contented infants and maintain almost continuous physical contact with infants (Morelli, Rogoff, Oppenheim, & Goldsmith, 1992) make extensive use of lullabies (Trehub & Trainor, 1998). Those that value infant vitality and expressiveness accord priority to play songs (Trehub et al, 1997).

23.2.5 Maternal singing style

Aside from a distinctive genre of songs for infants, mothers also use a distinctive performing style, which enables naïve adult listeners to distinguish ID performances from informal, non-ID versions of the same song both within and across cultures (Trehub, Unyk, & Trainor, 1993b; Trehub et al, 1997). Greater identification accuracy for same-culture performances implies culture-specific as well as culture-general features of the

ID singing style. Listeners also distinguish genuine ID performances (i.e. those sung directly to infants) by mothers and fathers from those in which parents attempt to reproduce their performances in the absence of infants (Trehub et al, 1997). In other words, the presence of an infant listener contributes to the expressiveness of parents' musical performances, in part, by providing an appropriate communicative context and, in part, by boosting the singers' level of arousal or engagement. Elevated arousal also contributes to the exuberance of pre-school and young schoolchildren's singing in the presence of their infant siblings (Trehub, Unyk, & Henderson, 1994).

In contrast to ID speech, which permits considerable flexibility in the use of intonation patterns, especially with pre-verbal listeners, ID singing generally involves well-known songs with defined pitch patterns and rhythms. As a result, maternal singers, who are typically untrained, have a limited range of expressive devices at their disposal. In general, their ID performances are higher in pitch level (1–2 semitones) and slower in tempo than their non-ID performances (Trainor, 1996; Trehub et al, 1997). Pitch level is also higher and words less clearly articulated when mothers perform a song for their infant than for their pre-school child (Bergeson & Trehub, 1999).

Maternal singing exhibits greater temporal stability than informal solo singing (i.e. no audience). Unlike solo singers, mothers forego expressive timing in favour of strict temporal regularity (Nakata & Trehub, 2008). This strategy is interesting in light of infants' enhanced processing of temporally regular music (Trehub & Hannon, in press). Perhaps to compensate for their lack of expressive timing, mothers give special emphasis to their dynamic accents. Specifically, pitch height and loudness are highly correlated in maternal singing, but not in solo singing (Nakata & Trehub, 2008).

ID singing is clearly distinguishable from non-ID singing, but the differences are much more modest than those between ID and AD speech. For example, ID speech is approximately 4–5 semitones higher than AD speech (Fernald, 1991), but ID singing is 1–2 semitones higher than non-ID singing (Trainor, 1996). Moreover, the dynamic range of ID speech, from whisper to shriek, greatly exceeds that of typical AD speech. In the case of singing, dynamic changes in ID renditions are more gradual than those in non-ID renditions (Nakata & Trehub, 2008). In many respects, then, ID singing is more predictable and less acoustically salient than ID speech.

Perhaps the most distinguishing feature of ID from AD singing—but the most elusive from a measurement perspective—is its vocal timbre, which conveys the singer's intense emotional engagement with the infant audience. Mothers' tendency to smile while singing to infants alters the shape of their vocal tract and the resulting vocal quality (Tartter & Braun, 1994). When naïve listeners attempt to distinguish ID from non-ID samples of singing, they often justify their judgements of ID singing on the basis of its 'smiling sound', 'soft voice', 'sense of involvement', or 'warm voice' (Trehub et al, 1997). These timbral differences may arise from micro-variations in frequency and amplitude that prevail in ID singing (Trainor, Clark, Huntley, & Adams, 1997).

23.2.6 Impact of maternal singing

Infants 6 months of age exhibit clear preferences for ID singing over non-ID singing (Trainor, 1996; see also Figure 23.1). In principle, this preference could be attributable to familiarity with the ID singing style, but comparable preferences have been demonstrated in hearing newborns with deaf, non-verbal parents (Masataka, 1999). The presumption is that elevated pitch level contributes to this preference (Trainor & Zacharias, 1998), but vocal timbre may be the critical feature. High pitch (relative to the singer's usual pitch level) may generate a vocal timbre that is suitable for arousing but not for soothing ID songs. For example, infants prefer lower-pitched versions of expressively sung lullabies (Volkova, Trehub, & Schellenberg, 2006), perhaps because such performances are consistent with the singer's soothing intentions.

Comparisons across studies reveal more sustained attention to vocal music (Trainor & Zacharias, 1998; Volkova et al, 2006) than to instrumental music (Plantinga & Trainor, 2005; Saffran, Loman, & Robertson, 2000). Greater engagement at the time of initial exposure to music should result in richer and more enduring memory for that music. Thus, although infants exhibit long-term memory for the tunes (i.e. relative pitch patterns) of synthesized folk melodies (Trainor, Wu, & Tsang, 2004), they fail to remember their pitch level (Plantinga & Trainor, 2005), as they do for expressively sung lullabies (Volkova et al, 2006). These findings confirm the importance of the voice (Vouloumanos & Werker, 2004, 2007) and of ecologically valid musical material for infants.

For the most part, the effects of ID music (and speech) have been examined with recorded auditory stimuli from unfamiliar women (i.e. the mothers of other infants). This contrasts with infants' usual experience of music as a familiar, multimodal stimulus. In fact, live maternal singing has important consequences for infant arousal (Shenfield, Trehub, & Nakata, 2003). The same type of singing can attenuate arousal levels for infants with higher initial levels and elevate arousal for infants with lower initial levels, raising the possibility that maternal singing optimizes infant arousal.

23.2.7 Relative impact of speech and singing

In contrast to repeated ID utterances, which typically differ in pitch level and tempo, ID songs are performed on different occasions at nearly identical pitch level and tempo (Bergeson & Trehub, 2002). In addition to specific ID songs being more stable than specific ID utterances in terms of timing, pitch patterning, and dynamics, the sound patterns of music in general are much more predictable than are those of speech. If acoustic salience underlies auditory preferences in early life, then infants should prefer ID speech to ID singing. Instead, they exhibit considerably greater attentiveness and engagement to audiovisual episodes of maternal singing than to comparable episodes of maternal speech (Nakata & Trehub, 2004). Infants' differential attentiveness to maternal singing is consistent with its suggested role as an arousal optimizer (Shenfield et al, 2003).

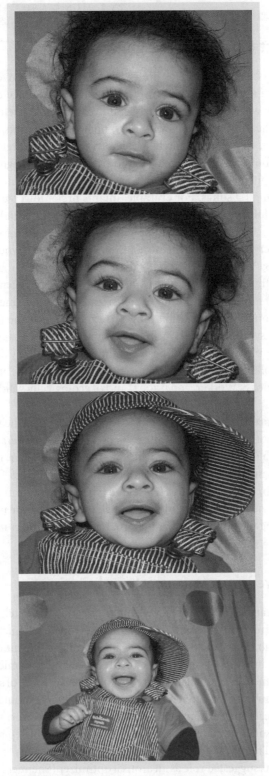

Fig. 23.1 Four photographs of an infant that indicate a gradation of emotional expressions from neutral to full smile during maternal singing.

23.2.8 Keeping in touch with infants

Just as Bachorowski and Owren (2003) have argued that selective pressures favoured vocal signals that influenced listener affect, Falk (2004) has argued for comparable selective pressures on ancestral mothers. She contends that productive activities such as foraging required mothers to release babies from their cradling arms, putting a premium on vocal signals that could maintain infant contentment in the absence of body contact or even visual contact.

Although maternal touch is a highly effective modulator of arousal (Montagu, 1986), its incidence is higher in Eastern cultures that make less use of ID speech than Western cultures do (Morikawa et al, 1988). This raises the possibility that different modes of maternal behaviour (e.g. ID speech, touch) could substitute for one another in managing infant arousal or affect. When mothers are briefly restricted from touching their 6-month-old infants, their ID speech becomes more expressive, as reflected in its elevated pitch and increased pitch range (Nakata & Trehub, 2002). This apparent compensation for restricted touch seems necessary for maintaining infant attention during maternal speech episodes. By contrast, mothers' singing style remains unchanged during bouts of restricted touch, yet infants' attention is comparable whether maternal touch is present or absent. The implication is that singing requires no special enhancement for situations in which caregivers are at a distance, perhaps even out of sight. These findings are consistent with Falk's (2004) claims of expressive maternal vocalization as a means of 'keeping in touch' with infants. It is fair to say, then, that infants are touched by expressive ID speech and singing.

23.3 CROSS-MODAL CORRESPONDENCES IN SPEECH AND SINGING

We know that adults automatically encode identity-specific cues from speech, and there are indications that infants do so as well (Houston & Jusczyk, 2003). For adults, individual differences in expressive timing (Lander, Hill, Kamachi, & Vatikiotis-Bateson, 2007) and articulatory style (Lachs & Pisoni, 2004; Rosenblum, Smith, Nichols, Hale, & Lee, 2006) provide cross-modal cues to the identity of unfamiliar speakers. When adults are exposed to a scripted utterance followed by dynamic but silent visual displays of two unfamiliar speakers, they succeed in matching the correct video to the previously heard speaker (Kamachi, Hill, Lander, & Vatikiotis-Bateson, 2003), but their level of accuracy is modest. Accuracy is greater when the samples are drawn from natural ID speech (Trehub & Brcic, 2008), which attests to the individuality of expressive cues in conversational speech (Lander et al, 2007).

Remarkably, 6-month-old infants succeed in linking silent videos of unfamiliar women to previously heard samples of ID speech (Trehub, Plantiga, & Brcic, 2009). They fail to match person-specific cues across modalities when the samples are drawn from different songs, succeeding, however, with different excerpts from the same song (Trehub et al, 2009). This finding may reflect mothers' use of different songs for different expressive intentions or the absence of a unique singing style in untrained singers. Nevertheless, it is clear that infants and adults automatically extract cues to the identity of unfamiliar speakers and singers—in some situations, at least—and that such identity cues are bimodal or multimodal.

23.4 Speculations about beginnings

It is possible that the precursors of music were affective vocal improvisations used in interpersonal contexts for social regulatory goals. We offer the highly speculative proposal that some of these affective communications became conventionalized and eventually elaborated into a code with discrete pitches and predictable timing that made synchronous activity possible. Although music continued to serve social regulatory goals, its reach extended from dyadic contexts to group contexts. With respect to language and its origins, there are speculations that multimodal, musical phrases, initially with holistic meanings, were subsequently subdivided into smaller meaningful units and combined, over time, in increasingly complex ways (Mithen, 2005; Wray, 1998, 2002). Some aspects of the ancestral vocal style may have been retained to serve as carriers of informational messages and, ultimately, spoken language.

Just as attachment to the primary caregiver provides the impetus for social-emotional development (Bowlby, 1968), affective responses to music may originate in infants' reactions to the vocalizations of caregivers. As noted, infants exhibit enhanced attention and affectively appropriate responses to maternal speech and song. To some extent, comparable cues drive affective reactions to spoken and sung performances, but song is more effective at comforting infants and sustaining their attention, perhaps because it combines positive emotional tone along with patterns of pitch and timing that have stood the test of time.

Elements from affective vocalizations, whether sung or spoken, predominate in the infant's musical environment. Most infants also experience some incidental exposure to non-vocal music, either by overhearing music intended for their parents or by parents' deliberate use of children's recordings. Exposure to recorded performances increases progressively during childhood. It is therefore useful to consider affective responses to non-vocal music in the early years, with the goal of identifying aspects of musical structure that trigger unlearned responses and others that depend on enculturation.

23.5 RESPONSES TO NON-VOCAL MUSIC

Most studies of musical emotion have been restricted to Western listeners and to Western musical materials. As a result, it is difficult to determine whether affective responses to music stem from universal reactions to acoustic patterns, music-specific knowledge, or extra-musical associations (i.e. links between specific musical structures and emotional experiences). There are suggestions, however, that pan-cultural interpretations of emotion in music are cued by specific acoustic features (e.g. tempo, loudness) and by subjective judgements of complexity (e.g. negative valence associated with complexity ratings). North American listeners use such cues to discern the intended emotions of joy, sadness, and anger in Hindustani musical passages (Balkwill & Thompson, 1999). Japanese listeners also apply those labels comparably to Hindustani, Western, and Japanese musical passages (Balkwill, Thompson, & Matsunaga, 2004; see also Chapter 27, this volume). Because the rich musical stimuli in these studies differ along multiple dimensions, a simple assignment of cues to specific emotion judgements is impossible. Moreover, the ubiquity of Western music raises the possibility that Western expressive devices influence musical performances in other cultures. Developmental research provides a unique opportunity to examine the responsiveness of listeners whose musical enculturation is in progress.

23.5.1 Consonance matters

Simultaneous or harmonic combinations of tones are considered consonant if their pitches blend smoothly to yield a pleasant sound. Such intervals are considered dissonant if their component pitches blend poorly, leading to fluctuations in amplitude that sound unpleasant to human listeners across cultures (Butler & Daston, 1968), but not to non-human primates (McDermott & Hauser, 2004). Although scholars consider the perceived consonance or dissonance of sequential or melodic intervals to result from musical exposure (e.g. Blacking, 1992), the wide cross-cultural distribution of the most consonant melodic intervals (Sachs, 1943), notably the octave, perfect fifth and perfect fourth, is unlikely to be coincidental. In other words, unlearned perceptual biases may have influenced the selection of melodic intervals across cultures.

The study of naïve listeners can address questions about the biological or cultural basis for consonance and dissonance and their associations with positive or negative valence. Infants (Schellenberg & Trehub, 1996a; Trainor, 1997) and young children (Schellenberg & Trehub, 1996a) show processing biases for consonant intervals or tone combinations. Specifically, they find consonant intervals more distinctive and more memorable than dissonant intervals. For example, they perceive the similarity of tones an octave apart (Demany & Armand, 1984), and they show enhanced processing of melodies with prominent perfect fifths (e.g. Cohen, Thorpe, & Trehub, 1987; Trainor & Trehub, 1993).

Like adults, infants show distinct preferences for consonant over dissonant patterns in the newborn period and thereafter (Masataka, 2006; Trainor & Heinmiller, 1998; Trainor, Tsang, & Cheung, 2002; Zentner & Kagan, 1996). Because the consonance/dissonance comparisons in the preference studies involved isolated harmonic intervals or harmonic intervals embedded in a musical piece, it is unclear whether infants would show comparable preferences for unaccompanied melodies with consonant component intervals. Such preferences may be restricted to non-vocal contexts. The pleasing harmonic quality of the human voice may override potentially negative responses to dissonant melodic intervals articulated in speech or song.

23.5.2 Timing matters

Intrinsic constraints may also influence responses to temporal aspects of music such as rhythm, metre, and tempo. Unpredictable or irregular rhythmic contexts compromise discrimination and memory in infants (Bergeson & Trehub, 2006; Hannon & Trehub, 2005; Trehub & Hannon, 2009) as well as adults (e.g. Jones, Johnston, & Puente, 2006). Temporal regularity may also have affective consequences. There are suggestions, for example, that infants prefer regular to irregular auditory sequences (Nakata & Mitani, 2005). For adults, unpredictable sound sequences can have unfavourable consequences on arousal (Herry et al, 2007), but expressive variations in timing may have more subtle and more favourable effects (Nair, Large, Steinberg, & Kelso, 2002).

23.6 ACQUIRING LABELS FOR
MUSICAL EMOTIONS

The ability to label musical emotions obviously depends on mastery of the emotion lexicon and linking appropriate labels to the intended musical emotions. To study age-related changes in this ability, children are typically required to judge the emotional intentions of musical samples by selecting a depicted facial expression or verbal label from two or more alternatives (see Chapter 8, this volume, for examples). The results across several studies converge in suggesting that children as young as 4 identify expressive intentions in music such as happiness and sadness, but they confuse fear and anger (Dolgin & Adelson, 1990; Terwogt & van Grinsven, 1991).

There is limited information about the cues that underlie age-related changes in children's judgements. Adults reliably interpret a range of emotional intentions in music on the basis of tempo, loudness, pitch, mode (major/minor), and consonance/dissonance (Chapters 14 and 17, this volume). In forced-choice tasks, Western adults judge music in the major mode and with rapid tempo as happy and music in the minor mode and with slow tempo as sad (e.g. Hevner, 1935; Peretz, Gagnon, & Bouchard, 1998). Mode differs in its usage across cultures and historical periods and is music-specific. By contrast, tempo is linked to arousal in speech and music across cultures. Accordingly, one would expect emotional interpretations based on tempo (fast or slow) to appear well before those based on modal contrast.

Most developmental studies of emotion perception in music have used orchestral excerpts from the classical repertoire (e.g. Cunningham & Sterling, 1988; Esposito & Serio, 2007; Nawrot, 2003), precluding the identification of specific cues underlying children's judgements. When tempo and loudness are held constant, children 8 and older associate the major mode with positive emotions and the minor mode with negative emotions (Gerardi & Gerken, 1995; Gregory, Worrall, & Sarge, 1996). When tempo and mode are varied systematically, 6- to 8-year-olds make conventional judgements of music as happy or sad on the basis of mode or tempo, 5-year-olds do so only on the basis of tempo, and 4-year-olds perform at chance levels on both dimensions (Dalla Bella, Peretz, Rousseau, & Gosselin, 2001).

Some insight into children's understanding of musical cues to positive and negative affect is provided by their own expressive performances. When 4- to 12-year-old children sing a well-known song ('Twinkle, Twinkle, Little Star'), their 'happy' renditions of the song are faster, louder, and at a higher pitch level than are their 'sad' portrayals (Adachi & Trehub, 1998). For the younger children, it is not at all clear that their contrastive performances arise from an understanding of the relevant expressive cues. In fact, requests for sad portrayals of songs often lead to confusion, hesitation, and highly unconventional performances. Nevertheless, child listeners within and across cultures successfully decode the intended emotion from performances of same-age children, and they do so more accurately than adults (Adachi & Trehub, 2000, Adachi, Trehub, & Abe, 2004).

In sung as opposed to instrumental music, words provide information about the singer's affective intentions. In most cases, the affective implications of the lyrics and performing style are consistent, making it difficult to disentangle their separate contributions to children's emotional interpretations. When 5- to 10-year-old children listen to novel excerpts sung in a stereotypically happy manner (fast tempo, major key) or sad manner (slow tempo, relative minor key), they judge the singer's feelings as happy when the lyrics depict positive events (e.g. 'Dad gave me a new bike for my birthday') and as sad when the lyrics depict negative events ('I lost all my money on the way to the store') (Morton & Trehub, 2007). Adults, by contrast, judge the singer's feelings on the basis of her expressive style. When the same tunes are sung with nonsense syllables rather than words, children's judgements match those of adults, confirming their ability to decode the non-verbal, expressive cues but underlining the dominance of verbal cues in their affective interpretations of songs.

In short, the ability to label discrete emotions in various types of music is evident in childhood, although the course of development of cue utilization remains unclear. Young children rely primarily on tempo and loudness when judging the intended emotion in musical performances (Adachi & Trehub, 2000; Adachi et al, 2004). Older children use pitch level, mode, and other cues arising from musical enculturation.

Multiple sources of information are available for the identification of emotions in music, but the relative weighting of cues is likely to change as children acquire greater understanding of the emotional implications of various musical structures. It remains to be determined, however, whether children's judgements of emotion in open-ended contexts would be similar to those in forced-choice contexts.

23.7 EXPECTATIONS

Music theorists consider the internal or deep structure of music, which generates expectations in listeners, as the principal source of emotional responses to music (Huron, 2006; Meyer, 1956; Narmour, 1990; Chapter 21, this volume). Musical expectations refer to the predictions that listeners implicitly generate about upcoming musical events, along with the confirmation or violation of such predictions over the course of listening. Violations of expectation are thought to generate affective reactions such as surprise, anxiety, or tension (i.e. the need for continuation). Confirmations of expectation are thought to generate resolution, repose, or relief.

Some expectations are thought to arise from universal principles of perceptual organization, but others stem from implicit knowledge of style-specific principles (Krumhansl, 2002; Narmour, 1990), including mental representations of the tonal hierarchy (Krumhansl, 1990). Implicit knowledge of the tonal hierarchy leads some pitches (e.g. tonic or reference tone, dominant or perfect fifth above the tonic) to sound stable and others (e.g. leading tone, tones outside the key) to sound unstable or incomplete. Violations of tonal expectation lead to changes in subjective judgements of emotion, physiological responses, and neural responses (Krumhansl, 1997; Sloboda, 1991; Steinbeis, Koelsch, & Sloboda, 2006).

Culture-specific expectations are necessarily shaped by musical exposure. In recent years, there has been increasing interest in mechanisms that underlie the acquisition of implicit knowledge about regularities in speech or music. Remarkably, after limited exposure to a sequence of tones, 7-month-old infants extract regularities based on the conditional probabilities between tones (Saffran, Johnson, Aslin, & Newport, 1999). In principle, infants could also learn about the complex hierarchical structure of Western tonal music, including the tonal hierarchy, from statistical regularities in Western musical pieces (Huron, 2006). Adults with little or no musical training exhibit implicit knowledge of this structure, which attests to the impact of incidental exposure (Tillman, Bharucha, & Bigand, 2000). The developmental timetable for emerging tonal knowledge and its consequences for responding affectively to music are of particular interest.

Although infants show enhanced learning in the context of consonant intervals (e.g. Schellenberg & Trehub, 1996b) and temporal regularity (e.g. Trehub & Hannon, 2009), which are common across cultures, no comparable advantages are evident for musical patterns that conform to Western tonal conventions (Lynch, Eilers, Oller, & Urbano, 1990; Trainor & Trehub, 1992; Schellenberg & Trehub, 1999). By 5 years of age, children show implicit knowledge of the component tones of a key (Trainor & Trehub, 1994), and by 7, they are sensitive to tonal stability and basic harmonic functions (Krumhansl & Keil, 1982; Schellenberg, Bigand, Poulin-Charronnat, Garnier, & Stevens, 2005; Speer & Meeks, 1988; Wilson, Wales, & Pattison, 1997).

Accordingly, children in the early school years could respond affectively to violations of expectation, as adults are presumed to do (Huron, 2006; Meyer, 1956). To date, however, no research has addressed this question. Even in the case of adults, it is unclear whether the tensions and resolutions that listeners perceive while listening to music result in distinctly affective experiences like those that arise from performance features (e.g. tempo, dynamics, timbre) or from extra-musical associations (e.g. Mendelssohn's *Wedding March*, national anthem). Perhaps the internal structure of music has its greatest affective impact on musically trained or highly experienced listeners who apprehend its aesthetic richness.

23.8 DEVELOPMENTAL DISORDERS

Research on children with developmental disorders has the potential to shed light on engagement with music in the face of severe intellectual, perceptual, or social challenges. *Autism* is defined principally by deficits in social interaction, communication, and cognitive flexibility. Aside from isolated cases of autistic musical savants (e.g. Treffert, 1989; Young & Nettelbeck, 1995), autistic individuals, on average, have more accurate pitch perception (Heaton, 2005; Järvinen-Pasly & Heaton, 2007) and pitch memory (Heaton, 2003; Heaton, Hermelin, & Pring, 1998) than the general population. Given their pronounced social deficits, one might expect delays or difficulty in recognizing the affective connotations of music. Nevertheless, autistic children 7 to 15 years of age identify conventional affective connotations of melodies in the major and minor mode much like their non-autistic peers (Heaton, Hermelin, & Pring, 1999). In stark contrast to the diminished sociability of autistic children, individuals with *Williams syndrome*, who have pronounced cognitive and spatial deficits, exhibit enhanced sociability. These children show greater engagement in music and a greater range of emotional responses to music than do normally developing children (Don, Schellenberg, & Rourke, 1999; Levitin et al, 2004).

Deaf listeners with cochlear implants are another population of interest. Their prostheses provide degraded pitch resolution that is adequate for the perception of speech in quiet environments but woefully inadequate for the transmission of musical pitch patterns. As a result, postlingually deafened adults tend to find familiar music unpleasant or unrecognizable in the post-implant period (Lazaletta et al, 2007; Leal et al, 2003). By contrast, most congenitally deaf children who receive their implants by 2 or 3 years of age find music highly engaging. They sing familiar songs with vim and vigour, preserving the timing but not the pitch contours of the songs (Nakata, Trehub, Mitani, & Kanda, 2006). Many child implant users listen regularly to pop music, which they recognize with or without the vocals but not from the melody alone (Vongpaisal, Trehub, & Schellenberg, 2006). They also recognize songs that accompany their favourite television programmes (Mitani et al, 2007). These child implant users successfully identify the valence (happy or sad) of musical pieces (piano renditions with multiple cues) from the Western classical repertoire (Hopyan-Misakyan, Gordon, Papsin, & Dennis, 2006), but the cues underlying their judgements have not been identified.

23.9 CONCLUSION

A number of scholars contend that musical emotions can be best understood as a process of sending and receiving discrete emotional messages (Juslin & Laukka, 2003). Although we concur with the perspective of music as communication, we dispute the notion that discrete emotional messages are involved. Instead, we view senders of musical messages as attempting to influence the affective state or actions of receivers, whether those receivers are infants, children, or adults. On the receiving end, we regard *interest* as the most basic and most important response to music, both for naïve listeners and for expert listeners. In the early years, intense interest in music motivates learning in this domain. For mature listeners, gradations of interest remain at the core of aesthetic emotions (Silvia, 2007).

Our contention is that affective responses to music arise within a social regulatory system in which caregivers use nonverbal vocal communication to modulate infants' arousal and engagement. Considerable social and musical enculturation is necessary before young listeners understand the conventions relating discrete emotional labels to music. Undoubtedly, the sound patterns of music give rise to a rich variety of affective experiences, with discrete emotional categories being among the many ways in which these experiences are described.

Although children eventually master the ability to interpret and express discrete emotions in music, they initially experience confusion about the cues that are relevant to specific emotional categories (Adachi & Trehub, 1998; Dalla Bella et al, 2001; Morton & Trehub, 2007). This confusion may reflect a broader problem, namely, the assumption that conventional emotion labels for music capture the essence of our emotional experiences. When adults are given a wide array of descriptors, they rarely select negative adjectives such as *sad, angry,* and *fearful* to describe their emotional responses to musical excerpts, opting instead for positive adjectives such as *relaxed, happy, dreamy, enchanted, nostalgic,* and *touched* (Juslin & Laukka, 2004, Table 4; Zentner, Grandjean, & Scherer, 2008, Table 2). Nevertheless, the same respondents select negative adjectives to denote emotions *expressed* by the music, which implies a fundamental disconnect between affective reactions to music, on the one hand, and labelling expressive intentions, on the other.

Obviously, listeners are often moved by music, but there is no compelling evidence that they are moved to discrete states of happiness, sadness, anger, or fear. Instead, being moved or touched by music may involve changes in affect arising, in part, from unlearned responses to acoustic cues, which would generate convergence across listeners and, in part, from listeners' personal and musical history, which should generate divergence. The indeterminate meaning of music, which gives listeners free rein to conjure up emotionally significant memories and fantasies, is likely to lead to further divergence.

Why, then, do listeners apply conventional emotion labels to music in typical experimental contexts? In general, they have few options because of the forced-choice format of responding. Even if they could respond freely, they might not choose to share their thoughts and feelings (e.g. imagining an amorous episode, wanting to escape from the laboratory without losing course credit or payment). It is also unlikely that experiences evoked by specific musical pieces in contextually appropriate settings would be elicited in the laboratory. Categorical labelling may result primarily from the demand characteristics of experiments on musical emotions. For situations in which listeners are genuinely moved by music, their feelings may be difficult, perhaps impossible, to describe in words. The default option is to use labels that are pervasive in everyday discourse about emotion.

In sum, we propose that musical emotions are best understood in the broad context of communication, with sound being used to influence the behaviour of others. Emotional responses arise, in part, from acoustic features such as amplitude, pitch variability, and temporal predictability and, in part, from domain-specific conventions and extra-musical associations. Exposure to emotionally meaningful music begins in the early days of life with the melodious speech and soft singing of the primary caregiver. Presumably, those sound patterns promote feelings of comfort, which are reinforced by the security of the dyadic context. They also enhance attention and arousal in ways that foster learning and strengthen interpersonal bonds. Such early responses to music may provide a foundation for subsequent emotional responses to music, which become more refined or differentiated over the course of development. Even in maturity, responses to music retain their basic social function of promoting emotional regulation, including self-regulation, and connections with others.[1]

[1] Preparation of this article was assisted by funding from the Social Sciences and Humanities Research Council and the Natural Sciences and Engineering Research Council of Canada.

Recommended further reading

1. Boone, R. T., & Cunningham, J. G. (2001). Children's expression of emotional meaning in music through expressive body movement. *Journal of Nonverbal Behavior, 25,* 21–41.
2. Falk, D. (2009). *Finding our tongues: Mothers, infants and the origins of language.* New York: Basic Books.
3. Heaton, P., Allen, R., Williams, K., Cummins, O., & Happe, F. (2008). Do social and cognitive deficits curtail musical understanding? Evidence from autism and Down syndrome. *British Journal of Developmental Psychology, 26,* 171–82.

References

Adachi, M., & Trehub, S. E. (1998). Children's expression of emotion in song. *Psychology of Music, 26,* 133–53.

Adachi, M., & Trehub, S. E. (2000). Decoding the expressive intentions in children's songs. *Music Perception, 18,* 213–24.

Adachi, M., Trehub, S. E., & Abe, J. (2004). Perceiving emotion in children's songs across age and culture. *Japanese Psychological Research, 46,* 322–36.

Bachorowski, J., & Owren, M. (2003). Sounds of emotion: The production and perception of affect-related vocal acoustics. *Annals of the New York Academy of Sciences, 1000,* 244–65.

Balkwill, L.-L., & Thompson, W. F. (1999). A cross-cultural investigation of the perception of emotion in music: Psychophysical and cultural cues. *Music Perception, 17,* 43–64.

Balkwill, L.-L., Thompson, W. F., & Matsunaga, R. (2004). Recognition of emotion in Japanese, Western, and Hindustani music by Japanese listeners. *Japanese Psychological Research, 46,* 337–49.

Bergeson, T. R., & Trehub, S. E. (1999). Mothers' singing to infants and preschool children. *Infant Behavior & Development, 22,* 51–64.

Bergeson, T. R., & Trehub, S. E. (2002). Absolute pitch and tempo in mothers' speech and song to infants. *Psychological Science, 13,* 72–5.

Bergeson, T. R., & Trehub, S. E. (2006). Infants' perception of rhythmic patterns. *Music Perception, 23,* 345–60.

Bergeson, T. R., & Trehub, S. E. (2007). Signature tunes in mothers' speech to infants. *Infant Behavior and Development, 30,* 648–54.

Blacking, J. (1992). The biology of music-making. In H. Myers (ed.), *Ethnomusicology: An introduction* (pp. 301–14). New York: Norton.

Bryant, G. A., & Barrett, H. C. (2007). Recognizing intentions in infant-directed speech: Evidence for universals. *Psychological Science, 18,* 746–51.

Bowlby, J. (1968). *Attachment and loss: Vol. 3. Attachment.* New York: Basic Books.

Burnham, D., Kitamura, C., & Vollmer-Conna, U. (2002). What's new, pussycat? On talking to babies and animals. *Science, 296,* 1435.

Butler, J. W., & Daston, P. G. (1968). Musical consonance as musical preference: A cross-cultural study. *Journal of General Psychology, 79,* 129–42.

Cohen, A. J., Thorpe, L. A., & Trehub, S. E. (1987). Infants' perception of musical relations in short transposed tone sequences. *Canadian Journal of Psychology, 41,* 33–47.

Cooper, R. P., & Aslin, R. N. (1994). Developmental differences in infant attention to the spectral properties of infant-directed speech. *Child Development, 65,* 1663–77.

Cunningham, J. G., & Sterling, R. (1988). Developmental analysis in the understanding of affective meaning in music. *Motivation and Emotion, 12,* 399–413.

Dalla Bella, S., Peretz, I., Rousseau, L., & Gosselin, N. (2001). A developmental study of the affective value of tempo and mode in music. *Cognition, 80,* B1–B10.

Demany, L., & Armand, F. (1984). The perceptual reality of tone chroma in early infancy. *Journal of the Acoustical Society of America, 76,* 57–66.

Dolgin, K. G., & Adelson, E. H. (1990). Age changes in the ability to interpret affect in sung and instrumentally-presented melodies. *Psychology of Music, 18,* 29–33.

Don, A. J., Schellenberg, E. G., & Rourke, B. P. (1999). Music and language skills of children with Williams syndrome. *Child Neuropsychology, 5,* 154–70.

Esposito, A., & Serio, M. (2007). Children's perception of musical emotional expressions. In A. Esposito et al (eds), *Verbal and nonverbal communication behaviors* (pp. 51–64). Berkeley, CA: Springer.

Falk, D. (2004). Prelinguistic evolution in early hominins: Whence motherese? *Behavioral and Brain Sciences, 27,* 491–503.

Fernald, A. (1985). Four-month-old infants prefer to listen to motherese. *Infant Behavior and Development, 8,* 181–95.

Fernald, A. (1991). Prosody in speech to children: Prelinguistic and linguistic functions. *Annals of Child Development, 8,* 43–80.

Fernald, A., & Kuhl, P. (1987). Acoustic determinants of infant preference for motherese speech. *Infant Behavior and Development, 10,* 279–93.

Fernald, A., Taeschner, T., Dunn, J., Papoušek, M., Boysson-Bardies, B., & Fukui, I. (1989). A cross-language study of prosodic modifications in mothers' and fathers' speech to pre-verbal infants. *Journal of Child Language, 16,* 477–501.

Gerardi, G. M., & Gerken, L. (1995). The development of affective responses to modality and melodic contour. *Music Perception, 12,* 279–90.

Gregory, A. H., Worrall, I., & Sarge, A. (1996). The development of emotional responses to music in young children. *Motivation and Emotion, 20,* 341–9.

Hannon, E. E., & Trehub, S. E. (2005). Tuning in to rhythms: Infants learn more readily than adults. *Proceedings of the National Academy of Sciences, 102,* 12639–43.

Hayashi, A., Tamekawa, Y., & Kiritani, S. (2001). Developmental change in auditory preference for speech stimuli in Japanese infants. *Journal of Speech and Hearing Disorders, 44,* 1189–1200.

Heaton, P. (2003). Pitch memory, labeling and disembedding in autism. *Journal of Child Psychology and Psychiatry, 44,* 543–51.

Heaton, P. (2005). Interval and contour processing in autism. *Journal of Autism and Developmental Disorders, 35,* 787–93.

Heaton, P., Hermelin, B., & Pring, L. (1998). Autism and pitch processing: A precursor for savant musical ability? *Music Perception, 154,* 291–305.

Heaton, P., Hermelin, B., & Pring, L. (1999). Can children with autistic spectrum disorders perceive affect in music? An experimental investigation. *Psychological Medicine, 29,* 1405–10.

Herry, C., Bach, D. R., Esposito, F., Di Salle, F., Perrig, W. J., Scheffler, K., et al (2007). Processing of temporal unpredictability in human and animal amygdala. *Journal of Neuroscience, 27,* 5958–66.

Hevner, K. (1935). The affective character of the major and minor modes in music. *American Journal of Psychology, 47,* 103–118.

Hopyan-Misakyan, T., Gordon, K., Papsin, B., & Dennis, M. (2006). *Identification of emotion in children with early onset deafness who use cochlear implants.* Paper presented at the International Conference of Music Perception and Cognition, Bologna, Italy, August 2006.

Houston, D. M., & Jusczyk, P. W. (2003). Infants' long-term memory for the sound patterns of words and voices. *Journal of Experimental Psychology: Human Perception and Performance, 29,* 1143–54.

Huron, D. (2006). *Sweet anticipation: Music and the psychology of expectation.* Cambridge, MA: MIT Press.

Järvinen-Pasly, A., & Heaton, P. (2007). Evidence of reduced domain-specificity in auditory processing in autism. *Developmental Science, 10,* 786–93.

Jones, M. R., Johnston, H. J., & Puente, J. (2006). Effects of auditory pattern structure on anticipatory and reactive attending. *Cognitive Psychology, 53,* 59–96.

Juslin, P. N., & Laukka, P. (2003). Communication of emotions in vocal expression and music performance: Different channels, same code? *Psychological Bulletin, 129,* 770–814.

Juslin, P. N., & Laukka, P. (2004). Expression, perception, and induction of musical emotions: A review and a questionnaire study of everyday listening. *Journal of New Music Research, 33,* 217–38.

Kamachi, M., Hill, H., Lander, K., & Vatikiotis-Bateson, E. (2003). Putting the face to the voice: Matching identity across modality. *Current Biology, 13,* 1709–14.

Kaplan, P. S., Bachorowski, J. A., Smoski, M. J., & Hudenko, W. J. (2002). Infants of depressed mothers, although competent learners, fail to learn in response to their own mothers' infant-directed speech. *Psychological Science, 13,* 268–71.

Krumhansl, C. L. (1990). *The cognitive foundations of musical pitch.* Oxford: Oxford University Press.

Krumhansl, C. L. (1997). An exploratory study of musical emotions and psychophysiology. *Canadian Journal of Experimental Psychology, 51,* 336–52.

Krumhansl, C. L. (2002). Music: A link between cognition and emotion. *Current Directions in Psychological Science, 11,* 45–50.

Krumhansl, C. L., & Keil, F. (1982). Acquisition of the hierarchy of tonal functions in music. *Memory & Cognition, 10,* 243–51.

Lachs, L., & Pisoni, D. B. (2004). Cross-modal source information and spoken word recognition. *Journal of Experimental Psychology: Human Perception and Performance, 30,* 378–96.

Lander, K., Hill, H., Kamachi, M., & Vatikiotis-Bateson, E. (2007). It's not what you say but the way you say it: Matching faces and voices. *Journal of Experimental Psychology: Human Perception and Performance, 33,* 905–914.

Lazaletta, L., Castro, A., Bastarrica, M., Pérez-Mora, R., Madero, R., De Sarriá, J., & Gavilán, J. (2007). Does music perception have an impact on quality of life following cochlear implantation? *Acta Oto-Laryngologica, 127,* 682–6.

Leal, M. C., Young, J., Laborde, M.-L., Calmels, M.-N., Verges, S., Lugardon, S., Andriew, S., Deguine, O., & Fraysse, B. (2003). Music perception in adult cochlear implant recipients. *Acta Oto-Laryngologica, 123,* 826–35.

Levitin, D. J., Cole, K., Chiles, M., Lai, Z., Lincoln, A., & Bellugi, U. (2004). Characterizing the musical phenotype in individuals with Williams Syndrome. *Child Neuropsychology, 10,* 223–47.

Lynch, M. P., Eilers, R. E., Oller, D. K., & Urbano, R. C. (1990). Innateness, experience, and music perception. *Psychological Science, 1,* 272–6.

Masataka, N. (1999). Preference for infant-directed singing in 2-day-old hearing infants of deaf parents. *Developmental Psychology, 35,* 1001–5.

Masataka, N. (2006). Preference for consonance over dissonance by hearing newborns of deaf parents and of hearing parents. *Developmental Science, 9,* 46–50.

McDermott, J., & Hauser, M. D. (2004). Are consonant intervals music to their ears? Spontaneous acoustic preferences in nonhuman primates. *Cognition, 94,* B11–B21.

Mehler, J., Bertoncini, J., Barriere, M., & Jassik-Gerschenfeld, D. (1978). Infant recognition of mother's voice. *Perception*, 7, 491–7.

Meyer, L. B. (1956). *Emotion and meaning in music.* Chicago, IL: Chicago University Press.

Mitani, C., Nakata, T., Trehub, S. E., Kanda, Y., Kumagami, H., Takasaki, K., Ikue Miyamoto, I., & Takahashi, H. (2007). Music recognition, music listening, and word recognition by deaf children with cochlear implants. *Ear & Hearing*, 28, 29S–33S.

Mithen, S. (2005). *The singing Neanderthals: The origins of music, language, mind and body.* London: Weidenfeld & Nicolson.

Montagu, A. (1986). *Touching: The human significance of the skin* (3rd edn). New York: Harper and Row.

Morelli, G., Rogoff, B., Oppenheim, D., & Goldsmith, D. (1992). Cultural variation in infants' sleeping arrangements: Questions of independence. *Developmental Psychology*, 28, 604–13.

Morikawa, H., Shand, N., & Kosawa, Y. (1988). Maternal speech to prelingual infants in Japan and the United States: Relationships among functions, forms, and referents. *Journal of Child Language*, 15, 237–56.

Morton, J. B., & Trehub, S. E. (2007). Children's perception of emotion in song. *Psychology of Music*, 35, 1–11.

Nair, D. G., Large, E. W., Steinberg, F., & Kelso, J. A. S. (2002). Perceiving emotion in expressive piano performance: A functional MRI study. In C. Stevens, D. Burnham, G. McPherson, E. Schubert, & J. Renwick (eds), *Proceedings of the 7th International Conference on Music Perception and Cognition, Sydney 2002* (CD rom). Adelaide, Australia: Causal Productions.

Nakata, T., & Mitani, C. (2005). Influences of temporal fluctuation on infant attention. *Music Perception*, 22, 401–9.

Nakata, T., & Trehub, S. E. (2002). *The potency of musical features in maternal speech to infants.* Paper presented at the Japanese Society of Music Perception and Cognition, Kyoto, Japan, 2002.

Nakata, T., & Trehub, S. E. (2004). Infants' responsiveness to maternal speech and singing. *Infant Behavior & Development*, 27, 455–64.

Nakata, T., & Trehub, E. E. (2008). *Timing and dynamics in infant-directed singing.* Paper presented at the International Conference on Music Perception and Cognition, Sapporo, Japan, August 2008.

Nakata, T., Trehub, S. E., Mitani, C., & Kanda, Y. (2006). Pitch and timing in the songs of deaf children with cochlear implants. *Music Perception*, 24, 147–54.

Narmour, E. (1990). *The analysis and cognition of basic melodic structures: The implication-realization model.* Chicago, IL: University of Chicago Press.

Nawrot, E. S. (2003). The perception of emotional expression in music: Evidence from infants, children, and adults. *Psychology of Music*, 31, 75–92.

Newman, R. S., & Hussain, I. (2006). Changes in preference for infant-directed speech in low and moderate noise. *Infancy*, 10, 61–86.

Papoušek, M., Bornstein, M. H., Nuzzo, C., Papoušek, H., & Symmes, D. (1990). Infant responses to prototypical melodic contours in parental speech. *Infant Behavior & Development*, 13, 539–45.

Peretz, I., Gagnon, L., & Bouchard, B. (1998). Music and emotion: Perceptual determinants, immediacy, and isolation after brain damage. *Cognition*, 68, 111–41.

Plantinga, J., & Trainor, L. J. (2005). Memory for melody: Infants use a relative pitch code. *Cognition*, 98, 1–11.

Rosenblum, L. D., Smith, N. M., Nichols, S. M., Hale, S., & Lee, J. (2006). Hearing a face: Cross-modal speaker matching using isolated visible speech. *Perception & Psychophysics*, 68, 84–93.

Sachs, C. (1943). *The rise of music in the ancient world. East and West.* New York: W. W. Norton and Co.

Saffran, J., Johnson, E., Aslin, R., & Newport, E. (1999). Statistical learning of tone sequences by human infants and adults. *Cognition, 70,* 27–52.

Saffran, J. R., Loman, M. M., & Robertson, R. R W. (2000). Infant memory for musical experiences. *Cognition, 77,* B15–B23.

Schachner, A. M., & Hannon, E. E. (2008). *Infant-directed speech modulates subsequent social preferences in 5-month-old infants.* Paper presented at the International Conference on Infant Studies, Vancouver, Canada, March 2008.

Schellenberg, E. G., Bigand, E., Poulin-Charronnat, B., Garnier, C., & Stevens, C. (2005). Children's implicit knowledge of harmony in Western music. *Developmental Science, 8,* 551–66.

Schellenberg, E. G., & Hallam, S. (2005). Music listening and cognitive abilities in 10 and 11 year olds: The Blur effect. *Annals of the New York Academy of Sciences, 1060,* 202–209.

Schellenberg, E. G., Nakata, T., Hunter, P. G., & Tamoto, S. (2007). Exposure to music and cognitive performance: Tests of children and adults. *Psychology of Music, 35,* 5–19.

Schellenberg, E. G., & Trehub, S. E. (1996a). Children's discrimination of melodic intervals. *Developmental Psychology, 32,* 1039–50.

Schellenberg, E. G., & Trehub, S. E. (1996b). Natural intervals in music: A perspective from infant listeners. *Psychological Science, 7,* 272–7.

Schellenberg, E. G., & Trehub, S. E. (1999). Culture-general and culture-specific factors in the discrimination of melodies. *Journal of Experimental Child Psychology, 74,* 107–27.

Shenfield, T., Trehub, S. E., & Nakata, T. (2003). Maternal singing modulates infant arousal. *Psychology of Music, 31,* 365–75.

Silvia, P. J. (2007). Interest—the curious emotion. *Current Directions in Psychological Science, 17,* 57–60.

Singh, L., Morgan, J. L., & Best, C. T. (2002). Infants' listening preferences: Baby talk or happy talk? *Infancy, 3,* 365–94.

Sloboda, J. A. (1991). Music structure and emotional response: Some empirical findings. *Psychology of Music, 19,* 110–120.

Speer, J., & Meeks, P. (1988). School children's perception of pitch in music. *Psychomusicology, 5,* 49–56.

Steinbeis, N., Koelsch, S., & Sloboda, J. A. (2006). The role of harmonic expectancy violations in musical emotions: evidence from subjective, physiological, and neural responses. *Journal of Cognitive Neuroscience, 18,* 1380–93.

Tartter, V. C., & Braun, D. (1994). Hearing smiles and frown in normal and whisper registers. *Journal of the Acoustical Society of America, 96,* 2101–7.

Terwogt, M. M., & van Grinsven, E. (1991). Musical expression and mood states. *Psychology of Music, 19,* 99–109.

Thiessen, E. D., Hill, E. A., & Saffran, J. R. (2005). Infant-directed speech facilitates word segmentation. *Infancy, 7,* 53–71.

Thompson, R. A. (1994). Emotion regulation: A theme in search of a definition. *Monographs of the Society for Research in Child Development (The Development of Emotion Regulation: Biological and behavioral considerations), 59,* 25–52.

Thompson, W. F., Schellenberg, E. G., & Husain, G. (2001). Arousal, mood, and the Mozart effect. *Psychological Science, 12,* 248–51.

Tillman, B., Bharucha, J. J., & Bigand, E. (2000). Implicit learning of tonality: a self-organizing approach. *Psychological Review, 107,* 885–913.

Trainor, L. J. (1996). Infant preferences for infant-directed versus noninfant-directed play-songs and lullabies. *Infant Behavior and Development*, 19, 83–92.

Trainor, L. J. (1997). Effect of frequency ratio on infants' and adults' discrimination of simultaneous intervals. *Journal of Experimental Psychology: Human Perception and Performance*, 23, 1427–38.

Trainor, L. J., Austin, C. M., & Desjardins, R. N. (2000). Is infant-directed speech prosody a result of the vocal expression of emotion? *Psychological Science*, 11, 188–95.

Trainor, L. J., Clark, E. D., Huntley, A., & Adams, B. A. (1997). The basis of preferences for infant-directed singing. *Infant Behavior and Development*, 20, 383–96.

Trainor, L. J., & Heinmiller, B. M. (1998). The development of evaluative responses to music: Infants prefer to listen to consonance over dissonance. *Infant Behavior and Development*, 21, 77–88.

Trainor, L., & Trehub, S. E. (1992). A comparison of infants' and adults' sensitivity to Western musical structure. *Journal of Experimental Psychology: Human Perception and Performance*, 18, 394–402.

Trainor, L. J., & Trehub, S. E. (1993). What mediates infants' and adults' superior processing of the major over the augmented triad? *Music Perception*, 11, 185–96.

Trainor, L. J., & Trehub, S. E. (1994). Key membership and implied harmony in Western tonal music: developmental perspectives. *Perception & Psychophysics*, 56, 125–32.

Trainor, L. J., Tsang, C. D., & Cheung, V. H. W. (2002). Preference for consonance in 2- and 4-month-old infants. *Music Perception*, 20, 187–94.

Trainor, L. J., Wu, L., & Tsang, C. D. (2004). Long-term memory for music: Infants remember tempo and timbre. *Developmental Science*, 7, 289–96.

Trainor, L. J., & Zacharias, C. A. (1998). Infants prefer higher-pitched singing. *Infant Behavior and Development*, 21, 799–805.

Treffert, D. (1989). *Extraordinary people: Understanding 'idiot savants'*. New York: Harper & Row.

Trehub, S. E., & Hannon, E. E. (2009). Conventional rhythms enhance infants' and adults' perception of musical patterns. *Cortex, 45*, 110–8.

Trehub, S. E., Plantinga, J., & Brcic, J. (2009). Infants detect cross-modal cues to identity in speech and singing. *Annals of the New York Academy of Sciences, 1169*, 508–11.

Trehub, S. E., & Trainor, L. J. (1998). Singing to infants: Lullabies and playsongs. *Advances in Infancy Research*, 12, 43–77.

Trehub, S. E., Unyk, A. M., & Henderson, J. L. (1994). Children's songs to infant siblings: Parallels with speech. *Journal of Child Language*, 21, 735–44.

Trehub, S. E., Unyk, A. M., & Trainor, L. J. (1993a). Adults identify infant-directed music across cultures. *Infant Behavior and Development*, 16, 193–211.

Trehub, S. E., Unyk, A. M., & Trainor, L. J. (1993b). Maternal singing in cross-cultural perspective. *Infant Behavior and Development*, 16, 285–95.

Trehub, S. E., Unyk, A. M., Kamenetsky, S. B., Hill, D. S., Trainor, L. J., Henderson, J. L., & Saraza, M. (1997). Mothers' and fathers' singing to infants. *Developmental Psychology*, 33, 500–7.

Unyk, A. M., Trehub, S. E., Trainor, L. J., & Schellenberg, E. G. (1992). Lullabies and simplicity: A cross-cultural perspective. *Psychology of Music*, 20, 15–28.

Volkova, A., Trehub, S. E., & Schellenberg, E. G. (2006). Infants' memory for musical performances. *Developmental Science*, 9, 583–9.

Vongpaisal, T., Trehub, S. E., & Schellenberg, E. G. (2006). Song recognition by children and adolescents with cochlear implants. *Journal of Speech, Language, and Hearing Research, 49*, 1091–1103.

Vouloumanos, A., & Werker, J. F. (2004). Tuned to the signal: The privileged status of speech for young infants. *Developmental Science*, 7, 270–6.

Vouloumanos, A., & Werker, J. F. (2007). Listening to language at birth: Evidence for a bias for speech in neonates. *Developmental Science, 10,* 170–2.

Werker, J. F., Pegg,, J. E., & McLeod, P. J. (1994). A cross-language investigation of infant preference for infant-directed communication. *Infant Behavior and Development, 17,* 321–31.

Wilson, S., Wales, R., & Pattison, P. (1997). The representation of tonality and meter in children aged 7 to 9. *Journal of Experimental Child Psychology, 64,* 42–66.

Wray, A. (1998). Protolanguage as a holistic system for social interaction. *Language and Communication, 18,* 47–67.

Wray, A. (2002). *Formulaic language and the lexicon.* Cambridge, UK: Cambridge University Press.

Young, R., & Nettelbeck, T. (1995). The abilities of a musical savant and his family. *Journal of Autism and Developmental Disorders, 25,* 229–45.

Zentner, M. R., Grandjean, D., & Scherer, K. R. (2008). Emotions evoked by the sound of music: Characterization, classification, and measurement. *Emotion, 8,* 494–521.

Zentner, M. R., & Kagan, J. (1996). Perception of music by infants. *Nature, 383,* 29.

CHAPTER 24

PREFERENCE, PERSONALITY, AND EMOTION

PETER J. RENTFROW AND JENNIFER A. MCDONALD

Barry proposed the idea of a questionnaire for prospective [dating] partners that covered all the music/film/TV/book bases . . . It amused us at the time . . . But there was an important and essential truth contained in the idea, and the truth was that these things matter and it's no good pretending that any relationship has a future if your record collections disagree violently . . .

Nick Hornby, High Fidelity

For Barry and his friends music was everything. From the moment they awoke to the second they fell asleep they listened to music, thought about it, and talked about it. Thus, it is no surprise why they supposed that a questionnaire asking about such things as music preferences would highlight valuable information about the character of a person. As it turns out, music aficionados are not the only ones who hold this belief. Research on lay theories of music indicates that many people believe music reflects important aspects of their personalities and the personalities of others (Rentfrow & Gosling, 2003, 2006). Does the music we prefer to listen to really reflect who we are?

Here, we attempt to shed some light on the notion that music preferences and personality are related. The chapter begins with a brief introduction to studying music preferences and to personality psychology, followed by an overview of contemporary issues in personality psychology and why it is relevant to consider individual differences in music listening. We then provide a review of studies that have connected music genre preferences to personality traits and examine alternative ways of assessing music preferences. The chapter concludes with a thorough discussion of the current gaps in the music and personality literature and suggestions for future research in this emerging sub-field of music psychology.

24.1 BRIEF INTRODUCTION TO THE STUDY OF MUSIC PREFERENCES

The definition of music preference is fairly self-explanatory—it refers to the extent to which a person prefers, or likes, a particular kind of music over another (e.g. Scherer & Zentner, 2001). Because music preference is usually seen as a long-term affective evaluation, it is usually described synonymously with musical taste, which has traditionally been defined as 'a person's overall attitude toward collective music phenomena' (Farnsworth, 1969, as cited by Radocy & Boyle, 1979, p. 221). Though music preference could also be perceived as transitory, potentially depending on the current state or context of the individual listener, much of the music-preference research has tended to consider stable evaluations over short-term evaluations, so the former will be the focus of the current chapter (for discussion related to preference in the form of music choice, see Chapter 25, this volume).

Stable music preferences were first measured by questionnaires that asked respondents to specify which types of music they enjoy hearing, from a list of a few styles like 'serious' (classical) or 'popular' (jazz; Farnsworth, 1949). Along these lines, sociologist Bourdieu (1984) notoriously measured tastes for different classes of classical music by asking respondents to indicate, from a list of works, which ones they know and like best. The most widely accepted means of studying music preferences, however, involves the rating of the *extent* to which individuals like particular musical styles or genres using a Likert-type scale. This approach was introduced by Cattell and Anderson (1953) in their creation of the IPAT music-preference test. This inventory consisted of 120 classical and jazz music excerpts, in which respondents reported how much they liked each excerpt. More recent music-preference measures (e.g. Litle & Zuckerman's Music Preference Scale, 1986; Rentfrow & Gosling's Short Test of Music Preferences, 2003, and their variations) have necessarily included a broader range of items (usually music genres) to rate to ensure a more complete range of musical evaluations. As we discuss below, these types of inventories have been helpful in not only measuring music preferences, but also determining underlying groupings of musical tastes and in examining relationships between musical likes and psychological constructs such as personality traits.

Studies have shown that knowing the types of music that people prefer can contribute to understanding characteristics of the individual and potentially signify their membership in certain groups. Past research in sociology has suggested, for instance, that social class is linked to music preferences, such that upper class and well-educated individuals tend to prefer 'highbrow' music genres (e.g. classical, opera, and big band), whereas working-class and less-educated individuals tend to prefer 'lowbrow' music (e.g. country, gospel, and rap; Katz-Gerro, 1999; Mark, 1998; Van Eijck, 2001). Newer studies using British and Israeli samples have emphasized, however, that social status is a better indicator of musical tastes or consumption than class (Chan & Goldthorpe, 2007; Katz-Gerro, Raz, & Yaish, 2007). Additionally, there is evidence that individuals living in urban environments tend to prefer jazz, classical, and contemporary rock music, whereas individuals in suburban and rural environments prefer classic rock, country, folk, and oldies (Fox & Wince, 1975; Katz-Gerro, 1999).

Other studies have demonstrated sex and gender differences in liking for different music genres. For instance, Colley (2008) found that male undergraduates assigned higher ratings to rock, folk, blues, reggae, and heavy metal music than did females, who were more inclined to prefer chart pop. Colley also found an association between self-reported masculinity and 'heavy'-sounding music and femininity and 'light'-sounding music. These results corroborate older findings related to gender differences in music choices (e.g. Christensen & Peterson, 1988). There are also reports of age and other demographic differences in music preferences, but these findings are relatively old and sparse (for a review, see Russell, 2007).

24.2 BRIEF INTRODUCTION TO PERSONALITY PSYCHOLOGY

Though the study of personality may be traced back over 2,000 years to Aristotle or his pupil, Theophrastus, by most accounts (see Goldberg, 1993), the current state of personality psychology owes much to the work of nineteenth- and twentieth-century lexical theorists. The lexical theory is based on the idea that those individual differences that are most important in human interactions will become encoded as single terms in language (Goldberg, 1993). Therefore, in order to identify the key dimensions on which individuals differ, it is necessary to examine the words people use to describe themselves and others. The lexical theorists perused dictionaries in search of words that could be used to describe a person, and developed extensive lists of personality-descriptive terms, or traits. For example, Allport and Odbert (1936) identified over 17,000 words that could be used to describe a person's personality.

A major advancement, which coincided with the expansion of the lexical approach, was the development of a statistical procedure called factor analysis. This provided a tool for empirically reducing the vast numbers of personality-descriptive terms down to common personality factors, or dimensions. Thurstone (1934), and later Cattell (1943), factor-analysed participants' ratings of themselves or others on descriptive personality terms, and identified factors that reflect broad dimensions of personality defined by what is most common among the descriptive terms on each factor. The application of factor analysis to the study of personality traits was a watershed moment in the field. Soon, researchers began factor-analysing responses to an assortment of personality and individual difference measures. However, confusion quickly arose as researchers began obtaining different results; whereas some found three personality factors, others found five, and still others found sixteen factors.

It was not until the early 1990s that a suitable conceptual and empirical framework for classifying and measuring personality dimensions emerged and began to garner scientific consensus. Factor analyses of tens of thousands of trait ratings made by hundreds of thousands of people provided evidence for the existence of five broad personality dimensions that can be reliably measured (e.g. Goldberg, 1992; John & Srivastava, 1999; McCrae & Costa, 1999; Ozer & Benet-Martínez, 2006; but see Ashton et al, 2004, and Block, 1995). Although there is less consensus about which labels best describe the 'Big Five' dimensions, the most popular labels spell the acronym OCEAN: Openness (also referred to as Culture or Intellect), Conscientiousness, Extraversion (or Energy), Agreeableness, and Neuroticism (or Emotional Instability). Openness refers to the degree to which a person is creative, curious, imaginative, broad minded, and unconventional. Conscientiousness is the tendency to be reliable, dependable, organized, efficient, and self-disciplined. Extraversion is defined by such terms as sociable, talkative, enthusiastic, active, and enterprising, and also by affect-laden terms such as happy, cheerful, and optimistic. Agreeableness reflects the extent to which someone is friendly, kind, trusting, generous, and sympathetic. And Neuroticism, which has a negative affect component, refers to such characteristics as anxious, moody, vulnerable, tense, and irritable. These factors reflect the basic dimensions that people use to describe themselves and others, and provide a useful framework for studying individual differences in personality.

Although the Big Five are not universally accepted in the field (e.g. Block, 1995), scores of studies indicate that these basic personality dimensions are rooted in biology (Jang, McCrae, Angleitner, Riemann, & Livesley, 1998; Loehlin, 1992; Plomin & Caspi, 1999), relatively stable throughout life (McCrae & Costa, 2003; Roberts, Walton, & Viechtbauer, 2006; Srivastava, John, Gosling, & Potter, 2003), and emerge in several cultures (e.g. Benet-Martínez & John, 2000; Saucier & Ostendorf, 1999; Church & Kaitigbak, 1989; McCrae & Costa, 1997). It should be pointed out, however, that recent cross-cultural studies of personality structure are beginning to converge and suggest the existence of a sixth personality dimension that resembles honesty and humility versus dishonesty and boastfulness (e.g. Ashton, Lee, & Goldberg, 2004; Ashton et al, 2004; De Raad, 1992).

Research has shown that the Big Five dimensions are associated with a variety of behaviours and important life outcomes. For example, Openness is positively related to possessing liberal attitudes, pursuing a career in the arts, and experimenting with illegal drugs; Conscientiousness has a positive effect on occupational performance and success, life expectancy, and satisfaction in romantic relationships; Extroversion is positively related to subjective well-being, social integration, and pursuing a career in social and enterprising industries (e.g. social work, sales, finance); Agreeableness is positively linked to religiousness, life expectancy, and volunteerism; and Neuroticism is negatively related to life expectancy, relationship satisfaction, and occupational satisfaction (Ozer & Benet-Martínez, 2006). How does personality become expressed in these domains?

Without doubt, the processes connecting personality and behaviour are complex, but explanations for the links are typically based on interactionist perspectives. Interactionist theories emphasize links between the person and the environment, and suggest that individuals select and create (sometimes unintentionally) social and physical environments that reinforce and reflect elements of their personalities, self-views, and values (e.g. Buss, 1987; Gosling, Ko, Mannarelli, & Morris, 2002; Rentfrow, Gosling, & Potter, 2008; Swann, Rentfrow, & Guinn, 2003). From this standpoint, we can therefore argue that highly open people, who are creative and curious, seek out careers that enable them to express their creativity, for instance; and that emotionally unstable people may experience dissatisfying relationships because their irritability upsets their relationship partners, which, in turn, creates an environment rife with tension.

In the light of recent work on the Big Five, personality can be defined as a multi-dimensional set of traits that contribute to individual differences in tendencies to think, feel, and behave in consistent ways throughout life (McCrae & Costa, 2003). As such, people's occupational aspirations, coping strategies, political orientations, and communication styles may be regarded, in part, as manifestations of underlying personality traits. Though the catalogue of documented connections between personality and behaviour is growing, the bulk of research has focused on connections with health, occupational performance, and interpersonal relationships. Those are important domains to examine, but they hardly capture the richness of people's daily lives. Every day, people pursue a variety of activities, from listening to music and reading books, to watching television and gardening, but the psychological functions these activities serve remain unclear. In fact, some researchers have expressed concern about the lack of information on relations between personality and the quotidian details of life (Funder, 2001; Rozin, 2001).

24.3 RESEARCH ON THE LINKS BETWEEN MUSIC PREFERENCES AND PERSONALITY

One pervasive phenomenon that deserves consideration but has failed to garner much attention in mainstream social and personality psychology is music. Though music pervades virtually every facet of people's daily lives, it has received relatively little attention in the field of personality psychology in comparison with other disciplines such as cognitive science (e.g. Radocy & Boyle, 1979; Sloboda, 1985; Zatorre, Belin, & Penhune, 2002), biological psychology (e.g. Fitch, 2006; Rider, Floyd, & Kirkpatrick, 1985; Todd 1999), clinical psychology (e.g. Hilliard, 2001; Wigram, Saperston, & West,

1995), and neuroscience (e.g. Blood & Zatorre 2001; Levitin, 2006; Levitin, Cole, Chiles, Lai, Lincoln, & Bellugi, 2004; Peretz & Hebert, 2000).

The lack of research in mainstream social and personality psychology on music preferences is surprising. Individuals clearly like to listen to some varieties of music more than others. And just as individuals seek out and create environments that satisfy their basic psychological needs, so too might they seek auditory, or musical, environments that reflect and reinforce aspects of their personalities. However, the psychological factors that underlie people's music preferences are not entirely clear. Are there certain individual differences linking people to certain styles of music? Do people prefer styles of music that reflect aspects of their personalities?

24.3.1 Early research on music preferences and personality

The bulk of research regarding music and personality factors has centred on the disposition of the musician rather than the listener. For example, one common finding has been that musicians are generally introverted and independent individuals (for a review, see Kemp, 1996, 1997; and Chapter 15, this volume). Though it is important to consider the relationships between personality and music preferences among musicians, the current review will focus only on work that has examined such connections among non-musicians.

There was some interest in individual differences in reactions to music listening in the early twentieth century (e.g. Myers, 1922), but the first well-documented studies suggesting that individual differences in music preferences and personality are linked did not occur until the 1950s, with the development of the IPAT Music Preference Test (Cattell & Anderson, 1953; Cattell & Saunders, 1954). In association with the Music Research Foundation, Cattell and colleagues were involved in a project investigating potential connections between personality and musical preference for the purposes of developing a new diagnostic procedure for assessing mental health (Wright, 1952). Among the various ideas considered was the notion that personality can be inferred from the types of music that people prefer; thus Cattell and Anderson (1953) created the IPAT with that in mind. Through factor analysis of liking for the classical and jazz excerpts presented, Cattell and Saunders (1954) identified 12 music preference factors that they interpreted as revealing unconscious aspects of personality. For example, they hypothesized that liking up-tempo jazz music reflected an upbeat personality, or surgency, whereas preferences for more sentimental classical music were regarded as reflecting a quality of sensitivity.

Although Cattell believed that preferences for music provided a key into the unconscious, most researchers regarded music preferences as a manifestation of more explicit, or conscious, personality traits. However, research in this area was minimal until the mid 1980s—more than 30 years after Cattell's pioneering work. One exception was Payne's (1967, 1980) investigation of factors involved in the appreciation of types of classical music. These studies did not, however, produce compelling evidence for the influence of personality on music appreciation. Instead, Payne (1980) argued that

other factors, such as musical training, were more important than personality dispositions. Nevertheless, there remained speculation that personality traits and preferences
for various music styles are related. And since classical music was clearly not the only
musical style that people enjoyed listening to at the time, it was necessary to examine
preferences for a range of music genres (e.g. Roe, 1985; Wheeler, 1985).

Litle and Zuckerman (1986) thus developed a Musical Preference Scale (MPS) with 60
genres belonging to broad categories, such as rock or popular music, that respondents
rated on a Likert-type scale ranging from 'dislike' to 'like very much'. Factor analyses of
preference ratings for the genres uncovered a few broad music factors, which were then
compared with one personality variable—sensation seeking. Though previous investigations did not establish meaningful relationships between sensation seeking and liking
for classical music (Glasgow, Cartier, & Wilson, 1985), Litle and Zuckerman found that
sensation seeking was related to preferences for particular musical styles. Specifically,
they ascertained that sensation seeking, measured by the Total score on the Sensation
Seeking Scale, was positively related to preferences for rock music and negatively related
to liking soundtrack music. Other sensation-seeking subscales were related to particular
genres as well. For example, scores on the experience-seeking subscale had a positive
relationship with rock, folk, and classical music. They interpreted the findings as being
consistent with theories of sensation seeking, which state that individuals with a need
for stimulation gravitate toward stimulating environments. Thus, high sensation seekers fulfil this need by listening to intense and complex music.

Litle and Zuckerman's (1986) work had a notable effect on subsequent research on
music preferences and personality. First, it was the first study to examine personality
and preferences for a broad array of music genres, not just preferences for classical or
jazz music. Second, it was the first to examine relationships between explicit personality traits and latent dimensions of music preferences. Third, the work provided a useful
and practical method for studying relationships between music and personality. And
fourth, Litle and Zuckerman provided a psychometrically sound measure for assessing
individual differences in music preferences.

Though other studies investigating sensation seeking and music preferences
provided considerable support for Litle and Zuckerman's results (e.g. Arnett, 1992;
McNamara & Ballard, 1999; Rawlings, Barrantes i Vidal, & Furnham, 2000), arguably the greatest influence of the study was in encouraging an exploration of additional personality traits in relation to genre preferences. For example, other studies
went on to correlate music-preference tendencies with personality characteristics such
as Machiavellianism and machismo (e.g. Hansen & Hansen, 1991), trait rebelliousness (e.g. Carpentier, Knobloch, & Zillmann, 2003), and Psychoticism (e.g. Rawlings,
Hodge, Sherr, & Dempsey, 1995); as well as the Big Five factors (e.g. Dollinger, 1993;
Rawlings & Ciancarelli, 1997; Rawlings et al, 2000; Weaver, 1991).

One of the first attempts to investigate connections between music preferences and
a broader set of personality traits was made by Dollinger (1993). Using an adapted version of the MPS, Dollinger factor-analysed the genre preference ratings provided by
58 participants. His analyses extracted six music-preference factors: country and western, jazz, classical, soul/rhythm and blues, traditional popular, and hard rock. He then

examined the relationships between participants' scores on the six music-preference factors and the NEO-PI (Costa & McCrae, 1985). Dollinger's results revealed that preferences for varied styles of music, as well as classical, jazz, and soul music correlated with Openness, and that preferences for hard rock were strongly related to the excitement-seeking facet of Extraversion. Though there were some limitations in the work, such as the small sample size and versions of the measures used, Dollinger's results were later replicated in a more rigorous study by Rawlings and Ciancarelli (1997).

Using a larger sample and more updated versions of the MPS and NEO-PI-R (Costa & McCrae, 1992), Rawlings and Ciancarelli (1997) replicated several of Dollinger's (1993) results. For example, they also found that Openness was related to preferences for classical, jazz, and unconventional music, and that excitement seeking was related to preferences for rock music. Rawlings and Ciancarelli also provided much more detailed explanations of the associations between music preferences and personality than did Dollinger (1993). They suggested that the relationship between Openness and 'breadth of musical preference' is driven by two particular facets of Openness— aesthetics and ideas (p. 130). In addition, they suggested that the relationships between preferences for rock music and the actions and values facets of Openness, which reflect rebelliousness and liberalism, respectively, stem from the tendency for rock music to emphasize themes of rebellion and liberal values. This interpretation is consistent with Carpentier et al's (2003) work, which found positive relationships between rebelliousness and preferences for rock and hip-hop music. Although Rawlings and Ciancarelli did not replicate all of Dollinger's (1993) findings (e.g. they did not find positive relationships between Agreeableness and classical music), the work highlighted the importance of Extraversion and Openness in understanding individual differences in music preferences. A few additional studies that used different personality measures, such as the Myers-Briggs Type Indicator and Eysenck's Personality Questionnaire, have similarly found that Extraversion and personality characteristics akin to Openness are consistently related to music preferences (e.g. Pearson & Dollinger, 2004; Rawlings et al, 2000). There is also evidence that other personality traits are related to preferences for other genres. For instance, Rawlings and colleagues (1995) found some support for the hypothesis that people who are 'tough-minded', or high on the Psychoticism scale of the EPQ-R, prefer hard rock or heavy metal music to easy-listening music.

Although early research on music preferences and personality generated some important findings and laid the foundation for future research (see Table 24.1 for a summary of key studies on music preferences and personality), the work generally lacked theoretical clarity and methodological rigour. First, the conceptual models of personality studied varied significantly. Whereas some researchers focused on psychoanalytic concepts and described music preferences in such terms (e.g. Cattell & Anderson, 1953; Cattell & Saunders, 1954), others focused on a handful of explicit traits and interpreted their relationships with music as reflections of those traits (Carpentier et al, 2003; Dollinger, 1993; Hansen & Hansen, 1991; Rawlings et al, 1995; Rawlings & Ciancarelli, 1997). Thus, there was no consensus about which personality constructs to assess. Second, there was very little consensus about which music genres to study. Although Litle and Zuckerman (1986) provided a thorough list of music genres for

Table 24.1 Studies on music preferences and personality

Study	Sample	Music genres measured	Personality traits measured	Key findings
Cattell & Saunders (1954)	384 (196 'normal' and 188 'abnormal' participants)	classical, jazz	warmth, reasoning, emotional stability, dominance, liveliness, rule-consciousness, social boldness, sensitivity, vigilance, abstractedness, privateness, apprehension, openness to change, self-reliance, perfectionism, tension	Identified music preference dimensions that resemble underlying personality dimensions
Litle & Zuckerman (1986)	82 US undergraduates	Broadway, classical, country and western, electronic, folk/ethnic, jazz, movie and TV soundtracks, popular, religious, rock, soul/R&B (with 60 subgenres)	sensation seeking	Established correlations between preferences for music genres and sensation seeking
Dollinger (1993)	58 US undergraduates	classical, country and western, disco, folk-ethnic, gospel, hard rock, jazz, light rock, new age, oldies, reggae, religious, soul/R&B, traditional popular	openness, extraversion (including excitement seeking)	Found correlations between preferences for music genres and two Big Five dimensions
Rawlings et al (1995)	Study 1: 133; 2: 53; 3: 161; 4: 44 Australian adolescents and undergraduates	Study 1: classical, dance, easy listening, hard rock/heavy metal; Study 2: same as Litle & Zuckerman, 1986; Study 3: consonant and dissonant chords; Study 4: classical, easy listening, hard rock/heavy metal, jazz	psychoticism, neuroticism, extraversion, impulsiveness, venturesomeness, empathy	Extended previous research by documenting relations between music-genre preferences (through both excerpts and music-preference questionnaires) and more personality traits; also investigated music attribute preferences related to consonant and dissonant chords
Rawlings & Ciancarelli (1997)	150 Australian undergraduates	Broadway, classical, country and western, electronic, folk/ethnic, jazz, popular, religious, rock, soul/R&B, and soundtracks	extraversion, agreeableness, conscientiousness, neuroticism, openness	Replicated and extended previous research by establishing relations between music-genre preferences and more personality traits

Table 24.1 Studies on music preferences and personality (continued)

Study	Sample	Music genres measured	Personality traits measured	Key findings
Rawlings, Barrantes i Vidal, & Furnham (2000)	76 Spanish and 79 British undergraduates	classical, country and western, dance/disco, easy listening, electronic, folk, hard rock, jazz, rap, religious, soft rock, soul/R&B, soundtracks, techno, top 40, world	Sensation seeking, openness to experience	Found cross-cultural evidence that personality is related to music preferences; the biggest predictor in both Spain and UK was the experience-seeking subscale of the sensation-seeking scale
Schwartz & Fouts (2003)	164 Canadian adolescents	13 qualities of music (e.g. 'soft and tender', 'upsetting and protesting')	introversive, inhibited, cooperative, sociable, confident, forceful, respectful, sensitive; scales to assess expressed concerns and behaviours	Assessed preferences for qualities of music instead of genres, and found associations between 'heavy' and 'light' music with different personality styles and developmental issues
Rentfrow & Gosling (2003)	Study 2: 1704; 3: 1383; 4: 500; 6: 3087 US undergraduates and young adults	alternative, blues, Christian, classical, country and western, electronica/dance, folk, heavy metal, jazz, pop, rap, rock, soul/R&B, soundtracks	extraversion, agreeableness, conscientiousness, emotional stability, openness, interpersonal dominance, social dominance, flirtatiousness, self-esteem, depression, political orientation, perceived physical attractiveness, perceived wealth, perceived athletic ability, perceived intelligence, verbal ability, analytical ability	Presented converging evidence across samples and methods for four music-preference dimensions; found correlations between music preference dimensions and personality that replicated across samples
Delsing et al (2008)	1044 Dutch adolescents	heavy metal, punk, gothic/wave, rock, jazz, classical, gospel, rap, soul/R&B, electronica/dance, pop	extraversion, agreeableness, conscientiousness, emotional stability, openness	Replicated the Rentfrow & Gosling (2003) music-preference dimensions and obtained similar links to personality in a Dutch sample
Zweigenhaft (2008)	83 US undergraduates (3 age groups)	same as Rentfrow & Gosling (2003) plus: bluegrass, funk, gospel, international, new age, oldies, opera, punk, reggae	extraversion, agreeableness, conscientiousness, emotional stability, openness and 30 personality facets	Identified links between the four music-preference dimensions and personality facets

assessing preferences, researchers seemed to pick and choose genres without providing any justification for doing so. Third, while the instruments used to assess individual differences in music preferences appeared valid, no attempt was made to actually assess their validity. Hence, with no unifying theory and no consensus about which personality dimensions or music genres to measure, comparisons of previous research on personality and music preferences is difficult.

24.3.2 Current directions in music preferences and personality research

Early research suggesting connections between certain music genres and personality characteristics was encouraging, but the picture provided was rather fragmented. Order and structure were needed to synthesize the field and facilitate further advancement. One line of work, which incorporated a broad and systematic approach to studying a range of personality variables and music genres, aimed to meet those demands.

In a series of studies using multiple methods, samples and regions, Rentfrow and Gosling (2003) set out to identify the structure of music preferences and the relationships between the music-preference dimensions and a host of personality variables. Just as Litle and Zuckerman (1986) had done, Rentfrow and Gosling developed an instrument that measured preferences for several music genres. However, they used a systematic procedure for selecting music genres, in which a group of participants were asked to indicate their level of familiarity with over 70 different music genres and sub-genres. The results from that study indicated that most people were not familiar with all of the sub-genres, suggesting that an extensive list of music genres may not actually be the ideal way to measure music preferences. However, the overwhelming majority of participants were familiar with all of the broader music genres. The broader genres thus provided an optimum level of analysis for studying music preferences. Those genres were used in the original version of the Short Test of Music Preferences (STOMP) and include: alternative, blues, classical, country, electronica, folk, heavy metal, rap, jazz, pop, religious, rock, soul/funk, and soundtracks. Unlike the MPS, the STOMP does not provide exemplar musicians or bands for each genre, as such information could potentially alter respondents' conception of the genre (Rentfrow & Gosling, 2003).

To determine whether there is a structure underlying music preferences, Rentfrow and Gosling (2003) factor-analysed music preference ratings from over 1,700 university students in the United States, and identified four basic music-preference dimensions. The generalizability of the factor structure was substantiated by confirmatory factor analysis in a follow-up study of over 1,300 undergraduates. Although the results were encouraging, the data from both studies were derived from self-reports of students in one geographic area. Thus, it was not entirely clear whether the results would generalize to other forms of music preference, such as people's music collections, or to people living in other regions. To address these limitations, they examined the contents of 500 online music libraries (ten from each state) to ascertain music genre preferences. Confirmatory factor analyses of these behaviourally-revealed preferences replicated the four-factor structure obtained, indicating that the dimensions do generalize across methods and geographic regions.

The first music-preference dimension, labelled *Reflective & Complex*, comprises preferences for classical, jazz, folk, and blues: music that tends to emphasize both positive and negative emotions, and is comparatively more complex than most other styles. The second dimension, *Intense & Rebellious*, contains preferences for rock, alternative, and heavy metal: music that tends to emphasize negative emotions and themes of disobedience. The third dimension, *Upbeat & Conventional*, comprises preferences for pop, soundtracks, religious, and country: music that tends to emphasize positive emotions and is comparatively less complex than other genres. The fourth dimension, *Energetic & Rhythmic*, contains preferences for rap, soul, and electronica; music that tends to emphasize energy and themes of self-gratification.

Subsequent analyses of the external correlates of these four music-preference dimensions revealed distinct associations with demographics, personality, political attitudes, and cognitive abilities. For example, preference for the *Reflective & Complex* dimension is positively related to Openness, as well as political liberalism and verbal ability, and negatively related to self-reported athletic ability. Additionally, preference for the *Intense & Rebellious* dimension is positively related to Openness, athletic ability, and verbal ability; and preference for the *Upbeat & Conventional* dimension is positively related to three of the Big Five traits—Extraversion, Agreeableness, and Conscientiousness—as well as to political conservatism and athleticism, and negatively related to Openness, social dominance, and verbal ability. Finally, preference for the *Energetic & Rhythmic* dimension is positively related to Extraversion, Agreeableness, verbal impulsivity, and political liberalism. The relationships between the music-preference dimensions and personality variables appear robust, as very similar patterns of relationships were observed across different samples.

Rentfrow and Gosling's (2003) findings are noteworthy because they are the first to suggest that there is a clear, robust, and meaningful structure underlying music preferences. The four-factor structure has since been replicated in a factor-analytic study of Dutch adolescents' music preferences, suggesting that the factors generalize to other cultures and younger ages (Delsing, ter Bogt, Engels, & Meeus, 2008). The four factors obtained in the Netherlands, which were labelled *Elite*, *Rock*, *Pop/Dance*, and *Urban*, corresponded almost perfectly with the Reflective & Complex, Intense & Rebellious, Upbeat & Conventional, and Energetic & Rhythmic dimensions obtained in the United States. Delsing and colleagues also found a pattern of correlations between the preference dimensions and personality characteristics comparable to the results obtained by Rentfrow and Gosling (2003). Colley (2008) has also reported obtaining a similar music preference structure to Rentfrow and Gosling, but noted that there were slight differences between females and males, especially in regard to perception of 'mainstream' music.

Taken as a whole, research on music preferences and personality has made it very clear that there is a structure underlying music preferences. That is, preferences for specific styles of music (e.g. classical) are closely related to preferences for other styles of music (jazz, blues, and folk). Moreover, this structure appears robust, as it has emerged in several samples, in different countries, and using different methods (Delsing et al, 2008; Rentfrow & Gosling, 2003; Wood, 2005). Individual differences in music preferences also appear to be linked to an array of psychological variables. Although the majority of studies concerned with relations between music preferences and personality have focused primarily on broad personality dimensions (e.g. the Big Five, sensation seeking), very little is known about how more specific personality traits relate to preferences for music. However, a recent study by Zweigenhaft (2008) examined connections between the four music-preference dimensions and the 30 personality facets assessed by the NEO-PI-R. The patterns of correlations converged with previous research, and also suggested that the music-preference dimensions are uniquely related to several facets of the Big Five.

24.3.3 Understanding the connections between music preferences and personality

The links between music preferences and personality are in line with interactionist perspectives, making it reasonable to suggest that people prefer styles of music that are consistent with their personalities. Accordingly, people high in sensation seeking are drawn to intense styles of music because such music may satisfy their need for physiological stimulation; extroverts enjoy music that is sociable and enthusiastic because it may feed their appetite for social stimulation and positive affect; open-minded people enjoy varied and creative styles of music because it may easily fulfil their need to experience new things; and highly intellectual people prefer styles of music that are abstract and complex because it may satisfy their need for cognitive stimulation. Thus, the music people enjoy listening to reinforces their basic psychological needs.

There has been a considerable amount of research indicating that people attribute certain psychological characteristics to the fans of particular musical styles, which makes it reasonable to suppose that preferences for music may be guided, at least partially, by people's desires to be seen as possessing such characteristics (Rentfrow & Gosling, 2006, 2007). Indeed, several researchers have proposed that music serves as a sort of badge to symbolize one's membership in a peer group or social category (Bryson, 1996; Dolfsma, 1999; Frith, 1981; Hakanen, & Wells, 1991, 1993; North & Hargreaves, 1999; Rentfrow & Gosling, 2007; Rentfrow, McDonald, & Oldmeadow, 2009; Tarrant et al, 2002). By expressing one's music preferences, individuals are effectively saying that they possess attitudes, values, and beliefs that are similar to those of other members with the same music preferences (North & Hargreaves, 1999). For example, North and Hargreaves (1999) examined the prototypical characteristics of the rap and pop music fan, and found that participants' music preferences were related to the degree to which their self-views matched the characteristics of the prototypical music fan with the same music preferences. Similar findings in different populations, age groups, and cultures provide additional support for the notion that the qualities associated with certain styles of music affect individuals' music preferences (North, Hargreaves, & O'Neill, 2000; Tarrant, North, & Hargreaves, 2000).

The work on music and social identity suggests that one of the reasons why music and personality are connected is because people see themselves, or would like to be seen by others, in ways that are consistent with the qualities associated with particular musical styles. For example, thrill seekers may have an affinity for death metal music because the qualities regarded as typical of death metal music are appealing to them. Thus, they may not only see themselves as embodying the qualities of the prototypical death metal fan, but they may also want others to see them as possessing such qualities. In this case, we might infer that the connections between personality and music preferences depend on the social representations of various musical styles.

There is certainly more that could underlie music preferences than normative beliefs about the fans of various music genres, though. Indeed, music in every given genre varies on an assortment of attributes—from tempo and instrumentation, to complexity and mood—and it is reasonable to suppose that just as individuals differ in their preferences for music genres, so too might they differ in preferences for specific qualities of music.

With very few exceptions, music preferences have typically been assessed using music genres, rather than music attributes or particular songs, as the unit of analysis (e.g. Litle & Zuckerman, 1986; Rentfrow & Gosling, 2003), whereby respondents indicate the extent to which they like various genres or broad music styles (e.g. classical, pop, rock, rap). As a result, there is little research available that has explicitly examined relationships between personality and preferences for music attributes. However, there is a smattering of work with music attributes that provides some potentially useful information. For example, Rentfrow and Gosling (2006) found that Extraversion was positively related to preferences for vocal (as opposed to instrumental) music; Weaver (1991) found a relationship between Neuroticism and preferences for 'downbeat' or slow music (as opposed to upbeat, fast music); Rawlings et al (1995) reported a correlation between Psychoticism and preferences for discordant triads; McCown, Keiser, Mulhearn, and Williamson (1997) found that Psychoticism and Extraversion were related to preferences for low-frequency tones (i.e. exaggerated bass); McNamara and Ballard (1999) suggested that sensation seeking was related to preferences for arousing or fast music (as opposed to less stimulating or slow music); and Schwartz and Fouts (2003) found that adolescents with preferences for 'tough', 'wild', and 'angry' (heavy) music displayed unstable identities and low self-esteem. Additionally, Kopacz (2005) indicated that Extraversion was related to preferences for songs that were fast and rich in melodic themes. Taken together, these studies provide convincing reasons to believe that the links between personality and music may also depend on specific music attributes.

There appear to be at least two processes connecting personality and music preferences. First, there is a considerable body of work indicating that individuals are drawn to certain styles of music because the psychological qualities associated with such music resonate with how they see themselves. Therefore, the image associated with music seems to play an important role in connecting people to their music of choice. Second, despite the limited number of studies, there appear to be sufficient reasons to believe that specific attributes of music may determine individuals' preferences.

The imbalance of attention paid to the role that social representations of music genres have on preferences, compared to the role of music attributes, stems from the fact that the majority of research has focused on the links between personality and preferences for genres. Thus, it is no surprise that we know very little about the connections between personality and preferences for attributes.

24.4 ISSUES AND FUTURE DIRECTIONS IN PERSONALITY AND MUSIC RESEARCH

Considerable progress has been made in our understanding of music preferences and personality. We now know that there is a latent structure underlying preferences for music genres, and that there are robust connections between personality and music-genre preferences that generalize across different geographic regions and age groups. There also appear to be some connections between personality and preferences for specific features of music. Of course, this increased understanding brings more questions. For example, what is the best way to assess music preferences? What role do music preferences play in interpersonal relationships? To what extent does the connection between music preferences and personality generalize across cultures? How stable are music preferences throughout life? How do people use music in their daily lives? It is important to mention and discuss future directions so that the study of music preferences and personality, a relatively small sub-field of music psychology, can flourish.

24.4.1 Measuring music preferences

There is a lack of consistency in the measures used to assess music preferences. This inconsistency impairs our ability to make cross-study comparisons, and ultimately limits the generalizability of the results. What is needed is a standard measure of music preferences that can be administered to individuals of different age groups, social classes, and cultures while still retaining the same psychometric characteristics.

The unit of analysis most commonly used for measuring music preferences is the genre, which tends to yield reliable and valid data, so one step toward developing a standard measure of music preferences could be to generate a comprehensive list of music genres. Preference data for each genre could then be analysed to obtain basic descriptive information for the genres as well as information about the structure of music-genre preferences. Such information would be valuable for developing shorter, and hence more efficient, measures that still retain the breadth of more comprehensive measures. Of course, such genre-based measures would be useful only in so far as respondents are familiar with and share a similar understanding of the genres included in the measure. For example, preferences for Lavani music may be informative, but how many people outside central India will be familiar with that style of music? Probably very few. However, if an excerpt of Lavani music is played, respondents who may have never heard such music before could easily indicate their preference for it. Thus, in addition to generating lists of music genres, a standard measure of music preferences could include excerpts of songs typical of each genre, so that familiarity with the genres is not a requirement.

Another limitation of music genres is that the social connotations that they evoke change over time. For example, jazz music now means something very different from what it did 80 years ago; whereas people currently associate jazz with sophistication and creativity, earlier generations considered it simplistic and crude. This raises important questions for the field. If, as we suggest in section 24.3.3, the social connotations associated with music genres shape people's preferences, and if those associations change over time, what are we to make of the links between music-genre preferences and personality? Are the personality characteristics of today's jazz music fans the same as the characteristics of those who listened to jazz 80 years ago? Is the current research on music preferences and personality merely providing us with a snapshot of music and personality links, or do those links generalize across generations?

It is conceivable that the relationships between specific styles of music and personality traits are not the same across generations. That, however, does not undermine this whole enterprise. Indeed, research on the structure of music preferences suggests that the dimensions are stable across methods, regardless of which genres are included, in different cultures, and across age groups (cf. Delsing et al, 2008). Thus, it is tempting to suppose that the dimensions of music preferences may be more stable and enduring than the genres that comprise them. Maybe there has been, and will continue to be, a music-preference dimension that possesses reflective and complex musical qualities, but in which the genres that comprise that dimension change over time. Perhaps there will also continue to be dimensions of music preferences that are intense and rebellious, upbeat and conventional, and energetic and rhythmic, but the genres that comprise those dimensions may change as their social connotations change. If so, then it is conceivable that the links between the preference dimensions and personality may be stable across generations, though this has yet to be empirically explored.

In light of the aforementioned limitations, we are currently developing an alternative assessment method for assessing music preferences that does not rely on knowledge or awareness of music genres. Specifically, we are creating a music-preference measure that uses excerpts of real songs as musical items, and respondents are asked to indicate their level of preference for each excerpt. This method avoids several of the limitations of music genres, yet still provides information about music-genre preferences. This method also provides an ecologically valid way to assess preferences for music attributes. By coding the music excerpts in our survey on various music attributes (e.g. tempo, instrumentation, romantic, complex), respondents' preference ratings for the music excerpts are weighted by the attribute ratings in order to generate music-attribute preference estimates. Preliminary analyses have revealed a number of interesting results. For instance, individuals high in Neuroticism tend to prefer music that is happy, slow, and simple; similarly people high in Extraversion tend to prefer music that is happy and has vocals (Rentfrow, 2008).

These results, although preliminary, are encouraging and provide a fruitful new direction in music-preference assessment. Indeed, just as early personality psychologists perused dictionaries to identify terms that people use to describe individuals, so too could music psychologists collect terms that people use to describe music. Such terms may not necessarily be the same ones that composers and musicians regard as most important, but they may nevertheless reflect the qualities that individuals attend to while listening to and evaluating music. Musical clips representing various music genres could then be coded on those music-descriptive terms, and analyses of music-attribute preferences could examine the structure of music-attribute preferences. Such analyses would help determine whether there is an interpretable structure of attribute preferences and, if so, identify which dimensions underlie individuals' perceptions and descriptions of music.

Essentially, what is needed is a framework for conceptualizing music preferences, just as we have an empirically-based framework for conceptualizing personality traits (i.e. the Big Five). As we see it, to develop that framework, it is crucial that we begin carefully constructing measures of music preferences. Thus, future research that includes a wider array of music genres, prototypical songs, and attributes will not only aid in the development of a measure of music preferences unbound by culture, age, or social class, but more importantly, such work will greatly inform our understanding of the nature of music preferences.

24.4.2 Music preferences and interpersonal relationships

Anecdotal evidence and empirical research clearly indicate that individuals use music in the service of self-expression. Indeed, it appears as though individuals use music as a badge to communicate information about themselves, and that individuals form impressions of others on the basis of their music preferences. For example, in a study concerned with personality judgements based on music preferences, Rentfrow and Gosling (2006) found that individuals talk a lot about their music preferences in the service of getting to know each other. Moreover, sharing information about music preferences appears to be an effective way to learn about others, as Rentfrow and Gosling also found that participants were able to form similar and accurate impressions of the personalities, values, and moods of target individuals on the basis of targets' top ten favourite songs.

Given that individuals place considerable importance on music, and that they are able to glean useful information about other people on the basis of their music preferences, it is interesting to consider the potential effects of such information on interpersonal relationships. For example, are people with similar music preferences more likely to get along and experience satisfying relationships with each other than individuals with radically different music preferences? Research on personality and romantic relationships suggests that this may be so. For example, a few studies suggest that romantic partners with similar personalities tend to experience more intimacy and satisfaction in their relationships than partners with different personalities (Luo & Klohnen, 2005).

Because music and personality are linked, it therefore seems reasonable to suppose that similarities in music preferences may contribute to relationship satisfaction. Indeed, if two people, whether romantic partners or room-mates, share similar preferences for music, they should agree more often about which music to listen to in the car or at home than people who enjoy listening to different styles of music. Thus, similar music preferences may lead to less conflict.

In a study concerning room-mate relationships, Wood (2005) found that university room-mates who had similar music preferences reported more satisfaction with their room-mates and a greater desire to continue living together than did room-mates with different music preferences. Additionally, a recent study found that close friends were more likely to share similar preferences for music than were less intimate friends (Selfhaut, Branje, ter Bogt, & Meeus, 2009). Together, these two studies provide encouraging evidence for the potential importance of music preferences in interpersonal relationships. Future research that explores the reasons why music influences the quality of relationships and whether such effects generalize across various types of relationships would be invaluable.

24.4.3 Music preferences and culture

It is also worth exploring whether the relationships between music preferences and personality generalize across cultures. For example, are people in East Asian cultures who enjoy jazz and classical music more open and intellectual than their compatriots who enjoy listening to popular conventional music, as is the case in Western cultures? Considerably less is known about the cross-cultural generalizability of music preferences and personality.

Individuals' preferences for music are probably shaped by their social interactions as well as exposure to popular media and cultural trends. Thus, the personality characteristics associated with preferences for a particular style of music may vary as a function of the person's social status, country of residence, and cohort, as well as the culture-specific associations with that style of music at that point in history. Thus, it is possible that the psychological characteristics linking people to a certain style of music in one culture may be different from the characteristics linked to that music in another culture. If so, that would suggest that the relations between music preferences and personality are driven more by the social representations of music genres than specific characteristics of the music. On the other hand, any cross-cultural similarities between music preferences and personality could suggest that music attributes play an integral role in determining music preferences.

Although most of the studies investigating the relationships between music and personality have been conducted in English-speaking countries, there is some evidence that similar personality and preference patterns exist in Spanish (Rawlings et al, 2000) and Dutch samples (Delsing et al, 2008). For example, in a study comparing participants from Spain and the UK, Rawlings and colleagues (2000) found that the strongest predictor of music preferences in both samples was the Experience Seeking subscale of the Sensation Seeking Scale. Also, Delsing et al's (2008) study of Dutch adolescents showed that the patterns of correlations between personality and the music preference dimensions were remarkably similar to those reported by Rentfrow and Gosling (2003), who studied North American undergraduates. Although the results suggest that the links between music and personality generalize across some Western cultures, future research on cultural differences in music preferences that uses assessment procedures that allow for the measurement of music genres and music attributes would greatly inform our understanding of the nature of music preferences.

24.4.4 Music preferences over time

We might also consider whether preferences for music are stable over time, and whether there are certain personality dispositions that contribute to the stability of music preferences. One might investigate, for example, whether the music preferences of highly open people are more likely to change throughout the life course than the preferences of less open people. As interest in the connections between music preferences and personality is still quite recent, there is hardly any information available that sheds light on the stability of music preferences. However, a recent longitudinal study by Delsing et al (2008) found that adolescents' music preferences are fairly stable over a period of three years. In that study, music-genre preferences were assessed, so it is interesting to consider whether preferences for music attributes are more or less stable than preferences for genres. Indeed, in every genre there are fast and intense songs, as well as dynamic and emotional songs. As individuals age, are they drawn to the same broad styles of music or to music that possesses similar musical attributes? Future research that examines the stability of preferences for both music genres and attributes will also illuminate our understanding of the precise characteristics of music that individuals find most appealing.

24.4.5 Music listening in context

Most of the research discussed has investigated the links between personality and stable music preferences by merely having respondents report their liking for a music genre or clip. To date, there are no known studies that have examined whether personality might influence how people use and interact with music in their daily lives. Of course, some research over the last decade has begun to call attention to the importance of studying how people actually select and use music in everyday life (e.g. DeNora, 1999, 2000; North, Hargreaves, & Hargreaves 2004; Sloboda, O'Neill, & Ivaldi, 2001; Chapter 18, this volume), as well as the importance of considering how situational or social factors and various arousal or affective states might influence music choices at a given time (e.g. Dodorico, 2006; Juslin & Laukka, 2004; North & Hargreaves 1996a, 1996b, 2000). As pointed out by Sloboda and O'Neill (2001), music is always heard in context, so it makes sense to consider contextual forces and state-preferences (actual selections) in addition to just trait-preferences or overall tastes.

A growing body of research has begun to identify some of the social psychological processes and roles of the environment that link people to their music preferences. Perhaps the most prominent figures leading the way in the social psychology of music are North and Hargreaves. In a series of studies, they have found that situations can influence people's preferences for certain types of music. For instance, in a study in which different styles of new-age music were played (low, moderate, and high complexity) in a dining area, participants reported preferring low and moderately complex music (North & Hargreaves, 1996a). Further, when individuals are in unpleasant arousal-provoking situations (e.g. driving in busy traffic), they tend to prefer relaxing music; yet in pleasant arousal-provoking situations (e.g. exercising), individuals tend to prefer music that is stimulating (North & Hargreaves, 1996b, 1997). Thus, it would appear as though music preferences are, to some degree, moderated by situational goals (see Chapter 19, this volume). But to what extent might personality moderate the types of music individuals listen to in certain situations?

A recent study by Chamorro-Premuzic and Furnham (2007) attempted to answer the question of whether traits can explain how people use music. Their results indicated that a more emotional function of music, in which the listener focuses on the content of the song, was positively related to Neuroticism. Furthermore, they found that Openness, intellectual engagement, and IQ were positively related to using music for cognitive stimulation, which involved focusing on the musical structure. Future research on personality that uses naturalistic methods to monitor individuals' music-listening habits, moods, and activities over a period of a few days would help to develop a much more ecologically valid depiction of the ways in which individuals interact with music.

24.4.6 Music preferences, emotion, and personality

Further exploration of music preferences in context should consider the emotional state of the individual prior to listening to music. Numerous studies have shown that music can elicit certain emotional reactions in the listener (Scherer & Zentner, 2001), but there is considerably less information about how mood might influence our music selections or how we respond to the music that we hear (see Chapter 25, this volume). For instance, do people in a sad mood prefer listening to happy music in order to change their mood? Or do they prefer listening to mood-consistent music? Ongoing research by Dodorico (2006) hypothesizes that the affective state of the individual prior to listening, as well as other contextual factors and individual difference variables, are connected to the types of music preferred at a given time—especially with regard to the emotional valence of the music.

One might interpret the aforementioned studies of context and initial mood as implying that stable personality characteristics do not play as large a role in determining music preferences if, in certain contexts, situational and emotional factors come into play. However, the environmental factors considered are still in agreement with the interactionist perspective of personality, since individuals tend to seek out situations that fit with their personalities. In addition, if we consider the affective aspects of music selections, such as using music to regulate mood, this is still consistent with the interactionist model. For instance, there are individual differences in how people regulate their emotions, and people seek out particular situations to affect how they feel, in accordance with their personalities (Gross, 1999). Therefore, individuals might choose to listen to different music when in a particular mood, and this is compatible with the interactionist theory. However, future research would need to consider potential interactions between the person and the affective environment more directly.

It would also be beneficial to expand research on music attributes to focus more on the affective aspects of music preferences. It is obvious that, in any one genre, there are a variety of different emotions expressed in the music—even one album could run the gamut of emotions. As mentioned, as long as research on music preferences and personality continues to restrict its focus to music genres, our understanding of the nature of music preferences will remain limited, because music attributes vary considerably within each genre. This point may be especially true when considering connections between affect-related traits and music preferences, as music-attribute preferences might be a more informative level of analysis with which to explore such connections.

For example, there is evidence that the traits of Extraversion and Neuroticism are related to positive affect and negative affect, respectively (e.g. Watson & Clark, 1992), yet the bulk of the research reviewed has not found meaningful links between Neuroticism and music-genre preferences. However, perhaps greater affective information can be gleaned from considering preferences for specific attributes. Even determining preferences for low-level music attributes, like tempo or pitch, might provide information about preferences for the emotions expressed in the music. Thus, further research might explore preferences for certain inherently affect-related musical elements in greater detail, to investigate whether there are any patterns of associations with persistent affect-laden traits, such as Neuroticism. In sum, examining music preferences at a more precise level might be helpful in exploring potential connections with other aspects of personality and affect.

24.5 CONCLUSION

It appears as though Barry and his friends are justified in believing that a questionnaire about music preferences will reveal valuable information about a person's character. Indeed, all of the research reviewed here indicates that there are clear connections between music preferences and personality. Although the relationships do tend to be somewhat small in magnitude, the patterns of relationships are very consistent across different measures of personality and music genres. What is more, there appears to be a robust structure underlying preferences for music genres. Very similar structures have been reported by different investigators from different countries and cultures.

In an attempt to guide future research on music and personality, we also identified several promising directions that will help illuminate our understanding of the nature of music preferences. In so doing, we hope it has become clear that research on music preferences has numerous implications for a wide range of psychological and social psychological processes.

RECOMMENDED FURTHER READING

1. Rentfrow, P. J., & Gosling, S. D. (2003). The do re mi's of everyday life: The structure and personality correlates of music preferences. *Journal of Personality and Social Psychology, 84,* 1236–56.
2. North, A. C., & Hargreaves, D. J. (2008). *The social and applied psychology of music.* Oxford: Oxford University Press. (Especially Chapter 3)
3. Gosling, S. D. (2008). *Snoop: What your stuff says about you.* New York: Basic Books.

REFERENCES

Allport, G. W., & Odbert, H. S. (1936). Trait-names: A psycho-lexical study. *Psychological Monographs, 47* (1, Whole No. 211).

Arnett, J. (1992). The soundtrack of recklessness: musical preferences and reckless behavior among adolescents. *Journal of Adolescent Research, 7,* 313–31.

Ashton, M. C., Lee, K., & Goldberg, L. R. (2004). A hierarchical analysis of 1,710 English personality-descriptive adjectives. *Journal of Personality and Social Psychology, 87,* 707–21.

Ashton, M. C., Lee, K., Perugini, M., Szarota, P., de Vries, R. E., Di Blas, L., Boies, K., & De Raad, B. (2004). A six-factor structure of personality-descriptive adjectives: Solutions from psycholexical studies in seven languages. *Journal of Personality and Social Psychology, 86,* 356–66.

Benet-Martínez, V., & John, O. P. (2000). Toward the development of quasi-indigenous personality constructs. *American Behavioral Scientist, 44,* 141–57.

Block, J. (1995). A contrarian view of the five-factor approach to personality description. *Psychological Bulletin, 117,* 187–215.

Blood, A. J., & Zatorre R. J. (2001). Intensely pleasurable responses to music correlates with activity in brain regions implicated in reward and emotion. *Proceedings of the National Academy of Sciences, 98,* 11818–23.

Bourdieu, P. (1984). *Distinction: A social critique of the judgement of taste.* London: Routledge.

Bryson, B. (1996). 'Anything but heavy metal': Symbolic exclusion and musical dislikes. *American Sociological Review, 61,* 884–99.

Buss, D. M. (1987). Selection, evocation, and manipulation. *Journal of Personality and Social Psychology, 53,* 1214–21.

Carpentier, F. D., Knobloch, S., & Zillmann, D. (2003). Rock, rap and rebellion: Comparisons of traits predicting selective exposure to defiant music. *Personality and Individual Differences, 35,* 1643–55.

Cattell, R. B. (1943). The description of personality: Basic traits resolved into clusters. *Journal of Abnormal and Social Psychology, 38,* 476–506.

Cattell, R. B., & Anderson, J. C. (1953). The measurement of personality and behavior disorders by the I.P.A.T. music preference test. *Journal of Applied Psychology*, *37*, 446–54.

Cattell, R. B., Eber, H. W., & Tatsuoka, M. M. (1970). *Handbook for the Sixteen Personality Factor Questionnaire (16 PF)*. Champaign, IL: Institute for Personality and Ability Testing.

Cattell, R. B., & Saunders D. R. (1954). Musical preferences and personality diagnosis: A factorization of one hundred and twenty themes. *Journal of Social Psychology*, *39*, 3–24.

Chamorro-Premuzic, T., & Furnham, A. (2007). Personality and music: Can traits explain how people use music in everyday life? *British Journal of Psychology*, *98*, 175–85.

Chan, T. W., & Goldthorpe, J. H. (2007). Social stratification and cultural consumption: Music in England. *European Sociological Review*, *23*, 1–19.

Christensen, P. G., & Peterson, J. B. (1988). Genre and gender in the structure of music preferences. *Communication Research*, *15*, 282–301.

Church, A. T., & Katigbak, M. S. (2002). The five-factor model in the Philippines: Investigating trait structure and levels across cultures. In R. R. McCrae & J. Allik (eds), *The five-factor model of personality across cultures* (pp. 129–54). New York: Kluwer Academic/Plenum.

Colley, A. (2008). Young people's musical taste: Relationship with gender and gender-related traits. *Journal of Applied Social Psychology*, *38*, 2039–55.

Costa, P. T., & McCrae, R. R. (1985). *The NEO Personality Inventory manual*. Odessa, FL: Psychological Assessment Resources.

Costa, P. T., Jr., & McCrae, R. R. (1992). *Revised NEO Personality Inventory (NEO-PI-R) and NEO Five-Factor Inventory (NEO-FFI) professional manual*. Odessa, FL: Psychological Assessment Resources.

DeNora, T. (1999). Music as a technology of self. *Poetics*, *27*, 31–56.

DeNora, T. (2000). *Music in everyday life*. Cambridge, UK: Cambridge University Press.

De Raad, B. (1992). The replicability of the Big Five personality dimensions in three word-classes of the Dutch language. *European Journal of Personality*, *6*, 15–29.

Delsing, M. J. M. H., ter Bogt, T. F. M., Engels, R. C. M. E., & Meeus, W. H. J. (2008). Adolescents' music preferences and personality characteristics. *European Journal of Personality*, *22*, 109–30.

Dodorico, J. A. (2006). *Emotionally 'tuned' in: The influence of mood on music preferences*. Unpublished master's thesis, University of Cambridge, England.

Dolfsma, W. (1999). The consumption of music and the expression of values: A social economic explanation for the advent of pop music. *American Journal of Economics and Sociology*, *58*, 1019–46.

Dollinger, S. J. (1993). Research note: Personality and music preference: Extraversion and excitement seeking or openness to experience? *Psychology of Music*, *21*, 73–7.

Farnsworth, P. R. (1949). Rating scales for musical interests. *Journal of Psychology*, *28*, 245–53.

Fitch, W. T. (2006). The biology and evolution of music: A comparative perspective. *Cognition*, *100*, 173–215.

Fox, W. A., & Wince, M. H. (1975). Musical taste cultures and taste publics. *Youth and Society*, *7*, 198–224.

Frith, S. (1981). *Sound effects: Youth, leisure, and the politics of rock 'n' roll*. New York: Pantheon.

Funder, D. C. (2001). Personality. *Annual Review of Psychology*, *52*, 197–221.

Galton, F. (1884). Measurement of character. *Fortnightly Review*, *36*, 179–85.

Glasgow, M. R., Cartier, A. M., & Wilson, G. D. (1985). Conservatism, sensation-seeking and music preferences. *Personality and Individual Differences*, *6*, 395–6.

Gosling, S. D., Ko, S. J., Mannarelli, T., & Morris, M. E. (2002). A room with a cue: Personality judgments based on offices and bedrooms. *Journal of Personality and Social Psychology*, *82*, 379–98.

Goldberg, L. R. (1992). The development of markers for the Big-Five factor structure. *Psychological Assessment, 4,* 26–42.

Goldberg, L. R. (1993). The structure of phenotypic personality traits. *American Psychologist, 48,* 26–34.

Gross, J. J. (1999). Emotion and emotion regulation. In In L. A. Pervin & O. P. John (eds), *Handbook of personality theory and research* (2nd edn, pp. 525–52). New York: Guilford Press.

Hakanen, E. A., & Wells, A. (1991). Adolescent music marginals: Who likes metal, jazz, country, and classical? *Popular Music and Society, 14,* 57–66.

Hakanen, E. A., & Wells A. (1993). Music preference and taste cultures among adolescents. *Popular Music and Society, 17,* 55–69.

Hansen, C. H., & Hansen, R. D. (1991). Constructing personality and social reality through music: Individual differences among fans of punk and heavy metal music. *Journal of Broadcasting & Electronic Media, 35,* 335–50.

Haven, S., & ten Berge, J. M. F. (1977). *Tucker's coefficient of congruence as a measure of factorial invariance: An empirical study (Heymans Bulletin No. 290 EX).* Groningen, The Netherlands: University of Groningen.

Hilliard, R. E. (2001). The use of cognitive-behavioral music therapy in the treatment of women with eating disorders. *Music Therapy Perspectives, 19,* 109–13.

Hornby, N. (1995). *High fidelity.* London: Penguin.

Jang, K. L., McCrae, R. R., Angleitner, A., Riemann, R., & Livesley, W. J. (1998). Heritability of facet-level traits in a cross-cultural twin sample: Support for a hierarchical model of personality. *Journal of Personality and Social Psychology, 74,* 1556–65.

John, O. P., & Srivastava, S. (1999). The Big Five trait taxonomy: History, measurement, and theoretical perspectives. In L. A. Pervin & O. P. John (eds), *Handbook of personality: Theory and research* (2nd edn, pp. 102–38). New York: Guilford Press.

Juslin, P. N., & Laukka, P. (2004). Expression, perception, and induction of musical emotions: A review and a questionnaire study of everyday listening. *Journal of New Music Research, 33,* 217–38.

Katz-Gerro, T. (1999). Cultural consumption and social stratification: Leisure activities, musical tastes, and social location. *Sociological Perspectives, 42,* 627–46.

Katz-Gerro, T., Raz, S., & Yaish, M. (2007). Class, status, and the intergenerational transmission of musical tastes in Israel. *Poetics, 35,* 152–67.

Kemp, A. E. (1996). *The musical temperament: Psychology and personality of musicians.* Oxford: Oxford University Press.

Kemp, A. E. (1997). Individual differences in musical behaviour. In D. J. Hargreaves & A. C. North (eds), *The social psychology of music* (pp. 25–45). Oxford: Oxford University Press.

Kopacz, M. (2005). Personality and music preferences: The influence of personality traits on preferences regarding musical elements. *Journal of Music Therapy, 42,* 216–39.

Levitin D. (2006). *This is your brain on music: The science of a human obsession.* New York: Dutton/Penguin.

Levitin, D. J., Cole, K., Chiles, M., Lai, Z., Lincoln, A., & Bellugi, U. (2004). Characterizing the musical phenotype in individuals with Williams Syndrome. *Child Neuropsychology, 10,* 223–47.

Litle, P., & Zuckerman, M. (1986). Sensation seeking and music preferences. *Personality and Individual Differences, 7,* 575–7.

Loehlin, J. C. (1992). *Genes and environment in personality development.* Newbury Park, CA: Sage.

Luo, S., & Klohnen, E. C. (2005). Assortative mating and marital quality in newlyweds: A couple-centered approach. *Journal of Personality and Social Psychology, 88,* 304–26.

Mark, N. (1998). Birds of a feather sing together. *Social Forces, 77*, 453–83.

McCown, W., Keiser, R., Mulhearn, S., & Williamson, D. (1997). The role of personality and gender in preference for exaggerated bass in music. *Personality and Individual Differences, 23*, 543–7.

McCrae, R. R., & Costa, P. T., Jr. (1997). Personality trait structure as a human universal. *American Psychologist, 52*, 509–16.

McCrae, R. R., & Costa, P. T., Jr. (1999). A five-factor theory of personality. In L. A. Pervin & O. P. John (eds), *Handbook of personality: Theory and research* (2nd edn, pp. 139–53). New York: Guilford Press.

McCrae, R. R., & Costa, P. T., Jr. (2003). *Personality in adulthood: A Five-Factor Theory perspective* (2nd edn). New York: Guilford Press.

McNamara, L., & Ballard, M. E. (1999). Resting arousal, sensation seeking, and music preference. *Genetic, Social, and General Psychology Monographs, 125*, 229–50.

Myers, C. S. (1922). Individual differences in listening to music. *British Journal of Psychology, 13*, 52–71.

Norman W. T. (1967). *2800 personality trait descriptors: Normative operating characteristics for a universal population.* Ann Arbor, MI: University of Michigan, Department of Psychology.

North, A. C., & Hargreaves, D. J. (1996a). Situational influences on reported musical preferences. *Psychomusicology, 15*, 30–45.

North, A. C., & Hargreaves, D. J. (1996b). Responses to music in aerobic exercise and yogic relaxation classes. *British Journal of Psychology, 87*, 535–47.

North, A. C., & Hargreaves, D. J. (1997). Liking, arousal potential, and the emotions expressed by music. *Scandinavian Journal of Psychology, 38*, 45–53.

North, A. C., & Hargreaves, D. J. (2000). Musical preferences during and after relaxation and exercise. *American Journal of Psychology, 113*, 43–67.

North, A. C., Hargreaves, D. J., & Hargreaves, J. J. (2004). Uses of music in everyday life. *Music Perception, 22*, 41–77.

North, A. C., Hargreaves, D. J., & O'Neill, S. A. (2000). The importance of music to adolescents. *British Journal of Educational Psychology, 70*, 255–72.

Ozer, D. J., & Benet-Martinez, V. (2006). Personality and the prediction of consequential outcomes. *Annual Review of Psychology, 57*, 401–21.

Payne, E. (1967). Musical taste and personality. *British Journal of Psychology, 58*, 133–8.

Payne, E. (1980). Towards an understanding of music appreciation. *Psychology of Music, 8*, 31–41.

Pearson, J. L., & Dollinger, S. J. (2004). Music preference correlates of Jungian types. *Personality and Individual Differences, 36*, 1005–8.

Peretz, I., & Hebert, S. (2000). Toward a biological account of music experience. *Brain and Cognition, 42*, 131–4.

Plomin, R., & Caspi, A. (1999). Behavioral genetics and personality. In L. A. Pervin & O. P. John (eds), *Handbook of personality theory and research* (2nd edn, pp. 251–77). New York: Guilford Press.

Radocy, R. E., & Boyle, J. D. (1979). *Psychological foundations of musical behavior.* Springfield, IL: Charles C. Thomas.

Rawlings, D., Barrantes i Vidal, N., & Furnham, A. (2000). Personality and aesthetic preference in Spain and England: Two studies relating sensation seeking and openness to experience to liking for paintings and music. *European Journal of Personality, 14*, 553–76.

Rawlings, D., & Ciancarelli, V. (1997). Music preference and the five-factor model of the NEO Personality Inventory, *Psychology of Music, 25*, 120–32.

Rawlings, D., Hodge, M., Sherr, D., & Dempsey, A. (1995). Toughmindedness and preference for musical excerpts, categories and triads. *Psychology of Music*, *23*, 63–80.

Rentfrow, P. J. (2008). *Development and validation of a musical music preference measure*. Manuscript in preparation.

Rentfrow, P. J., & Gosling, S. D. (2003). The do re mi's of everyday life: The structure and personality correlates of music preferences. *Journal of Personality and Social Psychology*, *84*, 1236–56.

Rentfrow, P. J., & Gosling, S. D. (2006). Message in a ballad: The role of music preferences in interpersonal perception. *Psychological Science*, *17*, 236–42.

Rentfrow, P. J., & Gosling, S. D. (2007). The content and validity of music-genre stereotypes among college students. *Psychology of Music*, *35*, 306–26.

Rentfrow, P. J., Gosling, S. D., & Potter, J. (2008). A theory of the emergence, persistence, and expression of regional variation in basic traits. *Perspectives on Psychological Science*, *3*, 339–69.

Rentfrow, P. J., McDonald, J. A., & Oldmeadow, J. A. (2009). You are what you listen to: Young people's stereotypes about music fans. *Group Processes and Intergroup Relations*, *12*, 329–44.

Rider, M. S., Floyd, J. W., & Kirkpatrick, J. (1985). The effect of music, imagery, and relaxation on adrenal corticoids and the re-entrainment of circadian rhythms. *Journal of Music Therapy*, *22*, 46–58.

Roberts, B. W., Kuncel, N., Shiner, R. N., Caspi, A., & Goldberg, L. R. (2007). The power of personality: The comparative validity of personality traits, socio-economic status, and cognitive ability for predicting important life outcomes. *Perspectives in Psychological Science*, *2*, 313–45.

Roe, K. (1985). Swedish youth and music: Listening patterns and motivation. *Communication Research*, *12*, 353–62.

Rozin, P. (2001). Social psychology and science: Some lessons from Solomon Asch. *Personality and Social Psychology Review*, *5*, 2–14.

Russell, P. A. (1997). Musical tastes and society. In D. J. Hargreaves & A. C. North (eds), *The social psychology of music* (pp. 141–58). Oxford: Oxford University Press.

Saucier, G., & Ostendorf, F. (1999). Hierarchical subcomponents of the Big Five personality factors: A cross-language replication. *Journal of Personality and Social Psychology*, *76*, 613–27.

Scherer, K. R., & Zentner, M. R. (2001). Emotional effects of music: Production rules. In P. N. Juslin & J. A. Sloboda (eds), *Music and emotion: Theory and research* (pp. 361–92). Oxford: Oxford University Press.

Schwartz, K. D., & Fouts, G. T. (2003). Music preferences, personality style, and developmental issues of adolescents. *Journal of Youth and Adolescence*, *32*, 205–13.

Selfhaut, M. H. W., Branje, S. J. T., ter Bogt, T. F. M., & Meeus, W. H. J. (2009). The role of music preferences in early adolescents' friendship formation and stability. *Journal of Adolescence*, *32*, 95–107.

Sloboda, J. A. (1985). *The musical mind: The cognitive psychology of music*. Oxford: Oxford University Press.

Sloboda, J. A., & O'Neill, S. A. (2001). Emotions in everyday listening to music. In P. N. Juslin & J. A. Sloboda (eds), *Music and emotion: Theory and research* (pp. 415–29). Oxford: Oxford University Press.

Sloboda, J. A., O'Neill, S. A., & Ivaldi, A. (2001). Functions of music in everyday life: An exploratory study using the Experience Sampling Method. *Musicae Scientiae*, *5*, 9–32.

Srivastava, S., John, O. P., Gosling, S. D., & Potter, J. (2003). Development of personality in early and middle adulthood: Set like plaster or persistent change? *Journal of Personality and Social Psychology, 84,* 1041–53.

Swann, W. B. Jr., Rentfrow, P. J., & Guinn, J. S. (2002). Self-verification: The search for coherence. In M. Leary & J. Tagney (eds), *Handbook of self and identity* (pp. 367–83). New York: Guilford Press.

Tarrant, M., North, A. C., & Hargreaves, D. J. (2000). English and American adolescents' reasons for listening to music. *Psychology of Music, 28,* 166–73.

Tarrant, M., North, A. C., & Hargreaves, D. J. (2002). Youth identity and music. In R. MacDonald, D. Hargreaves, & D. Miell (eds), *Musical identities* (pp. 134–50). Oxford: Oxford University Press.

Thurstone, L. L. (1934). The vectors of mind. *Psychological Review, 41,* 1–32.

Todd, N. P. M. (1999). Motion in music: A neurobiological perspective. *Music Perception, 17,* 115–26.

Van Eijck, K. (2001). Social differentiation in musical taste patterns. *Social Forces, 79,* 1163–84.

Watson, D., & Clark, L. (1992). On traits and temperament: General and specific factors of emotional experience and their relation to the five-factor model. *Journal of Personality, 60,* 441–76.

Weaver, J. B. (1991). Exploring the links between personality and media preferences. *Personality and Individual Differences, 12,* 1293–9.

Wheeler, B. L. (1985). The relationship of personal characteristics to mood and enjoyment after hearing live and recorded music and to musical taste. *Psychology of Music, 13,* 81–92.

Wigram, T., Saperston, B., & West, R. (1995). *The art and science of music therapy: A handbook.* Chur, Switzerland: Harwood Academic Publishers.

Wonderlic, E. F. (1977). *Wonderlic Personnel Test manual.* Northfield, IL: Wonderlic and Associates.

Wood (2005). *Music preferences and personality among college roommates.* Unpublished data, University of Illinois, Urbana Champaign, USA.

Wright, J. T. (1952). About the Music Research Foundation. In A. A. Capurso et al (eds), *Music and your emotions: A practical guide to music selections associated with desired emotional responses* (pp. 87–96). New York: Liveright.

Zatorre, R. J., Belin, P., & Penhune, V. B. (2002). Structure and function of auditory cortex: Music and speech. *Trends in Cognitive Sciences, 6,* 37–46.

Zweigenhaft, R. L. (2008). A do re mi encore: A closer look at the personality correlates of music preferences. *Journal of Individual Differences, 29,* 45–55.

CHAPTER 25

THE INFLUENCE OF AFFECT ON MUSIC CHOICE

VLADIMIR J. KONEČNI

25.1 INTRODUCTION

INTERACTIONS that one has on a virtually moment-by-moment basis with the social and physical environment frequently produce a change in affect; and so do cognitive representations of the past and expectations of the future interactive events. The complex mechanisms by which the physical and symbolic interactions with the environment give rise to affect, and the evolutionary reasons for this taking place, are for the most part not the subject of this chapter (but see Sections 25.3.2 and 25.5.2). Instead, the key question that it will address is: given that a change in affect has in fact been produced, by whatever means, is the experiencing person more likely to seek exposure to some environmental stimuli than others, and to choose one level or degree of those stimuli more than another? Therefore, when the discussion is additionally and of necessity limited to music as the stimulus, the purpose of the chapter becomes: is the choice of music to which to listen dependent on one's current affect?

In this chapter (and the handbook as a whole), the term 'affect' includes both emotion and mood. However, this classification simply reflects a reasonably justifiable convention and it will therefore be necessary, for theoretical and empirical reasons, that the two states (or processes, see Section 25.3; cf. Scherer, 2000, p. 70) under the 'affect' umbrella be clearly distinguished from each other.

The chapter consists of seven sections. An essential task is carried out first (Section 25.2): to place formally and accurately the topic of the present chapter in the constellation of relationships—or simple causal models—that constitute a significant portion of the handbook's music-and-emotion (M-E) domain (which, perhaps more accurately, ought to be referred to as the music-and-affect domain). The frequency with which the various categories of 'naïve' respondents endorse the importance and veracity of these causal relationships is also presented in this section, in tabular form.

Section 25.3 also has a foundational and definitional goal—that of specifying the author's theoretical assumptions concerning emotion (and, by implication, non-emotion, including mood). For this purpose, the author's prototypical emotion-episode model (or PEEM; Konečni, 1979, 1984, 1991) is reintroduced in updated form. In part, this section is meant to be a substantive contribution to the emotion literature. More importantly in the present context, the section on PEEM makes explicit the background for the author's interpretation of the research studies on the effects of emotion and mood on music choice (reviewed in Sections 25.4 and 25.6, respectively). Section 25.5 is devoted to a discussion of the concept of mood. Finally, the implications of the research on the effects of affect on music choice are discussed in section 25.7.

25.2 RELATIONSHIPS IN THE M-E DOMAIN

Music consists of many integrated components, including the composer, the score, the performer, the instrument, the sound, the listener, the listening environment—and the M-E domain is correspondingly broad and multi-faceted. In addition, when both researchers and lay people talk about the various relationships between music and emotion, they often fail to specify the extent to which the effect is direct, as opposed to mediated in some way, even though such mediation should often be of major theoretical interest.

25.2.1 Some causal models

Various aspects of M-E are presented in Table 25.1 in the form of simple causal models.[1] The two statements in the bottom part of the table (models 12 and 13) acknowledge the self-evident, but seldom mentioned, facts about M-E. First, much exposure

[1] Characteristics of the instruments, mood/tempo directions in the score, and the structural and acoustic features of the recorded or performed sound, among other features, may all contribute to the expression of emotion by music. These issues are not directly pertinent to the causal models in Table 25.1. Listeners generally can identify the expressive attributes of the music analytically without any concurrent emotional response. Respondents' statements (in Section 25.2.2) to the effect that music expresses, evokes, alludes to, or represents emotion—without any mention of the listener experiencing an emotional state—were classified under model 12.

Table 25.1 Relevant causal models in the relationship between music (M) and emotion (E), and the frequency (%) with which each model is mentioned

Causal Model	Frequency of mention by sample (%)					
	A	B	C	D	E	Mean
1. M → E	25	30	35	23	27	28
2. M → Associations → E	7	13	8	10	12	10
3. M → Dance → E	4	4	8	10	3	6
4. M → Physiological effects (No E)	11	2	0	3	7	5
5. M → Mood change (No E)	4	8	14	13	8	9
6. M → Contemplation, Analysis (No E)	4	2	11	0	2	4
7. $E_{composer}$ → $M_{attributes}$	0	4	0	0	6	2
8. $E_{performer}$ → $M_{attributes}$	0	6	0	3	2	2
9. $E_{listener}$ → M_{choice}	29	12	5	17	14	15
10. $E_{1\ listener}$ → M_1 → Assoc. → E_2 → M_2...	7	4	8	13	2	7
11. $E_{1\ listener\ time\ 1}$ → $M_{1\ time\ 1}$ $M_{1\ time\ 2,\ 3...n}$ → Assoc. → $E_{1\ time\ 2,\ 3...n}$	7	5	8	3	2	5
12. M → No discernible effect	4	9	3	3	10	6
13. E → No discernible effect on M_{choice}	0	0	0	0	5	1

Note: Without being presented with any of the above models, all participants anonymously completed the sentence 'My view of the relationship between music and emotion ...' and could make additional statements; up to three 'views' per participant were coded. In each column, entries are percentages (rounded to the nearest integer) of the total number of responses given by a sample. Sample A ($N = 12$, with a total of 28 responses; 2002) consisted of three faculty members and nine graduate students at a social psychology seminar. Sample B ($N = 44$, with 98 responses; 2002) were honours thesis candidates (junior-year undergraduates) at a lecture. Samples C and D ($N = 20$ and $N = 19$, with 37 and 30 responses, respectively, in 2004 and 2005): these participants were freshmen at the first meeting of a 'Music and Emotion' seminar. Sample E ($N = 71$, with 173 responses, 2006) consisted of upper-division students in a class on 'Psychology and the Arts' (prior to the lecture on music and emotion).

to music clearly does not have any discernible effect (model 12). It would seem that the very ubiquity of music in contemporary life ensures that much of it is ignored. For example, in a study using the experience-sampling method (Sloboda & O'Neill, 2001), it was found that although 44 per cent of the events somehow involved music, in only 2 per cent of the total was listening the principal activity. Second, it must be that people often do not choose to listen to music following the onset of an emotion (model 13 in Table 25.1; see Section 25.4).

The rest of the table is divided into two parts, the criterion of division being whether music listening (M) or emotion (E) is the causal agent. (The term 'emotion' is used in the table, rather than 'affect', in order to reflect the prevailing custom in the literature—even though this custom sometimes results in a lack of precision, if not dubious claims.)

$M \rightarrow E$ models

In the top part, the model stating the *direct* (proximal) causation of emotion by music listening ($1, M \rightarrow E$) is presented along with relevant alternatives. Models 4, 5, and 6 formalize the possibility that music may lead to contemplation and analysis, to a change in mood, and even to various physiological effects (e.g. Bartlett, 1996; Bernardi, Porta, & Sleight, 2006)—all without resulting in a genuine emotional state (as specified by PEEM, described in Section 25.3). For example, structural features of music may increase heart rate, but so may riding the bicycle. Music may make one feel 'good', but so does going for a walk. And for some people, especially musicians, music (with or without consulting the score) may be the equivalent of a mathematical or chess problem, and a way to deal with the concept of time (cf. Stravinsky, 1936/1998, pp. 53–54). It is important to note that in the literature on M-E, findings that support models 4 and 5 are sometimes uncritically interpreted as supporting model 1.

Model 3 acknowledges dance as possibly a major—most likely primordial—mediator between music and emotion (Konečni, 2005, 2008; Konečni, Brown, & Wanic, 2008). Dance allows the display of a person's physique, skill, and endurance. The young especially, and young women in particular, engage in it a great deal (Wells, 1990, Table III, p. 108). Dance makes possible the close observation of potential sexual partners and often involves physical proximity with them. It involves being courted, touched, encouraged—or slighted. Miller's (2000) case for the evolution of human music through sexual selection becomes more convincing when dance is proposed as one of the key mediators. It is therefore surprising that dance is almost universally ignored by music psychologists, except as a medium that can reflect the structural and expressive attributes of music (Krumhansl & Schenck, 1997). The chief reason may be music psychologists' relative neglect of the social context of music listening (Konečni, 1979, 1982; North & Hargreaves, 1997).

However, it is the idea that music gives rise to thoughts about significant others, about emotionally rich social situations, and one's past experiences and innermost strivings (model 2), that is here proposed as the central and necessary elaboration of $M \rightarrow E$ (model 1)—necessary from both the logical and evidentiary points of view. The temporal nature of music, its abstract quality (especially in comparison with other temporal arts, such as the theatre, or even to plotless choreography in dance), its blocking of other distractions when one is truly listening, and the fact that its structural features may affect motor behaviour and physiological responses—all play a part in the transformation of heard sound into emotional state via memories and contemplation (Konečni, 2008; Konečni et al, 2008; Konečni, Wanic, & Brown, 2007).

Krumhansl (2002, p. 45) has challenged a version of model 2 on the grounds that 'if this [that is, associations as the necessary mediators] were all, then emotional responses to music would vary greatly from individual to individual depending on their unique past experiences'. Actually, the available evidence indeed indicates that people's emotional reactions to the same piece of music are vastly different. Krumhansl (2002, p. 45) continues: 'But listeners agree remarkably well with one another in labeling musical emotions. Something in the music must produce this agreement . . . musical sounds may inherently have emotional meaning.' Indeed they may, but that is an issue of expression, not of induction, and the evidence for the former ought not to be marshalled as evidence for the latter. In other words, listeners' agreement about the expressive features of a piece of music does not favour model 1 over model 2—as Krumhansl apparently maintains.

$E \rightarrow M$ models

In the middle part of Table 25.1 (models 7–11) are models in which emotion, rather than music listening, is the causal agent. Models 7 and 8 refer to the possibility that the emotions experienced by the composer and performer, while composing and performing, influence the attributes of the composed and performed music. It is exceptionally difficult to investigate these possibilities experimentally (e.g. Gabrielsson & Lindström, 2001; Konečni, 2003; Persson, 2001; Simonton, 2001). Regarding the composers' emotions, when one considers, if nothing else, the length of most classical compositions, one would probably conclude that Gabrielsson and Lindström implicitly agree with at least some features of PEEM (in Section 25.3) when they strongly doubt (as did no less an 'emotivist', in the popular view, than P. I. Chaikovsky) that 'composers express their present feelings in their compositions' and instead think it much more likely that composers merely 'use various structural factors . . . to achieve certain intended expressions' (Gabrielsson & Lindström, 2001, p. 223).

As for the performers, model 8 may be correct for many of them, but in the limited sense of performance anxiety (or, perhaps more accurately, fear—as in 'stage fright') negatively affecting the attributes of performed music (e.g. Steptoe, 2001). The technical demands and concentration required especially in classical performance are so high that it is difficult to see how the performers' emotions can be part of the performance equation (except adversely), despite many music teachers' claims to the contrary. It is also important to note that experiments, such as Juslin's (2000), on performers' 'communication of emotion' do not necessarily address model 8, although they are sometimes cited as having done so: a skilled guitarist can, when instructed, perform a piece in an angry manner, without being in the least angry.[2]

Model 9 is, of course, the core of the chapter and the evidence for its feasibility will be examined in Section 25.4: when emotion is induced in people by non-musical means, which are the characteristics of the music to which they choose to listen (if music listening is indeed the behavioural option taken)? Finally, in models 10 and 11, examples are given of more complex scenarios that begin with $E_{listener} \rightarrow M_{choice}$; it will be argued in Section 25.4.3 that even though no empirical evidence exists for such multi-event sequences interweaving emotion, music choice, listening, and associations, they

---

[2] Note that PEEM (described in Section 25.3.2) allows the possibility that an 'angry' performance, coupled with associations, may produce genuine anger in the performer. Here one observes the grey area between a performer's faithful facial and bodily imitation of posture and gestures that are commonly assumed by genuinely angry people, on one hand, and a performer's subjective experience of genuine anger, on the other. This fine line is well known to actors and opera singers who encounter it in the 'method of physical action' within Stanislavski's 'system' (Konečni, 1991, 2008; Konijn, 2000; Stanislavski, 1936; Stanislavski & Rumyantsev, 1975).

are common in the lives of music listeners and contribute to the words 'music' and 'emotion' being spoken so often in the same breath.

25.2.2 Frequency of endorsement of causal models

The frequency of mention of various causal models by five different samples of respondents is also provided in Table 25.1; the samples are described in the note to the table. The respondents anonymously completed the sentence 'My view of the relationship between music and emotion . . .' and could make additional statements. Up to three different 'views' regarding M-E by each respondent were coded. Responses were collected at the beginning of a course, lecture, or seminar, without any introduction, guidance, or examples. The coders were two undergraduates who classified the responses in terms of the models in Table 25.1 with minimal additional instructions. The initial agreement between the two coders was 72 per cent, as determined by a third, independent, coder, who also resolved the disagreements.

As can be seen in Table 25.1, at least some respondents mentioned all 13 models used in the classification, with the M $\rightarrow$ E model by far the most popular ($M = 28$ per cent for all five samples). From freshmen (many with undeclared majors) to psychology graduate students and faculty, many people held the view that music directly induces emotion. Respondents who felt that music's effect on emotion is mediated by associations and dance (models 2 and 3, respectively) were far less numerous (10 per cent and 6 per cent), but also represented in all the samples.

The second most-mentioned causal relationship—that people's emotions determine their choice of music (model 9; overall $M = 15$ per cent)—was, perhaps not surprisingly, most frequently mentioned by the professional social psychologists in Sample A ($M = 29$ per cent). But they were not more likely than others to mention the more complex multi-stage causal models (10 and 11). This may be an indirect testimony to the conceptual and logistical difficulties that social and music psychology face in carrying out multi-stage experiments—even though such research may be sorely needed for the formulation of an adequate body of theory regarding M-E.

25.3 EMOTION IN THE M-E DOMAIN

In *Music and emotion* (Juslin & Sloboda, 2001), Scherer and Zentner (2001) published a chapter in which they carefully distinguished emotions from moods, preferences, attitudes, personality traits, and other concepts (Table 16.1, p. 363). The present approach shares their concern for these distinctions. In addition, it is in agreement with Gabrielsson's (2002) emphasis on subjective state as an essential component of an acceptable model of emotion (cf. Frijda, 2005). The latter point is important because— much as there is an emphasis in the present approach on the necessary role of the physiological response in emotion (an absence of the physiological response is equated with an absence of emotion)—indices of physiological fluctuations are considered to be insufficient when not corroborated by subjective report (i.e. when they are not the report's afferent underpinning; cf. Stemmler, Heldmann, Pauls, & T. Scherer, 2001).

25.3.1 Attributes of emotion

In the present view (cf. Konečni, 1991, 2003, 2008), emotions have an unambiguous cause or object, and because they guide and energize behaviour in key life situations, they have been subjected to considerable evolutionary pressures. Emotions are acute, physiologically and psychologically costly, and therefore reserved for emergencies. Typically there is an involvement of numerous bodily systems—in tandem and simultaneously. These states are readily identifiable by the experiencing person (and often, though not always, by observers), as well as nameable and reportable. Emotions flood consciousness and are probably universal in terms of expression and experience. In general, such criteria fit models of 'natural kinds' (Barrett, 2006) of both the basic-emotions (e.g. Buck, 1999; Ekman, 1973) and appraisal type (e.g. Frijda, 1988; Lazarus, 1991).

The real-world ecology—specifically with regard to the distribution and type of significant stimuli of social origin—limits the variety of emotional reactions (cf. Oatley & Duncan, 1994; Konečni, 2008). In fact, there are good conceptual reasons for reserving the term 'emotions' for the 'basic' ones—keeping in mind the criticisms by Ortony and Turner (1990) and Barrett (2006).

25.3.2 Prototypical emotion-episode model (PEEM)

The prototypical emotion-episode model, PEEM (Konečni, 1984; also see Konečni, 2008, for a more detailed account) is presented in Fig 25.1. This is a process model

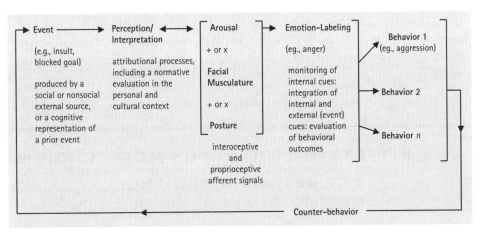

Fig. 25.1 The prototypical emotion–episode model, PEEM. From Konečni (2008), with permission of the American Psychological Association.

of emotion; the aim of its inclusion here is to facilitate the interpretation of various relevant findings. The event that initiates an episode is usually generated by another person (e.g. by an ego-thwarting insult), although it may consist exclusively of rumination related to prior events. Perception and interpretation (including a rapid attributional analysis) are linked by a feedback loop, and this initial stage necessarily precedes the occurrence of sympathetic arousal and facial and postural activity—with which it is, however, bidirectionally causally linked. In addition, arousal and facial expression influence each other (e.g. Ekman, Levenson, & Friesen, 1983; Lanzetta, Cartwright-Smith, & Kleck, 1976) and together (additively or multiplicatively) are subjected to a multi-faceted cognitive analysis that leads to the identification and labelling of one's emotion (the degree of deliberateness may differ).

Behaviour that follows emotion labelling depends on many factors, including the anticipated counter-behaviour by the social target of one's actions. That counter-behaviour is the event that begins the next passage through the emotion-episode sequence. Attributes of this second-generation event may cause the original state to diminish, intensify, or change dramatically—when the event's details require a re-labelling of emotion.

PEEM is conceptually and functionally broader (cf. Scherer, 2000) than models that are limited to a single subsystem (including various arousal models). Its treatment of an emotion episode as a process of multiple passages through a multi-component sequence, as well as the attention it devotes to the occurrence of misattribution and re-attribution, distinguish PEEM from other appraisal models and counter some of the criticisms that Barrett (2006) levels at natural-kinds models in general.

One of the assumptions of PEEM is that both a pronounced visceral response and an unambiguous subjective experience are necessary and probably sufficient for an authentic emotion episode to occur (Konečni, 2008; cf. Stemmler et al, 2001). There is a superficial similarity of this view with that of Schachter and Singer (1962), but also considerable differences in both scope and many significant details (Konečni, 1984). In addition, there is a kinship between certain features of the 'cognitive labelling' model (Konečni, 1975b, later incorporated into PEEM) and Zillmann's (1978) 'excitation transfer' model. It is with reference to PEEM and other criteria that have been described that the evidence for the effects of emotion and mood on music choice will be evaluated in Sections 25.4 and 25.6.

25.4 EFFECTS OF EMOTION ON MUSIC CHOICE: THE RESEARCH EVIDENCE

Because emotions often signify emergencies, it would seem, at first blush, unlikely that listening to music would be the experiencing person's primary option. But emergencies differ in their time course and in the modes of resolution that are possible, especially in contemporary social milieux, so that resorting to music listening when happy, angry, or sad (although presumably not when afraid) does not, on second thought, seem far-fetched. Unfortunately, this is mostly speculative reasoning, because, to the best of the author's knowledge, there exist no truly solid data collected in non-laboratory settings about the likelihood of persons choosing to listen to music (or read poetry, for that matter) immediately after an emotional state has been authentically induced. The diary, pager, interview, and survey studies provide some useful information, but have virtually insurmountable problems in trying to attain truthfulness, accuracy, and conceptual clarity (e.g. regarding the occurrence of emotion vs. mood), and to establish the direction of causality. Under normal circumstances, even though emotions are social, in that they often involve other human beings, they and their settings are private and intimate affairs to which researchers have very limited access.

25.4.1 Some methodological problems in the laboratory

Tightly controlled research in the laboratory has another set of problems. Perhaps the greatest and most relevant among these is that happiness and sadness (unlike anger and fear) cannot be *adequately* experimentally created. In the real world, these two key emotions of human bonding, separation, and loss, with immense reproductive-fitness implications, are generally induced by the rare significant others—something that cannot be replicated in the laboratory.[3] Perhaps the closest one can come to happiness and sadness in the laboratory is to ask people to recall real-life events (e.g. Konečni et al, 2008). Minor monetary winnings and losses, 'happy' or 'sad' three-minute film clips, praise from strangers, or the break-up of five-minute acquaintanceships—to mention just a few of the countless rather trivial events that have been engineered in the laboratory—do not result in emotions, or do so only as misnomers in scientific articles.

It is of interest that happiness and sadness are precisely the two emotions that music most readily and frequently *expresses*, for example, through the very structure of the classical sonata and the Catholic mass (including the *Requiem*); and it is perhaps the compelling nature of expression that has seduced researchers, such as Gaver and Mandler (1987), to recommend using music as a supposedly handy and simple method of inducing emotions in the laboratory (e.g. Koelsch, Fritz, von Cramon, Müller, & Friederici, 2006; and Chapter 12, this volume) with other research objectives in mind. Such advice seems doubly misplaced: music is a comparatively weak inducer of emotions even when the associative elements are introduced by the participants (Konečni et al, 2008); and once they are, (instrumental) music loses its apparent advantage as a

---

[3] That even the most advanced laboratory emotion-induction techniques, such as those described in Chapters 1–7 of the *Handbook of emotion elicitation and assessment* (Coan & Allen, 2007), come nowhere near the happiness- and sadness-inducing power of one's significant others can be easily ascertained by the discerning reader.

convenient 'appraisal-free' stimulus. In any case, as has been made clear, the focus of the present chapter is exclusively on the effects of non-musically induced emotions.

Authentic anger and fear can be induced very successfully in the laboratory. However, even though the procedures were safe, reliable, and humane, the truly adequate induction of these emotions in social-psychological and psychophysiological laboratories has been made, beginning with the early 1980s, next to impossible by the institutional boards overseeing research in both North America and Europe. For this reason, the review that follows is of data from laboratory studies conducted prior to what has been, in effect, an international ban on research on adequately induced negative emotions.

25.4.2 Data

A certain amount of solid evidence is available regarding the effect of listeners' emotional states on their choice among, and preference for, music-listening alternatives that differ on psychologically and aesthetically important dimensions, such as complexity, loudness, and rhythmic characteristics. The general finding is that the experience of negative emotional states leads people to sharply decrease their exposure to complex, novel, and loud music, and to complex rhythmic structures. The probable, mutually non-exclusive, and related explanations are that (a) coping with an acute, experientially demanding negative state decreases the amount of processing capacity that is available for the processing of music (Konečni & Sargent-Pollock, 1976) and other stimuli (Broadbent, 1971; Easterbrook, 1959; Kahneman, 1973; Posner, 1975; Sokolov, 1963), and (b) simple music at a soft listening level actively soothes negative emotions (Konečni, 1975b).

Anger

In a multi-purpose experiment, Konečni, Crozier, and Doob (1976) used an anger-induction procedure (originally developed by Konečni and Doob, 1972) to investigate the effect of this aversive emotional state on the choice between two computer-generated 'melodies' differing in complexity (or, in information theory terms, uncertainty). The effect of this powerful—naturalistic, yet standardized—anger-instilling procedure (with ego-thwarting remarks delivered by a covert assistant of the experimenter) is a considerable degree of authentic anger experienced by the (individually treated) research participants. In comparison to the neutrally treated control participants, those subjected to the experimental emotion manipulation exhibited anger in terms of self-report, facial configuration, and body posture (videotaped and later evaluated by raters unaware of the instigating condition), as well as cardiovascular response (cf. PEEM in Fig 25.1). The original research reports can be consulted for the evidence of extensive debriefing of participants and the efforts made to ensure their well-being during and after the experiment.

In the immediately following stage of the experiment, which was described to participants as an unrelated study, they chose on each of 50 ten-second trials to listen either to highly complex (9.17 bits/tone) or rather simple (4.00 bits/tone) tone sequences. Complexity was manipulated by varying the number of pitches, durations, and loudness levels of tones (keeping timbre constant), with 576 possible events in the pool for the complex, and only 16 in the pool for the simple, tone sequences that were randomly computer-selected within type (using sampling with replacement). These two complexity levels were used on the basis of pilot studies in which neutrally treated participants chose the two levels equally often over trials; this could be shown to be due to the different degrees of rated pleasingness and interestingness of the two 'melody pools' being perfectly balanced.

In the present context, the most relevant finding by Konečni et al (1976) was that the angry participants chose complex melodies on only 29 per cent of the trials, compared to about 50 per cent for the control group. The overall data pattern was in accord with Konečni's (1975a, 1975b) cognitive-labelling model, and showed that the active ingredients of the emotion that led participants to shun complex melodies were both the heightened physiological arousal and the cognitive processes (made explicit in PEEM) that were responsible for the interpretation and labelling of the heightened arousal level. A closely related issue is that coping with anger was presumably both physiologically and cognitively costly for the participants, and therefore reduced, as noted earlier, their processing capacity available for the reception and enjoyment of music. With regard to the impact on music choice, the difficulty of dealing with one's negative emotion seems to exceed that of coping with ordinary high-load tasks (see Figure 1 in Konečni, 1994; Konečni, 1975a; Niketta, 1990).

Complexity, a member of Berlyne's (1960, 1971) class of 'collative', or statistical, stimulus variables (along with novelty and surprisingness), is one of the relatively few major psychological and aesthetic dimensions by which both lay people and experts—spontaneously and analytically—describe musical compositions (and other works of art); it is therefore conceptually advantageous to relate a genuine emotion arising in dyadic social interaction to this attribute of music. (See Chapter 19, this volume, for a discussion of Berlyne's theory.) The results obtained by Konečni et al (1976) were perhaps the first in the literature to relate an emotional state induced by social stimuli (insulting words) to the choice of music to which to listen; the latter had been generally treated as if it occurs in a socio-emotional vacuum (cf. Konečni, 1979, 1982; North & Hargreaves, 1997).

Flath-Becker and Konečni (1984) were interested in the effects of the participants' anger and failure (including combined stress) on their preference for music pieces that differed radically in rhythmic complexity. The researchers' anger manipulation was modelled after a procedure developed by Hokanson and Shetler (1961). The participants were either repeatedly and sternly reprimanded to work faster on a task or neutrally treated. In addition, they either appeared to fail or to succeed on the task. In a counterbalanced research design, the participants then listened to portions of piano (Bach, Debussy, Bartók, Schönberg), orchestral (Bach, Ravel, Bartók, Schönberg), and percussion (Ginger Baker, Siegfried Fink-a, Fink-b, Cage) compositions characterized by different rhythmic structures (regular, ostinato, syncopated, and complex, respectively). As predicted, the more complex rhythmic structures were shunned in the anger and, especially, the anger combined with fail-ure, conditions. The preference for simple over complex rhythms in the combined stress condition was more pronounced in the piano and orchestral than in the per-cussion compositions (Flath-Becker, 1987). The additive effect of failure on angry people's already low preference for complex rhythm could be accounted for by an early version of PEEM (Fig 25.1).

In sum, Flath-Becker and Konečni (1984) were able to replicate and extend prior findings. Significantly, they obtained the predicted effects with composed, as opposed to computer-generated, music. That the effect of shunning complexity while experi-encing a negative emotional state was stronger for the piano and orchestral than for the percussion compositions is open to several interpretations. One is the relative rejection of contemporary percussion compositions by the non-musician participants, and their consequent lack of attention to the music's detailed attributes. Another is the degree of presence of the attention-maintaining melody in various compositions, which was confounded with their novelty. In any case, the extent to which emotions may *differ-entially* influence the processing of various attributes of music that contribute to the overall preference is a worthy subject for a renewed research effort.

Results theoretically analogous to, or supportive of, those for complexity have been obtained for loudness (one of Berlyne's, 1971, psychophysical stimulus dimensions), as both an independent and dependent variable, in studies by Konečni (1975b), and Konečni and Sargent-Pollock (1976, 1977; cf. North & Hargreaves, 1999). For exam-ple, Konečni and Sargent-Pollock (1976) showed that the significant reduction in the participants' choice of complex computer-generated melodies, following exposure to 95-dB/350-Hz squarewave stimulation, was mediated by a decrease in their processing capacity—lending support to one aspect of the previously mentioned interpretation of the overall $E_{listener} \rightarrow M_{choice}$ effect (Konečni, 1979, 1982, 1994).

Type A behaviour pattern

The manner in which anger influences a person's processing of music can be further clarified by considering the Type A coronary-prone behaviour pattern. In contrast to Type B, Type A behaviour is characterized by three main tendencies: time urgency, extreme competitiveness, and aggressiveness (Friedman & Rosenman, 1974; Jenkins, Rosenman, & Zyzanski, 1974). These tendencies result in Type A individuals being comparatively likely to focus on the central aspect of a task to the exclusion of periph-eral stimuli or information (Matthews & Brunson, 1979), even when the peripherally presented information can be helpful in the work on the central task (Strube, Turner, Patrick, & Perillo, 1983).

The Type A behaviour pattern therefore has precisely the same consequence on information processing as does the presence of a negative emotional state for people in general (cf. Easterbrook, 1959). Building on these ideas, Konečni and Gotlieb (1987) reasoned that (a) the differences in attention and processing between Type A and Type B individuals could be further augmented by the participants being sternly challenged (on an initial pseudo-task) and (b) one could gain additional knowledge about the effect of negative emotion on the processing of music by presenting to both types of participants, for the subsequent criterion tasks, a musical composition that authentically contains central and peripheral elements.

A fugue is such a musical form. The material for the experiment by Konečni and Gotlieb (1987) therefore consisted of three fugues (specially composed for the research, so that no participant would be familiar with them) and four variations on a segment of each fugue. A melodic phrase served as the central feature of each stimulus pattern, whereas the variations served as peripheral embellishments. There were two dependent measures: recall of the pitch contour of the central phrase (notes written on a music staff) and recognition of which of the four embellishments actually accompanied the central phrase. The results closely matched the predictions. Compared to other groups, the sternly challenged Type A individuals excelled on the recall test that dealt with the central features of each fugue and did poorly on the recognition test involving peripheral embellishments.

By having an intense, but excessively narrow, focus of attention, the angry Type A individuals simplified the array of musical stimuli to which they were listening. There is a clear conceptual link between this finding and those discussed in the previous section. Angry people in general, when given the choice between music pieces differing in complexity, prefer the simpler (computer-generated or authentic-music) options.

Consequences of angry people's exposure to music

It is helpful to shed more light on the preference that angry people have for simple melodies. Additional information comes from experiments on the *consequences* of angry people's (experimenter-imposed) exposure to simple melodies at a comfortable listening level, namely: (a) a reduction in the reported degree of anger; (b) a decline from an aversively high level of sympathetic arousal; and (c) a decrease in the probability and amount of aggressive behaviour (Konečni, 1975a, 1975b, 1979). Such findings make sense when one remembers that anger and a high level of arousal—the results of an unpleasant social exchange and characterized, for example, by a rise in systolic blood pressure of some 25 mm Hg over the baseline in the procedure used by Konečni and Doob (1972; cf. Hokanson & Shetler, 1961)—are reported by the participants as highly aversive. Meanwhile, simple melodies at a comfortable listening level are soothing and act faster than homeostatic processes. They are more effective than silence or reading or math tasks or complex melodies (Konečni, 1975a, 1975b; Strube et al, 1983) in ameliorating the aversive psychological consequences of anger, high arousal, and implied aggression.

Partly in this vein, Caspy, Peleg, Schlam, and Goldberg (1988) found that listening to 'sedative', as opposed to 'stimulative', composed music following a frustrating maze task helped the participants do better on Raven's matrices (cf. Rickard, Toukhsati, & Field, 2005, p. 236). Analogous results following mental arithmetic were obtained by Chafin, Roy, Gerin, and Christenfeld (2004)—a faster cardiovascular recovery due to music such as Pachelbel's *Canon* in comparison to less soothing music.

Fear

There are few real-world emergencies more compelling than those that succeed in inducing fear—and music listening is unlikely to be an adaptive response to them. Nevertheless, in what is perhaps the only laboratory experiment on this topic in the literature, Konečni (1979, section III.C., pp. 183–190) examined whether fear resulted in preference for simple melodies analogous to what has been observed for anger.

In the first stage of the experiment, participants assigned to the fear manipulation were told that at any time 'over a four-minute period they may be exposed to some extremely loud and aversive blasts of noise' (Konečni, 1979, p. 185; no noise was in fact administered to anyone in the experiment). During this four-minute period, some of the scared participants listened, on a pretext, for several minutes continuously to computer-generated simple melodies (4.00 bits/tone), whereas others spent the four minutes without anything at all happening. There were additional control groups of people who were not made afraid and of those who were neither afraid nor heard the music. After this initial stage, 15 minutes of rest filled with neutral activities followed for all groups. In the next stage, some participants underwent a similar fear manipulation for the second time, whereas for others fear was instilled at this point for the first time; and there were two no-fear control groups, one of which had heard the melodies in the initial stage, whereas the other had not. In conjunction with this stage, the dependent measure was collected: on each of 25 occasions signalled by a light, the participants could, if they wished, press a button—following which they would hear, for as long as they kept the button pressed (up to six seconds on each occasion), a simple computer-generated melody.

Turning to the results and examining first the music-exposure choices of the two no-fear groups as the baseline, one finds that the participants with prior experience of the melodies listened to them significantly longer when they were later given the choice than those without prior experience (means of 47.40 s vs. 34.40 s). A result in the same direction, but weaker (44.60 s vs. 39.30 s), was obtained for the two groups in which fear was experienced only once, in the final part of the study, with only the former group having prior experience with the music. So far, one can conclude that the simple melodies 'grow on one', to some extent, but that the people experiencing fear do not seek them more than those who are unafraid. However, the participants who chose to listen to the melodies more often, and for a longer total duration, than any other experimental group were those whose first (of two) fear experiences was accompanied by the melodies ($M = 73.10$ s of 150 s possible; whereas $M = 45.80$ s for the twice-afraid group without prior music experience).

On the basis of these results, it would seem that scared people's attraction to simple melodies is not as 'natural' as angry persons'. Judging from the choice behaviour of the two twice-afraid groups, with and without prior listening experience, people apparently need to learn that when one is afraid, simple melodies are psychologically soothing. However, once this knowledge has been acquired, scared people sought the melodies a great deal. Laboratory learning is not necessary for anger; perhaps the real-world ecology and dynamics of anger and fear differ in the extent to which people have the opportunity to learn about the soothing properties of certain kinds of music.

25.4.3 Implications of the $E_{listener} \rightarrow M_{choice}$ model

Although one would have preferred the evidence to come from a greater number of laboratories, it nevertheless seems convincing: The $E_{listener} \rightarrow M_{choice}$ model (9 in Table 25.1) is viable with regard to emotion as defined in PEEM (Fig 25.1), and in terms of choice among music-listening alternatives differing in complexity and some other collative and psychophysical variables. There is little doubt that people experiencing negative emotional states seek simple melodies. The evidence that such melodies are soothing ought to be appealing to researchers interested in the plausibility of the $M \rightarrow E$ model (1 in Table 25.1)—even if it should turn out that music has a stronger direct (proximal) impact on emotions by diminishing negative ones than by inducing positive (*or* negative) ones.

It should be noted that some of the mentioned findings hold for other art forms. For example, with regard to novelty, Konečni and Sargent-Pollock (1977) found that anger and aversively high physiological arousal lead people to shun little-known twentieth century paintings, and obtained additional support for the mediating role of limited processing capacity in the perception and enjoyment of aesthetic stimuli from different modalities (cf. Konečni's aesthetic-episode model, 1994). In fact, analogous findings have been obtained outside the domain of music and other arts. For example, Marlatt, Kosturn, and Lang (1975), using the identical anger-induction laboratory procedure that had been developed by Konečni and Doob (1972; and also used in the Konečni et al 1976 study described earlier), found that angered social drinkers consumed significantly more wine in the laboratory than those who had not been insulted. Alcohol intake and listening to simple melodies can apparently serve the same purpose—amelioration of negative emotion.

Findings that relate music choice by people experiencing certain emotional states to analogous preferences in other art forms and, especially, to non-aesthetic behaviours, hint at the desirability of studying music choice in the stream of daily activity (Konečni, 1979, 1982; North & Hargreaves, 1997). One research direction that implicates the $E_{listener} \rightarrow M_{choice}$ relationship as only the initial stage of complex, but more realistic, scenarios would utilize models 10 and 11 in Table 25.1. In model 10, a person experiencing a particular emotion chooses to listen to a suitable piece of music that gives rise to memories and associations (Juslin & Laukka, 2004, p. 225; Konečni et al, 2008) and these, in turn, lead the listener to replace the initial emotion by a different one; as a consequence, the person then chooses a different piece of music. In terms of PEEM (Fig 25.1), choosing to listen to soothing music when angry makes that event the initial stage of the next passage through the emotion-episode loop—one that is likely to result in a reduction of anger (Konečni, 1975a, 1979, 1982; Konečni et al, 1976) and the selection of different—presumably more complex or strident—music.

In contrast, model 11 formalizes the possibility that an emotion that led a person to choose a given piece of music can be reinstated, with the help of associations, when that same piece of music is heard (by choice or inadvertently) on subsequent occasions. In terms of PEEM, model 11 states that a piece of music, together with the associations to which it gives rise, may serve as the initial event in an emotion episode (cf. model 2 in Table 25.1). Note that the first part of model 11 makes explicit one of the possible sources of associations postulated in model 2. Despite its plausibility, testability and theoretical importance, only considerable literary and anecdotal material supports model 11 at this time.

25.5 MOOD IN THE M-E DOMAIN

Mood is emotion's unglamorous and unclamoring cousin—despite claims that 'mood is now recognized as a central element of human behavior' (Thayer, Newman, & McClain, 1994, p. 910). The latter statement presumably reflects ubiquity rather than impact, for there certainly seems to be a great deal of mood in the world—far more than emotion—and most of it is easily ignored or forgettable. Mood's omnipresence is associated with a great ease of occurrence and instilment in both the real world and the laboratory. There is therefore a myriad of simple laboratory procedures involving mood, many of which—music listening included—can be employed with a minimum of pre-testing and experimenter training. It follows that there is a large literature dealing with mood.

Since a mood does not 'press' like an emotion does, one may or may not be aware of it (authors—Thayer et al, 1994; Zillmann, 2000—differ on the necessity of awareness); but a mood's experiential component is clearly accessible to attention and analysis. Yet moods are so diffuse and subtly diversified that the term seems to have been expanded to cover most of what one can be consciously aware concerning one's inner state.

In the words of Parkinson, Totterdell, Briner, and Reynolds (1996, p. 5), 'mood may be something that is always with us but continually fluctuates over time'. In contemporary society, worldwide, 'mood' can be replaced by 'music' in the quoted sentence. One can see how the attributes of constant presence, diffuseness, subtlety, and diversity would make mood a natural partner for music—in everyday parlance, in social ecology, in lay theories, and in psychological research.

25.5.1 Some criteria for mood

Mood has been carefully distinguished from emotion by numerous authors including Ekman (1994, p. 56), Parkinson et al (1996, pp. 4–8, including Table 1.1, p. 8), Oatley, Keltner, and Jenkins (2006, p. 30), Larsen (2000, pp. 129–30), and Scherer and Zentner (2001, p. 363). Using these terms interchangeably—inadvertently or intentionally—is nevertheless rampant. Only rarely do authors who have engaged in the practice (Tice & Bratslavsky, 2000, p. 149) graciously issue a *mea culpa* (Tice & Wallace, 2000, p. 214).

There is agreement with regard to the dimensions on which moods and emotions can be distinguished. According to Parkinson et al (1996, pp. 4–8), these include (the mood pole in parentheses): duration (long), time pattern (gradual onset, continuous), intensity (low), and the specificity of cause (no particular event), and object (unspeci-fied). No wonder William James wasn't interested.

A key distinction—the extent of the physiological response—can be classified under the intensity dimension. As just one example, when participants' moods were instilled by film clips in the study by Cantor and Zillmann (1973, p. 101), the maximum systolic blood-pressure increase was 4.5 mm Hg; in contrast, the anger-induction procedure used by Konečni and Doob (1972) resulted in five times greater increases in pre-testing.

The difference between mood and emotion is perhaps the most striking when one considers the kind and number of laboratory procedures by which moods have been induced. One of them is Velten's (1968): participants read statements and are asked to experience the corresponding mood. Improbably, this technique is effective (cf. Parkinson et al, 1996, p. 51). In fact, in one study (Slyker & McNally, 1991), a simple instruction to 'get into a mood' (p. 37) was as effective as instruction + Velten, instruc-tion + music (Schönberg, Prokofiev), and instruction + Velten + music in inducing 'anxious' and 'depressed' moods.

25.5.2 Mood regulation

The central theme of mood research is the regulation of one's mood (e.g. Isen, 1984; Larsen, 2000; Zillmann, 1988, 2000), with most of the work devoted to the amelioration of bad mood. Thayer et al (1994) identified 32 categories of methods of repairing a bad mood; in the six-factor solution, music found its place alongside 'engage in hobby' and 'humour' in Factor 2, 'seeking pleasurable activities and distraction' (Table 2, p. 916). Parkinson et al (1996) similarly mentioned over a hundred strategies of mood mainte-nance and repair, among which was music.

With regard to theory, the initial work in mood regulation was limited to an excep-tionally simple version of hedonism, sharing it with pop psychology and the self-help industry.[4] Parrott's (1993) discussion of motives to inhibit good moods (cf. Knobloch, 2003), and the demonstration, by Erber, Wegner, and Therriault (1996), that people may adjust their moods downwards or upwards for the purpose of optimal self-presentation, have not been a serious threat. The 'hedonists' (e.g. Larsen, 2000; Oliver, 2003; Zillmann, 2000) somewhat belatedly invoked 'delay of gratification' and claimed that mood could be an instrument, rather than the end result: people prefer good total outcomes to good moods (cf. Martin & Davies, 1998). For example, purposefully main-taining a bad mood might help one offer condolences with more decorum. A pinch of hypocrisy is thus added to simple hedonism.

---

[4] Although the terms 'mood regulation' and 'emotion regulation' are often used interchangeably, there have been serious attempts, such as that by Gross (1998, p. 276), to distinguish between the two; moreover, Gross's (1998, Figure 4, p. 282) 'process model of emotion regulation' has some useful points of contact with PEEM (Figure 25.1 and Konečni, 1979, 1984, 2008). Another article on emotion regulation that is relevant for mood-regulation issues is that by Cole, Martin, and Dennis (2004)—especially in terms of these authors' cogent conceptual criticisms and sound methodological advice.

25.6 EFFECTS OF MOOD ON MUSIC CHOICE: THE RESEARCH EVIDENCE

25.6.1 Inclusion criteria

The literature on music preference is numerically dominated by studies (almost exclusively on adolescents or students) that report correlations between personality tests (e.g. extraversion, the five-factor model, sensation seeking; see Chapter 24, this volume) and music preference or music taste (reported retrospectively by paper and pencil). In many other studies, the correlations are between music preference (usually overall, but sometimes for a genre, or a theme, such as 'lost love', or an attribute, such as tempo or dynamics) and some verbal measure, retrospectively given, of an issue of interest to adolescents—drug use, loneliness, attitudes toward women and violence, being alone in their bedroom, suicide risk, 'romantic deprivation', recklessness. There have also been studies, starting in the 1950s and still going strong, that report correlations between music preference and popularity among peers, and generally discuss the role of music preference in young people's self-identity, clique membership, perception of others, and communication strategy. In many studies, music preference is related to some aspect of marketing or to shopping preferences (see Chapter 32, this volume). Since current mood plays no role in all these groups of music-preference studies—or at most a peripheral, causally remote, poorly measured one—they will not be discussed further.

Pager-style ('experience-sampling') studies dealing with mood and music listening are also outside the scope of the present chapter (see Chapter 18, this volume). Such studies are preferable to most mood-and-music paper-and-pencil work because they often yield useful information about the social ecology of music listening, but they cannot provide any information on the causal flow among the variables. Mood is obviously not experimentally manipulated. And it is pointless to discuss distinctions in the effects of mood, emotion, or attitude on the basis of such studies, because participants use their respective implicit 'theories' of what these terms mean. In only one study (Thompson & Larson, 1995, p. 735) was the focus exclusively on music listening as the primary activity.

A study by Saarikallio and Erkkilä (2007) attempted to develop a 'grounded theory' of mood regulation by music—relying exclusively on data collected in two 1.5-hour group interviews with eight adolescents (with follow-up forms). Such an approach shares many of the structural problems of the pager studies and has additional weaknesses. On balance, the richness of the collected anecdotal material seems more than offset by the drawbacks of the approach.

25.6.2 Data

In an important laboratory study that examined music preference as a function of induced moods, Cantor and Zillmann (1973) showed, in a 2 X 2 between-subjects design, pleasant vs. unpleasant X exciting vs. not exciting film clips to participants who then rated three songs (that were equally liked in pre-testing) in succession. In line with predictions that took the passage of time into account, hedonic contrast was obtained for the first song, excitation transfer for the second, and no effect of mood on preference for the third. The study showed how malleable, by mood, the liking for a short piece of music can be: preference apparently reflects the different rates of decay of components of mood. Note that the hedonic-contrast finding for the first song matches, for unpleasant mood, the result obtained by Konečni et al (1976) for negative emotion.

It is essential to distinguish between stable long-term preference for a genre and music attributes such as 'intense and rebellious' (Rentfrow & Gosling, 2003), on one hand, and people's choice among music alternatives in the presence of a mood, on the other. In what was perhaps the first laboratory experiment on what they called 'mood optimization', Breckler, Allen, and Konečni (1985) used a forced-choice paradigm in which participants listened to two minutes each of baroque music (mean ratings in pilot studies: complex, soothing), twentieth-century avant-garde music (complex, non-soothing), soft rock (simple, soothing), hard rock (simple, non-soothing), and a 350-Hz squarewave stimulus at 95 dB-A (rated aversive), for a ten-minutes total exposure. Participants made a choice every 15 s, were in complete control of the sequencing and chunking, and kept a tally of their choices; their individual pre-experiment liking for the four genres was known. Of main interest was the participants' strategy of self-exposure to the five alternatives, especially how they dealt with and offset the aversive stimulation.

The majority of participants chose the same mood-optimizing strategy: they listened to all of the aversive stimulation early in the session ('spinach first'), but did so in short runs interspersed with short runs of their 2nd, 3rd, and 4th most-liked music. It was, however, the 2nd most-liked soothing music that most frequently followed the aversive stimulus *immediately*. Sessions were typically ended by long runs of the best-liked music ('ice cream'), which for most participants was soft rock.[5]

In this impressively complex and fine-tuned strategy (which strongly implies non-automaticity of mood optimization), participants kept their most preferred music for the final listening pleasure, away from aversion, even though for most of them that final music was soothing *and* simple; they sacrificed the somewhat less-liked soothing *or* simple music to offset the negative impact directly. With familiar music—common in everyday life but absent in the Cantor and Zillmann (1973) study—there is clearly a constraint on the malleability of music preference by transient moods.

Experiments by North and Hargreaves (2000) supply another example of people's fine-tuned strategy of music choice. By varying tempo and loudness, two choice alternatives were created from the same music piece. *While* participants rode an exercise

---

[5] Analogous results were reported by Breckler et al (1985, Experiment 2) for visual stimuli. In a somewhat similar vein, Forgas and Ciarrochi (2002) found that people alternated their exposure between mood-congruent and mood-incongruent stimuli in order to maintain mood within reasonable limits.

bicycle or relaxed, they matched the 'energy' of the activity that was requested of them and chose predominantly 'high-arousal' music in the exercise group and 'low-arousal' in the relaxation condition. However, when (different) participants made selections immediately *after* exercise or relaxation, mood optimization replaced energy matching, so that people who had exercised chose 'low-arousal' music 71 per cent of the time (see also Chapter 19, this volume).

Analogous results were obtained by Lai (2004) with forced music exposure. Participants (elderly Taiwanese), who were apparently anxious prior to the period of relaxation that was coupled with listening to music, rated the music that was associated with the onset of recovery as the best. In addition, Dibben (2004), having exposed participants to four 40-second Haydn and Mozart excerpts, found that they gave higher ratings to their ensuing state if they had exercised prior to the music than relaxed; her results supported the cognitive labelling and excitation transfer models in the domain of mood.

Perhaps the most straightforward finding was obtained by Knobloch and Zillmann (2002). They placed participants in a bad, neutral, or good mood by false performance feedback, and then let them choose to what to listen over the next ten minutes; the options—which could be sampled ad libitum—were high vs. low 'energetic + joyful' (EJ) Top 30 songs. Mean exposure to high EJ music by people in bad, neutral, and good mood, respectively, was: 5.25, 4.82, and 3.78 minutes.

People in a bad mood, all else equal, will try to improve it (cf. Larsen, 2000)—including by music with commonsensical 'up' attributes of tempo and lyrics. People in a good mood can presumably afford to experiment—including with 'sad' music.

25.6.3 Mood and music: concluding remarks

There are constraints and subtleties in how mood influences music choice, but such findings should not obscure what is undoubtedly a central fact: good-mood maintenance is less important than bad-mood repair (cf. Tice & Wallace, 2000, p. 215). Whether one should therefore speak of a 'science of mood regulation' (Larsen, 2000, p. 129) is debatable. Knobloch and Mundorf (2003, p. 504) see it this way: 'A cynical speculation of future developments is the vision of a next generation of interfaces that will probably decode the user's mood and the corresponding music need from information such as heart rate, body heat, and pupil width.'

Measurable perturbation of the mentioned indices is not characteristic of mood—but there is no doubt that moods can be regulated, managed, adjusted, and optimized by music exposure and choice. Strategies may vary in complexity and the degree to which they are deliberate, habit-driven, or unconscious.

The deliberate choice of 'sad' music by listeners in neutral or sad moods has here been referred to only indirectly, in part because scarcely any solid data exist. It is ultimately an issue for (psychological) aesthetics that should include other art and entertainment forms, and more elaborate mood-optimization models (cf. Knobloch-Westerwick, 2006).

25.7 AFFECT AND MUSIC CHOICE: IMPLICATIONS

A chapter this author wrote 25 years ago (Konečni, 1982) emphasized the importance of studying emotional and cognitive factors in the social ecology of 'listening to music [given that listening] has become fully imbedded in the stream of daily life' (p. 500). The critique contained a call for music psychology to investigate ordinary people's interactions with music in the real world (pp. 497–502). It is gratifying to see that the recent experience-sampling studies, despite their shortcomings, have been successfully grappling with the social ecology of music, and that Chapter 18 in this volume is entitled 'Music in everyday life'.

However, in the domain of the present chapter, a recent consequence of going 'into the world' has been a paucity of ambitious laboratory studies. Large-scale studies are needed of the effects of socially induced affect on self-directed exposure to authentic music—categorized, on theoretical grounds, by structural and genre attributes. Also sorely lacking are carefully controlled experimental investigations of the *comparative* and *combined* effects of emotions and moods on the choice of music. As just one example, it is of great interest to study the combined effects of socially induced emotion and non-socially and semi-socially induced mood (by caffeine, alcohol, different types of exercise, news, Internet use, humour, music with and without lyrics). Because mood-driven exposure to music is a frequent (natural?) accompaniment to consumption, information, and physical and entertainment activities, studying their combined effects should be a profitable research endeavour.

Ekman (1994, pp. 56–7), Parkinson et al (1996, p. 9), Larsen (2000, p. 130), and Siemer (2005, p. 817) have discussed the connections between emotions and moods. Theoretically, of particular interest are similarly named states and situations in which, for example, a 'down' mood may be experimentally shown to lower the threshold for the full-blown emotion of sadness to develop when additional stimuli are presented.[6] However, when the down mood and sadness are separated by days, is amelioration more urgently sought in the case of emotion than mood? Is the 'arousal' aspect of a musical stimulus relatively more important for the optimization of mood and positive emotion, and its 'valence' more important in negative emotional experience? In addition to its intrinsic interest, people's choice among carefully constructed music alternatives may be the ideal vehicle by which to tease apart the subtle similarities and differences among affective processes.

---

[6] The idea that a mood may lower the threshold for the occurrence of a same-named emotion (cf. Konečni, 1975a, 1975b) should be distinguished from Ekman's view that 'it is as if the person is seeking an opportunity to indulge the emotion relevant to the mood' (1994, p. 57). The latter seems to go too far toward treating moods as causes of an active search for emotion-arousing stimuli. Note that in a study that appears to bear directly on these issues (Siemer, 2001), research participants who had been placed in qualitatively different moods later, unfortunately, only judged brief hypothetical 'emotional scenarios', rather than experienced any actual emotion.

Recommended further reading

1. North, A. C., & Hargreaves, D. J. (2008). *The social and applied psychology of music*. Oxford: Oxford University Press.
2. Konečni, V. J. (2008). Does music induce emotion? A theoretical and methodological analysis. *Psychology of Aesthetics, Creativity, and the Arts, 2*, 115–29.

References

Barrett, L. F. (2006). Are emotions natural kinds? *Perspectives on Psychological Science, 1*, 28–58.

Bartlett, D. L. (1996). Physiological responses to music and sound stimuli. In D. A. Hodges (ed.), *Handbook of music psychology* (2nd edn, pp. 343–85). San Antonio, TX: IMR Press.

Berlyne, D. E. (1960). *Conflict, arousal, and curiosity*. New York: McGraw-Hill.

Berlyne, D. E. (1971). *Aesthetics and psychobiology*. New York: Appleton-Century-Crofts.

Bernardi, L., Porta, C., & Sleight, P. (2006). Cardiovascular, cerebrovascular, and respiratory changes induced by different types of music in musicians and non-musicians: the importance of silence. *Heart, 92*, 445–52.

Breckler, S. J., Allen, R. B., & Konečni, V. J. (1985). Mood-optimizing strategies in aesthetic-choice behavior. *Music Perception, 2*, 459–70.

Broadbent, D. E. (1971). *Decision and stress*. London: Academic Press.

Buck, R. (1999). The biological affects: A typology. *Psychological Review, 106*, 301–36.

Cantor, J. P., & Zillmann, D. (1973). The effect of affective state and emotional arousal on music appreciation. *Journal of General Psychology, 89*, 97–108.

Caspy, T., Peleg, E., Schlam, D., & Goldberg, J. (1988). Sedative and stimulative music effects: Differential effects on performance impairment following frustration. *Motivation and Emotion, 12*, 123–38.

Chafin, S., Roy, M., Gerin, W., & Christenfeld, N. (2004). Music can facilitate blood pressure recovery from stress. *British Journal of Health Psychology, 9*, 393–403.

Coan, J. A., & Allen, J. B. (eds). (2007). *Handbook of emotion elicitation and assessment*. Oxford: Oxford University Press.

Cole, P. M., Martin, S. E., & Dennis, T. A. (2004). Emotion regulation as a scientific construct: Methodological challenges and directions for child development research. *Child Development, 75*, 317–33.

Dibben, N. (2004). The role of peripheral feedback in emotional experience with music. *Music Perception, 22*, 79–115.

Easterbrook, J. A. (1959). The effect of emotion on cue utilization and the organization of behavior. *Psychological Review, 66*, 183–201.

Ekman, P. (1973). Cross-cultural studies of facial expression. In P. Ekman (ed.), *Darwin and facial expression: A century of research in review* (pp. 169–222). New York: Academic Press.

Ekman, P. (1994). Moods, emotions, and traits. In P. Ekman & R. J. Davidson (eds), *The nature of emotion: Fundamental questions* (pp. 56–8). Oxford: Oxford University Press.

Ekman, P., Levenson, R. W., & Friesen, W. V. (1983). Autonomic nervous system activity distinguishes among emotions. *Science, 221*, 1208–10.

Erber, R., Wegner, D. M., & Therriault, N. (1996). On being cool and collected: Mood regulation in anticipation of social interaction. *Journal of Personality and Social Psychology, 70*, 757–66.

Flath-Becker, S. (1987). *Musikpräferenzen in Situationen psychischer Anspannung*. Frankfurt am Main, Germany: Lang.

Flath-Becker, S., & Konečni, V. J. (1984). Der Einfluss von Stress auf die Vorlieben für Musik. *Musikpsychologie, 1*, 23–52.

Forgas, J. P., & Ciarrochi, J. V. (2002). On managing moods: Evidence for the role of homeostatic cognitive strategies in affect regulation. *Personality and Social Psychology Bulletin, 28*, 336–45.

Friedman, M., & Rosenman, R. H. (1974). *Type A behavior and your heart*. New York: Knopf.

Frijda, N. H. (1988). The laws of emotion. *American Psychologist, 43*, 349–58.

Frijda, N. H. (2005). Emotion experience. *Cognition & Emotion, 19*, 473–97.

Gabrielsson, A. (2002). Perceived emotion and felt emotion: Same or different? *Musicae Scientiae, Special Issue 2001–2*, 123–47.

Gabrielsson, A., & Lindström, E. (2001). The influence of musical structure on emotional expression. In P. N. Juslin & J. A. Sloboda (eds), *Music and emotion: Theory and research* (pp. 223–48). Oxford: Oxford University Press.

Gaver, W. W., & Mandler, G. (1987). Play it again, Sam: On liking music. *Cognition & Emotion, 1*, 259–82.

Gross, J. J. (1998). The emerging field of emotion regulation: An integrative review. *Review of General Psychology, 2*, 271–99.

Hokanson, J. E., & Shetler, S. (1961). The effect of overt aggression on physiological arousal level. *Journal of Abnormal and Social Psychology, 63*, 446–8.

Isen, A. M. (1984). Toward understanding the role of affect in cognition. In R. S. Wyer & T. K. Srull (eds), *Handbook of social cognition* (Vol. 3, pp. 179–236). Hillsdale, NJ: Erlbaum.

Jenkins, C. D., Rosenman, R. H., & Zyzanski, S. J. (1974). Prediction of clinical coronary heart disease by a test for coronary-prone behavior pattern. *New England Journal of Medicine, 290*, 1271–5.

Juslin, P. N. (2000). Cue utilization in communication of emotion in music performance: Relating performance to perception. *Journal of Experimental Psychology: Human Perception and Performance, 26*, 1797–1813.

Juslin, P. N., & Laukka, P. (2004). Expression, perception, and induction of musical emotions: A review and a questionnaire study of everyday listening. *Journal of New Music Research, 33*, 217–38.

Juslin, P. N., & Sloboda, J. A. (eds). (2001). *Music and emotion: Theory and research*. Oxford: Oxford University Press.

Kahneman, D. (1973). *Attention and effort*. Englewood Cliffs, NJ: Prentice Hall.

Knobloch, S. (2003). Mood adjustment via mass communication. *Journal of Communication, 53*, 233–50.

Knobloch-Westerwick, S. (2006). Mood management theory, evidence, and advancements. In J. Bryant & P. Vorderer (eds), *Psychology of entertainment* (pp. 239–54). Mahwah, NJ: Erlbaum.

Knobloch, S., & Mundorf, N. (2003). Communication and emotion in the context of music and music television. In J. Bryant, D. Roskos-Ewoldsen, & J. Cantor (eds), *Communication and emotion: Essays in honor of Dolf Zillmann* (pp. 491–510). Mahwah, NJ: Erlbaum.

Knobloch, S., & Zillmann, D. (2002). Mood management via the digital jukebox. *Journal of Communication, 52*, 351–66.

Koelsch, S., Fritz, T., von Cramon, Y., Müller, K., & Friederici, A. D. (2006). Investigating emotion with music: An fMRI study. *Human Brain Mapping, 27*, 239–50.

Konečni, V. J. (1975a). Annoyance, type and duration of postannoyance activity, and aggression: The 'cathartic effect'. *Journal of Experimental Psychology: General, 104*, 76–102.

Konečni, V. J. (1975b). The mediation of aggressive behavior: Arousal level versus anger and cognitive labeling. *Journal of Personality and Social Psychology*, 32, 706–12.

Konečni, V. J. (1979). Determinants of aesthetic preference and effects of exposure to aesthetic stimuli: Social, emotional, and cognitive factors. In B. A. Maher (ed.), *Progress in experimental personality research* (Vol. 9, pp. 149–97). New York: Academic Press.

Konečni, V. J. (1982). Social interaction and musical preference. In D. Deutsch (ed.), *The psychology of music* (pp. 497–516). New York: Academic Press.

Konečni, V. J. (1984). Methodological issues in human aggression research. In R. M. Kaplan, V. J. Konečni, & R. W. Novaco (eds), *Aggression in children and youth* (pp. 1–43). The Hague, The Netherlands: Martinus Nijhoff.

Konečni, V. J. (1991). Psychological aspects of the expression of anger and violence on the stage. *Comparative Drama*, 25, 215–41.

Konečni, V. J. (1994). Interactive effects of music and visual art. In I. Deliège (ed.), *Proceedings of the 3rd International Conference for Music Perception and Cognition* (pp. 23–6). Liège, Belgium: ICMPC.

Konečni, V. J. (2003). Review of the book *Music and emotion: Theory and research*, P. N. Juslin & J. A. Sloboda (eds), 2001. *Music Perception*, 20, 332–41.

Konečni, V. J. (2005). The aesthetic trinity: Awe, being moved, thrills. *Bulletin of Psychology and the Arts*, 5, 27–44.

Konečni, V. J. (2008). Does music induce emotion? A theoretical and methodological analysis. *Psychology of Aesthetics, Creativity, and the Arts*, 2, 115–29.

Konečni, V. J., Brown, A., & Wanic, R. A. (2008). Comparative effects of music and recalled life-events on emotional state. *Psychology of Music*, 36, 289–308.

Konečni, V. J., Crozier, J. B., & Doob, A. N. (1976). Anger and expression of aggression: Effects on aesthetic preference. *Scientific Aesthetics*, 1, 47–55.

Konečni, V. J., & Doob, A. N. (1972). Catharsis through displacement of aggression. *Journal of Personality and Social Psychology*, 23, 379–87.

Konečni, V. J., & Gotlieb, H. (1987). Type A/Type B personality syndrome, attention, and music processing. In R. Spintge & R. Droh (eds), *Music in Medicine/Musik in der Medizin* (pp. 169–75). Berlin, Germany: Springer.

Konečni, V. J., & Sargent-Pollock, D. (1976). Choice between melodies differing in complexity under divided-attention conditions. *Journal of Experimental Psychology: Human Perception and Performance*, 2, 347–56.

Konečni, V. J., & Sargent-Pollock, D. (1977). Arousal, positive and negative affect, and preference for Renaissance and 20th-century paintings. *Motivation and Emotion*, 1, 75–94.

Konečni, V. J., Wanic, R. A., & Brown. A. (2007). Emotional and aesthetic antecedents and consequences of music-induced thrills. *American Journal of Psychology*, 120, 619–43.

Konijn, E. A. (2000). *Acting emotions*. Amsterdam, The Netherlands: Amsterdam University Press.

Krumhansl, C. L. (2002). Music: A link between cognition and emotion. *Current Directions in Psychological Science*, 11, 45–50.

Krumhansl, C. L., & Schenck, D. L. (1997). Can dance reflect the structural and expressive qualities of music? A perceptual experiment on Balanchine's choreography of Mozart's *Divertimento* No. 15. *Musicae Scientiae*, 1, 63–85.

Lai, H.-L. (2004). Music preference and relaxation in Taiwanese elderly people. *Geriatric Nursing*, 25, 286–91.

Lanzetta, J. T., Cartwright-Smith, J., & Kleck, R. E. (1976). Effects of nonverbal dissimulation on emotional experience and autonomic arousal. *Journal of Personality and Social Psychology*, 33, 354–70.

Larsen, R. J. (2000). Toward a science of mood regulation. *Psychological Inquiry*, 11, 129–41.

Lazarus, R. S. (1991). *Emotion and adaptation.* Oxford: Oxford University Press.

Marlatt, G. A., Kosturn, C. F., & Lang, A. B. (1975). Provocation to anger and opportunity for retaliation as determinants of alcohol consumption in social drinkers. *Journal of Abnormal Psychology, 84,* 652–9.

Martin, L. L., & Davies, B. (1998). Beyond hedonism and associationism: A configural view of the role of affect in evaluation, processing, and self-regulation. *Motivation and Emotion, 22,* 33–51.

Matthews, K. A., & Brunson, B. (1979). Allocation of attention and the Type A coronary-prone behavior pattern. *Journal of Personality and Social Psychology, 37,* 2081–90.

Miller, G. (2000). Evolution of human music through sexual selection. In N. L. Wallin, B. Merker, & S. Brown (eds), *The origins of music* (pp. 329–59). Cambridge, MA: MIT Press.

Niketta, R. (1990). Zum Einfluss kognitiver Belastung auf die Beurteilung von Musikstücken unterschiedlicher Komplexität. [The influence of cognitive load on the evaluation of music pieces of different complexity.] *Zeitschrift für experimentelle und angewandte Psychologie, 37,* 266–80.

North, A. C., & Hargreaves, D. J. (1997). Experimental aesthetics and everyday music listening. In D. J. Hargreaves & A. C. North (eds), *The social psychology of music* (pp. 84–103). Oxford: Oxford University Press.

North, A. C., & Hargreaves, D. J. (1999). Music and driving game performance. *Scandinavian Journal of Psychology, 40,* 285–92.

North, A. C., & Hargreaves, D. J. (2000). Musical preferences during and after relaxation and exercise. *American Journal of Psychology, 113,* 43–67.

Oatley, K., & Duncan, E. (1994). The experience of emotions in everyday life. *Cognition & Emotion, 8,* 369–81.

Oatley, K., Keltner, D., & Jenkins, J. M. (2006). *Understanding emotions* (2nd edn). Malden, MA: Blackwell.

Oliver, M. B. (2003). Mood management and selective exposure. In J. Bryant, D. Roskos-Ewoldsen, & J. Cantor (eds), *Communication and emotion: Essays in honor of Dolf Zillmann* (pp. 85–106). Mahwah, NJ: Erlbaum.

Ortony, A., & Turner, T. J. (1990). What's basic about basic emotions? *Psychological Review, 97,* 315–31.

Parkinson, B., Totterdell, P., Briner, R. B., & Reynolds, S. (1996). *Changing moods: The psychology of mood and mood regulation.* London: Longman.

Parrott, W. G. (1993). Beyond hedonism: Motives for inhibiting good moods and for maintaining bad mood. In D. M. Wegner & J. W. Pennebaker (eds), *Handbook of mental control* (pp. 278–305). Englewood Cliffs, NJ: Prentice Hall.

Persson, R. S. (2001). The subjective world of the performer. In P. N. Juslin & J. A. Sloboda (eds), *Music and emotion: Theory and research* (pp. 275–90). Oxford: Oxford University Press.

Posner, M. I. (1975). Psychobiology of attention. In M. S. Gazzaniga & C. Blakemore (eds), *Handbook of psychobiology* (pp. 441–80). New York: Academic Press.

Rentfrow, P. J., & Gosling, S. D. (2003). The do re mi's of everyday life: The structure and personality correlates of music preference. *Journal of Personality and Social Psychology, 84,* 1236–56.

Rickard, N. S., Toukhsati, S. R., & Field, S. E. (2005). The effect of music on cognitive performance: Insight from neurobiological and animal studies. *Behavioral and Cognitive Neuroscience Reviews, 4,* 235–61.

Saarikallio, S., & Erkkilä, J. (2007). The role of music in adolescents' mood regulation. *Psychology of Music, 35,* 88–109.

Schachter, S., & Singer, J. E. (1962). Cognitive, social, and physiological determinants of emotional state. *Psychological Review, 69,* 379–99.

Scherer, K. R. (2000). Emotions as episode of subsystem synchronization driven by nonlinear appraisal processes. In M. D. Lewis & I. Granic (eds), *Emotion, development, and self-organization: Dynamic systems approaches to emotional development* (pp. 70–99). Cambridge, UK: Cambridge University Press.

Scherer, K. R., & Zentner, M. R. (2001). Emotional effects of music: production rules. In P. N. Juslin & J. A. Sloboda (eds), *Music and emotion: Theory and research* (pp. 361–92). Oxford: Oxford University Press.

Siemer, M. (2001). Mood-specific effects on appraisal and emotion judgements. *Cognition & Emotion, 15,* 453–85.

Siemer, M. (2005). Moods as multiple-object directed and as objectless affective states: An examination of the dispositional theory of moods. *Cognition & Emotion, 19,* 815–45.

Simonton, D. K. (2001). Emotion and composition in classical music: historiometric perspectives. In P. N. Juslin & J. A. Sloboda (eds), *Music and emotion: Theory and research* (pp. 205–22). Oxford: Oxford University Press.

Sloboda, J. A., & O'Neill, S. A. (2001). Emotions in everyday listening to music. In P. N. Juslin & J. A. Sloboda (eds), *Music and emotion: Theory and research* (pp. 415–30). Oxford: Oxford University Press.

Slyker, J. P., & McNally, R. J. (1991). Experimental induction of anxious and depressed moods: Are Velten and musical procedures necessary? *Cognitive Therapy and Research, 15,* 33–45.

Sokolov, E. N. (1963). *Perception and the conditioned reflex.* New York: Macmillan.

Stanislavski, K. (1936). *An actor prepares* (trans. E. Reynolds Hapgood). New York: Theatre Arts Books.

Stanislavski, K., & Rumyantsev, P. (1975). *Stanislavski on opera.* New York: Theatre Arts Books.

Stemmler, G., Heldmann, M., Pauls, C. A., & Scherer, T. (2001). Constraints for emotion specificity in fear and anger: The context counts. *Psychophysiology, 38,* 275–91.

Steptoe, A. (2001). Negative emotions in music making: the problem of performance anxiety. In P. N. Juslin & J. A. Sloboda (eds), *Music and emotion: Theory and research* (pp. 291–308). Oxford: Oxford University Press.

Stravinsky, I. (1936/1998). *An autobiography.* New York: W. W. Norton.

Strube, M. J., Turner, C. W., Patrick, S., & Perrillo, R. (1983). Type A and Type B attentional responses to aesthetic stimuli: Effects on mood and performance. *Journal of Personality and Social Psychology, 45,* 1369–79.

Thayer, R. E., Newman, J. R., & McClain, T. M. (1994). Self-regulation of mood: Strategies for changing a bad mood, raising energy, and reducing tension. *Journal of Personality and Social Psychology, 67,* 910–25.

Thompson, R. L., & Larson, R. (1995). Social context and the subjective experience of different types of rock music. *Journal of Youth and Adolescence, 24,* 731–44.

Tice, D. M., & Bratslavsky, E. (2000). Giving in to feel good: The place of emotion regulation in the context of general self-control. *Psychological Inquiry, 11,* 149–59.

Tice, D. M., & Wallace, H. (2000). Mood and emotion control: Some thoughts on the state of the field. *Psychological Inquiry, 11,* 214–17.

Velten, E. (1968). A laboratory task for induction of mood states. *Behavior Research and Therapy, 6,* 473–82.

Wells, A. (1990). Popular music: Emotional use and management. *Journal of Popular Culture, 24,* 105–17.

Zillmann, D. (1978). Attribution and misattribution of excitatory reactions. In J. H. Harvey, W. J. Ickes, & R. F. Kidd (eds), *New directions in attribution research* (Vol. 2, pp. 335–68). Hillsdale, NJ: Erlbaum.

Zillmann, D. (1988). Mood management: Using entertainment to full advantage. In L. Donohew, H. E. Sypher, & E. T. Higgins (eds), *Communication, social cognition, and affect* (pp. 147–71). Hillsdale, NJ: Erlbaum.

Zillmann, D. (2000). Mood management in the context of selective exposure theory. In M. E. Roloff (ed.), *Communication yearbook 23* (pp. 103–23). Thousand Oaks, CA: Sage.

CHAPTER 26

POLITICS, MEDIATION, SOCIAL CONTEXT, AND PUBLIC USE

REEBEE GAROFALO

As this volume indicates, there has been a renewed interest in, as well as broad disagreement over, how music produces its emotional effects. Because the academic community is organized into a number of discrete disciplines, whose boundaries were initially defined centuries ago, each of these disciplinary strongholds has contributed its own unique perspective to this topic—most often one with a particular theoretical and/or methodological approach and, until recently, one that encouraged relatively little dialogue with other disciplines. As a result, the available data on music and emotion can be characterized as a kind of 'nature-nurture' continuum of findings with the so-called hard sciences at one end and the social sciences and humanities at the other.

Collaboration and synthesis across disciplinary lines, as is evident in this volume, is highly sought after, somewhat elusive, and still in its early stages. In the scientific community, for example, Peretz (2001) reports broad acceptance of Ekman's research that the facial expression of most basic emotions (happiness, sadness, anger, and fear) is universal, innate, and hard-wired (Ekman et al, 1987; cited in Peretz, 2001, p. 107). As regards musical emotions, however, conclusions quickly become more complicated and controversial, and there is not a hint of consensus as one moves across the continuum. Anthropologists, for instance, are likely to argue that 'emotional responses to music do not occur spontaneously, nor "naturally", but rather, take place within complex systems of thought and behaviour concerning what music means, what it is for, how it is to be perceived, and what might be appropriate kinds of expressive responses'

(Becker, 2001, p. 137). For anthropologists, the emotional response is culturally specific and socially constructed. It is evident, then, that the politics of how we conceptualize and theorize the connection between music and emotion begin with the very organization of knowledge. The resultant perspectives, as we shall see, selectively incorporate the received wisdom of the ages and extend to the ways in which music is used.

As to my own orientation, I would locate myself within the burgeoning and interdisciplinary field of popular music studies, which borrows variously from a number of fields such as sociology, political economics, communication, musicology, ethnomusicology, and cultural studies. Where cultural studies tends to limit itself to models of use and consumption, I gravitate toward an approach, borrowing from sociology, political economics, and communication, that includes a consideration of production and transmission, as well as reception and use. As I have written elsewhere, 'while the culturalists are to be credited with elevating culture to a position of greater significance on the political agenda, they can also be criticized for privileging the act of consumption in such a way as to ignore not only the political intentions of artists and cultural workers, but also the political economy of production and, in particular, the influential role of the culture industry itself' (Garofalo, 1992, p. 19).

In this essay, then, I intend to draw on an unorthodox and interdisciplinary range of sources, both scholarly and popular, to investigate the politics of music and emotion as they are affected by mediation, social context, and public use. My purpose is to broaden the scope of research that may be too narrowly focused, and suggest some avenues for further study. To this end, I examine the use of music in public contexts that seem particularly relevant to the current period—the construction of national identity, resistance to state power, political causes that espouse impulses as disparate as charity and hate, and various instances of social manipulation and control. The examples in this essay, which take the reader from the early twentieth century to the current period, have been chosen, not as an exhaustive list of possibilities, but rather as an instructive sample of intense emotional engagement with mass-mediated musics and/or large-scale social uses. To provide historical background, I begin by analysing some of the assumptions, definitions, and theories that have shaped our beliefs and practices regarding the affective power of music through the ages. This is the foundation upon which the politics of music and emotion rest.

26.1 ASSUMPTIONS, THEORIES, AND DEFINITIONS

26.1.1 The contradictory powers of music

No matter where one comes out on the specific mechanisms governing emotional responses to music, the one thing on which all observers seem to agree is that music is an incredibly powerful (emotional) force—and within Western modes of thought, such beliefs extend at least back to the ancient Greeks. But our understandings of the specificities of that power are often shaped by the assumptions we make about music, listeners, and the role of culture in society. Plato, of course, felt that music was powerful enough to undermine the state. He argued that 'any musical innovation is full of danger to the whole state, and ought to be prohibited . . . when modes of music change, the fundamental laws of the state always change with them' (cited in Portnoy, 1949, p. 240).

Plato's allegiance to continuity of musical practices was bound up with his particular view of the state as educator, protector, and moral guardian. He held music above the other arts in its ability to affect human emotions and the inner soul, and for this reason, believed that music had the power to educate and elevate the human spirit as well as to encourage the more debased aspects of human nature. Accordingly, he recommended the outright banishment of the newer and more innovative Ionian and Lydian modes, in favour of the traditional Dorian and Phrygian modes that he felt were more suitable to moral development and military training. While Plato certainly contemplated individual responses to music, his central concern was its effect on the collectivity. The fact that his ideas about music were not taken all that seriously in ancient Greece is less important than the fact that they provided the basis for subsequent beliefs about the power of music in Western culture.

Perhaps more importantly, Plato's ideas about music were also echoed in Eastern philosophy and throughout Christian, Jewish, and Muslim religious thought. Confucius noted music's power to 'bring about unity in the people's hearts and carry out the principles of political order', but he condemned 'sensual music' with the power to 'undermine people's character' (ibid, pp. 236–7). The Hebrew prophets told their followers 'that profane songs of love and lust are of sufficient cause to destroy the world and that Israel's religious songs can save it' (Idelsohn, 1929, p. 92). Although the Quran itself is silent on music and music making, comparable sentiments have been expressed in the Muslim world at least since the ninth century. Drawing a sharp distinction between 'art' music and various forms of religious music, musicologist Amnon Shiloah summarizes the Islamic ambivalence toward music: '[W]hen music is considered a spell inspired by the devil, it calls into question the basic concept of a transcendental divinity with absolute rule over the world and the deeds of men' (cited in Korpe et al, 2006, p. 249).

One can trace similar lines of reasoning across centuries of Christian religious thought from St Augustine to Luther to Calvin. Even the Quakers, in the formative stages of their development, expressed their opposition to music, as to all the arts, as a vain indulgence in the temptations of the secular world (Korpe et al, 2006, pp. 242–5). A number of contemporary Christian denominations have implicated popular musics from rock and heavy metal to R&B and rap, in everything from Satanism, to violence and delinquency, drug and alcohol abuse, and lewd and lascivious behaviour (Garofalo, 1994; Gray, 1993), even while others have embraced variations of these same musics to entice young people back to the church. Down through the centuries, then, people the world over have lived with and acted upon strong beliefs in music's power to redeem the human spirit and equally strong fears of its ability to arouse dangerous emotions and undermine rational behaviour.

26.1.2 Theoretical development

Though written from very different vantage points, most of the religious and philosophical tendencies cited above share a number of assumptions about music and the nature of listeners: namely, that music's power resides in the objective structures of the work itself; that listeners are passive receptacles ill equipped to resist this power; and that music is capable of producing significant and uniform emotions and behavioural effects.

Writing about 'popular music' in a very different historical context and with a very different orientation towards religion, the state, and the role of culture, Adorno, and many of his fellow critical theorists, came to the same gloomy conclusions regarding music and listeners. Adorno (1941a) described the dominant music of his era as 'pre-digested'. 'The composition hears for the listener,' he asserted. 'This is how popular music divests the listener of his spontaneity and promotes conditioned reflexes' (p. 23). In Adorno's analysis, listeners could overcome these obstacles only through disciplined engagement with serious music that challenged musical convention. But, as critical listening declined, music's emotional power took over and the way was open for conditioned responses and social control (DeNora, 2003, p. 87). Over the course of a couple of millennia, prevailing beliefs and attitudes about music's power (positive or negative) and about human nature in relation to it have routinely placed listeners in a relatively powerless position. As a result, questionable assumptions about the archetypal listener as still, silent, passive, and isolated have dominated most social science research on the subject (see Chapter 6, this volume).

More recently, a number of interdisciplinary interventions that could be lumped under the rubric of cultural studies have challenged objectivist notions of music's power and static conceptions of the listener, arguing that listeners play an *active* role in constructing their affective responses to music (see Chapter 7, this volume). In this regard, cultural studies embraces a premise of listener/consumer power—that once a piece of music enters the public arena/marketplace, the listener/consumer is free to reappropriate it, to resignify it, to use it in new and unintended ways (Chambers, 1985; Frith, 1981; Garofalo, 1987; Willis, 1978). In the cultural studies paradigm, for example, popular music was posited as a major element in the 'bricolage' of style used by British youth to construct the various subcultures of the sixties and seventies (Brake, 1980; Hebdige, 1979). In this tradition, Grossberg located the power of rock in its ability to create 'affective alliances' which define and 'encapsulate' the fans as 'different' (Grossberg, 1983, p. 84). Argued Grossberg: 'Rock and roll locates its fans as different even while they exist within the hegemony. The boundary is inscribed within the dominant culture. Rock and roll is an insider's art which functions to position its fans as outsiders' (Grossberg, 1984, p. 234). In this way, argued Grossberg, fans consciously use music and style as part of a strategy for empowerment and the construction of self-identity.

One of the most salient features of cultural studies is that it positioned the human subject as the motor of history, and for our purposes, as an active agent in using— indeed, producing—music's effects. In so doing, it drew crucially on Williams's (1961, 1977) important work regarding 'structures of feeling'. Applying this perspective to the social movements of the 1960s, Eyerman and Jamison (1998) have argued that music mobilizes tradition selectively, and enters the collective memory in ways that contribute to creating the 'structures of feeling' that Williams felt were so important to cultural formations and cultural change. Although Williams was not theorizing emotions per se—his concept embodied the complexity of 'a social experience which is still in progress'—he consciously chose the term 'feeling' over the term 'ideology' because he was concerned with 'meanings and values as they are actively lived and felt', and with the 'affective elements of consciousness and relationships' (Williams, 1977, p. 132). Echoing Eyerman and Jamison, DeNora (2003) has emphasized that 'there is a feeling component to movement activity' (p. 80).

Acknowledging a knowing, feeling, reflexive, self-aware actor, however, opens up questions of complex subjectivities—a topic taken up by Ortner (2005)—and herein lies the challenge to scientific researchers: to develop better models for incorporating subjectivity into social theory and research. At a social level, Kramer (2001) argues that 'the basic work of culture is to construct subject positions' (p. 156). Far from opening the door to an infinite array of possible ways of being, however, this notion is generally thought of in terms of a limited number of prospects, circumscribed by social conditions. Dibben (2006) elaborates that 'our sense of self develops within cultural narratives that are already extant. The idea of whom we are is not simply an abstract, disembodied notion that exists in the mind: rather, our sense of self is formed by the particular cultural narratives that are already present in the society within which we grow up' (p. 174). Used in this way, the notion of subject positions is an attempt to find a middle ground between 'the unconstrained relativism of . . . the idea that perceivers construct their own utterly individual and unpredictable meanings from an aesthetic object and the determinism . . . of rigid structuralism—the idea that meaning is entirely contained within the objective structures of the work itself' (Clarke, 2005, p. 93). Such formulations represent a theoretical advance that helps us to think about—if not measure—the complexity of the relationship between music and emotion.

26.1.3 What is music?

The literature on music and emotion is rife with discussions about the definition of emotions, and, in particular, musical emotions. Not so, with the other half of the equation. Like our stereotypic conceptions of listeners, historical notions about what constitutes music in the Western literature have tended most often to be drawn from examples from our European heritage. The intervals of the European diatonic scale, for example, are often so taken for granted that the scale appears to be almost natural. Seldom do we question how such an assumption might affect discussions of consonance and dissonance or a consideration of the emotional impact of music in cultures that utilize modes or microtone scales. Distinctions between music and speech that are evident in most Western cultures are less obvious in cultures where languages are tonal. According to Roberts (1974), there is an 'intimate connection between speech and melody in African music, which arises partly from the fact that so many African languages are tonal' (p. 189). Translating to the everyday, Jones (1974) has commented, 'The song you sing is what you mean to say' (p. 41). There are other aspects of the definition of music that bear even more directly on the present discussion.

Small (1987) defines music in part in terms of its 'organizing principles' (p. 25), and in this sense one can see an expanding definitional landscape in the trajectory of contemporary popular music from a conception of music as the organization of notes, to music as the organization of beats, to music as the organization of sound or noise. In Small's terminology, European musics can be defined in terms of the organization of notes (melody, chord patterns, harmony). Most African musics, he contends, are based on the central organizing principle of rhythm—a principle that extends beyond drums alone to encompass other instruments as well as vocal phrasing. In the history of popular music, at least in the United States, one can see a shift from melody to rhythm as the popular sounds of the commercial music industry enterprise known as Tin Pan Alley were displaced by the eruption of rock 'n' roll. Among the nuggets of wisdom passed on to young songwriters in the formative stages of Tin Pan Alley by veteran publisher and song writer Charles K. Harris were: 'Let your melody musically convey the character and sentiment of the lyrics' (cited in Hamm, 1983, p. 290). In all of his advice, there is not a mention of rhythm; indeed, his autobiography is subtitled: *Forty Years of Melody*.

Even after Tin Pan Alley began to incorporate more and more African-American elements, conservative culture critics felt reassured that these influences were 'limited by compromises with middle class conventions' and '"polished". . . so as to conform to the standards of European rendition' (Mooney, 1969, pp. 10–11). In contrast, the rhythm and blues of the late 1940s that led to the creation of rock 'n' roll was described by Baraka as 'huge rhythm units smashing away behind screaming blues singers', a decidedly different approach to music making (Jones, 1963, p. 168). Continued Baraka: 'Suddenly it was as if a great deal of the Euro-American humanist facade Afro-American music had taken on had been washed away by the war . . . And somehow the louder the instrumental accompaniment and the more harshly screamed the singing, the more expressive the music was' (ibid, p. 171). The strands of rock 'n' roll that flowed from this music were referred to as 'the Big Beat', calling further attention to this defining characteristic of the music. As the palette of sound that we call music expands, so too does the range of emotional responses it can produce.

The eruption of rock 'n' roll was significant not only because it signalled a paradigm shift toward African-American aesthetics and performance styles, but also because it embraced noise, as it incorporated the relentless pulse and sheer volume of the urban soundscape into the music itself. Gillett (1970) titled his classic study of the rise of rock 'n' roll *The Sound of the City* because it was 'the first form of popular culture to celebrate without reservation characteristics of city life that had been among the most criticized. In rock and roll, the strident, repetitive sounds of city life were, in effect, reproduced as melody and rhythm' (p. i). Punk, rap, and metal expanded the definition of music to include the dimension of noise even more explicitly.

When punk emerged in reaction to perceived excesses in rock in the mid 1970s, its task was to deconstruct rock, to strip it of all its bloat (including its African-American rhythmic influences). 'This music does not swing,' wrote Goldstein (1977). 'It advances in dense pneumatic chords' (p. 44). In so doing, punk reduced rock to the primal elements of texture and noise. Likewise, both rap and heavy metal have used the power of noise to assault traditional musical conventions and to trace the boundaries of youth culture. The sonic distortion that results when an amplifier is overdriven—through the creative use of feedback or voltage regulators, even vocal distortion boxes—has long been a defining element in the production of that 'heavy metal thunder'. Rap often assaults the listener with a dense mix of digital samples and synthesized noise. When Public Enemy's Chuck D. exhorts his fans to 'bring the noise', he is advocating a form of political resistance through the intentionally aggravating use of noise. But noise is most often thought of as an aversive stimulus. In emotional terms, then, incorporating noise into the definition of music, as we shall see, forces us to interrogate the relationship between pleasure and pain in music, as well as the distinction between emotions expressed in music and emotions aroused by music.

26.1.4 Words and music

There is another distinction in the definition of music that bears mentioning here: the distinction between instrumental music and music with lyrics. For Plato, this question was non-sequitur, since in his mind the poet and the musician were one, and musical form was subordinated to poetic text in his hierarchy of moral values. 'When there are no words,' wrote Plato, 'it is very difficult to recognize the meaning of the harmony and the rhythm . . .' (cited in Portnoy, 1949, p. 239). He was upset at the revolutionary tendency to create instrumental music that was beginning to take hold in ancient Greece, because he feared that this would lead to inappropriate moods and behaviours.

Privileging words over music as a necessary condition for proper moral and emotional development is also echoed in Christian, Jewish, and Muslim thought. In early Jewish and Christian music, the text was primary; melody and instrumental accompaniment were intended to embellish the message of the text (Portnoy, 1949, p. 239). This sense of the primacy of words also extended to Islamic music. 'As with Judaism (and probably because of Judaism),' explain Korpe et al (2006), 'Islam gives an overwhelming priority to "the word" and only sanctions those uses of music that enhance and glorify the word' (p. 249). Solely instrumental music was almost invariably linked to sensuousness, and sensuousness was almost invariably condemned, largely because of its associations with dangerous and uncontrollable emotions.

Certainly in Western culture, logo-centric rationality has generally been accorded a higher cultural value than emotion. To the extent that lyrics represent the rational element in music, perhaps the religious emphasis on the importance of 'the word' is a reflection of the need for control. Where popular musics have deviated from this formula, they have been vulnerable to criticism. Perhaps this is why the study of music and emotion has trailed behind other areas of musical science, such as music cognition or music development (Juslin & Sloboda, 2001, p. 4). Indeed, courses on music appreciation often focus on an intellectual understanding of, rather than an emotional response to, musical form. One result of this cognitive bias in the study of music has been that the body of the listener has been 'excised' as a site for further investigation (DeNora 2003, p. 84). This omission has serious implications for a thorough understanding of how we process music, particularly in sites, such as dance clubs, where music is 'heard' through the body as much as through the ears.

26.2 MEDIATION

A good deal of the received wisdom regarding the reception and emotional power of music predates the mass media. In the ideal, we often imagine music reception as an unmediated experience. It is a selling point of high-end speakers, for example, that they can faithfully reproduce the quality of a live performance. In reality, however, it is almost never the case that music is experienced in an unmediated way. Even in a live performance of acoustic music, instruments and vocals are likely to be fed through a microphone whose signal is amplified and transmitted via the speakers of a sound-reinforcement system. Music played on electric instruments and/or recorded in a studio can be subjected to a staggering panoply of effects such as echo, reverb, tremolo, delay, flanging, panning, fading, compression, equalization, multi-tracking, overdubbing, and pitch and tempo control, and then played on a variety of sound systems including hand-held devices and computers, home stereos and public address systems, and/or terrestrial and satellite radio, each of which can be heard in isolation through headphones or socially through loudspeakers. Each of these devices has a different social function, which mediates the experience of listening differently. Can we possibly imagine that such an array of alternatives would not affect our emotional state in different ways? Yet relatively little research on music and emotion foregrounds the effects of the technologies used in its creation, transmission, and/or reception.

The advent of the mass media changed our relationship to music in profound ways. Prior to the invention of sound recording, the subsequent popularization of the phonograph, and the introduction of commercial radio broadcasting, musical instruments provided the basis for musical home entertainment. Accordingly, listening to music required a live performance. In the popular image of collective playing and singing, music is 'consumed' only through the active participation of all concerned. Because there is no corresponding activity required to listen to a phonograph record or a radio broadcast, mass culture has been disparaged as directing society away from active music making toward passive music consumption. Lost in this equation is the notion that the teenagers who danced to rock 'n' roll records in the 1950s, for example, were as active and emotionally engaged as humanly possible.

In the realm of consumption, another cause for concern was the fact that audience size grew on a scale that increased by orders of magnitude. 'The transformation of an audience, once numbered in the thousands, to one of millions profoundly altered all the relationships involved,' wrote Handlin (1959, p. 67). For Handlin and others, the very process of mediation imposed greater and greater distances between artist and audience, which was often taken as an indicator of the 'alienation' of mass culture. But what about inventions like, say, the microphone? This tool of mediation revolution-ized the art of singing by enabling vocalists to be heard above the instrumental clamour of a large band without having to scream into an acoustic megaphone. It ushered in an era of 'crooning'—a more 'personal' style of singing that allowed for greater varia-tion in vocal nuance—creating the potential for experiencing feelings of intimacy at a sold-out concert in a crowded room. Far from leading to increased alienation, the microphone may well have created, in certain circumstances, the possibility of greater emotional engagement between artist and audience. Similarly, what about the dance club deejay who can 'peak' a crowd—propel them en masse toward a climactic moment of dance frenzy? These purveyors of commodified music are not only artists in their own right, they do serious emotional work on behalf of their audiences. Such examples are worthy of serious study.

In addition to transmitting music, technology can also play a role in its creation. With the advent of digital electronics, technology exists as an element of the music itself as never before. Musicians and listeners negotiate a complex relationship with the tools of music technology. Indeed, the very distinction between production and consumption has become less clear. Producers who make use of sampling devices in the creative process are acting as consumers of 'found' sounds. Conversely, consum-ers who 'burn' their own 'mix tapes' are creating new cultural products. Their value is evident in the popularity of such artefacts as consumer-generated iTunes playlists. Users of the original Napster network did not simply trade music files; they communi-cated with each other. They self-selected into communities of taste, sharing ideas and feelings, discussing music passionately, and suggesting new sounds to other users.

User preferences have now been systematized by enterprises like the Internet radio service Pandora's Music Genome Project (currently available only in the United States) and MusicBrainz's implementation of Linkara Música in Barcelona, Spain. Such services use a combination of file metadata, user recommendations, and audio fingerprinting to create sophisticated recommendation and identification engines. In addition, Pandora employs a team of professional listeners to rate each of the tens of thousands of songs in their database on hundreds of variables which, in addition to formal properties of music like beats per minute, also include measures like whether the singer's voice is 'gravelly or silky', whether the scope of the song is 'modest or epic', or whether the electric guitar sound is 'clean or distorted' (Leeds, 2006). Such mea-sures clearly bear on the realm of affect, and should be considered in research on music and emotion.

26.3 THE USES OF MUSIC

The observation that the historical research on music and emotion has been 'posed as speculation rather than as empirical enquiry' (DeNora, 2003, p. 84) has not stopped practitioners—from politicians and policy makers to activists and do gooders, not to mention advertisers, music corporations, and the military—from trying to apply the power of music to their own ends. Within our recent history, numerous attempts have been made to use music to rally the populace in support of elected officials and state policies, just as music has been used to protest against the actions of the state; music has been associated with everything from increasing productivity in the workplace and encouraging consumers to shop longer to defining and delimiting the boundaries of public space. This trajectory propels the research agenda toward a focus on what music 'does', and how it can be used (DeNora, 2001; Kramer, 2001).

There is some sense—particularly in the academic literature—that music is/should be a force for good. Whether deployed in the service of feel-good entertainment, intellectual stimulation, the bodily pleasure of dancing, protesting against an injustice, or supporting a just cause, there is a tendency to see music as a positive force in society (Cloonan & Johnson, 2002). But music also has a darker side: if it can promote feelings of love, so too can it fan the flames of hatred. Music is well known for its ability to gather, energize, even define, a group; it is also being used to disperse crowds. If music can provide pleasure—the most frequently reported emotional response to music is happiness—it can also be used to inflict pain. In short, if music can liberate the human spirit, it can also be used as a mechanism of regulation and social control.

We turn now to a discussion of these emotionally charged, and often contradictory, uses of and responses to music in the hope of shedding some light on the complexity of these processes and helping to point the way to future research.

26.3.1 Patriotism and national identity

Historical examples of using music to promote patriotism in the construction and reinforcement of national identity are legion—particularly in times of crisis and war—from bold, crisp marches that signify military power and precision to lyrics that extol the virtues of one's own society and/or denigrate the shortcomings of one's enemies. The most obvious examples of such practices involve the singing of national anthems at public events. The degree to which such anthems are deployed and the gusto with which they are sung—that is, the degree to which identity and ideology are reinforced at the emotional level—can often be taken as a measure of patriotic fervor. In those instances where the emotional investment in patriotism is perceived to be flagging (no pun intended), considerable resources may be expended in an effort to (re)establish a unified national identity, and the coercive underside of restoring hegemony can become apparent. The complexity of these processes in the modern world is most apparent in examples drawn from large-scale cultures.

One illustration of scale and complexity in promoting nationalism can be seen in the National Anthem Project, launched in the United States by the National Association for Music Education (MENC) in March 2005, as US support for the war in Iraq was beginning to wane. With then First Lady Laura Bush as its Honorary Chairman and sponsorship and/or financial support from more than a dozen organizations ranging from Jeep and Clear Channel to the Grammy Foundation and the Christian Educators Association, the National Anthem Project initially proposed a three-year national education campaign, which conflated singing 'The Star-Spangled Banner' with 'restoring America's voice through music education'—complete with a travelling national road show of ensemble performances and a climactic finale that involved eight to ten million children singing in unison at the twenty-first World's Largest Concert (Quigly, 2004).

The National Anthem Project created an elaborate and powerful network of public/private government, industry, and education partnerships that linked a value system and a way of life to a particular expressive act. To the extent that it proposed to renew national awareness of American traditions, promote the significance of 'The Star-Spangled Banner', and re-teach America to sing the national anthem (Lasko, 2004), its purpose was to engage its participants in ritualized practices that used music to mobilize tradition. Speaking to the importance of tradition, Eyerman and Jamison (1998) argue that 'traditions are more than texts which carry ideas; they also involve practical activities, forms of ritualized practice in and through which meaning and significance are embedded. Music, in particular, embodies tradition through the ritual of performance. It can empower, help create collective identity and a sense of movement in an emotional and almost physical sense' (p. 35). The degree to which music succeeds in such endeavours, however, often depends on perceptions of extra-musical contextual variables.

In its single-minded focus on one song and its explicit corporate and conservative ties, the National Anthem Project came under fire for its propagandistic bent and the fear that teachers might be coerced into adopting it (Hebert, 2006). That coercive potential, notes Hebert, had already become apparent in other places, which had experienced a resurgence of interest in patriotic music at the national level. In Japan, for instance, as a result of legislative changes in 2004, music teachers faced reprisals for 'failing to lead all students in singing their national anthem with sufficient enthusiasm', and school board inspectors were deployed to measure the intensity of their patriotism with decibel meters (ibid, pp. 23, 27). If, as Konečni (this volume) reminds us, different people experience vastly different emotional reactions to the same piece of music, then the emotions produced by singing in this instance might range from love (of country) to fear (of losing one's job).

Furthermore, we would do well to remember, as Brown (2006) argues, that 'if music is functioning to promote the solidarity of groups, it is very often doing so in order to fuel opposition to other groups, to create difference' (p. 12). Nowhere was this aspect of music's power more apparent than in Hitler's Germany, where music education became second in importance only to physical education in the schools. The Nazis had decided early on that music (and culture generally) would serve the propaganda machine at all levels of German society. Managers of music festivals, opera houses, and popular municipal venues found that their funding problems had all but disap-peared; all branches of the military sported marching bands; youth drum and bugle corps sprouted like mushrooms; workers enjoyed live orchestras and special radio broadcasts during scheduled breaks in the plant (Aber, 1944; Moller, 1980). All of these efforts were part of the Cultural Ministry's 'strength through joy' campaign, which required that art 'be full of fighting spirit' (Moller, 1980, p. 42). In this way, 'Hitler tried to use music's emotional power for political and social means in order to convince people that his ideology was true. Conventions, party rallies and feasts were carefully directed to provide intense musical experiences which supported the National Socialist ideology emotionally' (Kertz-Welzel, 2005, p. 4). Naturally, the more powerful the emotional connection, the more effective the propaganda.

The crowning touch in the Nazis' cultural strategy was their attempt to use the music of Germany's classical composers to link the Third Reich to the country's glori-ous cultural past. In this regard, Hitler's particular fondness for the music of Richard Wagner, often prominent at party functions, was telling, as was the fact that Wagner was widely regarded as a virulent anti-Semite. Welcomed by the composer's family, Hitler was able to use Wagner's operas to 'present the Nazi party and ideology as part and parcel of German history' (Horowitz, 1998). Wagner, more than any other clas-sical composer, used the power of music and spectacle to appeal to his audience at the level of immediate sensation. Wagner himself spoke of '*artistically conveying my purpose to the true Emotional* (not the Critical) *Understanding* of spectators' (Wagner, 1851, p. 391, emphasis his). Describing how this was accomplished, Finkelstein (1976) has noted: 'Everything was more gigantic, more overwhelming in sense appeal, than anything seen and heard before. The operas were longer, the orchestras twice the size, the singing louder, the stage spectacles more glamorous' (p. 78). In the hands of the Third Reich, Wagner's music 'created an overwhelming emotional atmosphere at mass meetings and on the radio ... The Germanic folk hero of the "glorious past" was literally drummed into all educational thought. Heroic struggle and war were glorified as a goal to be desired' (Moller, 1980, p. 42).

It was undoubtedly this sensibility that prompted director Francis Ford Coppola to select Wagner's 'Ride of the Valkyries' to orchestrate the napalm bombing of a Vietnamese village in *Apocalypse Now*, rather than the rock and soul music that domi-nates the rest of the film's soundtrack. The composition resonates immediately with the themes of violence and war, and its use in the film effectively links Wagner's own fascination with power to the statement Coppola wished to make about US involve-ment in Vietnam. In the hands of Coppola, however, the effects of Wagner's music become more ambiguous, as the scene confronts the viewer with a ballet of horror that arouses equal measures of fascination and disgust. In this way, Coppola's reappropria-tion of Wagner moves the composition into the realm of emotional turmoil and moral ambiguity, if not outright protest. If Coppola's use of Wagner produced conflicting emotional reactions that made it difficult to identify with the US attack, it also reminds us that Wagner must have been experienced very differently by Germans and Jews in Nazi Germany. Perhaps not surprisingly, performances of Wagner's music in Israel remain controversial to this day.

A more definitive use of patriotic music in the service of resistance and protest involves the Estonian struggle for independence. In what has come to be known as 'the Singing Revolution', Estonia drew on a long tradition of massive choral performances of patriotic music to mobilize a resistance sufficient to repel the occupying armies of the Soviet Union. Since 1869, Estonia has staged a music festival (known as Laulupidu), which meets roughly once every five years and involves as many as 25,000–30,000 singers in a single performance (Freemuse, 2007; see Figure 26.1). In 1947, during the first festival following the Soviet occupation, composer Gustav Ernesaks set to music a centuries-old poem—'*Mu isamaa on minu arm*' (Land of my fathers, land that I love)—which, escaping the notice of the Soviet censors, became an Estonian anthem of national pride and self-determination. A watershed moment in the history of the festival (and the country itself) came in 1969, at the centennial celebration of the festival, when the Soviets tried to ban the song. Tens of thousands of Estonians reportedly took to the stage and in defiance of the occupying forces, sang the song, not once, but again and again. 'This bold act reclaimed Estonian identity and set the stage for a series of increasingly daring rebellions' (Seitz, 2007) that eventually led to an independent Estonia in 1991.

In all such examples, serious inquiry must account for the role of scale and spectacle in the production of emotion, and in the ways in which music can be used to mobilize tradition and construct national identity. How are these variables, in turn, affected by mass mediation? (In the above examples, it is worth noting that Wagner certainly predated the mass media and that the Estonian tradition provides, paradoxically, one of the most powerful and least mediated examples of its kind.)

Fig. 26.1 The Singing Revolution: 25,000 performers on stage. Courtesy of The Singing Revolution.

Finally, given different emotional reactions to a particular piece of music among different constituencies—Japanese teachers vs. school board inspectors, Jews vs. Germans during the Third Reich, Estonian partisans vs. occupying Soviet troops—what are the precise variables that determine whether the music will be perceived or experienced as, say, propaganda, patriotism, or protest?

26.3.2 Popularizing protest

This essay draws on large-scale, complex cultures in part because the research on smaller, more homogeneous cultures has tended to focus on music's role in promoting group cooperation, solidarity, and affiliation; the anthropology literature is rife with discussions of the role of music in birth, death, courtship, marriage, worship, rites of passage, etc. Scale invariably increases the degree of difference, diversity, and stratification and, in many situations, as Brown (2006) reminds us, music can play a role maintaining—even producing—such differences. One need only witness the way the commercial music industry categorizes music and audiences to see this reality in action (Chapter 32, this volume). More germane to our purposes is the case of protest music. Often alongside patriotic musics there have existed various forms of protest music, which have been used to move audiences in similar ways, but toward radically different ends. Protest music has probably existed in some form since moans and groans were first used to indicate dissatisfaction. It was evident throughout the twentieth century in worker's choruses all over Europe, and in a developed body of labour, civil rights, and anti-war anthems in the United States. Strands of protest can be found in specific genres from Trinidadian calypso to Nigerian highlife, as well as in the 'new song' movements that swept Latin America in the 1960s, and the various forms of national rock and rap that took hold globally in the 1980s and beyond.

In the early 1900s, the International Workers of the World envisioned themselves as a 'singing union' with a simple formula. Familiarity and collective performance were key: make use of cultural forms already part of the collective memory, to which people already had a positive emotional connection, and encourage group singing in order to introduce new ideas. If the formula was simple, so too were the tools used to gauge its emotional impact. Denisoff (1972) distinguished between 'magnetic' and 'rhetorical' protest songs. The former were songs that were simple in structure, intended to be sung en masse with little preparation and little or no accompaniment, emphasized a collective identity in the use of the pronoun 'we', and were used to attract listeners to particular organizations or movements. Like the magnetic protest song, the rhetorical variant expressed dissatisfaction, but without pointing the way to any particular political solutions. Rhetorical protest placed some emphasis on lyrics, and allowed for greater latitude and sophistication musically (Denisoff, 1972). While either variety might have expressed, or aroused, particular emotions, only the magnetic attempted to draw people into active movement participation.

By the early 1960s, the folk revival that Denisoff was chronicling had begun to complete successfully in the commercial marketplace. In this way, the sound of protest music began to open up new possibilities for the depth and reach of popular music—even as it prolonged raging debates about mass culture, pitting 'authentic' folk music against 'commercial' pop—and it began to occupy a place in the national psyche that might once have been reserved for patriotic music. According to Denisoff, nearly all of the protest songs that entered the mainstream market were in the folk idiom and of the rhetorical variety, including all of Bob Dylan's early protest material. In songs like *Only a Pawn in Their Game* and *The Lonesome Death of Hattie Carroll*, Dylan appealed to the listener through a rational account of injustice, that is, through a cognitive input. Indeed, by the mid sixties, Dylan was well along the road to almost single-handedly transforming the lyric content of popular music—at least for the college-bound student population. But Denisoff concluded this line of reasoning prior to a watershed moment in Dylan's career.

In 1965, Dylan violated a sacred folk protocol by appearing on stage with an electric guitar—a solid-body, classic-rock Fender Stratocaster, no less. In so doing, he found himself on the receiving end of withering criticism in the mass culture debate, a subtext of which contrasted music that lent itself to engaged, participatory live performance with music that was perceived by folk purists as commodified, passively consumed, mass culture. But, in the move to electric, mass-mediated rock, Dylan effectively married his lyric poetry to the more primal urges that rock and roll had unleashed. At the same time, The Beatles and others infused rock with a lyric and musical sophistication that were rare for the mass market. The fact that these developments occurred within the context of the social movements of the 1960s suggested a larger, more complex, role for music than Denisoff's functionalist categories could accommodate, and demonstrated the limits of content analysis generally. It is here that Eyerman and Jamison (1998, p. 45) remind us of the importance of Williams's work.

Applying Williams's model to the 1960s, one could argue that the articulation of the rebelliousness that had always accompanied rock 'n' roll, the tradition of progressive protest in the United States, and the peace-and-love ethos of the counterculture created a structure of feeling wherein rock and other forms of mainstream popular music came to signify, and perhaps encourage, feelings of individual freedom and a collective opposition to oppression, even when the music was not, strictly speaking, 'about' such topics. It is this sense of the structure of feeling of the 1960s that allowed John Lennon to claim with some credibility that 'all our songs are anti-war' when asked if the Beatles planned to record any anti-war songs (Beatles, 2000, p. 145). Once music enters the collective memory in this way, it may be recalled as 'an embodied, emotive activity' (DeNora, 2003, p. 81) even after the social movements with which it is associated are no longer active. Eyerman and Jamison (1998, pp. 161–2) elaborate:

Such structures of feeling can be embodied and preserved in and through music, which is partly why music is such a powerful force in social movements and in social life generally. Music in a sense *is* a structure of feeling. It creates mood—bringing it all back home, as Dylan once said—and in this way can communicate a feeling of common purpose, even amongst actors who have no previous historical connection with one another. While such a sense may be fleeting and situational, it can be recorded and reproduced, and enter into memory, individual as well as collective, to such an extent that it can be recalled or remembered at other times and places. In such a fashion, music can recall not only the shared situationally bound experiences, but also a more general commitment to common cause and to collective action.

This formulation represents a considerable departure from the classical (Marxist) model of culture simply as determined by and reflective of economic interests and, as I have argued elsewhere, demands a conception of music as constitutive of identity and action, able to 'take the lead' in its own right (Garofalo, 1992).

26.3.3 Politicizing pleasure

There is another aspect of music as protest that became particularly salient in the context of the tumultuous 1960s: the fact that music has always been associated with (forbidden) pleasure(s). From sailors drawn irresistibly to the Siren's call and revellers at Dionysian festivals to blissful hippies, sweat-drenched disco dancers, and ecstatic ravers, images of individuals entranced by music have piqued our fascination with and fear of music's power. Losing oneself in the music, of course, is not quite the same thing as losing one's self. Quite the contrary, from hipsters and beats, to mods and rockers, to b-boys and headbangers, music has long figured prominently in the way people are defined and define themselves as individuals and as groups. As new genres and group formations have emerged, they have been met with impulses toward unrestrained participation by some and strict regulation by others. The eruption of rock 'n' roll in the 1950s was denounced by fearful adults as a Communist plot to encourage race mixing and undermine the moral fibre of the younger generation, even as youth were using the music to explore the sounds and textures of city life, embark on multicultural musical excursions, and engage in the sensuous public ritual of dancing.

In the 1960s, pleasure became a political demand, whether enacted in the psychedelic drug culture, the sexual revolution, or the joy of music making. Slogans such as 'Sex, drugs, and rock 'n' roll', 'Make love, not war,' and 'Turn on, tune in, and drop out,' which for some signified all of the excesses and destructive urges of the era, represented for many, and only half-jokingly, an affirmation of pleasure, of the body, of life—a conscious reaction to the rigidity and repression of the 1950s. According to Grossberg (1993), 'The field of struggle constructed by the various countermovements of the 1960s depended upon the articulation of politics and pleasure, of popular culture and social identity. Pleasure became a source of power and a political demand, enabled by the very marginality of those struggling' (p. 194). Pleasure, often realized in and through popular music, served as a form of resistance against state repression and regulated leisure.

Interestingly, the demand for pleasure as a political act reached its zenith in the unlikeliest of places—the disco dance floor (and, by extension, the myriad of dance club scenes that have followed in its wake). In focusing on rhythm to the extent that it did—'disco is insistently rhythmic in a way that popular song is not' (Dyer, 1979, p. 414)—disco emphasized the most physical aspects of music reception, those most associated with pleasure and the body. Nietzsche once observed that 'we listen to music through our muscles' (cited in Sachs, 2007, p. xi). No one who has been to a dance club in the last few decades would question this assertion. In these settings, music is clearly 'heard' physically: intense vibrations rattle the feet, rumbling bass pounds the chest, deafening volume warms the ears (Kassabian, 2007). For club goers, many of whom wear earplugs as protective gear, there is a thin line between ecstasy and agony, as the aspects of music that confer pleasure are realized only at the price of considerable pain. It is this aspect of the music that prompts Hughes (1994) to theorize disco as 'a form of discipline', which, for him, parallels a series of practices within gay male culture— 'bodybuilding, fashion, sadomasochism, and safe sex'—that 'combine pleasure with the discipline of the self' (p. 148).

It is worth noting that not even lyrics are exempt from this observation. As critic Greil Marcus has said, 'words are sounds we can feel before they are statements to understand' (quoted in Frith, 1983, p. 14). Applied to disco, 'language is subjugated to the beat, and drained of its pretensions to meaning; almost all traces of syntax or structure abandoned, reducing language to the simplest sequential repetition, a mere verbal echo of the beat itself' (Hughes, 1994, p. 149). The conflation of discipline and desire in disco brings into bold relief the difficulty of separating out our contradictory notions of music's power to produce order or Eros. As Hughes (1994, pp. 150–1) comments:

The power of music to master the individual has, of course, been regarded as, by turns, useful and dangerous in Western culture from ancient Greece onward. Martial music can create a disciplinary order in which the individual falls into step with his fellows, while erotic music can induce a lapse into sensuality and indulgence; but both useful and dangerous forms of music have roughly the same effect, as both are forces that overwhelm the will. Disco makes explicit the identity of the two seemingly opposed musical styles, which the Greeks distinguished as Dorian and Lydian: it takes the regular tattoo of the military march and puts it to the sensual purposes of dance music.

Again, the analysis suggests avenues for further inquiry. Do musics primarily heard through the body contribute differently to the emotional experience of the listener? What are the contextual variables that determine whether music will be perceived, experienced—indeed, felt—as uplifting or debased, or to use Hughes's terminology, 'useful' or 'dangerous'? Such questions become even more poignant when discussing hate music or the use of music in torture (see Sections 26.3.5 and 26.3.7).

26.3.4 Channelling charity

The principles of pleasure and identity formation in popular music were expanded and intensified in events like Woodstock. In the imagined community that came to be known as 'Woodstock Nation', one could see Grossberg's affective alliances at work on a grand scale. Mass mediation was a crucial variable in that Woodstock happened when it did in part because of advances in sound-reinforcement technology that could accommodate gatherings in the hundreds of thousands, granting audiences the simultaneous experience of live performance on a mass scale, and again challenging the notion of mass mediation as necessarily alienating. The sense of community engendered by the idea of a Woodstock Nation extended, in turn, to humanitarian causes like George Harrison's Concert for Bangladesh and to more radical political projects like the No Nukes concerts that halted the construction of nuclear power plants in the United States. Together, these strands of the 1960s/1970s experience prefigured the mega-events of the 1980s.

The sense of popular music as a defining cultural form connected to collective identity and progressive political ferment carried forward to the 1980s and beyond, even after it was primarily aligned with commercial entertainment and consumer culture. 'As the economy focuses less on production and more on consumption,' Lipsitz (1990) has argued, 'popular culture intervenes in the construction of individual and group identity more than ever before . . . while serious political issues such as homelessness and hunger seem to enter public consciousness most fully when acknowledged by popular musicians' (p. 630). Indeed, by the late 1980s, there was scarcely a social or political issue that had not been touched or inspired by the popular music phenomenon dubbed 'charity rock'—Band Aid, Live Aid, 'We Are The World', the Amnesty International Tours, two Nelson Mandela tribute concerts and all the rest (Garofalo, 1992; Omi, 1986). In these instances, the pleasure of popular music and the humanitarian impulse that accompanied it were harnessed in the service of changing attitudes, raising consciousness (and funds), and shaping behaviour toward progressive political ends.

To the extent that music events that are larger than life—which are designed to overwhelm—are associated with emotional power, then Live Aid (at the time the largest single event in human history) tapped the motherlode of human emotion, aided in no small measure by the wonders of satellite transmission, which helped to deliver an audience of 1.5 billion people. While Live Aid and defining charity rock songs like 'Do They Know It's Christmas?' and 'We Are The World' targeted the relatively safe issue of hunger, they also created an international focus on, and possibly an emotional connection to, Africa that was truly global. They also created the cultural space for more controversial projects. If Live Aid was designed to arouse the kind of sympathy, if not pity, that encourages listeners to open their hearts (and wallets), the Amnesty and Mandela concerts were directed more towards arousing and directing anger—anger that a system like South Africa's apartheid could exist, anger at the treatment of prisoners of conscience.

These latter projects also took steps to translate the affective connections that were made into concerted political action. In London, the first Nelson Mandela concert was designed to coincide with the political organizing of the local Anti-Apartheid Movement, which used the interest generated by the concert to mobilize activists for their 'Nelson Mandela: Freedom at Seventy' campaign. Concert goers at the first Amnesty tour were asked to sign up to be 'freedom writers' who participate in the letter-writing campaigns Amnesty uses to call attention to and advocate for the release of prisoners of conscience. As a result of their efforts, three of the six targeted prisoners were freed within two years. In addition, Amnesty USA added some 200,000 new volunteers to the organization. 'Previous to 1986, we were an organization post-forty,' said Amnesty USA's executive director. 'Music allowed us to change the very nature of our membership' (quoted in Garofalo, 1992, p. 35). In this instance, the affective connections generated by the mass cultural events were used to successfully recruit tens of thousands of volunteers into active, sustained political activity.

Clearly, there was a progressive slant to the causes and events outlined above. Indeed, the mega-events of the 1980s moved from simply humanitarian to overtly oppositional as they progressed. Explained at the time by Rockwell (1988): 'Rock's leftist bias arose from its origins as a music by outsiders . . . That bias was solidified by the 1960s, with its plethora of causes and concerns . . . Rock music was the anthem of that change—racial with the civil-rights movement, and also social, sexual, and political' (p. 23). Mega-events faded from view beginning in the early 1990s, only to be replaced by commercial festivals, albeit some with a political message, such as Peter Gabriel's globetrotting World of Music and Dance (WOMAD), and the Lollapalooza Tours and Lilith Fair in the United States. Interestingly, the disappearance of mega-events coincided with the disintegration of the Soviet Union, the failure of state socialism, and the establishment of global capitalism as a single worldwide economic system. It wasn't until opposition to the global consolidation of capital had reached mass-movement proportions that mega-events reappeared. But by then the contradictions involved in negotiating music's dual role as cultural force and commercial product had become all but unmanageable.

In 2005, Live Aid organizer Bob Geldof seized the opportunity of the twentieth anniversary of Live Aid to stage Live 8, an eleven-concert global extravaganza, designed to 'make poverty history' by pressuring the G8 to pledge increased aid and greater debt relief for Africa. Live 8 promoted itself as a movement-building exercise, announcing on its website: 'We don't want your money. We want you.' But the corporate presence, while evident at Live Aid, was more fully integrated into Live 8 (Chossudovsky, 2005). Rather than adopt the oppositional politics of the anti-globalization movement, Live 8 organizers chose to ally themselves with their corporate partners and use the momentum of the concerts as a lever to negotiate with the G8, leaving those in the audience to ponder their identities as consumers of the event more than their role as political activists (Elavsky, 2007).

Chief negotiator Bono's political stance and emotional tone in 2005 were rather different from those of the Bono who stalked the stage, ranting against war on *Sunday Bloody Sunday* in 1983. By 2005, Bono claimed friendships with politicians and policy makers with whom he would not have been in the same room 20 years earlier. Defending this strategy, Geldof intoned: 'Look, you can take a totally oppositional stance to everything . . . or you can use the platforms people give you' (Burkeman, 2005). For Geldof, the new reality of global capital dictated newly circumscribed subject positions. And although he saw Live 8 as the beginning of a protracted struggle, the commercial frame of the event served to undercut whatever affective political connections might have resulted from the performances. The experience of Live 8 highlights the importance of context in framing and shaping our affective responses to music.

It is clear that even the basic humanitarian impulse so often associated with rock and popular music festivals cannot be taken for granted. Moreover, as Eyerman and

Jamison (1998) are quick to remind us, 'these cultural political activities are not necessarily progressive nor need they always be morally commendable' (p. 10). So it is interesting to note that the heyday of charity rock in the 1980s was bracketed by periods in which popular music also served the cause of hate.

26.3.5 Hailing hate

Once one moves beyond the Platonic ideal of music as a transcendent force for good and conceives of music as an essentially social practice representing the full range of human emotion and interaction, then, as Keith Kahn-Harris (2003) points out, there is little reason not to expect hate to present itself as one more musical resource, no different in kind from love. Thus, for example, in its mission to disrupt the trajectory of popular music—indeed, the flow of everyday life—punk made widespread use of offensive and hateful symbols such as the swastika on both sides of the Atlantic. Often intended and defended as irony, such practices conveniently ignored the power of historical memory and nevertheless attracted racist Nazi skinheads to the scene, who developed a strand of the 'oi' sub-genre of punk as a music that came to be identified with the themes and practices of hatred, racism, and violence. In Great Britain in particular, more progressive elements organized the Rock Against Racism movement in opposition to such tendencies.

White power music—or white noise music, hate music, hatecore, or hate rock, as it is variously called—emerged as a major recruitment (and fundraising) tool for white supremacist organizations in the United States and neo-Nazi political parties in Australia, New Zealand, Canada, Brazil, and throughout Europe, particularly in the Scandinavian countries and in Germany after the fall of the Berlin Wall. It has expanded well beyond 'oi' to include other genres such as death metal, country and western, and various folk styles. 'Currently,' according to Corte and Edwards (2008), 'pinpointing a distinctive White Power musical genre is nearly impossible' (p. 12). Although Corte and Edwards maintain that the reinforcement of racist ideologies occurs primarily through the lyrics of the music, it is not clear that hateful lyrics alone are used to accomplish this task. 'Musicians may also deliberately set out to make musical sounds express hatred', argues Kahn-Harris (2003). 'Musicians often talk about their music as an expression of hatred and it would be inconceivable to think of Extreme Metal lyrics being accompanied by any other kind of music. Musical sounds are thus not "innocent" in the expression of hatred'.

White power music intentionally positions itself as rebellious and oppositional, taking on the mantle of authenticity so prized by other genres such as punk and certain strands of extreme metal, which are perceived by their adherents as operating outside commercial imperatives and mainstream success. 'Authentic music expresses the genuine feelings of the artist who feels the need to communicate his or her true emotions without constraints imposed by strictly financial or market forces' (Corte & Edwards, 2008, p. 8). By cultivating this aura of authenticity, and the selfless devotion of its artists to the cause (even while generating significant sums of money), white power music has been able to play a significant role in the formation of a group identity for the white supremacist movement. In addition to recruitment and fundraising, then, 'and perhaps most importantly', argues the Anti-Defamation League (ADL) on its website, 'hate music has been instrumental in the formation of a white supremacist subculture . . . In the 21st century . . . white supremacists around the world are linked not only by shared ideas, but by shared customs, fashions, and most crucially, music' (ADL, no date). Further research might interrogate the extent to which the emotional power of the music is strengthened and reinforced by the larger context of style and fashion.

While there is no question that white power music is used to promote racist and otherwise negative views of and feelings toward non-whites, immigrants, homosexuals, Jews, and other ethnic minorities, there is also another strategy that seeks to reframe the movement in more positive terms. Having learned that an explicitly racist message complicates the task of attracting new recruits, a number of white power music adherents have sought to 'reframe their core message from one of racial hatred to one of survival, pride and self-love' (Corte & Edwards, 2008, p. 14). In this formulation, white power activists are made over 'as the advocates for an embattled, self-loving and proud race actively pursuing the legitimate goals of self-defence and self-preservation against ascendant multiculturalism, immigration and race-mixing' (p. 7). This tack has the practical political advantage of making it easier to operate in countries with explicit laws against hate speech and holocaust denial. But for the purposes of the present paper we must ask: in what ways are the pathways from musical stimulus to emotional response altered when hate is framed in the language of love?

26.3.6 Music as a marker of public space

During the 1980s, hate was only one of the things that created controversy within popular music. It was precisely at the moment that charity rock claimed popular music for humanity that the Parents Music Resource Center in the United States launched its campaign to rescue the music from the evils of sex, drugs, violence, suicide, and Satanism (Garofalo, 1994; Gray, 1989; Grossberg, 1993). Grossberg (1993) saw this move as part of the continuing attack on the potentially subversive pleasures of music. 'The new conservatism clearly sees the need to regulate pleasure, to re-establish the discipline it believes necessary for the reproduction of the social order and the production of capital' (p. 194). Ultimately, the campaign was certainly about regulation and social control, as its main demand was for a warning label on controversial recordings. The genres that received the most scrutiny were rap and metal, interestingly the two musics that had most embraced the principle of organized noise as a mechanism for defining and demarcating the boundaries of youth culture. Viewed in this way, the PMRC campaign could be seen as an awkward and uneven attempt to reassert a vision of music as transcendent in the face of societal fears of its connections to the body. Ballinger (1995) elaborates: 'Embodied by the Enlightenment and 18th century classical music, societal sound began to be brought under control through dominant representations linking "music" to order/civilization/mind, and "noise" to chaos/the primitive/body'

(p. 13–14). Put another way, the struggle over which noises are culturally acceptable is one that has become a key component in establishing national identity, as well as one that defines public space as contested terrain.

It is part of the urban condition that the volume of noise (in both senses of the term) that comprises our daily lives has increased. This condition often erupts into conflict when private sounds spill over into public spaces. As Cloonan and Johnson (2003) claim: 'Part of the clamor of modernity is a public sonic brawling, as urban space becomes a site of acoustic conflict' (p. 31). Music, of course, is no exception to this dynamic, as can be the case with everything from the ubiquitous sounds of music in shopping malls, workplaces, and doctors' offices to the sound of music blaring from a private home with the windows open, a boombox flooding the sonic space of a sub-way car, or a public concert within earshot of a residential neighbourhood. 'In the era of the modern mass media,' Cloonan and Johnson (2003) continue, 'technology has amplified the projection of private musical tastes into the public sphere, thus col-lapsing a distinction that could be much more effectively maintained in a pre-urban, pre-industrial era' (p. 31).

The battle for sonic control of public space has been one of the most important cultural struggles of the last century and music has been deeply implicated in it. In this sense, music functions as a tool of social control to define what is culturally appropriate and to shape behaviour in a variety of social and public spaces. Even at its most unob-trusive, and whether or not the social manipulation appears benign, the connection to emotion is considered important. Muzak, the best known brand in programmed music, for example, claims on its website that its 'Audio Architecture is emotion by design . . . It bypasses the resistance of the mind and targets the receptiveness of the heart.' Typically, music services like Muzak have tried to realize this goal by using 'already-familiar musics', to which the listener may have a positive emotional con-nection, 'to engineer the acoustic dimensions of spaces and experiences for listeners' (Sterne, 2007). Muzak's intent, if not necessarily its effect, in this regard has been to use music as positive reinforcement, be it to increase productivity, reduce errors, make workers happier, or keep shoppers shopping. Founded as a 'background' music ser-vice, in the mid 1980s, Muzak partnered with Yesco, a 'foreground' music company. This coincided with the onset of a more dubious set of musical practices, in which Muzak and other programmed music services have been implicated, that Sterne (2007) has termed 'the nonaggressive music deterrent'.

Since the mid 1980s, there have been increasing instances of using music as negative reinforcement, to disperse crowds or discourage groups from assembling. The prac-tice can be traced back to a number of 7-Eleven stores, first in Canada and then in the United States, who were experiencing a problem with 'loitering teenagers' in the 1980s and 1990s and discovered that playing classical music (as well as some easy-listening pop) caused them to leave the area. At its height, about 150 stores adopted this prac-tice, and it soon extended to locations around the world, including various municipal buildings, public parks, and shopping malls, as well as subway systems in London, England, Sydney, Australia, and Boston, Massachusetts, some of which reported dramatic decreases in petty crime (Cloonan & Johnson, 2002, pp. 36–7; Hirsch,

2007, p. 348). According to Sterne (2007), such findings place these uses of music into the orbit of a much larger tradition of urban design known as Crime Prevention Through Environmental Design (CPTED), and extend the logic of CPTED into the acoustic realm.

Such practices, of course, are at odds with the exalted status as a 'civilizing force' that classical music has been accorded in the hierarchy of cultural values (Hirsch, 2007, p. 349). This, however, was certainly not its effect on the loitering teens, who were simply driven away. '[B]usiness and government leaders,' according to Hirsch (2007), 'are seizing on classical music not as a positive moralizing force, but as a marker of space' (p. 350). At stake for the teens in question—who are repelled not necessarily by the sound of classical music itself, but by the class and cultural baggage that attends it—are fears of identity disintegration and loss of status through negative associations. To the extent that music is used to construct the sonic boundaries of safe space and the symbolic aspects of achieved identity, then music which negates or challenges these functions can only be experienced as disruptive. In this way, 'sound is able to reinforce territory as a symbolic language by signaling to those who belong and rejecting those who do not, thanks to an encoded system of associations' (Hirsch, 2007, p. 352).

26.3.7 Music and torture

Crowe has identified the environmental factors that are used to control space in the CPTED schema as: heat, light, temperature, pressure, and sound (cited in Hirsch, 2007, p. 352). To the extent that music comprises the sonic element in such practices, music is being deployed as a kind of 'sonic weapon'. As definitional distinctions between music, sound, and noise blur, it does not require too long a journey down this road before one encounters a panoply of research and development efforts in the construction of 'acoustic weapons' by the defence industry over the past decade (Cusick, 2006). One product that has been deployed for military and police use is American Technology Corporation's Long Range Acoustic Device (LRAD), a highly directional 'hailing, warning, and deterrent system', capable of projecting 'high output music and deterrent tones' as a 15–30 inch wide 'strip of sound' for up to 1,000 meters in a way that can cause confusion, physical imbalance, and spatial disorientation (Cusick, 2006; see Figure 26.2).

While the intense blasts of sound themselves produce the physical symptoms, psychological operations specialists have long recognized the added value of the particular choice of music as an additional tool to further disorient, demean, and demoralize the enemy. General Manuel Noreiga was blasted out of the Vatican Embassy compound where he was holed up in Panama with barrages of high-volume rock in 1989. Rock has been used more recently by the US military in similar ways throughout the Middle East. In 2004, heavy metal tracks like AC/DC's 'Hell's Bells' were used to 'prepare' the battlefield for the occupation of Fallujah. In some sense, then, popular music has become the sound that the US military uses to announce its presence in foreign lands.

Fig. 26.2 The LRAD system deployed by the military.

Such practices, however, are limited to neither the United States nor the battlefield; they have also found their way into the interrogation room. When Knopf (2008) reminds his readers that places such as hospitals and prisons are 'public spaces', he is cautioning that they may be liable for royalty payments even in the case of torture, but that also means that the practices they engage in should be held up to public policy scrutiny. Human rights groups have noted the use of music in incidents in the former Yugoslavia, where Croat prisoners were forced to sing the Yugoslav national anthem while being beaten (Cloonan & Johnson, 2002, p. 34). In Iraq, uncooperative prisoners have been exposed for extended periods of time to rap, heavy metal, and children's music played at deafening volume. 'If you play it for 24 hours,' claimed one military spokesman, 'your brain and body functions start to slide, your train of thought slows down and your will is broken.' Once this physical and emotional deterioration is complete, 'That's when we come in and talk to them' (quoted in DeGregory, 2004).

Cusick (2006) reports that these techniques are neither new nor random, but rather the result of years of experimental research that are now enshrined in the policy of 'no touch torture', which includes 'hooding, stress positions, and sexual/cultural humiliation'. She speculates that this '*performative scene* in which music *is* the medium of ubiquitous, irresistible power that touches without touching' (ibid, emphasis hers) is, paradoxically, not unlike the dance club experience. The differences, of course, are to be found in context and use. In one instance, one willingly relinquishes control to achieve 'a deeply sensual, erotic . . . feeling of communion' with others, and in the other, one is forced 'to comply against one's will, against one's interests, because there is no way—not even a retreat to interiority—to escape the pain' (ibid).

The use of music as torture is premised on the notion that the music in question is antithetical to the cultural and emotional life of the victim—that it can dissolve the subjectivity of the person being tortured in the service of forced compliance. A less extreme version of this process is evident in the case of the unwanted teenagers in shopping malls. In both instances, however, the future could hold some unexpected ironies. What, for example, if the teenagers in question developed a liking for the music that now repels them? One is reminded of the Malcolm McDowell character in Stanley Kubrick's *A Clockwork Orange*, the leader of the young toughs who is completely invested in the music of Beethoven as the source of the inner strength that marks him as the leader of the gang and elevates him above the rest of the crowd. As the head of Boston's transit police speculated, classical music 'can lift the human spirit, even the spirit of a cynical teenager' (quoted in Hirsch, 2007, p. 349).

The particular characteristics that currently make some musics effective in military operations and torture could also change. Blasting rock at Noriega was effective only because the general was reportedly an opera lover who hated rock. 'Western music is not the Iraqis' thing,' says a spokesman for the US Army's psychological operations command. 'So our guys have been getting really creative in finding sounds they think would make the enemy upset' (quoted in DeGregory, 2004). But what if that situation changed? Given the globalization of the music industry and the global circulation of world cultures—described by Wallis and Malm (1984) as the two-way process of 'transculturation' (pp. 300–1)—an unprecedented range of musics is now available almost anywhere. Pareles (2007) reports that, with no more promotion than a mention on their website, Radiohead's *In Rainbows* album 'has been downloaded in places as far-flung—and largely unwired—as North Korea and Afghanistan'. Even some military spokesmen acknowledge that 'with the increasing globalization of the world, we know that some Iraqis do listen to American music, even heavy metal, on the Internet, the radio and TV. Even during the height of the Taliban, they could get Western music or videos' (quoted in DeGregory, 2004). What this means is that while some insurgents might be repelled by heavy metal attacks today, they could well be motivated differently by the same music at some point in the future. Such developments may never lead toward world peace; governments will always search for new ways to dominate (and others will continue to resist). Still, if it is important to look at use in determining how music works, we must also recognize that use is culturally and historically specific.

26.4 CONCLUDING THOUGHTS

The foregoing discussion offers a perspective that would probably be considered outside the mainstream of research on music and emotion. My purpose is to expand our understanding of and appreciation for the myriad of ways in which music is created, transmitted, received, experienced, and used in the real world, and to encourage other scholars to factor such knowledge into future research on the topic. Such an agenda can be limited by any number of practical constraints such as the compartmentalization of knowledge based on the disciplinary organization of the academy and an accompanying reward system that discourages dialogue and collaboration across disciplinary lines. Nevertheless, real-world applications and related social policies—some involving life-and-death decisions—continue apace, in the absence of a knowledge base, theoretical constructs, methodological procedures, and ethical considerations that are shared and/or agreed upon among the disciplines represented in this volume.

Artificial barriers to shared knowledge can frustrate fruitful dialogue on key issues as basic as the very definition of music. As the sounds we consider music expand to incorporate everything from the furious scratching of turntablists to the noise produced by technologies of sonic distortion, the repertoire of emotional responses varies accordingly. Yet much of the research in this area is biased towards an outmoded hierarchy of cultural practices that privileges the processes associated with the European classical tradition. As Juslin and Sloboda (2001) warn early on, 'much of the academic study of music takes as paradigmatic a very particular way of listening to music and talking about it that is enshrined in the narrow "classical concert culture" where . . . audiences are taught to listen "silently and respectfully" with minimum bodily movement or emotional expression' (p. 5). If the research on music and emotion is to realize its full potential, it must take into account the wildly divergent sounds, styles, and cultural practices that constitute the experience of music in the twenty-first century.

There are also challenges at the theoretical level. Theoretical constructs such as 'structures of feeling' or 'subject positions' are not likely to meet the rigorous requirements for measurement of the research scientist in the laboratory setting. But if the concept of culture writ large appears to be too unruly to be tamed by the scientific method, so too the laboratory setting can seem artificial and limiting by comparison. On balance, there is a relative paucity of research on music and emotion that foregrounds the effects of scale and spectacle, fashion and style, or the panoply of mediations associated with the creation, transmission, and reception of music. In a similar vein, it has to be acknowledged that different constituencies, employing different modes of listening, in different times and places, may well experience and react to the same piece of music differently. All of which is to say that social context matters, and is too often ignored. In the end, perhaps one of the most important contributions that the present volume can make is to foster a dialogue that encourages a balance between the artificiality of the laboratory situation and the complexity of the real world, and a consideration of the relationships among the biochemical determinants and socio-cultural variables that shape our emotional responses to music.

In this regard, it is worth noting that, to this day, popular perceptions regarding the power of music—and the policy recommendations and social uses that follow from them—derive as much from centuries-old philosophical positions and religious beliefs as from current scientific research and detailed cultural analysis. At the same time, recent breakthroughs in the science of digital imaging promise new and exciting developments in our understanding of neural stimulation, while social scientists are coming to understand the workings of culture in ever more complex ways. In the resulting clash of competing belief systems, it is important for scholars conducting research on music and emotion to be aware of and involved in the ways in which such research contributes to shaping state policy and ethical boundaries regarding the uses of music, to resist the efforts of those who would use such research crudely to reinforce previously held ideological positions, and to search for ways in which music can be used to promote intercultural communication and humanize the societies in which we live.

RECOMMENDED FURTHER READING

1. Grossberg, L. (1992). *We gotta get out of this place: popular conservatism and postmodern culture*. New York: Routledge.
2. Eyerman, R., & Jamison, A. (1998). *Music and social movements: mobilizing tradition in the twentieth century*. Cambridge, UK: Cambridge University Press.
3. Small, C. (1998). *Musicking: the meaning of performance and listening*. Hanover, VT: Wesleyan University Press.

REFERENCES

Aber, A. (1944). Music and politics in the third reich. *The Musical Times, June*, 179–80.

Adorno, T. W. (1941a). On popular music. *Studies in Philosophy and Social Science, IX*, 17–48.

Adorno, T. W. (1941b). The radio symphony: An experiment in theory. In P. Lazarsfeld & F. Stanton (eds), *Radio research, 1941* (pp. 110–39). New York: Duell, Sloan, and Pearce.

Beatles. (2000). *Anthology*. London: Chronicle Books.

Becker, J. (2001). Anthropological perspectives on music and emotion. In P. N. Juslin & J. A. Sloboda (eds), *Music and emotion: Theory and research* (pp. 135–60). Oxford: Oxford University Press.

Beegle, A. (2004). American music education 1941–1946: meeting needs and making adjustments during World War II. *Journal of Historical Research in Music Education, 26*, 54–67.

Benjamin, W. (1968). The work of art in the age of mechanical reproduction. In H. Zohn (trans.), *Illuminations: essays and reflections* (pp. 217–52). New York: Schocken.

Brake, M. (1980). *The sociology of youth and youth subcultures*. London: Routledge.

Brown, S., & Volgsten, U. (eds). (2006). *Music and manipulation: On the social uses and social control of music*. New York: Berghahn Books.

Brown, S. (2006). Introduction: 'How does music work?' Toward a pragmatics of musical communication. In S. Brown & U. Volgsten (eds), *Music and manipulation: On the social uses and social control of music* (pp. 1–27). New York: Berghahn Books.

Burkeman, O. (2005). Three months ago Bob Geldof declared Live 8 had achieved its aim. But what really happened next? *The Guardian, September 12*. Retrieved from: http:// www. guardian. co. uk/ world/ 2005/ sep/ 12/ hearafrica05. development

Chambers, I. (1985). *Urban rhythms: pop music and popular culture*. London: Macmillan.

Chossudovsky, M. (2005). Live 8: Corporate Media Bonanza. *Global Research, July 5*. Retrieved from: http://www.globalresearch.ca/index.php?context=viewArticle&code=CHO20050705&articleId=641

Clarke, E. F. (2005). *Ways of listening: an ecological approach to the perception of musical meaning*. Oxford: Oxford University Press.

Cloonan, M., & Johnson, B. (2002). Killing me softly with his song: an initial investigation into the use of popular music as a tool of oppression. *Popular Music, 21,* 27–39.

Corliss, R. (2001). That old christmas feeling: Irving America. *Time, December 24.* Retrieved from: http:// www. time. com/ time/ sampler/ article/ 0,8599,189846,00. html

Corte, U., & Edwards, B. (2008). White power music and the mobilization of racist social movements. *Music and Arts in Action, 1,* 1–18.

Cusick, S. G. (2006). Music as torture / music as weapon. *Transcultural Music Review, 10.* Retrieved from: http://www.sibetrans.com/trans/trans10/cusick_eng.htm

DeNora, T. (2001). Aesthetic agency and musical practice: New directions in the sociology of music and emotion. In P. N. Juslin & J. A. Sloboda (eds), *Music and emotion: Theory and research* (pp. 161–80). Oxford: Oxford University Press.

DeNora, T. (2003). *After Adorno: rethinking music sociology.* Cambridge, UK: Cambridge University Press.

DeGregory, L. (2004). Iraq 'n' roll. *St. Petersburg Times, Nov 21,* P. 1.E. Retrieved from: http:// www. sptimes. com/ 2004/ 11/ 21/ Floridian/ Iraq__ n__ roll. shtml

Denisoff, R. S. (1972). The evolution of the American protest song. In R. S. Denisoff & R. A. Peterson (eds), *The sounds of social change* (pp. 79–91). Chicago, IL: Rand McNally.

Dibben, N. (2006). Subjectivity and the construction of emotion in the music of Björk. *Music Analysis, 25,* 171–97.

Durie, B. (2005). Senses special: doors of perception. *New Scientist, 29 January.* Retrieved from: http://www.newscientist.com/channel/being-human/mg18524841.600-senses-special-doors-of-perception.html;jsessionid=LFEENMOOCPCN

Dyer, R. (1979). In defense of disco. In S. Frith & A. Goodwin (eds), *On record: Rock, pop and the written word* (pp. 410–18). New York: Pantheon.

Ekman, P., Friesen, W. V., O'Sullivan, M., Chan, A., Diacoyanni-Tarlatzis, I., Heider, K., Krause, R., LeCompte, W. A., Pitcairn, T., Ricci-Bitti, P. E., Scherer, K. R., Tomita, M., & Tzavaras, A. (1987). Universals and cultural differences in the judgments of facial expressions of emotion. *Journal of Personality and Social Psychology, 53,* 712–17.

Elavsky, C. M. (2007). *United as ONE: Live 8 and the politics of the global music spectacle.* Paper presented at the International Association for the Study of Popular Music—US Branch National Conference, Boston, USA, April 2007.

Eyerman, R., & Jamison, A. (1998). *Music and social movements: mobilizing tradition in the twentieth century.* Cambridge, UK: Cambridge University Press.

Finkelstein, S. (1976). *How music expresses ideas.* New York: International Publishers.

Frith, S. (1981). *Sound effects: youth, leisure, and the politics of rock 'n' roll.* New York: Pantheon.

Garofalo, R. (1987). How autonomous is relative: popular music, the social formation, and cultural struggle. *Popular Music, 6,* 77–92.

Garofalo, R. (ed.). (1992). *Rockin' the boat: mass music and mass movements.* Boston, MA: South End Press.

Garofalo, R. (1992). Understanding mega-events: if we are the world then how do we change it. In R. Garofao (ed.), *Rockin' the boat: mass music and mass movements* (pp. 15–36). Boston, MA: South End Press.

Garofalo, R. (1994). Setting the record straight: censorship and social responsibility in popular music. *Journal of Popular Music Studies, 6,* 1–37.

Gillett, C. (1970). *The sound of the city: the rise of rock and roll.* New York: Outerbridge and Dienstfry.

Goldstein, R. (1977). The possibilities of punk. *Village Voice, October 10,* 44.

Gray, H. (1989). Popular music as a social problem: a social history of claims against popular music. In J. Best (ed.), *Images of issues: Typifying contemporary social problems* (pp. 143–58). Hawthorne, NY: De Gruyter.

Grossberg, L. (1983). The politics of youth culture: some observations on rock and roll in American culture. *Social Text*, *8*, 104–26.

Grossberg, L. (1984). Another boring day in paradise: rock and roll and the empowerment of everyday life. *Popular Music*, *4*, 225–58.

Grossberg, L. (1993). The framing of rock: rock and the new conservatism. In T. Bennett, S. Frith, L. Grossberg, J. Shepard, & G. Turner (eds), *Rock and popular music: Politics, policies, institutions* (pp. 193–209). New York: Routledge.

Hall, S. (1980). Cultural studies: two paradigms. *Media, Culture, and Society*, *2*, 57–72.

Handlin, O. (1959). Comments on mass and popular culture. In N. Jacobs (ed.), *Culture for the millions? Mass media in modern society* (pp. 63–70). Boston, MA: Beacon.

Hamm, C. (1983). *Yesterdays: popular song in America*. New York: W. W. Norton.

Harris, C. K. (1926). *After the ball: forty years of melody*. New York: Frank-Maurice.

Hebdige, D. (1979). *Subculture: the meaning of style*. London: Methuen.

Hebert, D. (2006). Rethinking patriotism: national anthems in music education. *Asia-Pacific Journal for Arts Education*, *4*, 21–39.

Hirsch, L. E. (2007). Weaponizing classical music: crime prevention and symbolic power in the age of repetition. *Journal of Popular Music Studies*, *19*, 344–60.

Horowitz, J. (1998). The specter of Hitler in the music of Wagner. *New York Times, November 8*. Retrieved from: http:// query. nytimes. com/ gst/ fullpage. html? res= 9E07E5DF1E3F-F93BA35752C1A96 E958260

Hughes, W. (1994). In the empire of the beat: discipline and disco. In A. Ross & T. Rose (eds), *Microphone fiends: youth music and youth culture* (pp. 147–57). New York: Routledge.

Idelsohn, A. Z. (1929). *Jewish music, in its historical development*. New York: Holt.

Jones, H. (1974). *Big star fallin' mama*. New York: Dell.

Jones, L. (1963). *Blues people: Negro music in white America*. New York: William Morrow.

Juslin, P. N., & Sloboda, J. A. (2001). Music and emotion: Introduction. In P. N. Juslin & J. A. Sloboda (eds), *Music and emotion: Theory and research* (pp. 1–20). Oxford: Oxford University Press.

Kassabian, A. (2007). *Hearing as a contact sense*. Paper presented at the International Association for the Study of Popular Music, Mexico City, Mexico, June 2007.

Kahn-Harris, K. (2003). *The aesthetics of 'hate music'*. Institute for Jewish Policy Research. Retrieved from: http://www.axt.org.uk/HateMusic/KahnHarris.htm

Kertz-Welzel, A. (2005). The pied piper of Hamelin: Adorno on music education. *Research Studies in Music Education*, *25*, 1–12.

Knopf, H. (2008). Is torture by music a 'performance in public'. *Excess Copyright, July 3*. Retrieved from: http:// excesscopyright. blogspot. com/ 2008/ 07/ is- torture- by-music-performance- in. html

Korpe, M., Reitov, O., & Cloonan, M. (2006). Music censorship from Plato to the present. In S. Brown & U. Volgsten (eds), *Music and manipulation: On the social uses and social control of music* (pp. 239–63). New York: Berghahn Books.

Kramer, L. (2001). The history of animation: history, analysis, and musical subjectivity. *Music Analysis*, *20*, 153–78.

Lasko, E. (2004). First lady Laura Bush accepts position of honorary chair of the national anthem project. *MENC Press Release, May 21*. Retrieved from: http://www.menc.org/publication/press/releases/laurabush_may04.html

Leeds, J. (2006). The new tastemakers. *New York Times, September 3*. Retrieved from: http:// www. nytimes. com/ 2006/ 09/ 03/ arts/ music/ 03leed. html

Lester, P. M. (2002). Visual symbolism and stereotypes in the wake of 9-11. In P. M. Lester & S. Ross (eds), *Images that injure* (2nd edn). Westport, CT: Praeger Publishers. Retrieved from: http://commfaculty.fullerton.edu/lester/writings/visualsymbolism.html

Lipsitz, G. (1990). Listening to learn and learning to listen: popular culture, cultural theory, and American studies. *American Quarterly*, 42, 615–36.

Moller, L. E. (1980). Music in Germany during the Third Reich: the use of music for propaganda, *Music Educators Journal*, 67, 40–4.

Mooney, H. F. (1969). Popular music since the 1920s: the significance of shifting taste. In J. Eisen (ed.), *The age of rock* (pp. 9–29). New York: Vintage Books.

Omi, M. (1986). A positive noise: The charity rock phenomenon. *Socialist Review*, 16, 107–14.

Ortner, S. (2005). Subjectivity and cultural critique. *Anthropological Theory*, 5, 31–52.

Pareles, J. (2007). Pay what you want for this article. *New York Times, December 9*. Retrieved from: http:// www. nytimes. com/ 2007/ 12/ 09/ arts/ music/ 09parc. html?_ r= 1& ref= arts& oref= slo gin

Peretz, I. (2001). Listen to the brain: A biological perspective on musical emotions. In P. N. Juslin & J. A. Sloboda (eds), *Music and emotion: Theory and research* (pp. 105–34). Oxford: Oxford University Press.

Portnoy, J. (1949). Similarities of musical concepts in ancient and medieval philosophy. *Journal of Aesthetics and Art Criticism*, 7, 235–43.

Quigley, S. L. (2004). Project to rekindle singing of national anthem. *American Forces Press Service, November 5*. Retrieved from: http://www.defenselink.mil/news/newsarticle. aspx?id=24915

Roberts, J. S. (1974). *Black music of two worlds*. New York: William Morrow.

Rockwell, J. (1988). Leftist causes? Rock seconds those emotions. *New York Times, December 11*, 23.

Sachs, O. (2007). *Musicophillia: tales of music and the brain*. New York: Alfred Knopf.

Seitz, M. Z. (2007). Songs for a brighter tomorrow. *New York Times, December 14*. Retrieved from: http:// movies. nytimes. com/ 2007/ 12/ 14/ movies/ 14revo. html

Small, C. (1987). *Music of the common tongue: survival and celebration in Afro-American music*. New York: Riverrun Press.

Small, C. (1998). *Musicking: the meaning of performance and listening*. Hanover, NH: Wesleyan University Press.

Sterne, J. (2007). Urban media and the politics of sound space. *Open 9: Sound*. Retrieved from: http://www.skor.nl/article-2853-en.html

Wagner, R. (1851). A communication to my friends. In *Prose Works* (trans. W. A. Ellis). Retrieved from: http:// users. belgacom. net/ wagnerlibrary/ prose/ wagcomm. htm

Williams, R. (1965). *The long revolution*. New York: Penguin Books.

Williams, R. (1977). *Marxism and revolution*. Oxford: Oxford University Press.

Wallis, R., & Malm, K. (1984). *Big sounds from small peoples: the music industry in small countries*. London: Constable.

Willis, P. (1978). *Profane culture*. London: Routledge.

CHAPTER 27

CROSS-CULTURAL SIMILARITIES AND DIFFERENCES

WILLIAM FORDE THOMPSON AND LAURA-LEE BALKWILL

OVER the past century, research on the relationship between music and emotion has overwhelmingly focused on the perceptions and experiences of Western listeners in response to Western tonal music. This focus has largely been a pragmatic consequence of the challenges of carrying out research in non-Western contexts, but it has left many important questions unanswered. To what extent are emotional aspects of music similar across cultures? Are there general principles that might account for the connection between music and emotion in all (or most) cultures, or is that connection unique to each culture, and perhaps non-existent in some cultures? How might we conduct a cross-cultural study of emotion and music without the conclusions being corrupted by cultural biases?

In this chapter, we review empirical studies of music and emotion that involve a cross-cultural comparison, and we outline prevailing views on the implications of such studies. Cross-cultural investigations can provide important insights into the contribution of universal and cultural associations between music and emotion. They can also be used to validate psychological theories of music and emotion—which are overwhelmingly supported by research that privileges Western tonal music.

Reflecting the current state of research in this area, our focus is on the *perception* of emotion in music (decoding) rather than the induction of affective states by music. The question of whether individuals from different cultures have comparable affective experiences in response to music is largely unknown, but is a rich area for future research (see Chapter 6, this volume). We also discuss cross-cultural studies of emotional prosody. *Speech prosody* refers to the vocal qualities of speech and includes intonation (pitch variation), stress, and timing. It signals points of emphasis, indicates a statement or question, and conveys emotional connotations (Darwin, 1872; Frick, 1985; Juslin & Laukka, 2003). Prosodic communication of emotion can occur independently of verbal comprehension (Kitayama & Ishii, 2002).

We discuss research on speech prosody for two reasons. First, music and speech prosody share important acoustic attributes and may use a common 'code' for emotional communication (Juslin & Laukka, 2003). Second, current theory and evidence on cross-cultural emotional decoding is more advanced for prosodic materials than for musical materials and, as such, may provide a model for future cross-cultural research on music and emotion. We do not provide a detailed examination of ethnographic studies of specific musical traditions, as such discussions may be found in Chapters 6 and 7 (this volume).

We begin by discussing some theoretical implications of research on cross-cultural commonalities in the association between music and emotion. We note that cognitive, ethnomusicological, and sociological approaches complement each other by providing different levels of explanation and different perspectives on the concept of music. Section 27.2 reviews the central questions arising from cross-cultural research on emotion. In Section 27.3, we outline the *cue-redundancy model*, developed to account for cross-cultural similarities and differences in the expression and recognition of emotion in music. The model accounts for the balance of culture-transcendent and culture-specific emotional cues across musical genres. It can be used to frame research questions, and to communicate, compare, and integrate empirical findings.

Section 27.4 outlines a broader framework for summarizing existing data on emotional communication, referred to as *fractionating emotional systems* (FES). FES extends the cue-redundancy model by accounting for similarities and differences in emotional communication not only across cultures but also across the auditory channels of music and speech prosody. FES also accounts for the process of enculturation that permits the gradual division of musical and prosodic emotional coding systems as well as the emergence of distinctive systems across cultures. Section 27.5 provides a review of cross-cultural studies of music and emotion, while section 27.6 reviews cross-cultural studies of emotion in speech. Section 27.7 identifies some future prospects for the cross-cultural study of music and emotion.

27.1 MUSIC AS A CROSS-CULTURAL CONSTRUCT

In order to investigate music as a cross-cultural construct, one must confront the tasks of defining *music* on the one hand and *culture* on the other. Merriam (1964) characterized music as having three aspects: sound, behaviour, and concept. As sound, music can be defined as a class of auditory signals that are produced by performers and perceived by listeners. As behaviour, music is associated with tangible activities (e.g. performance, dance, ritual) that are often essential to music experience, and that can be subjected to rigorous psychological, social, and historical analyses. As concept, music is construed as having specific functions within any social group (Clayton, 2001; Cross, 2006; Dissanayake, 2001). To a large extent, cross-cultural music cognition has focused on music as sound, but there is increasing awareness that music is a multimodal phenomenon. The behavioural aspect of music cannot be treated as a distinct level of analysis, but is inseparable from perceptions and experiences of music. Indeed, the visual input from viewing the facial expressions and gestures of a music performer can profoundly influence a listener's emotional responses to music (Thompson, Graham, & Russo, 2005; Thompson, Russo, & Quinto, 2008).

The construct of *culture* has also been scrutinized and debated. It refers to the set of behaviours, beliefs, social structures, and technologies of a population that are passed down from generation to generation. It includes social conventions related to art, dress, manner, dance, music, religion, ritual, and morality. Like music, cultures can be examined on multiple levels, some of which are nested within others. For example, within any cultural environment (e.g. Northern India) there are many subcultures (Hebdige, 1979). Each subculture, in turn, is associated with its own distinctive *habitus*: the habits, beliefs, skills, schemas, and preferences that are tacitly acquired and that shape perceptions, behaviours, and experiences (see Chapter 6, this volume). The term culture is not equivalent to 'country' or 'continent', and is not always associated with any one geographical region. Moreover, most individuals do not 'belong' to a single culture. More typically, numerous cultural and sub-cultural influences can be detected for any one individual, colliding, merging, and making temporary appearances when the appropriate context arises. Thus, although cross-cultural studies have often involved an examination of music materials and practices within specific geographical regions (e.g. Europe, Japan, Northern India), it should be recognized that the construct of culture does not restrict studies to such strategies.

Most ethnomusicologists are sensitive to such challenges, and are dubious of attempts to characterize nations as singular cultures and compare them with one another. In order to appreciate this disciplinary perspective, it may be useful to note that 'ethnomusicology' was known as 'comparative musicology' at the turn of the twentieth century. This name was abandoned for three reasons. First, the 'comparative method' as practised at the beginning of the twentieth century was steeped in an implied cultural hierarchy. Many scholars at the time regarded Western art music as a cultural pinnacle, and they interpreted music from other cultures as earlier or more primitive stages of development in the evolution of music. Like the common distinctions between 'hunter-gatherer', 'agrarian society', and 'nation state', comparative musicologists at the time were preoccupied with characterizing the 'stage' of musical development for each culture. Second, any comparison involves the establishment of criteria for evaluating musical practices, and the question of which criteria to adopt raises thorny methodological issues. How does one compare cultures objectively without inadvertently using criteria that privilege the culture of the researcher? Most contemporary ethnomusicologists have concluded that there are no neutral criteria. Third, ethnomusicologists resolved that each culture should be understood on its own terms. The very act of comparing musical cultures is therefore suspect. The change in name from comparative musicology to ethnomusicology reflected these concerns.

Ethnomusicologists often point to the work of Alexander Ellis as a seminal event in the birth of their discipline (Ellis, 1885). At the time Ellis was working, many scholars believed that different musical cultures were progressing along a developmental path that approached Western European art music. Evidence of this could purportedly be found in the instruments of other cultures whose tuning was considered crude approximations of the more developed Western scale. The 'crude tuning' of these instruments was regarded as tacit evidence of the rudimentary listening skills of people in other cultures. Working at the British Museum, Ellis measured the tuning of instruments from different cultures, and observed that the varied tunings in other cultures were not merely poor approximations of Western tuning. Rather, he found that different instruments pointed to unique and stable tuning systems that were categorically 'different' from the Western scale. The instruments were not merely technologically naïve efforts along some path toward the Western scale, but sophisticated technological efforts in their own right. Ellis's results thereby conflicted with notions of a cultural hierarchy.

Although the abandonment of notions of cultural hierarchies was a welcome development, the abandonment of 'comparative' approaches altogether by ethnomusicology has been unfortunate. A full understanding of the cognitive basis of music is not possible unless similarities and differences across cultures in the perception, experience, and production of music are taken into account. Comparisons across cultures are difficult methodologically and susceptible to researcher bias, but renouncing all comparative research is hardly a productive response to such challenges. Ellis's own achievements depended on comparative measurements within and between cultures, and in recent years researchers have employed reciprocal or counterbalanced methods in which test materials and subjects are recruited from two or more cultures. These methods may not eliminate cultural bias entirely, but the empirical data provide useful grist for theorizing about the cognitive basis of music.

There are several approaches to the cross-cultural study of music, including ethnomusicological, anthropological, sociological, and cognitive. Among the most influential sociological approaches is that of Alan Lomax (1975, 1976, 1978). His method, called *cantometrics*, involved characterizing song styles from different cultures using rating scales for features such as intensity, tempo, rhythmic complexity, interval width, embellishment, register, and tension. The procedure allowed Lomax to analyse and compare song styles cross-culturally. This research led him to conclude that the emotional properties of music are central to understanding cross-cultural similarities and differences in musical behaviours: 'music somehow expresses emotion; therefore, when a distinctive and consistent musical style lives in a culture or runs through several cultures, one can posit the existence of a distinctive set of emotional needs or drives that are somehow satisfied or evoked by this music' (Lomax, 1962, p. 425). Put simply, song style mirrors and reinforces cultural style.

Cross-cultural music cognition may be defined as the exploration of similarities and differences in cognitive processes and emotional experiences for music across cultures, and can be used to differentiate universal and culture-specific determinants of mature forms of music understanding. In general, cross-cultural music cognition has a more restricted focus than ethnomusicology, which applies research strategies adapted from cultural anthropology, sociology, and other disciplines in order to understand specific musical systems and traditions within a social or cultural context (see Chapter 6, this volume).

All cross-cultural research has a specific set of challenges above and beyond those that are part of any research endeavour. The difficulties of identifying geographical correlates of culture, of isolating one culture from other cultural influences, and the potential for researcher bias have already been noted. How effectively a study addresses such pitfalls and challenges is an important factor in interpreting its findings. Of critical importance in cross-cultural research is an awareness of one's own cultural perspectives and how they can bias every facet of the research, from the question being asked, to the methodology employed, to the analysis strategy employed, to the interpretation of observations. Consulting with members of the cultures under investigation is one important way of increasing an awareness of one's biases.

Perhaps the greatest challenge to studies of the expression and recognition of emotion across cultures is establishing cross-cultural equivalence of conceptual and empirical variables. Much has been written about the use of emotion labels to conceptualize the communication of emotions (see Wierzbicka, 1992, for a review). Typically, researchers employ the strategy of back-translation to create an equivalent set of instructional materials in the language of each culture of interest. However, even when linguistic equivalence has been achieved, conceptual equivalence may still prove elusive. For example, the word for anger in English and the word for anger in Japanese may not be interpreted by members of these cultures with the same degree of intensity or as signifying the same situations or behaviours. Therefore, establishing equivalence must be handled with care and sensitivity to cultural mores.

Ethnomusicologists and anthropologists have drawn attention to many nuances of difference in musical understandings across cultures, but evidence from cross-cultural music cognition suggests that music experiences are also constrained in important ways by the nature of our physical environment, the structure of the auditory system, and evolved strategies of perceptual and cognitive processing (Huron, 2006; Patel, 2008; Thompson & Schellenberg, 2006). Such constraints provide a foundation upon which processes of enculturation lead to additional layers of culture-specific understandings of music. They are an important source of commonalities in music cognition across cultures, and may exert a powerful influence on emotional responses to music. They do not necessarily lead to musical 'universals' if environment-specific or culture-specific influences overwhelm their impact. However, the effects of constraints can sometimes lead to universal, or near-universal, aspects of music cognition or experience, giving rise to striking commonalities across cultures. The following observations have been proposed as likely candidates for musical universals:

- a processing advantage for music built on a small number of discrete pitch levels that are spaced unevenly (e.g. the major scale);
- greater sensitivity to pitch contour than to exact intervals;
- perceived similarity of pitches separated by an octave;

- greater sensitivity to pitch relations than to absolute pitch values;
- sensitivity to sensory consonance and dissonance;
- a tendency to perceive sequences of pitches that are proximal in pitch as part of the same group;
- a processing advantage for music that contains a regular temporal pattern of stress; and
- a tendency to perceive pitches as having different levels of stability, with one pitch class often acting as a point of reference for other pitch classes.

Such commonalities can be explained with reference to one or more cognitive, environmental, genetic, and biophysical constraints, which may be collectively referred to as *system constraints*. The similarity across cultures of sung phrase lengths, for example, may arise in part because human short-term memory has limited capacity and would be burdened by excessively long phrases (an evolved feature of cognitive architecture). In addition, the ability to produce a melodic phrase vocally is constrained by the biophysics of singing, in that air resistance, breathing apparatuses, and oxygen requirements of humans are similar across cultures.

Experience and learning invariably build upon, expand, and in some cases can counter the constraints imposed by cognitive, environmental, genetic, and biophysical factors. For example, there is considerable diversity in musical *scales* across cultures, including the amount of tonal material and the number of scale notes (e.g. 12 tones in the Western chromatic scale, seven tones in the Western major, Byzantine, Gypsy and Hungarian scales, five tones in Celtic, West African and Indonesian scales), the intervals formed by scale notes, and the tuning of scale notes (Patel, 2008). Indeed, the influence of experience and learning is vast and leads to patterns of thought, behaviour, and aesthetic sensibility that are often unique to specific subcultures, as documented by the *thick descriptions* provided by ethnomusicologists and anthropologists (Geertz, 1973; Nettl, 1983). When differences in musical systems, behaviours, and experiences are observed from one culture or subculture to the next, they can usually be interpreted as effects of enculturation.

Cross-cultural music cognition is a valuable strategy for understanding the complex interplay between early predispositions and enculturation, but other scientific approaches are also essential to a full understanding of the issues involved. In particular, developmental approaches, neuroscientific data, and evolutionary psychology are particularly important for interpreting the nature of culture-transcendent and culture-specific sources of musical understanding (see Cross, 2003; Livingstone & Thompson, in press; and Chapters 5, 12, and 23, this volume).

Considerable caution must be taken when attempting to draw conclusions from cross-cultural similarities in musical practices and structures. In particular, observations of apparent 'universals' in music have often been mistakenly interpreted as implicating the involvement of genetic (innate) or 'hard-wired' biological determinants of musical systems and behaviours. There are important qualifications that must accompany this interpretation. First, genetic constraints on musical behaviours that result from a process of *phylogenesis* represent just one of several potential system constraints. Commonalities in musical behaviours across cultures also arise from biophysical constraints, such as oxygen consumption requirements, or similarities across cultures in acoustic environments, such as the tendency for sequences of pitched sounds emanating from a single source to exhibit pitch proximity. Second, many apparent constraints on musical systems may not be specific to music. Some may arise as a by-product of general auditory processing or the limits of short-term memory (Justus & Hutsler, 2005; Patel, 2008). Third, commonalities in music behaviours across cultures frequently arise from transcultural diffusion and interaction. In the twenty-first century, it is difficult to find individuals who have not been exposed to a large number of musical styles and tuning systems from a wide range of cultures and subcultures. Therefore, arguments for innately determined constraints on musical systems are compelling only when they are grounded in evolutionary biology, when other potential constraints have been ruled out, or when accompanied by direct genetic evidence. Indeed, many phenomena that appear to be innate may prove to be learned, because learning takes place in an interaction between organisms and physical environments that is ubiquitous around the world. As such, many apparent 'universals' of music probably have no genetic basis.

Conversely, differences in musical practices across cultures do not imply that genetic or innate factors play no role in such practices. Rather, cultural differences result from *ontogenetic* processes, which are themselves products of natural selection that permit cognitive mechanisms to adapt to environmental conditions. Such processes are guided by knowledge and expectancies, and their operation changes with experience (Heyes, 2003). Ontogenetic processes account for differences across cultures in the communication of emotion in music, but they do not guarantee such differences because some environmental and biophysical influences on musical systems are ubiquitous and can lead to musical universals in the absence of any 'innate' influences on music cognition. This conception of phylogenetic and ontogenetic influences has the potential to resolve some of the abiding concerns surrounding the study of similarities and differences in the musical practices of different cultures.

The connection between music and emotion may be examined at several levels of analysis relevant to cross-cultural comparisons, with some levels relying more on phylogenetic determinants and other levels relying more on ontogenetic processes. Environmental signals that remain stable across geographical regions and over long periods of evolutionary time are most economically handled by phylogenetic determinants. For example, the startle response that follows an unexpected and intensely loud sound is instinctive; it is a genetically determined reflex that requires no process of learning. Other phylogenetically-determined mechanisms include early feature detection and orienting reflexes. More generally, psychological processes, including those associated with emotional responses to music, vary in the extent to which they permit adaptive modification in response to changing environmental conditions.

Environmental signals that are unstable across time or geographical location are most effectively handled by ontogenetic processes. Indeed, ethnomusicologists have revealed that there is a high degree of semiotic variability in our auditory environment, such that the role of learning and enculturation is indispensable to full (adult) understanding of the many connections between music and emotion. For example, the increased tension that is experienced by a North American listener following the occurrence of a nondiatonic tone results from an ontogenetic process: it requires a process of enculturation to a diatonic tonal system and is manifested only after a certain stage of development. Indeed, children are not sensitive to differences in mode until after the age of five (Dalla Bella, Peretz, Rousseau, & Gosselin, 2001).

Phylogenetic determinants are responsible for predispositions that shape initial perceptions of musical attributes, such as early sensitivity to the difference between consonent and dissonant intervals, and they exert culture-transcendent forces on the connection between music and emotion (Dowling & Harwood, 1986). Ontogenetic processes build upon such predispositions and permit cultural fractionation to occur in the emotional connotations of music across musical traditions, cultures, styles, and time periods. Examples include the banning of the tritone interval from Western tonal music in sacred music during the middle ages, and the characterization of certain kinds of music as socially or emotionally dangerous at various points in history (e.g. music composed in the mixolydian scale in 350 BC, ragtime in the 1900s, heavy metal in the 1980s). Mature forms of musical understanding reflect a network of cognitive processes that combine phylogenetic and ontogenetic sources of adaptive features. Adaptive features that have a phylogenetic source were favoured by natural selection and are specialized to respond to highly stable features in the environment. Adaptive features that have an ontogenetic source were not favoured by natural selection but are generated in the course of development, and vary across cultures.

All musical systems implicate a dense combination of emotional and structural signals, some of which are culture-transcendent and handled by phylogenetically determined cognitive mechanisms, others that are culture-transcendent but nonetheless handled by ontogenetically determined cognitive mechanisms, and still others that are historically and culturally specified and again handled by ontogenetically determined cognitive mechanisms. Phenomena that are culturally transcendent are often identified by experimental strategies developed in cognitive science. Behaviours that are historically and culturally specified are often identified through ethnographic strategies, commonly applied in ethnomusicology, sociology, and anthropology.

27.2 EMOTION AS A CROSS-CULTURAL CONSTRUCT

Emotions are, in an important sense, biological mechanisms of 'preparedness' (Darwin, 1872; Ekman, 1992; Huron, 2006; Lazarus, 1991; Tooby & Cosmides, 1990), and this functional property of emotions has important implications for cross-cultural comparisons. Emotional states often have tangible biological functions, facilitating survival responses such as fighting, fleeing, or freezing. Emotional experiences and behaviours are observed in all cultures, and may be interpreted as universal responses to significant events. Some events are significant regardless of one's cultural environment, and may generate consistent emotional responses across cultures. Being in imminent danger of attack by a wild animal is likely to generate heightened arousal and fear in any individual, whether from Bali, China, Finland, or Canada. Many events acquire meaning through social construction, however, and an understanding of their significance requires knowledge of cultural traditions. The convention of bowing as a signal of respect and politeness in some cultures can be very specific: bowing too briefly or for too long can have significant connotations that elicit a strong emotional response.

According to Matsumoto (1989), emotions are biologically programmed, but the process of learning to perceive and express emotions is dependent on enculturation. Categories of emotion are also influenced by cultural factors. Broad dimensions such as valence and arousal may be applicable across cultures, while specific emotional categories such as the Indian *rasa* 'adbhutam' (meaning wondrous) may not translate well across cultures (Deva, 1973 pp. 66–68; Russell, 1994). Moreover, the notion that typical interactions involve the communication of a singular definable emotion may be unrealistic. In many if not most contexts, people experience varying combinations of emotions, and musical expressions of human experience often reflect such mixed emotions. If decoding individual emotions across cultures is difficult, decoding expressions of mixed emotions is an even greater challenge. To our knowledge, investigations of sensitivity to mixed emotions across cultures have yet to be conducted.

Landmark studies by Ekman and colleagues suggested that facial emotion recognition is universal for a number of basic emotions (Biehl et al, 1997; Ekman, 1970, 1972; Ekman, Sorenson, & Friesen, 1969). Ekman also emphasized cultural differences in *display rules* for emotional communication, but it has nevertheless been suggested that many of the early studies of emotional communication underestimated the role of enculturation by relying on forced-choice response formats and posed expressions (Russell, 1994), and because the researchers chose to focus on agreement across cultures rather than disagreement. The challenge of interpretation inherent in such studies is exemplified by a study that revealed that members of Bahinemo tribes perceived all faces of Americans as 'angry' (Sorensen, 1975). Such findings underscore the difficulty of decoding emotions across cultural boundaries. Indeed, some scholars have even argued that certain emotions are unique to particular cultures, such that cross-cultural decoding is essentially impossible (Briggs, 1970; Lutz, 1988).

A number of researchers have emphasized the significance of such cross-cultural differences (Matsumoto, 1989; Mesquita & Frijda, 1992; Mesquita et al, 1997). This research has led to the speculation that many cultures have distinctive norms for displaying and decoding emotions, or even culture-specific emotions. Such norms may function to maintain positive social interactions, and are especially apparent for the expression and recognition of negative emotions, which have the greatest potential to disrupt social interactions (Matsumoto, 1989). The role of cultural norms can also explain the phenomenon of ethnic or in-group bias. For example, when emotional speech is recorded from an individual, decoding accuracy is often highest by members of the same cultural group from which the utterance was recorded (Kilbride

& Yarczower, 1983; Mesquita & Frijda, 1992). Although the study of ethnic bias has received considerable attention, a full understanding of the phenomenon is unlikely to emerge soon, because results are inconsistent across studies, emotional channels, and cultures under consideration (Elfenbein & Ambady, 2002).

Differences in emotion recognition across cultures may also arise from language differences. For example, some languages have highly expressive terms for certain emotional concepts and lack terms for expressing other emotional concepts. Such differences in language apply to the expression of emotion across communication channels. Note, however, that the lack of an emotional term does not imply the absence of that emotion in a culture, but reflects a lack of emphasis on a particular subordinate category (e.g. frustration) within a broader emotion category (e.g. anger) in the social discourse of that culture (Boucher, 1979; Johnson-Laird & Oatley, 1989; Russell, 1991).

In addition, each communication channel is associated with channel-specific properties that can sometimes interfere with cross-cultural emotional communication. With respect to speech prosody, differences in emotional decoding accuracy across cultures can also arise because culture-transcendent prosodic cues are masked differentially by attributes of voice quality that are unfamiliar to non-speakers of that language. As an example, pitch changes involved in tonal languages like Mandarin may confuse or mask the interpretation of emotional intent to individuals who are unfamiliar with that language. Similarly, difficulties in emotional decoding of music can arise because unfamiliar conventions of composition and performance overwhelm impressions of the music, masking culture-transcendent emotional cues.

27.3 THE CUE-REDUNDANCY MODEL

A basic property of music that is shared by all cultures is that it involves multiple features that must be analysed by the auditory system. Even silence is registered by the brain and contrasted with the possibility of sound. One or more acoustic features such as intensity, tempo, pitch height, timbre, sensory dissonance, rhythmic complexity, and harmony may be present in the music, and each feature varies with the emotional connotations of the music. Just as instrument membranes have resonant frequencies that allow them to vibrate in sympathy with different sounds, the various acoustic features of music can be said to 'resonate' to varying degrees with the emotional character of the music. In turn, the auditory receptors for these music features themselves resonate with the emotional character of the music.

Each emotion is correlated to some extent with different types of changes in acoustic features, but many of these associations are moderate or even weak, and so no individual feature can be relied upon to determine an intended emotion. Rather, the full set of features available must be evaluated in a probabilistic manner, with different features weighted according to the strength of their association with each emotion (see Chapter 17, this volume). A yet-to-be-discovered mechanism that summarizes the available evidence from multiple emotional cues determines the emotion that is ultimately perceived and experienced. Because cues overlap in their emotional implications, the process of emotional decoding has the advantage of cue redundancy, allowing emotional communication to occur through convergent evidence and appraisals based on 'family resemblances' rather than on defining features (Rosch & Mervis, 1975; Wittgenstein, 1953/2001).

Thus, for example, one might imagine two musicians from disparate cultures (A and B) each composing a piece of music on the theme of joy. They would probably compose in a scale they know to be associated with joy in their culture. Musician A might use intricate harmonies, a simple rhythm, and compose for a high-pitched wind instrument that is instantly recognized by her people as 'the joy flute'. Musician B might compose an unaccompanied melodic line, a complex rhythm, and compose for a stringed instrument that is widely associated with joy by his people. They might both perform their pieces at a fast tempo and moderate amplitude.

Although there would probably be many surface differences between the two compositions, each piece would contain psychophysical cues (e.g. rate, intensity, pitch height) that have similar emotional connotations across cultures, and culture-specific cues (e.g. cadences, specific instruments, harmonic progressions) that enhance the recognition process for members of the same culture. Balkwill and Thompson (1999) defined *psychophysical cues* as 'any property of sound that can be perceived independent of musical experience, knowledge, or enculturation' (p. 44). However, psychophysical cues are not merely the result of innate processes but also reflect other system constraints, as described earlier. For example, music that communicates high-arousal emotions may be characterized by attributes that reflect the increased oxygen requirements associated with high-arousal states. Because the connection between oxygen requirements and arousal states is ubiquitous, certain attributes of high-arousal music are likely to occur across cultures. The presence of such attributes is unlikely to be dictated by direct genetic encoding, but may emerge indirectly as a result of biophysical constraints.

Examples of psychophysical cues include sound intensity, rate (tempo), melodic complexity, melodic contour, pitch range, rhythmic complexity, dynamics, and timbre. Listeners have the advantage of 'cue redundancy' because most music communicates emotion through multiple redundant cues (e.g. Juslin, 2000, 2001; Thompson & Robitaille, 1992). Listeners who share cultural experiences with the singer/songwriter have additional benefits of cue redundancy, whereas listeners from another culture must rely on psychophysical cues in order to recognize the emotional connotation of the music.

Figure 27.1 illustrates the *cue-redundancy model* (CRM) proposed by Balkwill and Thompson (1999). A central tenet of the CRM is that listeners can appreciate affective qualities of unfamiliar music by attending to psychophysical cues. Consciously or intuitively, composers and performers draw upon these culture-transcendent cues as well as culture-specific conventions in order to express emotion in music. Listeners, in turn, attend to either or both sources of emotional meaning. When psychophysical

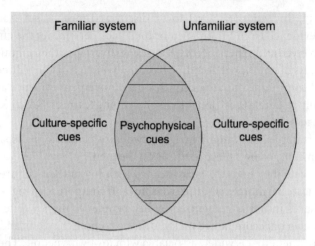

Fig. 27.1 The cue–redundancy model (CRM),
originally proposed by Balkwill & Thompson (1999).

cues in the music are not overwhelmed by culture-specific cues, listeners from outside
that culture are more likely to be able to decode the emotional intent.

Emotional decoding is affected by familiarity with the conventions of the tonal system and sensitivity to psychophysical cues. Listeners who are familiar with a musical
style should find it relatively easy to decode emotional meaning in that music, because
they can draw from both culture-specific and psychophysical cues. As such, in-group
advantages are a basic prediction of the CRM. However, because studies of in-group
advantages have yielded inconsistent results for other channels of emotional communication, their validity for emotional messages in music should be subjected to rigorous cross-cultural evaluation.

When culture-specific cues are unfamiliar or absent, listeners may still attend to
psychophysical cues such as tempo and intensity. These cues provide listeners with
a general understanding of the intended emotion even for unfamiliar musical styles.
Psychophysical cues are especially powerful signals because their interpretation
requires no knowledge of musical conventions. Indeed, cues such as tempo and intensity have emotional significance in other channels such as speech prosody, animal calls,
and alert signals.

The CRM can also be extended to the domain of speech prosody. Vocal expressions of anger are often marked by fast tempo and greater intensity; vocal expressions
of joy are often fast in tempo and have a large pitch range; and vocal expressions of
sadness are typically slow in tempo and low in pitch register (Juslin & Laukka, 2003).
When speech prosody and music convey the same emotion, they also tend to share
many of the same psychophysical cues (Ilie & Thompson, 2006). These commonalities suggest that emotions are communicated through psychophysical cues that

not only transcend cultural boundaries but are manifested in different channels of communication.

27.4 FRACTIONATING EMOTIONAL SYSTEMS

The concept of fractionating emotional systems (FES) extends the implications of the CRM, providing a broader framework for summarizing and interpreting cross-cultural data on emotional communication. Like the CRM, the FES framework acknowledges culture-transcendent and culture-specific influences on the emotional dimension of music and prosody. Ontogenetic processes allow for enculturation to occur, giving rise to culture-specific and domain-specific emotional cues and thereby differentiating or 'fractionating' emotional systems in different cultures and domains. Phylogenetic processes provide a point of convergence between emotional channels and cultural groups; ontogenetic processes provide a mechanism for distinguishing and focusing emotional channels and cultural groups.

Psychophysical cues are represented as a foundation for emotional communication that is common across cultures and auditory domains (music and speech prosody). This foundation is presumed to result from phylogenetic adaptations and other system constraints (ubiquitous environmental or biophysical influences), and is an important source of commonalities in emotional communication across cultures and auditory domains. For example, evidence suggests that infants prefer infant-directed song to infant-directed speech, just as they prefer infant-directed speech to affectively neutral speech (Nakata & Trehub, 2004; Singh et al, 2002). Such preferences may reflect early sensitivity to psychophysical cues along with an instinctive preference for positive emotional messages.

Emotional communication is maximally adaptive when it involves a combination of phylogenetic processes that handle stable acoustic features in the environment (e.g. the correlation between sound intensity and object proximity) and flexible ontogenetic processes for handling emotional signals that vary across environments. As displayed in Figure 27.2, enculturation builds culture-specific conventions and experiences of music from the foundations provided by phylogenetic contraints. The fanning out of triangular shapes represents the differentiating effects of ontogenetic processes, which promote the development of culture-specific experiences of the links between music and emotion, and between speech prosody and emotion.

Early in development, before enculturation has had the opportunity to exert a significant influence, there are few differences between individuals across cultures and few differences in the cues that must be used to decode emotional meaning in music and speech. With development, enculturation becomes increasingly evident, and leads to sensitivity to culture-specific and domain-specific emotional cues. This process

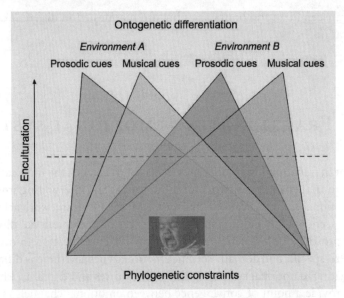

Fig. 27.2 An illustration of the concept of fractionating emotional systems (FES). The cue–redundancy model
addresses the distribution of psychophysical and culture-
specific cues for an enculturated individual, and may be
understood as a cross–section of FES (dotted line).

permits the partial fractionation of different systems of emotional communication
across cultures and emotional communication systems.

Throughout development, psychophysical cues bootstrap learning in complex
ways. For language acquisition, they interact with prosodic cues for segmentation and
syntactic understanding, and may be recruited to draw attention to statistical regularities in the transitional probabilities among acoustic events (Palmer & Hutchins, 2006;
Saffran, Aslin, & Newport, 1996). Moreover, different languages and musical styles permit different degrees of variation in psychophysical cues. For example, the use of pitch
variation for emotional communication is constrained in tone languages and in musical styles that reply on percussive instruments. Thus, the role of each psychophysical
cue for emotional communication varies as a function of the learning environment.

The cue redundancy model may be understood as a cross section of FES at any one
stage of development, from early development to full maturity. Early in development,
an individual will be predominantly sensitive to psychophysical cues that transcend
cultures and emotional channels. This stage would be represented in the CRM as a
relatively large proportion of overlap in the cues used for emotional communication
across domains and cultures. The process of enculturation leads to an increasing contribution of culture-specific and domain-specific cues to emotional meaning, and is
represented in the CRM by an increased proportion of such cues.

Nonetheless, a basic premise of FES is that psychophysical cues continue to exert an influence on emotional communication throughout the lifespan, providing a means for cross-cultural emotional communication and for commonalities between music and speech prosody in their use of emotional cues.

27.5 CROSS-CULTURAL STUDIES OF EMOTION AND MUSIC

Cross-cultural research on emotion and music includes studies that directly assess the capacity of individuals to interpret the emotional meaning of music across cultures, as well as studies that provide indirect evidence for cross-cultural commonalities in the association between music and emotion. The latter studies include developmental approaches and investigations of tension and complexity. These three sources of evidence will be reviewed in turn.

27.5.1 Direct assessments

Gundlach (1932) conducted one of the early psychological studies of emotional communication that considered music outside the Western classical tradition. His aim was to determine whether or not there are 'objective characteristics' of music in aboriginal cultures that form the basis of communicating specific moods. He analysed archives of songs collected from several North American aboriginal tribes. Songs were chosen for their correspondence with important aspects of aboriginal life (healing songs, love songs, and war songs) that were likely to express a specific emotion. Analyses of pitch, range, tempo, and rhythm revealed that war songs were typically low in pitch, fast in tempo, and wide in pitch range, whereas love songs were usually high in pitch, slow in tempo, and had a moderate pitch range. Healing songs often had the fewest number of rhythmic changes, whereas war songs had the greatest number of rhythmic changes. Gundlach concluded that there were measurable objective differences between these songs as a function of their emotional character.

In a later study, Gundlach (1935) presented a phrase from 40 different musical pieces to groups of listeners with varying levels of musical training. Their task was to select from a list of terms the verbal descriptor that best characterized the mood expressed by the composer, or to fill in their own description if they could not find an appropriate term. Agreement among participants was observed for each phrase (mean agreement $\geq .75$). Analyses of tempo, rhythm, intervals, range, intensity, mean pitch, and melody range revealed several 'objective' features of phrases associated with emotional communication. However, the extent to which such features can be decoded across cultures was not determined.

Morey (1940) extended this work by presenting samples of Western classical music (Schubert, Davies, Handel, and Wagner) to 11 male members of the Loma, a tribe in Liberia, West Africa. The pieces were selected on the basis that they conveyed emotions such as fear, reverence, rage, and love. Participants were teachers and students at the Holy Cross Mission School at Bolahun. They were asked to indicate which emotions were expressed by each music selection. Morey observed that the music often did not appear to elicit any emotions—or at least they did not evoke emotional judgements that are typical of Western listeners. In another experiment, Morey presented his music samples to 20 members of the Zealua Loma tribe outside the school. He reported that they did not find the music interesting and many of them left while it was still playing.

With ubiquitous media and increasing globalization in the twenty-first century, Western tonal music is so pervasive that it is rapidly losing its value as music stimuli in cross-cultural investigations. Research that involves Western tonal music therefore requires participants from extremely isolated cultures who are naïve to this music. Because radio and television are almost universally available, it is reasonable to wonder whether such cultures exist. Tom Fritz, together with Stefan Koelsch and colleagues, performed a cross-cultural study with participants from a native African population known as the Mafa (Fritz, Sammler, & Koelsch, 2006; Fritz et al, 2009). The Mafa are one of approximately 250 ethnic groups that make up the population of Cameroun. They are culturally isolated and live in the Extreme North Province in the Mandara mountain range. The remote Mafa settlements do not even have electrical supply, and are inhabited by individuals who pursue a traditional lifestyle and have not been exposed to Western music. Twenty German and 21 Mafa listeners judged the emotions conveyed in a sample of Western music. The music excerpts, which varied in duration (9–15 s), mode, tempo, pitch range, tone density, and rhythmic regularity, were composed to express the emotions happy, sad, and scary.

Music stimuli were classified using depictions of facial expressions from the Ekman archive (happy, sad, scary) (Ekman, 1976). Three Mafa participants could not recognize the facial expressions on the two-dimensional paper and were thus excluded from the test. Both German and Mafa listeners recognized all three emotions in the music samples at levels that were above chance performance (33 per cent). Among German listeners, recognition of happy music (99 per cent) was better than recognition of sad music (93 per cent) or scary music (81 per cent). Similarly, among the Mafa listeners, recognition of happy music (65 per cent) was better recognized than recognition of sad music (49 per cent) or scary music (48 per cent). This advantage for happy music did not arise because the two negative emotions were confused with one another: errors for each target emotion were distributed equally among the other two categories. Interestingly, the capacity to decode emotional expressions was significantly correlated with the degree of appreciation of the compositions. The authors proposed that 'meaningfulness' in music (clear emotional expression) leads to increased appreciation.

Hindustani music offers an ideal stimulus for cross-cultural comparisons, because of its strong association with emotional communication, and because it is easy to locate individuals who are unfamiliar with this music. Central to Hindustani music is the *raga-rasa* system in which each *raga* (set piece) is associated with one or more *rasas* (moods or essences). Each raga is also associated with a distinctive colour, season, and time of day. Deva and Virmani (1975) compared the intended mood of Hindustani ragas with mood ratings made by Indian listeners. In one experiment, four excerpts from ragas (roughly two minutes each) were played to 37 listeners, who were asked to choose from a list of mood adjectives the emotion that they believed was expressed. The authors reported that the perceptions of listeners often matched the intended mood of the ragas. In a second experiment, 228 listeners were asked to rate excerpts of a raga on expressed mood, associated colour, season, and time of day. Listeners judged the raga ('*Bhairav*') as dominant in empathy and compassion, and as reflecting vitality, positive affect, courage, and tranquillity. The majority of listeners associated the raga with the colour white or yellow, the season of autumn, and the time of day as early morning or early evening. According to Deva and Virmani, ratings generally approximated the intended mood of the raga.

In a later study, Gregory and Varney (1996) examined whether Western listeners who are unfamiliar with Hindustani music can interpret the emotional connotations of that music. Gregory and Varney asked British residents of Western and Indian heritage to judge the emotional messages implied in commercially recorded excerpts of Hindustani ragas, Western classical music, and Western new age music. After hearing each excerpt, listeners selected adjectives from a list developed by Hevner (1936; see Chapter 14, this volume). Western and Indian listeners were sensitive to intended emotions in Western music, but not Hindustani ragas. The finding suggests that emotional cues in unfamiliar music are not always interpretable, and suggests that culture-specific properties of music can mask culture-transcendent emotional cues.

Balkwill and Thompson (1999) performed a similar study, but observed far better emotional decoding of Hindustani music by Western listeners. They asked Canadian listeners to judge the emotional content of field recordings of Hindustani ragas, and to rate the presence of several psychophysical attributes in the music. Recordings were obtained of solo performances of Hindustani ragas that were explicitly intended to evoke specific emotions. Excerpts intended to convey joy/*hasya* were assigned high ratings of joy; excerpts intended to convey sadness/*karuna* were assigned high ratings of sadness; and excerpts intended to convey anger/*raudra* were assigned high ratings of anger. High ratings of joy were associated with high ratings of tempo and low ratings of melodic complexity. High ratings of sadness were associated with low ratings of tempo and high ratings of melodic complexity. Anger ratings were not significantly associated with ratings of tempo or complexity, but ragas performed on stringed instruments were rated much higher in anger than those performed on the flute.

A subsequent study conducted in Japan extended this work and provided additional evidence for the cue-redundancy model. Whereas Balkwill and Thompson (1999) examined judgements by Canadian listeners of Hindustani music, Balkwill, Thompson, and Matsunaga (2004) examined judgements by Japanese listeners of Japanese, Western, and Hindustani music. Music samples consisted of emotional music by two Canadian musicians in Toronto, Ontario, Canada, six Japanese musicians in Sapporo, Hokkaido, Japan, and the Hindustani music from Pune, India described in Balkwill and Thompson (1999). The music provided by the Canadian musicians was a compilation of improvisations on each target emotion. Each musician was asked to draw upon their musical experience and repertoire and to focus on the task of conveying each of the three specified emotions. This procedure was adopted to minimize extra-musical associations that many listeners may have formed between past pairings of familiar music with their own experiences. Because Japanese listeners are generally well acquainted with classical and popular Western music, the use of improvisations also served to decrease the level of familiarity with the Western music materials for this listener group.

The music provided by the Japanese musicians was a compilation of several genres of traditional composed music (*gagaku*, *shinto* and *minyo*). Each musician was asked to choose pieces from their repertoire that they felt would best convey each target emotion. These two stimulus sets, along with the Hindustani music previously collected (from Balkwill & Thompson, 1999) were then edited to create short excerpts (mean duration = 30 s) intended to evoke anger, joy, or sadness.

One hundred and forty-seven Japanese listeners (76 women, 71 men, mean age = 23.7) rated the degree of anger, joy, sadness, complexity, loudness, and tempo in each sample of music from Western, Japanese, and Hindustani stimulus sets. As expected, Japanese listeners were sensitive to the intended emotion of music from Japanese, Western, and Hindustani music, and their judgements were associated with the presence of psychophysical cues. High ratings of joy were associated with a fast tempo and a simple melody; high ratings of sadness were associated with a slow tempo and a complex melody; and high ratings of anger were associated with high intensity and a complex melody. The findings confirmed that Japanese listeners were sensitive to the emotions communicated in familiar and unfamiliar music, and their sensitivity was associated with the perception of psychophysical cues that transcended cultural boundaries.

More recently, we compared the judgements of Canadian and Japanese listeners for the same music stimuli (Balkwill, 2006). One hundred and thirty-nine Western listeners (82 women, 57 men, mean age = 25.7) participated in the study. As with Japanese listeners, the Canadian group was remarkably sensitive to intended emotions expressed in Japanese, Western, and Hindustani music, and their judgements were associated with the presence of psychophysical cues. Both groups were able to recognize music intended to evoke anger, joy, and sadness in all three tonal systems, and judgements for every emotion were significantly associated with at least one of the psychophysical attributes of complexity, intensity, tempo, and timbre.

An interesting difference observed between the Canadian and Japanese listener groups was the number of psychophysical cues associated with some emotion judgements. For example, in the case of anger ratings, the degree of perceived complexity, tempo, and intensity were all significant predictors for Japanese listeners, while for Canadian listeners, only degree of perceived intensity was significant. Previous research involving descriptions of visual stimuli have indicated that Japanese participants tend to process scenes more holistically, reporting more background stimuli than North American participants, who tend to focus on primary focal elements (Masuda & Nisbett, 2001). Whether similar differences between Japanese and North American groups in the quantity and quality of psychophysical cues associated with emotion recognition in this study can be attributed to cultural differences in attention focus or cognitive style is an intriguing question (see Nisbett, Peng, Choi, & Norenzayan, 2001, for a review). Further experiments with music and other auditory stimuli more clearly focused on this question may yield some interesting contributions to this area of research.

27.5.2 Developmental evidence

There is little doubt that long-term exposure to the music of one's culture has a powerful effect on our perceptions and experiences of music (Hannon & Trainor, 2007). Memory for music is better as a function of increasing age (Krumhansl & Keil, 1982; Trainor & Trehub, 1994) and of familiarity or conventionality of the music itself (Cuddy, Cohen, & Mewhort, 1981). Music processing is also enhanced by formal music training (Lynch & Eilers, 1991).

However, there is also considerable evidence that basic auditory skills are well developed at birth, and such skills are similar in all humans across cultures. Infants possess a number of perceptual skills for music that are remarkably similar to those of listeners who have had years of exposure to music. These apparent predispositions exert a significant influence on music experiences throughout the lifespan, including emotional responses to music and speech (Trehub, 2000, 2003; Trehub & Nakata, 2002). As examples, infants show evidence of processing advantages for contour patterns over precise intervals, for consonant over dissonant sounds, and for temporal pattern relations over absolute durations (Trehub & Hannon, 2006). Because these skills are observed very early in development, it is possible that their emergence reflects innate biases rather than environmental stimulation. In so far as such early skills do not rely heavily on processes of enculturation, they may form the basis for many important cross-cultural similarities in the perception of music.

It should be emphasized that it is not possible to rule out explanations of early auditory skills based on rapid adaptation of the auditory system to music exposure. To illustrate, the A1 tonotopic frequency map is fully developed (i.e. equivalent to adult organization) in rats two days after they are born (de Villers-Sidani, Chang, Bao, & Merzenich, 2007). If newborn rats are exposed to broadband noise for up to 90 days, no tonotopic map is evident. But within two days of turning off the noise, the A1 tonotopic map will be fully formed. Two conclusions may be drawn from these observations: (1) exposure to pitched tones is necessary for tonotopic perceptions to emerge, and (2) the rat learns pitch with only two days of auditory exposure. Clearly, the effects of learning can be unexpectedly rapid, such that one might be forgiven for assuming that the musical dispositions of newborns are innately determined.

An important influence on the emotional connotation of music is the relative balance of consonance and dissonance. In Western tonal music, consonance usually signals stability and positive emotional valence, whereas dissonance signifies tension, instability, and negative emotional valence. Musicologists have suggested that dissonance is understood and heard somewhat differently across different musical traditions, cultures, styles, and time periods, but evidence suggests that infants begin life with predispositions for processing consonance and dissonance, and these predispositions may remain influential into adulthood. Specifically, infants are highly sensitive to the distinction between consonance and dissonances, and even newborn infants prefer music that is consonant to music that is dissonant.

Zentner and Kagan (1996) exposed 4-month-old infants to consonant and dissonant versions of two melodies. Infants looked longer at the source of sound and moved less when consonant versions of melodies were played than when dissonant versions of melodies were played. Moreover, when the dissonant version was played, infants were more likely to fret and turn away from the music source. The researchers argued that infants are biologically predisposed to prefer consonance to dissonance (Crowder, Reznick, & Rosenkrantz, 1991; Trainor & Heinmiller, 1998).

Infant-directed singing (lullaby) is prevalent across cultures (Trehub, Unyk, & Trainor, 1993; Unyk, Trehub, Trainor, & Schellenberg, 1992), and plays many important functions in infant development, such as the acquisition of attentional skills, the maintenance of emotional stability, and the enhancement of infant–caregiver bonds (see also Chapter 23, this volume). These functions have implications for the survival of the infant, and are thought to have a biological basis. A number of researchers have proposed that all music may have ultimately originated from this form of musical activity, which conferred a survival advantage for ancestral populations. Unlike other primates, infants cannot cling to their mother's fur while the mother forages with both hands. Singing would have allowed mothers to soothe their infants (keeping them quiet to avoid predators) while foraging. If such conjectures are correct, then the diverse musical systems across all cultures should have a common foundation that is reflected in infant-directed songs. Moreover, cross-cultural similarities should be particularly evident for the emotional qualities of music.

In support of this view, Trehub and colleagues demonstrated that infants are naturally attracted to lullabies. Nakata and Trehub (2004) found that 6-month-old infants look longer at audio-visual recordings of their mother if she is singing a lullaby than if she is speaking, suggesting that lullabies generate positive affective states in infants. Moreover, cortisol levels (associated with stress) dropped significantly following infant-directed song, indicating that lullabies are naturally soothing.

Infant-directed song contains many of the emotional cues that are observed in infant-directed speech, including relatively high pitch, slow tempo, and simple and repeating contours (Fernald, 1991; Fernald & Simon, 1984). Is there a general connection between the emotional cues used in music and speech prosody? Evidence by Thompson, Schellenberg, and Husain (2004) suggests that there is. Musically trained and untrained adults were given a test of sensitivity to emotional prosody for phrases spoken in their own language (English) or in a foreign language (Tagalog, a language of the Philippines). The test required listeners to classify the emotional connotation of each utterance as happy, sad, fearful, or angry. Musically trained adults were significantly better than untrained adults at classifying the emotions, including those expressed in the unfamiliar language of Tagalog. That is, cross-cultural sensitivity to vocal emotions was enhanced for musically trained adults. The results suggest that psychophysical cues to emotion are instantiated in both music and speech prosody. Thus, long-term training in music gives rise to enhanced sensitivity to such cues, whether they occur in familiar music, unfamiliar music, familiar speech, or unfamiliar speech.

To address the possibility that the trained adults were naturally more sensitive to vocal emotions irrespective of their training, the researchers assessed the sensitivity of 6-year-olds to emotional prosody after one year of music lessons, drama lessons, or no lessons. The results revealed that both drama and keyboard lessons resulted in enhanced sensitivity to emotional prosody, including prosodic materials from an unfamiliar language (Tagalog). Thus, drama lessons, with their emphasis on learning to express different emotions, had a 'direct' effect on learning, whereas music lessons had a 'transfer effect' to the domain of speech prosody. One explanation for these findings is that music and speech prosody implicate the same acoustic cues to emotion. Music training may not only enhance sensitivity to culture-specific properties of a musical system; it may also engage and refine neural processes that respond to universal acoustic cues to emotion, thereby enhancing sensitivity to emotions in music and speech across cultures.

27.5.3 Tension and stability

Musical tension provides another source of emotional meaning in music. Tension can arise from several sources, including sensory dissonance, violations of expectations, complexity, and tonal instability. When we listen to music from an unfamiliar genre, our levels of uncertainty are generally higher, giving rise to perceived complexity and tension. Huron (2006) used a 'betting paradigm' to evaluate the level of uncertainty of continuations in a melody. Balinese and American musicians listened to an unfamiliar traditional Balinese melody and provided judgements, via a betting game, of their ability to anticipate future pitches. Not surprisingly, uncertainty was greater for American listeners than for Balinese listeners, but the levels of uncertainty also showed a different trajectory for the two groups. For Balinese listeners, the level of uncertainty was maximal in the middle of the melody, and minimal near the beginning and end of the melody. No such rising and falling pattern was observed for American listeners, who simply showed a subtle decline in uncertainty as the melody progressed.

In a series of studies of the *implication-realization* (I-R) model (Narmour, 1990), American and Chinese listeners were asked to provide ratings of continuation following fragments of British folk songs, Webern lieder, and Chinese pentatonic songs (Krumhansl, 1995; Schellenberg, 1996). Certain predictors based on the I-R model accounted for a significant proportion of the variance in ratings for the two listener groups and three musical styles, suggesting cross-cultural similarities in the formation of expectancies. For example, listeners tended to expect continuation tones that were close in pitch to preceding tones (see also Carlsen, 1981; Thompson & Stainton, 1998). If such expectancies are 'hard-wired', then they could provide a basis for emotional communication across cultures, whereby large changes in pitch in a melody universally give rise to heightened arousal (i.e. surprise) and increased tension.

Perceived tension in music can also be influenced by the overall complexity of the music. Cross-cultural comparisons suggest that a range of factors influence perceived complexity, and that these factors are weighted differently for judgements of familiar and unfamiliar music. Eerola, Himberg, Toiviainen, and Louhivuori (2006) asked Finnish and African listeners to judge the complex of Western and African folk songs. A range of melodic complexity measures was developed, including average interval size, entropy of interval distribution, entropy of note duration, rhythmic variability, note density, tonal ambiguity, and contour entropy (where entropy is a measure of uncertainty).

Overall patterns of judgements were similar for the two groups and the two styles of music, supporting the idea that complexity is a culture-transcendent construct. However, culture-specific influences on judgements of complexity were also evident. Whereas the style of the Western folk songs was familiar to both groups, the style of the African folk songs was familiar to only the African group. Complexity measures reflected these differences in familiarity, with differences in the predictive power of complexity variables differing between groups for the African folk songs. Taken together, the results suggest that melodic complexity transcends cultural boundaries, but musical enculturation still plays an important role.

Tension is also inversely related to tonal stability (Lerdahl & Krumhansl, 2007). Cross-cultural studies of tonal stability suggest that in the absence of knowledge of a tonal system, the relative stability of tones (tonal hierarchies) formed by non-native listeners were influenced mainly by pitch distribution. When Western listeners provide goodness-of-fit judgements for probe tones presented in the context of North Indian music (Castellano, Bharucha, & Krumhansl, 1984) and Balinese music (Kessler, Hansen, & Shepard, 1984), their judgements are primarily influenced by the frequency of occurrence of pitches. Similarly, when Western listeners provide judgements of North Sami yoiks the influence of Western schematic knowledge is strongly evident; when indiginous Sami listeners judge the same materials there is relatively little evidence for an influence of Western schematic knowledge (Krumhansl et al, 2000).

27.6 CROSS-CULTURAL STUDIES OF EMOTION AND PROSODY

Because emotion is expressed in music and speech prosody using very similar cues, cross-cultural studies of speech prosody are highly relevant to cross-cultural investigations of music and emotion (Ilie & Thompson, 2006; Juslin & Laukka, 2003; Patel, 2008). Indeed, tempo, intensity, and timbre affect judgements of emotion in both music and speech. For example, vocal expressions of anger are often marked by fast tempo and greater intensity (in the case of 'hot' anger); vocal expressions of joy are often fast in tempo with a higher pitch range; and vocal expressions of sadness are typically slow in tempo and low in pitch (Bachorowski & Owren, 1995; Frick, 1985; Scherer, 1986; Scherer & Oshinsky, 1977; Thompson & Balkwill, 2006).

Several investigations of emotional prosody have converged on the view that listeners are highly sensitive to the prosodic expression of anger, joy, and sadness (Juslin & Laukka, 2003). Conversely, a relatively low success rate has been reported for the recognition of fear and disgust in speech. Emotional sensitivity for prosodic materials is similar to emotional sensitivity for musical materials, although the two modalities differ in the emotions that are most commonly conveyed. Anger is commonly communicated through speech prosody, and it is often the best recognized emotion for spoken stimuli (e.g. Banse & Scherer, 1996). Interestingly, anger is also recognized rather well in music (Juslin & Laukka, 2003), even though this emotion is communicated in only certain genres of music, and composers have difficulty expressing anger with pitch or rhythmic structure (Thompson & Robitaille, 1992).

Although the CRM was developed to account for cross-cultural studies of music and emotion, it readily applies to emotional prosody, suggesting that a broader framework is needed to account for the emergence of emotional systems. The concept of fractionating emotional systems assumes that psychophysical cues provide a common point of departure for the development of emotional communication in music and speech prosody. According to FES, individuals should be able to recognize emotions expressed prosodically even when utterances are spoken in an unfamiliar language. Moreover, an ethnic bias should be observed for decoding emotional messages expressed prosodically, because of the presence of culture-specific cues.

Prosodic cues for emotion are well documented for English and some Western European languages (German, Dutch). Joy is expressed with a comparatively rapid speaking rate, high average pitch, large pitch range, and bright timbre; sadness is conveyed with a slow speaking rate, low average pitch, narrow pitch range, and low intensity; anger is expressed with a fast speaking rate, high average pitch, wide pitch range, high intensity, and rising pitch contours; and fear is conveyed with a fast speaking rate, high average pitch, large pitch variability, and varied loudness (Juslin & Laukka, 2003; Scherer, 1986).

Analyses of recognition rates indicate that prosodic cues alone allow listeners to identify the emotion being conveyed, with identification rates of roughly four to five times the rates that would be predicted by guessing (Banse & Scherer, 1996; Frick, 1985; Scherer, 1979, 1986; Standke, 1992; van Bezooijen et al, 1983). Not all emotions are decoded equally well from speech prosody, however. For example, anger and sadness are typically decoded more reliably than joy and fear (Banse & Scherer, 1996; Johnstone & Scherer, 2000).

A large number of studies have revealed sensitivity to emotional prosody across cultures and in unfamiliar languages. Kramer (1964) demonstrated that English-speaking American listeners could identify vocal expressions of emotion rendered in English and Japanese (content-filtered) at a rate better than chance. Beier and Zautra (1972) found that American, Polish, and Japanese listeners were able to identify emotion in American English speech. Similar positive results were reported by McCluskey and Albas (1981) for their study of Canadian and Mexican children and adult listeners judging vocally expressed emotion provided by Canadian and Mexican actors. In some cases, listeners were more accurate in recognizing the emotion in the unfamiliar language than in their own. In an experiment with samples of emotional speech spoken in Dutch, judges from the Netherlands, Taiwan, and Japan were also able to recognize each intended emotion with better-than-chance accuracy (van Bezooijen et al, 1983), although there were differences in level of accuracy as a function of emotion and language. More recently, Scherer et al (2001) recorded German actors (two male, two female) portraying five emotions (joy, anger, sadness, fear, and neutral). The voice samples were elicited using a scenario approach in which the actors were given text descriptions of emotional scenarios and asked to act them out (e.g. death of a loved one) in the performance of two standard sentences. These sentences were designed to circumvent the issue of semantic meaning by combining phonemes from six different languages (German, English, French, Italian, Spanish, and Danish; e.g. 'Fee gott laish jonkill gosterr').

By enlisting collaborators in nine countries (Germany, Switzerland, Great Britain, the Netherlands, Italy, France, Spain, the United States, and Indonesia), emotion judgements from groups of participants in each country were obtained (n ranged from 32 to 70, total = 428; age 18–30). All materials were translated into the language of each country. Participants were asked to focus on the emotion rather than the content of the sentence. After each utterance, they were given six seconds to select up to two emotion labels on the list of five target emotions. They were urged to select ones they thought best described the emotion the actor was trying to convey.

The authors reported an accuracy of 66 per cent across all emotions and all countries. Rate of accuracy was affected by country, type of emotion, and gender of the speakers. Confusion matrices were generated to assess patterns of errors as well as accuracy. German listeners had the highest rates of accuracy (Cohen's Kappa = .67, $p < .001$). Listeners from the other European countries also did well, with accuracy ranging from .52 to .62 (Cohen's Kappa, $p < .001$). Listeners from the one non-European country, Indonesia, had the lowest accuracy rate (Cohen's Kappa = .39, $p < .001$). The highest recognition rate was associated with expressions of anger; the lowest recognition rate was associated with expressions of joy.

Elfenbein and Ambady (2002) conducted a meta-analysis of 97 experiments exploring cross-cultural recognition of emotion in visual and auditory modes. In each study analysed, emotional stimuli (speech, facial expression) from at least one culture were presented to members and non-members of that culture. Cross-cultural emotion recognition accuracy was lower in studies of prosody than in studies of facial expression and body language, although most studies of prosody reported better-than-chance rates of recognition. Very few cross-cultural studies of emotional prosody have involved non-Western languages.

Examination of non-Western languages is important, because there is a long history of close contact between speakers of Western languages that might explain similar uses of prosody. Similar uses of prosody in Swedish and Norwegian, for example, can be explained by the history of interaction between speakers of these languages, and would not implicate universal principles of emotional prosody. Similar uses of prosody in

Western and non-Western languages, on the other hand, would provide compelling evidence for universal principles of emotional prosody.

Elfenbein and Ambady (2003) proposed a *cultural proximity hypothesis* to predict how well people of different cultures recognize emotional expression. According to their hypothesis, members of cultures who share cultural elements such as degree of individualism or collectivism, power structure, and gender roles, should be more successful at decoding each other's emotional expressions than members of cultures that are less similar. The cultural proximity hypothesis predicts, for example, that Japanese people should be better at recognizing the emotional expressions of Chinese people than the emotional expressions of North Americans, because Japanese and Chinese cultures are more similar to each other on relevant dimensions than Japanese and American cultures. Conversely, it predicts that English-speaking listeners should find it difficult to decode emotional prosody in Japanese and Chinese speech. This prediction contrasts with that of the cue-redundancy model, which suggests that psychophysical cues associated with emotions will allow individuals to decode emotions across cultural boundaries, including individualist and collectivist cultural boundaries.

Thompson and Balkwill (2006) investigated how well certain prosodic cues (frequency, intensity, and event density) were associated with the ability of English speakers to recognize emotion in five languages: English, German, Mandarin Chinese, Tagalog, and Japanese. Recordings were obtained of semantically neutral sentences (e.g. 'The bottle is on the table') spoken in a way that communicated each of four intended emotions: joy, sadness, anger, and fear. The use of prosody was not exaggerated or dramatic, but merely typical for speakers of each language. The five languages represent two members of the Germanic branch of the Indo-European language family (English and German), one language from the Sino-Tibetan family (Mandarin-Chinese), one language from the Altaic family (Japanese), and one from the Austronesian family (Tagalog) (Katsiavriades & Qureshi, 2003). German and English are Western languages spoken in individualistic societies, whereas Japanese and Chinese are Asian languages spoken in collectivist societies. Tagalog has been influenced by both the colonizing languages of Spanish and English, as well as by the languages of its Asian neighbours, Japan, Korea, and China.

Three predictions were evaluated. First, assuming that sensitivity to emotional prosody is partially dependent on psychophysical cues, listeners should be able to decode emotional prosody in any language at rates higher than that predicted by chance. Second, based on the idea that certain prosodic cues of emotion are culture specific, listeners should have higher rates of recognition for emotional prosody in their own language. Third, in view of previous research on emotional prosody, we predicted that listeners should be able to decode anger and sadness more reliably than joy and fear in all five languages (Johnstone & Scherer, 2000).

English-speaking listeners recognized the four emotions at a rate significantly better than chance in all five languages, achieving the highest recognition scores within their own language. The analysis of speech stimuli revealed several psychophysical cues associated with specific emotions, providing potential cues to the decoding of emotional meaning. Regression analyses confirmed the predictive power of these cues for emotional judgements. Across languages, the ability to decode emotions was associated with psychophysical cues such as mean frequency, intensity, and event density.

We also assessed the ability of adult, native speakers of Mandarin and Japanese to identify intended emotions in English, Mandarin, and Japanese speech samples (Balkwill & Thompson, 2005; Balkwill, 2006). Emotional decoding from these listeners was compared with the results from our English-speaking listeners. Again, semantically neutral sentences were used so that emotional intentions could be determined only by attending to prosodic aspects of speech.

Chinese and Japanese groups recognized anger, joy, and sadness at rates that were higher than chance performance in all three languages. Across languages and listener groups, the ability to decode emotions was associated with acoustic qualities such as mean frequency, intensity, and event density. Although both groups recognized fear above chance in English and Chinese, Japanese listeners' recognition of fear fell below chance in their own language. More data are needed to draw strong conclusions from such findings, but it is interesting to note that research on facial expressions indicates that Japanese judges also have difficulty decoding fear from Japanese facial expressions (Biehl et al, 1997; Matsumoto, 1992, 1996; Russell, Suzuki, & Ishida, 1993). It has been suggested that the emphasis in Japan on group cohesion and harmony discourages acknowledgement of emotions that threaten group harmony (Matsumoto, 1996).

We were able to address the cultural proximity hypothesis by comparing recognition rates for English, Chinese, and Japanese listeners. Support for the hypothesis would be evident if: (a) all listener groups are better at recognizing emotion in their own language than in other languages (even when verbal cues provide no information); (b) Chinese listeners are better than English-speaking listeners at recognizing emotion in Japanese speech; and (c) Japanese listeners are better than English listeners at recognizing emotion in Chinese speech. China and Japan have a long history of interaction between their peoples in times of peace and conflict (Rose, 2005). Emotional display rules in China and Japan are also similar in that negative emotions are considered inappropriate to display in public. North Americans, in contrast, have a higher tolerance of negative emotional displays (Eid & Deiner, 2001; Matsumoto, 1990).

Only our English-speaking listeners showed an in-group advantage across emotion categories. Chinese and Japanese listeners had an in-group advantage for the recognition of joy in their own language, but on the whole did not decode emotion better in their own language than in the English language. The high recognition of emotion in English speech by Chinese and Japanese listeners was not surprising, as all participants had exposure to English speech during their secondary school English-language training, as well as ongoing exposure through television, movies, and other media (Albas et al, 1976; Rosenthal et al, 1979; Scherer et al, 2001). That is, passive exposure to English speech among Japanese and Chinese listeners may have overwhelmed any decoding advantage arising from cultural proximity.

Across languages, judgements of joy were associated with greater range of fundamental frequency; judgements of sadness were associated with lower mean intensity, lower range of intensity, and lower event density; and judgements of anger were associated with greater mean and range of intensity, and greater event density.

Consistent with the cue-redundancy model, the type of acoustic parameter and the direction of association with emotion judgements were often similar in Canadian, Japanese, and Chinese listeners.

27.7 SUMMARY AND FUTURE PROSPECTS

Cross-cultural studies of music and speech prosody suggest that emotional communication occurs through a complex interplay between system-specific and psychophysical cues. Psychophysical cues have similar connotations across cultures (Balkwill & Thompson, 1999; Balkwill, Thompson, & Matsunaga, 2004) and similar functions in music and speech prosody (Ilie & Thompson, 2006; Juslin & Laukka, 2003; Patel, 2008). Reliance on psychophysical influences wanes throughout the lifespan, with enculturation gradually leading to increased sensitivity to culture-specific and channel-specific cues. Enculturation can lead to an understanding of abstract cues that have no psychophysical basis, but it can also influence the interpretation of psychophysical cues themselves, overlaying their significance with culture-specific nuance or altering their interpretation entirely.

To summarize, the FES model contains three components, as follows:

1. *Phylogenetic base.* Infants start life with an understanding of basic psychophysical cues to emotion. Psychophysical cues are determined by system constraints that may include genetic factors, but may also be determined by ubiquitous environmental and biophysical constraints. Musical and prosodic channels of communication share these psychophysical cues.
2. *Ontogenetic process.* Throughout development is a process of refinement and fractionation of different emotional communication systems. This fractionation applies not only to the modalities of music and prosody (which fractionate from each other), but also to musical and prosodic systems *across cultures*. That is, the process of fractionation permits the emergence of culture-specific systems of emotional coding, some prosodic and others musical. System-specific cues are learned through exposure to the conventions of one's culture, giving rise to culture-specific understandings of emotional communication.
3. *Cross-cultural communication.* Psychophysical cues remain available for decoding at all stages of development, with culture-specific and domain-specific cues overlaid increasingly throughout development. When an individual attempts to decode an emotional message (from prosody or music) across cultural boundaries, it is usually optimal to focus attention on psychophysical cues while ignoring culture-specific cues. Culture-specific cues can mask the ability to attend to psychophysical cues, and emotional communication is weaker across cultures than within cultures because psychophysical cues provide only one part of the

full emotional code. Nonetheless, it generally enables above-chance decoding of emotional messages.

Research is needed to evaluate the capacity for enculturation to alter the emotional connotation of psychophysical cues entirely. Existing data suggest that this capacity is either limited or seldom realized: individuals at all stages of development are capable of decoding basic emotions such as anger, joy, and sadness in unfamiliar music or speech, because both channels of emotional communication contain a number of psychophysical cues that transcend cultural boundaries, including pitch level and variability, sound intensity, rate (tempo), timbre, and complexity. Difficulties in decoding do occur, but they usually arise because culture-specific conventions and cues mask the detection of psychophysical cues. Training listeners to selectively attend to psychophysical cues may lead to improved cross-cultural emotional communication in music and speech prosody.

Further cross-cultural studies are also needed to classify the many known emotional cues as either psychophysical and having a phylogenetic basis, or culture-specific and having an ontogenetic basis. Juslin and Laukka (2003) have identified a large number of musical and prosodic cues such as jitter, vibrato, formant structure, the presence of pauses, onset characteristics, and articulation. More recently, Juslin and Västfjäll (2008) proposed a set of mechanisms for understanding emotional induction by music (see Chapter 22, this volume). One such mechanism—the *brain stem* response—is likely to respond in similar ways across all cultures to psychophysical features such as high intensity. Nonetheless, the potential role of this mechanism for cross-cultural emotional communication has yet to be fully understood.

How might one account for the existence of culture-transcendent connections between psychophysical cues and emotions? Huron (2006) provided a number of evolutionary explanations, and Scherer's (1986) *component process model* describes physiological changes that occur in the vocal apparatus during the expression of emotions. For example, speaking of something that is deeply unpleasant often manifests as faucal and pharyngeal constriction and a tensing of the vocal tract. The acoustic outcome is higher-frequency energy. Based on this model, Banse and Scherer (1996) predicted several associations between the acoustic attributes of speech and emotional intent.

Differences between expression and recognition of emotion in music and speech are also of interest. Are some emotions easy to convey through speech prosody, but difficult to convey in music? One might speculate that because speech carries the weight of semantic as well as emotional meaning, it may be more susceptible to within-culture norms as well as in-group and out-group biases. The FES framework accounts for the dynamic interplay between psychophysical cues and culture-specific conventions throughout development, and complements the CRM and other models of emotional communication. For example, the Brunswikian lens model (Brunswik, 1956) provides another valuable framework for understanding the ability to decode emotional meaning from either speech prosody (Scherer, 1982) or music (Juslin, 2000). Originally designed to describe visual perception, the model has been adapted to many types of human judgements (see also Chapter 17, this volume).

In a Brunswikian framework the intent of the encoder to express an emotion is facilitated by the use of a large set of cues that are probabilistic and partially redundant. Each cue by itself is not a reliable indicator of the expressed emotion, but combined with other cues, each one contributes in a cumulative fashion to the communication and recognition of emotion. The model incorporates the flexibility of the decoder to shift expectations from unavailable to available cues (Juslin, 2000). The CRM and FES are consistent with this model, but focus on the significance of psychophysical cues for the expression of emotions, their interaction with culture-specific convention that can enhance or hinder the ability of listeners to decode emotions across cultures, and the gradual fractionation of emotional communication systems across cognitive domains and cultural environments.

RECOMMENDED FURTHER READING

1. Elfenbein, H. A., & Ambady, N. (2002). On the universality and cultural specificity of emotion recognition: A meta-analysis. *Psychological Bulletin, 128,* 203–35.
2. Juslin, P. N., & Västfjäll, D. (2008a). Emotional responses to music: The need to consider underlying mechanisms. *Behavioral and Brain Sciences, 31,* 559–75.
3. Reyes, A. (2009). What do ethnomusicologists do? An old question for a new century. *Ethnomusicology, 53,* 1–17.

REFERENCES

Albas, D. C., McCluskey, K. W., & Albas, C. A. (1976). Perception of the emotional content of speech: A comparison of two Canadian groups. *Journal of Cross-Cultural Psychology 7,* 481–90.

Bachorowski, J., & Owren, M. (1995). Vocal expression of emotion: Acoustic properties of speech are associated with emotional intensity and context. *Psychological Science, 6,* 219–24.

Balkwill, L-L. (2006). *Perceptions of emotion in music across cultures.* Paper presented at Emotional Geographies: The Second International & Interdisciplinary Conference, May 2006, Queen's University, Kingston, Canada.

Balkwill, L-L., & Thompson, W. F. (1999). A cross-cultural investigation of the perception of emotion in music: Psychophysical and cultural cues. *Music Perception, 17,* 43–64.

Balkwill, L-L., & Thompson, W. F. (2005). *Recognition of emotion in five languages.* Paper presented at Auditory Perception Cognition and Action Meeting, November 2005, Toronto, Canada.

Balkwill, L-L., Thompson, W. F., & Matsunaga, R. (2004). Recognition of emotion in Japanese, North Indian and Western music by Japanese listeners. *Japanese Journal of Psychological Research, 46,* 337–49.

Banse, R., & Scherer, K. R. (1996). Acoustic profiles in vocal emotion expression. *Journal of Personality and Social Psychology, 70,* 614–36.

Beier, E. G., & Zautra, A. J. (1972). Identification of vocal communication of emotions across cultures. *Journal of Consulting and Clinical Psychology, 39,* 166.

Biehl, M., Matsumoto, D., Ekman, P., & Hearn, V. (1997). Matsumoto and Ekman's Japanese and Caucasian Facial Expressions of Emotion (JACFEE): Reliability data and cross-national differences. *Journal of Nonverbal Behavior, 21,* 3–21.

Bezooijen, R. van., Oto, S. A., & Heenan, T. A. (1983). Recognition of vocal expressions of emotion: A three-nation study to identify universal characteristics. *Journal of Cross-Cultural Psychology, 14,* 387–406.

Boucher, J. D. (1979). Culture and emotion. In A. J. Marsella, R. G. Tharp, & T. V. Ciborowski (eds), *Perspectives on cross-cultural psychology* (pp. 159–78). San Diego, CA: Academic Press.

Briggs, J. L. (1970). *Never in anger: Portrait of an Eskimo family.* Cambridge, MA: Harvard University Press.

Brunswik, E. (1956). *Perception and the representative design of psychological experiments.* Berkeley, CA: University of California Press.

Carlsen, J. C. (1981). Some factors which influence melodic expectancy. *Psychomusicology, 1,* 12–29.

Castellano, M. A., Bharucha, J. J., & Krumhansl, C. L. (1984). Tonal hierarchies in the music of North India. *Journal of Experimental Psychology: General, 113,* 394–412.

Clayton, M. (2001). Introduction: towards a theory of musical meaning (in India and elsewhere). *British Journal of Ethnomusicology, 10,* 1–18.

Cross, I. (2003). Music, cognition, culture and evolution. In I. Peretz & R. J. Zatorre (eds), *The cognitive neuroscience of music* (pp. 42–56). Oxford: Oxford University Press.

Cross, I. (2006). The origins of music: Some stipulations on theory. *Music Perception, 24,* 79–82.

Crowder, R. G., Resnick, J. S., & Rosenkrantz, S. L. (1991). Perception of the major/minor distinction: V. Preferences among infants. *Bulletin of the Psychonomic Society, 29,* 187–8.

Cuddy, L. L., Cohen, A., & Mewhort, D. J. (1981). Perception of structure in short melodic sequences. *Journal of Experimental Psychology: Human Perception and Performance, 7,* 869–83.

Dalla Bella, S., Peretz, I., Rousseau, L., & Gosselin, N. (2001). A developmental study of the affective value of tempo and mode in music. *Cognition, 80,* B1–B10.

Darwin, C. (1872). *Expression of the emotions in man and animals.* London: John Murray.

Deva, B. C. (1973). *An introduction to Indian music.* New Delhi, India: Publications Division, Ministry of Information and Broadcasting, Government of India.

Deva, B. C., & Virmani, K. G. (1975). *A study in the psychological response to ragas.* Research Report II of Sangeet Natak Akademi. New Delhi, India: Indian Musicological Society.

de Villiers-Sidani, E., Chang, E. F., Bao, S., & Merzenich, M. M. (2007). Critical period for spectral tuning defined in the primary auditory cortex (A1) in the rat. *Journal of Neuroscience, 27,* 180–9.

Dissanayake, E. (2001). Antecedents of the temporal arts in early mother-infant interaction. In N. L. Wallin, B. Merker, & S. Brown (eds), *The origins of music* (pp. 389–410). Cambridge, MA: MIT Press.

Dowling, W. J., & Harwood, D. L. (1986). *Music cognition.* New York: Academic Press.

Eerola, T., Himberg, T., Toiviainen, P., & Louhivuori, J. (2006). Perceived complexity of western and African folk melodies by western and African listeners. *Psychology of Music, 34,* 337–71.

Eid, M., & Diener, E. (2001). Norms for experiencing emotions in different cultures: Inter- and intranational differences. *Journal of Personality and Social Psychology, 81,* 869–85.

Ekman, P. (1970). Universal facial expressions of emotion. *California Mental Health Research Digest, 8,* 151–8.

Ekman, P. (1972). Universals and cultural differences in facial expressions of emotion. In J. Cole (ed.), *Nebraska symposium on motivation* (pp. 207–83). Lincoln, NE: University of Nebraska Press.

Ekman, P. (1976). *Pictures of facial affect*. Palo Alto, CA: Consulting Psychologists Press.

Ekman, P. (1992). An argument for basic emotions. *Cognition & Emotion, 6*, 169–200.

Ekman, P., Sorenson, E. R., & Friesen, W. V. (1969). Pan-cultural elements in facial displays of emotions. *Science, 164*, 86–8.

Elfenbein, H. A., & Ambady, N. (2002). On the universality and cultural specificity of emotion recognition: A meta-analysis. *Psychological Bulletin, 128*, 203–35.

Elfenbein, H. A., & Ambady, N. (2003). Cultural similarity's consequences: A distance perspective on cross-cultural differences in emotion recognition. *Journal of Cross Cultural Psychology, 34*, 92–109.

Ellis, A. (1885). On the musical scales of various nations. HTML transcription of the 1885 article in the now defunct. *Journal of the Society of Arts* (accessed 09/2009, http://stuart.sfa. googlepages.com/MSVN00.html)

Fernald, A. (1991). Prosody in speech to children: Prelinguistic and linguistic functions. *Annals of Child Development Psychology, 8*, 43–80.

Fernald, A., & Simon, T. (1984). Expanded intonation contours in mothers' speech to newborns. *Developmental Psychology, 20*, 104–13.

Frick, R. W. (1985). Communicating emotion: The role of prosodic features. *Psychological Bulletin, 97*, 412–29.

Fritz, T., Jentschke, S., Gosselin, N., Sammler, D., Peretz, I., Friederici, A. D., & Koelsch, S. (2009). Universal recognition of three basic emotions in music. *Current Biology, 19*, 573–76.

Fritz, T., Sammler, D., & Koelsch, S. (2006). How far is music universal? An intercultural comparison. In M. Baroni, A. R. Addessi, R. Caterina, & M. Costa (eds), *9th International Conference on Music Perception and Cognition* (p. 88). Bologna, Italy: Bononia University Press.

Geertz, C. (1973). Thick description: Toward an interpretive theory of culture. In *The interpretation of cultures: Selected essays* (pp. 3–30). New York: Basic Books.

Gregory, A. H., & Varney, N. (1996). Cross-cultural comparisons in the affective response to music. *Psychology of Music, 24*, 47–52.

Gundlach, R. H. (1932). A quantitative analysis of Indian music. *American Journal of Psychology, 44*, 133–45.

Gundlach, R. H. (1935). Factors determining the characterization of musical phrases. *American Journal of Psychology, 47*, 624–43.

Hannon, E. E., & Trainor, L. J. (2007). Music acquisition: Effects of enculturation and formal training on development. *Trends in Cognitive Sciences, 11*, 466–72.

Hebdige, D. (1979). *Subculture: The meaning of style*. London: Routledge.

Hevner, K. (1936). Experimental studies of the elements of expression in music. *American Journal of Psychology, 48*, 246–68.

Heyes, C. (2003). Four routes of cognitive evolution. *Psychological Review, 110*, 713–27.

Huron, D. (2006). *Sweet anticipation: Music and the psychology of expectation*. Cambridge, MA: MIT Press.

Ilie, G., & Thompson, W. F. (2006). A comparison of acoustic cues in music and speech for three dimensions of affect. *Music Perception, 23*, 319–29.

Johnson-Laird, P. N., & Oatley, K. (1989). The language of emotions: An analysis of a semantic field. *Cognition & Emotion, 3*, 81–123.

Johnstone, T., & Scherer, K. R. (2000). Vocal communication of emotion. In M. Lewis & J. M. Haviland-Jones (eds), *Handbook of emotions* (2nd edn, pp. 220–35). New York: Guilford Press.

Juslin, P. N. (2000). Cue utilization in communication of emotion in music performance: Relating performance to perception. *Journal of Experimental Psychology: Human Perception and Performance, 26,* 1797–813.

Juslin, P. N. (2001). Communicating emotion in music performance. A review and a theoretical framework. In P. N. Juslin & J. A. Sloboda (eds), *Music and emotion: Theory and research* (pp. 309–37). Oxford: Oxford University Press.

Juslin, P. N., & Laukka, P. (2003). Communication of emotions in vocal emotion and music performance: Different channels, same code? *Psychological Bulletin, 129,* 770–814.

Juslin, P. N., & Västfjäll, D. (2008). Emotional responses to music: The need to consider underlying mechanisms. *Behavioral and Brain Sciences, 31,* 559–75.

Justus, T., & Hutsler, J. J. (2005). Fundamental issues in the evolutionary psychology of music: Assessing innateness and domain-specificity. *Music Perception, 23,* 1–27.

Katsiavriades, K., & Qureshi, T. (2003). Ten language families in detail. Retrieved from: http://www.Krysstal.com

Kessler, E. J., Hansen, C., & Shepard, R. N. (1984). Tonal schemata in the perception of music in Bali and the west. *Music Perception, 2,* 131–65.

Kilbride, J. E., & Yarczower, M. (1983). Ethnic bias in the recognition of facial expressions. *Journal of Nonverbal Behavior, 8,* 27–41.

Kitayama, S., & Ishii, K. (2002). Word and voice: Spontaneous attention to emotional utterances in two languages. *Cognition & Emotion, 16,* 29–59.

Kramer, E. (1964). Elimination of verbal cues in judgments of emotion from voice. *Journal of Abnormal and Social Psychology, 68,* 390–96.

Krumhansl, C. L. (1995). Music psychology and music theory: Problems and prospects. *Music Theory Spectrum, 17,* 53–80.

Krumhansl, C. L., Toivanen, P., Eerola, T., Toiviainen, P., Järvinen, T., & Louhivuori, J. (2000). Cross-cultural music cognition: Cognitive methodology applied to North Sami yoiks. *Cognition, 76,* 13–58.

Krumhansl, C. L., & Keil, F. C. (1982). Acquisition of the hierarchy of tonal functions in music. *Memory & Cognition, 10,* 243–51.

Lazarus, R. S. (1991). *Emotion and adaptation.* Oxford: Oxford University Press.

Lerdahl, F., & Krumhansl, C. L. (2007). Modeling tonal tension. *Music Perception, 24,* 329–66.

Livingstone, S., & Thompson, W. F. (in press). The emergence of music from the Theory of Mind. *Musica Scientiae.*

Lomax, A. (1962). Song structure and social structure. *Ethnology, 1,* 425–51.

Lomax, A. (1975). The good and the beautiful in folksong. *Journal of American Folklore, 80,* 213–235.

Lomax, A. (1976). *Cantometrics: An approach to the anthropology of music. Audiocassettes and a handbook.* Berkeley, CA: University of California Media Extension Center.

Lomax, A. (1978). *Folk song style and culture.* Edison, NJ: Transaction Publishers.

Lutz, C. (1988). *Unnatural emotions: everyday sentiments on a Micronesian atoll and their challenge to western theory.* Chicago, IL: University of Chicago Press.

Lynch, M. P., & Eilers, R. E. (1991). Children's perception of native and nonnative musical scales. *Music Perception, 9,* 121–31.

Masuda, T., & Nisbett, R. E. (2001). Attending holistically versus analytically: Comparing the context sensitivity of Japanese and Americans. *Journal of Personality and Social Psychology, 81,* 922–34.

Matsumoto, D. (1989). Cultural influences on the perception of emotion. *Journal of Cross-Cultural Psychology, 20,* 92–105.

Matsumoto, D. (1990). Cultural similarities and differences in display rules. *Motivation and Emotion, 14,* 195–214.

Matsumoto, D. (1992). American-Japanese cultural differences in the recognition of universal facial expressions. *Journal of Cross-Cultural Psychology, 23*, 72–84.

Matsumoto, D. (1996). *Unmasking Japan: Myths and realities about the emotions of the Japanese.* Stanford, CA: Stanford University Press.

McCluskey, K. W., & Albas, D. C. (1981). Perception of the emotional content of speech by Canadian and Mexican children, adolescents, and adutls. *International Journal of Psychology, 16*, 119–32.

Merriam, A. P. (1964). *The anthropology of music.* Chicago, IL: Northwestern University Press.

Mesquita, B., & Frijda, N. H. (1992). Cultural variations in emotions: A review. *Psychological Bulletin, 112*, 197–204.

Mesquita, B., Frijda, N. H., & Scherer, K. R. (1997). Culture and emotion. In J. W. Berry, P. R. Dasen, & T. S. Saraswathi (eds), *Handbook of cross-cultural psychology, Vol. 2: Basic processes and human development* (2nd edn, pp. 255–97). Needham Heights, MA: Allyn & Bacon.

Morey, R. (1940). Upset in emotions. *Journal of Social Psychology, 12*, 333–56.

Nakata, T., & Trehub, S. E. (2004). Infants' responsiveness to maternal speech and singing. *Infant Behavior and Development, 27*, 455–64.

Narmour, E. (1990). *The analysis and cognition of basic melodic structures: the Implication-Realization Model.* Chicago, IL: Chicago University Press.

Nettl, B. (1983). *The study of ethnomusicology.* Chicago, IL: University of Illinois Press.

Nisbett, R. E., Peng, K., Choi, I., & Norenzayan, A. (2001). Culture and systems of thought: Holistic versus analytic cognition. *Psychological Review, 108*, 291–310.

Palmer, C., & Hutchins, S. (2006). What is musical prosody? *The Psychology of Learning and Motivation, 46*, 245–78.

Patel, A. D. (2008). *Music, language, and the brain.* Oxford: Oxford University Press.

Rosch E., & Mervis, C. (1975). Family resemblances: studies in the internal structure of categories. *Cognitive Psychology, 7*, 573–605.

Rose, C. (2005). *Sino-Japanese relations: facing the past, looking to the future.* London: Routledge.

Rosenthal, R., Hall, J. A., DiMatteo, M. R., Rogers, P. I., & Archer, D. (1979). *Sensitivity to non-verbal communication: the PONS test.* Baltimore, MD: Johns Hopkins University Press.

Russell, J. A. (1991). Culture and the categorization of emotions. *Psychological Bulletin, 110*, 426–50.

Russell, J. A. (1994). Is there universal recognition of emotion from facial expression? A review of cross-cultural studies. *Psychological Bulletin, 115*, 102–41.

Russell, J. A., Suzuki, N., & Ishida, N. (1993). Canadian, Greek, and Japanese freely produced emotion labels for facial expressions. *Motivation and Emotion, 17*, 337–51.

Saffran, J. R., Aslin, R. N., & Newport, E. L. (1996). Statistical learning by 8-month-old infants. *Science, 274*, 1926–8.

Schellenberg, E. G. (1996). Expectancy in melody: Tests of the implication-realization model, *Cognition, 58*, 75–125.

Scherer, K. R. (1979). Non-linguistic vocal indicators of emotion and psychopathology. In C. E. Izard (ed.), *Emotions in personality and psychopathology* (pp. 493–529). New York: Plenum Press.

Scherer, K. R. (1982). Methods of research on vocal communication: Paradigms and parameters. In K. R. Scherer & P. Ekman (eds), *Handbook of methods in nonverbal behavior research* (pp. 136–98). Cambridge, UK: Cambridge University Press.

Scherer, K. R. (1986). Vocal affect expression: A review and a model for future research. *Psychological Bulletin, 99*, 143–65.

Scherer, K. R. (1989). Vocal correlates of emotional arousal and affective disturbance. In H. Wagner & A. Manstead (eds), *Handbook of social psychophysiology* (pp. 165–97). New York: Wiley.

Scherer, K. R., & Oshinsky, J. S. (1977). Cue utilization in emotion attribution from auditory stimuli. *Motivation and Emotion, 1,* 331–46.

Singh, L., Morgan, J. L., & Best, C. T. (2002). Infants' listening preferences: Baby talk or happy talk? *Infancy, 3,* 365–94.

Sorenson, E. R. (1975). Culture and the expression of emotion. In T. R. Williams (ed.), *Psychological anthropology* (pp. 361–72). Chicago, IL: Aldine.

Standke, R. (1992). *Methods of digital speech analysis in research on vocal communication.* Frankfurt, Germany: Peter Lang.

Thompson, W. F., & Balkwill, L-L. (2006). Decoding speech prosody in five languages. *Semiotica, 158,* 407–24.

Thompson, W. F., Graham, P., & Russo, F. A. (2005). Seeing music performance: Visual influences on perception and experience. *Semiotica, 156,* 203–27.

Thompson, W. F., & Robitaille, B. (1992). Can composers express emotions through music? *Empirical Studies of the Arts, 10,* 79–89.

Thompson, W. F., Russo, F. A., & Quinto, L. (2008). Audio-visual integration of emotional cues in song. *Cognition & Emotion, 22,* 1457–70.

Thompson, W. F., & Schellenberg, E. G. (2006). Listening to music. In R. Colwell (ed.), *MENC handbook of music cognition & development* (pp. 72–123). Oxford: Oxford University Press.

Thompson, W. F., Schellenberg, E. G., & Husain, G. (2004). Decoding speech prosody: Do music lessons help? *Emotion, 4,* 46–64.

Thompson, W. F., & Stainton, M. (1998). Expectancy in Bohemian folksong melodies: Evaluation of implicative principles for implicative and closural intervals. *Music Perception, 15,* 231–52.

Tooby, J., & Cosmides, L. (1990). The past explains the present: Emotional adaptations and the structure of ancestral environments. *Ethology and Sociobiology, 11,* 375–424.

Trainor, L. J., & Trehub, S. E. (1994). Key membership and implied harmony in Western tonal music: Developmental perspectives. *Perception & Psychophysics, 56,* 125–32.

Trainor, L. J., & Heinmiller, B. M. (1998). The development of evaluative responses to music: Infants prefer to listen to consonance over dissonance. *Infant Behavior & Development, 21,* 77–88.

Trehub, S. E. (2000). Human processing predispositions and musical universals. In N. L. Wallin, B. Merker, & S. Brown (eds), *The origins of music* (pp. 427–48). Cambridge, MA: MIT Press.

Trehub, S. E. (2003). The developmental origins of musicality. *Nature Neuroscience, 6,* 669–73.

Trehub, S. E., & Hannon, E. E. (2006). Infant music perception: Domain-general or domain-specific mechanisms. *Cognition, 100,* 73–99.

Trehub, S. E., & Nakata, T. (2002). Emotion and music in infancy. *Musicae Scientiae, Special Issue 2001–2,* 37–61.

Trehub, S. E., Unyk, A., & Trainor, L. J. (1993). Maternal singing in cross-cultural perspective. *Infant Behaviour and Development, 16,* 285–95.

Unyk, A. M., Trehub, L. J., & Schellenberg, E. G. (1992). Lullabies and simplicity: A cross-cultural perspective. *Psychology of Music, 20,* 15–28.

Wierzbicka, A. (1992). Talking about emotions: Semantics, culture, and cognition. *Cognition & Emotion, 6,* 285–319.

Wittgenstein, L. (1953/2001). *Philosophical investigations.* Oxford: Blackwell.

Zentner, M. R., & Kagan, J. (1996). Perception of music by infants. *Nature, 383,* 29.

PART VII

APPLICATIONS

CHAPTER 28

MUSIC EDUCATION

THE ROLE OF AFFECT

SUSAN HALLAM

28.1 INTRODUCTION

MOST people engage with music throughout their lives. This may be through listening or active participation in music-making activities. Typically, this engagement has affective outcomes. Individuals use recorded music to manipulate personal moods, arouse emotions, and create environments that may influence the ways that other people feel and behave (DeNora, 2000; Sloboda & O'Neill, 2001; Sloboda et al, 2001). In the Western world, adults actively participate in making music for many reasons: for self-expression, self-improvement, recreation, and leisure; for a love of music, including performing for oneself and others and learning more about music; for the social values of meeting new people, being with friends, and having a sense of belonging (Coffman, 2002); and/or for spiritual reasons (Hinkle, 1988). The benefits and motives for all such participation include positive emotional, social, physical, health, intellectual, creative, and spiritual outcomes (Bailey & Davidson, 2002; Beck et al, 2000; Clift & Hancox, 2001; Kreutz et al, 2004).

Similarly, young people report that listening to music helps them to pass time, alleviate boredom, relieve tension, and distract themselves from worries (North et al, 2000). They perceive music as a multifaceted means for mood regulation, especially for controlling their feelings and making them feel good (Saarikallio & Erkkila, 2007). They may also play music loudly as an acceptable way to express anger towards parents. Playing an instrument is reported to provide a sense of achievement and confidence, and is also perceived as a means of communication, although it can also lead to frustration when aims are not attained (Tolfree & Hallam, 2007). Group music making with peers deepens musical knowledge and understanding, and develops social and personal skills, resulting in considerable personal satisfaction and enhanced confidence (Kokatsaki & Hallam, 2007). While there has been less research on young children's emotional responses to music, physiological, behavioural, and concentration changes have been demonstrated (Hallam & Price, 1998; Hallam et al, 2002; Savan, 1999). Overall, the evidence suggests that music plays an important role throughout our lives, and that typically the impact is affective rather than intellectual, with the widest range of benefits accruing to those who actively participate in making music. A number of studies have concluded that adult participation is an extension of engagement with active music making in childhood in the home or at school (Chiodo, 1998; Conda, 1997). Accordingly, the musical education offered during compulsory schooling should, at least in part, be concerned with inculcating a love of music.

With reference to the above, this chapter will synthesize the research evidence considering: the aims and provision of music education; opportunities for experiencing and expressing emotion in music education; students' affective experiences in music education; teaching to generate positive affective outcomes; the benefits of a greater emphasis on the emotions in music education; and directions for future research.

28.2 THE AIMS AND PROVISION OF MUSIC EDUCATION

The extent to which national and international education systems provide music education varies significantly, as do the means by which it is offered. Provision depends on the nature of the education system, economic wealth, political factors, and the perceived role and value placed on music in society. Some countries have a national music curriculum. In others, curricula are determined by states or provinces, while in others teachers determine the aims of the curriculum and how it is taught. In many countries, systems are in place for providing general music education for all pupils and specialized opportunities for those who show particular interest in or aptitude for music. Music may become optional as pupils progress through school; specialist selective schools may offer a full-time education with music at its core; extra-curricular music schools may operate out of school hours providing tuition and ensemble opportunities; centrally or locally funded music services may provide instrumental music tuition in schools during the school day in addition to a range of out-of-school music activities. Complementary to state-funded provision, private teachers and local community groups may offer further opportunities to develop musical skills. For those who wish to pursue careers in music, universities, colleges, and conservatoires provide opportunities to develop a range of academic, performing, creative, and technical skills.

There is a long-standing debate worldwide about the aims of music education—what should be taught, how it should be taught, and, indeed, whether it should be taught in school. It is therefore not surprising that the aims of formal music education vary over time (Cox, 2002) and between countries (Hargreaves & North, 2001; see Table 28.1 for some examples). All music curricula are embedded within the cultural philosophies pertaining in that place and at that time. Confucius, for instance, embraced the cultivation of honesty, love, and filial piety through the six arts, which included music. With this philosophical underpinning, in China, the notion of music education for its own sake is linked with morality, beauty, and good. Music is seen to join the various strata of society and family together in harmonious relationship, and also has a role in encouraging the Chinese people to conform to virtuous living, to reinforce self-control, and to improve behaviour. Currently, music education in China continues to fulfil this functional role, but is also a political and social tool (Yeh, 2001) (see Table 28.1). In Western cultures, the focus of music education has been hotly debated, and has been viewed as, for example, music appreciation (Scholes, 1935), aesthetic education (Abbs, 1994; Reimer, 1978), and more recently multicultural education (Campbell, 1991; Volk, 1998).

Table 28.1 International examples of music curricula

Australia

The prime purpose of arts education for most students is to enrich their educational experience generally: to foster confidence self-expression—the desire to have a go; to foster creative and innovative thinking that may have the benefit of carrying through into other school disciplines and other areas of life, both in and out of paid employment; to foster the habits of being self-directed and being involved—habits which will be ever more important to the self-esteem of many in a future of insecure job prospects and periods of unemployment as the traditional place of work in people's identity and self-esteem breaks down.

(Arts Education, 1995, p. 22, cited in McPherson & Dunbar-Hall, 2001)

State of Hessen, Federal Republic of Germany

Students are expected to attain the following goals:

- the ability to appreciate familiar and unfamiliar music with knowledge and understanding;
- the ability to understand the importance and effects of music on human beings in the past and present;
- the ability to critically reflect on the different forms in which music is presented, especially those forms used by the mass media;
- the ability to handle music technology productively and independently with an appropriate critical attitude;
- the ability to reproduce music using the voice and instruments;
- the ability to invent and form music, and to express oneself with music;
- the ability to read music.

(cited in Gembris, 2001)

Table 28.1 International examples of music curricula (continued)

Republic of China

To nourish pupils' love of country, people, work, science, socialism and unity through music education and let them be the ideal, moral, educated and disciplined successor and builder of socialism; to cultivate pupils' wisdom and aesthetic sense, so as to grow with physical and mental health; to nourish pupils' interest in music and to develop their basic knowledge, skill and reading ability in music; to nourish pupils' national pride and self-confidence through the teaching of representative Chinese folklore and widen their musical experiences with foreign musical compositions so as to enable them to feel and express through music.

(State Education Commission, 1994a, pp. 131 cited in Yeh, 2001)

United Kingdom

Learning and undertaking activities in music contribute to the achievement of the curriculum aims for all young people to become:

- successful learners who enjoy learning, make progress and achieve;
- confident individuals who are able to live safe, healthy and fulfilling lives;
- responsible citizens who make a positive contribution to society.

Music is an unique form of communication that changes the way that pupils feel, think and act. Music forms part of an individual's identity and positive interaction with music develops pupils' competence as learners and increases their self-esteem. It brings together intellect and feeling and enables personal expression, reflection and emotional development. As an integral part of culture past and present music helps pupils to understand themselves, relate to others, and develop their cultural understanding, forging important links between the home, school and the wider world.

(National Curriculum for England: Music (Key Stage 3) 11–14 year olds, 2007)

Reviews of music curricula adopting different levels of analysis have reached broadly similar conclusions about overall aims. Hargreaves and North (2001) suggest three main groups: musical; personal and social; and cultural. Pitts (2000) takes a historical perspective and suggests that music education is desirable for its cultural influence, for life and leisure, and for emotional and imaginative development. Taggart, Whitby, and Sharp (2004) found that of the 21 countries that they studied, most specified aims for arts education that included engaging with a variety of art forms; developing artistic skills, knowledge, and understanding; increasing cultural understanding; sharing arts experiences; and becoming discriminating arts consumers and contributors.

In a more fine-grained account, Cox (2002), drawing on 75 years of music in the school curriculum in the United Kingdom, outlined four overarching approaches to the curriculum: humanist, developmental, social meliorist, and social efficiency.

The *humanist* approach is associated with maintaining musical traditions and skills, belief in music as a spiritual or divine force, maintaining the academic status of music and what historically has been a rigid stratification between popular and classical genres, and providing opportunities for those perceived to be talented. Within this approach, emotional engagement with music is spiritual, 'connecting the generations through the at-once mystical and tangible phenomenon of music' (McCarthy, 1999, p. 195). Music in schools is seen as providing an outlet for the emotions and a means to stimulate imaginative play, particularly through folk tunes and dances.

In contrast, a *developmental* curriculum is in harmony with children's real interests, and music is seen as aesthetic education, self-enriching and creative. The emphasis is on pupils encountering music on its and their own terms. The musical and creative impulses of children are valued and the child is encouraged to express him- or herself through rhythm, melody and harmony.

The *social meliorist* approach to the curriculum views education as a major force for social change with the power to regenerate society. From this perspective, music is seen as having a refining influence on young people's lives. Historically, the concerts for children movement in the USA and UK illustrates this approach.

Social-efficiency approaches to the curriculum stress social utility as the supreme criterion against which the value of school subjects should be tested, with a direct connection between what is taught in schools and adult activities that are undertaken in society. Historically, this approach has often presented a threat to music education. But in the modern world, where the creative industries form a substantial element of developed economies, this is not necessarily the case. Most music curricula draw on aspects of all of these approaches.

Implicit in each of these approaches, with the exception of the social-efficiency approach, are beliefs about the affective power of music. These beliefs are rarely made explicit, although there are exceptions. For instance, Langer (1942, 1953) proposed that the aesthetic qualities of musical works capture and represent the general forms of human feelings. She defined music as the 'creation of forms symbolic of human feeling' and art education as 'the education of feeling' (1953, p. 8). Reimer (1970) further developed Langer's main proposal, arguing that 'music education is the education of human feeling through the development of responsiveness to the aesthetic quality of sound' (p. 39). He viewed music as a collection of aesthetic objects, the meaning and value of which are always internal (Reimer, 1970, p. 28).

Elliott (1995) challenged this approach. His 'praxial' philosophy of music rejected the idea of music as object, as a set of works, proposing music instead as a set of practices based on cognitive-affective constructive processes. For him, music is expressive of specific emotions that 'provide the artistic means to extend the range of our expressive powers beyond those we find naturally and ordinarily' (Elliott, 2005, p. 97). He outlines five kinds of knowing that apply to listening and creating music: *procedural knowing, verbal knowing, experiential knowing, intuitive knowing* and *supervisory knowing* (metacognition) (Elliott, 1995, pp. 49–106). He suggests that educators should refocus music education aims and support children to hear, interpret, and create musical expressions of emotion and the role of emotional meanings in their enjoyment of music (Elliott, 2005).

However, in a climate where education is seen as an important element in maintaining prosperity in a global economy, 'enjoyment' may be viewed as a luxury that cannot be afforded. A recent UK school inspector's report stated: 'Pupils are under-achieving in music because the teaching is unsatisfactory. It places too much emphasis on fun rather than learning.' This was despite the fact that 'the pupils' enthusiasm for the subject' had 'rocketed' and more children were continuing to engage in music education beyond what was compulsory (OFSTED, 2001).

In some cultures, there is no formal music education. Music is learned informally within the community through everyday life activities where it is a natural part of work, play, rituals, ceremonies, and religious and family occasions. Frequently in such cases, there is an aural-oral tradition. Where formal music education in the school curriculum is only recently developed, aural traditions can sit uneasily with notation and formal tuition methods (Primos, 2001). Whatever the nature of the formal school curriculum, informal music making occurs, to some extent, in all societies, forming an essential part of musical culture. Involvement of the wider musical community in music education is now being encouraged in some developed societies:

> Our aim is to give every child the chance to make music and enjoy the immense benefits it brings . . . Everyone involved in music education should work together to provide the framework and focus needed to deliver a universal music education offer to all children from early years onwards where they can take an active part in high quality music making. Children and young people do not care who provides the chance to make music. They just want that chance. This means putting the child at the heart of music education, providing the right opportunities, in the right way and at the right time.'
>
> (Department for Education and Skills and Department for Culture, Media and Sports, 2006, p. 7)

There has been less research about the aims of private instrumental teachers. Such evidence as there is suggests that a frequently cited aim is that learning to play an instrument should be fun and enjoyable (Hallam & Prince, 2000; Schenck, 1989). Whatever their stated aims, instrumental teachers perceive a wide range of benefits of learning to play an instrument, including enhanced social skills; love of music; team working; a sense of achievement; increased confidence and self-discipline; opportunities for relaxation; enhanced concentration, physical coordination, cognitive, listening, creative, and organizational skills; and giving enjoyment to others (Hallam & Prince, 2000).

Whatever the stated aims of the music curriculum, teachers may not adhere to them. Individual teachers may adopt different approaches to attaining the same aims. Teaching variously focuses on listening, understanding, and appreciation of music; performance; creativity; combinations of these; or has developed within a more general arts education where music, drama, literature, dance, film studies, and visual arts are components of a generic community which constitute a distinct category of aesthetic understanding (McPherson & Dunbar-Hall, 2001; Primos, 2001). Depending on the nature of the specified music curriculum, children may: learn to read musical notation; develop critical listening skills; acquire knowledge about the history of music, instruments, world musics, acoustics and the contribution of music to other art forms; learn to compose or improvise using a range of instruments or computer technology; develop technical skills in playing an instrument or singing; or develop performing and communication skills. These may be pursued through a focus on traditional national musics and cultures or western popular culture, the latter becoming a worldwide phenomenon.

28.3 OPPORTUNITIES FOR EXPERIENCING AND EXPRESSING EMOTION IN MUSIC EDUCATION

The activities that provide the greatest opportunities for children to experience and express emotion in their music education are those relating to listening and appraising, creating music (through improvisation or composition), and actively making music through playing an instrument or singing.

28.3.1 Experiencing emotion through listening and appraising

Listening is a fundamental musical skill. Despite this, it is one of the least studied aspects of music education (for a review, see Haack, 1992). The research has predominantly focused on perception and cognition relating to the formal elements and properties of music, and whether and at what age children can recognize different emotions as portrayed in music (e.g. Giomi, 1992; Rodriguez, 1998). The findings from this research are equivocal, unsurprisingly, as a wide range of different music and methodologies have been adopted (for a review, see Kopiez, 2002).

In relation to learners' experience of emotions in music education, rather than the recognition of them, there is a little research. Some insights come from the work of Finnäs (2006), exploring strong emotional experiences (see Chapter 20, this volume) in over 800 15- and 16-year-olds in Finland. They were asked to write a description of their recent strong experiences in relation to music and other aesthetic areas, for instance, literature, drama, and nature. Those living in the most urbanized areas experienced music as most frequently evoking strong emotional experiences, but for those living in rural areas and girls in moderately urban areas, emotional experiences related to natural phenomenon were more common. Although most strong musical experiences derived from listening, those rated most strongly tended to involve active music making. Strong musical experiences reported in a school context were rare, although some were reported in relation to school visits to concerts or musicals. Finnäs suggests that, although strong experiences in response to music were uncommon in schools, music education provided the adolescents with the necessary skills to facilitate such experiences. To date there is no evidence to support or refute this proposition.

28.3.2 Expressing emotion in music education

One recurring aim of music education is to facilitate opportunities for self-expression, allowing individuals to express their own emotions, feelings, and identity through music. This might be achieved through composing, improvisation, or the interpretation of music created by others. To what extent is this aim pursued and achieved?

Composition and improvisation

Research relating to children's improvisations and compositions has not tended to address issues of self-expression or emotion. The tendency has been to focus on creativity, its processes, the characteristics of creative children, and how to facilitate composition—the latter being particularly important as music teachers are often ambivalent about teaching creative activities in the classroom (Davies, 1986; Kratus, 1994). At primary level, the evidence suggests that creative music lessons are practical. That is, musical conventions, understandings, and skills are taught through participatory lessons in which an extra-musical theme provides the model for a structured composition or arrangement of sound effects based on a narrative. It is rare for teachers to allow pupils to approach musical creation in a meaningful way, and there is little reference to the possible emotional content of the music or its impact (Dogani, 2004).

Musical performance

Opportunities for personal expression of emotion are frequently found in instrumental and vocal music making, and there is considerable evidence that musicians see the musical communication of emotion as a key element of musical ability (Hallam & Prince, 2003) and performing (Laukka, 2004; Lindström et al, 2003). The outstanding performer is one who can play expressively and communicate emotion (Davidson & Coimbra, 2001). Teachers have been shown to perceive 'competent' instrumental performance in terms of technical proficiency, 'good' performance in terms of technical security with attention to emotion, fluency, and style, while at the 'exceptional' level, technique and accuracy are taken for granted with greater emphasis on communication with the audience, expression of emotion, inspiration, style, and fluency (Prince & Hallam, 1996). Pupils seem to share these perceptions, rating technical perfection in performance as only important or quite important and unimportant in relation to being able to play expressively (Prince & Hallam, 1996). Students also report spending considerable amounts of practice time in working on expressivity (Lindström et al, 2003), an activity that may enhance the effectiveness of practice leading to the adoption of a 'deep' approach to learning (Cantwell & Millard, 1994).

Given the high level of agreement that the communication of emotion is critical in musical performance, it might be expected that expressive skills would be given a high priority by music teachers in their teaching. However, several studies have suggested that music teaching tends to focus more on technique than expressivity (Hepler, 1986; Persson, 1993; Rostvall & West, 2001; Tait, 1992; Young et al, 2003). For instance, Rostvall and West (2001) made videos of lessons and coded the language used in terms of five educational functions: testing (questions), instructional (instructions, evaluations), analytical (explanations), accompanying (guiding the conversation), and expressive (related to the expressiveness of performance). The expressive aspects were not addressed by teachers.

Similarly, Karlsson and Juslin (2008) studied five instrumental teachers teaching 12 music students, and found that the pattern of language was primarily instructive for teachers and accompanying for students. The expressive aspects of performance were rarely explicitly considered by teachers; and where they were, instructions tended to be vague ('Play from the heart,' 'You have to move yourself to move others'). Overall, lessons were devoted mainly to technique and the musical score.

Detailed observation studies such as those described above are inevitably based on a small number of lessons with a limited sample of teachers and pupils. While this limits the generalizability of any single study, the cumulative evidence from research over time provides considerable support for the notion that teaching expressivity is frequently not explicit in music lessons and that teaching tends to focus on technique. Woody (2000) found that 48 per cent of students reported that they did not become seriously concerned with expressivity until they were well into high school or even at college. Overall, this is a neglected area in music education (Juslin & Persson, 2002).

Despite the evidence to the contrary, teachers perceive that they are spending time engaging with issues of expressivity in lessons (Laukka, 2004). Prince and Hallam (1996), in a study of teachers of pre-conservatoire students, found that 80 per cent of teachers indicated that they gave high emphasis to expressive elements in lessons (e.g. articulation, dynamics, feeling and imagination, tone quality, phrasing), with only 27 per cent indicating a high level focus on intellectual elements (discussing the background of the composer, analysis and discussion of meaning) and 17 per cent on technical elements (technique, accuracy, rhythm, fluency). The majority of pupils (67 per cent) supported their teachers in acknowledging the emphasis on expression, but 41 per cent also indicated that lessons had a high focus on technique and 11 per cent on intellectual elements. Despite teachers stating that they value expressive communication in lessons, pupils seem to perceive that technique is often emphasized at the expense of musical considerations.

Teaching students to communicate with emotion in music

There is considerable evidence that as a species, humans have a predisposition to respond to emotional communication in music. Infants have been shown to be able to distinguish between lullabies sung by mothers to their infants and lullabies sung without the infant present, preferring the former (Trainor, 1996, see also Chapter 23, this volume). Young children (aged 5 to 10) prefer folk songs played with expressive dynamics over those played without expression (Burnsed, 1998). Music is also perceived by adults to be a vehicle for the communication of emotion (Juslin & Laukka, 2004), and there is evidence that performers can communicate specific emotions to listeners with considerable accuracy (for reviews, see Juslin & Laukka, 2003, and Chapter 17, this volume). This process is enhanced by performers exaggerating expression (Sloboda, 1983), supported by appropriate bodily movement that draws the observers' attention to particular aspects of the music (Davidson, 1993).

Perhaps because of the ease with which music is perceived to communicate emotion, there is a tendency for teachers to see the ability to communicate expressively as a 'talent', which cannot be learned (Sloboda, 1996), although students themselves are more ambivalent about this (Lindström et al, 2003). Several authors have argued that expressive skills can benefit from instruction (Juslin et al, 2006; Woody, 1999), and there have been a number of attempts to explore the most effective ways of teaching expressivity (Dalgarno, 1997; Johnson, 1998; Marchand, 1975; Sloboda et al, 2003; Woody, 1999).

Despite this research, there is little information, which is easily accessible for teachers, explaining how to teach the communication of emotion. Various ideas have been proposed on the basis of the research. Having a clear internalized representation of what is to be learned is important (Hallam, 1997). Internalized representations develop through listening to music. Listening is therefore a frequently cited source of learning expressivity (Woody, 2000). However, there are unresolved questions about how expressive knowledge gained through listening can be transferred to the active process of communication of emotion in a specific performance.

Modelling is an effective teaching strategy, but teachers spend little time engaged with it (Dickey, 1992; Kostka, 1984; Rosenthal, 1984; Sang, 1987), and critics of this approach suggest that it may lead to copying rather than the development of personal expression—although there is little evidence that students have opportunities to develop self-expression in their lessons anyway. Even in individual instrumental tuition, the teacher usually dictates the curriculum, selects the repertoire, and how it is to be played, technically and musically (Hepler, 1986). Pupil activity in lessons is mainly playing, with much time taken up with teacher talk (Karlsson & Juslin, 2008; Kostka, 1984; Tait, 1992). This is almost exclusively uni-directional from teacher to student, although the ratio of teacher talk to student performance varies according to the lesson activity (Albrecht, 1991, cited in Schmidt, 1992). The teaching strategy most often adopted is raising students' attention to inaccuracies or areas that need improvement (Kennell, 1992). Even in higher education, where the apprenticeship model is perceived to underlie music-teaching practice (Persson, 1994), the evidence suggests that teachers may demand total compliance to suggestions and solutions that they offer, allowing students little opportunity to express themselves.

A common strategy used by teachers to focus on the emotional qualities of performance is metaphor (Barten, 1998; Rosenberg & Trusheim, 1989; see also Chapter 15, this volume). The difficulty with this is that it depends on the performer's personal experiences with words and images, and can be ambiguous (Persson, 1996). Despite this, Lindström et al (2003) found that 42 per cent of the students in their study reported the use of metaphor as being most effective in developing expressivity.

Another teaching strategy is to focus on the performer's felt emotions (Woody, 2000). Many students believe that it is necessary to *feel* the intended emotion while playing in order to convey it successfully to a listener (Lindström et al, 2003; Laukka, 2004), although some recognize that strongly felt emotion may interfere with the performance. There is evidence that students in higher education spend the greatest proportion of practice time on developing felt emotion for performance (Woody, 2000), the assumption being that felt emotions will turn into sound. Students also report preferring the use of experienced emotion and metaphor to teacher modelling (Lindström et al, 2003).

Teachers can also use verbal directions to support students in developing expressivity. Instruction, demonstrating graphically, and in prose, the nature of the sound properties and the rhythmic tendencies of rubato used by professionals to enhance expressivity, can enhance the performance of students (Woody, 1999).

One of the simplest ways in which learners could improve their communication of emotion would be to listen to recordings of their own playing. However, this occurs infrequently, much less often than listening to performances by others (Lindström et al, 2003). Another approach is to use computer feedback. Juslin et al (2006) have developed a program that aims to enhance a performer's communication of emotions by providing systematic feedback as a complement to traditional teaching strategies. It illustrates how musicians are able to communicate emotions by employing a set of acoustic cues such as tempo, sound level, articulation, and timbre, and provides explicit knowledge about the relationships among performers, cues, and listeners. This information is used to provide cognitive feedback allowing a performer to compare a regression model of his or her playing to an 'optimal' regression model of playing based on listeners' judgements (see Section 17.5, Chapter 17, this volume).

28.4 Students' affective experiences in music education

As we saw earlier, inculcating a love of music is sometimes cited as an aim of music education. However, the guidance received by teachers, in their training and through the resources available to them, frequently focuses on the practical ways in which they can develop pupils' skills, with no consideration of the affective outcomes of learning. This is reinforced by most formal systems of assessment. It is not surprising then that this becomes the focus of teachers' practice. So to what extent do students develop a love of music as a result of their musical experiences in education?

28.4.1 The perceived value of music

There have been a number of studies exploring the value that children place on music education and the extent to which they enjoy it. The outcomes of these vary depending on the age of the children participating, the value attributed to music within the specific culture, and the nature of the music curriculum pertaining at the time. For instance, 'Enquiry One' assessed students' perceptions of music education during the 1960s in the UK, and showed that it was judged to be irrelevant (Schools Council, 1968).

Later studies supported this, demonstrating that few pupils continued with music once it was not compulsory and that a substantial proportion of children discontinued playing an instrument when they transferred to secondary education (QCA, 2002; Harland et al, 2000). In contrast, a later study of almost 1,500 students aged 8–14 from 21 schools found that both teachers and pupils demonstrated very positive attitudes towards music (Lamont et al, 2003). Within music education systems there are also differences in responses between groups of children. In the USA, studies during the 1990s showed that the value that children placed on music declined more than for reading and mathematics (Austin & Vispoel, 2000; Eccles et al, 1993; Wigfield et al, 1997), but adolescents who played an instrument favoured this activity over almost all others that they rated (Wigfield et al, 1999).

28.4.2 The development of personal and social skills

Another frequently cited aim of music education is to develop a range of personal, social, and intellectual skills. Certainly, evidence is accumulating that active participation in music making can enhance aspects of IQ (see Schellenberg, 2004, 2006; and Hetland, 2000, for a review). In relation to affective outcomes, studies exploring the effects of increasing the amount of classroom music within the curriculum have found that children receiving extra music lessons show increased social cohesion within class, greater self-reliance, better social adjustment, and more positive attitudes. These effects were particularly marked in low-ability, disaffected pupils (Spychiger et al, 1993). A project using music to reduce anti-dark-skinned stereotyping among light-skinned Portuguese children also demonstrated positive outcomes (Sousa et al, 2005), and active engagement with instrumental music increased self-esteem compared with controls in children of low economic status (Costa-Giomi, 1999). Harland et al (2000) showed that the most frequent influences on pupils derived from engagement with music were awareness of others, social skills, well-being, and transfer effects. Some students perceived the benefits of music classes as listening to music and the development of musical skills, while others referred to the sheer fun and therapeutic nature of music, how it gave them confidence to perform in front of others, facilitated group work, and enabled them to learn to express themselves. Those who played instruments mentioned an increase in self-esteem and sense of identity. However, these findings were based on interviews with a relatively small sample of pupils from a small number of schools, and may thus not be generalizable.

28.4.3 The role of affect in motivation to actively engage with music

Although we typically think of learning as the deliberate acquisition of skills or knowledge, learning also occurs in relation to emotions, attitudes, and beliefs, including those about ourselves. Central to motivation to learn is self-perception and identity (see Hallam, 2009). Active engagement with music making can be a rewarding or punishing experience associated with negative or positive emotions. While we might expect that negative emotions, such as fear or frustration, might lead to an avoidance of learning, this may not always be the case. Where an individual's musical identity is sufficiently strong, his or her motivation may be such that he or she will persevere even if learning arouses negative emotions. For instance, Sudnow (1978), a highly skilled, adult, professional, classical musician, documented how tedious, effortful, frustrating, and time consuming was the experience of acquiring expertise in jazz improvisation, yet despite this he persevered. Kemp (1996), in his study of young musicians, found that those who emerged as the most highly accomplished were self-motivated almost to the point of obsession, as if they were unable to separate their developing self-perception from that of being a musician. Some children continue to play an instrument even though they are bullied as a result of their involvement with music (Howe & Sloboda, 1991). This high level of commitment may depend on the experience of intense, aesthetic, emotional reactions to music, initially occurring in early childhood (Sloboda, 1991); the ongoing intrinsic rewards—intellectual, physical, emotional, and social—of engaging in music making; the exhilaration of performing well; and the extrinsic rewards of praise in the form of teacher, parent and audience feedback. For children who are committed to playing an instrument, music becomes an important element of their identity (Wigfield et al, 1999).

If an individual does not have a musical identity as professional, amateur or listener, they are unlikely to maintain their interest in music. For many children, such an identity does not develop. Taking up an instrument is no different from participating in a team sport, or taking up a hobby, and is not seen as important in their long-term careers. Students who have a long-term commitment are more likely to express intrinsic motives for learning an instrument and find it pleasurable (McPherson & McCormick, 1999). A recent retrospective study of nine professional musicians showed that such commitment can develop early, and includes goal setting, career planning, dedication, determination, and a willingness to make sacrifices. The musicians reported that, as they progressed through secondary and higher education, self-belief became increasingly important as they encountered more critical appraisal and greater competition (MacNamara et al, 2006).

Intrinsic motivation is by its very nature underpinned by our internal emotional responses. In music, desire for achievement, curiosity, self-actualization, and overcoming detrimental performance anxiety have been found to be important elements influencing an individual's motivation to play an instrument (Motte-Haber, 1984). Nagel (1987) found that the music provided fulfilment of personal needs satisfied by the emotion-inducing quality of music, satisfaction of a positive social response within performance settings, exploration of aggressive drives through the exploitation of the motor skills entailed in musical performance, and some voyeuristic and exhibitionistic desires. Persson (1993; Persson et al, 1996), studying pianists, emphasized the importance of hedonic drive, alongside social and achievement motives, the latter based on the motive to achieve success but also the motive to avoid failure, which involves the fear of losing face. Gellrich and colleagues (1986) identified three types of achievement-related motives in music: a general achievement motivation; a specifically music-oriented achievement orientation; and a sensual-aesthetic motive, the pleasure and joy of playing certain pieces of music. Overall, active participation in music making provides rewards in many different ways.

Tasks that are intrinsically motivating share certain structural and emotional characteristics (Csikszentmihalyi, 1991), offering a level of challenge that is in balance with a person's current skills (Good & Brophy, 1991). When this occurs, an individual derives pleasure from the work and tends to continue with it. This is known as a state of *flow* (see also Chapters 15 and 20, this volume). If the task is too easy, the person becomes bored. If the work demands skills beyond the capabilities of the individual, anxiety is created and flow does not occur (O'Neill, 1999). Flow has been demonstrated in children as young as 4 and 5 years old undertaking musical activities in the classroom, and is associated with high self-concept or skill, perceived challenge, and active engagement (Custodero, 1999).

Intrinsic motivation is a crucial aspect of developing self-identity as a musician. Those who do not develop a musical identity and drop out of playing an instrument perceive themselves as less musically able, musically inadequate, and feel that they have greater strengths in other recreational activities (Frakes, 1984). The time costs of playing an instrument are too great in relation to the rewards they receive (Hurley, 1995). To engage with music in the long term, individuals need positive emotional experiences related to music in early life. Initially, the future musician exhibits acoustic-musical interests and preferences, enjoys being involved with music, and may have an intense musical experience. Later, the need to play with music develops into a need to learn, with strong requests for lessons. As not all of those studied are from musical backgrounds, this suggests powerful internal motivating forces. Finally, the individual commits to a musical career (Harnischmacher, 1997; Manturzewska, 1990; Sosniak, 1985).

The development of musical identity is closely linked to self-concept, which in turn is related to motivation, interest, and participation in school and out-of-school musical activities (Austin, 1990, 1991; Hedden, 1982; Klinedinst, 1991). Children are able to assess how well they are able to complete particular musical tasks (Greenberg, 1970). As they get older, engage with more musical experiences, make comparisons between themselves and others, and receive feedback from others, self-concept declines (Austin & Vispoel, 2000; Mota, 1999; Wigfield et al, 1997). Where comparisons are made with high-attaining others, self-concept is likely to be particularly deflated, so the context of learning is critical in determining how individuals perceive themselves (Marsh, 2005). Even if students believe that they have the potential to do well in music, this does not necessarily transfer to interest in it. Individuals can be highly competent or even outstanding in a field, but have greater interests elsewhere. Asmus and Harrison (1990), working with non-music major college students, found no relationship between music motivation and aptitude. They argue that interest stemmed from love of music.

28.4.4 Motivation to practise

Practising is not always a rewarding experience. Many children require parental encouragement to practise (Howe & Sloboda, 1991). They may also adopt a range of other motivating strategies, for instance, setting long- and short-term goals, playing favourite pieces, playing with others, or working to please teachers. Love of the instrument can also positively influence the amount of practice undertaken (Harnischmacher, 1997). To maintain motivation, high-achieving students tend to strike a balance between formal or required practice tasks and informal, creative, or enjoyable activities (McPherson & McCormick, 1999; Sloboda & Davidson, 1996).

Motivation to practise can be decreased by the interference of close relatives, dislike of particular music, and the distractions of leisure activities and the weather (Harnischmacher, 1997). Beginner instrumentalists tend to maintain motivation when motives are intrinsic, for instance, a focus on the instrument and the music. Where motives are extrinsic, for instance, participation in band or pleasing parents and friends, motivation is less strong (Pitts et al, 2000). Despite this, social rewards derived from parents and teachers do influence motivation (Pitts et al, 2000; Sloboda & Davidson, 1996) and there are additional benefits when students work in harmony with teachers and parents (Creech, 2006; Duke, 1999; Jørgensen, 1998).

28.4.5 Assessment processes and emotion

Assessment in music education frequently involves performance. For some students, performance is extremely anxiety-provoking (Prince, 1994). There has been little study of performance anxiety in younger students, most of the attention focusing on professional musicians or those aspiring to become professionals (see Chapter 16, this volume). Evidence to date suggests that young musicians demonstrate similar variability in reported nervousness to that of professionals. Papageorgi (2007) asked 410 students, aged 12–19, attending junior conservatoires or youth orchestras in the UK and Cyprus, to complete the Adolescent Musicians' Performance Anxiety Scale and a self-report questionnaire. Performance anxiety was found to be a multi-faceted phenomenon, dependent on self-perceptions, situational factors, identity, culture, and family environment. Female students and those with higher levels of expertise were more anxious, as were the Cypriot students, possibly because of the greater emphasis on educational attainment in Cyprus than the UK.

Young people experiencing anxiety adopt a range of coping strategies, but these tend to be less well developed than those of professionals, and are often focused on the reduction of feelings of fear rather than alleviating the detrimental effects on performance (Hallam, 1997). Some students enjoy performance, although the reasons for this may vary from the attention of the audience, the winning of competitions, or actual enjoyment of the music making (Howe & Sloboda, 1991).

28.5 TEACHING TO GENERATE POSITIVE
AFFECTIVE OUTCOMES

The affective outcomes of music education depend to a great extent on the quality and nature of the teaching to which students are exposed. Research on class music teacher effectiveness has largely focused on the teaching of knowledge or skills rather than pupils' emotional engagement with music (Goolsby, 1996; Rosenshine et al, 2002), although some research has demonstrated that frequent use of feedback leads to better performance and more positive attitudes towards learning (Dunn, 1997; Hendel, 1995). Music teachers tend to provide critical feedback in their teaching, despite the evidence that praise is more effective in motivating pupils and improving achievement (Carpenter, 1988; Price, 1989). Research studying conductors of musical groups has shown that where approval rates were raised, there were significant gains in the quality of performance (Humphreys et al, 1992). Praise rather than criticism engenders positive affect, motivation, and increased effort.

The literature on successful music teachers has shown that there are three broad categories of qualities that support their success: internal qualities, relating to others, and social/group management (Pembrook & Craig, 2002). These attributes need to be utilized at different times in relation to different learning and discipline situations and with different groups of students. They are overwhelmingly related to teachers' interpersonal skills, which impact on their relationships with pupils. For instance, internal qualities include emotional stability, energy, enthusiasm and enthusiasm about music, and being happy and optimistic. Relating to others includes being caring, empathetic, encouraging, friendly, people-oriented, interested in students, having emotional sensitivity, and having a sense of humour. These characteristics are also reflected in retrospective descriptions given by trainee music teachers of their own teachers (Cox, 2002). The ideal music teacher combined liveliness and friendliness with an evident desire to communicate a love of the subject:

She was quite free with ideas . . . she was quite happy to let you go out of the class . . . she'd quite happily let you go and play in the hall, she'd have people all over the place and it didn't worry her . . . she was very into composition, she wanted everybody to just go off and write pieces in groups. I frantically wrote songs . . . love songs, typical teenage girl.

(Cox, 2002, p. 101)

Some participants in the research were ambivalent or negative about their school music teachers. They reported fear of some teachers, and recalled unconstructive criticism and inappropriate teaching strategies, although these teachers were able to generate high standards. Despite these negative school experiences, the participants had chosen a career in music, indicating considerable intrinsic motivation to overcome these external demotivating factors.

In instrumental music, pupil–teacher relationships are a crucial element in determining commitment to music, and subsequently the level of musical expertise attained

(Manturzewska, 1990; Sosniak, 1990). The development of early motivation to engage with music requires teachers to be relatively uncritical, encouraging, and enthusiastic. As students progress, the relationship with the teacher changes from one of liking and admiration to respect for their expertise. Teacher–pupil relationships are heavily influenced by the teacher's own life histories, and in particular past relationships with their own teachers (Morgan, 1998). Student personality characteristics determine the way that teacher behaviours are perceived (Schmidt, 1989; Schmidt & Stephans, 1991). There may also be interpersonal dynamics operating between teachers and pupils of which teachers are not consciously aware (Gustafson, 1986). Defence mechanisms of projection and turning passive into active may be adopted by teachers to ward off unpleasant memories relating to their own experience as a learner. Past problems of the teacher in relation to their own learning can be projected on to the pupil.

28.6 THE BENEFITS OF A GREATER EMPHASIS ON AFFECT IN MUSIC EDUCATION

Through the twentieth century, music became more easily accessible until now it permeates almost everything that we do. Individuals are able to use music to manipulate their emotions and arousal levels and to a lesser extent those of others, and can choose to engage in active music making to meet musical, personal, or social needs. In formal music education, most curricula do not focus on the education of the emotions, or indeed the emotion in music. In the teaching of music, whether in classrooms or instrumental tuition, the focus is mainly on acquiring skills that facilitate participation in music or developing an intellectual understanding of it. There is little emphasis on the learning of emotional communication or dealing with the emotions relating to performance, despite the fact that learners and teachers agree that these are important.

In the Western world, the importance of what has come to be known as 'emotional intelligence' for individual success in life has been increasingly recognized, although the concept itself continues to be contested (Bar-On, 1997; Mayer & Salovey, 1997; Petrides & Furnham, 2001). Education systems in the USA and UK have initiated programmes to develop children's emotional and social skills, and these have had considerable success at least in the short term (e.g. Hallam et al, 2006). Such programmes aim to enhance learners' understandings of their own emotions and those of others and develop skills to improve social interaction and communication. If the importance of the emotions has been recognized more broadly in education, the time would seem ripe for it to play a more central role in music education. The possible benefits are significant. Fig 28.1 sets out a model of how a focus on inculcating a love of music could impact on children's well-being and their learning and performance in music. The model suggests that positive emotional experiences in lessons will lead to greater enthusiasm and motivation, which in turn heighten levels of engagement, enhance knowledge and

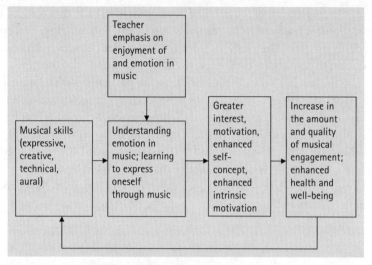

Fig. 28.1 How a focus on emotion could enhance commitment to and attainment in music.

skills, and promote the attainment of higher levels of expertise. Being able to engage with more complex music and having greater composition skills increases the level of challenge and pleasure when goals are attained. An emphasis on self-expression and the emotional elements of music may also facilitate the development of a musical identity. There are also benefits to the teacher, in that well-motivated students are easier and more rewarding to teach.

The evidence from the adult population regarding the positive benefits of music to health and well-being make a strong case for music education being compulsory for all children and for the emphasis within it being on developing a love of music through enjoyment and personal fulfilment. This requires those developing curricula and providing guidance for teachers to focus on the affective outcomes of engagement with music and for teachers themselves to make enjoyment of lessons a key priority.

28.7 DIRECTIONS FOR FUTURE RESEARCH

The reasons why learners do not sustain an ongoing active engagement with music making are multi-faceted and not entirely related to the quality and relevance of music education per se. Nevertheless, there are issues that need to be addressed to ensure that music education in all its forms is enjoyable, in addition to being intellectually stimulating and facilitating the development of a wide range of musical skills. Research needed to support this process includes that which:

- explores teachers' and pupils' perceptions of the role of emotion in music teaching and learning (listening, appraising, composing, and performing);
- explores the ways that teachers can develop emotional understanding of a range of music in learners, taking account of diversity in classrooms;
- explores the ways in which teachers can promote emotional communication in learners as they are composing, improvising, and performing;
- supports the development and evaluation of projects which make music in the school curriculum relevant and enjoyable;
- establishes whether music education contributes to learners' strong emotional experiences of music.

There is also a need for research on the long-term affective outcomes of different elements of music education in terms of pupils' personal and social development. The focus in recent years has tended to be on intellectual outcomes, particularly the enhancement of IQ. We need to understand what impact different kinds of engagement with music can have on subjective well-being, self-esteem, behaviour, social skills, and a range of transferable skills, for instance, concentration and self-discipline. More specifically, there are some interesting questions relating to why performers are reluctant to adopt effective ways of obtaining what has been demonstrated to be effective feedback on their performance, for instance, through self-recordings or computer feedback.

Recommended further reading

1. Hallam, S. (2009). Motivation to learn. In S. Hallam, I. Cross, & M. Thaut (eds), *Oxford handbook of music psychology* (pp. 285–94). Oxford: Oxford University Press.
2. Kopiez, R. (2002). Making music and making sense through music: Expressive performance and communication. In R. Colwell & C. Richardson (eds), *The new handbook of research on music teaching and learning* (pp. 522–41). Oxford: Oxford University Press.
3. Lines, D. K. (ed.). (2005). *Music education for the new millenium: Theory and practice futures for music teaching and learning.* Oxford: Blackwell.

References

Abbs, P. (1994). *The educational imperative: A defence of Socratic and aesthetic learning.* London: Falmer Press.

Asmus E. P., & Harrison C. S. (1990). Characteristics of motivation for music and musical aptitude of undergraduage nonmusic majors. *Journal of Research in Music Education,* 38, 258–68.

Austin, J. R. (1990). The relationship of music self-esteem to degree of participation in school and out-of-school music activities among upper elementary students. *Contributions to Music Education,* 17, 20–31.

Austin, J. R. (1991). Competitive and non-competitive goal structures: An analysis of motivation and achievement among elementary band students. *Psychology of Music*, 19, 142–58.

Austin, J. R., & Vispoel, W. P. (2000). Children's ability self-perceptions and interests:
Grade level, gender, and race differences for music, reading, and math. In R. G. Craven &
H. W. Marsh (eds), *Proceedings of the Inaugural Conference for Self-concept Theory, Research,
and Practice: Advances for the New Millennium* (pp. 133–42). Sydney, Australia: University
of Western Sydney.

Bailey, B. A., & Davidson, J. W. (2002). Adaptive characteristics of group singing: Perceptions
from members of a choir for homeless men. *Musicae Scientiae*, 6, 221–56.

Bar-On, R. (1997). *The Emotional Intelligence Inventory (EQ-i): Technical manual*. Toronto,
Canada: Multi-Health Systems.

Barten, S. S. (1998). Speaking of music: the use of motor-affective metaphors in music
instruction. *Journal of Aesthetic Education*, 32, 89–97.

Beck, R., Cesario, T., Yousefi, S., & Enamoto, H. (2000). Choral singing, performance
perception and immune system changes in salivary immunoglobulin and cortisol. *Music
Perception*, 18, 87–106.

Burnsed, V. (1998). The effects of expressive variation on the musical preferences of elementary school students. *Journal of Research in Music Education*, 46, 396–404.

Campbell, P. S. (1991). *Lessons from the world: A cross cultural guide to music teaching and learning*. New York: Schirmer.

Cantwell, R. H., & Millard, Y. (1994). The relationship between approach to learning and
learning strategies in learning music. *British Journal of Educational Psychology*, 64, 45–63.

Carpenter, R. (1988). A description of relationships between verbal behaviours of teacher-
conductors and ratings of selected junior and senior high school band rehearsals. *Update*,
7, 37–40.

Chiodo, P. A. (1998). The development of lifelong commitment: A qualitative study of adult
instrumental music participation. *Dissertation Abstracts International*, 58, 2578A.

Clift, S., & Hancox, G. (2001). The perceived benefits of singing: Findings from preliminary surveys of a university college choral society. *The Journal of the Royal Society for the
Promotion of Health*, 121, 248–56.

Coffman, D. D. (2002). Adult education. In R. Colwell & C. Richardson (eds), *The new handbook of research on music teaching and learning* (pp. 199–209). Oxford: Oxford University
Press.

Conda, J. M. (1997). The late bloomers piano club: A case study of a group in progress.
Dissertation Abstracts International, 58, 409A.

Costa-Giomi, E. (1999). The effects of three years of piano instruction on children's cognitive
development. *Journal of Research in Music Education*, 47, 198–212.

Cox, G. (2002). *Living music in schools 1923–99: Studies in the history of music education in
England*. Aldershot, UK: Ashgate.

Creech, A. (2006). *Dynamics, harmony and discord: A systems analysis of teacher-pupil-
parent interaction in instrumental learning*. Unpublished doctoral dissertation, Institute of
Education, University of London, UK.

Csikszentmihalyi, M. (1991). *Flow: the psychology of optimal experience*. New York: Harper Row.

Custodero, L.A. (1999). Constructing musical understandings: The cognition-flow interface.
Bulletin of the Council for Research in Music Education, 142, 79.

Dalgarno, G. (1997). Creating an expressive performance without being able to play a musical
instrument. *British Journal of Music Education*, 14, 163–71.

Davidson, J. W. (1993). Visual perception of performance manner in the movement of solo
musicians. *Psychology of Music*, 21, 103–13.

Davidson, J. W., & Coimbra, D. C. C. (2001). Investigating performance evaluation by assessors of singers in a music college setting. *Musicae Scientiae*, 5, 33–54.

Davies, C. D. (1986). Say it until a song comes (reflections on songs invented by children 3–13). *British Journal of Music Education*, 3, 279–93.

DeNora, T. (2000). *Music in everyday life*. Cambridge, UK: Cambridge University Press.

Department for Education and Skills and Department for Culture, Media and Sports. (2006). *Making every child's music matter: Music manifesto report no. 2. A consultation for action.* London: Department for Education and Skills.

Dickey, M. R. (1992). A review of research on modeling in music teaching and learning. *Bulletin of the Council for Research in Music Education*, 113, 27–40.

Dogani, K. (2004). Teachers' understanding of composing in the primary classroom. *Music Education Research*, 6, 263–80.

Duke, R. A. (1999/2000). Measures of instructional effectiveness in music research. *Bulletin of the Council for Research in Music Education*, 143, 1–49.

Dunn, D. E. (1997). Effect of rehearsal hierarchy and reinforcement on attention, achievement, and attitude of selected choirs. *Journal of Research in Music Education*, 45, 547–67.

Eccles, J., Wigfield, A., Harold, R. D., & Blumenfield, P. (1993). Age and gender differences in children's self- and task-perceptions during elementary school. *Child Development*, 64, 830–47.

Elliott, D. J. (1995). *Music matters: A new philosophy of music education*. Oxford: Oxford University Press.

Elliot, D. J. (2005). Musical understanding, musical works, and emotional expression: Implications for education. *Educational Philosophy and Theory*, 37, 93–103.

Finnäs, L. (2006). Ninth-grade pupils' significant experiences in aesthetic areas: the role of music and of different basic modes of confronting music. *British Journal of Music Education*, 23, 315–32.

Frakes, L. (1984). *Differences in music achievement, academic achievement and attitude among participants, dropouts and non-participants in secondary school music.* Unpublished doctoral dissertation, University of Iowa, USA.

Gellrich, M., Osterwold, M., & Schulz, J. (1986). Leistungsmotivation bei Kindern im Instumentalunterricht. Bericht uber eine erkundungsstudie (Children's performance motivation in instrumental teaching). *Musikpsychologie*, 3, 33–69.

Gembris, H. (2001). Federal Republic of Germany. In D. J. Hargreaves & A. C. North (eds), *Musical development and learning: The international perspective* (pp. 40–55). London: Continuum.

Giomi, C. J. (1992). The development of children's esthetic sensitivity to mood in music: An experimental study comparing five- and nine-year-olds using a non-verbal mode of response. *Dissertations Abstracts International*, 53, 1715-A.

Good, T. L., & Brophy, J. E. (1991). *Educational psychology*. New York: Longmans.

Goolsby, T. W. (1996). Time use in instrumental rehearsals: A comparison of experienced, novice, and student teachers. *Journal of Research in Music Education*, 44, 286–303.

Greenberg, M. (1970). Musical achievement and self-concept. *Journal of Research in Music Education*, 18, 57–64.

Gustafson, R. I. (1986). Effects of interpersonal dynamics in the student-teacher dyads in diagnostic and remedial content of four private violin lessons. *Psychology of Music*, 14, 130–39.

Haack, P. (1992). The acquisition of music listening skills. In R. Colwell (ed.), *Handbook of research on music teaching and learning* (pp. 451–65). New York: Schirmer Books.

Hallam. S. (1995). Professional musicians' approaches to the learning and interpretation of music. *Psychology of Music*, 23, 111–28.

Hallam, S. (1997). Approaches to instrumental music practice of experts and novices: Implications for education. In H. Jørgensen & A. C. Lehmann (eds), *Does practice make perfect? Current theory and research on instrumental music practice* (pp. 179–231). Oslo, Norway: Norges Musikkhøgskole.

Hallam, S. (2009). Motivation to learn. In S. Hallam, I. Cross, & M. Thaut (eds), *Oxford handbook of music psychology* (pp. 285–94). Oxford: Oxford University Press.

Hallam, S., Shaw, J., & Rhamie, J. (2006). *Evaluation of the primary behaviour and attendance pilot. Research report.* London: Department for Education and Skills.

Hallam, S., & Price, J. (1998). Can the use of background music improve the behaviour and academic performance of children with emotional and behavioural difficulties? *British Journal of Special Education, 25*, 87–90.

Hallam, S., & Prince, V. (2000). *Research into instrumental music services: Final report.* London: Department for Education and Employment.

Hallam, S., & Prince, V. (2003). Conceptions of musical ability. *Research Studies in Music Education, 20*, 2–22.

Hallam, S., Price, J., & Katsarou, G. (2002). The effects of background music on primary school pupils' task performance. *Educational Studies, 28*, 111–22.

Hargreaves, D. J., & North, A. C. (eds). (2001). *Musical development and learning: The international perspective.* London: Continuum.

Harland, J., Kinder, K., Lord, P., Stott, A., Schagen, I., & Haynes, J. (2000). *Arts education in secondary schools: Effects and effectiveness.* London: NFER/The Arts Council of England.

Harnischmacher, C. (1997). The effects of individual differences in motivation, volition, and maturational processes on practice behaviour of young instrumentalists. In H. Jørgensen & A. C. Lehmann (eds), *Does practice make perfect? Current theory and research on instrumental music practice* (pp. 71–88). Oslo, Norway: Norges Musikkhøgskole.

Heddon, S. K. (1982). Prediction of music achievement in the elementary school. *Journal of Research in Music Education, 30*, 61–8.

Hendel, C. (1995). Behavioural characteristics and instructional patterns of selected music teachers. *Journal of Research in Music Education, 47*, 174–87.

Hepler, L. E. (1986). The measurement of teacher/student interaction in private music lessons and its relation to do to do teacher field dependence/independence. *Dissertation Abstracts International, 47*, 2939-A.

Hetland, L. (2000). Learning to make music enhances spatial reasoning. *Journal of Aesthetic Education, 34*, 179–238.

Hinkle, L. B. (1988). The meaning of choral experience to the adult membership of the German singing societies comprising the United Singers Federation of Pennsylvania. *Dissertation Abstracts International, 48*, 2568A.

Howe, M., & Sloboda, J. A. (1991). Young musicians' accounts of significant influences in their early lives. 2. Teachers, practising and performing. *British Journal of Music Education, 8*, 53–63.

Humphreys, J. T., May, W. V., & Nelson, D. J. (1992). Research on music ensembles. In R. Colwell (ed.), *Handbook of research on music teaching and learning* (pp. 651–68). New York: Schirmer Books.

Hurley, C. G. (1995). Student motivations for beginning and continuing/discontinuing string music tuition. *Quarterly Journal of Music Teaching and Learning, 6*, 44–55.

Johnson, C. M. (1998). Effect of instruction in appropriate rubato usage on the onset timings and perceived musicianship of musical performances. *Journal of Research in Music Education, 46*, 436–45.

Jørgensen, E. (1998). Modeling aspects of type IV music instructional triads. *Bulletin of the Council for Research in Music Education, 137,* 43–56.

Juslin, P. N., & Laukka, P. (2003). Communication of emotions in vocal expression and music performance: Different channels, same code? *Psychological Bulletin, 129,* 770–814.

Juslin, P. N., & Laukka, P. (2004). Expression, perception, and induction of musical emotions: A review and a questionnaire study of everyday listening. *Journal of New Music Research, 33,* 217–38.

Juslin, P. N., & Persson, R. S. (2002). Emotional communication. In R. Parncutt & G. E. McPherson (eds), *The science and psychology of music performance. Creative strategies for teaching and learning* (pp. 219–36). Oxford: Oxford University Press.

Juslin, P. N., Karlsson, J., Lindström, E., Friberg, A., & Schoonderwaldt, E. (2006). Play it again with feeling: Computer feedback in musical communication of emotions. *Journal of Experimental Psychology: Applied, 12,* 79–95.

Karlsson, J., & Juslin, P.N. (2008). Musical expression: An observational study of instrumental teaching. *Psychology of Music, 36,* 309–34.

Kemp, A. E. (1996). *The musical temperament: Psychology and personality of musicians* Oxford: Oxford University Press.

Klinedinst, R. E. (1991). Predicting performance achievement and retention of fifth-grade instrumental students. *Journal of Research in Music Education, 39,* 225–38.

Kennell, R. (1992). Toward a theory of applied music instruction. *Quarterly Journal of Music Teaching and Learning, 3,* 5–16.

Kokotsaki, D., & Hallam, S. (2007). Higher education music students' perceptions of the benefits of participative music making. *Music Education Research, 9,* 93–109.

Kopiez, R. (2002). Making music and making sense through music: Expressive performance and communication. In R. Colwell & C. Richardson (eds), *The new handbook of research on music teaching and learning* (pp. 522–41). Oxford: Oxford University Press.

Kostka, M. J. (1984). An investigation of reinforcements, time use and student attention in piano lessons. *Journal of Research in Music Education, 32,* 113–22.

Kratus, J. (1989). A time analysis of the compositional processes used by children ages 7–11. *Journal of Research in Music Education, 37,* 5–20.

Kratus, J. (1994). Relationships among children's music audiation and their compositional processes and products. *Journal of Research in Music Education, 42,* 115–30.

Kreutz, G., Bongard, S., Rohrmann, S., Hodapp, V., & Grebe, D. (2004). Effects of choir singing or listening on secretory immunoglobulin A, cortisol, and emotional state. *Journal of Behavioural Medicine, 27,* 623–35.

Lamont, A. Hargreaves, D. J., Marshall, N. A., & Tarrant, M. (2003). Young people's music in and out of school. *British Journal of Music Education, 20,* 229–41.

Langer, S. (1942). *Philosophy in a new key.* Cambridge, MA: Harvard University Press.

Langer, S. (1953). *Feeling and form.* London: Routledge.

Laukka, P. (2004). Instrumental music teachers' views on expressivity: A report from music conservatoires. *Music Education Research, 6,* 45–56.

Lindström, E., Juslin, P. N., Bresin, R., & Williamon, A. (2003). 'Expressivity comes from within your soul': a questionnaire study of music students' perspectives on expressivity. *Research Studies in Music Education, 20,* 23–47.

Manturzewska, M. (1990). A biographical study of the life-span development of professional musicians. *Psychology of Music, 18,* 112–39.

Marchand, D. J. (1975). A study of two approaches to developing expressive performance. *Journal of Research in Music Education, 23,* 14–22.

Marsh, H. W. (2005). Big fish little pond effect on academic self-concept. *German Journal of Educational Psychology, 19,* 119–28.

Mayer, J. D., & Salovey, P. (1997). What is emotional intelligence? In P. Salovey & D. Sluyter (eds), *Emotional development and emotional intelligence: Implications for educators* (pp. 3–31). New York: Basic Books.

MacNamara, A., Holmes, P., & Collins, D. (2006). The pathway to excellence: the role of psychological characteristics in negotiating the challenges of musical development. *British Journal of Music Education, 23,* 285–302.

McCarthy, M. (1999). *Passing it on: the transmission of music in Irish culture.* Cork, Ireland: University of Cork.

McPherson, G. E., & Dunbar-Hall, P. (2001). Australia. In D. J. Hargreaves & A.C. North (eds), *Musical development and learning: The international perspective* (pp. 14– 26). London: Continuum.

McPherson, G. E., & McCormick, J. (1999). Motivational and self-regulated components of musical practice. *Bulletin of the Council for Research in Music Education, 141,* 98–102.

Mota, G. (1999). Young children's motivation in the context of classroom music: An exploratory study about the role of music content and teaching style. *Bulletin of the Council for Research in Music Education, 141,* 119–23.

Motte-Haber, H. de la (1984). Die Bedeutung der Motivation fur den Instrumentalbericht (The significance of motivation in instrumental reports). *Zeitschrift fur Musikpädagogik, 51,* 51–54.

Morgan, C. (1998). *Instrumental music teaching and learning: A life history approach.* Unpublished doctoral dissertation, University of Exeter, UK.

Nagel, J. J. (1987). An examination of commitment to career in music: Implications for alienation from vocational choice. *Dissertation Abstracts International, 42,* 1154–5.

National Curriculum for England: Music (Key Stage 3, 11–14 year olds) (2007). London: Qualifications and Curriculum Authority.

North, A. C., Hargreaves, D. J., & O'Neill, S. A. (2000). The importance of music to adolescents. *British Journal of Educational Psychology, 70,* 255–72.

OFSTED (2001). *Inspection report no. 199478.* London: Office for Standards in Education, Children's Services and Skills.

O'Neill, S. A. (1999). Flow theory and the development of musical performance skills. *Bulletin of the Council for Research in Music Education, 141,* 129–34.

Papageorgi, I. (2007). *Understanding performance anxiety in the adolescent musician.* Unpublished doctoral dissertation, Institute of Education, University of London, UK.

Pembrook, R., & Craig, C. (2002). Teaching as a profession. In R. Colwell (ed.), *Handbook of research on music teaching and learning* (pp. 786–817). New York: Schirmer books.

Persson, R. S. (1993). *The subjectivity of musical performance: An exploratory music-psychological real world enquiry into the determinants and education of musical reality.* Unpublished doctoral dissertation, School of Human and Health Sciences, Huddersfield University, Huddersfield, UK.

Persson, R. S. (1994). Control before shape—on mastering the clarinet: A case study on commonsense teaching. *British Journal of Music Education, 11,* 223–38.

Persson, R. S. (1996). Concert musicians as teachers: On good intentions falling short. In A. J. Cropley & D. Dehn (eds), *Fostering the growth of high ability: European perspectives* (pp. 303–20). Norwood, NJ: Ablex.

Persson, R. S., Pratt, G., & Robson, C. (1996). Motivational and influential components of musical performance: A qualitative analysis. In A. J. Cropley & D. Dehn (eds), *Fostering the growth of high ability: European perspectives* (pp. 287–301). Norwood, NJ: Ablex.

Petrides, K. V., & Furnham, A. (2001). Trait emotional intelligence: Psychometric investigation with reference to established trait taxonomies. *European Journal of Personality*, 15, 425–48.

Pitts, S. (2000). Reasons to teach music: establishing a place in the contemporary curriculum, *British Journal of Music Education*, 17, 33–42.

Pitts, S., Davidson, J. W., & McPherson, G. E. (2000). Developing effective practising strategies: Case studies of three young instrumentalists. *Music Education Research*, 2, 45–56.

Primos, K. (2001). Africa. In D. J. Hargreaves & A. C. North (eds), *Musical development and learning: The international perspective* (pp. 1–13). London: Continuum.

Price, H. E (1989). An effective way to do to do teach and rehearse: Research supports using sequential patterns. *Update*, 8, 42–6.

Prince, V. (1994). *Teachers' and pupils' conceptions of emotion in musical experience and their perceptions of he emphasis given to cognitive, technical and expressive aspects of instrumental lessons.* Unpublished MA dissertation, Institute of Education, University of London, UK.

Prince, V., & Hallam, S. (1996). *Cognitive, technical and expressive music skills: pupils' and teachers' perceptions of the relative emphasis given to each in instrumental music lessons.* Paper presented at the BPS Education Section Conference, November 1996, Reading, UK.

QCA (2002). *GCSE examination results, 1992–2001.* London: Qualifications and Curriculum Authority.

Reimer, B. (1970). *A philosophy of music education.* Englewood Cliffs, NJ: Prentice Hall.

Reimer, B. (1978). Education for aesthetic awareness: The Cleveland Area Project. *Music Educators Journal*, 64, 66–9.

Rodriguez, C. X. (1998). Children's perception, production, and description of musical expression. *Journal of Research in Music Education*, 46, 48–61.

Rosenberg, H. S., & Trusheim, W. (1989). Creative transformations: How visual artists, musicians, and dancers use mental imagery in their work. In P. Robin & J. E. Schorr (eds), *Imagery: Current perspectives* (pp. 55–75). New York: Plenum Press.

Rosenshine, B., Froehlich, H., & Fakhouri, I. (2002). Systematic instruction. In R. Colwell & C. Richardson (eds), *The new handbook of research on music teaching and learning* (pp. 299–314). New York: Schirmer books.

Rosenthal, R. K. (1984). The relative effects of guided model, model only, guide only, and practice only treatments on the accuracy of advanced instrumentalists' musical performance. *Journal of Research in Music Education*, 32, 265–73.

Rostvall, A-L., & West, T. (2001). *Interaktion och kunskapsutveckling (Interaction and learning. A study of music instrument teaching).* Unpublished doctoral dissertation, Royal College of Music, Stockholm, Sweden.

Saarikallio, S., & Erkkila, J. (2007). The role of music in adolescents' mood regulation. *Psychology of Music*, 35, 88–109.

Sang, R. C. (1987). A study of the relationship between instrumental teachers' modeling skills and pupils' performance behaviours. *Bulletin of the Council for Research in Music Education*, 91, 155–9.

Savan, A. (1999). The effect of background music on learning. *Psychology of Music*, 27, 138–46.

Schellenberg, E. G. (2004). Music lessons enhance IQ. *Psychological Science*, 15, 511–14.

Schellenberg, E. G. (2006). Long-term positive associations between music lessons and IQ. *Journal of Educational Psychology*, 98, 457–68.

Schenck, R. (1989). Above all, learning an instrument must be fun. *British Journal of Music Education*, 6, 3–35.

Schmidt, C. P. (1989). Individual differences in perception of applied music teaching feedback. *Psychology of Music*, 17, 110–12.

Schmidt, C. P. (1992). Systematic research in applied music instruction: A review of the literature. *Quarterly Journal of Music Teaching and Learning*, 3, 32–45.

Schmidt, C. P., & Stephans, R. (1991). Locus of control and field dependence as factors in
students evaluations of applied music instruction. *Perceptual and Motor Skills*, 73, 131–6.

Scholes, P. (1935). *Music, the child and the masterpiece: A comprehensive handbook of aims and
methods in all that is usually called musical appreciation.* London: Oxford University Press.

Schools Council (1968). *Enquiry one: Young school leavers.* London: HMSO.

Sloboda, J. A. (1983). The communication of musical metre in piano performance. *Quarterly
Journal of Experimental Psychology*, 35, 377–96.

Sloboda, J. A. (1991). Music structure and emotional response: Some empirical findings.
Psychology of Music, 19, 110–20.

Sloboda, J. A. (1996). The acquisition of musical performance expertise: Deconstructing the
'talent' account of individual differences in musical expressivity. In K. A. Ericsson (ed.),
The road to excellence (pp. 107–26). Mahwah, NJ: Erlbaum.

Sloboda, J. A., & Davidson, J. W. (1996). The young performing musician. In I. Deliege &
J. A. Sloboda (eds), *Musical beginnings: Origins and development of musical competence*
(pp. 171–90). Oxford: Oxford University Press.

Sloboda, J. A., & O'Neill, S. A. (2001). Emotions in everyday listening to music. In P. N. Juslin
& J. A. Sloboda (eds), *Music and emotion: Theory and research* (pp. 415–30). Oxford: Oxford
University Press.

Sloboda, J. A., O'Neill, S. A., & Ivaldi, A. (2001). Functions of music in everyday life: An exploratory study using the Experience Sampling Method. *Musicae Scientiae*, 5, 9–32.

Sloboda, J. A., Minassian, C., & Gayford, C. (2003). *Assisting advanced musicians to enhance
their expressivity: An intervention study.* Paper presented at the Fifth Triennial Conference
of the European Society for the Cognitive Sciences of Music, Hanover, Germany.

Sosniak, L. A. (1985). Learning to be a concert pianist. In B. S. Bloom (ed.), *Developing talent
in young people* (pp. 19–67). New York: Ballantine.

Sosniak, L. A (1990). The tortoise and the hare and the development of talent. In M. J. A. Howe
(ed.), *Encouraging the development of exceptional skills and talents* (pp. 149–64). Leicester,
UK: British Psychological Society.

Sousa, M., Neto, F., & Mullet, E. (2005). Can music change ethnic attitudes among children?
Psychology of Music, 33, 304–16.

Spychiger, M., Patry, J., Lauper, G., Zimmerman, E., & Weber, E. (1993). Does more music
teaching lead to a better social climate? In R. Olechowski & G. Svik (eds), *Experimental
research in teaching and learning* (pp. 322–6). Bern, Switzerland: Peter Lang.

Sudnow, D. (1978). *Ways of the hand: the organisation of improvised conduct.* London:
Routledge.

Taggart, G., Whitby, K., & Sharp, C. (2004). *International review of curriculum and assessment
frameworks: Curriculum and progression in the arts.* London: QCA.

Tait, M. (1992). Teaching strategies and styles. In R. Colwell (ed.), *Handbook of research on
music teaching and learning* (pp. 525–34). New York: Schirmer books.

Tolfree, E., & Hallam, S. (2007). *Young people's uses of and responses to music in their everyday lives.* Paper presented at the Conference of the Psychology of Education Section of the
British Psychological Society, University of Stafford, November 2007.

Trainor, L. J. (1996). Infant preferences for infant-directed versus non-infant-directed
playsongs and lullabies. *Infant Behavior and Development*, 19, 83–92.

Volk, T. (1998). *Music, education and multiculturalism. Foundations and principles.* Oxford:
Oxford University Press

Wigfield, A., Eccles, J. S., Yoon, K. S., Harold, R. D., Arbreton, A. J. A., Freedman-Doan, C., & Blumenfield, P. C. (1997). Changes in children's competence beliefs and subjective task values across the elementary school years: A 3-year study. *Journal of Educational Psychology*, *89*, 451–69.

Wigfield, A., O'Neill, S. A., & Eccles, J. S. (1999). *Children's achievement values in different domains: Developmental and cultural differences*. Paper presented at the Biennial Meeting of the Society for Research in Child Development, Albuquerque, USA, 1999.

Woody, R. H. (1999). The relationship between explicit planning and expressive performance of dynamic variations in an aural modelling task. *Journal of Research in Music Education*, *47*, 331–42.

Woody, R. H. (2000). Learning expressivity in music: an exploratory study. *Research Studies in Music Education*, *14*, 14–23.

Yeh, C-S. (2001). China. In D. J. Hargreaves & A. C. North (eds), *Musical development and learning: The international perspective* (pp. 27–39). London: Continuum.

Young, V., Burwell, K., & Pickup, D. (2003). Areas of study and teaching strategies in instrumental teaching: a case study research project. *Music Education Research*, *5*, 139–55.

CHAPTER 29

MUSIC THERAPY

MICHAEL H. THAUT AND
BARBARA L. WHEELER

Music affects us emotionally, physically, and aesthetically. These responses provide the basis for the use of music in therapy. Juslin and Sloboda (2001) described some of the emotional effects of music, noting that people's experience of music is often accompanied by an 'affective response of some sort (e.g. nostalgic recognition of a favorite song on the radio while driving a car, frustration directed at the music at the shops, joy when listening to an excellent performance at an evening concert, a sad mood created by the soundtrack of a late night movie)' (p. 3). Research into how music is processed by the brain has led to increased understanding of responses to music. Music influences physiological responses (i.e. changes in heart rate, electrical skin conductance, and breathing; Bartlett, 1996) and also affects motor responses (Thaut, 2005). With aesthetic responses, we experience the beauty and art of music (Aigen, 2005).

29.1 OVERVIEW OF MUSIC THERAPY

Music therapy is defined by the American Music Therapy Association (AMTA) as 'the clinical and evidence-based use of music interventions to accomplish individualized goals within a therapeutic relationship by a credentialed professional who has completed an approved music therapy program' (www.musictherapy.org). Bruscia (1998) says that 'music therapy is a systematic process of intervention wherein the therapist helps the client to promote health, using music experiences and the relationships that develop through them as dynamic forces of change' (p. 20). Music therapists use the unique qualities of music and a relationship with a therapist to access emotions and memories, structure behaviour, and provide social experiences in order to address clinical goals.

Music therapy may be used with children or adults with physical or emotional problems, or with healthy people to achieve higher level of awareness. According to the most recent figures on the employment of music therapists, music therapists serve the following client populations, with the first 19 being included here, arranged from more to less popular: developmentally disabled, school-age population, mental health, behavioural disorder, physically disabled, multiply disabled, elderly persons, Alzheimer's/dementia, autism spectrum disorder, speech-impaired, emotionally disturbed, learning-disabled, early childhood, neurologically impaired, dual-diagnosed, visually impaired, stroke, terminally ill, and hearing-impaired (AMTA, 2007).

Music therapists may work with any age group and people with a variety of disabilities. As a member of a therapeutic team or as a private practitioner, the music therapist participates in the analysis of individual problems and the establishment of treatment goals before planning and carrying out music-related treatment. The most common places for music therapists to work, according to information provided by members of AMTA, are children's facilities/schools (18 per cent), geriatric facilities (15 per cent), mental-health settings (13 per cent), self-employed and private practice (13 per cent), and medical settings (10 per cent), with other areas comprising the remainder (31 per cent) of respondents (AMTA, 2007).

Music therapy training is offered at the bachelor's level, although many music therapists have master's and doctoral degrees. The credential of Music Therapist-Board Certified (MT-BC) is awarded to people who have completed bachelor's level training and passed an examination. This is done through the Certification Board for Music Therapists (www.cbmt.org). Continuing education is required for renewal of the MT-BC.

Music therapy methods may be both active and receptive. Active methods involve the client *doing* something with the music; in receptive methods, the client is *receiving* the music, generally through some form of listening. All may include verbal processing of feelings and experiences, particularly with adults.

Bruscia (1998) divides the uses of music in therapy into four methods: improvising, performing or recreating, composing, and listening experiences. Improvisation occurs when the client makes up music vocally, instrumentally, or with a body part or other medium, individually or with others. Performing or recreating takes place when the client learns or performs pre-composed music (see Fig 29.1). Composing experiences involve the therapist helping the client write songs, lyrics, or instrumental pieces or create any kind of musical product. In listening experiences, the client listens to music of any type and responds silently, verbally, or in another modality. The music is selected and presented in a manner that targets the therapeutic goals of the client.

Music therapists use numerous methods and work in a wide variety of settings, and also conceptualize what they do in various ways. Bruscia (1998) has brought some order to the classification of what music therapists do, providing definitions for methods, procedures, and techniques, and suggesting that a *model* is 'a comprehensive approach to assessment, treatment, and evaluation which includes theoretical principles, clinical indications and contraindications, goals, methodological guidelines and

Fig. 29.1 Performance of pre-composed music within a music therapy session.

specifications, and the characteristic use of certain procedural sequences and techniques' (p. 115). Examples of improvisational models as defined by Bruscia (1987) include Creative Music Therapy (developed by Paul Nordoff and Clive Robbins, 2007) and Analytical Music Therapy (Mary Priestley, 1994).[1] Other accepted models in music therapy are The Bonny Method of Guided Imagery and Music (Helen Bonny, 2002) and Neurologic Music Therapy (Michael Thaut, 2005). We can also consider frameworks that underlie music therapy practice. Gfeller and Thaut (2008), for instance, divide psychiatric music therapy treatments into those that focus on cognition and those that focus on physical factors (biomedical model), as well as eclectic models. Outside psychiatric work, a behavioural and cognitive-behavioural framework provides the basis for much music therapy with children in schools in the United States. Some music therapists describe music therapy in terms of aesthetics (Aigen, 1995; Kenny, 2006, pp. 80–122), while still others focus on the meaning that is inherent in music therapy (Ruud, 1998; Stige, 2002). These are only some examples. Many music therapists practise an eclectic approach, drawing from various frameworks and models.

Emotion would seem to be involved in all or most music therapy, although the connections are not often articulated by music therapists, and little research examines this relationship. Emotion is core to some music therapy practices. Bruscia (1987), for instance, suggests that one type of music therapy (Priestley's Analytical Music Therapy) is referential, while another (Nordoff and Robbins' Creative Music Therapy) is non-referential or absolutist (Aigen, 2006). The exact role of emotion in most music therapy has not been considered in the literature. We may gain some understanding

---

[1] The dates listed by each model are of books that present them comprehensively; all models were developed many years earlier.

of its role by looking at the focus of the work. In music psychotherapy, the focus of the therapy *is* emotion, while in some other forms the focus is cognitive or physical functioning. However, just as people always have emotions, so music therapy always deals with emotion in one form or another.

As an example of music therapy in which emotion plays a central role, Bunt and Pavlicevic (2001) presented music and emotion within a general approach to music therapy labelled 'improvisational music therapy', and described the generation of emotional responses to help with therapy of a group of young children with language problems and limited attention, and a group of adults with mental health problems. They said (2001, p. 184):

> The group of language-delayed children may be so motivated to play the instruments and vocalize that their shifts in levels of excitement, quality of relationship, and emotional experiences and expressions may generalize outside of the sessions into further use of vocal sounds, gestures, and a corresponding rise in self-esteem. Likewise, the group of adults with mental health problems may be able to explore the shifting patterns of relating to one another and to the therapist in music and, with the therapist's help, draw analogies to more personal systems of interaction—both within and outside the music therapy setting.

29.2 BRIEF HISTORICAL-PHILOSOPHICAL REVIEW

Music and healing have been tied together throughout history. According to Moreno (1988), 'The continuing 30 thousand-year-old shamanic tradition of music and healing [is] still being practiced throughout the world' (p. 271). The Greek philosophers Plato and Aristotle wrote of how to use music to affect health and behaviour; music continued to be tied to healing throughout the Middle Ages (Boxberger, 1962) and later. Music has been used to treat both physical and mental problems in the United States since the late eighteenth century (Davis & Gfeller, 2008).

Formal music therapy in the United States had it roots during World War II, when musicians played their instruments in Veteran's Administration hospitals, playing for veterans with physical and emotional trauma from the war. Their music often had a positive effect on the hospitalized veterans, and the medical personnel began to request that hospitals hire the musicians. It became clear that the hospital musicians needed some training before entering the facilities, and the demand grew for a college curriculum. The first music therapy degree programme in the world began in 1944, followed by the first music therapy association in 1950. The American Music Therapy Association (AMTA), the current US association, was established in 1998 through the unification of two existing music therapy organizations.

Recent developments in brain research and the neurobiology of music are altering concepts of music therapy. As the neurological basis of music and the effect of music on brain plasticity are better understood, a new scientific framework for the ratio-nale of music in therapy is emerging. It is now clear that music can influence, shape, and educate cognitive, affective, and sensorimotor processes in the brain that can also be transferred and generalized to non-musical brain functions within a therapeutic model. These developments are beginning to change concepts of music in therapy and medicine (see also Chapter 30, this volume).

Emotion has always played an important role in explaining music's therapeutic effect, although scientifically based models for the role of music-evoked emotions in music therapy have been absent. Efforts are under way to develop a theoretical para-digm of music that can integrate musical response models in music perception and music cognition with concepts of music's influence on non-musical human behav-iour, psychologically and neurobiologically, as well as with concepts of behavioural learning and therapeutic change (Gaston, 1968; Thaut, 2005).

For the purpose of this chapter, and in keeping with the grand theme of music and emotion in this book, we will investigate the unique ability of music to access affective/motivational systems in the brain as a major mechanism of its therapeutic effective-ness.[2] This privileged access allows music to assume an effective role in influencing and modifying affective states. However, music also assumes a central role by way of affect modification in accessing the totality of a patient's cognitions and perceptions, feeling states, and behaviour organization. The paradigm of affect modification will serve as a useful theoretical foundation to put forth testable hypotheses for future research, which will allow music therapy to develop, validate, and modify specific functional interven-tions for non-musical behaviour learning and change, based on musical emotions.

Before we can assign to affect modification through music a critical role as an essen-tial modulatory component of behavioural learning and change in therapy, we must look at the genesis of affect and arousal in music, since this is where a transfer function of music to non-musical functions must begin.

29.3 THEORIES OF EMOTION AND AROUSAL IN MUSIC

What is the nature of our experience when we listen to or produce music? What thoughts and feelings are evoked through music perception? How do the physical attributes of the music stimulus influence our thinking and feeling in the perceptual process? Is it, per-haps, because music is essentially non-verbal and, unlike many other aesthetic media,

---

[2] The main portion of this chapter and the exposition of the relationship of emotion to music therapy were previously elaborated by Thaut (2002).

its patterns evolve in time—just as the content and form of our thoughts and feelings evolve in time and require temporal structure to be coherent and meaningful?

In order to justify the use of music in therapy, we have to develop a view of stimulus processing where the perception of stimulus properties is not an end in itself, but leads to transferable responses that can be meaningful determinants of non-musical behaviour as well. We will first review three classical theories that have formed the basis and springboard for multiple theoretical investigations to help in a conceptual development of the influence of music on behaviour: (a) Meyer's (1956) theory of emotion and meaning in music; (b) Mandler's (1984) cognitive theory of emotion; and (c) Berlyne's (1971) theory of emotion, arousal, and reward in aesthetic perception.

Meyer develops the view that meaning and emotion in music perception arise through the perception of patterns within the stimulus itself (i.e. the formal and structural components of a musical piece). He bases his theory on Dewey's conflict theory of emotion and McCurdy's theory that the tendency of an organism to respond needs to be blocked in order to arouse affect. Meyer transfers the tenets of these theories into music perception by postulating that listeners develop expectancy schemes when following musical patterns. A carefully crafted interruption of the expectation, followed by a period of suspension and resolution in the composition, will evoke an affective experience in the recipient.

In Meyer's view, meaning and emotion in music are a result of perceiving and building expectations within the syntax of the musical structures and the carefully planned manipulations thereof. He further contends that the genesis of emotional experience in music is similar to emotional experiences in daily life. Meyer acknowledges the existence of designated non-musical mood experiences, imagery, and memories in music perception, which can also cause emotional responses. However, since these responses are learned through association and not through perception of the stimulus patterns themselves, Meyer considers these responses of only secondary importance.

Mandler's theory (1984) resembles Meyer's account. Mandler develops a comprehensive view of the genesis of emotional experience in general, with special consideration to the biologically adaptive value of emotional reactions. An emotional reaction is preceded by biological arousal of the autonomic nervous system, caused by an interruption of expectancy or anticipation patterns that are based on perceptual-motor schemata. These schemata are created through human cognition in order to predict and plan for upcoming events. Thus for Mandler, human cognition unfolds in the continuous interplay between prediction and sensory confirmation. When something unexpected happens, arousal is triggered as an alerting signal to search for an interpretation of the interruption. In the interplay between arousal and interpretation, an emotional experience of a particular quality is produced. The cognitive interpretation of the arousal-triggering circumstances will define the quality of the emotional experience.

Mandler's theory can be applied to music stimuli when we look at the considerable evidence that emotional reactions to music involve strong arousal of the autonomic nervous system (Chapter 11, this volume) and also accept Meyer's account of how the process of interruption–suspension–resolution in perceiving musical structures induces emotional responses. For Mandler, emotion or affect is strictly post-cognitive.

Relevant to our inquiry into music perception, both Meyer and Mandler connect the process of assigning meaning with physiological arousal states, the interpretation of which results in an affective experience of a particular quality.

Berlyne's (1971) theory of emotion, arousal, and reward in aesthetic perception is similar to the previous views in its emphasis on the role of arousal in music perception. However, Berlyne expands and specifies the role and quality of arousal and its relationship to stimulus properties and corresponding affective response qualities. He views arousal not only as an alerting signal indicating an interruption in physiological homeostasis or cognitive prediction patterns. He proposes that the main process underlying healthy central nervous system functioning is to seek out sensory input. For example, moderate increases in arousal, decreases from extremely high arousal, or temporary increases followed by immediate decreases are perceived by an individual as pleasurable and rewarding. Changes in arousal—a measure of the state of alertness, wakefulness, excitement, stimulation, or readiness—are reflected in four psychophysiological response types: (a) central responses (e.g. EEG, evoked potential); (b) motor responses (e.g. motor neural activity, bodily movement); (c) sensory changes (e.g. change in sensitivity of sense organs and sensory pathways); and (d) autonomic responses (e.g. galvanic skin response, heart rate, respiration).

From a neurobiological view, it is known that physiological arousal states are mediated in part by brain structures in the thalamic, hypothalamic, and brain stem areas. In agreement with Meyer and Mandler, Berlyne contends that arousal states are the physiological accompaniment of emotional states and thus differentiates the latter from so-called non-emotional states. Berlyne has shown in great detail that artworks, including music, contain stimulus patterns that have specific arousal-influencing potential, which thus can induce affective experiences. A determination of music's arousal potential and influence on affective responses in regard to clinical populations is dependent upon identifying and analysing these stimulus patterns or properties and their corresponding property-specific responses in therapy settings. Three classes of stimulus properties have been studied extensively (Berlyne, 1971; McMullen, 1996). They are presented here as they pertain to music stimuli:

1. *Psychophysical properties*, including the perception of intensity, tempo, wave form, and rate of change (distribution of energy). These properties constitute the experience of activation (energy, excitement, stimulation) through the perceived stimulus object.
2. *Collative properties*, including the perception of structural elements in the composition. These properties are considered to constitute the experience of novelty, surprise, order, clarity, comprehension, and their respective opposites, through the perceived stimulus object.
3. *Ecological properties*, including the perception of elements in music that have acquired learned associations with extra-musical events and experiences. These properties are considered to constitute experience through associations triggered by music such as designated moods, connotations, memories, and private images.

Research measuring various aspects of listener responses to music stimuli has commonly substantiated similar dimensions of response (McMullen, 1996; Nagel et al, 2007; Schubert, 2003). Emotional experiences in music as a function of musical structures have also been demonstrated and analysed (Filipic & Bigand, 2005; Gomez & Danuser, 2007; Nielzén & Cesarec, 1982; Pallesen et al, 2005). The main findings of these studies support three basic arguments: (a) music is an efficient signal in transferring emotional messages; (b) factor analysis of musical structures and elements correlates with subjective emotional experiences; (c) communication of emotional meaning in music seems to be affected by complex interactions of personality traits with gender, age, mood, and musical selection.

29.4 CLASSIFICATION OF EMOTIONAL STATES

Theories presented in the preceding section gave an account of how emotion and meaning are perceived in music. Central to all is the concept that music can induce arousal, leading to affective experiences. Primarily the perception of patterns within the stimulus (the psychophysical and collative attributes) and secondarily extra-musical (ecological) learned associations with the actual stimulus induce arousal reactions and affective responses. In Berlyne's model, these responses are property-specific and may be subsumed under the terms activation/energy; novelty/surprise/order/clarity; and associations. Perceptual focus on specific attributes of the stimulus may thus facilitate affective responses within particular qualities. But how can these affective responses that are evoked within music be generalized, or functionally transferred to therapeutic processes in which nonmusical behaviour is the focus?

This question is closely linked to the critical question: how can the music-evoked feeling process be classified and interpreted as a source to modify behaviour in therapy that has no musical orientation? A quick review of psychological theories of how emotions are organized and related to one another may help to select the appropriate framework for a discussion of how music-induced emotions may function to modify non-musical behaviour (Ekman & Davidson, 1994; Panksepp, 1998; see also Chapter 4, this volume).

One prominent approach to emotion states distinguishes categories of basic and complex emotion states that can be verbally classified (e.g. anger, sadness, happiness, fear, disgust, surprise; Plutchik, 1962). Since music-evoked affective experiences refer only in specific instances to referential verbal classifications of affect and cannot directly express semantic content, this approach is of limited value to our discussion.

A second approach, originally based on Wundt's (1874) dimensional classification of affective states, offers better access to the relationship between music and affective experiences that build relevance for non-musical behaviour as well. Within the framework of this approach, all emotional states are located along a continuum of independent dimensions or qualities. A survey of the pertinent literature in regard to artworks (Berlyne, 1971; McMullen, 1996) reveals that all systems within this approach have two dimensions in common: *direction* (referring to the dimension of pleasantness vs. unpleasantness) and *intensity* (referring to the strength or level of activation of the perceived stimulus object). Following this dimensional viewpoint, every music-evoked affective experience can be classified and understood as an emotional state within a two-dimensional matrix that determines the direction and intensity of the experience.

In this context, Berlyne's theory on the connection among arousal, affect, and reward in aesthetic perception is of considerable importance. His contention is that aesthetic stimuli, depending on their arousal potential, are evaluated by the human organism in respect to their hedonic value—the experience of intrinsic reward, incentive value, motivation, attractiveness, and positive feedback when perceiving the stimulus in question. The reward value is the end product of the arousal-inducing stimulus properties and determines the quality of the affective experience as well as its function in influencing behaviour processes. The human organism is motivated to pursue behaviour and stimulation associated with strong reward experiences.

Berlyne relates reward experiences to the function of the brain reward system, because the centres in the brain controlling hedonic processes and the centres controlling the fluctuations of arousal overlap to a large extent in the limbic system (Olds, 1962). Since physiological research has shown that these same centres are activated while processing music stimuli (Chapter 12, this volume), it is reasonable to assume that music stimuli may influence those aspects of human behaviour that are related to the function of those brain areas (i.e. emotion, mood, motivation, alertness).

Following Berlyne a bit further, we can postulate five steps in which music exploits stimulus properties that facilitate perception by effectively controlling exploration, attention, motivation, and reinforcement. First, it has been shown that music stimuli entail arousal-influencing properties that can influence the state of readiness to perceive. Second, exploratory behaviour (i.e. seeking out new perceptual experiences) can be promoted by music stimuli, since the behaviour of perceptual curiosity is connected to and driven by the experience of reward through changes in arousal. Third, processes of selective attention and abstraction can be achieved by conveying stimulus information in a particular (musical) sensory modality that results in inhibition of information from stimuli in other modalities (Hernandez-Peon, 1961; Marteniuk, 1976) and can facilitate grouping or chunking of extra-musical information for perception, retention, and recall in learning processes (Claussen & Thaut, 1997; Wallace, 1994). Fourth, psychological and physiological research points to the fact that the perceptual process can have emotional accompaniments that may lead to the perception-enhancing experiences of pleasure, reward, and positive feedback, and may aid in promoting positive emotional experiences via their arousal-influencing potential (Berlyne, 1971). Fifth, music may function as a mediating response, adding distinctive stimulation to an external stimulus and facilitating discrimination learning.

Based on these models of emotion and meaning, it now becomes possible to propose mechanisms of how affective states in music can also effectively regulate and facilitate coherence in non-musical cognitive functions such as attention, memory, psychoso-cial, or executive processes in cognitive rehabilitation.

29.5 THE ROLE OF AFFECTIVE BEHAVIOUR IN BEHAVIOUR LEARNING AND CHANGE

Research in psychology and the neurosciences in regard to cognition and affect points increasingly to the important role affective states can play in determining behaviour and behavioural change (Dolan, 2002; Izard et al, 1984; Lane & Nadel, 2000; Strohsal & Linehan, 1986; see also reviews by Anderson, 2005; Purves et al, 2008). Research-based theoretical models (e.g. the associative network theory of memory and mood; Bower, 1981) have provided evidence for the influence of affective states and changes thereof on memory, learning, social behaviours, and cognitive executive functions (Blaney, 1986; Bower et al, 1978; Dalgleish & Power, 1999; Uttl et al, 2006). The associative net-work theory proposes that mood states serve as central 'nodes' to which all life events and cognitions that occur in a particular mood state become attached. By accessing and establishing a specific mood state—similar to an electronic circuit system—access to all events and cognitions associated with this mood state are facilitated in memory. In such a network model, affect becomes a primary agent for structuring cognitive orien-tation and information processing, memory recall, and learning strategies (Thaut & de L'Etoile, 1993). Emotional states have been shown to influence memory functions dur-ing encoding (Ruiz-Caballero & Gonzalez, 1994) and retrieval (Burke & Mathews, 1992; Eich, 1995; Kenealy, 1997; Rusting, 1999). The influence of emotion states on a variety of executive functions (e.g. problem solving and decision making) has also been shown (Carnevale & Isen, 1986; Hertel et al, 2000; Kavanagh, 1987; MacLeod et al, 1997).

Derryberry and Rothbart (1984) propose the central role of affective/motiva-tional processes to direct and organize behaviour within a neurophysiological model of emotion and sensory regulation. Affective/motivational states, evolving in the activation and interaction of cortico-limbic-brain stem systems, regulate, excite, atten-uate, and bias cortical pathways in regard to modulating sensory information process-ing and thus influence our subjective perceptions and cognitions. In other words, as Derryberry and Rothbart state, 'emotion influences the way we see and interpret the world' (p. 141).

The clinician's interest in developing methods that produce affective change as a means of achieving comprehensive behavioural change is thus only logical (Rachman, 1980). Several conceptual approaches exist in this respect, most notably cognitive therapies, which view affect as a result of cognitive processes and thus try to alter neg-ative thoughts or faulty perceptions to achieve emotional change (Beck et al, 1979).

Much research in cognitive psychology and neuroscience also demonstrates the strong reciprocal role of moods and emotions influencing cognitive functions such as memory, attention, learning, social behaviour, motivational states, and cognitive executive functions such as decision making, problem solving, and thoughts about self (e.g. Bower, 1981; Lane & Nadel, 2000; Markowitsch, 2000).

For example, in negative mood states, negative memories, destructive social behaviours, low self-esteem, and low levels of motivation are more likely to be accessible to one's cognitions and thus dominate one's behaviour. In positive mood states, positive materials and enhanced memory functions are more readily accessible (Fiedler, 1991; Teasdale & Fogarty, 1979). Positive emotional and mood states also seem to enhance memory function in regard to encoding and recall, regardless of mood congruency. In summary, a large amount of research has been accumulated, clearly demonstrating the critical role of emotional states in influencing perception, attention, learning, memory, and executive functions (Lane & Nadel, 2000; Purves et al, 2008).

Information processing in the brain occurs continuously against a dynamic filter of emotional-motivational states, which connects the saliency of emotional considerations to shaping higher cognitive functions. A distinct role for the emergence of music as a powerful language of emotion is provided by models that emphasize the iterative and integrative nature of emotional processing within the dynamic interplay between cognitive and emotional-motivational brain and behaviour functions. These models also provide the basis for music-induced emotion states to have regulatory influence on comprehensive non-musical cognitive and perceptual operations that can be functionally exploited in therapy and rehabilitation.

Furthermore, as research points to the efficiency of altering cognitions to alter mood states, it also documents the resistance of affective behaviours such as abnormal emotional experiences, certain mood states, and irrational fears and beliefs to cognitive change and the reciprocal influence of mood on cognitions (Teasdale, 1983). However, cognitions sometimes seem not to be accessible to therapeutic efforts, and at times interventions may be more practically aimed at the resultant affective components of behaviour. Several scientists have therefore suggested expanding the concept of behaviour modification to include techniques that feed directly into and/or facilitate change in the affective system (Rachman, 1981, 1984), to find another route to alter cognitions more effectively. The reciprocal role of affect/cognition is further emphasized by research evidence that cognitive-perceptual processes play a central role in the formation of emotion, and that feeling states and affect in most instances cannot exist in the absence of cognition (Lane & Nadel, 2000). These interactions may be particularly relevant for new neuropsychiatric models that begin to link neuroscience models of brain function more systematically with behavioural, learning-based treatment strategies as well as pharmacological interventions in psychiatric rehabilitation (Halligan & David, 2001).

Therefore, in accordance with previous models (Borod, 2000; Greenberg & Safran, 1984; Rachman, 1984), we suggest broadening the analysis of the relationship between affect and cognition to incorporate affect in the therapeutic process by methods that can evoke desirable affective tone and address affective change directly.

Thus, traditional methods of cognitive and behavioural interventions (e.g. verbal persuasion, behavioural regimens, insight orientation to change faulty perceptions) would be complemented by methods and stimuli that have unique qualities to evoke emotions and influence mood states.

29.6 MUSIC, AFFECT MODIFICATION, AND THERAPEUTIC CHANGE

The previous theoretical and empirical review of (a) music and emotion and (b) emotion and cognitive functions helps to locate music as a powerful language to engage the patient in a complex thinking–feeling process that can be directed towards non-musical functional rehabilitative goals. In this context, it has been suggested that both internal emotional 'feeling' experience and competence for emotional communication are critical for effective psychosocial functioning. Music therapy, as a powerful tool impacting affective behaviour processes, offers a specialized set of clinical techniques aimed at restoring and strengthening an individual's ability to organize emotional experience internally, as well as to conduct emotional communication verbally and non-verbally. A five-stage sequence of emotional behaviour training in therapy has been shown to be useful for applying music therapy techniques and activities to emotional processing (Thaut, 2002). Active and receptive therapeutic music exercises can be used very effectively to facilitate (a) the 'feeling' experience of emotion; (b) the identification of emotion; (c) the expression of emotion; (d) the understanding of emotional communication of others; and (e) the synthesis, control, and modulation of one's own emotional behaviour.

It has been suggested that an individual's capacity to interpret emotional communications of others, identify and/or modulate internal emotional experience, and communicate that experience to others non-verbally is one of the most important determinants of healthy ego function and social integration (Scherer & Ekman, 1984; Zajonc, 1984). By developing a clear understanding of the neuropsychological processes and effects of the stimulus properties of music that underlie the influence of music on behaviour, music therapy becomes an important and efficient treatment modality in which clinically significant emotional deficits are targeted for behavioural interventions. Lang (1970) suggests a three-system analysis of emotion, consisting of *subjective*, *behavioural*, and *physiological* behaviour components. This system could provide the music therapist with a conceptual understanding of how to target and select for assessment the most abnormally functioning components in a client's behaviour.

As discussed earlier, a strong research base supports the influence of affective states on comprehensive behaviour organization and cognitive functions. Based on this connection, it is suggested that affective states and modifications of affective states can have specific relevance in therapy processes. Rachman (1980) documents this relevance in a detailed survey of studies that show the effectiveness of emotional processing as prerequisite for behavioural change. Lang (1977) and Wolpe (1978) point out that a critical requirement in behaviour modification through imagery and emotional processing is that at least some of the emotional state that is the focus of therapy be present in the imagery process. Rachman (1981, 1984) discusses the relationship between cognitive and affective behaviours, their relevance in therapy processes, and their reciprocal relationship.

There are many examples of cognitive operations altering affective reactions (Beck et al, 1979; Meichenbaum, 1977). However, based on the premise that affective and cognitive processes are partially independent of and mutually influential on each other, Rachman proposes within a clinical paradigm the necessity to establish more direct therapy procedures for affect modification to facilitate behaviour modification. Affect modification is thus seen as prerequisite for certain types of behaviour modification.

Sutherland et al (1982) compared a verbal- and a music-based mood-induction procedure in a study comparing the influence of mood state on the ability to remove intrusive, unwanted cognitions. Unwanted thoughts in the form of distressing obsessions are prevalent in many psychiatric conditions and seem to be functionally related to fluctuations of mood states (Rachman & Hodgson, 1980). The results of the Sutherland study show that intrusive, unpleasant thoughts were harder to remove in an induced sad state than in a happy state. However, the music-based mood-induction procedure showed superior results compared to the verbal-based method in altering and sustaining mood states. Consequently, in the music-induced happy condition, unwanted cognitions were removed more efficiently.

Sutherland et al (1982), in interpreting the relationship between mood state and the ability to remove the unwanted thoughts, suggest that it is more difficult to replace a negative thought with a more pleasant thought in a dysphoric mood state. Teasdale and Taylor (1981) have argued from their research findings that in depressed mood, the accessibility of negative information is increased. Sutherland et al thus propose a sequential approach for therapy, in which existing mood states are the primary focus before specific distressing thoughts and behaviours are considered. The effectiveness of music to alter existing mood/emotional states in psychiatric imprisoned clients during group psychotherapy, measured via self-report scales, has also been shown by Thaut (1989).

The preceding discussion is of great importance for music therapy, because it points out directions in which the music-evoked affective response, capable of modifying affect, becomes relevant as an integral part of therapy processes directed towards comprehensive behaviour modification. The data that are presented suggest two different directions for applications of music in psychiatric rehabilitation:

1. Music induction of emotional responses which, through learned association, have specific significance for the behavioural state addressed in therapy;
2. Music induction of positive emotional/mood states, through perception of psychological/collative properties, which in turn facilitate cognitive reorientation and

behavioural reorganization resulting in changes in thinking and feeling states and overt behaviour.

The relationship between affect modification and behaviour modification, which has received renewed attention in the behavioural and therapy literature, implicates a search for efficient therapy techniques to access and modify affective behaviour. Not surprisingly, Rachman (1981) has pointed to music that is effective when fed into the affective system for therapy purposes. The understanding and appraisal of this function of music constitute the last link within a model that relates stimulus properties and neuropsychological processing in music to modification of thinking, feeling, and behaviour in therapy, and thus establishes music therapy as a neuropsychiatric treatment modality in a framework of cognitive psychiatric rehabilitation.

29.7 Music in therapy: The role of emotion

Considering the significant role of affect in modulating cognition and behaviour, research in neuropsychiatric music therapy can now use this role to generate a basic theoretical framework, in which the affective response in music is linked to the facilitation of functional therapeutic training and learning in a therapeutic context. The following survey and appraisal of related literature from music therapy, music psychology, and cognitive-behaviour research may help to introduce and define some of the most significant variables in such a theoretical framework.

Music may be described as an aesthetic, sensory-based language consisting of spectrally and temporally highly complex auditory patterns that perceptually engages cognitive, emotional, and motor functions in the brain. Musical behaviours comprise a broad range of diverse responses and experiences, such as emotional and mood responses, cognitive-analytical and aesthetic responses, and perceptual-motor responses (Jones & Holleran, 1992; Sloboda, 1985). The ability of music to evoke and alter emotional reactions is well documented (Harrer, 1975). Hodges (1996) has provided extensive surveys of the literature regarding affective responses to music. The majority of the surveyed studies provide strong evidence for the following four conclusions: (a) music evokes emotional and mood reactions, including emotional peak experiences; (b) music can alter a listener's mood; (c) emotional and mood responses to music are accompanied by physiological changes in the individual; and (d) existing mood, musical preference, cultural expectations, and arousal needs also play a role in determining affective responses to a given music stimulus. Despite these general agreements, no unified theories exist that explain the underlying neurophysiological and psychological mechanisms of affective responses in music perception (Berlyne, 1971; Jones & Holleran, 1992; Meyer, 1956; but see Chapter 22, this volume, for one attempt).

There are relatively few controlled studies using clinical populations, but results provide initial evidence for a relationship between music stimulation and affective responses that is therapeutically beneficial. A Cochrane review (Maratos et al, 2008) included four studies (Chen, 1992; Hanser & Thompson, 1994; Hendricks, 2001; Radulovic et al, 1997) that found greater reductions in symptoms of depression among those randomized to music therapy, and one study (Zerhusen et al, 1995) that found no change in mental state among those receiving music therapy compared to those who received standard care alone. Reinhardt and Lange (1982) found a positive change in affect and motivational states in clinically depressed patients as they listened to music selections that were familiar and liked by the patients. Thaut (1989), using guided listening and verbal interaction, instrumental group improvisation, and music relaxation as therapy techniques, found significantly improved scores for relaxation, mood, and thoughts about self in psychiatric prisoner-patients for all three therapy techniques on self-report scales. De L'Etoile (2002) found decreases in psychiatric symptomatology as a result of music group psychotherapy in patients with chronic mental illness. Other research (Andersson et al, 2006; Bouteloup, 1998; Evers, 1998; Gagner-Tjellesen et al, 2001; Kim et al, 2006; Ledger & Baker, 2007) has shown the positive effect of music therapy in various psychiatric settings. A Cochrane review of music therapy for people with schizophrenia and schizophrenia-like illnesses (Gold et al, 2005) found studies supporting the use of music therapy (Talwar et al, 2006; Tang et al, 1994; Ulrich et al, 2007; cited here in their published forms). The authors concluded that music therapy added to standard care helps people with schizophrenia to improve their global state, and that it may also improve mental state and functioning if a sufficient number of music therapy sessions are provided.

Of considerable importance for the evaluation of music as a stimulus to elicit affective responses and influence therapeutically relevant behaviours are the results of studies using music as mood induction technique (Albersnagel, 1988; Clark, 1983; Clark & Teasdale, 1985; Eifert et al, 1988; Martin et al, 1988; Pignatiello et al, 1986; Sutherland et al, 1982; Teasdale & Spencer, 1984). These studies document the efficiency of 'happy' and 'sad' music to induce depressed and elated mood states in normal subjects. Albersnagel (1988), Clark (1983), Clark and Teasdale (1985), and Sutherland et al (1982) reported larger groups of subjects reaching predetermined mood-change criteria as well as stronger subjective mood ratings using music mood induction compared to verbal methods (Velten, 1968). Pignatiello et al (1986) reported the superiority of music to induce mood without strong demand characteristics and gender differences associated with verbal induction.

As discussed previously, clinical applications of the transfer effects of musical mood induction substantiate the effect of affect on cognition and related behaviours. These include positive effects of elated mood in helping to remove intrusive, unwanted cognitions that were stronger for a music induction than a verbal induction (Sutherland et al, 1982); lower ratings of incentive to engage in pleasurable activities after having received a depression induction than after receiving an elation induction (Clark & Teasdale, 1985; Teasdale & Spencer, 1984); depressed mood using music induction associated with psychomotor retardation (Clark & Teasdale, 1985; Pignatiello et al,

1986; Teasdale & Spencer, 1984); a differential effect of mood on accessibility of positive and negative cognitions (Albersnagel, 1988; Clark & Teasdale, 1985); and subjects' estimates of their past success and future success on a task to be influenced by induced mood state (Teasdale & Spencer, 1984). Music was also found to be successful as a conditioning stimulus in decreasing fear during in vivo exposure to feared animals in the treatment of animal phobia (Eifert et al, 1988), and happy and sad music used to induce moods in chronic headache sufferers was found to decrease headache intensity during elated-mood induction and to have the reverse effect during despondency induction (Martin et al, 1988).

This brief review reveals initial evidence for the efficacy of music in eliciting and inducing differential emotional and mood states, which may subsequently influence the occurrence, frequency, and intensity of other behaviours, such as access to negative/positive cognitions about self, level of motivation, fear reduction, self-evaluation and self-image, experience of chronic pain, and ability to cope with intrusive, depressed thoughts. These behaviours are all found at the centre of clinical goals in therapeutic intervention strategies. We can summarize by saying that by accessing and modulating affective states, music not only addresses emotional and mood responses but also modulates a broad range of cognitive states regarding attention and perception, memory, psychosocial functions, and executive functions.

29.8 CLINICAL COMPONENTS

In this section, three major components of a clinical practice model for psychiatric music therapy using affect modification will be outlined. This chapter postulates that the core structure and content of every music therapy session should consist of music-based behaviour experiences that simulate real-life experiences and behaviours in need of therapeutic change. Thus, music therapy sessions turn into translational behaviour laboratories where clients experience, (re)learn, and train desired behaviours via music-based therapeutic exercises. The basic structure of this model of clinical practice is described in detail as the 'Transformational Design Model' in Thaut (2005). One of the unique contributions of the musical experience is the induction of affective/motivational qualities that provide positive affective tone within each behaviour experience and thus tune, attenuate, modulate, and positively bias a client's cognitions and perceptions toward change in the therapeutic learning process. The effect of therapeutic exercises in music focusing on coherence in executive functions (e.g. reasoning, problem solving, comprehension), reality orientation, decrease of fear and anxiety, social skills, emotional processing, problem solving, coping with unpleasant traumatic experiences, attitudes toward personal change, and so forth is mediated in part through the affective experience in music. In this mediation process, the client's affective/motivational system is accessed and positive mood/emotional/motivational changes are induced that enhance cognitive functions intrinsic to rehabilitative learning.

What are the mechanisms underlying the positive effect of music on affective change? It is postulated that an 'affective-evaluative response', which is a function of three inter-acting response systems, lies at the core of the emotional/mood reaction to music:

1. A primary affective response (Zajonc, 1984) or primary appraisal (Lazarus, 1984), which is a non-reflective, subjective response to a salient environmental stimulus expressed in terms of liked/disliked, pleasant/unpleasant, good/bad (Eifert et al, 1988).
2. Cognitive elaborations on the primary response determining the specific quality and meaning of the stimulus by analysing specific stimulus attributes and the context in which the stimulus is presented.
3. A differential neurophysiological arousal response based on lateralized brain hemispheric function (Davidson, 2000; Tucker, 1981) and autonomic, endocrine, and central arousal processes in different cortico-limbic-brain-stem-centred neural systems (Lane & Nadel, 2000).

It is further suggested that the affective-evaluative response determines the positive hedonic properties and reward value of the music, which in turn determines the quality of the mood/emotional experience of the music listener or performer. This sequence of information processing in therapeutic music perception contains three therapeutic effects:

1. The psychiatric music therapist designs music exercises for therapeutic learning and training (e.g. using specific forms and structures in group musical improvisa-tion to practise social skills of appropriate self-expression and executive functions regarding problem solving, comprehension, decision making, reality orientation, and to provide group-dynamic exercises for leading and following, cooperation, and group creative problem solving). The induction and temporal structuring and ordering of appropriate affective tone provided by therapeutic music experiences creates the central emotional context that enhances learning.
2. The affective qualities inherent in the process of music perception address relevant emotional materials in the therapeutic process directly—emotions and moods are experienced in the therapeutic music experience rather than only being verbalized. Emotional learning may be more efficient in music therapy due to the experiential emotional nature of the therapeutic experience.
3. Musical mood induction will access therapeutically desired associative memory networks, thus making mood-congruent cognitive information regarding one's self and one's environment more accessible to the client. For example, a system-atic employment of music to elevate a client's mood may render the client more accepting of positive cognitions and provide access to positive memories, thus breaking the vicious cycle of negative thoughts producing negative moods and vice versa. Positive mood/emotion states also enhance memory and attentional functions on a global level without mood congruency.

Thus, specific clinical music therapy techniques combined with verbal counselling techniques serve as 'training experiences' in which music-induced affect modification drives cognitive, affective, and behavioural change relevant to therapeutic goals. It is suggested that three of the most important areas where affect modification can contribute significantly to therapeutic change are: (a) social learning; (b) cognitive reorientation; and (c) emotional processing and emotional learning.

29.8.1 Social learning

Most psychiatric rehabilitation is concerned with the social aspects of behaviour. Many therapy methods offer and emphasize opportunities for social learning. Within the model of affect modification, music therapy methods offer two unique contributions to social experiences in therapy: (a) they organize social behaviours around the affective/motivational experience of social interaction using affect-evoking materials (i.e. music-based experiences; Zwerling, 1979); (b) they emphasize practice and learning of social skills experientially through performance in a positive emotional context (Thaut, 1989). Individuals who are socially aloof, fearful, or incompetent can experience in these activities motivating avenues to become interested in social situations.

Music, throughout history, has also functioned as a sociocultural agent, communicating group values, feelings of 'us', and mutually shared social norms, ideas, and conventions (Merriam, 1964). Music has always been used as a messenger for social, political, cultural, and religious ideas, but its particular strength and attractiveness as messenger were always found in the unique emotional quality and flavour that it added to the message. This potential of music to facilitate group building and communicate group feelings and values can be used as a powerful source of social learning in therapy.

Empirical and theoretical studies support the affective-social function of music in therapy. Thaut (1989) reports on the effect of music group therapy in promoting less hostile and more cooperative group-related behaviours in psychiatric prisoner-patients. Goldberg et al (1988) found that music therapy groups produce more therapeutic interaction among and emotional responses from patients than verbal therapy. Henderson (1983) found a positive effect for music therapy on awareness of mood in music, group cohesion, and self-esteem among adolescent psychiatric clients. Gaston (1968) and Feder and Feder (1981) stress music as a 'social' art that provides unique opportunities to integrate individuals in rewarding, non-threatening situations. According to Zwerling (1979), one of the primary offerings of music as creative arts therapy lies in its ability to provide actual social-emotional experiences that put into practice what can only be talked about in verbal therapies.

29.8.2 Cognitive reorientation

Considering the influence of mood on cognitions, a positive affective experience may render the individual accessible to cognitive change in therapy. Studies have shown that mood/emotional states are related to the quality and direction of one's self-perception, self-concept, self-esteem, motivation for change, and the ability to access skills such as problem solving and decision making efficiently (Teasdale & Spencer, 1984). A pleasant and rewarding affective experience in the therapeutic process may encourage reality focus and perceptual orientation. Topics such as rethinking personal problems, changing perceptions of others, learning new coping skills, processing significant life experiences, dealing with fears, and setting new goals may be presented in a new light in the framework of methods using an affective medium that organizes therapeutic experiences around their affective/motivational content and value for the individual (Gfeller, 2002).

Some clinical suggestions follow. For example, music mood-induction techniques may provide an intervention strategy to support cognitive therapies of depression by rendering the client more accessible to positive cognitions (Clark, 1983; Sutherland et al, 1982; Teasdale, 1983). Several behaviour therapy techniques can be accomplished efficiently using musical materials in conjunction with other therapy techniques. Music is an effective stimulus to facilitate imagery, a useful method to assess a client's reactions to a particular situation by having the client symbolically recreate a problematic life situation. Music, in this respect, not only helps elicit images from memory, based possibly on associative memory network operations (Bower, 1981), but also helps retrieve the mood/emotional quality of a particular life situation in the imaging process (Goldberg, 1992).

Cognitive coherence training in group or individual therapy (e.g. through music improvisation exercises, listening, or compositional exercises) can effectively address the (re)training of attention, memory, and executive functions such as comprehension, decision making, problem solving, reasoning, and behavioural organization (de L'Etoile, 2002).

Musical role playing in improvisational structures provides an affective medium to assess and teach interpersonal skills. The musical interaction may give opportunities to experience and practise new, healthy behaviours in an emotionally rewarding, enticing, and at the same time, sensory-ordered, reality-based therapy context.

Music can be an effective main or adjunct stimulus to practise relaxation techniques (Davis & Thaut, 1989). Eifert et al (1988) have shown that music can also be used as a positive affective stimulus in a classical conditioning paradigm to decrease fear reactions in phobia.

29.8.3 Emotional processing and emotional learning

Music cannot communicate human emotions directly in a semantic system, unless it is connected to emotional experiences through associative learning following the principles of classical conditioning. However, 'likeness' of the dynamics of a felt emotion and a musical pattern may be experienced by such things as perceiving the flow of musical patterns in a tension-resolution configuration, providing feelings of relief, pleasure, and reward. These, in turn, may be experienced as relief of emotional tension and conflict in one's feeling of self or perception of one's environment.

According to Langer's (1953) and Winner's (1982) theoretical views, the structure of music can mirror the structure and dynamics of human emotional experiences. The statement 'music sounds the way emotions feel' may summarize this view best. Music therapy can also offer methods to alter or induce desired mood states, which may directly influence feelings of depression, elation, anxiety, rest, relaxation, motivation, or levels of activation and energy (Thaut, 1989).

Zwerling (1979) has proposed that the arts (including music) have the unique ability to tap into the emotional component of behaviours, thoughts, and memories and elicit emotional reactions, thus making them powerful therapeutic stimuli to facilitate emotional processing in an actual or symbolic context in therapy. The need for emotional processing in therapy arises when emotions, consciously or unconsciously attached to maladaptive behaviours, hinder the development of more adaptive, healthier behaviours, or when emotional experiences (e.g. fear, trauma, loss) are not absorbed—that is, they return intermittently but persistently and disrupt normal behaviours. A broad gauge of successful emotional processing is a person's ability to talk about, see, listen to, or be reminded of the emotional event without experiencing distress or disruption of normal behaviour (Rachman, 1980).

Research points to the importance of affective behaviour to determine cognitive behaviour and behaviour change (Rachman, 1980, 1981). Therefore, we suggest exploring the potential of music to provide experiences of emotional learning using a five-step hierarchy. Emotional experiences through music can be guided and structured to help an individual to (a) experience, (b) identify, and (c) express different emotions verbally or nonverbally. Advanced emotional learning should help the individual to (d) perceive emotional communications of others and (e) be able to modulate (i.e. freely control, adjust, and adapt appropriately) emotional behaviour.

In a last reference to emotional learning, there is evidence that emotional experience through observation of emotional stimuli can be similar in nature to an actual emotional experience involving one's own actions (Alfert, 1966). Therefore, this chapter suggests that music may be used to promote experiences in the listener of empathy and feeling into the emotional content of a musical work to experience and understand emotions that represent or simulate real-life experiences (Gfeller, 2002).

Although the number of scientific investigations into musical responses of patients with psychiatric disorders is relatively limited, the available data support music as a perceptually meaningful therapeutic stimulus by showing evidence that the basic structural components in music perception/production of patients with psychiatric disorders are not disintegrated. For example, music-performance abilities seem to remain relatively intact in psychiatric patients (Steinberg et al, 1985), and expressive content in music is rated similar to that of healthy individuals by patients with mental illness (Nielzen & Cesarec, 1982).

29.9 AN INTEGRATIVE MODEL OF
MUSIC IN THERAPY

The model that follows depicts the variables of music stimulus properties, brain processing, evoked client responses, and clinical goals as they relate to one another in the
therapy process. The model identifies the three properties of music stimuli that evoke
arousal/affective responses within the specific experiential axes of activation energy;
novelty/surprise/clarity; and extra-musical associations. The character of these experiences determines their emotional, evaluative value for the client in terms of reward,
motivation, pleasure, positive feedback, tension relief, and insight. The outcome of
this evaluative process determines the consequences of the music therapy experience
in terms of perceived benefit, neurological change, and translation of the evoked affect
modification into behavioural goals. The three properties and experiences are:

1. *Psychophysical properties—experience in activation.* The positive influence of the
   psychophysical attributes of music stimuli on activation, energy level, excitement,
   and stimulation is particularly valuable in providing an immediate reward experience or reducing anxiety states for the client. It performs its function by stimulating residual, healthy, positive feelings and behaviours and providing motivation
   for behaviour change in supportive or short-term therapy settings.

2. *Collative properties—experience in structure.* The structural experience in music
   is central to several therapeutic goals in music therapy. The cognitive and affective areas of functional behaviour in terms of mental organization are stimulated through the experiences within musical perception. The experience of order,
   clarity, comprehension, and tension relief in musical structures will help the
   client perceive and respond cognitively and affectively to meaningful sensory
   stimulation. It is frequently observed that patients with severe mental illness who
   do not respond appropriately to verbal approaches will respond with functional
   behaviour in music-based therapy exercises. In addition, the feeling response that
   unfolds in the perceptual processing of musical events can be used to provide a
   directed feeling experience aimed at altering feeling states and promoting stress
   and anxiety reduction.

3. *Ecological properties—experience in associations.* The associative experience
   consists of designated mood or connotative experiences, memories, and private
   images that have acquired a learned association with the music stimulus. The
   client responds to an internal psychological event, not to anything that can be
   heard in the actual music stimulus. The occurrence of associative experiences,
   therefore, is difficult for the music therapist to control or predict, because it is
   an idiosyncratic response, shaped and stimulated by the client's past experiences
   or by very spontaneous private associations. Associative responses often reflect
   primary affective processes through recall of significant life experiences. Music

stimuli help to interpret the evoked experience in terms of emotional value for the client (Zwerling, 1979), and may facilitate awareness and recognition of significant feelings in life experiences. Thus awareness of suppressed feelings, recall of significant memories, designated mood experiences, and stress reduction through imagery are main therapeutic goals based on associative experiences in music.

29.10 APPLICATION TO OTHER MODELS OF MUSIC THERAPY

The model of emotion and music presented in this chapter was developed to apply to psychiatric music therapy, but as discussed in section 29.1, the relevance of emotion to music therapy applies beyond psychiatric work. Broader application of this model will be explored in this section. We will select three among many possibilities for applying the model.

29.10.1 Children with language delays

We will return to the earlier example (Bunt & Pavlicivec, 2001) in which the authors speak of the generation of emotional responses to help with therapy of a group of young children with language problems and limited attention. Goals with these children might be to increase their use of language and spontaneous communication. As stated earlier, 'The group of language-delayed children may be so motivated to play the instruments and vocalize that their shifts in levels of excitement, quality of relationship, and emotional experiences and expressions may generalize outside of the sessions into further use of vocal sounds, gestures, and a corresponding rise in self-esteem' (p. 184).

Applying the three steps from the model developed here—experience in activation, experience in structure, and experience in associations—to these children, we can see that the children were energized and stimulated by the musical activities (activation), making them receptive to the experiences. Structural experiences in music are likely to have facilitated stimulation of cognitive and affective areas to help the children to order their behaviour (structure). And the associations that the children make with the musical experiences will, as the authors suggest, generalize to further use of vocal sounds and gestures and also to a rise in self-esteem.

29.10.2 Adolescent hospitalized with burns

Robb (1996) describes a 15-year old girl who was hospitalized with burns to 95 per cent of her body. One difficult day when the girl was upset, a fill-in-the-blank format was used for a song that helped her express her frustrations and need for support.

The song, which she titled 'Hardest Day', used a melody taken from 'The River', written by Brooks and Smith and performed by Garth Brooks. She substituted some of her own words for those in the original song. Her composition spoke of the difficulties of her situation, feeling anger and feeling like giving up, and her decision to try her hardest to move forward.

Applying the three steps to this girl, we can see that the psychophysical attributes of music could help to reduce anxiety and provide immediate reward (experience in activation). The emotional and feeling responses that unfolded from the music may have been used to provide a directed feeling experience aimed at reducing her anxiety and stress (experience in structure). And the associations that she made with the music and the events that transpired would be helpful to her in future situations in which these feelings were evoked (experience in associations).

29.10.3 Adults with dementia and depression who had experienced neurological traumas

Scheiby (1999) discusses her work with supportive music psychotherapy following an Analytical Music Therapy model (as developed by Priestley, 1994). She writes about a session in which four clients, ages 42–92, have been receiving music therapy sessions three times a week for four weeks. In the session, clients support one member who has been experiencing feelings of loneliness by singing 'You've Got a Friend' with words changed to address the needs of the group member. Following that singing, the therapist asked them how they were feeling, but their answers did not seem to express their feelings with any depth. The therapist then suggested an 'action technique of free association by suggesting an improvisation theme: 'What we see and feel right now' (pp. 270–1). Scheiby describes the improvisation and what was accomplished, including getting in touch with anger that had been repressed, improved memory, improved speech, awareness of sense of humour, decreased social isolation, and improved interpersonal communication skills.

Here again, we can apply the three steps. Both the singing and the instrumental improvisation provided arousal for the clients' emotions, some of which they had been out of touch with and not able to express (activation). The emotional responses that unfolded in the perceptual processing of the music were essential to the therapy (structure). And the associations that the clients made to emotions and events both in and out of the session helped to accomplish the goals and provide for future success (associations).

29.11 SUMMARY AND CONCLUSION

The foregoing discussion has emphasized the treatment specificity of music stimuli in order to provide a systematic model for the use of music in therapy focusing on cognitive, affective, and perceptual aspects in the area of healthy psychological functioning in human personality. Both the discussion and model are intended to integrate an objective neurological basis for the effect of music stimuli, and their respective stimulus properties and associated responses, with the subjective variables of perceptual and evaluative music processing, in order to arrive at a predictable, analysable, and measurable treatment result.

We have attempted to outline some theoretical considerations about the importance of affective responses in behavioural learning and change, especially in a clinical context, and about one of music's central roles in therapy as a stimulus system uniquely qualified to modify affect. Considering the reciprocal relationship between cognition and affect, we can analyse emotion and meaning in music within a framework of theories of cognitive and affective processes. Fortunately, the scientific literature offers a considerable repertoire of procedures to assess affective behaviours that can be applied to clinical settings (Scherer & Ekman, 1982). Therapeutic music experiences, based on scientific mechanisms relating the perceptual experience in music to brain and behaviour, become meaningful therapeutic applications within an understanding of the biological basis and the role of affect-cognition processes in mental disorders, for instance, as beginning to be formulated in cognitive neuropsychiatry (Halligan & David, 2001). Within such a framework, music therapy is an effective core therapy modality in psychiatric rehabilitation as well as other areas.

RECOMMENDED FURTHER READING

1. Davis, W. B., Gfeller, K. E., & Thaut, M. H. (2008). *An introduction to music therapy: Theory and practice* (3rd edn). Silver Spring, MD: American Music Therapy Association.
2. Hallam, S., Cross, I., & Thaut, M. (eds). (2009). *Oxford handbook of music psychology*. Oxford: Oxford University Press. (Chapters 46–9)
3. Wheeler, B. L. (ed.). (2005). *Music therapy research* (2nd edn). Gilsum, NH: Barcelona Publishers.

REFERENCES

Aigen, K. (1995) An aesthetic foundation of clinical theory: An underlying basis of creative music therapy. In C. Kenny (ed.), *Listening, playing, creating: Essays on the power of sound* (pp. 233–57). Albany, NY: State University of NY Press.

Aigen, K. (2005). Philosophical inquiry. In B. L. Wheeler (ed.), *Music therapy research* (2nd edn, pp. 526–39). Gilsum, NH: Barcelona Publishers.

Aigen, K. (2006). *Music and emotions in music therapy: A philosophical inquiry into the meaning of expression in artistic and clinical contexts*. Paper presented at the Annual Conference of the American Music Therapy Association, Kansas City, USA, November 2006.

Albersnagel, F. A. (1988). Velten and musical mood induction procedures: A comparison with accessibility of thought associations. *Behavior Research and Therapy*, *26*, 79–96.

Alfert, E. (1966). Comparison of responses to a vicarious and a direct threat. *Journal of Experimental Research in Personality*, *1*, 179–86.

American Music Therapy Association. (2007). *The 2007 member sourcebook*. Silver Spring, MD: Author.

Anderson, J. R. (2005). *Cognitive psychology and its implications*. New York: Worth Publishers.

Andersson, G., Boalt Boethius, S., Svirsky, L., & Carlberg, G. (2006). Memories of significant episodes in child psychotherapy: An autobiographical memory approach. *Psychology & Psychotherapy*, *79*, 229–36.

Bartlett, D. L. (1996). Physiological reactions to music and acoustic stimuli. In D. A. Hodges (ed.), *Handbook of music psychology* (2nd edn, pp. 343–85). San Antonio, TX: IMR Press.

Beck, A. T., Rush, A. J., Shaw, B. F., & Emery, G. (1979). *Cognitive therapy of depression*. New York: Wiley.

Berlyne, D. E. (1971). *Aesthetics and psychobiology*. New York: Appleton-Century-Crofts.

Blaney, P. H. (1986). Affect and memory: A review. *Psychological Bulletin*, *99*, 229–46.

Bonny, H. (2002). *Music consciousness: The evolution of Guided Imagery and Music*. Gilsum, NH: Barcelona Publishers.

Borod, J. C. (ed.). (2000). *The neuropsychology of emotion*. Oxford: Oxford University Press.

Bouteloup, P. (1998). Music and pediatric psychiatry. *Soins, Pediatrie, Puericulture*, *182*, 7–12.

Bower, G. H. (1981). Mood and memory. *American Psychologist*, *36*, 129–48.

Bower, G. H., Monteiro, K. P., & Gilligan, S. C. (1978). Emotional mood as context of learning and recall. *Journal of Verbal Learning and Verbal Behavior*, *17*, 573–85.

Boxberger, R. (1962). Historical bases for the use of music in therapy. In E. H. Schneider (ed.), *Music therapy 1961* (pp. 125–66). Lawrence, KS: Allen Press.

Bruscia, K. E. (1987). *Improvisational models of music therapy*. Springfield, IL: Charles C. Thomas.

Bruscia, K. E. (1998). *Defining music therapy* (2nd edn). Gilsum, NH: Barcelona Publishers.

Bunt, L., & Pavlicevic, M. (2001). Music and emotion: Perspectives from music therapy. In P. N. Juslin & J. A. Sloboda (eds), *Music and emotion: Theory and research* (pp. 181–201). Oxford: Oxford University Press.

Burke, M., & Mathews, A. M. (1992). Autobiographical memory and clinical anxiety. *Cognition & Emotion*, *6*, 23–5.

Carnevale, J. D., & Isen, A. M. (1986). The influence of positive affect and visual access on the discovery of integrative solutions in bilateral negotiation. *Organizational Behavior and Human Decision Processes*, *37*, 1–13.

Clark, D. M. (1983). On the induction of depressed mood in the laboratory: Evaluation of the Velten and musical procedures. *Advances in Behavior Research and Therapy*, *5*, 27–49.

Clark, D., & Teasdale, J. (1985). Constraints of the effects of mood on memory. *Journal of Personality and Social Psychology*, *48*, 1595–1608.

Claussen, D., & Thaut, M. H. (1997). Music as a mnemonic device for children with learning disabilities. *Canadian Journal of Music Therapy*, *5*, 55–66.

Dalgleish, T., & Power, M. J. (eds). (1999). *The handbook of cognition and emotion*. Chichester, UK: Wiley.

Davidson, R. J. (2000). The functional neuroanatomy of affective style. In R. D. Lane & L. Nadel (eds), *Cognitive neuroscience of emotion* (pp. 371–88). Oxford: Oxford University Press.

Davis, W. B., & Gfeller, K. E. (2008). Music therapy: Historical perspective. In W. B. Davis, K. E. Gfeller, & M. H. Thaut (eds), *An introduction to music therapy: Theory and practice* (3rd edn, pp. 17–39). Silver Spring, MD: American Music Therapy Association.

Davis, W. B., & Thaut, M. H. (1989). The influence of preferred, relaxing music on measures of state anxiety, relaxation, and physiological responses. *Journal of Music Therapy*, 26, 168–87.

de L'Etoile, S. K. (2002). The effectiveness of music therapy in group psychotherapy for adults with mental illness. *The Arts in Psychotherapy*, 29, 69–78.

Derryberry, D., & Rothbart, M. K. (1984). Emotion, attention, and temperament. In C. Izard, J. Kagan, & R. Zajonc (eds), *Emotions, cognition, and behavior* (pp. 135–55). Cambridge, UK: Cambridge University Press.

Dolan, R. J. (2002). Emotion, cognition, and behavior. *Science*, 298, 1191–4.

Eich, E. (1995). Searching for mood-dependent memory. *Psychological Science*, 6, 67–75.

Eifert, G., Craill, L., Carey, E., & O'Connor, C. (1988). Affect modification through evaluative conditioning with music. *Behavior Research and Therapy*, 26, 321–30.

Ekman, P., & Davidson, R. J. (eds). (1994). *The nature of emotions: Fundamental questions.* Oxford: Oxford University Press.

Evers, S. (1998). Status of music therapy in inpatient pediatrics and child and adolescent psychiatry. *Praxis der Kinderpsychologie und Kinderpsychiatrie*, 47, 229–39.

Feder, E., & Feder, B. (1981). *The expressive arts therapies.* Englewood Cliffs, NJ: Prentice Hall.

Fiedler, K. (1991). On the task, the measures, and the mood in research on affect and social cognition. In J. P. Forgas (ed.), *Emotion and social judgment* (pp. 83–104). Oxford: Pergamon Press.

Filipic, S., & Bigand, E. (2005). Key processing precedes emotional categorization of Western music. *Annals of the New York Academy of Sciences*, 1060, 443–5.

Gagner-Tjellesen, D., Yurkovich, E. E., & Gragert, M. (2001). Use of music therapy and other ITNIs in acute care. *Journal of Psychosocial Nursing & Mental Health Services*, 39, 26–37.

Gaston, E. T. (1968). Man and music. In E. T. Gaston (ed.), *Music in therapy* (pp. 7–29). New York: Macmillan.

Gfeller, K. E. (2002). Music as therapeutic agent: historical and sociocultural perspectives. In R. F. Unkefer & M. H. Thaut (eds), *Music therapy in the treatment of adults with mental disorders* (pp. 60–7). Gilsum, NH: Barcelona Publishers.

Gfeller, K. E., & Thaut, M. H. (2008). Music therapy in the treatment of behavioral-emotional disorders. In W. B. Davis, K. E. Gfeller, & M. H. Thaut (eds), *An introduction to music therapy: Theory and practice* (3rd edn, pp. 209–46). Silver Spring, MD: American Music Therapy Association.

Gold, C., Heldal, T. O., Dahle, T. & Wigram, T. (2005). Music therapy for schizophrenia or schizophrenia-like illnesses. The Cochrane Database of Systematic Reviews 2005, Issue 2. Art. No.: CD004025.pub2. DOI: 10.1002/14651858.CD004025.pub2.

Goldberg, F. S. (1992). Images of emotion: The role of emotion in Guided Imagery and Music. *Journal of the Association for Music and Imagery*, 1, 5–17.

Goldberg, F., McNiel, D., & Binder, R. (1988). Therapeutic factors in two forms of inpatient group psychotherapy: Music therapy and verbal therapy. *Group*, 12, 145–56.

Gomez, P., & Danuser, B. (2007). Relationships between musical structure and psychophysiological measures of emotion. *Emotion*, 7, 377–87.

Greenberg, L., & Safran, J. (1984). Integrating affect and cognition: A perspective on the process of therapeutic change. *Cognitive Therapy and Research*, 8, 559–78.

Halligan, P. W., & David, A. S. (2001). Cognitive neuropsychiatry: Towards a scientific psychopathology. *Nature Reviews Neuroscience*, 2, 209–14.

Hanser, S. B., & Thompson, L. W. (1994). Effects of a music therapy strategy on depressed older adults. *Journal of Gerontology: Psychological Sciences*, 49, P265–9.

Harrer, G. (ed.). (1975). *Grundlagen der Musiktherapie und Musikpsychologie*. Stuttgart, Germany: Fischer.

Henderson, S. M. (1983). Effects of music therapy program upon awareness of mood in music, group cohesion, and self-esteem among hospitalized adolescent patients. *Journal of Music Therapy*, *20*, 14–20.

Hendricks, C. B. (2001). A study of the use of music therapy techniques in a group for the treatment of adolescent depression. *Dissertation Abstracts International*, *62(2-A)*, 472.

Hernandez-Peon, R. (1961). The efferent control of afferent signals entering the central nervous system. *Annals of New York Academy of Science*, *89*, 866–82.

Hertel, G., Neuhof, J., Theuer, T., & Kerr, N. L. (2000). Mood effects on cooperation in small groups: Does positive mood simply lead to more cooperation? *Cognition & Emotion*, *14*, 441–72.

Hodges, D. A. (ed.). (1996). *Handbook of music psychology* (2nd edn). San Antonio, TX: IMR Press.

Izard, C., Kagan, J., & Zajonc, R. (eds). (1984). *Emotions, cognition, and behavior*. Cambridge, UK: Cambridge University Press.

Jones, M. R., & Holleran, S. (eds). (1992). *Cognitive bases of musical communication*. Washington, DC: American Psychological Association.

Juslin, P. N., & Sloboda, J. A. (2001). Music and emotion: Introduction. In P. N. Juslin & J. A. Sloboda (eds), *Music and emotion: Theory and research* (pp. 3–20). Oxford: Oxford University Press.

Kavanaugh, D. J. (1987). Mood, persistence, and success. *Australian Journal of Psychology*, *39*, 307–18.

Kenealy, P. M. (1997). Mood-state dependent retrieval: The effects of induced mood on memory reconsidered. *Quarterly Journal of Experimental Psychology*, *50*, 290–317.

Kenny, C. (2006). *Music & life in the field of play: An anthology*. Gilsum, NH: Barcelona Publishers.

Kim, S., Kverno, K., Lee, E. M., Park, J. H., Lee, H. H., & Kim, H. L. (2006). Development of a music therapy group psychotherapy intervention for the primary prevention of adjustment difficulties in Korean adolescent girls. *Journal of Child & Adolescent Psychiatric Nursing*, *19*, 103–11.

Lane, R. D., & Nadel, L. (eds). (2000). *Cognitive neuroscience of emotion*. Oxford: Oxford University Press.

Lang, P. (1970). Stimulus control, response control and the desensitization of fear. In D. Levis (ed.), *Learning approaches to therapeutic behavior* (pp. 266–81). Chicago, IL: Aldine.

Lang, P. (1977). Imagery in therapy. *Behavior Therapy*, *8*, 862–86.

Langer, S. K. (1953). *Feeling and form*. New York: Scribners.

Lazarus, R. S. (1984). On the primacy of cognition. *American Psychologist*, *39*, 124–9.

Ledger, A. J., & Baker, F. A. (2007). An investigation of long-term effects of group music therapy on agitation levels of people with Alzheimer's disease. *Aging & Mental Health*, *11*, 330–8.

MacLeod, A. K., Tata, P., Kentish, J., & Jacobson, H. (1997). Retrospective and prospective cognitions in anxiety and depression. *Cognition & Emotion*, *11*, 467–79.

Mandler, G. (1984). *Mind and body*. New York: Norton.

Maratos, A. S., Gold, C., Wang, X., & Crawford, M. J. (2008). Music therapy for depression. [Cochrane Review], *The Cochrane Library*, *3*. Chichester, UK: John Wiley & Sons.

Markowitsch. H. J. (2000). Neuroanatomy of memory. In E. Tulving & F. I. M. Craik (eds), *Oxford handbook of memory* (pp. 465–84). Oxford: Oxford University Press.

Marteniuk, R. G. (1976). *Information processing in motor skills*. New York: Holt, Rinehart & Winston.

Martin, P., Nathan, P., Milech, D., & van Kappel, M. (1988). The relationship between head-aches and mood. *Behavior Research and Therapy, 26,* 353–6.

McMullen, P. (1996). Music as perceived stimulus object and affective responses: An alterna-tive theoretical framework. In D. A. Hodges (ed.), *Handbook of music psychology* (2nd edn, pp. 387–400). San Antonio, TX: IMR Press.

Meichenbaum, D. (1977). *Cognitive behavior modification.* New York: Plenum.

Merriam, A. P. (1964). *The anthropology of music.* Evanston, IL: Northwestern University Press.

Meyer, L. B. (1956). *Emotion and meaning in music.* Chicago, IL: Chicago University Press.

Moreno, J. J. (1988). The music therapist: Creative arts therapist and contemporary shaman. *The Arts in Psychotherapy, 15,* 271–80.

Nagel, F., Kopiez, R., Grewe, O., & Altenmüller, E. (2007). EmuJoy: Software for continuous measurement of perceived emotions in music. *Behavior Research Methods, 39,* 283–90.

Nielzén, S., & Cesarec, Z. (1982). Emotional experience of music by psychiatric patients compared with normal subjects. *Acta Psychiatrica Scandinavica, 65,* 450–60.

Nordoff, P., & Robbins, C. (2007). *Creative music therapy: A guide to fostering clinical musician-ship* (2nd edn). Gilsum, NH: Barcelona Publishers.

Olds, J. (1962). Hypothalamic substrates of reward. *Physiological Review, 42,* 554–604.

Pallesen, K. J., Brattico, E., Bailey, C., Korvenoja, A., Koivisto, J., Gjedde, A., & Carlson, S. (2005). Emotion processing of major, minor, and dissonant chords: A functional magnetic resonance imaging study. *Annals of the New York Academy of Sciences, 1060,* 450–3.

Panksepp, J. (1998). *Affective neuroscience: The foundations of human and animal emotions.* Oxford: Oxford University Press.

Pignatiello, M. F., Camp, C. J., & Rasar, L. (1986). Musical mood induction: An alternative to the Velten technique. *Journal of Abnormal Psychology, 95,* 295–7.

Plutchik, R. (1962). *The emotions: Facts, theories and a new model.* New York: Random House.

Priestley, M. (1994). *Essays on Analytical Music Therapy.* Gilsum, NH: Barcelona Publishers.

Purves, D., Brannon, E. M., Cabeza, R., Huettel, S. A., LaBar, K. S., Platt, M. L., & Woldorff, M. G. (2008). *Principles of neuroscience.* Sunderland, MA: Sinauer.

Rachman, S. (1980). Emotional processing. *Behavioral Research and Therapy, 18,* 51–60.

Rachman, S. (1981). The primacy of affect: Some theoretical implications. *Behavior Research and Therapy, 19,* 279–90.

Rachman, S. (1984). A reassessment of the 'primacy of affect'. *Cognitive Therapy and Research, 8,* 579–84.

Rachman, S., & Hodgson, R. (1980). *Obsessions and compulsions.* Englewood Cliffs, NJ: Prentice-Hall.

Radulovic, R., Cvetkovic, M., & Pejovic, M. (1997). *Complementary musical therapy and medi-camentous therapy in treatment of depressive disorders.* Paper presented at the WPA Thematic Conference, Jerusalem, Israel, November 1997.

Reinhardt, U., & Lange, E. (1982). Musikwirkungen bei Depressiven. *Psychiatrie, Neurologie und medizinische Psychologie, 34,* 414–21.

Robb, S. L. (1996). Techniques in song writing: Restoring emotional and physical well being in adolescents who have been traumatically injured. *Music Therapy Perspectives, 14,* 30–37.

Ruiz-Caballero, J. A., & Gonzalez, P. (1994). Implicit and explicit memory bias in depressed and non-depressed participants. *Cognition & Emotion, 8,* 555–70.

Rusting, C. L. (1999). Interactive effects of personality and mood on emotion-congruent memory and judgment. *Journal of Personality & Social Psychology, 77,* 1073–86.

Ruud, E. (1998). *Music therapy: Improvisation, communication, and culture.* Gilsum, NH: Barcelona Publishers.

Scheiby, B. B. (1999). Music as symbolic expression: Analytical Music Therapy. In D. J. Wiener (ed.), *Beyond talk therapy: Using movement and expressive techniques in clinical practice* (pp. 263–85). Washington, DC: American Psychological Association.

Scherer, K. R., & Ekman, P. (eds). (1982). *Handbook of methods in nonverbal behavior research.* Cambridge, UK: Cambridge University Press.

Scherer, K. R., & Ekman, P. (eds). (1984). *Approaches to emotion.* Hillsdale, NJ: Erlbaum.

Schubert, E. (2003). Update of the Hevner adjective checklist. *Perceptual and Motor Skills, 96,* 1117–22.

Sloboda, J. A. (1985). *The musical mind: The cognitive psychology of music.* Oxford: Clarendon Press.

Steinberg, R., Raith, L., Rossnagl, G., & Eben, E. (1985). Music psychopathology: III. Musical expression and psychiatric disease. *Psychopathology, 18,* 274–85.

Stige, B. (2002). *Culture-centered music therapy.* Gilsum, NH: Barcelona Publishers.

Strosahl, K. D., & Linehan, M. M. (1986). Basic issues in behavioral assessment. In A. Ciminero, K. S. Calhoun, & H. E. Adams (eds), *Handbook of behavioral assessment* (pp. 15–46). New York: Wiley.

Sutherland, G., Newman, B., & Rachman, S. (1982). Experimental investigations of the relations between mood and intrusive, unwanted cognitions. *British Journal of Medical Psychology, 55,* 127–38.

Talwar, N., Crawford, M. J., Maratos, A., Nur, U., McDermott, O., & Proctor, S. (2006). Music therapy for in-patients with schizophrenia: exploratory randomised controlled trial. *British Journal of Psychiatry, 189,* 405–9.

Tang, W., Yao, X., & Zheng, Z. (1994). Rehabilitative effect of music therapy for residual schizophrenia: A one-month randomized controlled trial in Shanghai. *British Journal of Psychiatry, 165(suppl. 24),* 38–44.

Tanguay, P. (1976). Clinical and electrophysiological research. In E. R. Ritvo (ed.), *Autism: diagnosis, current research and management* (pp. 75–84). New York: Spectrum.

Teasdale, J. (1983). Negative thinking in depression: Cause, effect, or reciprocal relationship? *Advances in Behavior Research and Therapy, 5,* 3–25.

Teasdale, J. D., & Fogarty, F. J. (1979). Differential effects of induced mood on retrieval of pleasant and unpleasant events from episodic memory. *Journal of Abnormal Psychology, 88,* 248–57.

Teasdale, J. D., & Spencer, P. (1984). Induced mood and estimates of past success. *British Journal of Clinical Psychology, 23,* 149–150.

Teasdale, J., & Taylor, R. (1981). Induced mood and accessibility of memories: An effect of mood state or of induction procedure? *British Journal of Clinical Psychology, 20,* 39–48.

Thaut, M. H. (1989). The influence of music therapy interventions on self-rated changes in relaxation, affect and thought in psychiatric prisoner-patients. *Journal of Music Therapy, 26,* 155–66.

Thaut, M. H. (2002). Neuropsychological processes in music perception and their relevance in music therapy. In R. F. Unkefer & M. H. Thaut (eds), *Music therapy in the treatment of adults with mental disorders: Theoretical bases and clinical interventions* (pp. 2–32). Gilsum, NH: Barcelona Publishers.

Thaut, M. H. (2005). *Rhythm, music, and the brain.* London: Taylor & Francis.

Thaut, M. H., & de L'Etoile, S. K. (1993). The effect of music on mood-state dependent recall. *Journal of Music Therapy, 30,* 70–80.

Tucker, D. (1981). Lateral brain function, emotion, and conceptualization. *Psychological Bulletin, 89,* 19–46.

Ulrich, G., Houtmans, T., & Gold, C. (2007). The additional therapeutic effect of group music therapy for schizophrenic patients: A randomized study. *Acta Psychiatrica Scandinavia*, 116, 362–70.

Uttl, B., Ohta, N., & Siegenthaler, S. L. (2006). *Memory and emotion: Interdisciplinary perspectives*. Malden, MA: Blackwell Sciences.

Velten, E. (1968). A laboratory task for induction of mood states. *Behavioral Research and Therapy*, 6, 607–17.

Wallace, W. T. (1994). Memory for music: Effect of melody on recall of text. *Journal of Experimental Psychology: Learning, Memory, and Cognition*, 20, 1471–85.

Winner, E. (1982). *Invented worlds*. Cambridge, MA: Harvard University Press.

Wolpe, J. (1978). Self-efficacy theory and psychotherapeutic change. *Advances in Behavior Research and Therapy*, 1, 231–6.

Wundt, W. M. (1874). *Grundzuege der physiologischen Psychologie*. Leipzig, Germany: Engelmann.

Zajonc, R. (1984). Feeling and thinking: Preferences need no inferences. *American Psychologist*, 35, 151–75.

Zerhusen, J. D., Boyle, K., & Wilson, W. (1995). Out of the darkness: Group cognitive therapy for depressed elderly. *Journal of Military Nursing Research*, 1, 28–32.

Zwerling, I. (1979). The creative arts therapies as 'real therapies'. *Hospital and Community Psychiatry*, 30, 841–4.

CHAPTER 30

MUSIC, HEALTH, AND WELL-BEING

SUZANNE B. HANSER

As a music therapist, my job is to use music in pursuit of the health and well-being of my clients. My clinical work and research have focused on the impact of music therapy on people who are confronted by stress, pain, and other vicissitudes of life. It is from this gestalt that I approach the topic. In this chapter, I explore the evolution of healthcare and emerging models of prevention, wellness, and integrative medicine that have allowed music therapists to become active partners with medical professionals in treating the whole person. Evidence of strong connections between mind and body has provided a foundation for understanding how engaging in musical experiences promotes health and well-being. I review contemporary approaches to the relaxation response and advances in health psychology to provide a vocabulary for describing how music affects well-being. Research has emphasized the impact of psychological factors, such as stress and the placebo response, on physical health, and I discuss the implications of these findings. I examine the effect of music on stress, pain, immune and neurologic function, and share a line of clinical outcome research that has circled my career as a music therapist. Four diverse conditions affecting health and well-being are covered: childbirth, depression, coronary heart disease, and cancer. Finally, new directions in theory, practice, and research relative to music, health, and well-being are predicted.

30.1 CONTEMPORARY HEALTHCARE

30.1.1 What is health?

The World Health Organization (1999) defines health as 'a state of complete physical, mental, and social well-being and not merely the absence of disease, or infirmity'.

Health is a broad term that refers to the comprehensive nature of one's physical and emotional status as it develops throughout a person's life. The phrase 'health and well-being' is not a technical term; therefore, it could encompass anything that an individual strives for in the process of becoming more whole, balanced, and positive in mind, body and spirit.

30.1.2 Developments in prevention and wellness

Healthcare services are slowly evolving from a disease and symptom model into one of prevention and wellness that emphasizes lifestyle in addition to medicine. Comprehensive medical centres are inviting practitioners of non-medical disciplines to join their teams in an attempt to provide holistic treatment plans for patients and healthy people who are at risk for a variety of diseases. Nutritionists educated in herbs and supplements, massage therapists, and acupuncturists are working with physicians and nurses to provide a compendium of techniques to improve overall health. Based on ground-breaking clinical research by physicians like Dean Ornish (Ornish et al, 1998), facilities such as the Preventive Medicine Research Institute in California have sprouted in order to inform medical professionals and consumers alike on the health benefits of proper diet, exercise, and reduction of stress. Ornish's colleagues have found strong evidence that these factors are significantly related to improvement in risk of a coronary incident for individuals who have coronary heart disease (Daubenmier et al, 2007). Increasingly, music therapy is becoming part of effective lifestyle enhancement programmes around the world that teach strategies for coping with stress and increasing pleasure in daily life (Son, 2008).

30.1.3 Health and fitness

Health and fitness centres are booming business enterprises as an increasing number of people learn that their well-being depends on fitness as well as general health. Background music is an integral part of the fitness centre, as it motivates people to remain on exercise equipment longer, step up their pace, or move in synchronization with the rhythm of the music (Gfeller, 1988). It is natural for people to find a musical way to regulate their moods, while they exercise, or at other times of the day.

The iPod and MP3 technologies have enabled people to have instant access to their favourite music with the flick of a finger. Not only can listeners select a piece of music to provide stimulation during a repetitive exercise, but they can also bring music to their morning routines, on their way to work, during an idle part of their day, or whenever they are alone and desire some auditory stimuli to attract their attention to something pleasant. As they listen, the memories and moods that are associated with the musical selection are triggered, allowing the listener to re-experience these moments in full regalia, that is, in vivid visual imagery or accompanied by goose bumps. At the very least, they can count on a massive mood change after listening to music that is meaningful to them.

Now that preferred music is easily available and portable, it is possible to prepare playlists for the purpose of changing feeling states. For example, listeners can search their memories for pieces of music that they have found relaxing. When they play this music again, they pay particular attention to the effect it has on them. If they corroborate the relaxing influence of this music, they add it to the 'peaceful' playlist. They might do the same for music that energized them and spurred them to keep moving, in order to construct an 'energy' playlist. Then, when drowsiness begins to seep in, after a night of sleeping too fitfully or a day of working too hard, they would have a remedy in their pockets, ready to plug in at a moment's notice.

This is precisely the prescription at Brigham and Women's Hospital in Boston, Massachusetts, where a new programme, 'Playlists for the Soul', is being piloted with patients who are referred for pain or palliative care services (Hanser, 2008). Here, patients receive iPods loaded with music from various genres and cultures. A music therapist meets with them individually to help categorize selections that will most likely elicit desired effects, such as 'relaxation' or 'sleep induction'. The music therapist uses an assessment protocol, which involves listening with the patients to the familiar pieces, observing their reactions, and questioning them about the thoughts, memories, associations, and images that are evoked. Using these data, the music therapist creates new playlists and burns compact discs for use after discharge from the hospital. In this way, patients can take control of their affective states back home, when they want to relax, sleep, or change their mood.

30.1.4 Integrative medicine

Providing iPods to patients is a simple, short-term strategy for coping with certain unpleasant mood states. But the burgeoning field of integrative medicine is opening up many alternative ways of meeting patients' long-term health needs through interventions by qualified professionals. Today, integrative medicine provides a new way to include both ancient and innovative practices in the resolution of disease. Responsive to the emotional and spiritual needs of patients in addition to the physical, it is also founded on evidence-based practice that weaves together the mind, body, and spirit heretofore separated in medical practice (Gilbert, 2003).

This emerging field has redefined the service of medicine and built an infrastructure to support the use of music, imagery, and other non-traditional forms of therapy (Remen, 2008). While non-traditional or non-Western therapies were once sought by consumers as alternatives to treatment, integrative medicine applies these services side by side with standard medical treatment in a holistic approach to health. The trend is continuing, and both the centres of integrative medicine and the professional journals covering the latest research on different integrative treatments are growing. Music therapy (see Chapter 29, this volume), as well as other mind-body therapies, are vital parts of such programmes.

30.2 THE CONNECTION BETWEEN
MIND AND BODY

30.2.1 Mind-body medicine

The synergistic relationship between mind and body provides a theoretical foundation for the use of music in health promotion. Mind-body medicine emphasizes the interactions between emotions, thoughts, relationships, behaviour, and spirituality in determining good health (Harrington, 2008). It also engages the individual or patient as an active participant in treatment or a personal growth plan. Its focus is wellness and health; its techniques involve empowering people to maximize the impact of the mind on the body and the body on the mind.

Cognitive-behavioural therapy contributes a constellation of methods, based on the assumption that thoughts affect feelings and behaviour. In this approach, people learn to change the way they think about unhealthy situations in order to change the feelings associated with them. While this therapy is extremely effective for a wide variety of conditions, a recent review of randomized, controlled trials with adults who have anxiety disorders offers convincing evidence (Hofmann & Smits, 2008).

In addition to traditional psychological treatments like cognitive-behavioural therapy, mind-body therapies also include many ayurvedic strategies designed to provide balance and peace (translated from the Hindu as science of life). Yoga, breathing techniques, and various forms of meditation are borrowed from this tradition. Tai chi and chi gong are other forms of Chinese medicine that are included in the armamentarium of mind-body techniques (Lu, 2005).

While there is a vast array of meditation models, including yoga and mindfulness, the purpose of meditation in contemporary health promotion is to suspend thought and judgement in an attempt to bring about relaxation or an altered state of awareness. Meditation is defined by Maison et al (1995, p. 39) as the 'self regulation of attention, in the service of self-inquiry, in the here and now'.

Other techniques that focus the attention in order to relax the body and mind include hypnosis, biofeedback, visual imagery and music therapy. In hypnosis, or *hypnotherapy*, the individual enters an altered state of consciousness by attending to a single object or thought. The resulting openness and responsiveness make one suggestible to certain feelings, like being relaxed or comfortable, even under conditions of anxiety or pain. One meta-analysis demonstrates a high degree of efficacy with children undergoing painful procedures (Uman, Chamber, McGrath, & Kisely, 2008). There is a growing literature supporting the effects on adults as well. *Biofeedback* is the use of data about one's physical condition to control and improve that condition (Schwartz & Andrasik, 2003). For example, blood pressure can be modified by individuals as they observe the monitor's reading, then change their thoughts, feelings, and behaviours and watch for concomitant changes in blood pressure. People can learn to recognize the internal stimuli that cause their blood pressure to change, then practise purposely engaging these thoughts and feelings, and in this way control their blood pressure. Similarly, individuals can alter activity in their hearts, sweat glands, or brain, as well as peripheral blood flow. *Imagery techniques* are another way of inducing relaxation. When people conjure up visual images of a peaceful place, or a familiar, calming picture, they can relax almost immediately.

Music therapy is another mind-body technique, which uses music to change mood, induce images, condition relaxation responses, increase contentment, or reduce stress. The effects of music therapy on selected health-related outcomes are described later in this chapter (see also Chapter 29, this volume).

30.2.2 The relaxation response

In his landmark book published in 1976, Dr. Herbert Benson described the relaxation response as a deeply restful state to fight the 'fight or flight response' by changing the physical and emotional responses to stress. By decreasing arousal of the sympathetic nervous system, the relaxation response benefits patients whose illnesses are related to stress. This list encompasses as many as 75 per cent of all medical conditions, including hypertension, cardiac illness, headache, arthritis, cancer, stroke, panic attacks, anxiety and depressive disorders, and chronic pain. Benson's research and, subsequently, hundreds of experimental research studies have established that learning to evoke the relaxation response positively affects a variety of health outcomes (Benson & Klipper, 2000; Benson & Proctor, 2003).

Functional magnetic resonance imaging (fMRI) has demonstrated that when a person meditates to evoke the relaxation response, parts of the brain that process attention and control the autonomic nervous system are activated (Lazar et al, 2000). Music has also been shown to evoke the relaxation response in special protocols (Hanser & Codding, 2008).

30.2.3 Health psychology

Research in the field of health psychology supports the use of behavioural interventions that improve quality of life for individuals and the quality of healthcare in society at large (Leventhal, Weinman, Levental, & Phillips, 2008). Two decades of experimentation have revealed a strong relationship between negative affect and the experience of physical symptoms (Mora, Halm, Leventhal, & Ceric, 2007).

Long-term effects of emotion may also affect susceptibility to infection. Smith and Nicholson (2001) found that individuals who reported high levels of negative mood or chronic stress developed more severe viruses and symptoms of asthma than those who claimed to have more positive moods and less stress in their lives. Cohen et al (2003) supported this finding with their own, that those who reported more positive emotions tended to show resistance to colds, when compared with individuals who reported experiencing more negative emotions. This line of research girds the theory that positive emotions build personal resources that can promote and protect good health.

30.2.4 Positive psychology

Ongoing research in mind-body medicine has given rise to a new way of looking at psychological well-being, called positive psychology. The 'broaden and build theory of positive emotions' (Frederickson, 2001) turns attention away from pathology, symptomatology, and abnormal behaviour in order to examine the impact of the positive and pleasant things people do. Resilience, positive emotions, and coping styles are the vocabulary of this approach. Tugade, Fredrickson, and Barrett (2004, p. 1161) posit:

Positive emotions can be an important factor that buffers individuals against maladaptive health outcomes. Emerging research indicates that finding ways to cultivate meaningful positive emotions is a critical necessity for optimal physical and psychological functioning. Indeed, positive emotions are good for your health. With increasing research, we continue to substantiate empirically age-old folk theories about positive emotions and health that have persisted through time.

'To flourish means to live within an optimal range of human functioning, one that connotes goodness, generativity, growth and resilience,' states Keyes (2002, p. 207). Mental health and well-being are considered here along an entire continuum, negative to positive. Research by Fredrickson and Losadis (2005) confirms: 'Results showed that the mean ratio of positive to negative affect was above 2.9 for individuals classified as flourishing and below that threshold for those not flourishing' (p. 678).

30.3 PSYCHOLOGICAL FACTORS THAT AFFECT HEALTH AND WELL-BEING

30.3.1 The influence of stress

In 1932, Walter Cannon published a book that summarized his research on the impact of stress on animals. He measured the neurochemical responses to stress in the sympathetic autonomic nervous system, and coined the term 'fight or flight' response to explain this heightened neurophysiological response in the presence of stress. This primitive reaction to a threat became 'hard-wired' into human brains when early humankind perceived a danger to their survival and had to run away or fight the approaching beast. Later, Hans Selye (1956) described how this early evolutionary survival mechanism led to or exacerbated diverse medical conditions. He proposed that when stress becomes chronic, the resulting heightened neurophysiological activity effectively begins to drain the body and brain of their energy and resources, causing a deterioration in immunologic function.

30.3.2 The placebo effect

A few years later, Henry Beecher (1959) documented the impact of a placebo in ameliorating pain, an outcome he observed personally while treating World War II soldiers. A shortage of morphine prompted him to suggest to soldiers that an injection would relieve their pain, even though they were receiving only a dose of salt solution. A high percentage of soldiers reported relief. Subsequently, the confidence in the ability of medical treatment to cure or benefit a condition has become known as the 'placebo effect' (Enck, Benedetti, & Schedlowski, 2008). More technically, it refers to the ability of an inert or benign substance to bring about healing, due to the person's belief or expectation that it will be effective. These psychological mechanisms may affect the progression of a disease as well as a response to therapy. This means that other factors, previously shunned as unsubstantiated, non-medical phenomena, such as sensory experiences, emotions, and even music are now recognized as significant influences on health and well-being. The placebo effect is estimated to be so great that clinical drug trials are required to include a treatment containing no active ingredients to compare with the treatment being investigated. It has now been documented that expectation can mediate powerful human perceptions, such as pain, motor function, and other conscious physiological experiences.

30.4 THE EFFECT OF MUSIC ON STRESS

In 2004, Pelletier conducted a meta-analysis of the effect of music on arousal due to stress. The initial search uncovered 74 articles, but 52 did not meet the following inclusion criteria: (1) included a pre-measure of stress or anxiety, (2) compared two contrasting conditions, (3) applied an experimental design, (4) used recorded music, (5) reported data sufficient for effect-size analysis, (6) included more than one subject, and (7) collected physiological, behavioural, or self-report data. Out of the 22 quantitative studies, 13 were conducted in medical settings (surgery, medical procedures, and childbirth preparation and delivery), two were on occupational stress, and six were conducted on college students. While the administration of music differed widely across these experiments, both music alone and music-facilitated relaxation were instrumental in decreasing arousal, with a statistically significant effect size ($d = .67$). Based on this review, Pelletier developed some specific recommendations for clinical practice (see Figure 30.1). But in addition to these suggestions based on the findings, it is revealing that so many studies failed to meet inclusion criteria.

Music Therapy Assisted Stress Reduction

1. Conduct individual sessions if possible, since there will be greater benefit. However, group sessions are still effective.
2. Be aware of that music is more effective with musicians than non-musicians.
3. Continue to use music with participants under 18 years since this age group received the greater benefit.
4. Use research supported music selections containing slower tempo, low pitches, containing primarily string composition, regular rhythmic patterns, no extreme changes in dynamics, and no lyrics. Research has used the following selections listed in order from most to least researched:
   - Steven Halpern—Several different musical selections (Guzzeta, 1988; Hamel, 2001; Liebman & MacLaren, 1991; Logan & Roberts, 1984; Van Fleet, 1985)
   - Debussy *Prelude to an Afternoon of a Faun* (Bolwerk, 1990; Ellis & Brighouse, 1952; Rider, Floyd, & Kirkpatrick, 1985)
   - Bach *Air on a G String* (Barger, 1979; Zimny & Weidenfeller, 1963)
   - John McLaughlin *Clouds* and *Peace of Mind* (Kibler & Rider, 1983; Rider, Floyd, & Kirkpatrick, 1985)
   - Ray Lynch *Deep Breakfast* (Standley, 1991)
   - Ocean waves with Baroque music in the background (Hoffman, 1974)
   - Faure—Harp chamber music, performed by Vito (Reynolds, 1984)
   - Daniel Kobialka *Fragrances of a Dream* and *Timeless Motion* Tanya Goodman *A Child's Gift of Lullabies* Platinum Disc Corporation's Relaxation Series *Cool Mountain Stream* (Robb et al., 1995)
   - Dvorak *New World Symphony* (*Symphony No. 9 in E Minor, Op. 95, Second Movement*) Sibelius *Swan of Tuonela* (Rohner & Miller, 1980)
5. While GIM is effective as a technique for stress reduction, avoid it if possible, since effects are minimal in comparison to other techniques.
6. Conduct multiple sessions if possible, otherwise provide a tape for later use since the more exposures to the music the greater relaxation response.
7. Use the most convenient of behavioral, self-report, or physiological recording procedures, since results demonstrated no significant difference between the three measures. However behavioral observation may reduce the distraction of stopping to take a pulse rate or complete self-assessment measures.
8. Use music assisted verbal suggestions procedures and vibrotactile stimulation when possible since these two procedures demonstrate the greatest effect size. Progressive relaxation procedures may be used initially to instruct how to relax, but then clinicians should move on to other procedures.

Fig. 30.1 Recommendations from Pelletier (2004) (reprinted with permission of the *Journal of Music Therapy*).

Indeed, Pelletier reviewed only investigations of recorded music, presumably because live music cannot be controlled or replicated easily, for research purposes. Music is, by its nature, a variable that defies objectivity, as it is produced by a unique human being or ensemble of humans. Research protocols that test interesting musical interventions, therefore, can be subjective and complex, challenging attempts at generalizing their impact to other audiences or participants. The paucity of experimental research indicates that while there is much discussion about engaging in musical activity for health and well-being, it is difficult to design research to test specific outcomes. Yet the disciplines of science and medicine demand rigorous and randomized clinical trials for music interventions to be considered evidence-based practice. This challenge exists, not only in examinations of the impact of music on stress and anxiety, but also in pain management research.

30.5 THE ROLE OF MUSIC IN PAIN MANAGEMENT

Because pain is actually a perception rather than a physical concept, it can be managed by mind-body techniques, such as music listening or music therapy. Musical experiences can affect the autonomic nervous system, and because it can reduce stress, focus attention, and change mood, it is instrumental in decreasing the perception of pain.

30.5.1 What is pain?

Pain is something that everyone experiences at some time. Yet relatively little is known about pain. Contrary to intuitive thinking, pain is a perception that is unique to the individual experiencing it. There is no single pain centre in the brain or universal response to a particular injury. Neither is there a particular sensation that defines pain. The IASP (2007) defines pain as 'an unpleasant sensory and emotional experience associated with actual or potential tissue damage, or described in terms of such damage'.

In most cases, there is an emotional element as well as a physical location for pain. Every person has a different threshold for pain; its severity is described along a wide continuum, even when the infliction is the same. In other words, a pin prick may elicit shrieks of distress in one person and hardly a notice in another individual. Remarkably, the response to a painful stimulus may be unrelated to its source.

This is why the most valuable source of pain assessment in hospitals is the patient's self-report. Unfortunately, the intensity of pain perceived by patients is underestimated by medical professionals, and pain medications are generally underutilized. The prevalence of pain led the Joint Commission on Accreditation of Healthcare Organizations in the United States to mandate its regular documentation in patients' charts.

The impact of pain on quality of life is substantial. It influences physical well-being and symptomatology, psychological well-being, social concerns, and spiritual well-being (Ferrell & Rhiner, 1991). The affective dimension of pain is the emotional response to pain, and the cognitive dimension reflects how the person thinks of the pain. However, pain is basically a cognitive experience.

Before 1965, pain was considered biological, the result of receptors (called nociceptors) that travelled up the spine to the brain. Then Melzack and Wall (1965) introduced the gate control theory of pain to explain the relationship of an ascending pain stimulus and the inhibitory stimulus descending from the brain. Pain signals from the source of inflammation or insult follow a neospinothalamic pathway for sharp or acute pain; they follow a paleospinothalamic tract for the throbbing, aching type of pain. As the names imply, the pain signals travel up the spine, through the medulla and pons, eventually reaching the thalamus, the relay station that resides in the limbic system of the brain. The thalamus and hypothalamus then send these pain signals to the cortex and other parts of the brain. Along their journey, the pain signals move through dorsal columns or gates where they encounter inhibitory pathways that are descending from the brain, through the dorsal horn, and down the spinal cord. The gate opens or closes at the dorsal horn, where impulses are facilitated or inhibited. More recently, Melzack (2001, p. 1379) introduced other factors into the theory:

The neuromatrix theory guides us away from the Cartesian concept of pain as a sensation produced by injury, inflammation, or other tissue pathology and toward the concept of pain as a multidimensional experience produced by multiple influences.

This neuromatrix theory of pain acknowledges the complexity of past history, culture, cognition, stress, immune function, emotion, and sensory input. It states that the perception of pain is determined by sensory-discriminative, affective-motivational, and evaluative-cognitive components. These correspond to the somatosensory, limbic, and thalamocortical systems of the brain. The autonomic nervous system, the response to stress, and immune function are also involved in this model. Neurotransmitters play a significant role.

Neurotransmitters are chemicals that are released from brain cells, or neurons. These chemicals cross over the gap, or synapse, between the axon of one neuron and the dendrite of another, facilitating the flow of information. Neurotransmitters are, obviously, essential for brain activity to occur. The types of chemicals are diverse, including acetylcholine, monoamines, purines, fatty acids, amino acids, peptides, hormones, histamines, and others. Trout (2004, p. 486) explains the role of certain neurotransmitters in pain perception:

Neurotransmitters (opioid peptides commonly called endorphins, serotonin, and norepinephrine) released in the dorsal horn from descending tracts that originate in the hypothalamus and brainstem inhibit the sensation of pain. The endogenous opioid peptides bind to opioid receptors on dorsal horn neurons, thus diminishing propagation of pain transmission. Serotonin and norepinephrine are activated by opioids and appear to have a synergistic effect with endogenous opioids. Studies have shown reduced analgesic effects of opioids when serotonin and norepinephrine antagonists are administered. These descending signals from the brain may explain the mechanism of action of many comfort measures commonly used by midwives, such as music therapy imagery and the comforting presence of a significant other.

This more comprehensive definition of pain perception accounts for the efficacy of mind-body approaches, including music therapy, in reducing pain. It implies that the cortex can ultimately modify and restrain the ascending pain signals by controlling the inhibitory messages. When musical stimuli enter the cortex through the auditory nerve and temporal lobe, they compete with incoming pain signals and contribute to the inhibitory effect. Because of the vast impact of music on mood, imagery, memory, and other processes related to affect, the potential for music and music therapy to affect pain is substantial.

30.5.2 Effects of music on pain

As demonstrated in a growing number of empirical studies, music listening and music therapy techniques have been effective in the clinical management of pain. Yet it has been immensely problematic to control the many extraneous variables that affect an individual's perception of pain. Although quantitative and qualitative investigations have been performed, only empirical studies that demonstrate high standards of scientific inquiry are included in systematic reviews, such as the Cochrane Library. The Cochrane Collaboration oversees the quality of healthcare research by upholding strict criteria for experimental methodology. However, even the most professionally executed research may not control the context for musical involvement, for instance the patient's preference and predicted emotional response to the music, or account for the diversity in the landscape of pain perception. These factors and others affected a review of 51 randomized controlled trials published by Cepeda et al (2006) in the Cochrane Library. These experiments dealt with pain during medical procedures, postoperative pain, labour pain, cancer pain, and other chronic pain conditions. Unfortunately, the analysis excluded 62 studies, 17 of which used music plus suggestion, an intervention that has a strong ideological and empirical foundation. The authors report that listening to music alone does reduce pain intensity and the necessity for opioid medication, but the magnitude of overall effects was small. This is not surprising, given the fact that individuals had some control over the choice of music in just over half of the reviewed studies (27); they did not choose the music in 15 studies, and criteria for music selection were unclear in seven studies. The remaining two experiments involved children.

Although the authors concluded that the clinical importance of music listening was unsubstantiated by their review, it is obvious that music interventions must be based on clear theoretical formulations involving the interrelationship of music and emotion. Furthermore, the methodological problems inherent in applied research, where individual differences and intervening variables abound, create a complex environment within which to identify significant changes in subjective measures, such as pain perception. The gap between laboratory studies and clinical outcome research, especially where the subjects engage in active and creative musical exploration, widens.

30.6 THE EFFECT OF MUSIC ON IMMUNE AND NEUROLOGIC FUNCTIONS

30.6.1 What activities enhance immune function?

Thanks to technological advances in neuroscience, immune function can be measured in an effort to predict the body's ability to resist disease and maintain health. In one study on the effects of meditation, the reaction to antibody titers in influenza vaccines was used as an indicator of immune function. Brain activity in the left side of the anterior brain indicated the presence of positive emotions while the subjects meditated. At the same time, an increase in antibody titers demonstrated a direct relationship between these positive emotions and improved immune function (Davidson et al, 2003).

There is also evidence that immune function is enhanced when laughter and humour intervene in stressful life experiences (Stone et al, 1987). Older adults are particularly talented at using humour to overcome crisis, and this was shown in a study by Mahoney et al (2002) to have positive impact on their health. In another investigation, positive emotions were directly linked to lower readmission rates to hospitals for older adults with cardiac illnesses (Middleton & Byrd, 1996).

30.6.2 How do neurotransmitters affect neurologic activity?

One significant aspect of the work of neurotransmitters was described within the neuromatrix theory of pain. But each type of neurotransmitter has a distinctive role in affecting health and well-being. Known as the 'feel good' chemical, *serotonin* is found in the central nervous system. It modulates mood, sleep, appetite, aggression, anger, and other emotions. The neurotransmitter and neurohormone *dopamine* has been found to be involved in sympathetic autonomic nervous system activity, and is also associated with pleasurable sensations when it is secreted.

For patients with Parkinson's disease, there is a shortage of dopamine, and so a dopamine precursor, levdopa (L-Dopa), is usually prescribed to reverse some of the effects of the disease. Interestingly, innovations in positron emission tomography (PET) have led to the detection of increased secretions of dopamine in the brains of individuals with Parkinson's disease as they experience the placebo effect (Fuente-Fernandez et al, 2002). This discovery demonstrates not only that the placebo effect activates the flow of dopamine, but that positive emotions or other rewarding activities may replace the need for dopamine-releasing pharmaceuticals.

30.6.3 Does music affect the release of neurotransmitters?

Evers and Suhr (2000) studied the effects of listening to pleasant and unpleasant music on the release of serotonin. They examined changes in the 5-HT content of platelets (a measure of serotonin), as a function of ten minutes of music listening. The content of 5-HT was higher when listeners rated music as pleasant, as opposed to unpleasant. This was the first experiment to investigate the changes in serotonin that could be elicited by music.

Music increased the release of dopamine in hypertensive rats in a study by Sutoo and Akiyama (2004). Systolic blood pressure was decreased while serum calcium and neostriatal dopamine levels increased during the music exposure. While this initial research is encouraging, the generalization from rats' to humans' perceptions of music raises questions beyond the scope of this chapter. Fortunately, experimentation on human dopamine release (Menon & Levitin, 2005) yielded confirmatory results. While subjects listened to pleasant music, activity in the hypothalamus also indicated a clear, physiological response. The same areas of the brain involved in reward, namely the nucleus accumbens, the ventral tegmental area, the hypothalamus, and insula, were also observed to be activated by music listening.

McKinney, Tims, Kumar, and Kumar (1997) examined a different neurotransmitter, plasma beta-endorphin. This chemical is an endogenous opioid peptide that is implicated in stress. The experimenters compared the effects of music imaging, silent imaging, music listening, and a control condition in 78 subjects. The music imaging group engaged in an adaptation of Guided Imagery and Music (GIM) methodology, including a progressive muscle relaxation exercise, and verbal suggestions for inducing imagery through the music. Subjects in the silent imaging condition heard similar suggestions for imagery, without any music. The music listening group heard 'Introduction and Allegro' by Maurice Ravel, as did the music imaging group, but the former did not hear imaging instructions. Individuals in the music imaging condition experienced a beneficial result, as evidenced by reduced levels of this peripheral beta-endorphin. However, the other three groups did not demonstrate such a change. Although replication of this finding is required, the research supports the importance of a combination of music and imagery techniques. The interpretation of these results is complicated by the recommendation by Pelletier (2004) that GIM demonstrates minor impact, compared with other music-facilitated stress reduction strategies. Clearly, researchers have yet to untangle the complex interactions between the manner in which music is presented, the subjective experience of the listener or participant, and the physical versus psychological modes of measuring their responses. The uniqueness of the human response to music challenges researchers in their attempts to standardize an experimental protocol and measure its influence on various aspects of functioning.

30.6.4 What is the effect of music on immune function?

There are several interesting studies of singing as it influences the immune system. Once again, the effect of singing is mediated by a variety of factors. Kreutz et al (2004) tested choral singers' immune function through their salivary immunoglobulin A and their stress levels through the stress hormone cortisol. Singing during rehearsals resulted in positive affect and enhanced immune function; listening to choral performances led to negative affect and a decrease in stress hormone levels. Kuhn (2002) compared the immune function of people singing while playing percussion with others who listened to live music. Immune function of individuals performing music was significantly greater than for those who listened and for those who did not participate with music at all. Support of the hypothesis that active music making has a more significant effect on the immune system than passive listening requires further investigation. Grape et al (2003) assessed heart rate variability (HRV), secretions of a variety of endocrinological and biochemical hormones, and verbal report of emotions in professional singers and amateurs during singing lessons. Both groups of singers displayed similar HRV over time, although the professionals showed a better ability to maintain HRV over the course of the lesson. Both professionals and amateurs increased their plasma oxytocin levels. As oxytocin inhibits the release of the stress hormone cortisol and affects the immune system, potentially relieving anxiety and pain, this is a very positive finding. Both groups also reported heightened energy and relaxation at the conclusion of the lesson. However, there were significant differences between the groups in serum concentrations of tumor necrosis factor (TNF-alpha), specifically, increased TNF-alpha in the professional singers, and decreased TNF-alpha in the amateur singers. The authors interpreted these results as demonstrating decreasing tension in the amateurs as opposed to increasing tension in the professionals. It is interesting that amateurs expressed increased joy at the end of the lesson, whereas the professional singers did not. The investigators concluded that the singing lessons resulted in decreased arousal and greater well-being for amateur singers, whereas the opposite was true for professional singers.

There is a growing number of studies examining the influence of different types of musical experiences on immune function. In one investigation, Guided Imagery and Music (GIM) resulted in decreases in cortisol and concomitant improvement in mood disturbance (McKinney, Antoni, Kumar, Tims, & McCabe, 1997). Another group of researchers reported positive effects of group drumming on a number of assessments of immune and neruoendocrine function (Bittman et al, 1994). One measure of immune function, salivary immunoglobulin A, was improved in a number of other music research studies (Charnetski, Brennan, & Harrison, 1998; Hucklebridge et al, 2000; McCray, Atkinson, Rein, & Watkins, 1996). Khalfa et al (2003) found that when subjects were engaged in a stressful task, salivary cortisol continued to rise for half an hour. A group of subjects listening to music, however, failed to display such an increase. Rider and Achterberg (1989) observed changes in specific white blood cells in the immune system when subjects experienced music-facilitated imagery. When they imagined fewer lymphocytes, changes were observed in these particular cells only; when they imagined fewer neutrophils, there was a concomitant decrease in these types of white blood cells. Bartlett, Kaufman, and Smeltekop (1993) were interested in the immune agent interleukin-1 (IL-1) as well as cortisol. In their research, subjects selected their preferred music from a sample of popular new age, classical, and classical jazz genres, chosen by the researchers as potentially relaxing. Music listening resulted in significant increases in IL-1 and significant decreases in cortisol, as opposed to the control group.

These promising studies are pointing the way for future research that will determine the specific impact of musical activity (see also Table 11.6 in Chapter 11, this volume). Now that markers of immune function and some neurochemical reactions are capable of measurement, researchers can focus more on musical variables such as preference, familiarity, associations, images elicited, and relationship of player to listener of the music. Exerting better control over these variables will be necessary to determine their true impact. Collaborative research between trained musicians or music therapists and scientists who understand the complex interrelationships between various measures of immunity and neurobiology will build a more accurate and complete music-stress-reduction-immunity paradigm.

30.6.5 What is the effect of music on other neurologic activity?

In a much-publicized experiment, Blood and Zatorre (2000) used positron emission tomography (PET) to observe changes in regional cerebral blood flow (rCBF) as listeners heard music that they predicted would evoke 'chills' or a sense of euphoria. The researchers summarize (p. 11823):

We have shown here that music recruits neural systems of reward and emotion similar to those known to respond specifically to biologically relevant stimuli, such as food and sex, and those that are artificially activated by drugs of abuse. This is quite remarkable, because music is neither strictly necessary for biological survival or reproduction, nor is it a pharmacological stimulus substance. Activation of these brain systems in response to a stimulus as abstract as music may represent an emergent property of the complexity of human cognition. Perhaps as formation of anatomical and functional links between phylogenically older, survival-related brain systems and newer, more cognitive systems increased our general capacity to assign meaning to abstract stimuli, our capacity to derive pleasure from these stimuli also increased. The ability of music to induce such intense pleasure and its putative stimulation of endogenous reward systems suggest that, although music may not be imperative for survival of the human species, it may indeed be of significant benefit to our mental and physical well-being.

30.6.6 How does music engage the autonomic nervous system?

It has been established that the sympathetic nervous system becomes active when the fight or flight response is triggered, due to stress or a threat to survival. In contrast, palliation and deep relaxation, such as are elicited by listening to soothing music, activate the parasympathetic nervous system, decreasing heart rate and blood pressure while enhancing blood flow to the vital organs. Now that advances in technology have enabled physiological, psychological, neurological, and immunological responses to music to be observed more closely, new theories arise regarding the basis for the response to music. It is clear that music behaviour influences both the sympathetic and parasympathetic parts of the autonomic nervous system (Chapter 11, this volume).

Engaging in the creation of music—active performance, improvising, or composing music—should trigger parts of both the sympathetic and parasympathetic autonomic nervous systems, effectively balancing the entire nervous system as few stimuli can. When physical movements necessitated by musical activity are paired with a positive psychological response, the results are an excitation of physiological activity (e.g. moderately heightened heart rate and blood pressure) that lacks the immunologic impact of negative stressors. This hypothesis carries implications for justifying the use of music to improve overall health, and requires scientific verification.

30.7 A SAMPLE OF CASES AND RESEARCH ON THE EFFECTS OF MUSIC

30.7.1 The case of childbirth

Before Western medicine introduced the hospital maternity ward and analgesic medication into the process of giving birth, every woman found a way to cope with the pain of contractions using her natural resources, particularly deep breathing, the social and physical support of other women, and the power of gravity. While the medical institution brought welcome good hygiene, Caesarian section surgery, anesthetics, and analgesia to birthing, it also minimized or eliminated the woman's control over this natural process. A return to natural childbirth allowed women to prepare themselves for labour and childbearing, and to seek methods that would assist them in managing their pain, while creating a more familiar and homelike setting.

Larson, O'Connell, and I (Hanser, Larson, & O'Connell, 1983) hypothesized that music could provide an auditory focal point similar in function to the visual focal point used to pinpoint concentration in many techniques of prepared childbirth. We engaged seven women in an investigation of the effects of music listening on the management of pain during labour. We met with each woman several months prior to expected delivery date, and helped her to select music that was meaningful to her. We observed her while she listened, and asked her to label the feeling state that the music induced. We created a compendium of musical selections, categorizing them by tempo and by the feeling evoked by the music. We encouraged her to listen to the slowest selections first, and to reserve the pieces that had a strict, rhythmic beat for transition, the period just before the birth.

Because of the variability of every woman's labour and delivery relative to length, complaints and complications, we were aware that it would require a very large number of women to garner the statistical power to test our hypotheses in a randomized controlled trial. We chose instead to have each woman act as her own control by alternating periods of music listening with periods of no music in the background. This procedure created a repeated-measures experimental design. Because it is very difficult to observe relaxation, we developed a pain behaviour rating scale to record pain-related behaviours, consisting of observed tension in different parts of the body, shifts in position (restlessness), vocalizations of pain, and requests for medication. We recorded the number of these behaviours during each contraction, and calculated a mean pain response score for each observation period. The results were that every woman experienced fewer pain responses while listening to her self-selected music than when no music was playing. Here is an account from one of the subjects:

I was panicky about going into labour. I was frightened about the needles, the IVs, and the problems I heard all about in our prepared childbirth classes. But I was most frightened about the contractions and the pain. What if I couldn't handle it? What if the pain was just too much? I didn't want drugs. I wanted so much to be awake and aware of everything that was going on. But I was just so scared.

So when I got to the hospital and the music therapist put on my favourite music, it was like I was home again, in my comfortable bed, with my husband, dreaming about this baby that was coming. I listened to the song played at our wedding and felt like I was at the ceremony again, kissing my husband and thinking it was the happiest day of my life. I told her to put on the music we danced to at the prom. I couldn't help smiling. I was practically giggling, and this was all while I was having contractions. And they were getting worse and worse, longer and stronger, and I was laughing and remembering the dances and the great times we had when we were together.

Then I was in transition, when the contractions kept up at their fiercest, and I was afraid I would lose it. That was when the music therapist played some really fast and rhythmic blues. The music was just what I needed. The rhythm kept on beating and I kept on breathing right in time. I got lost in the music while it told me when to breathe and got me caught up in the rhythm. The contractions felt like these huge waves, but the music gave me something to hold on to. I was inside the rhythm and it told me exactly what to do. I got through that labour, thanks to the music. I got to celebrate the birth of our baby, too, with a special piece, Handel's Hallelujah chorus.

Since the publication of this research, several experimental designs have evaluated the quality of the childbirth experience, and examined the role of music and its impact on the perception of pain (Durham & Collins, 1986; Phumdoung & Good, 2003). Few reports have considered the role of music in creating a soothing ambiance for the coach, medical team, and family, but anecdotal evidence is pervasive. The celebratory presence of music at the birth of a child is another aspect of the experience that bears documentation.

30.7.2 The case of depression

Depression is a common affective disorder, and is a major source of disability in over 121 million people throughout the world (World Health Organization, 2007). Approximately 5.8 per cent of males and 9.5 per cent of females will experience some depression in the course of a year. Untreated, it can lead to chronic disability, and globally it accounts for a high burden of disease. It can affect social relationships or the ability to live and work independently. When severe, it can lead to suicide. In clinical depression, affective symptoms may include depressed mood, loss of interest or pleasure, feelings of guilt, worthlessness, or hopelessness; somatic symptoms may appear as insomnia, loss of appetite, or headaches; behavioural symptoms may include isolation or agitation; cognitive symptoms may be problems in concentration or decision making.

For older adults, the problem of depression is exacerbated by the fact that medication is contraindicated for many of those who have physical illnesses, and that access to psychotherapy is limited when they themselves are ill or are caring for an ill family member. In response to these challenges, Larry Thompson, co-director of the Older Adults Research and Resource Center at Stanford University School of Medicine, and I embarked on a study to determine whether music-facilitated stress reduction was capable of relieving depression, anxiety, and distress while improving self-esteem and mood (Hanser & Thompson, 1994).

Thirty older adults seeking help for minor clinical depression were enrolled in this investigation, and were randomly assigned to one of three conditions. Ten were visited at home by me for one hour each week over eight weeks. During these individual sessions, I taught them eight stress-reduction strategies that were accompanied by listening to self-selected music. The techniques included: (1) movement to music; (2) gentle facial massage to music; (3) progressive muscle relaxation to music; (4) using music to induce visual imagery; (5) using music to visualize solving a problem; (6) using music to become energized; (7) using music to bring on sleep or deep relaxation; and (8) using music in some new creative way, such as painting, dancing, singing, or playing along to music. Ten other individuals received written instructions on how to perform the above activities and how to find music that would serve as a stimulus for these exercises. They received a weekly telephone call from me to assist them in administering the music programmes properly, but they never met me. They were instructed to listen to some music every day and practise one of the techniques while listening. Another ten individuals were on a waiting list to receive the intervention at the end of the eight-week treatment period, and served as the control group. All agreed to forego medication for depression during this time and were monitored for symptoms on a regular basis.

Standardized self-report measures of depression (Geriatric Depression Scale), anxiety (State-Trait Anxiety Inventory), overall distress (Brief Symptom Inventory), self-esteem (Rosenberg Self-Esteem Scale), and mood (Profile of Mood States) were administered pre-treatment, at four weeks, and after the eight-week protocol was completed. For those in the home visit and minimal therapist intervention groups, the same assessments were administered nine months after the end of treatment to determine any lasting effects. At the conclusion of the eight-week protocol, the two music-listening groups differed significantly from the control group on all assessments ($p < .05$). Not only was this difference statistically significant, but the improvement in depression from pre-treatment to post-treatment was clinically significant, such that this group of depressed older adults more closely resembled a non-depressed sample of people than they did other people with clinical depression. On follow-up nine months later, assessment results did not differ significantly from post-treatment results, and in some cases, further improvement was observed. Figure 30.2 shows the outcomes of each group on the Geriatric Depression Scale and the Anxious to Composed Subscale of the Profile of Mood States.

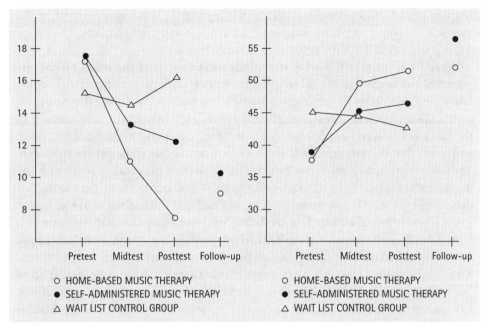

Fig. 30.2 Mean Geriatric Depression Scale (GDS) scores for the three conditions across four times of measurement (left). Mean Profile of Mood States (POMS) profiles, composed (top of graph) to anxious (bottom) scale, for the three conditions across four times of measurement (right). Reproduced by permission of the publisher from Hanser & Thompson (1994). Copyright (c) The Gerontological Society of America.

The following is the story of one of those subjects.

Judy was a 69-year-old female who was referred to the centre for a pathological bereavement reaction. Judy had lost her husband more than a year previously and she was still morose, despondent, and isolated. Her children were worried about her living alone because she was not eating regularly. She displayed a dysphoric mood, that is, one of hopelessness and lack of will to go on living. Judy was assigned to the home visit condition.

During our first visit, I encouraged Judy to identify music that she enjoyed, music that she associated with good times in her life, and music that tended to relax her. She thought for a moment, and replied that she really could not experience pleasure by listening to music, and that no particular music came to mind. When I prompted her further to consider albums she had once enjoyed, radio stations she turned on, or concerts she had attended, she told me that it was her husband, Bernard, who was the music lover.

Bernard had played the clarinet and loved the Big Band music that was popular when he and Judy were newly married. It turned out that there were boxes of records in the basement and a record player in good condition that had not been touched since

Bernard's death. Judy promised to ask her son to carry the boxes upstairs and to make sure that the player was in working order. I left her with the assignment to play some music every day and find a way to move to the music.

When I returned the following week, Judy was bright-eyed and much more energetic. She had listened to several recordings every day, and chose to listen while doing housework. She created a gentle exercise routine to perform, and continued to put on some of Bernard's favourites throughout the week. Judy enjoyed the facial massage in the next week's assignment. She listened to some recordings she had not heard in years, and found that they brought back wonderful memories that made her cry and laugh. The progressive muscle relaxation exercise was something Judy really appreciated. She discovered that a particular recording with Bennie Goodman as clarinetist soothed her deeply. She put it on before going to sleep, and said that she had not slept that well in many years. Judy was an excellent candidate for the imagery exercises. She imagined herself dancing with Bernard as she listened to 'Swing, Swing, Swing' with Gene Krupa on drums. She found that she could 'free her mind' when she listened and envisioned herself dancing with glee. Playing this music in the morning as she woke incited her to 'get up and face the day'. She had already experienced success with certain recordings to enhance sleep, so she asked her son to buy her some new records. During the final week of the treatment period, she attended a classical music concert with her son.

Judy improved on all measures of depression, anxiety, distress, self-esteem, and mood. Nine months later, she wrote some notes to accompany her answers to the psychological tests:

Before I took out all those records, I spent every day thinking that I would never see my husband again. I loved him so much. I couldn't bear to be without him. But now, when I put on his music, it feels like he is with me. I think about all the great times we had and how much we shared. I love the records and I love listening to his records. Thank you for giving me back my husband.

This transformative experience for Judy was captured best in the broad smile on her face. All of the psychological assessments revealed clinically significant improvement, and Judy continued to make music a part of her daily routine. Each person who participated in the research had a unique response to the music. It was functional in helping some of them sleep at night, in evoking optimism in others who looked forward to a special time for own relaxation, and in demonstrating to others how they could take control of their depression and make a difference in their overall mood.

Research on music and music therapy for depression and other psychiatric conditions has explored a variety of interventions. Gold (2007) undertook a systematic review of the experimental literature related to music therapy for people with psychoses and other psychiatric disorders, including affective disorders such as depression. His findings built on a previous Cochrane review regarding the effect of music therapy on schizophrenia and other psychotic disorders (Gold et al, 2005). The meta-analysis determined that music therapy had positive impact on global state, a variety of symptoms, and functioning in general. Further, the influence of music therapy increased directly with the number of sessions, and negative symptoms responded more quickly than global symptoms.

30.7.3 The case of coronary heart disease

Coronary heart disease (CHD) is the most common cause of death in the United Kingdom and the United States, as well as many countries around the world (American Heart Association, 2005; Peterson, Peto, & Rayner, 2004). By the year 2020, cardiovascular disease may account for as many as two-and-a-half million deaths. The physiological arousal that occurs with stress usually elevates heart and blood pressure. Over time, this results in hypertension, an enormous risk factor for cardiac illness.

In 2007, Mandel, Secic, Davis, and I published a study on the effects of music therapy on health-related outcomes in patients undergoing cardiac rehabilitation (Mandel, Hanser, Secic, & Davis, 2007). This was also a randomized, controlled trial with follow-up, and included 103 patients, 68 of whom completed the protocol. The patients were randomly assigned to cardiac rehabilitation only, or to music therapy plus cardiac rehabilitation. Music therapy included group activities that were designed to teach participants coping skills through *music-assisted relaxation and imagery* (MARI). Patients were instructed to practise listening to music and relaxing on a regular basis.

Immediate effects of individual sessions were assessed before and after every music therapy session through patients' reports of stress on a visual analogue scale and reports of anxiety on the State-Trait Anxiety Inventory. Significant improvements were reported on both assessments ($p < .001$).

Diastolic and systolic blood pressure were the physiological measurements that were compared from pre-treatment to post-treatment. Psychological measurements included self-reports of depression (Center for Epidemiologic Studies Depression Scale), anxiety (State-Trait Anxiety Scale), distress (Brief Symptom Inventory), and medical outcomes (Medical Outcomes Short—From Health Survey). All measurements were administered pre-treatment, post-treatment, and at one month, four months, and ten months post-treatment.

Results reflected a significantly larger decrease in systolic blood pressure for music therapy participants compared to the control group ($p < .05$). This outcome showed clinical significance through a calculation of effect size ($d = .58$). Although there were no significant differences between groups on psychological measures at post-treatment, significant differences were observed at four months' follow-up on anxiety, the general health subscale of the health survey, and on the social function subscale of the health survey (all p's $< .05$). At ten months post-treatment, 82 per cent of the music therapy participants reported that they continued to use music-assisted relaxation. The following is a case study by the principal author, Susan Mandel (2000):

Edward was a 75-year-old male who underwent coronary artery bypass graft surgery prior to his enrolment in cardiac rehabilitation. He was also diagnosed with an anxiety disorder. During his initial session, the music therapy clinician noted that Edward was very rigid, yet seemed to be fearful. He experienced difficulty sitting silently for five minutes while a blood pressure measurement was taken.

Edward seemed to benefit from his MARI compact disc (CD) listening experiences, describing his enjoyment of the suggestions with the music, and his experience of relaxation and pleasurable imagery. He reported, 'By the end of the time, you feel very, very calm and just very relaxed.' He seemed to have a total mind-body relaxation response to the MARI CD as noted in his listening log: 'Relaxes physical body. Slows down thinking too.' It seemed that Edward had not known this sense of complete relaxation prior to enrolling in the study. He stated: 'Getting a chance to just stay in one spot and listen to something that's slower and wants you to relax, tries to help you to relax makes a big difference . . . sometimes you think of things . . . you hadn't thought of for years.'

At the time of his final follow-up visit, seven months after baseline measurement, Edward's data indicated improved health-related quality of life, decreased depression and trait anxiety, as well as decreased systolic and diastolic blood pressure, with no reported change in medications. Anxiety was no longer indicated as a co-morbid condition. Edward reported almost daily home listening to the MARI CD and commented, 'I like the music and would like to find some CDs with similar quiet music.'

Mandel and I reviewed the research relevant to the influence of music for patients experiencing acute myocardial infarction (known commonly as heart attack), undergoing coronary artery bypass graft (CABG surgery), and recuperating in coronary care units (Hanser & Mandel, 2004). We found documentation of improvement in psychosocial, physiological, emotional, and overall health status as a function of music therapy interventions. Through the research and our own clinical experience, we found that individuals with cardiac conditions were able to take charge over the stress in their lives when they learned to recognize how music changed their heart rate and blood pressure.

30.7.4 The case of cancer

Cancer is a disease that occurs when abnormal cells inflate and multiply at an uncontrollable rate. The National Cancer Institute reports that there were 10.5 million Americans with a history of cancer in January 2003, and that over 1.4 million new cases would be diagnosed in 2007. These figures do not include carcinoma in situ (except in the bladder) or basal and squamous cell skin cancers. Over 1 million cases of these skin cancers were predicted for the year 2007 (American Cancer Society, 2007). People who have cancer may live with the fear of pain, of spread of disease, or of death. At the point of diagnosis, it is commonplace to see these patients evaluating the meaning of their lives, and trying to accept what it means to live with a chronic or terminal disease.

My colleagues at Dana-Farber Cancer Institute in Boston, Massachusetts and I were particularly interested in helping women with metastatic breast cancer cope with the distress, pain, fatigue, and shortness of breath that they often experience. Metastatic disease means that the cancer has advanced to other parts of the body, so there is a less optimistic prognosis compared with local or regional cancer. Another consideration was that, excluding the many varieties of skin cancer, breast cancer is the most common type in women. We wished to use a longitudinal, randomized controlled trial to investigate the effects of music therapy on psychological functioning, physiologic stress arousal, and quality of life (Hanser et al, 2006).

Seventy women were randomly assigned to music therapy or usual care. In three individual sessions that occurred while they were receiving chemotherapy, another music therapist or I provided the following musical experiences: (1) improvised or requested music on Native American flute, lyre, or guitar to encourage them to relax, (2) an invitation to have them improvise with me on hand chimes, rain stick, or other simple percussion instruments that required no previous experience or training, and (3) composition of a song that expressed something they wished to say to a loved one, or something about someone or something that was meaningful to them. Relaxation, comfort, and contentment, as reported on a visual analogue scale, improved significantly when immediate effects before and after each session were compared ($p < .0001$). Heart rate also decreased significantly ($p < .001$). No significant differences in depression, anxiety, or quality of life were observed between the music therapy and control group over time, but this finding may have been due to the attrition of participation in this very ill population.

After completing the three sessions, one of the patients wrote a personal letter, describing how she was able to use the techniques she had learned during the sessions:

I had to go up for a blood test that was particularly distressing to me. I had been having repeated problems with the test and had been overly emotional having it again. I was in tears as the nurse tried over and over to get my vein. She asked me to take a deep breath, but I knew that would not help. Without even thinking, my brain must have automatically felt that music would help me. I found myself singing 'God Bless America' to myself in my head. The music sounded so loud and powerful that I could not focus on the blood test and the singing at the same time. The music won, the test was over, and I was thrilled to realize that I had found a tool to help me with these kinds of procedures. I have tried it on a few other occasions, and it has been successful for me—even with other songs.

(quoted in Hanser, 2005, p. 42)

In a review of the literature on music therapy in adult oncology, both qualitative and quantitative research support the efficacy of music. Outcomes included pain management, symptom relief, reduction of distress, mood change, and enhanced quality of life. The most successful strategies included guided imagery and music, music with verbal suggestions, active music making, and live music by a music therapist (Hanser, 2006).

30.8 THE FUTURE OF MUSIC, HEALTH AND WELL-BEING

30.8.1 New directions in theory: the breakout principle

Now that the relaxation response has been documented, Herbert Benson has continued to generate theories about the factors that enhance well-being. The breakout refers to a decisive break in one's cognitive or emotional patterns. The principle is actually a four-stage process that takes advantage of the innate ability to heal oneself. It leads to creative solutions to problems or optimal performance through (1) a mental or physical struggle, (2) a letting go or release from the struggle, (3) a peak experience, and (4) a new state of improved performance and mind-body patterns (Benson & Proctor, 2003). The principle explains how a peak experience with music is capable of transforming a person's state of mind, body, and spirit.

Research on the neurology of the breakout principle documents the release of nitric oxide, a substance found in every human cell, in that second stage or release, just before a peak experience or breakout occurs. Nitric oxide has been associated with increased immune function, lower blood pressure, and other benefits to health (Stefano, Fricchione, Slingsby, & Benson, 2001). Surely the peak experiences described by Gabrielsson may have the same sort of impact (Chapter 20, this volume). Research has yet to be conducted on the effect of music on production of nitric oxide, but this offers an intriguing prospect for further investigation. Experimentation on the release of dopamine and other neurochemical agents and on various markers of immune function also hold promise for future research.

30.8.2 New directions in practice: Advance Music Directive

In order to construct the most potentially effective music strategy to bring about health and well-being, a person must be engaged in a deliberate process to identify and test the impact of different musical experiences. An innovation that empowers people to determine how they wish to use music in their care is the Advance Music Directive (Chadwick & Wacks, 2005). This concept is also known as the 'music living will' because of its similarity to the traditional legal document. The Advance Music Directive (AMD) is provided by a music therapist for persons of any age who wish to plan ahead, should a life-changing health event occur. After the therapist completes a review of the important music in the person's life, an extensive playlist is constructed, including selections targeted for their influence upon the person's physical and emotional condition. If individuals are not able to state their own preferences at the time when injury or catastrophic diagnosis occurs, the AMD, held in the records of the music therapist, physician, attorney, family and other designees, is enacted. A predetermined AMD treatment plan describes the use of the chosen music, which is then applied to energize and relax the patient, relieve emotional suffering, and elevate spiritual contentment. If one believes that music can affect health and well-being, then this process can ensure that the music which has the greatest impact will be accessible when the person needs it most.

30.8.3 New directions in society: the healing
empowerment centre

Recently a student in architecture and interior design at Parsons School of Design at New School University proposed the building of a healing empowerment centre.

The facility would offer education and services for healthy individuals in order to develop optimal functioning and help them realize their potential. The centre would contain four levels: the ground floor for meditation; the second floor for bodywork, massage, and exercise; the third floor for co-counselling and support groups; and the fourth floor for the staff to oversee operations. Nature, music, colour, light, and air are incorporated into the design (Hanser, 2004). It would be a place for people to concentrate on their mental, physical, and spiritual health and to apply their creativity towards self-actualization. Exploring emotion through music is one way that individuals could be empowered to live full lives and enjoy life. This vision is for a future that encourages the creative in every human being.

30.9 Conclusions

Health and well-being are being redefined as research uncovers former mysteries of mind and body. Psychoneuroimmunology has built a foundation for explaining the impact of music and emotion on health, and positive approaches to psychology have helped describe how music facilitates well-being. Engaging with music becomes a form of integrative medicine that benefits the whole person. As more sophisticated technology facilitates an understanding of human functioning in both the body and brain, there are more data to support the powerful impact of music. Yet, experimentation cannot control the numerous factors that affect a person's response to music (e.g. preference, familiarity, history, images generated, memories evoked). Indeed, scientific inquiry delves into those aspects of music that are capable of observation and description. This challenge has not daunted the many music psychologists, researchers and therapists who witness the benefits of music on health and well-being, and are devoting their careers to investigating new ways of exploring this extraordinary relationship.

Recommended further reading

1. Hanser, S. B. (1999). *The new music therapist's handbook*. Boston, MA: Berklee Press.
2. Levitin, D. J. (2006). *This is your brain on music*. New York: Dutton.
3. Sacks, O. (2007). *Musicophilia*. New York: Alfred A. Knopf.

References

American Cancer Society. (2007). *Cancer facts and figures 2007*. Retrieved from: www.cancer.org

American Heart Association. (2005). *Heart disease and stroke statistics—2005 update.* Retrieved from: http://americanheart.org/presenter.jhtml

Bartlett, D., Kaufman, D., & Smeltekop, R. (1993). The effects of music listening and perceived sensory experiences on the immune system as measured by interleukin-1 and cortisol. *Journal of Music Therapy, 30,* 194–209.

Beecher, H. (1959). *Measurement of subjective responses.* Oxford: Oxford University Press.

Benson, H. (1976). *The relaxation response.* New York: HarperCollins.

Benson, H., & Klipper, M. Z. (2000). *The relaxation response.* New York: HarperColllins.

Benson, H., & Proctor, W. (2003). *The breakout principle.* New York: Scribner.

Bittman, B. B., Berk, L. S., Felten, D. L. O., Westengard, J., Simonton, O. C., Pappas, J., & Ninehouser, M. (1994). Composite effects of group drumming music therapy on modulation of neuroendocrine-immune parameters in normal subjects. *European Journal of Applied Physiology, 69,* 451–9.

Blood, A. J., & Zatorre, R. J. (2001). Intensely pleasurable responses to music correlate with activity in brain regions implicated in reward and emotion. *Proceedings of National Academy of Sciences, 98,* 11818–23.

Cannon, W. B. (1932). *The wisdom of the body.* New York: Norton.

Cepeda, M. S., Carr, D. B., Lau, J., & Alvarez, H. (2006). Music for pain relief. *Cochrane database of systematic reviews 2006, Issue 2.* DOI: 10.1001/146651858.

Chadwick, D., & Wacks, K. (2005). *Music Advance Directives: Music choices for later life.* Paper presented at the 11th World Congress of Music Therapy, Brisbane, Australia, July 2005.

Charnetski, C. J, Brennan, F. X., & Harrison, J. F. (1998). Effects of music and auditory stimuli on secretory immunoglobulin. *Perceptual and Motor Skills, 87,* 1163–70.

Cohen, S., Doyle, W. J., Turner, R. B., Alper, C. M., & Skoner, D. P. (2003). Emotional style and susceptibility to the common cold. *Psychosomatic Medicine, 65,* 652–7.

Daubenmier, J. J., Weidner, G., Sumner, M. D., Mendell, N., Merritt-Worden, T., Studley, J., & Ornish, D. (2007). The contribution of changes in diet, exercise, and stress management to changes in coronary risk in women and men in the mnultisite cardiac lifestyle intervention program. *Annals of Behavioral Medicine, 33,* 57–68.

Davidson, R. J., Kabat-Zinn, J., Schumacher, J., Rosenkranz, M., Muller, D., Santorelli, S. F., Ubranowski, F., Harrington, A., Bonus, K., & Sheridan, J. F. (2003). Alterations in brain and immune function produced by mindfulness meditation. *Psychosomatic Medicine, 65,* 564–70.

Durham, L., & Collins, M. (1986). The effect of music as a conditioning aid in prepared childbirth education. *Journal of Obstetric, Gynecologic, and Neonatal Nursing, 15,* 268–70.

Elias, J., & Ketcham, K. (1998). *Chinese medicine for maximum immunity: Understanding the five elemental types for health and well-being.* New York: Three Rivers Press.

Enck, P., Benedetti, F., & Schedlowski, M. (2008). New insights into the placebo and nocebo responses. *Neuron, 59,* 195–206.

Evers, S., & Suhr, B. (2000). Changes of the neurotransmitter serotonin but not of hormones during short time music perception. *European Archives of Psychiatry and Clinical Neuroscience, 250,* 144–7.

Ferrell, B. R., & Rhiner, M. (1991). High-tech comfort: ethical issues in cancer pain management for the 1990s. *Journal of Clinical Ethics, 2,* 108–12.

Frederickson, B. L. (2001). The role of positive emotions in positive psychology: The broaden-and-build theory of positive emotions. *American Psychologist, 56,* 218–26.

Fredrickson, B. L., & Losadis, M. F. (2005). Positive affect and the complex dynamics of human flourishing. *American Psychologist, 60,* 678–86.

Fuente-Fernandez, R., Phillips, A. G., Zamburlini, M., Sossi, V., Calne, D. B., Ruth, T. J., & Stoessi, A. J. (2002). Dopamine release in human ventral striatum and expectation of reward. *Behavioural Brain Research*, 136, 359–63.

Gfeller, K. E. (1988). Musical components and styles preferred by young adults for aerobic fitness activities. *Journal of Music Therapy*, 25, 28–43.

Gilbert, M. D. (2003). Weaving medicine back together: Mind-body medicine in the twenty-first century. *Journal of Alternative and Complementary Medicine*, 9, 563–70.

Gold, C. (2007). *Effects of music therapy for people with psychoses and other psychiatric disorders: Systematic review and meta-analysis.* Paper presented at the 7th European Music Therapy Congress, Veldhoven, The Netherlands, August 2007.

Gold, C., Heidal, T. O., Dahle, T., & Wigram, T. (2005). Music therapy for schizophrenia and schizophrenia-like illnesses. *Cochrane database of systematic reviews 2005, Issue 2*, Chichester, UK: John Wiley & Sons.

Grape, C., Sandgren, M., Hansson, L., Ericson, M., & Theorell, T. (2003). Does singing promote well-being? An empirical study of professional and amateur singers during a singing lesson. *Integrative Physiological and Behavioral Science*, 38, 65–74.

Hanser, Samuel B. (2004). *The healing empowerment center: A radical vision for our future.* Unpublished senior thesis, Parsons School of Design, The New School University, New York, USA.

Hanser, S. B. (2005). Music therapy to enhance coping in terminally ill adult cancer patients. In C. Dileo & J. V. Loewy (eds), *Music therapy at the end of life* (pp. 33–42). Cherry Hill, NJ: Jeffrey Books.

Hanser, S. B. (2006). Music therapy research in adult oncology. *Journal of the Society for Integrative Oncology*, 4, 62–6.

Hanser, S. B. (2008). *Playlists for the soul.* Boston, MA: Dana-Farber Cancer Institute.

Hanser, S. B., Bauer-Wu, S., Kubicek, L., Healey, M., Manola, J., Hernandez, M., & Bunnell, C. (2006). Effects of a music therapy intervention on quality of life and distress in women with metastatic breast cancer. *Journal of the Society for Integrative Oncology*, 5, 14–23.

Hanser, S. B., & Codding, P. (2008). Music therapy. In M. I. Weintraub, R. Mamtani, & M. S. Micozzi (eds), *Complementary and integrative medicine in pain management* (pp. 41–68). New York: Springer.

Hanser, S. B., Larson, S. C., & O'Connell, A. S. (1983). The effect of music on relaxation of expectant mothers during labor. *Journal of Music Therapy*, 20, 50–8.

Hanser, S. B., & Mandel, S. E. (2004). The effects of music therapy on cardiac healthcare. *Cardiology in Review*, 13, 18–23.

Hanser, S. B., & Thompson, L. W. (1994). Effects of a music therapy strategy on depressed older adults. *Journal of Gerontology*, 49, 265–9.

Harrington, A. (2008). *The cure within: A history of mind-body medicine.* New York: Norton.

Hofmann, S., & Smits, J. (2008). Cognitive-behavioral therapy for adult anxiety disorders: a meta-analysis of randomized placebo-controlled trials. *Journal of Clinical Psychiatry*, 69, 621–32.

Hucklebridge, F., Lambert, S., Clow, A., Warburton, D. M., Evans, P. D., & Sherwood, N. (2000). Modulation of secretory immunoglobulin A in saliva: response to manipulation of mood. *Biological Psychology*, 53, 25–35.

International Association for the Study of Pain. (2007). *What is pain?* Retrieved from: www.iasp-pain.org/AM/Template.cfm?Section=Home&section=Pain_Clinical_Updates

Keyes, C. L. M. (2002). The mental health continuum: From languishing to flourishing in life. *Journal of Health and Social Behavior*, 45, 207–22.

Khalfa, S., Dalla Bella, S., Roy, M., Peretz, I., & Lupien, S. J. (2003). Effects of relaxing music on salivary cortisol level after psychological stress. *Annals of the New York Academy of Sciences*, 999, 374–6.

Kreutz, G., Bongard, S., Rohrmann, S., Hodapp, V., & Grebe, D. (2004). Effects of choir singing or listening on secretory immunoglobulin A, cortisol, and emotional state. *Journal of Behavioral Medicine*, 27, 623–35.

Kuhn, D. (2002). The effects of active and passive participation in musical activity on the immune system as measured by salivary immunoglobulin A. *Journal of Music Therapy*, 39, 30–9.

Lazar, S. W., Bush, G., Gollub, R. L., Randy, L., Fricchione, G. L., Khalsa, G., & Bensen, H. (2000). Functional brain mapping of the relaxation response and meditation. *Neuroreport*, 11, 1581–5.

Leventhal, H., Weinman, J., Leventhal, E., & Phillips, L. (2008). Health psychology: The search for pathways between behavior and health. *Annual Review of Psychology*, 59, 477–505.

Lu, H. C. (2005). *Traditional Chinese medicine: An authoritative and comprehensive guide*. Long Beach, CA: Basic Health Publications.

Mahoney, D. L., Burroughs, W. J., & Lippman, L. G. (2002). Perceived attributes of health-promoting laughter: A cross-generational comparison. *Journal of Psychology*, 136, 171–181.

Maison, A., Herbert, J. R., Werheimer, M. D., & Kabat-Zinn, J. (1995). Meditation, melatonin and breast/prostate cancer: hypothesis and preliminary data. *Medical Hypotheses*, 44, 39–46.

Mandel, S. E. (2007). *Effects of music-assisted relaxation and imagery (MARI) on health-related outcomes in cardiac rehabilitation: Follow-up study*. Unpublished doctoral dissertation, Union Institute & University, Cincinnati, OH, USA.

Mandel, S. E., Hanser, S. B., Secic, M, & Davis, B. A. (2007). Effects of music therapy on health-related outcomes in cardiac rehabilitation: A randomized controlled trial. *Journal of Music Therapy*, 44, 176–97.

McCraty, R., Atkinson, M., Rein, G., & Watkins, A. D. (1996). Music enhances the effect of positive emotional states on salivary IgA. *Stress Medicine*, 12, 167–75.

McKinney, C. H., Antoni, M. H., Kumar, M., Tims, F. C., & McCabe, P. M. (1997). Effects of guided imagery and music (GIM) therapy on mood and cortisol in healthy adults. *Health Psychology*, 16, 390–400.

McKinney, C. H., Tims, F. C., Kumar, A., & Kumar, M. (1997). The effect of selected classical music and spontaneous imagery on plasma beta-endorphin. *Journal of Behavioral Medicine*, 20, 85–99.

Melzack, R. (2001). Pain and the neuromatrix in the brain. *Journal of Dental Education*, 65, 1378–82.

Melzack, R., & Wall, P. D. (1965). Pain mechanisms: A new theory. *Science*, 150, 971–979.

Menon, V., & Levitin, D. (2005). The rewards of music listening: response and physiological connectivity of the mesolimbic system. *Neuroimage*, 28, 175–84.

Middleton, R. A., & Byrd, E. K. (1996). Psychosocial factors and hospital readmission status of older persons with cardiovascular disease. *Journal of Applied Rehabilitation Counseling*, 27, 3–10.

Mora, P., Halm, E., Leventhal, H., & Ceric, F. (2007). Elucidating the relationship between negative affectivity and symptoms: the role of illness-specific affective responses. *Annals of Behavioral Medicine*, 34, 77–86.

Ornish, D., Scherwitz, L. W., Billings, J. H., Brown, S. E., Gould, K. L., Merritt, T. A., Sparler, S., Armstrong, W. T., Ports, T. A., Kirkeeide, R. L., Hogeboom, C., & Brand, R. J. (1998). Intensive lifestyle changes for reversal or coronary heart disease. *Journal of the American Medical Association*, 280, 2001–7.

Pelletier, C. L. (2004). The effect of music on decreasing arousal due to stress: a meta-analysis. *Journal of Music Therapy*, 41, 192–214.

Peterson, S., Peto, V., & Rayner, M. (2004). Coronary heart disease statistics. Retrieved from: www. heartstats. org

Phundoung, S., & Good, M. (2003). Music reduces sensation and distress of labor pain. *Pain Management in Nursing*, 4, 54–61.

Remen, R. (2008). Practicing a medicine of the whole person: an opportunity for healing. *Hematology/Oncology Clinics of North America*, 22, 767.

Rider, M., & Achterberg, J. (1989). Effect of music-assisted imagery on neutrophils and lymphocytes. *Biofeedback and Self-Regulation*, 14, 247–57.

Schwartz, M. S., & Andrasik, F. (eds). (2003). *Biofeedback* (3rd edn). New York: Guilford Press.

Selye, H. (1956). *The stress of life*. New York: McGraw-Hill.

Smith, A., & Nicholson, K. (2001). Psychosocial factors, respiratory viruses and exacerbation of asthma. *Psychoneuroendocrinology*, 26, 411–20.

Son, Y. (2008). [The development and effects of an integrated symptom management program for prevention of recurrent cardiac events after percutaneous coronary intervention]. *Taehan Kanho Hakhoe Chi*, 38, 217–28.

Stefano, G. B., Fricchione, G. I., Slingsby, B. T., & Benson, H. (2001). The placebo effect and the relaxation response: Neural processes and their coupling to constitutive nitric oxide. *Brain Research Reviews*, 35, 1–19.

Stone, A. A., Cox, D. S., Valdimarsdottir, H., Jandorf, L., & Neale, J. M. (1987). Evidence that secretory IgA antibody is associated with daily mood. *Journal of Personality and Social Psychology*, 52, 988–93.

Sutoo, D., & Akiyama, K. (2004). Music improves dopaminergic neurotransmission: demonstration based on the effect of music on blood pressure regulation. *Brain Research*, 1016, 255–62.

Trout, K. K. (2004). The neuromatrix theory of pain: Implications of selected nonpharmacologic methods of pain relief for labor. *Journal of Midwifery & Women's Health*, 49, 482–8.

Tugade, M. M., Fredrickson, B. L., & Barrett, L. F. (2004). Psychological resilience and positive emotional granularity: Examining the benefits of positive emotions on coping and health. *Journal of Personality*, 72, 1161–90.

Uman, L., Chambers, C., McGrath, P., & Kisely, S. (2008). A systematic review of randomized controlled trials examining psychological interventions for needle-related procedural pain and distress in children and adolescents: an abbreviated Cochrane review. *Journal of Pediatric Psychology*, 33, 842–54.

World Health Organization. (2007). *Depression*. Retrieved from: www.who.int/mental_health/ management/depression/definition

World Health Organization. (1999). Ageing—exploding the myths. *Ageing and Health Programme (AHE)* (pp. 1–21). Geneva, Switzerland: World Health Organization.

....

CHAPTER 31

MUSIC AS A
SOURCE OF
EMOTION IN FILM

....

ANNABEL J. COHEN

EMOTION characterizes the experience of film as it does the experience of music. Because music almost always accompanies film, we may well ask what contribution music makes to the emotional aspects of film. The present chapter addresses this question.

Despite the integral role of music for film, film music has been largely neglected by the disciplines of both musicology and music psychology until recently (Cohen, 1994; Marks, 1997; Prendergast, 1992). The reasons for the neglect are complex, arising from social, technological, economic, historical, and cultural factors. Some of these factors also account for a parallel neglect by psychology of the study of film perception (Hochberg & Brooks, 1996a, 1996b). Moreover, unlike other types of popular or art music, much music for film has been composed with the understanding that it will not be consciously attended (Gorbman, 1987; Kassabian, 2001). Countering this neglect, the present chapter takes a psychological perspective on the sublime and remarkable emotional phenomena produced by music in the context of film. The chapter has the joint intent of supporting the argument that music is one of the strongest sources of emotion in film and of opening doors to further empirical work that explains why this is so.

The chapter is divided into five sections. Section 31.1 briefly establishes a context for discussing emotion in music and film. Section 31.2 focuses on music in film, first establishing a historical perspective and then examining the role of music at the interface of the fictional and non-fictional elements of film. It continues with empirical studies of music as a source of inference and structure, and it then summarizes functions that music serves for film. Section 31.3 presents a cognitive framework for understanding musical soundtrack phenomena previously described. Section 31.4 considers the role of the composer as the origin of the source of musical emotion for film. Conclusions are drawn and future directions are suggested in Section 31.5.

31.1 EMOTION: DEFINITIONS IN MUSIC AND FILM CONTEXTS

In the present chapter, the term film refers to the narrative dramas characteristic of movie theatres, television, and video with which most people are familiar as a source of entertainment. Music typically accompanies a considerable proportion of the duration of such films. Because of the relative novelty of the empirical study of film music in general, let alone the study of the emotional contribution of music in film, it would be premature to advocate a particular way of considering emotion in the present chapter. What is more important is to show how various 'music-alone' perspectives on emotion translate in the film context. These perspectives include the contribution of music to recognition of an emotion without necessarily feeling the emotion (e.g. Flores-Gutiérrez et al, 2007; Juslin, 1997; Levi, 1982), the establishment of subjective feeling (e.g. Pignatiello, Camp, & Rasar, 1986), and the experience of intense, affective reactions (Gabrielsson, 1998; Gabrielsson & Lindström; 1993; Sloboda, 1985, 1992).

The film context sometimes permits greater terminological clarity than the music-alone situation. For example, consider the terms *mood* and *emotion*, which are often differentiated with respect to the presence of an object (e.g. Barrett & Russell, 1999; Juslin & Västfjäll, 2008; Tan, 1996). Whereas both moods and emotions may be regarded as dispositions toward appraising emotional meaning structures and a readiness to respond in a certain manner, moods do not have objects; emotions do. For example, experiencing the emotion of relief requires an object of that emotion, such as a safe arrival after a treacherous journey. Experiencing a sad mood does not require an object of the sadness. Objects are not always evident in music-alone contexts, but, as argued by musicologist Nicholas Cook (1998), in a multimedia context, music readily finds an object. The emotional associations generated by music attach themselves automatically to the visual focus of attention or the implied topic of the narrative. Because film content provides the object of emotion generated by music, the film helps to control the definition of the object of the emotion experienced during the presence of music.

Considering music and emotion within the context of film also has the advantage of bringing knowledge from psychological studies of film to bear on questions regarding music and emotion. Based on the emotion theorist Frijda (1986), Tan (1996) for example, who refers to film as an 'emotion machine', addresses the question of the genuine nature of emotions in film, a topic that will be examined later in this chapter. Thus, research on music and emotion in the film context may benefit from research insights derived from studies of film and emotion. Conversely, our understanding of emotion associated with autonomous music may shed light on emotional processes that occur in the film context. All of this information may contribute to the understanding of both the unique accomplishment of composing music for film and the extent to which music provides an important source of emotion in film.

31.2 MUSIC AND CINEMA

31.2.1 Historical background

Beginnings. From the earliest days of film, music played a part. When silent film was first introduced at the turn of the century, music was enlisted to mask the extraneous noise of the film projector. While serving this function, music was also exploited to illustrate and explain the action (Palmer, 1980, p. 549). Kracauer (1960, p. 133) emphasizes that the noise problem of the film projection was relatively shortlived, and yet the importance of music remained. An entire music-for-the-silent-film industry developed to support this function of music (Limbacher, 1974; Thomas, 1997, pp. 37–40). It included publication of anthologies of music to represent various emotional settings, an increased demand for pianos in the thousands of small movie theatres that sprang up, and architectural plans for movie theatres that included places for pianists and sometimes other musicians.

Hugo Münsterberg. The first psychologist to direct attention to the new phenomenon of film was Hugo Münsterberg, a Harvard University professor (Figure 31.1). Between 1899 and 1916, he wrote 24 books, one of the last of which was *The Photoplay: A psychological study.* In what is regarded as the first book on film theory (Anderson, 1997), Münsterberg's views are enlightening. His experience of film was as fresh as a child's, although acquired as a highly intelligent adult. His understanding of both introspection and scientific method encourage our confidence in his record of and insight into film at that time:

Yes, it is a new art—and this is why it has such fascination for the psychologist who in a world of ready-made arts, each with a history of many centuries, suddenly finds a new form still undeveloped and hardly understood. For the first time the psychologist can observe the starting of an entirely new esthetic development, a new form of true beauty in the turmoil of a technical age, created by its very technique and yet more than any other art destined to overcome outer nature by the free and joyful play of the mind.

(Münsterberg, 1916/1970, pp. 232–3)

He did not live to experience the talking film, but his experience of film was not lacking in sound. There were sound effects—he describes a machine, the allefex, 'which can produce over fifty distinctive noises, fit for any photoplay emergency' (p. 205)—and there was music. In his view, music relieved tension, maintained interest ('keeps the

Fig. 31.1 Hugo Münsterberg (right) with members of the Vitagraph Co. The Psychologist is being shown the technique of moving pictures. (Circa 1915). [HUP Munsterberg, Hugo (1), Harvard University Archives].

attention awake'), provided comfort, reinforced emotion, and contributed to the aesthetic experience (pp. 204–5).

Münsterberg also used musical metaphor in describing the film experience (e.g. p. 120, pp. 128–9). For example, he recounts a narrative cliché of the period, a rapid alternation between three scenes: a jovial boss and his secretary enjoying a private after-hours party in the office, the dismal parents of the secretary awaiting their daughter's return, and the lonely wife awaiting her husband's attention. 'It is as if we saw one through another, as if three tones blended into one chord ... The photoplay alone gives us our chance for such omnipresence' (p. 105). Yet, to extend his metaphor of the musical chord, it is also music that can represent in rapid succession and perhaps simultaneously the emotional polyphony of these multiple messages.

Münsterberg directed attention to the importance of music within the film and to music as a means of understanding the psychological processes underlying film. Musical analogies to film were actually once common among film directors and theorists (e.g. Eisenstein, 1949; Mitry, 1963/1997). Münsterberg suggested that cinema is more similar to music than to photography and drama, which on the surface are arts that bear a more striking resemblance:

... we come nearer to the understanding of its [film's] true position in the aesthetic world, if we think at the same time of ... the art of the musical tones. They have overcome the outer world and social world entirely, they unfold our inner life, our mental play, with its feelings and emotions, its memories and fancies, in a material which seems exempt from the laws of the world of substance and material, tones which are fluttering and fleeting like our own mental states.

(p. 168)

Münsterberg's untimely death in 1916 (the year of his publication of *The Photoplay*) and the coincident advent of Behaviourism, focusing as it did on objectively observable behaviour, may in part account for the failure of psychological research in film and music to progress in parallel with the technological developments associated with these media. Instead, technology developed and its psychological study lagged behind in spite of a good start.

The sound film. In 1927, *The Jazz Singer* signalled the advent of the *talkies* and the demise of the film-music industry. With real voices and sound effects, music would no longer be needed to establish mood and emotional context—or would it? To the surprise of many, something was missing without music (Kracauer, 1960, p. 138). The screen had lost part of its vitality. As Kalinak (1992) says, 'when the possibility of synchronized speech and sound effects released sound film from its reliance upon continuous musical accompaniment, it initially rejected music entirely. But the life span of the all-talking picture was brief, the need that music filled quickly reasserting itself' (p. 45).

Several theorists have commented that music adds a third dimension to the two-dimensional film screen (Palmer, 1990; Rosar, 1994). Composers also shared this view. Aaron Copland (1941) stated 'the screen is a pretty cold proposition'. Film composer David Raksin (in Brown, 1994, p. 282) referred to Nietzsche's idea, 'without music, life would not be worth living'. His statement is extreme (deaf persons live worthwhile lives), but paraphrasing the maxim, few hearing people would deny that music contributes to their experience of film.

Since the early days of film, directors have recognized the contribution that film-editing made to the viewer, often referred to as *montage*. Viewers are typically unaware of the rapid changes in camera angle, the move from close-up to long-shot or from one part of the scene to another and back again. Nonetheless, viewers make sense of the world depicted by these juxtaposed shots. Theories of montage concern the audience's synthesis of juxtaposed information in the film. With the advent of the sound film, Russian director Sergei Eisenstein was among the first to extend the notion of visual montage to sound, and suggested that the listener incorporates the same synthetic process in making sense of the entire audiovisual cinematic presentation.

31.2.2 Music and the diegesis and the non-diegesis

Film theory commonly refers to the fictional, imagined, narrative world of the film as the *diegesis*. In contrast, the *non-diegesis* refers to the objective world of the audience, the world of artefact, of film screens, projectors, proficiency of actors, and technical aspects of the film. In terms of physical reality, music as acoustic vibrations belongs to the non-diegesis. Logically—unless such sound were part of a scene portrayed in a film, as in a film about a musical instrument, or the life of a great composer—these sounds of music should *detract from* rather than *add to* the sense of reality of the film. This point was well made in Mel Brooks's comedy *Blazing Saddles* (1974). A sheriff rides out on the desert—with seemingly appropriate music in the background—and meets face to face with the Count Basie Band performing the now inappropriate music 'April in Paris'. The fictional (diegetic) and the non-fictional (non-diegetic) realities collide and add to the humour of the scene. It is probably not coincidental that Brooks, the director and screenwriter of the film, is also a composer of music including some film scores, and so he would have been particularly sensitive to this film-score convention.

Thus, the audience selectively attends to only the part of the music that makes sense with the narrative. Selective attention is a common perceptual-cognitive operation. The phenomenon of 'inattentional blindness' is an example of it in the visual domain of film. Here it has been shown that people rarely noticed or were seldom distracted by impossible visual aspects represented in either a film or in their real-world experience. For example, viewers did not notice that a woman in a film clip began a short scene with a scarf and ended the scene without it (Levin & Simons, 2000). In another study, an experimenter positioned on a college campus solicited directions from unsuspecting students. Their conversation was interrupted by two confederates carrying a door. One of the confederates changed position with the experimenter who had initially asked for directions. The conversation about directions then continued. The student rarely realized that there were two different people to whom he or she had been conversing. Two facts are important here. First, the visual system is blind to much available information, and this inattentional blindness (cf. Mack & Rock, 1998) is equally characteristic of vision in the real and in the film world. Thus, the fact that audiences extract the emotional information in music and fail to attend to the acoustical aspects might be described as a case of inattentional deafness, a by-product of the fact that awareness depends on attention, and attentional capacity is limited. Indeed, the failure to notice a noxious sound (fingernails down a chalkboard) attests to the generality of the phenomenon to hearing (Wayand, Levin, & Varakin, 2005). A better parallel can be drawn to the role of prosody in speech perception, which shares with music a greater syntactic similarity than the visual or noise examples given. Here patterns of intensity and frequency from intonation systematically provide emotional meaning to a listener, yet the listener focuses on the meaning and is unconscious of this prosodic source of information (e.g. Banse & Scherer, 1996; Murray & Arnott, 1993).

Film-music scholar Claudia Gorbman (1987) has addressed the unconscious perception of film music in her book *Unheard melodies: Narrative film music*. Gorbman's perspective is well captured by Jeff Smith (1996): 'By veiling the lacks and deficiencies of other discursive structures, film music, according to Gorbman, lubricates the various cogs and pistons of the cinematic pleasure machine' (p. 234). Film-music theorist Anahid Kassabian (2001) challenges the notion of the either–or dichotomy—diegetic/non-diegetic—and argues that some film music is ambiguous in this regard. She also claims that in the absence of sound effects and dialogue, a music track draws attention to itself (p. 24). We may well ask why a director would choose music over meaningful dialogue or sound-effects at a critical point in the drama. A case in point is provided by the film *Witness*.

In *Witness*, a young Amish boy is the sole observer of a violent murder in a train station. He is directed to a noisy police station in order to search through a book of photographs of suspects for a match of his memory to the actual perpetrator of the crime. While left unattended momentarily, he wanders toward a display cabinet that holds a photograph of an honoured senior officer in the police force. As he views the photograph, Maurice Jarre's music replaces the background sound effects of the police station. The audience realizes that the boy becomes awestruck with the sudden recognition that the photograph of the police officer depicts the person who he saw commit the crime. The audience would be concerned now about the implications for the safety of the boy. This is one of the most critical points in the film, essential to the plot. Without it, the criminal in the police force would remain unknown and the boy could continue naïvely on his trip. Yet it is this crucial moment, a moment that must be comprehended by the audience, to which the unrealistic music is not merely added but is added at the expense of realistic, diegetic sound effects. But the audience, caught in the drama, is unlikely to note this departure from reality.

To examine whether music alone impacted the involvement in the film, Cohen, MacMillan, and Drew (2006) presented one minute of the *Witness* clip in a between-groups design so that participants saw the clip in only one of five soundtrack conditions: music-only, sound effects only, speech only, a combination of all three, and none. Participants were asked to rate their level of absorption (involvement) in the clip, their judged sense of reality, and the level of professional quality of the clip. The sound effects and speech tracks were composed especially for the experiment, and the music was the original soundtrack. A second set of clips was designed for an excerpt from *The Day of the Jackal*. The positive impact of the music on self-rated absorption in the film was evident for *Witness* but not for *Jackal*. The music-alone track for *Jackal* was perhaps not as effective because the original soundtrack in this case had contained music, dialogue, and sound effects, and the music-alone soundtrack that was developed from music used elsewhere in the film did not reach the same level of professional quality as the *Witness* excerpt. It is clear from this demonstration that music-alone can supersede the sound effects or dialogue in ability to involve the audience in the film. The extent to which an audience is actually aware of the music in a music-only soundtrack remains to be determined.

31.2.3 Music and inference: empirical studies

A number of studies have concerned the role of music in generating inferences, and often those inferences are associated with emotional meaning. Music presumably adds to the involvement in the diegesis while providing non-diegetic, acoustical information that is incompatible with the realism of the diegesis. At the interface of the diegetic and non-diegetic worlds, this typical use of music in film is paradoxical (Cohen, 1990). To escape the paradox, the analysis of the acoustical information can be regarded as a pre-attentive step that leads the listener to inferences consistent within the diegetic world of the film. From moment to moment, the audience member extracts information from non-diegetic sources to generate the emotional information he or she needs to make a coherent story in the diegesis. The successful director and film-score composer provide just the right cues to guide the attentional and inferences processes.

One attempt at understanding the phenemenon of diegetic inference comes from the context of psychological situation models described as 'vicarious experiences in narrative comprehension' (Zwaan, 1999, p. 15). Zwaan, for example, has focused on how literature enables readers to 'mentally leap into imagined worlds'. The information provided by the text is sufficient to enable a reader to place himself or herself at a spatial, temporal, and psychological vantage point from which events are vicariously experienced. The perspective is termed a deictic center.

Magliano, Dijkstra, and Zwaan (1996) extended the approach to the study of film. In their study, music was indirectly examined as one of six operationally defined film factors (such as montage) that might contribute to the psychological definition of the situation. In two experiments, they investigated visual, auditory, and discourse conditions that enable viewers to predict future events while viewing a James Bond movie, *Moonraker*. In Experiment 1, participants were instructed to generate predictions while watching the movie. In Experiment 2, participants provided 'think-aloud' protocols at different locations in the film. In both experiments, the presence of supporting visual and discourse information led to systematic predictions by the participant. Music significantly co-occurred with other cinematic sources of support such as montage and mise-en-scène, found to influence inference processes.[1]

The study by Magliano et al (1996) was not specifically designed to show the influence of music in the film context. Studies that have been so designed have been successful in showing this influence. Such studies typically require more conditions than do comparable studies in music-alone situations, because it is necessary to determine the effects of music-alone, film-alone, music judged in the context of film, and film judged in the context of music. The studies to be reported have often involved several if not all of these different comparison conditions.

In a study by Bullerjahn and Güldenring (1994), professional composers of film music (including Peer Rabin, composer for all Fassbinder films) created a total of five different backgrounds (e.g. crime, melodrama) for the same ten-minute film segment. Both quantitative and qualitative analysis showed that the different soundtracks led to different judgements of the appropriateness of emotional categories (e.g. sad, thrilling, sentimental, vivid), choice of genre (horror, comedy, thriller, crime, etc.), reasons for the actions of the protagonist, and expectations about the completion of the film. In some cases, these judgements and inferences could be attributed to specific aspects of the film. For example, the authors suggested that the final closure by the major chord of the melodrama music accounted for the presumed reconciliation, though it is preceded by an argument.

---

[1] When music was entered first into the regression equation, it too was found to be a significant predictor of inference, though accounting for only 6 per cent of the variance (J. P. Magliano, personal communication, June 6, 2000).

In a series of experiments, Thompson, Russo, and Sinclair (1994) specifically examined the effects of musical closure on perceived closure of a film. In their first experiment, a closed soundtrack ended with a traditional 'perfect' cadence (dominant chord to tonic chord ending). The unclosed soundtrack differed only with respect to the final bar, such that the ending was not on the tonic chord. Subjects viewed a short animation accompanied by one of the soundtracks, and were asked to rate the degree of closure represented by the clip. Judgements of closure were significantly higher for the condition in which the closed ending was presented. In a second experiment, a professional composer produced closed and unclosed soundtracks to accompany a short film clip produced by one of the experimenters. Closed soundtracks ended on the tonic chord, in contrast to the unclosed soundtracks. The effect of soundtrack closure was strong for only one of the film clips, suggesting that visual factors may take precedence over musical structure in some cases. In a final study, 12 separate soundtracks were composed for 12 clips from a commercial film, initially chosen for their assumed range in degree of closure. The soundtracks were also composed to represent a range of closure, and the degree of closure needed not to match that of the clip. Participants in the experiment judged the degree of closure of the soundtracks, the clips alone, and the soundtrack and clips together. The influence of independently judged visual and musical closure on judged closure of the film was shown through regression analysis, with a slightly greater contribution arising from visual than musical information. In addition to demonstrating a robust direct effect of musical structure on the feeling of closure of a film narrative, the authors also reported that the role of music was almost completely implicit. When participants were asked for the basis of their judgements, they almost always attributed their judgements to the visual information.

Boltz, Kantra, and Schulkind (1991) examined the role of music on inferences in a study that compared music that foreshadowed an outcome versus music that accompanied an outcome. Subjects viewed 20 different three- to four-minute clips from feature films and television dramas. Excerpts were selected that ultimately resolved in a happy (positive) or sad (e.g. tragic) way. Music emotionally consistent or inconsistent with these endings (as determined by music-alone ratings) either preceded (foreshadowed) or accompanied the video excerpt. Thus, in some cases the foreshadowing music correctly predicted the mood of the following video event and accompanying music was congruent with the mood of the video event, and in other cases foreshadowing music incorrectly predicted the subsequent event and accompanying music was incongruent with the event. Music accompanying an episode's outcome led to higher recall when the mood of the music and scene were congruent with each other. Conversely, mood-incongruent relations significantly lowered performance to a level comparable to that of the control condition in which no music had occurred. Foreshadowing, however, revealed the opposite pattern. Here, expectancy violations arising from mood-incongruent relations were significantly more memorable than were mood-congruent episodes in which viewers' expectancies were confirmed (pp. 597–8). Boltz et al (1991) concluded that their results supported the notion that viewers rely on the emotional expression of music to either generate expectancies about future scenarios or direct attending toward corresponding aspects of visual activities (p. 602).

In a further study (Boltz, 2004), participants were presented with the same clips accompanied by the congruent or incongruent soundtracks, and were asked to attend to the audio track, the video track, or to both tracks. Subsequently, they were tested for their memory of the visual film clips and the music. Performance in the mood-congruent condition was superior to that of the incongruent condition. Performance in the incongruent condition was good for the attended audio or visual medium, but did not extend to the unintended medium as it did when the mood of the music and video clip coincided. According to Boltz, congruence in mood of the music and film elicited a search for similar structural properties in the music and film, and the success of the search led to jointly encoding the music and visual material and an integrated music-video memory. Thus, memory for music information would mean memory for the visual information. However, without mood congruencies, attention to the entire music visual complex suffers as the focus is on only one of the modalities (as per instructions in the experiment) and attention directed to the other modality is not sustained due to incongruent meaning.

Marshall and Cohen (1988) also observed the ability of music to alter the interpretation of a simple visual presentation. They studied the effects of two different soundtracks on impressions about three geometric forms, a large and small triangle and a circle, in a short animation developed by Heider and Simmel (1944). In their experiment, subjects viewed the two-minute animation with one of two soundtracks or with no soundtrack (control condition). They then provided 12 ratings for the film overall and for the three figures. Other groups of subjects rated the music on these same scales. Each of the 12 scales represented a bipolar adjective pair (e.g. fast–slow, nice–awful) and specifically tapped one of the three dimensions of emotional meaning—activity, evaluation, and potency—comprising the semantic differential (Osgood, Suci, & Tannenbaum, 1957). The activity and evaluation dimensions are understood to represent the motivation (arousal) and appraisal (valence) dimensions associated with two-dimensional theories of emotion, on which many emotion theorists (Barrett & Russell, 1999; Lang, 1995; Storm & Storm, 1987) and music psychologists (Gregory, 1998; Madsen, 1997; Schubert, 1998) converge.

In Marshall and Cohen's (1988) study, two musical soundtracks were judged to have approximately the same activity level (measured by averaging responses on scales of fast–slow, active–passive, agitated–calm, restless–quiet). The relative activity levels of the three 'characters' in the film, however, differed for the two different musical backgrounds. For example, the large triangle was judged as the most active under one soundtrack, while the small triangle was judged as the most active in the other. Marshall and Cohen (1988) argued post hoc that shared accent patterns in the music and in the motion of the figures operated to focus attention on the temporally congruent part of the visual scene, and subsequently associations of the music were ascribed to this focus (see Figure 31.2). A similar accent-pattern/association breakdown in the processing of film and music was proposed by Lipscomb and Kendall (1994, p. 91).

Cook (1998), in his book *Analysis of musical multimedia*, has suggested the generality of Marshall and Cohen's (1988) theory to other multimedia examples in which musical meaning alters the interpretation of events that are at the focus of visual attention.

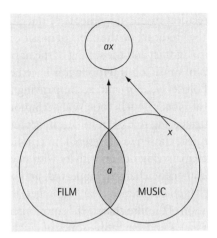

Fig. 31.2 Congruence–Associationist model based on that depicted by Marshall and Cohen (1988). The total meaning and structure of the music and film are presented by their respective circles. The overlap in music and film is depicted by the intersection of the circles (*a*). Attention is directed to this area of visual overlap in the film. Other associations of the music (*x*) are ascribed to this focus of attention (*ax*). Thus, music alters the meaning of a particular aspect of the film.

In advertisements for cars, for example, the car takes on both the vitality and the high-cultural associations of the classical music in the background. Music does more than provide an echo or counterpoint to a concept already present in the film. According to Cook, music can also direct attention to an object on the screen and establish emotionally laden inferences about that object.

Empirical evidence for the ability of music to focus attention is scant. It has been shown for simple geometric figures, but has not yet been demonstrated with more complex displays (cf. Lipscomb, 1999, 2005). Recent advances in the affordability of non-linear video editing equipment are facilitating the development of computer-generated isomorphic music and visual objects, leading to experiments that are showing that audiences are sensitive to temporal and formal congruencies, yet all experiment-defined congruencies are not necessarily picked up by the audience (Iwamiya, 2008; Kim & Iwamiya, 2008; Kendall, 2008).

Regarding the ability of music to focus attention, Bolivar, Cohen, and Fentress (1994), following Boltz et al (1991), noted that attention to a visual object might arise not only from structural congruencies, but also from semantic congruencies. Hypothetically, for example, a soundtrack featuring a lullaby might direct attention to a cradle rather than to a fishbowl when both objects were simultaneously depicted in a scene. Subsequently, additional associations from the lullaby would be ascribed to the cradle.

Shevy (2007) presented happy or ominous rock music or no music background for a video that featured a good (positive) character in a negative environment. Completion of rating scales by participants indicated that happy music had a positive influence on the interpretation of the environment, and that the presence of either kind of music increased the correlation in the judgements of the character and the environment. This study adds to the literature on the effect of music on interpretation in a film, here distinguishing the protagonist and the setting of the narrative.

Whereas the influences of music on interpretation have been shown for both fore-shadowing (Boltz, 2004; Boltz et al, 2001) and accompanying (Marshall & Cohen, 1988; Shevy, 2007; Thompson et al, 1994; Vitouch, 2001; Willis & Simons, 2005), Tan, Spackman, and Bezdek (2007) investigated the role of music on interpretation of an earlier event. Excerpts of 15 seconds of music chosen to represent four emotions were paired with four film clips of a film character carrying out an activity with neutral emotion. Music was presented either before or after the character appeared, and overlapped for only a few seconds. Music (conveing happiness, sadness, fear, and anger) in both positions systematically altered the interpretation of the film characters' emotions, as indicated by an analysis of the one-word emotion labels and the rating scales of eight emotions. Following the judgements of emotion, the participants rated the extent to which each of nine film factors (including presence of music) contributed to the depiction of the emotion of the film character. Participants ascribed their own judgements to two factors primarily: music and the facial expression of the film character, even though the facial expressions were neutral. Participants also rated aspects of the character's apparent physiological responses that were felt to portray emotion. These results clustered along two dimensions of action readiness and what the authors term 'valence' for terms 'energized' and 'trembling-shaking'. This two dimensional space led to the orderly placement of each music emotion (both pre- and post-film) in a distinct quadrant.

In another original study, Tan, Spackman, and Wakefield (2008) examined the effects of presenting the same piece of music diegetically or non-diegetically on viewers' interpretations of the film's narrative. They also explored the effects of non-diegetic music matching the mood of the scene (mood-congruent music) and non-diegetic music that was mood incongruent. An action sequence from Spielberg's *Minority Report* (2002) was paired with three soundtracks: (1) the original soundtrack, an orchestral rendition of the song 'Moon River' presented as if originating from within the environment of the characters (diegetic version); (2) the same recording of 'Moon River' presented as if a dramatic score (non-diegetic version), and (3) a third soundtrack, from a dramatic score accompanying a chase scene from *Empire of the Sun* (1987), serving as a mood-congruent condition to be compared with the mood-incongruent 'Moon River' soundtrack. In all versions, speech and sound effects remained intact, so that only the musical soundtrack was varied. Over 200 participants were asked to describe their interpretations of the film scene, and to rate various aspects of the film and music.

The mood of the film excerpt was rated as highest on a tense/antagonistic relationship between characters' dimensions and also highest on a 'calm' dimension when accompanied by the original score ('Moon River' diegetic); lowest on the calm dimension and highest on a tense/antagonistic relationship between characters' dimension when accompanied by the 'Moon River' non-diegetic music; and lowest on the calm dimension when accompanied by the non-diegetic congruent chase music. It was also found that participants' perceptions of the characters' emotions varied with musical soundtrack. For instance, the male character was seen as being less fearful and less excited and more romantically interested in the female character when the scene was accompanied by the non-diegetic version of 'Moon River' than the diegetic presentation of the same song. The study shows that audience perceptions of the emotions of film characters and overall emotion of the scene can differ significantly—depending on whether the music is presented diegetically or non-diegetically.

31.2.4 Functions of film music

Cohen (1999) described eight functions of music in a film or multimedia context. First, music masks extraneous noises. Second, it provides continuity between shots, for example, when the camera alternates between close-ups of two people who are presumably looking at each other (cf. Magliano et al, 1996, p. 205). Third, as Marshall and Cohen (1988) and Bolivar et al (1994) had argued, and as noted by Münsterberg (1916) and Cook (1998), it directs attention to important features of the screen through structural or associationist congruence. Fourth, it induces emotion, as often occurs during the opening credits of a film. The ability of music to induce mood has been shown experimentally (Pignatiello et al, 1986) and is used in music therapy (Albersnagel, 1988; see Chapter 29, this volume). Fifth, it communicates meaning and furthers the narrative, especially in ambiguous situations (Bullerjahn & Güldenring, 1994; Cohen, 1993; Kalinak, 1992; Levinson, 1996; Shevy, 2007; Tan, Spackman, & Bezdek, 2007; Vitouch, 2001). Sixth, through association in memory, music becomes integrated with the film (Boltz, 2004; Boltz et al, 1991), and enables the symbolization of past and future events through the technique of *leitmotif*. In leitmotif, a particular musical theme is continuously paired with a character or event so that eventually the theme conjures up the concept of the character or event in its absence (Kassabian, 2001; pp. 50–1; Palmer, 1980, p. 550). The composer Richard Wagner is typically regarded as the first to exploit this principle in opera. In an insightful article by the composer Saint-Saens (1903, p. 259), entitled 'The composer as psychologist', the author remarks that psychological principles must be responsible for the effectiveness of leitmotif. Mood-dependent memories can also be cued with the emotions established by music (Eich, 1995). Seventh, music heightens absorption in film, perhaps by augmenting arousal, and increasing attention to the entire film context and inattention to everything else (Cohen et al, 2008; cf. discussions of reality status by Preston, 1999; Qian, Preston, & House, 1999). Finally, music as an art form adds to the aesthetic effect of the film.

31.3 A COGNITIVE FRAMEWORK FOR UNDERSTANDING MUSICAL SOUNDTRACKS

Many of the functions of film music can be explained via notions of congruence or association, because these represent two primary ways in which the brain operates: through innate grouping principles (Bregman, 1990) and by learned connections (Cohen, 1993), respectively. Cohen (2005) presented a capacity-limited information-processing framework, which represented the congruence-association-ist concepts in a broad cognitive context. The model, referred to as the *Congruence-Associationist Model* (CAM), extends Marshall and Cohen's (1988) proposal of the importance of the congruence and associationist concepts to account for the influence of music on the interpretation of the Heider and Simmel (1944) film and film characters. The model has undergone several transformations to accommodate the growing empirical evidence specific to film music, as well as current perspectives in cognitive neuroscience.

The framework (see Figure 31.3) consists of five parallel channels along the vertical axis, each devoted to one of the significant domains of film as identified by the French film theorist Metz (described in Stam, 2000, p. 5 and p. 212): visual scenes, visual text, speech, sound effects (noise), and music. Each channel is hierarchically organized into four processing levels, with bottom-up levels (A and B) meeting the top-down level (D) at Level C, the level of conscious attention and working memory.

31.3.1 Bottom-up processes: levels A and B

Processing begins at level A with the analysis of physical features of the two visual and three auditory surfaces into components such as lines, phonemes, and frequencies.

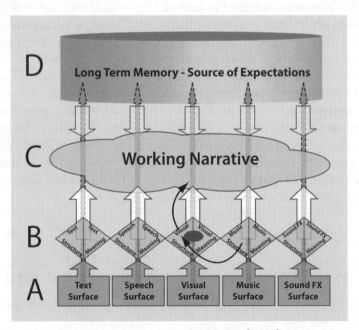

Fig. 31.3 Congruence–Associationist Model (CAM) for under-standing film–music communication (see text for explanation).

Within each of these domains, at the next level (B), groups of features are subsequently analysed into structural (gestalt-type) and semantic (associationist) information. For music, this means analysis into temporal structures (strong and weak beat patterns, segments, phrases) and categorization of cues of emotional meaning (e.g. pitch height, tempo, direction). For vision, this means motion-pattern analysis, segmentation, and analysis of temporal patterns, as well as assembly into meaningful objects. The outcome of analysis at level B affords the possibility for emergence of cross-modal congruencies, for example, shared accent patterns in audio and visual modalities, to lead pre-attention to only a portion of the visual information, shown here as the material within the oval in the visual channel. Some of the output from level B leaks through to level D, to be discussed in Section 31.3.2.

To further explain the concept of cross-modal congruence, cognitive psychologists have typically applied gestalt principles to visual pattern (Wertheimer, 1939) and later to auditory information (e.g. Bregman, 1990; Narmour, 1991). Rarely are the principles applied to the visual and auditory domains at once. But film music provides the necessity for such application (see Lipscomb, 2005; Kendall, 2008; Iwamiya, 2008). The simultaneous presentation of music and film automatically elicits bottom-up principles that entail perceptual grouping in both auditory and visual domains. When the auditory information and visual information are structurally congruent (e.g. share temporal accent patterns), the congruent information becomes the figure, the focus of attention (as originally argued by Marshall & Cohen, 1988). While usually in the film context that focus is visual, Boltz, Ebendorf, and Field (2009) have shown that the temporal format and emotional meaning of visual information can influence the intepretation and memory of ambiguous music.

As part of a larger study, Iwamiya (1994, pp. 134–5) showed that judgements of degree of audio-visual matching of four short film clips was lower when the original video and music components were desynchronized by 500 ms (the only delay examined), and more recently, Kim and Iwamiya (2008) have illustrated the impact of structural congruencies between telops (animated typographic letters) and auditory patterns. Thus, gestalt-theoretic ideas that are typically applied to visual or auditory domains independently can be applied to conjoint visual and auditory dynamic information. It follows that through innate or early-learned grouping processes, music can define the visual figure against the audiovisual background. According to CAM, music can sometimes determine the visual focus of attention.

More recently, a notion of temporal congruence, or temporal synchrony, has appeared in a solution to a general problem in cognition, that of consciousness. Cognitive scientists are focusing on the concept of 'binding' to explain how 'the unity of conscious perception is brought about by the distributed activities of the central nervous system' (Revonsuo & Newman, 1999, p. 123). Cognitive neuroscientists are attaching significance to neural synchronization (shared temporal patterning) across neural ensembles (Engel & Singer, 2001; Grossberg, 2007; Herrmann, Munk, & Engel, 2004; Kveraga, Ghuman, & Bar, 2007) following Grossberg (1980). Film music that shares patterns with visual information on the screen may therefore contribute to attention and consciousness by encouraging the elicitation of synchronous firing patterns of neurons that are measurable by EEG (electroencephalograph) or MEG (magnetoencephalograph), a more recent brain imaging technology. Indeed, neural oscillations have been proposed as necessary for information integration and the generation of the stream of consciousness characterizing working memory. Music is effective in generating synchronous firing patterns in the theta (4–8 Hz, Sammler, Grigutsch, Fritz, & Koelsch, 2007) and gamma range (>30 Hz, Bhattacharya & Petsche, 2005), the latter particularly for musicians. It is significant that music makes synchronous firing possible across disparate brain regions.

It is interesting to consider notions of congruent patterns in perceptual and cognitive psychology in relation to notions in the film-music literature on sensitivity to and effectiveness of synchronized musical and film structures. Kalinak (1992) suggests that it is this synchronization that contributes to the inaudibility of the music. Synchronization masks the real source of the sound (like ventriloquism):

The vocal track in classical cinema anchors diegetic sound to the image by synchronizing it, masking the actual source of sonic production, the speakers, and fostering the illusion that the diegesis itself produces the sounds. Mickey Mousing [synchronized music and visual accent] duplicates these conventions in terms of nondiegetic sound. Precisely synchronizing diegetic action to its musical accompaniment masks the actual source of sonic production, the offscreen orchestra, and renders the emanation of music natural and consequently inaudible. Musical accompaniment was thus positioned to effect perception, especially on semiconscious, without disrupting narrative credibility.

(Kalinak, 1992, p. 86)

31.3.2 Top-down processes: level D

We temporarily bypass level C because during bottom-up processing (A and B), some pre-attended information from all five channels leaks through to long-term memory (LTM) at D and begins a top-down inference process with the goal of constructing the narrative of the film—making the best story out of the two available sources of information, the surface information (A and B) and long-term memory (D). Thus, both bottom-up (A and B) and top-down (D) processes simultaneously generate information that meets at level C, which is referred to as the working narrative. In order to achieve consciousness of at least some of the information at A, matching of this information from B by inferences generated from LTM is necessary. The notion of such a matching process is found in theories of conscious attention (Grossberg's Adaptive Resonance Theory, ART; see Grossberg, 1995, 2007), comprehension (Kintsch, 1998, construction-integration), consciousness (Baars, 1997), and prediction of the environment (Kveraga et al, 2007). Each of these theories assumes or proposes that pre-attentive processes are sufficient to initiate the inference processes from LTM.[2]

[2] In Grossberg's (1996) theory, 'when both bottom-up and top-down signals are simultaneously active, only the bottom-up signals that receive top-down support can remain active ... Top-down matching hereby generates a focus of attention that can resonate across processing levels, including those that generate the top-down signals. Such a resonance acts as a trigger that activates learning

Kveraga et al (2007, p. 151) locate the source of the top-down predictions in the orbitofrontal cortex (OFC), 'a multimodal association area'. They propose that the brain extracts coarse gist information rapidly and sends it to OFC within 150 ms, time enough for it to establish predictions that can narrow down alternative interpretations of the original stimuli. Of particular interest to the present chapter, they connect the OFC to emotion via the amygdala and the medial prefrontal cortex, known for its involvement in the emotion of fear depicted by music (Gosselin et al, 2005). Kveraga et al (2007) suggest that this 'network employed in top-down facilitation of object perception may be part of an older system that evolved to quickly detect environmental stimuli with emotional significance' (p. 160). Similar proposals for predictive coding based on fast and slow gamma wave neural synchrony have been offered in Herrmann et al's (2004) match and utilization model (MUM). That model also incorporates the concept of binding of stimulus features through synchronous firing, and the engagement of long-term memory in perception.

From the perspective of film and film music, because everyday emotional experience associated with events is stored in LTM, inferences based on past experience would include emotion (e.g. how a protagonist would feel in a certain situation). These inferences generated by the LTM matching process accommodate the visual and emotional information from a film, but not the acoustical properties of the musical accompaniment that are the source of the emotional information. This explains why the acoustical aspects of the music are not generally attended: in the context of the rest of the narrative, the acoustical aspects of the music do not make sense to LTM (Where is that background music coming from?) and no hypotheses would be generated easily to include it (unless, of course, music were part of the diegesis, e.g. the portrayal in the film of attending a concert, or taking a music lesson). Indeed, Tan, Spackman, and Wakefield (2008) have shown different responses to the same music used in a film clip when the context of the presentation of the music was either diegetic or non-diegetic.

31.3.3 Working Narrative: level C

Returning to the remainder of the framework in Figure 31.3, information is transferred from level B to level C, the level of the working narrative. Priority of transfer is given to visual information in the grey oval at B, due to its cross-modal audiovisual congruence. Thus, not all of the visual sensory information that is potentially available is transferred. Also, information of musical meaning from B is transferred. The concept is that of constructing a narrative from the information gleaned simultaneously from the two visual and three auditory channels. The term working has a loose connection to Baddeley's notion of working memory, which includes audiovisual sources, capacity limitations, and conscious awareness. The present depiction illustrates how music transports various packages of information, be they structural or semantic, meeting the (diegetic and non-diegetic) goals of a film director and film-music composer for

processes within the system. Resonance is also proposed to be a necessary condition for conscious attention'.

the minds of the audience. The term narrative recognizes the audience aim of making sense of the presentation, using whatever information is at hand. Given the context of entertainment, added to the aim is the desire to make the best (most enjoyable) story possible. It is likely that the focus of attention is on the visual scene, as there is evidence for visual primacy and typical subservience of audio to vision (e.g. ventriloquism, cf. Driver, 1997; see also Bolivar et al, 1994; Thompson et al, 1994). However, conceivably contexts may be established where one of the other sensory channels dominates, and the rest are subservient (cf. Boltz et al, 2009). Thus, typically, the emotional meaning of the music is directed to this level because it is useful in determining the meaning of the visual scene. Components of the emotional meaning might fast-track to level D, however, as an aid to predictive coding of the rest of the film information. Consciousness of the musical meaning at level C arises only through correspondence with information from top-down processes based in long-term memory (LTM) arising from D.

An example of this attentional and inference process is provided by consideration of a portion of the film *Apollo 13*, the drama based on the dangerous technical difficulties within the spacecraft, Apollo 13, that prevented the planned landing on the moon and threatened a safe return to earth. Toward the end of the film, Apollo 13 hovers over the moon—so near and yet so far. The film depicts the fantasy of one of the astronauts, Jim Lovell (played by Tom Hanks), imagining his dream of having landed, taking several weightless steps, and slowly brushing his gloved fingers across the moon's surface. The audience has no trouble in inferring the anguish, awe, and exhilaration that he would have felt (in their working narrative at level C). Thanks to the composer, James Horner, the musical basis for such emotional information is carried by the musical soundtrack. On the other hand, the story gives no reason to predict that a full symphony orchestra is performing outside the spacecraft; hence, the acoustical aspect of the music (level A) is not transported to the working narrative. It is encoded by sensory memory, but it is not predicted by inferences derived from LTM (level D), and hence it is unattended.

Thus, the main phenomenal experience at the working narrative is one of a narrative with visual, verbal, and emotional components (but not music qua sound unless in specific contexts such as music videos or opening credits). Once attended in the working narrative, the information about the narrative can itself be stored in LTM and form the basis of new inferences. In parallel, acoustical aspects of the music can be processed at a conscious level (see levels C and D in the music column), as it is known that simultaneous tasks can co-occur (Neisser & Becklin, 1975), and there is evidence that background music is remembered (Boltz, 2004; Cohen, 2000; Smith, 1996). A similar process is envisioned for speech, sound effects, and text as well, but this is not the focus of the present chapter.

31.3.4 Emotion

Emotion cuts through seven of the eight functions of film music described in Section 31.2.4: contributing to the narrative's continuity; emotional meaning of events;

inducement of emotion; creation and activation of memory (state dependence, heightening attention to particular events, providing cues in leitmotif); maintenance of arousal, absorption or involvement; and finally, aesthetic experience. Emotion enters at every level of the proposed framework, analysis of structure and meaning, directing emotional meaning to the working narrative, cuing the inference process of LTM, and matching of LTM and stimulus representations in the working narrative.

Juslin and Västfjäll (2008) identify six classes of musical emotion, arising from brain stem reflexes, evaluative conditioning, emotional contagion, visual imagery, episodic memory, and musical expectancy. It seems reasonable to suggest that each of these can be found in the film context, for example, the use of rapidly changing basic acoustic characteristics, covariation between events (leitmotif), musical motion that mirrors activity of actors, visual imagery that is part of the envisioning of the film, the establishment of emotionally toned memories of the film that connect with its music and the particular events of the theatre visit, and surprise arising from unexpected aspects of the musical syntax.

Tan (1996) has raised the question whether emotion in film is genuine. He set out six criteria based on Frijda's (1986) laws of emotion, and again we can find examples from the situation of film music to establish that film music leads to genuine emotion, according to Tan's definition:[3]

1. *Control precedence.* Music controls emotion response (Thayer & Faith, 2000; Thayer & Levinson, 1983); hence, like other genuine emotions, emotion created by background music exerts control over the audience member. These effects can result simply from bottom-up analysis of the stimuli, although higher-order learned associations may also play a role.

2. *Law of concern: Emotion entails identifiable concern.* When music is combined with other media, the music readily finds an object. Cook (1998) provides clear examples of this with respect to advertising. Marshall and Cohen (1988) explained that music directed attention to an object and ascribed its meaning to that object. Attention is required for concern. Music directs such attention (see horizontal arrow from music to vision at level B in Figure 31.3).

3. *Law of situational meaning (or stimulus specificity).* Each emotion has a particular 'situational meaning structure', a set of critical characteristics of the stimulus. Characteristics of musical stimuli giving rise to particular perceived or evoked emotions have been identified by various researchers (e.g. Juslin, 1997; Juslin & Madison, 1999; Juslin & Västfjäll, 2008; Krumhansl, 1997; Rigg, 1964), and similarities between these characteristics and visually depicted emotions through gait, posture, and speech intonation have also been noted (see Boltz et al, 1991, for a summary). Some aspects of the emotional meaning of music transfer directly to film (Iwamiya, 1994; Sirius & Clarke, 1994; Smith, 1999).

---

[3] But see Russell and Barrett's (1999) practical guide to assessment of emotion, in which they claim that films do not induce true emotion, what they refer to as 'emotional episodes'.

4. *Law of apparent reality: the stimulus must represent some reality or other* (see also Tan, 1996, p. 67). Music contributes to the sense of reality of the narrative (first demonstrated in the 'talkies' in Steiner's score for *King Kong*; cf. Palmer, 1990, p. 28). It accentuates important events. The contribution of only the emotional components of the music to the diegesis has been described in Section 31.2 and explained via Figure 31.3 (see, in particular, the diagonal arrow between levels B and C).

5. *Law of change: emotion responds to changes in the situation* (see also Tan, 1996, p. 56). Music creates an ever-changing auditory environment that establishes expectations and implications, some of which are realized and some of which are violated. As such, it is a fertile source of emotion (see also Meyer, 1956).

6. *Law of closure: an emotion tends toward complete realization of its appraisal and action tendency, and is relatively immune to outside influences such as conscious control.* Music commands interest, especially in a darkened film theatre, as described by Münsterberg (1916). The emotion generated by music is governed by the tension and resolution established by the music of which the audience is unaware (cf. Thompson et al, 1994) and over which one seems to have little control, although this is a matter for further empirical work. Rehearing music reproduces emotional responses regardless of prior expectations (e.g. Jourdain, 1997).

Thus, having satisfied the six constraints described by Tan (1996), it can be concluded that music contributes genuine emotional experience in a film. Whereas Tan refers to film as an emotion machine, our analysis here suggests that music supplies a considerable portion of the fuel. The origin of the fuel, however, is the composer.

31.4 EMOTION AND THE FILM-SCORE COMPOSER

It is well to say that music is a source of emotion in film, but the ultimate source is the composer. The average theatre-goer appreciates the emotion established by film music, but would be hard pressed to know who composed this music. Whereas many classical composers have created film scores (e.g. Saint-Saens, Satie, Britten, Honegger, Milhaud, Prokofiev, Shostakovitch, Vaughan Williams, Bernstein, Copland, Schuller, and Corigliano), such composition is often regarded as a special talent and preoccupation, exemplified by George Steiner, Miklós Rósza, Erich Korngold, Bernard Hermann, Dimitri Tiomkin, John Williams, Rachel Portman, and Ennio Morricone among others. Composers known primarily for their film music have also been recognized for classical music composition as well, for example, Rósza and Korngold.

According to film-score composer Victor Young, the film-score composer is characterized by exceptional exactitude, diplomacy, and patience, in addition to music training (in Karlin, 1994, p. 310). Music composition for film differs from music composition for its own aesthetic sake. Typically, film music is music produced for the sake of the story. It is constrained by the intent of the director, narrative, time, and budget. Working within these constraints, the composer may be regarded as exploiting his or her metacognition of the operations described in the framework of Figure 31.3. The composer must know how shared audiovisual accent patterns can focus visual attention, how musical information avoids conscious attention, how mood is established, how musical associations provoke inferences through reinforcement or counterpoint, and how inferences are cued and generated via LTM to further the diegesis.

The composer is usually called upon at the end of the film production (Palmer, 1980; Rózsa, 1982, p. 191; some exceptions being Eisenstein and Hitchcock classics), and may be shown the film for the first time with recorded music already in place, known as temp tracks. The temp track indicates the director's wishes for type and placement of music, and therefore can restrict the composer's latitude considerably. In Henry Mancini's opinion, familiarity with the temp tracks may bias the director against new insights offered by the composer (Brown, 1994, p. 301). The composer's job is to replace the temp tracks with new material that must meet some or all of a number of constraints: time the music cue to a fraction of a second to coincide with the rhythm of the action of a particular frame of the film, match or create the mood or spirit of the film content, use affordable orchestration and rehearsal time, be unheard (unless the music is part of the diegesis) but be memorable, and never drown out the dialogue (cf. Burt, 1994, Ch. 6; Rozsa, 1982, pp. 69, 108, 110). In spite of these constraints, some composers such as classically trained John Barry claim that composing for film can be the ultimate freedom. Within these constraints, the composer can do whatever he or she wants and is assured of exposure.

Composing for film is one way of transmitting musical culture (e.g. Rozsa, 1982, p. 205), because, as shown in Figure 31.3, although the film music serves narrative function, it is also encoded in an information-processing channel devoted solely to music. Exposure to new compositional styles can be an added aspect of the film experience. For example, *The Red Violin* may provide one's first exposure to the work of the contemporary composer John Corigliano. Films provide a major source for transmission of a culture's musical conventions. Thus, composing for film is a two-way street: the composer learns to code music to match the visual and emotional information of a narrative; at the same time, the film provides the composer an opportunity to represent this emotional information in musically novel and creative ways, often to a large audience.

For a feature film, the composer may be given only a month of intensive work to score an hour of music. This pace is faster than that of a composer of 'music alone', but the genre is often, though not necessarily, redundant and characterized by cliché. The music does not have to stand independently, yet the possibility of (recent expectation for) a lucrative soundtrack album may create a challenge to compose music that lives on its own yet hardly reaches consciousness during the film.

Knowledge of the techniques and technology of film scoring can be acquired formally through courses, books, apprenticeships, or trial and error. The art of film music, however, perhaps more than other forms of music, requires 'taking the attitude of the other' (Meyer, 1956, Ch. 1). Specific messages must be communicated in an aesthetic package, but the aesthetic goals may be secondary, unlike composing music alone. Like other skills, such as chess, bridge, music performance, and knowledge of a discipline, expertise in film-music composition may follow the ten-year rule of concentrated practice (Ericsson, 1996). A student composer, Erin Hansen, in scoring an eight-minute film for a friend, spoke of the many hours of experimentation that were entailed until he achieved the effects he wanted. His work several years later went more quickly. Presumably, like learning any language after puberty, extensive effort is required to master the syntax and vocabulary. But the film-score language differs from languages learned from scratch, in that the grammar of the film-music language is already known implicitly from exposure to music and film-music conventions. The film score composer must turn that implicit knowledge into explicit knowledge, and in other words must become an expert of the rules.

Research by Lipscomb and Kendall (1994) corroborates the notion that the professional film-score composer has the knowledge to create a score that uniquely matches a portion of the film, and that the explicit knowledge of the composer is implicitly shared by the audience. Lipscomb and Kendall (1994) asked participants to select the best-fitting of five film scores for a feature film, *Star Trek IV: the Voyage Home*, with the music composed by Leonard Rosenman. One of the scores had been originally composed for the excerpt, and the remaining selections were by the same composer, but drawn from other excerpts in the film. Confirming the effectiveness of Rosenman's music, the most frequent choice of the subjects was the actual score he had composed for the segment, although not every subject made this choice. Similarly, we recall from research previously reviewed of Bullerjahn and Güldenring (1994) that the professional film-score composer can systematically manipulate the inferences generated by the viewer/listener. Likewise, in the study by Thompson et al (1994), the use of musical closure by the professional composer altered the judged closure in the film.

Some composers may be more suited to film-score composition than others in terms of both personality and motivation (which may play more of a role than talent, as is sometimes the case in regular musical achievement; see Sloboda, 1996). The film composer must have a dramatic sense (Rózsa in Brown, 1994, p. 278), an appreciation of the visual world of film, and a sensitivity to speech nuances. Unlike many other types of composition, the creation of a film score is a collaborative process. Generally, interpersonal intelligence (Gardner, 1983/1993) would be necessary on two fronts: appreciation of the demands of socially shared cognition and the accurate assessment of common ground (Krauss & Fussell, 1991) and the willingness to cooperate with the film production team (although the film composer Bernard Hermann was known to be irascible, according to Karlin, 1994, p. 270). Korngold describes his positive relations with executive producers and others responsible for the film (in Carroll, 1997, pp. 298–9) and claims that his artistry was not compromised in film composition. Similarly, Franz Waxman felt 'there was always room for fresh musical ideas in writing for the screen' (in Karlin, 1994, p. 307).

31.5 CONCLUSION

Emotion characterizes the primary experience of both music and film. Music typically plays an integral part of film. Kalinak's argument for the importance of music to the emotional experience in classical narrative film finds support in much of the information presented in this chapter:

Scenes that most typically elicited the accompaniment of music were those that contained emotion. The classical narrative model developed certain conventions to assist expressive acting in portraying the presence of emotion . . . close-up, diffuse lighting and focus, symmetrical mise-en-scène, and heightened vocal intonation. The focal point of this process became the music which externalized these codes through the collective resonance of musical associations. *Music is, arguably, the most efficient of these codes* [italics added], providing an audible definition of the emotion which the visual apparatus offers . . . Music's dual function of both articulator of screen expression and initiator of spectator response binds the spectator to the screen by resonating affect between them.

(Kalinak, 1992, p. 87)

Kalinak's is a strong statement regarding the role of music as a source of emotion. She has claimed that music is 'the most efficient code' for emotional expression in film. According to Kalinak (1992, p. 87), 'The lush, stringed passages accompanying a love scene are representations not only of the emotions of the diegetic characters but also of the spectator's own response which music prompts and reflects.' She is arguing that the simultaneity of both the representation and the elicitation of feeling is key. Though her analysis seems correct, more empirical research would be welcomed that compared the relative abilities of music and film to represent and elicit emotion. Recent neurophysiological research has begun to focus on music-visual stimuli. However, the visual material has been still affective pictures rather than moving pictures (EEG: Baumgartner, Esslen, & Jäncke, 2006; fMRI: Baumgartner, Lutz, Schmidt, & Jäncke, 2006; ERP: Spreckelmeyer, Kutas, Urbach, Altenmüller, & Münte, 2005). A study of gamma activation included music and video as two of eight types of stimuli presented, though the video itself had music in its soundtrack (Fitzgibbon, Pope, Mackenzie, Clark, & Willoughby, 2004). These examples provide a most promising foundation for future studies that examine behavioural and physiological responses to the joint presentation of music and video.

That music contributes to the emotional expression and experience of film seems logical, yet surprisingly, discussions of emotion in film often ignore music (e.g. Tan, 1996). Experimental evidence has shown that music influences the interpretation of film narrative and that the music becomes integrated in memory with the visual information. Music accomplishes other attentional functions through gestalt-structural and associationist principles. In addition, the fact that music requires cognitive resources probably plays a role in determining absorption, arousal, and general attention. Music also contributes to the aesthetic experience of the film. In conjunction with film, music can also satisfy Frijda's requirements, as identified by Tan (1996), of a stimulus that can support genuine emotion. In the new research framework for music and emotion of Juslin and Västfjäll (2008), the hypotheses that have been proposed for the study of the six mechanisms or types of musical emotion should be equally considered within the context of the moving image (e.g. their ontogenetic development, key brain regions, cultural dependency, induced affect, induction speed, degree of volitional influence).

Film-music composition can be regarded as a type of problem solving that exploits knowledge of the musical rules that express and create emotion through specific musical relations. There are many goals that must be satisfied by the film-score composer: providing continuation, directing attention, inducing mood, communicating meaning, cuing memory, creating a sense of reality, and contributing to the aesthetic experience. The ultimate compositional goal is to produce sound patterns that express the emotion consistent with the narrative, the emotion that is jointly recognized and experienced by the audience, binding the spectator to the screen (Kalinak, 1992, p. 87). The capacity of music to accomplish the emotional task, arguably far better than the screen itself as Kalinak has suggested, may be based on the ability of music to simultaneously carry many kinds of emotional information in its harmony, rhythm, melody, timbre, and tonality. Real life entails multiple emotions, simultaneously and in succession. Miraculously, yet systematically, these complex relations, this 'emotional polyphony', can be represented by the musical medium. An example is Korngold's music from the classic film *Sea Hawk* that links romantic love and the spirit of childhood adventure: 'The music for the love scenes still makes an indelible impression with its sweeping heroic lyricism, characterized by arching, repeated rising sevenths that dovetail perfectly with a hypnotic and unforgettable horn call that is redolent of every schoolboy's dream of pirate adventure' (Carroll, 1997, p. 254; other examples are provided by Steiner's ability to 'crystallize the essence of a film in a single theme'; Palmer, 1990, p. 29, p. 48).

As depicted by the Congruence-Associationist Model presented here, and as argued by Cook (1998), music is strong in the representation of emotion in the abstract, and the screen is strong in representing the object to which the emotion is directed. While more research is warranted to further examine the simultaneous contribution of music to emotional meaning, feeling, absorption, and memory, there is sufficient data available now to conclude that music, owing in large part to the explicit knowledge and skills of the composer, provides one of the strongest sources of emotion in film. The technical resources available for controlling musical and visual stimuli, and for measuring physiological and brain responses, provide enormous opportunities for empirical and theoretical advances in this area.[4]

[4] The Social Sciences and Humanities Research Council is acknowledged for its support of the author's programme of research in the psychology of film music. Appreciation is expressed to four anonymous reviewers and colleague Thomy Nilsson for their comments on an earlier version of this manuscript. The advice of editors Patrik Juslin and John Sloboda is also gratefully acknowledged.

Recommended further reading

1. Anderson, G. A., & Sadoff, R. H. (eds). *Music and the moving image* (online journal). Champaign, IL: University of Illinois Press.
2. Bordwell, D., & Thompson, K. (2007). *Film art: An introduction* (8th edn). New York: McGraw-Hill.
3. Buhler, J., Flinn, C., & Neumeyer, D. (eds). (2000). *Music and cinema*. Middletown, CT: Wesleyan University Press.

References

Albersnagel, F. (1988). Velten and musical mood induction procedures: A comparison with accessibility of thought associations. *Behavior Research Theory, 26,* 79–96.

Anderson, J. D. (1997). Introduction to the Symposium on Cognitive Science and the Future of Film Studies. In *Proceedings of Symposium on Cognitive Science and the Future of Film Studies* (pp. 2–6). Lawrence, KS: University of Kansas. Retrieved from: http://www.gsu.edu/~wwwcom/ccsmi/v3n1p1.htm

Baars, B. J. (1997). *In the theater of consciousness: The workspace of the mind*. Oxford: Oxford University Press.

Banse, R., & Scherer, K. R. (1996). Acoustic profiles in vocal emotion expression. *Journal of Personality and Social Psychology, 70,* 614–36.

Barrett, L. F., & Russell, J. A. (1999). The structure of current affect: Controversies and emerging consensus. *Current Directions in Psychological Science, 8,* 10–14.

Baumgartner, T., Esslen, M., & Jäncke, L. (2006). From emotion to perception to emotion experience: Emotions evoked by pictures and classical music. *International Journal of Psychophysiology, 60,* 34–43.

Baumgartner, T., Lutz, K., Schmidt, C. F., & Jäncke, L. (2006). The emotional power of music: How music enhances the feeling of affective pictures. *Brain Research, 1075,* 151–64.

Bhattacharya, J., & Petsche, H. (2005). Phase synchrony analysis of EEG during music perception reveals changes to functional connectivity due to musical expertise. *Signal Processing, 85,* 2161–77.

Bolivar, V. J., Cohen, A. J., & Fentress, J. C. (1994). Semantic and formal congruency in music and motion pictures: Effects on the interpretation of visual action. *Psychomusicology, 13,* 28–59.

Boltz, M. (2004). The cognitive processing of film and musical soundtracks. *Memory & Cognition, 32,* 1194–1205.

Boltz, M. G., Ebendorf, B., & Field, B. (2009). Audiovisual interactions: The impact of visual information on music perception and memory. *Music Perception, 27,* 43–59.

Boltz, M., Schulkind, M., & Kantra, S. (1991). Effects of background music on remembering of filmed events. *Memory and Cognition, 19,* 595–606.

Bregman, A. (1990). *Auditory scene analysis*. Cambridge, MA: MIT Press.

Brown, R. (1994). *Overtones and undertones: Reading film music*. Berkeley, CA: University of California.

Bullerjahn, C., & Güldenring, M. (1994). An empirical investigation of effects of film music using qualitative content analysis. *Psychomusicology, 13,* 99–118.

Burt, G. (1994). *The art of film music*. Boston, MA: Northeastern University Press.

Carroll, B. G. (1997). *The last prodigy: A biography of Erich Wolfgang Korngold*. Portland, OR: Amadeus.

Cohen, A. J. (1990). Understanding musical soundtracks. *Empirical Studies of the Arts, 8,* 111–24.

Cohen, A. J. (1993). Associationism and musical soundtrack phenomena. *Contemporary Music Review, 9,* 163–78.

Cohen, A. J. (1994). Introduction to the special volume on the psychology of film music. *Psychomusicology, 13,* 2–8.

Cohen, A. J. (1999). The functions of music in multimedia: A cognitive approach. In S. W. Yi (ed.), *Music, mind, and science* (pp. 53–69). Seoul, Korea: Seoul National University Press.

Cohen, A. J., MacMillan, K. A. & Drew, R. (2006). The role of music, sound effects & speech on absorption in a film: The congruence-associationist model of media cognition. *Canadian Acoustics, 34,* 40–1.

Cook, N. (1998). *Analysing musical multimedia*. Oxford: Clarendon Press.

Copland, A. (1941). *Our new music*. New York: McGraw-Hill.

Driver, J. (1997). Enhancement of selective listening by illusory mislocation of speech sounds due to lip-reading. *Nature, 381,* 66–8.

Eich, E. (1995). Searching for mood dependent memory. *Psychological Science, 6,* 67–75.

Eisenstein, S. (1949). *Film form: Essays in film theory* (J. Leyda, ed. & trans.). New York: Harcourt, Brace & World.

Engel, A. K., & Singer, W., (2001). Temporal binding and the neural correlates of sensory awareness. *Trends in Cognitive Sciences, 5,* 16–25.

Ericsson, K. A. (1996). The acquisition of expert performance: An introduction to some of the issues. In K. A. Ericsson (ed.), *The road to excellence: The acquisition of expert performance in the arts and sciences, sports and games* (pp. 1–50). Mahwah, NJ: Erlbaum.

Fitzgibbon, S. P., Pope, K. J., Mackenzie, L., Clark, C. R., & Willoughby, J. O. (2004). Cognitive tasks augment gamma EEG power. *Clinical Neurophysiology, 115,* 1802–9.

Flores-Gutiérrez, E. O., Díaz, J.-L., Barrios, F. A., Favila-Humara, R., Guevara, M. Á., del Rio Portilla, Y., & Corsi-Cabrera, M. (2007). Metabolic and electric brain patterns during pleasant and unpleasant emotions induced by music masterpieces. *International Journal of Psychophysiology, 65,* 69–84.

Frijda, N. H. (1986). *The emotions*. Cambridge, UK: Cambridge University Press.

Gabrielsson, A. (1998). Verbal description of music experience. In S. W. Yi (ed.), *Proceedings of the Fifth International Conference on Music Perception and Cognition* (pp. 271–6). Seoul, Korea: Seoul University.

Gabrielsson, A., & Lindström, S. (1993). On strong experiences of music. *Musikpsychologie. Jahrbuch der Deutschen Gesellschaft für Musikpsychologie, 10,* 118–39.

Gardner, H. (1983/1993). *Frames of mind: The theory of multiple intelligences*. New York: Basic Books.

Gorbman, C. (1987). *Unheard melodies: Narrative film music*. Bloomington, IN: Indiana University Press.

Gosselin, N., Peretz, I., Noulhiane, M., Hasboun, D., Beckett, C., Baulac, M., & Samson, S. (2005). Impaired recognition of scary music following unilateral temporal lobe excision. *Brain, 128,* 628–40.

Gregory, A. H. (1998). Tracking the emotional response to operatic arias. In S. W. Yi (ed.), *Proceedings of the Fifth International Conference on Music Perception and Cognition* (pp. 265–70). Seoul, Korea: Seoul University.

Grossberg, S. (1980). How does the brain build a cognitive code? *Psychological Review, 87,* 1–51.

Grossberg, S. (1995). The attentive brain. *American Scientist, 83,* 438–49.

Grossberg, S. (1996). The attentive brain: Perception, learning, and consciousness. [Abstract]. Retrieved from: http:// www- math. mit. edu/ amc/ fall96/ grossberg. html

Grossberg, S. (2007). Consciousness CLEARS the mind. *Neural Networks, 20,* 1040–53.

Heider, F., & Simmel, M. (1944). An experimental study of apparent behavior. *American Journal of Psychology, 57,* 243–59.

Herrmann, C. S., Munk, M. H. J., & Engel, A. K. (2004). Cognitive functions of gamma-band activity: memory match and utilization. *Trends in Cognitive Science, 8,* 347–55.

Hochberg, J., & Brooks, V. (1996a). Movies in the mind's eye. In D. Bordwell & N. Carroll (eds), *Post-Theory: Reconstructing film studies* (pp. 368–87). Madison, WI: University of Wisconsin Press.

Hochberg, J., & Brooks, V. (1996b). The perception of motion pictures. In M. P. Friedman & E. C. Carterette (eds), *Cognitive ecology* (pp. 205–92). New York: Academic Press.

Iwamiya, S. (1994). Interaction between auditory and visual processing when listening to music in an audio visual context. *Psychomusicology, 13,* 133–53.

Iwamiya, S. (2008). *Subjective congruence between moving picture and sound.* Paper presented at the Tenth International Conference on Music Perception and Cognition, Sapporo, Japan, August 2008.

Jourdain, R. (1997). *Music, the brain and ecstacy: How music captures our imagination.* New York: Morrow.

Juslin, P. N. (1997). Emotional communication in music performance: A functionalist perspective and some data. *Music Perception, 14,* 383–418.

Juslin, P. N., & Madison, G. (1999). The role of timing patterns in recognition of emotional expression from musical performance. *Music Perception, 17,* 197–221.

Juslin, P. N., & Västfjäll, D. (2008). Emotional responses to music: The need to consider underlying mechanisms. *Behavioral and Brain Sciences, 31,* 559–75.

Kalinak, K. (1992). *Settling the score.* Madison, WI: University of Wisconsin Press.

Karlin, F. (1994). *Listening to the movies.* New York: Schirmer.

Kassabian, A. (2001). *Hearing film: Tracking identifications in contemporary Hollywood film music.* New York: Routledge.

Kendall, R. (2008). *Stratification of musical and visual structures II: Visual and pitch contours.* Paper presented at the Tenth International Conference on Music Perception and Cognition, Sapporo, Japan, August 2008.

Kim, K-H., & Iwaymiya, S-I. (2008). Formal congruency between Telop patterns and sounds effects. *Music Perception, 25,* 429–48.

Kintsch, W. (1998). *Comprehension: A paradigm for cognition.* Cambridge, UK: Cambridge University Press.

Kracauer, S. (1960). *Theory of film: The redemption of physical reality.* Oxford: Oxford University Press.

Krauss, R. M., & Fussell, S. R. (1991). Constructing shared communicative environments. In L. Resnick, J. M. Levine, & S. D. Teasley (eds), *Socially shared cognition* (pp. 172–200). Washington, DC: American Psychological Association.

Krumhansl, C. L. (1997). An exploratory study of musical emotions and psychophysiology. *Canadian Journal of Psychology, 51,* 336–52.

Kveraga, K., Ghuman, A. S., & Bar, M. (2007). Top-down predictions in the cognitive brain. *Brain and Cognition, 65,* 145–68.

Lang, P. J. (1995). The emotion probe. *American Psychologist, 50,* 372–85.

Levi, D. S. (1982). The structural determinants of melodic expressive properties. *Journal of Phenomenological Psychology, 13,* 19–44.

Levin, D. T., & Simons, D. J. (2000). Perceiving stability in a changing world: Combining shots and integrating views in motion pictures and the real world. *Media Psychology, 2,* 357–80.

Levinson, J. (1996). Film music and narrative agency. In D. Bordwell & N. Carroll (eds), *Post-Theory: Reconstructing film studies* (pp. 248–82). Madison, WI: University of Wisconsin Press.

Limbacher, J. L. (1974). *Film music.* Metuchen, NJ: Scarecrow.

Lipscomb, S. D. (1999). Cross-modal integration: Synchronization of auditory and visual components in simple and complex media. In *Collected papers of the 137th Meeting of the Acoustical Society of America and the 2nd Convention of the European Acoustics Association* [CD-ROM]. New York: The Acoustical Society of America.

Lipscomb, S. D. (2005). The perception of audio-visual composites: Accent structure alignment of simple stimuli. *Selected Reports in Ethnomusicology, 12,* 37–67.

Lipscomb, S. D., & Kendall, R. (1994). Perceptual judgement of the relationship between musical and visual components in film. *Psychomusicology, 13,* 60–98.

Mack, A., & Rock, I. (1998). *Inattentional blindness.* Cambridge, MA: MIT Press.

Madsen, C. K. (1997). Emotional response to music. *Psychomusicology, 16,* 59–67.

Magliano, J. P., Dijkstra, K., & Zwaan, R. A. (1996). Generating predictive inferences while viewing a movie. *Discourse Processes, 22,* 199–224.

Marks, M. (1997). *Music and the silent film.* Oxford: Oxford University Press.

Marshall, S., & Cohen, A. J. (1988). Effects of musical soundtracks on attitudes to geometric figures. *Music Perception, 6,* 95–112.

Meyer, L. B. (1956). *Emotion and meaning in music.* Chicago, IL: Chicago University Press.

Mitry, J. (1997). *The aesthetics and psychology of the cinema* (C. King, trans). Bloomington, IN: Indiana University Press. (Originally published 1963)

Münsterberg, H. (1970). *The photoplay: A psychological study.* New York: Arno. (Originally published 1916)

Murray, I. R., & Arnott, J. L. (1993). Toward the simulation of emotion in synthetic speech: A review of the literature on human vocal emotion. *Journal of the Acoustical Society of America, 93,* 1097–108.

Narmour, E. (1991). The top-down and bottom-up systems of musical implication: Building on Meyer's theory of emotional syntax. *Music Perception, 9,* 1–26.

Neisser, U., & Becklen, R. (1975). Selective looking: Attending to visually significant events. *Cognitive Psychology, 7,* 480–94.

Osgood, C. E., Suci, G. J., & Tannenbaum, P. H. (1957). *The measurement of meaning.* Urbana, IL: University of Illinois Press.

Palmer, C. (1980). Film music. In S. Sadie (ed.), *New Grove dictionary of music and musicians* (Vol 6, pp. 549–556). Washington, DC: Macmillan.

Palmer, C. (1990). *The composer in Hollywood.* New York: Marion Boyars.

Pignatiello, M. F., Camp, C. J., & Rasar, L. (1986). Musical mood induction: An alternative to the Velten technique. *Journal of Abnormal Psychology, 95,* 295–7.

Prendergast, R. M. (1992). *Film music: A neglected art* (2nd edn). New York: Norton.

Preston, J. M. (1999). From mediated environments to the development of consciousness. In J. Gackenbach (ed.), *Psychology and the Internet: Intrapersonal, interpersonal, and transpersonal implications* (pp. 255–91). San Diego, CA: Academic Press.

Qian, J., Preston, J., & House, M. (1999). *Personality trait absorption and reality status evaluations of narrative mediated messages.* Paper presented at the Annual Meeting of the American Psychological Association, Boston, USA, August 1999.

Revonsuo, A., & Newman, J. (1999). Binding and consciousness. *Consciousness and Cognition, 8,* 123–7.

Rigg, M. G. (1964). The mood effects of music: A comparison of data from four investigations. *Journal of Psychology*, *58*, 427–38.

Rosar, W. (1994). Film music and Heinz Werner's theory of physionomic perception. *Psychomusicology*, *13*, 154–65.

Rozsa, M. (1982). *Double life*. New York: Hippocrene Books.

Russell, J. A., & Barrett, L. F. (1999). Core affect, prototypical emotional episodes, and other things called emotion: Dissecting the elephant. *Journal of Personality and Social Psychology*, *76*, 805–19.

Saint-Saens, C. (1951). The composer as psychologist. In J. Barzun (ed.), *Pleasures of music* (pp. 258–264). New York: Viking Press. (Originally published 1903)

Sammler, D., Grigutsch, M., Fritz, T., & Koelsch, S. (2007). Music and emotion: Electrophysiological correlates of the processing of pleasant and unpleasant music. *Psychophysiology*, *44*, 293–304.

Schubert, E. (1998). Time series analysis of emotion in music. In S. W. Yi (ed.). *Proceedings of the Fifth International Conference on Music Perception and Cognition* (pp. 257–63). Seoul, Korea: Seoul National University.

Shevy, M. (2007). The mood of rock music affects evaluation of video elements differing in valence and dominance. *Psychomusicology*, *19*, 57–78.

Sirius, G., & Clarke, E. F. (1994). The perception of audiovisual relationships: A preliminary study. *Psychomusicology*, *13*, 119–32.

Sloboda, J. A. (1985). *The musical mind*: *The cognitive psychology of music*. Oxford: Oxford University Press.

Sloboda, J. A. (1992). Empirical studies of emotional response to music. In M. R. Jones & S. Holleran (eds), *Cognitive bases of musical communication* (pp. 33–46). Washington, DC: American Psychological Association.

Sloboda, J. A. (1996). The acquisition of musical performance expertise: Deconstructing the 'talent' account of individual differences in musical expressivity. In K. A. Ericsson (ed.), *The road to excellence*: *The acquisition of expert performance in the arts and sciences, sports and games* (pp. 107–26). Mahwah, NJ: Erlbaum.

Smith, J. (1996). Unheard melodies? A critique of psychoanalytic theories of film music. In D. Bordwell & N. Carroll (eds), *Post-Theory*: *Reconstructing film studies* (pp. 230–48). Madison, WI: University of Wisconsin Press.

Smith, J. (1999). Movie music as moving music: Emotion, cognition, and the film score. In C. Plantinga & G. M. Smith (eds), *Passionate views* (pp. 146–67). Baltimore, MD: Johns Hopkins University Press.

Spreckelmeyer, K. N., Kutas, M., Urbach, T. P., Altenmüller, E., & Münte, T. F. (2006). Combined perception of emotion in pictures and musical sounds. *Brain Research*, *1070*, 160–70.

Stam, R. (2000). *Film theory*: *An introduction*. Malden, MA: Blackwell.

Storm, C., & Storm, T. (1987). A taxonomic study of the vocabulary of emotions. *Journal of Personality and Social Psychology*, *53*, 805–16.

Tan, E. S. (1996). *Emotion and the structure of narrative film*: *Film as an emotion machine* (B. Fasting, trans.). Mahwah, NJ: Erlbaum.

Tan, S-L., Spackman, M. P., & Bezdek, M. A. (2007). Viewers' interpretations of film characters' emotions: Effects of presenting film music before or after a character is shown. *Music Perception*, *25*, 135–52.

Tan, S-L., Spackman, M. P., & Wakefield, E. M. (2008). *Source of film music (diegetic or non-diegetic) affects viewers' interpretation of film*. Paper presented at the Tenth International Conference on Music Perception and Cognition, Sapporo, Japan, August 2008.

Thayer, J. F., & Faith, M. (2000). *A dynamical systems model of musically induced emotions*: *Physiological and self-report evidence.* Poster presented at New York Academy of Sciences Conference on The Biological Foundations of Music, New York, June 2000.

Thayer, J. F., & Levenson, R. (1983). Effects of music on psychophysiological responses to a stressful film. *Psychomusicology, 3,* 44–54.

Thomas, T. (1997). *Music for the movies* (2nd edn). Los Angeles, CA: Silman-James.

Thompson, W. F., Russo, F. A., & Sinclair, D. (1994). Effects of underscoring on the perception of closure in filmed events. *Psychomusicology, 13,* 9–27.

Wayand, J. F., Levin, D. T., & Varakin, A. (2005). Inattentional blindness for a noxious multi-modal stimulus. *American Journal of Psychology, 118,* 339–52.

Wertheimer, M. (1939). Laws of organization in perceptual forms. In W. D. Ellis (ed.), *A source book of gestalt psychology* (pp. 71–88). New York: Harcourt Brace.

Vitouch, O. (2001). When your ear sets the stage: Musical context effects in film perception. *Psychology of Music, 29,* 70–83.

Zwaan, R. A. (1999). Situation models: The mental leap into imagined worlds. *Current Directions in Psychological Science, 8,* 15–18.

CHAPTER 32

MUSIC AND MARKETING

ADRIAN C. NORTH AND DAVID J. HARGREAVES

THE traditional approach to music psychology takes as its focus the music itself, be this listening to music for enjoyment or a variety of other reasons, or the composition and performance of music at various levels of ability. This focus on the music itself inevitably shapes the kinds of topics that researchers are interested in. Cognitive psychologists will, for example, investigate the means by which music is perceived and processed, or the means by which musicians produce the skilled motor functions involved in performance. Physiological psychologists and neuroscientists have had considerable success in using imaging techniques to identify those areas of the brain that respond to music. Social psychologists will, for example, investigate people's motivations in playing a musical instrument, how their musical preferences might vary between different listening situations, or how inter-group processes might mediate both. Developmental psychologists might investigate how all of these processes change as a function of the ageing process. This chapter takes a different approach, however. Here the focus is not on music. Rather, in the context of marketing, music is viewed simply as a means to another end, namely profit.

In the course of everyday life, we hear music in a variety of settings. For example, we may listen to the radio as we drive to work, hear piped music in a restaurant or shopping mall, or listen to a CD at home during the evening. The one factor that ties together all these experiences of music is that somebody, somewhere is making money from them. For example, although some radio stations have a public-interest remit, we are able to listen to commercial radio stations in the car because somebody is using the music to sell advertising space to businesses. Music is played in restaurants and shopping malls to improve the ambience, but only then because the owners think that this attracts customers or encourages existing customers to spend more. Similarly, record companies only go through the financial risk of paying to record, distribute, and promote CDs because they expect to sell them for a profit.

To the music lover, such an approach can seem undoubtedly cynical and to even 'miss the point' of what music is 'about' or 'for'. This may well be true, but two other points are nonetheless undeniable. First, like it or not, the great majority of the music that we hear in everyday life was both brought into existence and presented to us for the purpose of profit. Second, although the focus of the research on music and marketing is not on the music itself, it is highly suggestive that researchers in the field have ended up using theoretical models that have a striking resemblance to those employed by researchers whose sole concern is with music per se. As such, it could be argued that it is simply naïve for music psychology to ignore the relationship between music and marketing, and that the study of the latter may well ultimately inform the former. There are several very negative stereotypes concerning music and marketing, such as the corrupt record company executive, the role of media who 'build up pop stars only to knock them down', the awfulness of the music played to us while we shop in a supermarket or wait on hold, or the notion that a well-loved song is 'ruined' through its use in a TV advert. However, our contention here is that a rounded understanding of the role of music in modern, everyday life simply cannot ignore the links between music and marketing.

Research on music and marketing can be found in many different domains, and in the present chapter we attempt to give an overview of these. We begin by considering what is commonly known as 'the music industry', and address the most overtly-commercial use of music in which people sell it in order to make money. Specifically, we look at how the structure of the music industry influences the number and type of musicians who achieve popularity; research on music purchasing (and piracy); and radio programming. In the second major section of the chapter, we address the role of music in advertising. Here we consider two approaches that have predominated research, concerning the use of music to elicit an emotional response among radio listeners and TV viewers; and the use of music to convey information about a product or to prime beliefs about the benefits of consuming it. In the final section of the chapter, we address the impact of music in retail and leisure settings. Here we describe research on how the pleasure and arousal elicited by music can mediate spending and patronage decisions; how the particular pieces of knowledge primed by certain pieces of music can predispose consumers to evaluate a product in a particular way or to purchase one product over another; and finally how music can impact upon time perception among consumers who are kept waiting in queues.

As this demonstrates, there are many ways in which researchers have made connections between music and marketing. Consistent with this, the research on the topic is published in journals based in a variety of disciplines, such as psychology, marketing, business studies, media and communication studies, or economics, to name just the most prevalent. Accordingly, we have deliberately adopted an eclectic approach in our coverage. Note also that we have only very recently attempted a much longer and more detailed review of this literature (North & Hargreaves, 2008), and the present chapter summarizes some of the arguments and evidence that we discussed during that.

32.1 THE MUSIC INDUSTRY

The Recording Industry Association of America (RIAA) reported that CD sales in the USA in 2007 were 20.5 per cent down on the 2006 figures. Similar figures from other recent years and other Western countries have received a great deal of media attention, with some speculating that the music industry itself is running into difficulties as a result of piracy and digital downloads. Of course, no business is happy to see its market shrinking, but before sounding the death knell for record companies, it is worth remembering that these reductions in sales are relative to a very high starting point. The same RIAA figures, for example, show that the market for pre-recorded CDs in the USA in 2007 was nonetheless worth US\$7.4 billion. The music industry is very big business, and likely to remain so for many years to come.

A brief inspection of the economics of the music industry leaves the reader feeling sometimes surprised that even larger amounts of money are not made, and sometimes surprised that the companies ever manage to turn a profit. With regard to the former, for example, royalty payments to successful musicians rarely exceed 15 per cent of the wholesale price of a CD and, before these royalties are paid, the record company subtracts costs incurred on behalf of the musician related to studio time, promotional videos, and any losses made by the musician's previous releases. But before we condemn the music industry for greed, remember also that it incurs massive financial risks on behalf of musicians. For example, only around 10 per cent of all releases actually make a profit (Vogel, 1998), and the costs of producing, distributing, and marketing a major new release are very high indeed (e.g. Wilson & Stokes, 2004).

The music industry has a long history of 'insulating itself' against these financial risks by buying up related businesses such as film studios, music retailers, or other record companies. This allows for cross-promotion (e.g. placement of songs into films, feature displays of a particular CD in prime high street retail space); introduces economies of scale; and perhaps most importantly of all, limits the amount of competition faced by any individual company (Fairchild, 1996). The result of this insulation process is, however, an oligopolistic market. For example, in 2001 over 75 per cent of album sales in the UK were accounted for by just six companies (Mintel, 2003). More simply, the financial risks involved in the music industry have led to individual record companies in the modern day having a small number of competitors, and arguably a reduced incentive to be innovative.

This relationship between lack of competition and reduced pressure to innovate manifests itself in one particularly interesting way. Specifically, the costs of producing and marketing a given CD are fairly constant, whether it sells 500 copies or 500,000 copies. It makes sense, therefore, for each individual record company to minimize the financial risk it faces by paying to produce and market a small number of recordings, and attempting to sell these in very large quantities. By paying to produce and market only a small number of recordings, the company in question minimizes its initial outlay and exposure to the risk of making a loss. The company can then maximize profits by, of course, selling more copies of these recordings. In apparent confirmation of this, several studies do indeed show that the smaller the number of record companies there are, the less choice in music that customers have. For example, Rothenbuhler and Dimmick (1982) showed that, in 1975, 21 different record companies had hit records in the USA, and that 37 different records reached number 1; in contrast, by 1980, only nine record companies had hit records in the USA, and only 17 different records reached number 1.

So if the music industry tries to release as few recordings as possible, how does it select particular songs and musicians? As we will see later, one crucial criterion is the extent to which the candidate songs correspond with the programming formats of radio stations, and thus obtain airplay. A second approach is the use of a small roster of 'star' performers, whose recordings are all but guaranteed to sell in large numbers. Economists have devoted a reasonable amount of time to what they call the 'superstar phenomenon' (e.g. Rosen, 1981, 1983). They argue that consumers rarely regard slightly inferior goods as substitutes for slightly better goods. For example, if somebody wanted to give you either £10 or £11, you would almost always take £11. It is not much better than £10, but nonetheless has a clear edge that means you always select it. In other words, in a perfect market, very small differences in the quality of two directly competing choices lead to massive differences in the number of consumers who select each of those goods, and so the very best musicians massively outsell those who are only slightly inferior to them. By 2001, for instance, Elvis Presley had 27 USA platinum singles, three times as many as Mariah Carey in second place (Fox & Kochanowski, 2004). Psychological factors also distort this process, however. Hamlen (1994), for example, provides data showing that the average 'cost' of being a black performer in the USA music charts between 1955 and 1987 was equivalent to approximately one hit album; and Salagniak, Dodds, and Watts (2006) found that the actual quality of a song was related poorly to its degree of success, whereas knowledge of other people's opinions of the music was related more closely.

32.1.1 Music purchasing and piracy

Despite the huge sums of money involved, it is surprising that very little research has actually addressed why people buy particular CDs. What research there is comes from disparate sources and is rather descriptive in nature, but can be grouped loosely under two subheadings concerning models of music consumption and individual differences. With regard to models of music consumption, several studies have indicated that variations in radio airplay precede variations in record sales (Erdelyi, 1940; Jacobovits, 1966; Wiebe, 1940). As such, these studies imply that the media determine rather than reflect musical taste. Lacher and Mizerski's (1994) model considered both analytical and more emotional factors that contribute to the decision to actually purchase music, finding that the need to re-experience the music was the strongest predictor. Meenaghan and Turnbull (1981) instead used radio airplay, record sales, and other data to illustrate the typical 'product life cycle' of successful pop singles. This life cycle was typically 16 weeks long, and progressed through five stages involving, respectively (1) initial selection of songs according to market potential; (2) pre-release promotion; (3) decisions by the media whether to grant airplay; (4) an 11-week period of actual heavy sales, in which sales are related closely to media airplay; and (5) a three-week period in which sales fall to almost zero. Crain and Tollison (1997) instead focused specifically on the socio-economic correlates of record sales. They found, for example, that the more radio stations there are—leading, presumably, to a greater range of music being played—so the greater the number of musicians whose music reached the charts; and, although it is harder to explain, that the length of songs was related negatively to the number of concurrent military deaths and positively to earnings.

A small number of other studies have instead adopted an individual-differences approach to music purchasing, and have focused in particular on opinion leadership. This refers to the tendency of some consumers to influence others directly by giving advice and directions for seeking out, buying, and using the music in question. This work is associated most closely with the team of Flynn, Goldsmith, and Eastman, whose 1996 study, for example, found that opinion leadership in music was related to various measures of commercial involvement such as buying music or reading music-related magazines. In a related line of work, a small number of other researchers have investigated 'just below' pricing strategies (e.g. £8.99 rather than £9), showing that these are used more for rap than classical music and more in-store than online, which in turn, they argue, indicates that they are employed with younger, less-educated music buyers (Mixon, Trevino, & Bales, 2004). Similarly, one conclusion to have emerged concerning online music purchasing is that consumers are impatient and unwilling to search. For example, Johnson, Moe, Fader, Bellman, and Lohse (2004) found that households that buy music online visit only 1.3 CD sites per month; and Rajala and Hantula (2000) found that delays of only 0.5 seconds led to perceptions of lower service quality, and that delays of four seconds were sufficient to reduce participants' inclination to return to the site in future.

Other researchers have investigated why people sometimes instead opt deliberately not to buy music and instead obtain counterfeit or 'pirate' copies of it. This issue came to particular prominence in the late 1990s, when the growth of the Internet led to peer-to-peer filesharing software and numerous illegal music download sites (Rothenbuhler & McCourt, 2004). Jones and Lenhart (2004) surveyed the extent to which people in the USA used the Internet to obtain pirated music between April 2000 and March 2001, finding that, over these dates, between 21 per cent and 29 per cent of participants had obtained music this way. Teston (2002) found even higher prevalence rates among school pupils. But only 13 per cent of the music downloaders identified by Jones and Lenhart regarded the practice as 'stealing', and the researchers used their data to estimate that, by summer 2000, there were 11 million users of illegal music downloading software in the USA alone, sharing approximately 1.5 billion songs. Similarly, Hui and Png's (2003) analysis of international CD sales from 1994 to 1998 led to their estimation that piracy had already led to a 6.6 per cent reduction in sales by as early as 1998.

Unfortunately, we know far less about why people should engage in music piracy. It is certainly possible to identify a demographic profile of the typical music downloader as someone who is male, an experienced Internet user, and from lower income and educational groups (Ang, Cheng, Lim, & Tambyah, 2001; Jones & Lenhart, 2004; Odell, Korgen, Schumacher, & Delucchi, 2000; Papadopoulos, 2003, 2004). However, it would be a mistake to regard music pirates as a homogeneous group, since numerous studies also highlight the role of an individual's morality and value systems, as well as the role of friendship networks, and attitudes towards the musicians concerned (e.g. Chiou, Huang, & Lee, 2005; Gopal, Sanders, Bhattacharjee, Agrawal, & Wagner, 2004; Molteni & Ordanini, 2003). Furthermore, North and Oishi (2006) found that (at least some of) these latter set of motivations were related to individual difference and cultural factors, such that, for example, the role of friendship differed between British and Japanese participants. What this shows is that the decision to obtain pirate copies of music is a complex one that involves psychological as well as economic factors. As such, simply reducing the price of legitimate CDs and prosecuting offenders seem overly simplistic as the main approaches to tackling piracy adopted by the music industry at present. Indeed, it would be interesting to directly compare the impact on piracy of price reductions versus an approach based on individual differences which accounts for other motivations.

31.1.2 Radio programming

Nowhere is the commercial, rather than aesthetic, motivation of the music industry more apparent than in the case of music radio programming. Let us be clear about this: commercial radio stations exist to broadcast adverts, not music. They attract a particular segment of the population through the use of a format, or a preponderance of a certain type of music that appeals to a particular subgroup of the population. The job of the radio station is then to deliver this target population to advertisers who promote products that should be of particular relevance to them (Hennion & Meadel, 1986; Rothenbuhler, 1985, 1987; Rothenbuhler & McCourt, 1992).

This focus on advertising and profit has numerous specific implications. First, different radio stations within a particular geographical area will adopt different formats to attract different parts of the overall population, and thus avoid competition. For example, a station playing contemporary pop music is not, strictly speaking, in competition with another station that plays music from the 1960s. The two stations are trying to attract very different subgroups of the population, who are being 'sold' to very different advertisers selling very different products. The greater the number of radio stations that exist in a particular area, so the more specific the format that each adopts as it tries to find an audience of its own and avoid truly direct competition. Second, since radio stations will only play songs that fit in with their format, record companies will only release songs that fit with the most prevalent formats. (This means that record companies are continually on the lookout for the most rare and precious song of all, the 'crossover hit', or a song that fits in with several radio station formats and that therefore receives maximum airplay.) Third, since the goal of a station is to keep people listening until the next advert break, they favour familiar and unobjectionable songs. The goal is not to play music that listeners like: rather, it is to avoid playing music that listeners dislike and that induces them to change stations, and this leads to very heavy airplay of a small number of 'safe' songs. Hendy (2000), for example, compared the number of pre-release songs played by Britain's publicly-funded BBC Radio 1 against the number played by commercial competitors Atlantic 252 and Virgin. Radio 1 was much more likely to play songs of, as yet, unproven public appeal since one in four songs it played had not yet been released, whereas the corresponding figures for the other two, commercial stations were one in 67 and one in 19 respectively.

Overall, this research on the music industry highlights two more general issues. First, it demonstrates the considerable importance of commercial and economic factors in determining the music that people hear. It is arguable that individuals have far less volition over the music they are exposed to than most of the research on the psychology of musical taste would suggest. For example, elsewhere in this volume (Chapter 19), we have written about theories of experimental aesthetics, and how these might explain people's preferences for one piece of music over another. However, in reality, the specific pieces of music that we are able to select between in everyday life are drawn from a small number of melodies that have already been pre-selected from a much wider pool, on our behalf, by the music industry. Commercial and economic factors 'weed out' a lot of the music that is ever produced before it reaches the public domain: in practice, psychological theories have the potential to explain variations in preference between only those pieces that survive this filtering process.

Second, rather paradoxically, there is considerable potential for research on the psychology of musical preference and taste within the context of the music industry. The increasing online (legal) availability of music and the proliferation of digital radio stations mean that, more than ever before, people have the opportunity to short circuit the control on what they listen to that is exerted currently by the music industry. If a wider range of music is available to us through digital media, this means that the music industry must, by definition, be playing a smaller role in 'filtering out' certain pieces before they reach the public domain. As individuals replace the music industry as the arbiters of what music becomes popular, so the more importance that we should attach to judgements of musical preference and taste made by those individuals. In blunt terms, the digitization of music means that psychological factors will become more important than economic factors in explaining the music that people listen to on a day-to-day level. In decades to come, we expect the psychology of music to make an increasing contribution to our understanding of the relationship between the music industry and its customers; and suspect that the importance of economic explanations may diminish. As we noted at the start of this chapter, links between music and marketing do not represent a challenge to psychological explanations of musical behaviour—they represent arguably the clearest opportunity for growth.

32.2 MUSIC AND ADVERTISING

Within the context of the music industry, music is a product, and it is selling this product that leads to financial gain. The remainder of the chapter focuses instead on instances in which music is used to sell other products. For instance, music can be used by advertisers for a variety of specific means, such as attracting attention, priming memory, carrying a message, avoiding barriers to communication imposed by different languages, or appealing to different age groups (e.g. Hecker, 1984; Scott, 2002; Taylor & Johnson, 2002). Academic research has focused on three particular uses that music might have in advertising, namely the classical conditioning of emotional responses; the use of information associated with the music to prime cognitions concerning the advertised product; and sonic branding/sponsorship.

Traditionally, advertising has aimed to influence purchasing by affecting beliefs about the consequences of consuming the product. Soap powder washes clothes whiter than white, bleach kills 99 per cent of all germs, and the correct choice of mouthwash can guarantee a good sex life. But Brown and Stayman's (1992) review highlighted a more recent approach to advertising that had begun to replace this 'attitude toward the brand' approach. The 'attitude toward the ad' approach did not attempt to influence beliefs about the benefits of consuming the product, but instead concentrated on simply ensuring that consumers liked a particular advert. Much of this approach can be traced to a landmark study by Gorn (1982), which showed that experimental participants' degree of liking for the music that was played while they saw a pen could itself mediate their subsequent preferences between two pens. As such, this and similar subsequent findings suggested that the music used in advertising should be liked by consumers, since this affective response to the music apparently conditioned responses to the advertised product itself.

However, there have been several failed attempts to use music to condition preferences for products, and the existing research has been criticized on various methodological grounds (see brief review by North & Hargreaves, 2008). The clearest contribution made by classical conditioning approaches to advertising has been within the context of the Elaboration Likelihood Model (ELM, Petty & Cacioppo, 1981; Petty, Cacioppo, & Schumann, 1983). The key concept in the ELM is the extent to which customers are involved with an advert, or have the motivation, opportunity, and ability to consider the messages it contains. Consumers who are highly involved consider the advert's messages (or more formally, there is a strong likelihood that they will elaborate on the messages); whereas consumers who are in a state of low involvement do not.

There is still very little research on this, but at the risk of over-generalizing we might expect that classical-conditioning effects of music might be found when customers are in a state of low involvement: because they are not really processing the advert messages, there is scope for the emotional aspects of the music contained in the advert to have an effect. However, when consumers are in a state of high involvement, then they are actively thinking about the claims made in the advert. Whether or not they like the music should be irrelevant to this active, fully conscious, and logical attempt to consider the product in question. A second experiment by Gorn (1982) confirmed this: when participants were told in advance that at the end of the experiment they would be asked to choose between two types of pen, their degree of liking for the music paired with the pens was unrelated to their subsequent choice. Instead, factual information about the relative merits of the two pens was more important in explaining their choice.

However, more recent research suggests that music can still have a positive impact in cases in which consumers are highly involved with advertising. This research has employed the concept of 'musical fit'. This involves using music to guide the way that consumers evaluate a product, such that the characteristics of the music fit with those of the brand. Using music to guide thinking in this manner may sometimes involve the use of quite explicit messages in the former. For example, MacInnis and Park (1991) found that using the song 'You make me feel like a natural woman' in an advert could influence beliefs about shampoo: the explicit message contained in the lyrics guided the manner in which viewers responded to the product. In other cases, the use of music to guide thinking may instead use subtler, implicit processes based on consumers' knowledge and stereotypes about the music employed. North, Hargreaves, MacKenzie, and Law (2004; see also Alpert, Alpert, & Maltz, 2005; Oakes & North, 2006), for example, played participants adverts for five products in which music (without lyrics) promoted the same notions as those encapsulated by the brand in question. For example, an advert for a sports drink featured dynamic, energetic, and youthful dance music that implicitly promoted the same brand values as the drink itself. Similarly, an advert for a bank featured old-fashioned, conservative, classical music that implicitly promoted the same values as the bank itself. Even though the music did not contain any explicit messages, it nonetheless had predictable effects on participants' perceptions of the advertised products. For example, the sports drink was perceived as more youthful and dynamic when the advert for it featured dance music than when other types of music were used. Furthermore, memory for the products was better when music 'fitted' the products than when either it did not or no music was used, and this suggests that the music had a direct impact on the way in which participants processed the information in the advert.

Other researchers have employed a dual-coding approach to effects such as these. Stewart and Punj (1998), for example, provide data to support their argument that music ought to prime the recall of non-verbal aspects of advertising specifically, whereas a verbal prompt should facilitate recall of its verbal information. Similarly, Miller and Marks (1992, 1997) found that congruent sound effects led to radio adverts producing more images in the minds of listeners and more information about the advert being learned. As these findings highlight, the precise mechanism by which musical-fit effects may occur is at present still under-specified, and may involve several complementary processes.

More generally, research on music and advertising faces four significant problems. First and most obvious is simply that the majority of the research is carried out under very artificial laboratory conditions. In particular, there is a need for research investigating the long-term impact of music in advertising on high street spending by the general public.

Second, researchers have proposed several complex theories that produce conflicting predictions, but that can, overall, explain almost any finding. For example, research on musical fit suggests that music can prime recall of products by encouraging consumers to think about them in a particular way. In contrast, Heckler and Childers (1992) argue that, instead, incongruous music should prime recall, because it leads to deeper processing as consumers try to resolve the incongruity between music and product. Furthermore, other researchers using a resource-matching approach (e.g. Olsen, 1997) have argued that the use of any music in advertising should reduce recall of the product, because the cognitive resources devoted to processing the music can no longer be devoted to processing the product itself. More simply, it is possible to produce a theoretical explanation of why memory for a product should be improved if the advert for it features congruous music, incongruous music, or no music at all. Clearly, a great deal of theoretical refinement and testing is required.

Third, data suggest that audiences will impose a coherent meaning on any combination of music and visuals, no matter how incongruous these are intended to be. Hung (2000), for example, found that when an advert for South American coffee featured supposedly incongruous avant garde music, viewers simply interpreted this as highlighting notions of 'adventure', which were in turn clearly regarded as congruous with the images of rainforests contained in the visual portion of the advert. What a researcher intends as 'incongruous' music may not be perceived as such by his or her research participants.

Finally, the notion of musical fit has been defined poorly by previous studies. As we have just seen, consumers may well impose their own interpretation on the role of music in any advert; and as such it may be difficult for advertisers to employ anything but the most unambiguous and crass connotations of music (such as, for instance, the notion that anything played on a distorted electric guitar is 'youthful' and 'rebellious'). Furthermore, in putting musical fit into practice, it is not clear exactly which aspects of the music should correspond with which aspects of the product. Should the music, for example, correspond with stereotypical notions of the general class of products in question, or the specific characteristics of the particular brand being advertised? TV adverts stereotypically portray cars as 'exciting', but music that highlighted this notion may be ineffective if the particular car being advertised is instead well known for its safety or fuel economy. What logical basis is there for using music to emphasize certain product attributes rather than others; and what logical basis is there for using certain musical attributes to do this to the neglect of others? These issues can be resolved by research, but this research is necessary before musical fit can be used by advertisers. Again, this is an area where research on music and marketing could benefit from research within mainstream music psychology. In particular, research on the relationship between musical preference and the listening situation has highlighted those aspects of particular types of music that lead to it being perceived as 'appropriate' for particular listening situations (Konečni, 1982; North & Hargreaves, 2000; North, Hargreaves, & Hargreaves, 2004; Sloboda, O'Neill, & Ivaldi, 2001). Although North, Hargreaves, MacKenzie, and Law (2004) made some attempt to draw on aspects of this research, it is not inconceivable that it could inform the debate on musical fit in commercial contexts more generally.

One other manifestation of the notion of musical fit in present-day advertising is sonic branding (e.g. Fulberg, 2003; Jackson, 2003). Sonic brands are very short bursts of music (or other sounds) that are intended to reflect key aspects of the brand in question and/or prime recognition of the brand. There is no direct evidence concerning sonic branding specifically, but we might expect that many of the above arguments concerning musical fit apply. Similarly, since it is also reasonable to regard sonic brands as examples of jingles, research that has demonstrated the effectiveness of the latter may be relevant. Tom (1990), for example, showed that jingles were more effective at promoting recall of products than were hit songs, and argued that this was because they had only ever been heard in the conext of advertising for the product in question. Precisely the same argument applies to sonic brands, of course. Similarly, Yalch (1991; see also Wallace, 1991) found that advertising slogans were remembered better when presented in the context of a jingle than when presented verbally. This again suggests that music may help people to recall a short message concerning a company, and again points to the potential effectiveness of sonic brands.

   Related to sonic branding are those more general instances in which businesses will deliberately associate themselves with particular pieces of music, musicians, or music festivals in an attempt to improve their corporate image. Pincus (2005), for instance, describes numerous instances in which particular brands have become associated with certain musical styles; and Phillips (2001) has described how musicians have allowed themselves, rather than just their music, to be used in adverts and other forms of marketing. Two studies, however, suggest that sponsorship practices such as these at least have the potential to backfire. Oakes (2003) found that attendees of a classical music and a jazz festival could remember an average of only .86 and .65 of the 57 and 18 sponsoring organizations respectively. Similarly, Englis and Pennell (1994) describe research showing directly that fans resent having 'their' music taken over by marketing campaigns. Branding and sponsorship may have commercial benefits, but clearly research is needed into those circumstances under which they will be less or more effective.

32.3 MUSIC IN COMMERCIAL ENVIRONMENTS

The third major way in which music is used for profit concerns those retail and leisure premises such as shops, bars, and hotels that play 'piped music' to their customers. Three clear strands of research on this concern musically induced pleasure and arousal, knowledge activation effects, and research on time perception among people who are waiting.

32.3.1 Pleasure and arousal-based effects

Several studies have indicated that the speed with which customers shop, dine, or drink is related positively to the tempo or volume of piped music. As long ago as 1966, Smith and Curnow reported that loud music played in a supermarket led to people moving more quickly between two points than did soft music. Similarly, Milliman (1986) found that slow music in a restaurant led to people eating their meals more slowly than did fast music, and as a consequence spending more money on drinks from the bar. McElrea and Standing (1992) asked lab participants to drink a can of soda (supposedly to rate its flavour), while music played in the background. Fast music playing in the background led to people drinking the soda more quickly. This has obvious commercial implications: when premises are quiet, managers should play slower, quieter music to encourage customers to linger; whereas at busy times, managers can relieve crowding by playing faster, louder music.

Findings such as these again highlight another area where mainstream music psychology and research on music and marketing might inform one another. One of the most heavily investigated theories of musical preference (Berlyne, 1971) has led to over 30 years of research on how aspects of music such as its complexity and familiarity, and crucially also its tempo and volume, can mediate arousal in the autonomic nervous system (see Chapters 19 and 29, this volume). While mainstream researchers have gone on to relate this to musical preference, it is clearly related closely also to the findings reported here, namely that musical properties that would be expected to increase arousal lead to consumers behaving in a manner consistent with elevated levels of arousal.

Other research has focused more directly on the affective impact of music experienced in retail environments and how this interacts with its arousal-evoking characteristics. Much of this work has been carried out explicitly within the context of Mehrabian and Russell's (1974) model of environmental psychology. Most research has concentrated on two aspects of the model. The first is that if people like an environment, then they should demonstrate approach behaviours; these include the desire to stay in, explore, communicate with others within, and be satisfied with tasks performed within that environment. The second is that higher levels of arousal should lead to the effects of pleasure (or displeasure) being amplified. Of course, if piped music is liked, then it should lead to people liking the environment more, and subsequent approach behaviours. Furthermore, as we have just seen, many researchers have argued that music can also influence the level of arousal that people experience, such that music that is loud, fast, or complex ought to amplify the effects of (dis)liked piped music on responses to commercial environments.

A reasonable number of studies support the contention of the model that liked piped music should lead to more approach behaviours. For example, North and Hargreaves (1996) found that, when liked music was played, diners in a student cafeteria were more likely to visit the source of the music, namely a stall offering advice on student-related issues; Caldwell and Hibbert (2002), Herrington and Capella (1996), and Sullivan (2002) all found that liking for the music played was related to the amount of time spent in commercial premises; Kerr, Yore, Ham, and Dietz (2004) and Boutelle, Jeffery, Murray, and Schmitz (2001) found that installing a music system on a stairwell could promote use of those stairs; and North, Tarrant, and Hargreaves (2004) found that uplifting rather than annoying music played in a gym could influence the extent to which people were prepared to be helpful (by offering to distribute leaflets on behalf of a charity for disabled athletes). Given this encouraging pattern of findings, it is unfortunate that research on the Mehrabian and Russell model concerning the effects of musically evoked arousal has led to results that can be most optimistically described as mixed (e.g. Dubé, Chebat, & Morin, 1995).

32.3.2 Knowledge activation effects

Other research has paralleled that concerning musical fit in advertising. Specifically, several researchers have studied how the specific pieces of knowledge activated by in-store music might influence three aspects of consumer behaviour, namely customers' perception of the premises, which premises they will visit, and the amount of money they spend. Research in the first of these areas supports the intuitive notion that customers' knowledge about, stereotypes concerning, and emotional responses to, in-store music generalize onto their perception of the premises in which they hear that music. For example, Baker, Grewal, and Parasuranam (1994) found that classical music was associated with the image of an upmarket store, and that, in conjunction with soft lighting, it led to people inferring that the store would provide higher-quality merchandise and service. Similarly, North, Hargreaves, and McKendrick (2000) played various musical styles in a bank and a bar, showing that perceptions of these influenced customers' perceptions of the premises. Furthermore, the nature of these perceptions grouped into three factors, namely how upbeat, aggressive, and dignified/cerebral the premises seemed. Four other studies indicate that music can influence which premises consumers are prepared to visit. Sirgy, Grewal, and Mangleburg (2000), for example, argue that music played in-store should be congruent with a customer's self-image in order to encourage patronage.

However, the most commercially relevant of all this research concerns the application of musical fit to in-store purchasing decisions. Several studies have addressed how the correspondence between the knowledge activated by in-store music and particular products and product attributes can promote beliefs about a product, raise the salience of products or product features, or increase actual purchasing. For example, North, Hargreaves, and McKendrick (1997, 1999) showed how playing stereotypically French and German music from a supermarket display could prime the purchase of French and German wines respectively. Areni and Kim (1993) argued that the upmarket, affluent, and sophisticated stereotype of classical music may explain why, relative to pop music, it led to people buying more expensive wine from a wine cellar. Other studies have followed from this, investigating whether this stereotype of classical music might lead to it promoting higher sales. North and Hargreaves (1998; see also Lammers, 2003; Wilson, 2003) found that playing classical music in a cafeteria led to people being prepared to spend more money on the same products than did other musical styles (and a 'no music' control condition); and North, Shilcock, and Hargreaves (2003) found much the same in a restaurant, where classical music again led to higher spending.

Such work is not without problems, however. First it could be argued that it is unethical to use music to such ends, since it could persuade customers to select products they would not necessarily want or pay so much for. While this may be true, we are not, however, convinced that using piped music to these ends is any more unethical than asking shopfloor staff to dress smartly or handing out advertising 'flyers' outside the main entrance. Nor do we believe that music could by itself persuade people to buy products they cannot afford: if you walked past a Porsche showroom would you really go inside and buy a car just because Germanic music was being piped onto the pavement outside?

This in turn leads to a second area of concern regarding musical fit and purchasing with which we do have more sympathy: as with research in the domain of advertising, it is by no means clear yet why musical fit should prime spending and the selection of certain products. If, as we suggested earlier, the effects are based on the ability of music to prime or raise the salience of certain thoughts and behaviours, then this could be measured via, for example, a reduction in the amount of time it takes customers to recognize products or reach a decision between two competing alternatives. As is clear from this, mainstream research on cognitive priming, heuristics, and schemata could make a valuable contribution to our understanding of music and marketing (e.g. Schwarz, 2004).

32.3.3 Time perception and waiting

A final group of studies has investigated the impact of music on customers as they wait. Businesses often play music when they ask customers to wait, be it while standing in a check-out queue or on hold on the telephone. Much of this practice is based on the old maxim that 'Time flies when you're having fun,' since the implicit position adopted by businesses is that if they use music to entertain customers, then the waiting period will be more pleasant and therefore pass more quickly. However, the existing research suggests that the true impact of music may be much more complex than this.

Researchers have focused on two particular approaches to conceptualizing the impact of music on time perception. The first approach draws on discrete-events models of time perception (e.g. Levin & Zackay, 1989; Ornstein, 1969). These state that the perception of how much time has elapsed is related positively to the number of events that are processed during the period in question: the more events that are perceived to have occurred, the more time is inferred to have passed. This effect occurs because, under conditions of uncertainty, the mind effectively invokes a heuristic that if a greater number of events have taken place, then more time must have passed. In the context of music and marketing, this means that pieces of music that require more cognitive processing lead to the perception of more events and therefore longer time-duration estimates. Such an argument is supported by studies showing that time perception estimates are longer when people are exposed to loud rather than quiet music (e.g. Kellaris & Altsech, 1992); that time perception is related positively to the tempo of music played to people while they queue (Oakes, 2003); and that time-duration estimates are longer when people hear eight short songs than when they hear four long songs (Bailey & Areni, 2006a).

Other research within the discrete-events model has gone a step further and related time-duration estimates to people's emotional responses to the music in question. People should pay more attention to music that they like, and try to avoid paying attention to music that they dislike. Accordingly, when people are exposed to music that they like, so they process more information, and longer time-duration estimates result than when disliked music is heard (e.g. Kellaris & Mantel, 1994).

Bailey and Areni (2006b) do not deny that discrete events processes can influence time perception. However, they argue that music can also influence time perception via so-called attentional models, by distracting people from their attempts to actively monitor the passage of time. The impact of music on time perception, they argue, depends on whether people who are kept waiting are actually interested in how much time has passed. Sometimes, people who are waiting will take the opportunity to simultaneously do some other task, such as think about something else, have a conversation, or simply draw a doodle on a pad. When these people then try to estimate how much time has passed, they have to reconstruct the events of the period and base their duration estimates on this. Under these circumstances, we would expect their estimates to be consistent with the predictions of discrete-events models. At other times, however, people will indeed monitor the passage of time. For example, a football fan stuck in traffic outside the ground just a few minutes before kick-off will be acutely aware of each passing moment. Attentional models become more important under these circumstances: the cognitive effort involved in processing any music that can be heard will distract people's attention from the passage of time, or reduce their ability to monitor time accurately. Since less temporal information is therefore available, perceived duration is shortened. Bailey and Areni (2006b) argue that the results of four published studies are consistent with this attentional model of the effects of music on time perception (Guéguen & Jacob, 2002; MacNay, 1996; North & Hargreaves, 1999; Roper & Manela, 2000).

Of course, the real test of Bailey and Areni's (2006b) arguments would be to contrast the time-duration estimates that result when two groups of experimental participants (or ideally, real customers) either are or are not focusing on the passage of time. In the meantime, this highlights one of the major problems with research on music and waiting time, namely that the theories that have been proposed are able to explain almost any apparent effect of music on time perception. If music leads to longer time-duration estimates, then it can be claimed that this is because the person concerned was not attempting to actively monitor time, was forced to use a discrete-events process, and therefore produced an excessively long time-duration estimate; if instead the same music leads to shorter time-duration estimates, then it can be claimed that this is because the person was instead attempting to focus on the passage of time, was distracted from these attempts by the music, and therefore had little temporal information on which to base their estimate, leading to excessively short judgements. While both approaches could well be accurate and true explanations of the impact of music on the perception of time under different circumstances, it is impossible to conclude this with confidence when we cannot be certain of the strategy that experimental participants followed as they waited. Whether or not a particular set of data supports either approach depends on whether or not we can trust participants' claims that they were (not) attempting to monitor the passage of time.

32.4 CONCLUDING REMARKS

This chapter has summarized the many ways in which music and marketing relate to one another. As we have seen repeatedly, there is the clear scope for research in the field to inform and be informed by developments in mainstream music psychology. But in addition to this, we would make several other concluding remarks. The first is simply that the range of the effects that music can have on consumer behaviour is striking. In addition to research on music purchasing and piracy per se, we have seen how music is crucial to radio station advertising; how the effectiveness of TV and radio adverts can be influenced by the extent to which viewers and listeners like the music they contain or respond to other aspects of the information provided by that music; how arousing music can lead to customers acting more quickly; that responses to piped music influence perceptions of the commercial premises in which it is played; that playing piped music that is well liked can lead to various approach behaviours towards commercial premises; that music with particular connotations can guide consumers towards purchasing certain products or spending more money on them than they would otherwise; and that music can influence the amount of time that customers believe they have been kept waiting or believe they have spent consuming a service. The available research suggests that the 'right' kinds of music can typically lead to increases in turnover of around 10 per cent, such that piped music makes clear commercial sense. Note also that different types of music very clearly have different effects. Businesses cannot regard music as a homogeneous sonic mass.

Second, nonetheless, although some areas of research (e.g. advertising) might benefit from more reductionist research designs, the majority of the research topics covered here can be faulted on the opposite grounds, namely that they consider short-term effects of music in the immediate environment. We are not aware of any research to date that has considered, for example, the longer-term impact of piped music on consumers' behaviour in other shops or their propensity to visit other branches of a chain store.

Third, it seems odd that so much social stigma should be associated with the use of music in marketing. The use of turquoise emulsion paint in supermarkets does not devalue Picasso's blue period, so why should piped music supposedly devalue 'real' music? Similarly, it is rare to hear of people complaining about the décor in a supermarket, yet it is perfectly acceptable to hear complaints about the music; and it is difficult to understand why this particular aspect of the aesthetics of commercial environments should be subject to such strong feelings. The relationship between music and marketing may be controversial, but it is important because it has the potential to boost income and to foster links between music psychology and the everyday circumstances in which people hear music.

Finally, as we noted at the beginning of the chapter, the focus of research in this field is rarely on the music itself, and so a critic might argue that the field has little to contribute to our understanding of music and emotion. We disagree. For instance, Juslin and Västfjäll (2008) highlight several specific mechanisms by which music might elicit emotion, which are addressed by the research reviewed here, albeit indirectly. For instance, Juslin and Västfjäll (2008) describe how some emotional reactions to music are the product of brain stem responses concerning arousal. As we noted in the section above on pleasure- and arousal-based effects, it is possible to conceptualize the impact of musical tempo and volume on the speed of customer behaviour in terms of, for example, Berlyne's theory of how these musical properties impact upon physiological alertness.

Second, Juslin and Västfjäll (2008) describe how music may elicit emotion through evaluative conditioning: 'This refers to a process whereby an emotion is induced by a piece of music simply because this stimulus has been paired repeatedly with other positive or negative stimuli' (p. 564). This may well relate to the research described earlier that has used music in adverts to condition responses to a product, or to that research that has used the pleasure evoked by music to evoke a positive response to a particular commercial environment. Juslin and Västfjäll's (2008) argument is of particular interest here, because they also highlight several characteristics of these kinds of emotional responses to music that may provide hypotheses for future work in specifically commercial contexts. For example, they argue that these effects may occur even if people are unaware of any link between the music and the stimulus it is conditioning responses to. This suggests, for example, that music may condition responses to a product or commercial environment without the awareness of the consumer, with obvious ethical implications. Moreover, Juslin and Västfjäll argue that this kind of conditioning is particularly robust, which suggests that the effects may remain over the long term.

A third mechanism cited by Juslin and Västfjäll (2008) that is apparently relevant to the commercial literature concerns what they term emotional contagion: 'This refers to a process whereby an emotion is induced by a piece of music because the listener perceives the emotional expression of the music, and then "mimics" this expression internally, which by means of either peripheral feedback from muscles, or a more direct activation of the relevant emotional representations in the brain, leads to an induction of the same emotion. For instance, the music might have a sad expression (e.g. slow tempo, low pitch, low sound level) that induces sadness in the listener' (p. 565). It is easy to see how such a process maps onto those knowledge activation effects in commercial contexts that are discussed in the present chapter, and a more detailed version of this in a specifically commercial context is set out by North, Hargreaves, MacKenzie, and Law (2004).

In short, it is the ability of research on music and marketing to foster links between music psychology and the everyday circumstances in which people hear music that makes it relevant to the present book. The ability of practitioners to apply many of the effects outlined in this chapter depends on their ability to reliably use music to produce emotional effects among consumers in everyday settings. As such, the commercial uses of music outlined here provide a clear opportunity for naturalistic testing and refinement of the more fundamental theories of music and emotion outlined elsewhere in this book. Furthermore, if the private sector can be persuaded of the financial advantages of being able to reliably influence customers' moods and emotions through music, this may open up a valuable source of research funding for theoretically oriented research.

Recommended further reading

1. Garlin, F. V., & Owen, K. (2006). Setting the tone with the tune: a meta-analytic review of the effects of background music in retail settings. *Journal of Business Research, 59,* 755–64.
2. Kellaris, J. J. (2008). Music and consumers. In C. P. Haugtvedt, P. M. Herr, & F. R. Kardes (eds), *Handbook of consumer psychology* (pp. 837–56). Mahwah, NJ: Erlbaum.
3. North, A. C., & Hargreaves, D. J. (2008). *The social and applied psychology of music.* Oxford: Oxford University Press.

References

Alpert, M. I., Alpert, J. I., & Maltz, E. N. (2005). Purchase occasion influence on the role of music in advertising. *Journal of Business Research, 58,* 369–76.

Ang, S. H., Cheng, P. S., Lim, E. A. C, & Tambyah, S. K. (2001). Spot the difference: consumer responses towards counterfeits. *Journal of Consumer Marketing, 18,* 219–35.

Areni, C. S., & Kim, D. (1993). The influence of background music on shopping behavior: classical versus top-forty music in a wine store. *Advances in Consumer Research, 20,* 336–40.

Bailey, N., & Areni, C. S. (2006a). Keeping time to the tune: background music as a quasi clock in retrospective duration judgments. *Perceptual and Motor Skills, 102,* 435–44.

Bailey, N., & Areni, C. S. (2006b). When a few minutes sound like a lifetime: does atmospheric music expand or contract perceived time? *Journal of Retailing, 82,* 189–202.

Baker, J., Grewal, D., & Parasuraman, A. (1994). The influence of store environment on quality inferences and store image. *Journal of the Academy of Marketing Science, 22,* 328–39.

Berlyne, D. E. (1971). *Aesthetics and psychobiology.* New York: Appleton-Century-Crofts.

Boutelle, K. N., Jeffery, R. W., Murray, D. M., & Schmitz, K. H. (2001). Using signs, artwork, and music to promote stair use in a public building. *American Journal of Public Health, 91,* 2004–6.

Brown, S. P., & Stayman, D. M. (1992). Antecedents and consequences of attitude toward the ad: a meta-analysis. *Journal of Consumer Research, 19,* 34–51.

Caldwell, C., & Hibbert, S. A. (2002). The influence of music tempo and musical preference on restaurant patrons' behavior. *Psychology and Marketing, 19,* 895–917.

Chiou, J. S., Huang, G., & Lee, H. (2005). The antecedents of music piracy attitudes and intentions. *Journal of Business Ethics, 57,* 161–74.

Crain, W. M., & Tollison, R. D. (1997). Economics and the architecture of popular music. *Journal of Economic Behavior and Organization, 32,* 185–205.

Dubé, L., Chebat, J. C., & Morin, S. (1995). The effects of background music on consumers' desire to affiliate in buyer seller interactions. *Psychology and Marketing, 12*, 305–319.

Englis, B. G., & Pennell, G. E. (1994). 'This note's for you': negative effects of the commercial use of popular music. *Advances in Consumer Research, 21*, 97.

Erdelyi, M. (1940). The relation between 'radio plugs' and sheet sales of popular music. *Journal of Applied Psychology, 24*, 696–702.

Fairchild, C. (1996). What you want when you want it: altering consumption and consuming alternatives. *Media, Culture and Society, 18*, 659–68.

Flynn, L. R., Goldsmith, R. E., & Eastman, J. K. (1996). Opinion leaders and opinion seekers: two new measurement scales. *Journal of the Academy of Marketing Science, 24*, 137–47.

Fox, M. A., & Kochanowski, P. (2004). Models of superstardom: an application of the Lotka and Yule distributions. *Popular Music and Society, 27*, 507–22.

Fulberg, P. (2003). Using sonic branding in the retail environment: an easy and effective way to create consumer brand loyalty while enhancing the in-store experience. *Journal of Consumer Behaviour, 3*, 193–8.

Gopal, R. D., Sanders, G. L., Bhattacharjee, S., Agrawal, M., & Wagner, S. C. (2004). A behavioral model of digital music piracy. *Journal of Organizational Computing and Electronic Commerce, 14*, 89–105.

Gorn, G. J. (1982). The effect of music in advertising on choice behavior: a classical conditioning approach. *Journal of Marketing, 46*, 94–101.

Guéguen, N., & Jacob, C. (2002). The influence of music on temporal perceptions in an on-hold waiting situation. *Psychology of Music, 30*, 210–214.

Hamlen, W. A. (1994). Variety and superstardom in popular music. *Economic Inquiry, 32*, 395–406.

Hecker, S. (1984). Music for advertising effect. *Psychology and Marketing, 1*, 3–8.

Heckler, S. E., & Childers, T. L. (1992). The role of expectancy and relevancy in memory for verbal and visual information: what is incongruency? *Journal of Consumer Research, 18*, 475–92.

Hendy, D. (2000). Pop music radio in the public service: BBC Radio 1 and new music in the 1990s. *Media, Culture and Society, 22*, 743–61.

Hennion, A., & Meadel, C. (1986). Programming music: radio as mediator. *Media, Culture and Society, 8*, 281–303.

Herrington, J. D., & Capella, L. M. (1996). Effects of music in service environments: a field study. *Journal of Services Marketing, 10*, 26–41.

Hui, K. L., & Png, I. (2003). Piracy and the legitimate demand for recorded music. *Contributions to Economic Analysis and Policy, 2*, article 11, 1–22.

Hung, K. (2000). Narrative music in congruent and incongruent TV advertising. *Journal of Advertising, 29*, 25–34.

Jackson, D. M. (2003). *Sonic branding: an essential guide to the art and science of sonic branding.* Basingstoke, UK: Palgrave Macmillan.

Jakobovits, L. A. (1966). Studies of fads: 1. The 'hit parade'. *Psychological Reports, 18*, 443–50.

Johnson, E. J., Moe, W. W., Fader, P. S., Bellman, S., & Lohse, G. L. (2004). On the depth and dynamics of online search behavior. *Management Science, 50*, 299–308.

Jones, S., & Lenhart, A (2004). Music downloading and listening: findings from the Pew Internet and American Life Project. *Popular Music and Society, 27*, 185–99.

Juslin, P. N., & Västfjäll, D. (2008). Emotional responses to music: the need to consider underlying mechanisms. *Behavioral and Brain Sciences, 31*, 559–621.

Kellaris, J. J., & Altsech, M. B. (1992). The experience of time as a function of musical loudness and gender of listener. *Advances in Consumer Research, 19*, 725–9.

Kellaris, J. J., & Mantel, S. P. (1994). The influence of mood and gender on consumers' time perceptions. *Advances in Consumer Research, 21,* 514–18.

Kerr, A. N., Yore, M. M., Ham, S. A., & Dietz, W. H. (2004). Increasing stair use in a worksite through environmental changes. *American Journal of Health Promotion, 18,* 312–15.

Konečni, V. J. (1982). Social interaction and musical preference. In D. Deutsch (Ed.), *The psychology of music* (pp. 497–516). New York: Academic Press.

Lacher, K. T., & Mizerski, R. (1994). An exploratory study of the responses and relationships involved in the evaluation of, and in the intention to purchase new rock music. *Journal of Consumer Research, 21,* 366–80.

Lammers, H. B. (2003). An oceanside field experiment on background music effects on the restaurant tab. *Perceptual and Motor Skills, 96,* 1025–6.

Levin, I., & Zackay, D. (eds). (1989). *Time and human cognition.* Amsterdam, The Netherlands: Elsevier Science.

MacInnis, D. J., & Park, C. W. (1991). The differential role of characteristics of music on high- and low-involvement consumers' processing of ads. *Journal of Consumer Research, 18,* 161–73.

MacNay, S. K. (1995). The influence of preferred music on the perceived exertion, mood, and time estimation scores of patients participating in a cardiac rehabilitation exercise program. *Therapy Perspectives, 13,* 91–6.

McElrea, H., & Standing, L. (1992). Fast music causes fast drinking. *Perceptual and Motor Skills, 75,* 362.

Meenaghan, A., & Turnbull, P. W. (1981). The application of product life cycle theory to popular record marketing. *European Journal of Marketing, 15,* 1–50.

Mehrabian, A., & Russell, J. A. (1974). *An approach to environmental psychology.* Cambridge, MA: MIT Press.

Miller, D. W., & Marks, L. J. (1992). Mental imagery and sound effects in radio commercials. *Journal of Advertising, 21,* 83–93.

Miller, D. W., & Marks, L. J. (1997). The effects of imagery-evoking radio advertising strategies on affective responses. *Psychology and Marketing, 14,* 337–60.

Milliman, R. E. (1986). The influence of background music on the behavior of restaurant patrons. *Journal of Consumer Research, 13,* 286–9.

Mintel. (2003). *Pre-recorded music, June 2003.* London: Mintel.

Mixon, F. G., Trevino, L. J., & Bales, A. R. (2004). Just-below pricing strategies in the music industry: empirical evidence. *International Journal of the Economics of Business, 11,* 165–74.

Molteni, L., & Ordanini, A. (2003). Consumption patterns, digital technology and music downloading. *Long Range Planning, 36,* 389–406.

North, A. C., & Hargreaves, D. J (1999). Can music move people? The effects of musical complexity and silence on waiting time. *Environment and Behavior, 31,* 136–49.

North, A. C., & Hargreaves, D. J. (1996). The effects of music on responses to a dining area. *Journal of Environmental Psychology, 16,* 55–64.

North, A. C., & Hargreaves, D. J. (1998). The effect of music on atmosphere and purchase intentions in a cafeteria. *Journal of Applied Social Psychology, 28,* 2254–73.

North, A. C., & Hargreaves, D. J. (2000). Musical preference during and after relaxation and exercise. *American Journal of Psychology, 113,* 43–67.

North, A. C., & Hargreaves, D. J. (2008). *The social and applied psychology of music.* Oxford: Oxford University Press.

North, A. C., & Oishi, A. (2006). Music CD purchase decisions. *Journal of Applied Social Psychology, 36,* 3043–84.

North, A. C., Hargreaves, D. J., & Hargreaves, J. J. (2004). The uses of music in everyday life. *Music Perception, 22,* 63–99.

North, A. C., Hargreaves, D. J., & McKendrick, J. (1997). In-store music affects product choice. *Nature, 390,* 132.

North, A. C., Hargreaves, D. J., & McKendrick, J. (1999). The effect of music on in-store wine selections. *Journal of Applied Psychology, 84,* 271–6.

North, A. C., Hargreaves, D. J., & McKendrick, J. (2000). The effects of music on atmosphere and purchase intentions in a bank and a bar. *Journal of Applied Social Psychology, 30,* 1504–22.

North, A. C., Hargreaves, D. J., MacKenzie, L., & Law, R. (2004). The effects of musical and voice 'fit' on responses to adverts. *Journal of Applied Social Psychology, 34,* 1675–1708.

North, A. C., Shilcock, A., & Hargreaves, D. J. (2003). The effect of musical style on restaurant customers' spending. *Environment and Behavior, 35,* 712–18.

North, A. C., Tarrant, M., & Hargreaves, D. J. (2004). The effects of music on helping behaviour: a field study. *Environment and Behavior, 36,* 266–75.

Oakes, S. (2003a). Demographic and sponsorship considerations for jazz and classical music festivals. *Service Industries Journal, 23,* 165–78.

Oakes, S. (2003b). Musical tempo and waiting perceptions. *Psychology and Marketing, 20,* 685–705.

Oakes, S., & North, A. C. (2006). The impact of background musical tempo and timbre congruity upon ad content recall and affective response. *Applied Cognitive Psychology, 20,* 505–20.

Odell, P. M., Korgen, K. O., Schumacher, P., & Delucchi, M. (2000). Internet use among female and male college students. *CyberPsychology and Behavior, 3,* 855–62.

Olsen, G. D. (1997). The impact of interstimulus interval and background silence on recall. *Journal of Consumer Research, 23,* 295–303.

Ornstein, R. E. (1969). *On the experience of time.* New York: Penguin.

Papadopoulos, T. (2003). Determinants of international sound recording piracy. *Economics Bulletin, 6,* 1–9.

Papadopoulos, T. (2004). Pricing and pirate product market formation. *Journal of Product and Brand Management, 13,* 56–63.

Petty, R. E., & Cacioppo, J. T. (1981). *Attitudes and persuasion: classic and contemporary approaches.* Dubuque, IA: William C. Brown.

Petty, R. E., Cacioppo, J. T., & Schumann, D. T. (1983). Central and peripheral routes to advertising effectiveness: the moderating effect of involvement. *Journal of Consumer Research, 10,* 135–46.

Phillips, D. (2001). Celebrity branding aims for the stars. *Brand Strategy, 154,* 10.

Pincus, B. (2005). Get in tune with consumers. *Brand Strategy, 190,* 46–7.

Rajala, A. K., & Hantula, D. A. (2000). Towards a behavioral ecology of consumption: delay-reduction effects on foraging in a simulated internet mall. *Managerial and Decision Economics, 21,* 145–8.

Roper, J. M., & Manela, J. (2000). Psychiatric patients' perceptions of waiting time in the psychiatric emergency service. *Journal of Psychosocial Nursing, 38,* 19–27.

Rosen, S. (1981). The economics of superstars. *American Economic Review, December,* 845–58.

Rosen, S. (1983). The economics of superstars. *American Scholar, Autumn,* 449–459.

Rothenbuhler, E. (1985). Programming decision making in popular music radio. *Communication Research, 12,* 209–32.

Rothenbuhler, E. (1987). Commercial radio and popular music: processes of selection and factors of influence. In J. Lull (ed.), *Popular music and communication* (pp. 78–95). London: Sage.

Rothenbuhler, E., & Dimmick, J. (1982). Popular music: concentration and diversity in the industry, 1974–1980. *Journal of Communication, 32,* 143–9.

Rothenbuhler, E., & McCourt, T. (1992). Commercial radio and popular music: processes of selection and factors of influence. In J. Lull (ed.), *Popular music and communication* (2nd edn, pp. 101–15). London: Sage.

Rothenbuhler, E. W., & McCourt, T. (2004). The economics of the recording industry. In A. Alexander, J. Owers, R. Carveth, C. A. Hollifield, & A. N. Greco (eds), *Media economics: theory and practice* (3rd edn, pp. 221–48). Mahwah, NJ: Erlbaum.

Salagniak, M. J., Dodds, P. S., & Watts, D. J. (2006). Experimental study of inequality and unpredictability in an artificial cultural market. *Science, 311*, 854–6.

Schwarz, N. (2004). Metacognitive experiences in consumer judgment and decision making. *Journal of Consumer Psychology, 14*, 332–48.

Scott, B. (2002). One tune no longer fits all. *International Journal of Advertising and Marketing to Children, 3*, 49–56.

Sirgy, M. J., Grewal, D., & Mangleburg, T. (2000). Retail environment, self-congruity, and retail patronage: an integrative model and a research agenda. *Journal of Business Research, 49*, 127–38.

Sloboda, J. A., O'Neill, S. A., & Ivaldi, A. (2001). Functions of music in everyday life: an exploratory study using the experience sampling method. *Musicae Scientiae, 5*, 9–32.

Smith, P. C., & Curnow, R. (1966). 'Arousal hypothesis' and the effects of music on purchasing behavior. *Journal of Applied Psychology, 50*, 255–6.

Stewart, D. W., & Punj, G. N. (1998). Effects of using a nonverbal (musical) cue on recall and playback of television advertising: implications for advertising tracking. *Journal of Business Research, 42*, 39–51.

Sullivan, M. (2002). The impact of pitch, volume and tempo on the atmospheric effects of music. *International Journal of Retail and Distribution Management, 30*, 323–30.

Taylor, C. R., & Johnson, C. M. (2002). Standardized vs. specialized international advertising campaigns: what we have learned from academic research in the 1990s. *New Directions in International Advertising Research, 12*, 45–66.

Teston, G. I. (2002). A developmental perspective of computer and information technology ethics: piracy of software and digital music by young adolescents. *Dissertation Abstracts International: Section B: The Sciences and Engineering, 62*, 5815.

Tom, G. (1990). Marketing with music. *Journal of Consumer Marketing, 7*, 49–53.

Vogel, H. (1998). *Entertainment industry economics* (4th edn). Cambridge, UK: Cambridge University Press.

Wallace, W. T. (1991). Jingles in advertisements: can they improve recall? *Advances in Consumer Research, 18*, 239–42.

Wiebe, G. (1940). The effect of radio plugging on students' opinions of popular songs. *Journal of Applied Psychology, 24*, 721–7.

Wilson, N. C., & Stokes, D. (2004). Laments and serenades: relationship marketing and legitimation strategies for the cultural entrepreneur. *Qualitative Market Research: An International Journal, 7*, 218–27.

Wilson, S. (2003). The effect of music on perceived atmosphere and purchase intentions in a restaurant. *Psychology of Music, 31*, 93–109.

Yalch, R. F. (1991). Memory in a jingle jungle: music as a mnemonic device in communicating advertising slogans. *Journal of Applied Psychology, 76*, 268–75.

PART VIII

ENCORE

CHAPTER 33

THE PAST, PRESENT, AND FUTURE OF MUSIC AND EMOTION RESEARCH

PATRIK N. JUSLIN AND JOHN A. SLOBODA

THE preceding 32 chapters of this volume reveal the healthy state of the current field of music and emotion. In this final chapter, we take the opportunity—benefiting from the overview that the volume is offering—to comment on the history of the field, summarize current trends, and propose future directions for research.

33.1 THE PAST

A comprehensive, multidisciplinary history of the field of music and emotion remains to be written and represents a major undertaking, which we leave for a possible chapter in a future volume. Budd (1985) offered a useful survey of some of the historical ideas in philosophical thought on the topic—which continue to resonate in current philosophical work (reviewed by Davies, this volume)—and Cook and Dibben (this volume) provide a whistle-stop tour of the key ideas in musicological thought since ancient times, especially since 1600. In this section, we will mainly restrict our comments to the development of music and emotion as a sub-field of music psychology. Even a cursory history of the field may be useful to explain the current state of the field and inform speculations about the future.

Despite the fact that the first studies of emotion in music coincided with the advent of psychology as an independent discipline in the late nineteenth century (e.g. Downey, 1897; Gilman, 1891; Weld, 1912), the emergence of music and emotion as a separate sub-field was not going to be easy: Apart from an early 'peak' of studies in the 1930s and 1940s, including the seminal work by Kate Hevner (1935), Melvin Rigg (1940), and Carl Seashore (1938), the area would soon be sidelined by other areas. The early work on musical emotions was mainly experimental, descriptive, and concerned with *perception* of emotion rather than induction of emotion (cf. Table 1.2, Chapter 1, this volume). Typical studies focused on self-report, asking subjects to match verbal labels to pieces of music—also relating such matching to individual differences (for reviews, see Gabrielsson & Juslin, 2003; and Gabrielsson & Lindström, this volume). However, the dominant trends in music psychology in the early twentieth century concerned more 'basic' psychophysical and perceptual processes, reflecting the regarding of the natural sciences as the ideal for 'the new behavioural science'. The strive for experimental control and the 'bottom-up' approach to psychology were not beneficial for an understanding of how listeners actually experience music (e.g. emotionally).

The subsequent trends in psychology more generally (for a recent review, see Goodwin, 2008) did little to change this situation: After first having to endure the 'emotion-banning' era of Behaviourism (e.g. Skinner, 1953), and then the 'cognitive revolution' (Gardner, 1985), the field barely survived until the eighties, when the tide slowly began to turn. During most of the history of music psychology, musical emotion studies were conducted by a few pioneers, with little or no connection to the broader field of affect. To be sure, each of the following decades would see the publication of what are today regarded as 'classic' books on the topic (by Meyer, 1956; Berlyne, 1960, 1971; Clynes, 1977). However, these books were largely isolated efforts which did not succeed in bringing music and emotion research into the 'mainstream' of music psychology; for instance, Meyer's work did not stimulate emotion-related work until the early 1990s (Sloboda, 1991) while Berlyne's work was not revived until the 1980s (Konečni, 1982) and 1990s (Hargreaves & North, 1997). Well into the 1980s, the *Zeitgeist* in music psychology was mainly characterized by experimental perceptual and cognitive research (as saluted in the influential book by Sloboda, 1985), in keeping with the origins of music psychology.

As noted by Sloboda and Juslin (this volume), the breakthrough came in the late 1980s and early 1990s—driven by many of the authors featured in the present book. Several factors contributed to this trend. One crucial factor was the blossoming of another, related field—the social psychology of music (e.g. Hargreaves & North, 1997)—which, arguably, moved music psychology away from the typical 1980s paradigm of laboratory-based experiments regarding cognitive processes to a broader exploration of the manifold ways in which music is used and experienced in everyday life—which in turn would contribute to the use of a broader range of methods in studying music experience. The music-emotion field also received a 'boost' from unexpected quarters, as the influential books by Damasio (1994) and LeDoux (1996; see also Panksepp, 1998) convinced neuroscientists that affect was perhaps after all worthy of serious attention—leading also to the initial neuroimaging studies of music and emotion (Blood et al, 1999). This trend culminated in the 'Geneva Emotion Week' 1998—devoted entirely to musical emotions—and the publication of the book *Music and emotion* (Juslin & Sloboda, 2001). The research carried out since then forms the basis for any current evaluation of the state of the field.

33.2 THE PRESENT

At the current stage, the topic of music and emotion has become a generally accepted field of research, as revealed by its inclusion in handbooks of music psychology (e.g. Hallam, Cross, & Thaut, 2009) and emotion psychology (e.g. Davidson, Scherer, & Goldsmith, 2003; Lewis, Haviland-Jones, & Barrett, 2008). (Even so, that 'music' is not taken *quite* as seriously as the other sub-topics is revealed by the fact that, although the other chapters in the last-mentioned handbook were written by experts in their respective fields, the chapter on music was written by two researchers who have not conducted any studies on emotion in music—Johnson-Laird & Oatley, 2008). At the time of writing, three conferences focusing on musical emotion were planned for the summer of 2009, testifying to the continuing high profile of the topic.[1]

What is the field of music and emotion of 2009 like? One characterization is obviously provided by preceding chapters of the present book. Judging from the content of this volume, how does the field of today differ from that of the past? Apart from the fact that it has grown in recent years, the field is characterized by a broader range of methods and genres of music than previously (the latter is presumably a result of a new generation of researchers entering the field); a stronger focus on induction of emotions, relative to perception of emotions; and increasing links to the developments in the 'affective sciences' more generally. One can also discern the emergence of further subdivisions of the field into areas such as 'measurement', 'performance', 'neuroscience', 'music experience', 'development', 'music in everyday life', 'music preference', and 'applications'.

However, the field is still mainly descriptive rather than hypothesis-driven, which may suggest that the field has not yet quite reached maturity. Theoretical work is less common in the music and emotion domain than in the emotion domain generally (Davidson, Scherer, & Goldsmith, 2003). As far as conceptualizations of emotion are

---

[1] The conferences were 'The Emotional Power of Music' (Geneva, June 2009), 'The International Conference on Music and Emotion' (Durham, September 2009), and 'Audio Mostly' (theme: 'Sound and Emotions'; Glasgow, September 2009).

concerned, both the dominant approaches (*categorical* and *dimensional*) continue to exist, side by side, in current research: for example, in the current volume, Hargreaves and North adopt a one-dimensional approach in terms of arousal; Thaut and Wheeler, and Schubert, adopt two-dimensional models; others such Zentner and Eerola, Sloboda, and Juslin et al adopt categorical models.[2] Furthermore, it can be noted that much current research is method-driven rather than issue-driven, suggesting the need to provide a broader methodological training to a new generation of musical emotion researchers; they need exposure to methods beyond their usual academic specialties by means of workshops and summer schools on specific techniques.

Moreover, despite calls for more cross-cultural research (see Sloboda & Juslin, 2001), there are still very few cross-cultural studies in the field; similarly, previous calls for further multidisciplinary research and integration have not yet been met—that is, there are still few clear cases of interdisciplinary collaboration. There are *some* examples of interdisciplinary influences, however, as in the adoption of Gibsonian ecological psychology in musicological and sociological work (Cook & Dibben, this volume; DeNora, this volume); the adoption of sociologically inspired approaches in British music psychology (Sloboda, this volume), and the increasing influence of neuroscientific research in music therapy (Thaut & Wheeler, this volume). However, intensely interdisciplinary research of the kind observed in neuroscience (Brehm, 2008) is still rare in the music and emotion field.

To be fair, multidisciplinary collaboration may not be quite as easy as it appears. This relates to the thorny issues of what counts as 'theory' and 'evidence' in different disciplines. For instance, Becker (this volume) is arguing forcefully for an integration of humanistic and scientific approaches to music and emotion; she notes that 'while the styles of argument and the criteria for evidence may remain distinct, the conclusions need to be comparable and not incommensurable' (p. 144). How the conclusions can ever be comparable and commensurable when the criteria for evidence remain distinct is unclear, however. Most of the 'dichotomies' or 'dimensions' that we used to characterize the field in a previous commentary (cf. Sloboda & Juslin, 2001) are still evident in the field; for example, the stimulus-driven biological view adopted by Peretz (this volume) is distant from the sociological listener-as-agent perspective adopted by DeNora (this volume). Still, Juslin et al (this volume) propose that some of these differences can be reconciled by noting that emotional reactions to music involve processing at multiple (and partly independent) levels of the brain (e.g. subcortical structures that enable 'automatic' processing as well as 'higher' cortical structures related to self-consciousness and imagination). On this view, different disciplines complement each other, by providing distinct parts of the overall puzzle. But the question remains just how far interdisciplinary integration is possible, or even desirable.

Another way to capture the nature of the field is in terms of the articles and books cited most widely in the field. Thus, Table 33.1 shows a subset of the most frequently

---

[2] The 'domain-specific' approach recommended by Zentner and Eerola (this volume) is actually a special case of the categorical approach, one in which the response categories were selected based on preliminary prevalence findings within a specific domain ('music').

Table 33.1 List of 20 frequently cited papers on music and emotion

Paper	Citations
Meyer (1956)	1,236
Berlyne (1971)	1,043
Blood & Zatorre (2001)	373
Blood et al (1999)	289
Juslin & Sloboda (2001)	266
Cooke (1959)	264
Clynes (1977)	243
Krumhansl (1997)	192
Sloboda (1991)	181
Juslin & Laukka (2003)	176
Bruner (1990)	153
Scherer & Oshinsky (1977)	152
Gabrielsson & Juslin (1996)	137
Juslin (2001)	132
Balkwill & Thompson (1999)	126
Peretz, Gagnon, & Bouchard (1998)	126
Gabrielsson & Lindström	120
Panksepp (1995)	119
Juslin (2000)	104

Source: Google Scholar; 12 May 2009

cited papers, as indicated by a Google Scholar search on 12 May 2009. We emphasize that such citation counts are imperfect measures of scientific impact, and that they may well tend to favour older publications and publications in relatively more 'active' sub-fields. Yet they offer some sense of which papers influence the field, one way or another. The articles and books listed in Table 33.1 could be—and probably already are—used as 'key reading materials' in courses on music and emotion. (These could be augmented by the 'recommended further readings' provided by the authors of the previous chapters in this book.)

33.3 THE FUTURE

What does the future hold for the music and emotion field? In this section, we propose future directions. However, instead of relying only on our own prejudices, we use the results from a mini-survey featuring several contributors to this volume as guidance. Who are better able to predict the future of the domain than the researchers at the forefront of the field? The authors were asked to indicate up to three priorities or main issues for the study of music and emotion to give particular attention to for the next five years. We were able to obtain a response from (at least) one author of every chapter in this book during the spring of 2009. Though there were individual differences and many authors understandably nominated issues close to their own sub-fields of research, there were nevertheless a number of recurrent themes in the responses (provided in full in the Appendix). In the following, we briefly discuss each theme, and then add some additional themes that, we believe, may be prominent in future research.

33.3.1 Measurement

The most frequent theme concerned measurement of musical emotions, addressed in at least ten of the responses. This was apparent, for instance, in calls for 'routine multiple-component measurement of emotion', 'objective measures of emotion', and 'a wider assessment palette'; and in the note that 'more attention needs to be given to develop reliable and valid measures of music-related behaviour'. One author voiced 'a plea for having researchers trying out new methods'. Another observed the need to develop 'more refined techniques for separating the perception of emotion in music from its emotional effects on listeners'. (Indeed, in our view, many researchers continue to confound these processes, causing confusion.) Another author emphasized the importance of longitudinal studies in evaluating developmental theories and, interestingly, suggested that 'one should view every study as possibly a developmental study that someone else, if not oneself, could carry out again on the same participants several years, or even decades down the road'. The same author also suggested that a digital database 'for sharing stimulus resources and data through the Internet' would benefit the field. In addition, increasing use of 'continuous response methods' was mentioned by some authors (discussed below in Section 33.3.7). Overall these comments suggest a need to broaden the researcher's methodological 'tool kit' in studies of music and emotion, including further development of novel measures, which may be especially useful in studies with special participants, such as infants (Trehub et al, this volume). Section 3 of this volume offers a useful starting point for such an endeavour. In addition to established measurement techniques in terms of self-report (Zentner & Eerola, Schubert), psychophysiology (Hodges) and neuroimaging (Koelsch et al), Västfjäll reviews a selection of 'indirect' or 'implicit' measures, many of which have not yet been used in regard to emotions in music, and Rentfrow and McDonald (this volume) discuss novel measures of music preference. Also useful is the *Handbook of emotion elicitation and assessment* (Coan & Allen, 2007), which (although it does not mainly concern music) offers further methodological recommendations and discussions of some of the caveats involved in interpreting data concerning emotional experience (Ch. 22) and brain activation (Ch. 26).

Developments in neighbouring disciplines can also be useful. Thus, for instance, in the context of product design, Diesmet (2002) has proposed the *Product Emotion measurement instrument* (PrEmo), by which participants can report their experienced emotions by using a set of expressive cartoon animations that portray each emotion using dynamic facial, bodily, and vocal expressions. The instrument can measure distinct as well as 'mixed' emotions and has been demonstrated to be cross-culturally reliable as well. Similar innovations—including ones that capture temporal aspects (see below)—will form a crucial part of future research.

33.3.2 Social contexts

Nine query responses concerned social processes related to music and emotion, as evident in various everyday and educational contexts. Thus, for instance, authors requested studies that 'capture naturalistic behaviours that occur in the "real" world', and that would explore 'social integration/disintegration'; 'collective action'; 'ethics and public policy implications of using music as a negative stimulus in situations ranging from crowd control to torture'; 'emotional consequences of joint music making', and 'integration of music-emotion theories with those concerning responses to other aspects of the environment' (making explicit the connection to environmental psychology). As noted by Sloboda (this volume), everyday emotions to music rarely if ever arise out of a decontextualized aesthetic relationship to the music as object.

In addition, several query responses emphasized aspects of emotion in music education contexts (see also Hallam, this volume): 'How can formal education better address the music–emotion relationship?' Thus, for example, one of the authors suggested 'a study exploring the perceptions of pupils and teachers of the role of emotion in classroom music and the ways in which this can be used to promote greater enjoyment of music and relevance to experiences outside the classroom', and also 'further work on the teaching of emotional communication in music performance', 'also extending it to include improvisation and composition'. Chapters by Simonton, Woody and McPherson, Juslin and Timmers, and Kenny (this volume) illustrate the crucial role of emotion in the work of musicians.

That the field has left its previous 'fixation' with laboratory studies is reflected in many chapters of this book (Becker; DeNora; Hargreaves & North; Sloboda; Juslin et al; Garofalo; and North & Hargreaves). Increasingly, studies of music are conducted in everyday contexts, and Sloboda (this volume) offers a review of the conceptual terrain and dimensions that must be considered in such an endeavour. This trend is likely to continue, as the social psychology of music (North & Hargreaves, 2008) and the new sociology of music (DeNora, this volume) continue to thrive.

33.3.3 Health

At least eight query responses concerned the role of musical emotions in health: 'well-being'; 'immunological changes'; 'management of emotional disorders (i.e. anxiety and depression)'; 'neurorehabilitation and psychiatry'; 'psychological and physiological health'; 'pain-reducing effects of music'. Several chapters in the present volume (Thaut & Wheeler; Hanser; DeNora; Koelsch et al; Juslin et al) discuss health aspects, which can be taken as further indication that this will be a salient topic in coming years (MacDonald, Kreutz, & Mitchell, in preparation).

Attempts to link music and health are, of course, not new. Shamans have explored the 'healing' qualities of music for 30,000 years (Moreno, 1991)—that is, long before the music therapy profession developed after the Second World War (see Thaut & Wheeler, this volume). What is new, however, is that this topic is now attracting increasing attention among 'basic' researchers—neuroscientists, psychologists, and sociologists. Current research on music and health involves both qualitative and quantitative approaches in a range of contexts including music therapy, community music, music education, surveys, as well as experimental studies (MacDonald & Mitchell, 2008).

Though a rather wide range of health effects of music have been demonstrated (see the reviews in Hanser, and Thaut and Wheeler, this volume), the underlying mechanisms are less well understood. Previous accounts have emphasized the roles of 'distraction and competing stimuli' and increases of 'perceived control' in explaining pain relief through music listening (see discussion in North & Hargreaves, 2008, pp. 305–11). More recent work has suggested that many of the health-beneficial effects of music (e.g. hormonal changes) are mediated by the *emotional* influences the music has on the listener. Accordingly, it becomes important to study the mechanisms that may produce such changes in emotions and stress (section 33.3.6 below). This will also comprise the emerging field of *emotion regulation* (e.g. Gross, 2007), as emotion and mood regulation using music has been widely documented (cf. Konečni, this volume; Sloboda, this volume).

33.3.4 The phenomenology of music experience

About seven query responses involved a theme described by one author as 'a focus on music experiences that do not clearly fall within the category of emotional responses'. It expresses a sense that 'emotion' and 'feeling', as normally defined, do not capture everything relevant in our experiences of music; that is, in addition to experienced emotions (feelings), there are 'flow' experiences, 'spirituality', 'altered states', 'vitality affects', 'perceptual and cognitive' aspects of music experience, as well as more complex 'aesthetic experiences'.

As shown in the descriptive system for strong experiences with music (SEM) outlined by Gabrielsson (this volume), 'emotion' is only one of several aspects that together make up music experiences. One might be tempted, as indeed appears to be the case with some of the authors, to expand the notions of 'emotion' and 'feeling' to embrace these other phenomena. However, for conceptual clarity, it is probably preferable to refer to these additional features using other terms. The perception of dynamic changes in musical form should not be labelled 'feeling' unless we want to confuse the phenomenon with feeling as a component of emotion. (This relates to the terminology problem raised by some authors in the questionnaire.)

Even in studies of 'emotion proper', there is a need to expand the number of emotions studied, especially to consider a wider range of positive emotions. Despite

Tomkins's (1963) argument many years ago that researchers have neglected positive emotion, there have been few advances thus far. It has been proposed that the positive emotions are fewer, less clearly differentiated, and less clearly associated with action tendencies than the negative emotions, but a more important reason for the previous neglect is probably psychology's general focus on emotional problems (e.g. anxiety, depression). Hence, studies of music and emotion may help to 'restore the balance' between positive and negative emotion in the affective sciences. Positive emotions dominate in musical experiences, as noted in several chapters of this book (cf. Sloboda & Juslin; Becker; Juslin et al; Sloboda; Gabrielsson), and this must be reflected in self-report instruments used to measure subjective feeling (Zentner & Eerola, this volume). It is further necessary to distinguish among the 'raw' feeling and the reflective consciousness that follows (e.g. Lambie & Marcel, 2002). Verbal self-report can only access the experience if reflective cognitions are involved—yet mere 'raw' feeling is important in many applications (e.g. marketing, film, health), which may require other measures of emotion.

Ultimately, it could be fairly difficult to establish clear boundaries between feelings of emotions and other experiential qualia in music listening. One might predict then, that in the long term, the field of music and emotion may eventually be subsumed under the far broader heading of 'music experience', in a concerted attempt to explain more comprehensively how music is experienced, emotionally and otherwise. (To be fair, however, exploring phenomena other than emotions will not necessarily contribute much to our understanding of emotions.)

33.3.5 Cross-cultural comparisons

One further common theme in the query responses was a request for cross-cultural studies of music and emotion—occurring in six responses. One author requested 'more genuinely cross-cultural studies, involving cultures with no prior exposure to each other's music (so excluding Westerners)', and as a follow-up, 'studies about how rapidly they improve through increased exposure or training'. Another author emphasized the need for emotion researchers to 'forge links with sympathetic anthropologists and ethnomusicologists in order to carry out studies in a wide range of non-Western cultures', and also added that funding agencies must 'ignore the objections' of those anthropologists and ethnomusicologists who are ideologically opposed to cross-cultural experimentation.

Cross-cultural studies are crucial to test the generalizability of results, as observed by one author, and also have implications for theory (see hypotheses about 'cultural impact' in Juslin et al, this volume). As already noted, there are few cross-cultural studies in the field. One probable reason is the practical difficulties of conducting such studies. Thompson and Balkwill (this volume) offer a useful survey of the many problems that confront the music researcher interested in cross-cultural comparison (see also Matsumoto & Yoo, 2007), and also review the (few) music-psychological studies conducted to date. Becker (this volume) provides a thought-provoking review of more ethnographic approaches to investigating the 'habitus' of music listening in distant cultures. Both contributions will hopefully encourage researchers to embark on further cross-cultural explorations that can establish the boundary conditions of current theories and findings obtained mainly in Western contexts. An urgent need for cross-cultural research has been recognized in psychology more generally, and the current process of internationalization of psychology—with national associations in over 90 countries (Brehm, 2008)—will probably benefit such goals.

33.3.6 Underlying mechanisms

Six query responses mentioned the importance of further work on the underlying mechanisms through which music arouses emotions. This is the question of what is happening between the musical event (input) and the emotion (output). Sloboda and Juslin (this volume) mention the fact that remarkably few studies thus far have proposed or tested possible mechanisms. Juslin and Västfjäll (2008) recently attempted to draw more attention to this issue. They argued that the dominant approach to explaining emotion causation in emotion research more generally—'appraisal theory' (e.g. Scherer, 1999)—is insufficient to account for musical emotions. (It is important, however, in accounts of music performance anxiety; see Kenny, this volume). It is notable that only a few of the (eight) mechanisms theorized by Juslin et al (this volume) have been considered by mainstream researchers (for a recent review, see Moors, 2009). Further, many of the 'classic' theories of emotion typically featured in textbooks (e.g. the theories by James and Schacter & Singer) do not actually address the details of emotion causation. Hence, further hypothesis-driven work in this area could be illuminating for musical emotions as well as emotions in general, provided that experimental paradigms are created that reliably activate each mechanism (procedures manipulating musical expectancies—see Huron & Margulis, this volume—seem especially well developed). This may go some way toward achieving what one author in the questionnaire described as: 'integration of theories concerning music with more general theories of emotion'. In addition, a multiple-mechanism theory could help to resolve some of the current controversies in the field, by showing that different researchers focus on different mechanisms with different associated characteristics (see Juslin et al, this volume). Sooner or later, theories of underlying mechanisms will also have to address the relationship between 'liking' (i.e. preference, Table 1.2, Chapter 1, this volume) or 'aesthetic appreciation' and 'emotion' (as observed in two query responses).

33.3.7 Temporal aspects

Five query responses raised the issue of temporal aspects of musical emotions. Music always exists in time, and technological advances have made it easier to capture the dynamic aspects of our responses to music. Hence, authors noted the need to 'shed more light on the temporal dynamics of emotions'; 'examining music emotions in longer pieces of music that may have varying expressive content'; and conducting studies on 'emotional sequencing (in long pieces of music—what is the emotional result of listening, say, to a symphony, during the course of which you may experience many different emotions?)'.

Achieving this will require 'further development of efficient techniques for continuous recording of perceived and/or felt emotion'. Here one author noted that 'continuous-response research is in need of tools that are easily available and easy to use', and worried that 'many people interested in continuous-response methods are too timid to use it because it seems too new and complicated. By having some tools that help them collect and/or help them analyse such data, they may start feeling brave enough to explore continuous-response approaches'. The review by Schubert (this volume) provides a natural point of departure for exploring this area further, but the importance of dynamic measures extends to psychophysiology and brain imaging also, as highlighted by Hodges and Koelsch et al in this volume.

33.3.8 Neuroimaging

One final theme in the author query was 'neuroimaging', which was considered in five of the responses. One author requested more research on 'the neurological changes as a function of engaging in musical experiences'; another author noted the need to identify 'brain signatures underlying different emotions' (see Damasio et al, 2000). A third author noted that the noise problems associated with fMRI need to be eliminated, and that when that happens, 'the basic fMRI studies will need to be redone to see if the results are the same'. Neuroscience research on musical emotions has blossomed since *Music and emotion* was published (as shown in the chapters in the present book by Peretz and Koelsch et al). The 1990s, during which the music and emotion field truly emerged, has been called 'the decade of the brain' and involved some major advances in our understanding of brain–behaviour relations. Still, trend analyses indicate that neuroscience has seen only a modest increase in prominence in 'mainstream' psychology, despite evidence for its conspicuous growth in general (Tracy, Robins, & Gosling, 2004). The same is perhaps true of the music and emotion field: despite increasing numbers of studies, it is not altogether clear how neuroimaging studies thus far have increased our understanding of emotional responses to music. Much has been made of the fact that it could be shown that the pleasant experiences of music activate dopamine-rich areas of the brain associated with other pleasure-inducing stimuli, yet this finding was neither particularly surprising, nor contributed to a deeper understanding of the underlying process. Juslin and Zentner (2002) proposed that the coupling of theoretically precise psychological predictions with brain imaging techniques 'promises to be one of the most important domains in the new millennium' (p. 15). However, it is perhaps fair to say that this promise remains to be fulfilled: for instance, Juslin et al (this volume) argue that most current neuroscientific studies of music and emotion (like several of the psychophysiological studies reviewed by Hodges, this volume) look for simple and direct links between music (e.g. pleasant vs. unpleasant music) and brain response (somewhat akin to a modern behaviourist paradigm), without taking into account the underlying psychological process (or mechanism) that explains this relationship. In a similar fashion, one author in our author survey noted that 'considerable progress has been made with imaging technology, but also added that: 'We need to be a lot cleverer if we want to address the neurophysiology and neurochemistry involved in the sorts of subtle emotions that are found in music listening and creation.'

33.3.9 Additional directions

In addition to the above directions, we think the following topics may be salient in the future. First, *technological* approaches to music and emotion (e.g. in computer science, engineering, sound design) are currently increasing and may eventually be sufficient to motivate a separate chapter in a possible future volume on music and emotion. Most of this research is concerned with automatic analysis and synthesis of emotions in music (for overviews, see Friberg, 2008; van de Laar, 2006). In automatic analysis of audio or MIDI data, various acoustic features are first extracted and then combined to predict the (perceived) mood or emotion (e.g. Lu, Liu, & Zhang, 2006). Such algorithms can be used for Music Information Retrieval on the Internet. A wide range of analytic methods can be used, such as neural networks, Bayesian modeling, and Hidden Markow Models. Though some of the studies may appear to merely replicate previous psychological studies (ignoring the theoretical issues, but retaining the statistics), other studies may break new ground, and lead to novel applications—for instance, in music education, music-browsing systems, and computer games. Much can presumably be learned in this context from already well established applications of music and emotion in various media contexts such as music in film (see Cohen, this volume). Somewhat related is the current interest in emotion in *sound design*. It is recognized that a large part of our emotions in everyday life are evoked by cultural products (besides music), and that designers should therefore include emotions in the intentions of their design, in order to achieve products and interfaces that are richer and more challenging (Diesmet, 2002). The recent 'Design & Emotion' conference in Hong Kong (2008) featured a number of theoretical and methodological debates of interest to music and emotion researchers also.

Another promising avenue for future research might involve 'special' subsets of musical emotions. For instance, music does not only evoke emotions at the individual level, but also at the interpersonal and intergroup level. Such 'collective emotions' have been little investigated in the emotion field and even less in music and emotion research. When people go to concerts or make music together, their emotions are in part influenced by the emotions of *other* people present in the context, whether through rhythmic entrainment, emotional contagion, or shared concerns. These emotions can be considered part of 'dynamic social systems', and could even involve 'collective emotion regulation' (for an overview, see Parkinson, Fischer, & Manstead, 2005). Another special subset of emotions can be called 'meta-musical emotions': people may experience a range of emotions only indirectly related to music—such as longing for a concert or experiencing excitement over one's record collection. The kind of in-depth interviews used in sociological studies (e.g. DeNora, this volume) may be ideal to explore the highly personal ways in which listeners relate to their music in daily life. One final type of emotion that might be fruitful to explore in future studies is 'refined emotions' (see Frijda & Sundararajan, 2007). The notion does not actually refer to a subset of emotions (e.g. that anger is 'coarse' and love is 'refined'), but rather to a *mode* of experiencing all the ordinary emotions, one characterized by attitudes of detachment, restraint, self-reflexivity and savouring. The idea, partly inspired by Confucian philosophy and Chinese poetics, is somewhat speculative, but could help to explain more 'profound' experiences that involve music and emotion.

33.4 CONCLUDING REMARKS

We finished our last commentary (Sloboda & Juslin, 2001) with the hope that a future book would report progress in a rather more self-conscious and self-confident manner (p. 462). In some ways, at least, we think this is true of the present volume: the music and emotion field of 2009 is more advanced than it was in 2001. But make no mistake, the field is still fraught with disagreement about many issues, such as which emotions music induces, whether there are uniquely *musical* emotions, and whether a categorical or dimensional approach provides the best account of such emotions. Because the topic of music and emotion is so close to the heart of why most of us engage with music, one sometimes gets the feeling that scholars are motivated by what they *want* musical emotions to be—rather than what they actually *are* for most people. Such motives may partly underlie oversimplified debates about whether music evokes 'basic' or 'refined' emotions. We predict that the field will slowly move away from such basic issues, similarly to what has happened in the 'affective sciences' more generally (Davidson et al, 2003). Perhaps we do not need to resolve the age-old question of whether emotions are discrete or dimensional, but rather can focus on under what circumstances they manifest as one or the other, or are most usefully measured in terms of one or the other. We believe that music-emotion researchers will soon begin to focus on more limited, but more precisely defined, topics which will, eventually, help to resolve some of the 'grander' issues that currently define (or perhaps stifle) the field.

One consideration, which could guide us more explicitly away from 'time-honoured' questions, is the notion of benefit: which groups or constituencies stand to benefit from the results of specific pieces of research? There is a tendency, which is by no means confined to music-emotion research, for researchers to define the goals in terms of their own professional worlds—the need to be innovative, rigorous, peer-appreciated, and understandable within the institutional and professional constraints and incentives that determine how research resources are allocated. There is of course nothing unacceptable about any of these goals, but if research is governed mainly by these goals, it will tend to be of relevance or interest primarily to other scholars. Perhaps music and emotion researchers could frame more research programmes in light of their potential benefit to a particular constituency within the world of music or within the wider worlds of education, health and healing, business and industry, culture and religion. Although there are some notable exceptions (particularly in the areas of health and therapy), the general impression is that applicability is either not considered at all, or is bolted on at the end—in the form of a rather tokenistic afterthought.

Sloboda (2005) argued that applicability should be a more explicit factor in strategic research planning—both at an individual and an institutional level. Is there music-emotion research that could be framed around specific practical concerns of composers, performing musicians, audiences, or music broadcasters? Can music-emotion research address important issues of human and cultural development? As Sloboda (2005) noted, the situation is not so much that disputed answers have been given to such questions. Rather, it is the case that most researchers do not even bother to pose or answer them in a serious way.

Retrospectively, it may turn out that the second half of the twentieth century was a rather privileged moment in the history of research, where many researchers were left free to 'follow their noses' wherever their individual interests took them. There are signs that the world may be entering a phase of its history when the opportunities and resources for rigorous research become significantly more constrained. As this happens, stakeholders (including taxpayers and governments) may ask more searching questions about the value of specific areas of research. Music-emotion researchers perhaps need to be ready with better answers than are currently apparent from most of their outputs!

Despite all this, the fact that our emotional experiences with music can be so incredibly rich, multi-faceted, and difficult to capture in any straightforward fashion is perhaps partly the reason why the field of music and emotion remains endlessly fascinating—and why we can be quite certain that this book will not be the last on this topic.

APPENDIX

Responses to questionnaire about the top priorities for the field from 27 authors

1

A. Strategies for bringing together scientific and cultural approaches to music and emotion.
B. Music and altered states.
C. Music and spirituality.

2

A. For understanding the role of music on emotion in the film/video context, developmental studies and longitudinal studies would be important in sorting out effects of declining plasticity with age versus effects of particular critical periods for acquiring representations of certain kinds of information.

B. Emotion research benefits from fMRI, but the problem of the noise of the magnet and the small claustraphobia-inducing chamber provoke an unnatural emotional baseline. Emotion research will benefit when these two problems are eliminated. When this happens (which I expect it might in 5 years) the basic fMRI studies will need to be redone to see if in fact the results are the same. There are no (or very few) studies of the effects of music and video under fMRI, and these need to be done (some may be currently in progress, which would begin to pave the way).

C. Longitudinal studies (that one as a researcher could begin early in life) would assist developmental models, and one should view every study as possibly a developmental study that someone else, if not oneself, could carry out again on the same participants several years, or even decades, down the road.

D. The development of a system (digital database) for sharing stimulus resources and data through the Internet will also benefit progress on emotion research.

3

A. How far emotions are verbally (or even critically/musicologically) constructed.

B. If emotional interpretations are constructed in the course of performance, the extent to which they are constrained by structural/referential/other features of the composition.

C. How far emotions have a history, and the extent to which the study of music (scores, recordings, written responses, etc.) might shed light on that history (another way to put this: how far the study of music and emotion is a psychological or a musicological enterprise).

4

A. In terms of research I would like to see done: I'd be interested in more genuinely cross-cultural studies of expressiveness, involving cultures with no prior exposure to each other's music (so excluding Westerners). The examples would have to be endorsed as clearly expressive by composers/performers of the music's home culture. The questions would be about what if any emotions the music expresses (not what participants feel or what it makes them think of). And as follow-up, there could be studies about if and how rapidly they improve through increased exposure or training from those of the music's home culture.

B. I also have a reservation about the methodology of your (Juslin's) experiments that this excludes the contribution of dynamic/structural elements in music's expressiveness by holding the tune constant. So I'd be interested in experiments that reversed yours, by holding many of the prosodic elements constant but varying the dynamic/structural features of the music in appropriate ways.

5

A. Music, emotions, and collective action.

B. Music, emotions, and health.

C. Music, emotions, and social integration/disintegration.

6

A. Research should focus more on 'vitality affects' in music, that is, dynamic features such as crescendo/diminuendo, accelerando/ritardando, glissando, changes of timbre, and other types of sudden or gradual changes, further on the effects of formal features such as repetition, variation, condensation or transposition of the musical material. This requires further development of efficient techniques for continuous recording of perceived and/or felt emotion as well as refinement of the meaning of the concept 'vitality affects' in music.

B. Free phenomenological ('subjective') description should be used much more as it often provides much more depth, insight, and explanation of the listener's experience than crude techniques such as choice among adjectives, simple rating scales, etc.

C. Research has so far mainly dealt with 'basic' emotions, but many 'feelings' are much more complex and include perceptual and cognitive components. The concept of 'feelings' has to be further analysed and refined.

7

A. The ethics and public policy implications of using music as a negative stimulus in situations ranging from crowd control to torture.

B. More cross-cultural comparison of how the brain processes 'consonance' and 'dissonance' in societies that use scales with different musical intervals and have different sonic expectations.

C. More research on the effects of different kinds of mediation in shaping the emotional response to the same piece of music.

8

A. A study on the long-term affective outcomes of active engagement with music during compulsory education through making or listening to music with particular reference to well-being, self-esteem, social skills, and a range of transferable skills including concentration, self-discipline, and being able to manage motivation.

B. A study exploring the perceptions of pupils and teachers of the role of emotion in classroom music and the ways in which this can be used to promote greater enjoyment of music and relevance to experiences outside the classroom.

C. Further work on the teaching of emotional communication in music performance, also extending it to include improvisation and composition.

9

A. Studies of neurological changes as a function of engaging in musical experiences.

B. Studies of immunologial changes as a function of engaging in musical experiences.

C. Analyses of correlations between psychological and physiological measurement of emotions as they are affected by music.

10

A. Examining relationships among specific music emotions and overarching terms such as Konečni's 'aesthetic awe' or 'being moved'. Could one be moved by the music without being able to identify specific emotions and, if so, is that still an emotional response? Embedded in this is a call for a movement away from simpler emotion words such as happy/sad toward more nuanced, complex emotions.

B. Examining music emotions in longer pieces of music that may have varying expressive content (e.g. a Mahler symphony instead of a 30-second excerpt). If one can 'track' the various emotions in a complex piece as they shift suddenly or even overlap, does that support a cognitivist position, since it would be unlikely that a listener would actually experience a series of short-lived, changing emotions? Or, as above, could one be moved in general while being aware that many other emotions are being expressed?

C. Increasing the naturalistic context of the listening situation.

11

A. Collaborative cross-cultural research. Too little emotion research addresses questions of cultural difference and similarity. Emotion researchers need to forge links with sympathetic anthropologists and ethnomusicologists in order to carry out studies in a wide range of non-Western cultures. Granting agencies need to be sympathetic to requests for travel funds and ignore the objections of those anthropologists/ethnomusicologists who are ideologically opposed to cross-cultural experimentation.

B. Better non-animal behavioural research methods. Whether one thinks ill or well of animal research, the field of emotion has benefited enormously from the study of rats, mice and cats (e.g. Panksepp, 1998). Invasive neurosurgery and neurochemistry simply cannot be used with human participants. Unfortunately, animals cannot tell us how they are feeling, so researchers must rely on explicit overt behaviours (such as licking, stratching, sniffing, nursing, fleeing, etc.) in order to infer the affective state of the animal. As a consequence, animal research has addressed only a handful of 'major' emotions such as fear, panic, anger, hunger, social bonding, seeking, etc. Especially if we want to avoid research with primates, we simply can't use animals to study emotions like jealousy, envy, pride, loyalty, joy, gratitude, sadness, schadenfreude, optimism, humour, etc. Considerable progress has been made with imaging technology, but we need to be a lot cleverer if we want to address the neurophysiology and neurochemistry involved in the sorts of subtle emotions that are found in music listening and creation.
C. Attending to qualia: Better connection with phenomenology. Feelings are the proximal reason people listen to music. Emotion research will benefit by working more closely with those engaged in detailed description of the phenomenology of musical experience.

12
A. Resolving problems concerning terminology and distinctions.
B. Improving the measurement of emotional responses to music.
C. Focusing more systematically on the underlying mechanisms (i.e. on how, exactly, emotions are evoked by music).

13
A. Psychological and physical care of young musicians (e.g. avoidance of early and/or excessive exposure; suitable repertoire, etc.).
B. Development of evidence-based treatments for music-performance anxiety.
C. Music as an adjunctive tool in the management of emotional disorders (i.e. anxiety and depression).

14
A. Identify the brain signatures underlying different emotions.
B. Shed more light on the temporal dynamics of emotions (also with regard to the activity if the brain structures underlying these emotions).
C. Investigate how we can use the emotion-modulating effects of music for the treatment of disorders, and to improve both psychological and physiological health.

15
A. A concerted return is overdue of both laboratory and field-research attention to the effects of emotion and mood on the choice among music-listening alternatives.
B. What is required is a complex comparative examination of causal paths and mediation that are involved in the effects of music and other art stimuli, as well as a routine multi-component measurement of emotion.
C. A detailed investigation of the states/concepts of *being moved* and *aesthetic awe* has been initiated in several laboratories; such redirection of some of the research effort that is currently invested in the alleged effects of music on the fundamental emotions, and on 'states' that exist only as linguistic 'emotional' labels in verbal reports, would be advantageous to the field.

16
A. Integration of theories concerning music with more general theories of emotion.
B. Integration of theories concerning emotional response to music with those concerning 'like–dislike' responses.

C. (From a more selfish perspective) Integration of theories of emotional response to music with theories concerning responses to other aspects of the environment.

17

I think the field is mature enough to conduct:

A. cross-domain (e.g. music and language); and

B. cross-cultural comparisons.

18

A. Assessment: I think more attention needs to be given to developing reliable and valid measures of music-related behaviour (from music preferences to uses of music).

B. Methods: I think it is important for the field to conduct studies that capture people's everyday involvement and experiences with music (studies that capture naturalistic behaviours that occur in the 'real world').

C. Generalizability: One concern I have about some of the music research out there (especially my own) is that it provides a snapshot of the connections between music and psychology among young people born in Western societies that speak English. The findings may not generalize to younger or older generations or to people in other cultures. Collecting data from more diverse samples would be very helpful in this regard.

19

A. The Wittgensteinian tenet holds that language is our greatest problem. Misunderstandings and misinterpretations of words from one field that have a similar meaning in another, or with a different word, are perhaps our biggest challenges. But they always have been, especially as the various silos of research feel compelled to talk to one another without having genuine time to do so thoroughly. I don't mean that in a derogatory way. We all have limited time, and we do our best. So, it is not really an issue for the next five years, but a continuing challenge. Authors and teachers simply need to keep reminding us of how to handle the problems. An example is this very volume: while you have asked authors to pay careful attention to the definitions you have provided, my reading of at least one other chapter, and indeed my own writing, cannot be said to precisely fit them.

B. Continuous-response research is in need of tools that are easily available and easy to use. My suspicion is that many people interested in continuous-response methods are too timid to use it because it seems too new and complicated. By having some tools that help them collect and/or help them analyse such data, they may start feeling brave enough to explore continuous-response approaches. At the same time, those who have more experience in statistics and mathematics may start entering the field, providing more technically 'high-end' contributions.

C. We also need a lot more reliability and validity testing of continuous-response approaches—for example, how do we know for how long a listener remains on task when making continuous emotional responses? We can't or perhaps shouldn't simply interrupt them and ask them if they were concentrating. Well, maybe we could. But the challenge will be to come up with non-intrusive ways of addressing this and similar issues. So I think the period of (rather exciting) exploration with continuous emotional response will continue. But sooner or later, the approach will be taken more seriously, and become more refined when these checks are made, repeated and compared.

20

Wow! A big, even intimidating request.

From my standpoint, the number one question is: What is the relation between emotion and appreciation in music? This question includes several subsidiary questions. For example, is emotion essential for music appreciation or can a purely cognitive or intellectual experience be equally valid? And if emotion does make a significant contribution, whether separately or in conjunction with cognitive appraisals, then what kinds of emotions make that contribution? For instance, are the emotions generic, such as the 'arousal potential' of the old 'new' experimental aesthetics, or are they in some way music specific? We seem to have distinctive modules for the cognitive processing of music. Do we have similar modules for affective appreciation of musical compositions? Or is the emotional experience of listening to Beethoven's Fifth comparable to that of reading a great work of literature or painting? And permeating all these questions is the precise form of the emotion–appreciation relation: is it linear or curvilinear? And does the relation depend on emotional content or type?

21
A. More research on psychological mechanisms.
B. More research into emotional sequencing (in long pieces of music)—what is the emotional result of listening, say, to a symphony, during the course of which you experience many different emotions?
C. Individual differences in emotional responses to music (e.g. are there some people who don't experience much emotion in music—and why?).

22
A. Revisit experimental aesthetics and Berlyne's early attempts at building a basis for an understanding of a biological aesthetics. We have a better neuroscience base now but many of his perceptual and philosophical insights were ahead of their time.
B. More rigorous research into the role of musical emotion in neurorehabilitation and psychiatry—contrary to popular belief, a field with a weak research record.

23
A. Investigations that promote a greater sensitivity to cross-cultural similarities and differences in the relation between music and emotion.
B. A focus on music experiences that do not fall clearly within the category of emotional responses.
C. A focus on experiments designed to elucidate psychological mechanisms underlying emotional responses to music.

24
A. Gaining greater insight into the contribution of language, cognition, and culture to the development of musical emotions.
B. Developing more refined techniques for separating the perception of emotion in music from its emotional effects on listeners.
C. Exploration of the emotional consequences of joint music making.

25
A. Research on mechanisms.
B. Research on the relation between music, emotion, and health.
C. A wider assessment palette.

26
A. A better understanding of the emotionalizing of performers. What is happening cognitively when performers use a mood-induction strategy in performance? Do the emotional language and imagery examples so prominent in instruction promote the idea that performers themselves must feel what they hope to convey to audiences?
B. Objective measures of emotion in performing and listening. Perhaps using brain-scan technology to understand if emotion centres are activated in expressive performance conditions. Or using other physiological indicators (heart rate, skin conductance) to study emotional experiences with music, and compare with self-reports.

C. How can formal education better address the music–emotion relationship? For example, conventional instruction is largely analytical in nature. Music-listening instruction often involves identifying discrete properties (melody, timbre, form). This goes against the natural desire to listen to be emotionally moved. Do such instructional experiences affect student understanding of the emotional nature of music?

27

A. The first is that self-reports of emotion to music need to become more subtle, systematic and musically 'intelligent'. I see it as a plea for having researchers trying out new methods, including similarity judgements of emotional music that do not require any verbal labelling and that can be analysed by cluster analysis or multi-dimensional scaling techniques.

B. A second issue is that more attention needs to be paid to mechanisms and moderators of musical emotion induction. Moderators are aspects of performance, of listeners, and contexts (such as room acoustics) in addition to the traditional focus on musical structure as emotion-driving forces.

C. Finally, music therapy should grow out of its impressionistic phase and become a real clinical science, in which any study needs to involve rigorous control groups that make findings interpretable. For example, is there more to the pain-reducing effects of music than simple distraction? Amazingly, we don't know.

Note: A few responses have been edited for brevity or to preserve the anonymity of the respondent.

REFERENCES

Balkwill, L-L, & Thompson, W. F. (1999). A cross-cultural investigation of the perception of emotion in music: Psychophysical and cultural cues. *Music Perception*, *17*, 43–64.

Berlyne, D. E. (1960). *Conflict, arousal, and curiosity*. New York: McGraw Hill.

Berlyne, D. E. (1971). *Aesthetics and psychobiology*. New York: Appleton Century Crofts.

Blood, A., & Zatorre, R. J. (2001). Intensely pleasurable responses to music correlate with activity in brain regions implicated in reward and emotion. *Proceedings of the National Academy of Sciences*, *98*, 11818–23.

Blood, A. J., Zatorre, R. J., Bermudez, P., & Evans, A. C. (1999). Emotional responses to pleasant and unpleasant music correlate with activity in paralimbic brain regions. *Nature Neuroscience*, *2*, 382–7.

Brehm, S. S. (2008). Looking ahead: The future of psychology and APA. *American Psychologist*, *63*, 337–44.

Budd, M. (1985). *Music and the emotions. The philosophical theories*. London: Routledge.

Clynes, M. (1977). *Sentics: The touch of emotions*. New York: Doubleday.

Coan, J. A., & Allen, J. B. (eds). (2007). *Handbook of emotion elicitation and assessment*. Oxford: Oxford University Press.

Cooke, D. (1959). *The language of music*. London: Oxford University Press.

Damasio, A. (1994). *Descartes' error: Emotion, reason, and the human brain*. New York: Avon Books.

Damasio, A. R., Grabowski, T. J., Bechara, A., Damasio, H., Ponto, L. L. B., Parvizi, J., & Hichwa, R. D. (2000). Subcortical and cortical brain activity during the feeling of self-generated emotions. *Nature Neuroscience*, *3*, 1049–56.

Davidson, R. J., Scherer, K. R., & Goldsmith, H. H. (eds). (2003). *Handbook of affective sciences*. Oxford: Oxford University Press.

Diesmet, P. (2002). *Designing emotions*. Doctoral dissertation, Delft University of Technology, The Netherlands.

Downey, J. E. (1897). A musical experiment. *American Journal of Psychology, 9*, 63–9.

Friberg, A. (2008). Digital audio emotions: An overview of computer analysis and synthesis of emotional expression in music. In *Proceedings of the 11th International Conference on Digital Audio Effects*. Espoo, Finland: DAFx-08.

Frijda, N. H., & Sundararajan, L. (2007). Emotion refinement: A theory inspired by Chinese poetics. *Perspectives on Psychological Science, 2*, 227–41.

Gabrielsson, A., & Juslin, P. N. (1996). Emotional expression in music performance: Between the performer's intention and the listener's experience. *Psychology of Music, 24*, 68–91.

Gabrielsson, A., & Juslin, P. N. (2003). Emotional expression in music. In R. J. Davidson, K. R. Scherer, & H. H. Goldsmith (eds), *Handbook of affective sciences* (pp. 503–34). Oxford: Oxford University Press.

Gabrielsson, A., & Lindström, E. (2001). The influence of musical structure on emotional expression. In P. N. Juslin & J. A. Sloboda (eds), *Music and emotion: Theory and research* (pp. 223–48). Oxford: Oxford University Press.

Gardner, H. (1985). *The mind's new science. A history of the cognitive revolution*. New York: Basic books.

Gilman, B. I. (1891). Report on an experimental test of musical expressiveness. *American Journal of Psychology, 4*, 558–76.

Goodwin, C. J. (2008). *A history of modern psychology* (3rd edn). New York: John Wiley & Sons.

Gross, J. J. (ed.). (2007). *Handbook of emotion regulation*. New York: Guilford Press.

Hallam, S., Cross, I., & Thaut, M. (eds). (2009). *Oxford handbook of music psychology*. Oxford: Oxford University Press.

Hargreaves, D. J., & North, A. C. (eds). (1997). *The social psychology of music*. Oxford: Oxford University Press.

Hevner, K. (1935). Expression in music: A discussion of experimental studies and theories. *Psychological Review, 42*, 186–204.

Johnson-Laird, P. N., & Oatley, K. (2008). Emotions, music, and literature. In M. Lewis, J. M. Haviland-Jones, & L. F. Barrett (eds), *Handbook of emotions* (3rd edn, pp. 102–13). New York: Guilford Press.

Juslin, P. N. (2000). Cue utilization in communication of emotion in music performance: Relating performance to perception. *Journal of Experimental Psychology: Human Perception and Performance, 26*, 1797–1813.

Juslin, P. N. (2001). Communicating emotion in music performance: A review and a theoretical framework. In P. N. Juslin & J. A. Sloboda (eds), *Music and emotion: Theory and research* (pp. 309–37). Oxford: Oxford University Press.

Juslin, P. N., & Laukka, P. (2003). Communication of emotions in vocal expression and music performance: Different channels, same code? *Psychological Bulletin, 129*, 770–814.

Juslin, P. N., & Sloboda, J. A. (eds). (2001). *Music and emotion: Theory and research*. Oxford: Oxford University Press.

Juslin, P. N., & Västfjäll, D. (2008). Emotional responses to music: The need to consider underlying mechanisms. *Behavioral and Brain Sciences, 31*, 559–75.

Juslin, P. N., & Zentner, M. R. (2002). Current trends in the study of music and emotion: Overture. *Musicae Scientiae, Special Issue 2001–2*, 3–21.

Konečni, V. J. (1982). Social interaction and musical preference. In D. Deutsch (ed.), *The psychology of music* (pp. 497–516). New York: Academic Press.

Krumhansl, C. L. (1997). An exploratory study of musical emotions and psychophysiology. *Canadian Journal of Experimental Psychology, 51*, 336–52.

Lambie, J. A., & Marcel, A. J. (2002). Consciousness and the varieties of emotion experience: A theoretical framework. *Psychological Review, 109*, 219–59.

LeDoux, J. E. (1996). *The emotional brain.* New York: Simon & Schuster.

Lewis, M., Haviland-Jones, J. M., & Barrett, L. F. (eds). (2008). *Handbook of emotions* (3rd edn). New York: Guilford Press.

Lu, L., Liu, D., & Zhang, H. (2006). Automatic mood detection and tracking of music audio signals. *IEEE Transaction on Audio, Speech, and Language Processing, 14*, 5–18.

MacDonald, R., & Mitchell, L. (2008). *Researching the relationship between music and health: An overview of published research and key themes.* Paper presented at the 10th International Conference on Music Perception and Cognition, Sapporo, Japan, 2008.

Matsumoto, D., & Yoo, S. H. (2007). Methodological considerations in the study of emotions across cultures. In J. A. Coan & J. B. Allen (eds), *Handbook of emotion elicitation and assessment* (pp. 332–48). Oxford: Oxford University Press.

Meyer, L. B. (1956). *Emotion and meaning in music.* Chicago, IL: Chicago University Press.

Moors, A. (2009). Theories of emotion causation: A review. *Cognition & Emotion, 23*, 625–62.

Moreno, J. (1991). The music therapist: Creative arts therapist and contemporary shaman. In D. Campbell (ed.), *Music physician for times to come* (pp. 167–85). Wheaton, IL: Quest books.

North, A. C., & Hargreaves, D. J. (2008). *The social and applied psychology of music.* Oxford: Oxford University Press.

Panksepp, J. (1995). The emotional sources of 'chills' induced by music. *Music Perception, 13*, 171–208.

Panksepp, J. (1998). *Affective neuroscience: The foundations of human and animal emotions.* New York: Oxford University Press.

Parkinson, B., Fischer, A. H., & Manstead, A. S. R. (2005). *Emotions in social relations: Cultural, group, and interpersonal processes.* New York: Psychology Press.

Peretz, I., Gagnon, L., & Bouchard, B. (1998). Music and emotion: Perceptual determinants, immediacy, and isolation after brain damage. *Cognition, 68*, 111–41.

Rigg, M. G. (1940). Speed as a determiner of musical mood. *Journal of Experimental Psychology, 27*, 566–71.

Scherer, K. R. (1999). Appraisal theories. In T. Dalgleish & M. Power (eds), *Handbook of cognition and emotion* (pp. 637–63). Chichester, UK: Wiley.

Scherer, K. R., & Oshinsky, J. S. (1977). Cue utilisation in emotion attribution from auditory stimuli. *Motivation and Emotion, 1*, 331–46.

Seashore, C. E. (1938). *The psychology of music.* New York: McGraw-Hill.

Skinner, B. F. (1953). *Science and human behavior.* New York: MacMillan.

Sloboda, J. A. (1985). *The musical mind. The cognitive psychology of music.* Oxford: Oxford University Press.

Sloboda, J. A. (1991). Music structure and emotional response: Some empirical findings. *Psychology of Music, 19*, 110–20.

Sloboda, J. A. (2005). Assessing music psychology research: Values, priorities, and outcomes. In J. A. Sloboda (ed.), *Exploring the musical mind: Cognition, emotion, ability, function* (pp. 395–419). Oxford: Oxford University Press.

Sloboda, J. A., & Juslin, P. N. (2001). Commentary. In P. N. Juslin & J. A. Sloboda (eds), *Music and emotion: Theory and research* (pp. 453–62). Oxford: Oxford University Press.

Tomkins, S. S. (1962). *Affect, imagery, consciousness: Vol. 1. The positive affects.* New York: Springer.

Tracy, J. L., Robins, R. W., & Gosling, S. D. (2004). Exploring the roots of contemporary psychology: Using empirical indices to identify scientific trends. In T. C. Dalton & R. B. Evans (eds), *The lifecycle of psychological ideas: Understanding prominence and the dynamics of intellectual change* (pp. 105–30). Dordrecht, The Netherlands: Kluwer.

van de Laar, B. (2006). Emotion detection in music: a survey. In *Proceedings of the Fifth Twente Student Conference on Information Technology* (1:700). Enschede, The Netherlands: Twente University Press.

Weld, H. P. (1912), An experimental study of musical enjoyment. *American Journal of Psychology*, 23, 245–308.

INDEX

absorption 557
accent structures 381
achievement 472–3
acoustic cues 394, 460, 461–2, 472, 473, 481
actions 63, 556
activation 78, 392–3
Activation–Deactivation Adjective
    Check List 189–90
activation–deactivation continuums 198
activity 394, 888
    arousal 240–1, 377
    level 462
adjective checklist 227, 228
adjective circle 377, 378
adjective clock 202–3
adjective ratings 459, 460
Adolescent Musicians' Performance
    Anxiety Scale 805
Advance Music Directive 872
advertising and music 910, 914, 915–19
aesthetic consequences 354–8
    compositional impact 354–6
    stylistic transformations 356–8
aesthetic contribution 456
aesthetic emotions 211, 634–5
aesthetic properties 635
aesthetic response 517, 634–8
aesthetic rewards 403–4
aesthetics:
    new empirical 635
    speculative 515
aesthetic value 635
affect 9, 10, 261, 270
    induced 627
    modification and therapeutic
        change 830–2
    negative 78, 198, 258–9, 262–3, 264,
        266, 268, 657
    positive 78, 258–9, 262–3, 264, 266,
        268, 657, 806–7
    vitality 393–4
    see also education: role of affect;
        Positive and Negative Affect Schedule
Affect Grid 190
Affect Intensity Measure (AIM) 189, 190
affection 207

affective aspects 519
affective behaviour, role of in behaviour
    learning and change 828–30
affective circumplex see dimensional
    model of emotion
affective dimension 161
affective memory 266
affective priming 268
affective prosody 115
affective response 517
affective science 4
affect and music choice 697–717
    attributes of emotion 703
    data 706–10
    emotion–and–music (E–M) model 711–12
    implications 717
    methodological problems in laboratory
        setting 705–6
    mood 714–16
    mood in the Music–and–Emotion (M–E)
        domain 712–13
    Music–and–Emotion (M–E)
        domain 698–702
    prototypical emotion–episode
        model (PEEM) 703–4
affordance 165, 207–8
age: aesthetic responses to music across
    lifespan 533–8
agency 165
Agreeableness 672–3, 676, 680
alcohol use 416
American Music Therapy Association 819–20,
    822
Amnesty concert 742–3
amplitude envelope 384, 391
AMUSE project (Appraisal in Music and
    Emotion) 607–8
amygdala 107, 108, 109, 110, 116–17,
    316–18, 336
    involvement in positive emotions 320–2
    sub–regions and connected
        networks 319–20
Analytical Music Therapy 821
anger 78, 103, 138, 200, 208, 269, 706–9
    cross–cultural similarities and
        differences 777–8, 779, 780, 782

anger (continued)
  expression and communication in
        performance 459, 460, 462, 463, 464, 466,
        468, 470
Anglo–American analytic philosophy 18
anterior cingulate cortex 322, 326–8
anthropological perspectives 127–51,
        759–60, 941
  arousal 137–44
  cultural construct, emotion as 130–2
  cultural construct, person as 133–4
  culturally inflected listening 128–30
  habitus of listening: culture and
        biology 146–50
  habitus of listening, person and
        emotion in 134–7
  single–brain/–body approaches 144–5
  supra–individual biological
        approaches 145–6
anticipation 270
anxiety 866, 869
anxious apprehension 427
apparent reality, law of 898
appraisal 589, 598, 629, 634, 797, 888, 942
  see also valence
appreciation 517
arousal 10, 137–44, 198–9, 202, 227,
        361, 527–9
  aesthetic consequences 354, 357
  autonomic 410
  –based effects 919–21
  biographical antecedents 358
  dimensional approaches 78
  ecstasy: Sufis 138–9, 140
  effects 919–21
  energy 198–9, 200, 381
  evaluative misattribution 268
  experimental aesthetics and liking for
        music 520, 522–3, 525
  functional neuroimaging 328
  goals 521, 529–30
  heart or pulse rate 285
  multivariate approaches for
        emotion–specific patterns 296
  muscular tension 291
  and music therapy 823–6
  optimal–arousal model 361
  Pentecostal 143–4
  physiological 296, 427, 517
  rage: Balinese bebuten trancing 139–42
  response to loudness 226
  and reward in aesthetic perception
        theory 824–5, 827
  theory 29–30
  time series analysis 238
  see also activity arousal; motivation;
        tension arousal

arousalists 33, 36–7
arpeggio 466–7
articulation 171–2, 384, 391, 393, 454
  expression and communication in
        performance 461
  legato 461, 463, 465
  manipulation of structural factors 379–80
  performer motivation 414
  staccato 461, 465
art music 502
ascending reticular activating
        system (ARAS) 522
assessment processes and emotion 805
associations 558
association speed task 263
associative network theory of memory and
        mood 828
associative sources 480–1
athletic ability 680
attack 461
attention/attentional 519
  conscious 894
  focusing 889
  measures 264
  models 923
attitude, changed/special 557
attraction 207, 587
attributes of emotion 703
audience size 733
audio–visuo–motor mechanism 294
auditory perception 556
autism 105, 659
autobiographical memories 266
autocorrelation diagnostics 236–7
autonomic nervous system 282, 863–4
autonomic subcomponent 85
autoregression 237–8
Autoregressive Integrated Moving
        Average (ARIMA) 231, 237–8
availability and brain emotion circuit
        invasion 117–18
availability to consciousness 627
averaged parametric correlation (PAC) 245–6
awareness of emotion, limitations of 210–11
awe 207

background music 174, 850
Balinese bebuten trancing 139, 141–2
baroque music 53
bar position 466, 467, 468
basic emotions 76–7, 101, 105, 199,
        331–2, 503, 945
  decoding 471
  expression and communication in
        performance 462, 464, 470, 471
  functional neuroimaging 314, 331
  measures and findings 195–8

model/theory 201–2, 209
  privileged 470
battle music 172
behaviour 296, 556
behavioural component 830
behavioural effects 521
behavioural framework 821
behavioural measures 261, 269
  see also indirect, perceptual,
      cognitive and behavioural measures
behavioural subcomponent 85
beta–endorphin 861
betting paradigm 582
bias 505
Big Five factors 675, 681
biochemical processes 286, 287–8
biofeedback 852–3
biographical antecedents 358–61
  biographical stress 358–60
  late–life effects 360–1
biological vulnerability 435
biology 146–51
biomedical model 821
bipolar disorder 416–17
blended space 68n
bliss 207
blood–oxygen level dependent (BOLD) 316, 319,
      333, 334–5, 336
blood–oxygen saturation 293
blood pressure 290, 296
blood volume 292
bodily responses 75
body movements 293–4
body temperature 291–2
Bonny Method of Guided Imagery and Music 821
bottom–up processes: levels A and B 892–4
brain regions 624
brain stem reflex 620–1, 625–6
brain stem response 615, 616, 782
breakout principle 871–2
BRECVEM 619–23
  brain stem reflex 620–1
  emotional contagion 622
  episodic memory 623
  evaluative conditioning (EC) 622
  musical expectancy 623
  rhythmic entrainment 621
  visual imagery 622–3
Brief Symptom Inventory 866, 869
Brunswikian lens model 471–3, 474–5,
      782–3
burnout 405–6

calm–contentment 91
cancer 870–1
cantometrics 758
caregiving 102–3, 647–53

maternal singing 102–3, 649–50,
      651, 652
maternal vocalization as means of 'keeping
      in touch' 653
  musical speech 647, 648–9
categorical approaches 76–7, 188, 196n,
      199, 462, 936
categorical data 228
categorical emotion theory see basic emotions
catharsis 47, 50, 564
causal explanations 73
causal influences on musical emotions 611–12
causal models 698–702
causal relationships testing 618–30
  ongoing experiments 628–30
  theoretical predictions 624–8
  see also BRECVEM
Center for Epidemiologic Studies Depression
      Scale 869
centrality of music to experience 500–2
central nervous system 281–2
chamber compositions 352
change, law of: emotion responds to changes
      in the situation 898
charity music 741–4
childbirth 864–5
children and adolescents 428–9, 431, 437–8,
      440, 533, 577
  see also infants
children with language delays 840
chills 292, 297, 316, 329, 550, 863
choice 498–9
  see also affect and music choice
chromaticism 359, 361
cinema see film/cinema
circumplex model 78, 198, 200, 227,
      377, 614
classical conditioning models 440, 443
classical music: historiometric
      perspectives 347–63
  aesthetic consequences 354–8
  biographical antecedents 358–61
  melodic originality 348–53
classic approaches 52–60, 164–7
classification of emotional states 826–8
closed–response formats 193–4
closure, law of 898
coarse emotions 211, 212
Cochrane Collaboration 859
Cochrane Library 859
Cochrane review 833, 868
code description 460–4
code descriptions, verification of 468–9
code, functionalist origins of 470–1
coding, alternative forms of 480
cognition 557–9
  and anxiety 426–8

cognitive appraisal 434, 477, 616, 619–20, 628
cognitive aspects 519
cognitive–behavioural framework 821
cognitive–behavioural therapy 425, 852
cognitive content of hope 62
cognitive exhilaration 587
cognitive feedback 479
cognitive framework and musical
    soundtracks 891–8
    bottom–up processes: levels A and B 892–4
    emotion 896–8
    top–down processes: level D 894–5
    working narrative: level C 895–6
cognitive irony 587
cognitive measures 264–6
    see also indirect, perceptual, cognitive
       and behavioural measures
cognitive psychology 519, 909
cognitive reorientation 836–7
cognitive shock 587
cognitive subsystem 426
cognitive theory 21–2, 36, 37, 50, 55, 824
cognitive therapy 425
cognitivist view 32, 99–100, 296, 628
    see also perceived emotion
coherence 74
collative properties 825, 839
collective action – striving and
    contention 176–8
collective emotions 944
collinearity 238
communication 10, 565
    see also expression and communication
       in performance
communicative musicality 412
community 565
comparative emotion model checklist 209
complex emotions 464
complexity 391, 466–7, 468, 525–6, 528,
    772, 776
    subjective 523–4
compliance 530–2
component process model/theories 77, 782
composer 898–900
composition 798
compositional impact 354–6
comprehension 894
computerized measurement: two–note transition
    probabilities 349–51
computer software 460, 462, 479, 481
Conceptual Act Model 200–1
conceptual blending theory 68–9
conceptual integration framework 68n
conceptual symmetry 163–4
concern, law of 897
condensation 391
conditioned response (CR) 439–40, 480

conditioned stimulus (CS) 439
conditioning 617
confirmation 564–5
conflict–resolution 177
conflict theory of emotion 824
conformity: compliance and prestige 530–2
congenitally deaf listeners 659–60
Congruence–Associationist Model (CAM) 889,
    891–2, 893, 902
congruent music 888, 890–1
connection with others, emotional 404–5
connectivity analyses 335
Conscientiousness 672, 680
conscious attention theories 894
consciousness 894
consistency 81–2, 473
consonance 105, 108, 317, 324,
    393, 655–6
    cross–cultural similarities and
       differences 773–4
    intervals 389
construction of emotion 163
contagion, emotional 37–8, 440, 615,
    616, 622, 625–6, 629, 632–3
    expression and communication in
       performance 477
    marketing 925
contexts 87, 92, 500–2, 521, 529
    ordinariness versus specialness 495–7
    performance 520
    see also social contexts
Continental philosophy 18
continuous recording of emotional
    expression 373–4
continuous response 459, 460
Continuous Response Digital Interface
    (CRDI) 228, 231–2, 373
continuous scanning 335
continuous self–report methods 223–48
    comparing different performances of
       the same piece 242–3
    continuous and post–performance response,
       relationship between 243–4
    continuous response definition 224–5
    felt versus perceived emotion 244–5
    functional data analysis versus traditional
       time–series 242
    insights 239–40
    interfaces based on dimensional
       models 240–1
    measurement of emotions 226–8
    response collection interfaces 228–9
    sampling rate and response
       latency 225–6
    serial correlation 245–6
    time domain or frequency domain 246
    see also data analysis

contour theory 31–3, 34, 470
contradictory powers of music 726–8
Contrastive Valence theory 598–600
control, loss of 558
control precedence 897
coronary heart disease 869–70
correlations, general with compositional
    characteristics 352
correlations, specific with emotional
    expression and impact 353
cortex 108
cortical emotional pathway 111–13, 117
cortisol 861–2
counterstatement 47
Creative Music Therapy 821
Crime Prevention Through Environmental
    Design 747
cross–cultural similarities and differences 34, 101,
    127–9, 755–83, 941–2
  anthropology 759–60
  communication 781–2
  cue–redundancy model 764–7
  developmental evidence 773–5
  direct assessments 769–73
  ethnomusicology 757–60
  fractionating emotional systems
      (FES) 767–9
  future prospects 781–3
  music cognition 758–9
  ontogenesis 761–2
  phylogenesis 760–2
  speech prosody 776–81
  subcultures 757
  tension and stability 775–6
cross–modal congruence 893
cue–redundancy 764–7, 768, 771, 777,
    779, 781, 782–3
  expression and communication in
      performance 472, 474
cue utilization 463, 473, 475
cue weight 473
cultural construct, emotion as 130–2
cultural construct, person as 133–4
cultural impact and learning 624, 627
cultural influences see social and cultural
    influences
culturally inflected listening 128–30
cultural proximity hypothesis 779–80
culture 146–51
  and preference 686–7
  –specific cues 766, 767–8, 777
  see also cross–cultural similarities and
      differences

da capo aria 53–4
dance 700
data 706–10

data analysis of continuous self–report
    methods 229–39
  autocorrelation diagnostics 236–7
  comparison of magnitude of response across
      different parts of same time series 235
  comparison of two or more time–series 235–6
  descriptive approaches 231–2
  functional data analysis 239
  inferential approaches 233
  reliability and second–order deviation
      threshold 233–5
  time series analysis and ARIMA–based
      models 237–8
deaf listeners with cochlear implants 659–60
deceptive cadence 584–5
decibel 461
decision time task 263
decoding emotions 471, 472
decoratio 53–4
default mode 579
defining emotions 74, 75
definition of music 729–31
deictic center 886
demand characteristics 75, 75n,210
  and strategic responding 256–7
dementia 841
denial–tension 587
density 466–7
depression 416, 435, 833, 841, 865–8, 869
descriptive approaches 231–2
descriptive system for Strong Experiences
    with Music (SEM–DS) 554–66, 569–70
  cognition 557–9
  existential aspects 562
  feelings/emotion 559–62
  general characteristics 554
  interplay of music, person and situation 569
  musical factors 568
  perception 556–7
  performers 566
  personal factors 563–5, 568
  physical reactions and behaviours 554, 556
  religious experiences 563
  situational factors, physical and
      social 568–9
  social aspects 563–5
  transcendental aspects 562–3
designative meaning 60
developmental curriculum 795
developmental disorders 659–60
developmental psychologists 909
developmental theory of coping 434
'deviations' 461
diary studies 192
diegesis 883–5
difference transformation 238
Differential Emotion Scale (DES) 189, 190

differentiation 586
different performances of the same piece,
    comparison of 242–3
dimensional models 77–8, 187–8, 195,
    196n, 202, 209, 227, 936
    data 228
    expression and communication in
        performance 462
    interfaces based on 240–1
    measures and findings 198–201
    see also one–dimensional; two–dimensional;
        three–dimensional
direction 466, 468
direction dimension 827
disapproval 498–9
discord 20
discrete emotion theory 187, 227
    see also basic emotions
discrete–events models of time
        perception 922–3
dislike 498–9
display rules 763
dispositions 130, 135
dissonance 110, 317, 324, 393
    aversion 208
    caregivers 655
    cross–cultural similarities and
        differences 773–4
    intervals 389
    sensory 108–9
distinguishing emotional processes 76
distraction 90, 508–9
distress 866, 869
domain–specific approaches 197n,201–8,
        209, 767, 936n
dominant approaches 241, 936, 942
dopamine 580–1, 860, 861
dot probe task 264
double appoggiatura 466–7
down–sampling 226
dropout 405–6
drug use 416
DSM–IV 430
DSM–IV–TR 430, 431
dual–coding approach 917
duration 466–7
    contrasts 461
    neglect 244
dynamic causal modelling (DCM) 335
dynamic concepts 393
dynamic qualities 59
dynamics 380, 454, 464
dynamic structure 27–8
dynamism 391

eclectic models 821
ecological approach to perception 69

ecological properties 825, 839–40
ecological validity versus experimental
        control 370
ecstasy 138–9, 140, 143, 548–9
education: role of affect 791–809
    aims and provision 792–7
    assessment processes and emotion 805
    benefits of greater emphasis on affect 807–8
    composition and improvisation 798
    directions for future research 808–9
    listening and appraising 797
    motivation and active engagement 802–4
    motivation to practise 805
    perceived value of music 801–2
    performance 798–9
    personal and social skills
        development 802
    positive affective outcomes 806–7
    teaching students to communicate with
        emotion 799–801
education and emotional expression 478–9
efficacy and brain emotion circuit
        invasion 118–19
ego–involved goals 410–11
Elaboration Likelihood Model 916
electrocardiogram (ECG) 284
electroencephalogram (EEG) 111
electromyography (EMG) 290–1, 296
embodied meaning 60
emergent meaning 68
eminence 537–8
emotional problems 415–17
emotional Stroop task 264
EmotionSpace Lab 228, 237
emotion–to–music (E–M) models 701–2
emotivists 83, 99–100, 297, 628
    see also induced emotion
empirical aesthetics 515
empirical research in expression and
        communication 457–69
    standard paradigm 458–9
EMuJoy 229, 230
enchantment 207
encoding habits 349
Energetic & Rhythmic dimension 680
energizing 90, 509
energy 462
    arousal 198–9, 200, 381
entrainment 86, 509
    see also rhythmic entrainment
episodic associations 89
episodic memory 266, 609–10, 615–17,
        623, 625–6, 629, 632–3
ethnomusicology 127, 128, 757–8, 941
evaluation dimension in cinema/film 888
evaluative conditioning (EC) 615, 617, 622, 625–6,
        629, 636

evaluative misattribution 261, 266–9, 270
evaluative responding measures 264
event–related potentials 583
events 63
everyday life and music 493–512
    centrality of music to experience and salience
        of context 500–2
    circumstance of exposure: role of
        choice 498–9
    contextual specificity of judgement
        obtained 508–10
    intellectual stance of writer/researcher 506–8
    investigation, method of 503–6
    location of occurrence 497
    nature of music 502–3
    occurrence, frequency of 494–5
    ordinariness versus specialness of context or
        experience 495–7
    scope and purpose 493–4
    transmission, nature of 499–500
everyday musical activity 175–6
evoked emotions 82–4, 92
    and activation of mechanisms incorporating
        information processing 89–90
    positive 87–9
    and 'synchronized' responses 85–6
existential aspects 562
exosemantic correspondences 172
expanded lens model 475–6, 479
expectancy 90, 110, 477, 557, 616,
        625–6, 629
    bias 412
    and emotional responses 329–30
    experimental aesthetics and liking for
        music 519
    generalized (schematic) 590–1
    infants and music 658–9
    structural 89
    –tension 587
expectancy and thrills 575–600
    affective consequences 580–1
    biological origins 576–7
    explicit approaches 582
    Huron's ITPRA theory 688–9
    implicit approaches 583
    Margulis's attraction and tension
        theory 587
    memory 579–80
    mental representations 578–9
    Meyer's *Emotion and meaning in
        music* 584–6
    musical examples 589–91
    Narmour's Implication–Realization
        theory 586–7
    prediction effect 581
    statistical learning 577–8
    see also frisson

experience:
    ordinariness versus specialness of 495–7
    subjective 353
experienced emotions 297
Experience–Sampling Methodology (ESM) 88,
        92, 192, 505, 612–18, 633
experiencing subjects: composers, listeners
        and imagined personas 28–31
experiential subcomponent 85
experimental aesthetics and liking for
        music 515–41
    definitions and methods 517–18
    reciprocal feedback model 518–21
    structural factors and situational
        influences 521–6
    see also social and cultural influences
experimental control versus ecological
        validity 370
expression 64–5
    as function of many factors 392
    theory 29, 30
expression and communication in
        performance 453–82
    accuracy of communication 459–60
    code description 460–4
    code descriptions, verification of:
        synthesis 468–9
    expressive patterns and
        ornamentation 464–8
    felt emotion in performers 478
    felt emotions in listeners 476–7
    future research directions 479–82
    GERMS model 456
    music education 478–9
    working definition of expression 454–5
    see also empirical research; functionalist
        perspective
expression, emotional 454, 456
expressive analysis 63–4
expressive behaviour 75
expressive gestures 464–5, 481
expressive intention 472
expressive vocabularies 60–5
Extraversion 415, 613, 672, 676, 680,
        682, 689
extreme metal 744
Eysenck's Personality Questionnaire 676

Facial Action Coding System (FACS) 291
facial emotion recognition 763
facial expressions 291
facial muscle activity 296
factor analysis 671–2, 674, 675, 679
factorial design 469
factorial experiment 89–90
false alarms 437–9, 440, 441, 443
familiarity 523–4, 597

fear 78, 103, 200, 710, 895
  absence 208
  cross–cultural similarities and
      differences 777, 779, 780
  expression and communication in
      performance 459, 460, 462, 463, 470
  instructed 440
  structure 433–4
feedback delivery 479
Feedback–learning of Musical Expressivity
    (Feel–ME) 479
feedback production 479
feelings/emotion 10, 161, 210, 559–62, 940
  different (mixed, conflicting, changed) 561
  functional neuroimaging 327
  intense/powerful 559
  mood 561–2
  negative 560–1
  positive 559–60
  subjective 296
Feeltrace 230
felt emotion 83, 188, 244–5, 411–13,
    414, 500, 800–1
  in listeners 476–7
  in performers 478
  see also induced emotion
film/cinema and music 879–902
  diegesis and non–diegesis 883–5
  film–score composer 898–900
  functions of music 891
  historical background 881–3
  inference 885–91
  see also cognitive framework and
    musical soundtracks
finger temperature 291–2
fitness 850–1
flow 403–4, 549, 804
  group 405
fMRI 76, 145, 313, 316–17, 333–4, 632, 943
  amygdala 319
  anterior cingulate cortex 328
  BRECVEM 622
  interleaved silent steady state
    imaging 336
  limbic and paralimbic structures 336–7
  relaxation response 853
  ventral striatum 326
forced choice 192, 459, 460
foreshadowing an outcome versus
    accompanying an outcome 887, 890
form 383, 387, 391
  position 466, 467, 468
formal aspects of practice 407
formalism 48, 50, 51
  errors 66
fractionating emotional systems (FES) 767–9, 777,
    781, 782–3

free descriptions and choice among descriptive
    terms 370–1
free labelling 459, 460
frequency domain 246
frequency spectrum 379–80
frisson 591–600
  causes 593–4
  examples 594–5
  Huron's Contrastive Valence theory 598–600
  individual differences 592–3
  Pankepp's Separation Distress theory 596–8
  physiological correlates 595–6
F tests 235, 242
'fun centres' 326
functional connectivity 335
functional data analysis (FDA) 231, 239
  versus traditional time–series 242
functionalist perspective 469–76
  Brunswickian lens model 471–3
  code, functionalist origins of 470–1
  expanded lens model 475–6
  implications and findings 474–5
  Lens Model Equation (LME) 473–4
functional level 75
functional neuroimaging 313–38
  activation/activity changes within limbic and
    paralimbic structures 336–7
  amygdala 319–22
  analysis of data 334–5
  anterior cingulate cortex and insular
    cortex 326–8
  basic emotions 331–2
  everyday and music–evoked sadness 332
  expectations and emotional responses 329–30
  hippocampus 322–5
  interleaved silent steady state imaging 336
  parahippocampal gyrus 324–5
  'real' emotions 331–3
  sparse temporal sampling versus continuous
    scanning 335
  subject selection 337
  survival functions 332
  temporal poles 324–5
  time course of emotion 328–9
  ventral striatum 325–6
  see also fMRI; PET
fundamental frequency 461
fusion–emotional ecstasy 549
future research directions 479–82

gaiety versus gloom 202
gastric motility 293
gate control theory of pain 858
gaze 129
gender differences 174–5, 428–9, 538–9,
    592, 671, 680
generative rules 454, 456

generic space 68n
Geneva Emotional Music Scales
    (GEMS) 190, 206, 209, 212
genres of music 683–4
Geriatric Depression Scale 866, 867
GERMS model 454–5, 456, 481
Gestalt principles 58, 893
gestures 53–4, 171, 464–5
    see also expressive gestures
global content 434
global form, disruption of 391
goals:
    achievement 508–10
    congruence 434
    of listener 90–1
    relevance 434
gooseflesh (piloerection) 591–2, 598, 599
Granger causality mapping (GCM) 335
group flow 405
Guided Imagery and Music (GIM) 623, 633,
    821, 861, 862

habituation 356–7
habitus of listening 129–30, 145, 757, 942
    culture and biology 146–51
    person and emotion in 134–7
happiness 102, 110, 138, 270, 316, 318
    –elation 91
    expression and communication in
        performance 460, 462–3, 464–5,
        466, 468, 470
happy music 103, 106, 112–13, 291, 833–4
hard–to–describe experience, words
        insufficient 554
hardware level 75
harmony/harmonic 171, 377, 384, 389, 390,
    393, 466, 468
    progressions 381
    structures 172
    surprise 595
hate music 744–5
headaches 834
healing empowerment centre 872–3
health and well–being 175–6, 849–73, 939–40
    Advance Music Directive 872
    autonomic nervous system 863–4
    breakout principle 871–2
    cancer 870–1
    childbirth 864–5
    coronary heart disease 869–70
    definition of health 849–50
    depression 865–8
    developments in prevention and wellness 850
    fitness and health 850–1
    healing empowerment centre 872–3
    immune function 859–63
    integrative medicine 851

    mind–body medicine 852–3
    neurotransmitters and neurologic
        activity 860–1, 863
    pain management 857–9
    positive psychology 854
    psychological factors 853–5
    relaxation response 853
    research 633
    stress 855–7
heart rate 284–6, 296
heavy metal music 208, 731
hedonic motive 403
helpless–oriented patterns of motivation 408
hemispheric specialization 111–12
hermeneutical approach 50, 52, 60, 63
Hierarchical Linear Models 617–18
Hindustani music 101, 135–7, 381, 655, 770–2
hippocampus 316–18, 321, 322–3, 324–5
historical background 46–52
historiometric perspectives *see* classical music:
        historiometric perspectives
holding form 177
hospitalization 840–1
humanist approach 794–5
humour 591
Huron, D. 598–600
hydraulic theory 21
hypnosis/hypnotherapy 852
hypothalamus 322

IASP 857
iconic associations 89
identified regulation 407
identity 133, 134, 165, 734–8, 803–4
imagery 413–14, 558–9, 853
imagination 415, 577
immune function 859–63
immunoglobulin A 861–2
Implication–Realization theory 586–7, 775
Implicit Association Test 265, 271
implicit measures 75
improvisation 798
    and music therapy 822
inattentional blindness 884
inclinations 135
incongruent music 888, 890–1
index 89, 480
indirect measures 271
indirect, perceptual, cognitive and
        behavioural measures 255–72
    affect regulation measures 270
    behavioural measures 269
    cognitive measures 264–6
    evaluative misattribution measures 266–9
    indirect measures, classes of 260–1
    indirect measures, logic of 258–60
    memory measures 266

indirect, perceptual, cognitive and
        behavioural measures (continued)
    perceptual measures 263–4
    psycho–motor measures 261–3
    self reports of affect, problems with 256–8
individual difference factors 521
individual differences in response 532–41
    age: aesthetic responses to music across
            lifespan 533–8
induced affect 627
induction of emotion 10, 76, 83–4, 209, 280,
        296–7, 627, 632–3
infants and music 19, 645–62
    consonance 655–6
    cross–cultural similarities and
            differences 773–4
    cross–modal correspondences in speech
            and singing 653–4
    developmental disorders 659–60
    expectations 658–9
    infant–directed singing (lullabies) 774
    infant–directed speech 470, 647
    labels for emotions 656–8
    timing 656
    see also caregiving
inferential approaches 231, 233, 885–91
inferior colliculus 321
informal aspects of practice 407
information:
    focus 624
    impoverishment principle 629
    processing measures 261
    theory 585
inhibitory synaptic processes 336
insights 563–4
institutional contexts 520–1
instrumental music 48, 49, 352, 731–2
insula 322, 327–8
insular cortex 326–8
integral 237–8
integrated approaches 298
integrated regulation 407
integrative medicine 851
integrative studies 81
intellectual engagement 688
intelligence quotient (IQ) 688
Intense & Rebellious dimension 680
intensity dimension 381, 389, 392–3,
        461, 470, 495, 827
interfaces based on dimensional
        models 240–1
interference principle 629–30
interleaved silent steady state imaging 336
interleukin–1 (IL–1) 862
internal process, limited access to 257–8
internal sources of emotion 480–1
International Workers of the World 738

inter–objective comparison (IOC) 56–7
interpersonal relationships and
        preferences 685–6
interpretation of an earlier event 890
inter–subjective comparison 56
intervallic motion 586
intervals 374–5, 379, 380–1, 384, 385,
        389, 393, 454
intonation 461
introjected regulation 407
introversion 415
intuition 415
invasion hypothesis 118
inverted–U relationship 522–4
investigation, method of 503–6
IPAT Music Preference Test 670, 674
iPods 850, 851
irritation 208, 498–9
iso principle 633
ITPRA (Imagination, Tension, Prediction,
        Reaction and Appraisal) theory 598, 688–9

Japanese music 101, 655
Joint Commission on Accreditation of Healthcare
        Organizations (United States) 857
joy 207, 211, 777–8, 779, 780, 782
    expression and communication in
            performance 459

key 382–3, 388
knowledge:
    activation effects 921–2
    dependence 456

lag structure 226, 239–40, 241, 247
language 338
    delays, children with 840
    differences 764
late–life effects 360–1
learning, emotional 438, 837–8
Lens Model Equation (LME) 473–4
levodopa (L–Dopa) 860
lexical approach 55, 57
Likert method 192, 194
liking see preference
limbic structures/system 106–7, 336–7
linear component 473
linear dilation 243
linear regression models 475
listener/listening 134–5, 518
    accessibility 356
    consistency 473
    focused emotions 506–8
    judgement 472
    music education 797
Live 8 743
Live Aid 742

location of occurrence 497
Long Range Acoustic Device 747–8
long–term memory 894–5, 896, 897, 899
loudness 384, 389, 392–3, 454
    caregivers 657
    cross–cultural similarities and
        differences 772
    expression and communication in
        performance 461, 463, 469
    manipulation of structural
        factors 379–80, 381
    performer motivation 414
    see also intensity
love and courtship 174, 207
love/tenderness 460, 462, 463, 466, 470
lyrics 611, 731–2

Mahler inefficiency argument 244
Mandela concert 742
marketing and music 909–25
    advertising 915–19
    knowledge activation effects 921–2
    music industry 911–15
    pleasure and arousal–based effects 919–21
    time perception and waiting 922–4
MARSYAS 238
mass media 732–3
mastery–oriented patterns of motivation 408
matching 473, 474
match and utilization model (MUM) 895
maternal speech/songs see caregiving
meaning and emotion in music theory 824
meaning enhancement 90, 509
measurement 74–5, 938–9
mediation see politics, mediation, social
    context and public use
medical outcomes 869
Medical Outcomes Short–Form Health
    Survey 869
meditation 852
melodic contour 381
melodic direction 377, 381, 385
melodic motion 385
melodic originality 348–53, 361–2
    aesthetic consequences 354–5, 356–8
    biographical antecedents 359, 360
    computerized measurement: two–note
        transition probabilities 349–51
    measure validation 351–3
melodic properties 376
melodic range 385
melody 390, 611
memorability 496–7
memory 519, 558
    affective 266
    expectancy and thrills 579–80
    factors 611

measures 261, 266
    semantic 609–10
    see also episodic; long–term
mental illness, chronic 833
mental representations and expectancy and
    thrills 578–9
mere exposure effect 581, 622
mere exposure hypothesis 523–4
meta–musical emotions 944–5
metaphor 413–14, 800, 882
meter 466, 467, 468
    bias 578
metric complexity 352
Meyer, L.B. 584–6
MIDI data 944
mimesis 47, 50, 138
mimicry 37–8
mind–body medicine 852–3
minority influences 531
minor key themes 353
mirroring responses to music's
    expressiveness 35–8
mirror neurons 622
mode 101, 103, 106, 129, 375–6, 382–3,
    385, 388
    of agency 171–2
    caregivers 656–7
    of looking 129
    manipulation of structural factors 377,
        378–9, 380–1
modelling 800
moderation 529
modularity 627
mood 10, 23, 76, 561–2, 714–16, 866
    cinema/film 880
    congruence 258, 414
    disorders 416–17
    induction and performer motivation 412
    manipulation of structural factors 382–3
    music 174
    in the Music–Emotion (M–E)
        domain 712–13
    pre–existing 611
    regulation 509
mordent 466–7
Motherese 27
motion principles 454, 456
motivation 63, 401–19
    and active engagement with
        music 802–4
    choosing and sustaining musical
        involvement 402–6
    dimension in cinema/film 888
    emotional problems 415–17
    helpless–oriented patterns 408
    imagery and metaphor 413–14
    intrinsic 803–4

motivation (continued)
  personality traits 415
  and practice 406–8, 805
  preparing for performance 409–11
  self–induced felt emotion 411–13
motivational subsystem 426
motives of listener 90–1
motor/behavioural subsystem 426
motor response 296
moving average (MA) 237
MP3 player 850
multi–dimensional phenomenon 454
multi–movement compositions, outer
  movements of 352
Multiple Affect Checklist Revised
  (MAACL–R) 190
multiple emotions 397
multivariate analysis techniques and ratings 371–3
multivariate approaches and
  emotion–specific patterns 294–6
Münsterberg, H. 881–3
muscular tension 290–1
musemes 56–7
musical closure on perceived closure of a
  film, effects of 887
musical factors 568
musical fit 917–19
musical fragment 468
Musical Preference Scale (MPS) 670, 675, 676
musical savants 105, 659
music–assisted relaxation and imagery
  (MARI) 869–70
music industry 910, 911–15
Music Information Retrieval on
  the Internet 944
musicking 149
musicology, perspectives from 45–69
  classic approaches 52–60
  defining musicology 45–6
  historical background 46–52
  structural and expressive vocabularies 60–5
music space 68n
Music Therapist–Board Certified
  (MT–BC) 820
music–to–emotion (M–E) models 698–702, 711
Muzak 746
Myers–Briggs Type Indicator 676

Narmour, E. 586–7
narrative method 193
National Anthem Project 735
National Cancer Institute 870
naturalistic approaches 518
naturalistic settings 299
nature of music 502–3
Nazi Germany 735–6
needs 563–4

negative emotions 88–9, 295, 336, 338,
  498–9, 941
negative emotions and performance
  anxiety 425–44
  biological vulnerability 435
  cognition 426–8
  cognitive appraisal 434
  developmental theory of coping 434
  emotional–based theoretical
    model 441–4
  emotional contagion 440
  epidemiology of anxiety disorders 428–9
  false alarms 437–9, 440
  fear structure 433–4
  generalized psychological
    vulnerability 435
  instructed fear 440
  reciprocal determinism 441
  reinforcement 440
  social phobia 429–33
  true alarms 438–9
  unpredictability and
    uncontrollability 435–6
negative reinforcement 440, 746–7
negative responses 38–40
NEO–PI 676
NEO–PI–R 337, 613, 676, 681
neural pathway 104–6, 115–16
neurobiological subsystem 426
neurobiology 99–120
  cortical emotional pathway 111–13
  implications of brain emotion circuit
    invasion 117–19
  neural pathway 104–6
  subcortical route 106–11
  universality and predispositions 100–4
  vocal emotions: brain
    organization 115–17
neuroimaging 110, 943–4
  see also functional neuroimaging
neurologic activity 860, 863
neurological traumas 841
Neurologic Music Therapy 821
neuromatrix theory 858
neuroscientists 909
Neuroticism 415, 618, 672, 673, 682,
  688, 689
neurotransmitters and neurologic
  activity 858, 860–1
New musicology 60, 62, 67
non–appraisal emotions 634
non–diegesis 883–5
nostalgia 207, 211, 212
note:
  density 383, 387–8
  emphasis 464–5
nucleus accumbens 107, 108, 325–6

objective complexity 523–4
objective ratings 354–5
occurrence, frequency of 494–5
OCEAN acronym 672
one–dimensional models 78, 936
on–timing 466–7
ontogenesis 624, 761–2, 767, 781–2
open–earedness 534–5
open–ended formats 193
Openness 613, 672, 676, 680, 688
opera 47
operant conditioning 440, 443
optimal–arousal model 361
optimal complexity model 523
orbitofrontal cortex 112–13, 321, 330, 895
organismic explanations 73
originality see melodic originality
ornamentation 464–8
'outcome feedback' 478
oxytocin 862

pain management 857–9
Panksepp, J. 596–8
parahippocampal gyrus 109, 317–18, 321, 324
paralimbic structures 336–7
parallel enrichment procedure 193, 460
parasympathetic nervous system 282, 863
Parents Music Resource Center 745–6
pARF 230
Parkinson's disease 860
patriotism 734–8
pattern:
    classification analysis 335
    nature of 456
    origin of 456
    processing and brain regions 456
pauses/rests 385, 391
    see also intervals
peacefulness 110, 208, 211
peak activations 76
peak experience 403, 548, 549, 551
peak performance 549
peer culture 165
perceived emotion 82–4, 92, 188, 209,
        212, 280, 394, 480–1
    psychophysiological processes 297
    underlying mechanisms of evoked
        emotions 606
    versus felt emotion 244–5
perceived expression 369
perceived stability 381
perceived value of music 801–2
perception 10, 76, 83–4, 556–7
    and induction, relationship
        between 632–3
perceptual coding 519
perceptual effects 456

perceptual–imaginative routes 619
perceptual measures 261, 263–4
    see also indirect, perceptual, cognitive
        and behavioural measures
perceptual properties 635
perfectionism 415
performance 27, 798–9
    anxiety see negative emotions and
        performance anxiety
    contexts 520
    see also expression and communication
        in performance
performative approach 66–7
performer consistency 473
performers 566
peripheral skin temperature 291–2
personal aspects 563–5
personal emotional meaning of non–musical
        context 501–2
personal factors 87, 568
personality 538–40
    factors 300
    questionnaires 337
    traits 10, 415
    see also preference and personality
personal skills development 802
personal variables 300
personhood 133, 135–6
persuasion 47
perturbations 148
PET 313, 316, 318, 333–4, 632, 860, 863
    limbic and paralimbic structures 336–7
    peak activations 76
    single–brain/–body approaches 145
    ventral striatum 326
phenomenological level 75
phenomenological method 193
phenomenology of music experience 940–1
philosophical perspectives 15–40, 727, 728
    contour theory 31–3
    experiencing subjects: composers,
        listeners and imagined personas 28–31
    mirroring responses to music's
        expressiveness 35–8
    negative responses 38–40
    philosophy and its methods 15–21
    qualified listener 24
    symbol, music as 25–8
    theories of emotions 21–3
    theory constraints 23–4
    universalism 34–5
phylogenesis 760–2, 781–2
physical reactions and behaviours 554, 556
physiological component 830
physiological measures 518
physiological psychologists 909
physiological reactions 296, 554, 556

physiological signatures 198
physiological subsystem 426
piracy 912–14
pitch 385–6, 389, 393, 651
    contour 390
    expression and communication in
        performance 461, 470
    manipulation of structural factors 377, 379,
        380, 381
pity 37
placebo effect 855
place marker approaches 229
'Playlists for the Soul' 851
play songs 649
pleasant music/stimuli 268, 316, 319,
        320–1, 323, 326, 329, 336–7
pleasure 78, 919–21
    –displeasure continuums 198
    politicizing 740–1
plugging 523
political conservatism/liberalism 680
politics, mediation, social context and public
        use 725–51
    contradictory powers of music 726–8
    definition of music 729–31
    lyrics 731–2
    mediation 732–3
    theoretical development 728–9
    see also uses of music
polygraph 373
popular music 502, 681
Positive Affective dimension 198
positive emotions 88, 295, 320–2, 336,
        337, 338, 941
Positive and Negative Affect Schedule
        (PANAS, PANAS–X) 189, 190, 198
positive psychology 854
positive reinforcement 440, 746
positivity bias 610
possibilities 563–4
post–outcome phase 588–9
post–performance response 247
post–skip reversal 578–9
potency 381, 888
power 78
PRAAT software 462
practice 805
    and motivation 406–8
prediction 81–2, 577, 581, 589
    of environment 894
predispositions 100–4
preference 10, 517, 521, 523–4, 531,
        534, 537, 636
preference and personality 669–90
    culture and preference 686–7
    current directions in research 679–81
    early research on links between 674–9

interpersonal relationships and
        preferences 685–6
    listening to music in context 687–8
    measurement of preferences 683–5
    preferences over time 687
    understanding connections between 681–3
pre–outcome phase 588
preparing for performance 409–11
prestige 530–2
prevalence of musical emotions 606,
        608–11, 612–15
pride 464
Priestley's Analytical Music Therapy 821
probe–tone methodology 582
'problem music' styles 540
processing, emotional 837–8
processing styles 258–9
Product Emotion measurement instrument
        (PrEmo) 938–9
Profile of Mood States (POMS) 189, 190, 866
propaganda 530
prosodic cues 27, 116
protest music 738–40
prototype approaches 79, 80, 520, 524–6
prototypical emotion–episode model
        (PEEM) 701, 703–4, 707–8, 711, 713n
prototypical exemplars 79
psychological factors 854–5
psychological mechanisms 75, 619
psychological perspectives 73–92
    categorical approaches 76–7
    complex interactions between music,
        listener and situation 86–7
    consistency and predictability 81–2
    defining emotions 74, 75
    dimensional approaches 77–8
    distinguishing emotional processes 76
    evoked emotions and activation of
        mechanisms incorporating information
        processing 89–90
    evoked emotions and 'synchronized'
        responses 85–6
    evoked positive emotions 87–9
    goals and motives of listener 90–1
    implications and directions for future
        research 91–2
    measuring emotions 74–5
    perceived and evoked emotion 82–4
    prototype approaches 79, 80
psychology of health 853–4
psycho–motor measures 261–3
psychophysical cues 765–8, 772–5, 779–82
psychophysical properties 825, 839
psycho–physiological interaction (PPI)
        analysis 335
psycho–physiological measures 279–300
    biochemical processes 286, 287–8

blood–oxygen saturation 293
blood pressure 290
blood volume 292
body movements 293–4
chills 292
finger, peripheral skin or body
    temperature 291–2
gastric motility 293
heart or pulse rate 284–6
induced emotions 296–7
integrated approaches 298
literature overview 280–1, 282
multivariate approaches and
    emotion–specific patterns 294–6
muscular tension 290–1
naturalistic settings 299
personal variables 300
pupillary reflex and startle eye blink reflex 293
respiration 289–90
skin conductance 286, 289
structural features of music 299–300
timing issues 298–9
Psychoticism 682
PsySound 238
public space, music as a marker of 745–7
public use see politics, mediation, social
    context and public use
pulse rate 284–6
punk music 731, 744
pupillary reflex 293
purchasing music 912–14

qualified listener 24
quasi–physical reactions 556
questionnaire about top priorities for the
    field 946–52
questionnaire studies 608–12

radio programming 914–15
rage: Balinese bebuten trancing 139, 141–2
random fluctuations 454, 456
rap music 681, 731
rate see tempo
ratings and multivariate analysis techniques 371–3
reaction 589, 598, 606
'real' emotions 314, 316, 320, 330
receptivity 557
reciprocal determinism 441
reciprocal feedback model 516, 518–21, 529
reconfigurability and brain emotion circuit
    invasion 118
Recording Industry Association of
    America 911
refined emotions 211, 945
Reflective & Complex dimension 680
regional cerebral blood flow (rCBF) 316, 318, 334,
    336, 863

registral direction 586
registration 243
regression models 473–4, 479
regression to the mean 578–9
regulation of emotion 940
reinforcement 440, 746–7
relation to music, special/changed 558
relaxation 208, 853
relief 208
religious ecstasy 143
religious experiences 563
religious thought 727, 728, 731
renewal ecstasy 548
repeated exposure paradigm 523
Repeated Measures Analysis of
    Variance 235
repetition 47, 391, 523–4
representative design 468
residual variance 474
respiration 289–90
response collection interfaces 228–9
response latency 225–6
retrospective self–report 504–6
rhythm 110, 171, 386, 391
    expression and communication in
        performance 461
    manipulation of structural factors 376, 377,
        379, 380, 381
rhythmic entrainment 149, 621, 624,
    625–6
rhythmic structures 172
right hemisphere hypothesis 111–12
rock 'n' roll music 730–1
Rorschach inkblot test 266–7
Rosenberg Self–Esteem Scale 866
rostral cingulate zone 327
RTCRR 229, 230

sad music 38, 103, 105, 106, 112–13
    muscular tension 291
    musical therapy 833–4
sadness 37, 102
    affect regulation measures 270
    cross–cultural similarities and
        differences 777, 779, 780, 782
    everyday and music–evoked 332
    expression and communication in
        performance 460, 462–3, 464–5, 466,
        468, 470
    functional neuroimaging 318
    –melancholgy 91
sampling rate and response latency 225–6
sampling theorem (Nyquist) 225
scales 760
scary music 105, 109–11, 116
schizophrenia 833
second–order deviation threshold 233–5

second–order deviation threshold, reliability
of 233–5
sedative music 285, 290, 291
seduction 207
self–actualization 564–5
Self–Assessment Manikin scales 190, 191
self–concept 804
self–determination theory 407
self–efficacy 411
self–esteem 866
self–induced felt emotion 411–13
self–perception 803
self–presentation bias 210, 257, 260
self–referring emotions 499–500
self–report measures and models 75, 187–213, 271,
296, 609
of affect, problems with 256–8
basic emotion model 195–8
comparisons of models 209–10
dimensional emotion models 198–201
domain–specific approaches 201–8
naturalistic approaches 192–3
problems and considerations 210–13
questionnaire 805
real–time assessment 194–5
response format and language 193–4
retrospective 194–5, 504–6
standard instruments 189–92
see also continuous self–report methods
semantic elements 57
semantic memory 609–10
semiotic theory 26, 28, 55–6, 64
Sensation Seeking Scale 593, 675
Experience Seeking subscale 687
sensitivity 415
sensory route 619
sentograph 229, 374
Separation Distress theory 596–8
sequential approach 69
sequential development 391
serial correlation 245–6
serotonin 860
setting 175
shivers 550
short–lived emotions 397
Short Test of Music Preferences
(STOMP) 670, 679–80
signification 172
similarity 26, 586
singer's formant 462, 597
'Singing Revolution' (Estonia) 737
single appoggiatura 466–7, 468
single–brain/–body approaches 144–5
single rating scale 228
sitar 135–7
situational cues 436
situational factors 568–9, 611

situational influences 521–6
situational meaning, law of (stimulus
specificity) 897
situations 520, 521, 529
changed experiences 557–8
skin conductance 286, 289, 296, 297
slide 466–7
social aspects 563–5
social class 538–9, 671
social contexts 87, 520–1, 939
see also politics, mediation, social context
and public use
social and cultural influences 432–41, 526–32
arousal–state goals 529–30
conformity: compliance and prestige 530–2
Konečni's arousal–based approach 527–9
see also cross–cultural similarities and
differences
social dominance 680
social–efficiency approaches 795
social learning 470, 836
social meliorist approach 795
social movement activity 176
social phobia 429–33, 441
social psychology 520, 909
Social Readjustment Rating Scale 359
social skills development 802
social status 671
social sui generis 161
sociobiologic translations 163
sociological approach 159–79, 758
close interactions 174–5
collective action – striving and
contention 176–8
everyday musical activity and everyday
health practice 175–6
rediscovery of emotion within
sociology 160–2
social structures: towards conceptual
symmetry 163–4
subjectivity – classic models 164–7
tacit practice and emotional
work 171–4
technology of emotion construction, music
as 168–70
solemnity versus triviality 202
somatic nervous system 282
somatovisceral activity 295
sonic branding 919
sorrow 459
sound design 944
sound level see loudness
sparse temporal sampling versus continuous
scanning 335
Spearman rank correlation 245–6
spectrum 392
speculative aesthetics 515

speech prosody 756, 764, 766, 767, 775, 776–81, 782
speed *see* tempo
Spencer's law 470
sphygmomanometer 290
stability 775–6
standard conditions 29
standard paradigm 458–9, 464, 481
startle eye blink reflex 293
startle outliers 226
startle reflex 108
State–Trait Anxiety Inventory/Scale 866, 869
statistical learning 577–8
stimulative music:
    blood pressure 290
    heart or pulse rate 285
    muscular tension 291
    respiration 289
stimuli 369
stimulus specificity 897
strategic responding 256–7
stress 358, 416, 854–7
    biographical 361
Strong Experiences with Music (SEM)
        project 193, 547–71, 940
    analysis 552–3
    data collection 551–2
    earlier research 548–51
    general results and example 533–4
    subjects 552
    see also descriptive system
structural analysis 63–4
structural coupling 146–8
structural equation modelling 335
structural vocabularies 60–5
structure 58, 64–5, 299–300, 367–95, 521–6
    amplitude envelope 391
    analysis of structure–emotion
        relationships 369–70
    articulation 391
    continuous recording of emotional
        expression 373–4
    dependence on 627–8
    expectancies 89
    experimental control versus ecological
        validity 370
    expression as function of many factors 392
    form 383, 391
    free descriptions and choice among
        descriptive terms 370–1
    harmony 390
    intervals 374–5, 389
    key 382–3, 388
    loudness (intensity) 389
    manipulation of several factors 377–81
    melody 376, 390
    mode 375–6, 382–3, 388

non–verbal responses 374
note density 383, 387–8
pauses/rests 391
perceived expression 369
pitch 389
psychophysiological processes 297
ratings and multivariate analysis
        techniques 371–3
rhythm 376, 391
shared 68
specially composed music 374
stimuli 369
synthesized tone sequences 376–7
tempo 376, 382, 383, 387–8
timbre 389
tonality 390
style sensitivity 534
styles of listening 130, 171
stylistic transformations 356–8
stylistic unexpectedness 455
subcortical pathway of vocal
        emotions 116–17
subcortical route 106–11
    scary music 109–11
    sensory dissonance 108–9
    startle reflex 108
subcultures 757
subjective complexity 523–4
subjective component 830
subjective experiences 353
subjective feeling 296
subjective ratings 356
subjectivity 133–4, 135–6, 164–7, 173–4
subordinate level 79
substance abuse 416
substitute 466–7
Sufis 138–9, 140
superordinate level 79
supra–individual biological
        approaches 145–6
surprise 208, 589–90, 595
    temporal 595
    –tension 587
survival functions 332
survival value of brain function 624
swan–song phenomenon 360–1
symbolism 25–8, 89
symbol–number test 263
sympathetic nervous system 282, 863
synaesthetic perception 557
synchronization 74, 85–6
    of subsystems 327
synthesis 468–9
synthesized tone sequences 376–7
systematic design 468
system constraints 760
system identification 238

tabla 135–7
tacit practice and emotional work 171–4
tactile perception 556
tambura 135–7
task–involved goals 410–11
tastes 517–18, 521, 534
technological approaches 944
technology 733
   of emotion construction,
      music as 168–70
tempo 103, 106, 376, 382–3, 386–8, 392 3
   caregivers 651, 656–7
   cross–cultural similarities and
      differences 772
   expression and communication in
      performance 454, 461, 463, 464,
      469, 470, 472
   heart or pulse rate 285
   manipulation of structural factors 377,
      379, 380, 381
   performer motivation 414
temporal aspects 942–3
temporal congruence 893
temporal features 461
temporal poles 317–18, 322, 324–5
temporal structures 172
temporal surprise 595
temporal synchrony 893
tenderness 207, 211, 463
   see also love/tenderness
tension 202, 208, 587, 775–6
   arousal 198–9, 200, 240–1, 381
   muscular 290–1
   versus relaxation 202
text space 68n
thalamus 321
Thematic Apperception Test (TAT) 267
theories of emotions 21–3
theory constraints 23–4
therapy 208, 323, 633, 819–42
   adolescent hospitalized with burns 840–1
   affective behaviour, role of in behaviour
      learning and change 828–30
   affect modification and therapeutic
      change 830–2
   children with language delays 840
   classification of emotional states 826–8
   clinical components 834–8
   dementia and depression and neurological
      traumas 841
   historical–philosophical review 822–3
   integrative model 839–40
   overview 819–22
   theories of emotion and
      arousal 823–6
thoughts 558
three–dimensional models 78, 200–1

three–note transition probabilities 351
thrills 550
   see also expectancy and thrills
timbre 381, 386, 389, 392, 393, 462,
      463, 469
   vocal 650, 651
time course of emotion 328–9
time domain 246
time perception and waiting 922–4
time series analysis and ARIMA–based
      models 237–8
timing 298–9, 454, 461, 464, 656
tonal expectation 658–9
tonal stability 776
tone 379–80, 386, 389, 390, 391, 463
   onsets, rapidity of 461
top–down processes: level D 894–5
Toronto Alexithymia Scale 337
torture and music 747–9
traditional time–series versus functional
      data analysis 242
training 538, 540–1
trait anxiety 415, 866, 869
trancing 139, 141–2
transcendence 207
transcendental aspects 562–3
transcendent ecstasy 549
transcendent move 48
transcranial magnetic stimulation 630
Transformational Design Model 834
transmission, nature of 499–500
triangulation approach 271
trill 466–7
true alarms 438–9, 441, 443
t tests 236
turn 466–7
two–dimensional approach/models 78,
      198–200, 228–9, 888, 936
Two–Dimensional Emotion–Space
      (2DES) 228, 237
two–note transition probabilities 349–51,
      353, 355, 362
type A behaviour pattern 708–9

ubiquity of music 163
uncertainty 585
unconditioned stimulus (UCS) 439–40
uncontrollability 435–6
underlying mechanisms for evoking
      emotions 605–38, 942
   aesthetic response 634–8
   AMUSE project (Appraisal in Music and
      Emotion) 607–8
   Experience–Sampling Methodology
      (ESM) 612–18
   implications and directions for future
      research 630–3

questionnaire studies 608–12
see also causal relationships testing
unimodal musical stimuli 298
unique experience 554
universalism 34–5
universality 100–4
unmodelled component of communicative
  process 474
unpleasant music/stimuli 316, 319, 323,
  329, 336–7
unpredictability 435–6
Upbeat & Conventional dimension 680
urban/rural environments 671
uses of music 734–49
  charity music 741–4
  hate music 744–5
  as marker of public space 745–7
  patriotism and national identity 734–8
  pleasure, politicizing of 740–1
  protest music 738–40
  torture 747–9
utilitarian emotions 211, 634–5
UWIST Mood Adjective Checklist 190

valence 78, 111–12, 198–9, 200, 202,
  227, 238, 394
  expression and communication in
    performance 462
  functional neuroimaging 319, 328
  manipulation of structural
    factors 377, 381
  multivariate approaches for emotion–specific
    patterns 296
variant model 200
variation 47
vegetative activity 326–8
velocity 461
ventral striatum 107, 322, 325–6
ventromedial prefrontal cortex 112–13

verbal ability 680
verbal directions 801
verbal impulsivity 680
verbalization of emotions, difficulties
    in 211–12
verbal reports 518
vestibulomotor mechanism 293–4
vibrato 461
vicarious experiences in narrative
    comprehension models 886
vicarious functioning 474
Visual Analogue Scale (VAS) 190
visual features of performers 480
visual imagery 615, 617, 622–3, 625–6
visual perception 557
visual response formats 191
vitality affects 393–4
vocal emotions: brain organization 115–17
vocal music 47
vocal timbre and caregivers 650, 651
volitional influence 627
voluntary control 456
vulnerability 435

war and music 358
well–being *see* health and well–being
Western music 101, 770–2
white power music *see* hate music
Williams syndrome 659
withdrawal ecstasy 549
Wittgenstein's puzzle 580
wonder 207
Woodstock Nation 741–2
working narrative: level C 895–6
work–specific (veridical)
    expectations 590–1
World Health Organization 849
wrong–note harmonies/melodies 590
Wundt curve 354–5, 356, 361, 522